135 150 165 180 165

ARCTIC CIRCLE

60

45

30

TROPIC OF CANCER

15

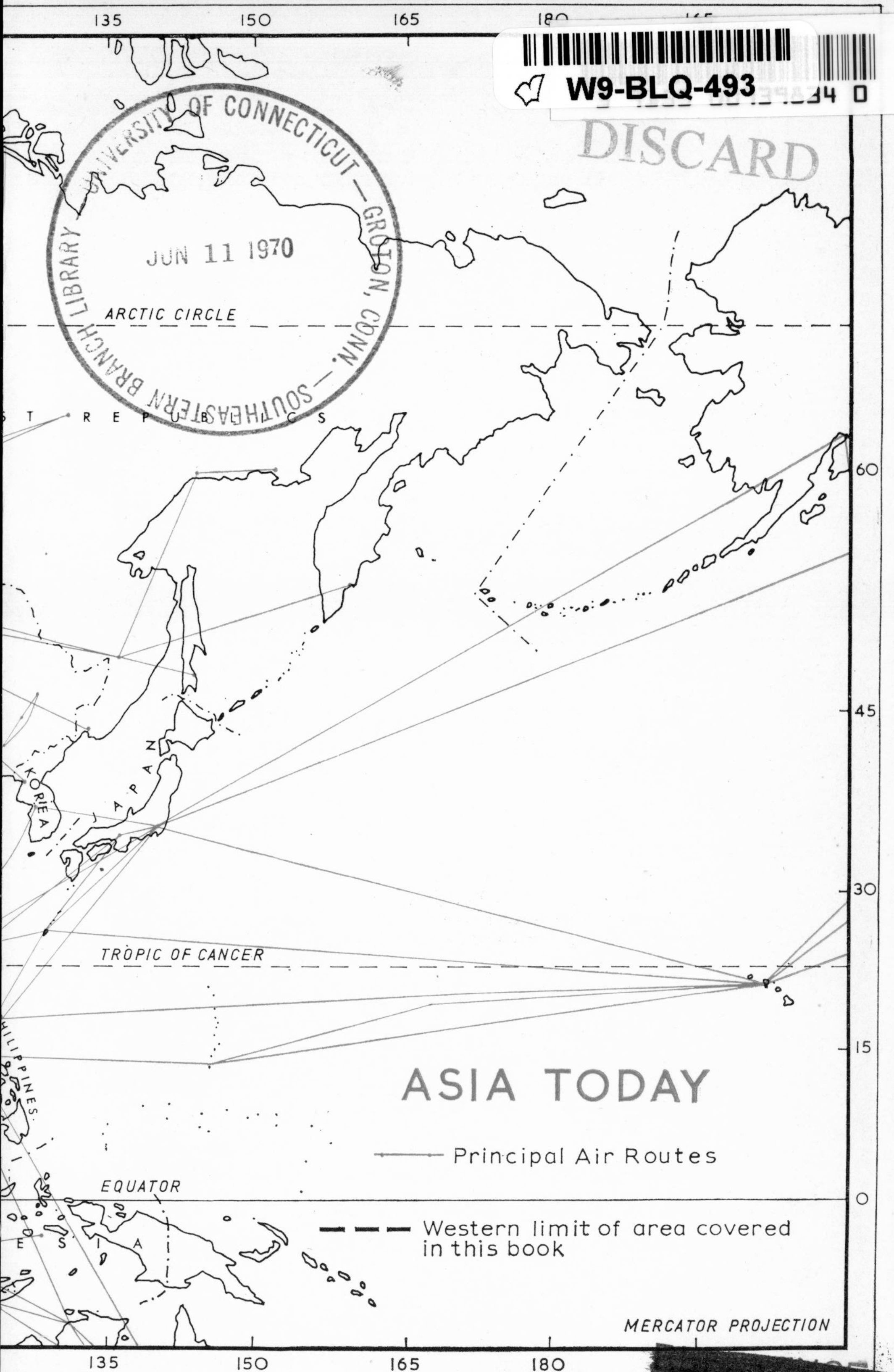

ASIA TODAY

———— Principal Air Routes

EQUATOR

0

— — — Western limit of area covered
in this book

MERCATOR PROJECTION

135 150 165 180

© ANTHONY BLOND

ASIA: A HANDBOOK

ASIA

A HANDBOOK

Edited by

GUY WINT

FREDERICK A. PRAEGER, *Publishers*

New York · Washington

BOOKS THAT MATTER
Published in the United States of America in 1966
by Frederick A. Praeger, Inc., Publishers
111 Fourth Avenue, New York 10003, N.Y.

Third printing 1967

Library of Congress Catalog Card Number: 65 - 13263

Printed in Great Britain

CONTENTS

PAGE

PART TWO: THE COUNTRIES

South Asia

Central Asia

The Far East

South-East Asia

PART THREE: GENERAL

Religion

MAPS

FOREWORD

This book is concerned with a huge area containing over half the world's population. In the last half century much of it has undergone great political and social change, and the remainder seems destined for upheaval no less drastic, whether by revolution or by more orderly processes.

In a continent thus torn by *Sturm und Drang* three areas naturally distinguish themselves. First there is China, so huge a part of Asia, which has become Communist. Its revolution is perhaps the most weighty event of this age. China's vicissitudes, its ambition and its fate will decide much of the future of Asia and of the rest of the world.

Japan is outstanding because, though its history has been tempestuous, it has so far escaped violent revolution and a complete break with its old society. But radical change has fast been taking place. Japan has had such a peculiar history since the Meiji Restoration that it faces problems of an order different from that of other countries in Asia. First in the field as a great power, alone among Asian countries it can claim that it is fully developed. The psychology, outlook and problems of its people are different from those of the rest of Asia.

In most of the other countries of Asia the picture is of the end of colonialism. A row of nations have been reborn, and enter on a restless new life. These new nations show all the signs of growth—over-confidence and lack of confidence, assertiveness and anxiety, adventurousness and conservatism. In each case politics is controlled by nationalism, that simple, rather primitive but all-moving principle that has been incomparably the most pressing force of our time.

All these new states exist in the shadow of their colonial past. They have become free with extraordinary rapidity. Not unnaturally their cultural life has not yet caught up with the political facts, and much of Asia is still weighed down by the Westernization it has gone through in the past three centuries. Part of the Western legacy is of great value, and will not lightly be dissipated. In particular, the British achievement in India still dominates the life of that country and is likely to continue to do so, as the Roman Empire hung over Europe long after it was dissolved.

Much of this book is about relations between the new Asian states and the rest of the world. One fact stands out: Europe, which used to exercise such precedence in world affairs, has been abruptly dwarfed. Today the countries of Asia have asserted themselves and redressed the balance, so that the old inequality is being rapidly removed. Obsequiousness has disappeared, to be replaced by the determination that, in the next century, the east wind, if it does not prevail over the west, will at least blow with equal vigour.

Only in one way has the new Asia so far failed to contribute its share to world civilization. This is in ideas. Asia has borrowed, adapted, synthesized; it has not initiated. For this non-creativity there is undoubtedly an explanation, and it may lie in the fact that so much of the civilization of modern Asia is hybrid, and that the national soul of each of the various countries suffered a deep wound from the thrusting of new philosophies and ways of life upon them.

While writing this introduction I have been reading the superb memoirs of Chateaubriand. At the following passage I stopped. Chateaubriand speaks of the Europe of his day, but does it not equally fit the Asia of ours?—

'Is it possible for a political system to subsist, in which some individuals have so many millions a year, while other individuals are dying of hunger, when religion is no longer there with its other-worldly hopes to explain the sacrifice? There are children whom their mothers feed at their withered breasts for want of a mouthful of bread to give their dying babies; there are families whose members are reduced to huddling together at night for want of blankets to warm them.

'As education reaches down to the lower classes, the latter gradually discover the secret canker which gnaws away at the irreligious social order. The excessive disproportion of conditions and fortunes was endurable as long as it remained concealed; but as soon as this disproportion was generally perceived, the old order received its death blow. Try to convince the poor man, once he has learned to read and ceased to believe, once he has become as well informed as yourself, try to convince him that he must submit to every sort of privation, while his neighbour possesses a thousand times what he needs: in the last resort you would have to kill him.[1]'

The final sentence sounds ominous for the future of Asia. But at least one great cause of killing and convulsion, over-population, may be halted. The devastating torrent of babies, for which until recently no check was possible, seems suddenly likely to be brought under control. The effectiveness and cheapness of new devices of birth control may prove tremendously important.

At present only a minority of the people of Asia takes a part in politics. What will happen when the continent really wakes? In the coming century Asia is to undergo, too, the revolution of the disappearance of distance as it adopts the various devices that speed up communication. The Asiatic continent will be equipped with atomic power, and the countless miracles of material progress will be available to its needs.

The countries of Asia teem with history; it is a very old continent. Though Asia is renascent, in almost none of its countries is there a sense of starting out on a new career. All are more or less sophisticated; in this Asia differs from Africa. That is why in this book so much space is allotted to history, along with the data of the present and surmises about the future. Nobody who wishes to study the future of the continent dare turn his back upon the past.

This book omits the region that has come to be called the Middle East. Political geography has become rather disconnected from the geography

[1] *The Memoirs of Chateaubriand*, ed. and trans. Betty Radice and Robert Baldick, Hamish Hamilton, London, 1961.

taught at school. The Middle East is now a unit which has detached itself from Asia and exists as a kind of sixth continent between Asia and Europe, with fairly well defined boundaries. This book therefore deals with Asia east of Afghanistan. It is true that Pakistan seems to exist in both the Middle East and in Asia; but by and large the division chosen is sharp and definite.

A great variety of facts is set out in this book—in the form of country-by-country basic information and surveys, essays on political, social, economic, cultural and religious aspects of Asia, maps, and extracts from treaties and agreements signed since the last war. Contributors have been deliberately left free to describe the picture as they see it; no attempt has been made to induce a unity of view. It is hoped both that information has been presented in a businesslike manner and that what has been lost in uniformity has been gained in variety and vividness. The guiding principle in editing has been to produce an 'encyclopaedia' that can be read. Asia's problems are exciting, and this book attempts to mirror them.

It has taken longer than expected to get this book through the press, and meanwhile events have occurred remorselessly. Any reference book is bound to be a little out of date as soon as it appears. As this foreword is being written, events are happening in Vietnam, in Kashmir and on the frontiers between India and Pakistan, in Indonesia, Malaysia and China, any one of which could change the whole future of Asia. But the book cannot be held up until the outlook is clear; the most that can be offered is that it may be brought up to date and re-issued from time to time. In the meantime events have been covered up to the end of March 1965.

In committing this book to the press the editor is conscious of the huge amount of work that has gone into it and that is not reflected in the authorship of the contributions. To name everyone who has helped would mean a long list.

To George Patterson I owe a special debt. Himself the author of stimulating books about Asia, he has been responsible for the inclusion of much that is of human interest among the records of fact. I should like to express my deep gratitude to Dr. Werner Klatt for his conscientious and scholarly labours in compiling the Basic Information, and to Miss E. M. J. Campbell of Birkbeck College and Mr. G. R. Versey of University College, University of London, who devoted much time and patience to the preparation of the maps. Also I owe much to the imagination and courtesy of my publisher, Anthony Blond, and his house editor, Antony Wood.

Oxford, September, 1965 GUY WINT

ASIA: A HANDBOOK

PART ONE

BASIC INFORMATION

BASIC INFORMATION

INTRODUCTION

The information here contained has been collected from many sources. International sources have been used wherever available, in order to make possible comparisons from country to country. Preference has been given to the reference books of the United Nations and its specialized agencies; this organization has devoted great efforts, over a number of years, to the collection and standardization of facts and figures derived from national sources of varying validity and quality. Where original sources are lacking or contradictory, not even the United Nations has been able to fill gaps or to eliminate uncertainties. Even such vital data as population figures are unobtainable for some countries, large as well as small.

This section cannot hope to be more informative than its sources. Where a selection has had to be made, all possible bias has been avoided. The interests of this book's likely users have been given priority over all else. As it is intended in this section to provide an international dossier, national weights and measures, be they British, American or the country's own, have had to give way to those used in the publications of the United Nations. However, as this book is a publication in the English language, English weights and measures have been added wherever possible. Asia's trade with Britain and the United States has been shown in every case side by side with that of the largest other trading partner. Wherever possible figures relate to the year 1962; per capita figures are not, however, necessarily based on the 1962 total population figures given. Slight discrepancies between information to be found elsewhere in this book and that given in this section are due to differences in sources and periods covered.

Some of the information here contained, such as the size and location of countries, will remain valid as long as those countries retain their national identity and present boundaries. Other information, such as the size of the population of a given country and its industrial efforts, is bound to become out of date in the not too distant future. Indeed, some of the latest data available has already been superseded by events. Preference has been given to information likely to remain relevant for some time after publication. The list of sources on the next page will enable the user of this book to find new information where that given has become out of date.

Tibet is not included in Part One as insufficient data is available since the country was incorporated in China following the entry of the Chinese Army in 1950. Bhutan, Sikkim, Brunei, Sabah, Sarawak and Macao are also excluded for lack of factual information.

MAIN SOURCES

United Nations Publications

Yearbook of the United Nations, 1963, New York, 1965
Statistical Yearbook, 1963, New York, 1964
Yearbook of National Accounts Statistics, 1963, New York, 1964
Yearbook of International Trade Statistics, 1962, New York, 1964
World Economic Survey, 1964, New York, 1965
UN Economic Survey of Asia and the Far East, 1964, Bangkok, 1965
UN Economic Bulletin for Asia and the Far East, 1964, Bangkok, 1964
Production Yearbook, 1964 (FAO), Rome, 1964
Yearbook of Labour Statistics, 1964 (ILO), Geneva, 1964
Statistical Yearbook, 1963 (UNESCO), Paris, 1964
World Communications (UNESCO), Paris, 1964
Report on the World Health Situaton (WHO), Geneva, 1963

Other Sources

ABC, *World Airways Guide*, London, 1965
Agency for International Development, *US Foreign Assistance, 1945-1963*, Washington, 1963
Central Statistical Office (London), *Annual Abstract of Statistics, 1964*, London, 1964
S. H. Steinberg (ed.), *The Statesman's Yearbook, 1964-1965*, London, 1964
US Department of State, *Profiles of Newly Independent States*, Washington, 1964
US Department of State, *Status of the World's Nations*, Washington, 1965
Meteorological Office, London, *Tables of Temperature, Relative Humidity and Precipitation for the World—Part V: Asia* (MO 617E), London, 1958

KEY TO TERMS AND ABBREVIATIONS USED

comm. = commercial
Food, etc. = Food, Drink and Tobacco
Foreign Aid = Civilian Aid
GNP = Gross National Product
GRT = Gross Registered Ton(s)
ha. = hectare(s)
inh. = inhabitants
kW = kilowatt(s)
kWh = kilowatthour(s)
mill. = million
milliard (UK) = billion (US)
n.a. = not available
N,P_2O_5,K_2O = Nutrient Content
NRT = Net Registered Ton(s)
per head of population (pop.) = not always based on latest data
ton = metric ton
$=US $
— = nil or none

EQUIVALENT WEIGHTS AND MEASURES

1 kilometre	= 0·62 mile
1 square kilometre	= 0·39 square mile
1 hectare	= 0·47 acre
1 centimetre	= 0·39 inch
1 kilogram	= 2·20 lbs
1 metric ton	= 0·98 long ton
1 metric ton	= 1·10 short tons
1 mile	= 1·61 kilometres
1 square mile	= 2·59 square kilometres
1 acre	= 0·40 hectare
1 inch	= 2·54 centimetres
1 lb	= 0·45 kilogram
1 long ton	= 1·02 metric tons
1 short ton	= 0·91 metric ton

SOUTH ASIA

INDIA

1. *Area:* 3·04 mill. sq. km. (1·17 mill. sq. miles).
2. *Population:* 449·5 mill. (excl. Pakistan-occupied Jammu and Kashmir).
3. *Density of Population:* 148 per sq. km. (383 per sq. mile).
4. *Rate of Population Increase:* 1·93 per cent.
5. *Birth Rate:* 3·83 per cent.
6. *Death Rate:* 1·9 per cent.
7. *Geographical Location:* 8°N–33°N; 68°E–97°E.
8. *Capital:* Delhi (2·15 mill.). Other principal towns: Bombay (4·31 mill.) Calcutta (2·96 mill.); Madras (1·77 mill.).
9. *Mean Temperature:* Delhi (714 ft.) 57°F (14°C) Jan., 92°F (33°C) June; Bombay (37 ft.) 75°F (24°C) Jan., 85°F (29°C) May; Calcutta (21 ft.) 67°F (19°C) Jan., 86°F (30°C) May; Madras (51 ft.) 76F° (24°C) Jan., 91°F (33°C) May.
10. *Mean Annual Rainfall:* Delhi 25·2 in. (640 mm.); Bombay 71·2 in. (1,783 mm.) Calcutta 63 in. (1,600 mm.); Madras 50 in. (1,270 mm.).
11. *Political Status:* Democratic Republic Union of States since 26/1/1950; independent since 15/8/1947.
12. *International Affiliations:* United Nations; British Commonwealth; Sterling Area; Colombo Plan.
13. *Head of State:* Dr. Sarvepalli Radhakrishnan, President of the Republic.
14. *Head of Government:* Lal Bahadur Shastri, Prime Minister.
15. *Political Institutions:* House of the People (Lower House); Council of States (Upper House).
16. *Political Parties:* House of People, 1963: Congress 359; Communists 33; Swatantra 26; Jan Sangh 13; Praja Socialists 12; others 33; Independent 15.
17. *Languages:* Hindi (of the Devenagari script). English (due for review in 1975). 13 other approved languages.
18. *Religions:* Hindus 366·5 mill.; Sikhs 7·8 mill.; Jains 2 mill.; Buddhists 3·2 mill.; Muslims 46·9 mill.; Christians 10·7 mill.
19. *Working Population:* 43 per cent of total.
20. *Urban Population:* 18 per cent of total.
21. *Illiteracy:* 77 per cent of over 10 years of age.
22. *Expenditure on Education:* 2·4 per cent of GNP.
23. *Primary Schools:* 319,000 schools; 732,000 teachers; 32 mill. pupils.
24. *Secondary Schools:* 57,600 schools; 562,000 teachers; 9 mill. pupils.
25. *School Enrolment:* 31 per cent of 5-19 years.
26. *Students (Higher Education):* 1·44 mill.
27. *Physicians:* 85,000; 1 per 5,300 inh.
28. *Hospital Beds:* 98,000; 0·2 per thous. inh.
29. *Newspapers:* 465; circ. of 313: 4·6 mill.; 11 per thous.
30. *Newsprint:* 0·3 kilos per head.
31. *Newspapers:* In Hindi, English and 11 other languages.
32. *News Agencies:* Press Trust—PTI; United News—UNI.
33. *Radio Transmitters:* 60; 1,373 kW.
34. *Broadcasting:* All-India Radio.
35. *Radio Licences:* 3·1 mill.; 6 per thous.
36. *TV Licences:* 750.
37. *Cinemas:* 3,400; seating capacity 2·4 mill.; 6 seats per thous.
38. *Cinema Attendance:* 1·4 mill.; 3 per head of pop.

39. *Net Domestic Product:* 154·8 milliard Rupees; Growth Rate: 3·5 per cent p.a.

40. *Gross Domestic Product:* $32·5 milliard; GNP: $73 per head of pop.

41. *Private Consumption:* n.a.

42. *Wages Fund:* n.a.

43. *Expenditure on Food, etc.*: n.a.

44. *Expenditure on Household Goods:* n.a.

45. *Agricultural Population:* 70 per cent of working pop. Farms under 5 ha. (12·5 acres): 80 per cent of holdings; 40 per cent of area.

46. *Arable Land:* 160·9 mill. ha. (402 mill. acres); 0·35 ha. (0·85 acres) per head. Irrigated Land: 24·4 mill. ha.

47. *Production of Paddy:* 34·8 mill. ha. (87 mill. acres); 48 mill. tons; 1·38 tons per ha. (0·55 tons per acre).

48. *Production of Grains:* 84·7 mill. tons. 188 kilos per head of pop.

49. *Production of Sugar:* 2·3 mill. tons; Tea 343,000 tons; Cotton 944,000 tons.

50. *Livestock:* Cattle 176 mill.; Pigs 5 mill.; Sheep and Goats 101 mill.

51. *Production of Fertilizers* (thous. tons): N:194, P_2O_5:88.

52. *Consumption of Fertilizers* (thous. tons): N:426; P_2O_5: 92; K_2O: 36. Total: 3·5 kilos per ha. (3 lb. per acre).

53. *Development Programme:* Fourth Five-Year Plan 1965/66-70/71.

54. *Development Projects:* heavy industry (public); light industry (private); irrigation; communications; social services.

55. *Energy Production:* 64·2 mill. tons coal equivalent.

56. *Energy Consumption:* 73·1 mill. tons coal equivalent; 162 kilos per head.

57. *Electricity Installed:* 6·7 mill. kW.

58. *Electricity Output:* 25·8 milliard kWh.

59. *Production of Coal:* 61·4 mill. tons.

60. *Production of Mineral Oil:* 1 mill. tons.

61. *Production of Iron Ore:* 8·1 mill. tons.

62. *Production of Manganese Ore:* 0·5 mill. tons.

63. *Production of Steel:* 5·1 mill. tons.

64. *Consumption of Steel:* 6·4 mill. tons; 14 kilos per head of pop.

65. *Production of Cotton:* 14 mill. spindles; 860,000 tons cotton yarn.

66. *Consumption of Cotton:* 1·07 mill. tons; 2·4 kilos per head of pop.

67. *Production of Cement:* 8·6 mill. tons.

68. *Production of Petrol*: 6·1 mill. tons.

69. *Production of Motor Vehicles:* 31,000 pass. cars; 27,000 comm. vehicles.

70. *Production of Merchant Vessels:* 22,000 GRT.

71. *Telephones Installed:* 593,500.

72. *Letters Received:* 3,859 mill.; 9 per head of pop.

73. *Railway Transport:* 85 mill. pass./km.; 83 mill. ton/km.

74. *Motor Transport:* 312,000 pass. cars; 274,000 comm. vehicles in use.

75. *Sea Transport:* 16·6 mill. NRT entered; 12·0 mill. NRT cleared. Merchant Fleet: 1·2 mill. GRT.

76. *Sea Transport:* 6·7 mill. tons loaded; 16·6 mill. tons unloaded.

77. *Civilian Airlines:* Air India International, Bombay; Indian Airlines Corporation, New Delhi.

78. *Air Transport:* 1,461 mill. pass./km; 47 mill. ton/km.

79. *Foreign Trade* (mill. R.): Imports 10,771; Exports 6,937; Balance −3,834.

80. *Foreign Trade:* Imports $5 per head; Exports $3 per head.

81. *Foreign Trade* (mill. R.): Imports: UK 1,783; USA 3,153; W. Germany 965. Exports: UK 1,627; USA 1,170; USSR 383.

82. *Foreign Trade* (mill. R.): Imports: Machines 3,724; Other Manuf. 1,985; Foods 1,523. Exports: Manuf. 2,722; Raw Mat. 1,117; Tea 1,292.

83. *Foreign Aid:* USA: 1946-63: $4,718 mill. UK: 1945-63: £48 mill.

84. *Foreign Aid:* Sino-Soviet: 1956-63: $1,250 mill. offered; $500 mill. drawn.

85. *Public Finance:* (lacks R.): Revenue 1,500,25; Expenditure 1,522,31.

86. *Government Obligations* (crores R.): 7,700.

87. *Foreign Exchange:* £1 sterling = 13·33 Rupees; US $1 = 4·76 Rupees.

88. *Foreign Exchange:* 1 Rupee = 1s. 6d.; 1 Rupee = US $0·21.

89. *Tourism:* 150,000 tourists. Tourist Centres: Delhi; Amritsar; Chandigarh; Benares; Srinagar; Bombay; Calcutta; Darjeeling; Madras.

90. *Visa Requirements:* British subjects: no visa. US citizens: visa required. Import and export of Indian currency limited to 75 Rupees.

NEPAL

1. *Area:* 141,000 sq. km. (54,000 sq. miles).
2. *Population:* 9·5 mill.
3. *Density of Population:* 68 per sq. km. (177 per sq. mile).
4. *Rate of Population Increase:* 1·5 per cent.
5. *Birth Rate:* 4·5 per cent.
6. *Death Rate:* 3 per cent.
7. *Geographical Location:* 26° 30′N–30° 30′N; 80°E–88° 30′E.
8. *Capital:* Katmandu (0·2 mill.).
9. *Mean Temperature:* Katmandu (2,592 ft.) 30°F (−1°C) Jan., 68°F (20°C) July.
10. *Mean Annual Rainfall:* Katmandu 17·4 in. (442 mm.).
11. *Political Status:* Constitutional Monarchical Hindu State.
12. *International Affiliations:* United Nations; Colombo Plan.
13. *Head of State:* Mahendra Bir Bikram Jang Sha Deva, ruling King.
14. *Head of Government:* Surya Bahadur Thapa, Chairman of Council of Ministers.
15. *Political Institutions:* National Guidance Council.
16. *Political Parties:* Banned in December 1960.
17. *Languages:* Nepali; English.
18. *Religions:* Sanatan Hinduism; Buddhism.
19. *Working Population:* 49 per cent of total.
20. *Urban Population:* 3 per cent of total.
21. *Illiteracy:* 95 per cent of over 10 years of age.
22. *Expenditure on Education:* n.a.
23. *Primary Schools:* 3,200 schools; 4,000 teachers; 150,000 pupils.
24. *Secondary Schools:* 550 schools, 3,000 teachers; 60,000 pupils.
25. *School Enrolment:* 10 per cent of 5-19 years.
26. *Students (Higher Education):* 6,000.
27. *Physicians:* 130; 1 per 73,000.
28. *Hospital Beds:* 1,140; 0·1 per thous.
29. *Newspapers:* 13; circ. 7,000. 0·8 per thous.
30. *Newsprint:* 0·01 kilos per head.
31. *Newspapers:* In English, Nepali, Hindi.
32. *News Agency:* Rashtrija Sambad Samiti.
33. *Radio Transmitters:* 2; 25 kW.
34. *Broadcasting:* Radio Nepal.
35. *Radio Receivers:* 13,000; 1 per thous.
36. *TV Receivers:* —
37. *Cinemas:* n.a.
38. *Cinema Attendance:* n.a.
39. *Gross National Product:* n.a.
40. *Gross Domestic Product:* \$446 mill.; GNP: \$50 per head of pop.
41. *Private Consumption:* n.a.
42. *Wages Fund:* n.a.
43. *Expenditure on Food, etc.:* n.a.
44. *Expenditure on Household Goods:* n.a.
45. *Agricultural Population:* 93 per cent of working pop.
46. *Arable Land:* 3·9 mill. ha. (9·8 mill. acres); 0·4 ha. (1 acre) per head.
47. *Production of Paddy:* 1·4 mill. ha. (3·5 mill. acres); 1·2 mill. tons; 0·9 ton per ha. (0·35 ton per acre).
48. *Production of Grains:* 1·2 mill. tons; 130 kilos per head of pop.
49. *Production of Sugar:* —
50. *Livestock:* n.a.
51. *Production of Fertilizers:* —
52. *Consumption of Fertilizers:* n.a.
53. *Development Programme:* Three-year Plan, 1962-65.
54. *Development Projects:* Priority to industry, transport and communications.
55. *Energy Production:* —
56. *Energy Consumption:* 0·04 mill. tons coal equivalent; 4 kilos per head.
57. *Electricity Installed:* 6,000 kW.
58. *Electricity Output:* 11 million kWh.
59. *Production of Coal:* —
60. *Production of Mineral Oil:* —
61. *Production of Iron Ore:* —
62. *Production of Manganese Ore:* —
63. *Production of Steel:* —
64. *Consumption of Steel:* —

65. *Production of Cotton:* —
66. *Consumption of Cotton:* n.a.
67. *Production of Cement:* —
68. *Production of Petrol:* —
69. *Production of Motor Vehicles:* —
70. *Production of Merchant Vessels:* —
71. *Telephones Installed:* 1,200.
72. *Letters Received:* n.a.
73. *Railway Transport:* n.a.
74. *Motor Transport:* n.a.
75. *Sea Transport:* —
76. *Sea Transport:* —
77. *Civilian Airline:* Royal Nepal Airline Corporation (RNAC).
78. *Air Transport:* n.a.
79. *Foreign Trade:* n.a.
80. *Foreign Trade:* n.a.
81. *Foreign Trade:* n.a.
82. *Foreign Trade:* n.a.
83. *Foreign Aid:* USA: 1946-63: $53 mill.
84. *Foreign Aid:* Sino-Soviet: 1956-63: $65 mill. offered; $15 mill. drawn.
85. *Public Finance:* n.a.
86. *Government Obligations:* n.a.
87. *Foreign Exchange:* £1 sterling = 21·30 Rupie; US $1 = 7·60 Rupie.
88. *Foreign Exchange:* 1 Rupie = 11d; 1 Rupie = US$0·13.
89. *Tourism:* Tourist centres: Katmandu; Katmandu Valley.
90. *Visa Requirements:* Tourist visa obtainable with minimum of formality (valid for 7 days).

PAKISTAN

1. *Area:* 947,000 sq. km. (366,000 sq. miles).
2. *Population:* 96·6 mill.
3. *Density of Population:* 102 per sq. km. (265 per sq. mile).
4. *Rate of Population Increase:* 2·1 per cent.
5. *Birth Rate:* n.a.
6. *Death Rate:* n.a.
7. *Geographical Location:* West Pakistan: 23° 30′N–38° 30′N; 61° 30′E–75° 45′E. East Pakistan: 20° 30′N–26° 30′N; 88°E–92° 30′E.
8. *Capital:* Rawalpindi (0·34 mill.). Other principal towns: Karachi (1·91 mill.); Lahore (1·3 mill.); Dacca (East Pak.) (0·56 mill.).
9. *Mean Temperature:* Karachi (13 ft.) 66°F (19°C) Jan., 87°F (31°C) June ; Lahore (702 ft.) 54°F (12°C) Jan., 92°F (33°C) June; Dacca (35 ft.) 65°F (18°C) Jan., 83°F (28°C) May; Chittagong (87 ft.) 67°F (19°C) Jan., 82°F (28°C) June.
10. *Mean Annual Rainfall:* Karachi 7·7 in. (196 mm.); Lahore 19·8 in. (503 mm.); Dacca 74·2 in. (1,885 mm.); Chittagong 107·5 in. (2,731 mm.).
11. *Political Status:* Islamic Republic since 23/3/1956; independent since 14/8/1947.
12. *International Affiliations:* United Nations; British Commonwealth; Sterling Area; Colombo Plan; CENTO and SEATO.
13. *Head of State:* Mohammed Ayub Khan, President.
14. *Head of Government:* Mohammed Ayub Khan, Field-Marshal, Commander in Chief, Minister of Defence.
15. *Political Institutions:* Constitution abrogated 7/10/1958; New Constitution 1/3/1962. National Assembly.
16. *Political Parties:* 1965: Pakistan Muslim League 119; Combined Opposition Parties 15; Independent 16.
17. *Languages:* Urdu (West Pakistan); Bengali (East Pakistan); English (until 1972). Also Sindhi; Punjabi; Pashto; Balochi.
18. *Religions:* Muslims 86 per cent; Hindus 12 per cent; Buddhists 1 per cent; Christians 1 per cent.
19. *Working Population:* 33 per cent of total.
20. *Urban Population:* 13 per cent of total.
21. *Illiteracy:* 72 per cent of over 10 years of age.
22. *Expenditure on Education:* 1·2 per cent of GNP.
23. *Primary Schools:* 48,000 schools; 130,000 teachers; 5 mill. pupils.
24. *Secondary Schools:* 6,000 schools; 63,000 teachers; 1·5 mill. pupils.
25. *School Enrolment:* 26 per cent of 5-19 years.
26. *Students (Higher Education):* 175,000.
27. *Physicians:* n.a.
28. *Hospital Beds:* n.a.
29. *Newspapers:* 99; circ. 500,000; 5 per thous.
30. *Newsprint:* 0·3 kilos per head.
31. *Newspapers:* In Urdu, English, Sindhi, Bengali.
32. *News Agencies:* APP; PPA.
33. *Radio Transmitters:* 23; 223 kW.
34. *Broadcasting:* Radio Pakistan.
35. *Radio Licences:* 280,000; 3 per thous.
36. *TV Licences:* —
37. *Cinemas:* 390; seating capacity 195,000; 2 seats per thous.
38. *Cinema Attendance:* 80 mill.; 1 per head of pop.
39. *Net Domestic Product:* 32·6 milliard Rupees; Growth Rate: 2·7 per cent p.a.
40. *Gross Domestic Product:* $7 milliard; GNP: $74 per head of pop.
41. *Private Consumption:* 75 per cent of GNP.
42. *Wages Fund:* n.a.
43. *Expenditure on Food, etc.*: n.a.
44. *Expenditure on Household Goods:* n.a.

45. *Agricultural Population:* 75 per cent of working pop. Farms under 5 ha. (12·5 acres): 89 per cent of holdings; 47 per cent of area.

46. *Arable Land:* 25·5 mill. ha. (64 mill. acres); 0·25 ha. (0·65 acres) per head. Irrigated Land: 11 mill. ha.

47. *Production of Paddy:* 10 mill. ha. (25 mill. acres); 14·8 mill. tons; 1·5 tons per ha. (0·6 ton per acre).

48. *Production of Grains:* 20 mill. tons; 210 kilos per head of pop.

49. *Production of Sugar:* 300,000 tons; Jute 950,000 tons; Cotton 350,000 tons.

50. *Livestock:* Cattle 24 mill.; Pigs 0·1 mill.; Sheep and Goats 18 mill.

51. *Production of Fertilizers* (thous. tons): N: 24.

52. *Consumption of Fertilizers* (thous. tons): N:62; P_2O_5: 11; K_2O: 6. Total: 3 kilos per ha. (3 lbs per acre).

53. *Development Programme:* Five-Year Plan 1960-65.

54. *Development Projects:* Industry 26 per cent; Agriculture 27 per cent; Public Utilities 25 per cent; Services 22 per cent of Gross Investment.

55. *Energy Production:* 3 mill. tons coal equivalent.

56. *Energy Consumption:* 7·3 mill. tons coal equivalent; 75 kilos per head.

57. *Electricity Installed:* 0·8 mill. kW.

58. *Electricity Output:* 2·3 milliard kWh.

59. *Production of Coal:* 1 mill. tons.

60. *Production of Mineral Oil:* 0·4 mill. tons.

61. *Production of Iron Ore:* 1,000 tons.

62. *Production of Manganese Ore:* —

63. *Production of Steel:* 7,000 tons.

64. *Consumption of Steel:* 0·65 mill. tons; 7 kilos per head of pop.

65. *Production of Cotton:* 2·1 mill. spindles; 200,000 tons cotton yarn.

66. *Consumption of Cotton:* 250,000 tons; 2·6 kilos per head of pop.

67. *Production of Cement:* 1·4 mill. tons.

68. *Production of Petrol:* 0·6 mill. tons.

69. *Production of Motor Vehicles:* —

70. *Production of Merchant Vessels:* —

71. *Telephones Installed:* 94,200.

72. *Letters Received:* 718 mill.; 7 per head.

73. *Railway Transport:* 12 millard pass./km.; 8·8 milliard ton/km.

74. *Motor Transport:* 60,000 pass. cars; 31,000 comm. vehicles in use.

75. *Sea Transport:* 9·1 mill. NRT entered; 7·8 mill. NRT cleared. Merchant Fleet: 0·3 mill. GRT.

76. *Sea Transport:* 2·3 mill. tons loaded; 5·8 mill. tons unloaded.

77. *Civilian Airline:* Pakistan International Airlines (PIA), Karachi.

78. *Air Transport:* 642 mill. pass./km.; 26·4 mill. ton/km.

79. *Foreign Trade* (mill. R.): Imports 3,515; Exports 1,892; Balance −1,623.

80. *Foreign Trade:* Imports \$8 per head; Exports \$4 per head.

81. *Foreign Trade* (mill. R.): Imports: UK 627; USA 1,334; W. Germany 330. Exports: UK 329; USA 173: India 189.

82. *Foreign Trade* (mill. R.): Imports: Machines 1,377: Manuf. 757; Foods 293. Exports: Jute 774; Jute Fabrics 310; Rice 116.

83. *Foreign Aid:* USA: 1946-63: \$2,227 mill. UK: 1945-63: £39 mill.

84. *Foreign Aid:* Sino-Soviet: 1956-63: \$125 mill. offered; \$25 mill. drawn.

85. *Public Finance:* n.a.

86. *Government Obligations:* n.a.

87. *Foreign Exchange:* £1 sterling = 13·33 Rupees; US\$1 = 4·76 Rupees.

88. *Foreign Exchange:* 1 Rupee = 1s. 6d; 1 Rupee = US\$0·21.

89. *Tourism:* Tourist centres: West Pakistan: Karachi; Lahore; Peshawar; Khyber Pass. East Pakistan: Dacca; Chittagong.

90. *Visa Requirements:* British subjects: no visa. US citizens: visa required.

CEYLON

1. *Area:* 66,000 sq. km. (25,000 sq. miles).
2. *Population:* 10·4 mill.
3. *Density of Population:* 159 per sq. km. (413 per sq. mile).
4. *Rate of Population Increase:* 2·8 per cent.
5. *Birth Rate:* 3·66 per cent.
6. *Death Rate:* 0·86 per cent.
7. *Geographical Location:* 5°N–10°N; 78°E–82°E.
8. *Capital:* Colombo (0·5 mill.).
9. *Mean Temperature:* Colombo (24 ft.) 79°F (26°C) Jan., 82°F (28°C) May; Nuwara Eliya (6,168 ft.) 57°F (14°C) Jan., 61°F (16°C) May.
10. *Mean Annual Rainfall:* Colombo 93·1 in. (2,365 mm.); Nuwara Eliya 91·8 in. (2,332 mm.).
11. *Political Status:* Dominion of Ceylon; independent since 4/2/1948.
12. *International Affiliations:* United Nations; British Commonwealth; Sterling Area; Colombo Plan.
13. *Head of State:* William Gopallawa, Governor-General.
14. *Head of Government:* Dudley Senanayake, Prime Minister.
15. *Political Institutions:* House of Representatives (Lower House); Senate (Upper House).
16. *Political Parties:* House of Reps, 1965: United National Party 66; Sri Lanka Freedom Party 41; Lanka Sama Samaji Party 24; Communist Party 9; Independent 3.
17. *Languages:* Sinhalese; Tamil; English.
18. *Religions:* Buddhists 5·2 mill.; Hindus 1·6 mill.; Christians 0·8 mill.; Muslims 0·5 mill.
19. *Working Population:* 37 per cent of total.
20. *Urban Population:* 15 per cent of total.
21. *Illiteracy:* 24 per cent of over 10 years of age.
22. *Expenditure on Education:* 4·5 per cent of GNP.
23. *Primary Schools:* 8,400 schools; 76,000 teachers; 2·3 mill. pupils.
24. *Secondary Schools:* Included under *Primary Schools.*
25. *School Enrolment:* 74 per cent of 5-19 years.
26. *Students (Higher Education):* 12,000.
27. *Physicians:* 2,000; 1 per 4,700 inh.
28. *Hospital Beds:* 30,600; 3 per thous.
29. *Newspapers:* 8; circ. 350,000; 37 per thous.
30. *Newsprint:* 1·2 kilos per head.
31. *Newspapers:* In Sinhalese, Tamil, English.
32. *News Agency:* Press Trust.
33. *Radio Transmitters:* 23; 463 kW.
34. *Broadcasting:* Radio Ceylon.
35. *Radio Licences:* 390,000; 38 per thous.
36. *TV Licences:* —
37. *Cinemas:* 318; seating capacity 180,000; 20 seats per thous.
38. *Cinema Attendance:* 27 mill.; 3 per head of pop.
39. *Gross National Product:* 6·8 milliard Rupees; Growth Rate: 3·7 per cent p.a.
40. *Gross Domestic Product:* $1·3 milliard; GNP: $129 per head of pop.
41. *Private Consumption:* 73 per cent of GNP.
42. *Wages Fund:* 49 per cent of Nat. Inc.
43. *Expenditure on Food, etc.:* 60 per cent of private consumption.
44. *Expenditure on Household Goods:* 9 per cent of private consumption.
45. *Agricultural Population:* 53 per cent of working pop.
46. *Arable Land:* 1·5 mill. ha. (3·7 mill. acres); 0·15 ha. (0·35 acres) per head. Irrigated Land: 370,000 ha.

47. *Production of Paddy:* 0·6 mill. ha. (1·5 mill. acres); 1 mill. tons; 1·66 tons per ha. (0·65 tons per acre).

49. *Production of Tea:* 200,000 tons.

51. *Production of Fertilizers:* —

53. *Development Programme:* Ten-Year Plan 1959-68.

55. *Energy Production:* —

57. *Electricity Installed:* 94,000 kW.

59. *Production of Coal:* —

61. *Production of Iron Ore:* —

63. *Production of Steel:* —

65. *Production of Cotton:* —

67. *Production of Cement:* 85,000 tons.

69. *Production of Motor Vehicles:* —

71. *Telephones Installed:* 38,600.

73. *Railway Transport:* 2 milliard pass./km. 300 mill. ton/km.

75. *Sea Transport:* 5 mill. NRT entered; 4·4 mill. NRT cleared.

77. *Civilian Airline:* Air Ceylon, Colombo.

79. *Foreign Trade* (mill. R.): Imports 1,660; Exports 1,808; Balance +148.

81. *Foreign Trade* (mill. R.): Imports: UK 342; USA 47; Burma 189. Exports: UK 529; USA 152; China 133.

83. *Foreign Aid:* USA: 1946-63: $88 mill.

85. *Public Finance:* n.a.

87. *Foreign Exchange:* £1 sterling = 13·33 Rupees. US$1 = 4·76 Rupees.

89. *Tourism:* Colombo; Kandy; Nuwara Eliya; Anuradhapura; Polonnaruwa.

48. *Production of Grains:* 1 mill. tons; 100 kilos per head of pop.

50. *Livestock:* Cattle 1·3 mill.; Sheep and Goats 0·5 mill.

52. *Consumption of Fertilizers* (thous. tons): N:40; P_2O_5:1; K_2O:30. Total: 48 kilos per ha. (42 lbs. per acre).

54. *Development Projects:* Emphasis on agriculture, manufacturing and services. Gross Investment to double in 10 years.

56. *Energy Consumption:* 1·2 mill. tons coal equivalent; 118 kilos per head.

58. *Electricity Output:* 328 mill. kWh.

60. *Production of Mineral Oil:* —

62. *Production of Manganese Ore:* —

64. *Consumption of Steel:* 0·2 mill. tons; 19 kilos per head of pop.

66. *Consumption of Cotton:* n.a.

68. *Production of Petrol:* —

70. *Production of Merchant Vessels:* —

72. *Letters Received:* 335 mill.; 32 per head.

74. *Motor Transport:* 83,000 pass. cars; 35,000 comm. vehicles in use.

76. *Sea Transport:* 1 mill. tons loaded; 4·5 mill. tons unloaded.

78. *Air Transport:* 38·7 mill. pass./km.; 0·7 mill. ton/km.

80. *Foreign Trade:* Imports $34 per head; Exports $37 per head.

82. *Foreign Trade* (mill. R.): Imports: Foods 629; Manuf. 408; Machines 215. Exports: Tea 1,148; Rubber 290; Veg. Oils 112.

84. *Foreign Aid:* Sino-Soviet: 1956-63: $80 mill. offered; $25 mill. drawn.

86. *Government Obligations:* n.a.

88. *Foreign Exchange:* 1 Rupee = 1s. 6d; 1 Rupee = US$0·21.

90. *Visa Requirements:* British and US American tourists: no visa. Import of Rupees limited to 75 in Indian, Pakistani or Ceylon currency.

CENTRAL ASIA

MONGOLIA

1. *Area:* 1·55 mill. sq. km. (0·6 mill. sq. miles).
2. *Population:* 1 mill.
3. *Density of Population:* 0·6 per sq. km. (2 per sq. mile).
4. *Rate of Population Increase:* 2·8 per cent.
5. *Birth Rate:* 3·92 per cent.
6. *Death Rate:* 1·12 per cent.
7. *Geographical Location:* 42°N–52°N; 87°E–120°E.
8. *Capital:* Ulan Bator (0·2 mill.).
9. *Mean Temperature:* Ulan Bator (4,347 ft.) −14°F (−26°C) Jan., 61°F (16°C) July.
10. *Mean Annual Rainfall:* Ulan Bator 8·2 in. (208 mm.).
11. *Political Status:* People's Republic; independent since 5/1/1946.
12. *International Affiliations:* United Nations; Treaties with the Soviet Union and the People's Republic of China; COMECON.
13. *Head of State:* Zsamsarangin Sambu, Chairman of Presidium, Great People's Khural.
14. *Head of Government:* Yumjaagin Tsedenbal, Chairman of Council of Ministers.
15. *Political Institutions:* Great People's Khural.
16. *Political Party:* Mongolian People's Revolutionary (Communist) Party (50,000 members).
17. *Language:* Mongol.
18. *Religion:* Buddhism (Lamaism).
19. *Working Population:* n.a.
20. *Urban Population:* n.a.
21. *Illiteracy:* n.a.
22. *Expenditure on Education:* n.a.
23. *Primary Schools:* 400 schools; 100,000 pupils.
24. *Secondary Schools:* 40 schools; 7,000 pupils.
25. *School Enrolment:* 46 per cent of 5-19 years.
26. *Students (Higher Education):* n.a.
27. *Physicians:* n.a.
28. *Hospital Beds:* n.a.
29. *Newspapers:* 3; circ. 100,000; 103 per thous.
30. *Newsprint:* n.a.
31. *Newspapers:* In Mongol.
32. *News Agency:* Monsame.
33. *Radio Transmitters:* 3; 225 kW.
34. *Broadcasting:* Ulan Bator Radio.
35. *Radio Receivers:* 25,000; 25 per thous.
36. *TV Receivers:* —
37. *Cinemas:* 10.
38. *Cinema Attendance:* n.a.
39. *Gross National Product:* n.a.
40. *Gross Domestic Product:* n.a.
41. *Private Consumption:* n.a.
42. *Wages Fund:* n.a.
43. *Expenditure on Food, etc.:* n.a.
44. *Expenditure on Household Goods:* n.a.
45. *Agricultural Population:* n.a.
46. *Arable Land:* n.a.
47. *Production of Paddy:* n.a.
48. *Production of Grains:* 0·3 mill. tons; 300 kilos per head of pop.
49. *Production of Sugar:* —
50. *Livestock:* Sheep 12 mill.; Goats 5·5 mill.; Horses, Cattle and Camels 5·5 mill.
51. *Production of Fertilizers:* —
52. *Consumption of Fertilizers:* n.a.

53. *Development Programme:* Five-Year Plan 1961-65.

54. *Development Projects:* Industrial centres (Ulan Bator and Darhan Region); food industries.

55. *Energy Production:* n.a.

56. *Energy Consumption:* n.a.

57. *Electricity Installed:* n.a.

58. *Electricity Output:* 150 million kWh.

59. *Production of Coal:* 0·8 mill. tons.

60. *Production of Mineral Oil:* —

61. *Production of Iron Ore:* —

62. *Production of Manganese Ore:* —

63. *Production of Steel:* —

64. *Consumption of Steel:* —

65. *Production of Cotton:* —

66. *Consumption of Cotton:* n.a.

67. *Production of Cement:* 50,000 tons.

68. *Production of Petrol:* —

69. *Production of Motor Vehicles:* —

70. *Production of Merchant Vessels:* —

71. *Telephones Installed:* 10,500.

72. *Letters Received:* n.a.

73. *Railway Transport:* n.a.

74. *Motor Transport:* n.a.

75. *Sea Transport:* —

76. *Sea Transport:* —

77. *Civilian Airline:* Air Transport Administration (UVS–MNR), Ulan Bator.

78. *Air Transport:* n.a.

79. *Foreign Trade:* n.a.

80. *Foreign Trade:* n.a.

81. *Foreign Trade:* n.a.

82. *Foreign Trade:* n.a.

83. *Foreign Aid:* Western: —

84. *Foreign Aid:* Sino-Soviet: 1956-63: \$630 mill. (Soviet \$485 mill.; Chinese \$115 mill.) offered.

85. *Public Finance:* n.a.

86. *Government Obligations:* n.a.

87. *Foreign Exchange:* £1 sterling = 11·20 Tughrik; US\$1 = 4 Tughrik.

88. *Foreign Exchange:* 1 Tughrik = 1s. 9d; 1 Tughrik = US\$0.25.

89. *Tourism:* Tourist centres: Ulan Bator; Gobi Desert.

90. *Visa Requirements:* Tourist visa (two weeks' validity). Entry from Russia or China.

RUSSIAN CENTRAL ASIA[1]

1. *Area:* 3·99 mill. sq. km. (1·55 mill. sq. miles).
2. *Population:* 27·2 mill. (Kazakhstan 40 per cent; Uzbekistan 35 per cent; Kirgizia 9 per cent; Tadzhikistan 9 per cent; Turkmenistan 7 per cent).
3. *Density of Population:* 7 per sq. km. (18 per sq. mile).
4. *Rate of Population Increase:* n.a.
5. *Birth Rate:* n.a.
6. *Death Rate:* n.a.
7. *Geographical Location:* 35° 30′N–55° 30′N; 52°E–89°E.
8. *Capitals:* Tashkent (0·9 mill.)—Uzbekistan; Alma-Ata (0·5 mill.)—Kazakhstan; Frunze (0·2 mill.)—Kirgizia; Dushanbe (0·2 mill.)—Tadzhikistan; Ashkhabad (0·2 mill.)—Turkmenistan.
9. *Mean Temperature:* Alma-Ata (2,543 ft.) 16°F (−9°C) Jan., 72°F (22°C) July; Ashkhabad (741 ft.) 32°F (0°C) Jan., 84°F (29°C) July; Dushanbe (2,673 ft.) 31°F (−1°C) Jan., 81°F (27°C) July; Frunze (2,461 ft.) 46°F (8°C) Jan., 74°F (23°C) July; Tashkent (1,569 ft.) 29°F (−2°C) Jan., 78°F (26°C) July.
10. *Mean Annual Rainfall:* Alma-Ata 23·5 in. (597 mm.); Ashkhabad 8·9 in. (226 mm.); Dushanbe 21·5 in. (546 mm.); Frunze 15·1 in. (384 mm.); Tashkent 14·7 in. (373 mm.).
11. *Political Status:* Russian Central Asia consisting of five Soviet Socialist Republics (see under *2* above).
12. *International Affiliations:* —
13. *Head of State:* A. I. Mikoyan, Chairman of the Presidium of the Supreme Soviet.
14. *Head of Government:* A. N. Kosygin, Prime Minister.
15. *Political Institutions:* Representation in Supreme Soviet and Soviets of the five Soviet Republics.
16. *Political Party:* Communist Party of the Soviet Union.
17. *Languages:* Turkic languages (55 per cent); Russian; Iranian.
18. *Religions:* Muslims (60 per cent); Russian Orthodox; Jews.
19. *Working Population:* n.a.
20. *Urban Population:* 40 per cent of total.
21. *Illiteracy:* negl.
22. *Expenditure on Education:* n.a.
23. *Primary Schools:* 25,200 schools; 5·4 mill. pupils.
24. *Secondary Schools:* 108,000 pupils.
25. *School Enrolment:* n.a.
26. *Students (Higher Education):* 143,000.
27. *Physicians:* 39,000; 1 per 700 inh.
28. *Hospital Beds:* 226,000; 8 per thous.
29. *Newspapers:* 2·8 mill.
30. *Newsprint:* n.a.
31. *Newspapers:* In Russian; local languages.
32. *News Agency:* Tass.
33. *Radio Transmitters:* n.a.
34. *Broadcasting:* Tashkent; Alma-Ata; Frunze; Dushanbe; Askhabad; and other local stations.
35. *Radio Receivers:* 6 mill.; 220 per thous.
36. *TV Licences:* —
37. *Cinemas:* 10,500.
38. *Cinema Attendance:* 353 mill.; 13 per head of pop.
39. *Gross National Product:* n.a.
40. *Gross Domestic Product:* n.a.
41. *Private Consumption:* n.a.
42. *Wages Fund:* n.a.
43. *Expenditure on Food, etc.:* n.a.
44. *Expenditure on Household Goods:* n.a.

[1]In many cases no figures are available for this area as a separate part of the Soviet Union.

45. *Agricultural Population:* n.a.

47. *Production of Grains:* 27·2 mill. ha. (68 mill. acres); 18 mill. tons; 0·66 tons per ha. (0·26 tons per acre).

49. *Production of Sugar Beet:* 2·8 mill. tons; Cotton: 4 mill. tons.

51. *Production of Fertilizers:* n.a.

53. *Development Programme:* Five-Year Plan 1966-70.

55. *Energy Production:* n.a.

57. *Electricity Installed:* n.a.

59. *Production of Coal:* 46·2 mill. tons.

61. *Production of Iron Ore:* n.a.

63. *Production of Steel:* 0·8 mill. tons.

65. *Production of Cotton:* n.a.

67. *Production of Cement:* 5·9 mill. tons.

69. *Production of Motor Vehicles:* n.a.

71. *Telephones Installed:* n.a.

73. *Railway Transport:* n.a.

75. *Sea Transport:* n.a.

77. *Civilian Airline:* Aeroflot, Moscow.

79. *Foreign Trade:* n.a.

81. *Foreign Trade:* n.a.

83. *Foreign Aid:* —

85. *Public Finance:* n.a.

87. *Foreign Exchange:* £1 sterling = 2·52 Rubles; US$1 = 0·90 Rubles.

89. *Tourism:* Arrangements through Intourist.

46. *Arable Land:* 39·5 mill. ha. (98 mill. acres); 1·5 ha. (3·7 acres) per head.

48. *Production of Grains:* 18 mill. tons; 665 kilos per head of pop.

50. *Livestock:* n.a.

52. *Consumption of Fertilizers:* n.a.

54. *Development Projects:* Details to be published in 1966.

56. *Energy Consumption:* n.a.

58. *Electricity Output:* 24·6 milliard kWh.

60. *Production of Mineral Oil:* 10·7 mill. tons.

62. *Production of Manganese Ore:* —

64. *Consumption of Steel:* n.a.

66. *Consumption of Cotton:* n.a.

68. *Production of Petrol:* n.a.

70. *Production of Merchant Vessels:* n.a.

72. *Letters Received:* n.a.

74. *Motor Transport:* n.a.

76. *Sea Transport:* n.a.

78. *Air Transport:* n.a.

80. *Foreign Trade:* n.a.

82. *Foreign Trade:* n.a.

84. *Foreign Aid:* —

86. *Government Obligations:* n.a.

88. *Foreign Exchange:* 1 Ruble = 8s.; 1 Ruble = US$1·10.

90. *Visa Requirements:* Visa required by all foreign visitors. Import and export of Rubles illegal. Police registration through Intourist hotels.

THE FAR EAST

CHINA

1. *Area:* 9·76 mill. sq. km. (3·77 mill. sq. miles).
2. *Population:* (est.) 680-730 mill.
3. *Density of Population:* 70-75 per sq. km. (182-195 per sq. mile).
4. *Rate of Population Increase:* 2·3 per cent.
5. *Birth Rate:* 3·4 per cent.
6. *Death Rate:* 1·1 per cent.
7. *Geographical Location:* 18° 30′N–55°N; 70°E–133°E.
8. *Capital:* Peking (5·5 mill.). Other principal towns: Shanghai (6·9 mill.); Tientsin (3·22 mill.); Shenyang, Mukden (2·41 mill.); Wuhan (2·15 mill.); Chungking (2·12 mill.).
9. *Mean Temperature:* Peking (125 ft.) 25°F (−4°C) Jan., 80°F (27°C) July; Chungking (755 ft.) 45°F (7°C) Jan., 86°F (30°C) August; Kwangchow, Canton (29 ft.) 56°F (13°C) Jan., 84°F (29°C) July; Wuhan (121 ft.) 40°F (4°C) Jan., 86°F (30°C) July; Shenyang, Mukden (141 ft.) 11°F (−12°C) Jan., 78°F (26°C) July.
10. *Mean Annual Rainfall:* Peking 24·1 in. (612 mm.); Chungking 41·5 in. (1,054 mm.); Kwangchow, Canton 64·7 in. (1,643 mm.); Wuhan 49·5 in. (1,257 mm.); Shenyang, Mukden 27·9 in. (709 mm.)
11. *Political Status:* People's Republic since 1/10/1949.
12. *International Affiliations:* —
13. *Head of State:* Liu Shao-chi, Chairman of People's Republic of China.
14. *Head of Government:* Chou En-lai, Prime Minister.
15. *Political Institutions:* National People's Congress (NPC).
16. *Political Parties:* Chinese Communist Party (CCP) (18 mill. members). Chairman of Central Committee: Mao Tse-tung. Minority parties attending People's Political Consultative Conference.
17. *Languages:* Chinese dialects: Cantonese, Hakka, Swatow, Foochow, Wenchow, Ning-po, Wu, Mandarin.
18. *Religions:* Confucianism; Buddhism; Taoism; Islam (10 mill. minority); Christians (4 mill.).
19. *Working Population:* n.a.
20. *Urban Population:* 13 per cent of total.
21. *Illiteracy:* n.a.
22. *Expenditure on Education:* n.a.
23. *Primary Schools:* 90 mill. pupils.
24. *Secondary Schools:* 8·5 mill. pupils.
25. *School Enrolment:* n.a.
26. *Students (Higher Education):* 2·3 mill.
27. *Physicians:* n.a.
28. *Hospital Beds:* n.a.
29. *Newspapers:* 392; circ. (est.) 12 mill.; 20 per thous.
30. *Newsprint:* n.a.
31. *Newspapers:* In Chinese, English.
32. *News Agency:* NCNA.
33. *Radio Transmitters:* 233.
34. *Broadcasting:* Central People's Broadcasting Service.
35. *Radio Receivers:* 7 million; 10 per thous.
36. *TV Receivers:* 20,000.
37. *Cinemas:* 1,200.
38. *Cinema Attendance:* 4,000 mill.; 6 per head of pop.

39. *Net National Product:* 152 milliard Yuan; Growth Rate: 12·6 per cent p.a.
41. *Private Consumption:* n.a.
43. *Expenditure on Food, etc.:* n.a.
45. *Agricultural Population:* n.a.
47. *Production of Paddy:* n.a.
49. *Production of Tea:* 150,000 tons.
51. *Production of Fertilizers:* 3 mill. tons (commercial weight).
53. *Development Programme:* Five-Year Plan 1966-70.
55. *Energy Production:* 405 mill. tons coal equivalent.
57. *Electricity Installed:* n.a.
59. *Production of Coal:* (est.) 200 mill. tons.
61. *Production of Iron Ore:* n.a.
63. *Production of Steel:* (est.) 10 mill. tons.
65. *Production of Cotton:* 10 mill. spindles.
67. *Production of Cement:* (est.) 8 mill. tons.
69. *Production of Motor Vehicles:* n.a.
71. *Telephones Installed:* n.a.
73. *Railway Transport:* 46 milliard pass./km.; 265 milliard ton/km.
75. *Sea Transport:* n.a.
77. *Civilian Airline:* Civil Aviation Administration of China (CAAC), Peking.
79. *Foreign Trade* ($ milliard) (est.): Imports 1·2; Exports 1·5; Balance +0·3.
81. *Foreign Trade* ($ milliard) (est.): Imports: Non-Communist Countries 0·8; USSR 0·2. Exports: Non-Communist Countries 0·7; USSR 0·4.
83. *Foreign Aid:* Western: —
85. *Public Finance:* n.a.
87. *Foreign Exchange:* £1 sterling = 6·90 Yuan; US$1 = 2·45 Yuan.
89. *Tourism:* Peking: Forbidden City; Ming Tombs; Shanghai; Tientsin; Wuhan.

40. *Gross Domestic Product:* n.a.
42. *Wages Fund:* n.a.
44. *Expenditure on Household Goods:* n.a.
46. *Arable Land:* 109 mill. ha. (272 mill. acres); 0·15 ha. (0·35 acres) per head.
48. *Production of Grains:* (est.) 190 mill. tons; 270 kilos per head of pop.
50. *Livestock:* Cattle 45 mill.; Pigs 180 mill.; Sheep and Goats 100 mill.
52. *Consumption of Fertilizers:* n.a.
54. *Development Projects:* Agriculture the foundation; industry the leading sector.
56. *Energy Consumption:* n.a.
58. *Electricity Output:* (est.) 30 milliard kWh.
60. *Production of Mineral Oil:* (est.) 6 mill. tons.
62. *Production of Manganese Ore:* n.a.
64. *Consumption of Steel:* 10 mill. tons; 15 kilos per head of pop.
66. *Consumption of Cotton:* 1·2 mill. tons.
68. *Production of Petrol:* n.a.
70. *Production of Merchant Vessels:* n.a.
72. *Letters Received:* n.a.
74. *Motor Transport:* n.a.
76. *Sea Transport:* n.a.
78. *Air Transport:* n.a.
80. *Foreign Trade* (est.): Imports $2 per head; Exports $2 per head.
82. *Foreign Trade* ($ mill.) (est.): Imports: Grains 350; Raw Mat. 350. Exports: Textiles 500; Raw Mat. 300.
84. *Foreign Aid:* Soviet: 1956-63: $430 mill.
86. *Government Obligations:* n.a.
88. *Foreign Exchange:* 1 Yuan = 2s. 9d; 1 Yuan = US$0·41.
90. *Visa Requirements:* Visa required by all foreign travellers. Import and export of Yuan (YMP) illegal.

TAIWAN

1. *Area:* 36,000 sq. km. (14,000 sq. miles).

2. *Population:* 11·3 mill.

3. *Density of Population:* 315 per sq. km. (819 per sq. mile).

4. *Rate of Population Increase:* 3·1 per cent.

5. *Birth Rate:* 3·74 per cent.

6. *Death Rate:* 0·64 per cent.

7. *Geographical Location:* 22°N–24°N; 120°E–122°E.

8. *Capital:* Taipei (0·96 mill.).

9. *Mean Temperature:* Taipei (30 ft.) 55°F (13°C) Jan., 84°F (29°C) July.

10. *Mean Annual Rainfall:* Taipei 83·8 in. (2,129 mm.).

11. *Political Status:* National Republic.

12. *International Affiliations:* United Nations; Security Treaty with USA.

13. *Head of State:* Chiang Kai-shek, President.

14. *Head of Government:* Dr. Yen Chia-kan, President of the Executive Yuan.

15. *Political Institutions:* Legislative Yuan.

16. *Political Parties:* 1963: Kuomintang (90 per cent of seats); Young China Party; Democratic Socialist Party.

17. *Language:* Chinese (Amoy and Mandarin dialects).

18. *Religions:* Confucianism; Buddhism; Taoism.

19. *Working Population:* 30 per cent of total.

20. *Urban Population:* n.a.

21. *Illiteracy:* 16 per cent of over 12 years of age.

22. *Expenditure on Education:* 3·3 per cent of GNP.

23. *Primary Schools:* 1,900 schools; 47,000 teachers; 2 mill. pupils.

24. *Secondary Schools:* 300 schools; 13,000 teachers; 300,000 pupils.

25. *School Enrolment:* 74 per cent of 5-19 years.

26. *Students (Higher Education):* 135,000.

27. *Physicians:* 6,900; 1 per 1,550 inh.

28. *Hospital Beds:* 4,800; 0·5 per thous.

29. *Newspapers:* 31; circ. 720,000; 66 per thous.

30. *Newsprint:* 0·9 kilos per head.

31. *Newspapers:* In Chinese, English.

32. *News Agency:* CNA.

33. *Radio Transmitters:* 156; 600 kW.

34. *Broadcasting:* Broadcasting Corporation of China.

35. *Radio Licences:* 763,000; 72 per thous.

36. *TV Licences:* 5,000.

37. *Cinemas:* 550; seating capacity 410,000; 40 seats per thous.

38. *Cinema Attendance:* 70 mill. 7 per head of pop.

39. *Net Domestic Product:* NT$72·4 milliard; Growth Rate: 7·1 per cent p.a.

40. *Gross Domestic Product:* $1·2 milliard; GNP: $115 per head of pop.

41. *Private Consumption:* 67 per cent of GNP.

42. *Wages Fund:* 49 per cent of Nat. Inc.

43. *Expenditure on Food, etc.:* 56 per cent of private consumption.

44. *Expenditure on Household Goods:* 8 per cent of private consumption.

45. *Agricultural Population:* 50 per cent of working pop.

46. *Arable Land:* 870,000 ha. (2·2 mill. acres); 0·08 ha. (0·2 acres) per head of pop. Irrigated Land: 500,000 ha.

47. *Production of Paddy:* 0·8 mill. ha. (2 mill. acres); 2·6 mill. tons; 3·3 tons per ha. (1·3 tons per acre).

48. *Production of Grains:* 2·7 mill. tons; 240 kilos per head of pop.

49. *Production of Sugar:* 800,000 tons; Tea 20,000 tons.

50. *Livestock:* Cattle 0·1 mill.; Pigs 3·1 mill.

51. *Production of Fertilizers* (thous. tons): N:77; P_2O_5:29.

52. *Consumption of Fertilizers* (thous. tons): N:111; P_2O_5:30; K_2O:24. Total: 190 kilos per ha. (165 lbs. per acre).

53. *Development Programme:* Four-Year Plan 1961-4.

54. *Development Projects:* Manufacturing industries; power projects; services.

55. *Energy Production:* 4·9 mill. tons coal equivalent.

56. *Energy Consumption:* 6·4 mill. tons coal equivalent: 568 kilos per head.

57. *Electricity Installed:* 1 mill. kW.

58. *Electricity Output:* 4·8 milliard kWh.

59. *Production of Coal:* 4·6 mill. tons.

60. *Production of Mineral Oil:* —

61. *Production of Iron Ore:* —

62. *Production of Manganese Ore:* —

63. *Production of Steel:* 0·2 mill. tons

64. *Consumption of Steel:* 0·35 mill. tons; 29 kilos per head of pop.

65. *Production of Cotton:* 465,000 spindles; 52,000 tons cotton yarn.

66. *Consumption of Cotton:* 54,000 tons; 4·8 kilos per head of pop.

67. *Production of Cement:* 1·85 mill. tons.

68. *Production of Petrol:* 1·2 mill. tons.

69. *Production of Motor Vehicles:* —

70. *Production of Merchant Vessels:* —

71. *Telephones Installed:* 120,300.

72. *Letters Received:* 348 mill.; 31 per head.

73. *Railway Transport:* 3·5 milliard pass./km.; 2 milliard ton/km.

74. *Motor Transport:* 10,000 pass. cars; 12,000 comm. vehicles in use.

75. *Sea Transport:* 8·5 mill. NRT entered. Merchant Fleet: 0·5 mill. GRT.

76. *Sea Transport:* 2·3 tons loaded; 3·2 mill. tons unloaded.

77. *Civilian Airline:* Civil Air Transport (CAT), Taipei.

78. *Air Transport:* 107·2 mill. pass./km.; 1·4 mill. ton/km.

79. *Foreign Trade* (NT$ mill.): Imports 12,174; Exports 8,735; Balance −3,439.

80. *Foreign Trade:* Imports $27 per head; Exports $19 per head.

81. *Foreign Trade* (NT$ mill.): Imports: UK 125; USA 4,621; Japan 4,157. Exports: UK 140; USA 2,132; Japan 2,083.

82. *Foreign Trade* (NT$ mill.): Imports: Cotton 1,154; Min. Oil 805; Wheat 769. Exports: Sugar 1,810; Fruits 816; Cotton Goods 494.

83. *Foreign Aid:* USA: 1946-63: $4,524 mill.

84. *Foreign Aid:* Sino-Soviet: —

85. *Public Finance* (NT$ mill.): Revenue 15,006; Expenditure 13,527.

86. *Government Obligations:* n.a.

87. *Foreign Exchange:* £1 sterling = NT$112; US$1 = NT$40.

88. *Foreign Exchange:* NT$1 = 2d; NT$100 = US$2·50.

89. *Tourism:* Tourist Centres: Taipei; Tamsui; Taichung: Sun Moon Lake.

90. *Visa Requirements:* Tourist visa. Money declaration on entry.

HONG KONG

1. *Area:* 1,033 sq. km. (398 sq. miles).
2. *Population:* 3·4 mill.
3. *Density of Population*: 3,300 per sq. km. (8,600 per sq. mile).
4. *Rate of Population Increase:* 2·68 per cent.
5. *Birth Rate:* 3·28 per cent.
6. *Death Rate:* 0·6 per cent.
7. *Geographical Location:* 22°N; 114°E.
8. *Capital:* Victoria (0·63 mill.).
9. *Mean Temperature:* Hong Kong (109 ft.) 60°F (16°C) Jan., 82°F (28°C) July.
10. *Mean Annual Rainfall:* Hong Kong 90 in. (2,286 mm.).
11. *Political Status:* British Crown Colony.
12. *International Affiliations:* British Commonwealth; Sterling Area.
13. *Head of State:* Sir David Trench, Governor and Commander-in-Chief.
14. *Head of Government:* M. D. I. Gass, Colonial Secretary.
15. *Political Institutions:* Executive Council; Legislative Council; Urban Council (partly elected).
16. *Political Parties:* Civic Association; Reform Club; Democratic Self-Government Party.
17. *Languages:* English (official); Chinese dialects.
18. *Religions:* Confucianism; Buddhism; Taoism.
19. *Working Population:* 39 per cent of total.
20. *Urban Population:* 76 per cent of total.
21. *Illiteracy:* 9 per cent of over 10 years of age.
22. *Expenditure on Education:* n.a.
23. *Primary Schools:* 1,600 schools; 17,000 teachers; 500,000 pupils.
24. *Secondary Schools:* 300 schools; 4,700 teachers; 100,000 pupils.
25. *School Enrolment:* 66 per cent of 5-19 years.
26. *Students (Higher Education):* 17,000.
27. *Physicians:* 935; 1 per 3,200 inh.
28. *Hospital Beds:* 7,200; 2·4 per thous.
29. *Newspapers:* 44; circ. 750,000; 226 per thous.
30. *Newsprint:* 6·8 kilos per head.
31. *Newspapers:* In Chinese, English.
32. *News Agency:* Pananews.
33. *Radio Transmitters:* 7; 18 kW.
34. *Broadcasting:* Radio Hong Kong.
35. *Radio Licences:* 172,000; 58 per thous.
36. *TV Licences:* 16,000; 7 per thous.
37. *Cinemas:* 73; seating capacity 78,000; 26 seats per thous.
38. *Cinema Attendance:* 65 mill.; 23 per head of pop.
39. *Gross National Product:* n.a.
40. *Gross Domestic Product:* $736 million; GNP: $258 per head of pop.
41. *Private Consumption:* n.a.
42. *Wages Fund:* n.a.
43. *Expenditure on Food, etc.:* n.a.
44. *Expenditure on Household Goods:* n.a.
45. *Agricultural Population:* 7 per cent of working pop.
46. *Arable Land:* 14,000 ha. (35,000 acres); 0·01 acre per head.
47. *Production of Paddy:* 11,000 ha. (27,000 acres); 19,000 tons; 1·7 ton per ha. (0·7 ton per acre).
48. *Production of Grains:* 19,000 tons; 5 kilos per head of pop.
49. *Production of Sugar:* —
50. *Livestock:* Cattle 12,000; Pigs 300,000.
51. *Production of Fertilizers:* —
52. *Consumption of Fertilizers:* n.a.
53. *Development Programme:* —
54. *Development Projects:* Industry; public utilities; housing projects.
55. *Energy Production:* —
56. *Energy Consumption:* 1·8 mill. tons coal equivalent; 517 kilos per head.
57. *Electricity Installed:* 0·5 mill. kW.
58. *Electricity Output:* 1·5 milliard kWh.
59. *Production of Coal:* —
60. *Production of Mineral Oil:* —
61. *Production of Iron Ore:* 65,000 tons.
62. *Production of Manganese Ore:* —

63. *Production of Steel:* —

64. *Consumption of Steel:* 0·45 mill. tons; 130 kilos per head of pop.

65. *Production of Cotton:* 0·6 mill. spindles; 107,000 tons cotton yarn.

66. *Consumption of Cotton:* 113,000 tons; 33 kilos per head of pop.

67. *Production of Cement:* 0·2 mill. tons.

68. *Production of Petrol:* —

69. *Production of Motor Vehicles:* —

70. *Production of Merchant Vessels:* —

71. *Telephones Installed:* 145,700.

72. *Letters Received:* 106 mill.; 31 per head.

73. *Railway Transport:* 146 mill. pass./km.; 13 mill. ton/km.

74. *Motor Transport:* 42,000 pass. cars; 12,000 comm. vehicles in use.

75. *Sea Transport:* 22·2 mill. NRT entered. Merchant Fleet: 0·8 mill. GRT.

76. *Sea Transport:* 2·2 mill. tons loaded; 7·3 mill. tons unloaded.

77. *Civilian Airline:* Cathay Pacific Airways (CPA), Hong Kong.

78. *Air Transport:* n.a.

79. *Foreign Trade* (HK$ mill.): Imports 6,657; Exports 4,387; Balance −2,270.

80. *Foreign Trade:* Imports $340 per head; Exports $225 per head.

81. *Foreign Trade* (HK$ mill.): Imports: UK 760; USA 792; China 1,213. Exports: UK 737; USA 908; Malaya 451.

82. *Foreign Trade* (HK$ mill.): Imports: Foods 1,609; Manuf. 1,995; Machines 711. Exports: Manuf. 2,206; Foods 380; Raw Mat. 231.

83. *Foreign Aid:* USA: 1946-63: $36 mill.

84. *Foreign Aid:* Sino-Soviet: —

85. *Public Finance:* n.a.

86. *Government Obligations:* n.a.

87. *Foreign Exchange:* £1 sterling = HK$16; US$1 = HK$5·75.

88. *Foreign Exchange:* HK$1 = 1s. 3d; HK$1 = US$0·17.

89. *Tourism:* 400,000 tourists. Tourist Centres: Aberdeen, Repulse Bay; Kowloon: New Territories.

90. *Visa Requirements:* British subjects: no visa. US citizens: visa required. No restrictions on import or export of money.

JAPAN

1. *Area:* 370,000 sq. km. (143,000 sq. miles). (Excl. Kurile Islands (Soviet administration) and Ryukyu Islands (US Administration)).

2. *Population:* 94·9 mill. (Excl. Kurile and Ryukyu Islands.)

3. *Density of Population:* 257 per sq. km. (668 per sq. mile).

4. *Rate of Population Increase:* 0·95 per cent.

5. *Birth Rate:* 1·7 per cent.

6. *Death Rate:* 0·75 per cent.

7. *Geographical Location:* 23° 30′N–45° 30′N; 128° 30′E–146°E.

8. *Capital:* Tokyo (Municipal Area 8·48 mill.; Greater Tokyo 9·9 mill.). Other principal towns: Osaka (3·1 mill.); Nagoya (1·64 mill.); Yokohama (1·44 mill.); Kyoto (1·3 mill.); Kobe (1·15 mill.).

9. *Mean Temperature:* Tokyo (19 ft.) 38°F (3°C) Jan., 76°F (24°C) July; Nagasaki (436 ft.) 20°F (−7°C) Jan., 66°F (19°C) July; Sapporo (56 ft.) 42°F (6°C) Jan., 79°F (26°C) July.

10. *Mean Annual Rainfall:* Tokyo 61·6 in. (1,565 mm.); Nagasaki 75·5 in. (1,918 mm.); Sapporo 41·1 in. (1,041 mm.).

11. *Political Status:* Constitutional Democracy; Emperor deprived of all political power.

12. *International Affiliations:* Member of United Nations; Colombo Plan; Security Treaty with USA.

13. *Head of State:* Hirohito, Emperor (Nihonkoku Tenno).

14. *Head of Government:* Eisaku Sato, Prime Minister.

15. *Political Institutions:* Diet consisting of House of Representatives (Lower House) and House of Councillors (Upper House).

16. *Political Parties:* House of Reps, 1964: Liberal Democratic Party 140; Socialist Party 366; Democratic Socialist Party 10; Communist Party 3; Others 22.

17. *Language:* Japanese.

18. *Religions:* Shintoists 78 mill.; Buddhists 61 mill.; Christians 0·7 mill.

19. *Working Population:* 50 per cent of total.

20. *Urban Population:* 63·5 per cent of total.

21. *Illiteracy:* negl.

22. *Expenditure on Education:* 6·5 per cent of GNP.

23. *Primary Schools:* 26,700 schools; 351,000 teachers; 11·8 mill. pupils.

24. *Secondary Schools:* 16,800 schools; 398,000 teachers; 8·7 mill. pupils.

25. *School Enrolment:* 91 per cent of 5-19 years.

26. *Students (Higher Education):* 2·1 mill.

27. *Physicians:* 101,400; 1 per 915 inh.

28. *Hospital Beds:* 687,000; 7 per thous.

29. *Newspapers:* 157; circ. 39·1 mill.; 416 per thous.

30. *Newsprint:* 9·5 kilos per head.

31. *Newspapers:* In Japanese.

32. *News Agencies:* Kyodo; Jiji Press.

33. *Radio Transmitters:* 400; 2,318 kW.

34. *Broadcasting:* Japan Broadcasting Corp.

35. *Radio Licences:* 18·6 mill.; 196 per thous.

36. *TV Receivers:* 12·6 mill.; 133 per thous.

37. *Cinemas:* 7,200; seating capacity 3·2 mill.; 35 seats per thous.

38. *Cinema Attendance:* 863 mill.; 9 per head of pop.

39. *Gross National Product:* 19,000 milliard Yen; Growth Rate: 9·9 per cent p.a.

40. *Gross Domestic Product:* $47·8 milliard; GNP: $504 per head of pop.

41. *Private Consumption:* 52 per cent of GNP.

42. *Wages Fund:* 58 per cent of Nat. Inc.

43. *Expenditure on Food, etc.:* 44 per cent of private consumption.

44. *Expenditure on Household Goods:* 9 per cent of private consumption.

45. *Agricultural Population:* 30 per cent of working pop. Farms under 5 ha. (12·5 acres): 98 per cent of holdings; 84 per cent of area.

46. *Arable Land:* 6·1 mill. ha. (15 mill. acres); 0·07 ha. (0·16 acres) per head. Irrigated Land: 3·4 mill. ha.

47. *Production of Paddy:* 3·3 mill. ha. (8·2 mill. acres); 17 mill. tons; 5·26 tons per ha. (2·13 tons per acre).

48. *Production of Grains:* 21 mill. tons; 221 kilos per head of pop.

49. *Production of Sugar:* 213,000 tons; Tea: 77,000 tons.

50. *Livestock:* Cattle 3·3 mill.; Pigs 4 mill.; Sheep and Goats 1 mill.

51. *Production of Fertilizers* (thous. tons): N:1,151; P_2O_5:490.

52. *Consumption of Fertilizers* (thous. tons): N:669; P_2O_5:465; K_2O:506. Total: 269 kilos per ha. (237 lb. per acre).

53. *Development Programme:* Ten-Year Plan 1961-70.

54. *Development Projects:* Two-fold increase of per capita Nat. Inc.

55. *Energy Production:* 65·4 mill. tons coal equivalent.

56. *Energy Consumption:* 131·8 mill. tons coal equivalent; 1,390 kilos per head.

57. *Electricity Installed:* 29·14 mill. kW.

58. *Electricity Output:* 140·4 milliard kWh.

59. *Production of Coal:* 54·4 mill. tons.

60. *Production of Mineral Oil:* 0·8 mill. tons.

61. *Production of Iron Ore:* 2 mill. tons.

62. *Production of Manganese Ore:* 104,000 tons.

63. *Production of Steel:* 27·5 mill. tons.

64. *Consumption of Steel:* 23 mill. tons; 242 kilos per head of pop.

65. *Production of Cotton:* 13·3 mill. spindles; 490,000 tons cotton yarn.

66. *Consumption of Cotton:* 653,000 tons; 6·9 kilos per head of pop.

67. *Production of Cement:* 28·8 mill. tons.

68. *Production of Petrol:* 35·1 mill. tons.

69. *Production of Motor Vehicles:* 269,000 pass. cars; 856,000 comm. vehicles.

70. *Production of Merchant Vessels:* 2·2 mill. GRT.

71. *Telephones Installed:* 7·4 mill.

72. *Letters Received:* 7,928 mill.; 83 per head.

73. *Railway Transport:* 207 milliard pass./km.; 57·5 milliard ton/km.

74. *Motor Transport:* 743,000 pass. cars; 1·8 mill. comm. vehicles in use.

75. *Sea Transport:* 69 mill. NRT entered. Merchant Fleet: 10 mill. GRT; Tankers: 2·8 mill. GRT.

76. *Sea Transport:* 19 mill. tons loaded; 123 mill. tons unloaded.

77. *Civilian Airlines:* Japan Air Lines (JAL); All Nippon Airways, Tokyo.

78. *Air Transport:* 2,240 mill. pass/km.; 34 mill. ton/km.

79. *Foreign Trade* ($ mill.): Imports 5,637; Exports 4,917; Balance −720.

80. *Foreign Trade:* Imports $59 per head; Exports $52 per head.

81. *Foreign Trade* ($ mill.): Imports: UK 146; USA 1,809; Australia 436. Exports: UK 192; USA 1,411; Hong Kong 192.

82. *Foreign Trade* ($ mill.): Imports: Raw Mat. 2,362; Fuels 1,041; Machines 771. Exports: Machines 1,253; Other Manuf. 2,859; Foods 330.

83. *Foreign Aid:* USA: 1946-63: $3,824 mill.

84. *Foreign Aid:* Granted: $300 mill.

85. *Public Finance* (milliard Yen): Revenue 2,447: Expenditure 2,974.

86. *Net Public Debt* (milliard Yen): 462.

87. *Foreign Exchange:* £1 sterling = 1,010 Yen; US$1 = 360 Yen.

88. *Foreign Exchange:* 100 Yen = 2s. 0d; 100 Yen = US$0·28.

89. *Tourism:* 350,000 tourists. Tourist Centres: Tokyo; Kamakura; Nikko; Kyoto; Nara; Fuji-Hakone.

90. *Visa Requirements:* Visa for 15 days transit or 60 days tourist stay.

SOUTH KOREA

1. *Area:* 98,000 sq. km. (38,000 sq. miles).
2. *Population:* 26·1 mill.
3. *Density of Population:* 265 per sq. km. (690 per sq. mile).
4. *Rate of Population Increase:* 2·9 per cent.
5. *Birth Rate:* n.a.
6. *Death Rate:* n.a.
7. *Geographical Location:* 33°N– 38° 30'N; 125°E–130°E.
8. *Capital:* Seoul (2·45 mill.). Other principal towns: Pusan (1·16 mill.).
9. *Mean Temperature:* Seoul (285 ft.) 24°F (−4°C) Jan., 77°F (25°C) July.
10. *Mean Annual Rainfall:* Seoul 49·2 in. (1,250 mm.).
11. *Political Status:* Republic; independent since 15/8/1948. Armistice with North Korea 27/7/1953.
12. *International Affiliations:* Colombo Plan; Security Treaty with USA.
13. *Head of State:* Pak Chong-hui (Park Chung Hee), President.
14. *Head of Government:* Chong Il-kwon, Prime Minister.
15. *Political Institutions:* National Assembly.
16. *Political Parties:* 1963: Democratic Republican Party 110; Civil Rule Party 41; Democratic Party 13; Others 11.
17. *Language:* Korean (Hanguk script).
18. *Religions:* Confucianism; Buddhism; Animism; 3 mill. Christians.
19. *Working Population:* 32 per cent of total.
20. *Urban Population:* 28 per cent of total.
21. *Illiteracy:* 29 per cent of over 10 years of age.
22. *Expenditure on Education:* 4 per cent of GNP.
23. *Primary Schools:* 4,700 schools; 63,000 teachers; 3·9 mill. pupils.
24. *Secondary Schools:* 1,400 schools; 19,000 teachers; 800,000 pupils.
25. *School Enrolment:* 64 per cent of 5-19 years.
26. *Students (Higher Education):* 270,000.
27. *Physicians:* 7,300; 1 per 3,100 inh.
28. *Hospital Beds:* 33,900; 1·5 per thous.
29. *Newspapers:* 45; circ. 1·8 mill.; 69 per thous.
30. *Newsprint:* 1·8 kilos per head.
31. *Newspapers:* In Korean, Chinese, English.
32. *News Agencies:* Hapdong NA; Donghwa NA.
33. *Radio Transmitters:* 64; 512 kW.
34. *Broadcasting:* Korean Broadcasting System.
35. *Radio Receivers:* 1·2 mill.; 46 per thous.
36. *TV Receivers:* 40,000.
37. *Cinemas:* 265; seating capacity 175,000; 8 seats per thous.
38. *Cinema Attendance:* 98 mill.; 4 per head of pop.
39. *Gross National Product:* 281·5 milliard Won; Growth Rate: 4·4 per cent p.a.
40. *Gross Domestic Product* (est.): $2·5 milliard; GNP: $105 per head of pop.
41. *Private Consumption*: n.a.
42. *Wages Fund:* 40 per cent of Nat. Inc.
43. *Expenditure on Food, etc.*: 61 per cent of private consumption.
44. *Expenditure on Household Goods:* 4 per cent of private consumption.
45. *Agricultural Population:* 58 per cent of working pop.
46. *Arable Land:* 2·1 mill. ha. (5·1 mill. acres); 0·08 ha. (0·2 acres) per head.
47. *Production of Paddy:* 1·1 mill. ha. (2·8 mill. acres); 3 mill. tons; 2·75 tons per ha. (1·1 ton per acre).
48. *Production of Grains:* 4·2 mill. tons; 165 kilos per head of pop.
49. *Production of Sugar:* —
50. *Livestock:* Cattle 1·1 mill.; Pigs 1·3 mill.
51. *Production of Fertilizers* (thous. tons): N:36.
52. *Consumption of Fertilizers* (thous. tons): N:127; P_2O_5:82; K_2O:17. Total: 150 kilos per ha. (135 lb. per acre).

53. *Development Programme:* Five-Year Plan 1962-66.

54. *Development Projects:* 5 per cent Annual Growth Rate, with emphasis on industrial development and export.

55. *Energy Production:* 7·5 mill. tons coal equivalent.

56. *Energy Consumption:* 8·6 mill. tons coal equivalent; 328 kilos per head.

57. *Electricity Installed:* 0·5 mill. kW.

58. *Electricity Output:* 1·8 milliard kWh.

59. *Production of Coal:* —

60. *Production of Mineral Oil:* —

61. *Production of Iron Ore:* 0·2 mill. tons.

62. *Production of Manganese Ore:* —

63. *Production of Steel:* 0·1 mill. tons.

64. *Consumption of Steel:* —

65. *Production of Cotton:* 0·55 mill. spindles; 52,000 tons cotton yarn.

66. *Consumption of Cotton:* 69,000 tons; 2·6 kilos per head of pop.

67. *Production of Cement:* 0·8 mill. tons.

68. *Production of Petrol:* —

69. *Production of Motor Vehicles:* —

70. *Production of Merchant Vessels:* —

71. *Telephones Installed:* 139,300.

72. *Letters Received:* 210 mill.; 8 per head.

73. *Railway Transport:* 5·9 milliard pass./km.; 4 milliard ton/km.

74. *Motor Transport:* 11,000 pass. cars; 22,000 comm. vehicles in use.

75. *Sea Transport:* 5·6 mill. NRT entered.

76. *Sea Transport:* 0·8 mill. tons loaded; 3·7 mill. tons unloaded.

77. *Civilian Airline:* Korean National Airlines, Seoul.

78. *Air Transport:* 14·6 mill. pass./km.

79. *Foreign Trade* ($ mill.): Imports 415; Exports 55; Balance −360.

80. *Foreign Trade:* Imports $16 per head; Exports $2 per head.

81. *Foreign Trade* ($ mill.): Imports: UK 6; USA 214; Japan 109. Exports: UK 2; USA 12; Japan 23.

82. *Foreign Trade* ($ mill.): Imports: Chemicals 94; Other Raw Mat. 90; Manuf. 73. Exports: Foods 22; Raw Mat. 19; Manuf. 6.

83. *Foreign Aid:* USA: 1946-63: $5,674 mill.

84. *Foreign Aid:* Sino-Soviet: —

85. *Public Finance* (mill. Won): Revenue 69,090; Expenditure 55,080.

86. *Government Obligations:* n.a.

87. *Foreign Exchange:* £1 sterling = 715 Won; US$1 = 255 Won.

88. *Foreign Exchange:* 100 Won = 2s. 9d; 100 Won = US$0·40.

89. *Tourism:* Tourist Centres: Seoul: Inchon; Kyongju.

90. *Visa Requirements:* Tourist visa obtainable with minimum formality. No currency restrictions.

NORTH KOREA

1. *Area:* 122,000 sq. km. (47,000 sq. miles).
2. *Population:* (est.) 10·5 mill.
3. *Density of Population:* 70-86 per sq. km. (182-224 per sq. mile).
4. *Rate of Population Increase:* 3·3 per cent.
5. *Birth Rate:* 4·65 per cent.
6. *Death Rate:* 1·35 per cent.
7. *Geographical Location:* 37° 59′N–43°N; 124° 3°′E–130° 30′E.
8. *Capital:* Pyongyang (0·94 mill.).
9. *Mean Temperature:* Pyongyang (138 ft.) (18°F (−8°C) Jan., 76°F (24°C) July.
10. *Mean Annual Rainfall:* Pyongyang 37 in. (940 mm.).
11. *Political Status:* Democratic People's Republic since 8/9/1948. Armistice with South Korea 27/7/1953.
12. *International Affiliations:* Treaties with the Soviet Union and the People's Republic of China.
13. *Head of State:* Ch'oe Yong-kon, Chairman of Presidium, Supreme People's Assembly.
14. *Head of Government:* Kim Il-song, Marshal, Prime Minister and Supreme Commander of the Armed Forces.
15. *Political Institutions:* Supreme People's Assembly.
16. *Political Party:* Korean Workers' (Communist) Party (1·3 million members). Chairman of Central Committee: Marshal Kim Il-song.
17. *Language:* Korean (Hangul script).
18. *Religions:* Confucianism; Buddhism; Animism.
19. *Working Population:* n.a.
20. *Urban Population:* n.a.
21. *Illiteracy:* n.a.
22. *Expenditure on Education:* n.a.
23. *Primary Schools:* n.a.
24. *Secondary Schools:* n.a.
25. *School Enrolment:* n.a.
26. *Students (Higher Education):* n.a.
27. *Physicians:* n.a.
28. *Hospital Beds:* n.a.
29. *Newspapers:* n.a.
30. *Newsprint:* n.a.
31. *Newspapers:* In Korean.
32. *News Agency:* KCNA.
33. *Radio Transmitters:* 8.
34. *Broadcasting:* Korean Central Broadcasting Committee.
35. *Radio Receivers:* 600,000; 72 per thous.
36. *TV Receivers:* —
37. *Cinemas:* n.a.
38. *Cinema Attendance:* n.a.
39. *Gross National Product:* n.a.
40. *Gross Domestic Product:* n.a.
41. *Private Consumption:* n.a.
42. *Wages Fund:* n.a.
43. *Expenditure on Food, etc.:* n.a.
44. *Expenditure on Household Goods:* n.a.
45. *Agricultural Population:* n.a.
46. *Arable Land:* n.a.
47. *Production of Paddy:* n.a.
48. *Production of Grains:* (est.) 4 mill. tons; 380 kilos per head of pop.
49. *Production of Sugar:* —
50. *Livestock:* n.a.
51. *Production of Fertilizers:* 0·9 mill. tons (commercial weight).
52. *Consumption of Fertilizers:* n.a.
53. *Development Programme:* Seven-Year Plan 1961-67.
54. *Development Projects:* 1961-64: raw material basis; 1965-67: heavy industry.
55. *Energy Production:* n.a.
56. *Energy Consumption:* n.a.
57. *Electricity Installed:* n.a.
58. *Electricity Output:* 11·9 milliard kWh.
59. *Production of Coal:* 14 mill. tons.
60. *Production of Mineral Oil:* —
61. *Production of Iron Ore:* n.a.
62. *Production of Manganese Ore:* n.a.
63. *Production of Steel:* 1 mill. tons.
64. *Consumption of Steel:* n.a.
65. *Production of Cotton:* —
66. *Consumption of Cotton:* n.a.
67. *Production of Cement:* 2·4 mill. tons.
68. *Production of Petrol:* —

69. *Production of Motor Vehicles:* —
70. *Production of Merchant Vessels:* —
71. *Telephones Installed:* n.a.
72. *Letters Received:* n.a.
73. *Railway Transport:* n.a.
74. *Motor Transport:* n.a.
75. *Sea Transport:* n.a.
76. *Sea Transport:* n.a.
77. *Civilian Airline:* —
78. *Air Transport:* —
79. *Foreign Trade* ($ mill.) (est.): Imports 150; Exports 150.
80. *Foreign Trade* (est.): Imports $14 per head; Exports $14 per head.
81. *Foreign Trade* ($ mill.) (est.): Imports: USSR 80; China 70. Exports: USSR 90; China 60.
82. *Foreign Trade* ($ mill.) (est.): Imports Foods 20; Fuels 20. Exports: Metals 75.
83. *Foreign Aid:* Western: —
84. *Foreign Aid:* Sino-Soviet; 1956-63: $260 mill. (Soviet $115 mill.; Chinese $130 mill.) offered.
85. *Public Finance:* n.a.
86. *Government Obligations:* n.a.
87. *Foreign Exchange:* £1 sterling = 7·15 Won; US$1 = 2·55 Won.
88. *Foreign Exchange:* 1 Won = 2s 10d; 1 Won = US$0.45.
89. *Tourism:* —
90. *Visa Requirements:* Tourist visa difficult to obtain. Entry from China.

RUSSIAN SIBERIA AND FAR EAST[1]

1. *Area:* 11·33 mill. sq. km. (4·4 mill. sq. miles).
2. *Population:* 22·9 mill.
3. *Density of Population:* 2 per sq. km. (5 per sq. mile).
4. *Rate of Population Increase:* n.a.
5. *Birth Rate:* n.a.
6. *Death Rate:* n.a.
7. *Geographical Location:* 49°N–90°N (land); 60°E–170°W.
8. *Towns:* Novosibirsk (1 mill.); Omsk (0·7 mill.); Krasnoyarsk (0·5 mill.); Vladivostok (0·3 mill.).
9. *Mean Temperature:* Irkutsk (1,532 ft.) −6°F (−21°C) Jan., 60°F (16°C) July; Tomsk (399 ft.) −6°F (−21°C) Jan., 63°F (17°C) July; Verkhoyansk (330 ft.) −58°F (−50°C) Jan., 56°F (13°C) July; Vladivostok (94 ft.) 6°F (−14°C) Jan., 65°F (18°C) July.
10. *Mean Annual Rainfall:* Irkutsk 14·9 in. (379 mm.); Tomsk 19·9 in. (506 mm.); Verkhoyansk 5·3 in. (135 mm.); Vladivostok 23·6 in. (599 mm.).
11. *Political Status:* Russian Siberia and Far East consisting of Economic Regions within the Russian Soviet Federal Socialist Republic (RSFSR).
12. *International Affiliations:* —
13. *Head of State:* A. I. Mikoyan. Chairman of Presidium of Supreme Soviet.
14. *Head of Government:* A. N. Kosygin, Prime Minister.
15. *Political Institutions:* Representation in Soviet of RSFSR as Siberian and Far Eastern Krays.
16. *Political Party:* Communist Party of the Soviet Union.
17. *Languages:* Russian majority; German 0·25 mill.; Turkic 0·3 mill.; Yakut 0·2 mill.; Tuva 0·1 mill.
18. *Religions:* Russian Orthodox (majority); Muslims; Jews; Buddhists; Baptists; Lutherans.
19. *Working Population:* n.a.
20. *Urban Population:* 60 per cent of total.
21. *Illiteracy:* negl.
22. *Expenditure on Education:* n.a.
23. *Primary Schools:* 22,400 schools; 4·4 mill. pupils.
24. *Secondary Schools:* 375 schools; 250,000 pupils.
25. *School Enrolment:* n.a.
26. *Students (Higher Education):* 200,000.
27. *Physicians:* 42,500; 1 per 540 inh.
28. *Hospital Beds:* 217,000; 9 per thous.
29. *NNespapers:* n.a.
30. *Newsprint:* n.a.
31. *NNespapers:* n.a.
32. *News Agency:* n.a.
33. *Radio Transmitters:* n.a.
34. *Broadcasting:* Novosibirsk, Irkutsk; and other local stations.
35. *Radio Receivers:* n.a.
36. *TV Licences:* —
37. *Cinemas:* 16,400.
38. *Cinema Attendance:* n.a.
39. *Gross National Product:* n.a.
40. *Gross Domestic Product:* n.a.
41. *Private Consumption:* n.a.
42. *Wages Fund:* n.a.
43. *Expenditure on Food, etc.:* n.a.
44. *Expenditure on Household Goods:* n.a.
45. *Agricultural Population:* n.a.
46. *Arable Land:* n.a.
47. *Production of Grains:* 19·8 mill. ha. (49 mill. acres); 14·6 mill. tons; 0·74 tons per ha. (0·3 tons per acre).
48. *Production of Grains:* 14·6 mill. tons; 635 kilos per head of pop.
49. *Production of Sugar Beet:* 0·3 mill. tons.
50. *Livestock:* n.a.
51. *Production of Fertilizers:* n.a.
52. *Consumption of Fertilizers:* n.a.

[1]In many cases no figures are available for this area as a separate part of the Soviet Union.

53. *Development Programme:* Five-Year Plan 1966-70.
54. *Development Projects:* Details to be published in 1966.
55. *Energy Production:* n.a.
56. *Energy Consumption:* n.a.
57. *Electricity Installed:* n.a.
58. *Electricity Output:* n.a.
59. *Production of Coal:* n.a.
60. *Production of Mineral Oil:* n.a.
61. *Production of Iron Ore:* n.a.
62. *Production of Manganese Ore:* —
63. *Production of Steel:* n.a.
64. *Consumption of Steel:* n.a.
65. *Production of Cotton:* n.a.
66. *Consumption of Cotton:* n.a.
67. *Production of Cement:* 6·9 mill. tons.
68. *Production of Petrol:* n.a.
69. *Production of Motor Vehicles:* n.a.
70. *Production of Merchant Vessels:* n.a.
71. *Telephones Installed:* n.a.
72. *Letters Received:* n.a.
73. *Railway Transport:* n.a.
74. *Motor Transport:* n.a.
75. *Sea Transport:* n.a.
76. *Sea Transport:* n.a.
77. *Civilian Airline:* Aeroflot, Moscow.
78. *Air Transport:* n.a.
79. *Foreign Trade:* n.a.
80. *Foreign Trade:* n.a.
81. *Foreign Trade:* n.a.
82. *Foreign Trade:* n.a.
83. *Foreign Aid:* —
84. *Foreign Aid:* —
85. *Public Finance:* n.a.
86. *Government Obligations:* n.a.
87. *Foreign Exchange:* £1 sterling = 2·52 Rubles; US$1 = 0·90 Rubles.
88. *Foreign Exchange:* 1 Ruble = 8s.; 1 Ruble = US$1·10.
89. *Tourism:* Arrangements through Intourist.
90. *Visa Requirements:* Visas required by all foreign visitors. Import and export of Rubles illegal. Police registration through Intourist hotels.

SOUTH-EAST ASIA

BURMA

1. *Area:* 678,000 sq. km. (260,000 sq. miles).
2. *Population:* 23·2 mill.
3. *Density of Population:* 34 per sq. km. (88 per sq. mile).
4. *Rate of Population Increase:* 1·5 per cent.
5. *Birth Rate:* 5 per cent.
6. *Death Rate:* 3·5 per cent.
7. *Geographical Location:* 15°N–28° 30'N; 91°E–102°E.
8. *Capital:* Rangoon (0·69 mill.). Other principal towns: Mandalay (0·21 mill.), Moulmein (0·12 mill.).
9. *Mean Temperature:* Rangoon (18 ft.) 77°F (25°C) Jan., 86°F (30°C) April; Mandalay (252 ft.) 68°F (20°C) Jan., 89°F (32°C) April; Akyab (29 ft.) 70°F (21°C) Jan., 84°F (29°C) May.
10. *Mean Annual Rainfall:* Rangoon 103 in. (2,616 mm.); Mandalay 32·6 in. (828 mm.); Akyab 202·9 in. (5,154 mm.).
11. *Political Status:* Union of Burma; independent since 17/10/1947.
12. *International Affiliations:* United Nations; Sterling Area; Colombo Plan.
13. *Head of State:* Ne Win, General, Chairman of Revolutionary Council.
14. *Head of Government:* Ne Win, General; Minister of National Planning and Defence.
15. *Political Institutions:* Government by Revolutionary Council, State Supreme Councils.
16. *Political Parties:* Parliament and State Councils dissolved since 2/3/1962.
17. *Languages:* Burmese (official); English (permitted); over 60 other languages.
18. *Religions:* Buddhism (no longer State religion); 1·3 mill. Christians.
19. *Working Population:* n.a.
20. *Urban Population:* n.a.
21. *Illiteracy:* 26 per cent of over 11 years of age.
22. *Expenditure on Education:* 3·6 per cent of GNP.
23. *Primary Schools:* 13,000 schools; 36,000 teachers; 1·6 mill. pupils.
24. *Secondary Schools:* 1,400 schools; 8,000 teachers; 300,000 pupils.
25. *School Enrolment:* 43 per cent of 5-19 years.
26. *Students (Higher Education):* 17,000.
27. *Physicians:* 1,150; 1 per 18,000 inh.
28. *Hospital Beds:* 12,400; 0·6 per thous.
29. *Newspapers:* 39; circ. 250,000; 12 per thous.
30. *Newsprint:* 0·6 kilos per head.
31. *Newspapers:* In Burmese, English, Indian, Chinese.
32. *News Agency:* NAB.
33. *Radio Transmitters:* 5; 205 kW.
34. *Broadcasting:* Burma Broadcasting Service.
35. *Radio Licences:* 117,000; 6 per thous.
36. *TV Licences:* —
37. *Cinemas:* 386; seating capacity 270,000; 13 seats per thous.
38. *Cinema Attendance:* 115 mill.; 5 per head of pop.
39. *Gross National Product:* 6·5 milliard Kyats; Growth Rate: 4·7 per cent p.a.
40. *Gross Domestic Product:* $1·2 milliard; GNP: $52 per head of pop.
41. *Private Consumption:* 67 per cent of GNP.
42. *Wages Fund:* n.a.
43. *Expenditure on Food, etc.:* n.a.
44. *Expenditure on Household Goods:* n.a.

45. *Agricultural Population:* n.a.

46. *Arable Land:* 6 mill. ha. (15 mill. acres); 0·26 ha. (0·65 acres) per head. Irrigated Land: 0·6 mill. ha.

47. *Production of Paddy:* 4·7 mill. ha. (11·7 mill. acres); 7·5 mill. tons; 1·6 tons per ha. (0·65 ton per acre).

48. *Production of Grains:* 7·5 mill. tons; 323 kilos per head of pop.

49. *Production of Sugar:* 200,000 tons; Cotton: 20,000 tons.

50. *Livestock:* Cattle 5·3 mill.; Pigs 0·6 mill.; Sheep and Goats 0·5 mill.

51. *Production of Fertilizers:* —

52. *Consumption of Fertilizers* (thous. tons): N:4; P_2O_5:1. Total: 0·7 kilos per ha. (0·6 lb. per acre).

53. *Development Programme:* Second Four-Year Plan 1961/62-1964/65.

54. *Development Projects:* Mining and industrial projects.

55. *Energy Production:* 0·8 mill. tons coal equivalent.

56. *Energy Consumption:* 1·16 mill. tons coal equivalent; 50 kilos per head.

57. *Electricity Installed:* 0·25 mill. kW.

58. *Electricity Output:* 500 mill. kWh.

59. *Production of Coal:* —

60. *Production of Mineral Oil:* 0·6 mill. tons.

61. *Production of Iron Ore:* —

62. *Production of Manganese Ore:* —

63. *Production of Steel:* —

64. *Consumption of Steel:* —

65. *Production of Cotton:* 5,000 tons cotton yarn.

66. *Consumption of Cotton:* n.a.

67. *Production of Cement:* 53,000 tons.

68. *Production of Petrol:* 0·5 mill. tons.

69. *Production of Motor Vehicles:* —

70. *Production of Merchant Vessels:* —

71. *Telephones Installed:* 18,800.

72. *Letters Received:* n.a.

73. *Railway Transport:* 1·5 milliard pass./km.; 750 mill. ton/km.

74. *Motor Transport:* 22,000 pass. cars; 20,000 comm. vehicles in use.

75. *Sea Transport:* 1·7 million NRT entered; 2·1 mill. NRT cleared.

76. *Sea Transport:* 2·1 mill. tons loaded; 1 mill. tons unloaded.

77. *Civilian Airline:* Union of Burma Airways, Rangoon.

78. *Air Transport:* 64·6 mill. pass./km.; 1·2 mill. ton/km.

79. *Foreign Trade* (mill. Kyats): Imports 1,042; Exports 1,261; Balance +219.

80. *Foreign Trade:* Imports $11 per head; Exports $14 per head.

81. *Foreign Trade* (mill. Kyats): Imports: UK 156; USA 46; Japan 206. Exports: UK 123; USA 4; Indonesia 151.

82. *Foreign Trade* (mill. Kyats): Imports: Manuf. 460; Machines 200; Foods 113. Exports: Foods 965; Raw Mat. 253.

83. *Foreign Aid:* USA: 1946-63: $108 mill. UK: 1945-1963: £37 mill.

84. *Foreign Aid:* Sino-Soviet: 1956-63: $100 mill. offered; $20 mill. drawn.

85. *Public Finance* (mill. Kyats): Revenue 1,302; Expenditure 1,054.

86. *Government Obligations:* n.a.

87. *Foreign Exchange:* £1 sterling = 13·33 Kyats; US$1 = 4·76 Kyats.

88. *Foreign Exchange:* 1 Kyat = 1s 6d; 1 Kyat = US$0·21.

89. *Tourism:* Tourist Centres: Rangoon; Mandalay; Shan States (Inle Lake).

90. *Visa Requirements:* Tourist visa. Import of Kyats illegal.

THAILAND

1. *Area:* 514,000 sq. km. (198,000 sq. miles).
2. *Population:* 28 mill.
3. *Density of Population:* 54 per sq. km. (140 per sq. mile).
4. *Rate of Population Increase:* 2·64 per cent.
5. *Birth Rate:* 3·48 per cent.
6. *Death Rate:* 0·84 per cent.
7. *Geographical Location:* 5° 30′N–20° 30′N; 98° 30′E–106°E.
8. *Capital:* Bangkok (1·33 mill.).
9. *Mean Temperature:* Bangkok (7 ft.) 78°F (26°C) Jan., 86°F (30°C) April.
10. *Mean Annual Rainfall:* Bangkok 55·5 in. (1,410 mm.).
11. *Political Status:* Constitutional Monarchy.
12. *International Affiliations:* United Nations; Colombo Plan; SEATO.
13. *Head of State:* King Bhumibol Adulyadej.
14. *Head of Government:* Thanom Kittikachorn, Field-Marshal, Prime Minister and Minister of Defence.
15. *Political Institutions:* Constituent Assembly (appointed by the King).
16. *Political Parties:* —
17. *Languages:* Thai; English.
18. *Religions:* Buddhists 16 mill.; Muslims 0·7 mill.; Animists; Christians 0·15 mill.
19. *Working Population:* 53 per cent of total.
20. *Urban Population:* 12 per cent of total.
21. *Illiteracy:* 14 per cent of over 10 years of age.
22. *Expenditure on Education:* 2·5 per cent of GNP.
23. *Primary Schools:* 26,000 schools; 112,000 teachers; 4 million pupils.
24. *Secondary Schools:* 1,600 schools; 14,000 teachers; 300,000 pupils.
25. *School Enrolment:* 58 per cent of 5-19 years.
26. *Students (Higher Education):* 140,000.
27. *Physicians:* 3,400; 1 per 7,500 inh.
28. *Hospital Beds:* 21,400; 0·8 per thous.
29. *Newspapers:* 27; circ. 300,000; 11 per thous.
30. *Newsprint:* 0·7 kilos per head.
31. *Newspapers:* In Thai, English, Chinese.
32. *News Agencies:* —
33. *Radio Transmitters:* 20; 126 kW.
34. *Broadcasting:* Thai National Broadcasting.
35. *Radio Receivers:* 163,000; 6 per thous.
36. *TV Receivers:* 160,000; 6 per thous.
37. *Cinemas:* 230; seating capacity 138,000; 5 seats per thous.
38. *Cinema Attendance:* n.a.
39. *Gross National Product:* 63·1 milliard Baht; Growth Rate: 5·4 per cent p.a.
40. *Gross Domestic Product:* $2·5 milliard; GNP: $93 per head of pop.
41. *Private Consumption:* 73 per cent of GNP.
42. *Wages Fund:* n.a.
43. *Expenditure on Food, etc.:* 51 per cent of private consumption.
44. *Expenditure on Household Goods:* 8 per cent of private consumption.
45. *Agricultural Population:* 82 per cent of working pop. Farms under 5 ha. (12·5 acres): 70 per cent of holdings.
46. *Arable Land:* 10·3 mill. ha. (26 mill. acres); 0·4 ha. (1 acre) per head. Irrigated Land: 1·9 mill. ha.
47. *Production of Paddy:* 6·2 mill. ha. (15·5 mill. acres); 9 million tons; 1·5 tons per ha. (0·6 ton per acre).
48. *Production of Grains:* 9·8 mill. tons; 350 kilos per head of pop.
49. *Production of Sugar:* 250,000 tons.
50. *Livestock:* Cattle 5·5 mill.; Pigs 4·9 mill.
51. *Production of Fertilizers:* —
52. *Consumption of Fertilizers* (thous. tons): N:12; P_2O_5:7; K_2O:3. Total: 2 kilos per ha. (2 lb. per acre).

53. *Development Programme:* National Economic Development Plan 1961-66.

54. *Development Projects:* Industrial projects primarily in the Bangkok area.

55. *Energy Production:* —

56. *Energy Consumption:* 2·2 mill. tons coal equivalent; 77 kilos per head.

57. *Electricity Installed:* 0·3 mill. kW.

58. *Electricity Output:* 0·7 milliard kWh.

59. *Production of Coal:* —

60. *Production of Mineral Ore:* —

61. *Production of Iron Ore:* 30,000 tons.

62. *Production of Manganese Ore:* 2,000 tons.

63. *Production of Steel:* —

64. *Consumption of Steel:* 0·3 mill. tons; 11 kilos per head of pop.

65. *Production of Cotton:* 0·1 mill. spindles.

66. *Consumption of Cotton:* 20,000 tons; 0·7 kilos per head of pop.

67. *Production of Cement:* 1 mill. tons.

68. *Production of Petrol:* —

69. *Production of Motor Vehicles:* —

70. *Production of Merchant Vessels:* —

71. *Telephones Installed:* 49,700.

72. *Letters Received:* n.a.

73. *Railway Transport:* 2·5 milliard pass./km.; 1·3 milliard ton/km.

74. *Motor Transport:* 52,000 pass. cars; 64,000 comm. vehicles in use.

75. *Sea Transport:* 4·6 mill. NRT entered; 4·3 mill. NRT cleared.

76. *Sea Transport:* 3·1 mill. tons loaded; 2·7 mill. tons unloaded.

77. *Civilian Airline:* Thai Airways, Bangkok.

78. *Air Transport:* 133·7 mill. pass./km.; 1·9 mill. ton/km.

79. *Foreign Trade* (mill. Bahts): Imports 11,348; Exports 9,529; Balance −1,819.

80. *Foreign Trade:* Imports $19 per head. Exports $16 per head.

81. *Foreign Trade* (mill. Bahts): Imports: UK 1,024; USA 1,951; Japan 3,357. Exports: UK 466; USA 818; Malaya 1,379.

82. *Foreign Trade* (mill. Bahts): Imports: Manuf. 3,872; Machines 3,156; Fuels 1,224. Exports: Rice 3,240; Rubber 2,111; Tin 685.

83. *Foreign Aid:* USA: 1946-63: $869 mill.

84. *Foreign Aid:* Sino-Soviet: —

85. *Public Finance:* n.a.

86. *Government Obligations:* n.a.

87. *Foreign Exchange:* £1 sterling = 60 Bahts; US$1 = 20·85 Bahts.

88. *Foreign Exchange:* 1 Baht = 4d; 1 Baht = US$0·05.

89. *Tourism:* 225,000 tourists. Tourist Centres: Bangkok: Palace, Temples, Floating Market; Ayuthya; Chiang Mai.

90. *Visa Requirements:* British citizens: visa required. US citizens: no visa required.

CAMBODIA

1. *Area:* 181,000 sq. km. (70,000 sq. miles).
2. *Population:* 5·7 mill.
3. *Density of Population:* 32 per sq. km. (83 per sq. mile).
4. *Rate of Population Increase:* 2·17 per cent.
5. *Birth Rate:* 4·14 per cent.
6. *Death Rate:* 1·97 per cent.
7. *Geographical Location:* 8° 30'N–14° 30'N; 102° 30'E–107° 15'E.
8. *Capital:* Phnôm-Penh (0·4 mill.).
9. *Mean Temperature:* Phnôm-Penh (43 ft.) 82°F (28°C) Jan., 84°F (29°C) July.
10. *Mean Annual Rainfall:* Phnôm-Penh 57·5 in. (1,461 mm.).
11. *Political Status:* Constitutional Monarchy; independent since 8/11/1949 (29/12/1954).
12. *International Affiliations:* United Nations; Colombo Plan.
13. *Head of State:* Norodom Sihanouk, Chief of State.
14. *Head of Government:* Norodom Kantol, Prime Minister.
15. *Political Institutions:* National Assembly.
16. *Political Party:* 1962: Popular Socialist Community 77.
17. *Languages:* Cambodian (Khmer); French.
18. *Religions:* Theravada Buddhism; 100,000 Christians.
19. *Working Population:* n.a.
20. *Urban Population:* 13 per cent of total.
21. *Illiteracy:* 67 per cent of over 15 years of age.
22. *Expenditure on Education:* 4·8 per cent of GNP.
23. *Primary Schools:* 3,600 schools; 16,000 teachers; 600,000 pupils.
24. *Secondary Schools:* 50 schools, 900 teachers; 28,000 pupils.
25. *School Enrolment:* 41 per cent of 5-19 years.
26. *Students (Higher Education):* 4,000.
27. *Physicians:* 56; 1 per 32,000 inh.
28. *Hospital Beds:* 1,350; 0·6 per thous.
29. *Newspapers:* 9; circ. 28,000; 6 per thous.
30. *Newsprint:* 0·3 kilos per head.
31. *Newspapers:* In Khmer, Chinese, French.
32. *News Agency:* AKP.
33. *Radio Transmitters:* 2; 35 kW.
34. *Broadcasting:* Radio Cambodia.
35. *Radio Receivers:* 32,000; 6 per thous.
36. *TV Licences:* 300.
37. *Cinemas:* 18; seating capacity 12,300; 2 seats per thous.
38. *Cinema Attendance:* 3 mill.; 0·6 per head of pop.
39. *Gross National Product:* 16 milliard Riels. Growth Rate: 3·8 per cent p.a.
40. *Gross Domestic Product:* $433 mill.; GNP: $91 per head of pop.
41. *Private Consumption:* n.a.
42. *Wages Fund:* n.a.
43. *Expenditure on Food, etc.:* n.a.
44. *Expenditure on Household Goods:* n.a.
45. *Agricultural Population:* (est.) 70 per cent of working pop.
46. *Arable Land:* 2·4 mill. ha. (5·9 mill. acres); 0·4 ha. (1 acre) per head. Irrigated Land: 60,000 ha.
47. *Production of Paddy:* 1·6 mill. ha. (4 mill. acres); 1·6 mill. tons; 1 ton per ha. (0·4 ton per acre).
48. *Production of Grains:* 1·7 mill. tons; 300 kilos per head of pop.
49. *Production of Sugar:* —
50. *Livestock:* Cattle 1·3 mill.; Pigs 0·7 mill.
51. *Production of Fertilizers:* —
52. *Consumption of Fertilizers:* —
53. *Development Programme:* Five-Year Plan 1960-64.
54. *Development Projects:* To reduce the country's dependence on foreign assistance.
55. *Energy Production:* —
56. *Energy Consumption:* 0·2 mill. tons coal equivalent; 37 kilos per head.
57. *Electricity Installed:* 23,000 kW.
58. *Electricity Output:* 79 mill. kWh.

59. *Production of Coal:* —
61. *Production of Iron Ore:* —
63. *Production of Steel:* —
65. *Production of Cotton:* —
67. *Production of Cement:* —
69. *Production of Motor Vehicles:* —
71. *Telephones Installed:* 3,500.
73. *Railway Transport:* 72 mill. pass./km.; 55 mill. ton/km.
75. *Sea Transport:* n.a.
77. *Civilian Airline:* Royal Air Cambodge, Phnôm-Penh.
79. *Foreign Trade* (mill. Riels): Imports 3,583; Exports 1,903; Balance −1,680.
81. *Foreign Trade* (mill. Riels): Imports: UK 99; USA 484; France 658. Exports: UK 211; USA 181; France 493.
83. *Foreign Aid:* USA: 1946-63: $367 mill.
85. *Public Finance:* n.a.
87. *Foreign Exchange:* £1 sterling = 98 Riels; US$1 = 35 Riels.
89. *Tourism:* Phnôm-Penh; Angkor.
60. *Production of Mineral Oil:* —
62. *Production of Manganese Ore:* —
64. *Consumption of Steel:* —
66. *Consumption of Cotton:* n.a.
68. *Production of Petrol:* —
70. *Production of Merchant Vessels:* —
72. *Letters Received:* n.a.
74. *Motor Transport:* 14,000 pass. cars; 8,000 comm. vehicles in use.
76. *Sea Transport:* 410,000 tons loaded; 480,000 tons unloaded.
78. *Air Transport:* n.a.
80. *Foreign Trade:* Imports $18 per head; Exports $10 per head.
82. *Foreign Trade* (mill. Riels): Imports: Iron and Steel 394; Cars 332. Exports: Rubber 744; Rice 515.
84. *Foreign Aid:* Sino-Soviet: 1956-63: $75 mill. offered; $50 mill. drawn.
86. *Government Obligations:* n.a.
88. *Foreign Exchange:* 1 Riel = 2½d; 100 Riels = US$2·85.
90. *Visa Requirements:* Tourist visa. Import of Cambodian currency limited to 400 Riels.

LAOS

1. *Area:* 237,000 sq. km. (91,000 sq. miles).
2. *Population:* 1·9 mill.
3. *Density of Population:* 8 per sq. km. (21 per sq. mile).
4. *Rate of Population Increase:* n.a.
5. *Birth Rate:* n.a.
6. *Death Rate:* n.a.
7. *Geographical Location:* 14°N–22° 30′N; 100°E–107° 30′ E.
8. *Capital:* Vientiane (0·16 mill.).
9. *Mean Temperature:* Vientiane (531 ft.) 70°F (21°C) Jan., 81°F (27°C) July; Luang Prabang (942 ft.) 69°F (21°C) Jan., 85°F (29°C) July.
10. *Mean Annual Rainfall:* Vientiane 67·5 in. (1,715 mm.); Luang Prabang 51·5 in. (1,308 mm.).
11. *Political Status:* Constitutional Monarchy; independent since 19/7/1949; neutrality guaranteed 23/7/1962. Government of National Union.
12. *International Affiliations:* United Nations; Colombo Plan.
13. *Head of State:* King Savang Vatthana Sri.
14. *Head of Government:* Prince Souvanna Phouma, Prime Minister and Minister of Defence, Foreign Affairs, Veteran Affairs and Social Action.
15. *Political Institutions:* National Assembly.
16. *Political Parties:* 1962: Neutralists 13; 'Les Jeunes' 12; Southern Right Wing 10; Rassemblement du Peuple Lao 6; Independent 15.
17. *Languages:* Lao; French.
18. *Religions:* Theravada Buddhism.
19. *Working Population:* n.a.
20. *Urban Population:* n.a.
21. *Illiteracy:* n.a.
22. *Expenditure on Education:* n.a.
23. *Primary Schools:* 1,700 schools; 3,200 teachers; 100,000 pupils.
24. *Secondary Schools:* 3,000 pupils.
25. *School Enrolment:* 17 per cent of 5-19 years.
26. *Students (Higher Education):* 1,000.
27. *Physicians:* 42; 1 per 55,600 inh.
28. *Hospital Beds:* 620; 0·3 per thous.
29. *Newspapers:* 1; circ. 1,000; 0·6 per thous.
30. *Newsprint:* n.a.
31. *Newspapers:* In Laotian.
32. *News Agency:* Laos Press.
33. *Radio Transmitters:* 4; 17 kW.
34. *Broadcasting:* Radiodiffusion Nationale Lao.
35. *Radio Receivers:* 20,000; 11 per thous.
36. *TV Receivers:* 80,000.
37. *Cinemas:* 16; seating capacity 5,000; 3 seats per thous.
38. *Cinema Attendance:* n.a.
39. *Gross National Product:* n.a.
40. *Gross Domestic Product:* $137 mill.; GNP: $80 per head of pop.
41. *Private Consumption:* n.a.
42. *Wages Fund:* n.a.
43. *Expenditure on Food, etc.:* n.a.
44. *Expenditure on Household Goods:* n.a.
45. *Agricultural Population:* n.a.
46. *Arable Land:* 1 mill. ha. (2·5 mill. acres); 0·5 ha. (1·2 acres) per head. Irrigated Land: 750,000 ha.
47. *Production of Paddy:* 0·6 mill. ha. (1·5 mill. acres); 0·5 mill. tons; 0·9 ton per ha. (0·35 ton per acre).
48. *Production of Grains:* 0·6 mill. tons; 293 kilos per head of pop.
49. *Production of Sugar:* —
50. *Livestock:* Cattle 0·3 mill.; Pigs 0·6 mill.
51. *Production of Fertilizers:* —
52. *Consumption of Fertilizers:* —

53. *Development Programme:* —
54. *Development Projects:* —
55. *Energy Production:* —
56. *Energy Consumption:* 0·05 mill. tons coal equivalent; 27 kilos per head.
57. *Electricity Installed:* n.a.
58. *Electricity Output:* n.a.
59. *Production of Coal:* —
60. *Production of Mineral Oil:* —
61. *Production of Iron Ore:* —
62. *Production of Manganese Ore:* —
63. *Production of Steel:* —
64. *Consumption of Steel:* —
65. *Production of Cotton:* —
66. *Consumption of Cotton:* n.a.
67. *Production of Cement:* —
68. *Production of Petrol:* —
69. *Production of Motor Vehicles:* —
70. *Production of Merchant Vessels:* —
71. *Telephones Installed:* 1,000.
72. *Letters Received:* n.a.
73. *Railway Transport:* n.a.
74. *Motor Transport:* 5,000 pass. cars; 2,000 comm. vehicles in use.
75. *Sea Transport:* n.a.
76. *Sea Transport:* n.a.
77. *Civilian Airline:* Air Laos, Vientiane.
78. *Air Transport:* n.a.
79. *Foreign Trade:* n.a.
80. *Foreign Trade:* n.a.
81. *Foreign Trade:* n.a.
82. *Foreign Trade:* n.a.
83. *Foreign Aid:* USA: 1946-63: $328 mill.
84. *Foreign Aid:* Sino-Soviet: 1956-63: $10 mill. offered; $5 mill. drawn.
85. *Public Finance:* n.a.
86. *Government Obligations:* n.a.
87. *Foreign Exchange:* £1 sterling = 672 Kip; US$1 = 240 Kip.
88. *Foreign Exchange:* 100 Kip = 3s. 0d; 100 Kip = US$0·40.
89. *Tourism:* Tourist Centres: Vientiane; Luang Prabang.
90. *Visa Requirements:* Entry and exit visa.

SOUTH VIETNAM

1. *Area:* 170,000 sq. km. (66,000 sq. miles).
2. *Population:* 14·9 mill.
3. *Density of Population:* 87 per sq. km. (226 per sq. mile).
4. *Rate of Population Increase:* 2·45 per cent.
5. *Birth Rate:* 3·1 per cent.
6. *Death Rate:* 0·66 per cent.
7. *Geographical Location:* 8°N–17°N; 104°E–109°E.
8. *Capital:* Saigon (1·4 mill.).
9. *Mean Temperature:* Saigon (30 ft.) 78°F (26°C) Jan., 80°F (27°C) July.
10. *Mean Annual Rainfall:* Saigon 79·2 in. (2,009 mm.).
11. *Political Status:* Republic since 26/10/1955; independent since 8/3/1949 (29/12/1954).
12. *International Affiliations:* Colombo Plan.
13. *Head of State:* Nguyen Van Thien, Major-General, Chairman of National Directory Committee.
14. *Head of Government:* Nguyen Cao Ky, Brigadier, Chairman of Executive Committee.
15. *Political Institutions:* National Assembly.
16. *Political Parties:* Suspended.
17. *Languages:* Vietnamese; French; English.
18. *Religions:* Buddhism; Taoism; Animism; 1 mill. Christians.
19. *Working Population:* n.a.
20. *Urban Population:* n.a.
21. *Illiteracy:* n.a.
22. *Expenditure on Education:* n.a.
23. *Primary Schools:* 6,300 schools; 26,000 teachers; 1·4 mill. pupils.
24. *Secondary Schools:* 500 schools; 7,600 teachers; 230,000 pupils.
25. *School Enrolment:* 47 per cent of 5-19 years.
26. *Students (Higher Education):* 20,000.
27. *Physicians:* 490; 1 per 28,000 inh.
28. *Hospital Beds:* 20,660; 1·5 per thous.
29. *Newspapers:* 26; circ. 350,000; 28 per thous.
30. *Newsprint:* 0·4 kilos per head.
31. *Newspapers:* In Vietnamese, French, Chinese, English.
32. *News Agency:* VP.
33. *Radio Transmitters:* 18; 161 kW.
34. *Broadcasting:* Vietnamese National Broadcasting Service.
35. *Radio Licences:* 125,000; 9 per thous.
36. *TV Licences:* —
37. *Cinemas:* 153; seating capacity 83,000; 6 seats per thous.
38. *Cinema Attendance:* 18 mill.; 1·2 per head of pop.
39. *Gross National Product:* 68·7 milliard Dong.
40. *Gross Domestic Product:* $1·1 milliard; GNP: $88 per head of pop.
41. *Private Consumption:* n.a.
42. *Wages Fund:* n.a.
43. *Expenditure on Food, etc.:* n.a.
44. *Expenditure on Household Goods:* n.a.
45. *Agricultural Population:* n.a.
46. *Arable Land:* 3·1 mill. ha. (8 mill. acres); 0·2 ha. (0·5 acres) per head of pop. Irrigated Land: 600,000 ha.
47. *Production of Paddy:* 2·5 mill. ha. (6·2 mill. acres); 5·2 mill. tons; 2·1 tons per ha. (0·85 ton per acre).
48. *Production of Grains:* 5·2 mill. tons; 350 kilos per head of pop.
49. *Production of Sugar:* 100,000 tons.
50. *Livestock:* Cattle 1·1 mill.; Pigs 3·3 mill.
51. *Production of Fertilizers:* —
52. *Consumption of Fertilizers* (thous tons): N:17: P_2O_5:3; K_2O:3. Total: 7 kilos per ha. (6 lb. per acre).
53. *Development Programme:* Five-Year Plan 1962-6.
54. *Development Projects:* Agriculture, fuel and power, communications.

55. *Energy Production:* 0·1 mill. tons coal equivalent.
56. *Energy Consumption:* 0·8 mill. tons coal equivalent; 55 kilos per head.
57. *Electricity Installed:* 110,000 kW.
58. *Electricity Output:* 0·35 milliard kWh.
59. *Production of Coal:* 0·1 mill. tons.
60. *Production of Mineral Oil:* —
61. *Production of Iron Ore:* —
62. *Production of Manganese Ore:* —
63. *Production of Steel:* —
64. *Consumption of Steel:* 0·1 mill. tons; 6 kilos per head of pop.
65. *Production of Cotton:* 5,000 tons cotton yarn.
66. *Consumption of Cotton:* n.a.
67. *Production of Cement:* —
68. *Production of Petrol:* —
69. *Production of Motor Vehicles:* —
70. *Production of Merchant Vessels:* —
71. *Telephones Installed:* 18,100.
72. *Letters Received:* 58 mill.; 4 per head of pop.
73. *Railway Transport:* 339 mill. pass./km.; 150 mill. ton/km.
74. *Motor Transport:* 29,000 pass. cars; 26,000 comm. vehicles in use.
75. *Sea Transport:* 3·6 mill. NRT entered.
76. *Sea Transport:* 0·4 mill. tons loaded; 2·1 mill. tons unloaded.
77. *Civilian Airline:* Air Vietnam, Saigon.
78. *Air Transport:* 79·5 mill. pass./km.; 0·6 mill. ton/km.
79. *Foreign Trade* (mill. Piastres): Imports 9,235; Exports 1,962; Balance −7,273.
80. *Foreign Trade:* Imports $15 per head; Exports $3 per head.
81. *Foreign Trade* (mill. Piastres): Imports: UK 159; USA 3,397; Japan 15,562. Exports: UK 307; USA 64; France 714.
82. *Foreign Trade* (mill. Piastres): Imports: Machines 1,606; Metals 713; Min. Oil 615. Exports: Rubber 1,327; Rice 254; Tea 62.
83. *Foreign Aid:* USA: 1946-63: $1,896 mill.
84. *Foreign Aid:* Sino-Soviet: —
85. *Public Finance:* n.a.
86. *Government Obligations:* n.a.
87. *Foreign Exchange:* £1 sterling = 205 Piastres; US$1 = 73·50 Piastres.
88. *Foreign Exchange:* 1 Piastre = 1½d; 100 Piastres = US$1·67.
89. *Tourism:* Tourist Centres: Saigon; Cholon; Dalat; Hué. Travel outside the capital dependent on security arrangements.
90. *Visa Requirements:* Tourist visa, except US citizens staying up to 7 days. Currency registration.

NORTH VIETNAM

1. *Area:* 159,000 sq. km. (65,000 sq. miles).
2. *Population:* (est.) 17·2 mill.
3. *Density of Population:* 108 per sq. km. (280 per sq. mile).
4. *Rate of Population Increase:* n.a.
5. *Birth Rate:* n.a.
6. *Death Rate:* n.a.
7. *Geographical Location:* 17°N–24°N; 102°E–108°E.
8. *Capital:* Hanoi (Municipal Area: 0·64 mill.; Greater Hanoi: 0·85 mill.).
9. *Mean Temperature:* Hanoi (53 ft.) 62°F (17°C) Jan., 85°F (29°C) June.
10. *Mean Annual Rainfall:* Hanoi 69·9 in. (1,776 mm.).
11. *Political Status:* Democratic Republic.
12. *International Affiliations:* Treaties with the Soviet Union and the People's Republic of China.
13. *Head of State:* Ho Chi Minh, President.
14. *Head of Government:* Pham Van Dong, Prime Minister.
15. *Political Institutions:* National Assembly.
16. *Political Party:* Workers' (Communist) Party (600,000 members). Chairman of Central Committee: Ho Chi Minh.
17. *Languages:* Vietnamese; French.
18. *Religions:* Buddhism; Taoism; Animism.
19. *Working Population:* n.a.
20. *Urban Population:* 10 per cent of total.
21. *Illiteracy:* n.a.
22. *Expenditure on Education:* n.a.
23. *Primary Schools:* 5,500 schools; 1 mill. pupils.
24. *Secondary Schools:* 30 schools; 15,000 pupils.
25. *School Enrolment:* n.a.
26. *Students (Higher Education):* n.a.
27. *Physicians:* n.a.
28. *Hospital Beds:* n.a.
29. *Newspapers:* n.a.
30. *Newsprint:* n.a.
31. *Newspapers:* In Vietnamese.
32. *News Agency:* AVI.
33. *Radio Transmitters:* 9.
34. *Broadcasting:* Voice of Vietnam.
35. *Radio Receivers:* n.a.
36. *TV Receivers:* —
37. *Cinemas:* n.a.
38. *Cinema Attendance:* n.a.
39. *Gross National Product:* n.a.
40. *Gross Domestic Product:* n.a.
41. *Private Consumption:* n.a.
42. *Wages Fund:* n.a.
43. *Expenditure on Food, etc.:* n.a.
44. *Expenditure on Household Goods:* n.a.
45. *Agricultural Population:* n.a.
46. *Arable Land:* n.a.
47. *Production of Paddy:* 2·3 mill. ha. (5·6 mill. acres); 4·6 mill. tons; 2 tons per ha. (0·8 ton per acre).
48. *Production of Grains:* 4·7 mill. tons; 275 kilos per head of pop.
49. *Production of Sugar:* 20,000 tons; Cotton: 6,000 tons.
50. *Livestock:* Cattle 0·8 mill.; Pigs 4·2 mill.
51. *Production of Fertilizers:* —
52. *Consumption of Fertilizers:* n.a.
53. *Development Programme:* Five-Year Plan 1961-65.
54. *Development Projects:* Priority on industrial targets: downward revision of targets in 1963.
55. *Energy Production:* n.a.
56. *Energy Consumption:* n.a.
57. *Electricity Installed:* n.a.
58. *Electricity Output:* 0·3 milliard kWh.
59. *Production of Coal:* 2·6 mill. tons.
60. *Production of Mineral Oil:* —
61. *Production of Iron Ore:* n.a.
62. *Production of Manganese Ore:* n.a.
63. *Production of Steel:* —
64. *Consumption of Steel:* 0·05 mill. tons; 3 kilos per head of pop.
65. *Production of Cotton:* n.a.
66. *Consumption of Cotton:* n.a.
67. *Production of Cement:* 0·5 mill. tons.
68. *Production of Petrol:* —

69. *Production of Motor Vehicles:* —
71. *Telephones Installed:* n.a.
73. *Railway Transport:* n.a.
75. *Sea Transport:* n.a.
77. *Civilian Airline:* —
79. *Foreign Trade* ($ mill.) (est.): Imports 150; Exports 100; Balance −50.
81. *Foreign Trade:* n.a.
83. *Foreign Aid:* Western: —
85. *Public Finance:* n.a.
87. *Foreign Exchange:* £1 sterling = 10·10 Dong; US$1 = 3·60 Dong.
89. *Tourism:* —

70. *Production of Merchant Vessels:* —
72. *Letters Received:* n.a.
74. *Motor Transport:* n.a.
76. *Sea Transport:* n.a.
78. *Air Transport:* —
80. *Foreign Trade* (est.): Imports $9 per head; Exports $6 per head.
82. *Foreign Trade:* n.a.
84. *Foreign Aid:* Sino-Soviet: 1956-63: $600 mill. (Soviet: $270 mill.; Chinese: $260 mill.) offered.
86. *Government Obligations:* n.a.
88. *Foreign Exchange:* 1 Dong = 2s. 0d; 1 Dong = US$0·28.
90. *Visa Requirements:* Tourist visa difficult to obtain. Entry from China.

MALAYA

1. *Area:* 131,000 sq. km. (51,000 sq. miles).
2. *Population:* 7·4 mill.
3. *Density of Population:* 56 per sq. km. (146 per sq. mile).
4. *Rate of Population Increase:* 3·1 per cent.
5. *Birth Rate:* 4·03 per cent.
6. *Death Rate:* 0·93 per cent.
7. *Geographical Location:* 1° 17′N-6° 30′N; 99°E–105°E.
8. *Capital:* Kuala Lumpur (0·32 mill.)
9. *Mean Temperature:* Kuala Lumpur (127 ft.) and Penang (23 ft.) 81°F (27°C).
10. *Mean Annual Rainfall:* Kuala Lumpur 96·1 in. (2,441 mm.); Penang 109·3 in. (2,776 mm.).
11. *Political Status:* Federation; Member of Federation of Malaysia since 16/9/1963.
12. *International Affiliations:* United Nations; British Commonwealth; Sterling Area; Colombo Plan.
13. *Head of State:* Syed Raja Putra, Paramount Ruler.
14. *Head of Government:* Tungku Abdul Rahman, Prime Minister, Minister of External Affairs, and Minister of Culture, Youth and Sports.
15. *Political Institutions:* Federal Parliament: House of Representatives (Lower House) and Senate (Upper House).
16. *Political Parties:* House of Reps, 1962: Alliance Party 74; Pan Malayan Islam Party 12; Socialist Front 8; People's Progressive Party 5; Independent 4.
17. *Languages:* Malay; Chinese; Tamil; English.
18. *Religions:* Islam (official); Taoism; Confucianism; Buddhism; 300,000 Christians.
19. *Working Population:* 34 per cent of total.
20. *Urban Population:* 42 per cent of total.
21. *Illiteracy:* 29 per cent of over 10 years of age.
22. *Expenditure on Education:* n.a.
23. *Primary Schools:* 4,900 schools; 42,000 teachers; 1·1 mill. pupils.
24. *Secondary Schools:* 700 schools; 7,000 teachers; 200,000 pupils.
25. *School Enrolment:* 62 per cent of 5-19 years.
26. *Students (Higher Education):* 19,000.
27. *Physicians:* 925; 1 per 7,000 inh.
28. *Hospital Beds:* 26,700; 4·3 per thous.
29. *Newspapers:* 28; circ. 470,000; 67 per thous.
30. *Newsprint:* 0·8 kilos per head.
31. *Newspapers:* In English, Malay, Chinese, Tamil.
32. *News Agencies:* Bernama.
33. *Radio Transmitters:* 21; 185 kW.
34. *Broadcasting:* Radio Malaya.
35. *Radio Licences:* 292,000; 41 per thous.
36 *TV Licences:* —
37. *Cinemas:* 287; seating capacity 150,000; 22 seats per thous.
38. *Cinema Attendance:* 62 mill.; 9 per head of pop.
39. *Gross National Product:* M$6·9 milliard; Growth Rate: 4·1 per cent p.a.
40. *Gross Domestic Product:* $1·7 milliard; GNP: $241 per head of pop.
41. *Private Consumption:* 65 per cent of GNP.
42. *Wages Fund:* 47 per cent of Nat. Inc.
43. *Expenditure on Food. etc.:* 57 per cent of private consumption.
44. *Expenditure on Household Goods:* 7 per cent of private consumption.
45. *Agricultural Population:* 58 per cent of working pop. Farms under 5 ha. (12·5 acres): 90 per cent of holdings.
46. *Arable Land:* 2·5 mill. ha. (6·2 mill. acres); 0·35 ha. (0·85 acres) per head of pop. Irrigated Land: 220,000 ha.
47. *Production of Paddy:* 0·4 mill. ha. (1 mill. acres); 1 mill. tons; 2·5 tons per ha. (1 ton per acre).
48. *Production of Grains:* 1 mill. tons; 135 kilos per head of pop.

49. *Production of Sugar:* —

50. *Livestock:* Cattle 0·3 mill.; Pigs 0·5 mill.; Sheep and Goats 0·3 mill.

51. *Production of Fertilizers:* —

52. *Consumption of Fertilizers* (thous. tons): N:26; P_2O_5:6; K_2O:12. Total: 17 kilos per ha. (15 lbs. per acre).

53. *Development Programme:* Five-Year Plan 1961-65.

54. *Development Projects:* Land resettlement, communications and social services.

55. *Energy Production:* —

56. *Energy Consumption:* 1·9 mill. tons coal equivalent; 260 kilos per head.

57. *Electricity Installed:* 0·3 mill. kW.

58. *Electricity Output:* 1·5 milliard kWh.

59. *Production of Coal:* —

60. *Production of Mineral Oil:* —

61. *Production of Iron Ore:* 3·7 mill. tons.

62. *Production of Manganese Ore:* —

63. *Production of Steel:* —

64. *Consumption of Steel:* 0·3 mill. tons; 37 kilos per head of pop.

65. *Production of Cotton:* —

66. *Consumption of Cotton:* n.a.

67. *Production of Cement:* 0·3 mill. tons.

68. *Production of Petrol:* —

69. *Production of Motor Vehicles:* —

70. *Production of Merchant Vessels:* —

71. *Telephones Installed:* 90,200.

72. *Letters Received:* 135 mill.; 18 per head.

73. *Railway Transport:* 595 mill. pass./km.; 707 mill. ton/km.

74. *Motor Transport:* 118,000 pass. cars; 37,000 comm. vehicles in use.

75. *Sea Transport:* 14·9 mill. NRT entered; 15·7 mill. tons cleared.

76. *Sea Transport:* 7·7 mill. tons loaded; 3·7 mill. tons unloaded.

77. *Civilian Airline:* Malayan Airways, Kuala Lumpur.

78. *Air Transport:* 50·8 mill. pass./km.; 0·9 mill. ton/km.

79. *Foreign Trade* (M$ mill.): Imports 2,447; Exports 2,626; Balance +179.

80. *Foreign Trade:* Imports $110 per head. Exports $118 per head.

81. *Foreign Trade* (M$ mill.): Imports: UK 534; USA 144; Indonesia 294. Exports: UK 246; USA 383; Singapore 519.

82. *Foreign Trade* (M$ mill.): Imports: Foods 563; Machines 482; Manuf. 472. Exports: Rubber 1,368; Tin 616; Other Metals 184.

83. *Foreign Aid:* USA: 1946-63: $25 mill. UK: 1945-63: £56 mill.

84. *Foreign Aid:* Sino-Soviet: —

85. *Public Finance:* n.a.

86. *Government Obligations:* n.a.

87. *Foreign Exchange:* £1 sterling = M$8·57; US$1 = M$3·05.

88. *Foreign Exchange:* M$1 = 2s 4d; M$1 = US$0·33.

89. *Tourism:* Tourist Centres: Kuala Lumpur; Penang.

90. *Visa Requirements:* British and US citizens: no visa required. Liberal currency regulations.

SINGAPORE

1. *Area:* 580 sq. km. (224 sq. miles).
2. *Population:* 1·7 mill.
3. *Density of Population:* 2,980 per sq. km. (7,750 per sq. mile).
4. *Rate of Population Increase:* 2·92 per cent.
5. *Birth Rate:* 3·51 per cent.
6. *Death Rate:* 0·59 per cent.
7. *Geographical Location:* 1° 17′N–103° 51′E.
8. *Capital:* Singapore (1·71 mill.).
9. *Mean Temperature:* Singapore (33 ft.) 80°F (27°C).
10. *Mean Annual Rainfall:* Singapore 95 in. (2,413 mm.).
11. *Political Status:* Member of Federation of Malaysia 16/9/1963-9/8/1965 (date of secession).
12. *International Affiliations:* British Commonwealth; Sterling Area; Colombo Plan.
13. *Head of State:* Inche Yusof bin Ishak, Chief of State.
14. *Head of Government:* Lee Kuan Yew, Prime Minister.
15. *Political Institutions:* Legislative Assembly.
16. *Political Parties:* 1963: People's Action Party 37; Barisan Socialists 13; United People's Party 1.
17. *Languages:* Chinese; English; Malay.
18. *Religions:* Confucianism; Taoism; Islam.
19. *Working Population:* n.a.
20. *Urban Population:* 63 per cent of total.
21. *Illiteracy:* 31 per cent of over 10 years of age.
22. *Expenditure on Education:* n.a.
23. *Primary Schools:* 500 schools; 9,700 teachers; 300,000 pupils.
24. *Secondary Schools:* 90 schools; 2,300 teachers; 70,000 pupils.
25. *School Enrolment:* 77 per cent of 5-19 years.
26. *Students (Higher Education):* 13,000.
27. *Physicians:* 640; 1 per 2,500 inh.
28. *Hospital Beds:* 6,740; 4 per thous.
29. *Newspapers:* 8; circ. 500,000; 286 per thous.
30. *Newsprint:* 6·3 kilos per head.
31. *Newspapers:* In Malay, Chinese, English, Tamil.
32. *News Agencies:* —
33. *Radio Transmitters:* 8; 80 kW.
34. *Broadcasting:* Radio Singapore.
35. *Radio Licences:* 150,000; 90 per thous.
36. *TV Licences:* 30,000; 19 per thous.
37. *Cinemas:* 62; seating capacity 44,000; 27 seats per thousand.
38. *Cinema Attendance:* 23 mill.; 14 per head of pop.
39. *Gross National Product:* n.a.
40. *Gross Domestic Product:* $546 mill. GNP: $361 per head of pop.
41. *Private Consumption:* n.a.
42. *Wages Fund:* n.a.
43. *Expenditure on Food, etc.:* 51 per cent of private consumption.
44. *Expenditure on Household Goods:* 5 per cent of private consumption.
45. *Agricultural Population:* 8 per cent of working pop.
46. *Arable Land:* 14,000 ha. (35,000 acres); 0·01 ha. (0·02 acres) per head.
47. *Production of Paddy:* —
48. *Production of Grains:* —
49. *Production of Sugar:* —
50. *Livestock:* Cattle 7,000; Pigs 400,000.
51. *Production of Fertilizers:* —
52. *Consumption of Fertilizers* (thous. tons): N:7; K_2O:4.
53. *Development Programme:* Four-Year Plan 1961-65.
54. *Development Projects:* Infrastructure for industrial development.
55. *Energy Production:* —
56. *Energy Consumption:* 1·2 mill. tons coal equivalent; 722 kilos per head.
57. *Electricity Installed:* 0·2 mill. kW.
58. *Electricity Output:* 0·8 milliard kWh.
59. *Production of Coal:* —
60. *Production of Mineral Oil:* —

61. *Production of Iron Ore:* —

62. *Production of Manganese Ore:* —

63. *Production of Steel:* —

64. *Consumption of Steel:* n.a.

65. *Production of Cotton:* —

66. *Consumption of Cotton:* n.a.

67. *Production of Cement:* —

68. *Production of Petrol:* —

69. *Production of Motor Vehicles:* —

70. *Production of Merchant Vessels:* —

71. *Telephones Installed:* 67,500.

72. *Letters Received:* 65 mill.; 38 per head.

73. *Railway Transport:* n.a.

74. *Motor Transport:* 81,000 pass. cars; 17,000 comm. vehicles in use.

75. *Sea Transport:* n.a.

76. *Sea Transport:* 7·8 mill. tons loaded; 13·6 mill. tons unloaded.

77. *Civilian Airline:* Malayan Airways, Singapore.

78. *Air Transport:* n.a.

79. *Foreign Trade* (M$ mill.): Imports 4,036; Exports 3,417; Balance −619.

80. *Foreign Trade:* Imports $791 per head. Exports $670 per head.

81. *Foreign Trade* (M$ mill.): Imports: UK 385; USA 201; Indonesia 804. Exports: UK 217; USA 284; Malaya 942.

82. *Foreign Trade* (M$ mill.): Imports: Rubber 970; Min. Oil 601; Manuf. 573. Exports: Rubber 1,099; Foods 495; Min. Oil 416.

83. *Foreign Aid:* —

84. *Foreign Aid:* —

85. *Public Finance:* n.a.

86. *Government Obligations:* n.a.

87. *Foreign Exchange:* £1 sterling = M$8·57; US$1 = M$3·05.

88. *Foreign Exchange:* M$1 = 2s 4d; M$1 = US$0·33.

89. *Tourism:* Tourist attractions: Chinatown; Trips to Brunei, Sarawak and Sabah.

90. *Visa Requirements:* British and US citizens: no visa required. No currency restrictions.

INDONESIA

1. *Area:* 1·49 mill. sq. km. (0·57 mill. sq. miles).
2. *Population:* 97·8 mill.
3. *Density of Population:* 66 per sq. km. (172 per sq. mile).
4. *Rate of Population Increase:* 2 per cent.
5. *Birth Rate:* 4 per cent.
6. *Death Rate:* 2 per cent.
7. *Geographical Location:* 6°N–11°S; 95° 30′E–140° 30′E.
8. *Capital:* Djakarta (2·9 mill.). Other principal towns: Surabaja (1 mill.); Bandung (1 mill.).
9. *Mean Temperature:* Djakarta (26 ft.) 80°F (27°C).
10. *Mean Annual Rainfall:* Djakarta 71·3 in. (1,811 mm.).
11. *Political Status:* Republic since 17/8/1945; independent since 2/11/1949.
12. *International Affiliations:* United Nations; Colombo Plan.
13. *Head of State:* Dr. Sukarno, President.
14. *Head of Government:* Dr. Sukarno, Prime Minister.
15. *Political Institutions:* 'Guided Democracy': Mutual Co-operation House of Representatives.
16. *Political Parties:* 1960–; Indonesian Nationalist Party (PNI) 44; Muslim Scholars (NU) 36; Indonesian Communist Party (PKI) 30; Others 20; Functional Groups (without political affiliation) 153.
17. *Languages:* Bahasa Indonesia (official); Chinese; Dutch; English.
18. *Religions:* Muslims 90 per cent (approx.); Christians 7 mill.; Buddhists 1 mill., Hindus (island of Bali).
19. *Working Population:* 34 per cent of total.
20. *Urban Population:* 15 per cent of total.
21. *Illiteracy:* 82 per cent of over 10 years of age.
22. *Expenditure on Education:* 1·3 per cent of GNP.
23. *Primary Schools:* 40,000 schools; 240,000 teachers; 9·6 mill. pupils.
24. *Secondary Schools:* 5,500 schools; 35,000 teachers; 750,000 pupils.
25. *School Enrolment:* 40 per cent of 5-19 years.
26. *Students (Higher Education):* 250,000.
27. *Physicians:* 1,940; 1 per 10,000 inh.
28. *Hospital Beds:* 73,600; 0·8 per thous.
29. *Newspapers:* 95; circ. 1 mill.; 11 per thous.
30. *Newsprint:* 0·2 kilos per head.
31. *Newspapers:* In Indonesian, Chinese, English.
32. *News Agencies:* Antara.
33. *Radio Transmitters:* 69; 400 kW.
34. *Broadcasting:* Radio Republic Indonesia.
35. *Radio Receivers:* 1·2 mill.; 13 per thous.
36. *TV Receivers:* —
37. *Cinemas:* 675; seating capacity 513,000; 5 seats per thous.
38. *Cinema Attendance:* 257 million; 3 per head of pop.
39. *Gross National Product:* 210 milliard Rupiah; Growth Rate: 3·9 per cent p.a.
40. *Gross Domestic Product:* $6·2 milliard; GNP: $69 per head of pop.
41. *Private Consumption:* n.a.
42. *Wages Fund:* n.a.
43. *Expenditure on Food, etc.:* n.a.
44. *Expenditure on Household Goods:* n.a.
45. *Agricultural Population:* 72 per cent of working pop.
46. *Arable Land:* 17·7 mill. ha. (44 mill. acres); 0·17 ha. (0·4 acres) per head. Irrigated Land: 5·5 mill. ha.
47. *Production of Paddy:* 7·3 mill. ha. (18 mill. acres); 13·4 mill. tons; 1·85 tons per ha. (0·75 ton per acre).
48. *Production of Grains:* 16·6 mill. tons; 170 kilos per head of pop.

49. *Production of Sugar:* 600,000 tons; Tea: 65,000 tons.

50. *Livestock:* Cattle 6·4 mill.; Pigs 2·7 mill.; Sheep and Goats 7·7 mill.

51. *Production of Fertilizers:* —

52. *Consumption of Fertilizers* (thous. tons): N:99; P_2O_5:46; K_2O:5. Total: 8 kilos. per ha. (7 lbs. per acre).

53. *Development Programme:* Eight-Year Development Plan 1961-68.

54. *Development Projects:* Increased industrial and agricultural output; improvements in distribution.

55. *Energy Production:* 34 mill. tons coal equivalent.

56. *Energy Consumption:* 11·5 mill. tons coal equivalent; 117 kilos per head.

57. *Electricity Installed:* 0·4 mill. kW.

58. *Electricity Output:* 1·2 milliard kWh.

59. *Production of Coal:* 0·5 mill. tons.

60. *Production of Mineral Oil:* 22·8 mill. tons.

61. *Production of Iron Ore:* —

62. *Production of Manganese Ore:* 6,000 tons.

63. *Production of Steel:* —

64. *Consumption of Steel:* 0·25 mill. tons; 2 kilos per head of pop.

65. *Production of Cotton:* 0·25 mill. spindles; 10,000 tons of cotton yarn.

66. *Consumption of Cotton:* n.a.

67. *Production of Cement:* 0·5 mill. tons.

68. *Production of Petrol:* 11·6 mill. tons.

69. *Production of Motor Vehicles:* —

70. *Production of Merchant Vessels:* —

71. *Telephones Installed:* 139,600.

72. *Letters Received:* 220 mill.; 2 per head of pop.

73. *Railway Transport:* 7·6 milliard pass./km.; 1·2 milliard ton/km.

74. *Motor Transport:* 141,000 pass. cars; 98,000 comm. vehicles in use.

75. *Sea Transport:* n.a.

76. *Sea Transport:* 17·8 mill. tons loaded; 5·5 mill. tons unloaded.

77. *Civilian Airline:* Garuda Indonesian Airways, Djakarta.

78. *Air Transport:* 302·8 mill. pass./km.; 4·7 mill. ton/km.

79. *Foreign Trade* (mill. Rupiahs): Imports 29,133; Exports 30,532; Balance +1,399

80. *Foreign Trade:* Imports: $7 per head. Exports: $7 per head.

81. *Foreign Trade* (mill. Rupiahs): Imports: UK 2,263; USA 6,132; Japan 6,405. Exports: UK 2,281; USA 8,392; Singapore 7,353.

82. *Foreign Trade* (mill. Rupiahs): Imports: Manuf. 10,338; Machines 8,304; Foods 3,519. Exports: Rubber 13,464; Min. Oil 9,711; Tin 1,571.

83. *Foreign Aid:* USA: 1946-63: $880 mill.

84. *Foreign Aid:* Sino-Soviet: 1956-63: $650 mill. offered; $200 mill. drawn.

85. *Public Finance:* n.a.

86. *Government Obligations:* n.a.

87. *Foreign Exchange:* Official rate not operative.

88. *Foreign Exchange:* Official rate not operative.

89. *Tourism:* Tourist Centres: Djakarta; Jogjakarta; Bogor; Bandung; Bali.

90. *Visa Requirements:* Tourist visa. Police registration. Travel permit outside capital. Import and export of Rupiahs illegal.

THE PHILIPPINES

1. *Area:* 297,000 sq. km. (115,000 sq. miles).
2. *Population:* 29·3 mill.
3. *Density of Population:* 98 per sq. km. (255 per sq. mile).
4. *Rate of Population Increase:* 2·15 per cent.
5. *Birth Rate:* 2·92 per cent.
6. *Death Rate:* 0·77 per cent.
7. *Geographical Location:* 5°N–22°N; 117°E-127°E.
8. *Capital:* Manila (1·14 mill.). Other principal towns: Quezon City (0·4 mill.).
9. *Mean Temperature:* Manila (47 ft.) 77°F (25°C) Jan., 84°F (29°C) May; Baguio (4,954 ft.) 64°F (18°C) Jan., 69°F (21°C) April-May.
10. *Mean Annual Rainfall:* Manila 82 in. (2,083 mm.); Baguio 183 in. (4,748 mm.).
11. *Political Status:* Republic; independent since 4/7/1946.
12. *International Affiliations:* United Nations; Colombo Plan; SEATO; Security Treaty with USA.
13. *Head of State:* Diosdado Macapagal, President.
14. *Head of Government:* Ramon Diaz, Executive Secretary.
15. *Political Institutions:* Congress: House of Representatives (Lower House) and Senate (Upper House).
16. *Political Parties:* House of Reps, 1963: Liberal 55; Nacionalista 44; vacant 5.
17. *Languages:* Tagalog (official language); English 10·7 mill.; Spanish 0·6 mill.; 70 other languages.
18. *Religions:* Roman Catholics 83 per cent; Other Christians 3·2 mill.; Muslims 0·8 mill.; Pagans 0·4 mill.
19. *Working Population:* 38 per cent of total.
20. *Urban Population:* 35 per cent of total.
21. *Illiteracy:* 24 per cent of over 10 years of age.
22. *Expenditure on Education:* 3·2 per cent of GNP.
23. *Primary Schools:* 31,000 schools; 117,000 teachers; 4·2 mill. pupils.
24. *Secondary Schools:* 1,600 schools; 22,000 teachers; 600,000 pupils.
25. *School Enrolment:* 70 per cent of 5-19 years.
26. *Students (Higher Education):* 900,000.
27. *Physicians:* 3,950; 1 per 7,000 inh.
28. *Hospital Beds:* 13,650; 0·5 per thous.
29. *Newspapers:* 22; circ. 450,000; 16 per thous.
30. *Newsprint:* 1·3 kilos per head.
31. *Newspapers:* In English, Tagalog, Chinese, Spanish.
32. *News Agencies:* PNS.
33. *Radio Transmitters:* 127; 458 kW.
34. *Broadcasting:* Philippines Broadcasting Service.
35. *Radio Receivers:* 700,000; 24 per thous.
36. *TV Receivers:* 150,000; 6 per thous.
37. *Cinemas:* 776; seating capacity 613,000; 26 seats per thous.
38. *Cinema Attendance:* 15 mill.; 0·6 per head of pop.
39. *Gross National Product:* 14·8 milliard Pesos; Growth Rate: 5·2 per cent p.a.
40. *Gross Domestic Product* (est.): $4·9 milliard; GNP: $191 per head of pop.
41. *Private Consumption:* 78 per cent of GNP.
42. *Wages Fund:* 42 per cent of Nat. Inc.
43. *Expenditure on Food, etc.:* 50 per cent of private consumption.
44. *Expenditure on Household Goods:* n.a.
45. *Agricultural Population:* 58 per cent of working pop. Farms under 5 ha. (12·5 acres): 84 per cent of holdings; 42 per cent of area.
46. *Arable Land:* 11·2 mill. ha. (28 mill. acres); 0·4 ha. (1 acre) per head. Irrigated Land: 800,000 ha.

47. *Production of Paddy:* 3·2 mill. ha. (8 mill. acres); 4 mill. tons; 1·25 tons per ha. (0·5 ton per acre).

48. *Production of Grains:* 5·2 mill. tons; 175 kilos per head of pop.

49. *Production of Sugar:* 1·6 mill. tons.

50. *Livestock:* Cattle 1·1 mill.; Pigs 6·7 mill.; Sheep and Goats 0·6 mill.

51. *Production of Fertilizers:* —

52. *Consumption of Fertilizers* (thous tons): N:48; P_2O_5:25; K_2O:32. Total: 9 kilos per ha. (8 lb. per acre).

53. *Development Programme:* Five-Year Integrated Socio-Economic Programme 1962-67.

54. *Development Projects:* Priority on industry and transport.

55. *Energy Production:* 0·3 mill. tons coal equivalent.

56. *Energy Consumption:* 5 mill. tons coal equivalent; 169 kilos per head.

57. *Electricity Installed:* 0·9 mill. kW.

58. *Electricity Output:* 3·7 milliard kWh.

59. *Production of Coal:* 0·2 mill. tons.

60. *Production of Mineral Oil:* —

61. *Production of Iron Ore:* 0·8 mill. tons.

62. *Production of Manganese Ore:* 5,000 tons.

63. *Production of Steel:* —

64. *Consumption of Steel:* 0·4 mill. tons; 13 kilos per head of pop.

65. *Production of Cotton:* 0·6 mill. spindles; 13,000 tons cotton yarn.

66. *Consumption of Cotton:* 35,000 tons; 1·2 kilos per head of pop.

67. *Production of Cement:* 1 mill. tons.

68. *Production of Petrol:* 2·9 mill. tons.

69. *Production of Motor Vehicles:* —

70. *Production of Merchant Vessels:* —

71. *Telephones Installed:* 139,700.

72. *Letters Received:* n.a.

73. *Railway Transport:* 1 milliard pass./km.; 185 mill. ton/km.

74. *Motor Transport:* 100,000 pass. cars; 90,000 comm. vehicles in use.

75. *Sea Transport:* 9·1 mill. NRT entered; 16·1 mill. NRT cleared. Merchant Fleet: 0·4 mill. GRT.

76. *Sea Transport:* 7·2 mill. tons loaded; 5·1 mill. tons unloaded.

77. *Civilian Airline:* Philippine Airlines (PAL), Manila.

78. *Air Transport:* 388·1 mill. pass/km.; 5 mill. ton/km.

79. *Foreign Trade* ($ mill.): Imports 584; Exports 562; Balance —22.

80. *Foreign Trade:* Imports $20 per head. Exports $19 per head.

81. *Foreign Trade* ($ mill.): Imports: UK 25; USA 257; Japan 103; Exports: UK 7; USA 290; Japan 133.

82. *Foreign Trade* ($ mill.): Imports: Machines 159; Manuf. 134: Foods 79. Exports: Sugar 131; Copra 116; Wood 108.

83. *Foreign Aid:* USA: 1946-63: $1,850 mill.

84. *Foreign Aid:* Sino-Soviet: —

85. *Public Finance* (mill. Pesos): Revenue 1,829; Expenditure 1,500.

86. *Government Obligations:* n.a.

87. *Foreign Exchange:* £1 sterling = 10·90 Peso; US$1 = 3·90 Peso.

88. *Foreign Exchange:* 1 Peso = 1s. 10d; 1 Peso = US$0·26.

89. *Tourism:* Tourist Centres: Manila; Baguio; Legaspi; Cebu; Mindanao.

90. *Visa Requirements:* Tourist visa obtainable with minimum of formality. Currency declaration.

ASIAN MEMBERS OF THE UNITED NATIONS

Country	Date of Admission	United Nations	IAEA	ILO	FAO	UNESCO	WHO	Fund
India	30/10/1945	*	*	*	*	*	*	*
Nepal	14/12/1955	*			*	*	*	*
Pakistan	30/ 9/1947	*	*	*	*	*	*	*
Ceylon	14/12/1955	*	*	*	*	*	*	*
Mongolia	27/10/1961	*				*	*	
China (Taiwan)	24/10/1945	*	*	*		*	*	*
Japan	18/12/1956	*	*	*	*	*	*	*
South Korea			*		*	*	*	*
Burma	19/ 4/1948	*	*	*	*	*	*	*
Thailand	16/12/1946	*	*	*	*	*	*	*
Cambodia	14/12/1955	*	*		*	*	*	
Laos	14/12/1955	*	*	*	*	*	*	*
South Vietnam			*	*	*	*	*	*
Malaysia	17/9/1957	*		*	*	*	*	*
Indonesia	28/ 9/1950[1]		*	*	*	*	*	*
Philippines	24/10/1955	*	*	*	*	*	*	*

Country	Bank	IFC	IDA	ICAO	UPU	ITU	WMO	IMCO
India	*	*	*	*	*	*	*	*
Nepal	*		*	*	*	*		
Pakistan	*	*	*	*	*	*	*	*
Ceylon	*	*	*	*	*	*	*	
Mongolia					*		*	
China (Taiwan)	*		*	*	*	*	*	*
Japan	*	*	*	*	*	*	*	*
South Korea	*		*	*	*	*	*	*
Burma	*	*	*	*	*	*	*	*
Thailand	*	*	*	*	*	*	*	
Cambodia				*	*	*	*	*
Laos	*		*	*	*	*	*	
South Vietnam	*		*	*	*	*	*	
Malaysia	*	*	*	*	*	*	*	
Indonesia[1]	*			*	*	*	*	*
Philippines	*	*	*	*	*	*	*	

[1]Indonesia ceased to be a member of the United Nations in March 1965.

Key to Organizations

Bank—International Bank for Reconstruction and Development
FAO—Food and Agriculture Organization
Fund—International Monetary Fund
IAEA—International Atomic Energy Agency
ICAO—International Civil Aviation Organization
IDA—International Development Association
IFC—International Finance Corporation
ILO—International Labour Organization
IMCO—Inter-Governmental Maritime Consultative Organization
ITU—International Telecommunications Union
UNESCO—UN Education, Scientific and Cultural Organization
UPU—Universal Postal Union
WHO—World Health Organization
WMO—World Meteorological Organization

Source: United Nations, *Yearbook of the United Nations, 1963*, NewYork, 1965

PART TWO

THE COUNTRIES

SOUTH ASIA

INDIA
The Political History

by

PERCIVAL SPEAR

Geography

On the map of Asia, India hangs like an inverted spire or stalactite cutting into the Arabian sea. It hangs from a slanting wedge which is the Ganges valley and the Punjab, which in turn is attached to the Himalayan range, called by the early English the Great Snowy Range. From these fastnesses, where the great Hindu gods are said to dwell, India stretches out over 1,174,000 square miles, an area thirteen times as large as Great Britain but five-twelfths that of the United States. It would go into Africa nearly ten times. This region forms a compact geographical area, a sub-continent of its own, which is now divided politically into the States of India, Pakistan and Nepal with the island of Ceylon as a pendant at its tip. This area contains all varieties of climate, from the Arctic of the higher mountains to the lush tropical of Bengal and the south west corner. Physically as well as culturally, it is a microcosm of the world as a whole.

Shape

The shape of the country and the nature of its entrances and exits have determined much of its history and the make-up of the people today; it is therefore worth examining more closely. The mountains of the north, leading on to the barren plateau of Tibet, have proved an effective barrier to intercourse with China. Physically, they have acted as a great catchment area for the annual monsoon rains. They produce the water which fertilizes the great plains of the north and provides irrigation for rainless tracts. The forests of the mountainsides are the symbols of the prosperity of the plains. To the north-east the hills are lower and more broken, but their rain-sodden and fever-haunted nature have made them as effective a barrier to human relations as their greater neighbours to the north. Until World War II no road or railway had been built between eastern India and Burma. The retreat from Burma in 1942 had to be conducted through forest-entangled and fever-stricken passes; even today the normal route is by sea from Calcutta to Rangoon.

To the north-west the story is different. Here the mountains are as high as those bordering Burma, but they are bare and barren, and they are broken by well defined passes. Moreover, the passes do not lead merely to another river valley as in Burma, itself encased in further mountains, but to the Iranian plateau which stretches to the great seats of civilization in the Middle East and to the wastes of Central Asia where nomads wandered and periodically swarmed. Here was India's window on the world, the door of access by which the stranger entered.

The Northern Corridor

The traveller debouching from the north-west passes found himself in the Indus valley running roughly north and south. To travel down it was to enter a blind alley, for waterless lands crossed the route and the sea lay at its end. Progress eastward was barred by the deserts of Rajasthan, more effective, until modern times, than the highest range of mountains. But in the north an easy route led south-eastward into the northern Indian plain. The Punjab is still in the Indus basin and from the Sutlej to the Jumna valleys the transition is imperceptible. This plain, like a great diagonal cylinder on the map, stretches to the Bay of Bengal. It is so flat that there is no tunnel on the railway between Calcutta and Lahore; the land rises only 600 feet between Calcutta and Delhi. It is so fertile that fine crops will grow wherever there is a sufficiency of rain and two a year wherever there is a good monsoon.

This corridor skirts Rajasthan in its western portion. Rajasthan is a large arid region, running to complete desert in the west, which divides Sind and the Indus valley from the rest of India. It has been an historic citadel of Hinduism against Islamic invaders and is noted for its Rajput prowess, its conservative ways, its romantic castles and marble palaces set in azure lakes. From the practical point of view it is hot, infertile, poor and backward.

On the line of the Jumna where Delhi and Agra stand the corridor branches out to the plains and hills of central India. This is the route taken by all invaders of the south and this junction of routes is the factor which has given the two cities their strategic importance. On this strip of land seven decisive Indian battles have been fought. The river Narbada is the natural boundary of Hindustan and central India. Central India itself is a vast area of mingled hill and plain, forest and river. Its eastern half, stretching to Behar and Orissa, has proved an almost complete barrier in the past. Its central portion has fertile areas; it is easy enough to provide the passage of armies and difficult enough to make their reinforcement difficult. Hence the historic fact that it was far easier to conquer south India than to retain it.

The South

Central India leads on to the Deccan plateau rising steeply from the west and sloping gradually to the east. It is a picturesque and stony region, a land of vistas rather than of wealth; with the rain of the western monsoon held by the western *ghats*. On each side of the Deccan run coastal plains with typical tropical climates. That on the west is narrow and rain-drenched, running down to the elephant-rearing forests of Malabar. Only at Cochin in the extreme south does it open out to the plain of Travancore, brilliant with palm trees and historically prosperous from their products and pepper growing. To the east the plain is wider and no less fertile until it turns due south along the Coromandel coast. Madras is set in a cotton growing country, the land of the Tamils which has been famous since pre-Christian times for its textiles and its wealth. With the fertile region of Gujarat on the angle of western coast where it turns westward in the Gulf of Cambay our survey is completed. Gujarat is hot and fertile and famous for its cotton and indigo.

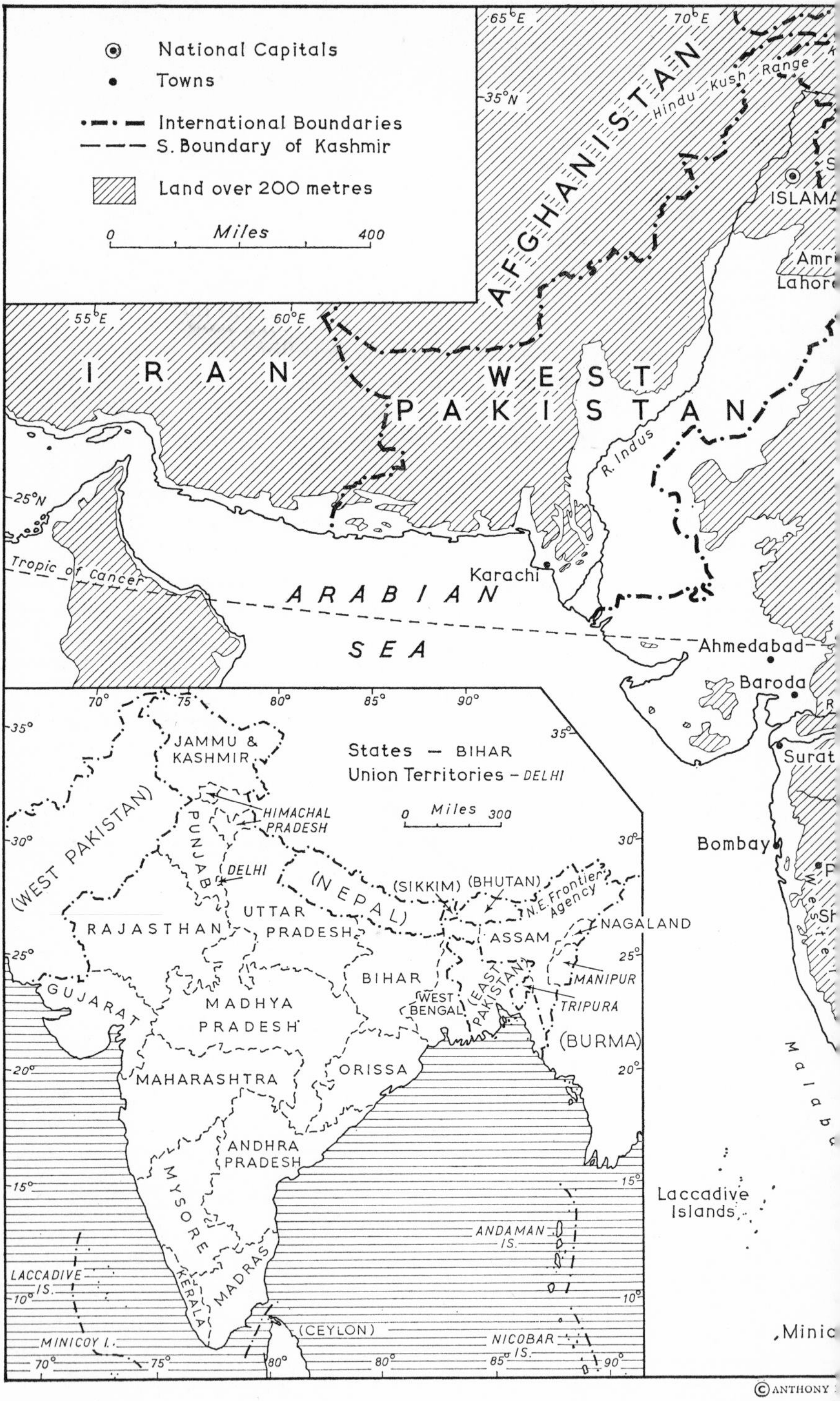
National Capitals
Towns
International Boundaries
S. Boundary of Kashmir
Land over 200 metres
0 Miles 400
65°E
70°E
35°N
55°E
60°E
25°N
AFGHANISTAN
Hindu Kush Range
ISLAMA
Amri
Lahore
IRAN
WEST PAKISTAN
R. Indus
Karachi
Tropic of Cancer
ARABIAN SEA
Ahmedabad
Baroda
Surat
Bombay
Laccadive Islands
Minic
Malaba
States — BIHAR
Union Territories — DELHI
0 Miles 300
JAMMU & KASHMIR
HIMACHAL PRADESH
PUNJAB
DELHI
(WEST PAKISTAN)
RAJASTHAN
UTTAR PRADESH
(NEPAL)
(SIKKIM)
(BHUTAN)
N.E. Frontier Agency
NAGALAND
ASSAM
MANIPUR
TRIPURA
BIHAR
WEST BENGAL
(EAST PAKISTAN)
(BURMA)
GUJARAT
MADHYA PRADESH
MAHARASHTRA
ORISSA
ANDHRA PRADESH
MYSORE
MADRAS
KERALA
(CEYLON)
LACCADIVE IS.
MINICOY I.
ANDAMAN IS.
NICOBAR IS.
70°
75°
80°
85°
90°
35°
30°
25°
20°
15°
10°

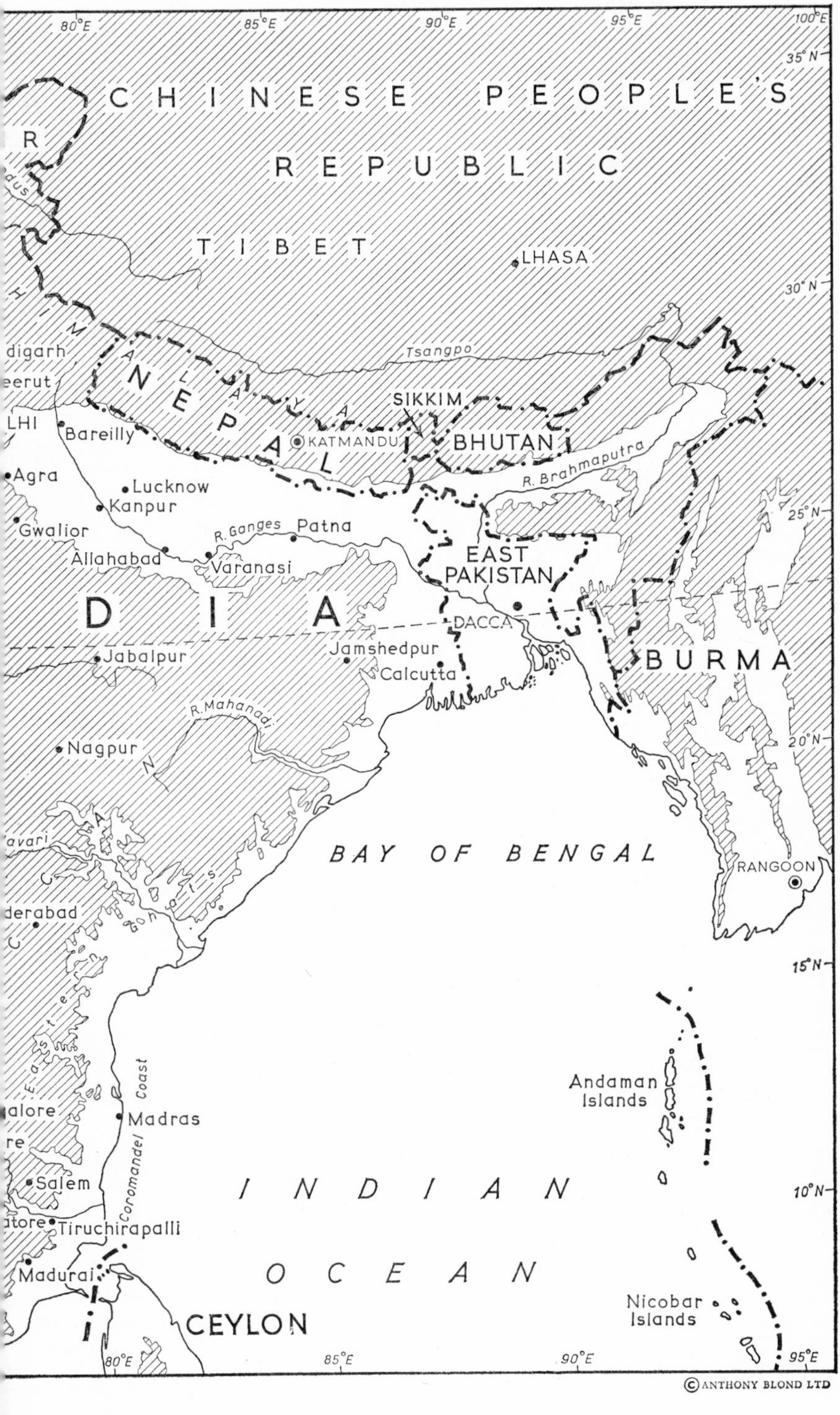
CHINESE PEOPLE'S REPUBLIC
TIBET
LHASA
NEPAL
HIMALAYA
KATMANDU
SIKKIM
BHUTAN
Tsangpo
R. Brahmaputra
EAST PAKISTAN
DACCA
BURMA
RANGOON
DIA
Bareilly
Agra
Lucknow
Kanpur
Gwalior
R. Ganges
Patna
Allahabad
Varanasi
Jamshedpur
Calcutta
Jabalpur
R. Mahanadi
Nagpur
Eastern Ghats
Coromandel Coast
Madras
Salem
Tiruchirapalli
Madurai
CEYLON
BAY OF BENGAL
INDIAN OCEAN
Andaman Islands
Nicobar Islands
80°E
85°E
90°E
95°E
100°E
35°N
30°N
25°N
20°N
15°N
10°N
©ANTHONY BLOND LTD

The Monsoon

India is a land of periodic rains or monsoons. The south-east monsoon sweeps up the Ganges valley until (in normal years) it meets the south-west monsoon which, breaking in Ceylon early in May, reaches the hills beyond Delhi about the middle of June. The north-west has winter rains which are scanty, unpredictable but invaluable. The vagaries of these monsoons still determine the happiness of the majority of Indians. Too much rain means floods and destruction; too little, famine and death. In the northern lands of frequent droughts 'fine weather' means rainy weather.

The most fertile regions of India have traditionally been the richest; hence the concentration of political power in the north and its periodic dominations of the south. But with the advent of industrialism these conditions have changed. The sites of manufacture may now be said to be the seats of power. Two such concentrations are Bombay with Sholapur to the south, and Ahmedabad in Gujarat, where the cotton of the Deccan is made into cloth for the Indian market and exported to the Middle East, Africa and South-East Asia. Another is the iron- and coalfield of South Behar, where the Parsi Tata built the first great Indian steel plant. Development has been assisted by transport, of which the railway system is a legacy of the British period. Generally speaking this ran eastwards and westwards, to connect the ports of Calcutta, Bombay and Madras with the interior centres of production. But north-south lines were added giving India a network which enabled her in the Second World War both to sustain a great army on her eastern frontier and to distribute food from north to south in the absence of sea transport and food imports.

India has a wealth of agricultural products, both temperate and tropical; she has all the main industrial components in quantity, except oil; and she has a transport system which enables her to make use of them. These things, joined to the skill of her people, should give her a bright future.

History

India is an amalgam of peoples and civilizations which together produced a social and cultural body which is unique in some of its characteristics and unsurpassed for its resilience and powers of absorption. The first peoples of whom we know anything concrete are the Dravidians who perhaps replaced forest-dwelling Australoid groups, of whom traces are still to be found in the south. From about the mid-third to the mid-second millennium B.C. a civilization flourished in the Indus valley, the Punjab and Gujarat, related to though not identical with the Sumerian culture of Mesopotamia. This civilization vanished without a trace until rediscovered by archaeologists in 1923, but we now know that it had an important influence upon the make-up of what was later called Hinduism. We can only surmise that the Dravidians were responsible for this culture, because human remains are few and have not yet been fully analysed. But we do know that in the late first millennium B.C. these people, in their Tamil section, produced another civilization in the south. Though later overlaid by influences from the north, Tamil culture has been an important factor in the make-up of south Indian Hinduism.

The Indus valley dwellers were probably overthrown and certainly replaced in north-west India about the middle of the second millennium B.C. by Aryan-speaking pastoral tribes entering by the north-western passes. They were tall and blond, lovers of sport, gambling and good living, worshippers of the sun and powers of nature, poets and philosophers. Their tongue developed into the classical language of Sanskrit, related to the Aryan family which includes Greek and Latin, the Teutonic and Slav languages. Their hymns of the Rigveda constitute some of the oldest literature in the world and begin the development of its longest lived systems of philosophy. These gifted people gradually spread over north India, assimilating more from the conquered aboriginals than they cared to admit, and developing kingdoms and philosophies with equal celerity. About 1000 B.C. occurred some conflict which caught posterity's imagination and provided the occasion for the composition of the great epic the *Mahabharata*. This, with its twin the *Ramayana*, still lies close to the heart of Indian life today.

Caste, Religions and Empires

The first millennium B.C. saw the social development of the caste system, the momentous development of world religions and the political development of great empires. The Aryans brought with them the usual classes of king, chiefs and freemen, and they also had priests. Over the centuries and for causes which may include race and colour feeling and the conqueror-conquered relationship, but which are still largely obscure, these groups became stratified into four orders of priest, warrior, merchant and farmer, with 'outcastes' for menial tasks beyond. These orders in their turn became hereditary and subdivided until today there are some two thousand groups, each with their own social status, duties, privileges and disabilities, their rules of marriage, contact and diet. Caste is officially abolished today and is not easily to be seen in the cities, but it remains a ruling social force in rural India, that reservoir of Indian continuity.

As Hindu religion developed in the hands of the priests or Brahmins, it led to schism and creative action. Two world religions derive from this time: Jainism, an important influence within India to this day with its non-violent doctrine (an influence on Mahatma Gandhi, too) and Buddhism. Gautama the Buddha or Enlightened One was born about 560 B.C. and died about 480 B.C. His cult died out of India after flourishing for more than a thousand years, but it profoundly influenced Hinduism in the process and is still active in Ceylon, Burma, South-East Asia and Japan.

With the first of the great empires India enters upon recorded history. Alexander the Great, with his invasion of 326-5 B.C. gave the impulse. The Mauryan Empire which followed for a century and a half was the first attempt to unify India politically and gave the first Indian world figure in the person of Asoka. He repented of conquest, preached non-violence, and engraved moralizing edicts on pillars and rocks. A second empire flourished under the Guptas in the 4th and 5th centuries A.D. when ancient Indian culture reached its full stature. It was then, with the possible exception of China, the most advanced civilization in the world with its corpus of Sanskrit literature, its great systems of philosophy (the Vedanta), its scientific and mathematical knowledge (zero and the decimal point were invented in India).

Before this time the Indian stock and culture were enriched by a number of invaders, from the Greek adventurers from what is now modern Turkestan to the mysterious Kushans, who have left mounds all over north India, and under whom Buddhism assumed a new form and winged its way across Central Asia to China. After the Guptas came fresh barbarian hordes who first fatally injured Indian Buddhism and then coalesced with the inhabitants to form the north Indian pattern recognizable today. From Brahminical compromise and barbarian might arose the Rajput clans as we know them, who were to form the life-blood of militant Hinduism in the centuries to come.

The Muslims

In A.D. 712 India was invaded by Arab adherents of the new Muslim religion, who conquered Sind. Three centuries later Turkish Muslims raided deep into India, and overran the Punjab, establishing a reputation for temple destruction and intolerance. But nearly two more centuries passed before a fresh wave of Turks burst over north India and established the first Muslim empire at Delhi. Henceforth was established a rhythm of conquest and recovery, of attraction and repulsion which lasted for more than seven hundred years and was only ended with partition. It was seven hundred and fifty-five years before the Hindus regained Delhi after the Muslim conquest. Islam gave India many of the arts and graces of life, many fine buildings (including the Taj Mahal) and exquisite paintings and an impetus to monotheism. It captured one-quarter of its people. The Delhi Empire was overthrown by the world-conqueror Taimur in 1298. It was followed by the Mogul Empire in the 16th century, founded by the inimitable Babur and cemented by India's second secular world figure, the Emperor Akbar. The Mogul Empire provided a Persian cultural mantle for the Indian governing classes. Apart from this, with its Persianized bureaucracy, it was a working model of orderly administration upon which others could build.

India and the West

The Mogul power broke up in the 18th century; the year of its death as an empire is 1761. Its would-be successors were the freedom-loving and tenacious Marathas of western India. But their triumph was forestalled by a world movement into whose orbit India was now moving. This was the expansion of the West with its scientific revolution now leading into the first industrial revolution with its accompaniments of new economic and military power. The first agents of the West were the Portuguese whose attempts to introduce the Europe of the Catholic renaissance foundered upon the rocks of intolerance and cruelty, insufficient power and Spanish conquest. Their successors were European commercial agents, Dutch, English and French mainly. These men counted their rupees and jockeyed for privileges; they had no idea that they were presently to be used as levers of a cultural destiny. Political confusion in India prompted the European companies to seek their own defence; commercial rivalry led them into war and the use of Indian allies. The new superiority of Western arms soon gave them a corner in king-making. Once the British had eliminated French power in the south they marched speedily to the dominion of all India to the river Sutlej in 1818. This success was made possible, not only by military superiority but because of the distracted state of India at the time. There was no will to resist an empire; in fact a disposition to accept one.

Britain and the New India

The British Empire in India resembled its Mogul predecessor in many ways; it provided a dignified and static framework beneath which traditional society might revive and trade proceed. But in the 1830s a radical change occurred, which marks the birth of the India we know today. Radical and moral reforming zeal in England determined on introducing Western culture into India, believing that Indians would accept it once they were aware of it, and confident in its mission whatever the effect on political dominion. So English became the official language and Western ideas and techniques were poured into the country through educational, official and commercial channels. Traditional India made a last convulsive effort to throw off the Western incubus in the so-called Mutiny of 1857. Thereafter there was a tacit acceptance of the Western challenge. The gifts of the West must be accepted, but the heirlooms of the past must not be abandoned. The two must be arranged in a harmonious pattern in the halls of Indian society.

One sign of this process was the educational 'explosion' which occurred about the middle of the second half of the 19th century. Then Indian individuals and groups began to set up Western style colleges and schools themselves, thereafter providing a demand behind which government achievement lagged. A second feature was the rise of Indian machine industry, pre-eminently of cotton. A third feature was the nationalist movement, openly imported from the West, but early blending itself with local and indigenous currents of feeling. The Indian National Congress was founded in 1885. Twenty years later it was able to withstand the government's administrative partition of Bengal in a hurricane campaign which aroused mass emotion. But it was still an essentially middle class body, divided into 'moderate' and 'extremist' wings. Thence began another rhythm of concessions by the Government to rising national sentiment and demands for more rapid advance. The first sign was the Morley-Minto reforms of 1909, a first symbol the removal of the capital from Calcutta to Delhi in 1911.

The Nationalist Movement

The First World War was a turning point in development. It stimulated Indian consciousness of and demand for political rights; it restricted British power and modified Britain's attitude; it provided in general discontent a fertile soil for the growth of political turmoil. The political fruit was the Montford constitution which gave India the beginnings of parliamentary government under the device of dyarchy. It also saw the steady estrangement of Hindus and Muslims into hostile camps as they saw the sceptre drawing nearer and mused as to who should grasp it first. The Congress had showed its power, but it was still a middle class body which could not be described as an alternative government. The man who turned the Congress into a mass national organization and its executive into a potential government was

Mahatma Gandhi. After a career in South Africa where he crossed swords with the late General Smuts, Gandhi returned to India in 1915 full of nationalist fervour, zeal for social reform, and ideas of 'non-violence' culled from Hindu, Jain and Christian sources. His opportunity came in the post-war unrest of 1919. He used the indignation aroused by European sympathy with the savage Government action of Amritsar in 1919 along with Muslim anger at the treatment of Turkey to launch a non-co-operation movement. It shook the Government but did not overthrow it and on its collapse Gandhi retired to social reform activity. The episode was none the less the writing on the wall for the British *raj*. Gandhi led a second and much better organized movement in 1930-31. Again it was defeated. But in 1937 when provincial autonomy was introduced, the Congress found itself in control of seven out of eleven provinces. A promising experiment ended with the Second World War which led on directly to independence. The Congress refused to co-operate except on terms of political advance. The Cripps offer of 1942 would have made Congress the virtual ruler of post-war India. Its rejection left the way clear for the Muslims, now led by the consummate and embittered tactician Jinnah, and fearful of the effects of Hindu domination. Jinnah declared for Pakistan, or a separate Muslim state, in 1940, but it was not until 1946 that he won the support of Muslims as a whole. Henceforth he bargained from strength and through a series of conferences, riots and massacres forced his way to partition and independence. Then in the two years after the war the Congress were faced with a double front of their former opponents, the British, now anxious to hand over, and their former compatriots, the Muslims, now insisting on separation. The division of India was the result of successive Congress errors but in perspective we may see that it had one important advantage. A united India on any terms conceivable in 1945 would have been so weak at the centre and so hampered with mutual suspicion that the great developments of Nehru's India would have been impossible.

Mahatma Gandhi

Gandhi's political mission was to turn a middle class national movement into a mass national sentiment. In a real sense he was the creator of the Indian nation as distinct from a body of nationalists amongst the people. That he was able to do this was largely the result of the other side of his complex character and the way he combined his politics with his religion and his ethics. Starting out as an English-trained lawyer he served his community in South Africa for many years as a lawyer and champion. Here he acquired his distaste for Western civilization, his belief in reconciliation and non-violence, of 'soul-force' as he later expressed it, and here he practised his dietetic experiments. To this he added a fervent nationalism which meant that India should be free. On returning to India he identified himself with the peasant masses. It was this thought which caused him to wear, not the saffron robe of the ascetic, but the loincloth of the peasant. The people responded by making him a saint or 'great soul'. He never converted all India to non-violence, but his belief in and practice of it gave him a moral ascendancy which made his position unique and unassailable. To the peasant he was a saint who guaranteed that the Nationalist movement would not overturn their cherished Hindu way of life; to the middle classes he was a gifted politician whose eccentricities (like fasting and insisting on hand spinning as a qualification of Congress membership) were condoned because he had the double knack of dealing with the British and arousing the masses. For them independence and parity with the West were worth a spinning wheel. This analysis is confirmed by the fact that today Gandhi is still a Mahatma or great soul for the masses while he is forgotten or disregarded by the classes.

Independence

As the twenties and thirties were Gandhi's India, the years of independence have been Nehru's India. The new Government, inaugurated with enthusiasm on August 15th, 1947 after the whirlwind Viceroyalty of Lord Mountbatten, was at once beset with difficulties. The first arose from the massacres in the Punjab which accompanied partition. These were mutual between Sikhs, Hindus and Muslims and may have cost up to half-a-million lives. These in turn set in motion the great migrations, which led some six million people on either side to cross the border in the next few months seeking new homes. The tide of exasperated refugees reached Delhi at the end of August. New massacres broke out and for a time threatened the existence of the Government itself. When quelled they left behind a great body of refugees to be absorbed, a large body of uprooted Muslims awaiting transport in improvized camps and general bitterness. Not until Gandhi intervened to insist, at the cost of a threatened fast to death, on the evacuation of the Delhi mosques and security for Muslims, was confidence restored. This intervention outraged certain militant Hindus and cost Gandhi his life on January 30th, 1948. The sacrifice was not in vain for it produced such a revulsion against militant Hindu groups that they have been politically insignificant ever since.

Hard on the heels of the Punjab massacres came the Pathan incursion into the Muslim majority State of Kashmir with the Hindu ruler's consequent accession to India. For a time there were hostilities between the two Dominions until a truce was arranged in April 1948. In this matter India has insisted on the ruler's legal right of accession, and though she offered a plebiscite in the early days of the dispute has rejected every proposal by successive United Nations missions for implementing the suggestion. The first Kashmiri leader, Sheikh Abdullah, was in prison without trial for nine years with one short break. Kashmir has now been given a constitution by its own constituent assembly which has proclaimed its union with India. But Pakistan remains unreconciled and the issue remains a running sore in the relations of the two countries. India occupies Hindu and Sikh Jammu, the coveted vale of Kashmir with Ladakh and Little Tibet to the north-east, while Pakistan has a fringe round the southern border and the regions in the north-west.

The Indian States

The next question was the future of the Indian States, some 562 in number, of which Hyderabad, the largest, had a population of seventeen millions. The British had withdrawn their claims to paramountcy and advised all rulers to join one or other new State. In fact all of them did so except Kashmir, Hyderabad in the south and Junagarh, a small State on the Kathiawar coast. India justified the occupation of Junagarh on the ground of the popular will and of Hyderabad in 1948 as a 'police action', an action indeed, to which the folly of its ruler, the Nizam, contributed. But the problem of integration of these often backward territories remained. This was carried through with mingled rigour and skill by Sardar Patel. The completeness of his success should not hide the greatness of the achievement. In less skilful hands this problem might have wrecked the new State.

The Constitution

The new Government next proceeded to draft a constitution. This came into force in January 1950 and has proved so far a successful instrument of government. With a president in the place of a constitutional sovereign the Constitution is of the parliamentary type, with two houses of legislature, a prime minister and a cabinet responsible to the lower house. The structure of state, or Indian Union, is federal, the constituent units now being broadly arranged on a linguistic pattern. The chief exception is the Punjab with its mixed Sikhs and Hindus. The states thus have a life of their own, but enough authority is concentrated at the centre to enable the federal authority to dominate the country. There is universal suffrage with an electorate of 175 millions, the largest in the world. Within this constitution political life is still dominated by the National Congress compared to which other parties appear more as splinter groups. The most active of these is the Communists, but it can hardly yet be said that India has evolved a party system, let alone a two-party one. As a corollary to the constitution came the question of relationship to the British Commonwealth. Indian patriotism was satisfied by the declaration of an independent Republic and the desire not to cut adrift by continued membership with recognition of the Queen as the Head of the Commonwealth.

Nehru's India

Since that time the years that have passed have been those of Nehru's India. At first the government was in effect a duumvirate of Nehru and the west Indian political boss Patel. Patel died at the end of 1950 and after 1951 Nehru's supremacy remained unchallenged until his death. He led Congress to victory at three general elections and Congress knew that it could not do without him. Nehru used this ascendancy to attempt the modernization of his country. In 1950 a Planning Commission was set up from which have stemmed three successive Five-Year plans of development. The economy has been divided into public and private sectors, agricultural and industrial fields. Broadly speaking, established industries remained in the private sector while public utilities, new projects like the three steel plants, irrigation and power plants are in the public one. The first plan, aided by the Colombo plan, emphasized agricultural production which was increased by about 25 per cent. Along with this went power plants and irrigation schemes. The second plan was much more ambitious, involving the raising of two billion pounds outside the country, and of the national income by five per cent p.a. The third plan, still larger, is encountering certain difficulties. This was Nehru's bid to solve the problem of Indian poverty, to make India economically self-sufficient and the industrial centre of South Asia.

Along with industrial activity has gone development in other directions. Education has been pushed forward. The number of universities is now over 60 though primary education has lagged behind. In the field of social reform a series of Hindu Code bills have modified the traditional code of Manu to give women more equal property and personal rights with men. The English language has been retained as an alternative official language to Hindi, but seems unlikely to remain so. In commerce the decimal system has been adopted for the currency.

Indian foreign policy has been peculiarly Nehru's own; he was his own Foreign Minister ever since independence and until his death his handling of affairs was unquestioned. Mr. Nehru was responsible for India's basic policy of 'non-alignment' with the power blocs, a term which he preferred to 'neutralism'. The larger the uncommitted world, he thought, the less the chance of a catastrophic atomic war which would inevitably suck India in. India has maintained good relations with both Russia and the West (with some reservations during the Dulles period) and has accepted help from both camps in her development plans. For example, Britain, Germany and Russia are each responsible for steel plants now completed. In the last years of his life Mr. Nehru found China difficult to manage. After coining the *Panch Shila* or five principles of good relations in 1954 with Mr. Chou En-lai, relations deteriorated following China's seizure of Tibet. As a result of her uncommitted attitude India has frequently been able to mediate in international affairs. One such instance was the Korean War of 1950. More recently she has been actively engaged in the U.N.O. operations in the Congo. She has taken a great interest in the development of Africa and may be described as the unofficial mentor of the Afro-Asian group of nations.

In recent years India's position has undergone a radical change in consequence of her dispute with China. From 1949 Mr. Nehru cultivated good relations with the new Communist Government of China. His efforts reached high water mark with the enunciation with Mr. Chou-en-lai of the *Panch Shila* or five principles of good neighbourliness in 1954, which were accepted at the Bandung conference in the following year. Tibet has been the cause of steady deterioration since then. The Chinese take-over of Tibet in 1951 was resented by Indian opinion which was in turn resented by the Chinese. The flight of the Dalai Lama in 1959 deeply stirred Indian opinion and the hospitality accorded to Tibetan refugees led to Chinese charges of a breach of the *Panch Shila*. Whatever weight is attached to these matters, the tangible cause of the present situation is the current Chinese road programme in Tibet. This has involved the driving of a road from Tibet into Sinkiang across a corner of Indian Ladakh. Some 12,000 square miles seem to have been quietly occupied by the Chinese. Indian protests and refusal to consider a frontier revision led to Chinese denunciations of the 'MacMahon' frontier line further east as an imperialist hangover. The situation boiled over in October 1962 when the Chinese suddenly advanced towards Assam in the north-eastern mountain tract and came within striking distance of Tezpur; their sudden halt and retirement was almost more embarrassing to India than the advance had been. Western offers of help and suggestions of negotiations with Pakistan followed.

On 26th May, 1964, Mr. Nehru died in office. Though increasingly critical, India had become so dependent on his leadership that she has not yet recovered her sense of direction. Nehru had been utterly disillusioned by the Chinese and depressed by his failure to impart more impetus to the national effort. He was hoping for a revival of national spirit in response to the Chinese challenge and was feeling for new solutions, particularly in Kashmir.

His successor, Mr. Lal Bahadur Shastri, is a man of integrity noted for his powers of conciliation, but he has yet to give evidence of drive. The new government has to meet some serious internal problems: food shortages resulting from the mounting population (140 millions in 18 years), lack of foreign exchange in honouring the current Five-Year plan and consequent inflation, and a rising north-south tension connected with the language question. Externally it is confronted by China and Pakistan and pressure for a choice of friends between east and west. The immediate future is likely to be critical and to see the beginning of a new stage in Indian development.

BIBLIOGRAPHY

A. L. Basham. *The Wonder that was India.* (Sidgwick and Jackson, London, 1956.)

F. Bernier (ed. A. Constable and V. A. Smith). *Travels in the Moghul Empire.* (Oxford Univ. Press, London, 2nd. ed., 1934.)

M. Brecher. *Nehru.* (Oxford Univ. Press, London, 1959.)

G. T. Garrett (ed.). *The Legacy of India.* (Oxford Univ. Press, London, 1934.)

B. G. Gokhale. *The Making of the Indian Nation.* (Asia Publishing House, London, 1959.)

Sir P. J. Griffiths. *Modern India.* (Ernest Benn, London, 1957.)

J. L. Nehru. *Autobiography.* (John Lane the Bodley Head, London, 1936.)

K. M. Panikkar. *A Survey of Indian History.* (Asia Publishing House, London, 4th ed., 1964.)

H. S. L. Polak, H. N. Brailsford and Lord Pethick-Lawrence. *Mahatma Gandhi.* (Odhams, London, 1949.)

H. G. Rawlinson. *India, a Short Cultural History.* (Cresset Press, London, 1943.)

P. Sittaramaya. *History of the National Congress,* 2 vols. (Allahabad, 1946.)

D. E. Smith. *India as a Secular State.* (Princeton Univ. Press, Princeton and London, 1963.)

Percival Spear. *India, A Modern History.* (Univ. of Michigan Press, Ann Arbor, 1961.)
(Ed.) *The Oxford History of India.* (Oxford Univ. Press, London, 3rd ed., 1958.)

BIOGRAPHICAL NOTE

Percival Spear took a B.A. in History from St. Catharine's College, Cambridge and then proceeded to India, where he was a Lecturer in History at St. Stephen's College, Delhi and an honorary Reader in the University of Delhi between the years 1924 and 1940. In 1937 he received a Leverhulme Research Fellowship for work on Indian history. In 1940 he joined the Government of India and became Deputy Secretary in the Department of Information and Broadcasting. Since the War he has been Fellow and Bursar of Selwyn College, Cambridge and has divided his time between administrative duties and Indian historical studies. In 1957-8 he was a visiting Professor in Indian History at the University of California (Berkeley).

Dr. Spear's published works are as follows: *The Nabobs: English Social Life in India in the 18th century* (Oxford Univ. Press, 1932; Oxford paperback ed., 1962.); *Delhi: A Historical Sketch* (Oxford Univ. Press, London, 1937); *India, Pakistan and the West* (Oxford Univ. Press, 3rd ed., 1958); *The Twilight of the Mughals* (Cambridge Univ. Press, London, 1951); *The Oxford History of India* (Oxford Univ. Press, London, 3rd ed., 1958); *India: A Modern History* (Univ. of Michigan Press, Ann Arbor, 1961).

INDIA
The Land and the People

by

TAYA ZINKIN

THE impression India makes upon the visitor is at first one of incredible poverty, a poverty so compelling that it brings tears to the eyes of those who see slums, rickety pot-bellied children and skeletal cattle for the first time. The first reaction of such people is to wonder why India has not gone Communist.

The pressure of population is tangible everywhere, in the crammed city streets, in the crowded village lanes, in the myriad of stamp-sized fields. In Calcutta sad-eyed cattle graze the pavement while hundreds of thousands of people live on that very same pavement. Everywhere the newcomer is oppressed by the combination of poverty and overcrowding. Yet to the Indians themselves the picture does not appear quite so bad.

Indians may be poor, they may lack lebensraum, but much of their misery is made bearable by the extraordinarily strong warmth of belonging which characterizes the Indian way of life and is rooted in the very caste system India's well-wishers want to destroy. This warmth of belonging which is very real is not apparent to the naked eye, it has to be experienced to be understood; it is to this warmth of belonging that India owes that social and political stability which so surprises the visitor from the affluent society.

After poverty and overcrowding the visitor begins to notice the extraordinary diversity of India, a diversity as apparent to the unobservant eye as the poverty. Everybody looks different and dresses differently. Complexions range from white to black coffee; noses from Biblical spurs to mongolian pugs; some people are very tall, others very short. Dress, like a botanical classification, reveals the exact identity of the bearer, his or her religion, caste, region and occupation. The variety is endless. Thus an urban Sikh from Patiala rolls his beard inward, not to be confused with an urban Sikh from the Punjab who rolls his beard outward, while rural Sikhs wear their beards loose. Catholic untouchable women from Kerala wear their earrings through the top of their ears, their caste sisters through the lobe. In India there are as many turbans as there are makes of cars in the West and I once counted 20 different ways of draping the sari; and many men wear hats, caps, bonnets, toppers of all shapes instead of turbans just as many women wear pyjamas, lungis, skirts or sarongs. Some people wear next to nothing, others are overdressed, some women display their breasts, others their legs, but all of them, unless they be widows, wear some sort of jewellery, be it nose rings or toe rings, glass or gold.

The unity which exists underneath the apparent diversity is as real as the warmth of belonging, and like the warmth of belonging it eludes the visitor, though he will notice that everybody has black hair and dark eyes, that everybody eats with his fingers and that many people wear unstitched clothes. Yet, in India, everybody feels Indian, because Hinduism, like Christianity in Europe, has provided a continent with an underlying attitude and a civilization which is quite different from that of Africa or China. Everybody in India, even the Muslims and the Jews, has been deeply affected by the Hindu way of looking at life. This is because of the extraordinary all-embracing pervasiveness of Hinduism, which transforms everything it touches. Thus caste, the key institution of Hinduism, has affected all religious institutions in India; even the Jews have their untouchables who cannot enter high caste synagogues and there are Catholic churches in Kerala with special benches at the back for their untouchable parishioners.

The unity which runs through a society divided by latitude, longitude, language, race, habits, cannot be described in a few words. One has to go to India to feel it, and to feel too the contrast between rich and poor, town and country, modernity and the Middle Ages, between what Mr. Nehru liked to call the cowdung age and the atomic age. In this contrast lies the core of Indian politics.

Politics

India is overwhelmingly in the cowdung age; its leaders are determined to bring it into the atomic age, and to do so democratically. Under the British there could be no such attempt, democratic or otherwise, because it would have cut too deeply across the fabric of tradition. Indeed, Gandhi was propelled into politics by the realization that only a government of the people by their own people could attempt to reform Indian society; Gandhi was above all a social reformer dedicated to making Indians equal, be they untouchables or women; Pandit Jawaharlal Nehru, his political heir, being a Socialist, was further fired by the desire to give equality economic content. In India, since independence, the urge to equality and modernity has dominated politics. The task of modernization and equalization was not easy in a country as poor, as overcrowded and as backward as India; it was further complicated by a series of man-made cataclysms which overtook India at the time of birth. Had those cataclysms not been dealt with successfully, independent India might have been still-born.

The emergencies which faced the Government of India at independence were so enormous that for the first few years they used up most of the Government's energies. As a result of the partition of India and Pakistan there was immense dislocation in the country. This dislocation was further aggravated by the vivisection of the Punjab and Bengal and the ensuing riots with their human hecatomb and the flooding of refugees across the border by the millions. Millions of Hindu refugees from Pakistan had to be rehabilitated, a new capital had to be built for the Indian Punjab, the assets of undivided India had to be partitioned and Indian troops had to be sent to Kashmir to rescue the Maharajah from invasion, firstly by tribes from Pakistan, later by the Pakistan Army. In addition 562 independent Princely States, covering two-fifths of India and 90 million people, had to be integrated into the framework of the Indian Union. All this was done. Except for a few hundred thousand refugees from East Pakistan and for the Kashmir question, everything has been settled, leaving the Government free to introduce equality, people's democratic participation and economic progress. Of these economic progress is dealt with elsewhere.

From 1950 onwards the Government of India has been steadily engaged in a programme of development, of education, of democratization, and of bringing about social and human equality.

Democracy

First a Constitution had to be framed. This Constitution, which made it possible for India to be a Republic within the Commonwealth, had to embody the federal structure of the State, guarantee fundamental rights, protect minorities, select the official language and make it impossible for the Government to be arbitrary while at the same time leaving it strong enough to rule in cases of emergency. No wonder therefore that the Indian Constitution is the longest in the world with its eight schedules and its 400 articles. Its provisions are largely taken from the American and the British Constitutions. Typical of the spirit of the new India are the fundamental rights which guarantee equality before the law, equality of opportunity regardless of sex, caste or creed and the abolition of untouchability.

The Constitution provided for universal adult suffrage. Since the Constitution was adopted in 1950 there have been three general elections—1951-52, 1957, 1962. Each time some 60 per cent, 100 million people, have voted. Each time the Congress has won three-quarters of the seats at the Centre, two-thirds of the seats in the States and nearly half the votes. Each time the Congress did badly in a couple of States,—Rajasthan and Pepsu in 1952; Kerala and Orissa in 1957; Madhya Pradesh and Rajasthan in 1962. Each time the Communists came poor seconds with 180-odd seats in the States and under 30 seats at the Centre and under 10 per cent of the vote. In 1957 the Communists won the election in Kerala by one seat, but after 28 months of misrule they were unseated by the President of India and defeated in an election by the Democratic Front; in the inconclusive 1965 election they won more seats than any other single party.

The stability of Indian politics comes largely from the structure of Indian society. India is basically a society of microscopic owners with a vested interest in the status quo. When it has been made clear to them that the status quo cannot endure, they vote in favour of gradual change; evolution replaces revolution, and this evolution, in India, is the product of consent. The voters have to agree before a major reform can become law; and the leaders never fail to consult them, just as when the electorate has made its wishes clear, the leaders do not fail to abide by the wishes of the people. It is this revolution by consent which is called Nehruism because Mr. Nehru always insisted on taking the people into his confidence and always responded to their expressed desires, even when they were not in agreement with his own. Thus he dropped the compulsory joint cooperative farming programme dear to his heart the moment he realized it would lose the Congress Party votes, and he gave way to the popular demand for Linguistic

States despite his own fear that a division of India on linguistic lines would accentuate fissiparous tendencies and end in the balkanization of the motherland. Indeed, now that India has been divided into linguistic states, the Government of India is doing its best to avoid exacerbating regionalism's potential threat to unity. Careful thought is constantly given so that no State should feel left out, whether it is over development or the appointment of central ministers. However, one major threat to Indian unity still remains because of the chauvinistic insistence of many northern Indians that Hindi—their mother tongue—should become the national language. The South does not speak Hindi and wants English to have a place equal to Hindi's as the Government of India has already promised that it will.

To make democracy more real, to give power to the villagers, the Congress Party has been developing the village councils, vesting increasing powers in them and grouping them into pyramids with an increasing say in local self-government. These elected village councils, the Panchayats, a feature of ancient India, had lost their raison d'être once the Pax Britannica had made the villager feel that the Government was his 'Ma, Bap'—Mother and Father—responsible for his welfare. The Government of India has been making every possible effort to foster local leadership and to break the old apathy of expecting the Government to do everything. Besides reviving the Panchayat system it has created Community Projects—India's counterpart of American Agricultural Extension—which have the twofold function of bringing new techniques to the villages and of eliciting local leadership.

The Community Projects have only begun to stir the villages out of their old apathy; there has been considerable response to agricultural improvements but little induction of spontaneous leadership. Nevertheless, the effect of the Community Projects on the administration itself has been revolutionary; for the first time administrators have had to solicit the cooperation of the villagers instead of ordering it. Indeed, the most striking change I have seen in India in the last generation has been the change of position of the administrator from a demi-god to a common mortal, sure sign that democracy is taking roots.

The administrator has not been the only one to step down from his authoritarian pedestal; the politician has had to step down also. During the days of struggle against the British, martyrdom in gaol, sacrifice, and agitation earned the Congress leaders halos. Nothing tarnishes a halo faster than office when the people learn from experience that the leaders are there to implement national policies, not to lay down the law. The politicians have, like the administrators, had to learn that they are there to serve the people, not to order them about, and that if they fail to convince them it is they, the politicians, who have to give up their schemes.

Equality

There has been nothing this democracy has been keener on than equality, economic equality as well as social equality.

Economic equality is being introduced, gradually, through land reforms and a crippling system of taxation; nearly one-tenth of the income even of the poorest goes in taxation, and the very rich are taxed so heavily that they have to spend some of their capital every year in order to pay all their taxes.

Beside taxation, land reforms are lopping off the tall poppies. Over 200 Acts have been passed or are in the process of being passed. When they have all been put into effect, nobody will be able to hold more than a quite small quantity of land, 30 unirrigated acres in most States. The land reforms have been slow; because of State autonomy each State has had to pass its own legislation; at times the acts have been challenged in the courts; sometimes they have had to be modified, and the Constitution has once had to be amended. The delays have, however, reduced friction because people had enough warning of the ceilings to dispose of their land either by selling it to their sitting tenant or by distributing it amongst their kin. At the end of it all, land reforms will produce equality in two ways.

First of all, the income that will be left from the land once the ceiling is enforced will rarely exceed £300 per annum; moreover the land reforms are breaking the hold of the merchant and the money lender on the peasant. In addition, land reforms have an effect on the caste structure in the countryside. The very big landlords tended to belong to the top castes or to be Muslims; ceilings have meant that the land has gone from them to the middle castes which are in fact the cultivating castes and are numerically the majority everywhere in India, although the particular caste varies from place to place. Thus land reforms have in a sense given further economic strength to those to whom adult franchise was already giving political power. Moreover, wherever new lands have been reclaimed by the Government the untouchables have been given preference for settlement.

The Untouchables

The Congress was pledged to make all Indians equals, so the untouchables whom Gandhi named 'Harijans', the children of God, came very high on the Government's list. The practice of untouchability was made a criminal offence under the Constitution. There are some 60 million untouchables in India. They are born outside the caste system and contact with them was considered so polluting that they were debarred access to any place where they might touch others or their food or water, caste temples, wells and hotels for instance. They have now been given access by law to all public places; any obstruction of them is a criminal offence. The Government of India has done as much to abolish untouchability as the American Government to make its negroes equals. But this still does not mean that untouchables have become full citizens everywhere in India.

The untouchables get special electoral weightage through reserved untouchable seats; they get preference for Government jobs, Government lands, and for admission to schools and colleges. Each Government has at least one untouchable senior Minister; the Congress President in 1962, Mr. Sanjivaya, is an untouchable who has been Chief Minister of Andhra. Grants, loans, scholarships, housing schemes have all been mobilized in the fight against untouchability; £40 million have been earmarked during the Third Plan Period for untouchable uplift. However, legislation, even backed by money, is not enough. Untouchables can become full citizens only when they have the will and the means to insist on their legal due. So long as he is not economically emancipated, an untouchable would be foolish to enter one of the caste temples of his village. It would only annoy his caste patrons and deprive him of his job. Nobody minds when untouchables go into the big caste temples of the cities, eat in urban restaurants or live in the better part of the suburbs; but in the village where everybody knows everybody's grandfather and where tradition is paramount, every attempt to enforce the law leads to tension. Education, urbanization and industrialization are the shears with which to cut through the prejudice of millennia.

The untouchables were not alone in their need of assistance; under Hindu law women did not exist; they were minors always under the guardianship of their men; first of their father, then of their husband, and, if he died, of their sons. Women were highly respected in India, but they did not run their own affairs. The greatest feminists who have ever lived, Gandhi and Nehru, set out to change the status of the Hindu woman. Gandhi brought women into politics; he was so successful that they now quite often take the lead when it comes to courting arrest, whether it is to get rid of the communists, or to get Bombay city incorporated into Maharashtra. Nehru piloted the reform of Hindu Law first through a general election and then through Parliament. He thus redeemed Gandhi's pledge that 'Hindu women should not suffer any disability not suffered by man'. Monogamy has been enforced, divorce is now permissible for much the same reasons as in Britain, daughters now inherit from their father, widows from their husband, mothers from their sons. Widows have been given the guardianship of their children and can claim a share of the paternal house if they do not want to remain with their in-laws. Nehru has insisted that 15 per cent of the Congress candidates for elections must be women, and in every ministry there is at least one woman minister. Women get full opportunity in Government posts except for a few obvious ones like the Defence Services, and during the last decade the number of women who have gone out to work in all walks of life has been very large.

There has also been a very sharp increase in female education; in the old India women were normally illiterate, but in 1960 there were no less than 200,000 girls at college. Indeed education has become a status symbol for girls; a literate daughter requires a smaller dowry than an illiterate one; this has been pushing up the age of marriage and in the case of college graduates it has been displacing arranged marriages or prepared marriages. Traditionally Indian marriages are arranged by the parents according to caste, horoscope and custom. The children have, theoretically, always enjoyed the right of veto; but since they did not meet their mate until the betrothal they had little reason or opportunity to exercise this veto; after all they knew that their parents had their interests at heart and were the best judges. But now, with education and its resultant increase in the age of marriage, children have become more discriminating. Amongst the educated, the parents now have to prepare the marriage instead of merely arranging it; that is, they must find out what their children expect out of marriage and arrange for the couple to meet before finalizing the wedding. But the old style of arranged marriage with no real say for the children is still very frequent in the villages. Love marriages, of course, are virtually unknown outside a few big cities.

In the past change was often made difficult by the existence of the joint family, which tied the younger generation to the speed at which grandmother was willing to move. Today the joint family is rapidly breaking up. Now that girls are so much more often educated and that marriages occur in the teens rather than in childhood, daughters-in-law press for their own house more often; nor are earning members of the family quite as willing as they used to be to share with the idle and the jobless. Above all, the joint family is disappearing amongst the peasantry. Those whom the increase in population has reduced to a fragment of land want to keep the pittance they earn as labourers to themselves. Those who have large farms have been frightened by the legislation imposing ceilings on landholdings into breaking their farms up amongst the different members of the family. Even in business, the joint family is being worn away by high taxation; Indian taxes are always severe, and they are especially severe on non-agricultural joint families.

If people are to be equal, they have to be educated. Only one Indian out of four is literate; illiteracy goes up with age as there used to be fewer schools in the past, and many semi-literates have become illiterate for lack of practice.

The Government of India has embarked upon an education programme which it is hoped will see two-thirds of the children in the age group 6-11 at school by the end of 1966. The problem is not to persuade the parents to send their children to school but to find enough money, buildings, teachers and trainers of teachers. The size of the problem is forbidding: there are in India 558,000 villages and the total population will be around 600,000,000 by 1980.

The Government of India has allocated nearly £20 million for family planning in the Third Five-Year Plan. The difficulty will be to spend that amount so long as a safe, cheap oral contraceptive is not available, but clinics are spreading rapidly, and in peninsular India there have been thousands of sterilizations, though it is rare for such sterilization to occur before the family has four or five living children.

At the beginning of the Third Plan there were some 34 million children at primary school; there should be some 50 million by 1966. One child in five goes to middle school; there were one million children at secondary school in 1951; there were three million ten years later and the number is expected to go up to four million by 1966. Every third child goes on from secondary school to college and there is a steady shift at the university from arts to science. India has over 1,000 colleges and their number goes up every year, but the standard of education has suffered severely since 1947 from a lowering of the standard of admission and from a decline of the standard of school English; English is still the language of instruction in most colleges, although Hindi is the official language and English is only an associate language under the constitution. The regional language, not Hindi—except where it is the regional language—has been displacing English at school. The attempts that have been made to replace English in the colleges raise grave problems: there are not the textbooks in the regional languages, and the disappearance of English would tie university teachers and students to their own linguistic region.

But still not enough has been done. India's need for technicians is endless. Only £360 million is allotted to educational expansion in the Third Plan, and the emphasis is still too often on cram books and memorizing.

Caste and Politics

Caste is the dominant feature of Indian life, the feature which makes Indian civilization different from any other. While everybody has heard of untouchables, not many people realize that untouchability is only an extension of caste and that there are as many watertight compartments within the caste system as there are cells in a bee-hive. In theory there are only four main castes and the outcastes. In practice there are innumerable Brahmin sub-castes, as many untouchable sub-castes and a myriad of sub-castes in between, which all tend in their exclusiveness to behave as if they were castes, instead of sub-castes.

A caste has been defined as a group of people who can eat, sit and marry with each other without considering themselves polluted. Under the Indian social system almost everybody is polluted by almost everybody else so that sub-castes tend to be very small. For instance, a Maharashtrian potter who uses a big wheel to turn his pots will not eat with or marry into the family of a Maharashtrian potter who uses a small wheel to turn his pots; each potter thinks himself better than the other and neither has any desire to pollute himself by fraternizing. The caste system, like all hierarchy, has to be based upon a clear-cut recognition of hierarchical gradations. The Indian caste system is sufficiently prolific for so many gradations to have emerged that everybody can find comfort in the thought that there is someone lower than himself; in any case so long as distance is kept, there is little cause for conflict; nobody else cares whether the potter with the big wheel or the potter with the little wheel ranks higher, since nobody else is planning to marry into their family.

In the past what mattered was to be a big fish in a small pond; therefore sub-castes multiplied with tropical exuberance, making it possible for almost everybody to be a leader of sorts. Adult franchise has dealt a mortal blow to sub-caste. Once a leader has to represent an electorate of 75,000 people for the local Assembly, and three-quarters of a million for Parliament, he has to appeal to the largest possible number. Caste has become polarized into a sandwich. Everywhere at the bottom there is the layer of untouchable bread, everywhere at the top there is the thin layer of Brahmin bread, and in the middle there is the filling which is made up by the dominant cultivator and artisan castes of the area which vary from region to region but everywhere represent perhaps two-thirds of the electorate and hold political power.

As political power has shifted from the Brahmins to the major cultivating and artisan castes, the Brahmins have tended to move to the key positions of economic and technological power. Thanks to their tradition of education they provide the administrators, the engineers, the economists, the managers without whom India cannot progress from the cowdung to the atomic age;

thus everybody, except the landless labourers and the untouchables who are a numerical minority everywhere, has been provided with enough power and participation in his destiny and that of his country to make Nehruism, revolution by consent, attractive and India stable.

BIBLIOGRAPHY

Horace Alexander. *Consider India.* (Asia Publishing House, London, 1961.)

G. M. Carstairs. *The Twice Born.* (Hogarth Press, London, 1957.)

L. del Vasto. *Gandhi to Vinoba.* (Rider, London, 1956.)

S. C. Dube. *Indian Village.* (Routledge and Kegan Paul, London, 1955.)

M. K. Gandhi. *An Autobiography.* (Phoenix, London, 1949.)

J. H. Hutton. *Caste in India.* (Oxford Univ. Press, London, 1961.)

R. K. Karanjia. *The Mind of Mr. Nehru.* (Allen and Unwin, London, 1960.)

D. N. Majumdar. *Caste and Communication in an Indian Village.* (Asia Publishing House, London, 1958.)

McKim Marriott (ed.). *Village India.* A collection of essays. (Chicago Univ. Press, Berkeley, 1958.)

A. C. Mayer. *Caste and Kinship in Central India.* (Routledge and Kegan Paul, London, 1960.)

A. C. Mayer and others. *Pilot Project India.* (Univ. of California Press, Berkley, 1958.)

T. Mende. *Conversations with Nehru.* (Secker and Warburg, London, 1956.)

B. B. Misra. *The Indian Middle Class.* (Oxford Univ. Press, London, 1961.)

P. Moon. *Divide and Quit.* (Chatto and Windus, London, 1961.)

W. H. Morris-Jones. *The Government and Politics of India.* (Hutchinson, London, 1964.)

N. V. Sovani and V. M. Dandekar (eds.) *Changing India.* A collection of essays. (Asia Publishing House, London, 1961.)

Maurice and Taya Zinkin. *Britain and India: Requiem for Empire.* (Chatto and Windus, London, 1964.)

Taya Zinkin. *Caste Today.* (Oxford Univ. Press, London, 1962.) *India Changes!* (Chatto and Windus, London, 1958.) *Reporting India.* (Chatto and Windus, London, 1962.)

BIOGRAPHICAL NOTE

TAYA ZINKIN. B. 1918; studied medicine in Paris; researched in bio-chemistry at the University of Wisconsin; married Maurice Zinkin, I.C.S. in 1945; lived in India from 1945 to 1960. From 1950 to 1960 correspondent from India for *The Economist* and *The Guardian*, and from 1955 to 1960 for *Le Monde.* Author of: *India Changes!* (Chatto and Windus, London, 1958); *Rishi* (Methuen, London, 1960); *Rishi Returns* (Methuen, London, 1961); *Caste Today*(O.U.P., London, 1962); *Reporting India* (Chatto and Windus, London, 1962); *India* (O.U.P., London, 1963); and in collaboration with Maurice Zinkin *Britain and India: Requiem for Empire* (Chatto and Windus, London, 1964).

THE INDIAN BORDER

by

GEORGE N. PATTERSON

INDIA has approximately 2,000 miles of northern border with what is described as the 'Tibet region of China'. But over 1,000 miles of this territory is outside the effective control of India. India has no jurisdiction over Nepal and Bhutan—except for her assurances that any act of aggression against these countries would be taken as aggression against India. Since 1947 Pakistan has been in occupation of 'Azad Kashmir'. And since October 1962 the Chinese have forcibly seized some of this border territory.

LADAKH

Ladakh has never had a properly defined boundary. In or about the year A.D. 900, during one of the many revolutions in Tibet's history, a Tibetan known as Ni-ma-mgon emigrated to western Tibet, married a local chieftain's daughter and brought the area under his control, including Ladakh, or 'Maryul' as it was known at that time. This territory, with some exceptions at different times, for several centuries remained under the jurisdiction of his descendants, the 'Kings of Ladakh'.

In 1664–65 Ladakh accepted the sovereignty of the Mogul Emperor of India, Aurangzeb. In 1680, after being invaded by Kalmuks sent by the Regent of Tibet, the Ladakhis appealed to the Mogul Governor of Kashmir for help, and in this way defeated the Tibetan army. A Treaty was signed which was the last formal definition of the Ladakh-Tibet frontier 'at the time of the Ladakhi Kings'.

When Kashmir, under the Dogra, Maharajah Gulab Singh, feudatory of Maharajah Ranjit Singh, attacked Ladakh in 1834 in an attempt to include it within his own boundaries, the Ladakhis appealed to the Tibetan Government for assistance. A Tibetan army, including Chinese troops, was sent to their aid. After varying success in different areas, the Dogras out-manoeuvred the Tibetans by flooding their main camp and a Peace Treaty in 1842 was signed broadly recognizing 'the frontiers it had during the times of the Ladakhi Kings'.

Following the First Sikh War between Britain and the Sikhs another Treaty was signed, the Treaty of Lahore, in which 'the hill countries . . . including the provinces of Kashmir and Hazara' were annexed to British India. Later, in 1846, in the Treaty of Lahore, Britain sold to Gulab Singh, while remaining paramount, 'all the hilly and mountainous country with its dependences situated to the eastward of the river Indus and westward of the River Ravi, including Chumba and excluding Lahul'. Article 2 of this

Treaty laid down that the eastern frontier of Kashmir—the frontier between Ladakh and Tibet—was to be defined by the Commissioners appointed by Britain and Maharajah Gulab Singh.

The following is part of the statement drawn up by the Commissioners:

> 'As regards the Ladakh-Tibet boundary, the Commissioners owing to Immamudin's rebellion in Kashmir were unable to reach the Tibet border. One of the Commissioners, however, wrote a memorandum in which he pointed out that the line was, as he thought, already sufficiently defined by nature, and recognized by custom, with the exception of the two extremities. On the appointment of the Second Commission (1847) steps were taken to secure the co-operation of the Chinese and Kashmir officials, *but the Chinese delegate never appeared and the demarcation of the frontier had to be abandoned* and the northern as well as the eastern boundary of the Kashmir state is still undefined.' (Italics—ed.)

On the basis of these treaties the Indian Government claim that the whole of the Aksai Chin plateau, the Chang-chungmo Valley and the Rangong, Rupshu and Hanle areas belong to India. However, Chinese maps show their boundary in this area much further to the west, and include about 4,000 square miles—the greater part of the Aksai Chin, parts of the Chang-chungmo valley, and the Pangong, Spanggur Tso and Chang-lo areas in Tibet.

The Chinese authorities contend:

(1) That the then Peking Government did not participate in this Treaty and that, therefore, their successors were not bound by it.

(2) That the frontiers were never delimited, and that in any case they did not include the big bulge, which was part of Sinkiang and not of Tibet.

It must be stated against this, however, that the Chinese authorities in Sinkiang had set up a border pillar at a point 64 miles south of Suket, that is to say *well to the north of the territory now under dispute*, and a map published by Peking University in 1925, showing the Chinese Empire at its widest extent under the Manchu Dynasty, *excluded the Aksai Chin from China's frontiers*.

Before the dispute with China Ladakh was classified geographically as being 45,762 square miles in area with a population of 183,476. But since 1954 China has been quietly occupying 14,000 square miles of this barren north-eastern bulge of Kashmir, with India since 1960 desperately building roads and multiplying military outposts to stop the Chinese advance. According to the Indian Note of July 12th, 1962, the Indian Government protests that seven of the Chinese military outposts are 'outside the Chinese claim line as shown in their 1956 map'. The Chinese boundary in this sector, according to the 1956 map, is a concave line from the Karakoram Pass to the Konka Pass, skirting the origins of the Chip Chap and Galwan rivers. But in the 1960 map the boundary has advanced to include a much wider area. South of the Konka Pass the Chinese claims have also advanced from 1956 to 1960 to include Khurnak Fort and part of the Pangong Lake. Without going into confusing details of which country's outposts are where—often they are behind each other—it is obvious that the Chinese are now well beyond their 1956 line on the entire Ladakh front.

Between Ladakh and Nepal there is also disputed territory but while this might be used as a bargaining counter in any overall settlement there is no wide area of controversy, although the territory is militarily important.

Sikkim

In Sikkim, a small 1800-square-mile protectorate of India with a population of 165,000, there are almost 100,000 Nepalis subject to political influence from Nepal; the remainder of the population is divided between Lepchas, Bhutias and Tibetans. The ruling family is of Tibetan extraction in its origin some two centuries ago, and by inter-marriage since, and the late Maharajah was a younger brother installed by Britain in 1914. India has taken over the British agreement recognizing Sikkim as a 'protectorate' but added some points of her own. When in 1949 the political parties emerged and looked like removing the unpopular Maharajah, India stepped in at the Maharajah's request with troops to 'restore law and order', and also added a Dewan, or Chief Minister, to 'advise' the Maharajah. Sikkim receives considerable economic aid from India, and Indian technicians and engineers are assisting in the development of the country.

Bhutan

Bhutan is larger than Sikkim and its original inhabitants are of Tibetan extraction with only a slight admixture from North Assam. But in the past century there has been a great influx of Nepalis, and while the Bhutanese try to minimise the numbers and admit to 25 per cent the local Nepali organization claims 64 per cent; the true figure is probably somewhere between. The Maharajah is young, but the victim of a serious ailment, and is opposed by relatives and other factions. The Government is composed of 130 district head-men and meets once a year—or oftener in emergency.

Bhutan's relations with India are different from Sikkim's in that Bhutan has full control over her internal affairs and an understanding regarding India handling her external affairs. There has in fact been no officially announced agreement about their dispute over the term in the Indo-Bhutanese Treaty, 'guided by the advice of the Indian Government'. India claims that this gives her the right of control of Bhutan's external affairs, while Bhutan maintains that India can proffer advice but it is not incumbent on Bhutan to accept it. Bhutan has only a minuscule militia scattered thinly across 18,000 square miles of mountains, to protect a population of 700,000 heavily infiltrated by Tibetan refugees with Chinese agents among them. It has a network of roads in the south under Indian supervision built with aid given by India. China has repudiated India's claims to special relationships with Sikkim and Bhutan, and has made alternative offers to both countries—such as part of a 'Federation of Himalayan States', sovereignty, diplomatic representation, and considerable economic aid. China's invasion of Indian territory in October 1962 has put a new complexion on these offers.

The North-East Frontier Agency

The North East Frontier Agency, between Bhutan and Burma, is also claimed by China, which occupied some of it in 1960 and has since invaded the whole territory. Despite intense military preparations since 1960 this is the most vulnerable part of India's border.

The segregation of the N.E.F.A. as a separate tribal area was really begun by the implementation of the '*Inner Line Regulations*' in 1873. At the same time the geographical conformation of the territory, with its savage mountains and impenetrable forests, contributed to the separate development of distinctive tribal groupings. South of the Inner Line the territory comprising the six districts of Goalpara—Kameng, Darrang, Nowgong, Lackimpur and Sibsagar—was raised to the status of a province, known as Assam.

Throughout the period of British administration little was done in the N.E.F.A. other than sending in punitive expeditions to restrain the marauding tribes. A weak China and a weak Burma presented no external threats to the North-East. It was through the two routes from Tibet, Tawang and Rima, or Walong, that the Tibetans had come to first trade then inhabit the northern areas of the territory. It was through the Pangsu Pass in the eastern section that the earlier Ahom conquerors had come; then the later northern Burmese tribes and, finally, the Burmese Army. It was through this same Pass that the Indian Army passed to defeat the Japanese. It is chiefly from this area that the Nagas have conducted their decade-long revolt against Indian forces. The movement of tribes over the centuries has left this area with a predominant Tibeto-Burmese people of Mongolian origin, and only a slight sprinkling of Assam admixture.

Historically, the N.E.F.A. is wide open to the claims of any of the neighbouring countries, depending on the particular basis of the claim advanced. Ethnically and economically, until the twentieth century, its associations were mostly with the north. According to one historian, in the 5th century a local Rajah sent an embassy to the Chinese Court. A Muslim invasion was unsuccessful, but a more powerful invasion by the Ahoms of North Burma in the 14th century succeeded in conquering a large area, extending right up to the border of Tibet. The Ahom rulers remained in power in Assam until replaced by the British in 1839. But even the Ahoms were only able to control their territory with the help of Naga warriors.

With the coming of the British, and the rapid expansion of the tea industry in North Assam, new opportunities for trade in the south were opened up to the N.E.F.A. tribes. But, also, new confusions were introduced as independent arrangements regarding the buying and selling of land were entered into between the various tribes and European tea-planters. To safeguard the rich tea interests it became necessary to extend British administration in the area, and this was done sporadically, without a central policy, and reluctantly. District Commissioners and Political Officers on the plains of Assam interfered as little as possible with the hill people, except when there was a serious outbreak of fighting or when specifically asked to do so by the tribal councils.

When China's forceful and ambitious Frontier Commissioner, General Chao-Erh-feng, entered Tibet in 1905 with a Chinese Army bent on subjugating the country, and then turned southwards to claim 'China's' territory in N.E.F.A., in 1910, the British Government awoke to the possible dangers threatening Assam and India in this move. With Chao Erh-feng's death in 1911, and the subsequent Tibetan defeat of the Chinese, the threat was diminished, but in 1913 the British Government convened a meeting to discuss the status of Tibet and stabilize the situation. This Conference was attended by the plenipotentiaries of Britain, Tibet and China, and known as the Simla Convention. At first China objected to a Tibetan representative having equal status with the Chinese representative, but later agreed to attend. However, the terms finally proved unacceptable to China, especially those relating to the proposed boundaries between Tibet and China, and between Tibet and the N.E.F.A. The chief Chinese objections to signing the Simla Convention, according to Ivan Chen, the Chinese plenipotentiary, were:

(1) 'Tibet should be recognized as a region of China'.
(2) 'All the places west of the Salween shall be placed within the limits of the autonomy of Tibet but any question which may arise there of political territorial or international nature, shall be discussed between China and Great Britain'.
(3) 'The imposing of a time limit on the Tibetan and Chinese representatives by Sir Henry MacMahon in which they had to give a definite answer'.

When China refused to sign, Britain and Tibet went ahead and signed the Convention. They also signed a declaration by which they agreed to regard the third party, China, as excluded from the benefits which would have accrued to her had she signed the Convention.

Indo-Chinese Border Dispute

The border dispute between China and India is being conducted on three levels: (1) from Kashmir to Burma, and including the border states; (2) the MacMahon Line, as just described, from Bhutan to Burma; and (3) the limited N.E.F.A. districts of Tawang, or Chedong, and Longju. The Chinese policy is to try to win (1) and (2) by emphasizing (3), for if she can succeed in this then her case on the first two will be difficult to refute. For this reason we shall now concentrate on (3) in some detail to show the basis of China's claims—but this should not be taken as supporting either of them.

In 1914, as a result of the Simla Convention between Britain and Tibet, the India-Tibetan frontier was delimited from the eastern boundary of Bhutan to the Isurazi Pass on the Irawaddy-Salween water parting. This became known as the 'MacMahon Line'. Sir Henry MacMahon, who was the British representative, recommended that while great care should be taken to avoid friction with the Tibetan Government (who had objected to the proposed alterations in the Tawang area), and the vested interests of the Tawang Monastery, an experienced British official should proceed to the western part of the Line to settle its future administration. Tawang, the area of the heaviest fighting between China and India, is in what is now known as the 'Kameng Frontier Tract' of the North-East Frontier Agency, which was created by Britain in 1912; before then it was vaguely termed 'Western Section of the North-East Frontier'. The importance of this is stressed in the following excerpt from a report of the Chief Secretary of Assam to the Political Officer, Balipara Frontier Tract, dated 17th September 1936:

'. . . It amounts to this, that while the Chinese already claim a large stretch of territory East of Tawang as part of the Sikang Province of China, the Tibetan Government, over whom the Chinese Government claim suzerainty, are collecting revenue and exercising jurisdiction in the Tawang area many miles south of the international frontier. The Government of India consider that some effective steps should be taken to challenge activities which may be extended to a claim on behalf of China to Tawang itself, or even Bhutan and Sikkim. . . . *The continued exercise of jurisdiction by Tibet in Tawang, and the area south of Tawang, might enable China . . . to claim prescriptive rights over part of the territory recognized as within India by the* 1914 *Convention. . . .*' (Italics—ed.)

In the autumn of 1936 the British Political Officer in Sikkim, Sir Basil Gould, had an interview with the Tibetan Government in Lhasa at which Tawang was discussed. The Tibetan Government's attitude was that: (1) up to 1914 Tawang had been undoubtedly Tibetan; (2) they regarded the adjustment of the Tibeto-Indian border as part and parcel of the general adjustment and determination of boundaries contemplated in the 1914 Convention; if they could, with British help, secure a definite Sino-Tibetan boundary they would, of course, be glad to observe the Indo-Tibetan border as defined in 1914; (3) they had been encouraged in thinking that the British Government of India sympathized with this way of regarding the matter owing to the fact that at no time since the Convention and Declaration of 1914 had the Indian Government taken steps to question Tibetan, or to assert British, authority in the Tawang area.

In 1938, a small expedition under a Captain Lightfoot was sent to Tawang, and in his report to the Government of India, dated 7th September, 1938, he also warned that unless regular tours were undertaken, and some effective measures to establish administration were introduced, British authority over the area would be lost. The Central Government in reply said that a second tour could not be allowed as it 'might result in the Government of India having to undertake permanent occupation in order to fulfil their obligations . . . .' It was decided subsequently, in July, 1939, that the question of future policy should be decided after the expiry of one year. World War II intervened, and in 1947 India became independent, but the last British Political Officer there in 1947 has told the present writer that there was no alteration in the position when he was there and that it was still necessary to obtain permission from the Tibetan authorities in Tawang to travel in that area, that Indian authority extended only to the Se-la Sub Agency, south of Tawang, and that token tribute was paid to Tibet in recognition of this.

When India became independent in 1947 the Indian Government was almost immediately presented with a problem involving the N.E.F.A. and other border territories. The Tibetan Government, choosing the time when the Kuomintang in China was in decline, and a new Indian policy imminent, sent a telegram to the Indian Government on October 16th, 1947 demanding recognition of her claims to the former territories:

'. . . such as Zayul and Walong and in the direction of Pemako, Lonag, Lapa, Mon, Bhutan, Sikkim, Darjeeling and others on this side of the river Ganges and Lowo, Ladakh, etc., up to the boundary of Yarkhim'.

The Indian Government sent a reply (published in White Paper No. 2) as follows:

'The Government of India would be glad to have an assurance that it is the intention of the Tibetan Government to continue relations on the existing basis until new Agreements are reached on matters which either party would wish to take up. This is the procedure adopted by all other countries with which India has inherited Treaty relations from his Majesty's Government. . . .'

In 1950 the Chinese Army invaded Tibet and India recognized her right to do so under China's pre-1914 Simla Convention claims of 'suzerainty' over Tibet.

Between the earlier period of China's invasion of Tibet in 1905, and the later invasion in 1950, only fitful interest in the N.E.F.A. had been taken, as has been noted. Prior to 1914 the N.E.F.A. was divided into two sections, the Western and Eastern, each under the nominal charge of a distant Political Officer. In 1912 these sections were named as Balipara and Sadiya respectively. In 1912 units of the Assam Rifles began penetrating some of the valleys in Lohit and Siang, but Subansiri and Tawang were left as administrative voids—although several letters were sent by Assam Governor and Secretaries to the Central Government warning that this lack of administration was in danger of letting the territory go to China by default. In 1942 another Frontier Tract was created out of the Sadiya Tract and named Tirap Frontier Tract; and in 1946 the Balipara Frontier Tract was divided into the Se-La Sub Agency and Subansiri Area. In 1949 the remaining parts of the Sadiya Frontier Tract were divided into the two divisions of Abor Hills and Mishmi Hills. In 1949, the Subansiri Divisional Headquarters was established and Tawang was brought under Indian administration for the first time in February 1951. In 1951, also, Naga Hills was formed into a separate district and in 1953 it was named the Tuensang Frontier District. Finally, in 1954, the Divisions were given the names of Kameng (2,000 sq. miles), Subansiri, (7,950 sq. miles), Siang (8,392 sq. miles), Lohit (5,800 sq. miles), and Tirap (2,657 sq. miles) and brought under a specially created administrative unit of some 31,438 sq. miles under the Foreign Ministry, with the Governor of Assam acting as the agent of the President of India.

The greatest, and most immediate, threat to India lies in the recent Chinese invasion of the N.E.F.A., in October 1962, and her claims to this territory—according to the Chinese Government, 'illegally' occupied by Indian administrators and troops. In the 'Report of the Officials of the Government of India and the Chinese People's Republic on Boundary Questions' published in February, 1961, the Chinese officials deliberately excluded Sikkim and Bhutan and equivocated on the N.E.F.A. In an exchange of diplomatic Notes the Chinese Government made clear its claims:

'The traditional, customary Sino-Indian boundary east of Bhutan follows in the main the southern foot of the Himalayas, and Chinese maps published throughout the years have all shown the location of this line. The unilateral claim about the boundary in this sector put forward by the Indian Government in its memorandum has never been accepted by the Chinese Government. In view of the fact that the Sino-Indian boundary has never been formally delimited . . . and that moreover . . . what is in dispute is not the question of the location of individual parts on the boundary but involves the question of larger tracts of territory, the Chinese Government has always hoped to have friendly discussions . . . so as to seek a reasonable settlement of the boundary question . . . (*But*) *the unshakeable fact remains that it is only the boundary line running along the southern foot of the Himalayas . . . which is the true, traditional, customary line of the boundary between China and India in the eastern section. . . .*' (Italics—ed.)

This was categorically refuted by India.

To sum up the basis of the dispute: (1) Until the 20th century the territory belonged to no sovereign power; (2) Britain established her claim in the early 20th century, particularly through the 1914 Simla Convention, but did not take 'effective steps' to bring large parts of it within her administration, which would have been sufficient to give her right to the territory under international law; (3) from 1947 to 1950 the Government of India began to bring the territory under her administrative control, but seriously jeopardized her claims to the territory, by (a) recognizing China's claim to a suzerainty over, and armed conquest of, Tibet in 1950, which suzerainty could be extended to include those other areas; and (b) recognizing Tibet as 'a region of China' in 1954 (which negated her own claims that she would have inherited under the 1914 Simla Convention, because these were agreed between Britain and a sovereign treaty-making Tibet).

There are two distinct schools of thought among objective scholars studying this difficult problem. One is that India lost nothing by claiming the MacMahon Line while repudiating Tibet's right as an independent nation to negotiate the Convention which produced the boundary; the argument being that Tibet was in a position to negotiate such a treaty *at the time*, but that circumstances in 1950, 1954, and 1962 were such that China was the dominant power and so in a position to dictate her own interpretations.

The other school argues that the Tibetan Government was the effective administration controlling Tibet and some parts of N.E.F.A. from 1914 to 1950, that both Britain and the later Governments recognized this in their official dealings with Tibet, and that India's claims to the MacMahon Line can only be on the basis of recognizing Tibet as an independent sovereign state.

Whatever may be the final outcome India's position has been strengthened by the late Mr. Nehru's offer to take the matter to the International Court for a decision and by accepting the Afro-Asian moderated interpretation of China's cease-fire 'offer' contained in the 'Colombo proposals'. But in the light of N.E.F.A.'s history, and China's own categorical claims, it is highly unlikely that the Chinese Government will agree to India's counter-proposal.

A recent proposal of China is for a 'Confederation of Himalayan States'—to include Nepal, Sikkim, Bhutan, N.E.F.A. and Nagaland. This proposal, like previous ones, is unacceptable to India. No solution to the Sino-Indian border dispute seems in sight.

BIBLIOGRAPHY

S. K. Blugai. *Anglo-Assamese Relations.* (Gurhati, Assam, 1949.)
W. J. Buchanan. *Notes on Tours in Darjeeling and Sikkim.* (Darjeeling, 1961.)
Ivan Chen. *China-Tibet-U.K.* Account of the Simla Conference, 1913-14. (Peking, 1940.)
Sir Edward Gait. *A History of Assam.* (Thacker, Spink and Co., Calcutta, 2nd ed., 1926.)
Alistair Lamb. *The China-India Border: The Origins of the Disputed Boundaries.* (Chatham House Essays, Oxford Univ. Press, London, 1946.)
W. Leifer. *Himalaya: Mountains of Destiny.* (Galley Press, London, 1962.)
Sir Robert Reid. *The Frontier Areas Bordering on Assam.* (Shillong, 1942.)
Vincent A. Smith. *The Early History of India.* (Clarendon Press, Oxford, 4th ed., 1924.) *The Oxford Student's History of India.* (Oxford Univ. Press, London, 15th ed., revised by H. G. Rawlinson, 1951.)

BIOGRAPHICAL NOTE

George Patterson went to China as a missionary in 1946 and from 1947 to 1950 worked among the Khambas of East Tibet. When China invaded Tibet he remained on the Indo-Tibetan border studying and writing on the political affairs of the Himalayan countries and tribes. He has been a free-lance journalist, correspondent for *The Daily Telegraph* and *The Observer* and contributor to leading international journals. He has also lectured and broadcast on Asian affairs. His publications (all by Faber and Faber, London) include: *Tibetan Journey* (1954), *God's Fool* (1956), *Up and Down Asia* (1958), *Tragic Destiny* (1959), *Tibet in Revolt* (1960) and *Peking versus Delhi* (1963).

NEPAL

by

GEORGE N. PATTERSON

NEPAL is an independent kingdom, situated on the southern slopes of the Himalayas, and thus occupying a key position between the Republic of India and Communist China. It is bounded on the north by Tibet, on the east by Sikkim and west Bengal, and on the south and west by the two Indian Provinces of Bihar and Uttar Pradesh. The country is about 500 miles long by 100 miles wide and falls away from the near-30,000 feet Himalayan peaks in three distinct terraces to the plains of India. Between Nepal and the plains of India there is no natural frontier or barrier of any kind.

In this strategic area of mountains, valleys and jungles live nine million Nepalis, the most martial being the Limbus, Rais, Magars and Gurungs, better known outside Nepal as 'Gurkhas'. Most of the nine million inhabitants are scattered in remote valleys throughout the country, with little or no contact between them. The Katmandu Valley, which contains the capital of that name, is the largest 'valley' in Nepal, covering an area of 242 square miles at a height of 4,500 feet, and has the largest concentrated population of 415,000. Most Nepalese are Hindus. Many aristocratic families have matrimonial connections with Indian princes. The Gurkhas constitute one of the most important sections of the Indian Army and are being recruited in increasingly large numbers in the mountain divisions raised to combat the Chinese threat from the north.

The modern history of Nepal has been shaped by three important periods. First, the conquest of the Katmandu Valley by Prithvi Narayan Shah in the 1760s that led to the unification of Nepal under one rule. The Shah dynasty continues to rule in Nepal until the present day. Secondly, the usurpation of power by Jung Bahadur in 1846, which resulted in the hegemony of the Rana family for 104 years without a break. Even today some Ranas are a significant factor in the kingdom's social and economic life. Finally, the sequence of events from 1950 onwards.

Nepal leapt from feudalism into the 20th century in 1951. That was the year when its unique agnate system of rule by a Prime Minister Rana dynasty was replaced by a form of constitutional monarchy with democracy. But Nepal was nowhere near prepared for modern democratic methods, for in addition to the lack of administrative machinery and means of transport and communications there was no national consciousness but only primitive tribal loyalties. The old order had been disrupted too suddenly for the speedy creation of a country-wide social, economic and political base which might have supported democratic institutions. There was no bridge between the disgruntled aristocrats used to absolute power and the idealistic Congress Party with theories and little experience. To further complicate the situation, many Nepalis are extremely sensitive to India's interest in Nepal's affairs; they question the loyalties of the Congress leaders whose associations have all been with India and who owe their positions to India's intervention on their behalf in 1951.

In 1952 a militant nationalist, Dr. K. I. Singh, led a revolt against the Government, but fled to Tibet and China. Following this there was a period of maladministration, corruption and nepotism which culminated, under the threat of a national demonstration, in the King dissolving the Royal Council of State and vesting all Royal prerogatives in the then Crown Prince, now King, Mahendra.

King Mahendra began his reign in 1955 by denouncing the previous four years of democracy as 'shameful', and tried to govern by 'direct rule', but was forced by the political parties to hold elections in 1959. The Congress Party emerged clear winners with a majority of 74 seats in a House of 109. But the King, who had said at his coronation that there would never be 'two sovereigns in Nepal', quickly tired of the continued bickering, corruption and maladministration and on December 15th, 1960, he announced that once again he had taken over direct rule and had imprisoned the political leaders.

The earlier attitude of superiority and contempt of the martial Nepalis for the plain-dwelling Indians had been temporarily modified by the help India had given to the Nepali Congress leaders in overthrowing the Rana regime. But this quickly disappeared. To assert their independence of India the Nepalese leaders turned to China and in 1956 a Sino-Nepalese Treaty was signed, and China gave to Nepal considerable economic aid. This friendly beginning was continued by both sides, and after agreeing to a Sino-Nepalese boundary settlement favourable to Nepal the Nepalese Government agreed to China building a strategic road from Lhasa, in Tibet, to Katmandu, thereby offsetting Indian advantages. In addition, China is now contributing over 20 crores of rupees (£15½ million) in aid of various kinds. India has also increased its aid to Nepal.

In the first two years after the King took over, according to the report of the King's hand-picked 'Intellectuals' Conference' held in June, 1962, there was little change. Dr. K. I. Singh, who led the abortive revolt in 1952 and returned in 1956 to be Prime Minister, declared that if the King did not change his policies he would lead another revolt against him. His chief fear was that the King's vacillating direction of Nepalese affairs was opening the way for a return of the exiled Nepali Congress Party under threat of arms and committed to a pro-Indian policy, which in turn would bring in the Chinese from the north to 'help' pro-Chinese elements—and so make Nepal into another Korea.

China's attitude towards Nepal was summed up in Mao Tse-tung's ominous words a few years ago: 'In defeating China in war the imperialists have taken away *many Chinese dependent states and parts of her territories* . . . England seized Burma, Bhutan, *Nepal* . . .' It is this fear of China's long-term intentions in Nepal, together with the deterioration in Indo-Nepal relations, which led in March 1963 to a visit to Nepal by the then Indian Home Minister, Mr. Lal Bahadur Shastri. China's invasion of Indian territory in October 1962 virtually altered Nepal's attitude toward its southern neighbour, dissipating much of the anti-Indian feeling that had been allowed to develop in the country and bringing about a realization that if Nepal is to remain independent it should develop closer ties with India.

The Economic Situation

Over 90 per cent of the population is engaged in subsistence farming. Whilst the country is normally self-sufficient in foodstuffs, in good years the Terai region in the south provides a grain surplus for export to India. In years when the rains fail, on the other hand, and in case of wide-spread flooding rice or wheat has to be imported. In the sherpa regions the introduction of the potato has helped to supplement grain production and farm income.

Farming is carried out mostly by small-holders under the traditional Zamindari (intermediary) system and on rent-free Birta land. A Land Reform Commission has been set up to control rents and interest rates in agriculture and to prohibit evictions except where rents have not been paid or land has been left idle.

Nepal's foreign trade—imports of approximately 300 million rupees and exports approximately 150 million rupees—is primarily, if not exclusively, with India. In the past Indian rupees used to circulate freely, side by side with Nepalese rupees, but in 1964 the Government took steps to restrict the circulation of Indian currency. The official rate of exchange is 160 NRs to 100 IRs. Government revenue and expenditure runs at an annual rate of 300 million rupees.

Nepal's industry is in its infancy. Hydro-electric projects are given a certain priority in long-term planning, designed to improve communications, intensify farming and create the basis of an indigenous industry. However, the consumption of energy (1962: 4 kilogrammes of coal equivalent per head of population) is still the lowest on record for countries listed by the Statistical Office of the United Nations. Among the limited range of goods produced are sugar, jute bags, matches and cigarettes.

No official information is available on Nepal's national income, but it is believed to be no higher than U.S. $50 (£18) per head of population. The current development plan, running from 1962-65, aims at raising the level of economic performance and the standard of living. Of the 670 million rupees (£32 million) set aside for development during the Three-Year Plan, 560 million are expected to become available in the form of foreign aid and foreign loans. The three sectors which are given priority are industry and mining (150 million), transport, communications and public works (145 million) and agriculture, irrigation and village development (110 million). Two-fifths of the grants-in-aid which are used in support of the development plan are provided by the United States (Rs. 210 million); India has offered two-thirds as much (140 million) and Russia and China two-fifths (80 million) and one-fifth (40 million) respectively. Britain offered

Nepal in 1960 a programme of aid to the value of £1 million, spread over five years and including diesel generating, hydro-electric and road building equipment. In 1952 Nepal became a member of the Consultative Committee of the Colombo Plan, under which technical and training assistance has been given.

BIBLIOGRAPHY

Karl Eskelund. *The Forgotten Valley.* (Alvin Redman, London, 1959).
Girilal Jain. *India Meets China in Nepal.* (Asia Publishing House, London, 1960.)
David Snellgrove. *Himalayan Pilgrimage.* (Bruno Cassirer, Oxford, 1961.)
Francis Tuker. *Gorkha. The Story of the Gurkhas of Nepal.* (Constable, London, 1957.)

BIOGRAPHICAL NOTE

GEORGE PATTERSON went to China as a missionary in 1946 and from 1947 to 1950 worked among the Khambas of East Tibet. When China invaded Tibet he remained on the Indo-Tibetan border studying and writing on the political affairs of the Himalayan countries and tribes. He has been a free-lance journalist, correspondent for *The Daily Telegraph* and *The Observer* and contributor to leading international journals. He has also lectured and broadcast on Asian affairs. His publications (all by Faber and Faber, London) include: *Tibetan Journey* (1954), *God's Fool* (1956), *Up and Down Asia* (1958), *Tragic Destiny* (1959), *Tibet in Revolt* (1960), and *Peking versus Delhi* (1963).

PAKISTAN

by

GUY WINT

PAKISTAN was born out of the decision by the British Government that it could not compel the parts of India in which there was a Muslim majority to accept an All-Indian government which, reflecting the composition of the rest of the sub-continent, was predominantly Hindu. The decision was not reached in a hurry. For years there was discussion, and a long and painful attempt to reassure the Muslims by providing safeguards which would limit the power of the executive over them. Much of the most adroit political intelligence of England was directed for some years to this effort. The conciliation was in vain, and in June 1947, the British Government accepted the demand of the leader of the Muslim League, Mr. Jinnah, for a separate state.

Pakistan consisted of the North-West Frontier Province, Sind, Baluchistan, part of the Punjab, part of Bengal, and certain Moslem States.[1] Divided into two parts, West and East, with 1,000 miles of Hindu territory between, it was the part of the sub-continent in which the Muslims, according to the census reports, formed a clear majority. This fell short of Mr. Jinnah's claims, which were roughly that it should include as the homeland of the Muslims all the territory ruled by Muslims before the coming of the British. By the settlement actually reached, a large section of the Muslims, over 30,000,000, were left in India. These lived in areas in which they were a minority, even though, as in the U.P., they had enjoyed an exceptionally favoured position in recruitment to government service. For this section the creation of Pakistan was no triumph. They were immeasurably weakened by the secession of the major part of the Muslim community to form their own state; they were forced to lower their claims, and to be satisfied by the tolerance accorded them by the Hindus.

The first result of the setting up of the new state was a violent explosion in the Punjab, due largely to the situation of the Sikh minority, which emigrated en masse to India; in the excitement caused by the movement of population, law and order broke down, old scores were settled, trains were ambushed, and there was mass plunder. The worst was over within a month.

[1] The idea of Pakistan was first invented by Rahmat Ali, a student at Cambridge, and was first aired in 1933. He explained the name as follows: 'The name "Pakistan" is composed of letters taken from the names of its component parts—Panjab, Afghans (inhabitants of the North-West Frontier Province), Kashmir, Sindh, and Beluchistan.' Rahmat Ali also derived the name from the word Pak (which means Pure or Clear). The word therefore means the land of all that is noble or sacred in life for a Muslim.

U.S.S.R.
IRAN
AFGHANISTAN
Kashmir
CHINESE PEOPLE'S REPUBLIC
NEPAL
WEST PAKISTAN
INDIA
BURMA
EAST PAKISTAN
INDIAN OCEAN
CEYLON
CHINA
Khyber Pass
Peshawar
ISLAMABAD
Rawalpindi
Sialkot
Gujranwala
Lahore
Lyallpur
Chenab
Multan
Sutlej
Indus
Kalat
Sukkur
DELHI
Hyderabad
Karachi
ARABIAN SEA
SIKKIM
BHUTAN
R. Brahmaputra
ASSAM
R. Ganges
EAST BENGAL
TRIPURA
DACCA
WEST BENGAL
Sundarbans
Chittagong
BAY OF BENGAL
National Capitals
Towns
International Boundaries
S. Boundary of Kashmir
Land over 200 metres
Miles
0
300
25 N
70 E
20 N
90 E

In the meanwhile, the civil servants had performed a remarkable feat in putting together the apparatus of a modern government. This was in spite of the fact that the number of civil servants who opted to work for the new state was far too small. They worked under great physical handicaps, having often no offices or furniture. But somehow they managed to bring order out of chaos.

Geography and Climate

In its ultimate shape Pakistan had a territory of 365,000 square miles. With its population of 100 million it ranks among the major powers. As the majority of the population are Muslim, Pakistan counts among the leading nations in the world of Islam.

The country consists of two geographically separate parts, West Pakistan and East Pakistan. The capitals of the two wings are almost 1,500 miles apart, and while Dacca can be reached by fast aeroplane from Karachi in three hours, it takes six days by sea to go from Karachi to Chittagong, the seaport on the Bay of Bengal.

West Pakistan borders in the west and north on Iran and Afghanistan and it is thus interested in the affairs of the Middle East; in the south it reaches to the shores of the Arabian sea; and in the east India is its neighbour. East Pakistan (East Bengal) borders in the west, north and north-east on India, in the south-east on Burma and in the south on the Bay of Bengal. It thus looks eastwards and its interests are closely tied to events and developments in West Bengal and elsewhere in South and South-East Asia.

West Pakistan absorbs some 85 per cent of the territory of the whole country, but only 45 per cent of the total population. Some of the country's internal difficulties derive from these disproportions in territory and population; whereas others are due to racial and linguistic differences. The chief language of West Pakistan is Urdu; in East Pakistan Bengali is spoken. English continues to be the medium of communication between officials and intellectuals of the two parts of the country.

The landscape of Pakistan varies from the mountainous regions in the north and north-west to the arid plains of West Pakistan and the alluvial plains of East Bengal. In the west the river system which embraces the Indus, Chenab, Jhelum, Ravi and Sutlej provides the irrigation without which the country would be barren. In the east the Ganges and Brahmaputra and their tributaries form an extensive network of waterways.

The interior of West Pakistan has a continental climate with cold winters and hot summers. Early in the year frost occurs whilst in mid-summer temperatures up to 120°F. are recorded. Some 20 inches of rain are the most that can be expected in the three summer months, not enough to sustain farming without irrigation. East Bengal has a sub-tropical climate with high temperatures and a degree of humidity which can be trying to the indigenous population, let alone to Europeans. During the winter months the rainfall is usually slight and temperatures are tolerable.

The geographical separation, following independence, of the two parts of the country called for two capitals. Karachi, at first the capital of the country, is to be replaced by a new capital which is being built north of

Rawalpindi and which will be called Islamabad. In the interim Rawalpindi serves as the seat of government. In East Pakistan, Dacca will be replaced by Tejgaon, lying four miles outside the present administrative centre.

Early History: Breakdown of Government

The state was unfortunate to lose early its President and founder, Mr. Jinnah; he died, exhausted, a year after setting it up. In the beginning the government was carried on by a Cabinet responsible to a National Parliament and Constituent Assembly which, in addition to members representing the Pakistan constituencies, included also the Muslim members from the former Parliament of India; those who chose to throw in their lot with Pakistan were provided with seats in the new Pakistan Parliament. Unlike India, Pakistan made slow progress in drafting its constitution. It was said that time was deliberately spun out by the representatives from the Indian constituencies, who were in danger of ending their career when the constituent assembly finished its work. The most serious issue of the time was the bid by the orthodox and the mullahs to gain a political privilege guaranteed by the constitution. They agitated for boards to be set up consisting of Muslim divines, and these boards would have had the power to veto any legislation of either the national or provincial legislature if they thought this inconsistent with the principles of Islam.

While these discussions took place, there was a serious deterioration in the standards of government; and corruption became a national scandal. The main cause of the malaise was alleged to be the nature of the political parties. The Muslim League, the militant party which had created Pakistan, began soon to break up, first in East Pakistan and then in the West, and totally failed to produce a vision or a leadership which could hold the state together. It had been obvious from the start that there would be tension between East and West. There was little bond of union except the glaring one of religion. The East, which considered itself more progressive because more practised in parliamentary government, resented the favoured position of the Punjabis in the civil service and armed services. Politics were haunted by the struggle between these two wings of the state, and this further frustrated the making of the constitution.

For these reasons, parliamentary government in Pakistan broke down. It was the first failure of the parliamentary system in the Commonwealth; its crash was therefore regarded as momentous. The country moved towards its crises by stages. There was an interval of high-handed intervention by the Governor-General, Ghulam Mohammed; then a return to the constitution, under which the parties lurched further onwards to discredit; gradually the public came to look to the Governor-General—or President, as he was when Pakistan followed India and became a Republic—as a more reliable repository of power than the Prime Minister, who was a shifting figure at the mercy of Parliament. In October 1958 the President, who at this time was Sikander Mirza, a former diplomat of the old Indian Political Service, declared that Parliament was abolished, and that Pakistan was to be governed by its civil servants, their authority guaranteed by the Army.

The event which precipitated the crisis was a squalid brawl on the floor of the legislature in East Bengal, in which the Deputy Speaker was killed. The party system was discredited. Within a month Mirza was replaced by the Army Commander in Chief, Ayub Khan. Mirza himself was too much tainted with the corruption of the previous regime.

Ayub Khan's Constitution

It quickly became clear that the new system of government, though called a military dictatorship, was different from old-fashioned ones. After the first days the army was kept very much in the background. The Government turned its attention to urgent matters which had been scandalously neglected by its parliamentary predecessor, such as re-housing the refugees who had been left in frightful squalor ever since the foundation of the state, and remedying the economic administration which had produced a foreign exchange crisis. The civil service was purged of those members who had made it corrupt. A modest land reform was carried out, important because of the excessive power of the landed class in North West Pakistan. But after this start, the Government was preoccupied with the problem of the constitution: how this should be reformed so that some form of democracy could be resumed, but without the instability of government which the Westminster type of democracy seemed fatally to engender in Pakistan.

President Ayub Khan appointed a Commission which was instructed to review the constitutional issue by a fixed time. The drafting of the new constitution was the work chiefly of Mr. Manzur Quadir, an able lawyer who had had no part at all in politics until he was invited into the Cabinet by President Ayub. It was published early in 1962. The guiding principle of the constitution was to prevent the continued existence of the political parties which according to the judgment of the regime had been responsible for the squalid life of the past. The constitution therefore prohibited political parties. There would be Legislatures, both at the centre, and for the East and West halves of the state, and they were to be indirectly elected by eighty thousand local councils called Basic Democracies. These local councils had been already brought into existence in the previous year. Candidates were to be chosen on a personal basis, and not as members of a party.

The elections were held in the spring. They went against the Government plan. For, though formally the candidates stood as individuals, and there was no mention of party ties, in fact many stood as the veiled supporters of the parties which had existed before the Presidential coup. The prospect opened up of a struggle between the President and Parliament, the issue being the legitimization of the parties.

In the result, President Ayub did not contest the coming to life of the parties. He abandoned the attempt to organize a parliament without parties. He accepted the fact that wherever there is a parliament, parties are bound to come into existence. He therefore concentrated on patching up parliamentary support in such a way as to guarantee the executive a long term of life, and to remove it from the danger of being made and unmade so frequently, in which he saw the root cause of all the weaknesses of the parliamentary system. In order to obtain influence in Parliament, he applied for membership of one of the two halves into which the old Moslem League had divided.

The leadership of the politicians passed chiefly to Mr. Suhrawardy, a former Prime Minister (and former Prime Minister of Bengal in the last days of the British Raj). His own party, the Awami League, was very small; but he had the best political head in the country, and the course of future events looked like taking the shape of a long political duel between him and President Ayub. Suhrawardy had, however, the handicap of being a Bengali, and the old regionalism of the country was likely to frustrate him. Broadly speaking the aim of the politicians was to sabotage the President, and to compel elections held on the old party basis and with unrestricted franchise. Suhrawardy died in the autumn of 1963.

The Presidential government of Ayub Khan has been notable for efficiency, and for a humanity that is rare in military dictatorships. The Government realized that the threat of repression was enough to enforce its will upon a rather timid opposition: it did not need to employ coercive methods. Freedom of opinion was only half-heartedly controlled. Here and there the Government has been arbitrary. But it has been able to govern with few political prisoners. There has been little interference by the executive with the law courts. Ayub Khan's government has been especially notable for redressing the balance between the West Pakistanis and the Bengalis. The long-standing grievance of the Bengalis, that they paid an undue share of the cost of the state and received far too few of its benefits, has been removed.

Recently the Government has been losing its sureness of touch. It has given the impression that it is no longer in control of its circumstances. And, with this, rumours have begun to circulate of corruption. To check these the Government has taken powers to curb the press.

At the end of 1964 and the New Year of 1965 a Presidential election was held. The opposition parties combined, and chose Miss Jinnah as their candidate. She is the sister of the founder of the State, and she enjoys much of the veneration belonging to him. For a time her candidature seemed to endanger the popularity of Ayub Khan, but in the result he was safely re-elected by nearly two-thirds of the votes. His election, by a procedure which was not seriously branded as unfair, considerably increased his prestige.[1]

Foreign Policy

In foreign relations Pakistan, throughout its life, has been obsessed with the quarrel with India over Kashmir. The details of the dispute are set out elsewhere in this book. It can scarcely be said that Pakistan's concern was unreasonable. The greater part of the Indian Army was massed on its frontier, and leading Indian statesmen, such as Mr. Krishna Menon, did not hesitate to describe Pakistan as 'India's enemy No. 1'; Mr. Krishna Menon continued to say this even when fighting had begun with China on India's northern border. The need to woo the support of great powers against India led Pakistan to throw in its lot with both SEATO and the

[1] For details see page 407.

CENTO alliance (formerly the Baghdad Pact). In the times when public opinion could be expressed in the newspapers, it has been clear however that this policy is not altogether popular and that there is a strong current of opinion in favour of Pakistan going neutralist. Recently, the Pakistan Government has veered towards China in its dispute with India, and has taken the advantage of China's cordiality to get a favourable settlement of the part of its border which used to be undemarcated.

Pakistan has followed this by an exploration of its relations with China over the whole field, and has caused anxiety in India that it may enter into an understanding with Peking which would be directed against India. Presumably this would come about as the result of a favourable attitude by China over Kashmir. Pakistan has also caused anxiety in the United States, and doubts have grown about the permanence of its membership of SEATO and CENTO. In March 1965 President Ayub Khan paid a visit to Peking, where he was treated as an honoured guest. But he followed this by a visit to Russia, which is interested in preserving a framework favourable to India. Evidently the foreign policy of Pakistan is becoming freer, and its Government sees the chances of manoeuvre.

Pakistan has a feather in its cap for its settlement of its quarrels with the tribal peoples of the North-West Frontier. During the British period this region was continually disturbed. The people of the Frontier were not directly administered by the Government. They were continually raiding the administered areas. The first act of Mr. Jinnah was to withdraw the army with which the Government had been accustomed to overawe the tribal people, and to appeal to them on the score of Islam to live at peace with Pakistan. The success of this bold gesture surprised the former British administrators. It was backed up by an economic policy of aid to help the Pathans of the region in developing small industry. Reward for enlightened policy came later when Afghanistan tried to stir up the tribes in an anti-Pakistan movement (see page 472). By and large Afghanistan has had an extremely limited success.

Less satisfactory was Pakistan's record with its minorities. The main trouble was relations with the Hindus. In West Pakistan these fled the country in 1947; but in the East a very large Hindu minority remain, including the middle class who dominated the economic life. It is hard to acquit the Government of deliberate squeezing out of the Hindu inhabitants. There was in any case a popular feeling against them, and it did nothing to discourage this. Tension came to a head in 1950 when there were savage riots in East Pakistan (as there were corresponding riots in West Bengal in India). Opinion throughout Pakistan was bitterly roused, and there was more likelihood of war with India in 1950 than at any other time. The Hindus interpreted the signs of the times, and most of the more prosperous members of the community migrated to India. In 1963 tension again rose, and there were savage riots in East Bengal, which caused equal savagery in Bihar. The disorders rose out of the eviction of Muslims—who according to India had settled unlawfully—from Assam.

Pakistan has pursued a firm policy which may be divided clearly into separate phases. In the first years of independence it placed its trust in membership of the Commonwealth. It was disappointed when the Commonwealth was deaf to its appeal to rectify matters over Kashmir. There followed an attempt to exploit its position as the largest Muslim country in the world, and to align itself with the Muslim states of the Middle East. This move was rebuffed, partly because it was countered by skilful Indian propaganda, chiefly in Cairo. Pakistan, in its search for security against India, then availed itself of the offer by America of alliances with the countries which could give it a foothold on the Asian continent. But it sought to give the alliance an anti-Indian slant, while America tended all along to treat it as directed against Russia. It was fear that America was providing too great an arms supply for India, following on the invasion by China, that led Pakistan to reconsider its loyalties towards America.

Before events took this turn, Ayub Khan had made an attempt to come to terms with India, proposing a joint direction of their armed forces. The offer was made under the shadow of Chinese aggression. It was rebuffed by India.

The Economic Situation

Pakistan, not unlike other countries in South and South-East Asia, is still a predominantly agrarian community, and it is likely to remain so for some time to come. Four out of every five Pakistani live in villages, and three out of four are engaged in farming, forestry and fishing which contribute half the national income. Agriculture supplies the chief subsistence crops: wheat in the west and paddy (rice) in the east of the country. Moreover, some of the principal commercial and export products are of agricultural origin; i.e. jute, cotton, tea, wool and hides. Before the war, East Bengal held the world monopoly in raw jute production. Since the partition of the sub-continent India has developed in West Bengal the cultivation of jute as a raw material basis of her jute mills, whilst East Pakistan has built mills for her raw jute so as to become independent of Indian processing.

The means of exploitation known in the 19th and early 20th centuries held out little hope that Pakistan would lend itself readily to industrial development. The means of transportation and modern machinery developed during the last war and thereafter have eased the problems of development which, however, remain formidable. Pakistan does not appear to be endowed with rich mineral resources, though deposits of coal, iron, manganese, lead, chromite, tungsten, limestone and gypsum have been found. Natural gas has been discovered in large quantities. Some mineral oil is also produced and intensive oil exploration is carried out in various parts of the country.

At present less than half the country's energy requirements and only one per cent of its steel consumption are met from indigenous sources. The use of energy and steel per head of population may be taken as a measure of the distance which Pakistan has to go before she will rank among the industrial countries of the world. In Japan, the only industrialized country in Asia, the supplies of energy and steel per person are approximately twenty and thirty times respectively as large as in Pakistan.

While manpower and manual skills are not lacking, the high rate of illiteracy and the shortage of teachers and skilled technicians of all kinds present serious problems in any programme of development. Only one-quarter of those eligible are enrolled in primary and secondary schools, and only a little over one per cent of the nation's income is spent on education (against six per cent in Japan and in the United States). Only two per cent of all students train in agriculture (against 10 per cent in Taiwan). As almost half the population is under 14 or over 65 years of age (against 35 per cent in Britain) and many women are still in purdah, the active population accounts for one-third only (against over half in the Soviet Union).

In an effort to overcome the inhibitions that stand in the way of progress, a National Planning Board was founded following the declaration of independence. A Six-Year Plan was formulated in 1950. The year 1965 will see the end of the second Five-Year Plan under which a total of Rs. 19,000 million (£1,400 m.) is to be spent at the rate of 3 : 2 in the public and private sectors of the economy: 60 per cent of the expenditure is expected to be mobilized from indigenous sources and the remainder is to come from overseas aid, foreign credits and investors. Foreign assistance has been available multilaterally under the Colombo Plan, by a Western consortium, by the specialised agencies of the United Nations, and bilaterally by the United States (over $700 million), by Britain (nearly £40 million) and, more recently, by the Soviet Union ($45 million) and China ($60 million).

One of the chief objectives of the Plan is to attain self-sufficiency in food grains. Irrigation schemes, flood controls and multi-purpose projects (irrigation and electric power development) are designed to this end; so are plans to reduce the salinity of the soils in West Pakistan and to extend the fishing fleet as well as the marketing and procuring of fish as a major source of animal protein.

The contribution of industry and construction is still less than one-fifth of the national income. Not unnaturally industries based on the traditional indigenous raw materials, such as jute, cotton, sugar and leather are still in the forefront; but cement, paper and chemicals have been added in recent years. Hydro-electric projects and natural gas have provided industry with much needed energy, but the fuel and power economy represents a bottleneck in the process of development.

The replacement of imports by domestically produced goods is a prime target of the Plan: by comparison, any scheme designed to contribute to international or intra-regional divisions of labour ranks low among the priorities of the Plan. The Pakistan Industrial Development Corporation (PIDC) has the task of promoting industries essential for the development of the country. It is supported by an Industrial Finance Corporation (PIFC) as well as an Industrial Credit and Investment Corporation (PICIC).

As a member of the sterling area Pakistan has been able to draw on her sterling accounts accumulated during the last war, but currency reserves have declined greatly and the balance of payments position is tight. Britain is still Pakistan's main export market, but the United States is her main supplier of imports. In 1955 Pakistan devalued her currency and this brought it into line with those members of the sterling area who devalued their currency, together with Britain, in 1949.

BIBLIOGRAPHY

J. Russell Andrus and Azizali F. Mohammed. *The Economy of Pakistan.* (Oxford Univ. Press, London, 1958.)

L. Binder. *Religion and Politics in Pakistan.* (Univ. of California Press, Berkeley and Los Angeles, 1961.)

Keith Callard. *Pakistan: A Political Study.* (George Allen and Unwin, London, 1957.)

Robert D. Campbell. *Pakistan: Emerging Democracy.* (Princeton Univ. Press, Princeton, New Jersey.)

Fazl Al-Rahman. *New Education in the Making in Pakistan.* (Cassell, London, 1953.)

A History of the Freedom Movement, 3 vols. (Pakistan Historical Society, Karachi, 1960).

Sir William Ivor Jennings. *Constitutional Problems of Pakistan.* (Cambridge Univ. Press, 1957.)

Mahbub ul Haq. *The Strategy of Economic Planning.* (Oxford Univ. Press, London, 1963.)

W. N. Peach, M. Uzair and G. W. Rucker. *Basic Data of the Economy of Pakistan.* (Oxford Univ. Press, Karachi, 1959.)

Rahmat Ali. *The Pakistan National Movement and the British Verdict in India.* (Pakistan National Movement, Cambridge, 1946.)

Ian Stephens. *Pakistan.* (Ernest Benn, London, 1963.)

Richard Symonds. *The Making of Pakistan.* (Faber, London, 3rd ed. 1951.)

The Second Five-Year Plan, 1960-65. (Government of Pakistan, Planning Commission, Karachi, 1960.)

Hugh Tinker. *India and Pakistan: A short Political Guide.* (Pall Mall Press, London and Dunmow 1962.)

L. F. Rushbrook-Williams. *The State of Pakistan.* (Faber and Faber, London, 1962).

BIOGRAPHICAL NOTE

Guy Wint. B. London, 1910. Educated at Dulwich College, Oriel College, Oxford, and Berlin University. Member of St. Antony's College, Oxford since 1957. Formerly leader-writer for *The Manchester Guardian:* now writes for *The Observer* on Asian affairs. His publications include *Spotlight on Asia* (Penguin, London, 1955); (with Peter Calvocoressi) *Middle East Crisis* (Penguin, London, 1957); *Common Sense About China* (Gollancz, London, 1960) and *China's Communist Crusade* (Praeger, New York, 1965).

CEYLON

by

B. H. FARMER

CEYLON is a tropical island with a marked individuality and strong internal contrasts. Although its culture embodies many Indian traits, the survival and dominance of Buddhism is alone sufficient to mark it off from the mainland. Internally, the contrast between Wet Zone and Dry Zone has been of great significance throughout history. The Wet Zone of the south-west is liable to rain at all seasons; but the Dry Zone, which covers most of the lowlands in the north and east and extends in modified form into the eastern part of the central highlands, is subject to searing drought during the months from May to September, or longer, and to unreliability of rainfall at other seasons.

THE EARLY HISTORY OF CEYLON

In the closing centuries of the era before Christ the Sinhalese (who seem to have come from north India) established a high level of civilization in the Dry Zone, especially in the north-centre around Anuradhapura, and in the south-east. This was based on the skilful use of irrigation; and its surviving memorials, in the shape not only of irrigation works but of Buddhist shrines, are most impressive.

The Sinhalese Kingdom was often rent by internal dissension and troubled by the threat of the Tamils from south India. The first contacts of these Hindu people with the Sinhalese seem to have been peaceful; but from the second century B.C. onwards there were repeated armed invasions by Tamil rulers. The centre of gravity of Sinhalese settlement moved southward from the Anuradhapura region towards and eventually into the Wet Zone and the hills, whose thick jungles had been avoided in earlier centuries. The Dry Zone declined, its irrigation works fell into disrepair and decay, and (apparently) malaria came in; by the time of European contact in the 15th century it was a region of occasional malaria-ridden villages, except in the Tamil-occupied Jaffna Peninsula and along the east coast.

But Buddhist monks had written down the story of the ancient glories, as they saw them; and what they wrote has had a profound influence on the modern Sinhalese. Ceylon is seen as Sri Lanka, 'holy Ceylon', the Island with a unique role in the preservation of Buddhism; and the Tamils are identified as the enemies of the heroes of old and, even, as the destroyers of the glory of ancient Ceylon.

INDIA

PALK STRAIT

80 E

10 N

National Capital
Towns
International Boundary
Boundary of Lowland
Dry Zone
Land over 300 metres

Miles
0 50

81 E 82

Jaffna Peninsula

Jaffna

Talaimannar

Adam's Bridge

Mannar

GULF OF
MANNAR

Parangi Aru

Malwatu Oya

9 N

9

Trincomalee

Anuradhapura

Kala Oya

Mahaweli Ganga

Pattalam

8 N

C E Y L O N

8

Batticalo

Chilaw

Kurunegala

Matale

Kandy

Gal Oya

Negombo

Badulla

7 N

COLOMBO

Nuwara Eliya

ADAM'S PEAK

7

Ratnapura

Walawe Ganga

INDIAN OCEAN

Gin Ganga

6 N

Galle

Hambantota

6 N

80 E 81 E 82

© ANTHONY BLOND LT

The Portuguese Period

Ceylon has fallen during the last 450 years successively under Portuguese, Dutch and British rule. During the earlier part of their period from 1505 to 1597 the Portuguese maintained the fiction that the Sinhalese king was the sovereign, though increasingly he was their puppet. From 1597 until 1658, the King of Portugal claimed the sovereignty, though he never exercised it in the Up-country kingdom of Kandy. The Portuguese had a lasting effect on the maritime regions, beginning that process of differentiation which still sets the 'Low Country' Sinhalese apart from the 'Kandyans'. The Roman Catholicism which they implanted is still dominant in some coastal areas, especially among the Karava, the fisher caste. These and other formerly lowly castes owe to the Portuguese the beginning of their rise in status. The commercial influence of Portugal was less lasting.

The Dutch Period

The Dutch East India Company had for some time been the ally of the Kandyan king before they finally ousted the Portuguese in 1658. From then till 1795 they held undisputed sway in the Low Country and in Jaffna, and in 1766 extracted from the Kandyan king (with whom they had been in conflict) the cession of the entire seaboard. The Dutch continued the concentration on the lowlands of the Wet Zone that had been a feature of Portuguese rule, though they were also interested in Jaffna; in their time, however, seekers after cinnamon penetrated into the Kandyan kingdom. The cinnamon trade was to the Dutch 'the great industry', and plantations were established. Castes such as the Karava (already mentioned) and the Salagama (cinnamon peelers) benefited greatly from this interest of the Dutch. The Dutch Company further encouraged the settlement of persons in its service, and there remains to this day a sizeable community of 'Burghers'. Roman-Dutch law is an important element in the legal system of Ceylon.

The British Period

The British, after one or two preliminary skirmishes, moved into Ceylon in 1795-96, mainly in order to deny Trincomalee and other bases to the French during the Napoleonic Wars. After a period of uncertainty, Ceylon became a Crown Colony in 1802. The British soon succeeded where their predecessors had failed; for, in 1815, the Kandyan Kingdom finally became British territory, a treaty being signed which guaranteed the integrity, laws and religion of the Kingdom and which further differentiated the Kandyan from the Low-country Sinhalese.

The British period was one of revolutionary change, much of it centring on the introduction of plantation, first of coffee Up-country, then of tea when coffee was stricken by disease, and later of coconut and rubber on rather lower ground (though still almost entirely in the Wet Zone, for climatic reasons). European plantations and enterprise were rapidly imitated by Ceylonese land-owners and small-holders who planted nearly all of Ceylon's million acres of coconuts. Great social changes were set in train and the economy of the country was transformed, so that it came to import much of its food and almost all of its manufactures in exchange for exports of plantation products.

With the development of plantations came the immigration of Indian Tamil labour, the construction of roads and railways, the improvement of the port of Colombo, the growth of towns, the spread of Ceylon Tamils from Jaffna into southern Ceylon, and apparently a rise in average living standards until the 1930s. But little of all this (apart from the construction of a road network) affected the Dry Zone. Something was done from 1870 on to restore irrigation works, but only locally did this have much effect on settlement until, after 1932, serious efforts were made to encourage colonization. But much of the effort here was made under the influence of Ceylonese Ministers, notably D. S. Senanayake, and success depended on malaria control with DDT.

The British period also saw the establishment of an educational system which was particularly potent in its effect on those who became the English-educated upper middle class, and the development of a modern administration and judiciary.

Ceylon is of course the classic case of a colony which slid gently and with very little disturbance through a sequence of constitutional changes to independence. It had by 1923 a Legislative Council in which unofficial members were in the majority. In 1931 under the so-called 'Donoughmore Constitution', universal adult franchise was introduced and Ceylonese Ministers were for the first time placed in charge of departments of government. There were further constitutional changes in May, 1947, most of whose Westminster-style provisions have survived into the era of independence.

Ceylon Since Independence

During the first eight years of independence the United National Party (U.N.P.) dominated the scene. The Party had been founded by D. S. Senanayake in 1945-46, and had won the elections under the Soulbury Constitution (1947) which provided the first Parliament of independent Ceylon. The U.N.P. brought together Sinhalese who had been associated with Senanayake in the Ceylon National Congress, a number of Ceylon Tamils, the Ceylon Muslim League, and, until 1951, S.W.R.D. Bandaranaike's Sinhala Maha Sabha (Bandaranaike crossed the floor in that year), while in 1948 even G. G. Ponnambalam, leader of the Tamil Congress, joined Senanayake's Cabinet.

D. S. Senanayake died in March 1952 and the Governor-General called on his son, Dudley, who had been Minister of Agriculture and Lands, to form a Government. The U.N.P. easily won the elections of May, 1952. Dudley Senanayake resigned in October, 1953, and was succeeded by his uncle, Sir John Kotelawala.

Under U.N.P. rule, in spite of strikes and other troubles, Ceylon seemed to many western observers to have discovered not only how to maintain law and order and to work a Westminster-style constitution but also how to contain communal disharmonies. They expected U.N.P. rule to continue after the elections of April, 1956, but in the event that party limped home with eight seats only, decisively defeated by Bandaranaike's coalition, the Mahajana Eksath Peramuna (M.E.P.). There followed a period of instability which cannot unfortunately be said to have passed. Much labour unrest; severe communal disturbances in 1956 and 1958 (following Government moves to implement the declared policy of establishing Sinhalese as the sole 'national language'); a number of periods of rule under a state of emergency; unprecedented Cabinet dissension which broke up the M.E.P. coalition in 1959; the assassination of Bandaranaike on 25th September of the same year; a period of indecisive rule by a Cabinet rent by quarrels under his successor, W. Dahanayake; an election in April, 1960, which very briefly returned Dudley Senanayake and the U.N.P. to power; a further election in July, 1960, which brought back the Sri Lanka Freedom Party (S.L.F.P.), Bandaranaike's own party and the main constituent of the former M.E.P., his widow being called upon to form the Government; an attempted coup by police and military early in 1962; the defeat of Mrs. Bandaranaike's government in December, 1964 (mainly because of the defection of some of her erstwhile supporters); the three months of uncertainty, realignment and increasing bitterness preceding the ensuing elections: such is the catalogue of main events, and it does not need much imagination to sense the political instability and the inevitable shelving of major economic issues which lie behind it.

What had happened to the power and apparent stability of the U.N.P.? What new forces were at work? The initial defeat of the U.N.P. in 1956 owed something, of course, to the untimely loss of D. S. Senanayake, to the personal unpopularity of Kotelawala (who was very insensitive to public opinion) and to the passing of the wave of sympathy that had helped to return Dudley Senanayake to power on the death of his father. It owed something to the feeling that the U.N.P. had been in office long enough and had grown indolent if not corrupt; and to the skill with which Bandaranaike brought into his M.E.P. coalition not only his own S.L.F.P. but the Viplavakari Lanka Sama Samaja Party (V.S.L.S.P.), the more extreme of Ceylon's two Trotskyite parties, with other smaller groups and with which he engineered a 'no contest pact' with other anti-U.N.P. groups, notably the Nava Lanka Sama Samaja Party (N.L.S.S.P., the other Trotskyite party), and the Communists.

But there was more to it than personalities, or the swing of the pendulum, or Bandaranaike's tactical skill. The U.N.P., unlike the Indian Congress Party, was essentially narrowly-based, for all D. S. Senanayake's genuine desire to create a united nation and for all his efforts to weld other groups to his own. It was essentially the party of the English-educated affluent middle class families who had formed the spearhead of the nationalist movement in the 1920s, 1930s and 1940s. Many members of this group had by 1956 lost whatever touch they had ever had with the growing urban working-class, with the small but articulate intelligentsia, and with the social movement that was developing in the villages. This movement was, in fact, a complex social revolution compounded of a Buddhist revival and an associated resurgence of Sinhalese language and culture, largely in reaction against the West but stimulated also by *Buddha Jayanti* (the 2,500th anniversary of the Buddha's attainment of *nirvana*) and sustained by that sense of historic destiny to which reference has already been made; and compounded also of the frustration of vernacular-educated Sinhalese (especially Buddhist priests, school-masters, ayurvedic physicians and the like) who found that jobs went to the English-educated, and who felt hostile not only to the English-educated and to the U.N.P. but also to the Tamils, who were alleged to have more than their share of Government jobs and who anyway were seen as the historic enemy. Bandaranaike, sensing what was abroad in the villages, was able to canalize these and other complex grievances and in doing so to amplify them. The U.N.P. on the other hand adopted its Sinhalese-only policy too late.

Not surprisingly, the reaction of a large proportion of the Ceylon Tamils to this new Sinhalese nationalism has been to unite, behind the most extreme of the Tamil parties, the Federal Party, which as its name implies wishes a federal solution to the problems of the Tamil-populated northern and eastern provinces. The Indian Tamils are mostly disenfranchized by Ceylon's citizenship legislation; there have, however, been moments of acute tension when it seemed that the Indian and Ceylon Tamils were about to make common cause. And the Sinhalese are aware, of course, that, although a majority in their own island, they face the Dravidian mass of south India across Palk Strait. Not surprisingly, then, but most unfortunately, no politician in Ceylon today can afford to neglect communal feeling. The poor showing of the N.L.S.S.P. and the Communists in the 1960 elections, widely interpreted in the West as a defeat for the left, was in the main due to their support for parity in the language issue. But the left, as the West knows it, may gain in future in urban electorates, or more widely if economic conditions deteriorate further; while the coalition between the S.L.F.P. and the N.L.S.S.P. effected in June, 1964 certainly increased the influence of the left until the fall of the Government (mentioned above) for reasons that included suspicion by some S.L.F.P. members of their leftish allies.

The position of the press in Ceylon should perhaps be mentioned here. The Ceylon press has sometimes been irresponsible and considerable sections of it were, at the time of Mr. Bandaranaike's struggle for power in 1956, in the hands of interests generally favourable to the U.N.P. The S.L.F.P. Government returned to power in July 1960 announced its intention of taking over the two principal companies concerned. But it has proved difficult to draft legislation which would satisfy on the one hand members of the Government Parliamentary Party, thirsting for control, and, on the other, critical opinion at home and abroad, anxious for the freedom of the press. Just before the Coalition Government fell in December, 1964 two Bills which seemed inconsistent with the freedom of the press as understood in the West were suffering a stormy passage.

Economic Situation

But what, meanwhile, has happened to the economy of the Island? Ceylon became independent with an economy which, while narrow-based and hence very liable to booms and slumps, made possible an average standard of living higher than that of most Asian countries; and a start had been made with the agricultural colonization of the Dry Zone and with industrialization. In the years since independence booms and slumps have continued: in 1951, for example, came the post-Korean boom, while since 1961, Ceylon has suffered severely from low commodity prices and foreign-exchange problems.

The possibility of the nationalization of foreign-owned enterprises in Ceylon, and, in particular, of tea estates, is an aspect of Ceylon politics that has attracted attention and created nervousness in some quarters. Nationalization of this sort has always formed part of the programme of the various left-wing parties in Ceylon, and Mr. Bandaranaike, in engineering the coalition and the 'no contest pact' that brought him victory in 1956, followed suit, no doubt largely in order to win left support. He did, in fact, nationalize public road passenger transport, which had aroused a great deal of public dissatisfaction and whose magnates were supposed for the most part to be U.N.P. supporters. He also nationalized the port of Colombo. But he made it reasonably but not perhaps unambiguously clear that he intended to leave foreign estates well alone; and the same line has been pursued by his successors in office. Foreign enterprises have not escaped entirely however, for in May 1961 a State Oil Corporation was formed and took over compulsorily certain installations previously owned by foreign oil firms. It is always possible, of course, that a shift of policy, or a victory of the left, or a coalition such as that formed in June, 1964 could once more bring the nationalization of estates into view.

And ever more insistent looms the shadow of a runaway increase in population: there were 5.3 million people in Ceylon in 1921, there were about 11 million in 1962, there may well be 21 million by 1981. A considerable amount of thought has been given to the consequent economic problems: the Planning Secretariat put out a Six-Year Programme of Investment in 1955 (though this was not much more than a collection of departmental estimates); a World Bank Mission reported in 1953; and the present Government is committed to the Ten-Year Plan, 1959-68 and to subsequent short-term implementation proposals. The cornerstone of the Plan is progressive industrialization, leaning heavily on the development of agriculture both for home production and for export. The general strategy seems sound, though some of the targets are optimistic, especially in view of the political situation. But it is worth recording that agricultural yields seem to be rising and a cash economy spreading.

BIBLIOGRAPHY

Sydney D. Bailey. *Ceylon.* (Hutchinson, London, 1952.)

H. W. Codrington. *A Short History of Ceylon.* (Macmillan, London, revised ed., 1939.)

The Economic Development of Ceylon. World Bank mission report. (Cumberlege, London, 1953.)

B. H. Farmer. 'Ceylon'. (In O.H.K. Spate, *India and Pakistan*, Methuen, London, 2nd ed., 1957.) *Ceylon: A Divided Nation.* (Oxford University Press for Institute of Race Relations, London, 1963.), *Pioneer Peasant Colonization in Ceylon.* (Oxford University Press for Royal Institute of International Affairs, London, 1957.)

Sir Ivor Jennings. *The Economy of Ceylon.* (Oxford University Press, Madras, 2nd ed., 1951.)

E. F. C. Ludowyk. *The Story of Ceylon.* (Faber and Faber, London, 1962.)

L. H. Horace Perera. *Additional Chapters to H. W. Codrington's 'A Short History of Ceylon'.* (Macmillan, London, 1952.)

The Ten-Year Plan. (Planning Secretariat, Colombo, 1959.)

W. Howard Wriggins. *Ceylon, Dilemmas of a New Nation.* (Princeton Univ. Press, Princeton, N.J., 1960.)

BIOGRAPHICAL NOTE

Bertram H. Farmer. B. 1916. Fellow of St. John's College, Cambridge and University Lecturer in Geography, University of Cambridge. Honorary Editor, Institute of British Geographers. Publications include: 'Ceylon' in O.H.K. Spate, *India and Pakistan* (Methuen, London, 2nd ed., 1957); 'Rainfall and Water Supply in the Dry Zone of Ceylon' in R. W. Steel and C. A. Fisher (eds.) *Geographical Essays on British Tropical Lands* (George Phillip, London, 1956); *Pioneer Peasant Colonization in Ceylon* (Oxford Univ. Press for Royal Institute of International Affairs, London, 1957); *Ceylon: a Divided Nation* (Oxford Univ. Press for Institute of Race Relations, London, 1963).

CENTRAL ASIA

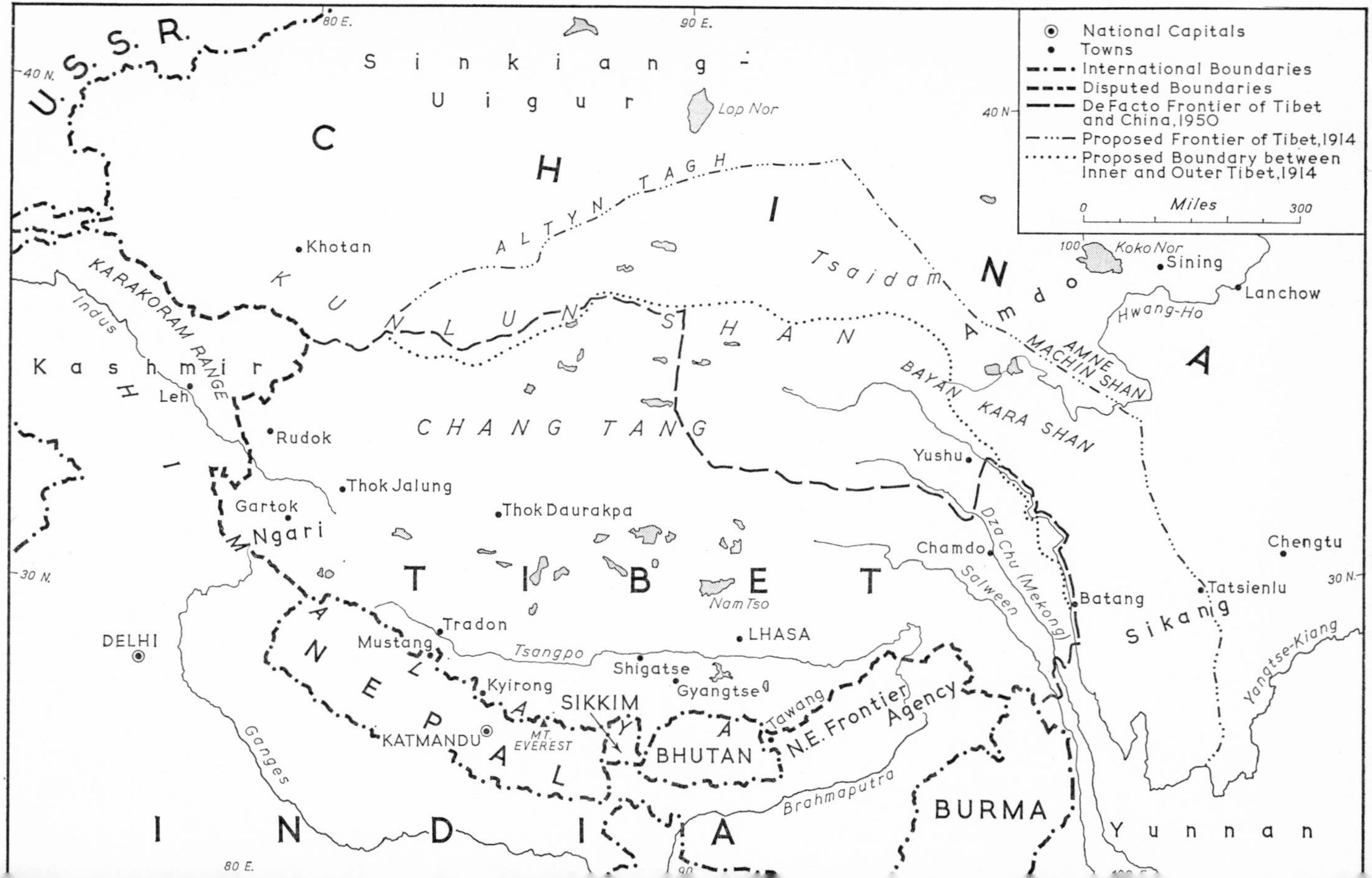
National Capitals
Towns
International Boundaries
Disputed Boundaries
De Facto Frontier of Tibet and China, 1950
Proposed Frontier of Tibet, 1914
Proposed Boundary between Inner and Outer Tibet, 1914
Miles
0
300
U.S.S.R.
Sinkiang-Uigur
CHINA
Amdo
Lop Nor
Koko Nor
Sining
Lanchow
Hwang-Ho
ALTYN TAGH
KUNLUN SHAN
Tsaidam
AMNE MACHIN SHAN
BAYAN KARA SHAN
CHANG TANG
Khotan
Rudok
Thok Jalung
Thok Daurakpa
Gartok
Ngari
Kashmir
KARAKORAM RANGE
Indus
Leh
HIMALAYA
TIBET
Nam Tso
LHASA
Yushu
Chamdo
Dza Chu (Mekong)
Salween
Batang
Sikang
Tatsienlu
Chengtu
Yangtse-Kiang
Yunnan
Tradon
Mustang
Tsangpo
Shigatse
Gyangtse
Kyirong
SIKKIM
MT. EVEREST
KATMANDU
NEPAL
BHUTAN
Tawang
N.E. Frontier Agency
Brahmaputra
BURMA
DELHI
Ganges
INDIA
40 N.
30 N.
80 E.
90 E.
100

TIBET

by

GEORGE N. PATTERSON

Tibet a Powerful Nation

It was in the 7th century that Tibet as a nation, and a powerful one at that, emerged from the realm of legend and entered history. A Tibetan king, Srong-tsen Gampo, conquered regions in north Burma and western China and exacted tribute from the Emperor of China, including the marriage of the Emperor's daughter. The same king was equally successful in his attacks on the Indian border, subjugating large parts of Nepal and taking a princess from that country also as tribute. These two queens were Buddhists and converted the King to their faith, and in the years that followed he extended the Buddhist religion throughout the whole of Tibet. Until this time Tibet had only had an oral language, derived from the same linguistic family as the Burmese; but Buddhist scriptures were now brought from India and a written character adapted from the Sanskrit to fit the Tibetan language.

Peace Treaty with China

In the 8th century Tibet became a great military power in Asia, reaching from the Chinese capital of Changan, which its armies had captured, to near the River Ganges in India, and from Turkestan to Burma. In the 9th century, after over 100 missions had passed between the two countries, a peace treaty was signed on the basis of equality.

In the 13th century Tibet became a vassal state of the Mongols under Genghis Khan, but later Kublai Khan appointed a favourite Tibetan priest as Priest-King of Tibet and constituted ruler of (1) Tibet Proper, comprising the 13 states of U-Tsang Province; (2) Kham, and (3) Amdo. In the 17th century when the Great Fifth Dalai Lama visited Peking Tibetan records claim that he was received as an independent sovereign.

China's Claim to Suzerainty

After the death of the Sixth Dalai Lama there was a period of considerable intrigue. At one point the Chinese Emperor sent three armies into Tibet which were eventually successful in defeating the Mongols who were then in possession, and he installed a Seventh Dalai Lama of his own choice. China's claim to suzerainty over Tibet appears to date from this invasion. Following it, a Manchu resident and a garrison force of 3,000 Chinese troops were left behind and communication with China was kept open by stationing small detachments of troops along the Lhasa-Chamdo-Batang-Tachienlu 'road'. The new boundary between China and Tibet was demarcated by a pillar, erected in 1727 on the Bum-La south-west of Batang. (See map).

Tibet recovers 'Greater Tibet'

The absolute rule claimed by the Chinese residents in Lhasa was not maintained. When inter-tribal war broke out in Kham Province in 1860, rapidly involving the whole of East Tibet, the inhabitants appealed to both the Chinese and Tibetan Governments for help. The former were in no position to help because of their involvement with foreign powers, but the Dalai Lama responded by sending a Tibetan Army which suppressed the fighting in 1863. The Tibetan claim to the reconquered territory dates from this time, when the Chinese Imperial Court confirmed the claim. When the Younghusband expedition marched on Lhasa in 1904 the Chinese reacted to this threat to their interests in Tibet by appointing an 'Imperial Resident' in East Tibet. The Khambas revolted, the Chinese sent in an army under General 'Butcher' Chao Erh-feng, and he ruthlessly brought the whole country under the direct control of the Chinese Government. Chao was killed in 1911, but his assistant proposed that East Tibet should be converted into a new Chinese province to be called '(H)Si-kang', or 'Western Kham'. Following the revolution in China the Kham Tibetans again revolted, defeated the Chinese, but agreed under pressure from Britain not to invade west China.

The Simla Convention

In 1913 a Conference was held in Simla between China, Tibet and India, from which emerged an agreement to divide Tibet into two zones, 'Outer Tibet', nearer India, including Lhasa, Shigatse and Chamdo; and 'Inner Tibet', nearer China, including Batang, Litang, Tatsienlu and a large part of East Tibet. Chinese suzerainty over the whole of Tibet was recognized, but China agreed not to convert Tibet into a Chinese province. Two days after China had initialled the draft, she repudiated it, objecting to the boundary between 'Inner' and 'Outer' Tibet, but Tibet and Britain recognized it as binding upon themselves, with China, having repudiated the Conference, entitled to none of the advantages which the Convention would have conferred upon her. The agreement included the fixing of the boundary between Tibet and India, known as the 'MacMahon Line'.

Little of major historical importance occurred in Sino-Tibetan relations between the Simla Convention and the Chinese Communist invasion in 1950. In the war between China and Japan Tibet maintained a neutral position. Following the end of World War II and the deteriorating political situation in China, arms and ammunition on a large scale became available to the East Tibetan leaders and brought the possibility of a successful revolt against the central Lhasa Government—a long-cherished ambition of the East Tibetans, or Khambas, as they are known—within reach.

Chinese Communist 'Liberation' of Tibet

On October 25th, 1950, Peking radio broadcast that the process of 'liberating' Tibet had begun. However, it was still not publicly admitted to be a military action. At this time the Chinese were almost certainly sincere in their desire for a 'peaceful liberation'. As the historical record indicates, while there was some ground for Chinese claims to Tibet based on their conquests of the country at various times, there was an equally sound basis for Tibet's claim to independence through having ultimately expelled the Chinese from the country. It was this uncertainty as to Tibet's actual historical status which accounted for the early hesitation of the Chinese in their 'liberation' action, while at the same time loudly insisting on their 'right' to liberate. But when the Dalai Lama's brother dramatically escaped to the United States, and a copy of a top-secret American military briefing booklet was discovered to be circulating on the border disclosing alarming plans, the Chinese must have decided that 'peaceful measures' were no longer practicable.

On receiving the report that Chinese troops were entering Tibet the Tibetan Government approached the Government of India to raise the matter of China's aggression on Tibet's behalf in the United Nations, but the Indian Government advised the Tibetan Government to approach the United Nations directly. This they did on November 11th, 1950, and an 'unofficial note' was circulated to members of the Security Council. On November 17th the El Salvador delegate formally raised the complaint against China in a letter to the Secretary-General. But both the Governments of the United Kingdom and India opposed the Tibetan appeal.

China Ignores 17-point Agreement

The Tibetan Government appealed to the U.N. and prepared four delegations to proceed to Britain, the U.S., India and Nepal, to seek support. The appeal to the U.N. was shelved and the delegation discouraged from proceeding by the countries concerned. The Tibetan Government were forced by this isolation into submitting to the Chinese take-over of Tibet. The Chinese Government proposed that a Tibetan delegation be sent to Peking, and on arrival this delegation, according to their report and the Dalai Lama's later statement, were forced to sign a 17-Point Agreement, in May, 1951. Armed with this 'Agreement' the Chinese authorities and occupation army proceeded to take over the whole of Tibet. However, they met considerable resistance from the Tibetan people at all levels and were forced into ruthless methods of coercion; this in turn caused sporadic outbreaks of protest and even armed revolt. A Report on Tibet published by the International Commission of Jurists in 1961 established that from 1950 to 1959 there were over 90,000 deaths in Tibet. Most were killed in the savage fighting, but some were killed after trials which were conducted in public for their opposition to Chinese measures. According to the Dalai Lama many were beaten to death, crucified, burnt alive, drowned, starved, strangled, hanged, buried alive, disembowelled, beheaded. Thousands were rounded up, imprisoned, taken to labour camps, or forcibly expatriated to China. To cope with the growing revolt the Chinese were forced to put more troops into Tibet until there were a reputed 250,000 in various parts of the country. In addition hundreds of thousands of Chinese 'settlers' were also sent to Tibet in a programme of enforced colonization.

Such a large and unexpected influx of people in the precariously balanced food situation which obtained in Tibet forced the Chinese to make drastic 'reforms' of Tibet's archaic methods of food storage, supply and distribution.

As these methods were intimately connected with the rights of monasteries as granaries, landowners and tax levies this inevitably resulted in protests and scattered riots. The policy of land reform was at first restricted to east Tibet. But while the remote character of this territory may have lent itself to facilitating an unwitnessed and rigorous enforcement of land reforms, the policy itself, in an area that was notoriously hostile to the Chinese, was bound to be an explosive issue. In 1952-53 widespread fighting of a sporadic character broke out in Kham and Amdo.

Reforms and Demonstrations

In Lhasa itself the Chinese proceeded much more cautiously, but even in the capital there were anti-Chinese demonstrations from as early as 1952. Many of the issues raised by the anti-Chinese groups were apparently inspired by feudal officials who wanted little or no change at all and were only using popular sentiment to oppose reforms of any kind. This feeling, to a great extent, was due to the irritating presence of tens of thousands—some reports put the figure at about 250,000—of Chinese troops in Tibet which, with the famine due to floods and other causes, roused resentment. Finally, the Chinese policy of imposing the Chinese language, dress and customs in the schools, and the enforced expansion of Communist Party cadres, sparked the Tibetans into revolt. The revolt began in Kham, in East Tibet, in 1956, but by mid-1958 20,000 Khambas, short of food and ammunition, had fallen back on central Tibet. Here Lhasa Government sympathizers had access to secret stocks of arms, ammunition and food never declared to the Chinese, and the fighting spread rapidly to south and south-west Tibet and the local revolts had become a national uprising. On March 17th, 1959, fighting broke out in Lhasa, and the Dalai Lama and members of his Government left the capital secretly and fled to India. A few months later the Tibetan rebels ran out of ammunition and the revolt ended.

On his arrival in India the Dalai Lama repudiated the 17-point Agreement of 1951 as being signed under duress. He was given asylum in India, but was not permitted to set up a government in exile. However, a third attempt to raise the matter of Chinese aggression in the United Nations was successful, when Ireland and Malaya acted as sponsors, in 1959, and a mildly worded resolution was passed.

Institutional Integration with China

Following on the ruthless suppression of the revolt in the accessible areas of Tibet—even by Chinese figures at least 20,000 rebels were still free in the inaccessible mountains—the Chinese authorities took over complete control. Hitherto, they had sought to retain a façade of control through the Dalai Lama, Tibetan institutions and officials; but now Chinese personnel were appointed over Chinese institutions reorganized on a Chinese pattern through Chinese heads of departments and Chinese cadres, as in China itself. Towards the end of 1960 the Panchen Lama was so little in evidence at the many Chinese-organized public demonstrations that it was widely rumoured both inside and outside Tibet that he was either under strict house arrest or dead. For ten months he was kept in Peking before being permitted to return to Lhasa. In December 1964 the Dalai Lama was formally dismissed from his official positions in Tibet under the Chinese regime and in January 1965 the Panchen Lama was also so dismissed.

In the meantime, the primary target of the Chinese was the monasteries and the complete destruction of all that pertained to the priestly feudal system. Tens of thousands of lamas were sent into forced labour. The monasteries were first of all denuded of their treasures, then used as centres of indoctrination. The monastic system which had dominated Tibet for centuries was broken up, and even in the event of the Dalai Lama and his Government returning to Tibet it is now unlikely that the priests will ever return to their former influence.

Shortage of Food

After the revolt, all Tibetans, both priest and lay, were given just adequate supplies of food if they completed their labour quotas, but after a few months even this was cut down and ration cards were issued. There seems no doubt that the initial starving was a punitive measure. But the growing food crisis in China, together with the new tactics of the Tibetan guerillas, who destroyed all crops within reach of the Chinese and blew up lines of supply, created a situation in which the Chinese troops might have mutinied. The Chinese retaliated by depriving the Tibetans of food in towns and villages under their control. This, in turn, drove these Tibetans to join the guerillas in their inaccessible mountain hide-outs with more attacks and local uprisings.

Economic Situation

In a desperate attempt to suppress another revolt the Chinese have ruthlessly re-organized the economy of the whole country. The 'Eight-Point Charter' for agricultural production used in China has been imposed in Tibet, but while this may look impressive on paper, in Tibet it has not solved any problems. Since 1959 Tibet has had good harvests, it is true, but this cannot be directly attributed to the 'Charter' since this was only introduced post-1959—and, in any case, the food has been requisitioned under duress and sent to China. Confiscated estates have been taken from monasteries and landowners under a 'redemption policy' but promissory notes have not been honoured.

Every town and village in the country has been divided into four zones and each zone is supervised by a branch committee of the municipality organization of the Chinese Communist Party. Supply and market co-operatives were introduced into every district under Chinese jurisdiction and under the guidance of the state trading companies set up in urban centres.

Schools had already been introduced before the revolt, but after the revolt they were introduced on a large scale. In the three years since March, 1959 Peking reported that 1,941 schools of all kinds had been set up, with an enrolment of 59,877. Peking did not mention, of course, the many thousands of Tibetan children who had been taken forcibly to China for 'education'.

Chinese reports also claim 157 medical institutions, with a hospital to every special administrative region. These have a reported staff of 560 professional medical workers and 643 spare-time health workers.

Surface mines are being opened in and around Lhasa, and small factories for tanning are springing up around large towns. Along the main China-Tibet highway the heavy military traffic has created the demand for garages and repair shops. In addition, small factories for farm implements and small tools are being encouraged and subsidized.

The Future

At one time it looked as if Tibet would have no future, but recently, with the widening breach between India and China, Tibetans have been hopeful that this will mean a relenting of India's previous policy of non-commitment. They see this in terms of supplies of arms, officially or otherwise, for the guerillas, and in this event they are optimistic that what they almost succeeded in doing in 1959 with a minimum of arms they will successfully accomplish next time. Certainly, any influx of arms to the guerillas will mean a long and costly engagement for the Chinese, with all the disadvantages on their side—plus the possibility of the revolt spreading into west China.

BIBLIOGRAPHY

Sir Charles Bell. *Tibet Past and Present.* (Oxford Univ. Press, London, 1924.)

Concerning the Question of Tibet. (Foreign Languages Press, Peking, 1959.)

David Howarth (ed.). *My Land and My People. The Autobiography of His Holiness the Dalai Lama* (XIV). (Weidenfeld and Nicolson, London, 1962.)

A Lamb. 'Tibet in Anglo-Chinese Relations'. (Royal Central Asian Journal, London, 1957-58.)

Thubten Norbu. *Tibet Is My Country.* (Rupert Hart-Davis, London, 1960.)

George N. Patterson. *Tibet in Revolt.* (Faber and Faber, London, 1960.)

H. E. Richardson. *Tibet and its History.* (Oxford Univ. Press, London, 1962.)

The Question of Tibet and the Rule of Law. (International Commission of Jurists, Geneva, 1959.)

Chanakya Sen. *Tibet Disappears.* (Asia Publishing House, London, 1960.)

Sir Eric Teichman. *Travels of a Consulate Officer in Eastern Tibet.* (University Press, Cambridge, 1922.)

Tsung-lien Shen and Sheng-ch'i Liu. *Tibet and the Tibetans.* (Stanford Univ. Press, Stanford, 1953.)

L. A. Waddell. *The Buddhism of Tibet.* (W. Heffer, Cambridge, 2nd ed., 1934.)

BIOGRAPHICAL NOTE

George Patterson went to China as a missionary in 1946 and from 1947 to 1950 worked among the Khambas of East Tibet. When China invaded Tibet he remained on the Indo-Tibetan border studying and writing on the political affairs of the Himalayan countries and tribes. He has been a free-lance journalist, correspondent for *The Daily Telegraph* and *The Observer* and contributor to leading international journals. He has also lectured and broadcast on Asian affairs. His publications (all by Faber and Faber, London) include: *Tibetan Journey* (1954), *God's Fool* (1956), *Up and Down Asia* (1958), *Tragic Destiny* (1959), *Tibet in Revolt* (1960) and *Peking versus Delhi* (1963).

MONGOLIA

by

OWEN LATTIMORE

Geography and History

Mongolia—the Mongolian People's Republic—is a little over 600,000 square miles in area; roughly the combined area of France, Germany, Italy, and Great Britain. It has a population slightly over one million, or double the number of half a century ago. In 1960 the death rate was 10·5, birth rate 43·2 per thousand. Its northernmost point—52° 15′ N.—is not quite as far north as Moscow, or Edmonton, Alberta; its southernmost point —41° 32′ N.—not quite as far south as New York city. An average elevation of 4,800 feet adds to the severe continentality of the climate. The highest mountain peak is over 15,000 feet. The average all-year-round temperature at Ulan Bator, the capital (population 160,000) is a little below freezing, with extremes of over 90°F. in summer and below 50° below zero in winter. The 'gobi' or desert regions in the south represent the zone of maximum aridity, not reached by precipitation from Siberia in the north or China in the south. In the north there is a considerable river system—Selenge, Orkhon, Tola (Tuul) and Kerulen—and here, with a rainfall approaching 20 inches per annum, wheat growing is possible and is being rapidly expanded.

The Mongolian People's Republic is considerably smaller than historical Mongolia. In the late 16th and early 17th century the Manchus conquered the eastern and southern fringes of Mongolia and used its tribal levies in the conquest of China (1644). This is the origin of 'Inner' Mongolia (meaning Mongolia nearer to the Great Wall of China), which today under the Communist government of the Chinese People's Republic survives in part as an Inner Mongolian Autonomous Area, but has partly been absorbed into several Chinese provinces. The Mongolian People's Republic is the historical 'Outer' ('more distant') Mongolia, finally conquered by the Manchus only in the 18th century. West of Inner and Outer Mongolia, also under Manchu rule, were Mongol tribal groups in Sinkiang province and in Tibet. The Kalmuk Mongols of the lower Volga, near Stalingrad (now Volgograd) were migrants from Sinkiang. Finally there are the Buryats, or Buryat-Mongols, of Siberia, mostly east of Lake Baikal, who were never conquered by the Manchus and were not fully integrated among the Mongol people even in the time of Chingis (Genghis) Khan.

Religion

In the period of the Mongol Empire over China and most of Central Asia, Mongolia was only lightly touched by Buddhism. 'Lama' Buddhism, a

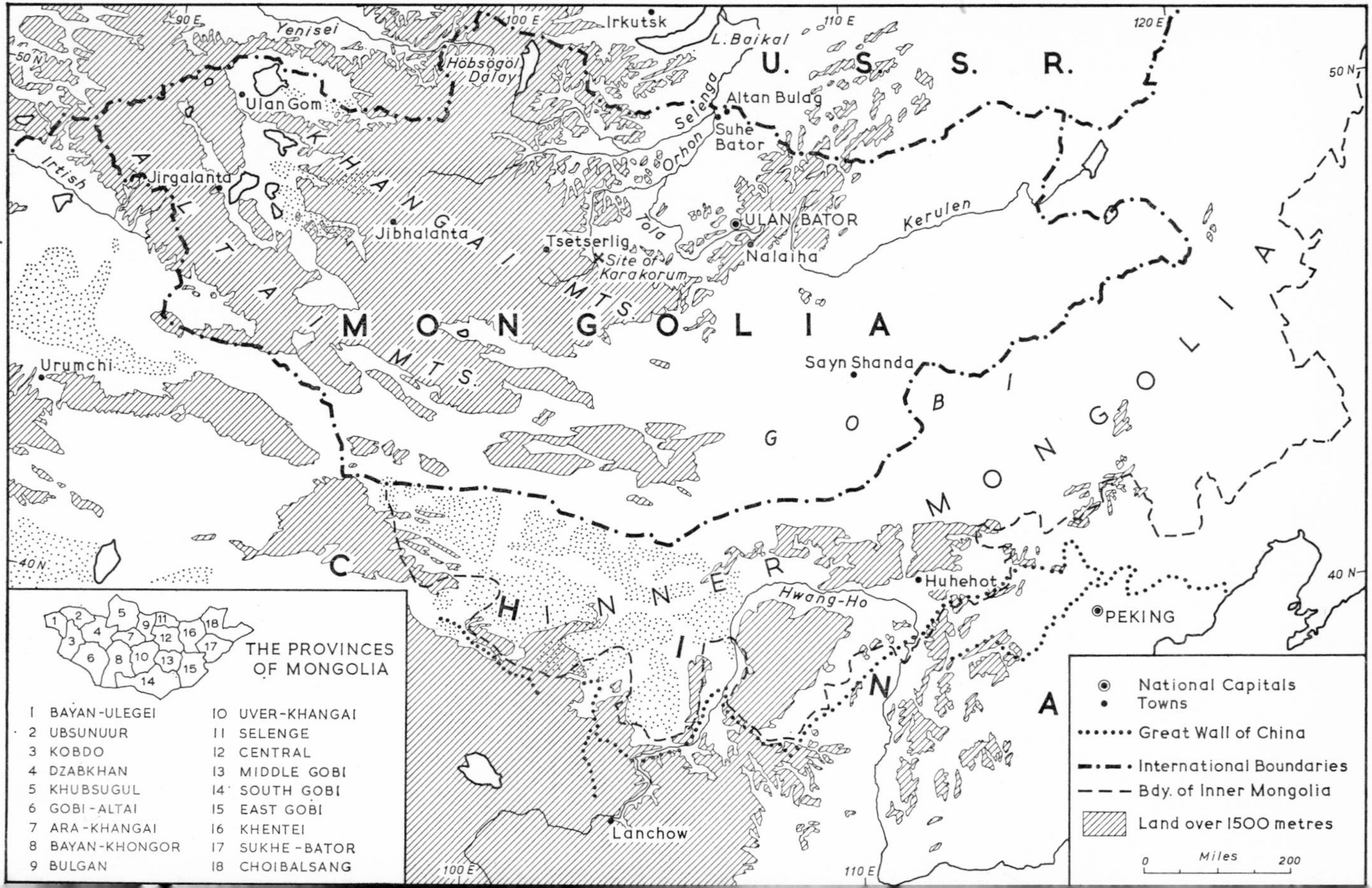
U. S. S. R.
MONGOLIA
INNER MONGOLIA
CHINA
GOBI
ALTAI MTS.
KHANGAI MTS.
Irkutsk
L. Baikal
Yenisei
Höbsögöl Dalay
Ulan Gom
Irtish
Jirgalanta
Jibhalanta
Tsetserlig
Site of Karakorum
Tola
Orhon
Selenga
Altan Bulag
Suhe Bator
ULAN BATOR
Nalaiha
Kerulen
Sayn Shanda
Urumchi
Huhehot
Hwang-Ho
PEKING
Lanchow
90 E
100 E
110 E
120 E
50 N
40 N
THE PROVINCES OF MONGOLIA
1 BAYAN-ULEGEI
2 UBSUNUUR
3 KOBDO
4 DZABKHAN
5 KHUBSUGUL
6 GOBI-ALTAI
7 ARA-KHANGAI
8 BAYAN-KHONGOR
9 BULGAN
10 UVER-KHANGAI
11 SELENGE
12 CENTRAL
13 MIDDLE GOBI
14 SOUTH GOBI
15 EAST GOBI
16 KHENTEI
17 SUKHE-BATOR
18 CHOIBALSANG
National Capitals
Towns
Great Wall of China
International Boundaries
Bdy. of Inner Mongolia
Land over 1500 metres
0 Miles 200

branch of Mahayana Buddhism, coming from Tibet, began the conversion of the Mongols in the late 16th century. One of its important features is the theory that certain aspects or manifestations of the historical Buddha are 'reincarnated' in priestly representatives. At the death of the incumbent, the manifestation is 'reincarnated' in a new body, that of an infant born at or soon after the death of the previous embodiment. The new incarnation is identified by priestcraft, a procedure which retains authority within the ecclesiastical establishment.

Until the Manchu conquest, there was a tendency for princes claiming descent from Chingis Khan to be 'discovered' or 'recognized' as reincarnations, thus effecting a convergence of secular and ecclesiastical authority. The Manchus, by forbidding this practice, were able to use religion to prevent political unity. Monasteries were allowed to acquire, by endowment, territories whose inhabitants were under their jurisdiction. A dual system of princely or feudal authority and monastic authority was thus instituted. The most important reincarnation in Outer Mongolia was the Jebtsundamba Hutukhtu. His residence or 'household', *eruge* in written Mongol, *örgöo* in modern Mongol, 'Urga' in Russian pronunciation, became the capital of Mongolia (now Ulan Bator).

Political History—Tsarist Period

In 1911, the year of the Chinese Revolution, Outer Mongolia (but not Inner Mongolia) succeeded in breaking away from China. The theory (only crudely formulated, since Mongolia had no international lawyers), was that the only bond of union had been the Manchu dynasty. With the fall of the dynasty, Chinese and Mongols were each free to go their own way. The Mongols, wanting complete independence, turned to Tsarist Russia for support. Russia, unwilling to upset the international balance, negotiated a tripartite agreement under which China was to have sovereignty (or 'suzerainty'), Mongolia was to have autonomy, and Russia a protectorate with—in effect—a dual veto: to prevent Outer Mongolia from adding Inner Mongolia, and to prevent China from trying to reassert control. Since there were four main lines of princes claiming descent from Chinghis Khan, the Jebtsundamba Hutukhtu was recognized as simultaneously spiritual and secular sovereign, to prevent jealousy among them.

History—Second Revolution

With the outbreak of the Russian Revolution in 1917 autonomous Mongolia lost its Tsarist support. A Chinese warlord of a Japanese-supported clique captured Urga and forced the Mongols to sign a renunciation of autonomy. Anti-Bolshevik Russians then retreated into Mongolia and the Chinese were ousted, but a reign of terror began under the 'mad Baron' Ungern-Sternberg. This led to a second revolution, now celebrated by the Mongols as their 'real' revolution, in 1921, led by an ex-soldier, Sukebator, and an ex-student-interpreter, Choibalsang, who was already in secret contact with Russian Communists. Partisans were organized who asked and received help from the Bolsheviks. Scattered bands of Chinese were driven out and Ungern-Sternberg captured and executed. Soviet troops were stationed at Urga (later withdrawn), but Soviet policy was restrained, in order not to force a crisis with China. The Hutukhtu was continued as a limited monarch, with real power in the hands of the revolutionaries.

Sukebator died in 1923 and the Hutukhtu in 1924. No successor was proclaimed, and Mongolia became, historically, the first of the 'People's Republics' outside of the Soviet Union but within the Soviet sphere. The issue of international recognition of Mongolia's independence from China was still kept in the background. There was some contact with the more Left Wing of the Chinese Nationalists, but not with the Chinese Communists, who were geographically remote. Right Wing and Left Wing tendencies alternated in Mongolian internal politics. Choibalsang, the Communist-oriented companion of Sukebator, achieved complete ascendancy only about 1935.

Recent History

The dominating consideration was by then the danger of Japanese invasion. With Soviet support more openly proclaimed in successive declarations, and after severe border fighting in which Soviet forces took part, Japanese invasion was staved off. In 1945 Mongol troops joined Russian forces in routing the Japanese in Manchuria and Inner Mongolia. In 1946, pursuant to one of the clauses in the Yalta agreements, Chiang Kai-shek consented to a plebiscite in which the Mongols chose full independence in preference to federation with China, and China then formally sponsored Mongolia's first application for membership in the United Nations. The next year this support was withdrawn, nominally because of a frontier dispute, and from then until 1961, through Chiang Kai-shek's influence with the United States, Mongolia's membership in the United Nations was successfully blocked.

Present Status and Conditions

Besides being a member of the United Nations, and recognized of course by all nations of the Soviet-Chinese block, Mongolia has diplomatic relations with India, Burma, and Indonesia and since 1963, with the United Kingdom. Victory of the Chinese Communists in 1949 made possible demobilization of most of the Mongolian army, since Mongolia has frontiers with only two states, China and the Soviet Union. The resultant savings in manpower and budget speeded up economic development. Defence expenditure fell from 46·6 per cent of the budget in 1940 to 2·6 per cent in 1959, but increased again to 6·4 in 1960.

The Mongolian People's Republic (Bügd Nairamdakh Mongol Ard Uls) is a one-party state. Unlike China, no minority parties are even nominally recognized. Unlike Poland and several other countries, the single party, the Mongolian People's Revolutionary Party (Mongol Ardyn Khuv'sgalt Nam) was not formed by even nominal coalition with one or more previously existing parties. It began as a pre-Communist, nationalist revolutionary party which by successive changes in membership requirements transmuted itself into what is essentially a Communist Party. Choibalsang died in 1952, ending a period of personal supremacy now stigmatized as a 'cult of personality,' though the condemnations have not been as severe as in the case of Stalin.

Two policies underlie present conditions. (1) The campaign against religion, which led to bloodshed and failure in the 1930s, was resumed successfully by persuasion and by organized provision of alternative occupations for priests. The number of lamas (priests) was reduced from about 100,000 to about 200, and most ex-priests are now married. One large and several small monasteries are now under state protection. (2) Education was pushed to the point where there is now virtually no illiteracy, though the proclaimed minimum 10-year (8-18) schooling has not everywhere been achieved. In 1921 there was only one elementary school; by 1960 there were 419, with 15 'secondary specialized schools'. A university was founded in 1947; it now has an enrolment of about 2,000, and there are seven other 'higher' schools, for medicine, agriculture, teacher training, etc.

Economic Situation

The economy is approximately 70 per cent pastoral, with an animal population of some 23 million, about 50 per cent sheep, 25 per cent goats, and the remainder horses, horned cattle (including yaks), and camels. Livestock has been historically subject to heavy losses, even more through storms than disease, but the increase of agriculture, to provide hay and fodder, the building of winter shelters, and a great increase in veterinary services, is remedying this instability. The pastoral economy is organized under co-operatives which have some of the features of Soviet collectives, but under complicated regulations which take account of small children and old people, families may privately own up to 75 head of stock. The former export economy of raw wool, hides, and live animals is being modified by a new industry of textile manufacture, tanning, bootmaking, and meat canning. Flour mills make it no longer necessary to import flour.

Existing industrial energy is largely supplied by the Nalaikha coal mines (highly mechanized) near Ulan Bator; for this reason the political capital is also the main industrial centre. A large oilfield has been discovered in the south, near the Chinese frontier, and refining has begun. The oilfield (which may extend well into Chinese territory) has access to the main railway (opened for through-traffic in 1956) which links the Soviet trans-Siberian system with the north China rail net. The next planned step in heavy industry under the current (1961-65) Five-Year Plan is an iron-steel complex in the north-west.

Mineral resources—iron, coal, and probably oil—are large. There are also rarer metals, like tungsten and gold. Other resources, as yet little exploited, include fisheries and timber. Industrial development of these resources is limited by a factor rare in Asia—underpopulation. There is not a large surplus of manpower to be transferred at will from the traditional pastoral occupations to industry. At present, there are Soviet experts in considerable numbers and Chinese, East German, Czechoslovak and other experts in smaller numbers, but the master-plan appears to call for expansion only at a rate which allows executive as well as lower ranks to be filled by Mongols, as fast as they can be trained. The object appears to be to avoid developments which would involve the permanent settlement in Mongolia of alien minorities difficult to assimilate.

A further aim appears to be the creation, step by step with industrial development, of a 'socialist élite' proletariat. In the new industries, labour is recruited only from young men and girls who have completed the ten-year (8-18) school course. As employment includes not only further on-the-job training, leading to promotion, but housing, health, and recreational privileges, the result is to create an industrial labour force which is enthusiastically committed to support of the regime.

Economic development is backed mainly by the Soviet Union with outright gifts and low-interest loans for machinery, technicians, etc. An important aspect of Chinese aid is labour-battalions. Under the initial agreement, the labourers had the right to settle in Mongolia, but this option appears to be rarely exercised. Recent Mongol official statements have been critical of China. All official expressions of gratitude for aid list the Soviet Union first and then East Germany, Czechoslovakia, China, 'and others', in varying order of precedence. Chinese economic aid has recently sharply decreased.

Mongolia has practically no national minority problems, an advantage possessed by few other countries in Asia. Most Chinese fled or were driven out in the 1920s. Their descendants (usually Chinese father, Mongol mother) are now thoroughly Mongol. Less than two per cent are listed as 'Chinese'. Kazakhs (4·3 per cent) are the largest minority. They are pastoral nomads, Turkish by language, related to the Kazakhs of Chinese Sinkiang and Soviet Kazakhstan. There are a few Buryats (2·9 per cent), mainly in north-east Mongolia and a few reindeer-herders, speaking a Turkish language, west of Lake Khubsugol.

BIBLIOGRAPHY

Gerard M. Friters. *Outer Mongolia and its International Position.* (Johns Hopkins Univ. Press, Baltimore, 1949.)

Owen Lattimore. *Nomads and Commissars.* (Oxford Univ. Press, London, 1962).

Ivor Montagu. *Land of Blue Sky.* (Dobson, London, 1956.)

National Economy of the Mongolian People's Republic for 40 Years. (State Publishers, Ulan Bator, 1961.)

BIOGRAPHICAL NOTE

Owen Lattimore (b. 1900) spent his early life in China engaged in business, journalism and research. Research Student at Harvard University, 1929. Fellow of Harvard-Yenching Institute in Peiping, 1930-31. Research Fellow, Guggenheim Foundation, Peking, 1931-33. Editor, *Pacific Affairs*, 1934-41. Lecturer, Johns Hopkins University, 1938-63. Director, School of International Relations, Johns Hopkins University, 1939-53. Political Adviser to Generalissimo Chiang Kai-shek, 1941-42. Director, Pacific Operations, Office of War Information, San Francisco, 1943. Economic Consultant, American Reparations Commission in Japan, 1945. Visiting lecturer at Ecole Pratique des Hautes Etudes, Sorbonne, 1958-59 and University of Copenhagen, 1961. Professor and Head of Department of Chinese Studies and Centre for Research on China, University of Leeds. Author of many books on Asia.

RUSSIAN CENTRAL ASIA

by

G. E. WHEELER

The Geographical Background

Russian or Soviet Central Asia is the name usually given to the area bounded on the north by Western Siberia, on the south by Persia and Afghanistan, on the east by the Sinkiang-Uygur Autonomous Region of China and on the west by the Caspian Sea. It consists of the five Soviet Socialist Republics of Kazakhstan, Turkmenistan, Uzbekistan, Kirgizia and Tadzhikistan. Soviet geographers include only the last four in the term 'Soviet Central Asia', Kazakhstan being regarded as a separate geographical region.

The northern part of the area occupied by Kazakhstan consists of steppe and semi-desert bordered by a mountain belt in the south-east. To the south of this is a desert belt known as the Turan lowland and containing the two great sandy deserts of Karakum and Kyzylkum separated from each other by the Amu-Dar'ya (Oxus) River. Further south again there is another desert strip consisting of sandy steppes and oases which in the west runs along the Soviet-Persian frontier. The south-east consists of some of the largest, highest and most glaciated mountain ranges in the world—the Tien-Shan and Pamirs. The climate is dry and continental with hot summers and cold winters. Dry farming is extensively practised in the north, farming in the south being mainly irrigated. The most important economic asset of the area is cotton, mainly grown in the Fergana and Vakhsh valleys. Cereals are now grown extensively in Kazakhstan and many other crops in the semi-desert and desert regions. There are important mineral resources including iron, copper and lead.

The population of 27 million is about 67 per cent Asian and 33 per cent European, mainly Russian and Ukrainian.

Early History

Since the 5th century A.D. Central Asia has been repeatedly invaded both from east and west. Turkic nomads swept over the whole area in the 6th century and remained in possession of Kazakhstan until the coming of the Russians. Transoxania, the land between the Amu-Dar'ya and Syr-Dar'ya rivers, was conquered in the 8th century by the Arabs who challenged and overcame paramount Chinese influence. During the 9th century most of Transoxania became part of the Persian Samanid Empire which had succeeded Arab rule. From the overthrow of the Samanids in 999 up to the Mongol invasion which began in 1220, the desert and oasis regions were mainly ruled by various Turkic Muslim dynasties, the most important being

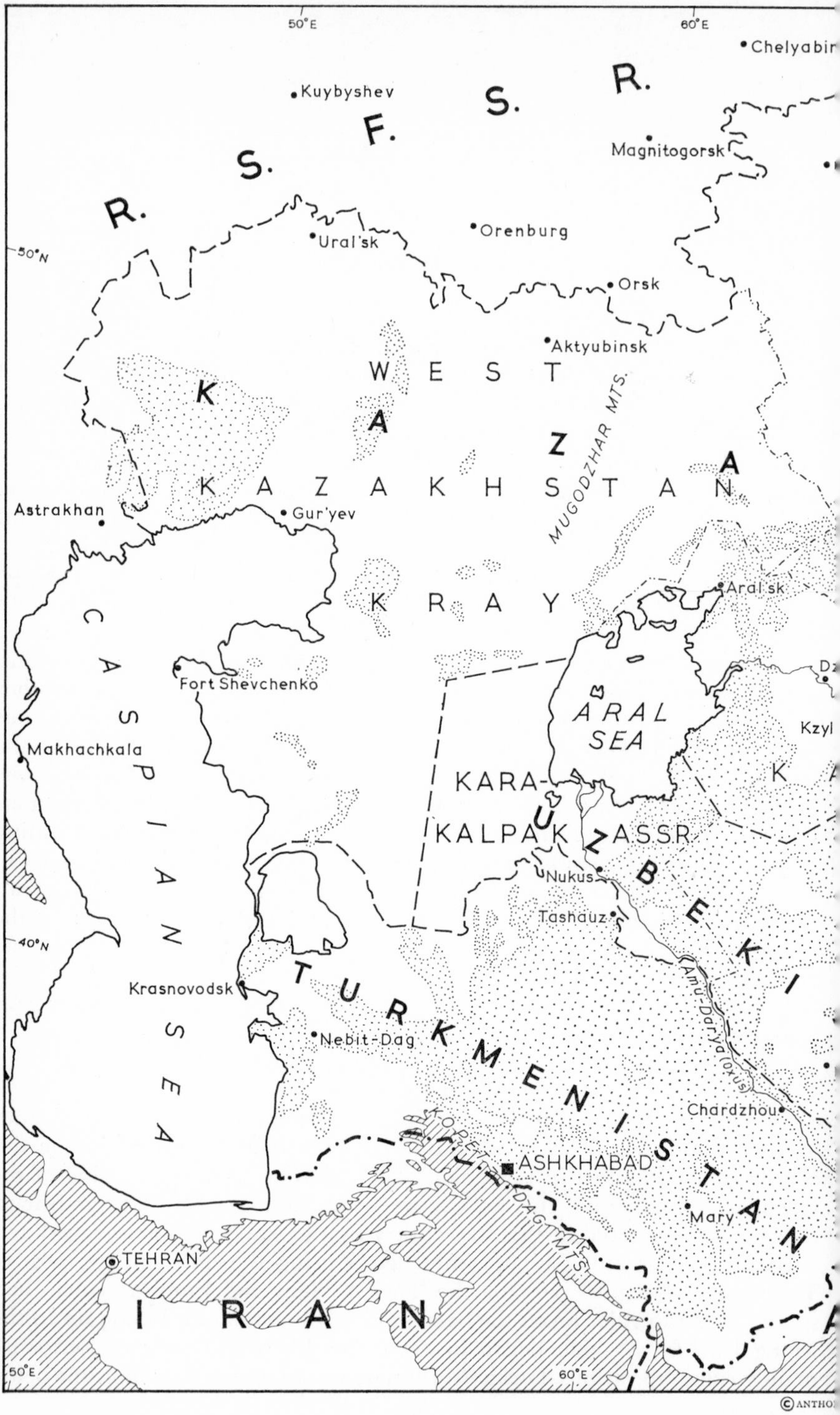
50°E
60°E
Chelyabir
Kuybyshev
R. S. F. S. R.
Magnitogorsk
Orenburg
Ural'sk
50°N
Orsk
Aktyubinsk
WEST
KAZAKHSTAN
KRAY
MUGODZHAR MTS.
Astrakhan
Gur'yev
Aral'sk
CASPIAN SEA
Fort Shevchenko
ARAL SEA
Makhachkala
Kzyl
KARA-KALPAK ZASSR
UZBEKI
Nukus
Tashauz
40°N
Amu-Darya (Oxus)
Krasnovodsk
TURKMENISTAN
Nebit-Dag
Chardzhou
KOPET-DAG MTS.
ASHKHABAD
Mary
TEHRAN
IRAN
50°E
60°E
©ANTHO

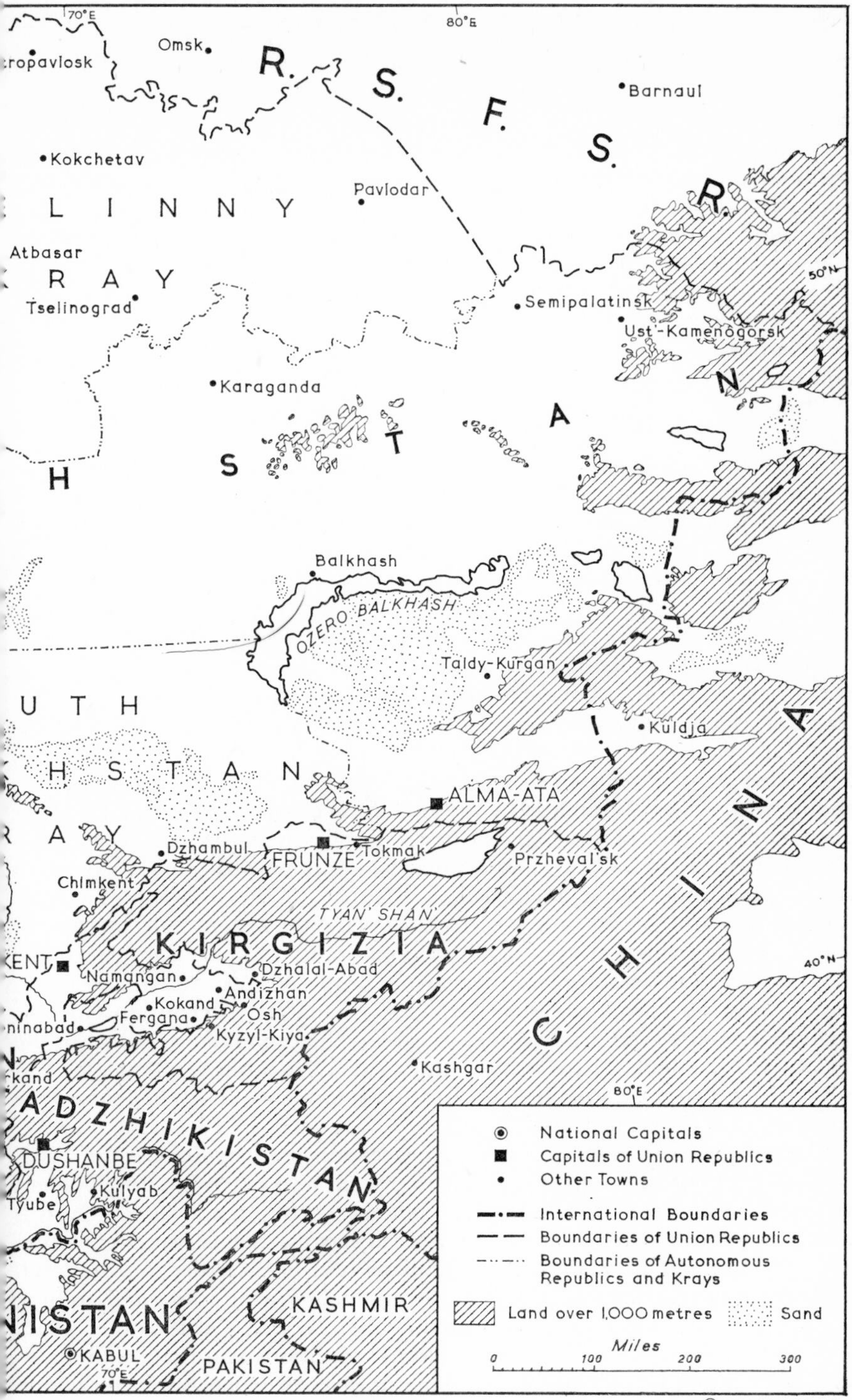
70°E
80°E
Omsk
ropavlosk
R. S. F. S. R.
Barnaul
Kokchetav
Pavlodar
LINNY
Atbasar
RAY
Tselinograd
Semipalatinsk
Ust'-Kamenogorsk
50°N
Karaganda
H S T A N
Balkhash
OZERO BALKHASH
Taldy-Kurgan
UTH
Kuldja
HSTAN
ALMA-ATA
RAY
Dzhambul
FRUNZE
Tokmak
Przheval'sk
CHINA
Chimkent
TYAN' SHAN'
KIRGIZIA
KENT
Namangan
Dzhalal-Abad
40°N
Andizhan
Kokand
Fergana
Osh
ninabad
Kyzyl-Kiya
Kashgar
kand
80°E
ADZHIKISTAN
DUSHANBE
Kulyab
Tyube
KASHMIR
NISTAN
KABUL
70°E
PAKISTAN
National Capitals
Capitals of Union Republics
Other Towns
International Boundaries
Boundaries of Union Republics
Boundaries of Autonomous Republics and Krays
Land over 1,000 metres
Sand
Miles
0
100
200
300

the Seljuks, who ruled the whole of Muslim Asia up to 1157, and the Khorezm Shahs, who reached the zenith of their power at the beginning of the 13th century. From 1137 to 1212 Transoxania and Semirech'ye (now W. Kirgizia and the Alma-Ata and East-Kazakhstan Oblasts of Kazakhstan), were dominated by a Tungusic or (possibly) Mongolian people, the Kara-Kitays, who came from the East and never embraced Islam although they were tolerant of it. The Mongol invasion and subsequent domination included the whole of the desert and oasis regions and a part of the Kazakh steppe. The greater part of the Mongol forces was composed of locally recruited Turks and the number of Mongols who settled in the area was negligible. By the middle of the 14th century all the Mongol rulers had become Turkicized and embraced Islam.

From the middle of the 14th to the beginning of the 16th century the desert and oasis regions, and particularly Transoxania, were under Timur (Timurlane) and his successors. During the 15th century the nomad Kazakhs began to embrace Islam and a part of them, the Uzbeks, came south to overturn the Timurid Empire and establish an Uzbek Empire which remained in power until 1510 when it broke up into various khanates of which the principal were Bukhara and Khiva.

The Coming Of The Russians

The first phase of Russian expansion in Asia had been a movement due east from the Urals to the Pacific, which began at the end of the 16th century. The second phase was the gradual spread over what is now Kazakhstan. This was begun by Peter the Great at the beginning of the 18th century. The third phase was the advance into the semi-desert and desert regions ending with the establishment by the end of the century of Russian rule over the whole area now occupied by the five Republics, with the partial exception of the Khanates of Bukhara and Khiva, which remained semi-independent vassal states until 1921. The Russian advance to the frontiers of China, Afghanistan and Persia and the establishment of Russian rule in Central Asia were motivated by political, economic and military considerations: it was desired to establish frontiers with 'properly constituted states' e.g. Persia, as distinct from the semi-barbarous khanates; the Russian Government and commercial firms wished to exploit the economic resources of the region and particularly its cotton, and to deny it both economically and militarily to Britain, whose hold on India and influence in Afghanistan were regarded as a threat to Russia.

Russian rule did much to ensure peace and security in Central Asia. Communications and irrigation were improved and extensive development was planned for the future. Little was done in education and discontent was caused by widespread colonization by Europeans. Before the Revolution some two million Russians and Ukrainians had been settled on the land. Little account was taken of nationality or nationalist aspirations and nothing was done to build up a trained indigenous civil service. On the other hand, there was little interference with established traditions and the local inhabitants were exempt from military service until 1916 when the introduction of labour conscription caused widespread revolt. This measure and the suppression of the revolt to some extent predisposed the population in favour of the Revolution of 1917.

The Revolution And The Civil War

In 1917, after the 'February' Revolution, the Muslims of Russia, entirely on their own initiative, had moved some way towards unity on the basis of their common culture. Various Muslim Congresses were created throughout the Empire, but although one of them, held in Orenburg in April 1917, raised the idea of territorial autonomy, most of the Muslim intelligentsia were concerned with cultural rather than political matters and were prepared to leave their political future to an all-Russian Constituent Assembly. The Soviet leaders were at first ready to treat the Muslims as a cultural and even, perhaps, as a political entity and one of their first acts (December 1917) was to declare the Muslim 'national and cultural institutions' free and inviolable in future. A Commissariat of Muslim Affairs was formed, and in June 1919 a 'Russian Party of Muslim Communists'. Shortly afterwards, however, this was dissolved and its functions taken over by a Central Bureau of Muslim Organizations of the Russian Communist Party. By the middle of 1919 the Commissariat of Muslim Affairs itself was dissolved and the whole concept of Islam was removed from Soviet political parlance, never to return.

During the Civil War there were some manifestations of political as distinct from cultural nationalism in Central Asia. Since, however, this nationalism was concerned mainly with getting rid of foreign influence, and particularly of foreign settlers, and was not interested in the class war and socialism, it was quickly suppressed by the Soviet authorities. This resulted in intense friction between the Muslims and Russian colonists. A purely Muslim Government created in Kokand was soon liquidated by Russian military force in January 1918, and in April an Autonomous Soviet Socialist Republic of Turkestan was created. After considerable resistance by a Social Revolutionary Government in Ashkhabad (now capital of Turkmenistan) the Tashkent Government, which was almost entirely Russian with only nominal Muslim participation, gained virtual control of the whole of Turkestan by the end of 1919, except for the Khanates of Bukhara and Khiva. But resistance to the Soviet regime now became widespread in the form of the Basmachi movement, which can best be described as the despairing reaction of the people to the inefficient and oppressive authority exercised by the Tashkent Government. A so-called Turkestan Commission despatched from Moscow to deal with the situation brought into being a number of palliative measures designed to humour the Muslims, and as a result of this the Basmachi movement began to collapse in 1922. By this time Khiva and Bukhara had become the Khorezmian and Bukharan 'People's Soviet Republics' and remained nominally independent until 1923 and 1924 when they became the Khorezmian and Bukharan Soviet Socialist Republics. In 1924 the administrative frontiers of Turkestan and Kazakhstan were realigned, the Republics of Turkestan, Khorezm (Khiva), and Bukhara were abolished, and the whole area was divided into the five Republics of Uzbekistan, Tadzhikistan, Kirgizia, Turkmenistan and Kazakhstan.

The Nationalities Policy and History to 1962

The nationalities policy of the Communist Party can best be seen as an expedient designed to compromise between the total disruption of the Russian Empire, which would have deprived the Russian state of vital natural resources, and the formal perpetuation of that empire, which would have run directly counter to the principles of Communism. By creating a so-called federal structure under the overriding control of the Communist Party it was hoped to ensure the economic and military security of the Empire, while at the same time giving world, and particularly Asian, opinion the impression that the non-Russian nationalities of the Soviet Union were being granted self-determination.

As stated earlier, the Tsarist Government had taken little account of nationalities in Central Asia. The social structure was in fact clan and tribal rather than national, the only peoples whose homogeneity and territorial concentration gave them any sense of national consciousness being the Kazakhs and Turkmens. Generally speaking the distinction was not as between peoples, but as between nomads and settled peoples. As a result, however, of the nationalist sentiment aroused during the Civil War, it was possible to arrive at a more or less precise labelling of nationalities, largely on the basis of language. Ostensibly language was the deciding factor in the delimitation of 1924; but in effect any territorial division on the basis of language was and is impossible, particularly in respect of the Fergana and Zeravshan Valleys, where the Uzbeks and Tadzhiks are culturally and historically one people. In the new delimitation the primary consideration was without doubt economic and administrative: by parcelling out the economic resources of the region as far as possible the Soviet authorities ensured that none of the Republics would have economic predominance. At the same time, by emphasizing what were in many cases very slight linguistic and cultural differences, the possibility of the various nationalities 'ganging up' against the Soviet regime was appreciably diminished.

After the collapse of the Basmachi movement active opposition to the new regime was only sporadic. In 1937 there occurred in Uzbekistan what was described by the authorities as a nationalist conspiracy. The Prime Minister and the First Secretary of the Uzbek Communist Party were accused of nationalism and of being British agents and were executed with a number of their alleged supporters. They admitted having worked for the independence of Turkestan from Soviet rule but not to collusion with Britain, of which no proof was forthcoming. It has never been established whether there was a real plot; the numerous arrests and executions may simply have been part of Stalin's Union-wide purge of so-called enemies of the people. During the Second World War large numbers of Muslim prisoners and deserters fought for the Germans against the Soviet army.

As elsewhere in the USSR, post-war reconstruction was very rapid and the material condition of the people greatly improved. After Stalin's death there was some posthumous rehabilitation of the victims of his purges. Although the authorities continued to inveigh against 'bourgeois nationalism', survivals of the past and religion, there were no overt signs of active opposition to the regime. From about 1954 onwards there has been a steady stream of delegations from the independent Asian and African countries to the larger cities of Uzbekistan, Tadzhikistan and Turkmenistan, delegations to Kazakhstan and Kirgizia being much less frequent. Up to 1962 foreign visitors were not free to visit rural areas.

Political Status and System of Government

Under the 1936 Soviet Constitution, the five Republics are regarded as fully sovereign Soviet Socialist states forming part of the USSR. The system of government and administration is uniform, each Republic having a President, a Council of Ministers and an elected Supreme Soviet or Parliament. Overriding control of all political, economic and cultural activities is exercised by the Communist Party, either the First or the Second Secretary of each Republic Party always being a non-native, usually a Russian. Although the Republics are nominally self-governing, responsibility for defence and security, foreign affairs, communications and a large range of economic and financial subjects is vested in the Central Government in Moscow. Generally speaking the Republics are divided into oblasts or provinces, but in Kazakhstan the northern oblasts have been grouped into the Tselinniy Kray or New Lands Region. The Autonomous Soviet Socialist Republic of Kara-Kalpakia is included in Uzbekistan and the Autonomous Oblast of Gorno-Badakhshan (the Pamirs) in Tadzhikistan. Conscription into the Soviet armed forces is universal. There are no national formations and conscripts are liable for service anywhere in the Soviet Union or abroad.

The Economy

Before the Revolution the economy of the whole region was almost entirely agricultural, industry being confined to cotton ginning and a small amount of copper and coal mining. Since the Revolution, and particularly since 1950, expansion in all branches of the economy has been very great, although many of the irrigation and other projects had been visualized by the Tsarist Government. Collectivization was introduced between 1928 and 1932 and resulted in a great increase in cotton (a mono-culture); it had disastrous effects on stock-breeding, mainly in Kazakhstan, and on the supply of meat and dairy produce. In 1954 the New Lands campaign was launched and a vast area of virgin land was put under cultivation in Kazakhstan, the main crop being wheat. For this purpose hundreds of thousands of Russians and Ukrainians were brought in from the west of the USSR and the proportion of Kazakhs has now dropped to 29 per cent of the total population of the Kazakh SSR.

During World War II a large number of factories with their trained personnel were transferred to Central Asia from the west and this gave a great fillip to the industrialization of the whole region. The output of coal, oil, natural gas, lead and steel has enormously increased, and light industries such as food packing and textiles have been greatly developed. In a survey carried out during 1957 by the secretariat of the United Nations Economic Commission for Europe, it was established that while cultivation and export of raw cotton and silk naturally remained the mainstay of the region's economy, not only cotton ginning and the production of cotton-seed oil but also the manufacture of fertilizers, of cotton picking machines, and of 60 per cent of the Soviet Union's output of spinning machinery were among its major industries. Cotton spinning and weaving account for 4 per cent and 5 per cent respectively of the Soviet Union's total output. Both steel and an increasing range of engineering products are now made in Central Asia; and a wide range of industries producing building materials and light consumer goods show a share of total Soviet output that does not fall far short of the share of population. As a result, Soviet Central Asia can be characterized as a region equipped with a fairly broad range of consumer-goods industries producing for the local market, but dependent on imports for nearly all capital goods. The 1957 survey reported favourably on living standards which it found were 'on much higher levels than in the neighbouring Asian countries'; it estimated that the average living standards for the region as a whole were probably one-fifth to one-fourth lower than the Soviet average, but found that this disparity could not be regarded as large compared with that found in other countries.

Social Conditions

Although Soviet Central Asia has many affinities—ethnic, cultural and climatic—with the Middle Eastern and South Asian countries adjoining it, the Republics have no direct diplomatic, commercial or social contacts with them. The earlier Soviet policy of trying to attract to the Central Asian republics people belonging to the same ethnic groups across the Soviet border—Azerbaijanis and Turkmens in Persia, and Uzbeks, Tadzhiks and Turkmens in Afghanistan—has long been discontinued. Whereas in Tsarist times there was continual movement across the Russian frontier by nomad tribes, traders and pilgrims to the holy cities of Persia and beyond, the frontiers are now firmly closed. Westernization in respect of living and work habits, general and technical education, the status of women and the breakdown of the old tribal, clan and family groupings and loyalties has proceeded much further in Central Asia than in any other part of the continent. An important factor has been the enormous increase in white settlement since the Revolution. The number is now more than three times what it was in 1917 and the Russians (excluding the Ukrainians and Belorussians) are now the most numerous nationality in the whole region. Nevertheless, the white settlers tend to live side by side with rather than among the native population: there has been very little inter-marriage, that between Muslim girls and European men being virtually nil. In the arts, and particularly the theatre, music and painting, there is a tendency to hark back to the past and this evokes strong and constant criticism by the Soviet authorities.

Culture and Education

After the Arab conquests of Transoxania in the 8th century, Islamic culture spread rapidly throughout the settled districts and by the end of the 10th century had obtained a firm hold, Bukhara and Samarkand becoming two of the most important theological strongholds of the Muslim world of that time. The effect of Islam on the nomad Kazakhs, Turkmens and Kirgiz was more gradual and much less marked; it gathered strength, however, under Tsarist rule, since the Russians regarded it as a stabilizing and civilizing factor. Although the actual conquest of Transoxania had been carried out by Arab forces, the administration of the region became to a large extent Persianized, and today the still predominantly Islamic culture of Central Asia and Kazakhstan is Iranian rather than Arab.

The main effects of Islam were on law, social customs and language. Muslim canon law (*shari'at*) and customary law (*'adat*) were already widely practised in the settled districts before the Mongol conquest. The canon law had little vogue among the nomads until the Russian conquests brought some degree of stabilization, but Muslim customary law began to take a hold during the 17th century. Before the Mongol conquest the written official and literary language had been Arabic and, to a minor extent, Persian, but during the 13th and 14th centuries under the Timurid Dynasty a written Turkic language called Chaghatay (after one of Chingis Khan's sons) was developed. This used the Perso-Arabic script, which remained the only script used for Central Asian languages until the introduction of a Latin in 1930, and later a modified Cyrillic alphabet from about 1940. From the Arab conquests up to the Russian Revolution of 1917 all the Central Asian languages borrowed extensively from Arabic and Persian, but hardly at all from Mongolian. Since 1917 borrowing has been confined to Russian and international words.

Unlike the Tsarist Government which interfered little with native culture, religion and languages, the Soviet Government from the beginning pursued an active policy in all these matters. The arts have been greatly encouraged and largely remodelled on Soviet and Russian lines. Languages have been systematized and developed, and great efforts have been made to build up national literatures on standard Soviet lines. At first the tendency was to emphasize the often slight differences in native cultures and languages; but with the intensification of the declared official policy of uprooting all traces of nationalism, more emphasis has recently been laid on similarity and inter-resemblance than on differences. The Soviet attitude towards Islam, the prevailing religion, has been consistently hostile, particularly in respect of practices thought to interfere with economic productivity. Of the vast number of mosques which existed before the Revolution only a very few remain in operation and religious instruction has been totally excluded from education.

In education progress has been remarkable; illiteracy, which stood at over 95 per cent before the Revolution, has been virtually stamped out; in addition to the primary and secondary schools, each republic has at least one university and large numbers of technological and other training colleges. Local languages are the medium of instruction in the primary and secondary schools, but the study of Russian is greatly encouraged since it is largely used in higher and technical education and training.

The Future

It is reasonable to expect that the great material progress achieved during the last 15 years will be maintained and extended. There is, however, no prospect of the peoples of Central Asia attaining independence or self-determination of the kind now enjoyed by such former colonial territories as India, Pakistan and the Arab countries. Indeed, it is probable that even the nominal national status of the republics will eventually disappear if the present plans of the Soviet regime are realized. During the past three years it has been increasingly emphasized that the present so-called federal structure of the Soviet Union is a temporary one from which a unitary multinational state will ultimately evolve. There will be an intermediate phase known as 'coming together' (*sblizheniye*) in which national distinctions such as frontiers and languages will fade away to prepare for the final phase of 'fusion' (*sliyaniye*). The process of coming together now said to be in progress is clearly meeting with considerable passive resistance which is being countered by what is called 'international education'. In addition, the steady increase in Russian and other Slav settlement will serve to lessen the chances of active nationalist opposition.

BIBLIOGRAPHY

A. Bennigsen and C. Quelquejay. *The Evolution of the Muslim Nationalities of the USSR and their Linguistic Problems.* (Central Asian Research Centre, London, 1961.)

Olaf Caroe. *Soviet Empire.* (Macmillan, London, 1953.)

Nathaniel Curzon. *The Russians in Central Asia.* (Longmans, London, 1889.)

M. Holdsworth. *Turkestan in the Nineteenth Century.* (Central Asian Research Centre, London, 1959).

Alexander Park. *Bolshevism in Turkestan* 1917-1927. (Colombia Univ. Press, New York, 1957.)

Richard Pierce. *Russian Central Asia (1867-1917).* (Univ. of California Press, Berkeley, 1960.)

Richard Pipes. *The Formation of the Soviet Union.* (Harvard Univ. Press, Cambridge, Mass., 1954.)

E. Schuyler. *Turkistan* (2 vols.). (Sampson Low, London, 1876.)

F. H. B. Skrine and E. D. Ross. *The Heart of Asia.* (Methuen, London, 1899.)

N. A. Smirnov. *Islam and Russia.* (Central Asian Research Centre, London, 1956.)

Geoffrey Wheeler. *Racial Problems in Soviet Muslim Asia.* (Oxford Univ. Press, 2nd ed., 1962.). *The Modern History of Soviet Central Asia.* (Weidenfeld and Nicolson, London, 1964.)

S. A. L. Zenkovsky. *Pan-Turkism and Islam in Russia.* (Harvard Univ. Press, 1960.)

Map of Soviet Central Asia and Kazakhstan (four sheets and gazetteer, 60 miles to 1 inch). (Central Asian Research Centre, London, 1962.)

Central Asian Review. (London: quarterly since 1953.)

BIOGRAPHICAL NOTE

GEOFFREY WHEELER has been Director of the Central Asian Research Centre, London, since 1953. He served for 33 years in the Army and Indian Political Service and was Counsellor in the British Embassy in Tehran from 1946-50. Author of *Racial Problems in Soviet Muslim Asia* and *The Modern History of Soviet Central Asia*, and Joint Editor of *Central Asian Review* (see above).

THE FAR EAST

CHINA

by

GEOFFREY HUDSON

Geography

China to-day covers the same area as the so-called Chinese Empire at the end of the nineteenth century except for Outer Mongolia, which has become an independent state, and Tannu-Tuva, which has been annexed by the Soviet Union. The old Chinese Empire comprised within its borders both Chinese in the strict sense—speakers of one of the dialects of the Chinese language—and certain non-Chinese peoples of whom the most important were the Tibetans, Mongols and Turkis (now known as Uigurs). The Chinese were, and are, the overwhelming majority of the total population—over 93 per cent—but an ethnographic map shows more of a balance between the Chinese and other nationalities, because the Chinese predominate in all areas of high population density, whereas the non-Chinese elements prevail in vast areas of mountain and desert where population density is very low. The extent of the territories they occupy has thus made the non-Chinese peoples of China more important, both historically and at the present time, than their numbers would indicate.

Three thousand years ago the Chinese occupied only a small part of the area which they now inhabit. It was confined to the middle and lower basin of the Yellow River, including both the loess-soil uplands of Shansi and Shensi and the alluvial lands of the North China Plain. From this homeland they have expanded their ethnic range in historical times in three directions; the main one southward to the Yangtse, the south China coastlands, the West River basin and Yunnan; the second westward into the borderlands of Tibet and Turkestan; and the third north-eastward into Manchuria. There have also been scattered settlements further afield within the range of Chinese political authority, and in recent times the large emigration to the south beyond the confines of Chinese territory, which has produced the communities known as the Overseas Chinese. In this demographic expansion the Chinese, while retaining their language and strongly marked culture traits formed in their Yellow River valley homeland, have mingled with earlier inhabitants and adapted themselves to a variety of climatic conditions. The Yellow River basin is a region of relatively low rainfall and temperate-zone continental climate with hot summers and cold winters; Manchuria and the north-western borderlands are even drier with greater extremes of temperature; the Yangtse valley and south China, on the other hand, are regions of high rainfall and subtropical climate with mild winters and humid summers. The climate differences are reflected in the prevailing forms of agri-

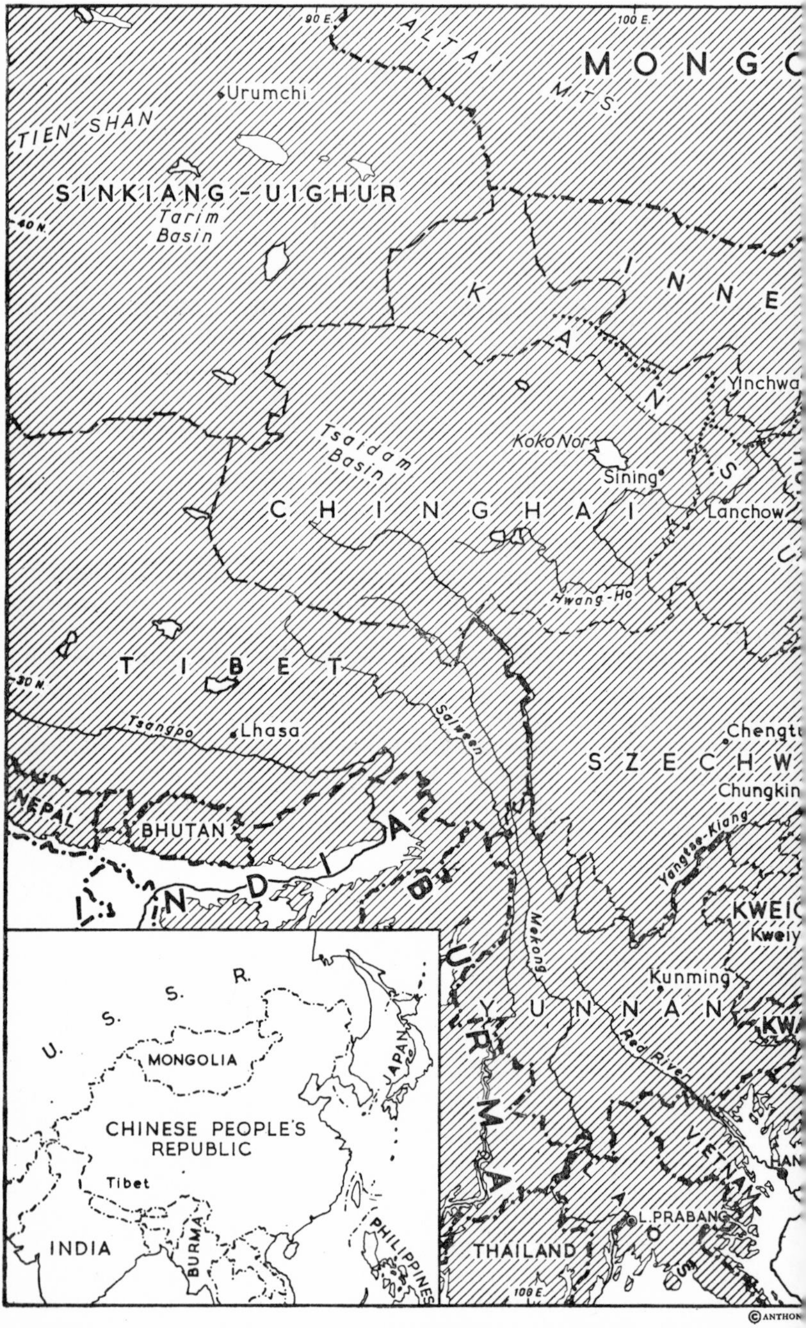
90 E.
100 E.
ALTAI MTS.
MONGO
Urumchi
TIEN SHAN
SINKIANG-UIGHUR
Tarim Basin
40 N.
KANSU
INNE
Ynchwa
Tsaidam Basin
Koko Nor
Sining
CHINGHAI
Lanchow
Hwang-Ho
TIBET
30 N.
Tsangpo
Lhasa
Salween
Chengtu
SZECHW
Chungkin
NEPAL
BHUTAN
INDIA
Yangtse-Kiang
BURMA
Mekong
KWEIC
Kweiy
Kunming
YUNNAN
Red River
VIETNAM
L. PRABANG
THAILAND
LAOS
108 E.
U. S. S. R.
MONGOLIA
JAPAN
CHINESE PEOPLE'S REPUBLIC
Tibet
INDIA
BURMA
PHILIPPINES

HEILUNGKIANG
Harbin
130 E
U.S.S.R.
GT. KHINGAN MTS
Changchun
Vladivostok
KIRIN
MONGOLIA
Shenyang
LIAONING
40 N.
Huhehot
PEKING
PYŎNGYANG
KOREA
Lushun
Talien
(Port Darien)
Tientsin
SŎUL
HOPEI
SHANSI
Taiyuan
Tsinan
SHANTUNG
Tsingtao
JAPAN
Hwang Ho
Chengchow
KIANGSU
HONAN
ANHWEI
Hofei
Nanking
Shanghai
30 N.
HUPEI
Hangchow
Wuhan
EAST
CHINA SEA
CHEKIANG
Nanchang
KIANGSI
Changsha
HUNAN
Foochow
FUKIEN
TAIPEI
Amoy
Taichung
Quemoy
TAIWAN
KWANGTUNG
Pescadores
Tainan
Swatow
Kwangchow
Kaohsiung
HONG KONG
MACAO
SOUTH
CHINA SEA
Haikow
HAINAN
110 E.
120 E
National Capitals
Towns
Great Wall of China
International Boundaries
Disputed Boundaries
Boundaries of Autonomous Regions
Provincial Boundaries
Land over 200 metres
0
Miles
300

culture; in the north wheat, millet and sorghum are the principal grain crops, whereas all China south of the divide between the Yellow River and the Yangtse is primarily a zone of wet rice cultivation.

The Chinese ethnic region has a coastline on the east side of Asia looking out towards the Pacific Ocean or rather the inner seas separated from the main ocean by the island chain made up of Japan, the Ryukyu Islands, Formosa and the Philippines. On the landward side the region is surrounded on the north, west and south-west by great tracts of mountain and desert which have in the past acted as barriers secluding China from close contacts with other main regions of civilization in South and West Asia and Europe. To the north is the arid plateau land of Mongolia, with a surface varying from uninhabitable desert (the Gobi or Shamo, 'Sea of Sand') through short-grass steppe suitable only for the pasture of animals to long-grass steppe which can be cultivated, but at the risk of producing 'dust-bowl' conditions. To the north-west is Sinkiang, or East Turkestan, as it used to be called—an even more arid region, but enclosed and traversed by high mountain ranges which feed fertile piedmont oases from their snows and glaciers. East Turkestan has more desert than Mongolia, but has always, nevertheless, had a more settled population because of the possibility of intensive agriculture in the oases. It has also in the past been the main avenue of overland trade between China and West Asia and even India (in spite of the roundabout routes involved); the ancient 'silk road' from China ran this way and Roman merchants from Syria used to buy Chinese silk at a place in the Pamirs, the mountains which mark what is to-day the western extremity of China's territory.

South of East Turkestan lies Tibet, a country of high plateau, much of it 15,000 or 16,000 feet above sea-level and uninhabitable because of the combination of aridity and altitude. The lower ground provides pasture for animals, and agriculture can be carried on in a few sheltered valleys, particularly in the south-east, but Tibet as a whole must be reckoned a desert country sharply contrasted with both China proper to the east of it and with India to the south and south-west. From India Tibet is separated by the great curving range of the Himalayas, which not only comprises many of the highest mountains in the world, but also divides two different climatic zones; the Tibetan plateau to the north of the range is almost entirely treeless, whereas the southern slopes of the Himalayas descending to the plains of India receive a heavy summer monsoon rainfall and are clothed with dense forest. Tibet is a very difficult country for anyone to enter or cross, but it is somewhat more accessible from China than from India—a fact which has helped to determine its history in modern times. It is a natural barrier and buffer between India and China, and formerly, even when it was controlled by China, it was hard for a government in Peking to exert power on the Indian border because of the inadequacy of communications; it is the penetration of Tibet by motor road and air transport which has made China a much nearer neighbour to India as a result of the recent reconquest than it was in the eighteenth and nineteenth centuries.

Finally, there are to the south-west of China, forming natural frontiers with Burma, Laos and Vietnam, mountain ranges which, although of low altitude as compared with the Himalayas, are for the most part covered with thick jungle and very difficult to cross. These mountains have in the past effectively separated China by land from the countries of South-East Asia—though less from Vietnam than from Laos and Burma—and communication with these countries has always been mainly by sea, so that they have come to be known collectively to the Chinese as the 'South Seas'. Sea routes from China in the days of sail led southwards to Cambodia and the Gulf of Siam, to the Moluccas, Borneo, Java and the Malay Peninsula, with further access onwards through the Straits of Malacca into the Indian Ocean. But the enormous distances by sea round Malaya from the ports of China to the Bay of Bengal or the Persian Gulf greatly reduced the possibilities of contacts with India, Persia or Arabia through maritime trade.

The Shang Dynasty

The earliest Chinese civilization of which we have knowledge flourished in the plains of northern Honan close to the Yellow River in the second millennium B.C. It can be identified with the period of the Shang Dynasty, which was mentioned in ancient Chinese historical records, but was believed by critical Western scholars to be mythical until its material remains were revealed by archaeological excavation from about 1930 onwards. Shang society was based on intense agriculture and its capital was a town of some size. Since the Shang people lived in the midst of relatively primitive tribes and had no knowledge of any civilization as materially advanced as their own, they called their land *Chung Kuo* or 'the Central Country', which remains to this day the Chinese name for China. The implications of such a name—that China is the centre of the world, a country of unique civilization surrounded by inferior peoples on the periphery—has never ceased to affect the Chinese outlook. Foreigners naturally were not inclined to accept this Chinese estimate of their own pre-eminence and tended to call their country by the name of the dynasty reigning over it when they first had knowledge of it. Thus the Arabs used the name of the Ch'in or Ts'in Dynasty which ruled China during the later part of the third century B.C.; this passed into Latin as Sinae, and ultimately into English as 'China'. The Russians, on the other hand, who first became aware of the existence of China by overland trade routes during the Middle Ages, called it Kitai—the Cathay of Marco Polo and other medieval travellers from Western Europe—which was the name of a Mongol tribe dominant in north China in the eleventh century A.D., and this is still the name used in Russian.

The Shang period in China is memorable particularly for the magnificent bronze vessels, which are often great works of art and exhibit a highly developed technique of working in metal. Most characteristic of the archaeological finds, however, are the so-called 'oracle bones'; these bones were used for divination and the questions and answers were inscribed on them. Thus we have specimens of the earliest forms of Chinese writing; this was a 'picture-writing' developing into an 'ideographic' script, similar in some ways to Egyptian hieroglyphics and other pre-alphabetic scripts of other ancient civilizations. But, whereas these comparable modes of writing were elsewhere superseded by alphabets, derived ultimately from a single model created in the region of the East Mediterranean, the Chinese have retained their ideographic script to the present day, though the individual signs have been so far altered from the forms of Shang times as to be usually unrecognizable. The Chinese system of writing has always indeed been one of the most characteristic features of Chinese civilization, and at the present day the question whether to retain it—in a simplified form—or to discard it is still a matter of controversy in China, for the script is too cumbrous for an age which aims at streamlined efficiency, yet its total abolition would make too great a break with China's cultural heritage to be easily acceptable to those—even if they are Communists—who set store by China's separate national identity.

The Chou Dynasty

The Shang period was followed by that of the Chou, a dynasty originally based on the Wei valley in what is now Shensi province to the west of the Shang country in Honan. The Chou kings ruled over a much larger area than the Shang and greatly increased it by the conquest of non-Chinese tribes round the fringes of the Chinese homeland; these conquered lands were settled by Chinese colonists who absorbed the native inhabitants and thus extended the territory of the Chinese race. The Dynasty was unable, however, to govern so large an area effectively from a single centre and parcelled it out into fiefs, which, as central control was relaxed, developed into independent states, often at war with one another and paying only nominal allegiance to their suzerain. The period from 403 to 221 B.C. is known in Chinese history as the Era of the Warring States. In spite of the incessant warfare it was a time of economic expansion, as rival local rulers sought to increase their revenues, and of intellectual development, stimulated by the decay of old religious and social institutions and the quest for new norms of government and morals.

Confucius, Taoists and Legists

Among a number of philosophical schools which then arose three were outstanding. One was that of Confucius, which taught a humanist ethic not unlike that of Greek Stoicism; men should be educated in virtue in preparation for the public service, and the ruler who was himself virtuous would also be successful because his good administration would make his subjects contented and attract others to his side. In contrast to the Confucians, the Taoists held that wisdom and happiness for man came through a mystical inner illumination; politically they were anarchists and considered that the best thing a ruler could do for his subjects was to lead them back to a state of primeval innocence where they would not need any more government. The third school, that of the so-called Legists, shared the Taoists' disregard of the Confucian virtues, but taught that salvation lay, not in the reduction, but in the enhancement, of the power of the state; the ruler who, through rigorously enforced laws, strengthened his own state sufficiently would subdue all his rivals and establish universal peace through a universal empire.

The Ch'in Dynasty

The Ch'in state, which heeded the advice of the Legists, finally succeeded in destroying all the other Chinese states and creating a universal empire between the Tibetan border mountains and the Pacific coast in 221 B.C. The Ch'in ruler adopted a title rendered in English as 'emperor' and subsequently used by all Chinese monarchs, but hitherto applied only to gods. He governed his empire, which now extended from the plateau of Mongolia—where he built the Great Wall to stop the raids of nomadic tribes—southward to Canton, through a centralized bureaucracy of appointed officials, suppressing the hereditary aristocracy which had sustained the feudal system of Chou times. He persecuted the Confucians because of their association with the old political order, but failed to find any other moral or religious basis for the empire which he had established by the ruthless use of force. After his death his dynasty disappeared almost immediately in a series of political convulsions which convinced educated Chinese of the insufficiency of Legist principles.

The Han Dynasty

The next dynasty, the Han, which, except for a short interval of usurpation, reigned for four centuries (206 B.C. to A.D. 220), established a compromise on which Chinese society and government continued to be based in essentials down to the overthrow of the imperial monarchy in 1912. The Han Emperors maintained the centralized bureaucracy created by the Ch'in for governing an even more extensive territory—to the Ch'in dominions they added what is now Sinkiang and also northern Vietnam—but instead of opposing traditional learning, they patronized it, and turned the Confucian school, which had become the equivalent of a religious sect, into a pillar of their rule. The Confucians accepted the autocracy of the Emperor, but held that he should administer the empire through officials who had been specially educated for their task through study of Confucian philosophical writings and other literature regarded by the Confucians as morally edifying.

Origin of the Civil Service

The test of qualification for office was thus some kind of examination which conferred an academic degree, and this was the origin of the system of public competitive examinations for the civil service which became the most distinctive social and political feature of Chinese civilization. The system was not perfected all at once; it evolved over many centuries. Its tendency was to substitute merit—though merit according to a special criterion—for birth or wealth as a qualification for administrative office, and it became possible for a man of the most humble origin to rise to the highest position in the state if he had the required ability and could acquire the necessary education. The latter condition was, of course, always a limiting factor, for the bulk of the population was too poor to be able to afford the education for its sons, except in so far as promising boys might be helped by charitable 'clan' or village endowments. But the numbers of those competing in the examinations grew ever greater as time went on, and from the eleventh century was indirectly increased by the development of printing, which made books more easily available.

The 'scholar' class overlapped with the landowning class and the term 'gentry' is usually applied to that element of Chinese society which combined academic qualifications with landed property and was able, when not actually holding appointments in the imperial civil service, to live a life of cultivated leisure on income from rents and take part in local government, thus supplementing the work of the central bureaucracy and forming such 'public opinion' as existed under a monarchy not restricted by any kind of parliamentary or municipal rights. There were always, however, landlords who were not scholars, thus lacking the social status which belonged to the scholar class, and also scholars who had no landed or other property and made a living, when not in government service, as teachers, secretaries, clerks and even letter-writers for the illiterate. The number of qualified scholars was always much greater than the number of civil service jobs available for them, so that they had to rely on alternative sources of income; their aspiration, however, was to serve in the greater offices of state, as ministers of the central government or as governors of provinces; these were the 'mandarins', who lived in grand style and had great opportunities of acquiring wealth, but were always liable to dismissal, degradation or even execution if they incurred the displeasure of the Emperor.

The scholar class was officially Confucian, but its members, especially when they were living in retirement, were often addicted to the mystical practices of Taoism, which, when carried to an extreme, involved an ascetic life as a recluse in the mountains. Thus the Chinese cultural tradition has both a worldly side, in which the individual is subordinated to family duties and the service of the state, and an unworldly one, so often represented in Chinese art, in which he can achieve spiritual emancipation in a mountain hermitage—where, as a Chinese saying has it, the sage 'regards the affairs of the world as so much duckweed'. From the first century A.D. the Taoist opposition to Confucianism was reinforced by that of Buddhism, which was introduced into China from India by way of Central Asia. Buddhism, with its monastic ideal, its doctrines of reincarnation and *nirvana*, its subtle epistemology and its emphasis on personal salvation rather than on social duty, ran counter to Confucian philosophy, and Buddhism never succeeded in establishing itself as a state religion in China, but in its popular form it gained a strong hold on the masses of the people. Buddhism and Taoism—which had in the meantime developed into a popular religion with its own gods, ritual worship and magical beliefs—were rivals, but they also influenced each other and a product of this interaction was Ch'an Buddhism, better known under its Japanese name of Zen, which concentrated on a technique of meditation designed to produce an inner enlightenment. Educated Chinese often combined Confucianism, as a system of mundane ethics, with Ch'an Buddhism, as a means to spiritual illumination; and although the more orthodox Confucians strongly disapproved of both Taoism and Buddhism, there was a prevailing tendency in Chinese thought to regard them all as complementary rather than incompatible, and one of the stock themes of Chinese pictorial art represents Confucius, Lao Tzu and the Buddha engaged in an amicable intellectual discussion.

The Chinese upper class of landlords, scholars and government officials was sustained by rents and taxes from the production of the masses of peasants and artisans who made up the bulk of the population. In periods of good administration and freedom from external or civil war, when the pressure of population was not too great, these classes enjoyed tolerable conditions of life, but even at the best times China was exceptionally liable to famine brought on either by droughts, when the uncertain spring rains were insufficient to nourish the crops, or by floods, when the great rivers swollen by melting snows on the mountains of Tibet overflowed their banks in the flat plains and inundated vast areas of cultivated land. There were moreover two human factors which aggravated these natural conditions. The unchecked growth of population in times of peace tended to force a surplus of the peasantry on to marginal lands, to drive them into the towns as casual labour usually unemployed, or make them tenants of landlords who thus acquired more and more land. At the same time the decline of a dynasty, which so often followed its early period of energy and good administration, led to official corruption and abuses of power imposing additional burdens on the people. According to Confucian theory a dynasty reigned because it held the 'Mandate of Heaven', a divine commission to govern, but it lost this mandate if the descendants of the founder proved unworthy, and the displeasure of Heaven was manifested by an increase of natural calamities. This belief was more than the primitive idea that monarchs should be responsible for the weather; one of the symptoms of a breakdown of administration was that officials neglected the care of dykes and dams, so that floods, when they came, were far more devastating than when such public works were well maintained. In circumstances of over-population, governmental maladministration and widespread famine, the combination of social discontents with the belief that the reigning dynasty has lost its mandate has often in Chinese history been sufficient to cause large-scale popular revolts and a change of dynasty, a new dynasty being founded sometimes by the leader of the revolt and sometimes by a general who takes advantage of the disorder to install himself in power. Such upheavals were never, however, until 1912, real revolutions, for the political structure and methods of government remained in essentials the same from one dynasty to another.

The Han Dynasty and the Roman Empire

The Chinese Empire of the Han was contemporary with the Roman Empire in Europe and the lands round the Mediterranean, and the two great political units were roughly comparable in size and population, but their historical destinies were widely divergent. The Roman Empire broke up, never to be reconstituted in its original shape; even apart from its Asian and African lands, its European territories are to-day partitioned between seventeen sovereign states. On the other hand, all the territory held by the Han Dynasty, except for Vietnam, remains to-day within the frontiers of China. For most of the twenty-one centuries between the founding of the Han Dynasty in 206 B.C. and the fall of the Ch'ing in A.D. 1912 China was politically united under a single government, and even in periods of political division its cultural unity remained virtually intact. But if China thus excelled Europe in the stability and continuity of its civilization, it was the divisions and mutations of Europe which opened the way to more progressive modes of economic and intellectual life. In China the weight of ancient tradition, the prestige of the 'classics' and the authority of a conservatively indoctrinated bureaucracy were adverse to advance in the sciences and to economic and political innovations. There were some remarkable developments of natural science and technology in China in the early centuries, but Confucian orthodoxy was unfavourable to scientific enquiry, and progress in this field had virtually ceased long before the great advances of Western science which ushered in the modern age of mankind. Similarly the vast Chinese Empire produced a flourishing internal commerce and a considerable foreign trade, but social and political conditions obstructed the rise of a genuine capitalist economy. The Chinese merchant might become rich, but politically he remained at the mercy of the imperial bureaucracy; he could give his son an education to enable him to compete in the civil service examinations, and himself could purchase a nominal degree which would admit him to the ranks of the 'gentry', but he had no municipal or parliamentary representation which would have given him political power.

The main factors in the history of Chinese civilization before the nineteenth century were internal, but there were two important external factors. One of these was Buddhism, which has already been mentioned; this was an entirely peaceful influence. But the other factor was the permanent threat of the nomadic peoples, few in numbers and spread out over vast expanses of steppe and desert, who were nevertheless highly mobile, and, accustomed as they were to herding on horseback, formed natural cavalry armies which under a capable military leadership could become potent instruments either for predatory raiding or for permanent conquest. To hold the northern nomads at bay was always the primary strategic concern of a Chinese government, but on several occasions in history the defence failed and a part or the whole of China was overrun.

The Mongol and Manchu Conquests

The two most notable conquests were those made by the Mongols in the thirteenth century and by the Manchus in the seventeenth. The invasions of these plundering barbarians caused much suffering and humiliation to the Chinese people; nevertheless, the Chinese cultural tradition was little affected, for the northern nomads had no higher culture of their own and were unable to draw regular revenues from conquered China without employing Chinese civil servants, with the result that the conquerors became gradually assimilated to the civilization of the conquered. This happened especially to the Manchus, whose dynasty, the Ch'ing, replaced the native Chinese house of Ming in the imperial capital of Peking in 1644. The Ch'ing Emperors learned to speak and write Chinese, and the Manchu language fell into disuse; certain government posts were reserved for Manchus, but the Chinese element in the administration became more and more predominant, so that by the nineteenth century there was little to distinguish the Ch'ing from a pure Chinese dynasty. In one respect, however, it was more effective than a purely Chinese dynasty would have been. The military organization of the Manchus combined with the resources of China sufficed to add Mongolia, Sinkiang and Tibet to the Manchu–Chinese Empire; none of these three territories had been held by the Ming Dynasty, nor had any previous purely

Chinese dynasty controlled Tibet. Thus the China that confronted Europeans in the Far East in the early nineteenth century was more than twice as large territorially as that which the Portuguese voyagers found when they first reached China in the sixteenth century.

Beginning of Western Trade with China

The voyage of Vasco da Gama, who reached India round Africa in 1498, had opened the Indian Ocean to European navigation, and after the Portuguese capture of Malacca in 1511 it could not be long before they reached China as well. The first voyage there was in 1516. At first there was little to distinguish the Portuguese in Chinese eyes from the Arab and Malay traders who had long visited Chinese ports; for their services to the Chinese Government in suppressing piracy they were granted the right to establish a trading settlement at Macao. But neither the Portuguese nor the Dutch, French and English merchants, who followed them to the China Seas, made any real impression on China until the second quarter of the nineteenth century. They were allowed to trade in certain ports—from 1757 only at Canton—but they were not permitted to travel in the interior or to have any contacts with the Chinese people except for merchants officially licensed to have dealings with them. Nor was the Chinese court willing to enter into diplomatic relations on a basis of equality with envoys of the European maritime nations; it would receive diplomatic missions only if they came to offer homage and tribute to the Chinese Emperor. Only with Russia was some sort of diplomatic contact established; this was because, while the other states of Europe had made contact with China only through merchant shipping, Russia had a land frontier with the Chinese Empire to the north of Manchuria and Mongolia, and negotiations were required in order to settle frontier disputes and keep Russia from aiding rebellious Mongol tribes. But neither the Russian outposts in Siberia nor the European traders coming to Canton impressed the Chinese as bearers of a civilization comparable to their own.

The First Jesuit Missionaries

A stronger impression was made by the Catholic missionaries, especially the Jesuits, who penetrated into China from the beginning of the seventeenth century. They were respected by the Chinese for their mathematical knowledge and employed by the Government for certain purposes such as astronomical observations for regulating the calendar—a matter of great importance for Chinese state rituals—and geographical surveys. Their opportunities for making converts were, however, severely restricted, particularly after the Pope had decided against the Jesuit policy of accepting the Confucian cult of ancestors as a civil observance compatible with Christianity. The influence of the missionaries was thus a very limited one, and their presence in China did little to stimulate curiosity about the West in the minds of the Confucian scholar-officials, whose outlook had become imperviously ethnocentric and self-sufficient. Only a great shock, or series of shocks, could arouse China from the complacency of an immobile traditionalism in a rapidly changing world.

The 'Opium War' and The Treaty of Nanking

The first great shock was administered by defeat in the Anglo-Chinese war of 1839–42, the so-called 'Opium War'. The occasion of this was the action taken by a commissioner of the Chinese Government to enforce a prohibition of the import of opium which was being violated by British merchants with the connivance of the local authorities. But even without this particular issue an armed conflict was imminent because the British, as the principal European traders at Canton, were unwilling to put up any longer with the conditions imposed on the trade there. The fighting which then took place suddenly revealed the Chinese Empire as incapable of standing up to even a small expeditionary force of a European power, and the Treaty of Nanking which concluded the war was a great humiliation for China. Britain obtained the opening of additional ports, including Shanghai, a fixed customs tariff instead of arbitrary taxation on trade, rights of residence in the ports with extra-territorial jurisdiction of British consuls, and the cession of the island of Hong Kong. Other Western nations hastened to conclude similar treaties on behalf of their merchants. China could no longer be secluded from contact with the West; the Western 'barbarians' were now in Chinese ports no more on sufferance, but as of right which they had the power to enforce.

The T'ai P'ing Rebellion

The loss of prestige suffered by the Ch'ing Dynasty, added to the factors which, as we have seen, tended to undermine all Chinese dynasties after the first few generations, produced the great T'ai P'ing rebellion, which began in 1851 under the leadership of a convert to Protestant Christianity. The rebels overran a large part of south China, captured Nanking and advanced as far north as Tientsin, but were driven back and finally crushed by forces loyal to the Ch'ing. The Manchu garrisons in China had proved incapable of resisting the rebels, but the religious fanaticism of the latter—the first manifestation of the new Western influence in China—set the Confucian scholar class against them, and this was their undoing. In the last phase of the civil war the Ch'ing cause was aided by the Western powers, whose trade was suffering from the extension of T'ai P'ing military operations into the neighbourhood of Shanghai, and the fame of General Gordon and his 'Ever-Victorious Army' led to a widespread popular belief in the West that his campaign had decided the issue of the civil war, but in fact the T'ai P'ing had already lost nearly all their territory outside Kiangsu province before the Western intervention took place. While the civil war was in progress Britain and France had carried on a war of their own against the Ch'ing Government resulting in new treaties which gave foreigners unlimited rights of travel in the interior of China and provided for the residence of foreign diplomatic missions in Peking and diplomatic relations with China on terms of equality—a concession which the Chinese Court had hitherto denied on principle to 'barbarians'.

Expansion of Western Influence

British and French troops entered Peking in 1860 to enforce the demands of their Governments, but withdrew after the ratification of the new treaties

China remained an independent state—reunified after the collapse of the T'ai P'ing revolt in 1864—but subject to servitudes on its sovereignty through extra-territorial rights of foreigners within its borders and to economic pressures which began slowly, but surely, to transform the basis of its social order. The foreign merchants brought with them their banks and insurance companies; their commercial operations were immune from the exactions of Chinese officials, and increasingly covered Chinese domestic as well as foreign trade; Western shipping predominated not only on the overseas routes but also in coastwise navigation and on inland waters such as the Yangtse river. Foreign capital was invested in harbour facilities and public utilities in the ports and found a new field with the beginning of railway construction in China. The general policy of the Chinese Government towards these innovations was to make concessions under pressure to foreign interests, but to obstruct economic development wherever possible. The first railway in China was constructed from Shanghai to Woosung in 1876, but in the following year the Government bought it, tore up the rails and demolished the rolling stock.

The new conditions nevertheless forced the government itself to open the door to the modern world, if only a little way. It needed men with knowledge of foreign languages and international law for the diplomatic service which it had been compelled to create; it needed men with mathematical and scientific qualifications in order to build the modern army and navy which after the defeats China had suffered were recognized as essential for national defence. It was believed by leading Chinese statesmen of the time that it was possible thus to train experts without damage to the Confucian ideology or to the existing structure of the state. But the young diplomats and officers drank in Western political ideas with their languages and sciences and became violently discontented with their environment. The vogue of Western education grew rapidly and a new Western-educated intelligentsia was formed.

The Period of Reforms

In 1895 China suffered a shock greater than any previously undergone. A war with Japan which began in the previous year ended in utter defeat for China. Such humiliation at the hands of the Japanese was a greater blow to Chinese pride than had been inflicted by the wars with Britain and France, because Japan had been a cultural satellite of China and her new naval and military superiority over China was manifestly due to the fact that she had modernized her whole state system on Western lines, which China had not tried to do. Patriotic indignation in China—further stimulated by extortions of leasehold territories and railway concessions by Germany, Russia, Britain and France—now took shape in an agitation for sweeping reforms which, through the advocacy of a scholar named K'ang Yu-wei, converted the reigning Emperor Kwang Hsu and caused him to issue a series of Reform Edicts in 1898. But the reforms antagonized too many vested interests, and the Dowager Empress Tzu Hsi, whose sympathies were with the conservatives, carried out a *coup d'état*, whereby the Emperor was made a prisoner in his own palace and the reform party suppressed. The sequel was the rising of the so-called 'Boxers', a popular anti-foreign movement through which the emotions generated by China's degradation were diverted from the agitation for reform into attacks on foreign residents, particularly missionaries. Although the Boxers were supported by a Court faction and joined by part of the army, their attempt to drive the Western nations out of China by force was foredoomed to failure; an international army composed of contingents from all the principal Western powers and Japan marched in the summer of 1900 to Peking where the legations had been besieged by the Boxers, and the Court had to flee from the capital. For the Ch'ing Dynasty and for the *ancien régime* this was the beginning of the end. Although the Dowager Empress continued to hold the reins of power for another eight years, she now accepted the inevitability of reforms, and entrusted her political henchman Yuan Shih-k'ai with the task of putting them into effect. His primary concern was with the re-organization of the army, but of even greater importance than his military measures was the abolition of the old system of examinations for the civil service. A Western education and not Chinese classical learning henceforth became the key to the public service, and this had the most profound effect on the Chinese mind, for the whole range of ideas and values on which Chinese society and government had traditionally been based was now discredited overnight. The monarchy itself only survived by six years the passing of the examination system. Republican ideas had already become current among young army officers, reflecting the predominant American influence in Western education in China. In October 1911, at Hankow on the middle Yangtse, the garrison troops mutinied and proclaimed a Republic; other army units made common cause with them, and after some indecisive fighting the Regent for the last Ch'ing Emperor, then still a child, signed an edict of abdication.

The Chinese Republic

The Chinese Republic, which thus came into existence, was dedicated in theory to the principles of popular sovereignty and liberal democracy which the intelligentsia and young officers had imbibed from the West, but the reality of the new regime was something very different. Since the army had made the Revolution, effective power rested with the generals, and since revenue to pay the troops was raised on a provincial basis, the military governor of each province had an opportunity to exercise political power on his own. The masses of the people were bewildered and apathetic; they had lost faith in the old order of things, but the new ideas meant nothing to them. China was threatened with serious internal disorder and at the same time with the loss of the outer territories of the old empire, for Outer Mongolia and Tibet now declared themselves independent, claiming that their allegiance had been to the Manchu Dynasty and that they had no other ties with China. The Chinese garrisons in Outer Mongolia and Tibet were driven out, and the new Chinese Republic was unable to undertake the reconquest of these territories; it had its hands full with trying to restore the authority of the central government in the provinces of China itself. The leading personality of the new regime was Yuan Shih-k'ai, who, having abandoned the cause of the Ch'ing Dynasty, had been elected President of the Republic and proceeded to try to convert his office into a personal dictatorship. His real aim vas to restore the monarchy in his own person and found a new dynasty, but ıis control over the army was insufficient; he had himself proclaimed Emperor n 1915, but was overthrown by a revolt in which the republican intelli-gentsia combined with generals whose only motive was jealousy of Yuan. The elimination of Yuan and his death in 1916 left China without any out-tanding leader, and the forces of disintegration now gained the upper hand. The years from 1916 to 1928 are known as the 'war-lords period' because of he predominance of the provincial military governors who tore China apart vith their civil wars and intrigues; there was no longer a national army and he Government in Peking, composed of adherents of the strongest military action, ceased to exercise more than a nominal authority.

Sun Yat-sen and the Kuomintang

In opposition to the phantom government in Peking—which continued to be ecognized internationally as the legal government, since it was established in he capital—a government of the Kuomintang Party was set up at Canton n the extreme south of China under the leadership of Sun Yat-sen, who had played an important part, though a far from decisive one, in the Revolution of 1911. The Kuomintang was a party of liberal and progressive ideas drawing its support mainly from the commercial middle class in Canton and Shanghai and also from 'Overseas Chinese' in Singapore, San Francisco and elsewhere. As a prophet of republican democracy, Sun had supposed that China could pass directly from the bureaucratic absolutism of the Ch'ing to a political system on the American model; he was sadly disillusioned by what actually happened after 1911 and came to the conclusion that a period of tutelage' or party dictatorship would be necessary to re-unify China, sup-press the war-lords and establish an effective central administration before iberal democratic institutions could function in China. It was no simple natter, however, to undertake such a task, for the Kuomintang had no army of its own and was dependent on pacts with the local war-lords of south China. It was, above all, in the hope of obtaining military assistance that Sun vas finally induced to turn for support to the Government of Soviet Russia, although he was not himself a Communist nor was his party a Marxist one.

The key to this development lay in the international situation in which China was involved after the First World War. China took no direct part n the war, but its indirect effects were far-reaching. The absorption of the Western powers in the mutual slaughter in Europe left Japan free to act in the Far East, and in 1915 Japan addressed to China the notorious Twenty-one Demands, which, if accepted in full, would have turned China into a Japanese protectorate. With encouragement from the United States, China rejected some of the demands, but accepted others, including a provision for transfer to Japan of the Germany-leased territory of Kiaochow in Shantung, which had been captured by a Japanese expeditionary force soon after the outbreak of war. Japan's claim was confirmed by Britain and France in secret treaties in return for Japanese naval assistance against German sub-marines in the later stages of the war. After the end of the war, however, there was an intense nationalist agitation in China against the transfer of Kiaochow to Japan, and a delegation was sent to the Paris Peace Conference

—China having formally declared war on Germany—representing both the Peking and Canton Governments but acting less as a team of Government officials than as an agency of unofficial nationalist opinion. Britain and France supported Japan at the Conference; President Wilson protested at the secret treaties, but allowed the transfer of Kiaochow to be written into the Treaty of Versailles, which the Chinese delegation then refused to sign.

At the Washington Conference two years later Japan at length agreed to restore Kiaochow to China, but in the meantime Chinese sentiment had become extremely hostile not only towards Japan, but towards all the Western powers with the exception of the new Soviet Government of Russia, which had not taken part in the Paris Peace Conference and had demonstratively renounced as a matter of principle all extra-territorial rights and other concessions acquired by Tsarist Russia in China. Nationalist public opinion in China thus came to regard the new regime in Russia as China's only friend in opposition to Western and Japanese imperialism, and it was in these circumstances that the Chinese Communist party was founded in 1921. Its following was at first mainly in Shanghai and Canton, the cities where the Kuomintang was already most strongly established and where there were larger numbers of industrial workers than anywhere else in China. The Chinese Communists adhered to the orthodox doctrine of Marxism-Leninism which held that only the urban proletariat could make a socialist revolution and concentrated their efforts on winning the support of this class in the places where it existed. They also, however, in accordance with Lenin's principle of a worker-peasant alliance, extended their activity to the countryside where conditions were ripe for an agrarian revolt. To an increasing congestion of population on the land had been added oppressive taxation by the war-lords for the upkeep of their private armies and the rapacity of landlords who were the only source of credit for a peasantry living on the margin of subsistence. Among the peasant masses the preaching of Communism was unexpectedly successful, but as yet the party leadership had no inkling that the decisive action of the Chinese Communist Revolution was to take place entirely in rural areas.

While the Communists were building up their party in China the Soviet Government made direct contact with the Kuomintang. Joffe, its envoy to China, met Sun Yat-sen and agreed on terms of co-operation whereby the Soviet Union would render political and military assistance to the Canton government. In accordance with this agreement Michael Borodin was sent to Canton in the autumn of 1923 as a political adviser, and a little later General Galen (Blücher) with a team of Russian officers to train cadets for a Kuomintang party army at a military academy set up at Whampoa. The Kuomintang reached an agreement with the Chinese Communist party for a united front against the war-lords and foreign imperialism, and Communists were permitted to enrol individually as members of the Kuomintang. A certain Chiang Kai-shek was appointed Director of the Whampoa Academy with a Communist, Chou En-lai, as his deputy in charge of political education.

Chiang Kai-shek and the Kuomintang

Sun Yat-sen died in March 1925, and three months later an incident in Shanghai, when International Settlement police under the command of a British sergeant opened fire on rioting Chinese strikers from a Japanese textile factory, was used by the Kuomintang-Communist alliance to start a nation-wide agitation against British and Japanese imperialism. The foreign concessions in Canton were blockaded and Hong Kong was paralysed by strikes instigated from Canton. Meanwhile there was a struggle for power in succession to Sun within the Kuomintang and Chiang Kai-shek emerged as the supreme leader. In July 1926 he led the Kuomintang army, now officered by Russian-trained Whampoa cadets, northward from Canton to the Yangtse. It won a series of easy victories over the mercenary armies of the war-lords, the ardour and efficiency of the new Kuomintang military force being supplemented by the propaganda of the Communists which everywhere 'mobilized the masses' in support of the revolutionary drive. The Kuomintang captured Hankow, where the British Concession was overrun, and Nanking, where a number of foreigners were killed, and entered Shanghai, where British troops were landed to guard the International Settlement. The movement now reached a point of crisis. Further attacks on foreigners and their property would have involved open war with Britain and perhaps other Western nations. Chiang Kai-shek suspected that it was the object of the Russian advisers and the Communists to embroil him in such a war; he was also alarmed at the success of the Communists in 'mobilizing the masses' and feared that they would soon try to take over power from the Kuomintang. Moscow, on the other hand, wished to maintain the Kuomintang-Communist alliance as a means of pressure on Britain and Japan, and dissuaded the Chinese Communists from taking independent action. Chiang was thus able to move first, and in April 1927 he carried out a *coup d'état* against the Communists in Shanghai; this was repeated in other cities where the Communists had a following, so that the party was broken up and suppressed, with many of its members imprisoned or executed.

What survived from the wreck of the Communist movement was a peasant revolt which had broken out in remote rural areas of Kiangsi and Hunan provinces under the leadership of Mao Tse-tung, himself sprung from a Hunan peasant family. Mao had diverged from other Chinese Communist leaders in the importance he attached to the agrarian *jacquerie*; in a report he wrote in February 1927 he declared that the poorer peasants were providing seven-tenths of the forces of the revolution. The party leadership, however, was reluctant to accept a situation which was so different from the Russian model in which the proletariat had made the revolution in Petrograd and Moscow and the peasants had been only auxiliaries in the civil war. They kept on trying to capture cities and provide the revolution with its proper proletarian base. But all these attempts failed, while Mao's peasant guerillas held their own in the mountains of south China and a large area of southern Kiangsi was brought under a 'soviet 'administration.

The Kuomintang, after its break with the Communists, moved politically towards the right. It refrained from further direct attacks on foreign treaty rights in China and obtained international recognition as the *de jure* Government of China after its capture of Peking—which, however, it downgrade from its status as capital, making Nanking the new seat of government. I compromised with the war-lord system, allowing several of the provincia generals to retain a private military power on condition of acknowledgin the supremacy of the central government. All this was indeed an anti climax after the intense revolutionary impetus of 1926. But there had bee real progress; there was now a genuine national authority in China instead o the anarchy of the previous decade and a sense of purpose which had bee lacking in the freebooting generals who had made the history of the war-lor period. The Kuomintang aimed at creating an effective state administratio and building up a modern industry in China; in foreign policy it hope gradually to obtain revision of the 'unequal treaties' and get rid of extra territoriality and foreign leaseholds by various forms of pressure, but withou war.

Had twenty years of peace been granted to Chiang Kai-shek's government it might have achieved much in unifying and modernizing China and raisin the country's international status. But it had to cope with two great Japanes invasions, the first in 1931 which tore away Manchuria from China, and th second beginning in 1937 which brought vast areas of China from the Grea Wall in the north down to Canton and the island of Hainan in the sout under hostile military occupation. The loss of Manchuria deprived China o what was then its most industrially developed area; during the eight years o war which began in 1937 China was first partially, and then totally, blockade by sea and six of her seven largest cities were captured by the enemy. Agains these invaders, greatly superior in military organization and armaments China could only fight a war of 'resistance', retreating into the interior of th country and trying to exhaust the enemy by a protracted opposition an refusal to accept dictated terms of peace. Such a struggle involved immens suffering, devastation and disruption of normal life for the Chinese people and it was no wonder that the newly erected fabric of central government an reformed fiscal administration cracked under the strain. The currency wen into high inflation, and it was only possible to maintain armies in the field b allowing generals to requisition supplies in their respective 'war zones'— practice which inevitably revived the habits of war-lordism. The commercia middle classes of the larger cities, who had provided the liberal element i the Kuomintang, fell under Japanese occupation or became refugees; th government became dependent on the co-operation of the landlords fo carrying on its administration and its politics became increasingly reaction ary. Meanwhile in the Japanese-occupied areas the Kuomintang official either fled or collaborated with the enemy, and a political vacuum was thu created into which guerilla resistance forces could infiltrate. Since the Com munists were specialists in guerilla tactics, it was they who were able to tak advantage of this situation.

The Rise of Communism

From 1927 to 1937 the Communists, without ever being able to captur cities, had preserved a local independent state of their own, first in souther Kiangsi in south China, and then, after being driven out of that area by th

Kuomintang, in northern Shensi in the north-west, which they reached by the famous 'Long March'. This Communist state within China, complete with government and army, schools and even a university, was always confined to rural territory; having expropriated landlords for the benefit of the peasants, it had the support of the latter, but it controlled no industrial areas, and was dependent for its arms on the most primitive kind of production upplemented by captures from the Kuomintang or the Japanese. Such an agrarian regime was obviously far removed from the original Communist idea of an urban proletarian revolution, but it was held that since the Communist party was by definition the vanguard of the proletariat, peasants under Communist direction were really acting under the leadership of the proletariat even though the movement in the cities had almost ceased to exist. From this trange situation the idea later arose in the West that the Chinese Communists were not real Communists, but merely 'agrarian reformers'. But as far as their principles went they were orthodox Marxist-Leninists; their ruralism had been imposed on them by force of circumstances, not by their own choice. It did, however, have the effect of bringing to the top men such as Mao Tse-tung, who were best able to adapt themselves to the conditions imposed on the party by the course of events.

The civil war between the Kuomintang and the Communists went on simultaneously with the Japanese campaigns in Manchuria from 1931 to 1933, and after these were ended by the so-called Tangku Truce, Chiang Kai-shek concentrated his military forces against the Communists. But Japanese encroachments continued, and Chinese public opinion began to demand a cessation of the civil war and the formation of a national united front to resist Japan. On a visit to Sian at the end of 1936 Chiang Kai-shek was kidnapped by a local commander who insisted that he call off the struggle against the Communists and lead a united front. When Japan renewed the war in the summer of 1937 an agreement for joint action against the Japanese was reached by the two parties; operations by the Communist army were to be subject to orders from Chiang Kai-shek as supreme commander of all Chinese armed forces. In practice their operations were those of mutually distrustful allies rather than of components of a single national army, and t soon became evident to the Kuomintang that the war was working to the advantage of the Communists, because, as experienced guerillas, they were better able to infiltrate behind the Japanese lines. The Kuomintang, therefore,—or rather the Chinese Government headed by Chiang Kai-shek in its war-time capital of Chungking, in the west of China,—instituted a blockade of the Communists' territory to prevent them from obtaining supplies of arms. This met with strong objection from General Stilwell, who after the outbreak of war between Japan and America was sent by President Roosevelt as military adviser to Chiang Kai-shek. Stilwell wanted to send American arms to the Communists and use them for an offensive against the Japanese in north China; Chiang's opposition to the scheme culminated in a demand to Roosevelt for Stilwell's recall. Roosevelt complied and replaced Stilwell with another American general, Wedemeyer, who dropped the idea of arming the Communists.

China Policies of the U.S.A. and U.S.S.R.

The war against Japan was brought to an end, not by the Chinese themselves, who in spite of their obstinate resistance were incapable of driving the Japanese from their territory, but by the Americans, who had destroyed Japanese sea-power in the Pacific and finally brought Japan to surrender with two atomic bombs, and by the Russians, who overwhelmed the Japanese army in Manchuria in a brief campaign in the last week of the war. It was with the aid of these two powers that China was now to regain her lost territory and take the surrender of the Japanese forces which remained on her soil. The political aims of the two powers, however, were divergent, and neither was free from contradictions. The Americans provided shipping and transport aircraft to enable Chinese government troops to take over Nanking, Shanghai, Peking, Tientsin and other cities from the Japanese, thus also forestalling the Communists, who but for this logistical support for the Kuomintang might have reached them first. The Americans were not, on the other hand, willing to back the Chinese Government in a new civil war against the Communists and put pressure on it to form a political coalition with them. The Russians, for their part, were ready to give limited aid to the Communists but not to repudiate Chiang's regime as the legal Government of China; they turned over to the Communists the stocks of arms they had captured from the Japanese in Manchuria and thus greatly strengthened the Communist army, but they continued to negotiate with Chiang and concurred in the American idea of a coalition. In December 1945 President Truman sent General Marshall to China as his personal representative to mediate between the two sides in what was again developing into a civil war. His task was doomed to failure from the start, for both sides aimed at dictatorial power and neither had any trust in the other; the Marshall mission achieved nothing except to bring odium on America for uninvited interference in Chinese internal affairs. The civil war was renewed and after a period of deadlock ended in the collapse of the Kuomintang army and the decisive victory of the Communists. Chiang Kai-shek with the remnant of his army and a number of civilian Kuomintang supporters with their families took refuge in the island of Formosa, where they were for the moment safe, since the Communists had no fleet with which to pursue them. The whole mainland of China, however, submitted to Communist rule, and in October 1949 a new government, that of the Chinese People's Republic, was proclaimed in Peking. The Soviet Union hastened to extend *de jure* recognition to it, and Mao Tse-tung went to Moscow, where he concluded a treaty of military alliance with the Soviet Union.

The Korean War

Of the non-Communist powers Britain extended recognition after a brief interval, partly in accordance with the British practice of recognizing any government which appeared to have stable control of a nation's territory, and partly in the hope of preserving British commercial interests in China. The American Government would have followed suit but for a crisis in domestic politics. The American people had long been accustomed to regard China as a special friend and ally of the United States and were dismayed at the emergence of a new Communist China allied with Russia; they were critical of the Truman Administration for what was considered its failure to give adequate support to the government of Chiang Kai-shek—a failure which was widely believed to be due to pro-Communist influences in the State Department. President Truman, therefore, decided to postpone recognition of the new regime in China until after the mid-term Congressional elections in November of 1950, but in the meantime the Korean War broke out, and before the end of the year the United States and Communist China were engaged in large-scale hostilities. Korea, liberated from Japanese rule by the Allied victory in 1945, had been divided into American and Russian zones of military occupation pending the establishment of an independent Korean state; in the outcome a Communist government had been set up in the Russian zone and an anti-Communist one in the American, so that when the Russian and American forces withdrew, the two rival Korean factions were left confronting each other, the Communists being the better armed. In June 1950 the North Koreans attacked, and Truman took a decision to send American forces to the assistance of South Korea. Since the elections which had been held in South Korea had been supervised by the United Nations, South Korea was in a sense a ward of the latter, and a decision of the Security Council in the absence of the Soviet Union (which was boycotting Council meetings at the time) turned the aid to South Korea into a United Nations war, but although fifteen other nations sent contingents to take part in the war, the bulk of the troops committed—and the casualties incurred—were always American. As a supplement to the action being taken in Korea—regarded in America as a war for the containment of Communism—the American Government sent a fleet to protect Formosa against a threatened invasion from the Chinese mainland. Chiang Kai-shek's government was thus not only secured in its possession of Formosa, but remained in full diplomatic relations with the United States and with American support retained China's seat in the United Nations.

Communist China intervened in the Korean war after the North Korean forces had been decisively defeated by the United Nations army, which then advanced to the Yalu river separating Korea from Manchuria. The Chinese drove the United Nations army out of North Korea, but were unable to dislodge it from a fortified line established across the middle of the peninsula close to the parallel of latitude which had divided the former Russian and American occupation zones. After three years of fighting—which cost a million military casualties for the belligerents and the lives of a similar number of Korean civilians—the war was ended by an armistice, but was followed neither by a peace treaty nor by any reconciliation between Communist China and the United States. The Chinese Communists now regarded America as their mortal enemy, the conflicts which had arisen over Korea and Formosa being in line with the ideological view that America, as the strongest capitalist power, must be the principal foe of the 'socialist' world. The Americans, on their side, were embittered by the war and convinced that the new China would try to extend its power all over the Far East unless firmly held in check; American defensive alliances were concluded with Japan, South Korea and Formosa to safeguard them against Communist penetration or attack.

Consolidation of the Communist Regime

Internally the Korean war helped to consolidate the Communist regime ir China, for it enhanced Chinese military prestige and enabled the Govern ment to evoke patriotic emotions in the Chinese people over and above support for Communism; it also provided pretexts for a reign of terror ir which great numbers of former supporters of the Kuomintang were put to death as alleged agents of America. After the war the Communist Governmen took in hand the economic and social transformation of China in accordance with its principles. It had already brought the whole country—except for inaccessible Formosa—under a firm central control, and through its omni present party organization and the universal use of radio loud-speaker extended its directives and exhortations into every village. By ending the civil war it had enabled agriculture and industry to revive and it had stabi lized the currency; the war in Korea, which did not touch the territory o China itself or even its coastwise shipping—since the Americans in fear o Russian intervention had kept the war confined to Korea—did not reverse this progress. Socially the land reforms which the Communists had already carried out had eliminated the landlords as a class—and often physically destroyed them—but the Chinese bourgeoisie was not at first expropriated From 1954 onwards, however, new measures were undertaken. Plans were formulated for raising national productivity and carrying out the long over due industrialization of China in the shortest possible time. Together with the direction of the economy by the state to bring about rapid economic growth private business was to be nationalized and the peasants induced to merge their individual holdings of land into collective farms. These aims were vigorously pursued during the mid-fifties and met with remarkably little resistance; this success was mainly due to the tactical skill with which the measures were carried out. Owners of business enterprises received some compensation for their loss of their property, and the peasants were led on by stages to collectivization, the advantages of collective farming being demon strated by the fact that agricultural credits and other state facilities were available only to collectives.

The 'Hundred Flowers' and the 'Great Leap Forward'

The Communists had more trouble, however, with the intellectuals; these had been generally sympathetic to Communism in the days of Kuomintang rule, but their addiction to ideas of personal and academic freedom caused them to chafe at the authoritarian controls now imposed in every sphere of Chinese life. The use of techniques of 'brain-washing' had only a limited success in converting the educated class to Communism, and in an attempt to conciliate the intellectuals and obtain their co-operation Mao Tse-tung proclaimed a new era of freedom of speech known as the 'Hundred Flowers' movement. But this produced so much criticism of the party that the policy was reversed and the critics persecuted for 'rightism.' This reaction coincided with an economic crisis; bottlenecks had developed in industrial production and economic growth was being slowed down. The answer of the Com munists was to proclaim the 'Great Leap Forward' in which the mobiliza tion of China's immense man-power—and woman-power—for urgent conomic tasks was to make up for lack of capital and overcome all diffi-ulties. The Great Leap was urged on with propaganda which gave it all the motional accompaniments of a religious revival and the whole Chinese eople were stirred to extraordinary efforts. Groups of collectives were ombined to form 'communes', work was carried on under a kind of military iscipline, and steel was produced in backyard furnaces all over the country. ut the pace could not be kept up, and the neglect of agriculture for the sake f high-speed industrialization exacted its penalty when bad weather pro-uced crop failures in three successive years. The whole economic structure vas threatened by food shortages and precious foreign exchange had to be ised to buy grain abroad; priority had to be given to agriculture and new in-entives found for peasants to produce more. The Great Leap Forward ended n something of an anti-climax; its results were quite disproportionate to its romises and the efforts it exacted, yet the economy was gradually developing nd the time when China would be one of the great industrial nations was in ight.

Foreign Policy: Sino-Soviet and Sino-Indian Disputes

n foreign policy Communist China, without bettering its relations with merica, began to have trouble with its Russian ally from 1958 onwards. 'he Chinese suspected—and not without reason—that the Russians were eluctant to give China as much aid as they could, particularly in the nilitary field, because of a fear of the increase of Chinese power which would esult if the most numerous people in the world were to attain their full trength. They were also alarmed at Russian attempts under Khrushchev to eek a *rapprochement* with America because they were afraid that China would e left out of any deal that might thus be concluded. Further, the Chinese esented the Russian favours shown to India, which, as a bourgeois and non-ligned power, the Chinese considered to be a dangerous rival for influence 1 Asia. The Chinese expressed their sense of grievance and their anxieties by n ideological campaign designed to convince the world Communist move-nent that any Russian deal with America would be a betrayal of the Com-nunist cause, that 'imperialism' was incorrigible, and that Nehru was one of s stooges. The Russians replied by denunciations of 'dogmatism' and of hose who would provoke nuclear war by provocative policies. The quarrel ose to its height at the time of the Khrushchev-Eisenhower exchanges of 959–60, was allayed during the next year or so, and then flared up again in onnection with China's border disputes with India and the Chinese nilitary campaign against India in the autumn of 1962. In July 1963 an ttempt to resolve ideological difficulties by discussions between Russian and Chinese Communist Party representatives in Moscow failed completely, and 1 August Peking bitterly denounced the Nuclear Test Ban Treaty which ppeared to the Chinese to be an attempt to maintain an exclusive 'nuclear lub'. The Chinese press also revealed that Russia had promised to help China produce nuclear weapons but had gone back on the promise at the me of Khrushchev's visit to the United States in 1959. It was clear that vhatever the strains on the Chinese economy, and whatever China's weakness might still be in a conflict with a nuclear power, the rulers in Peking were resolved that China should play the part of a Great Power in world affairs and compensate for political isolation by a bold and vigorous self-confidence.

BIBLIOGRAPHY

Theodore H. E. Chen. *Thought Reform of the Chinese Intellectuals.* (Hong Kong Univ. Press, Hong Kong, 1960.)

H. G. Creel. *Chinese Thought from Confucius to Mao Tse-tung.* (Eyre and Spottiswoode, London, 1954.)

C. P. Fitzgerald. *China: A Short Cultural History.* (Cresset Press, London, revised ed., 1954.)

Geoffrey Hudson, Richard Lowenthal and Roderick MacFarquhar. *The Sino-Soviet Dispute.* Documents and Commentary. (*The China Quarterly*, London, 1961.)

Owen Lattimore. *The Inner Asian Frontiers of China.* (American Geographical Society, New York, 2nd ed., 1951.)

Mao Tse-tung on Guerilla Warfare. Translated with an Introduction by Samuel B. Griffith. (Cassell, London, 1962.)

Edwin O. Reischauer and John K. Fairbank. *East Asia: the Great Tradition.* (Allen and Unwin, London, 1961.)

Benjamin I. Schwartz. *Chinese Communism and the Rise of Mao.* (Harvard Univ. Press, Cambridge, Mass., 1951.)

Ssu-yu Teng and John K. Fairbank. *China's Response to the West. A Documentary Survey, 1839-1923.* (Harvard Univ. Press, Cambridge, Mass., 1954.)

BIOGRAPHICAL NOTE

GEOFFREY HUDSON. Fellow of All Souls College, Oxford 1926-54. Served in the Research Department of the Foreign Office 1939-46. Worked part-time on the editorial staff of *The Economist* 1946-54. Fellow and Director of Far Eastern Studies at St. Antony's College, Oxford, since 1954. Advisory Editor of *The China Quarterly* since 1960. Author of *Europe and China: a Survey of their Relations in History to 1800* (Edward Arnold, London, 1931); *The Far East in World Politics* (Oxford Univ. Press, London, 2nd. ed., 1939).

TAIWAN

by

RICHARD HARRIS

TAIWAN presents many problems according to whether it is seen through Chinese eyes (mainland Communist or Nationalist), through American eyes or through the eyes of those other countries concerned with which government to recognize and with the rival claims of each government to occupy China's seat in the United Nations, a seat which includes permanent membership of the Security Council as one of the wartime five Great Powers.

In the Chinese mind Taiwan is primarily one of those territories lost to Chinese control during a century of weakness and humiliation, a century whose memory they are anxious to expunge. To the government in Peking Taiwan remains the outstanding territory in this task of restoration. The attainment of this goal is hindered in part by the Nationalist Government with its rival claim to be the Government of China: in part by American policy which supports that claim militarily and politically. In the early stages after 1949 Peking's hostility to the remnant force of their Nationalist enemy was as great as to the Americans, but time has concentrated this hatred wholly on the Americans. Proposals made or hinted at by Peking for a resolution of this issue—the restoration of Taiwan to mainland sovereignty—have gradually got more and more tolerant to the point of accepting as a first step no more than a recognition of Peking's sovereignty, leaving the Nationalist Government intact, though of course demanding as a counterpart of this temporary independence of the Kuomintang Government, a total American withdrawal from this piece of Chinese territory in which the United States has no business to interfere.

From the Nationalist viewpoint the unity of Taiwan and the mainland is also a sacred fact. While the Nationalists remain recognized by the Americans and others as the Government of China their raison d'être has to be maintained by annual declarations of a forthcoming return to the mainland where the Chinese suffering under the Communist yoke would, they claim, welcome them. This is the view maintained by Chiang Kai-shek and his closest colleagues. Of the refugee mainland population of about two million now settled on the island the status quo is as much as they can hope for. The population of Taiwan who are Chinese, though alienated by circumstances—as the brief history following shows—have little interest in the national issue and would probably prefer to be independent. The claim to independence is made by Taiwanese exiled in Japan, tacitly supported by many in the island itself.

The outside world sees Taiwan in terms of recognition of one Chinese government as against another. But in this respect it is not to be compare with East and West Germany or other states divided in terms of the cold war For one thing the balance of territory under the control of each side is to small to sustain any Nationalist claim. In any case the situation in Chin was such in 1946-49 that Britain and other Western countries recognized th Communist Government set up in Peking in 1949. Many of the countrie which still in theory recognize the Nationalist Government in Taiwan as th Government of China do so in deference to American policy which has sinc the Korean war regarded a change by any government as something of a unfriendly act. The argument for the admission of the Peking Government t China's seat in the United Nations is a stronger and more active issue an of greater concern to the world than the issue of recognition, which is matter for each government to decide. It is the American policy over this rather than its choice of which government to recognize, which has cause such a prolonged crisis.

A separate issue is the future of the island itself, irrespective of its govern ment; the question whether it should be independent of the mainland—as it inhabitants would probably prefer—or whether it is inalienably part o China. International opinion on this varies from those who sustain Chian Kai-shek's claim to be the Government of China, through those who whil dismissing this claim and anxious to see the Peking Government seated in th U.N. would nevertheless argue that Taiwan has a claim for independence to those who support not merely Peking's admission to the U.N. but th return of Taiwan to control by the mainland as a just concomitant of suc admission. Even this last position would divide those who think this retur should be peacefully arranged by international agreement and those— confined to China's Communist allies—who accept the Chinese argumen that the return of Taiwan is their affair to be arranged as they think fit including if needed an invasion to drive Chiang Kai-shek from power.

Before analysing all these various opinions, the facts on Taiwan must b set out. How just is the claim that it is a part of China and what have bee the international events leading to the present position?

Historical Summary

Taiwan was not appreciably populated by Chinese or ruled as part of Chin before the 17th century. Its aboriginal inhabitants had been raided from tim to time, beginning as far back as the 7th century, from both the Chines mainland and, in later centuries, from Japan. The Portuguese gave it th name of Formosa; the Dutch set up trading stations and built forts in 1624 being driven there by trading competition from the Spaniards and Portugues who were then in occupation of the Philippines and Macao. The Dutch in turn were driven out by the powerful Chinese sealord Chen Ch'eng-kung He came of a Fukien family who created their own pocket of resistance to th conquest of China by the Manchus. He was known in Europe as Koxinga (from the local dialect pronunciation of his assumed name as a resistanc leader, Kuo Hsing-yeh). Heavily pressed on the mainland he and hi followers retreated to Taiwan as a base and thus considerably increased th Chinese emigrant population. For 20 years after 1662 he and his successors uled the island. Eventually the established Ch'ing (Manchu) Dynasty ended his exiled opposition and in 1683 Taiwan came under Chinese rule.

Emigration from Fukien province and to a less extent from Kuangtung gradually filled up the island with Chinese settlers during the following centuries—a period during which it was administered loosely as a prefecture of Fukien. It was not until 1885 that the island became a Chinese province and not merely an adjunct of Fukien across the straits. Japanese aggression meanwhile had grown and concentrated on the island. After the war against China of 1894-95 the island was ceded to Japan. Under Japanese rule it was developed through improved agriculture and its inhabitants began to enjoy higher standards of living than those of the mainland. But they were of course Chinese, speaking the non-Mandarin minority dialects of Fukien province, even though by 1945 they had been somewhat alienated by time and circumstance from their Chinese past.

The present population is 11 million of whom only about 200,000 of aboriginal stock remain.

Under the Cairo declaration of 1943 it was agreed that all territories occupied by Japan since 1894 should be given up. This was formalized in the Potsdam agreement in 1945 where it was laid down that Taiwan should be returned to the Republic of China. After the Japanese surrender the island therefore returned to the administration of the Nationalist Government under a provincial governor. If anything Taiwan suffered even more than the mainland from the exactions and misrule of these post-war years, though in the early stages there was some welcome from the Taiwanese for the mainland Chinese as liberators from Japanese rule. This soon changed when prominent Taiwanese were treated as collaborators, assets were seized and made Government monopolies, and the economy of the island quickly reduced to ruin by carpet-bagging mainland officials. In February, 1947, the despairing Taiwanese broke out in revolt but the provincial governor gave an assurance of reforms. A month later, when he had got sufficient reinforcements from the mainland, the leaders of the revolt were massacred and opposition was ruthlessly suppressed throughout the island; in all some ten thousand Taiwanese were killed. After American protests a new provincial governor was appointed and some reforms were introduced. In 1948, Chiang Kai-shek began to prepare the island as a retreat for his government and sent General Chen Cheng as governor. Martial law was re-established and members of the left-wing opposition were arrested and executed. While temporarily stepping down from the Chinese Presidency Chiang Kai-shek transferred assets to the island, including American military aid, and himself moved there in 1949, the Nationalist Government of China formally establishing itself in December of that year. Although American economic aid continued, in accordance with programmes already initiated, military aid declined with the end of the civil war on the mainland. Hainan island fell to the Communists in April, 1950 and it was expected that an assault on Taiwan would soon follow. In addition the Nationalists had retained control of some islands off the mainland, the most important being Quemoy and Matsu. A hastily mounted assault on the former had already been beaten off at the end of 1949 when Communist armies were pushing southwards. In January 1950 President

Truman declined any further involvement in the Chinese civil war and refused any further military aid. Chiang Kai-shek's precarious position was suddenly transformed in 1950 after the outbreak of the Korean war when President Truman ordered the American Seventh Fleet to prevent any attack on Taiwan from the mainland, at the same time ordering the Nationalists on the island to cease attacks on the mainland. He declared that the legal status of Taiwan must await a peace treaty with Japan. Although in theory this move was intended to be temporary, American military, political and economic commitment to the island and the chastened Nationalist Government steadily grew. A military advisory group was sent in 1951, pressures for reform were more readily accepted than they had been on the mainland and gradually the island's economy was restored. Continued recognition of the Nationalist Government as the Government of China was reaffirmed by Dean Rusk, Assistant Secretary of State, in May, 1951. In 1952 President Eisenhower's new administration removed the restriction that had been put on Nationalist attacks on the mainland (though in the form of minor guerilla raids these had never ceased).

At the San Francisco conference of 1951 (to which neither the Peking nor Taiwan Governments were invited as participants) a peace treaty was signed with Japan by the Western powers and in it Japan renounced all rights to Taiwan. Later a subsidiary peace treaty was signed between Japan and the Nationalist Chinese Government, though this did not cede any specified legal title to the island. In December, 1954 a further measure of American alliance was a mutual security pact signed with the Nationalist Government, thereby ensuring American defence of the island (and the subsidiary Pescadores islands near the west coast) against any attack from the mainland. Heavy shelling attacks on Quemoy and Matsu from the mainland occurred in September, 1954 and again in October, 1958. American statements at the latter time implied that the defence of these offshore islands might be undertaken by American forces only if such an attack was considered to be preliminary to an attack on Taiwan itself. But apart from this ambiguous position no American commitment to defend these islands has been made.

Since the signing of the security pact in 1954 American military aid to the Nationalist army has given it modern equipment and efficient training. In spite of the Sino-American ambassadorial talks which began in 1955 and have since continued in Warsaw, no agreement has been reached on the Taiwan issue which has been one item on the agenda. The Chinese argue that Taiwan being part of China any action there is an internal Chinese matter and that they cannot give an undertaking not to use force in a matter in which the United States has no rightful part.

Any change in the status of Taiwan will arise from one of two things: a change in American policy or a vote in the United Nations giving China's seat to the Peking Government.

Taiwan at the United Nations

Some change in American policy was foreshadowed with the election of President Kennedy but the impetus fell away, and under President Johnson's administration American involvement in South Vietnam precluded any possibility, in American eyes, of a new policy towards Peking. This may, of course, be forced on the United States if support for the administration of the Peking Government at the United Nations gains a majority. The United States had until 1961 always postponed discussion of the China issue at the United Nations by means of a moratorium on which it was able to get a majority vote. In 1961—perhaps foreseeing that a majority vote would no longer be possible—the decision was taken to allow discussion of the issue, but to regard it as 'an important matter' thus requiring a two-thirds majority for any change. The procedural motion to define the issue as important was passed by 61 to 34 with 7 abstentions (Britain voting with the majority). A Soviet resolution was then submitted coupling admission of Peking with the expulsion of the Taiwan Government from the United Nations. This won 37 votes against 48 with 19 abstentions. A similar resolution, amended by neutral countries to cover only the admission of Peking, also failed to be passed. Britain voted in favour of both resolutions. The voting in the second case was 21 for, 41 against and 39 abstaining. (Since the latter resolution made no mention of Taiwan, the Communist bloc countries all abstained.)

Early in 1965 shifts of recognition by some of the smaller African states had almost brought support for Peking level with support for the Nationalist Government in Taiwan but the postponement of the United Nations General Assembly prevented the matter being brought to the vote.

If and when a vote for the admission of Peking's representation looks like gaining the required two-thirds majority the future of the Nationalist Government will then become a live issue. The admission of the Peking representative would not in itself demand a settlement of the Taiwan issue but a solution much canvassed in the United States has come to be known as the 'two Chinas' policy. The aim is to have both governments in the United Nations leaving the territorial status quo. The refusal of both governments to entertain it makes this policy highly unreal. If Peking's representative were admitted to the United Nations the possibilities would then be:

The dismissal of the Nationalist Government from the United Nations, thereby reversing the situation that has obtained for the past 13 years. This would not mean any alteration in Taiwan's status though it is probable that many countries now recognizing Chiang Kai-shek's government as the Government of China would switch to recognition of Peking.

Or: a seat in the General Assembly could be reserved for the Taiwan Government—described as China—while giving the permanent seat on the Security Council to the Peking Government. (This amounts to the 'two Chinas' solution.)

Or: a seat in the General Assembly could be reserved for the Taiwan Government described as such and not as China. (This would probably be supported by many neutralist countries which would not accept the 'two Chinas' solution.)

If present attitudes are maintained, the Communist Government in Peking would not take its seat in the Security Council unless the Nationalist Government ceased to be represented at all. Equally the Nationalist Government would refuse a seat in the General Assembly if the Communists were admitted to the Security Council and would certainly refuse if they were described as Taiwan and not as China. No simple solution to the problem of United Nations seating is therefore likely, in so far as any fulfilment of the United Nations' declared wishes are concerned; nor is there any policy that looks like getting the necessary majority in the United Nations.

Apart from the issue as seen from the United Nations, however, we must consider as a separate political question the future of the Nationalist Government of Chiang Kai-shek. Once its claim to be the Government of China is no longer admitted by the United Nations and the majority of governments now so recognizing it, then its future as the Government of Taiwan naturally will come up for consideration. Among its mainland supporters there are no doubt those who would be willing to accept a share in ruling an independent Taiwan, though Chiang Kai-shek personally would refuse such a reduction of his status. But if an independent Taiwan was agreed to then the indigenous population would certainly press their claim to elect or nominate that government from among their own number. In any case, in the event of Chiang Kai-shek's death or retirement we may expect to see a gradual loosening of the cohesion of the Nationalist (Kuomintang) party and a gradual taking over of power by Taiwanese.

American Policy Towards Taiwan

The difficulty of the issue really stems from American policy towards China, which has in the past been highly emotional and which looks on China increasingly as the source of all revolutionary disorder in Asia. While these conditions continue, a wholly new policy towards China is unlikely. There has, however, in recent years been a distinct decline in interest in the Nationalist Government in Taiwan as a factor in this policy. During Mr. Dulles' days it was admitted that Chiang Kai-shek was indeed maintained as an alternative government which might regain power one day on the mainland, and thus Peking could argue that a government dedicated to its overthrow was militarily supported by the United States. This threat had some substance in the years after the Korean war but it is no longer a reality on either side now. But there can be no settlement of the Taiwan issue while the status quo is maintained. American policy can only change step by step and the first step to break up the jam would be the withdrawal of American recognition from Chiang Kai-shek's government as the Government of China while recognizing its continued authority in Taiwan. This would open the way eventually for a more widely supported government to emerge on the island and need not affect any American decision over the recognition of Peking.

Otherwise the prospect is that with the death of Chiang Kai-shek the break-up of the Kuomintang as a party would begin; the prospect of any return to the mainland would then be formally and not merely tacitly dropped. At the same time there might be renewed offers from the mainland for an accommodation in the knowledge that a struggle for power in the KMT could revolve round such factors. Such tensions certainly exist in the KMT party but circumstances have not been favourable for the mainland's claim and it is impossible to tell what following it might be able to gather from the ranks of a crumbling Kuomintang. Equally there is no means of estimating what sympathy for a link with the mainland exists among the native Taiwanese. Nationalist rule has at least had the effect of ending their alienation from Chinese ways under Japanese rule. The national language (Kuo Yu or Mandarin) is taught in schools and the sense of Chinese nationalism is inculcated. But even with this advantage, conditions on the mainland both political and economic must confine support for their case to such few dedicated Communists as survive underground in Taiwan.

Certainly while China's present leaders remain there will be no dropping of the Taiwan issue. The determination to restore it to Peking's rule will be unaltered. On the other hand a change in Taiwan towards regarding Taiwan as Taiwan and not as a part of China could result from the retirement or death of Chiang Kai-shek or a change in American policy.

BIBLIOGRAPHY

Mark Mancall (ed.). *Formosa Today.* (Pall Mall Press, London, 1964.)
Robert P. Newman. *Recognition of Communist China?* (Macmillan, New York, 1961.)

BIOGRAPHICAL NOTE

RICHARD HARRIS. B. 1914 in China; lived there until 1928. Returned to China on war service, 1945; with British Embassy in China, 1947-50; joined *The Times* as correspondent in Hong Kong 1951-53, and Singapore 1953-55. Since 1955 leader-writer on Asian affairs on *The Times* editorial staff in London. Author of *Independence and After* (Oxford Univ. Press, London. 1962). Has also taken part in broadcasting and television on Asian subjects.

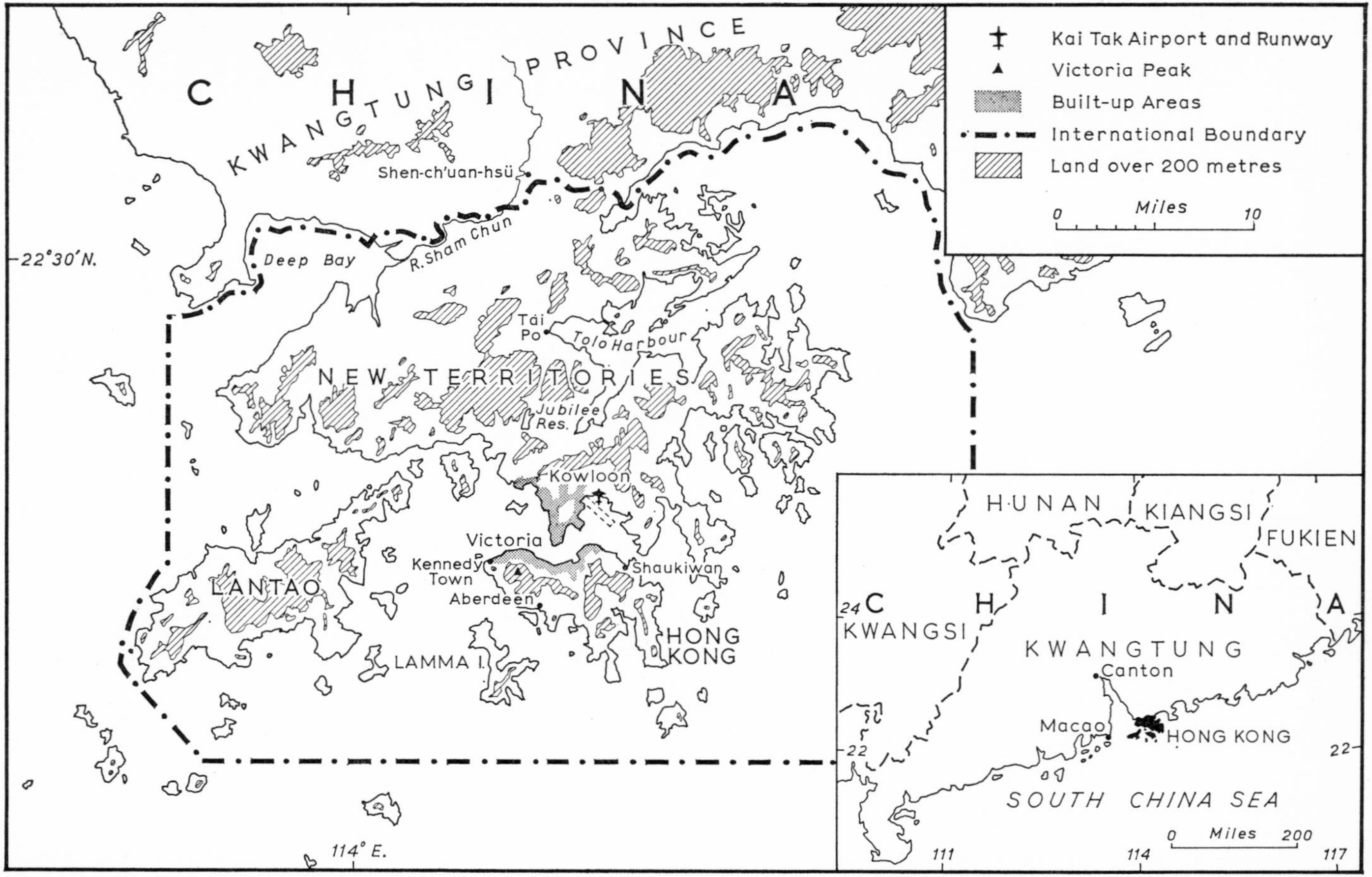

Kai Tak Airport and Runway
Victoria Peak
Built-up Areas
International Boundary
Land over 200 metres
0 Miles 10
CHINA
KWANGTUNG PROVINCE
Shen-ch'uan-hsü
R. Sham Chun
Deep Bay
22°30′N.
Tai Po
Tolo Harbour
NEW TERRITORIES
Jubilee Res.
Kowloon
Victoria
Kennedy Town
Shaukiwan
Aberdeen
LANTAO
LAMMA I.
HONG KONG
114° E.
HUNAN
KIANGSI
FUKIEN
KWANGSI
KWANGTUNG
Canton
Macao
HONG KONG
SOUTH CHINA SEA
0 Miles 200
24
22
111
114
117

HONG KONG

by

W. A. C. ADIE

Origin

Hong Kong sprang into being out of the clash between two worlds—Europe and China—which had developed civilizations that were self-sufficient, but so different that each regarded the other more or less as barbarians. The declining Manchu Dynasty was concerned to insulate its alien Chinese subjects from any contact with other foreigners, for fear that new ideas might subvert them. At the same time, the Emperors and their mandarins clung to an unrealistic, sinocentric view of the world. They could not conceive of the existence of independent foreign states with which diplomatic relations on a basis of equality could be possible, or trade relations desirable. Chien Lung wrote to George III that 'Our dynasty's majestic virtue has penetrated every country under Heaven, and kings of all nations have offered their costly tribute by land and sea . . . we possess all things'.

Although the Portuguese were allowed to settle in Macao in 1557, the main representatives of Europe eventually became the British, whose East India Company set up a trading post in Canton in 1715. Their ideology, as expressed by men like Wilberforce and Adam Smith, could not be reconciled with the feudal outlook of a Chien Lung; they were convinced that Christianity and commerce were the true creators of liberty and welfare for all races. But after 1757, foreign traders in China were confined to a sort of ghetto in Canton under severe restrictions—for example, no one was allowed to teach them Chinese on pain of death. In fact, although the Manchu Government was able to frustrate diplomatic and cultural contacts, it could not prevent the spontaneous growth of commercial intercourse, which in the circumstances largely took the form of blatant smuggling with the connivance of the very officials who were supposed to restrict the foreigners' activities. After the expiry of the East India Company's monopoly of the China trade in 1834, the British Government became seriously concerned to find some way of normalizing the situation in Canton and controlling its own subjects' behaviour. But Lord Napier's attempt to establish contact with the Manchu authorities was frustrated, like all previous attempts, owing to their unrealistic beliefs about the world as described above. Shortly after this, the Emperor sent down the energetic and honest Commissioner Lin Tse-hsu, who drove the British out of Canton and Macao; they took refuge in Hong Kong and fighting broke out, as a result of which negotiations were at last opened with the Manchu authorities. The evidence indicates that it was Keshen, their representative, who suggested the cession of

Hong Kong to Britain; his motives are uncertain, but Elliott, on the British side, explained his own as follows: 'The palpable impossibility of trusting our Merchants at Canton and the utter hopelessness of finding efficient and avowed protection or liberal arrangements at Macao have cast upon me the absolute necessity of providing a secure seat for the trade'—and this meant establishing a colony in Hong Kong. The plenipotentiaries agreed to this on 20th January, 1841 and a few days later the foundation of the Colony was proclaimed. However, neither side accepted the agreement, and hostilities continued.

Even so, the development of the settlement there was carried on with such energy by those on the spot that London eventually abandoned its discouraging attitude, the cession to Britain being confirmed by the Treaty of Nanking, which ended the war. The traumatic effects of defeat in this war on Chinese national pride cannot be overestimated; it has always been played up in both Communist and Nationalist anti-foreign propaganda as the unjust and aggressive 'Opium War', and it was widely so condemned in Britain too; in fact, to pretend that opium was the issue at stake is as naïve as to say that the American War of Independence was fought over tea. But the attitude of many Chinese and others towards Hong Kong is undoubtedly affected by such emotive connotations to this day.

Population and Land Problems

From such an inauspicious beginning, Hong Kong has grown to be a modern city state of three millions—more than the population of New Zealand—with flourishing industries and high standards of public administration and welfare, in spite of the fact that old-fashioned *laissez-faire* capitalism and sheer Victorian 'colonialism' are its twin foundation-stones.

To maintain its large population, Hong Kong disposes of a land area of only 398¼ square miles, the greater part of which consists of steep hillsides which provide little beyond beautiful scenery. Many of the paradoxes of Hong Kong stem from the fact that it was not originally intended to be a colony in the usual sense of the word, the influx of population being unforeseen. Further complications arise from the fact that 365½ square miles of its area—the New Territories, on the mainland—are only held on a 99-year lease granted by the Manchu Emperor on July 1st, 1898, although they are very important for the colony's life. Almost all possible land in the New Territories (about 50 square miles) is under intensive cultivation, and in the last few years new industrial towns have been built there, partly on land reclaimed by tipping hills into the sea. Both in the city of Victoria on Hong Kong island and in Kowloon, which faces it across the harbour, there has been a spectacular building boom since the war; owing to the shortage of land the ultra-modern blocks of flats, hotels, banks and offices must either cling to the cliffs or tower up from the strip of land reclaimed from the harbour. About 500,000 people, many of them immigrants from China, had been rehoused in eleven Government-built resettlement estates by the end of 1962 and another 500,000 will be rehoused by 1967. In 1962 the Government adopted a 10-year plan to build flats for more than 150,000. Nevertheless, many still live in improvised shacks on the hillsides or on the roofs of large buildings. Although the annual value of agricultural production is HK $200,000,000 or more, and of fisheries HK $60,000,000, much of the food must be imported from China, and under an agreement signed in November, 1960, China also sells 5,000 million gallons of water a year to Hong Kong. The provision of an adequate water supply has always been difficult because there are no large rivers or underground springs. At present, the reservoirs can store 10,500 gallons of rainwater, and when the building programme now underway is completed, conventional sources of supply will be pretty well exhausted and the use of nuclear power to distil sea-water may have to be considered. Apart from the influx of refugees, Hong Kong's birth rate is the second highest in Asia, at 32·8 per 1,000.

Hong Kong's Industrial Revolution

At the outbreak of World War II, Hong Kong's population was estimated at 1,600,000, of whom about a quarter were sleeping on the streets. Japanese occupation brought it down to about 600,000 but by the end of 1950 it had risen to 2,360,000 again.

Next year the Korean War trade boom came to an end, and the embargo on export of strategic goods to China dealt a severe blow at Hong Kong's traditional entrepot trade; trade with China was also considerably reduced because of the Chinese Government's own decision to cut imports of consumer goods, and import capital goods mainly from the Soviet bloc.

As a result, the refugees could not find employment in the declining entrepot trade, while primary production—agriculture and fisheries and a little mining—could only absorb a few. But among them were many businessmen from Shanghai and Canton who brought with them their capital and experience. Thus, a new 'entrepreneurial élite', as described by W. W. Rostow, arrived ready-made to help prepare the 'take-off into economic growth' which all underdeveloped countries dream of. The necessary preconditions for industrialization—efficient administration and financial arrangements, an adequate infrastructure of communications, public utilities, education and welfare services, port facilities, the shipbuilding industry and so forth—had already been provided.

Among the factors contributing to Hong Kong's spectacular economic growth must be noted, first of all, the high quality of the managerial and labour force and the rarity of industrial unrest. This may be partly owing to the fact that the trade union movement is split between Communists and Nationalists, but is mainly due to some characteristics of Chinese social structure, such as the prevalence of family firms and of the recruitment of the foreman's own clansmen as workers. Such factors also tend to limit bureaucratic wastefulness in business, and to reinforce the effects of traditional Chinese thrift, industriousness and skill. Savings have been high, and apart from remittances to relatives in China they have usually been ploughed back into equipment for further production. Compared to private capital formed locally or transferred from unsettled areas abroad, the grants from the Colonial Development and Welfare Fund have been negligible. Hong Kong has received no 'aid' under the Colombo plan, or any other such scheme.

A most important factor, however, has been the survival of *laissez-faire* capitalism in Hong Kong owing to its origin as a free port; while some of the inherent evils of capitalism have been mitigated by the Chinese social system or by Government action, economic planning and controls have been almost non-existent, and the much-maligned profit motive has reigned supreme.

The Problem of the Refugees

At the last census, in March 1961, the population was found to be 3,133,131, over 99 per cent of whom were Chinese; what has the industrial revolution done for them? Studies carried out by economists have shown that the standard of living of the average worker, low as it still is, is far higher than in mainland China (where industrialization started at about the same time) and compares favourably with other developing countries. The workers themselves evidently prefer Hong Kong, though they could return to China any time. Many of those who did leave to help 'build socialism' there have since trickled back to Hong Kong. It is still easy to find squatters without proper houses, and almost as easy to find people who look underfed; but this is not the fault of the Hong Kong Government, which has made superhuman efforts to keep up with the influx of refugees, and has resettled many hundreds of thousands in modern multi-storey blocks during the last few years.

When the island was ceded, a supplementary treaty provided that all Chinese would have unrestricted access to it; moreover the status of Chinese residents in Hong Kong has all along been ambiguous, since according to the Chinese principle of *ius sanguinis* they remain Chinese nationals even though they may be, from the British point of view, citizens of the United Kingdom and colonies by birth. This situation has caused many complications; in May, 1950 the Government was finally compelled to restrict entry from the mainland, except for local traffic to and from Kwangtung: China immediately protested. When a relaxation was tried in 1956, control had to be reimposed after three months because the inflow was again getting out of hand. An official quota of fifty a day is still allowed in. In May, 1962 the Canton authorities relaxed their own border controls, and in a few days about 50,000 had crossed over illegally. If the flow had been encouraged, it would have swamped the Colony's resources entirely; for one thing, the precarious water situation was emphasized a few days later when the Chinese were obliged by the drought to cut off the water they were supplying across the border. Most of the escapees had to be sent back.

The Future

Although, in theory, the New Territories will revert to China in 1997, leaving only the ceded territory of Kowloon ($3\frac{1}{4}$ square miles) and Hong Kong island, building and investment continue apace and few appear to think that far ahead. At present, Hong Kongites seem more worried about the limitations lately imposed by various countries on the imports of Hong Kong-manufactured goods, especially textiles.

Though Hong Kong's unique situation has so far precluded the normal colonial development towards self-government, it would seem that some political provision must be worked out to regularize its continued existence, perhaps as a member of a South-East Asian Federation and/or under international guarantee. Peking would probably not wish, for some time to come, to lose such a fruitful source of foreign exchange; while Hong Kong's potentialities as a 'shop window' of an alternative way of life, and for bridging the present artificial and dangerous political, cultural and ideological gulf which again yawns between China and the rest of the world could, if properly handled, prove increasingly important for world peace in the coming years—whether or not China's efforts to achieve Great (and nuclear) Power status are crowned with rapid success. It must be noted that by proposing the establishment of a Chinese Consulate in Hong Kong, Peking has clearly recognized British sovereignty; though since such a Consulate could claim authority over the majority of the inhabitants, these proposals have so far been turned down.

The interests of the world at large require that Hong Kong should on the one hand receive adequate outside assistance in solving its economic problems, and on the other, that the anomalies in its status, and that of its residents, should be removed by suitable international arrangements and internal political development. Three million Chinese demonstrating the arts of democratic self-government might give Asia an example in the political field, which would be even more instructive and valuable than Hong Kong's existing economic success.

BIBLIOGRAPHY

G. C. Allen and A. G. Donnithorne. *Western Enterprise in Far Eastern Economic Development.* (Allen and Unwin, London, 1954.)

Sir Charles Collins. *Public Administration in Hong Kong.* (Royal Institute of International Affairs, London, 1952.)

Maurice Collis. *Foreign Mud.* (Faber and Faber, London, 1946.)

S. G. Davis. *Hong Kong in its Geographical Setting.* (Collins, London, 1949.)

G. B. Endacott. *A History of Hong Kong.* (Oxford Univ. Press, London, 1958.)

E. Hambro. *Hong Kong Refugees Survey Mission.* (Report to the UN High Commissioner for Refugees.) (Leyden, 1955.)

E. R. Hughes. *The Invasion of China by the Western World.* (A. and C. Black, London, 1937.)

E. V. G. Kiernan. *British Diplomacy in China 1880-85.* (University Press, Cambridge, 1939.)

Sir F. Lugard. *Memorandum regarding the restrictions of opium in Hong Kong and China.* (Hong Kong, 1908.)

E. Luard. *Britain and China.* (Chatto and Windus, London, 1962).

A. Mills. *British Rule in Eastern Asia.* (Humphrey Milford, London, 1942.)

M. Perham. *Lugard, The Years of Authority, 1898-1945.* (Collins, London, 1960.)

G. R. Sayer. *Hong Kong: Birth, Adolescence and Coming of Age.* (Oxford Univ. Press, London, 1937.)

E. F. Szczepanik. *The Economic Growth of Hong Kong.* (Oxford Univ. Press, London and Hong Kong Univ. Press, Hong Kong, 1958.)

A. Waley. *The Opium War Through Chinese Eyes.* (Allen and Unwin, London, 1958.)

See also Hong Kong Government Annual Reports. (H.M. Stationery Office, London or Government Publications Bureau, Hong Kong.)

BIOGRAPHICAL NOTE

W. A. C. Adie, M.A. Formerly worked on Far Eastern and South-East Asian affairs at the Foreign Office and at posts in the area. Now engaged in research on recent and contemporary history of China. Author of articles in *China Quarterly*, *Political Quarterly*, *Political Studies*, etc. (London) and member of the Royal Institute of International Affairs Working Group on China and the World.

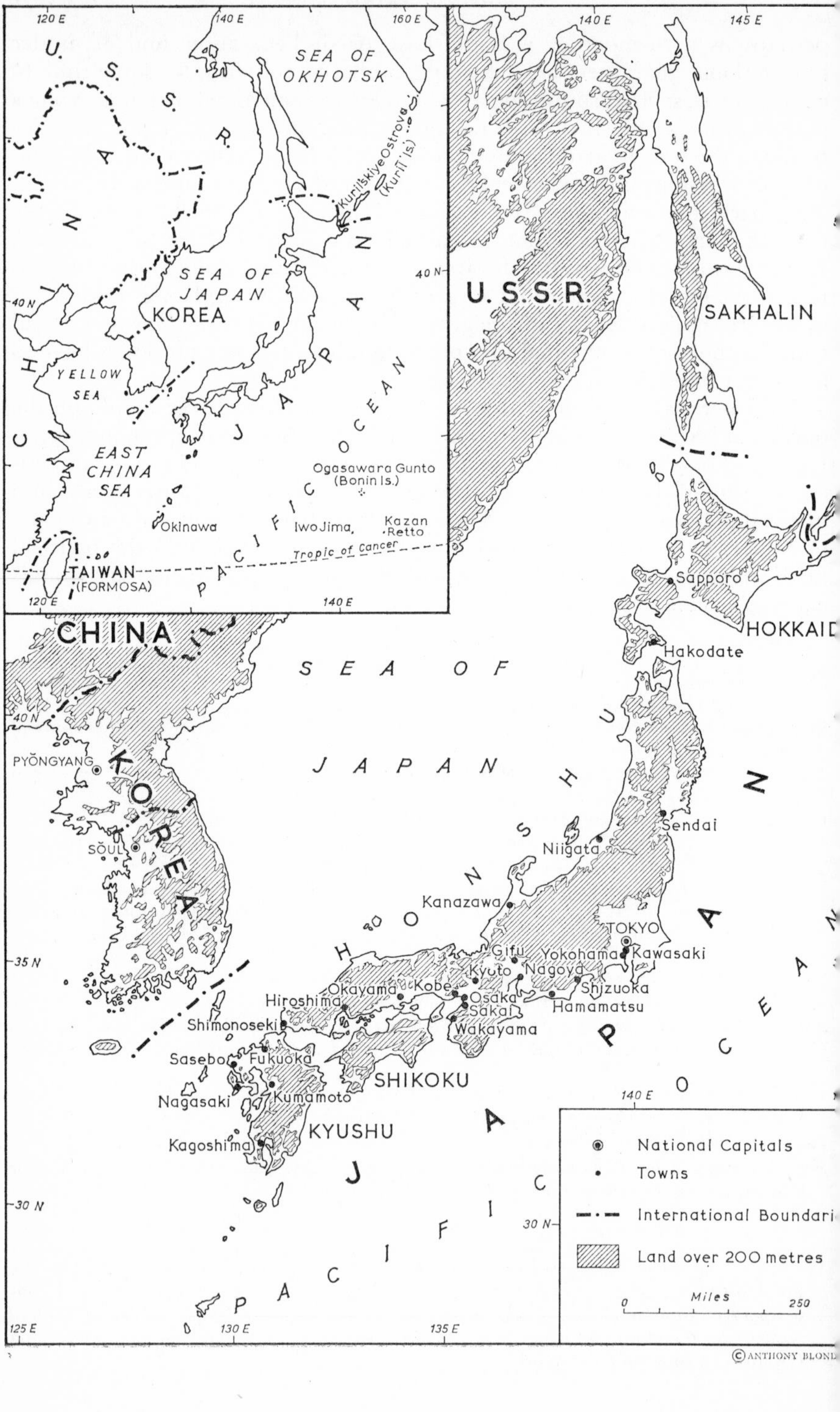

U.S.S.R.

SEA OF
OKHOTSK

Kurilskiye Ostrova
(Kuril is.)

SEA OF
JAPAN

KOREA

YELLOW
SEA

EAST
CHINA
SEA

Okinawa

Ogasawara Gunto
(Bonin Is.)

Iwo Jima

Kazan
Retto

Tropic of Cancer

TAIWAN
(FORMOSA)

PACIFIC OCEAN

120 E 140 E 160 E

40 N

40 N

120 E

140 E

U.S.S.R.

SAKHALIN

140 E 145 E

Sapporo

HOKKAIDO

Hakodate

CHINA

SEA OF

JAPAN

PYŎNGYANG

KOREA

SŎUL

Sendai

Niigata

Kanazawa

Gifu

TOKYO

Yokohama

Kawasaki

Kyoto

Nagoya

Osaka

Shizuoka

Kobe

Hamamatsu

Okayama

Sakai

Hiroshima

Wakayama

Shimonoseki

SHIKOKU

Sasebo

Fukuoka

Nagasaki

Kumamoto

KYUSHU

Kagoshima

HONSHU

JAPAN

PACIFIC OCEAN

40 N

35 N

30 N

30 N

125 E 130 E 135 E

140 E

	National Capitals
•	Towns
—·—·—	International Boundaries
▨	Land over 200 metres

Miles

0 250

© ANTHONY BLOND

JAPAN

by

RICHARD STORRY

Early History

The remote ancestors of the present inhabitants of the four major and nearly 3,000 minor islands of Japan almost certainly came from the mainland of Asia; from China, Manchuria, and Korea. It may be that there was also some immigration from the region of South-East Asia. But no records exist of these early movements of peoples. There is only a substantial and elaborate body of myths, suggesting that invaders from overseas gradually supplanted the existing inhabitants of Japan, the Ainu (of whom a few descendants survive in the northern island of Hokkaido).

Mythology alleged that the Japanese islands were created by the gods; that the grandson of the sun goddess came down, at her command, to rule Japan; that he was the progenitor of a line of semi-deities destined to be the Emperors of Japan, his own great-grandson being the first. Nothing more need be said about such legends, except to note two things: first, that this mythology was intimately connected with a cult of the sun; secondly, that the myths of national origin were taught in Japanese schools as factual history until soon after the end of the Pacific War, in 1945. Japanese nationalist sentiment rested squarely on a belief in this mythology; and for anyone to express public disbelief in it could lead to a popular outcry and, occasionally, to unpleasant consequences to the person concerned.

Japan, an intensely mountainous country, has two important plains. One is in the east, in what is known as the Kanto area. Here today are to be found Tokyo—the largest city in the world—and the conurbations of Yokohama and Kawasaki. The other main plain is in the west, in what is called the Kansai region, at the head of the Inland Sea. This area, in which have grown up the cities of Kyoto, Osaka, and Kobe, is the heartland of the historical Empire. The ancient capitals, changing with every new Emperor, were all in this Kansai area. A permanent capital was established in A.D. 794 at Heian-kyo, later to be known as Miyako or Kyoto. This city remained, in name at any rate, the metropolis until 1868.

In early times it was natural that the Japanese should have been profoundly impressed by the culture of China, the country that represented the very acme of civilization and power in the Asian world. Two importations from China deserve special mention—the ideographic script and the Buddhist religion. The former gave structure and style to the spoken language, although through the years the Japanese evolved syllabic ideographs of their own. Buddhism, introduced about the middle of the 6th century, dazzled minds and hearts with the range of its metaphysical beliefs and the colour and variety of its artistic traditions. All the same, the Buddhist faith, even when patronized by the Throne, did not supplant the indigenous religion of the Japanese, namely Shinto, bound up as this was with the myths surrounding the creation of Japan and the establishment of the Imperial dynasty.

Confucianism, too, entered Japan, with profound effects upon the thought and behaviour of succeeding generations. Chinese ideas of government, like so much that came into Japan from abroad, were remoulded along distinctively Japanese lines. For example, it was a basic concept among the Chinese that their Emperor enjoyed the favour of Heaven only so long as his rule was virtuous. If Emperors became vicious and incompetent, then others had the right to overthrow them. Thus the sometimes bloody changes of dynasty were justified in the eyes of sages and people alike. The Japanese, however, never saw their own hereditary sovereigns in this light. The Emperor of Japan was the Son of Heaven by virtue of divine descent. He could not fail to be virtuous by the very nature of his unique inheritance. So any idea of overthrowing the traditional line of Emperors and replacing it by another was so impious as to be almost unthinkable.

In practice, only very few Emperors of Japan exercised any real governmental powers. From the 8th century to the 12th these were in the hands of a gifted family of courtiers, the Fujiwara. From the 12th century until more than half-way through the 19th, government was carried on, in the Emperor's name, by a succession of Shoguns, or their representatives. The name 'Shogun' is an abbreviation of a long Japanese compound word meaning, in essence, 'generalissimo'. The Shogun's government was basically a military affair, conducted in the main by and for the warrior class.

The last great family of Shoguns, the Tokugawa, adopted in the 17th century a policy of strict national seclusion. The Dutch and Chinese were permitted to engage in a severely limited amount of trade in a confined part of a single port, Nagasaki. No other foreigners were allowed to enter the country; and the Japanese themselves were forbidden to go abroad. Christianity, introduced by Portuguese Jesuits in the 16th century, was suppressed.

Arrival of Commodore Perry

The inevitable intrusion of the outside world occurred in the 1850s. Commodore Perry of the United States Navy, with a powerful squadron, was the first to compel the reluctant Japanese to open their doors. This happened in 1854. Within the next 20 years other powerful countries had followed suit and under the impact of their pressure a number of changes took place; and these were almost as revolutionary as those which followed Japan's surrender in 1945.

The Shogun's government was overthrown by a combination of feudal lords and their retainers from south-west Japan. The new masters of the country declared that the Emperor would be restored to the full dignity of sovereign ruler, and in what is known as the Meiji Restoration the reigning Emperor, a young man in his teens, moved from Kyoto to a new capital in the east, the modern Tokyo. The seclusion policy was wholly abandoned, the national aim now being to modernize Japan with all possible speed.

Japan as Pupil of the West

The small group of able retainers of the lords from south-western Japan carried out the policy of modernization with single-minded determination. They were indeed the founding fathers of modern Japan. Under their authoritarian direction a system of compulsory state education was established as the necessary basis of future progress. The machinery of government was reshaped on Western lines. A programme of industrialization was put in motion, as quickly as men could be trained in the use of new techniques. Railways, steamships, harbours, banks, printing presses, and post-offices—these and other typical appurtenances of Western industrial culture were soon established on Japanese soil. Needless to say, a modern army and navy also came into being; and by 1894 Japan was strong enough to engage in war with China. By the following year China, having suffered a series of defeats, signed a treaty of peace by which Japan obtained Formosa and other gains.

Only 10 years later Japan inflicted defeat on Russia by land and sea; and thus in 1905, after this success, Japan was one of the Great Powers; a status confirmed after World War I, when the Japanese obtained a permanent seat on the Council of the League of Nations. The Japanese Empire now included not only the Kurile Islands, South Sakhalin, Korea, Formosa, and part of South Manchuria, but also the former German islands in the Pacific north of the Equator. Such a rapid rise to world power, in terms of economic as well as military and political strength, had not been known in modern times. Even the history of Prussia and Germany in the second half of the 19th century seemed less impressive.

At first, Japan's rise to power was welcomed by most of the people of Asia. Here was an Asian country, after all, that had defeated Imperial Russia and thus exploded the myth of white invincibility. This was how millions in India, Burma, Java, and in China too, interpreted Japan's victory in 1905.

Imperialist Japan

It was not long, however, before Japan began to be regarded as an imperialist nation as proud and overbearing as Britain, France, Holland, and the United States. This was due, in the main, to the course taken by Japanese-Chinese relations.

These had always been ambivalent. On the one hand the Japanese gave shelter and help to radical Chinese in their early struggles—to Sun Yat-sen, for example. On the other, the Chinese discovered that Japan regarded China, especially Manchuria and north China, as her sphere of political and economic influence. The Japanese, having consolidated their modernization, were in an expansive mood; and after 1905 China appeared to be the natural target for Japan's expansion. The confused state of China's polity after the collapse of the Manchu Dynasty in 1912 was in itself almost an invitation to the Japanese to take a hand, overtly or behind the scenes, in Chinese affairs.

Throughout the period of World War I and the 1920s Japan's relations with China were always tense, often stormy, sometimes deceptively calm. The breaking point came in the 1930s.

In September, 1931, Japanese forces in south Manchuria seized the city of Mukden and then set about the conquest of all Manchuria. This action, in its initial stages at all events, was carried out without the approval of the Japanese Government. But once the army was committed to its course of aggression the cabinet in Tokyo could do little to restrain it. For by constitutional practice the cabinet had no jurisdiction over the operations of the fighting services. This was the province of the Supreme Command—in other words the Army and Navy General Staffs. Moreover the Army and Navy Ministers, invariably generals and admirals, always felt that their first obligation was to their respective services. It was unusual for them to be aware of any binding ties to their cabinet colleagues.

In defiance of a large body of opinion both inside Japan and outside—for Japan's action was condemned by the League of Nations and the United States—the army not only completed the occupation of Manchuria but also transformed the country into a nominally independent state, Manchukuo. In fact Manchukuo was wholly controlled by Japan.

Fascism

There now followed a period which Japanese historians have labelled as 'fascist'; although the Japanese brand of fascism lacked a Duce or Führer, and there was never a single mass party in Japan, as in Italy and Nazi Germany.

In a sense it was a quasi-revolutionary period. For the World Depression had hit Japan very hard, bringing great distress to a large proportion of the farming community, which was drastically affected by the collapse of Japanese silk exports. The processing of silk cocoons was a vital household occupation for many hundreds of thousands of households.

Amid the general misery and discontent Japan's still weak parliamentary system, often disturbed by unsavoury corruption scandals, hardly showed to advantage. Confucian traditions, the strongly ethnocentric nationalist training implanted by school and family alike, the rigorous watchfulness of the ubiquitous police—these prevented grievances seeking an outlet in Marxist agitation. The eruptions took the form of ultra-nationalist militancy. No fewer than three Premiers and ex-Premiers were assassinated by nationalist fanatics in uniform between the spring of 1932 and the spring of 1936. Other public men also were killed in the same period; and a number of bloody conspiracies failed only because of timely discovery by the police. Even so, in February, 1936, a group of young officers at the head of over a thousand troops, after carrying out a series of assassinations, occupied buildings in the heart of Tokyo and only surrendered after four days of defiance. The city was fortunate in being spared the sight of Japanese soldiers fighting each other, the mutineers being persuaded to lay down their arms peacefully.

The views and purposes of these extreme nationalists were not always clear. But they claimed to be passionately loyal to the Emperor—this was somewhat ironic, since the Emperor was a quiet, liberal-minded scholar with no time for extremism of any sort—and most of them declared that the Emperor was given evil advice by selfish and corrupt courtiers and politicians, and that these must be liquidated in summary fashion if Japan were to be saved from further ruin. There was a pronounced National Socialist flavour to much of this agitation. Many young officers, sincerely concerned by the plight of the farming districts from which most of them came, were bitterly hostile to the great capitalist combines, the so-called *zaibatsu* ('financial cliques'), which dominated the economy. The young officers despised the Diet, which they regarded as little more than a stage for marionettes operated by the *zaibatsu*. Some officers advocated the nationalization of all private property in excess of a certain figure. Yet Marxism and orthodox Socialism in general were suspect in their eyes. The ultra-Nationalists, then, tended to be both anti-capitalist and anti-Marxist. On the conduct of foreign policy their views were usually chauvinist in the extreme.

This kind of unrest enabled the leaders of the army to exert a form of blackmail on the Japanese Establishment. For example, the Minister of War would tell the cabinet that unless the army's wishes on some matter of policy were adopted, he and the other generals could not guarantee that their subordinates would behave themselves. In such manner the already considerable political influence of the army was greatly enhanced. Thus in 1937, when fighting broke out between a detachment of Japanese troops and Chinese forces near Peking, the cabinet felt unable to refuse a demand from the Minister of War that reinforcements should be sent to north China.

In this way a local Sino-Japanese clash developed into a full-scale undeclared war, the so-called 'China Incident'. This struggle outraged both the British and the Americans, whose interests were destroyed, purloined, or disrupted by the Japanese armies as these occupied the coastal cities of China and advanced into the interior.

European Alliance

Between Japanese militarism and European fascism there was a certain climate of opinion in common and a growing identity of purpose. For Germany, Italy, and Japan thought of themselves, in the horrible jargon of the day, as 'Have-Not Nations'.

But it was not until September, 1940—after Germany's spectacular victories in Europe—that the three formerly allied themselves in the Tripartite Axis Pact.

Thenceforward relations between Japan and the Anglo-Saxon Powers became steadily worse; until in July, 1941, a serious crisis arose after Japan had persuaded the Vichy Government to permit the establishment of Japanese military, naval, and air bases in the southern part of French Indo-China. This move was interpreted in Washington and London as implying a clear threat to the security of both Malaya and the Dutch East Indies. Accordingly the United States Government placed a virtual embargo on trade with Japan. Similar action was taken by the Governments of Britain and Holland.

The Americans insisted, in talks with the Japanese at Washington, that they would raise the embargo only in return for a firm promise that Japan would withdraw from both Indo-China and China proper. The Japanese now faced a serious situation—one brought upon them by the folly and ambition of their own military nationalists. For imports from South-East Asia—notably oil from Dutch Borneo—were essential to Japan's economy, now being placed on a wartime basis.

The Japanese Premier of the day, Prince Konoye, was prepared to bow to Washington's demand. The alternatives, after all, were economic strangulation or war. But Lieutenant-General Tojo, the War Minister, was adamant in rejecting any idea of a military withdrawal from China. The result of this clash of views was Konoye's resignation in mid-October, 1941, Tojo succeeding him as Prime Minister. It had already been decided in secret, at a conference of the highest military and civilian leaders in Tokyo, that, if talks with the Americans were not successful by the late autumn, then war must come.

Pearl Harbour

It came on 7th December 1941, when Japanese forces suddenly attacked the American Pacific fleet in Pearl Harbour, Hawaii, the British at Hong Kong, Malaya and Singapore, and American airfields in the Philippines. The Japanese assault preceded their declaration of war. They had adopted the same surprise tactics in their struggles with China in 1894 and with Russia in 1904.

For the next six months, until the early summer of 1942, the Japanese were overwhelmingly victorious. A vast area from the Indo-Burmese border to the Solomons Sea fell into their hands.

The tide turned very slowly at first. But the ebb quickened in 1944, with defeats for the Japanese in the Pacific, on the frontiers of India and Burma, and in the Philippines. Shipping losses and increasingly heavy and frequent air raids began to cripple the Japanese economy; and so by the summer of 1945 the situation was becoming desperate indeed.

In July, 1945, the Japanese asked the Soviet Government to mediate for peace; but the response in Moscow was evasive. The Russians in fact were preparing to enter the war against Japan; for this had been agreed upon by secret accord with the British and Americans at Yalta at the beginning of the year.

Hiroshima

The dropping of the first atomic bomb over Hiroshima on 6th August 1945, followed within the next three days by Russia's attack and the dropping of a second atomic bomb over Nagasaki, enabled the Emperor of Japan to resolve a deadlock that had developed in the counsels of his military and civilian leaders. Half of them were ready to admit defeat. The other half maintained that the war must continue. Both sides turned to the Emperor, asking him in effect to give the casting vote. The Emperor, who had never acted except on the advice of his government or high command, now declared that Japan ought to accept the terms of the Potsdam Proclamation—by Truman, Churchill, and Chiang Kai-shek—which demanded the unconditional surrender of all Japan's armed forces. This decision was broadcast, in the Emperor's own words, on 15th August 1945.

The Occupation of Japan

Although in name an Allied responsibility, the Occupation of Japan, which lasted for a little over six and a half years, was primarily an American affair. In fact General MacArthur, the Supreme Commander, would brook little interference from Washington or elsewhere with the way in which he and his staff conducted their business. They governed indirectly, through the Japanese cabinet, passing on to the latter a stream of instructions which were usually executed without cavil or delay.

In his official announcement of Japan's decision to surrender, the Emperor had admonished his subjects 'to beware most strictly of any outbursts of emotion that may engender needless complications'. Thus it was clearly understood by all officers of the state that cooperation with the Americans was now the national policy. Mr. Yoshida, Prime Minister during most of the Occupation period, tells us in his Memoirs that Admiral Suzuki, Premier at the time of the surrender, observed that while it was important to be a good winner in a war it was equally important to be a good loser. The Japanese as a whole seemed to be of this mind. Relations between the Japanese and the Americans, then, were remarkably harmonious.

Having disarmed Japan the prime aim of the Occupation authorities was to reform the social and political life of the country—or, in a word, to 'democratize' it. And under prompting from the Americans something not far short of a real, though bloodless, revolution took place during the Occupation years. The Japanese, dazed and disillusioned by their national collapse, were ready, often eager, to accept 'democracy' as the talismanic word of the new era.

The vote was given to all men and women of 21 and over. In a new constitution, drafted by MacArthur's staff, sovereignty was formally vested in the people, and the Diet became the 'highest organ of the state', the Lower House having much greater power than the Upper House. As for the Emperor, he became 'the symbol of the unity of the people'. Women were given full equality with men in such matters as property rights, inheritance, and divorce. Millions of tenant farmers were granted possession of the land they tilled. The oppressive, centralized authority of the police was radically curtailed. The teaching of Japanese history in schools came to a stop, pending the introduction of new text-books purged of ethnocentric bias.

With these and other reforms Japan became a free society almost overnight. Individualism began to outweigh community and family ties. Pacifism replaced belligerence. Samurai ideals of self-sacrifice gave way to hedonism. An entire structure of traditional ideas about the Emperor, about Japan and the Japanese race, about the obligations of the individual to society, came toppling down. In its place stood two modest but satisfying ideals—hard work and the pursuit of personal happiness.

On 8th September 1951, Japan signed a Treaty of Peace with 48 other nations in San Francisco. No doubt because wartime ill-feeling had to some extent subsided, and thanks to the foresight and resolution of Mr. Foster Dulles as chief architect of the Treaty, the peace settlement was not ungenerous. No crippling reparations were imposed on Japan; no limitations were imposed on Japanese economy and trade. All the same, the Treaty formally liquidated a colonial empire, from south Sakhalin to Formosa, already lost.

Together with the Treaty of Peace Japan signed another document, a Security Pact with the United States, whereby the latter could retain her forces in and around Japanese territory in order to protect it from attack. Moreover, the Americans continued to have jurisdiction over the Ryukyu and Bonin Islands immediately south of Japan.

The Peace Treaty came into force on 28th April 1952. Japan was once again, in an official sense, an independent nation.

Japan Since 1952

The most striking development since the Peace Treaty came into force has been Japan's economic growth. This is examined in another section of this book. But its important political and social effects should be mentioned here.

The rise in the standard of living, though unevenly spread, has immensely increased the number of those Japanese who regard themselves as belonging to the middle class, the bourgeoisie and petty bourgeoisie as opposed to the urban and rural proletariat. Indeed some sociologists claim that probably more than 70 per cent of the Japanese people feel that they are members of this broad middle class, since they now own property in the form of land or savings.

In political terms this has meant that in every general election since the Peace Treaty the Conservatives, represented by the present Liberal-Democratic Party, have contrived to win a majority of seats in the all-important lower house—the House of Representatives—of the National Diet. There have been five of these elections between the beginning of 1952 and the middle of 1962. On each occasion the Socialist and other parties of the left have increased their percentage of the total number of votes cast; and this figure was just over 39 per cent in the election of November, 1960. But they are still hardly within sight of winning power. In 1962, for example, the Conservatives held 296 seats in the House of Representatives. Their opponents, combined, held 181 seats.

Indeed, so far there has only been one Socialist cabinet in Japanese history—the Katayama administration, which held office—in coalition with a group of Conservatives, be it noted—from May, 1947, to March, 1948.

Yet the leading organs of the press and the greater part of the academic world, a very articulate section of Japanese society, favour the Socialists. The powerful trade union movement is also closely tied to the main Socialist party. Furthermore, it is probable that younger voters, especially in the cities and towns, support the Socialists. But the countryside on the whole is Conservative. This is not so much because traditions are always stronger in country districts than in towns; rather, it is due to the Occupation land reform, and to the food and agricultural policy of successive governments which has meant that the farmers have had an assured market and a guaranteed price for rice, the staple crop.

The long years in opposition have been very frustrating for the Socialists. Hence a certain bitterness in the tone, and an air of irresponsibility in the content, of many of their pronouncements and electoral manifestoes. Equally its continued success at the polls has often tempted the government party to display an unedifying ruthlessness in the Diet, an almost flippant lack of consideration for the rights of the Opposition; and this has stunted the proper growth of the parliamentary spirit in Japan. For in response to such tactics by the Conservatives the Socialists have on many occasions resorted to a form of violence inside the Diet; one typical method being to sit on the floor of the corridor leading to the Lower House, thus preventing the Speaker from taking his chair. This produces inevitable countermeasures from the Liberal-Democrats, who with the help of the Diet police set about the physical ejection of their opponents.

The most notorious of these 'battles' took place on 19th May 1960, at the crisis of the debate over the ratification of the revised Japanese-American Security Pact. On this occasion some five hundred policemen were called in to remove the far from passive 'sit-down' Socialists. The Conservative rump then hastened to ratify the new Pact, although the entire Opposition and even several Government supporters were absent from the chamber.

Foreign Relations

These have been dominated by the Cold War. The Japanese as a whole would prefer to be committed to neither side in this great East-West struggle. Nevertheless they value their association with the United States. After all Japan's prosperity is based on a capitalist economy, and Japan's present political structure has been deeply influenced by American example. On the official level Japanese foreign policy is closely tied to that of the United States; and the economic bonds with America are multifarious and are intimately related to Japan's own standard of living. For example, the export of high-class consumer goods to America has greatly helped to promote the domestic demand for these commodities. Thus the Japanese home market has become increasingly Americanized. Any serious rift with the United States would be regarded as an almost unmitigated disaster.

Japan, then, is the ally of the United States—but a somewhat fearful and sometimes reluctant ally. The Japanese—perhaps even more than most people in the modern world—dread the prospect of nuclear war; and one of the most effective points that the Socialists make in their appeal to the Japanese people is that American bases may attract Communist rockets. This particular fear lay behind the great demonstrations against the revised Security Pact that took place in Tokyo in May and June, 1960.

In many respects the new Pact was an improvement, from the Japanese point of view, on the old. For the old Pact, signed together with the San Francisco Peace Treaty, had no limit set to its validity; and there were other elements in it which retained something of the flavour of the Occupation, when Japan lacked independence. For instance, American forces in Japan under the terms of the old Pact could be used to quell serious disorders on an invitation from the Japanese Government.

The revised Security Pact of 1960 is an agreement, formally at any rate, between two equal and independent powers. Its duration is 10 years.

But this term is regarded as too long, not only by Japanese Socialists but also by some Conservatives. Furthermore, the revised Pact was negotiated and signed a few months before the U-2 incident; and the Americans were forced to admit that some U-2 planes were based on airfields in Japan, although it was asserted that these planes had been used exclusively for weather observations. The U-2 affair and the disruption of the Paris 'Summit' talks occurred before the revised Security Pact had been ratified by the Japanese Diet. It was only a few days after ratification by the Lower House, amid the rude violence that has been described, that Khrushchev warned Japan that American bases would be dealt 'a shattering blow' if they were employed for intelligence flights over Soviet territory.

The physical struggle inside the Diet, followed by the hasty and undignified ratification of the new Pact by the Liberal-Democratic rump, scandalized the Japanese public. Khrushchev's message thoroughly alarmed it. There followed the massive demonstrations in Tokyo that attracted the attention of the world. Moreover, an official visit to Tokyo by President Eisenhower was cancelled, only a very short time before it was due to take place, by the Americans at the request of the Japanese Government.

This was misinterpreted outside Japan, and especially in the United States as the result of some skilfully organized Communist plot.

But it should be noted that the Pact was ratified by both Houses of the Diet, that although the Prime Minister, Mr. Kishi, resigned—in July, 1960, when the storm of agitation was already dying down—he was succeeded by Mr. Ikeda, of the Government's party; and in the next general election, of November, 1960, this party, as we have seen, obtained a substantial majority of seats.

The new Premier diverted public attention from foreign affairs by promising to double personal income, in terms of real purchasing power, within 10 years.

Relations with the Communist Bloc

What, then, has been Japan's relationship with the Communist Bloc, with the Soviet Union and the People's Republic of China?

The Soviet Union refused to sign the Treaty of Peace at San Francisco; and there is still no formal and official peace agreement between the Soviet Union and Japan. But in October, 1956, after long months of negotiations the two countries agreed to resume diplomatic relations. Trade between the two has not reached formidable proportions; but Japanese businessmen hope that they may be able to contribute to the development of Siberia by furnishing industrial machinery and other manufactured products. There is in fact the possibility that at least some of this hope may be gratified, the Russians bartering oil for machinery.

As one would expect, the Soviet Union, as the country of Lenin and the pioneer Communist state, enjoys what is now almost a traditional prestige in the eyes of the far left. But it must be said that, except among the members of the Japan Communist Party and the ranks of its fellow travellers, the Soviet Union is an object of widespread suspicion and dislike in Japan; and such feelings are not unmixed with fear. For the Russians, in addition to extending their territorial waters from three to twelve miles, have for many years drastically restricted Japanese fishing in the seas north of Hokkaido. The Russians retain not only the Kurile Islands and South Sakhalin but also certain small islands geographically grouped with the Kuriles, which were administratively part of Hokkaido up to the summer of 1945. These particular islands, the Habomais and Shikotan, are very close indeed to Hokkaido. Yet their shores and nearby waters are entirely closed to Japanese fishermen.

The treatment of Japanese prisoners in Siberia after the War and the Soviet slowness to repatriate them—as late as 1957 it was alleged that there were still about 11,000 Japanese prisoners-of-war in Russian hands—caused deep resentment, as did the barbarous way in which Japanese residents were expelled from South Sakhalin in 1945.

Communist China, however, is by no means the object of comparable antipathy. On the contrary, the People's Republic of China attracts a good deal of sympathetic interest in Japan. This is due to a variety of factors. First, every educated Japanese is aware of his country's cultural debt to China in the past. This, however, is no doubt a minor factor. Of more importance is the feeling, particularly strong among intellectuals, that a tradition of co-operation with 'progressive' Chinese was shamefully betrayed by Japan's aggression against China between the two World Wars and especially from 1937 onwards. Indeed everyone in Japan knows that the attack on China was accompanied by all manner of abominations; for these matters, heavily censored up to 1945, have been given great publicity through Japanese magazines and books in the post-war years. So among educated people there is a feeling akin to guilt in their attitude to the Chinese. The racial factor, too, works in favour of the Chinese and against the Russians.

Ideology, of course, also plays a significant part. While it is true that in the left-wing student movement there is a substantial faction which criticizes Mao Tse-tung, Japanese intellectuals in general—teachers, students, artists, writers, actors, and journalists—are to some extent fascinated by the spectacle of the People's Republic, even if many of them disapprove of the restrictions on personal liberty that the regime has imposed. There can be no doubt, too, that a proportion of the industrial working population admires Communist China. For such people Communism in operation in China has something resembling a moral appeal. Yet here we might note that when Japanese scholars write about the people's communes they rarely advocate this type of organization for Japan. The Japanese farmer, indeed, is very unlikely to be attracted to the idea of compulsory collectivization.

It is worth remarking, also, that in contrast to Soviet Russia the People's China adopted a lenient policy towards Japanese war criminals and was not slow to send back to Japan those Japanese in China whom the Nationalist Government had not yet repatriated before its exodus to Formosa.

But it is perhaps the pull of economic interests that makes Japanese of all shades of opinion keenly interested in what goes on in China. The Japanese business world is prepared to ignore ideology when it comes to the prospect of trade with Red China. For undoubtedly the Government's policy of doubling incomes within ten years will mean much larger imports of raw materials. This must lead to more persistent demands by Japanese businessmen for access to Chinese iron ore, coal, and other resources.

However, until very recently the Peking Government has made it plain that any enlargement of Sino-Japanese trade depends on a change in Japan's diplomatic policy towards the two Chinas. For Japan—thanks to American insistence during the winter of 1951-52—recognizes the Nationalist Government in Formosa as the legitimate government of China.

So an official gulf separates Japan from the People's Republic; and, since China's foreign trade is controlled by a commission of the Peking Government, commercial dealings with Japan can be cut off at any moment—as occurred in 1958 when, on the excuse of an insult given to their trade delegation in Nagasaki, the Chinese abruptly cancelled all outstanding contracts and severed economic relations with Japan.

Nevertheless the Chinese have welcomed various deputations from Japan. One of these, representing the Socialist Party, achieved some notoriety. The deputation was headed by the party's Secretary-General, Mr. Asanuma. He was moved, while in Peking, to make a speech in which he referred to the United States as 'the common enemy' of Japan and of the People's Government. This was in 1959. In the autumn of the following year, at a public meeting in Tokyo and in full view of the audience and of a battery of television cameras Asanuma was stabbed to death by a youth belonging to one of the small extreme right-wing groups that still poison the political atmosphere in Japan. The young man—who later committed suicide while in detention—declared that it was Asanuma's speech at Peking which made him a deserving victim of assassination.

Relations with South Korea

An even nearer neighbour than either Soviet Siberia or mainland China has yet to come to terms with Japan. This is Korea, or more strictly South Korea. Here the many years of Japanese rule left a legacy of active dislike. This is to some extent reciprocated. For a minority of the Koreans in Japan, for years little esteemed by the Japanese among whom they lived, behaved with possibly pardonable arrogance, and sometimes with inexcusable lawlessness, as soon as Japan surrendered and the restraints imposed by the overbearing police were removed. There was no doubt greater resentment in Japan over the so-called Rhee Line, which denied Japanese fishermen access to waters within fifty miles of the Korean coast. Syngman Rhee himself, while he was in office, would allow no Japanese economic repenetration of his country; and it is only very recently that Japanese-Korean negotiations, renewed after a break, have shown signs of bringing mutual amity.

Relations with Britain

With Britain and the Commonwealth Japan's relations have improved in slow, undramatic, solid fashion. Hydrogen bomb explosions over Christmas

Island have drawn protests from Tokyo, in the form of diplomatic notes and large but orderly crowds in processional demonstration outside the British Embassy. In general, however, Japanese-British relations have begun to prosper, notably since the late 1950s. For British exports to Japan have been rising steadily, and in 1962 a Trade Treaty was signed by the two countries.

As for Asia outside China, Japan once again occupies the position, in terms of prestige, that she held for a few years after the defeat of Imperial Russia in 1905. For the developing countries of Asia, and of Africa and the Middle East also, see in Japan an example of rapid economic growth achieved without revolution or the complete suspension of parliamentary government.

Yet, considering her status as the most technologically advanced country in Asia, and one of the most industrialized nations of the world, with her literate population of not far short of a hundred million, Japan has not played the part on the stage of world diplomacy—at the United Nations, for example—that her innate and potential strength might require. For one thing no really outstanding Japanese statesman has impressed his image on the world in post-war times, in the manner, let us say, of Nehru or Adenauer. The fact is that since the death of the last of those who created modern Japan in the 19th century Japanese leadership has been both collective and curiously undramatic. It has also been a shifting leadership—between civilians and soldiers (and sailors) before the War; between factions of Conservative politicians since. The one constant has been the energy of the Japanese people, harnessed or guided by a devoted and capable bureaucracy.

Japan's professional foreign service, for example, is an admirable organization which suffered greatly from its comparative impotence during the 1930s and during the Pacific War. The Occupation purges affected it much less than other branches of the bureaucratic machine, such as the Home Ministry. But the masterly conduct of foreign policy requires more than able ambassadors and Foreign Office officials. It needs the drive and inspiration that only a statesman of the first magnitude can provide. This figure has yet to make his appearance in post-war Japan.

Defence

Article 9 of the Japanese Constitution clearly states that 'the Japanese people forever renounce war as a sovereign right of the nation and the threat and use of force as means of settling international disputes'. It goes on to say that 'land, sea, and air forces, as well as other war potential, will never be maintained'.

There can be no doubt that this clause of the Constitution was generally welcomed when the people of Japan were introduced to it, and that it has retained great popularity ever since.

The Japanese have not shed their ethnocentric prejudices so thoroughly as to be indifferent to the charm of being thought unique in the world. To be the only nation without any armed forces would certainly confer a unique status on Japan. Armed neutrality, like that of Switzerland, is one thing; unarmed neutrality quite another.

However, under strong pressure from the United States Japan embarked upon a measure of rearmament even before the Peace Treaty was signed. This was the creation in 1950 of a body of infantry, some 75,000 strong, known as the National Police Reserve. The Peace Treaty itself specifically recognized Japan's right to self-defence in accordance with the principles of the United Nations Charter.

Today, Japan possesses an army, navy, and air force—known respectively as the Ground, Maritime, and Air Self-Defence Force. They are not equipped for offensive purposes. The Air Self-Defence Force has no bombers; and the Maritime Force contains no vessel larger than a destroyer. None of the services has nuclear weapons.

Still, it is difficult to see how this situation can be squared with Article 9 of the Constitution. Japanese governments have tried to get round this issue by a variety of legal fictions. They have argued that the requirements of the United Nations Charter, including the right of collective self-defence acknowledged in Article 51 of the Charter, must take precedence over a clause in a national Constitution. They have also contended that armed services without nuclear weapons and offensive aircraft do not constitute 'war potential'. It may be observed, however, that old Mr. Yoshida, still powerful in his retirement, was reported to have stated in the summer of 1962 that Japan needs nuclear weapons for her defence.

At all events, modest but by no means negligible armed services exist for Japan's defence; and so far the Japanese Supreme Court has avoided, or been spared, the need to give a verdict on their constitutional legality.

The Japanese Islands

The Kuriles stretch, a long string of them, from the north-east of Hokkaido to the southern tip of Kamchatka. The Habomais are very small islands lying immediately north-east of the Nemuro Peninsula of Hokkaido; north-east of the Habomais, and close to them, is the island of Shikotan.

The Kurile and Habomai Islands; Shikotan

Until the 19th century even Hokkaido (then known as Yezo) was by no means well colonized by the Japanese; as for the Kuriles, few Japanese penetrated as far north in feudal times. All the same, it was generally recognized that Hokkaido and its adjacent islands were under Japanese jurisdiction. The local inhabitants were the unsophisticated Ainu, who were hunters and fishermen. The Ainu on the nearer Kuriles and in the southern part of Sakhalin would see Japanese traders and officials from time to time. Nevertheless the Shogunate did not become seriously concerned to exercise its authority in the northern islands until Russian penetration became manifest early in the 19th century. When in 1853 and 1854 the Russians tried to force open the doors of Japan—simultaneously with Perry's arrival in Yedo Bay—the Shogun's representative told the Russians that 'all the Chishima Islands of Yezo (the Kuriles) are Japanese territory . . . In olden times our territory extended as far as Kamchatka, and it was inhabited only by the Ainu. It was only in later times that your country took possession of some of those islands'.

In 1855, however, the first Russo-Japanese Treaty recognized Japanese possession of Kunashir and Etorop, the two large Kurile Islands nearest to Hokkaido, and Russian possession of the other Kuriles stretching north-east to Kamchatka. The Habomai group and Shikotan were not discussed in the Treaty; for these clearly belonged to Japan. Twenty years later, by another treaty, Japan surrendered all claim to Sakhalin and in exchange obtained the rest of the Kuriles. Then in 1905 by the Treaty of Portsmouth Japan, as part of her prize for her victory over Russia, obtained the southern half of Sakhalin.

Forty years later these arrangements were again disturbed. With Japan's surrender in 1945 Russian forces occupied not only South Sakhalin and the Kuriles but also Shikotan and the Habomais.

South Sakhalin and the Kuriles had been promised to the Soviet Union by secret agreement at Yalta in February, 1945. Moreover, the Cairo Declaration of December, 1943, had made it clear that after her submission Japan would be reduced to her four main islands and such minor islands as the Allies should determine. Again, by Article 2 of the San Francisco Peace Treaty, 1951, Japan renounced all claims on South Sakhalin and the Kuriles. Meanwhile, in 1947, the Russians had made the Kuriles, Habomais and Shikotan part of Sakhalin Oblast.

But the Japanese do not regard the Habomais and Shikotan as part of the Kuriles. Furthermore, they make a distinction between the South Kuriles and the rest of the Kurile chain. They tend to claim that the renunciation made in Article 2 of the Peace Treaty cannot properly apply to Kunashir and Etorop—still less to the Habomais and Shikotan—since these islands were recognized, by the Russians, as belonging to Japan as long ago as 1855.

It is not so much the islands themselves as the seas in their vicinity that are important to the Japanese. For in pre-war years these northern waters provided half of Japan's total catch of salmon and 30 per cent of the nation's crab fisheries.

Since 1945, however, the Soviet Union has placed stringent restrictions on Japanese fishing in these seas.

In recent years the Russians have hinted that they might be willing to consider returning the Habomais and Shikotan to Japan, provided the latter formerly recognize Russia's legal sovereignty over the Kuriles.

The Ryukyu and Bonin Islands (Okinawa)

The long chain of 55 islands known as the Ryukyus extend from Kyushu in south-west Japan to a point about 100 miles off the north-east coast of Formosa. The largest island is Okinawa; and this contains the only substantial town, Naha, and 80 per cent of the entire population of the Ryukyus.

From the early 17th century onwards the ruler of the Ryukyus paid tribute not only to the Emperor of China but also the Lords of Satsuma in Kyushu, Japan. In 1879, however, the Japanese government, ignoring Chinese protests, dethroned the ruler and incorporated the islands, as Okinawa Prefecture, in the national administrative system.

The Ryukyus fell into American hands during the last year of the Pacific War, when Okinawa was captured after a bitter and costly struggle lasting for two and a half months. American government of the Ryukyus was recognized by the San Francisco Peace Treaty.

Nevertheless, the Americans have acknowledged that Japan has residual sovereignty over the islands; and in 1954 the most northerly islands were restored to full Japanese control. Over the rest of the islands an American High Commissioner (the commanding general) exercises ultimate authority. This was slightly modified in 1962, when President Kennedy, by Executive Order, gave a measure of greater self-government to Okinawa Legislature (of 29 elected members). The President declared on this occasion that he recognized the Ryukyus 'to be part of the Japanese homeland', that he looked forward to the day 'when the security interests of the free world will permit their restoration to full Japanese sovereignty.'

The Bonins are four groups of small islands in the Pacific south of Japan, the principal island being Chichishima and the most famous, Iwojima. Sparsely populated—'Bonin' is said to be a corruption of the Japanese expression, *munin* ('devoid of people')—the islands were formally annexed by Japan in 1876. In February, 1945, the United States Marines fought a gruelling campaign for possession of tiny Iwojima (eight square miles in area) which the Japanese had heavily fortified. The Japanese garrison of over 20,000 died almost to the last man in its defence. Since 1945 the Bonins have been under American military administration.

A Glance at the Future

Nothing is more uncertain than prediction. Only fools make guesses. But a few judicious and highly tentative speculations seem in order, even in the case of a people as volatile as the Japanese. Given two basic conditions—peace and economic well-being—the Japanese, though never safe from the natural hazards of earthquakes and typhoons, will surely not risk the artificial disasters that might follow the loss of a free parliament and a free press. For some years after the War there were many, in Japan as well as outside, who forecast that the free, almost licentiously free, society of the post-war era would not long endure. So far their forebodings have not been justified, in spite of pressures and threats from the extremes of right and left in political and social life. These have been resisted with success, and indeed with apparent ease.

It is doubtful, for example, whether a Conservative government will ever obtain the necessary two-thirds majority in the Diet to carry out a revision of the Constitution, in order to give the Emperor a more positive status and to bring Article 9 into closer touch with existing realities. Extremism, then, is not likely to prevail, provided that war or economic recession are avoided. It is the sudden pressure of an international crisis, such as the U-2 affair and its immediate aftermath, when the people of Japan feel the breath of World War III on their necks, that creates the panic in which a group, representing one political extreme or another, might see some chance of grasping power. Short of the sudden appearance of such turbulence the barometer for Japan appears to be set at Fair.

BIBLIOGRAPHY

Sir Esler Dening. *Japan.* (Ernest Benn, London, 1960.)

Donald Keene. *Living Japan.* (Heinemann, London, 1959.)

James Kirkup. *These Horned Islands. A Journal of Japan.* (Collins, London, 1962.)

John M. Maki. *Government and Politics in Japan.* (Thames and Hudson, London, 1962.)

George B. Sansom. *A History of Japan.* 3 vols. To 1334, 1334-1615, 1615-1867. (Cresset Press, London, 1958, 1961, and 1964.) *Japan, A Short Cultural History.* (Cresset Press, London, 1946.)

Richard Storry. *A History of Modern Japan.* (Penguin, London, 1960).

Glenn T. Trewartha. *Japan, A Physical, Cultural and Regional Geography.* (Methuen, London, 1960.)

BIOGRAPHICAL NOTE

RICHARD STORRY. B. 1913 at Doncaster, Yorkshire. Educated at Repton and Merton College, Oxford. Lecturer at Otaru College of Commerce, Hokkaido, Japan, 1937-40. Army Officer in Egypt, Singapore, India, Burma and London, 1941-46. Research Scholar of the Australian National University, 1948-52. Research Fellow of the Australian National University, 1952-55. Roger Heyworth Memorial Research Fellow of St. Antony's College, Oxford, 1955-60. Official Fellow of St. Antony's College since 1960. Lecturer in Far Eastern Studies, University of Oxford since 1962. Visited post-war Japan in 1949, 1953-54, 1959-60, 1961. Publications: *The Double Patriots: A Study of Japanese Nationalism* (Chatto and Windus, London, 1957), *A History of Modern Japan* (Penguin, London, 1960) and *Japan* (Oxford Univ. Press, London, 1965).

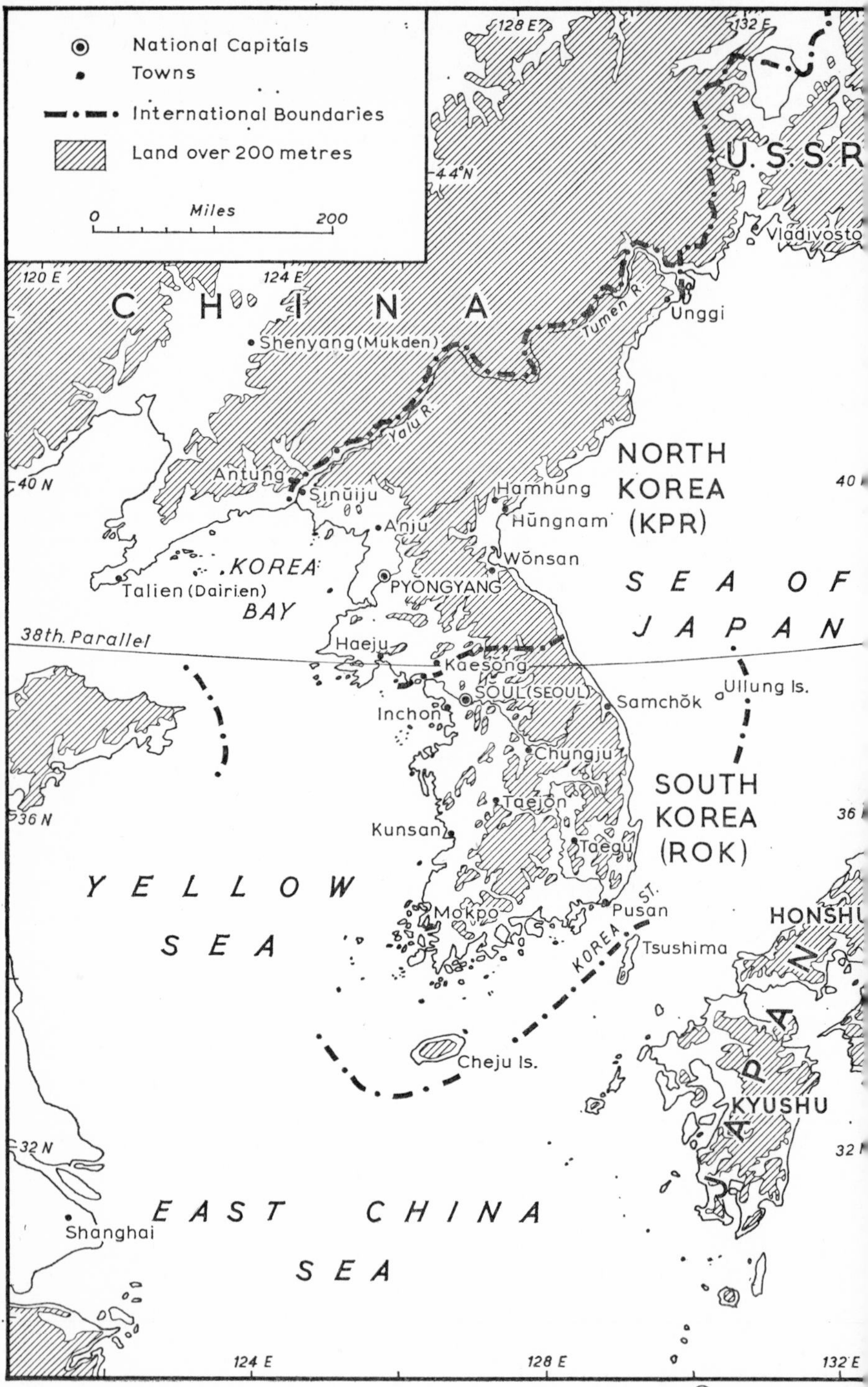

National Capitals
Towns
International Boundaries
Land over 200 metres

Miles
0 200

128 E? 132 E

U.S.S.R

44°N

120 E 124 E

C H I N A

Shenyang(Mukden)

Tumen R

Unggi

Vladivosto

40 N

Antung Yalu R.

Sinūiju

Anju

NORTH
KOREA
(KPR)

40

Hamhùng

Hūngnam

Wōnsan

KOREA
BAY

Talien (Dairien)

Haeju

PYONGYANG

SEA OF

JAPAN

38th. Parallel

Kaesŏng

SŎUL (SEOUL)

Inchŏn

Samchŏk

Ullung Is.

36 N

Chungju

Taejŏn

Kunsan

Taegu

SOUTH
KOREA
(ROK)

36

YELLOW

SEA

Mokpo

Pusan

KOREA ST.

HONSHU

Tsushima

Cheju Is.

KYUSHU

32 N

32

EAST CHINA

Shanghai

SEA

124 E 128 E 132 E

© ANTHONY BLOND LT

SOUTH KOREA

by

WALTER FRANK CHOINSKI

Historical Summary

The Koreans trace their origin back some 43 centuries, the year 1966 being 4299 on the Korean calendar.

Except for the mythical Tan-Gun, the earliest known Korean ruler is reputedly a former Chinese Minister of the Chou Dynasty (China) who in 1200 B.C. migrated to north-west Korea as a result of political upheavals in China between the Shang Dynasty and the Chou Dynasty.

In 193 B.C. the Ki Ja Dynasty was overthrown, and succeeding governments interfered with overland trade routes between China and South Korea. Irritated by this interference, Chinese armies attacked and in 108 B.C. north-west Korea capitulated. Chinese power in the peninsula disintegrated rapidly and by 37 B.C. north-west Korea was once more under non-Chinese rule.

With the fading of Chinese control began the period of the Three Kingdoms which were to dominate the peninsula for the next 1,000 years.

The beginning of the 13th century saw the rise of Mongol power, and in 1208 Genghis Khan embarked on his imperialistic career. Initially, by virtue of having lent some aid to the Mongols, Koryo stood in a favourable position for an alliance. However, the opportunity vanished when the Koreans snubbed the Great Khan's friendly but uncouth envoys and made it clear that they wanted no association with the northern barbarians. This attitude led ultimately to a Mongol attack, and in 1252 the Koryo King fled to the island of Kangwha where he was safe from the invader who had no boats. In 1240 the Mongols withdrew but returned in 1253 to invade the country more ruthlessly than before. Finally, with the capitulation of the Koryo king and his subsequent death in 1259, the occupation by the Mongols was complete. In 1260, Kublai Khan inherited the empire.

Rebellions in China during the last half of the 14th century signalled the wane of Mongol power, and the Ming dynasty came to power in 1368.

The Ming Emperor recognized the new King and approved the name Chaohsien (Choson) for Korea. Yi selected Hanyang (Seoul) as his capital. The following 200 years were punctuated by border incidents and Japanese pirate depredations, against both of which the Koreans were uniformly successful. Korean culture reached its highest point during the reign of Chong-jong (1506-44).

At this time, in Japan, a very capable military leader named Hideyoshi became Shogun, and immediately set out to satisfy his ambition to conquer China. This took the form of a request that Korea join Japan in attacking the Chinese. In the spring of 1592, a Japanese army landed in Pusan and Korea became a stepping stone to invasion. After a succession of sieges and bribed escapes, the Japanese were pocketed in the south in 1593, and a four year truce was observed. In 1597 Hideyoshi launched a second invasion. Admiral Yi was reinstated, but too late to prevent the landing of the Japanese fleet. The year 1598 found the Japanese bottled up in the fortress of Ulsan, but once more they bribed their way out and set sail for home.

While the Koreans were still recovering from the destructive Japanese invasion, the Manchus to the north were growing in power and threatening China. Once again Korean respect for the Ming and her contempt for the uncultured Mongol barbarians led Korea into trouble. In 1619 a Korean army sent to aid the Ming Emperor was defeated, and in 1627 the Manchus, with their Mongol allies, invaded Korea. The Korean rulers unwisely maintained their attitude of contempt for the Manchus and thereby provoked a second invasion in 1636. The court was besieged in Namhan, the ancient Paekche capital 17 miles south-east of Seoul, and Manchu troops again ravished the country. Finally the Koreans capitulated.

The Japanese, who in 1872 had managed to exchange envoys with the Koreans, in 1884 engineered a revolt by Korean aggressives who took over the palace. The Chinese supported the Korean conservatives and a conflict ensued which ended in the Tientsin agreement in 1885, with promises by both Chinese and Japanese to evacuate their military forces. This agreement was violated when, in 1894, Chinese troops were brought into the peninsula to help suppress a revolt in the south. This provoked the Japanese and a war between China and Japan started on Korean soil. In successive battles, the Japanese defeated the Chinese, concluding the war in a Japanese victory on Chinese territory in 1895. Following this victory, the Japanese adopted a stronger attitude toward Korea. For seven years the Russians and Japanese sparred for political domination of the Korean peninsula, and in 1904 Japan finally declared war. Korea was forced into the position of being Japan's ally. After the war, and in the flush of military success (1905), a Japanese Resident-General was established to rule the country. Two years later the King was forced to abdicate in favour of his feeble-minded son, and finally in August, 1910 annexation by Japan formally ended Korean independence and the Yi dynasty, which had ruled for over 500 years.

The Koreans did not accept Japanese annexation placidly, and for ten years Korean patriots carried on armed resistance which the Japanese sought to suppress with military force.

On 1st March 1919 thirty of the most prominent Koreans signed a proclamation of independence and sent it to the Governor-General. This is popularly known as the 'Mansei Uprising'. Arrest followed swiftly, and great crowds joined the demonstration irrespective of class, age, religion or sex; all had the single common bond of nationality.

The Japanese were infuriated that the subjugated people should dare to seek liberty from the benevolent imperial plan for their social and political salvation, and the Governor directed all the power at his command toward crushing the populace by force. In August, 1919 a new Governor-General was sent out from Japan, and a plan of wholesale reform in the administration was inaugurated. With increased Japanese involvement in military 'incidents' economic pressure increased until, during the last years of World War II, every effort was made to force maximum Korean production for the war effort. The conclusion of World War II brought an end to Japanese rule.

In December 1943 the Cairo Declaration promised Korea its independence 'in due course'. A provisional Korean government was formed in Chungking in 1944 and at the Potsdam Conference in July 1945 the Allies declared that 'the terms of the Cairo Declaration shall be carried out'. The USSR committed itself to support the independence of Korea when it declared war on Japan on 8th August 1945. Russian troops entered Korea from the north on 12th August 1945, and United States troops from the south on 8th September 1945.

With the end of Japanese rule, a political vacuum existed in both the Soviet and United States zones. In South Korea, two separated political forces presented themselves to the United States Occupation authorities. The first, the Korean People's Republic, was proclaimed on 6th September 1945. It was Communist-dominated and was opposed to the United States Military Government. The other was the exiled Korean Provisional Government which returned to Korea from the United States and China after the Japanese surrender. United States authorities maintained the Military Government was the only government in South Korea. In February 1946, the United States Military Government created the Representative Democratic Council, an all-Korean body which was to act in an advisory capacity to the Commanding General of the American Forces. Syngman Rhee was made Chairman. This was replaced in October 1946 by the Korean Interim Legislative Assembly, which was created to give the Koreans control of their government with United States authorities retaining the power to dissolve the assembly and to appoint half its members.

The first effort to unite Korea came at the Moscow Conference of December 1945 at which the United States, the United Kingdom and the USSR (with China abstaining) agreed that the United States and USSR commands in Korea were to form a joint commission which was to make recommendations to the Four Powers regarding the organization of a provisional Korean democratic government. The 'joint commission' provided for by the Moscow agreement met from 20th March to 8th May 1946, but was unable to reach agreement. It reconvened a year later but the discussions were stalemated.

The United States referred the Korean question to the United Nations and, on 14th November 1947, the General Assembly adopted a resolution calling for elections throughout Korea under the observation of the United Nations Temporary Commission on Korea. The elections were to select a national assembly, to draft a democratic constitution, and establish a national government. The Soviet Command, however, denied the United Nations Commission entry to its zone.

Elections were held in South Korea on 10th May 1948, under the supervision of the United Nations Commission, and the National Assembly met for the first time on 31st May 1948 and elected Syngman Rhee Chairman. Subsequently, on 20th July 1948, he was elected President.

The Republic of Korea was inaugurated on 15th August 1948. On the same day the United States Military Government in Korea came to an end.

The Korean Conflict

On 25th June 1950, well trained and experienced North Korean Communist forces invaded South Korea with massed armour and heavy artillery supported by tactical aircraft. It was the relatively small army of South Korea, immature, without trained and experienced leaders, operating under the untried government of an impoverished country, that bore the brunt of the sweep of the Red forces across the 38th parallel.

Overwhelmed by vastly superior Communist forces the South Koreans fought as best they could but were forced to retreat. However, less than twenty-four hours after the surprise attack, the Security Council of the United Nations (which the Soviet Union had boycotted at the time) branded the North Koreans as guilty of a 'breach of the peace' and demanded an immediate cessation of hostilities and withdrawal of North Korean forces. When the invader failed to comply, the United Nations Council called upon other member nations to give all possible help to the Republic of Korea to repel the attack and restore peace and security in the area.

On 27th June, President Truman announced that the United States would send air and sea forces 'to give the South Korean Government troops air cover and support', and on 30th June he ordered Occupation troops to be flown from Japan to Korea.

Material contributions to aid the Republic of Korea were made by more than forty countries, sixteen of which contributed ground, naval and air forces. A United Nations Command was created and General of the Army Douglas MacArthur was appointed Commander in Chief.

It was apparent by 5th July 1950 that only maximum support and effort by the United Nations could stave off the total collapse of the Republic of Korea. The ROK Army had been forced to withdraw so fast that vast quantities of arms and ammunition fell into the hands of the invaders, and resistance was offered only in the form of hasty road blocks and light defensive positions at the Han River. The announcement of United Nations aid and the arrival of American air and ground support from Japan brought new hope to the South Koreans.

By the first of October the situation was definitely in Allied hands. Seoul was again occupied by friendly forces, and most of the elements of the United Nations forces and ROK Army were on or north of the 38th parallel. Following the decision to clear all Korea of the Communist threat, a determined drive to the north was begun in all sectors, and by 7th October, the drive towards the Yalu River was begun. However, by this time Chinese Communist Forces (CCF) under the guise of volunteer forces, were committed to assist the army of North Korea. The full effect of this intervention was felt on 26th November when the ROK forces collapsed completely under a direct frontal attack. All attempts to coordinate the defence of the area failed. The majority of the units were able to avoid annihilation by escaping through the mountains, but at the expense of their heavy equipment.

Late on New Year's Eve of 1950, the enemy began a general offensive across the entire front with an attack directed at Yonchon. As the drive gained momentum across the Imjin River, the Eighth United States Army, now supporting ROK forces, and the ROK forces were forced to withdraw until all reached Yongwol where the Chinese Communist forces' drive to the south was stopped dead.

Late in January 1951, the American Eighth Army began to launch limited offensives designed to inflict maximum damage to the enemy with a minimum of United Nations casualties. Operation Thunderbolt was the first of the offensives under the new doctrine. Playing a leading role in this attack were the ROK forces. United Nations forces were again on the Han River by 12th of February and from then on friendly forces remained in a favourable position. A secure front, passing through Hongchon, was established across the entire Korean Peninsula by 15th of March. By the end of April of 1951 the entire army was in line across 116 miles of commanding terrain, almost entirely north of the 38th parallel.

The long awaited spring offensive of the Chinese Communist forces came on 22nd April. Although there were heavy losses in ground, the first attempt of the Communist-termed 'fifth phase offensive' was halted. By 1st June United Nations forces were again north of the 38th parallel, which, with minor changes, is the present United Nations defensive position.

The Soviet delegate at the United Nations, on 23rd June 1951, proposed negotiations for a truce. The United Nations agreed to negotiate because its original objective—that of repelling aggression against the Republic of Korea—had been achieved. Truce negotiations began in July, were suspended first by the Communists, then resumed, suspended next by the United Nations delegation, resumed again, and finally brought to a conclusion two years later when an armistice was signed on 27th July 1953.

During those two years of frustrating, deadlocked negotiations, some of the hardest fighting of the Korean conflict took place, for both sides considered it necessary that military operations continue until an armistice agreement was signed. There were patrol clashes, raids and bitter small-unit struggles, and hard-fought battles involving many divisions. The air-war over Korea was intensified, and large-scale United Nations air attacks, naval bombardments, and strikes by carrier-based planes, as well as fierce ground fighting finally convinced the Communists that they could not conquer the Republic of Korea.

The stumbling block to a truce was the question of the repatriation of prisoners of war. The Communists demanded that all POWs be returned to the countries from which they had come. The United Nations Command, which held about eight times as many POWs as the Communists, insisted on voluntary repatriation of prisoners, on the principle that no one who did not wish to return to his homeland should be compelled to return.

Finally, the Communists agreed to voluntary repatriation of prisoners, and the armistice was signed. Under the agreement, a demarcation line across the Korean peninsula was established along the final battle line. Most of it runs north of the 38th parallel, with a short dip below the parallel at the western terminal. The troops of both sides were withdrawn leaving a two-and-a-half mile demilitarized zone between them. The agreement provided for the reunification of Korea to be brought about through political negotiations. But the negotiations failed because the Communists refused, among other things, to agree to elections supervised by the United Nations.

In the Korean conflict, 58,000 Koreans were killed and 176,000 wounded, more than a million civilians were killed, and another million wounded or injured. The tides of war left 100,000 Koreans orphans and more than 284,000 widows with 517,000 dependent children. About eight million South Koreans were driven from their homes.

The cost in lives, wounded, money and effort by United Nations forces reached monumental figures.

First Government: Presidential System

South Korea's first government had similarities to both the American presidential system and the British parliamentary system.

The Constitution provided for popular sovereignty, defined a separation of powers, but awarded the President a preponderance of authority, especially in time of economic 'crisis'.

Legislative power was vested in the National Assembly of which the House of Representatives was the only existing body. Each member represented approximately 100,000 people. A House of Councillors, or upper house, was specified in the constitution as a part of the National Assembly, but was never formed.

Provincial government was an administrative subdivision of the executive branch of the Central Government. The nine provinces in the ROK, and Seoul as a 'Special City', were administered by the Ministry of Home Affairs. Provincial Governors and the Mayor of Seoul were appointed by the President. County administrators were appointed by the President of the Republic on recommendation of the Provincial Governor through the Minister of Home Affairs. Chiefs of ward offices in Seoul were appointed by the President of the Republic on the recommendation of the Mayor through the Minister of Home Affairs.

The cities, towns, and townships were governed by elected local councils, who in turn elected their own chief executives. These local councils had the power to enact and repeal local ordinances and also were required to carry out the tasks assigned them by the Minister of Home Affairs.

All policemen were appointed by the National Government and were under the supervision of their Provincial Governor, and were not subordinate to local officials.

All the above factors were instrumental in enabling the Syngman Rhee Government to control the outcome of elections and the enforcement, or non-enforcement, of legal provisions. As the time for the second election approached, in 1952, it appeared that incumbent President Syngman Rhee would not be re-elected. However, strong pressures were brought on the National Assembly by the executive branch and the elections, required on or before 23rd June 1952, were postponed; martial law was declared and 13 Assemblymen were arrested by the Government. After boycotts of the Assembly by various factions, the Assembly, on 4th July 1952, unanimously adopted four amendments to the Constitution: (1) the President should be elected by popular vote; (2) the National Assembly should be reorganized into a bicameral body; (3) Cabinet members should be appointed by the President upon the recommendation of the Prime Minister instead of by the President on his own initiative; and (4) the Cabinet may be dissolved by a vote of no-confidence by the Assembly.

Syngman Rhee was re-elected on 5th August 1952, for a new term beginning August 15th.

A second constitutional change was undertaken in November 1954. Three important points in the amendment were (1) the abolition of the office of Prime Minister and authorization for the President to preside directly over the State Council and appoint its members; (2) incumbent President Rhee was exempted from the constitutional limitation of two consecutive four-year terms; (3) provision was made for the Vice-President to succeed the President should the latter die in office.

Syngman Rhee was re-elected in 1956 and for the presidential race of 1960 the Liberal Party again nominated him for a fourth term. He was again elected President. On election night major demonstrations occurred throughout South Korea against the election results.

On April 19th and thereafter a very large demonstration by university and high school students occurred demanding the resignation of President Rhee and the holding of new elections, and, as a result, the Cabinet resigned and President Rhee tendered his resignation.

New Constitution: Assembly-Responsible Government

On June 15th the House of Representatives adopted a new Constitution, substituting a straight parliamentary system for the previous presidential system. The post of President was continued, but it was transformed into a ceremonial position without executive authority. The executive power was placed in the hands of a State Council headed by a Prime Minister. The Prime Minister appointed his own Cabinet, and was required to resign if he received a vote of no-confidence in the House of Representatives on a major issue.

Following adoption of the new Constitution, the old Assembly dissolved itself, designating July 29th as the date for a new general election. Provisions were made also, for the first time since passage of the 1952 constitutional amendment, to elect the House of Councillors.

In the July election, the Democratic Party won a majority of seats in the House of Representatives. President Yun, under pressure, nominated Dr. John M. Chang, Head of the Democratic Party, for the position of Prime Minister. He was elected on August 19th.

No sooner had the 25 million Korean people observed the first anniversary of the student-led uprising of April 1960 than another revolution struck the discontented country. On 16th May 1961, a closely-knit group of younger generals and colonels overthrew the strife-torn but freely elected government of Prime Minister John M. Chang. The new Government, under the title of 'The Revolutionary Military Committee', announced a six-point declaration of 'Revolutionary Pledges' which emphasized anti-Communism, observance of the United Nations Charter, strengthening of ties with the United States and other friendly nations, elimination of political corruption and social evils, advancement toward economic self-support, building up of national strength to excel Communism, and return of the governmental authority to 'new and conscientious' politicians upon completion of its 'revolutionary tasks'.

The military junta, which was renamed 'The Supreme Council for National Reconstruction', let it be known that there would be heavy punishment for any violations of the new regulations, declared an 'emergency' martial law and ordered the arrest of the Chang Cabinet, a blockade of the sea and air ports, freezing of banking, dissolution of the National Assembly and all local legislatures, press censorship, prohibition of assemblage, and a 1900 to 0500 curfew.

A Revolutionary Court and a Revolutionary Prosecution were organized in July to administer the revolutionary laws, mostly applicable retroactively. Close to 40,000 government officials were found to be corrupt, guilty of partisan politics, patronizing mistresses, or excessive use of foreign luxuries (which were banned).

General Park Chung Hee, who had remained in the background in the initial stages of the *coup d'état*, took over control of the SCNR on 1st July, arrested Lieutenant-General Chang Do Yung, and placed him under trial with forty other military officers on charges of being 'counter-revolutionary'. In December, Park announced his intention to run as a candidate for election to the presidency, but in March of 1963 he renounced this intention and declared that he was going to extend his military regime until 1967.

Anti-Government demonstrations, without precedent as to violence, broke out in major cities in spite of an array of 150 admirals and generals avowing support of General Park. The American Ambassador informed the 'Military Junta' and General Park that they should 'work together' with major political groups on a procedure for transition from the incumbent military rule to a civilian government acceptable to the 'South Korean Nation' as a whole. The impression was left that the American Government might be inclined to consider withholding its economic aid.

General Park announced his agreement to the demands of existing political parties, stated that elections would be held within the year 1963, and that he would be a candidate, as a civilian. As Mr. Park he was elected and formally inaugurated on 17th December 1963 as the first President of the 'Third Republic of Korea', and thus ended the 945 days of military rule in South Korea.

South Korea is currently administered by Park's Democratic Republican Party which occupies 110 of the 175 seats in the one-house Parliament. The Minjung (Civil Rule) Party is the largest minority party with 41 seats, followed by the Democratic Party with 15 seats. There are in all 12 parties, the organization and functions of which are now regulated by law. Each promises the constituency the benefits of social security, long-range economic development programmes, adherence to the United Nations Charter, and unification of the two Koreas under United Nations-sponsored general elections

The Democratic Republican Party, led by Park Chung Hee, is committed to revolutionary ideals, and a popularly elected president with powers to control the executive branch as provided by the Constitution drafted by the

Military Junta. It is the strongest party, with a powerful secretariat, the first of its kind in Korean political history. The Minjung (Civil Rule) Party, led by Yun Po Sun, successor party of former Premier John M. Chang ousted by the Military Junta, has pledged revision of the constitution to curb presidential powers. The Democratic Party, led by Mrs. Park Sun Chon, ranked high in elections, perhaps owing to the fact that it is the successor to the Democratic Party ousted by the Military Junta Revolution of 1961. The Party of the People, led by Huh Chung, is a coalition of many pre-revolutionary groups now under the leadership of the man who was Premier for three months following the downfall of Syngman Rhee. The Liberal Democratic Party, led by Kim Do Yun, consists of dissidents who broke away from their pre-revolutionary associates. It presumes to share in the revolutionary objectives of the party in power. The Liberal Party, led by Chang Taik Sang, comprises a conglomeration of former Syngman Rhee liberals. The Chungmin Ho (Right Citizens) Party, League of Pyun Yung Tai (former Prime Minister), Chupung Ho (Autumn Breeze) Party and Society of Oh Jae Yung and Sin Heung (New Development) Party are splinter groups with great hopes of attaining political significance under a civilian government.

Considering the fact that in 1948 there were 48 parties which participated in the general elections supervised by the United Nations, it may be concluded that the Republic of Korea may be approaching a degree of political integrity.

Programme for Economic Development

For the past several years the economy has been gradually sinking into a downward trend with the gross national product falling from 4·0 per cent in 1955, to 2·3 per cent in 1960. The outbreak of the April Revolution (1960) and the May Revolution (1961) aggravated the depression as a whole.

However, with the enactment of the Foreign Investment Encouragement Law and the devaluation of the currency (won), economic prospects began to recover until in 1964 they reached proportions not known since the establishment of the Republic. To make the plan more realistic, the 1962-66 Five-Year Plan was readjusted to the extent that the original 7 per cent annual growth rate was reduced to 5 per cent. The production of grains, coal, cement, power and industrial consumer goods has since advanced to the degree that South Korea now seems capable of permanent industrial development for home consumption and export.

Exports have shown remarkable increases in the last few years and, with industrial 'know-how' increasing, neighbour countries are looking to South Korea for low-priced consumer goods—the wage scale being about one-half that of Japan. During 1964 approximately 50 per cent of South Korea's exports (about U.S. $60 million) comprised consumer goods. South Korea's prospects for extended private and U.S. Government capital and markets, through its Industrial Development Agency, seems promising.

If Korea and Japan can return to normal economic relations, a healthy and viable South Korean economy will vie for a share of world trade. The resumption of trade with Japan continues to be deterred by the demands of South Korea that Japan places its 600,000 Korean expatriates under South Korean citizenship, renounces its claims to Tokto Island and settles the dispute over Korean-Japanese offshore fishing rights.

Although the growth rate of South Korea's gross national product has risen to 7 per cent (1964), the increase of the population is such that growth rate of the country's GNP per capita is only 4 per cent.

If industrial ambitions are fully realized, the once under-developed 'Land of the Morning Calm' may yet become the 'Land of the Morning Smog'.

Basic Issues

The major problem besetting the Republic of Korea is the military and political division of Korea into North and South. This separation colours and intensifies all other problems.

Korea had been developed by the Japanese on an agricultural pattern in the south, and on an industrial pattern in the north. Much of this pattern has continued to exist. The south is overpopulated, the north underpopulated. The division impedes the development of a self-sustaining economy in the south. In reaction to this artificial situation, unification has become the central theme of ROK politics. The division of Korea presents a formidable security problem to the Republic of Korea, requiring it to maintain an extremely large and costly army. In spite of this situation, the Communists are constantly seeking to infiltrate the government, the police, and the armed forces, and the Republic of Korea must be alert continually for espionage and subversion. The north-south split divides families and natural trade areas, and perpetuates a state of suspended hostilities in Korea.

The Republic of Korea's problems are intensified by the task of remedying the destruction which occurred in the Korean War, in which 400,000 homes and many factories and mines were demolished, many agricultural fields and paddies damaged, and millions made refugees. This repair and rebuilding work has overtaxed the resources of the Government and the economy, despite the large amounts of aid given by the United States.

If the ROK is to cope with its 26 million population, it must have financial resources to continue rehabilitation, to expand factories and mines, to improve agriculture, and grant the people greater participation in the affairs of their government. This the new Government promises to accomplish.

BIBLIOGRAPHY

Walter Choinski. *The Republic of Korea.* (Military Assistance Institute, Arlington, Virginia, 1964.)

Chong-Sik Lee. *The Politics of Korean Nationalism.* (Berkeley Univ. Press, California, 1963.)

Economic Statistics Yearbook. (Bank of Korea, Seoul, 1964.)

Korea, Its Land, People and Culture of all Ages. (Ministry of Public Information, Republic of Korea, Seoul, 1963.)

Military Revolution in Korea. (Supreme Council for National Reconstruction, Seoul, 1961.)

Miryok Lee. *The Yalu Flows: a Korean Childhood.* (Harvill, London, 1954.)

W. D. Reeve. *The Republic of Korea: a Political and Economic Study.* (Oxford Univ. Press, London, 1963.)

Republic of Korea. (Far Eastern Economic Review Yearbook, Hong Kong, 1965.)

BIOGRAPHICAL NOTE

WALTER FRANK CHOINSKI. Educated in letters and law at the University of Wisconsin. On active duty in United States Army 1939-58: retired with rank of Colonel. Since 1958 associated with the American Institutes for Research in the Behavioral Sciences, Pittsburgh, Pennsylvania, where now Director of Research for the Military Assistance Institute of Washington, D.C. and Arlington, Virginia. Has lived and travelled extensively in Poland, Germany, Italy, France, North and South Korea, Laos, Cambodia, Vietnam, Thailand, Kashmir and Mexico. Has written books on 14 countries which are now in use at the Military Assistance Institute by student officers assigned to duty in overseas areas.

NORTH KOREA

by

CHONG-SIK LEE

THE Democratic People's Republic of Korea, which is the official designation of the North Korean regime, is in firm control of the Korean peninsula north of the armistice line drawn in 1953. Just as the Republic of Korea government in the south, the Pyongyang regime has claimed itself to be the only legitimate sovereign government in Korea, although in more recent years it has acknowledged the *de facto* power of the South Korean regime by proposing negotiations on unification.

North Korea, in theory, is still in the stage of the people's dictatorship. Thus the regime has kept its three 'major' political parties, i.e., the Korean Workers' Party, the Korean Democratic Party, and the Ch'ondogyo Youth Fraternal Party, and has been allocating a certain number of seats in the Supreme People's Assembly to the two latter groups. But, in fact, North Korea has long been under the complete control of the Workers' Party, particularly its supreme leader, Kim Il-song (born 1912).

Political developments in North Korea since 1945 have clearly manifested Kim Il-song's shrewdness and lack of any scruples in political engineering. Although the future premier did have some revolutionary record behind him, as a Communist partisan in Manchuria during World War II, he was a relatively unknown figure in 1945 when he returned to Korea at the tail of the Russian forces invading Japanese-occupied Korea. Since then Kim has been intent on establishing himself as the unequivocal leader of the Korean Communist movement. He was able to depend upon support from the Russian command in Pyongyang in the early stages of postwar political struggle. He was 'elected' premier in 1948.

In his struggle for the mastery over North Korean politics Kim used the tactics of amalgamation of rival groups, purges, and occasional violence. As is to be expected, massive propaganda accompanied each move.

FOUNDATION OF THE COMMUNIST PARTY

Thus in October, 1945, soon after Kim's arrival in Korea, the 'North Korean Central Bureau of the Korean Communist Party' was created in Pyongyang and all the indigenous Communists were forced to submit to it. There were throughout Korea at this time numbers of Communists and Communist sympathizers organized by indigenous leaders who had emerged from their underground dormancy after the liberation of Korea but were independent of Kim Il-song. Having, with Russian help, established himself as the first secretary of the new organization, Kim proceeded to execute a sweeping purge in December to remove the 'undesirable elements' in the party. One of the strongest contenders for power against Kim, Hyon Chunhyok, had already been assassinated in broad daylight in September.

Six months later, in July, 1946, the Central Bureau annexed the New People's Party, headed by Korean returnees from north-west China. The returnees, generally known as the Yenan faction because of their close association with the Chinese Communists in Yenan, included such prominent figures as Kim Tu-bong, Mu Chong, Kim Ch'ang-man, Ch'oe Ch'ang-ik and Han Pin among others, and added considerably to the prestige and strength of the Communist camp as a whole. The newly amalgamated party was named the North Korean Workers' Party, and the alliance of the two groups lasted a number of years.

Finally, in June, 1949, the North Korean Communists absorbed the Communist 'exiles' from South Korea, merging the North and South Korean Workers' Parties into the Korean Workers' Party (Choson Nodong-dang). Pak Hon-yong, one of the few survivors from the earliest stage of the Korean Communist movement in 1921 and the leader of the South Korean Workers' Party in 1949, in effect surrendered himself and his followers from the south to the young leader who became the chairman of the new, united party of Korea.

The purge of the possible contenders for power against Kim Il-song continued during and after the Korean War. Thus in December, 1950, the third plenum of the Central Committee of the Workers' Party dismissed Mu Chong from the command of the Second Army Corps on the grounds that his neglect of duties during the retreat inflicted grave damage on the army. The significance of this episode goes beyond the fact that one of the major leaders of the Yenan faction was purged. It shows Kim Il-song's political ingenuity and skill, in that Mu had been a close comrade of P'eng Teh-huai since the 1930s and that P'eng was in command of the 'Chinese People's Volunteers in Korea', who had just joined the Korean War in late October. Was there, perhaps, a fear on the part of Kim Il-song that Mu Chong might subvert his power in an alliance with P'eng Teh-huai, and was the purge merely a scheme to prevent this outcome? This hypothesis is substantiated partly by the fact that at least three known comrades of Kim Il-song from the partisan days, Kim Il, Yim Ch'un-ch'u, and Ch'oe Kwang, were purged or reprimanded at this conference on similar charges with Mu and were all reinstated shortly afterwards. Kim Il since then has attained the lofty position of First Vice-premier and Minister of Agriculture, in charge of carrying out the all-important collectivization programme; Yim Ch'un-ch'u was made ambassador to Albania and Bulgaria; Ch'oe was later promoted to be a full general in the North Korean Air Force.

Another major purge occurred in 1953 when Pak Hon-yong (Vice-premier and Foreign Minister), Yi Sung-yop (former Minister of Justice), Chu Nyong-ha (former ambassador to Russia and Vice-minister of Foreign Affairs), Kwon O-jik (ambassador to China), and several other important leaders of the 'domestic faction' were implicated. Official charges advanced against them were that they had actively engaged in espionage for the United States occupation forces while they were in South Korea, furnished information about North Korean political and economic conditions to enemy agents, and attempted to overthrow the existing government in North Korea. It has been surmised in the West, however, that the real reason for the purge was the discovery of an attempt to obstruct the armistice at Panmunjom, and that the Government may also have sought to put the responsibility for starting the war upon the shoulders of the purged group. Be that as it may, another significant segment of the Korean Workers' Party that posed a potential threat to Kim Il-song was eliminated.

The de-Stalinization campaign in Russia also had its impact in North Korea. Although Khrushchev's secret speech itself had not been printed in the North Korean papers, the regime made it known to the public that the twentieth congress of the Communist Party of the Soviet Union had denounced Stalin's 'cult of personality'. In these circumstances, it was natural for some of the leading elements to decide to bring about a change in Pyongyang similar to that in Moscow—for the cult of personality practised by Kim Il-song had gone to extremes.

An attempt was made by two leading figures in the 'Yenan faction', Yun Kong-hum, the Minister of Commerce, and Ch'oe Ch'ang-ik, the Vice-premier, in alliance with a 'Soviet faction' man, Pak Ch'ang-ok, Minister of Mechanical Industry, to denounce Kim Il-song. At the August, 1956, plenum of the party's Central Committee, which had been called to hear the premier's report on his visit to the Soviet Union and Eastern Europe, Yun Kong-hum criticized the authoritarianism of Kim and the 'anti-people' nature of Kim's policies. Other critics of the premier joined in support of Yun, and a major crisis developed at the plenum. The supporters of Kim, however, outnumbered the dissidents and branded the critics as anti-party reactionary elements. According to one source, the three major critics had been expelled from the Central Committee and stripped of their official functions when P'eng Teh-huai, the Chinese Defence Minister, and Anastas I. Mikoyan intervened and secured their restoration to the Central Committee.

Party Purges

The last major purge known to the West was revealed at a plenum of the Korean Workers' Party in March, 1958. The premier stated that the sixty-nine-year-old Kim Tu-bong—the elder statesman of the Yenan group, who had been chairman of the presidium of the North Korean Supreme People's Assembly since its establishment in 1948—together with Vice-premier Pak Ui-wan and the former secretary of the North Korean Communist Party, O Ki-sop, had conceived of (not actually plotted) overthrowing the party although no evidence was 'as yet obtained' to prove that they had participated in an 'anti-revolutionary riot'. The premier also stated that although the party had been 'patient in educating' these persons for the past year and a half, they were not earnest enough to confess their past mistakes and correct them. In the same speech Kim Il-song denounced Ch'oe Ch'ang-ik, Kim Ung (former general commander of the war front and Vice-minister of Defence), and others for engaging in sectarian activities. It has been asserted by independent observers that General Chang P'yong-san, one of the lelegates at Panmunjom, and other influential military men of the Yenan action were purged in May, 1958, on account of an alleged *coup d'état* planned for May Day. The Yenan faction virtually disappeared from North Korean politics in 1958.

A review of political developments of the last two decades thus clearly eveals that the authoritarian leader of North Korea effectively squashed all his opponents and rivals and put the party and the regime firmly under his control. Kim Il-song did not hesitate to purge members of the domestic and Yenan factions, and even some of the Russian faction, but he has been most ledicated to nurturing the strength of his personal followers. It is significant n this connection that the histories published in North Korea after 1958 omit all mention of the Korean revolutionaries in North China (the Yenan group) and have nothing but contempt and invective for the Communist movement n Korea before 1931, in which year Kim Il-song allegedly started his evolutionary career. It is now stated that the illustrious Marshal Kim Il-song and his personal followers were the only true Communists Korea produced during the early, pre-World War II years of the movement.

Economic Planning

The extremism and fervour with which the personal power of Kim Il-song was consolidated was reflected in the economic programmes adopted by the regime after the armistice that concluded the Korean War in July, 1953. Three years of war had virtually ruined all industry and the country was plagued by severe food shortages. According to North Korean sources, he output of various industries in 1953 in comparison with the pre-war evel in 1949 was as follows: electrical, 26 per cent; fuel, 11 per cent; metallurgy, 10 per cent; chemical, 22 per cent. Many mining and industrial facilities were completely destroyed. Damage to irrigation facilities and river lams affected some 900,000 acres of farm land and reduced the area of arable land by about 200,000 acres out of about 5.5 million acres normally cultivated. Grain production in 1953 was reduced to 88 per cent of the 1949 total.

At the conclusion of the armistice, the regime immediately began to econstruct ruined industries and rehabilitate the economy as a whole. The Three-Year Plan (1954-56) aimed at the recovery of the pre-war production level. The First Five-Year Plan (1956–60) was designed to build the foundation of socialist industry', and the Seven-Year Plan (1961–67) is o turn North Korea into an 'advanced socialist industrial country'.

In the process of planning economic rehabilitation and development, the egime placed the main emphasis upon the reconstruction and further development of heavy industries. Thus during the three-year rehabilitation period the regime allocated approximately 49·6 per cent (or 39,900 million *won*) of a total investment of 80,600 million *won* to industry and only 7,400 million *won*, or 8·6 per cent, to agricultural reconstruction. Approximately 81 per cent of the funds for industry went to heavy industries. At the end of he three-year plan, the premier reported that machine production and metal processing had increased by more than three times the pre-war level, and construction materials by 2·8 times, while mining and metallurgy had reached the pre-war level, but the most essential electrical, fuel, and chemica industries were still below the pre-war level. At the end of the five-year pla in 1960, however, the regime declared that even these industries had over taken the pre-war level, electric production having increased 1·5 times, fue production twice, and chemical production four times. Allegedly, Nort Korea was in 1960 sufficiently industrialized and its economy so wel diversified as to be totally rid of all the characteristics of a colonial economy

The regime launched the seven-year plan with great fanfares in 1961 an has continuously asserted that progress is being made on schedule to reac the heights of Socialism. The following table taken from an official Nort Korean publication illustrates the volume of production and the rate c growth contemplated by the regime:

	Production Goals for 1967	
	Physical Units	*Times 1960*
Electric power	17,000 million kw-h.	2·4
Coal	25 million tons	2·4
Iron ore	7·2 million tons	2·3
Pig iron	2·3 million tons	2·7
Steel	2·3 million tons	3·6
Hydraulic and thermal turbines	448,000 kw.	106
Tractors (in terms of 15 h.p. unit)	17,100 units	5
Automobiles	10,000 units	3·2
Chemical fertilizers	1·7 million tons	3
Cement	4·3 million tons	1·9
Fabrics	500 million metres	2·6
Underwear	65 million pieces	3·9
Footwear	40·7 million pairs	1·8
Grain	6,600,000 tons	1·7
Meat	350,000 tons	3·9
Eggs	800 million	6·4

Economic Organization

It must be noted in this connection that North Korea suffered a heav loss in population during the war owing not only to war casualties, but als to the heavy outflow of refugees to South Korea. In order to bring abou rapid industrialization and to meet the labour shortage, the regime move large numbers of farmers to urban areas, requiring all these men and wome to participate in industrial activities. Of the total population of 10,789,00 as of December 31, 1960 (48·4 per cent male), 38·3 per cent were classifie as labourers and factory workers, 13·7 per cent as office (or 'white collar' workers, and 44·4 per cent as farmers. At the end of 1953, when the popula tion was 8,491,000, farmers accounted for 66·4 per cent. The annual rate o population growth is reported to be approximately 3 per cent.

The regime has been requiring each worker to perform an incredibl amount of work each day, and since April, 1959, has used the system o *Chŏllima* or 'flying-horse' teams granting awards for the overfulfilment of as signed quotas. Instead of providing material incentives, the regime resorted t nore indoctrination and discipline accompanied by occasional purges, to en-ure the increase in production. The following quotation from Kim Il-song's peech of February 26, 1959 applies not only in the context of economic levelopment, to which he was referring, but also in other spheres of life:

> In some of the factories the social groups carry out few educational activities. 'urthermore, even the party organizations neglect this, and hence the economic luties are performed through sheer coercion. What is done instead, day and night, ; ideological investigation. The guiding group from the central party will investigate ne's ideology, and so on. Nothing but complaints will result from these investi-ations.

The entire agricultural population in North Korea has been collectivized, eing placed in cooperative farms as Socialist workers. After a brief 'experi-nental stage' in 1953 and 1954, the party undertook a full-scale collectiviza-ion programme in November, 1954. Within three years, by December, 957, 95·6 per cent of the farmers were organized into 16,000 cooperatives. n October, 1958, only two months after the Chinese Communist regime aunched its commune movement, the North Korean regime amalgamated he small cooperatives into 3,843 large cooperatives with an average of some oo households each.

The farmers in each cooperative are organized in work teams, and heir daily work is supervised and evaluated by team leaders who, in onsultation with other officers of the cooperatives, issue points to the farmers t the end of the day. The farmers are paid (or given a share of the products) t the end of the year according to the total points they have earned. vailable information indicates that the state and the cooperatives take a ion's share of the products in the form of taxes, various fees, and 'common eserves of the cooperatives', allowing much less than a half of the products o the farmers.

The cooperatives have provided the regime with a convenient channel for egimenting and disciplining the people. The farmers in a cooperative are rganized into a number of 'party-policy study groups' to receive proper Communist indoctrination in their spare time. Each cooperative is equipped vith a number of 'Party history study rooms', 'agitators', and 'conversation eaders' to provide proper 'guidance'. North Korean sources indicate that concentrated guidance groups' from various party hierarchies make frequent ounds at the cooperatives and that the farmers receive their 'education' and ndoctrination at their place of work during the rest period.

In spite of the official pronouncements to the contrary, there are signs of onsiderable strain in North Korean agriculture. For example, even the fficial publications admitted a drop in agricultural production in 1959, the rst year after the agricultural cooperatives were merged into larger units. North Korean newspapers (which are under complete state control) also ccasionally print articles written by reporters and letters from readers hat severely criticize the 'mistakes and tardiness' of the local officials. In December, 1961, the regime took the extreme measure of removing the gricultural cooperatives from the jurisdiction of the prefectural (*kun*) overnments on the ground that the 'administrative methods of the prefectural people's committees could not smoothly guide the agricultural co-operatives'. The cooperatives are now placed under newly created 'management committees' at the prefectural level staffed by agricultural experts dispatched by the central government. Since the agricultural cooperative was, in fact, the only administrative unit of local government under the prefectural level in rural areas, and since the cooperatives are pervasive in their functions, the decision of December, 1961, did not leave much to the prefectural governments. It is reasonable to surmise, therefore, that the regime was compelled to resort to this drastic action by some unexplained but serious defects in the cooperatives.

Prospects of Unification of Korea

Practically every political speaker in North Korea today ends his speech by referring to the goal of 'peaceful unification' of Korea. The Pyongyang regime has also conducted a ceaseless propaganda campaign in recent years to attribute all responsibility for the prolongation of the division of the country to the South Korean leaders and the 'American imperialists'. The North Korean proposals on unification have the air of reasonableness. First of all, so goes the argument, the Korean problem must be solved by the Koreans alone, i.e., without interference by the United Nations Commission for the Unification and Rehabilitation of Korea or by the United States. The North Korean regime demands, therefore, the immediate withdrawal of the United Nations agency and the United States military forces from South Korea (where there are two infantry divisions), as well as the cancellation of the mutual defence agreement between the Republic of Korea and the United States, as the first requirements for unification. When these conditions are met, the two Governments are to send their representatives to establish the 'Supreme National Committee', which will bring about a unified policy on economic and cultural developments while at the same time preparing for a 'free election' to be held throughout Korea. In the event that the establishment of the Committee should not be feasible, the North Korean premier has proposed that a committee consisting of 'representatives of industry and commerce' shall be allowed to meet in order that they may agree on trade and 'assistance' matters.

The North Korean rulers, however, are obviously aware that it would be impossible for the United States to withdraw its troops from South Korea and to cancel the mutual defence agreement with the Republic of Korea Government. A mere hint of this nature on the part of Washington would create unrest in the South, and actual American withdrawal would probably cause another Korean War. In the face of such conditions, the Pyongyang regime seems to have adopted a basic tactic of steady propaganda (1) to influence the South Korean populace in order that they may turn against the United States and (2) to consolidate the 'democratic basis' in North Korea. Every economic measure taken in North Korea, therefore, is presented as being justified in the name of 'peaceful unification of the fatherland'.

The regime of Kim Il-song emerged in its early period under the auspices of the Russian army, but it has lately been strongly identified with Communist China in the Sino-Soviet ideological dispute. Norht Korean literature attacking 'international revisionism' began to appear about 1958 and in the same year the agricultural programmes in China were also imitated. In recent years the Pyongyang regime has consistently sided with China on such issues as the Sino-Indian border dispute and the arming of Cuba. The North Korean party has been attacked along with the Chinese and Albanian parties by some of the Eastern European Communist parties. Although the causes and the meaning of the North Korean position in the current intra-bloc dispute are yet to be explored, some explanations are possible.

First, the North Korean Communists have always found it difficult to accept the principle of 'peaceful coexistence' advanced by the Soviet Union. As early as August, 1953, the premier had declared that it was dangerous and harmful to think that North Korea could coexist with South Korea. He accepted the correctness of the principle in the international sphere at that time, but one gained the impression that Kim Il-song was not fully convinced of the validity of the Russian argument. Full acceptance of the principle of coexistence would mean a reduction of intensity in the anti-American campaign which was an essential part of the 'peaceful unification' movement. It would also weaken the argument for radical economic programmes in North Korea, in that the construction of the 'democratic base' is an integral part of the 'peaceful unification' movement. Thus the desire for the rapid recovery and development of the economy of North Korea and the existence of anti-Communist regimes in Nationalist China and South Korea may have drawn North Korea closer to Peking. The latter factor would in particular draw the two regimes closer to attack 'American imperialism' as the prime enemy of the 'peace-loving peoples.' It is perhaps relevant to remind readers that the Korean War was launched in 1950 in the midst of the North Korean campaign for 'peaceful unification.'

These factors alone, however, would not justify and hence would not explain the extent to which Pyongyang has aligned itself with Peking. The present writer believes that the stronger cause for the seemingly sudden change in the North Korean attitude around 1958 lies in Kim Il-song's discovery that the anti-party plot by Ch'oe Ch'ang-ik and his group, i.e., the 1956 denunciation of the premier, had received encouragement and support from Moscow. It would certainly be difficult to relegate the North Korean identification of the Ch'oe group with 'international revisionism' to a mere coincidence. It can be argued, then, that the North Korean leadership is united with the Chinese and Albanian comrades in their resentment of the Soviet interference in domestic politics. Will the pro-Chinese trend of the North Korean regime continue? Will the Soviet Union impose economic and other sanctions against North Korea? Can the North Korean leadership successfully steer the treacherous course of international Communism while opposing 'revisionism, dogmatism, and all other opportunism'? Only time will tell.

BIBLIOGRAPHY

The China Quarterly, London, April-June, 1963. A Symposium on North Korea.

Chong-Sik Lee. *The Politics of Korean Nationalism*. (Univ. of California Press, Berkeley and Los Angeles, 1963.)

North Korea: A Case in the Techniques of Takeover. (U.S. Department of State, Washington, 1961.)

Philip Rudolph. *North Korea's Political and Economic Structure*. (Institute of Pacific Relations, New York, 1959.)

BIOGRAPHICAL NOTE

CHONG-SIK LEE is a native of Korea and an assistant professor of political science at the University of Pennsylvania. He is the author of *The Politics of Korean Nationalism* and has contributed a number of articles on the Korean Communist movement and the North Korean regime to scholarly journals.

RUSSIA IN SIBERIA AND THE FAR EAST

by

S. V. UTECHIN

THE BEGINNING

THE most significant feature of Siberia and the Russian Far East, underlying all economic, social and political developments, is that it has been an area of gradual Russian colonization since the late 16th century. The small and mostly primitive indigenous peoples were easily subdued by small Cossack detachments, which, within a few decades, occupied and annexed to Russia the whole vast territory from the Ural Mountains to the Pacific. The main attractions for the Russian colonists were at first the precious furs, then (from the 18th century) the lead and silver to be mined in the Altay area and in Transbaykalia, and from the 1830s also gold which was found in many places in central and eastern Siberia. There was little agricultural colonization in the early period except in so far as it was necessary to provide food for the Russian traders, miners and military and administrative personnel (the latter of necessity including a very considerable number of people engaged in transport and communications). Almost from the very beginning of Russian colonization, Siberia was used as a place of banishment for common criminals, religious dissenters and political offenders. Of the latter, two comparatively numerous groups played an important role in the intellectual development of the area—the Decembrists from the late 1820s and the Poles after the Polish uprising of 1863. Siberia never knew serfdom, but many of the mine-workers in the 18th century were state peasants who, together with their families, were compulsorily settled there to work in the mines; and in the 19th century the mines were partly worked by convicts.

The indigenous peoples were at first largely left alone, provided they paid tribute (later taxes) and did not interfere with the Russian colonists. In the 1830s a more ordered system of indirect rule was introduced, with either tribal or district assemblies electing headmen who had the double function of internal administration according to customary law and of representing their people with the Russian authorities. Assimilation was comparatively easy, since there was no racial prejudice on the Russian side, and the majority of the indigenous peoples were, at least formally, Christianized (though Buddhism was at the same time making headway among the Buryats).

The Great Reforms of the 1860s and '70s, which profoundly transformed European Russia, did not affect Siberia to the same extent, partly because there were no serfs to be emancipated, but also because there was no local

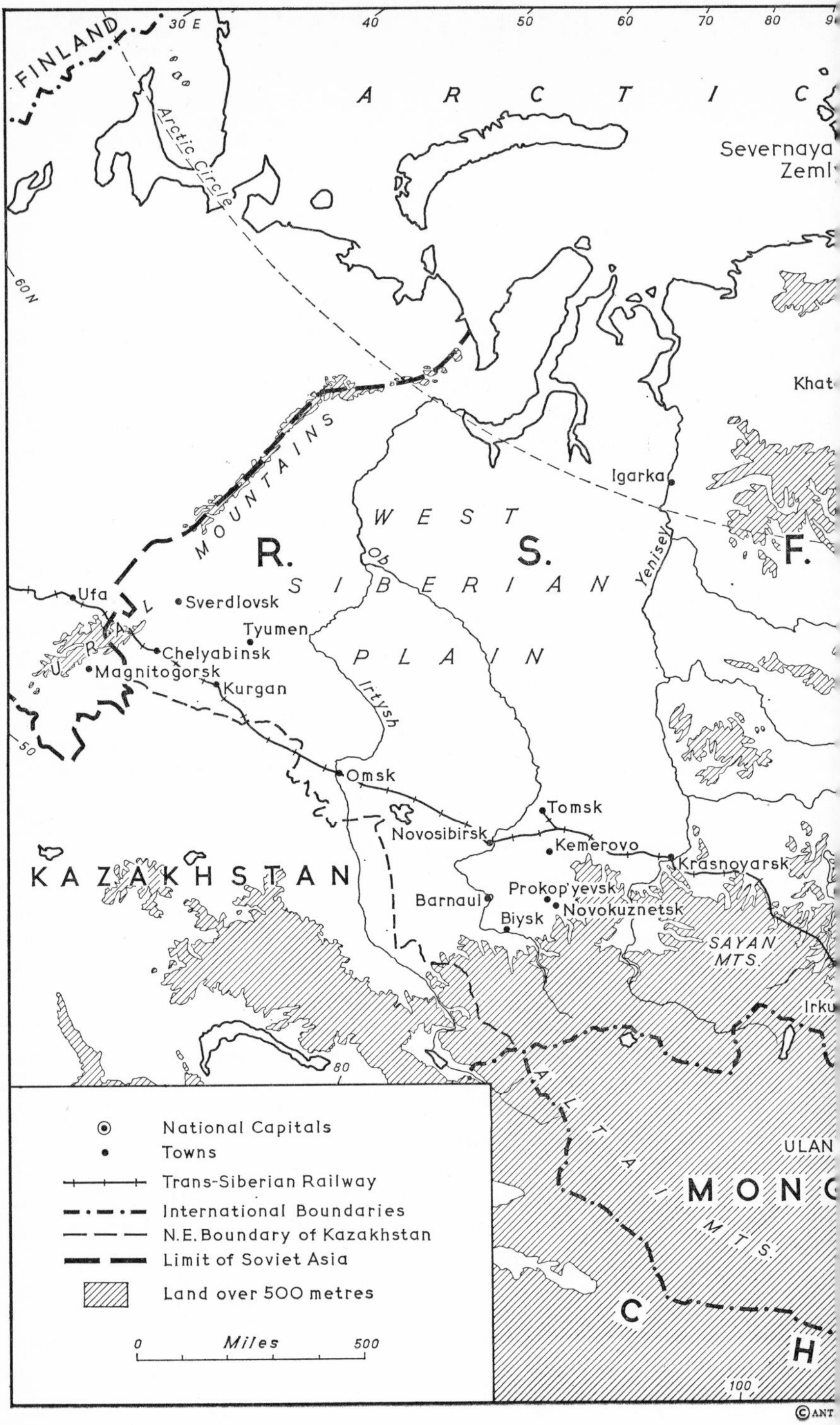

FINLAND
30 E
40
50
60
70
80
A R C T I C
Severnaya Zeml
Arctic Circle
60N
Khat
Igarka
MOUNTAINS
W E S T
R.
S.
F.
Ob
S I B E R I A N
Yenisey
Ufa
Sverdlovsk
U R A L
Tyumen
Chelyabinsk
P L A I N
Magnitogorsk
Kurgan
Irtysh
50
Omsk
Tomsk
Novosibirsk
Kemerovo
Krasnoyarsk
KAZAKHSTAN
Barnaul
Prokop'yevsk
Novokuznetsk
Biysk
SAYAN MTS.
Irku
80
ALTAI MTS.
ULAN
MONG
C
H
100
National Capitals
Towns
Trans-Siberian Railway
International Boundaries
N.E. Boundary of Kazakhstan
Limit of Soviet Asia
Land over 500 metres
0 Miles 500
©ANT

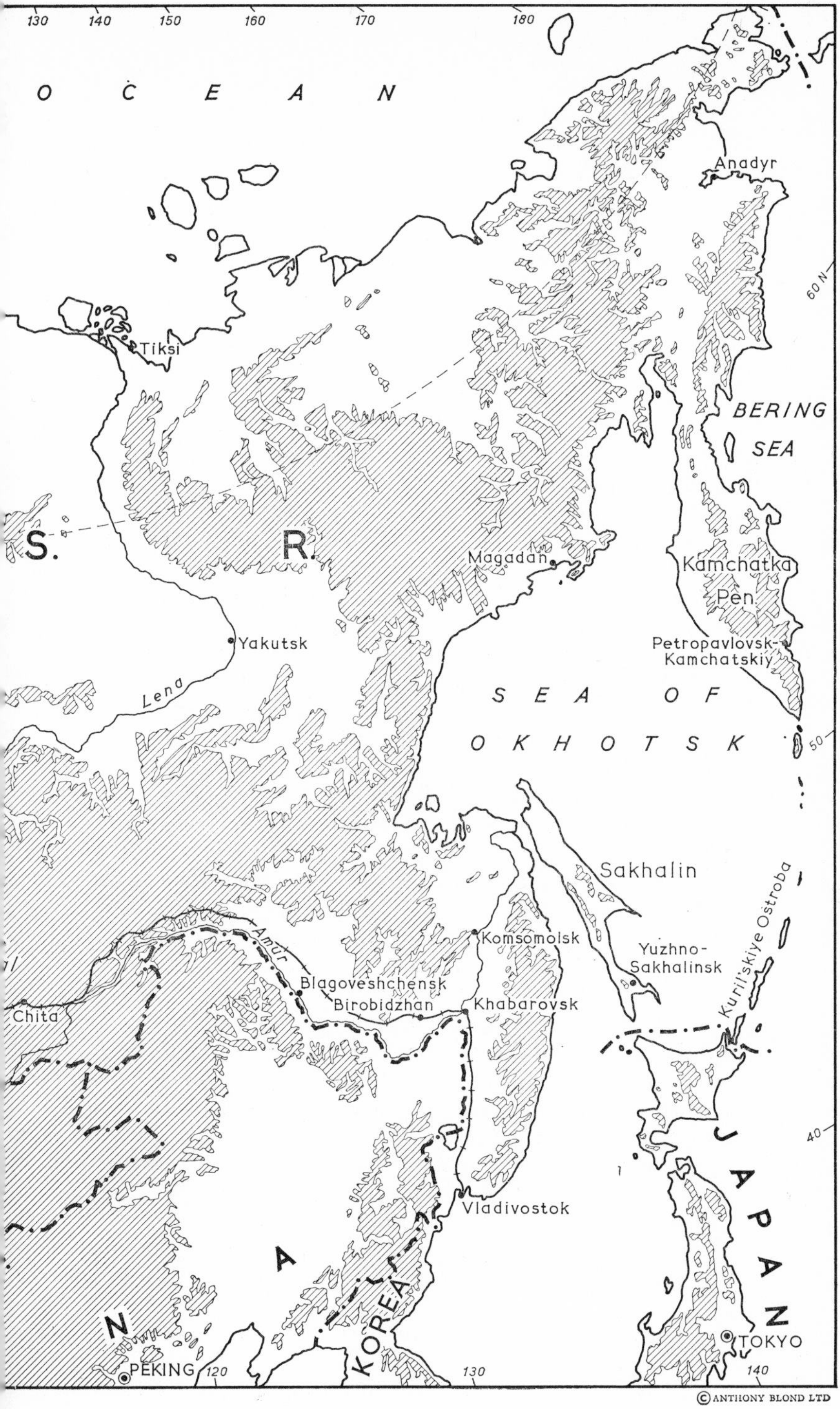
130
140
150
160
170
180
O C E A N
Tiksi
Anadyr
60 N
BERING
SEA
S.
R.
Magadan
Kamchatka
Pen.
Yakutsk
Petropavlovsk-
Kamchatskiy
Lena
S E A O F
O K H O T S K
50
Sakhalin
Kuril'skiye Ostroba
Komsomolsk
Yuzhno-
Sakhalinsk
Amur
Blagoveshchensk
Birobidzhan
Khabarovsk
Chita
40
JAPAN
Vladivostok
A
KOREA
N
TOKYO
PEKING
120
130
140

nobility either, and with this class lacking and the small educated stratum consisting mainly of banished revolutionaries the St. Petersburg authorities were reluctant to introduce local government and the reformed judiciary. This was resented by the more enlightened among the merchants (especially in Irkutsk and Tomsk) and the more prosperous among the peasants, and a Siberian 'regionalist' movement developed from the 1870s. A similar tendency began to develop towards the end of the century in the Far East, where the Amur and Maritime areas had been annexed by Russia following the treaties with China in 1857 and 1860, and Vladivostok, founded in 1862, had rapidly developed into a prosperous port with a cosmopolitan (Russian, Chinese and Korean) population and wide trading contacts in the Pacific area.

The Railway

A new era in the life of Siberia and the Russian Far East opened with the construction of the Trans-Siberian Railway in 1891-99, the eastern section of which was at first formed by the Chinese Eastern Railway built by the Russians in Manchuria in 1896-1903. The immediate effects of the new ease of communications were twofold: a rapid increase in agricultural colonization, and a more intensive Russian involvement in Far Eastern affairs in general, especially as regards China and Korea. Colonization was now primarily motivated not by the needs of Siberia but by agricultural over-population in European Russia. This peasant settlement was put on a systematic and rational, though very bureaucratic, basis, the whole operation being directed from the Resettlement Board in St. Petersburg. The tempo of colonization was further accelerated by the agricultural reforms of Stolypin in 1907. On the eve of the 1917 revolution the peasant population of Siberia and the Far East was not homogeneous, being divided on the one hand into the 'old inhabitants' and the 'new settlers', and the latter in turn into those who had done well and those who had not succeeded in creating viable farms. Dairy farming was the most profitable enterprise, and through a cooperative butter-making and marketing organization Siberian butter went as far afield as England.

The Revolution

Siberia and the Far East had their share of revolutionary events, during both the 1905 and the 1917 Russian revolutions, and in both cases it was the railwaymen and the soldiers who were the most responsive to the call of the revolutionary parties. During the Civil War the area was for the most part in the hands of various, usually ephemeral, anti-Bolshevik regimes, one of which was a Siberian Government formed in Tomsk in 1918 by the regionalists. In 1919-20 Omsk in Western Siberia was the residence of Admiral Kolchak, recognized by the other White governments as the 'Supreme Ruler' of Russia. The Bolshevik victory in 1920 was socially a victory for the poorer elements among the 'new settlers', who now benefited most from the redistribution of land. Until the mid-1930s most of Siberia was ruled by the Bolsheviks as a single unit, first by the Siberian Revolutionary Committee, then by the Siberian Bureau of the Central Committee of the Communist

Party, and at the end as one administrative area—the Siberian *kray* (territory). The Far East was not at once incorporated into the Russian Soviet Federative Socialist Republic, but a Far Eastern Republic was formed in 1920 (with Chita as its capital) as a kind of buffer state between Communist Russia and Japan. It was one of the first examples of a 'people's democratic' regime controlled by the Bolsheviks. The Far Eastern Republic existed until 1922, when it ostensibly dissolved itself and was admitted into the RSFSR as the Far Eastern *kray*. The indigenous peoples of the area, of which some of the larger tried to organize autonomous regimes of their own in 1917 and during the Civil War, were subjected to the usual Soviet policy of fictitious territorial autonomy (there are now three Autonomous Republics, three Autonomous Oblasts and six National Okrugs in Siberia and the Far East) and encouragement for the development of cultures 'national in form and socialist in content'.

Collectivization of Agriculture

Collectivization of agriculture in 1929-34 put an end to the class of prosperous Siberian farmers, and dairy farming was so severely hit that it has still not recovered. The peasants put up strong resistance to collectivization, and there were several uprisings, one of them (in the Altay area) lasting for four years. On the other hand, industrialization, which had begun with the construction of the Trans-Siberian Railway and had received some slight impetus from the First World War, was again taken up during the First Five-Year Plan period (1929-32), and the Kuznetsk coal-mining basin became second in importance in the whole USSR. Throughout the period of Stalin's rule in Russia most construction projects in Siberia and the Far East, as well as timber-felling and the mining of precious metals, were largely worked by the forced labour of concentration camp inmates and 'special settlers' (people deported from European Russia and from the territories in the west which were annexed between 1939 and 1946). During the Second World War, when many factories were evacuated to Siberia from the west, and throughout the post-war period, Siberian industry has been growing very rapidly, especially in western Siberia. The Virgin Land Campaign of 1953-56, and the emphasis in the current Seven-Year Plan on accelerated development of the eastern parts of the USSR, have created boom conditions in western and central Siberia: the cities are growing rapidly, Novosibirsk having reached the million mark; the Trans-Siberian Railway has been electrified as far as Irkutsk; a Siberian Division of the USSR Academy of Sciences has been established which appears to be very vigorous and somewhat freer from ideological shackles than older academic establishments.

The Far East (including the Kurile Islands and the southern half of Sakhalin, which were annexed from Japan after the end of the war and from which all Japanese were expelled) has so far been little affected by this new expansion, and its rate of economic development in recent years has been lower than the USSR average, though it too has to some extent benefited from the freer conditions of the post-Stalin era—e.g. the Far Eastern University in Vladivostok, which had been closed in consequence of the Great Purge of the late 1930s, was re-opened in 1956, and there have been signs in the last year or two that there is some realization of the Far East's potentialities as a supplier of industrial goods to the under-developed countries of Eastern Asia.

The Great Purge

The Great Purge of 1937-38 affected Siberia and the Far East at least as severely as the rest of the Soviet Union. Among the people who were shot or died in concentration camps were the leading members of all the Party and administrative apparatus in the area, including Marshal Blyukher, who, as commander of the Soviet armed forces in the Far East, had for a decade exercised something like vice-regal powers. All the Chinese, and those Koreans who were not Soviet citizens, who for more than half a century had lived in Vladivostok and other parts of the Far East, were expelled from the USSR, while Koreans who were Soviet citizens were deported to Kazakhstan and Central Asia. The Siberian and Far Eastern concentration camp areas, which included some of the most notorious in the country—copper and uranium mining in Noril'sk on the lower Yenisey and gold, platinum and tin mining in the *Dal'stroy* camp system in the extreme north-east centred on Magadan—were the scenes of some of the most important strikes and uprisings of camp inmates in 1953-55. Since the release of the prisoners in 1955-57, the industries of these areas have declined and now appear to be stagnant.

Economic Prospects

The economic outlook for Siberia, especially its southern parts along the Trans-Siberian Railway, is bright thanks to its mineral riches, great rivers and abundance of forests. The known plans for the next two decades foresee the building of several huge hydro-electric and thermal power stations, a further great expansion of the iron and steel industry and engineering, and the creation of aluminium and chemical industries. These plans are likely to be fulfilled, provided, of course, that Siberia continues to enjoy the priority that has been given to its development in recent years. A difficult problem is that of labour, since the natural increase of the population will provide only a small fraction of what is required. Since the forced labour of camp inmates and the large-scale deportation of people to Siberia as 'special settlers' have now ceased, the authorities have to rely for attracting settlers from European Russia upon a combination of material incentives (which have to be very substantial, because of the adverse climatic and living conditions) and all sorts of pressures short of actual deportation. This last category of semi-voluntary labour consists mainly of young people who are recruited soon after they leave school, and they form rather an unstable element in Siberia. On the one hand they are often enthusiastic and selfless in work, caring little about the difficult conditions, but on the other hand many soon return home, unwilling to stick it out for long, while those who do remain are often difficult to handle and strikes occur frequently. The prospects for Siberian agriculture are much less promising than those for industry. The Virgin Land Campaign has brought under cultivation large areas and western Siberia has become one of the chief producers of grain in the country;

but mono-culture and bad management have already led to soil erosion, the yields, even at first not very high, are falling, and in view of the generally irrational agricultural policy of the Soviet leadership (under-investment and restrictions upon initiative) little improvement can be expected in the foreseeable future.

Racial Assimilation

The native peoples, apart from the Mongol-speaking Buryats and the Turkic-speaking Yakuts (perhaps also the Tuvinians, whose country was quietly annexed in 1944), are expected to become assimilated, though this is not often stated openly. Far more important is the question of whether the Soviet Government (or any Russian government) will be able or willing to maintain the policy of exclusively white settlement in the Russian Far East pursued since the 1930s, or whether it will be forced (not least by the need for labour, which is already critical) to re-open the doors to Chinese immigration.

BIBLIOGRAPHY

J. P. Cole and F. C. German. *A Geography of the U.S.S.R. The Background to a Planned Economy.* (Butterworth, London, 1961.)

D. J. Dallin. *The Rise of Russia in Asia.* (Hollis and Carter, London, 1950.) *Soviet Russia and the Far East.* (Hollis and Carter, London, 1948.)

G. Kennan. *Siberia and the Exile System*, 2 vols. (The Century Co., New York, 1891.)

R. J. Kerner. *The Urge to the Sea. The Course of Russian History: The Role of Rivers, Portages, Ostrogs, Monastries and Furs.* (University of California Press, Berkeley and Los Angeles, 1946.)

W. Kolarz. *The Peoples of the Soviet Far East.* (George Phillip, London, 1954.)

C. Krypton. *The Northern Sea Route and the Economy of the Soviet Union.* (Methuen, London, 1956.)

G. V. Lantzeff. *Siberia in the Seventeenth Century.* (Univ. of California Press, Berkeley, 1943.)

E. Lipper. *Eleven Years in Soviet Prison Camps.* (Hollis and Carter, London, 1951.)

M. A. Novomeysky. *My Siberian Life.* (Max Parrish, London, 1956.)

V. Petrov. *It Happens in Russia. Seven Years Forced Labour in the Siberian Goldfields.* (Eyre and Spottiswoode, London, 1951.)

M. Raeff. *Siberia and the Reforms of 1822.* (University of Washington Press, Seattle, 1956.)

Y. Semyonov. *The Conquest of Siberia.* (Routledge, London, 1944.)

E. Thiel. *The Soviet Far East. A Survey of its Physical and Economic Geography.* (Methuen, London, 1957.)

D. W. Treadgold. *The Great Siberian Migration: Government and Peasant in Resettlement from Emancipation to the First World War.* (Princeton Univ. Press, Princeton, N.J., 1957.)

BIOGRAPHICAL NOTE

S. V. Utechin. B. 1921 in Russia; educated at Moscow University (Faculty of History), Kiel University and Oxford (B. Litt.). Senior Research Officer in Soviet Studies at the London School of Economics and Political Science 1958-62; Research Fellow at St. Antony's College, Oxford since 1962. Publications: *Everyman's Concise Encyclopaedia of Russia* (Dent, London, 1961), *Russian Political Thought: A Concise History* (Dent, London, 1964), and many articles on modern Russian history and Soviet affairs.

SOUTH-EAST ASIA

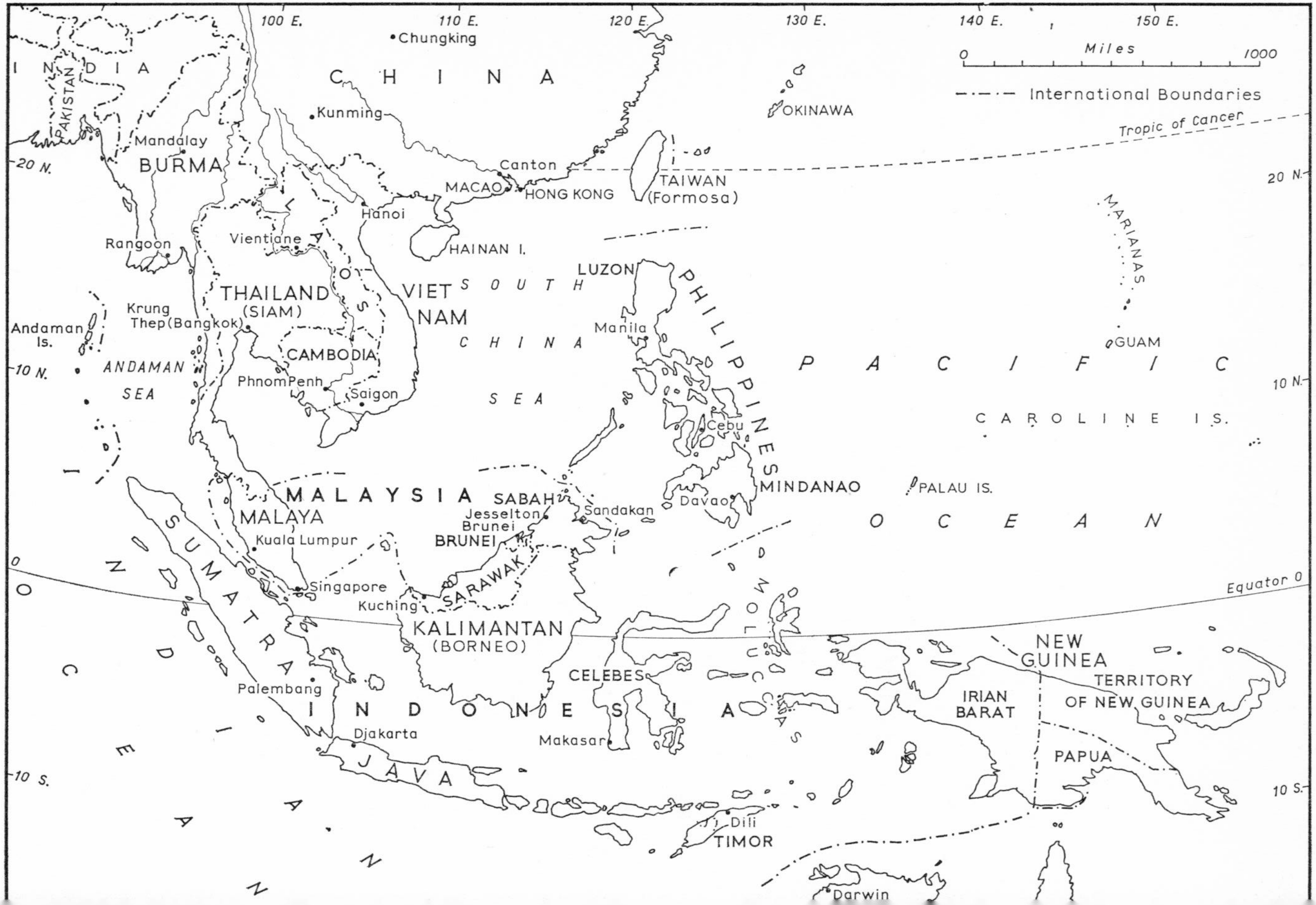
100 E.
110 E.
120 E.
130 E.
140 E.
150 E.
Miles
0
1000
International Boundaries
Tropic of Cancer
20 N.
10 N.
Equator 0
10 S.
0
INDIA
PAKISTAN
CHINA
Chungking
Kunming
Mandalay
BURMA
Rangoon
Canton
MACAO
HONG KONG
TAIWAN (Formosa)
OKINAWA
MARIANAS
GUAM
Hanoi
HAINAN I.
LAOS
Vientiane
THAILAND (SIAM)
Krung Thep (Bangkok)
Andaman Is.
ANDAMAN SEA
CAMBODIA
Phnom Penh
Saigon
VIET NAM
SOUTH CHINA SEA
LUZON
Manila
PHILIPPINES
Cebu
MINDANAO
Davao
PACIFIC OCEAN
CAROLINE IS.
PALAU IS.
MALAYSIA
MALAYA
Kuala Lumpur
Singapore
SABAH
Jesselton
Brunei
BRUNEI
Sandakan
SARAWAK
Kuching
KALIMANTAN (BORNEO)
CELEBES
Makasar
MOLUCCAS
SUMATRA
Palembang
INDONESIA
Djakarta
JAVA
Dili
TIMOR
NEW GUINEA
IRIAN BARAT
TERRITORY OF NEW GUINEA
PAPUA
Darwin
INDIAN OCEAN

SOUTH-EAST ASIA

by

SAUL ROSE

Lands and Peoples

South-East Asia, which stretches from Burma's western frontier to the most easterly island of Indonesia, consists of a peninsula of the Asian continent together with an archipelago lying between Australia and the China coast. These geographical features have given it the character of a crossroads. It has provided stepping-stones for the migration of peoples making their way down from the mainland, while through the Straits of Malacca—'the gateway to the Pacific'—has lain the main sea route to the East.

Most of the population of the area, which is estimated to total more than 200 million, can be classified as belonging to the 'Indonesian' type. Their ancestors are believed to have originated from more northerly climes, and to have made their way southward in two major migrations between 2500 and 1500 B.C. Descendants of earlier inhabitants are still to be found in tribes such as the Sakai, which live in the jungles of Malaya; and there were later arrivals, notably the Annamites, the Thai and the Burmans, who also moved down from the north. Thence too came the overseas Chinese who are scattered about the region in considerable numbers, amounting to 12-13 million. As a result of these migrations the region presents a kaleidoscope of peoples, and each country is confronted with the problems of a 'plural' or multi-racial society.

Cultural Influences

In addition, the cultural pattern was strongly marked by external influences. South-East Asia has been an area of overlap between the Indian and Chinese spheres. In the first phase Indian influence predominated. Brahmanism and Buddhism were imported by Indian merchants, and the impress was visible in various forms ranging from styles of architecture to systems of government. Indianized kingdoms rose and fell during the first fifteen centuries of the Christian era. Some of them paid tribute to the Emperor of China from time to time, but the Chinese cultural impact was felt mainly in the area adjacent to the Empire, particularly in Annam.

In the 14th and 15th centuries Islam reached South-East Asia, brought by Muslim traders from the Middle East and from India, and made rapid headway. Malacca, through its key position dominating the Straits, became both the main *entrepôt* for trade and also the centre for the propagation of the faith.

In the 16th century began the era of Western dominance. The Portuguese and Spaniards sought not only 'Christians and spices' but also political supremacy. The Portuguese captured Malacca in 1511 and secured control of the valuable Spice Islands, while the Spaniards established themselves in the Philippines. The Portuguese in their turn were ousted by the Dutch in the following century. The East Indies, despite British efforts to intervene, fell under Dutch control, and Portugal was left with the vestigial possession of half the island of Timor.

The wave of imperialism in the 19th century brought the British back on the scene. Burma was conquered; Singapore was founded and soon outstripped Malacca which was acquired from the Dutch; the rest of the Malay peninsula was brought under British protection, which was extended to Sarawak, North Borneo and Brunei. The French established their ascendancy in Indochina, and Siam was left as a buffer state between French and British spheres of influence, owing its survival to their rivalry. Then at the end of the century, after their victory over Spain, the U.S.A. took possession of the Philippines.

By 1900, therefore, almost the whole of the area had fallen under Western sway. Even Siam's nominal independence was subject to strong Western influence. This state of affairs lasted for 40 years. It would have gone on considerably longer had it not been for the Japanese onslaught which overthrew the Western positions in a matter of a few months. From 1942 to 1945 the Japanese 'New Order' replaced Western dominance, but made very few converts. The interregnum, however, had two decisive effects: it showed that Western rule was not unalterable, and it encouraged the growth of nationalism in resistance to foreign domination from any quarter. Ironically the concept of nationhood was in many cases the result of colonial conquest. The political boundaries in South-East Asia are largely the result of accidents of acquisition. It was out of the idea of combined resistance to alien rule that the concept of common nationhood grew.

Western Withdrawal

At first the policy of the Western Powers, returning to South-East Asia as the end of the Japanese war approached, was essentially the restoration of the *status quo ante bellum*; but this was found to be impossible. The U.S.A. had promised independence to the Philippines, and fulfilled that undertaking in 1946. In the British sphere a process of decolonization set in, starting with the Indian Empire and spreading inexorably eastward. In the event the only question was whether the Western Powers would go gracefully or be ejected. Britain parted with Burma on friendly terms; and then Malaya attained independence, leaving the State of Singapore with a large measure of internal self-government and the dependencies of Sarawak, North Borneo and Brunei as the last outposts of empire. The Dutch, however, had to be expelled by the combined forces of the Indonesian nationalist movement and world opinion, although they retained Western New Guinea until 1962 despite continual complaints from Indonesia. The anti-Western movement was reinforced from 1949 by the Communist triumph in China. This was felt particularly in Indochina; and the French, after a grim and costly war, were obliged to quit. Laos and Cambodia became independent states, but Vietnam was divided between a Communist regime in the north and an anti-Communist regime in the south.

The Indochina crisis in 1954 led to the Western proposal for a regional defence arrangement, which was accepted by some of the countries in the area. The South-East Asia Treaty Organization, which was set up by Pakistan, Thailand, the Philippines, Australia, New Zealand, Britain, France and the U.S.A., extended its protection to the Indochina settlement reached at the Geneva Conference. While SEATO has proved effective in preventing any open Communist aggression it has shown itself unable to cope with subversion in areas bordering on the Communist sector. Laos and South Vietnam have been subjected to infiltration and Cambodia has been under pressure. Communist guerilla activity was successfully combated in Malaya, but it had no direct line of communication with its main base in China and, even so, it took ten years of considerable military effort. The border zone is much more vulnerable to penetration.

Communism and Nationalism

The spread of Communism elsewhere in the region has been inhibited partly by the unassimilated character of overseas Chinese society. Often unpopular because of their role as moneylenders and middlemen, they are sometimes regarded with suspicion as a potential 'fifth column' for Chinese imperialism. To the extent that Communism is now identified with China its appeal to the other communities is diminished.

The force of nationalism is still predominant. In the colonial period the Communists could exploit the nationalist movement for their own ends, since for both of them the immediate aim was to shake off the foreign yoke. Once independence was achieved, however, a Communist movement which showed itself subservient to alien control lost the support of nationalists. Even when the current of nationalism has run counter to Communism it has not led to a pro-Western stand, partly because the memory of the independence struggle dies hard, and partly because in some places Western rule still persists. So long as the Dutch held onto Western New Guinea President Sukarno could maintain a state of 'permanent revolution', with advantage to the Indonesian Communist Party and sympathy from his Asian neighbours. The Portuguese in Timor may not be left undisturbed much longer. For Britain a problem was posed by Singapore and the Borneo territories. The solution that was propounded was to merge them with the Federation of Malaya in a 'New Malaysia'. This project only became feasible after Malaya had attained independence and showed its capacity for self-government. The scheme was accepted by Singapore with its predominantly Chinese population; but in the Borneo territories, where public opinion had only rudimentary means of political expression, the situation was more obscure. The Sultan of Brunei declined to join. The two British colonies of Sarawak and North Borneo (now called Sabah) were incorporated in the new Malaysia in September 1963 after a UN commission of enquiry had found that most of the population favoured the project. But the new creation aroused hostility from neighbouring Indonesia which embarked on a policy of 'confrontation' designed to intimidate and 'crush' Malaysia.

To the problem of insecurity is added the question of whether the countries of South-East Asia can be made politically and economically viable. Most of them adopted forms of Western democracy as their model, partly because of familiarity and partly because their claim to independence had been based on democratic principles. Whether Western-style institutions, even though modified, are suited to South-East Asian conditions is open to question. In South Vietnam, under constant Communist threat, they merely veiled the dictatorship of President Diem and his successors. President Sukarno has instituted 'guided democracy' in Indonesia. Siam experimented briefly with a limited form of democracy until Marshal Sarit put a stop to it. In Burma a much more promising experiment has also been halted by the Army. In several countries the attainment of independence has been followed by an increase in communal tensions, previously overlaid by the nationalist movement, and a need has been felt for more discipline and cohesion, which the Army has been ready and willing to supply.

Politics and Economics

Although there is a trend towards more authoritarian rule, this does not imply any abatement of the spirit of national independence. But Communism might find an opening if the new countries cannot supply the material needs of their peoples. They occupy an extensive and productive portion of the globe, comprising a land area of more than $1\frac{1}{2}$ million square miles. Although there are some dense concentrations, particularly on the islands of Java and Luzon and in the Red River delta of Vietnam, the region as a whole is not very thickly populated and has traditionally provided a surplus of food, particularly rice, for export. Among the other major products entering into international trade are rubber, tin, timber and oil. The region is 'under-developed' although the standard of living is generally higher than in China or India. The economy is mainly agricultural, and not greatly diversified. It is consequently vulnerable to economic fluctuations. There is competition between East and West in the supply of economic and technical assistance; but the new states are sensitive, and suspicious of 'strings' being attached. They are torn between the desire for foreign investment and their resolve to avoid any form of 'colonialism'. Economic development is subordinated to political considerations.

The Colombo Plan

In 1950 the Colombo Plan was launched, under Commonwealth auspices, with the aim of bringing assistance to the countries of South and South-East Asia, partly by mutual aid. This project was so successful that it was extended and expanded: it is still continuing and includes every country in the region except North Vietnam. But the amounts supplied are relatively small. Much greater quantities are being provided by the U.S.A. directly to individual countries through bilateral arrangements.

Partly through economic influence and partly for reasons of strategy the U.S. role in South-East Asia has been enhanced while that of the European

Powers has declined. America has assumed some of the responsibility—and also some of the odium—which previously attached to the Colonial Powers. Australia too is taking a growing part in the affairs of her 'Near North', while China under the new regime has clearly not lost her traditional interest in the 'Southern Ocean'. These attentions are unwelcome in some quarters, but they are unavoidable. Neither side can afford to relinquish the region to the other.

Several of the South-East Asian countries, for their part, refuse to be committed and prefer a policy of non-alignment. Similarly, in their domestic affairs, presented with a choice between Communist and Western models they decline the option and are trying their own methods. These experiments may sometimes appear misguided, but they are a mark of independence; and perhaps there may emerge from them a new contribution towards solving the problems of South-East Asia.

BIBLIOGRAPHY

J. H. Brimmell. *Communism in South-East Asia.* (O.U.P., London, 1959).

R. H. Fifield. *Diplomacy of Southeast Asia, 1945-58.* (Harper, New York, 1958.)

D. G. E. Hall. *History of South-East Asia.* (Macmillan, London, 1955.)

B. Harrison. *South-East Asia.* (Macmillan, London, 1955.)

G. McT. Kahin (ed.). *Governments and Politics of South-East Asia.* (Cornell Univ. Press, New York, 1959.)

BIOGRAPHICAL NOTE

SAUL ROSE, M.A., D.Phil. Fellow of New College, Oxford. Lecturer in International Relations at Aberdeen University, 1949-52. International Secretary of the Labour Party, 1952-55. Fellow of St. Antony's College, Oxford, 1955-63. Publications: *Socialism in Southern Asia.* (Oxford Univ. Press, London, 1959). *Britain and South-East Asia* (Chatto and Windus, London, 1963). Editor of *Politics in Southern Asia* (Macmillan, London, 1963.)

CHINA
BHUTAN
INDIA
EAST PAKISTAN
DACCA
BAY OF BENGAL
Akyab
Kaladan
UPPER BURMA
Myitkyina
Bhamo
Lashio
Mandalay
Irrawaddy
Salween
BURMA
ARAKAN YOMA
Magwe
PEGU YOMA
Sittang
Prome
LOWER BURMA
Bassein
RANGOON
Moulmein
LAOS
Luang Prabang
VIENTIANE
THAILAND
ANDAMAN SEA
ANDAMAN IS.
Tavoy
TENASSERIM
Mergui
KRUNG THEP
(Bangkok)
GULF OF SIAM
KACHIN STATE
CHIN DIVISION
BURMA PROPER
SHAN STATES
KAYEN
KAREN
INTERNAL DIVISIONS
90 E.
100 E.
20 N.
10 N.
National Capitals
Towns
International Boundaries
Disputed Boundary
Land over 200 metres
0 Miles 200

BURMA

by

HUGH TINKER

ORIGIN

MORE than most countries, Burma is a complex of antitheses. A national unity and a tribalistic disunity; the cult of serenity and withdrawal, and the cult of force and violence; the worship of absolute authority, together with an absence of social barriers; relaxed and easy personal relations, constantly exploding into tension and schizophrenia: these are some of the attributes of this puzzling country. Burma has undergone invasion, colonial occupation, foreign economic exploitation, the ravages of 20th-century war, the intoxication of a Socialist-style democracy, and the drab regimentation of military rule. While foreign observers have constantly predicted disintegration and collapse, Burma has survived all these experiences with the essence of its social and religious life unimpaired. This resilience is, perhaps, the key to this paradoxical, indeed Gilbertian country.

Burmans are fond of recalling that their national unity predates the Norman conquest of England. King Anawrahta (A.D 1044-77) ruled an empire that included most of modern Burma within its boundaries, from his capital, Pagan. The Burmese race had penetrated the northern and eastern mountain boundaries about the year A.D. 700. They gradually displaced earlier inhabitants, the Pyu and the Mons, though their settlements did not penetrate into the region of Lower Burma. The Burmese were followed by branches of the great Thai race, known in Burma as Shans. Between 1287 and 1531, the Shans dominated Upper Burma. All these peoples adopted wet-rice cultivation, using irrigation, and embraced (to greater or lesser extent) the teaching of the Theravada school of Buddhism, gained from Ceylon. They occupied the level lands of the Irrawaddy plain, and the valley country in east and north Burma. The hills remained the domain of tribes who largely practised shifting, dry-rice cultivation, and who remained Animists. Among the more prominent were the Kachins, the Karens, and the Chins. Remaining outside Buddhism, they did not acquire a literary culture and they did not imitate Hindu ideas of kingship, as did the plain-dwellers.

The Prime Minister of Burma between 1947 and 1962, U Nu, in his appeals for national unity constantly reminded his countrymen that Burma had never long sustained a unified polity. Nu recalled: 'The evil tradition of wresting power by force. Burmese history is full of instances where a king is overthrown by a contender by force, and who in turn is similarly ousted by a still more forceful rival. Except for the glorious period of Anawrahta,

Bayinnaung and Alaungpaya, Burma has been a battlefield of warring states.' Bayinnaung reigned from 1551 to 1581; Alaungpaya from 1752 to 1760. Both unified Burma by military conquest, but neither created a unitary state. Alaungpaya's dynasty ruled until 1885, when Burma finally passed under British rule; but not even its most able kings created a regular system of administration, while under the worst the country degenerated into anarchy.

Burma Annexed to British India

Burma was annexed to British India between 1826 and 1885; it was governed as an Indian province, and its administration, educational system, laws, and economic structure were largely conditioned by the Indian connexion. Immigration, much from south and east India, led to the growth of an Indian community of half a million, and the most important sectors of commerce were in Indian hands. The export-import trade was dominated by British and Indian companies. Whereas in India the experience of British rule created, virtually, a new class—a middle class with an all-India outlook who formulated a demand for political autonomy and independence—in Burma, no such transformation came about. The small professional middle class was drawn almost entirely from the small group of official families which had served the Burmese Kings. They failed to establish any kind of leadership, or contact with the peasant mass. In the aftermath of the Dyarchy reforms in India, Burma received instalments of political devolution: a legislature, ministerial government, and responsibility for many aspects of administration.

The 'Thakins'

But the middle-class lawyer-politicians remained cocooned in their own little world, and mass political leadership passed to itinerant monks (not unlike the hedge-priest, John Ball), of whom U Wisara was foremost. Theirs was a crude, rabble-rousing appeal, and their programme was little more than preaching hatred of the foreigners and a return to the good old days. In the 1930s, they gave way to an extremist group, the *Dobama Asi-ayone*, commonly called *Thakins*, or 'Masters'. The Thakins attracted a following among a group of students at Rangoon University. Drawn from the rural lower middle class, for the most part backward in their studies, these rustic students decided to invest in political agitation. In 1936, they contrived a strike, which involved about half the undergraduates. Under pressure from the Minister for Education, Dr. Ba Maw, the university authorities capitulated. Thenceforward, the militant strike was the master-weapon in Burmese politics.

The 1930s in Burma opened with the Saya San rebellion, a primitive, messianic revolt, and with the anti-Indian riots; the decade closed with student riots and the formation of political private armies on the Fascist model: the Thakin Army was known as the Steel Corps. The Thakins linked up with Japanese agents, and thirty young men, headed by Aung San, the 1936 strike leader, went to Japan for military training. Early in 1942, they re-entered Burma with the Japanese invader. Having driven out the British forces, the Japanese granted a façade of independence to Burma. They appointed Dr. Ba Maw as Head of State, *Adipati*, or Generalissimo. His principal lieutenants were drawn from the Thakins, with Aung San as *Bogyoke*, or chief of the Japanese-controlled 'Burma National Army', Thakin Nu as head of the Foreign Office, and Than Tun (a Communist Thakin) as minister for agriculture. Gradually, the Thakins became disillusioned with their Japanese masters, and they made contact with British military intelligence agencies. In 1944 the tide of war turned; the Japanese suffered their most severe military disaster in any theatre in an abortive advance into India; in the early months of 1945, British-Indian forces swept down into the plain of the Irrawaddy. Aung San led his Burma National Army into hiding, and subsequently made his way to British military headquarters.

Recognition of Aung San

After hostilities ceased, Burma came under British military government, and events were considerably influenced by the decision taken by Admiral Mountbatten as Supreme Commander to recognize Aung San and his colleagues as leaders of the 'Patriotic Burmese Forces'. In the post-war political settlement, Aung San successfully outplayed other contenders for power. He kept together his erstwhile soldiers in a quasi-military association, the 'People's Volunteer Organization' or PVO, and he held together a significant political following in the 'Anti-Fascist People's Freedom League' or AFPFL. This included the growing Communist movement led by Than Tun. Aung San's demand was nothing less than full control over the Government. Taking advantage of police grievances, he was able to launch a national general strike which immobilized all the public services. His demands were accepted, and on 9th January 1947 he came to London to negotiate an agreement with Mr. Attlee, the import of which may be summarized as 'full independence within one year'.

Although there was much that was ignoble in his makeup, Aung San was a man of vision: he saw that an essential prerequisite of independence was national unity, and he realized that the Shans and the hill tribes still nourished ancient enmities, arising out of a thousand years of conflict. In February 1947, he negotiated an agreement with leaders of the frontier peoples which largely secured their confidence. In June, a constitution was introduced—which entailed Burma quitting the British Commonwealth—and then, in July, Aung San and most of his Cabinet were assassinated. At the invitation of the last British Governor, Sir Hubert Rance, Thakin Nu took his place as Prime Minister, and led his country into independence on 4th January 1948.

Independence and After

During the following months, the Union of Burma seemed unlikely to have any lasting duration. Revolts broke out on every hand. First, Than Tun and the Communists 'went underground'; they were followed by the now leaderless PVO; finally, in February 1949, a large section of the Karen minority joined the rebellion. Many of the Karens had become Christians, many had served in the army, and they had formed by far the most effective war-time resistance movement; now they came close to capturing Rangoon, but they divided their forces in order to take secondary objectives, such as Mandalay, and their moment faded. In the hour of crisis, Nu was deserted by his Socialist colleagues in the Cabinet, Ba Swe and Kyaw Nyein; he was compelled to form a non-partisan government of national emergency, in which his principal lieutenants were Justice E Maung (Foreign Minister) and the Commander of the Armed Forces, General Ne Win (Deputy Premier, Minister for Home Affairs and Defence). Gradually, the insurgents were thrown back; first, the principal towns were retaken; then, lines of communication were re-established; and at last the rebels were driven into the hills and the jungle. But they could not be completely finished off, as were the Communist guerillas in Malaya.

General Elections and the AFPFL

The first general elections after independence took place in 1951. Because of continuing insecurity, they were staggered over the months June-October. The AFPFL, as the ruling coalition, secured 85 per cent of the seats in parliament on 60 per cent of the popular vote. The only element of opposition came from a small group representing Arakan; which region considered itself underprivileged after independence. Following the elections, the AFPFL Government made strenuous efforts to further its programme for economic development. The philosophy of the AFPFL leaders was, originally, thorough-going in its Marxism. Soon after independence, measures of nationalization (that is, expropriation) of foreign-owned utilities were pushed through. The insurrections slowed down the process of nationalization, and the flight of foreign capital gave the Government food for thought. A team of American economists and technicians were invited to make a survey of Burma's resources and to prepare a blue-print for future economic development. This team presented a preliminary report in May 1952, and on its recommendations the Government launched a development programme (July 1952) under the slogan 'Towards a Welfare State'. In Burmese this was called *Pyidawtha* (literally, 'sacred-pleasant-country'). The next year, the American team presented a 2,000-page *Comprehensive Report*, which purported to provide a recipe for all Burma's problems, economic and administrative. There was to be an investment programme, to be completed by 1960, to cost 7,500,000,000 Kyats or £562,500,000. The attitude of those who drafted this plan is summarized in their declaration:

> There is no known limit to possible improvements in materials, methods, and products . . . Burma must become a progressive nation, so that her people not only live better in 1960, but look forward to continued improvement without limit.

All this was very much to the liking of politicians who had preached that their British rulers had deliberately kept them poor. Unfortunately, not one forecast made in the plan was ever implemented. A number of new industrial undertakings were launched: textile mills, a steel mill, a pharmaceutical plant. All swallowed up foreign exchange, all ran into difficulties, and none was made to run at a profit. During the same period, the international terms of trade shifted, to Burma's disadvantage. The world price of rice, upon which Burma mainly depended, came tumbling down; imports increased in volume, but receipts steadily fell. By 1955, Burma was suffering from an acute balance of payments crisis. Attempts to alleviate the position by a series of barter agreements with Communist countries proved highly disadvantageous. The industrialization programme was first curtailed, and then largely liquidated. All this was intensely frustrating to the Marxist-Socialist members of the Cabinet.

Buddhism as Solution to Nation's Problems

Meanwhile, Nu as Prime Minister was steadily putting more and more emphasis upon religion, upon Buddhism, as the solution to the nation's problems. Between 1954 and 1956 an international Buddhist Council held conclave at Rangoon, and much merit accrued to the Prime Minister and to Burma. A second general election took place in April 1956. Again, the AFPFL was confirmed in power: but with a considerably reduced majority. Nu decided to take a year's sabbatical leave from the premiership, in order to reorganize and rejuvenate the AFPFL. Ba Swe, the Socialist boss, became Prime Minister *ad interim*. When Nu returned to office, it became clear that a breach was opening between his supporters and the Socialists. This became acute when, in January 1958, at an All-Burma Congress of the AFPFL, Nu delivered a long statement of policy in which he concluded 'the AFPFL rejects Marxism as a guiding philosophy or as the ideology of the AFPFL'. This was taken by Ba Swe and Kyaw Nyein as a direct challenge to their Marxist-Socialist position. On 4th June 1958, these two resigned from the Government, along with all their following. To confront the well-organized Socialist parliamentary faction, Nu had only the rump of the so-called 'Clean' AFPFL. He obtained reinforcements from the Arakanese bloc, and from ex-Justice E Maung and others. Faced with a Socialist motion of no confidence, he obtained a majority of seven. To break this near-deadlock, Nu announced that fresh elections would be held in November. But this was not to be.

The Army Takes Over

On 28th October, Parliament was assembled, and Nu announced that he was handing over power to General Ne Win and the Army. Constitutional proprieties were observed, and the General secured the assent of Parliament to his actions. He announced his intention of restoring national order and stability, in order to create a situation in which fair elections could take place. The military regime carried through a number of reforms, but earned increasing unpopularity.

Elections were fixed for February 1960. Most observers favoured the chances of the Swe-Nyein group, called the 'Stable' AFPFL. They were known to have the support of influential army leaders, such as Brigadier Aung Gyi, the Chief of Staff. Nu enjoyed the support of a handful of front-rank politicians, but behind them stood a raggle-taggle party. Undaunted, Nu flung himself into a political campaign reminiscent of Franklin Roosevelt in his prime. He made two sweeping promises: he declared that Buddhism should be declared as the state religion, and he undertook to extend the principle of separate State or regional autonomy, already enjoyed by the Shans, Kachins, Chins, and Karens, to two other minorities: the Arakanese and the Mons. When polling day came, Nu won a landslide victory; out of 250 seats in the Chamber of Deputies, his party won 166 seats; his Socialist opponents gained a mere 34 seats, and both Ba Swe and Kyaw Nyein were unseated.

General Ne Win promptly handed back the premiership to Nu, and withdrew his military men from the ministries and public corporations. Nu now named his party the *Pyidaungsu Ahphwe-gyok* or Union League, leaving to the Swe-Nyein group the discredited name of the AFPFL. His government redeemed its pre-election promises circumspectly, but showed no great readiness to tackle the problems facing the nation. One long-term problem was student unrest; the 1936 pattern of the militant strike was constantly repeated. A reforming Rector, Dr. Hla Myint, attempted to tighten discipline and raise the lax academic standards. Nu compromised and conciliated, and Dr. Hla Myint resigned. Another urgent problem was the continuing suspicion of many of the frontier peoples of the policies of the central government. The Shans, especially, included a section which desired to secede from the Union of Burma, as the 1947 Constitution entitled them to do. The Army had exercised a heavy hand in the Shan States, and in 1959 a new revolt broke out in the Shan hills.

The Revolutionary Council

Among the army leaders, an influential group had never accepted the desirability of a return to parliamentary government. This group became steadily more powerful, and eventually they prevailed upon General Ne Win to intervene. On 2nd March 1962 the army moved into Rangoon. The Prime Minister, the President, the Chief Justice, and a number of prominent persons were arrested. The 1947 Constitution was abolished, and General Ne Win became chairman of a revolutionary council. With one exception, the new government was drawn exclusively from the armed forces. The country's constabulary was absorbed into the army. The Supreme Court and the High Court were dissolved. A draconian policy of national discipline was instituted; the only serious protest came from the student body. A riot on the usual model in July 1962 was suppressed by military force, with the death of fifteen student agitators. Measures to discipline the ebullient, pleasure-loving Burmese were accompanied by measures to control and exclude foreigners. Xenophobia, endemic in Burma, arose again. In the past Burma had many times slammed the door in the face of the outside world. But in the 1960s there was one power which Burma could not hope to shut out: Communist China. The conclusion of an agreement with China on 28th January 1960 over the disputed boundary was in many respects an achievement for Burma. In return for the transfer of about fifty square miles of territory to China, Burma secured a recognized frontier line, and China abandoned long-standing claims to all the country north of Myitkyina. But the tacit price of this concession was Burma's acceptance of a neutrality which allowed for no association with countries inimical to China, especially India.

Economic Situation

Such an attitude of isolation accorded with the philosophy of Ne Win's administration, expressed in the manifesto *Burma's Way to Socialism*. This may be summarized as State control and management in all sectors of the economy. The last vestiges of British participation in banking and industry were eliminated. The Indians were entirely excluded from commerce, and the domiciled Indian community was almost entirely driven out of the country. Economic development has virtually come to a standstill. Between 70 and 80 per cent of the export trade depends upon the sale of rice, for which world demand appears to be inelastic. It is calculated that in real terms the per capita income in Burma in the 1960s is some 15 per cent below the pre-war level.

BIBLIOGRAPHY

J. R. Andrus. *Burmese Economic Life.* (Stanford Univ. Press, Stanford, 1947.)

J. F. Cady. *A History of Modern Burma.* (Cornell Univ. Press, Ithaca, New York, 1958.)

J. L. Christian. *Modern Burma.* (California Univ. Press, Berkeley, 1942.) Re-issued with additional chapters as *Burma and the Japanese Invader* (Bombay, 1945.)

J. S. Furnivall. *The Governance of Modern Burma.* (Institute of Pacific Relations, New York, 1958.)

D. G. E. Hall. *Burma.* (Hutchinson, London, 2nd ed. 1956.)

W. C. Johnstone. *Burma's Foreign Policy: a study in Neutralism.* (Harvard Univ. Press, Cambridge, Mass., 1963.)

Maung Maung. *Burma's Constitution.* (The Hague, Nijhoff, 2nd ed. 1961.)

L. W. Pye. *Politics, Personality, and Nation Building: Burma's Search for Identity.* (Yale Univ. Press, New Haven, 1962.)

Thakin Nu. *Burma under the Japanese.* (Macmillan, London, 1954.)

H. Tinker (ed.). *U Hla Pe's Narrative of the Japanese Occupation of Burma.* (Cornell Data Paper, Ithaca, New York, 1961.)

H. Tinker. *The Union of Burma: A Study of the First Years of Independence.* (Oxford Univ. Press for Royal Institute of International Affairs, London, 3rd ed., 1961.)

BIOGRAPHICAL NOTE

Hugh Tinker served on the Assam-Burma border in 1942. Professor of History, University of Rangoon, 1954-55. Now Professor of Government and Politics in the University of London.

BURMA
LAOS
VIETNAM
THAILAND
CAMBODIA
ANDAMAN SEA
GULF OF SIAM
M. Chiang Rai
Chiang Mai
M. Lampang
Luang Prabang
VIENTIANE
Nong Khai
Udon Thani
Tak
M. Phitsanulok
Khonkaen
Nakhon Sawan
Chao Phraya
Lopburi
Nakhon Ratchasima
M. Ubon
Ayuthya
KRUNG THEP (Bangkok)
Mekong
PHNOM PENH
Isthmus of Kra
Songkhla
20 N.
15 N.
10 N.
100
100 E
105 E.
20
National Capitals
Towns
International Boundaries
Land over 200 metres
Miles
0
200

THAILAND

by

D. INSOR

Origin

Thai tribes started their migration from south-west China about a thousand years ago. Some advanced along the Salween river, others along the Mekong: these areas form the present-day Shan States of Burma and the Kingdom of Laos. Only the Thais, reaching the headwaters of the Menam Chao Phraya, finally penetrated to the sea.

In the 13th century the Thais drove out the Khmers (Cambodians), whose empire extended over much of the 'golden peninsula', and founded the Kingdom of Sukhotai. Ayuthaya became the capital of a new and powerful dynasty a hundred years later. This city, until its capture and total destruction by the Burmese in the mid-18th century, rivalled London in size and magnificence. In 1782 the victorious general Chakri founded the present ruling dynasty with its capital at Bangkok.

Two Remarkable Kings

From a remarkable line of kings two stand out. The wise and noble Mongkut —27 years a monk, he travelled the country, learned English and was devoted to astronomy—was succeeded in 1868 by Chulalongkorn, the 'beloved monarch', who in the 42 years of his reign revolutionized, with the help of foreign advisers, the laws, administration and customs of the Kingdom. It is a tribute to the reforms of these kings—and to the rivalry between Britain and France—that Siam (now Thailand) alone in South-East Asia was never a colony.

Free of foreign control the Thai people also preserved their independence at home. Land was made available to all who might farm it. No peasant wars have been recorded in Thai history—though invasion, forced resettlement, disease, slavery and the *corvée* (up to the end of the 19th century) exacted their toll. It is a peasant, and not a landlord, economy which accounts for the ease and stability of Thailand—the envy of less fortunate peoples.

Religion

The Thais, like their neighbours—except the Malays—are Buddhists. The influence of this compassionate yet reasonable and 'detached' religion is deeply marked. There have been no Buddhist crusades and no Buddhist persecutions, either of heretics or unbelievers. Tolerance, acceptance of 'fate' (*karma*, the result of one's own actions), even non-violence, are characteristic. Thai people are cheerful, easy going, friendly, hospitable; sometimes quick-tempered, often indolent; for they live in a climate that is warm and relaxing, in a land generally fertile and well watered, suited to the traditional rice culture.

Revolt and Counter-Revolt

The Thai people, more than 80 per cent of whom live in villages, are naturally conservative, either ignorant of politics or indifferent. Thus when in 1932 absolute monarchy was overthrown by a group of young civilians and officers, the people remained largely untouched and unmoved. Under the Constitution half the deputies were elected and half appointed, but few of the electors bothered to vote. The Army, which had defeated a royalist counter-revolt, gained more and more control over the civilians. Japan's role in the 'thirties had a strong attraction for the military leader, Colonel (later Field-Marshal) Pibun Songkram, who became Prime Minister in 1938. His civilian rival, Pridi Panomyong, a young lawyer, in succession Minister of the Interior, Foreign Affairs and Finance, was powerless to reverse the prevailing trend which, in 1941, culminated in virtual military dictatorship and alliance with Japan.

The Pridi Regime

Thailand bowed to the inevitable. But Pridi secretly organized a 'Free Thai' resistance movement with the help of the Allies and of Thais in Britain and America. In 1944 Pibun was compelled to resign and Pridi took over behind the scenes. Thailand was spared the devastation of other countries of South-East Asia but suffered serious moral deterioration. Remarkably free of corruption (or brutality) before the war, the Thai administration at that time faced few complicated problems and had been strengthened by the numerous foreign advisers recruited by King Chulalongkorn and his successors. Severely hit by the inflation of the war and post-war years, officials, politicians (and later, soldiers) succumbed to the temptations offered by government-controlled schemes, notably, in those years, the rice trade—Thailand's major export.

The Pridi regime might have endured the financial crisis, the responsibility of providing rice reparations to Malaya and the cession of parts of Burma, Malaya, Laos and Cambodia seized by Pibun, but for a tragic occurrence: the death in June 1946 of the young King. The mystery—whether it was accident, suicide or murder—has never been solved. But Pridi was blamed for failing to investigate promptly, and was even accused by his opponents of instigating the 'murder'. For over a year the parliamentary regime hung on until in November 1947 it was forcibly overthrown.

Marshal Pibun's Take-over

Thus failed the second attempt at democracy in Thailand. With the support of the Army, Marshal Pibun regained power for the next 10 years. Police General Phao Sriyanond, Pibun's aide, controlled parliamentary elections, suppressed 'subversive' opposition, expanded the police and inaugurated—among other profitable activities—an opium-smuggling network. The Army crushed an attempted *coup d'état* by followers of Pridi in

1949—Pridi had fled the country—and a revolt by the Navy in 1951. Later that year Pibun staged his own coup, in reply to a Communist 'plot'. Such plots were uncovered almost yearly, and hundreds of suspects, especially Chinese, were arrested. From 1950 the regime received economic and military aid from the United States. In 1954 Thailand signed the South-East Asia Collective Defence Treaty and SEATO Headquarters were set up in Bangkok two years later. The Thai Government sought security in commitment to the West.

Internally, Pibun tried to balance between the rival—and growing—power of the Army, led by Field-Marshal Sarit, and the Police. Attempting to secure wider support, Pibun turned in 1956 to a new-found belief in democracy. Political parties, trade unions, free speech (at a 'Hyde Park' by the Grand Palace), were duly authorized. But when elections were still framed, students demonstrated in protest. The Army also came out in opposition and a few months later (September 1957) the tottering regime fell. Pibun fled to Japan, Phao to Switzerland, where they later died.

Democracy Ended

Democracy briefly flourished. Free elections were held in December 1957 and the opposition grew—Socialists in the impoverished north-east and the independent Democratic Party in Bangkok. Alarmed at the disintegration of authority Marshal Sarit descended on Bangkok (from convalescence, after a serious operation abroad) and carried out, not a *coup d'état* (he emphasized), but a revolution. The Constitution was abrogated, Parliament dismissed, parties and trade unions disbanded, Communist suspects rounded up and the country placed under martial law (as it still is). 'Evils and corrupt practices had multiplied', declared Marshal Sarit. 'Subversion of the Government was the order of the day . . . The nation's economic situation was highly precarious, with thousands of millions of *baht* of debts . . . The garb of democracy was weighing down Thailand . . . Consequently the Revolutionary Party has to seize power.'

Marshal Sarit's Regime

Six years of discipline and enforced political stability have shown striking economic results. A six-year economic development plan, from October 1961, aims to increase the national income at the rate of five per cent a year. Large-scale irrigation and hydro-electric projects, including the Yanhee Dam, the biggest in South-East Asia, have been completed. Highways and feeder roads (to bring farmers' produce to market) are being constructed. Wide streets, fountains, new offices, shops and hotels give Bangkok an air of prosperity.

Under Sarit politics were kept under firm control. Under martial law what he said was law. Leftist politicians were put in gaol. Demonstrations were not permitted and the press was subdued. The Government formed under a provisional Constitution was headed by Sarit, the Supreme Commander of the Armed Forces. His Army deputies, Generals Thanom and Prapart, were Ministers of Defence and of the Interior respectively. Yet enterprising civil servants joined the Cabinet, notably Thanat Khoman,

Minister of Foreign Affairs, and Sunthorn Hongladarom, Minister of Finance. And the monarchy was highly regarded—more so than in former times. On more than one important occasion the reasoned views of King Bhumibol Adulyadej prevailed. Although the Constitution was gradually taking form, Sarit was reluctant to jeopardize economic progress by an early 'relapse' into democracy.

The New Era

The death of Marshal Sarit in December 1963 marks the end of an era. With his heavy hand removed there have been new stirrings towards democracy and away from arbitrary rule. Exposure of the amount of state funds—some £10 millions—misappropriated by the late leader shocked the Thai people, who are normally tolerant to a fault. General (now Field-Marshal) Thanom became the new Prime Minister. His position is not as secure as his predecessor's: his main rival is General Prapart, who as his deputy and Minister of the Interior controls both the Army and the Police. Thanom brought into his government the able and respected Pote Sarasin, Secretary-General of SEATO, as Minister of National Development, and hastened the drafting of the Constitution for approval, early in 1965, by the Constituent Assembly. Both Thanom and his ambitious deputy accepted—with some misgivings—elections later in the year.

Communism

Communism is the greatest danger, judging by ministerial pronouncements: Communists appear to be at the root of all disorders. In reality Communism has little appeal to most Thais, who are reasonably contented, Buddhist by religion and monarchist by inclination. It is true that some students, labour leaders, journalists and politicians have shown themselves susceptible to Communism, or at least neutralism—often, in Government circles, considered the same thing. But in general the Thais, unlike the large and industrious Chinese minority (over 3 million out of a total population of nearly 30 million), are simply not affected. The exception, and it is an important one, is the people of the north-east. This is the poorest, least fertile and most neglected area of the country. Its people consider themselves Lao, akin to the inhabitants of Laos just across the Mekong. Separatism, economic discontent, Communist propaganda and the influence of the Pathet Lao together form a major problem for Bangkok.

Relations with Neighbours

The Government is urgently developing the north-east and improving the calibre of officials. But the situation in Laos, which remains disturbing, is now recognized to be beyond its control. In return for the United States' commitment to defend Thailand, without waiting for a decision by the other SEATO members, the Thai Government has reluctantly come out in support of America's 'neutralist' policy in Laos. Relations with Burma, the traditional enemy, are remarkably good; with Cambodia, bad (diplomatic relations were broken off, for the second time in three years, in October 1961). Malaysia, however, is a new friend, a partner with Thailand

and the Philippines in the Association of South-East Asia for Economic and Cultural Cooperation. China, of course, is the greatest problem, for the resurgence of her imperial sway—whether it be harsh or benevolent—cannot be long delayed.

Present and Future Prospects

To sum up: the Government is not popular, especially among the intellectuals, but neither can it be called oppressive. The Thai people traditionally respect authority; most of them are not interested in politics and so long as they are left alone hardly object to the system by which they are ruled. The local Chinese, in particular, find the favourable opportunities for making money well worth the abstention from politics. 'Sino-Thai co-operation'—the watchword of the Chinese Chamber of Commerce—takes the sensible form of Chinese directorships being offered to prominent Thai officers or officials in return for 'security of tenure'. But what the Chinese think privately, they keep to themselves.

What are the prospects for democracy? Ironically, the very success with which Thailand warded off colonialism in the past has contributed to the failure of democracy in the present. There was no colonial power to oppose, hence no national movement, uniting all sections of the population, could grow and develop. (Thailand, on the other hand, is pleasantly free from feelings of inferiority or prejudice towards the West. Encouragement of foreign investment and the constructive use of American aid are noticeable, at least compared with several other countries in Asia.) Democracy in Thailand started at the top, with the successful coup—precursor of many others—against absolute monarchy: it never took root. Popular indifference—the voting record ranged from 20 to 40 per cent of the electorate—and the influence of personality rather than policy, led to rule by isolated cliques. These could be—and were—easily overthrown by armed force.

The 'military group' is still dominant in the country even if its power is qualified—outwardly at least—by a new Constitution and new elections. But, in the longer view, the economic progress sponsored by Sarit and continued by his successor must strengthen—in number, quality and effect—the very middle class (and even the richer peasantry) whose former instability and weakness permitted the military to take command.

Economic Situation

From the sea, south of Bangkok, almost to the northern foot-hills near Burma and Laos, extends the great Central Plain of Thailand. The countryside is flat, paddy fields stretching to the horizon; only a few trees and clumps of bamboo indicate the occasional farm house, raised on stilts to avoid flooding during the five or six months of the rainy season. Villagers catch fish in the ponds and swamps; boats pass by along the rivers and canals; children tend grazing buffaloes. 'There is rice in the fields, fish in the water'—this is the way the people have expressed it since the days of Sukhotai.

Agriculture still accounts for almost half the national income and for 85 to 90 per cent of exports. Almost three-quarters of the cultivated land is under rice. More than half the total crop comes from the Central Plain—

which provides most of the yearly export of 1 to 1½ million tons—while le than one-third comes from the same amount of land in the north-eas Rubber and tin from the southern peninsula, bordering Malaya, are majc exports; also teak from the northern forests around Chiangmai; and, recentl upland crops successfully grown in the north-east—chiefly maize, jute an kenaf, and tapioca.

Thailand lacks the basic fuel and metal resources for heavy industry there is no coal, a little oil, some lignite, and small deposits of iron ore. Le than one in ten of the active population works in industry. Up-country ther are saw mills and rice mills—nearly all owned by Chinese, who also bu transport and export rice. In and around Bangkok, cement, tobacco, spirit soap and textiles are produced. At Sriracha, south-east of Bangkok, an o refinery has been completed. New projects—encouraged by the Board c Investment—include a large oil refinery, a big textile works, a jute mil various car assembly plants and highway construction in the south.

Much progress has been made in attracting industry, and developin power and communications, but for Thailand the needs of agriculture ar and will long remain, decisive.

BIBLIOGRAPHY

Wendell Blanchard (ed.) *Thailand: Its People, its Society, its Culture.* (Human Relations Are Files, New Haven, 1957.)

John Blofeld. *People of the Sun: Encounters in Siam.* (Hutchinson, London, 1960.)

Noel Busch. *Thailand: an Introduction to Modern Siam.* (D. Van Nostrand, New York, 1959.)

Chula-Chakrabongse. *Lords of Life.* (Alvin Redman, London, 1960.)

Richard J. Coughlin. *Double Identity: The Chinese in Modern Thailand.* (Hong Kong Uni Press, Hong Kong, 1960.)

John de Young. *Village Life in Modern Thailand.* (Univ. of California Press, Berkeley, 1955.)

W. A. Graham. *Siam*, 2 vols. (de la More Press, London, 1924.)

James C. Ingram. *Economic Change in Thailand Since 1850.* (Stanford Univ. Press, Stanforc 1955.)

D. Insor. *Thailand: a Political, Social and Economic Analysis.* (Allen and Unwin, London, 1963.

Alexander Macdonald. *Bangkok Editor.* (Macmillan, London and New York, 1949.)

Robert L. Pendleton. *Thailand: Aspects of Landscape and Life.* (Duell, Sloan and Pearce, Ne York, 1962.)

A Public Development Program for Thailand. (Johns Hopkins Univ. Press for International Ban for Reconstruction and Development, Baltimore, 1959.)

W. D. Reeve. *Public Administration in Siam.* (Royal Institute of International Affairs, Londor 1951.)

William G. Skinner. *Chinese Society in Thailand: an Analytical History.* (Cornell Univ. Pres Ithaca, New York, 1957.)

W. A. R. Wood. *History of Siam.* (Siam Barnakich Press, Bangkok, 1933.)

BIOGRAPHICAL NOTE

D. Insor has lived a number of years in Thailand and has written the only comprehensiv account so far of present conditions (see above). He has contributed articles to *The Guardia* on South-East Asian affairs.

CAMBODIA, LAOS AND VIETNAM

by

P. J. HONEY

CAMBODIA

General

The English name 'Cambodia' is a corruption of 'Kambuja', itself derived from the Hindu 'Kambu', the mythical founder of the Khmer people. The country was subject to strong Indian religious and cultural influence through the Empire of Funan, between the 2nd and 6th centuries A.D. The Khmer kingdom of Angkor was founded by Jayavarman II in A.D. 802 and reached the zenith of its development between A.D. 1000 and A.D. 1200, the period during which the unparalleled Khmer architectural masterpieces were constructed. Subjected to continual Siamese military pressure from the 14th century onwards, Cambodia was assailed on the other flank by the southward advance of the Vietnamese in the 17th century. Much Cambodian territory was annexed by the Vietnamese during the 17th and 18th centuries, and she became the centre of Siamese-Vietnamese rivalries during the 18th and 19th centuries. In 1863, following the establishment of French power in neighbouring Cochin China, King Norodom placed Cambodia under the protection of France, and her status of protectorate was recognized by Siam four years later. A further treaty of 1884 reduced the King's power and permitted the introduction of French administrators. The two provinces of Siem Reap and Battambang have long been the subject of disputes with Siam and have changed hands several times, but they were finally restored to Cambodia in 1945.

Under Japanese pressure, Prince Norodom Sihanouk declared Cambodia independent in 1945 but, in January 1946, concluded an agreement with France whereby Cambodia continued to enjoy internal autonomy but left foreign affairs and national defence in French hands. During the Indo-Chinese war, a Cambodian resistance movement, the Khmer Issaraks, fought for full independence, but the movement was small and lacked prestige because it was directed by the Vietnamese Communists. The Geneva agreements of 1954 placed the whole country under King Norodom Sihanouk, although formal independence of France was not achieved until December of that year.

Political

Impulsive and unconventional by nature, Norodom Sihanouk clashed with the International Control Commission appointed to supervise the carrying out of the Geneva agreements when he sought to alter the electoral provisions

100 E

C H I N A

119

Red River

Mekong

Lao Kay

Tuyen Quang · Lang Son

Phong
Saly · Dien Bien Phu

T O N K I N

HANOI

Hai Duong

Haiphong

Sam Neua

Nam Dinh

20

Luang Prabang
Plaine
des Jarres

Xieng Khouang

A N N A M R A N G E

L A O S

VIENTIANE

NORTH
VIETNAM

Hainan

Vinh

2

Dong Hoi

17th. Parallel

Savannakhet

Quang Tri

Hué

Tourane

T H A I L A N D

V I E T N A M

Paské

KRUNG THEP
(Bangkok)

Site of
Angkor
×

Qui Nhon

Battambang

Tonle Sap
(Great Lake)

Mekong

C A M B O D I A

Kompong Chhnang

Kompong Cham

S E A

Nha Trang

GULF OF
SIAM

Sihanoukville

PHNOM-PENH

Dalat

Bien Hoa

SAIGON

SOUTH
VIETNAM

10 N.

Plain of
Reeds

Cholon

My Tho

S O U T H C H I N A S E A

⊚ National Capitals
· Towns
—·—·— International Boundaries
▨ Land over 200 metres

0 Miles 200

Delta of the
Mekong

110 E.

© ANTHONY BLOND LTD

of the 1947 constitution. In Shavian fashion, he abdicated in favour of his father, Norodom Suramarit, on 2nd March 1955 and organized a political party, the Popular Socialists, which won an overwhelming majority in the September 1955 elections. Since then, Norodom Sihanouk has continued to play the dominant role in Cambodian politics and has shaped the country's policies irrespective of whether he was in or out of office. In December 1955 Cambodia was admitted to membership of the United Nations Organization.

Norodom Sihanouk has accorded recognition to Communist China and has established diplomatic relations with countries of the Communist bloc. Though professing neutralism, he has rejected the protection offered by SEATO and inclines his foreign policy to meet the wishes of China. Cambodia's refusal to accept further United States aid has subjected her formerly stable economy to severe strains. Her friendly relations with the Communist world have proved a source of great friction between Cambodia and her immediate neighbours, South Vietnam and Thailand, and have caused the severing of diplomatic relations with these states. They accuse Cambodia of providing Communism with a base in South-East Asia, and there is much evidence to show that the Communist insurgents in South Vietnam regularly operate from Cambodian territory.

Future Prospects

Cambodia is a small country, weaker than either South Vietnam or Thailand, and would certainly have been annexed by one or other of these states had it not been for the intervention of France during the 19th century. Since the departure of the French in 1954, she has survived, thanks to the balance of power between the Communist and anti-Communist forces in the world. Norodom Sihanouk has acquired prestige and influence far in excess of what the mere size and importance of Cambodia would seem to justify. So long as the equilibrium of world power remains undisturbed, Cambodia will almost certainly continue to play an important role in Asia. If, however, that balance is disturbed, or if Communism should prevail in South Vietnam or Thailand, then there is little likelihood that Cambodia would survive as an independent state. Her own resources are totally inadequate for her defence and she places increasing reliance upon China to afford her protection against any threat from her immediate neighbours.

LAOS

General

A country of jungle-covered hills and valleys, with few roads and no railway, whose principal highway is the river Mekong, Laos is the least developed of the former states of French Indo-China. Most of its people—less than half of them are Laos, the rest being hill tribesmen—live by subsistence rice farming in the lowlands or by slash and burn cultivation in the hills.

Laotian history, recorded since the 14th century, is a story of internal dissension between rival princes and foreign interference or domination.

Laos has enjoyed unity and independence only when there has been a power equilibrium between her neighbours or when these have been weak, and when she has been governed by a ruler powerful enough to impose his own control over all the regions. The country split into its constituent principalities in 1711 and, following the Siamese conquest of Vientiane in 1828, fell largely under Siamese control. French control replaced Siamese later in the 19th century and, in 1899, France reunited the kingdom. Present frontiers were established as a result of Franco-Siamese treaties between 1893 and 1907. King Sisavang Vong, acceding to Japanese pressure, proclaimed the independence of Laos in March 1945, but later revoked the proclamation after the return of the French.

War

A Laotian resistance movement, Lao Issara, defied the King and set up an independent government but, when it was defeated by French troops in March 1946, its leaders retired to Bangkok. There a split developed between the extremists, led by Prince Souphanouvong, and the moderates, who later returned peacefully to Laos. In 1949 France granted Laos independence within the French Union, and the Lao Issara was dissolved.

The key figure in subsequent Laotian disorders was Prince Souphanouvong. Although a Laotian prince, he was educated in Vietnam and France, worked as an engineer in Vietnam, and married a Vietnamese Communist. He has lived longer in Vietnam than in Laos and depends largely upon the Vietnamese Communists for support. Under Vietnamese direction he formed the Pathet Lao, nominally a Laotian resistance movement, but in fact comprising many hill tribesmen and Vietnamese as well as Laotians, and under Vietnamese Communist control. From its base at Sam Neua in northern Laos, the Pathet Lao declared itself the only legal government of Laos and its claim was, not unnaturally, supported by the Vietnamese Communists.

The Aftermath

The Geneva agreements of 1954, which ended the war in Indo-China, accorded sovereignty over the whole of Laos to the Royal Government. The Pathet Lao were, however, given temporary control of two provinces, Phong Saly and Sam Neua, pending their integration with the Royal Government. Foreign troops were to be withdrawn except for a small French military training group.

Imprecise wording in section 14 of the agreements was exploited by the Vietnamese Communists, not only to prevent Pathet Lao integration, but to strengthen and enlarge the movement. The United States provided aid on a massive scale to the Royal Government and the struggle for supremacy between the two rival Laotian parties assumed a Communist/anti-Communist aspect. Until December 1955 the Royal Government sought unsuccessfully to impose a military solution and then changed its tactics, attempting to form a democratic coalition government together with the Pathet Lao. This lasted until 1958 and was followed by a less tolerant attitude towards the Pathet Lao. After the *coup d'état* of Captain Kong Le in

August 1960, a neutralist, Prince Souvanna Phouma, formed a government and civil war broke out.

The deposed right wing government of Prince Boun Oum re-established itself in Vientiane while Souvanna Phouma's supporters joined forces with the Pathet Lao in the resistance. Communist North Vietnam and the USSR poured in aid to the Pathet Lao with the result that the military campaign went against Boun Oum's government and the Pathet Lao overran northern and much of central Laos. A 14-nation conference met at Geneva in the spring of 1961 and, after lengthy deliberations, reached agreement in June 1962. A neutralist coalition government, comprising the three rival factions, was set up but failed to function effectively. After disputes with the Pathet Lao, the neutralist faction joined forces with the right wing and fighting was resumed. North Vietnamese use of Laotian territory to supply the insurgents in South Vietnam has provoked American bombing of points along the route.

Future Prospects

Laos shares common frontiers with Communist China and Communist North Vietnam, both of whom materially support the Pathet Lao, the Vietnamese contributing regular military formations. Armed Communist take-over of the whole country has been prevented primarily by fear of United States and Thai intervention which might result. North Vietnam regards Laos as a secondary objective, the main one being South Vietnam. Consequently, the future of Laos depends upon the outcome of the war in South Vietnam. If Communism prevails there, it is likely to do so in Laos as well. Should Communist North Vietnam be forced to desist from her military efforts in South Vietnam, it is likely she would also withdraw her support from the Pathet Lao. The future prospects of Laos are therefore overshadowed by events in Vietnam.

VIETNAM

Chinese Domination

The very early history of Vietnam is mythical and little is certain before 111 B.C., when Han Wu-ti captured the Kingdom of Nam Viet for China and renamed it the Province of Giao Chi. From then until A.D. 939 it remained part of the Chinese Empire and was profoundly influenced by Chinese civilization, still everywhere in evidence today. Chinese religions, philosophy, writing, social and administrative patterns, and much else besides were adopted by the Vietnamese people during this millennium of subjugation. Ngo Quyen drove out the Chinese in A.D. 939 to re-establish Vietnamese independence, which was maintained, with the exception of one short period (1413-27) of Ming domination, until the French conquest during the second half of the 19th century. Even Kublai Khan's Mongol hordes were defeated by General Tran Hung Dao in 1284 and driven back into China.

Independence

In the 10th century A.D. Vietnam occupied only the northern part of her present territory, but a relentless—if gradual—expansion southward engulfed the Kingdom of Champa and part of Cambodia until, by 1780, its frontiers reached the southern tip of Ca-mau in the Gulf of Siam. National unity failed to survive this territorial expansion and the country split into two mutually hostile states early in the 17th century, the dividing line being close to the present frontier between North and South Vietnam. Two centuries later, in 1802, the land was re-united under a single Emperor, Gia Long, the founder of the later Nguyen Dynasty which survived until 1945.

French Domination

France attacked Vietnam in 1858 and established the colony of Cochin China in 1867. Under the treaties of 1874, 1884, and 1885, Annam and Tonking became French protectorates, thus completing French domination over the whole of Vietnam. Cities, roads, railways, bridges, and ports were constructed by the French, who transformed the archaic imperial system of government into a modern colonial one. Great changes took place in the Vietnamese social structure, system of education, and national economy. In 1940 the French colonial government submitted to Japanese might and Vietnam, Laos, and Cambodia, which together formed the Indo-Chinese Union, were brought under Japanese domination. The French continued to administer the territory under Japanese control until March, 1945. After Japan's surrender to the Allies, northern Vietnam was occupied by Chinese Kuomintang troops and the south by British troops, but by then political change was already taking place.

War

Clandestine Nationalist political activity was prevalent during the 1920s and 1930s in Vietnam but most indigenous leaders, lacking training and experience, were ineffectual. Only Ho Chi Minh, a dedicated Russian-trained Communist, had these qualifications, but he devoted himself to the service of his ideology rather than his country. He formed the Vietnamese Revolutionary Youth League in China, indoctrinating young Vietnamese patriots at Whampoa Military Academy and returning them to Vietnam to form Communist cells. In 1930 he founded the Indo-Chinese Communist Party.

When Japan occupied Vietnam in 1940, the leading Vietnamese Communists fled to southern China, where Ho Chi Minh joined them. There they formed the Viet Minh League, ostensibly a Nationalist coalition but in reality a Communist-dominated body, and induced the Allies to supply its guerilla force inside Vietnam. Immediately following the Japanese surrender in 1945, the Viet Minh occupied Hanoi and proclaimed the independent Democratic Republic of Vietnam. The French were in prison, where they had been placed by the Japanese, and no other Vietnamese group was armed, so the Viet Minh encountered little resistance. The Emperor, Bao Dai, abdicated in its favour.

A period of confusion followed when the British released the imprisoned French in the south and the Chinese-supported Vietnamese Nationalists opposed the Viet Minh in the north. Following the withdrawal of the British and Chinese occupation forces, confusion was further confounded with the French, the Viet Minh, and the Nationalists all striving to win control of Vietnam. French efforts were baulked by the inability of France to send reinforcements, while the Nationalists proved no match for the Viet Minh. After inconclusive fighting and fruitless negotiations, the Viet Minh commenced open warfare in December 1946.

Despite American military aid and the support of a Nationalist government to which they granted increasing independence, the French were defeated. Communism's victory in neighbouring China enabled massive military aid to be given to the Viet Minh. In the spring of 1954, with the main French force besieged at Dien-bien-phu, an international conference met at Geneva to decide the future of French Indo-China.

Peace

The Geneva conference negotiated an armistice and split Vietnam into two at the 17th parallel, according control of the northern zone to the Communists and the southern to the Nationalists. The French withdrew and an International Control Commission (Chairman India; members Canada and Poland) was sent to supervise the truce. National elections and reunification were envisaged for July 1956, but these did not take place. Nearly a million refugees fled south from the Communists, and the frontier was closed.

South Vietnam—The Republic of Vietnam

Agriculturally rich but industrially poor, South Vietnam was given little chance of survival in 1954. Premier Ngo Dinh Diem faced a land ravaged by war, torn by internal dissensions between armed politico-religious sects, riddled with Communist agents, filled with penniless refugees, and defended by a defeated, demoralized army. With American financial aid he accomplished a seeming miracle by breaking the power of the sects—army morale and prestige were restored by these victories—establishing control over the whole territory, and resettling the refugees successfully. By 1956 he was ready to dispose of the absentee Chief of State, Bao Dai, through a popular referendum and to declare a Republic with himself as President. A democratic constitution was promulgated and a parliament was elected.

With order and peace restored, the countryside returned to normal and abandoned lands were reoccupied. New settlements were established in the uplands and, thanks to generous United States monetary and technical help, the foundations of a light industry were laid. But the Communist threat obliged the Government to maintain very large armed forces, a big drain on the economy, and to impose strict security measures which generated increasing resentment among the population. The absence of full political freedom antagonized the educated élite in towns and cities, while the arrogance and corruption of many provincial administrations displeased the peasantry. Nevertheless, much real economic progress was made between

1956 and 1959 and agrarian reforms improved the lot of the poorer peasants. In mid-1959, however, Communist subversion commenced and spread rapidly.

During 1960, Communist terrorism and guerilla warfare increased dramatically and some areas fell under the control of the insurgents. Terrorists and military supplies reached South Vietnam in ever larger numbers, infiltrated from the North through Laos, Cambodia, or by sea. Government forces encountered continuing setbacks and President Diem produced no new solution save the *agroville*, or large defended village, many of which were hastily built. In November three battalions of parachute troops rebelled in Saigon, almost overthrowing the Government thanks to the inaction of the other troops there. Their declared object was to replace Diem with a more effective leader against the Communists, but the revolt was crushed.

American military help was increased during 1961, but the strength of the Communist insurgents also grew, so that it was not until early 1962, when helicopters and aircraft flown by United States pilots were used and United States officers accompanied army units on operations, that the military situation improved. Britain despatched the Thompson Mission, comprising veterans of the Malayan emergency, while Australia sent army officers to train the Vietnamese in jungle warfare. A programme of defending villagers from Communist insurgents inside strategic hamlets met with initial success, but the scheme was pushed ahead too quickly without sufficient preparation and lost much of its effectiveness. Increasing Communist infiltration and ever more stringent repression by the Government created rising tension. An incident at Hué in May 1963 set in motion a series of anti-Government demonstrations which could not be suppressed. Buddhist monks achieved most notoriety by their self-immolation, but the movement was nation-wide and embraced all religions. On 1st November the Government of Ngo Dinh Diem was overthrown by an Army *coup d'état* in which the President and his brother were murdered. During the months that followed, one military regime replaced another as rivalries among generals increased and political stability was eroded. In August 1964, agitation led by a clique of politically ambitious Buddhist monks began and, throughout the remainder of 1964, made stable government almost impossible. Nevertheless, the war against the Communist insurgents was waged with varying fortunes, though the scale of fighting escalated steadily, and it still continues.

South Vietnam's future depends entirely upon the outcome of the war. Three possible solutions are envisaged. Firstly a withdrawal of United States forces after an international commission has agreed upon some form of neutral status for the country. Communist terms are likely to be so stiff, however, that they would render subsequent Communist annexation of South Vietnam inevitable, which renders this the least likely of the three. Secondly, the committal of larger American aid, and possibly American troops, to enable the war to be won, but that would necessitate further years of fighting. Finally, United States bombing of North Vietnamese industry and communications so as to cause severe economic hardship and orce North Vietnam to abandon the war. It is impossible to tell which policy will eventually be adopted, which makes the future of South Vietnam uncertain and difficult to predict.

North Vietnam—The Democratic Republic of Vietnam

North Vietnam is largely mountainous and, although it possesses most of Vietnam's limited industry and almost all her mineral wealth—coal, apatite, metals—it is a densely populated food deficit area. When the Vietnamese Communist regime assumed control in 1954 it had three principal objectives: to impose Communism; to reunify Vietnam so as to acquire South Vietnam's rice surplus; to industrialize rapidly. Of these, the first was considered the most important since South Vietnam appeared likely to collapse under the weight of her own dissensions and industrialization would require some time to achieve. Consequently, Chinese-style agrarian reforms were carried out with great ruthlessness. The ferocity of the campaign and the numbers killed by the people's courts led to scattered revolts, so that a 'correction of errors' campaign had to be instituted. Nevertheless, a typically Communist regime was imposed upon the country, but Communism lost most of its popular appeal and prestige in the process. Since then, the unpopularity of the regime has continued to grow.

Great efforts were made to solve the food shortage by putting new land under cultivation, but much of the benefit was lost through the rigid imposition of collectivization. This proved distasteful to the peasantry and adversely affected agricultural production. A series of good harvests up to 1959 enabled the population to be fed, albeit at a very low level, but between 1960 and 1964 harvests were poor and severe food shortages persisted. In some areas famine caused many deaths and the pressures for reunification so as to obtain access to South Vietnam's rice have become progressively greater.

Aid was provided by countries of the Communist bloc from 1954 onwards, with China the largest individual contributor. With its help war damage was repaired and a start was made on the programme of industrialization, but progress was far slower than the Vietnamese Communists had anticipated. The basic economic plan, reduced to its simplest terms, was to build factories for the production of manufactured articles which would be sold abroad. The foreign exchange thus earned would be used to purchase rice to feed the population. Poor planning, bad management, and the lack of experienced personnel all contributed to the relative failure of this plan, with the result that industry has been unable to bridge the food gap and will not be capable of doing so in the foreseeable future.

Sino-Soviet differences in recent years have proved a source of great embarrassment to North Vietnam. Vietnamese Communist leaders remained acutely aware of the geographical proximity of China, Vietnam's traditional enemy, and they went to great lengths to avoid causing her any offence. Russia, on the other hand, and Eastern Europe are the only available sources of industrial equipment which North Vietnam so badly needs. Moreover, the Russian presence is regarded by the Vietnamese as a safeguard against possible Chinese encroachment, so that it was important to avoid offending Russia. Until August 1963, North Vietnam maintained a neutral position in the dispute and benefited economically from the attempts of the two Communist giants to woo her support. At that date, Moscow demanded she sign the partial nuclear test-ban treaty while China insisted that she denounce it. Neutrality was no longer possible, so the Vietnamese denounced the treaty, aligned themselves with China, and suffered cuts in Soviet aid and technicians. Since the overthrow of Khrushchev, however, North Vietnam has tried to improve relations with Russia and to return to a posture of neutrality in the dispute.

Food shortages, the lamentably slow progress of industrialization, and the inability of the Communist countries to supply food all combined to persuade North Vietnam that the only solution to her difficulties lay in the annexation of South Vietnam. The campaign of armed subversion began in 1959 and its scale increased rapidly under the pressures imposed by a series of bad harvests. United States military aid to South Vietnam also increased to enable the growing Communist threat to be resisted. Dangers of escalation are inherent in the situation since the major power blocs support opposing sides in Vietnam and would be reluctant to see their protégés defeated. The United States bombed North Vietnamese naval bases in August 1964 by way of retaliation for attacks on her shipping, but since that time has shown a less determined attitude. Both China and Russia have exploited apparent American vacillation by pledging support for North Vietnam in the event of an attack upon its territory. North Vietnam has also provided military aid to the Communist Pathet Lao in Laos and has used territory controlled by that faction in eastern Laos to infiltrate soldiers, arms, and other supplies into South Vietnam.

The future of North Vietnam is dependent upon a number of different factors. Government stability has so far been ensured by President Ho Chi Minh, but he is now 75 years old and reported to be showing signs of senility. His retirement or death could well cause a power struggle. The war in South Vietnam has now escalated to the point where American military action against North Vietnam has become a real possibility, and disagreements about the future course of the struggle are known to exist between the North Vietnamese, the Chinese, and the Russians. Industrialization has progressed, but slowly, and agricultural area has been expanded by new irrigation. However, an annual population growth of 3·4 per cent has offset the benefits of this expansion. Late in 1964 North Vietnam sought to establish closer relations with the Soviet Union and her initiative led to the visit of a large Soviet delegation led by Premier Kosygin in February 1965. The process of lessening her dependence upon China may be a long and difficult one. Because of these factors, some of them external, it is not possible to make any appraisal of what may happen in the future.

The Economic Situation

North Vietnam possesses the bulk of the country's mineral resources, with coal and anthracite deposits estimated at 20 billion tons and iron deposits estimated at 250 million tons. The country is overpopulated in relation to available agricultural land—an imbalance likely to become greater as a result of rapid population growth—so that economic planning has aimed at industrialization. Planners hope to export manufactured products and to import food so as to bridge the existing deficit. Economic assistance, credits and technical aid have been provided by the Communist bloc, with China as the largest individual donor state, followed by the Soviet Union and the East European countries. Among the most notable of North Vietnam's industrial projects are the Thai-nguyen iron and steel complex, with a planned production of 200,000 tons in 1965, the electro-chemical complex at Viet-tri, and the fertilizer industry centred about Lam-thao, which is supplied from large apatite deposits at Lao-kay. There are textile mills at Nam-dinh and Hanoi, a cement factory at Haiphong, and machine tools factories close to Hanoi. Heavy emphasis has been placed on the construction of thermal electricity generating stations to remedy the inadequacy of present electrical power supply. Progress in industrialization has been hampered, however, by a number of factors, among the most important being poor initial planning, inefficient management, lack of a skilled labour force, lax control of quality, and the adverse effects upon supplies of political factors.

South Vietnam's large agricultural areas are capable of producing over 5 million tons of rice annually, enough to supply home needs and to provide a large surplus for export. The country's most valuable export is rubber, with a potential annual production of about 80,000 tons. Sugar and coffee are other important agricultural products. A large industrial complex is under construction at An-hoa, which will draw its power from the coal deposits at Nong-son nearby. Much of the investment emphasis in recent years has been upon manufacturing, and considerable progress has been made, particularly in cotton fabric production. Other manufactures include jute bags, wood products, brown sugar, paper, glass, beer and soft drinks, and tobacco. A 160,000-kW hydro-electric scheme is nearing completion at Da-nhim, and it will more than double the present capacity of 142,000 kW. Much disruption has been caused to both agriculture and industry by the Viet Cong insurgents, who have interrupted communications, carried out sabotage, spread terrorism, and forced large numbers of farmers to seek safety in town and cities. Uncertainty about the future has virtually halted private investment, and the country's economy is sustained by American aid, currently running at the rate of 2 million dollars per day.

BIBLIOGRAPHY

C—Cambodia L—Laos V—Vietnam

C—Lawrence Palmer Briggs. *The Ancient Khmer Empire.* (*Transactions of the American Philosophical Society*, Vol. 41 Part 1, Philadelphia, 1951.)

C—G. Coedes. *Les Etats hindouises d'Indochine et d'Indonésie.* (F. de Boccard, Paris, 1948.)

V—Allan B. Cole. *Conflict in Indo-China and International Repercussions.* (Cornell Univ. Press, New York, 1956.)

L—Lucien de Reinach. *Le Laos*, 2 vols. (A. Charles, Paris, 1901.)

V—Philippe Devillers. *Histoire du Viet-Nam de 1940 à 1952.* (Editions du Seuil, Paris, 1952.)

L—Henri Deydier. *Introduction à la Connaissance du Laos.* (Imprimerie Française d'Outre-Mer, Saigon, 1952.)

V—Bernard Fall. *Le Viet-Minh, 1945-1960.* (Armand Colin, Paris, 1960.) *The Two Vietnams.* (Praeger, New York, 1963.)

C—Thomas FitzSimmons (ed.). *Cambodia, its People, its Society, its Culture.* (HRAF Press, New Haven, Conn., 1959.)

V—Ellen J. Hammer. *The Struggle for Indochina* (Stanford Univ. Press, Stanford, 1954.)

V—P. J. Honey (ed.) *North Vietnam Today* (Praeger, New York, 1962.)

V—P. J. Honey. *Communism in North Vietnam.* (Ampersand Books, Allen and Unwin, London, 1965.)

V—Pierre Huard and Maurice Durand. *Connaissance du Viet-Nam.* (Imprimerie Nationale, Paris, 1954.)

V—Jean Lacouture and Philippe Devillers. *La fin d'une guerre: Indochine 1954.* (Editions du Seuil, Paris, 1960.)

V—Donald Lancaster. *The Emancipation of French Indo-China.* (Oxford Univ. Press for Royal Institute of International Affairs, London, 1961.)

L—Paul le Boulanger. *Histoire du Laos Français.* (Librairie Plon, Paris, 1931.)

L—Frank M. Lebar (ed.). *Laos, its People, its Society, its Culture.* (HRAF Press, New Haven, Conn., 1960.)

V.—Charles Robequain. *The Economic Development of French Indo-China.* (Oxford Univ. Press, London, 1944.)

L—Katay D. Sasorith. *Le Laos, Son evolution politique: Sa place dans l'Union Francaise.* (Editions Berger Levrault, Paris, 1953.)

V—Georges Taboulet. *La geste française en Indochine,* 2 vols. (Maisonneuve, Paris, 1955.)

V.—Virginia Thompson. *French Indo-China.* (Macmillan, New York, 1937.)

V—Gerard Tongas. *L'Enfer Communiste au Nord Vietnam* (Nouvelles Editions Debresse, Paris, 1960.)

BIOGRAPHICAL NOTE

P. J. Honey is Lecturer in Vietnamese at the School of Oriental and African Studies, University of London. Most of his published work is in the form of articles, but he has recently written two books, *North Vietnam Today* and *Communism in North Vietnam* (see above). He has also lectured and broadcast extensively.

MALAYSIA

by

DERRICK SINGTON

History

UNTIL the 19th century the world importance of the little kingdoms of the Malay Peninsula and North Borneo was only as stepping-stones on the great sea-route between India and China. Indian penetration began about 100 B.C. and superimposed Hinduism, Buddhism, and then Islam on the earlier animism of the Malay peoples who had come out of Central Asia in about 9000 B.C. and 2000 B.C. In the 8th century A.D. the Malay kingdoms were conquered by the Kings of Sri Vijaya in Sumatra; and in the 15th century Malacca conquered the whole peninsula and much of Sumatra. The Malacca dynasty fell in 1511 to Portugal, which lost the lucrative trade beyond India to Holland in the 17th century. Based on Java, the Dutch East Indian Company monopolized the trade in tin from the Malay west-coast kingdoms for 130 years.

Meanwhile the British East India Company in 1773 set up an outpost on Balambangan, North Borneo, which however was soon overrun by Sulu pirates. Thirteen years later Francis Light, a merchant sea-captain, got the East India Company to lease Penang Island from the Sultan of Kedah. In 1795 the Dutch asked British forces to take over Malacca to prevent it from falling into French hands. The scene was set for the establishment of the most successful of the Company's three Straits Settlements by the gifted Stamford Raffles, who had become Governor of Java (1811-15) when that island was taken from the Dutch, after Holland had fallen to Napoleon. Following the restoration of Java to the Netherlands Raffles, who burned to extend enlightened British rule, persuaded the Governor-General of India, against the wishes of the British Government, to allow him in 1819 to found Singapore.

He took advantage of rivalry to the throne of Johore, and an agreement was signed giving the East India Company rights to establish trading-stations in Singapore. By 1825 the trade of the port had quintupled as a result of Raffles' policy of 'opening it to ships of every nation free of duty'. Meanwhile Holland recognized Malaya as a British sphere of influence in return for British recognition of Dutch interest in Indonesia. Malacca was re-transferred to the British East India Company (1824). For nearly 50 years the British Government and the Company aimed at non-intervention in the kingdoms of Malaya. But Siam's attempts to assert dominion caused limited intervention. In 1821 the Siamese seized Kedah (whose Sultan fled to Penang). Four years later, in the Burney Treaty, Siam promised not to attack Perak or Selangor in return for a British guarantee not to interfere in Kedah. In

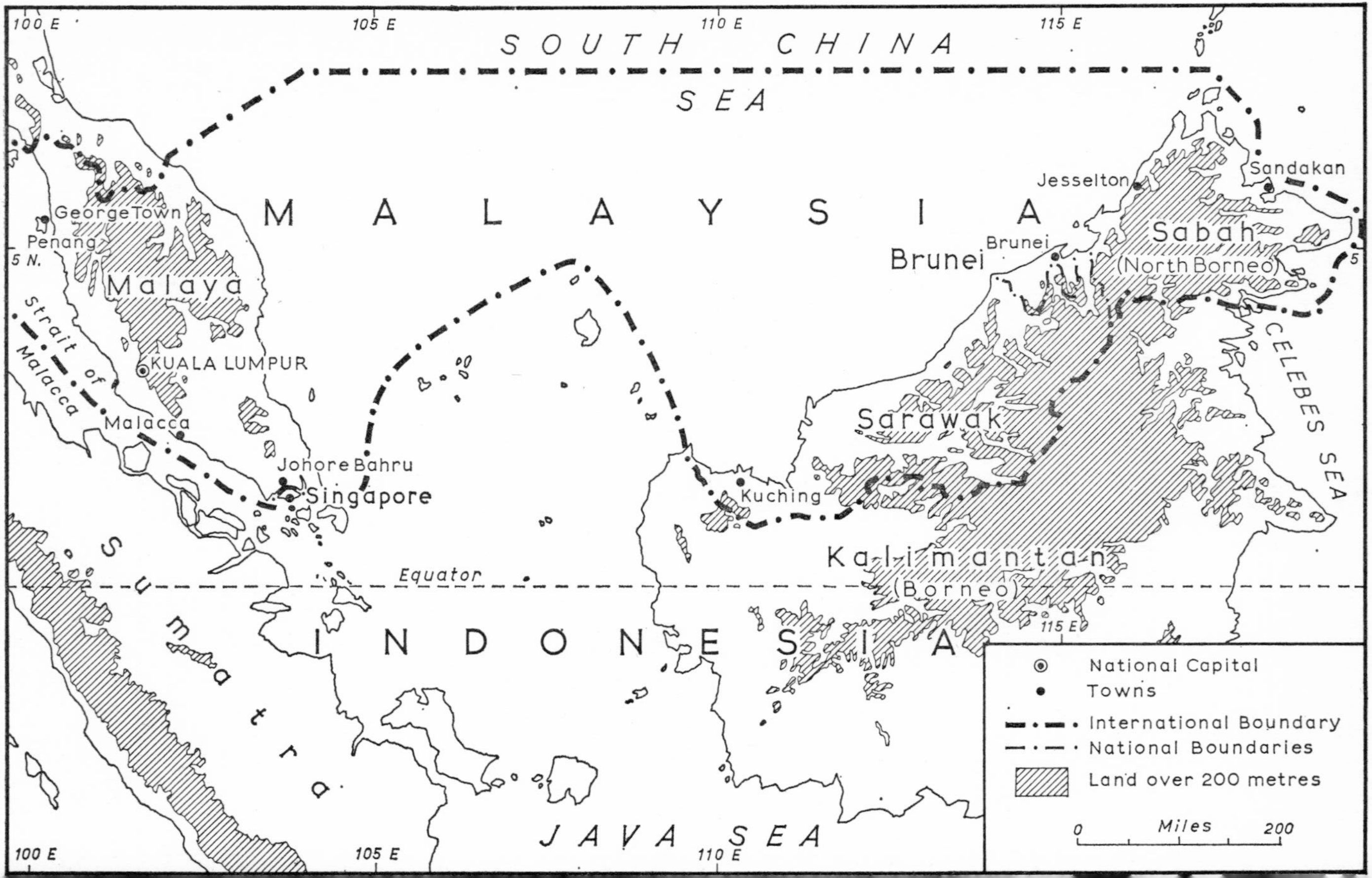
SOUTH CHINA SEA
MALAYSIA
INDONESIA
Malaya
GeorgeTown
Penang
KUALA LUMPUR
Malacca
Strait of Malacca
Johore Bahru
Singapore
Sumatra
Equator
JAVA SEA
Kuching
Sarawak
Brunei
Jesselton
Sandakan
Sabah (North Borneo)
Kalimantan (Borneo)
CELEBES SEA
100 E
105 E
110 E
115 E
5 N.
National Capital
Towns
International Boundary
National Boundaries
Land over 200 metres
0 Miles 200

1842, with British diplomatic help, the Kedah Sultan was restored to his throne by the Siamese.

Meanwhile (1839) an adventurous young British officer—ignoring East India Company policies of non-intervention—landed in Borneo, helped the Sultan of Brunei to quell a Dayak rebellion, and was awarded the Governorship of Sarawak. For 27 years James Brooke ruled as White Rajah, suppressing piracy along the Borneo coast with the help of Singapore naval forces. In 1846 the British Government authorized him to accept the Brunei Sultan's offer of Labuan Island as a coaling station for the new steamships on the China route. The Straits Settlements Governor, Colonel Cavenagh, shelled the Trengganu coast, where a pretender to the throne was being supported by Siam (1862); and he blockaded Perak's tin exports to enforce compensation to Penang-born Chinese who had suffered violence there.

The Colonial Office had assumed responsibility for the three Straits Settlements, Penang, Malacca and Singapore, in 1869, but the British Government remained opposed to intervention in neighbouring Malaya until 1873 when Lord Kimberley, as Colonial Secretary, enjoined the Governor, Sir Andrew Clarke, to 'consider appointing' British advisers to the Malay States, in order to restore order and protect commerce. In 1874 the Governor met the Malay leaders of Perak on Pangkor Island and persuaded Raja Abdullah to accept a British Resident. The appointee to the post, James Birch, tried to abolish slavery and tax-extortion by direct action and was stabbed to death by Malay chiefs on 2nd November 1874. After a British punitive expedition the murderers were hanged.

When, however, the Sultan of Selangor agreed to accept a Resident, the man appointed, J. G. Davidson, won Malay approval; and Hugh Low, who became Resident of Perak in 1877, successfully established 'indirect rule', abolishing abuses, gradually, by working through, not against, the Malay Sultan and his chiefs and headmen.

In 1874 Sungei Ujong, a small tin-producing State, accepted British protection. The neighbouring miniature kingdoms, after eleven years of disorders, asked for British officials, and in 1895 all nine States were merged under one king to form the State of Negri Sembilan to which a British Resident was appointed. Pahang in 1887 accepted a British Agent, Hugh Clifford, and in 1888 a Resident. But his attempts to establish a rule of law and to stop chiefly extortions resulted in a rebellion which was put down after four years (1895). In 1896, Selangor, Perak, Pahang and Negri Sembilan were federated under a Resident-General, Frank Swettenham. The Malay Sultans remained rulers only in name and appurtenances. A modern central administration was built up in Kuala Lumpur. Economic development went ahead. Population in the Federated States increased by 60 per cent between 1891 and 1901. Revenue trebled between 1895 and 1905. But Malay—and European business—opposition to the power of the Resident-General of the Federation grew. In 1909 a Federal Council was set up under the Governor of the Straits Settlements.

In the same year Siam, no longer expansionist, ceded Kedah, Perlis, Kelantan and Trengganu to British control. But the Rulers of these States and of Johore preferred to remain outside the Federation. Each Unfederated

State accepted a British Adviser. The great transforming force of Malaya, rubber, was brought from Brazil and planted experimentally in Singapore in 1877. Two hundred tons of it were exported from Malaya's 50,000 acres in 1905. By 1920 Malaya exported 196,000 tons, or 53 per cent of total world production. During the 1890s large-scale excavation techniques developed in tin-mining. Malaya's tin exports almost trebled between 1890 and 1930. She produced half the world output.

The 1930s saw a shift of power from the Federal Government to the governments of the individual States, whose Malay Sultans had continued to urge this. Control over agriculture, education, health and public works was given to the States. But the Federal Council retained the purse-strings. The four Unfederated Malay States were more loosely controlled and, with the exception of Johore, less developed economically. The three Straits Settlements, largely Chinese-populated, remained under a British Governor and Residents, with Legislative and Executive Councils composed of officials and nominated unofficials. Thus no democratic representation had come to Malaya by the time the Japanese erupted into the territories in 1942. Racial antagonism was still dormant because of the presence of the ruling European power.

In the reign of Sir Charles Brooke, the second White Rajah of Sarawak, between 1868 and 1917, piracy was finally put down and tribal head-hunting reduced. Revenue rose from about £14,000 to £200,000 a year, through orderly conditions, improved communications, and increases in trade and production. Sir Charles Brooke could not prevent the Brunei Sultan from making over large tracts of North Borneo in 1877 to the Austrian Baron Overbeck who was financed by Alfred Dent. Overbeck leased other areas of North Borneo from the Sultan of Sulu. In 1881 Dent secured a Royal Charter from the British Government, to form the North Borneo Company. In 1888 North Borneo, together with Brunei and Sarawak, came under British protection. Fifteen years later much land was leased to companies and smallholders for rubber-planting. The Japanese invasion of 1942 devastated many of the towns of North Borneo. Sarawak suffered less. In 1941 the third Brooke abrogated his absolute powers in Sarawak and set up an advisory council.

War and Civil War

The rapid Japanese conquest of Malaya in 1942 broke the confidence of the inhabitants in the invincibility and permanence of British rule; it also stimulated Malay nationalism, because the Japanese tried to join Malaya with Sumatra, thus helping forward a Pan-Malay movement linked to Indonesia. But Japanese rule awoke inter-racial antagonisms in Malaya. It evoked armed resistance by the Chinese Communist Malayan People's Anti-Japanese Army (MPAJA) which fought a tough guerilla war from the jungle. Before the British returned in 1945 the MPAJA tried to take over areas of the country, with consequent clashes between Chinese elements and Malays, many of whom had 'collaborated' with the Japanese. The British Military Administration restored order. But the Malayan Union which Britain then tried to create, based on equal citizenship for all races, and on centralized control of the nine Malay States, aroused bitter Malay opposition which crystallized around Dato Onn bin Ja'afar and his United Malays National Organization (UMNO). In 1948 a looser Federation was substituted, in which the Malay States retained important powers. Singapore was excluded because of Malay fears that the accession of its million Chinese would mean Chinese domination of the country. Malayan citizenship was made available to all races, but under stiff qualifications so that even many second-generation Chinese did not qualify.

The resultant Chinese disappointment provided a favourable moment for a Chinese-led Communist insurrection, launched in June 1948. At first the revolt looked like disrupting the machinery of government. It was conducted by about 7,000 men from deep-jungle bases. They had support from 50,000 Chinese peasants who supplied them, and they tried, by intimidation, assassination and destruction, to wreck the Malayan tin and rubber industries. At the peak of the insurrection some 30,000 troops and 60,000 police were deployed against the rebels. They were gradually mastered largely as a result of the systematic cutting off of their supplies through General Briggs's planned resettlement of half a million scattered Chinese 'squatter' cultivators. By the time the British High Commissioner, Sir Henry Gurney, was ambushed and killed in 1951 the Communist leaders had realized that their terror tactics could not bring victory, especially since the Malay half of the population hated and feared this Chinese bid for power. But only after General Templer's energetic period as High Commissioner (1952-54) was it clear that the Communist rebellion had failed.

Ultimate fiasco that it was, the Communist insurrection none the less indirectly brought independent nationhood to Malaya. It sharpened nationalist feeling; and it caused the British Government to seize courageously the opportunity of appealing to a nationalism which was inevitably Malay-led, but which constituted a counter-force that was too strong for the Communists. This involved taking a considerable risk. Although Malcolm Macdonald, as British Commissioner-General in South-East Asia, had successfully brought the leaders of the different races together in a Communities Liaison Committee no democratic election had yet been held in Malaya. On the other hand, an attempt by Dato Onn to launch an all-races nationalist party had come to grief. The Malay leader had overestimated the extent to which Malays and Chinese were prepared to bury their differences within a single organization. Later Tungku Abdul Rahman, Onn's successor as UMNO leader, succeeded in forming an Alliance between UMNO and the Malayan Chinese Association. In 1954 a Malayan-British committee drafted a plan for a largely elected assembly. The first general election was held in 1955, and the victors were the all-races Alliance which immediately pressed for full independence.

PARTY POLITICS

From their position of nationalist strength Abdul Rahman and his colleagues met the Communist guerilla leader, Chin Peng, and offered him an amnesty in return for surrender and the abandonment of Communism. The offer was rejected, and the Malayan leaders then secured a promise of independence from the British Government at a London conference (1956). A Commonwealth commission, including Australian, Indian and Pakistani representatives, under Lord Reid, drafted a constitution. Malaya became a sovereign independent nation on 31st August 1957. Under the Reid Constitution qualifications for citizenship were much eased, but Malay predominance in the civil service was safeguarded. In a second general election, in 1959, the Alliance won again, but with a reduced majority. The Communist rebellion had petered out.

Singapore, with its 75 per cent of Chinese, had progressed to self-government by easier stages. Already in 1953 the legislative council was one-third elected. But the ferment of Chinese Communism was strong in the trade unions and the Chinese schools. The first Chief Minister, David Marshall, and his successor, Lim Yew Hock, had to face violent rioting, in 1955 and 1956, which could only be put down by British troops. The risk of a Communist take-over was considered too great, both by the British Government and by neighbouring Malaya, for an independent Singapore to be contemplated. And the Malay leaders were adamant against the incorporation of the politically unstable territory into Malaya. Lee Kuan Yew's anti-colonialist, non-Communist, Socialist People's Action Party (PAP) easily won the Singapore elections of 1959, and he became the first Prime Minister under a self-government constitution which left foreign policy and defence under Britain, and internal security under a mixed council of British, Malayans, and Singaporeans.

The PAP Government set about eradicating Chinese Communism and chauvinism in Singapore by educating the people to live with, and understand, the neighbouring races. But Lee Kuan Yew warned the Malay leaders that the Singapore political danger would only pass if the island were integrated with independent Malaya. His warning was suddenly re-inforced in 1961. Three 'ex-Communists' in the PAP, including Lim Sin Siong, whose release from detention Lee had insisted on—believing them converted from Communism—campaigned against the PAP candidate at a by-election, and caused Lee a reverse. In a political landslide thousands left the PAP and joined a new 'Socialist Front' formed by the Communist front-man, Lim Sin Siong. The Government's majority in the Assembly dwindled to one. Seeing the 'red light', Tungku Abdul Rahman decided that Malaya would be safer with Singapore inside it than if she stayed separate. In August 1961 Lee and Abdul Rahman agreed that Singapore should join Malaya, sending 15 members to a parliament of 119, and retaining autonomy in Labour and Education. But the Malayan premier stipulated at the same time that Sarawak, Brunei and North Borneo must also join Greater Malaysia since, with their large non-Chinese majorities, including Dayaks, Melanaus, Kayans, Dusuns and Muruts, these territories would counterbalance the accession of Singapore's 1¼ million Chinese to the new State.

The Singapore Socialist Front denounced the Malaysia plan as a 'sell-out' of Singapore to a 'reactionary, British-manipulated' Malayan leadership. But the British Government assented to the Malaysia project (November 1961), resigning itself to the consequent transfer of the Singapore base to a sovereign Malaysia. This would subject the base to the Anglo-Malayan

Defence Agreement of 1957 which, literally interpreted, precluded its automatic use for the purposes of the South-East Asia Treaty Organization of which Britain was a member.

SOVEREIGNTY AND FEDERATION

In August 1962 the British Government agreed with the Prime Minister of Malaya to transfer sovereignty over Singapore, Sarawak and North Borneo to the new Malaysian Federation by 31st August 1963. Detailed constitutional arrangements for the accession of the Borneo territories were to be drawn up by an inter-governmental committee. The Brunei Protectorate was expected to accede as well. The Cobbold Commission, which had visited the Borneo territories in February 1962, had found misgivings among the tribal majority about coming under a predominantly Malay government, and there were some local Chinese mercantile objections to joining Malaysia. An indefinite transition period was therefore arranged during which as many British administrators as possible were to stay for as long as possible in Sarawak and North Borneo.

On 1st September 1962, in a referendum, the people of Singapore voted, by a large majority, in favour of the PAP Government's proposals for joining Malaysia. The arrangements under which the referendum was held had been denounced as undemocratic by the Socialist Front. The provisions for a separate Singapore citizenship inside Malaysia, which had been insisted on by the Malayan leaders in order to prevent left-wing Singaporeans from standing for parliamentary election outside Singapore, were likewise bitterly attacked by the Socialist Front.

The final negotiations between the Governments of Singapore and Malaya over the structure of Malaysia, held in Kuala Lumpur and London in 1963, were tense and long. Having accepted disproportionately low representation for Singapore in the Malaysian Assembly, Lee Kuan Yew bargained hard, and successfully, to ensure that provision for a Malaysian Common Market—essential for Singapore's industrialisation—should be incorporated in the Federal Constitution. There was also stiff bargaining over Singapore's contribution to Federal revenues and to the economic development of the relatively backward Borneo territories. The former was eventually fixed at 40 per cent of the island's tax-receipts, and the latter took the form of a £17·5 million loan. (Malaya was committed to providing £60 million over five years for the development of the two Borneo territories.) The final agreements to set up Malaysia were signed in London on 8th July 1963. On 21st September Lee Kuan Yew's People's Action Party won a decisive victory in Singapore's elections, securing 37 out of 51 seats in the new Assembly.

A new prospect thus opened for the ring of territories colonized by Britain around the South China Sea. With the birth of Malaysia its leaders would face the problem of welding a nation out of 4 million economically and politically thrustful Chinese, 3¾ million leisurely and less sophisticated Malays, ¾ million backward Borneo tribesmen, and about the same number of Indians. For a time the Malays would be the dominant partners. But the restless, modernizing Chinese would eventually demand full political equality. Yet Chinese economic efficiency would be feared as long as the Malay peasants and the Borneo tribesmen remained backward.

The Economic Situation

Rapid economic development is essential in Malaysia. Annual population increases are very large—over 3 per cent in Malaya, 3 per cent in Singapore, and not much less in the Borneo territories. In Malaya 68,000 additional workers enter the labour market each year. Malaya's major economic resource is rubber which brings a third of the country's revenue and about 60 per cent of its export earnings. Second comes tin-mining which produces 15 per cent of the revenue, but offers little prospect of expansion; present deposits are being gradually worked out. Malaya's future depends on a reasonable and stable world rubber-price, and upon natural rubber remaining competitive with synthetic. Measures to diversify the crop pattern by encouraging oil-palms, manila-hemp and cocoa are in hand, but they take time to bear fruit. The Malayan Second Five-Year Plan 1961-65 provides for the annual settlement of about 30,000 families on newly opened-up land, much of it under rubber. About 40 per cent of Plan expenditure will be on communications and social services. One-fifth of the development finance is to come from external loans and grants. Foreign investment for new industries is satisfactory because Malaya is considered one of the most stable countries of Asia.

In Singapore's Four-Year Plan 1961-65, 53 per cent of expenditure is on industrial estates and other infra-structure to attract new investment. But political instability almost halted the latter. The hope is that with Singapore part of Malaysia, political troubles will end. With its skilled labour force and developed amenities the island should be well-placed to attract foreign and domestic capital. But revenue will continue to depend mainly on the massive entrepôt trade which, in spite of Indonesian 'confrontation' (see below), remains at a high level. About 30 per cent of Government finance for the Singapore Plan must come from foreign loans and grants.

Sarawak and North Borneo, much less advanced than Malaya and Singapore, have their development plans. Timber and rubber are important exports from both. But, with present population increases, a faster opening up of new land for peasant settlement is needed. Industrialization will be necessary too. Brunei is uniquely fortunate in having oil deposits which were struck in 1929. Her resultant financial surpluses, far too great for her own requirements, should be more freely available for investment in the rest of Malaysia, if she joins eventually. But as important as anything for Malaysia will be the development of peasant co-operatives. The Malay cultivators, and the tribespeople of Borneo, in order to be on equal terms with the resourceful Chinese, will need to emerge from primitive agriculture and financial fecklessness. Only through co-operative banking and marketing are they likely to be able to build up the resources necessary to do this.

The Brunei Rebellion

The winter of 1962 produced sharp surprises. Unexpectedly, in the tiny British-protected Sultanate of Brunei, an insurrection broke out against accession to Malaysia. The population of Brunei was only 83,000, with Malays numerically the largest race. But the oil which had been struck in 1929 meanwhile yielded some five million tons annually and accounted for 92 per cent of the Sultanate's exports; and Brunei's financial surpluses had, for years, been so great that it could, if necessary, have lived entirely on the interest accumulated from investment abroad. Since 1955 the Sultan, Sir Omar Saifuddin, had been under considerable pressure from the Ra'ayat Party, led by A. M. Azahari, to democratise his state and make a bid to become the constitutional monarch of a smaller federation of the three Bornean territories. In 1959, after talks in London, the Sultan promised indirect elections for a central legislature within two years. But he retained a nominated majority in the Assembly, and the elections were postponed repeatedly before they were held in August 1962. By that time Tungku Abdul Rahman's Malaysia project had been agreed with Britain; but Brunei's accession to Malaysia depended on her Sultan. However Azahari's Ra'ayat Party won all the elected seats in the Brunei elections, fighting on a platform which was opposed to a link-up with Malaya in a Malaysian Federation. (In 1961 there had already been violent demonstrations in Brunei against certain Malays from the peninsula who had been appointed as officials. The Ra'ayat Party had been able to convince Bruneians that these Malays were coming in to monopolize key-posts and to appropriate the wealth from Brunei's oil.)

However, Tungku Abdul Rahman had won the Sultan of Brunei over to his Malaysia plan; and, after it became clear that the Sultan intended to take Brunei into Malaysia, Azahari withdrew to Manila in the Philippines and launched his rebellion on 8th December 1962. But the revolt was doomed when the rebels failed to secure the person of the Sultan. Nor did the peoples of North Borneo and Sarawak support the 'Northern Borneo National Army' as Azahari had hoped. By 14th December the revolt had been virtually suppressed. Altogether 3,000 British troops had been involved. Several hundred insurgents escaped into the jungle near the Brunei-Sarawak border. On 20th December the Brunei Sultan suspended the 1959 Constitution and appointed an Emergency Council.

It soon became known that the Brunei rebels had been trained in Malinau and Tarakan in neighbouring Indonesia. On 19th December President Sukarno urged Indonesians to support the Brunei rebellion; three weeks later an Indonesian Government spokesman said that requests by Azahari for help in men and arms would be seriously considered. Finally, on 11th February 1963 the Indonesian Foreign Minister declared that the creation of a Malaysian Federation would be resisted by all means short of war. Indonesian leaders criticized the Malaysia project as 'neo-colonialist' (British bases would remain to protect it). Also during the 1958-61 insurrection in Indonesia the anti-Sukarno rebels had bought arms and supplies through a large illicit trade with Singapore and Malaya. Indonesian rebel leaders had found asylum in Malaya. Yet President Sukarno's threats did not prevent the birth of Malaysia. The London agreements of 8th July took Sarawak and North Borneo into the new Federation but with special safeguards against Malay domination. They retained a veto on immigration, had their own heads of state, controlled for a period their own education systems and public service appointments, and retained English as official language for ten years. North Borneo and Sarawak were to have no state religions. The Sultan of Brunei, however, decided not to take his state into Malaysia.

Indonesia's hostility had placed the Malaysia project squarely in a wide international context. It was clear that, without resorting to direct aggression, Indonesia could foment guerilla war in Northern Borneo from her own adjoining territory. Indonesia's two-million-strong Communist Party was evidently eager to do this. Since the Indonesian forces were largely Russian armed and aided, this would obviously have Great Power repercussions. More unexpected than the Indonesian political intervention was the unanimous resolution by the Filipino House of Representatives in April 1962 asking President Macapagal to claim North Borneo from Britain. The claim, lodged in June, was based on the contention that the Sultan of Sulu had not been sovereign, but subject to Spain, when he had leased North Borneo to the British business concern of Alfred Dent in 1878; or, alternatively, that this lease of North Borneo had been revocable and not a cession of sovereignty. The British Government rejected the claim in 1962 and during talks with the Vice-President of the Philippines in London during January 1963. But the claim continued to be pressed.

In January 1963 the United Nations Secretary-General, U Thant, expressed concern over the Malaysia situation, and his willingness to help diplomatically. His chief political adviser, Mr. C. V. Narasimhan, visited Malaya, Indonesia and Borneo, and suggested tentatively that referendums might be held in Sarawak, North Borneo and Brunei to settle the issue of joining Malaysia. Following diplomatic activity by Britain and Australia, Indonesia and the Philippines became more conciliatory. President Sukarno and Tungku Abdul Rahman met in Tokyo in June and declared that they would try to settle their differences in a spirit of neighbourliness. But after the London signing of the Malaysia agreements (8th July) Sukarno declared that the Malayan Prime Minister had broken a promise made at Tokyo to consult the peoples of Borneo before creating Malaysia. The Indonesian and Filipino Presidents and the Malayan Premier met in Manila (30th July-6th August) and decided to set up a concert of their three nations to be known as Maphilindo. The Filipino claim to North Borneo was to be taken up after Malaysia had come into being. A postponement of the creation of Malaysia was agreed on, so that the United Nations Secretary-General could ascertain the wishes of the people of North Borneo and Sarawak. A nine-man United Nations Commission visited the two territories and confirmed that elections held in North Borneo (December 1962) and Sarawak (June 1963) had represented a free and fair vote on the Malaysia issue. The Indonesian and Filipino governments refused to accept this verdict; and when Malaysia was launched on 16th September they declined to recognize it. Indonesia broke off commercial relations with Malaysia (25th September).

Intervention and Confrontation

On 18th September the British Embassy in Jakarta was burned down by a mob; and British firms in Indonesia were seized, though allegedly only as a temporary measure. Indonesian-fomented guerilla activity in Sarawak increased. Britain, Australia and New Zealand remained committed under the 1957 Defence Treaty to help protect the Borneo territories; and by January 1965 some 12,000 Commonwealth troops and considerable naval forces were committed to Malaysia. In March 1964, following mediation by Mr. Robert Kennedy, the Indonesian, Filipino and Malaysian Foreign Ministers met in Bangkok but failed to reach agreement. A summit meeting of the three took place in Tokyo in June and, although there was a declaration in favour of setting up an Afro-Asian commission of inquiry, the talks broke down. Indonesia insisted that further withdrawals of Indonesian forces from Malaysia should be geared to the progress of political talks. President Sukarno's aim seemed to be to force Malaysia out of its special relationship with Britain and to secure new plebiscites in Sabah (North Borneo) and Sarawak on the Malaysia issue.

From August 1964 onwards the Indonesians staged raids on the Malayan mainland both by sea and air. These were militarily ineffective, and Malaysia took the matter to the UN Security Council where a Norwegian resolution deploring the Indonesian landings was only frustrated by the Soviet veto. In July and September 1964 serious race riots broke out in Singapore, provoked, so the Malaysian Government alleged, by Indonesia. More and more it seemed that, under these pressures, harmony between Malaysia's main races was absolutely essential to the survival of the new Federation.

BIBLIOGRAPHY

F. Spencer Chapman. *The Jungle is Neutral.* (Chatto and Windus, London, 1950.)
H. P. Clodd. *Malaya's First British Pioneer (Francis Light).* (Luzac, London, 1948.)
Reginald Coupland. *Raffles of Singapore.* (Oxford Univ. Press, London, 1946.)
C. D. Cowan. *Nineteenth Century Malaya.* (Oxford Univ. Press, London, 1961.)
Rupert Emerson. *Malaysia, A Study in Direct and Indirect Rule.* (Macmillan, New York, 1937.)
Emily Hahn. *James Brooke of Sarawak.* (Arthur Barker, London, 1953.)
D. G. E. Hall. *A History of South East Asia.* (Macmillan, London, 1958.)
Brian Harrison. *South East Asia.* (Macmillan, London, 1954.)
J. Kennedy. *A History of Malaya 1400-1959.* (Macmillan, London, 1962.)
John Lowe. *The Malayan Experiment.* (A Fabian Pamphlet, London, 1960.)
C. Northcote Parkinson. *British Intervention in Malaya.* (Univ. of Malaya Press, Kuala Lumpur, 1960.)
Robert Payne. *The White Rajahs of Sarawak.* (Robert Hale, London, 1960.)
Victor Purcell. *The Chinese in Malaya.* (Oxford Univ. Press, London, 1948.) *Malaya Communist or Free?* (Victor Gollancz, London, 1954.)
T. E. Silock. *The Economy of Malaya.* (Donald Moore, Singapore, 1956.)
Sir Frank Swettenham. *British Malaya.* (Allen and Unwin, London, 1948.)
K. G. Tregonning. *North Borneo.* (H.M.S.O., London, 1960.)
Paul Wheatley. *The Golden Khersonese.* (Univ. of Malaya Press, Kuala Lumpur, 1961.)
Sir Richard Winstedt. *Malaya and its History.* (Hutchinson, London, 1948.)
C. E. Wurtzburg. *Raffles of the Eastern Isles.* (Hodder and Stoughton, London, 1954.)

BIOGRAPHICAL NOTE

DERRICK SINGTON. B. 1908; educated Wellington College and Trinity College, Oxford; free-lance journalist; commanded propaganda unit in North-West Europe campaign in Second World War; Deputy-Controller of *Die Welt*, the British-launched West German newspaper (1946-50); *Manchester Guardian* correspondent in South-East Asia, covering the war in Indo-China and the Malayan Communist insurrection (1950-52); Staff leader-writer of *Manchester Guardian* (1952-54). Publications: *The Goebbels Experiment* (with Arthur Weidenfeld) (1942); *Belsen Uncovered* (1947); *The Offenders*, a book against capital punishment (with Giles Playfair) (1957); and *Malayan Perspective* (1952), a Fabian brochure.

INDONESIA

by

LESLIE PALMIER

Origins

The earliest Indonesians were the last great group of migrants from the Asian mainland, the Malays. Before A.D. 200 they had evolved the highly productive technique of swamp rice cultivation. Their subsequent history shows control of the archipelago oscillating between states based on sea-trade with foreign ideologies, and land-based states with local adaptations of the ideologies.

Thus, the Hindu-Buddhist trading empire of Srivijaya, based on south Sumatra, 670-1350, was succeeded by Mojopahit, centred on eastern Java, 1294-1500, whose Hindu-Buddhism had much more Javanese content, and whose power was based on production of a surplus of rice. Similarly, the coming of Islam led to the rise of Malacca as a major trading centre from about 1400; but the next major Islamic state was the Javanese inland empire of Mataram, established about 1580.

The West

An era of sea-based power opened in 1511 when the Portuguese captured Malacca. They lost it to the Dutch, however, and by 1667 the latter had complete control of the spice-bearing Moluccas.

With the passage of time the Dutch shifted their interest to the produce of Java. That island was briefly in British hands from 1811 to 1815, when T. S. Raffles attempted to institute reforms; they would have created a market for British manufacturers. The Dutch needed rather to develop the island's produce to meet their financial exigencies. Their solution was the famous (or notorious) *cultuurstelsel* or forced cultivation system, instituted in 1830. The wealth it produced gave rise to a strong middle class in the Netherlands, who made the government abandon forced cultivation in favour of free enterprise. From the 1870s both estate agriculture and mineral resources began to be developed.

It was only at the turn of the century that Western enterprise turned to develop the islands round Java, with the Government simultaneously extending the area of its administration. These 'outer islands' have therefore had a relatively short period of exposure to Western influence.

Western enterprise in the Netherlands Indies, however, was insulated in enclaves. The way of life of the Indonesian cultivator was unimproved by any modernizing influences. Indeed, the growth of population, a consequence of the pacification of the islands and improvements in hygiene, had lowered his standard of living. In an attempt to remedy the situation, an 'ethical

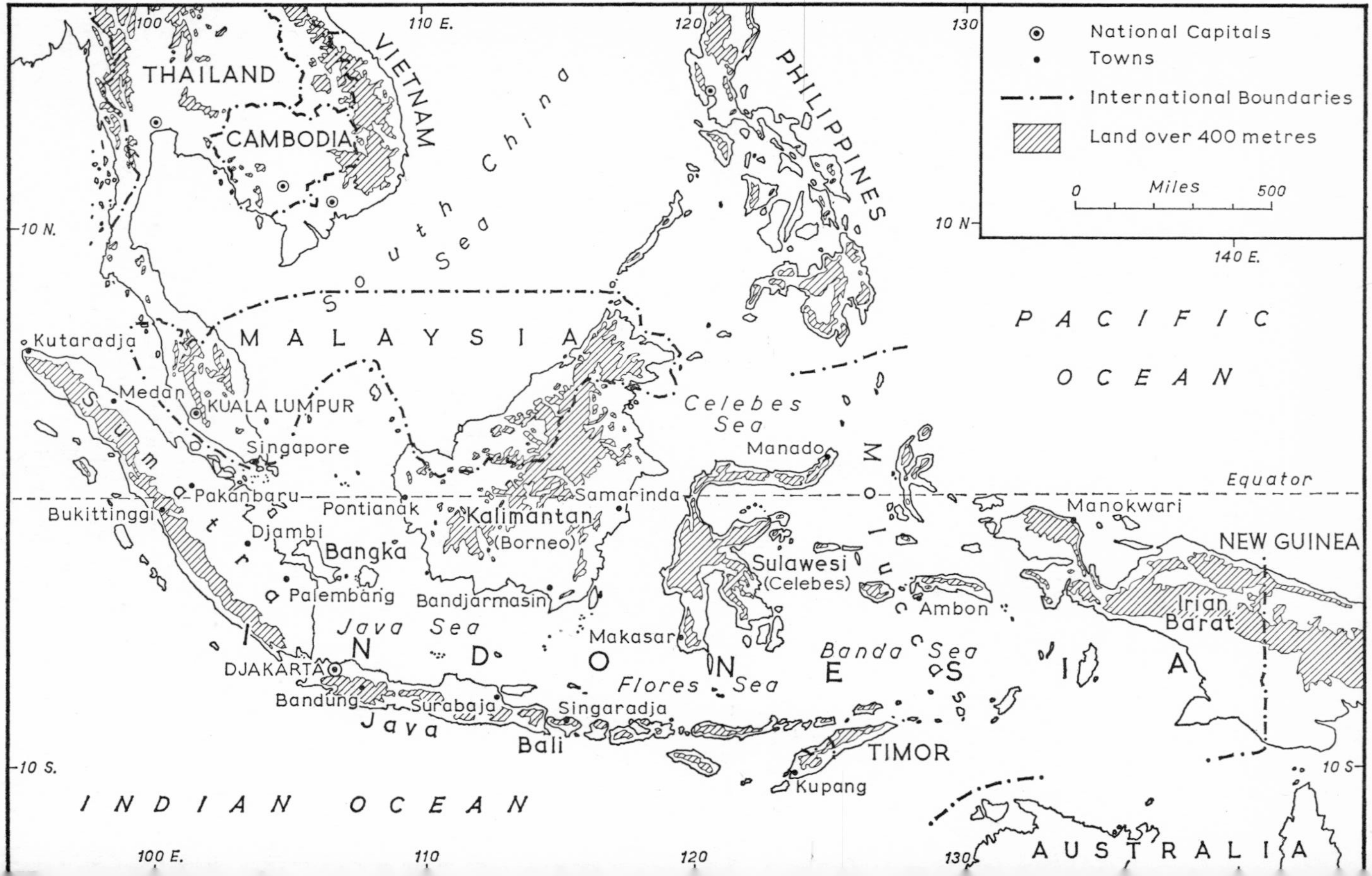
National Capitals
Towns
International Boundaries
Land over 400 metres
0 Miles 500
THAILAND
CAMBODIA
VIETNAM
PHILIPPINES
South China Sea
MALAYSIA
PACIFIC OCEAN
INDIAN OCEAN
INDONESIA
Moluccas
AUSTRALIA
NEW GUINEA
Irian Barat
Kalimantan (Borneo)
Sulawesi (Celebes)
Sumatra
Java
Bali
TIMOR
Bangka
Celebes Sea
Java Sea
Flores Sea
Banda Sea
Equator
Kutaradja
Medan
KUALA LUMPUR
Singapore
Pakanbaru
Bukittinggi
Djambi
Palembang
Pontianak
Samarinda
Bandjarmasin
Makasar
Manado
Manokwari
Ambon
Kupang
DJAKARTA
Bandung
Surabaja
Singaradja
100 E.
110 E.
120
130
140 E.
10 N.
10 S.

policy' was inaugurated in 1900, designed to fulfil a moral obligation to help the people of the Indies.

Western education was introduced in the latter half of the 19th century, but very few Indonesians acquired it, and many of those who did were not given the social positions commensurate with their qualifications. They naturally felt resentful at the colonial dispensation.

Nationalism

In addition, new ideas from Muslim modernists in the Middle East, the rise of nationalist movements in Asia, the spectacular Japanese victory over Russia in 1905, and after 1917 the influence of Marxism-Leninism from the Soviet Union, all helped to arouse political interest.

The establishment, beginning in 1903, of urban and district councils on which some Indonesians sat, provided experience in politics. It was only a matter of time before modern organizations began to develop. The first to do so was the *Budi Utomo* (High Endeavour), founded in 1908; it aimed at revivifying Javanese culture and further spreading Western education. Somewhat similarly, in 1911 modernist Islam took shape in Indonesia in the form of the *Muhammadiyah*, which adopted the methods of Christian missions and undertook much social welfare work. In the same year, the first mass movement among Indonesians, and the only one before World War II, was founded: the *Sarekat Islam* (Muslim Association). It faded into insignificance in the early 1920s, disrupted by its Marxist faction.

A *Volksraad* (People's Council) was set up in 1918, but the Government did not treat it seriously, and so led Indonesians to despair of constitutional methods.

In 1920, the customary, or *adat*, law of the islands was revived; this had the effect of emphasizing the division between Westernized and other Indonesians. In addition, Indonesian political activity was strongly restricted. As a result, the new nationalist movements of the 1920s were limited to the Westernized.

The leaders of these movements emerged from the *Perhimpunan Indonesia* (Indonesian Association), a student organization in the Netherlands, which in 1922 turned to advocate independence through non-co-operation with the Dutch. Many of its members joined the Bandung Study Club, organized in 1925 by Sukarno, which became the nucleus of the Indonesian Nationalist Party (*P.N.I.*) founded in 1927, and had the same aims as the Association.

At the end of 1926 the Communist Party (*P.K.I.*), which had come into being in 1920, attempted a revolt; the Dutch had no difficulty in crushing it. They then took a strong line against all non-co-operative and revolutionary organizations. Sukarno was arrested in 1929, released in 1931, and re-arrested in 1933; he was set free only by the Japanese in 1942. In his absence the non-co-operative Nationalist groups, disunited, had little influence, while many Nationalists began to co-operate with the Government. It is perhaps from this period, if not earlier, that one may date the opening of the bitter breach between co-operators and non-co-operators.

Japan Intervenes

In February-March 1942 the Japanese Army overran the Indies. To ensure their control, the conquerors played off against one another the civil servants, the Nationalists, and the fervent Muslims (whose strength the Japanese built up through a village-based organization known as the Masjumi). Then, in October 1943, the Japanese created an Indonesian Army; it was to render invaluable service to the Nationalist cause.

Japan surrendered to the Allies on 15th August 1945; and on the 17th the Indonesian Nationalist leaders proclaimed independence. Sukarno was named President of the new Republic. From the end of that year to late 1949 it was in conflict with the Dutch, who sought to re-establish their dominion. The Republic was most strongly based in central Java, as well as in some parts of Sumatra. Despite two military actions against them, in 1946 and 1948, the Republicans remained unsubdued, and survived two internal revolts, left-wing in 1946, Communist in 1948.

The Dutch Depart

The Dutch were however able to establish states in the areas not controlled by the Republic. Those Indonesians who served in their administrations came to be known as Federalists and were branded by the Republicans as co-operators.

Finally, at the Round-Table Conference at The Hague, held between August and November, 1949, the Dutch agreed to leave. The only issue left undecided was the government of Western New Guinea. Sovereignty over the territory, as over the rest of Indonesia, went to the new state, the *Republik Indonesia Serikat*, or United States of Indonesia, composed of the Republic of Indonesia, based on central Java, and the Dutch-created states. It was agreed that for one year Western New Guinea would be governed by the Netherlands and discussions would be held to decide its political future. Since Western New Guinea lay in their area, this agreement lowered the standing of the Federalists who had co-operated with the Dutch.

Triumph of the Unitary State

The United States of Indonesia's life was ill-starred. The Republicans, mostly Javanese, considered the Federalists, who were all non-Javanese, as little short of traitors. Yet the latter were drawn from the richer areas of Indonesia, which in the aggregate held the majority of the population. The Javanese homelands are the centre and east of Java. These are deficit areas, for which food itself has to be bought from the proceeds of the sale of non-Javanese produce. Thus, though the Javanese were dominant politically they were dependent economically, and lived in fear of losing their control. However, though in a slight minority in the population, they were united; the other Indonesians consisted of several disparate peoples.

Javanese history and culture have emphasized the role of the state; other Indonesians have much more sympathy for, and ability in, private trade. In addition, the Javanese are considerably more xenophobic than other Indonesians. So ideological differences compounded conflicts of interest.

Post-independence politics in Indonesia may be divided into three phases.

First, the conversion of the state from federal to unitary, thus giving the Republicans dominance. Second, attempts at co-operation between the Javanese and the other-Indonesian factions. (The term faction indicates all those, whether of the ethnic group indicated or not, who supported its aims. Within either faction there were some of the same ethnic origin as those in the opposed camp.) Third, the establishment of an authoritarian state which would maintain Javanese control.

Indonesia's first three cabinets were either formed by the *Masjumi* (Islamic) party alone, or by a coalition between the *Masjumi* and the *P.N.I.* (Nationalists). The latter was predominantly a Javanese party, but the *Masjumi* then also included the *Nahdatul Ulama* (Muslim Scholars), or *N.U.*, who were largely based on east Java.

Javanese Leadership

With the fall of the third Cabinet on 1st August 1953, the first attempt at co-operation ended. The *N.U.* had withdrawn from the *Masjumi* in mid-1952, and thereafter that party, as the 1955 elections were to show, spoke mainly for the other-Indonesians, and no party spoke for both factions. Politics became a battle in which the Javanese factions, consisting of the President, the *P.N.I.*, the *N.U.*, and the *P.K.I.* (Communists), sought to keep the *Masjumi* and the small but able *P.S.I.* (Socialists), the main voices of the other-Indonesian faction, out of power.

The next Cabinet included only the Javanese faction; the *Masjumi* was in opposition. Despite manifest ineptitude and widespread corruption, the Cabinet enjoyed Presidential support and remained in office. It used its patronage to cripple the *Masjumi's* chances in the forthcoming elections. Its main positive contribution was the holding of the Bandung Conference of Afro-Asian nations. The President, whose influence in Government increased considerably, exerted himself to build up the Communist Party to offset the village-level support enjoyed by the *Masjumi*. His unsuccessful attempt to impose a chief of staff on the Army led to the fall of the Cabinet on 12th August 1955.

Indonesia held its first elections towards the end of that year; they gave a clear majority to the three major Javanese parties. One, however, was the *P.K.I.*, and the threat it represented led to another attempt at co-operation. A Cabinet composed of the major non-Communist parties took office at the end of March 1956.

Guided Democracy

The exclusion of Communists from government was not to Sukarno's liking, and he called for a 'guided democracy', in which the Cabinet would include all major parties, and there would be a National Council, representing every organized interest in the community, to 'advise' the Cabinet. The Javanese faction supported these proposals, the other-Indonesians did not, and on 1st December 1956 Mohammed Hatta resigned his Vice-Presidency.

The favouring of Java by the Government had long been resented by the people of the other islands, as well as by their military units, who often found themselves without pay or food. As a result, in mid-1956 military commanders began to barter copra and rubber from their islands with Singapore. After Hatta's resignation, army-led councils took over provincial governments in Sumatra, Sulawesi, and Kalimantan. The Cabinet declared martial law and resigned.

The next Cabinet represented principally the Javanese faction, and was Sukarno's instrument. The National Council was established in May 1957. A National Conference, organized in November, failed to bridge the gulf between the two factions, and an attempt was made on Sukarno's life on the 30th.

Revolt of the Non-Javanese

The previous day, the United Nations had rejected Indonesia's demand that the Netherlands be compelled to discuss Western New Guinea with her (transfer being a precondition). In December Dutch concerns were taken over and their personnel ejected from Indonesia; this assured the Javanese faction of support. Some in the other-Indonesian faction protested against the irrationality of the measures taken; they were threatened and beaten up. A number fled to Central Sumatra, where they formed a Revolutionary Council. In February 1958 they issued an ultimatum to Sukarno insisting that he abandon 'guided democracy'. When this was rejected, they declared a Provisional Government. They received little support, however, and by September Government forces had subdued all organized resistance. In August the President dissolved the *Masjumi* and the *P.S.I.*

The Constituent Assembly had been sitting since its election in 1955, and seemed on the point of reaching a decision in favour of a bicameral constitution, with the upper house reserved for regional representation. This would, of course, have safeguarded the other-Indonesians against Javanese hegemony, and did not please Sukarno. He therefore asked the Assembly to accept the still-born Constitution of 1945, which enshrined a strong Presidential Cabinet. When it refused he sent it home (on 5th July 1959); and decreed the 1945 Constitution. He then formed a Presidential Cabinet, and also went through the formality of rechristening the National Council as the Supreme Advisory Council provided for in the new Constitution.

Sukarno's Constitution

Sukarno's ideas involved the creation of governing bodies which included several major groups, but no formal opposition. The groups were to be 'regional and functional'; the latter including the armed forces, farmers, labour, religious groups, and co-operatives. Since the functional groups had a predominance of Javanese, the formula ensured their majority. All such representatives were in any case directly or indirectly selected by the President. One may regard this either as a means of ensuring Javanese dominance, or as a recognition of the fact that the Javanese were the most advanced people in the archipelago.

This formula was applied in the creation of various new governing organs. In March 1960 the elected Parliament was replaced by a 'Mutual Help' Parliament. Half its seats were allotted to members of political parties, the remainder to members of functional groups. Only parties of the Javanese faction were given seats: the *Masjumi* and the *P.S.I.* were excluded. (Indeed, a year later Sukarno ordained that only eight political parties were to exist; the *Masjumi* and the *P.S.I.* were not among them.) No votes were to be taken; the President himself would decide in case of disagreement. The following year Regional Assemblies were established on the same basis as the Parliament.

A People's Consultative Assembly was set up as supreme body. Parliament was included as one of its 'functional groups'. It met for the first time in November-December 1960; it conferred the title of 'Great Leader of the Revolution' on Sukarno, and decided to form a National Front to arouse the populace about Western New Guinea.

Sukarno also introduced a number of slogans, including USDEK, MANIPOL, and NEKAD, in which Indonesians are indoctrinated. MANIPOL is the Political Manifesto, in which Sukarno explains 'Guided Democracy'. USDEK stands for the initial letters of its five statements of principle, namely: return to the 1945 Constitution, Indonesian socialism, guided democracy, guided economy, Indonesian identity. Similarly, NEKAD represents maintaining the unitarian form of the Republic, socialist economy, restoration of security, supporting religious faith, loyalty to democratic principles.

Relations with the Chinese

The expropriation of the Dutch was simply the first step towards 'Indonesian socialism'. The next to be dispossessed were the *K.M.T.* (Nationalist) Chinese in September 1958; the following year Chinese engaged in rural trade, many of whom followed the Communist star, were deprived of their livelihood. Urban firms and plantations thus acquired were taken over by the state; rural trade was handed over to co-operatives. Friction with Communist China ensued, but in January 1960 the two countries finally exchanged ratifications of the 1955 treaty regulating citizenship of those of Chinese descent. The process did not stop with the foreigners. Both imports and exports were taken over by the state, forcing some 3,400 out of the 4,000 Indonesian importers out of business.

The New Order

After all these changes, three centres of power were visible in Indonesia, none in the constitutional bodies. They were the President himself, whose position depended upon a strong personal following, and upon his ability to play off the other two centres of power against one another. These were the federation of military units known as the Indonesian Army, under the Chief of Staff of the Armed Forces, General Abdul Haris Nasution; and the Communist Party, the Secretary of whose Politburo was Dipa Nusantara Aidit.

The new order now set itself three priority tasks: restoration of security; incorporation of Western New Guinea; and provision of enough food and clothing. It achieved its first task. By the end of 1961, most of the 1958 rebels had 'returned to the Republic'; in some instances this meant that they replaced Government forces as the legitimate authority in their areas. In mid-1962 the surrender was announced of the Darul Islam rebels, active since 1949. The Indonesian Army was thus able to concentrate its energies on the Western New Guinea Campaign.

The Western New Guinea Dispute

The dispute between Indonesia and the Netherlands over the western half of the island of New Guinea arose from the Round Table Conference held at The Hague in 1949. The Dutch were prepared to agree that a new Federated Republic of Indonesia was to receive sovereignty over the Netherlands Indies only if Western New Guinea were excluded. The Indonesians refused to accept sovereignty over anything less than the whole of the Dutch colony. Eventually, both sides accepted an ambiguous compromise to the effect that whilst sovereignty over the whole of the Indies was to be transferred to Indonesia, the Netherlands was to continue to govern Western New Guinea for a year, during which its political future would be settled by discussions between Dutch and Indonesians.

This ambiguity permitted the Dutch to believe that since government was to remain in their hands, so was sovereignty unless the discussions concluded otherwise; and the Indonesians to hold that sovereignty was theirs, but that the Dutch were permitted to govern the territory for a year, during which talks would take place about its future government.

The discussions held in 1950 came to nothing. The incorporation of Western New Guinea thereafter became Indonesia's main aim. It seemed to her rulers that to permit one part of the former Netherlands Indies to remain outside its recognized successor would invite other parts to secede. In addition, animosity to colonialism helped to silence critics of Javanese dominance in government, and to divert the people's attention from their continuous impoverishment.

Western New Guinea consists of some 60,000 square miles of extremely mountainous and barren terrain, providing a bare existence to some 700,000 Stone-Age tribesmen. Strategically it has no value without command of the sea.

The Dutch initially thought that control of Western New Guinea would enable them to remain a world power, as well as to provide both a home for the Eurasians from Indonesia and a field for missionary endeavour. Though they were disappointed on all counts, they still refused to transfer the territory, but instead decided to prepare it for independence; a Representative Assembly was set up in 1961.

Faced with Dutch obduracy, Indonesia in 1956 abrogated the Netherlands-Indonesian Union formed at the Round-Table Conference, and repudiated her debts to the Netherlands. She tried to gain the backing of the United Nations Assembly for her claim, but could not muster the necessary two-thirds majority in her favour. After her third failure, in 1957, she expropriated all Dutch firms and expelled nearly all Netherlands nationals. From 1959 she proceeded to acquire large quantities of arms, mainly Soviet. In 1962 Indonesian and Dutch naval craft clashed in the waters of Western New Guinea, and Indonesian paratroops were dropped in coastal regions.

At about the same time the United States intervened, and in March talks between Netherlands and Indonesian representatives began outside Washington, with a previous American ambassador to India, Mr. Ellsworth Bunker, acting as third party. Agreement was reached on 16th August. From 1st October, Western New Guinea was administered by the United Nations, which handed the territory over to Indonesia on 7th May. Indonesia promised to hold a plebiscite before the end of 1969 to enable the Papuan inhabitants to decide the future status of Western New Guinea.

Malaysia

The incorporation of Western New Guinea came too late to heal the rift in the Indonesian body politic. The Javanese faction were firmly in the saddle. To their need for an external enemy was now added the interest of the Army (in which the Javanese were of course the largest single component) in justifying its large size and its great share of the national budget.

With the dispute over Western New Guinea settled, President Sukarno opposed the plan to form a Federation of Malaysia from Malaya, Singapore, and the British Borneo territories. However, he met the Prime Minister of Malaya, Tungku Abdul Rahman, and President Macapagal of the Philippines in Manila in August 1963 and all these resolved to ask for, and to accept, a United Nations verification of whether the people in British North Borneo and Sarawak wanted to join Malaysia. The UN accordingly carried out a survey and on 14th September announced a positive finding. Two days later, when the new State came into existence, Sukarno refused to recognize it. Malaysia therefore broke off diplomatic relations with Indonesia. Indonesian troops were moved to the Indonesian frontier with Sarawak and engaged in hit and run fights with Commonwealth troops; they achieved no great success.

Both the United States and the Philippines attempted a settlement of the dispute: though Sukarno promised much, he fulfilled little. A meeting with Tungku Abdul Rahman in Tokyo in June 1964 failed when Sukarno refused to end hostilities. The next month Anastas Mikoyan, then Soviet Deputy Prime Minister, visited Indonesia. He reaffirmed Soviet support for Indonesia, and a series of landings by sea and air of guerrillas began on the Malayan Peninsula proper (which Indonesia had recognized as independent since 1957). With the assistance of the local population, the invaders were quickly killed or captured.

Malaysia complained of Indonesian aggression to the Security Council which in September voted in favour of a Norwegian motion deploring the Indonesian action; the Soviet Union, however, exercised its veto. Both Britain and the United States suspended all aid to Indonesia, with the sole exception of the latter's surplus farm products.

By April 1964 nearly all British firms had been expropriated. In March 1963, however, the Indonesian government restored its diplomatic relations with the Netherlands, and in July trade began again. A technical cooperation agreement followed in April 1964. The Dutch Foreign Minister, Dr. Luns, visited Djakarta in July, and agreed to extend an export credit for 30 million dollars for 1965, in return for certain concessions from Indonesia.

In August 1964, the Communist Party's Deputy Chairman was appointed to the Presidential Cabinet, which thus finally embodied Sukarno's combination of NASAKOM, or Nationalism, and Communism. Indonesian foreign policy thereafter increasingly assimilated itself to the Chinese line.

The Economic Situation

The new order's successes in its political tasks were not paralleled by its performance in the economic field. Agriculture is the most important occupation in the country, taking up the energies of some 70 per cent of the population; it provides more than half the national income and nearly two-thirds of the exports. Before the war, the islands were self-sufficient in food; since then, population has increased more quickly than rice. The Government met with little success in its attempts to have enough grown.

Most export crops are produced by estate agriculture; smallholders are responsible for subsistence farming as well as some cash crops for export. In consequence of war, insecurity, and political instability, production of export crops has still not reached the prewar level. Among them was rubber, which in 1961 constituted 39 per cent (the largest single portion) of the total value of Indonesia's exports.

Indonesia is the largest South-East Asian producer of crude oil, which is her other principal foreign exchange earner (34 per cent of total exports in 1961). Since November 1960 the three foreign oil companies have acted as contractors to the Government, with whom they are negotiating their share in the proceeds. (The term 'contractor' is considered less offensive to Nationalist ears than 'foreign investor'.) Production of petroleum shows a steady rise.

The country's extreme dependence on these two sources of foreign revenue has accentuated the pre-war 'colonial' character of her economy, despite the efforts of successive governments to diversify it. Most of her other exports, in any case, are also primary products. Among them is tin, of which Indonesia is also a major producer. The industry, which is Government-owned, has been neglected; production of tin shows a continuous decline. Only the high tin prices obtaining in the early sixties have induced the Government belatedly to re-equip the mines.

Large and small industry in Indonesia accounts for about 10 per cent of the national product, but its growth has been hampered by shortage of foreign exchange. Government attempts to have it produce enough cloth for the population have not met with success.

In January 1961, in an attempt to arrest the economic decline, an Eight Year Development Plan was launched. It aimed at spending over the period 1961-68 Rp.240,000 (about $5,400 m.), of which it was hoped that a quarter would be provided in foreign aid. The chief object was to increase the national income, which was estimated at Rp.2·6 bn. in 1960, by 12 per cent by the end of the plan period. Nearly half the amount allocated was to be spent on increasing production, and a quarter on improving distribution (including communications).

For the plan to work would have required the Government to halt its reckless inflation, initially brought about by the Western New Guinea campaign. With the decision to commence hostilities against Malaysia, however, the inflation accelerated, the plan became obsolete, and the economy continued its decline. The Consumer Index in the capital, Djakarta, rose twenty-one times between 1958 and April 1964. Matters were no better in the countryside. In February 1964 the Deputy Governor of Central Java estimated that one million people were starving.

BIBLIOGRAPHY

R. C. Bone. *The Dynamics of the Western New Guinea (Irian Barat) Problems.* (Cornell Univ. Press, Ithaca, New York, 1958.)
H. Feith. *The Wilopo Cabinet, 1952-53.* (Cornell Univ. Press, Ithaca, New York, 1958.)
L. Fischer. *The Story of Indonesia.* (Hamish Hamilton, London, 1959.)
P. S. Gerbrandy. *Indonesia.* (Hutchinson, London, 1950.)
D. G. E. Hall. *A History of South-East Asia.* (Macmillan, London, 1955.)
W. A. Hanna. *Bung Karno's Indonesia.* (American Universities Field Staff, New York, 1960.)
B. Harrison. *South-East Asia.* (Macmillan, London, 1957.)
G. McT. Kahin. *Nationalism and Revolution in Indonesia.* (Cornell Univ. Press, Ithaca, New York, 1952.)
G. McT. Kahin (ed.). *Major Governments of Asia.* (Cornell Univ. Press, Ithaca, New York, 1958.)
R. Kennedy. *The Ageless Indies.* (John Day, New York, 1942.)
Leslie Palmier. *Indonesia and the Dutch.* (Oxford Univ. Press, for Institute of Race Relations, London, 1962.)
Statistical Pocket Book of Indonesia. (Central Office of Statistics, Djakarta, annually.)
J. M. van der Kroef. *The West New Guinea Dispute.* (Institute of Pacific Relations, New York, 1958.)
H. J. van Monk. *The Stakes of Democracy in South-East Asia.* (Allen and Unwin, London, 1950.)
B. H. M. Vlekke. *Nusantara.* (W. van Hoeve, The Hague and Bandung, 1960.)
Dorothy Woodman. *The Republic of Indonesia.* (Cresset Press, London, 1955.)

BIOGRAPHICAL NOTE

LESLIE PALMIER made the first of several visits to Indonesia in 1951, as part of his graduate studies at the London School of Economics. He took his Ph.D. in 1956, and spent the next academic year as Research Fellow in Southeast Asia Studies at Yale University. From 1957 to 1962 he headed the first university department of Asian Studies in New Zealand, and then joined a Southern Asian research centre in the social sciences, located in India, of which he is now deputy director. He has published *Social Status and Power in Java* (London, Athlone Press, 1960), *Indonesia and the Dutch* (London, Oxford University Press, 1962), and *Indonesia* (London, Thames and Hudson, 1965).

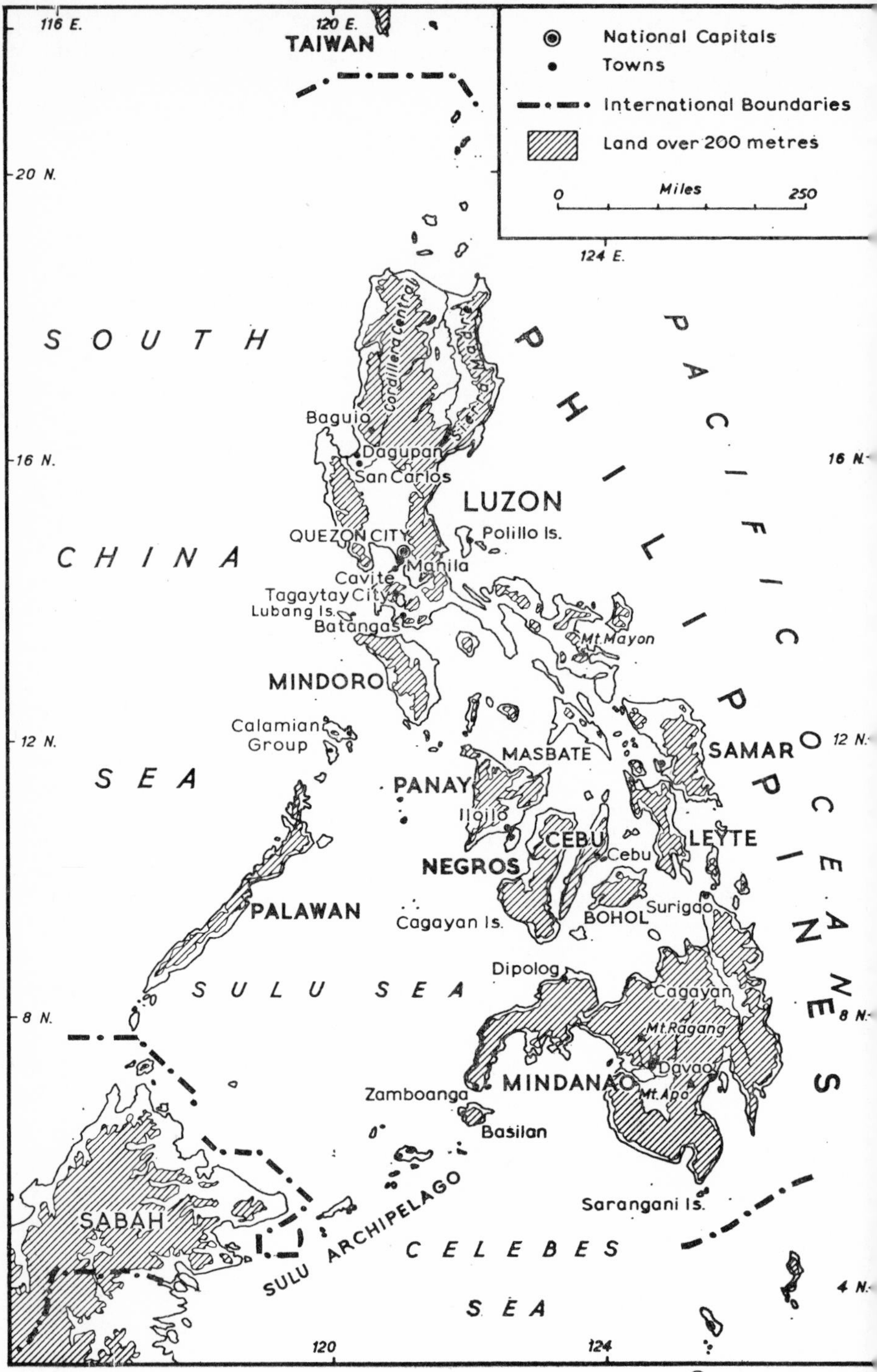
116 E.
120 E.
TAIWAN
National Capitals
Towns
International Boundaries
Land over 200 metres
0
Miles
250
124 E.
20 N.
16 N.
12 N.
8 N.
4 N.
SOUTH CHINA SEA
PHILIPPINES
PACIFIC OCEAN
Cordillera Central
Sierra Madre
Baguio
Dagupan
San Carlos
LUZON
Polillo Is.
QUEZON CITY
Manila
Cavite
Tagaytay City
Lubang Is.
Batangas
Mt.Mayon
MINDORO
Calamian Group
MASBATE
SAMAR
PANAY
Iloilo
CEBU
LEYTE
NEGROS
Cebu
PALAWAN
Cagayan Is.
BOHOL
Surigao
Dipolog
SULU SEA
Cagayan
Mt.Ragang
Davao
MINDANAO
Mt.Apo
Zamboanga
Basilan
SABAH
SULU ARCHIPELAGO
CELEBES SEA
Sarangani Is.
120
124

THE PHILIPPINES

by

WALTER FRANK CHOINSKI

Geography

The islands comprising the Republic of the Philippines are at the crossroads of intercontinental and regional travel lanes, off the south-east coast of Asia. They stretch from 5° to 22° north latitude, and from 117° to 127° east longitude. The island chain is in the form of a sprawling triangle, 1,152 miles from north to south, and 688 miles from east to west at the base. The irregular coastline of 10,850 miles is twice as long as that of the United States. The immense archipelago consists of 7,107 islands and islets, of which only 2,773 are named. The total land area is 114,830 square miles.

The 11 main islands have a land area exceeding 1,000 square miles each. Luzon is the largest with 40,814 square miles. Manila Bay, which has an area of 770 square miles, is one of the finest natural harbours in the world.

Ethnic Origin and Minorities

The official census of the Philippines places the population of the Republic at 29·3 million persons. The Philippines may truly be referred to as an oriental melting pot, where all races and nationalities mingle steadily with the original inhabitants.

The Indonesians who migrated to the Philippines in two waves from about 8,000 to 3,000 years ago were of Mongoloid stock with Caucasian strains. They are of slender build, with light complexions, thin faces, high aquiline nose, broad forehead, and deep-set eyes. The Ilongots of the Sierra Madre and the Carballo Mountains in central Luzon are descendants of the early Indonesians.

Following the Indonesians were the Malays, who came to the Philippines in several waves, starting about 200 B.C. The Malays are brown, of medium height, with slender bodies, flat noses, black hair, and brown eyes. Before coming to the Philippines the Malays had extensive cultural contacts with India, China, and Arabia.

About 58 per cent of today's population of the Philippines are descended from the Indonesians and the Malays. Europeans and Americans contribute only about three per cent to the population. It is estimated that there are about 250,000 Chinese in the Philippines.

Religion

The Republic of the Philippines is unique in that it is the only Christian nation in the Far East. Christian Filipinos constitute 93·3 per cent of the population, while of the remaining 6·7 per cent a considerable portion are

Muslims, and the rest pagans. Roman Catholics make up 82·9 per cent of the Christian population, the remainder belonging to the Filipino Independent (Aglipayan) Church, or Protestant churches of various denominations.

The Muslim faith is the principal non-Christian religion of the country. The Muslim Filipinos (commonly called Moros) are concentrated in the Sulu Archipelago, southern and western Mindanao, and southern Palawan. The solidarity of this group results in their having a considerable influence in national affairs.

Rituals vary among the pagan groups. Basically animistic, they have little influence on the national scene.

Language

The Philippines is commonly referred to as the third largest English-speaking country in the world, next only to the United States and Great Britain. It is the language of the leading newspapers and magazines, and most of the radio stations. It is the language of government, trade, and commerce. It is used as the medium of instruction in all the schools (with some exceptions in the primary grades in the provinces) and hence must be considered as the leading language despite the fact that only about one-third of the population speaks English.

Tagalog, the official Filipino language, is spoken by about one-third of the population. It is being taught in all schools.

In all, there are 68 known dialects spoken in the Philippines, though only eight dialects provide the language for 90 per cent of the people. In addition to Tagalog, the leading dialects are Hiligayon, Cebuano, Bikol, Samareno, Ilocano, Pampanga, and Pangasinan.

Historical Summary

Although the existence of the Philippines was known to the Portuguese through their trade contacts for many years before the arrival of the Spaniards, the discovery of the archipelago is traditionally credited to Ferdinand Magellan, the Portuguese explorer in the service of Charles I of Spain. On 17th March 1521, Magellan landed on an uninhabited islet south of Samar and shortly thereafter sailed westward to Cebu. He was slain on 27th April 1521, less than six weeks after his arrival, by Lapulapu who recently has become a symbol of Philippine independence and is hailed as 'the first Filipino to have repelled European aggression'.

It was not until the arrival of Legaspi, in April 1565, that the actual conquest of the islands began. On 8th May of that year what is now Cebu City was founded and served as a hub for further exploration and expansion, which resulted in the selection of the Moro-dominated town of Maynila, renamed Manila, as the permanent centre of operations on 24th June 1571.

As education progressed and as contact with other nations increased, the dissatisfaction of the Filipinos with their colonial status became increasingly evident. The most significant events prior to independence took place between the years 1872 and 1899, when strong undercurrents advocating reform and independence first rose to the surface. The Cavite revolt of 1872, although quickly and ruthlessly suppressed, became a popular symbol and resulted in a propaganda campaign against the Spanish Government which grew with the years. Perhaps the best known of all Filipino heroes is José Rizal, who, although stimulated by intellectual activities, was saddened by the general apathy towards Philippine issues which he found among his intellectual countrymen. While completing courses at the Central University of Madrid for his doctorate in Philosophy and Letters, Rizal wrote his first political novel, *Noli Me Tangere*, which was more than well received by the Filipinos, but not by the Spaniards. Against the advice of his associates in Europe he returned to the Philippines in 1887. A year later he left for Europe, and in 1889, in Paris, he formed a group of Filipino patriots; he then moved to Madrid and Biarritz where he finished his second novel, *El Filibusterismo*. In 1890 he went to Hong Kong, whence he founded a colony within the territory of British North Borneo for dispossessed Filipinos.

Rizal returned to Manila in June 1892 with a draft constitution for a Liga Filipina which had as its aim the unification of the Filipinos. The Liga was formed on 2 July 1892, and four days later Rizal was taken into custody, imprisoned at Fort Santiago, Manila, and ordered into banishment to 'one of the islands in the south'. He went to Dapitan, Mindanao, but left for Spain in September 1896. As the steamer entered the Mediterranean he was placed under arrest by the ship's master and returned to the Philippines and Fort Santiago, where he was tried before a military court for sedition and rebellion. One and a half hours after he was married to Josephine Bracken, at 0700 hours on 30th December 1896, he was executed, ironically, by four Filipino soldiers.

Spanish reaction to this movement was so inflexible that its place was soon taken by another, still stronger movement, that advocated, not reform, but independence—the Sons of the People, better known as the Katipunan. This organization, formed in 1892 under the leadership of Andres Bonifacio and Aguinaldo, first raised the cry of Philippine independence on 26th August 1896.

Successes in the south by Aguinaldo led to a rivalry between him and Bonifacio which weakened the movement. It was not resolved until May of the following year, when Bonifacio, having refused to recognize the leadership of Aguinaldo, was executed by Aguinaldo's orders as a traitor to the revolutionary cause. By June 1897, Aguinaldo's forces were confined to an area around Biak-na-Bato. It was here, on 1st November 1897, that the Biak-na-Bato Republic was proclaimed, with Aguinaldo as the first President. A constitution was adopted with a preamble stating the intent to establish a Philippine Republic separate from Spain.

The military campaign, however, continued to favour the government troops, and on 14th December, following a series of negotiations, an agreement was signed which brought the revolution temporarily to an end. Under the terms of the agreement, Aguinaldo and approximately 40 of his companions were exiled to Hong Kong. The revolution ended on 31st December 1897, following the arrival of Aguinaldo in Hong Kong.

As an action in the American war against Spain, an American fleet under Commodore George Dewey destroyed the Spanish fleet in Manila Bay on 1st May 1898. Aguinaldo and his companions returned to the Philippines on

19th May aboard the American warship McCulloch. The Filipinos drove the Spaniards from many provinces and besieged Manila itself. Aguinaldo recalled many of his officers and generally cooperated with the American forces in suppressing Spanish authority. At this juncture the American military authorities concluded an understanding with the Spanish military commander to stage a mock battle for Manila, which surrendered on 13th August 1898.

On 10th December 1898 the United States Congress ratified the Treaty of Paris, under which Spain ceded the Philippines to the United States. Misunderstandings arose between the Americans and the Filipinos, and an incident at the San Juan Bridge in Manila touched off hostilities on 4th February 1899.

Under Aguinaldo's leadership a republic had been proclaimed on 23rd January 1899. The open phase of the insurrection lasted approximately nine months, although guerrilla activity continued for nearly another year. The major fighting ceased with the capture of Aguinaldo on 23rd March 1901. Organized Filipino resistance collapsed in 1902 with the surrender of the Philippine General Miguel Malvar to American forces.

Upon the surrender of Manila, the Americans established a military government with General Wesley Merritt as the first Military Governor. Local government was immediately organized in those towns that had fallen into American hands. In 1900, however, the Spooner Amendment was passed by the United States Congress authorizing the President to establish civil government in the Philippines. On 4th July 1901, William Howard Taft was inaugurated Civil Governor of the Islands.

In 1931, Senator Sergio Osmena and Speaker Manuel A. Roxas led a mission to the United States, which secured the passage of a law granting independence to the Philippines ten years after the establishment of the Commonwealth. This was called the Hare-Hawes-Cutting Law. It was adopted by the United States Congress in 1932, vetoed and passed again by Congress over the veto on 17th January 1933.

However, Senate President Manuel L. Quezon, the Filipino leader, objected to some of its provisions. The law was rejected by the Philippine legislature. Quezon led another mission to the United States and in 1934 secured the passage of a new independence law (the Tydings-McDuffie Law) more favourable to the Philippines.

This law provided, among other things, for the establishment of a Commonwealth of the Philippines preparatory to the granting of complete independence. An American High Commissioner was to reside in Manila to represent the President of the United States during the life of the Commonwealth.

A Constitutional Convention was called to frame an organic law. It met from 30th July 1934 to 19th February 1935, when it adopted the Constitution of the Philippines. President Franklin D. Roosevelt approved this Constitution on 23rd March 1935. It was then submitted to the Filipino people for approval. In a plebiscite held on 14th May 1935, the Constitution was ratified by the Philippine electorate. Four months later, Manuel L. Quezon was elected President.

The Commonwealth of the Philippines was inaugurated on 15th November 1935.

On 8th December 1941, the Philippines were invaded by Japanese forces. The outnumbered Philippine-American forces fought a series of heroic battles culminating in the historic defence of Corregidor and Bataan. On 9th April 1942, Bataan fell and on 6th May Corregidor was overrun.

On 20th October 1944, the American forces under General Douglas MacArthur landed on Leyte Island. On 23rd October, the Commonwealth Government was re-established on Philippine soil under President Sergio Osmena who had succeeded to the Presidency upon the death of Manuel L. Quezon on 1st August 1944. The liberation of Manila started on 3rd February 1945, when the first United States forces entered the city. Public administration was transferred to the Commonwealth Government on 27th February 1945.

After the war, the Philippine Government was saddled with crushing problems of rehabilitation and reconstruction. In the elections that followed the liberation of the Philippines, President Osmena was defeated by Senate President Manuel A. Roxas. Roxas became the first President of the Republic of the Philippines, which was inaugurated on 4th July 1946.

President Roxas died in office in 1948, and was succeeded by Vice-President Elpidio Quirino.

In the elections of 1953, Quirino was defeated by the former Secretary of National Defence, Ramon Magsaysay.

Under the energetic leadership of President Magsaysay, the Filipino people embarked on a concerted effort to achieve peace and prosperity at home as well as security from external dangers.

The untimely death of President Magsaysay in a plane crash on the island of Cebu on 17th March 1957 was a great blow to the Republic. He was widely loved and admired as a man of the people, and a true leader. Vice-President Carlos Garcia was sworn in as President the next day, and in the November elections was chosen to retain that post.

Under President Garcia, the Republic continued to face numerous problems, the outstanding of which were basically 'personal economy' and corruption. Although the gross national product rose steadily throughout his administration, the economic level of the Filipino worker was such that three out of four 'barrio' people had but a cash earning of about P100 per year (US $24·00), while the wealth of the country concentrated around Manila and fell to those who managed to be 'in on the deal'.

It was no surprise then that when the national elections were held on 14th November, 1961, President Garcia was defeated by Vice-President Diosdado Macapagal in what may be considered a landslide vote in his favour. Macapagal has expanded public housing facilities and reduced unemployment by 2.4 per cent but has failed to implement the land reform programme, improve workers' wages or stabilize the peso. His opposition to Communism, support of the United Nations, extension of relations with Japan and Taiwan, retention of American bases on the island and support of British bases in South-East Asia may counter accusations of vindictiveness against political enemies and business men who failed to support him, and assure him success in the presidential elections of November 1965.

Political Parties

Although embryonic political parties appeared in the Philippines prior to the Spanish-American War, it was not until 1906 that viable political parties began to emerge.

Before the establishment of the Commonwealth in 1935, the two major parties active on the political scene were the Nationalist Collectivist Party led by Manuel Quezon and the Unipersonalist Nationalist Party of Sergio Osmena, Senior. Following the Nationalist Collectivist victory in the 1922 legislative elections these two parties joined to form the Nacionalista Consolidada Party. In 1935, after Quezon and Osmena were elected President and Vice-President, respectively, of the new Commonwealth Government, the party assumed the name of the Nacionalista Party, which, under Quezon's leadership, retained firm political control until the evacuation of the Government to the United States in early 1942 under the threat of Japanese occupation.

The Commonwealth Government under the Nacionalista Party returned to the islands in October 1944 and remained in office until 1946, when it was unseated by the newly formed Liberal Party under Manuel Roxas. The Liberals remained in power until the 1953 elections, when the Nacionalistas, led by Ramon Magsaysay as their presidential candidate, swept into office once more. Although weakened by the sudden death of President Magsaysay in 1957, the Nacionalista Party, under the leadership of President Carlos P. Garcia, former Vice-President under Magsaysay, was successful in the November 1957 campaign and dominates Philippine politics today.

There are five significant political parties functioning in the Republic at present: the Nacionalista, Liberal, Democratic, Nationalist-Citizens, and Progressive Parties. In addition, there are a number of minor political splinter groups, including the officially outlawed Communist Party, which have only a slight influence on the political scene.

The Nacionalista Party initially gained predominance in Philippine politics owing to its outstanding leadership and to its maintenance of a practical monopoly of the independence issue. Out of office during the period from 1946-53, its return to power was attributable primarily to the broad popularity of its 1953 candidate, Ramon Magsaysay, actually a Liberal turned Nacionalista for election purposes. Under President Magsaysay, and now under President Garcia, the party has been concerned mainly with internal problems which centre around the weak Philippine economic base. It is generally pro-Western in its international orientation although it maintains considerable flexibility in its approach to problems of primarily Asian concern.

The Liberal Party was formed in 1945 from among members of the Liberal wing of the Nacionalista Party. Under the leadership of Manuel Roxas, the party offered the electorate a new and vigorous approach to the many postwar problems. It also answered the public's desires on the collaboration issue stemming from Philippine relations with Japan during the

Japanese occupation, and easily unseated the Nacionalista Party in the 1946 election. President Roxas died on 15th April 1948 and was succeeded by Vice-President Quirino. Opposition charges of graft and corruption were used effectively in the defeat of the party in the 1953 campaign, and the party continues to suffer politically from such charges.

Today the party platform centres around cooperation with the United States on the international scene, and clean government with increased opportunities for foreign investors at home. The incumbent President of the Republic, Diosdado Macapagal, is a member of the Liberal Party, having been elected to the office of Vice-President in the 1957 campaign, defeating the Nacionalista Party candidate, José P. Laurel, Jr.

The Democratic Party was organized from a Liberal Party faction which unsuccessfully sought the presidential nomination for Carlos P. Romulo in 1953. In the campaign which followed, the Democrats supported the Nationalista Party and have continued the support, with only minor variations, since that time.

The Nationalist-Citizens Party was formed by Senator Lorenzo Tanada of the Liberal Party in 1947 under the name of the Citizens Party. Initially a small and ineffective group politically, it gained somewhat by its support of the Nacionalista Party in the 1953 campaign. This gain was more than offset by losses incurred in supporting Senator Claro Recto for President in 1957, during which time its name was changed to the Nationalist-Citizens Party to indicate Senator Recto's Nationalist-oriented programme.

The Progressive Party is the newest political party in the Republic. It was formed shortly after President Magsaysay's death from a nucleus of the 'Magsaysay-for-President' movement active in the 1953 elections.

Rumours of a 'third force' and the possibility of a third major political party to overcome the shortcomings of the present political system are linked with the names of Senators Manuel Manahan and Raul Manglapus, both Jesuit-trained politicians. Thus far potential supporters have remained silent and the likelihood of success appears doubtful.

Principal Industries

Primary economic gains appear to be possible in the expansion of firms engaged in producing goods for domestic consumption and in expanding facilities for further processing of materials in the extractive industries of the country before these goods are placed in the export market. However, cheap electric energy is lacking. When hydro-electric power becomes available in quantity and at a low price, metal ore concentrates may be smelted domestically, adding considerably to the unit value of such exports. A basic steel industry does not appear economically feasible at the moment, since coking coal and other necessary agents are lacking.

A further problem in Philippine industrial expansion is created by the reluctance of those with savings to invest in industrial ventures in which gains might be small and long in coming, and in which the risks are relatively high. Land, particularly agricultural land for tenant farming, is preferred as a high-return investment. Recent trends in national legislation toward Filipinization of certain sectors of the economy (Retail Trade Nationalization Act) have not encouraged needed investment from abroad, although an awareness of this problem has given rise to discussion in the national legislature of the problem of foreign investment funds.

Industrial Development

Principal impediments to industrial development in the Philippines have been the general shortage of managerial and technical know-how, shortage of power facilities in certain areas, some fear of competition from government-operated enterprises in certain lines of production, lack of basic information for planning new enterprises, and lack of domestic capital for financing new industries. Domestic investors have been reluctant to venture into the relatively new field of manufacturing, preferring to invest their capital in trade and real estate as in the past. The same preference has been displayed by the commercial banking system in its lending operations.

The Government has gone ahead with plans to establish an integrated steel industry at Iligan (Mindanao), where it now has some steel mills which produce a limited variety of products using ingots made from local scrap. The projected iron and steel complex is to include facilities for making most types of steel items and a large smelter to supply pig iron, produced from domestic ore. Some tentative contracts have been awarded for equipment, and the Philippine Republic is looking abroad—primarily in the United States—for assistance in financing the project.

Basic Issues

Since the inauguration of the Republic of the Philippines on 4th July 1946, the pattern of development has been similar in many respects to that of any other new nation. There have been numerous social, economic, and political issues which have required adjustment and change, and which in general have been met and resolved successfully. There are certain recurrent aspects which in a basic sense have had, and probably will continue to have, considerable influence on the national development.

The widespread destruction and devastation of the islands during World War II have presented formidable problems. These have been met primarily by an ambitious development programme which has as its goal a viable national economy with strong growth potential. In many respects, the results have been remarkably good, but in other respects it is evident that further adjustments remain to be made. This is particularly true in the matter of Government control procedures designed to channel development into worthwhile efforts that will aid in stabilizing and balancing the economy.

Certain minority groups continue to require considerable understanding and effort. In the southern part of the country, particularly in the Sulu Archipelago area, the Moro minority is a proven source of irritation and concern. Because the Moro element is largely indifferent to customs regulations, the national Government is constantly involved in anti-smuggling drives to halt the illegal trade which continues between this area and the islands of Indonesia.

The Chinese minority element in the Republic, which is centred in the Manila area, for many years has been one of the dominant influences on the business life of the islands. In many respects, the Chinese represent a stabilizing group financially, which is beneficial to the national Government. Inherent Filipino distrust of this element continues to result in Government action to encourage Filipino participation in parallel business ventures, thereby curtailing Chinese opportunities for investment and growth. This problem will require a reasonable solution if the Government is to avail itself of the proven business and trade acumen of the 250,000 Chinese resident in the Philippines.

Communist influence, formerly a serious threat to the Government and to the welfare of the people, has been reduced greatly. The Hukbalahap (Huk) military potential is no longer considered to be a threat to the Government, although the extent of infiltration into the various political, social, and economic areas of Philippine society, particularly the school system, may prove to be a matter of concern in the future. Rather than operate as a 'liberation army', the Huks are now involved in all types of nefarious business and have assumed political aspirations under the guidance of prize-fighter Faustino Del Mundo and Luis Taruc's cousin Pedro. It is believed that these two have the support of half a million farmers whose votes may be cast *en masse* in favour of candidates for the offices of mayor, municipal councillor and national congressman. These followers of Sumulong ('to go forward'), the nickname of Del Mundo, adopt typical subversive tactics.

BIBLIOGRAPHY

T. A. Agoncillo. *Malolos, The Crisis of the Republic.* (University Philosophical Review, Quezon City, 1960.)

José Maminta Aruego. *Philippine Government in Action.* (University Publishing Co., Manila, 1953.)

Conrado Benitez. *History of the Philippines.* (Ginn, Boston, 1954.)

Howard Boyce. *The Philippines.* (Military Assistance Institute, Arlington, Virginia, 1964.)

Carlos Quirino. *Magsaysay of the Philippines.* (Alemars, Manila, 1958.)

The Philippines 1965. (Far Eastern Economic Review Yearbook, Hong Kong, 1965.)

BIOGRAPHICAL NOTE

WALTER FRANK CHOINSKI. Educated in letters and law at the University of Wisconsin. On active duty in United States Army 1939-58; retired with rank of Colonel. Since 1958 associated with the American Institutes for Research in the Behavioral Sciences, Pittsburgh, Pennsylvania, where now Director of Research for the Military Assistance Institute of Washington, D.C. and Arlington, Virginia. Has lived and travelled extensively in Poland, Germany, Italy, France, North and South Korea, Laos, Cambodia, Vietnam, Thailand, Kashmir and Mexico. Has written books on 14 countries which are now in use at the Military Assistance Institute by student officers assigned to duty in overseas areas.

PART THREE

GENERAL

RELIGION

HINDUISM

by

K. M. PANIKKAR

OF all the great religions of the world Hinduism is the least known outside India. It is also only recently that its claim to be a great religion has come to be recognized in the West. Formerly, while Indian philosophy was generally accepted among scholars and students as an independent and valuable contribution to the thought of mankind, Hindu religion was considered as a complex of superstitions, irrational customs, primitive beliefs and magical formulae, with innumerable divinities, grotesquely figured with many heads and arms, and even with animal shapes. Apart from the worship of images, always a difficult matter to understand for those professing religions of Semitic origin, the wider prevalence of the worship of the mother goddess (Kali) with rituals involving animal sacrifice gave the impression that Hinduism was one of the lower religions, which, it could be assumed, would break down with the spread of modern knowledge. Not much interest was, therefore, taken in it, except in an anthropological sense.

The fact that Hinduism was able to resist the onslaught of Islam for over 750 years, and has emerged stronger after over 150 years of challenge by Christianity, has now made the West realize that what it had previously considered to be no more than primitive superstitions, held together by a strange system of social organization which was termed 'caste', must have some inherent values of high significance. The Hindu religion has thus for the first time come to be studied as a religion, with a desire to understand its teachings and to discover its essential values.

Many factors add to the difficulty of understanding the Hindu religion. Unlike most other religions it has no founder. No Buddha, no Christ, no Mohammed taught a definable set of Hindu doctrines, at least to start with. Consequently it has no beginning. The Hindus define their religion as *Sanatana Dharma* or eternal truth. Secondly there is no scripture, no authoritative text to which the enquirer can turn. The Vedas (circa 1500 B.C.) are a collection of hymns, some philosophical, some ritual, which throw much light on the religious practices of early Indians, and also on the origins of their philosophical thought. But they provide no consistent body of doctrine, which may be formulated as a creed. The *upanishads* which constitute the next great group of religious writings deal with some of the major problems of religion, the nature of *Brahman* (the ultimate power), of *atman* (the soul) etc. But here also, though a consistent philosophical system is taught in many of the texts, the characteristics of a religion as the West understands it do not emerge. Again the popular religion preached in the *puranas* (another set of sacred writings) would seem to the outsider to be at variance with the high philosophical teachings of the *upanishads*. When it comes to later times Hindu religious thought sub-divides itself into many sects, varying from the worship of minor local deities to the two great philosophical forms of Saivism and Vaishnavism, with numerous sub-cults of their own. No wonder that an outside student is confused and troubled, as there is neither a church to declare, define and teach the faith, nor a universally accepted scripture which could be studied as authoritative.

It is the historical and evolutionary character of the Hindu religion that makes it look like a tropical jungle to one who views it from outside. During the last 3,500 years of its existence every generation has left a sediment of ideas, opinions and practices in Hinduism. Nothing was ever totally discarded. The rituals and the *yajnas* (sacrifices) prescribed in the Vedas and the worship of gods long since forgotten are still followed with the same meticulous regard for details, by different groups in different parts of India. The upanishadic doctrines continue to be taught and contemplated upon. The stories in the *puranas* of demons with many heads and kings with many hands are accepted as miracles, side by side with the highest speculations and the deepest religious feelings. Also, one can see in the popular religion everywhere the survivals of primitive religions and totemic practices. This diversity makes Hinduism difficult for the outsider to understand.

Doctrine

With such a confusing variety of sects, doctrines, and practices the question may well be asked whether Hinduism is a religion. It was a commonplace in European writing in the past to say that the only possible definition of a Hindu is one who has been born of parents claiming to be Hindu. It was generally said that no definition of Hinduism on the basis of dogmas or beliefs was possible. Belief in Christ was a minimum requirement for a person to claim to be a Christian. It was necessary for all Muslims to believe in Allah as the sole God and Mohammed as His prophet. But no such dogma could be postulated for Hinduism. A formulation, however widely made, would exclude groups of sects which are recognized as orthodox. Similar is the position in regard to Hindu social structure. Often it is held that caste is a characteristic of Hinduism and yet there are recognized sects like the Lingayats, the Arya Samaj and the Brahmo Samaj which do not accept the caste system and openly deny the superiority of the Brahmins.

However, in spite of this extreme diversity there is a framework of ideas and doctrines which could be considered as characteristically Hindu. It is within this framework that the different sects and creeds flourish and they are generally accepted as a common background for all Hindu systems. These ideas and doctrines may be broadly divided as falling within three categories: (1) conceptions relating to God and man's relations with God; (2) conceptions relating to the world; and (3) conceptions relating to man's life in society. In respect of all these Hinduism has an attitude which is different from that of all other religions.

The Hindu conception of God is on three planes: as the Absolute—*Brahman*—the supreme Reality which is undefinable, without qualities, beyond predication; as *Isvara* or God with qualities, all powerful, all merciful, etc., conceived generally as Brahma, Vishnu and Siva, representing the three aspects of creation, maintenance and destruction; and as *Ishta Devata*, the God of choice, a representation according to one's special aptitude, as Krishna, Kali, Durga, Hanuman, Ganes, etc.

The only Reality that Hinduism accepts is the undefinable Absolute—*Nirguna Brahman*—or *paramatman*, a force which comprehends everything and to which no qualities could be assigned. *Neti* (not like this) was the way in which ancient teachers tried to convey the idea of Brahman. The whole universe *samsara* is but a reflection of this one Reality through the veil of *Maya*. Maya is generally translated into Western languages as illusion. It actually means the veil which conceals the Absolute. The phenomenal world is that veil, but it is no illusion. It is an empirical reality: something which exists but is subject to decay, death and transformation. Its true nature could only be understood in relation to the Supreme Reality, and that understanding is the ultimate object of human endeavour.

The *paramatman*—the universal soul, Brahman, is reflected in every sentient being as *jivatman* or the individual soul. This is the meaning of the supreme thought of Hindu religion, *Tat tvam asi*, *That art Thou*, which puts in a nutshell the doctrine of the relationship of the universal soul with the individual. The identity of the two is concealed by the enveloping veil of *Maya* and once that is penetrated the duality ceases to exist and the individual attains realization.

Brahman is without qualities, and therefore, judged by the conceptions of other religions, it may even be denied that it has anything to do with the idea of God. But the conception of *Isvara* meets this point. Brahman manifests itself as *Isvara*, possessing *gunas*, or qualities. The creation of the world, its maintenance and its continuous renovation are the primary functions which are associated with the *Isvara* conception. Though these are considered the separate attributes of Brahma, Vishnu and Siva—the Triad of Hinduism—it is always emphasized that they are merely three aspects of the same Brahman viewed as endowed with *gunas* or qualities. The function of Brahma is creation; of Vishnu is the upholding of the world; of Siva is the work of destruction and renovation. Brahma as the god of creation is not worshipped. But Vishnu and Siva are the 'gods' of Hinduism in the popular sense of the word. They are the manifestations of Brahman, whose worship leads one to the realization of the ultimate truth.

Another conception, which is most significant for the understanding of Hinduism, is that of *Ishta Devata*, or the God of Choice. Hinduism offers a variety to choose from, but the most popular are the various aspects of *Devi* (the mother goddess) and Krishna. Though the Devi cult may have had a non-Indian origin and may be connected with the worship of Ishtar, Isis and other goddesses of ancient times, in India it is well integrated with the rest of Hindu thought. The Devi in whatever form conceived, represents *prakriti*, or energy, which, operating through *purusha*, or matter, sets in force all the activity in the world. All *Ishta Devatas* are conceived as involving this dual principle, of *prakriti* (energy) and *purusha* (matter) expressed in terms of male and female counterparts. This is the doctrine behind Hindu ideas of gods and goddesses in combination, an idea which leads to a great deal of misunderstanding in the Western world. Every manifestation of god, as *Isvara* or *Ishta Devata* has its male and female counterpart; Siva and Parvati, Vishnu and Lakshmi, Brahma and Sarasvati, Krishna and Radha. In fact this conception is carried to its logical conclusion in the idea of Siva as *Ardha Narisvara* or god who is half man, half woman.

The doctrine of *Ishta Devata* has a special significance in Hinduism as it enables the worshipper to identify himself with a special aspect of god, with which he is in sympathy, to develop qualities of devotion, *bhakti*, and cultivate a sense of personal relationship.

This triple approach to God is the special characteristic of Hinduism, it being always emphasized that the worship of *Ishta Devata* is only a method of realizing union with *Saguna Brahman* or the ultimate God, of identification with Brahman or the Supreme Reality.

The Individual and the World

The Hindu view of life is as a succession of rebirths based on the idea that till the individual soul obtains its release by cutting through the bonds of *Maya*, and attains realization with the Absolute, it must be born over and over again. The chain of births (which is a doctrine which Hinduism has in common with Buddhism) is determined by our individual *karma*. Karma literally means action. In this context it means the cumulative effect of a man's actions. The Hindu doctrine is that every action must have its effect, and the cumulative effect of a man's actions shapes his life. This is not a doctrine of fatalism for it is open to a man to change his future by shaping his *karma*. As *karma* is a continuous process, man is building up his own future. In order to break the chain of rebirth, man has to control his *karma* by a discipline of the mind and body, which is defined in Hindu philosophy as his *dharma*.

This discipline is the division of life into four *asramas:* study and preparation, life in society, life in retirement and finally renunciation. According to Hindu religion this is the ideal way of life. Every man must prepare himself for life by proper education and training (*brahmacharya*). Then he should fulfil his obligations to society (*grihastha*). The third stage is of retirement when he makes way for younger people contenting himself with advice and guidance, and he finally renounces the world and its activities. This division into four stages is no doubt only an ideal, but it is a universally accepted ideal among the Hindus, though but a few may follow it in practice.

Complementary to this idea of *asramas* is the definition of the objects of worldly life. The ultimate object is of course deliverance from the chain of rebirths and the attainment of union with the Absolute. But in life, there are three objects a man must seek to achieve; *dharma*, righteous conduct, *artha*, the acquisition of economic welfare and *kama*, life in senses. A right balance between these three objects is what men should aim at. Both *artha*, economic welfare, and *kama*, worldly pleasure, should be subject to righteous conduct, as otherwise it will only accumulate evil *karma* and thus prevent the final objective of liberation. A text in the Mahabharata declares that *artha* and *kama* to exclusion of *dharma* should be shunned; but *dharma* without *artha* and *kama* is also not desirable. A proper harmony of these three objectives is what is taught as the ideal life in Hinduism.

'Dharma'

Artha and *kama* are easily understood. The first is the life of earthly prosperity, the second the life of enjoyment. But *dharma* which is to govern both and is the basic religious and ethical conception of Hinduism is not so easy to define. One of the difficulties of defining *dharma* is the various meanings in which the word has come to be used. *Dharma* means duty, law, religion, ethical obligations, moral principles. The *dharma sastra* of Manu, for example, deals with law and morals; *rajadharma* means the duties of kings; *stridharma* means the duty of women. Each sect in a way elaborates the *dharma* a little differently. Broadly speaking, from the point of Hindu religious thought, *dharma* means the moral order. Now this conception of moral order is complicated by two ideas of *varna* and *guna*—caste and inherited qualities. *Varna*, which the West translates as caste, is a notional division of society in four orders, the Brahmins, Kshatriyas, Vaisyas and Sudras, based as Krishna says on *guna*, and *karma*, i.e., inherent qualities and actions. The four-fold division is theoretically on the basis of those devoted to intellectual, mental and spiritual pursuits (Brahmins); those concerned with upholding social order, leaders in temporal life—the arm of society (Kshatriyas); those concerned with economic welfare (Vaisyas); and the working classes. This broad division is expressed allegorically in the Vedas in a famous hymn which says that the Brahmins emerged from the face, the Kshatriyas from the arms, the Vaisyas from the stomach and the Sudras from the feet of *Purusha*. This division was originally not based on birth, but in due course came to be considered hereditary, though at all times, there have been Brahmins who were engaged in non-intellectual professions, and Sudras who were scholars, saints and statesmen. The division was effective only in a broad sense and in the *samskaras* or rituals.

The doctrine of *varnas* or caste however had a great influence on the conception of *dharma*. Normally speaking, the varna or caste was said to decide a man's *dharma*, or duties in life. *Svadharma* or the individual's duty came to be interpreted in terms of his caste. The Brahmin's *dharma* was theoretically to lead a disciplined religious life. The Kshatriya's *dharma* of upholding society authorized him to do many things which would be sinful for a Brahmin to do: killing in battle, taking of life in hunting to mention only two examples. Similarly in the case of Vaisyas and Sudras. This was a popular and widely accepted view of *dharma* which provided a theoretical justification for caste.

'Guna'

Apart from the idea of *dharma* based on *varna*, there is also the doctrine of *dharma* based on *guna*. The doctrine of *guna* is one of the basic notions of Hindu thought and pervades every aspect of it. Briefly stated, it means that there are three basic qualities—*satva*, *rajas* and *tamas* which constitute human personality. *Satva* may be defined as harmony of qualities, an even balance; *rajas* where the egoistic characteristics predominate; *tamas* represents evil qualities. These are compounded in different proportions in all individuals, as a result of one's *karma*, inherited qualities, environments, etc.

This conception of *guna* affects all Hindu thought. Only the Ultimate, the *Brahman*, is without *guna*, and the highest expression of Hindu religion is in terms of *Nirguna Brahman*—that is *Brahman* without qualities. But when he manifests himself as *Isvara*—as God—he is endowed with *gunas*. The gods who are worshipped are necessarily conceived as having *gunas*.

'Avatar'

There is one further conception in Hinduism which also differentiates it from all other religions: that is the doctrine of *avatar* or incarnation. In essence this doctrine is simple. At every critical stage in human history God incarnates in this world to serve mankind. Such incarnations may be for specific purposes or limited objectives but may also be for the general uplift of mankind. The theory of *avatars* is stated by Krishna himself in the *Bhagavad Gita* in the following two verses:

> Whenever there is a decline of *dharma* and rise
> of *adharma* (unrighteousness) I incarnate myself.
>
> For the protection of the good, for the destruction
> of the wicked and for the establishment of
> righteousness, I come into being from age to age.
> (Gita, IV—Verses 7 and 8).

The god of *avatars* is *Vishnu*, the sustainer of the world in the Hindu Triad. There are no *avatars* of Brahma or Siva as the functions of creation and destruction *ex hypothesi* do not require incarnations. Vishnu's *avatars* include such unlikely manifestations of divine power as fish, tortoise, boar, man-lion, etc., each of which was, however, only for a specific purpose. The only full *avatar*, i.e. the incarnation of God with the totality of divine powers, is Krishna himself, who, therefore, is an object of worship. The Buddha, it may be mentioned, was also included among the *avatars* at least by the 10th century A.D.

The doctrine of *avatar* has, however, undergone a very significant evolution, which may be traced to the text in the Gita quoted above. When it is assumed that when *dharma* declines, and *adharma* is powerful, God will show himself in every age, for the reorganization of society, this easily lends itself to the view that every major reformer of religion is in a sense an *avatar*. As Hinduism holds that every individual has a spark of the divine in him, it is but logical to assume that some have it in a greater degree and that others by spiritual discipline leading to greater realization of God may become the instruments of His Will. Thus the Hindus accept without serious question the prophets of all religions as manifestations of God, as *avatars* for re-establishing *dharma*. The Hindu attitude to Christ, Mohammed and other founders of religion is governed by this idea of *avatars*.

Also, the number of minor *avatars* in Hinduism has no limits. Sri Ramakrishna Paramahamsa (19th century) and Sri Aurobindo (died middle of the 20th century) to mention only two among others, are looked upon by their followers as *avatars*, and according to the doctrine of God manifesting Himself to rescue faith in times of degeneration, the claim could only be judged in the light of their success in their mission.

Variety and Tolerance

It is this general body of beliefs that provides the framework of Hindu religion. Within that framework the greatest variety is permitted. Primitive beliefs and doctrines are easily adjusted, for the local gods and saints of tribes and racial groups come to be looked upon and accepted as manifestations and *avatars* of the supreme Godhead. There is no doctrine, except that of a complete denial of God and the *atman*, that could not be fitted within Hinduism.

One consequence of this is the wide tolerance that Hinduism teaches. Tolerance of other faiths is not with the Hindus a question of convenience; it is an article of faith, for has not Krishna himself said it: 'I give to each one according to his belief'. A higher belief may be recommended but worship of God under any form is considered by the Hindus as leading to a knowledge of Truth.

BIBLIOGRAPHY

Sir Edwin Arnold. *The Song Celestial* (verse translation of the *Bhagavad Gita*). (Kegan Paul, Trench, Trubner, London, 8th ed., 1897.)

G. Morris Carstairs. *A Study of a Community of High-Caste Hindus.* (Hogarth Press, London, 1957.)

Paul Deussen. *System of Vedanta*, trans. Charles Johnstone. (Open Court Publishing Co., Chicago, 1912.)

Sir Charles Eliot. *Hinduism and Buddhism.* (Edward Arnold, London, 1921.)

John Farquhar. *An Outline of the Religious Literature of India.* (Humphrey Milford, London, 1920.)

P. D. Mehta. *Early Indian Religious Thought.* (Luzac, London, 1956.)

Sir Sarvepalli Radhakrishnan. *The Hindu View of Life.* (Allen and Unwin, London, 1927.) *Indian Philosophy*, 2 vols. (Allen and Unwin, London, 1923.)

Swami Nikhilananda. *Hinduism: Its Meaning for the Liberation of the Spirit.* (Allen and Unwin, London, 1959.)

Yadunatha Simha. *A History of Indian Philosophy*, 2 vols. (Simha Publishing House, Calcutta, 1956.)

BIOGRAPHICAL NOTE

Kavalam Madhava Panikkar. B. 1895, d. 1963. Vice-Chancellor, Jammu and Kashmir University, ex-M.P. (Rajya Sabha). Educated at Madras, Oxford; Scholar of Christ Church, Bar-at-Law (Middle Temple). D.Litt. (Delhi), LL.D. Member of the National Academy of Letters, India. Official Career: Editor, *Hindustan Times*, New Delhi; Minister, Patiala State; Prime Minister, Bikaner State; Member, Constituent Assembly of India; Vice-President, Royal India Society, London; Vice-President, Indian Council for Cultural Relations; Member, Indian Academy of Letters; Ambassador in China (1948-52); Ambassador in Egypt (1952-53); Member, States Reorganisation Commission (1954-56); Ambassador in France (1956-59); Member, Rajya Sabha (Upper House of Parliament) (1959-61). Invited to deliver lectures at the University of Paris, University of Oxford, St. Gallen (Switzerland), and at different Indian universities. Author of numerous books on Asia; has also published novels, plays and poems in Malayalam.

ISLAM

by

PETER PARTNER

THE religion of Islam (which means 'submission') derives from the teaching of Muhammad, in the third decade of the 7th century, to the tribes of Arabia. It is in essence a prophetic revelation, revealed not continuously through an historic church, but once and for all through an historic personage. There is however some element of continued revelation in the development of Islamic law, which allows a certain discretion in the interpretation of the revealed laws transmitted by the Prophet in the Quran.

HISTORICAL

There is no distinction in Islam between the community of believers, the Dar ul-Islam, and the state. The society brought into being by the Muslim conquests, which in the early Middle Ages embraced half of the world known to Europeans, was a theocracy. The Caliph of Islam was not a sort of Pope, but the main prayer leader of a society whose entire organization was, in theory, religious. There was therefore no distinction between religious law and any other kind of law; the *sharia* embraces the whole life of man.

The great handicap of Islamic society was that its universality depended on its political supremacy. When the Islamic Empire began in the high Middle Ages to break up, to disintegrate into warring caliphates, and to suffer defeat at the hands of Christians and Mongols, the religious prestige of the theocratic society suffered a corresponding depression. When the Arab Empires finally disintegrated in the late Middle Ages, and were replaced by the Ottoman Turkish, Mogul and Safavid Empires, the institutions of Islam suffered changes which were not compatible with the religious idealism of their origins. When, finally, in the modern period, these Empires in their turn succumbed in the face of Western technical progress and imperialism, Islam was left to become the religion of the conquered instead of that of the conquerors.

MODERN ISLAM

The institutions, the law, the outlook of Islam all derive from an Islamic past of conquest and theocratic rule. Contrasting this with their present state, modern Muslims have sometimes become disorientated and bewildered. 'Why' (to quote the title of an influential pamphlet) 'have the Muslims become backward?' The reaction of modern Muslims has taken two principal forms. On the one hand there has been a return to the sources: an attempt to cleanse and renew the fundamental tradition and law of Islam. On the other there has been a complex attempt at mimesis, sometimes in the shape of direct imitation or 'Westernization', sometimes by seeking parallels from Islamic history and tradition in the Western world, and so covertly importing Western things into a supposedly Islamic synthesis. Of this last tendency 'Islamic social justice' and 'Islamic democracy' are important examples.

Measuring the external characteristics of Muslim movements by their apparent distance from Western culture, Westerners have described some as 'extreme' or 'fundamentalist' (e.g., Muslim Brethren in Egypt, Jamaat-e-Islami in Pakistan, Dar-ul-Islam in western Java); others as 'Islamic moderate' (Masjumi party in Indonesia); and others as 'Westernizing' or 'secularist' (the ruling groups in Pakistan and Indonesia). Such classifications are useful for following the political rough-and-tumble. But as soon as one comes to any single major Islamic thinker they tend to break down. Naturally enough, most of the more important figures in Islamic thought of the past century have spoken both of an inward spiritual renewal which looks back to classical Islam, and of coming to terms at least in some degree with Western culture. Muhammad Iqbal in India, Muhammad Abdu in Egypt, the leaders of the Muhammadiyah movement in Indonesia, have all looked both ways. Plainly, some Islamic thinkers are more Western in outlook than others. But plainly also, Islam should not be judged or measured only by the degree to which it manages to approximate to Western ideas. Just as useful, and more interesting, than a spectrum of Muslim opinion which runs from 'fundamentalist' to 'Westernizer' would be a spectrum related to *ijtihad* or the faculty allowed by Muslim doctrine to the community of believers to interpret Muslim law. This faculty is not claimed in a wholesale or indiscriminate way save by a few; for most the exercise of *ijtihad* is reserved to a small group of those learned in the law, and the most conservative would claim that the gates of *ijtihad* are closed, and no further modification of Islamic law allowable. Such a spectrum would be very different; Muhammad Iqbal, whose philosophy is often counted as Westernized, is on the whole conservative as regards *ijtihad*.

It is a paradox that Islam, this universalist religion, should have contributed so powerfully to the setting up of new national states. The Islamic revival stands behind Pakistani and Indonesian nationalism, just as it does behind Arab nationalism. But this association does not mean identity. The religious reformer Sayyid Abul Ala Maududi asked before Pakistan was brought into existence: 'Why should we foolishly waste our time in expediting the so-called Muslim national state and fritter away our energies in setting it up, when we know that it will not only be useless for our purpose but will rather prove an obstacle in our path?' At the other extreme Sukarno warned his nationalist followers that: 'It is useless to wait for help from an airplane from Moscow or a caliph from Istanbul'.

Pakistan

In Pakistan, the child of Islam, the demand for an Islamic state has so far been disappointed. The Muslim League was the party of Indian Muslims and not the party of north-west India and East Bengal; in 1945 Jinna sacrificed the possibility of compromise in order to maintain just this principle. But when Pakistan was set up it became apparent that there was a great gulf between the Muslim League politicians, who thought primarily in Western political terms, and the orthodox Muslim *ulama* or religious leaders; and that operating on both these political forces there was a regionalism which no one knew quite how to control.

The 1949 Objectives Resolution of the Muslim League announced as an objective of the future constitution of Pakistan that: 'Muslims shall be enabled to live their lives in the individual and collective spheres in accord with the teaching and requirements of Islam as set out in the Holy Quran and the Sunna' (Sunna means 'prophetic tradition'). This was cautious, but it opened the door to a movement for imposing Islamic law upon the state. Seven years of wrangling followed, in which the *ulama* to achieve this end became more and more deeply involved in national and regional politics. The disastrous riots which the *ulama* abetted against the heretical Ahmadiyah sect in the Punjab in 1953, and the involvement of the religious leaders in the regionalist demands of East Bengal, both contributed to the breakdown of parliamentary government in Pakistan. By that breakdown the movement for an Islamic state has been the loser. The 1956 constitution went far towards satisfying the *ulama's* desires in the 'repugnancy' clause which declared that no law be enacted which is contrary to the injunctions of Islam, and that existing laws be made to conform with these injunctions.

The bureaucracy and the Army, which have ruled Pakistan for the past few years, have been hostile to the idea of a religious state. President Ayub Khan has pronounced himself in favour of the separation of religion from government, just as General Iskander Mirza did earlier. There is only a very evasive equivalent to the 'repugnancy' clause in the Constitution of March 1962, and the Council of *ulama* and Muslim scholars for which it provides has a merely advisory function. For the moment the viewpoint which prevails is that expressed by the Pakistan Judges in 1954: 'The sublime faith called Islam will live even if our leaders are not there to enforce it . . . our politicians should understand that if Divine commands cannot make or keep a man a Musalman, their statutes will not'. It would be wrong to say of Pakistan that the Islamic state has been defeated by Westernizers; perhaps it would be more correct to say that the Islamic state has proved to be a source of division rather than a principle of unity. Whatever solution is found for Islam in Pakistan will closely influence the forty million Muslims in India—the largest Muslim minority in the world. Although the Indian state protects the rights of this great but depressed group, their condition is inevitably precarious, and affected by the relations of Pakistan with India.

Indonesia

Indonesian Islam is the heir to a syncretist tradition, in which Islam has lain rather lightly on earlier Hindu and Buddhist elements, and in which mysticism has from the earliest times been more important than law. As compared with Pakistan which looks back ultimately to the authoritarian Abassid Caliphate, Indonesia has a looser and less monolithic inheritance.

Islam was adopted in the East Indies in the 15th and 16th centuries by plurality of local rulers. Islamic law has been confined in the area largel to the law of personal status, and indigenous custom, *adat*, has—as in Malay —always been more important than the *sharia* or body of Islamic law. Thu although Islam is probably the religion of nine out of ten Indonesians, an is in an important sense the great unifying force of the tribal and regiona particularisms of this huge area, it is not a religion which has ever bee imposed on the islands in a single and unified manner. When the moder Indonesian nationalists have sought a national myth, they have gone bac beyond the Muslim period to the Hindu Kingdom of Majapahit and th Javanese pre-Islamic social ideal of 'Ratu Adil' (righteous king).

Nevertheless, Indonesian nationalism cannot be separated from Islami revival. Although the Sarekat Islam party was Islamic in the political sens of representing Muslims as against Dutch or Chinese, and not in the re ligious sense, it would not have been so important had it not been for th currents of Islamic modernism which were circulating in Indonesia early i this century. Having already been influenced by the Arabian Wahhab movement, Indonesia was early and profoundly influenced by the Egyptia 'Salafiyah' school of modernism, whose leader Muhammad Abdu also stoo behind much of the thought of Arab nationalism. The instrument of Salafiya ideas in Indonesia was the Muhammadiyah movement, which became wealthy educational and social reformist force, with some two thousan schools and many other cultural institutions under its control. In this en vironment of the Muhammadiyah the group later known as 'Religiou Socialists' formed their ideas.

In the Second World War the Islamic organizations were an importan part of the Japanese scheme for penetrating Indonesian society and using i for their own ends. The Muhammadiyah, the Council of *ulama* and th Council of Muslim Associations were merged into a single Council supervise by the Japanese Religious Affairs Office. In the later stages this Council wa involved in the 'Independence' movement sponsored by Japan. Thus th religious bodies were involved from the very beginnings of the setting up of a national Indonesian state.

Sukarno has attempted to preserve a bridge between secular nationalism and Muslim feeling. His Five Points (Pantja Sila) include 'Faith in God', but he interprets this in a sense which seems merely to include Islam among the other religions. The Ministry of Religion set up by the Indonesian Government might also be described as a Ministry of Religions, in that it is concerned with religious freedom and the relations between the religious communities, besides Muslim law and *waqfs* (charitable foundations).

Relations between the Government and the Muslim groups have not been good. In the mountains of Western Java the Dar-ul-Islam movement has maintained itself by terrorism and military action since the immediate post-war period. The doctrine of the Dar-ul-Islam differs only in degree from that of the *ulama;* what has kept it in being seems to have been social and regional rather than religious forces. More important was the rebellion led by some of the Religious Socialists of the Muslim Masjumi party (heir of the Muham-madiyah) in Celebes and Sumatra in 1958-61. The *ulama* on the other hand have remained loyal to the Government. Here as in the case of Pakistan it seems that the great obstacle to Muslim unity and progress is not ideological nationalism but regionalism.

Other Islamic Communities

Islam has penetrated less deeply into Malayan society than into that of Indonesia, and Islamic law has been operative in Malaya only in matters narrowly concerning personal status. India and Indonesia have influenced Malayan Islam in the modern period, but not profoundly, and although the Ahmadiyah sect and the Indonesian Muhammadiyah have made some impact on Malaya, there has been so far no development in depth.

Twenty million Muslims live in the U.S.S.R., about three-quarters of them in the six Union Republics of Azerbaidjan, Turkmenistan, Uzbekistan, Tadzhikistan, Kirgizia and Kazakhstan. The attitude of the Soviet Government towards these Muslims is determined partly by the official hostility of Communist doctrine to all religions, but far more by the problem of the subject nationalities, and of the period of Russian colonial history which preceded the Revolution. At the time of the Revolution there was a short period of cautious collaboration between the Communist party and both the Islamic and the minority movements (notably the Turkic one). This was over by 1920, but even after this Sultan Galiev was able to get a hearing for his doctrine of an alliance between Communism and Pan-Islamic nationalism, based on a Muslim state on the middle Volga, and even for an alliance between Communism and eastern 'bourgeois' nationalism. This doctrine was condemned by Stalin, and although some of its elements have in practice been present in Russian policy in oriental countries since the war, the doctrine itself has never been rehabilitated. On the whole the temptation to use the Russian Muslim minorities as a bridge to Muslims outside the Soviet Union has been resisted because of fear that it might awaken the minorities against Russian rule. There has been a notable softening of the official attitude to Islam in the past ten years, but it has not gone far.

The Chinese Muslim minority ('Hui') numbers about ten millions, of whom roughly half are in the province of Chinese Turkestan or Sinkiang (now called the Sinkian Uighur Autonomous Region). It is made up of several ethnic groups, of which the most important are the Uighur and Kazakh. Chinese policy towards the Muslims has in late years been conciliatory; religious lands have escaped confiscation in Sinkiang. Like the U.S.S.R., China thinks to use the Muslims as pawns in foreign policy in Asia and the Near East. A Chinese *imam* accompanied Chou En-lai to Bandung in 1955.

BIBLIOGRAPHY

Leonard Binder. *Religion and Politics in Pakistan.* (Cambridge Univ. Press, London, 1961.)

G. McT. Kahin. *Nationalism and Revolution in Indonesia.* Oxford Univ. Press, London, 1952.)

Walter Kolarz. *Russia and Her Colonies.* (Philip, London, 1952.)

W. Z. Laqueur (ed.) *The Middle East in Transition.* (Routledge and Kegan Paul, London 1958.)

Louis Massignon. *Annuaire du Monde Musulman: 1954.* (Paris, 1955.)

Wilfrid Cantwell Smith. *Modern Islam in India.* (Gollancz, London, 1946.) *Islam in Modern History.* (Oxford Univ. Press, London, 1957.)

C. A. O. Van Nieuwenhuijze. *Aspects of Islam in Post-Colonial Indonesia.* (W. Van Hoeve, The Hague and Bandung, 1958.)

Geoffrey Wheeler. *Racial Problems in Soviet Muslim Asia.* (Oxford Univ. Press, London, 1960.)

S. A. Zenkovsky. *Pan-Turkism and Islam in Russia.* (Oxford Univ. Press, London, 1960.)

BIOGRAPHICAL NOTE

Peter Partner (b. 1924) is the author of *A Short Political Guide to the Arab World* (Pall Mall Press, London, 1960), and of various works on European medieval history. Teaches history at Winchester College.

BUDDHISM

by

EDWARD CONZE

SLIGHTLY more than a century ago the great bastions of Buddhism first experienced the ruthless onslaught of modern civilization. The Buddhist religion, quiescent since about A.D. 1400, initiated nothing of its own between 1850 and 1960, remained on the defensive and constantly retreated before hostile forces. The societies in which it flourished, notably China, Tibet and Japan, had for a time sought safety in withdrawing upon themselves. The Buddhists have on the whole maintained the old behaviour pattern and prefer to ignore the new and unwelcome developments.

To appreciate their feelings we just have to look at the blows which this ancient religion has had to endure. In China, soon after the Opium War in 1842 forced the Manchus to admit the foreign invader, the 'long-haired Christians' of the T'ai P'ing rebellion between 1850 and 1864 destroyed countless temples and monasteries, and Chinese Buddhism has been a shadow of its former self ever since. In Japan the threatened American invasion of 1853 was followed about 1870 by the disestablishment of the Buddhist Church and the burning or confiscation of innumerable temples, while the actual invasion of 1945 brought financial ruin through MacArthur's 'land reform' of 1947-50, and led to a 'general trend towards profanity' and to rather widespread religious apathy. In Tibet the day of reckoning came only in 1950, and in 1959 the Dalai Lama was forced once more to flee the country. In Mongolia between 1935 and 1937 Soviet troops demolished the lamaseries and killed most of their inhabitants. Less openly brutal, the English in Ceylon and Burma did immense damage to the Buddhist Order. Unwilling to take over the ecclesiastical functions of the native kings they promoted indiscipline in the monasteries, drove monks into politics and disorganized monastic finances, while in addition the temple schools could no longer provide a socially advantageous education. These are only a few of the more dramatic blows which have reduced Buddhism to impotence. They are as nothing compared with the slow-working antagonistic forces which grind it down from day to day.

For there was little to attract Buddhists in the amalgam of ideas which the gunboats, soldiers, traders and missionaries from Europe and North America forced so assiduously upon Asian lands. Militarism, the backbone of the whole system and the only reason for the presence of these intruders in Asia, was extremely distasteful to them, as involving the deliberate, habitual and large-scale taking of life. Commercialism likewise displeased them because it increases greed and makes people discontented with what they have got.

Modern medicine has its conveniences, but the wholesale multiplication suffering and dissatisfied human beings is a doubtful boon. And to systema cally increase the wants of the poor means to kindle an all-consuming furna of discontent which is bound to destroy established authority everywhe beyond repair. Nor was the message of salvation through Jesus Chri presented to the Buddhists in a way likely to win their hearts. Missionari remained profoundly ignorant of even the elementary tenets of the doctrin To modern scholars their misconceptions seem almost grotesque, and y they normally used the most offensive language when speaking of Buddhi beliefs and practices, or of monks and particularly nuns. To a Buddhi the way of life of these 'Western barbarians' could only appear as a comple abomination, as a fulfilment of the worst prophecies about the Kali Yuga— complete lack of serenity and contentment, of beauty and charm, of manne and deportment, of peace and quiet, of respect for holy men and sacred thing

The present situation of Buddhism is the outcome of the deadly an irreconcilable conflict between Buddhist traditions and the main forces the modern age. The pressure of modern life is threefold, and affect 1) monastic institutions; 2) doctrinal integrity; and 3) the co-operatio between monks and laity.

Monastic Institutions

Monastic institutions are the powerhouses which generate the though force that sustains the Buddhist community. In their absence the religio must die, as it has nearly done in Nepal. History has everywhere shown tha congregations of contemplatives must first be suppressed before 'Progres can really begin. Once the 'needs' of the 'masses', as interpreted by the capitalist or bureaucratic sponsors, set the tone of society, monks must appea as mere idlers, 'useful' in no way whatsoever. And monks are, of course, ver vulnerable, and can be eliminated by removing either their physiological c their economic basis. Direct slaughter was the method adopted in Mongoli and Tibet. In China and Japan economic pressure sufficed. China has pre served a number of monasteries as 'living museums'. In Japan man thousands of priests survive, but they could not protect their sanctuaries fror invasion by the turmoil of the outside world. It is only in the Theravad countries that the state has taken concrete measures to further the dignit and security of the monks, and to assist the dissemination of their messag among the population.

Doctrinal Integrity

The doctrinal integrity of the Buddhists is subjected to many pressures, o which it will be sufficient to mention four.

(a) Although Asian *nationalism* is an inevitable reaction to man years of humiliation and ill-treatment, it does not go very well wit Buddhism. On closer consideration it must appear slightly ridiculou to compensate for one's own sense of inferiority by boasting abou the achievements of one's ancestors. Nevertheless, in taking this de tached point of view, Asian Buddhists would lose touch with thei supporters. So we find them often buying survival by howling with th wolves, and in Ceylon, Burma and Japan they habitually recommend their religion for reasons of national pride. This is a departure which, if unchecked, must in due course degrade a universal religion into a conglomeration of frantic tribal cults.

(b) Basically the '*cold war*' is a matter of indifference to Buddhists. Nevertheless political issues seem at present in Asia to be so much more urgent than religious considerations that many Buddhists have become willing tools of the rival forces. The primacy of politics has nearly ruined the 'World Fellowship of Buddhists'. Thai monks sprinkle holy water on American tanks. After 1950 both the USSR and China have regularly sent high dignitaries on propaganda tours into Asia. Numerous prominent Buddhists have proclaimed the compatibility of Buddhism and Communism, while others have as vociferously demonstrated their incongruity. In other words, on these issues Buddhists have forgotten how to speak with a voice of their own.

(c) The corroding effects of *modern 'science'* on the Buddhist faith have barely begun. Minor frictions have arisen from European geography, and Buddhist monks feel uneasy and embarrassed when asked to find Mount Sumeru or the land of Shambala on a modern globe. Likewise the prestige of science has undermined traditional beliefs by making a surprising number of Asian Buddhists ashamed of the magical elements in their religion. But up to now the deadly challenge has been so little understood that Asian Buddhists like to indulge in euphoric statements to the effect that Buddhism is the only religion which has nothing to fear from science. The future will bring a sad awakening.

(d) The concern for the '*standard of living*' and the urge to constantly increase the consumption of industrial commodities is also none too helpful to the Buddhist way of life. There is no more deadly poison to spiritual insight than bodily comfort. All this preoccupation with material possessions and social position must seem a complete misdirection of energy which keeps people so busy that they have not much time left for religion. In consequence in all industrialized countries people eschew doctrinal complications, and prefer simple and 'straightforward' doctrines, such as that of the Jodo Shinshu in Japan.

Monks and Laity

The new age furthermore presents the monks with some *technical* problems. In the village communities their mass support was assured, but now they have to find it in the big cities. New institutions must therefore be evolved, such as the YMBA, and so on. Much more important, however, is the fact that the monks' *social ideals* are out of date. Religious bodies are intensely conservative, and dislike it if one social system suddenly replaces another. Perfectly adjusted to feudalism, the Catholic Church has made gigantic intellectual and organizational efforts to adapt itself to an industrial society, and yet it has succeeded only imperfectly. For over two millennia Buddhism has subsisted within a relatively stable society, agricultural or nomadic, headed by an absolute ruler who was consecrated by the monks in return for his obedience to the Dharma and who established a harmony between society and the cosmic and spiritual forces on which its prosperit depended. None of this makes much sense in the modern world, and generall speaking the Buddhists have watched the change of events in a kind o stupor, without producing men like Lamennais or Marc Sangier, or docu ments like the encyclical *Rerum Novarum*. The one exception is U Nu, the on ruler who is also a sage, and who has tried to temper economic progress wit an insistence on Buddhist values.

Future Prospects

As to the future prospects of Buddhism, the short term outlook is extremel bad. Not one aspect of the present situation favours it as a religious force. I industrialization, militarization and national self-assertiveness are the thre most powerful factors in Asian society at present, then the first two are un compromisingly hostile to everything that Buddhists stand for, and the thir favours them only on condition that they become untrue to themselves Whether Buddhism be persecuted by the State or not, for quite a time tc come increasing inanition will be its fate.

The long-term prospects are slightly better. And this for three reasons: 1) Modern communications have re-established contact between the variou branches of Buddhism which had been separated for so long. Narrow sectarianism will therefore be slowly worn down, some cross-fertilization will take place, and a deeper understanding of the Buddha's message will thus emerge. 2) In the Communist countries Buddhism will in due course profit from the astounding similarities which exist between dialectical materialism and Mahayana philosophy. Many observers have commented on these analogies, and over the heads of both priests and commissars a new synthesis may well be created within the next century or so. 3) The glory of Asia is bound up with Buddhism as a cultural force. Everywhere the finest periods were precisely those in which it was in the ascendant. Once the threat from the outside world is removed, once Asia is either united or tolerably secure, Buddhism may well recommend itself as the most suitable ideology. So many Asian empire-builders have in the past turned to it as the ideal cement of vast societies. A religion which has tamed the descendants of Genghis Khan need not necessarily fail with the successors of Mao Tse-Tung.

It must be borne in mind that Buddhism has never sought survival through self-assertive competitiveness. Though it has endured many persecutions, it has never resisted, and yet it is still there. Spiritual trends operate on levels too deep for historians to reach, and we must always be prepared for surprises. Some of them may be triggered off by something as intangible as the recent revival of Buddhist meditation.

BIBLIOGRAPHY

Bhikkhu Amritananda. *Buddhist activities in socialist countries.* (New World Press, Peking, 1961.)
Charles Bawden. 'Mongolia Revisited.' (*Journal of the Royal Central Asian Society*, London, XLVII, 1960.)
Buddhists in New China. (Chinese Buddhist Association, Peking, 1956.)
W. K. Bunce. *Religions in Japan.* (Charles Tuttle, Tokyo, 1955.)

P. Carrasco. *Land and Polity in Tibet.* (Univ. of Washington Press, Seattle, 1959.)
Edward Conze. *Buddhism. Its Essence and Development.* (Oxford Univ. Press, paperback ed., London, 1960.) *Buddhist Scriptures.* (Penguin, London, 1959.) *A Short History of Buddhism.* (Chetan, Bombay, 1960.) *Buddhist Thought in India.* (Allen and Unwin, London, 1962.)
W. L. King. 'An experience in Buddhist meditation (in Burma).' (*Journal of Religion*, XLI, 1961.)
W. Kolarz. *Religion in the Soviet Union.* (Macmillan, London, 1961.)
C. McDougall. *Buddhism in Malaya.* (Donald Moore, Singapore, 1956.)
E. M. Mendelson. 'Religion and authority in modern Burma' in *The World Today.* (Oxford Univ. Press, London, 1960.)
D. E. Pfanner and J. Ingersoll. 'Theravada Buddhism and village economic behaviour. A Burmese and Thai comparison.' (*Journal of Asian Studies*, New York, XXI, 1962.)
D. C. Vijayavardhana. *Dharma-Vijaya or The Revolt in the Temple.* (Colombo, 1953.)
O. H. de A. Wijesekera. *Buddhism and Society.* (Bauddha Sahitya Sabha, Colombo, 1954.)
A. Winnington. *Tibet. Record of a Journey.* (Lawrence and Wishart, London, 1957.)

BIOGRAPHICAL NOTE

EDWARD CONZE. B. 1904, London. Educated in Germany; studied philosophy at various German universities, and obtained the degree of Ph.D. at Cologne in 1928. In 1933 he returned to England, where he has conducted extra-mural classes for twenty-five years and written a number of books on Buddhism. In 1963-4 he went to the University of Wisconsin as a Distinguished Visiting Professor of Buddhist Studies. He is at present a Research Fellow at Manchester College, Oxford. He is a Vice-President of the Buddhist Society, London.

RELIGION IN CHINA

by

C. P. FITZGERALD

The history and state of religion in China differ profoundly from the European and Western Asian experience. In the regions now Christian or Muhammadan these universal creeds have superseded the ancient paganism which preceded them, not only in its popular polytheistic manifestations, but also in its refined and sophisticated ethical and philosophical schools. In China nothing has finally perished: the ancient cults and the classical school of Confucian ethical teaching persisted side by side, until very recent times, with the new universal religion of Buddhism: new, that is, to China, about 1800 years ago.

In broad general terms it might be said that the people were both Buddhist and followers of the old polytheism which came to be known as Taoism: the scholars were Confucians. In harsher terms a modern, but not a Communist, Chinese writer once said 'in China the uneducated believe in everything, the educated in nothing'. The statement is indeed accurate enough; the ordinary, often illiterate, people both in the country and in cities worshipped indiscriminately at Buddhist monasteries and Taoist temples. To them there was no clear distinction between the Boddhisatvas and the Gods. The fact that the theology of Buddhism conflicted sharply with many of the beliefs grouped under 'Taoism' was either unrealised or ignored. Ancestor worship, or reverence to the spirits of the dead, who were at least in theory believed to have both survival in another world and influence upon the fate of their descendants, continued as perhaps the most widespread and persistent religious cult. Yet the belief in a link between the dead and their living descendants is quite incompatible with Buddhist theology which teaches the transmigration of souls and the unimportance of the earthly condition.

Confucianism, Buddhism and Taoism

Popular religion was thus confused and inchoate, lacking any accepted overall theology, or central organization. 'Three Ways to One Goal', the common saying has it, meaning that the Goal is not Eternal Life, or Salvation, but the Good Life here on earth, and the three ways, which are equally valid approaches to this end, are rational ethical Confucianism (with ancestor worship as a kind of auxiliary rite), Buddhism, and Taoism.

For several centuries, since at least the 10th century of the Christian era, the Confucians, the educated class of scholars, have had no God at all. Ancient, classical Confucianism as taught by the Sage himself and his disciples, did indeed admit the existence of the gods, and acknowledged in a vague way the primacy of T'ien, 'Heaven,' who had in high antiquity been a sky and weather deity. But when the Sung Confucian philosophers in the 10th century and later began to reshape Confucian doctrine to meet a more sophisticated age, they pruned away every vestige of theistic belief, leaving only Moral Law as the impersonal prime mover of the Universe. Chu Hsi, the greatest of the Sung philosophers (1137-1200 A.D.), said in reply to a question 'there is no man in Heaven judging sin'. Confucianism since his time has borne the deep imprint of his thought, and the view he held has been the accepted teaching of the scholars.

As such it can hardly be claimed that Confucianism is a religion at all in the Western sense; it is an ethical system to which were attached some very ancient imperial ceremonies, the worship of Heaven by the Emperor, the ancestral rites practised by most Chinese families. The imperial rites fell into disuse with the fall of the monarchy in 1912; ancestor worship has continued until the present time; but under the People's Republic the rapid social changes which are replacing the old Chinese great family of many relations living together by the small 'biological' family of parents and children, and the constant spread of state education teaching Marxism-Leninism as the only form of ethical instruction are, no doubt, quickly eroding the active practice of ancestral rites. Confucian ethical teaching is also at a discount; it is 'reactionary', 'feudalistic' and outmoded: the modern intellectual is brought up as a Marxist.

Buddhism was not in origin a Chinese religion; it was introduced to China in the 3rd century A.D. from India, and its first teachers in China were Indian monks. It was only very gradually that the new religion took hold among the Chinese people. A long and laborious process of translation from Sanskrit to Chinese—two very different languages—was necessary before the Chinese could read the Buddhist scriptures or master the theology. By the 5th century Buddhism had won a large following both among the educated class and the common people. New schools, some of Indian origin, others evolved in China, arose and active disputes among them stimulated intellectual interest. But these ideas did not reach far down; the people had never abandoned their own ancient cults, the gods of the wind, the sea, the mountains and rivers, of war and wealth. Innumerable and ancient, local and various, these cults took refuge under the umbrella of Taoism, which had in origin been the quietist philosphy of profound minds. Later Taoism turned increasingly to alchemy, magic, and the pseudo-science of astrology, making contact with the old popular polytheism, and, in open competition with Buddhism, adopting a monastic order. During the 6th and 7th centuries, when Confucian teaching was much neglected, the two popular creeds gained great power and influence, but never ousted Confucianism nor resolved their contest by the victory of one religion.

Thus the 'Three Ways' became co-existent, and gradually the fire and dynamism went out of them. After the T'ang period (7th to 9th centuries A.D.) Buddhism fell into a slow decline; while Taoism at the same period, the early Sung, was reorganized as a state cult in which every deity was given rank and function in a heavenly hierarchy modelled closely on the imperial civil service, and ruled, as on earth, by the Jade Emperor, a divine absolute monarch. The Chinese ruling class, themselves agnostic or atheist Confucians, were deeply distrustful of any popular religion which seemed to be gaining many converts and inspiring them with faith and zeal. Such movements all too easily turned from religious to political ends, engendered rebellions and stirred up unrest among the peasantry. It was thought better to extend imperial patronage to the two officially recognized religions of Buddhism and state Taoism, subsidize their great shrines, permit their great festivals, and keep them under surveillance and control. When, as happened from time to time, the Emperor himself, or the ladies of the Palace became ardently addicted to Buddhism, the Confucian officials strongly remonstrated and recalled the monarch to his duty. Such memorials are treasured among the gems of later Chinese literature.

Thus the condition of religion in imperial China, down to the end of the 19th century, was almost the exact opposite of that with which the European peoples were familiar either at home with Christianity or among their traditional antagonists the Muslims. Agnosticism instead of being a rare and unpopular attitude only safely adopted by the rich and powerful, was the acknowledged and proclaimed view of the ruling class, the basis of higher education, indeed of all education. Popular religion was not under the guidance and inspiration of dedicated men of learning, but left to persons of little education and often of less probity. A few unworldly men of letters retired, often after an active life as Confucian officials, to the peace of a mountain Buddhist monastery. A few retired scholars studied the works of the ancient Taoist philosophers. The two religions themselves had sunk into a mutual and apathetic tolerance, no longer attempting to instruct their followers in the niceties, or even the principles, of their theologies, and accepting the offerings and the worship of all indiscriminately.

The Christian Missions

To the early Christian missionaries who began to reach China from the middle of the 17th century this seemed a wide open field. Here was the same degenerated paganism, the same detached, perhaps devitalized, philosophy as the early Christians had overcome in the late Roman Empire. What was needed was to find a Chinese Constantine and the triumph of the Church would be assured. The Jesuits laboured assiduously at both the Court of the Ming and then the Manchu Dynasty to achieve this aim. Portents for a time seemed favourable. Jesuits, men of great learning, were employed in the Government service. They reformed the calendar. They improved the Chinese artillery, they made some distinguished converts. But they did not convert an Emperor. In the middle of the 18th century a violent dispute between Jesuits and Benedictines, known as the rites controversy, ruined the chances of the Roman Catholic missions. The Emperor K'ang Hsi, incensed to find foreign priests appealing to distant Rome to settle the religious practices of some small minority of his subjects, forbade further missionary work.

Just as the Chinese Government had always suppressed Buddhist sects which became dangerously popular and active, so now when the Christian missionaries strayed beyond the field of their immediate usefulness to the

Court, the tolerance of their mission was abruptly terminated. Catholicism languished for a century, retaining a hard core of faithful converts, but making no progress.

In the mid-19th century, the Protestant nations, led by Britain, and allied to Catholic France, defeated the Chinese in war and imposed on her the first 'Unequal Treaties'. Among the provisions of these instruments were some which obliged the Chinese Government to permit the free preaching of the Christian religion, the free movement of missionaries, and their right to build churches, establish residences, schools, and hospitals wherever they chose. The era of great missionary activity had begun. It lasted almost exactly one hundred years, until in 1950 the Communist Government of the People's Republic having won total power in China put into effect policies which led to the withdrawal of all Protestant missionaries and the expulsion of all foreign Catholic priests and missionaries.

During this century the number of Protestant Christian converts, of many separate sects, attained a maximum of about two million, and the number of Catholic Chinese also reached approximately the same figure. By the end of the missionary era the total population of China was six hundred million. From these figures it is evident that although the influence of the Christian Chinese, by reason of their connections with the outside world and the high educational average of the Protestant community, was out of proportion to their numbers, they still remained a tiny minority among the Chinese people, the vast majority of whom were wholly ignorant of Christian doctrine and belief, and not at all attracted to a religion which was deemed 'foreign'. Buddhism, after nearly two thousand years of life in China, still suffers from this stigma in the eyes of the Confucian scholar.

Policy of the Present Government

It is with a realization of the marginal importance of the Chinese Christian Churches to the nation as a whole that the policy of the present Government towards them must be considered. That policy is simply to confine religious activity purely to ritual observance and acts of worship. No social activity whatever, no schools, hospitals or orphanages, no active evangelism can be conducted or controlled by a Christian Church. Citizens of the Republic are, according to the constitution, permitted freedom of religious worship and belief. The Churches have had to sever all connections with foreign churches or missionary societies. The Chinese Protestant Churches have since tended to amalgamate, encouraged to do so by the Government, and to ignore or slur over the doctrinal differences which separated Anglican from Presbyterian or Baptist from Methodist.

The Catholic Church resisted this policy until all the hierarchy had in consequence been put in prison, or if foreign, expelled. The uncompromising anti-Communism of the Vatican left the Church in China no alternative. Many of the lower clergy preferred, or were by the pressure of their flock induced to submit to Government control, and a schismatic Church has now arisen which while in doctrine conforming with Rome accepts the authority in all lay matters of the Chinese Government. Since no bishops remain in China to ordain new priests, and since those whom the Vatican might appoint would not be accepted by the Chinese Government, there is no apparent end to this situation other than an interruption of the Apostolic Succession. It would appear that in general while a reduced number of Christians still practise their religion under these conditions in the cities, the rural mission churches in villages where the converts were few have been closed. The Catholic villages which existed in some parts of China continue under priests who are in the view of the Vatican schismatic.

Islam in China was always a small sect, and recognized as an alien religion. There are about ten million Muhammadans, now treated as a national minority; although in origin, in the 8th century, of Western Asian descent, they have intermingled with Chinese and are Chinese in speech and custom, apart from religion. Mainly concentrated in the north west and south west of the country, Muslim communities are found in all parts, and formerly specialized in certain trades such as caravan transport, eating houses and the curio trade. Respected and permitted to live their own religious life as a national minority, they make no converts and exercise little influence as a community, except in the few areas where they are a local majority.

The present state of religion thus in some ways resembles the position under the Emperors. Buddhism is tolerated as a popular religion with, it is estimated, about fifty million ardent followers, and many more occasional supporters. Christianity is strictly controlled, but is a very small minority. Islam is given local special status; and the ruling class, although acknowledging a new ethic, Marxism, as their guide, remain, as before, openly atheist.

BIBLIOGRAPHY

K. S. Latourette. *A History of Christian Missions in China.* (Society for Promoting Christian Knowledge, London, 1929.)

Moslems in China. (Foreign Languages Press, Peking, 1953.)

W. E. Soothill. *The Three Religions of China.* (Oxford Univ. Press, London, 3rd ed., 1929.)

A. F. Wright. *Buddhism in Chinese History.* (Stanford Univ. Press, Stanford, 1959.)

A. F. Wright (ed.). *Confucianism in Action.* (Stanford Univ. Press, Stanford, 1959.) *The Confucian Persuasion.* (Stanford Univ. Press, Stanford, 1960.)

BIOGRAPHICAL NOTE

C. P. FITZGERALD. B. 1902, London; educated at Clifton College, Bristol. Lived in China, 1923-1939, with brief breaks, and for four years after the war, 1946-50. Has subsequently paid two visits to China (1956 and 1958). Leverhulme Fellowship for anthropological research in China, 1936-1939. Worked at Tali, Yunnan province. Representative of the British Council in North China, 1946-1950. Author of many books on China, including *The Birth of Communist China* (Penguin, London, 1955), *China: A Short Cultural History* (Cresset Press, London, revised ed., 1961) and *The Chinese View of their Place in the World* (The Royal Institute of International Affairs, London, 1964.) 1965

RELIGION IN JAPAN

by

CARMEN BLACKER

SINCE the beginning of historical records in Japan the religious life of the Japanese has been dominated by two cults, diverse but intermingled. The loosely connected complex of cults and practices that now goes under the name of Shinto was the native religion, stretching back into the remote prehistoric period when the present Japanese race was formed. On to the strong background colour of this folk religion was imprinted, from the 6th century A.D. onwards, the doctrines of Buddhism in various of the Mahayana sects. Although Buddhism is universally acknowledged to be a religion of an altogether 'higher' type than early Shinto, it has never attempted, as did Christianity in Europe, to stamp out the older folk cults. A commingling of the two has therefore, with brief interludes, been the religion of the great majority of Japanese for some thirteen centuries.

EARLY SHINTO

In its earliest form Shinto seems to have been largely a recognition of the mystery, power and 'otherness' manifested in those things which lie beyond the competence of primitive man. The coming of spring, the onset of the rains, the growth of crops, the fertility of animals and women, the unaccountable effect which something beautiful has on the mind, a man with extra majesty and skill—all these are beyond his control and understanding and operate in ways utterly mysterious. The mystery which inhered in these things and which seemed to betoken a more powerful world beyond his own, was shadowily personified and called *kami*. There were thus myriads of *kami*, who were given long names but who had no shape of their own. In order to manifest themselves they had to be 'called down' into an object—usually a tall thin shape such as a tree or a stone or a banner—or even better into a human being trained to act as a medium. Thus summoned, they could be invoked for help and advice on problems which are usually humanly insoluble. The purpose of the *matsuri* or festival, celebrated in all villages on certain fixed days, was to call down the god, to feast him and entertain him, and then if possible to persuade him to pronounce, through an appointed medium, on the prospects during the coming year for the rice harvest, the rains, the storms, the epidemics.

But the power of these superior beings was not uniformly benign. If they could grant blessings when duly reverenced, they could also blast with curses (*tatari*) when offended. Broadly, they were offended by death and blood. Anyone who had been in contact with a corpse, with a woman in childbirth, a wounded man or any other of the recognized sources of pollution, was considered contaminated and must undergo a ritual isolation from his fellow men for a stated period, and for an even longer time refrain from approaching a shrine. Any violation of these rules could incur the danger of a sudden *tatari*, striking in the form of sickness, madness, accident or fire.

In this early period such injunctions towards ceremonial purity were all that was required in the way of 'moral' conduct in the sight of the *kami*. *Tsumi*, the modern word for sin, indicated anciently only this physical pollution. The development of an ethical code in Shinto came only later, with the influence of Buddhism and Confucianism from China. Indeed, scarcely any Japanese word for moral qualities, with the exception of a single term meaning something like 'sincerity', is of native origin. Benevolence, justice, propriety, compassion—words for these qualities appeared in the Japanese language only with the arrival of the Confucian classics and Buddhist scriptures.

Buddhism

When in the course of the 6th century Buddhism made its first appearance in Japan from Korea, it is scarcely surprising that a religion so remote from such beliefs as those of early Shinto should have been at first misunderstood. The *kami* had after all been regarded as a superior source of power capable of bestowing worldly benefits beyond human grasp—a good rice harvest, recovery from sickness, easy childbirth, male children. The Buddha had taught that worldly prosperity, the accumulation of what seem to be the blessings of this world, was in the long run of little account. The world as experienced in the ordinary human manner was invariably full of suffering. Only by a profound internal transformation of consciousness achieved through meditational disciplines and moral purification could one arrive at the illumination which comes from knowledge of the reality lying behind the veil of appearances.

It was some time, therefore, before the Japanese understood Buddhism to be anything more than a new version of their old religion. The figure of the Buddha and his attendant Bodhisattvas were seen not as images symbolizing a different state of consciousness, but as potential bestowers of worldly boons. The sutras too, the Lotus Sutra, the Large Prajnaparamita Sutra, the Suvarna-prabhasa Sutra, were during the early centuries used not as guides to an internal transformation revealing the vanity of the world, but as spells for rain, for the Emperor's recovery from sickness, for the birth of a male heir.

In the course of time the true purport of Buddhism was understood by a minority of Japanese, who inaugurated a distinctive and powerful spiritual tradition as well as a noble and moving school of Buddhist art. But even today it is still true that for the average Japanese Buddhism has but two main functions, neither of which finds any place in the original teachings of the Buddha.

The first is the disposal of the dead and the pacification of ghosts and spirits. The ancient Shinto cult, with its abhorrence of the pollution of death, had provided no means for the repose of the dead, and little in the way of a comforting eschatology. From the burial mounds of the pre-Buddhist period it is clear, indeed, that the dead were greatly feared. All dead spirits were apparently potentially harmful, but especially those that had died a violent or untimely death. It was Buddhism which came to provide the special requiem masses necessary to enable the spirit to settle down and join the benevolent ranks of 'the ancestors', to whom offerings were daily made in household shrines to ensure a constant benign protection. Although in the early Buddhist doctrine in India such steps were irrelevant, since the dead person was believed to be soon reborn in the state prescribed by his past karma, Japanese Buddhism has always provided the means, so insistently demanded by the folk religion, for the living to help the dead to final peace.

The second main function of Buddhism in Japan is still to provide magical spells for the production of mundane benefits. Even as new sects of Buddhism found their way during the medieval period from China to Japan, this stress on productive magic still persisted. The Tendai and Shingon sects, dominant from the 9th to the end of the 12th century, answered this need very well with their Tantric derivations, providing spells for warding off plague, fire, drought and malevolent ghosts. Indeed today it is only the Amidist Jodo and Shin sects which require from the faithful a complete self-surrender to the mercy of Amida Buddha, and which, together with the Rinzai sect of Zen, entirely eschew spells for worldly benefits. Even in the Soto sect of Zen the richest and most renowned temples are not those which shelter a wise teacher capable of guiding disciples towards spiritual illumination, but those which enshrine an image reputed to be efficacious in granting, for a stated sum of money, such boons as prosperity in business, harmony in the family or freedom from traffic accidents.

On a less popular level the Buddhist sects which have taken root in Japan have fallen roughly into two categories. The *tariki* or 'other strength' sects rely completely on the overwhelmingly superior power of Amida Buddha to enable all beings who call on his name to be reborn in his Pure Land, a paradise where eventually they can be sure of attaining the Buddhist goal of nirvana. The Jodo and Shin sects, which arose in Japan during the 13th century, thus deny the efficacy of any effort which the disciple himself may make towards his own enlightenment. All that is required of him is complete faith and trust in Amida, expressed in recitations of the sacred invocation *Namu Amida Butsu.*

The *jiriki* or 'self strength' school on the other hand, is eminently exemplified by the Rinzai sect of Zen. Here the disciple is taught that through strenuous *zazen*, sitting and struggling with various meditational exercises designed to lead the mind to hitherto unsuspected depths, he can by his own efforts, aided by the guidance of a qualified master, bring about in himself successively deepening experiences of illumination. It is here that we find the most profound and distinctive indication of Japanese spirituality. The Zen sect, with its unique and practical teaching towards 'sudden enlightenment', has deeply influenced much of the best of Japanese art.

State Shinto

Until the Meiji Restoration in 1868 inaugurated a new era of contact with the West, most Japanese had without difficulty subscribed to both Shinto and Buddhism. Various philosophical amalgamations of the two religions had at various times been proposed, but the solution most generally accepted was that the Shinto *kami* acted as local guardians or occasionally as temporary manifestations of Buddhist deities. Hence every Buddhist temple invariably contained also a Shinto shrine, and in most people's minds the two supernatural orders were only vaguely distinguished. This was a true *shimbutsu-shugo*, joining of gods and Buddhas.

The policy of the Meiji Government in the early 1870s however was to foster a spirit of national identity and enthusiasm centring on the Emperor. They hence set about a drastic policy of forcibly separating Shinto and Buddhism (*shimbutsu-bunri*) and of persecuting Buddhism as a foreign and undesirably other-worldly creed. Buddhist temples were converted into Shinto shrines. Monks and nuns were forced to return to lay life. At the same time the Meiji Government was concerned to stamp out those aspects of the old Shinto which seemed primitive and 'uncivilized'—which in effect meant a great deal of the folk religion. All those cults in which Shinto and Buddhist elements were indissolubly mixed, such as the mountain cult of the Shugendo, together with survivals such as the *miko*, women who made themselves mediums for deities or spirits to speak through their mouths, were suppressed.

In their place a largely artificial cult of State Shinto was fostered, wherein the Emperor, who had hitherto lived a revered but shadowy existence in the confines of his palace in Kyoto, was elevated to the position of focal point of loyalty and blind reverence. At the same time the exceedingly ancient myths contained in the early chronicles, which for centuries had remained in virtual oblivion, were resuscitated to the position of divine scriptures, and forced to yield the exhilarating doctrine of the divine destiny of Japan to pre-eminence over all other nations.

With the promotion of the cult of State Shinto to its climax in the final catastrophe of the war went an increasingly severe policy of repression of all other religious cults. Those attempting to found new cults, whether in sympathy with State Shinto or not, were flung into prison and their organizations dissolved. It was only in 1945 when the American occupation disestablished State Shinto that the Japanese were for the first time since the early 1870s granted complete religious freedom.

The Post-war Scene

The immediate result of the removal of restrictive legislation was the extraordinary upsurge of what are known as the *shinko-shukyo*, the new religions. All over the country new cults sprang up, until by 1951 the number reached the remarkable figure of 720. With the weeding out of obviously fraudulent cases and the collapse of others through the death of the original founder, the number has now dropped. But the new cults are still a striking feature of the post-war religious scene in Japan, and their increasing wealth, converted into huge concrete cathedrals and powerful networks of propaganda, is in marked contrast to the increasingly dilapidated state of many temples of the more traditional Buddhist sects.

Undoubtedly these new sects have arisen to fill the void which resulted from the collapse of the reputedly invincible State Shinto. In most cases they are messianic in character, promising to the faithful a millenarian rain of divine blessings and worldly favours. Those crushed by defeat, poverty and total loss of any directing purpose in life were roused to ardent faith, hope and sometimes charity by powerful figures claiming unique divine revelation and promising unique divine rewards. Such figures as the founders of these new cults are not new in Japanese religion. Their counterparts can be traced back to the 7th and 8th centuries. What is new, of course, is the appearance of modern methods of propaganda and organization, so that we find the curious combination of religious cults in shape and inspiration of great antiquity, adorned with vast concrete edifices of bizarre modern design, missionary tours to Hawaii and California, private broadcasting stations, huge rallies reminiscent of an American football match. Most of the new cults are tolerant and innocuous, providing genuine comfort, fellowship and hope in otherwise humdrum lives. Only Soka Gakkai, with its intolerance, its militancy, its ruthlessly threatening methods of propaganda and its obscure political ambitions, strikes an increasingly fanatical and sinister note.

It should be noted, however, that these cults seldom appeal to Japanese with claims to academic or intellectual respectability. For them, as for most university students, a slightly melancholy agnosticism seems to be the approved order.

Christianity, it may be remarked, has largely failed to make much mark on the post-war scene. Perhaps one of its most moving triumphs was the discovery after the war of small communities in Kyushu who since the beginning of the persecution in the 17th century had succeeded in remaining 'hidden Christians', undiscovered and unsuspected by either the persecutors of the feudal regime or by the later and more virulent inquisitors of State Shinto.

BIBLIOGRAPHY

W. G. Aston. *Shinto.* (Longmans, London, 1907.)

W. T. de Bary (ed.) *Sources of the Japanese Tradition.* (Columbia University Press, New York, 1958.)

Sir Charles Eliot. *Japanese Buddhism.* (Edward Arnold, London, 1935.)

D. C. Holtom. *The National Faith of Japan: a Study in Modern Shinto.* (Kegan Paul, London, 1938.) *Modern Japan and Shinto Nationalism: a Study of Present-day Trends in Japanese Religions.* (University of Chicago Press, Chicago, 2nd ed., 1947.)

E. Dale Saunders. *Buddhism in Japan.* (University of Pennsylvania Press, Philadelphia, 1964.)

D. T. Suzuki. *Essays in Zen Buddhism*, 3 vols. (Reprinted by Rider, London, 1950.) *Zen Buddhism and its Influence on Japanese Culture.* (Eastern Buddhist Society, Kyoto, 1938.)

Harry Thomsen. *The New Religions of Japan.* (Charles E. Tuttle, Tokyo, 1963.)

BIOGRAPHICAL NOTE

CARMEN BLACKER read Modern Greats at Somerville College, Oxford and studied Japanese at the School of Oriental and African Studies, University of London and at Keio University, Tokyo. Lecturer in Japanese at the University of Cambridge from 1958. A practising Buddhist.

CHRISTIAN MISSIONS IN ASIA

by

DAVID M. PATON

Christianity in Asia, considered relatively to the antiquity of its cultures, is a new-comer; and, relatively to the population, Christians are few. There are of course exceptions. Outside the Near Eastern homelands of Christianity (where the Churches today are the sadly attenuated but direct descendants of those planted by the apostles), the Christians of Malabar in South India trace their origin to one of the twelve, St Thomas; and although this claim is not usually conceded by historians, it is likely that Christianity arrived there in the second or third century. But Nestorian Churches have died out which once stretched from modern Iraq to the China Sea. Recent archaeological evidence shows them to have been more widespread in China than was suspected. The missionary work of the Franciscan John of Montecorvino and others in India and China in the Mongol period was also without permanent result. Living Christianity today largely descends from the work of Roman Catholic missionaries which started in various places around the year 1500 but was not on a large scale till the nineteenth century; or of Protestant missionaries beginning in India in 1706, in China in 1807, and in Japan in 1859. The much smaller Russian Orthodox effort, most successful in Japan, began there in 1861. South India apart, Christianity in Asia is usually not more than one hundred and fifty years old, and may be much younger. If there were Christian communities before, today's Christianity is not connected with them, but is the result of a fresh impetus from outside Asia.

Christian Communities Compared

Christian communities in Asia are usually very small. The figures for selected countries (extracted from the *World Christian Handbook*, 1962) on the next page tell their own story.

Except in the Philippines, in the most Christian parts of South India, in parts of Indonesia, and in Korea, Christians of all sorts taken together are normally a tiny fraction of the population—seldom more than five per cent, often less than one per cent. Moreover, for purposes other than statistical they usually cannot be 'taken together', because of the divisions between them. Most of these have been imported from the West; and if there have been Asian additions, it is also the case that the most significant project in Christian reunion—the Church of South India, inaugurated in 1957—originated in Asia.

Country	Population	Roman Catholics	Protestants and others	Christians (% of Pop.)
Burma	20,477,000	183,713	1,137,084	6·4
Cambodia	4,845,000	52,632	46,000	2·0
Ceylon	9,388,000	737,259	92,533	8·9
China	669,000,000	3,266,000	1,000,000	0·6
India	402,750,000	5,620,054	8,875,336	3·6
Indonesia	89,600,000	1,176,693	6,231,803	8·3
Japan	92,740,000	266,262	676,719	1·0
Korea	31,400,000	413,485	2,687,451	9·9
Malaya	6,515,000	151,565	124,453	4·2
Pakistan	86,823,000	304,561	416,265	0·9
Philippines	24,718,000	17,397,000	3,228,150	83·5
Thailand	21,881,000	110,000	33,598	0·7

There are also between two and three million Orthodox Christians in Asia, for the most part of different race and culture from the bulk of the population. This qualification applies also to certain other Churches and Christian denominations, e.g. in Malaya the Christians are mostly Chinese or Indian, not Malay, and in Burma not Burman but Karen or Chin.

Doubtful Progress

Christianity in Asia shares with certain other aspects of Western culture the stigma of being the result of the imperialist expansion of the West in what Sardar K. M. Panikkar has called 'the age of Vasco da Gama'. Dr. Pannikkar has concluded from his review of Asian history that the Christian missions in Asia have 'definitely failed'. He is not alone in this judgment, which appears to be common form among Asian intellectuals. Churchmen in the West—Fr. Gabriel Hebert SSM, for example, in *God's Kingdom and Ours*—have made considerable use of his *Asia and Western Dominance* in their analysis of missionary weaknesses without necessarily accepting either his presuppositions or his conclusions. It may well be that there are Asian Christians who come to much the same conclusion in practice—Christianity is their religion, but they do not believe that it will conquer and they are not certain it is true. If they so think, their thoughts run on lines very much like those of many respectable English Christians.

This is not the place to argue the Christian case (which is, *pace* Dr Panikkar and Dr Toynbee, inevitably 'exclusive'). One may, however, note that a Christian may have a clear-sighted, even disillusioned, view of the present condition and immediate prospects of Asian Christianity, and at the same time maintain a matter-of-fact and cheerful confidence in the future.

Christianity and the Asian Religions

A recurring theme in the writings of Asian Christians concerns the necessity of a dialogue with the great Asian religions. Christianity has been present in the homelands of Hinduism, Buddhism and Islam for several centuries, and has not been without its effect on them; yet no real meeting between the religions has yet taken place. All the signs are that this encounter is about to begin. In the West, Christians will have to face Hindu and Buddhist missions from the East, and argue afresh about the 'scandal of particularity' involved in the incarnation of the Son of God. In the East, Asian intellectuals will have to consider that same 'scandal' when it is put to them, free of its association with 'Western notions of superiority', by fellow intellectuals, also Asians, who are fully orthodox Christians. Preparing for this encounter is the principal preoccupation of institutes for the study of religion and society (such as that at Bangalore, presided over, until his recent death, by Paul Devanandan).

This intellectual activity will include, for virtually the first time, profound theological effort. In the days when the Asian Churches were wholly dependent on Western missions, theology tended to be laid down by missionaries and accepted by nationals. Today—China is the extreme example of a general trend—the Church is coming to the realization that it is itself responsible both for the purity of the Church's faith and the intelligibility with which it communicates that faith. Out of this double concern is born theology—a theology which is no more simply a copybook learning of other people's formulations but a struggle to express the truth of God in terms that writer and reader can make their own. In a sense, it is the enemies of Christianity who are the midwives of a truly Asian, truly Christian, theology.

Another prime concern is about the proper social role of Christians in Asia. Once upon a time, they were, in the Chinese phrase, 'running dogs of imperialism'. From that situation they must escape. But Christians cannot legitimately escape from subservience to the West merely to climb on to a nationalist bandwagon—there are too many awful warnings in the recent history of the West of the results of bestowing an uncritical blessing upon nationalist aims.

'Asian Christianity'

Voices can be heard now of leaders, of men and women committed to the quest for a Christian Church which is united or at least moving purposefully towards union and away from the multiplicity of Western-originated denominations. They are leaders who seek for such an indigenous Church and as part of its self-hood a new relationship with the nation. They seek for the same reasons to remain a true part of the world Christian community, building on the foundations bequeathed from the old era of dependence on the mission a new relation of mutuality and interdependence. They want Christianity in Asia to be a genuinely Asian Christianity.

This new reformation of the Asian Churches is expressed organisationally for the non-Roman Churches in the East Asia Christian Conference. There are similar stirrings on the Roman Catholic side. Bishops from Asia and Africa have spoken and voted on the 'progressive' side in the Vatican Council. Protestant and Anglican leaders, however, must also reckon in some countries with an influx of independent and often sectarian missionaries, and with new division caused by the profound suspicion entertained by 'fundamentalists' of the theological and political reliability of the ecumenical leadership; the division between 'liberals' and 'fundamentalists' is at its deepest and most bitter in parts of Asia. This evangelical zeal may sometimes become united with a nationalist suspicion of the missionary and result in independent churches; in China one of these, known as 'the Little Flock', was reported a few years ago to be larger than any of the Protestant Churches founded by the Missions.

Future Prospects

The majority of Asian Christians may be assumed to be preoccupied with more immediate matters. Many, perhaps most, so fear absorption into the dominant religious culture—be it Hindu, or Buddhist, or Islamic, or Maoist—that they are tempted to retire into a nostalgic self-enclosed Christian world, ready to be incapsulated in the larger society as a sub-caste in a ghetto. Dr. D. T. Niles, of Ceylon, has recorded his belief that this ghettoism is a more pressing danger to the Church in Asia than the syncretism that is more feared.

The detached modern observer, especially if he be of humanist cast of mind, may concede that some churches in some Asian countries may survive perhaps for centuries in this socially uncreative manner: he is not likely to expect any brighter future for Christianity in Asia. A Christian must needs be a more emotionally committed observer, but he must recognize that Christianity has not yet engaged the soul of Asia, and that what happened to Nestorian and Franciscan could happen in our time also. He need not accept that it *will* happen—indeed, if he remains a Christian he will not.

More than any others, Asians have explored the nature of religion. Now Asia moves with the rest of us into a world where religion is at a discount—a world 'come of age' in which men are 'religionless' (the phrases are Dietrich Bonhoeffer's). What in the depths of her being Asia will do with this secular world and what part Christianity (in whose bosom the modern world originated, and which is not *primarily* a religion for men to practise, but a message from the living God) will play in the drama does not yet appear. As usual the facts allow of several interpretations; and the prophecy any observer makes is likely to be determined as much by his prior assumptions as by his empirical analysis.

BIBLIOGRAPHY

P. D. Devanandan. *The Gospel and Renascent Hinduism.* (S.C.M. Press, London, 1959.)
K. S. Latourette. *History of the Expansion of Christianity,* 7 vols. (Eyre and Spottiswoode London, 1937-45.)
D. T. Niles. *Upon the Earth.* (S.C.M. Press, London, 1962.)
Kavalam Panikkar. *Asia and Western Dominance.* (Allen and Unwin, London, 1953.)
David M. Paton. *Christian Missions and the Judgment of God.* (S.C.M. Press, London, 1953.)
M. A. C. Warren (ed.). *Christian Presence Series.* (S.C.M. Press, London.)

BIOGRAPHICAL NOTE

The Rev. David M. Paton was an Anglican Missionary in China. Author of *Christian Missions and the Judgment of God* (S.C.M. Press, London, 1953) and *Anglicans and Unity* (Mowbrays, London, 1962), and editor of *Essays in Anglican Self-Criticism* (S.C.M. Press, London, 1958) and *Church and Race in South Africa* (S.C.M. Press, London, 1958).

ART

INDIAN ART

by

PHILIP S. RAWSON

INDIA's present-day artistic independence, as well as the problems of that independence, are the product of a long period of conquest, suffering and splendour. India's artistic difficulties are no nearer solution than the political. There have been parts of India which were never in fact touched by conquest, even in relatively recent times. But the major areas underwent drastic political changes for some four or five centuries before the establishment of the British Raj. These changes had a profound effect on the arts.

From the 11th century A.D. onwards the various Islamic invaders from the north-west brought with them Islamic styles of art, architecture and painting. But following the custom of Islam, the invaders relied for the detailed execution of buildings conceived in the Islamic style upon craftsmen native to the conquered country—so that there was plenty of opportunity for a genuine Indo-Islamic style to evolve. The mosque and the tomb, which are the prime forms of Islamic architecture, achieved on Indian soil an idiosyncratic magnificence unexcelled in the Islamic world. In the various sultanates set up at Delhi, in central and eastern India and in the Deccan from the 13th century on, mosques and tombs were built in profusion. Painters and calligraphers from Persia, and perhaps other countries, were employed at the courts. It was by no means rare for an Islamic ruler to develop so deep a sympathy with his Hindu subjects as to discountenance his Muslim ministers and fellow rulers. But orthodox Islamic iconoclasm very often did, in fact, result in the virtual destruction of traditional Indian court arts.

MOGUL ART

The greatest Muslim dynasty in India was the Mogul. Its earlier members played as important a part in the physical destruction of native works of art as some of its later members did in building up new arts. For during the 16th century the long history of Muslim rapine and destruction reached its apogee. The great temples in the areas accessible to the Muslim armies were looted and often totally destroyed. When the Hindu Kingdom of Vijaynagar fell in 1565 an army of men was kept for a full year at the work of the destruction of the capital. Great temples which were not destroyed relapsed into the oblivion of the jungle as the geographical pattern of life changed—there to await rediscovery by Western-style archaeology. Only in those areas whose Hindu rulers by the luck of their land, by military prowess or diplomacy evaded conquest, did Hindu artistic traditions survive intact into the modern era. Madras, Kerala, Orissa, and parts of Bengal were the most fortunate in this respect. Certain Rajput states in Rajasthan and the Punjab made successful artistic compromises.

The first two rulers of the Mogul Dynasty were adventurers chiefly occupied in carving out for themselves a base kingdom in the north-west of India against the rivalry of others of their own kind. It was the third, Akbar (1556-1605), who converted this kingdom into a true empire by his military, diplomatic and administrative genius. During his long reign he created an administrative system which, with suitable modifications, has served successive Governments of India ever since. And he was passionately interested in the arts. Carefully he fostered schools of architects and painters, organising them into well-run official bureaux, which oversaw both their training and their ultimate output. Many of his artists and craftsmen must have come to him from the Deccan sultanates, where both architecture and painting had reached a high degree of achievement during the 16th century. Some of his leading painters had come from Persia as full-fledged artists. But Akbar recruited Hindus and Muslims alike into his ateliers—a fact of great importance for the history of the arts.

The building projects of Akbar were unique. It was his architects who evolved from the traditional massive Persian mosque gateway the Indian form of Muslim tomb of which the later Taj Mahal is the triumphant culmination. The tomb he built his father Humayun, in Delhi, is an outstanding example. The pink stone of the Delhi region is used with white Rajasthan marble, in bands and panels, to set off the colossal cubical simplicity of the main masses with their crowning pointed domes, huge arcades, and corner minarets. Akbar's most ambitious project, however, was the new city he built near Agra of the same pink stone, starting from scratch on a waterless site—later abandoned and now a noted tourist spot. The palace-courts, mosques and public buildings of Fatehpur Sikri, with their pierced screens, their serpentine brackets, deep eaves and passages of vigorous ornament that is far more organic than most Muslim design, represent a new and totally original style. Some extraordinary architectural inventions were included. Generally construction by pillar and canopy was favoured, with deep eaves. One five-storey building, the Panch Mahal, is without walls. The doorway of the Jami mosque is 176 feet high. But the most striking structure of all is the throne of the Diwan-i-khas. From the floor of the audience-hall rises a single fretted column that spreads with thirty-six moulded stalactite brackets to support the throne-platform. From this to the corners of the gallery running around the hall four fretted bridges fly.

Under Akbar's successors, Jehangir (d. 1628) and Shah Jehan (1628-1658), many more mosques and tombs were constructed, refining the Akbar tradition. White stone came more and more into favour. The most famous and influential of the mosques is the Moti Masjid, at Agra (1650). It represents a style that became the basis for innumerable buildings throughout the succeeding centuries, and even influenced the architecture of the British in India. Its low-pitched scalloped arches on square piers, and eaves-like drip-mouldings can be recognized everywhere. The most famous of the tombs, of course, is the great Taj Mahal at Agra, built to receive the body of Shah Jehan's wife. Its colossal size, its white perfection of proportion, its elegant and restrained ornament, are universally admired. Shah Jehan so beggared his empire in building it that the even larger tomb he projected for himself came to nothing. He lies by his wife, in hers. The Taj was built by a Turk to the design of an architect from Lahore, and its calligraphic ornament was prepared by an artist from Shiraz. A truly international monument three centuries before Chandigarh!

The art of painting was no less thoroughly transformed under the Moguls. Akbar set up an imperial atelier where a corps of painters worked continuously. Mural work *was* done, but only one example, in a little hunting lodge as yet unphotographed, survives. The surviving Mogul works are miniatures. They are mostly either records of historical events or illustrations of Muslim or Hindu literature. For Akbar desired that his Hindu and Muslim subjects should understand each other. He therefore distributed to his leading subjects of each faith illustrated copies of the chief works of the other faith's literature. The Muslim and Hindu artists worked side by side in the atelier; indeed each individual painting was usually the joint work of several artists—one doing the portraits, another the costume and colour, a third the landscape, and so on. In this way elements of several different traditions were thoroughly blended, and a style was evolved which was basically Persian, but was marked by characteristics of Indian art and by a stern and vigorous new naturalism.

This last element came partly from European painting. Akbar, interested in everything, had begun to collect European pictures, engravings and objets d'art. These were lodged in the atelier for the painters to study. We know Mogul copies of many works of European art; others appear portrayed in Mogul paintings. And there are many motives and technical devices which Akbar's painters adopted from Western art.

Under Jehangir and Shah Jehan the atelier continued to flourish. Jehangir added a quasi-botanical element to its subject matter—flowers, animals and birds executed in isolation, in jewel-like colours. Under Shah Jehan the repertoire became wider, with an emphasis on secular subjects. But it also became formalized and somewhat repetitive—the enamelled colours and delicate contours lack the conviction and strength of earlier work. Under Aurangzeb (d. 1666), the last Mogul, a bigoted puritan dedicated to warfare, the atelier was abolished. The artists thus deprived of their livelihood were ejected to find what living they could. Some took to free-lance work in the bazaars, turning out exceedingly skilful and polished versions of those subjects from the repertoire which were most likely to appeal to the casual buyer—including especially series of portraits of famous men, hunting scenes, night pieces and erotic scenes. The tradition of this kind of art continued down to the present century; it is usually called, for convenience, the Delhi school, since its chief centre was perhaps Delhi. For a very long time Delhi pictures were believed to represent the true Mogul style, both by British and Indian collectors.

Other members of the Mogul atelier, however, found employment at the courts of Rajput princes in the Hindu states of Rajasthan and the Punjab. Fine indigenous styles of painting, orientated towards the miniature, had flourished in many of these states through the 16th and 17th centuries. Certainly some influence had already reached a few such centres from the Mogul capital. But the new wave of influence was decisive, and magnificent schools of sophisticated miniature painting developed at many of these courts during the later 17th century, to evolve and flourish throughout the 18th century, and in many cases to continue through the 19th. The outstanding schools were at Udaipur, Jaipur, Kishangarh, Bundi, Kotah, Jammu, Basohli, Guler and Kangra. Since the work of these schools has become recognized in the last twenty years, artists have frequently attempted to recapture their charm and brilliance.

The British Period

During the British period the native arts were more or less ignored by the ruling class. A great deal of architecture was executed in India for the British, in the form of commercial buildings for the East India Company, houses for rich merchants, fortifications and funerary monuments. Most of them were interesting variants of the Palladian and Georgian styles prevailing in Britain, and have been far too little studied. Many have now vanished; but they were often depicted in watercolours and prints. There were, too, monuments in the various styles of Victorian architecture. Many of these adapted features of Mogul architecture (in the characteristic manner of Victorian architects). One of the outstanding examples is the Victoria Memorial Hall in Calcutta. This, a huge, centralized and dome-crowned museum, is constructed of white Jaipur stone. There were, too, during the British period, many unfortunate travesties both of Western and Indian styles erected, and many unhappy marriages of styles. It must be mentioned, too, that a very high proportion of the output of 19th-century British academic sculptors—including John Flaxman—was destined for India. The present Indian Government has been in general solicitous of this work. Where political expediency has dictated the removal of memorials to the British Raj, the works themselves have often been carefully preserved in a place of safety.

Painting and sculpture during the British epoch falls into two main groups. First there is the group which comprises the survivals of old traditions. These are associated with regions where Hindu culture has remained intact since the Middle Ages until today. Such are the hill-regions of Nepal, Sikkim and Bhutan, and even parts of the far south such as Malabar and Travancore. Here there still survive styles of building, sculpture and painting which are unbroken lineal descendants of mediaeval styles. In Orissa and Madras there are sculptors engaged on restoration of the 10th-13th century temples, who also produce individual pieces of sculpture for sale in a style remarkably like that of the Middle Ages. The famous temples of Mount Abu are continuously restored, and large sections of them are actually modern reworkings. Recently the Government has instituted at several centres training schools where young stonemasons are trained in the exact imitation of classical sculptures. This is said to be intended to insure the continuous restoration of the temples. It seems, however, as if alumni of these schools may well contribute to the flourishing international market in almost unidentifiable forgeries. It is probably not with this sort of activity that the future lies.

Many folk arts survived in a healthy condition into the present century. At the present day religious emblems are still used, and on the walls of houses in cities and country towns, traditional magical diagrams, or, say, Sita and Rama, are still painted in versions of traditional styles. In fact the 'people' of India still display their traditional affection for pure decoration; houses, shops, cafés and lorries may have crude versions of traditional motives, e.g. a peacock or a vase of flowers, painted on them. Many hand-painted shop-signs testify to the survival of older traditions.

The second group of painting and sculpture during the British epoch comprises post-Muslim traditions which, after the disastrous reign of Aurangzeb, who attempted to proscribe the arts altogether, adapted themselves to new conditions in order to survive. Painting here was the most successful art. Many families of artists—for art was a family occupation—settled down to the bazaar life, producing pictures to sell. Some of them continued to produce such faithful replicas of 'Delhi school' work in the present century that they have, in fact, deceived quite practised eyes as to their age. Some of them produced sets of portraits of family ancestors on commission, some sets of portraits of Sikh, Maratha or Afghan kings. Some worked up sets of Hindu subjects, devotional, martial and erotic. But the characteristic feature of all this art was that it was repetitive. Pictures were based on sets of master-designs, which were family or school property. Many painters went to work in the scriptoria of Kashmir, where through the 18th and 19th centuries illustrated volumes of Persian and Indian classics were produced.

Another activity which these painters undertook was the painting of houses. The old monumental tradition of wall painting, as exemplified at Ajanta or Ellora, had, of course, been only the religious manifestation of a flourishing secular art tradition. And it had more or less vanished, save in those areas where Hindu traditions survived intact. But post-Mogul painters developed a particular kind of miniature interior decoration, exemplified by the Chamba Palace murals (National Museum, New Delhi) and especially by the rooms of the Tambekarwada house at Baroda. Here the entire interior—walls, door and window panels, ceilings—is covered with what are in effect slightly enlarged miniature paintings covering the whole range of Hindu subject matter. Incidentally, types and motives from European art are also assimilated; so that one may encounter, say, a Victorian lady with her parasol amongst the prancing mounted maharajas and their courtiers.

Under the British Raj many wealthy and successful Indians attempted to adapt themselves to the outlook of their rulers. Artistically speaking, however, the effect of the British upon the artistic life of India was catastrophic. They patronized native bazaar art, for the sake of souvenirs of India to be pasted into scrap books. During the 19th century sets of 'Indian costumes', 'Indian customs' (especially hook-swinging and Sati), 'Indian idols' were produced, and sets of erotica for the licentious British soldiery and India's own segregated youth, which can be far from negligible work. Under the patronage of the British, Indians also learned Western methods of architectural drawing and miniature painting. Ravi Varma, with great financial but very little artistic success, made adaptations of European oil painting and oleograph technique to Indian subject matter. At the same time an almost incredibly complacent contempt for native Indian art was frequently and forcibly expressed by British officials. In order to 'civilize' Indian taste art-schools were set up during the 1850's following the conservative British pattern, with figure drawings from casts and from the nude as the basis of teaching. From these, generations of careful academic artists have emerged, though few have found outlets for their talents. During this period of British cultural imperialism Indians never saw any originals of first-class Western art. This fact, more perhaps than anything else, has conditioned the opinions of Indian chauvinist critics. Indians laboured under the narrow academic regime which Europe itself was even then in the act of rejecting. This regime they identified with 'European art'. The nationalist rejection of European influence, when it set in, threw out the European baby with the British bathwater to such effect that it is still very hard for even the best-intentioned Indian critic to appreciate the virtues of much of Europe's greatest art.

Bengal Renaissance

The Bengali cultural 'Renaissance' was centred on the Tagore family in Calcutta with its supporting clique. A moving spirit was E. B. Havell, who came to Calcutta in 1896 as Principal of the Calcutta School of Art and immediately abolished the academic teaching schedule. During the 1880's and '90's the writing of Rabindranath Tagore had done much to promote a faith amongst Bengalis in their own cultural future. A few progressive Englishmen had begun to plead for some kind of cultural self-determination for India. And finally the Theosophists began to stir up amongst Indians and Europeans a wave of uncritical enthusiasm for the achievements of Indian philosophy and theology. Havell himself was not a Theosophist, but from his contact with Adyar his writings are deeply imbued with theosophical ideas and the admiration he conceived for Indian art was directed towards its expression of literary spiritual concepts. In this he remained an academician at heart. His books established a pattern for the appreciation of Indian art as a vehicle for theosophical philosophy which has dominated much criticism and art in India right down to the end of the last war. Only recently have some Indian artists tried to escape from its grip.

Influence of Archaeology

One further element in the artistic situation at the turn of the century is important. This is the work of the archaeological survey of India, Cunningham's brainchild, set up in 1862 and operated for years on a shoe-string budget with the greatest devotion by a handful of dedicated men. They were interested not so much in art as in India's past, and they conceived their task as being part of the general 19th-century pursuit of human origins. Through their scientific publications India became aware of the extent of the richness of her art.

Abanindranath Tagore

The closest and most important of Havell's pupils was the painter Abanindranath Tagore, Rabindranath's nephew. Together they sought Indian examples both for subject matter and style. Indian legends and incidents from Indian history supplied the first, 'Mogul miniatures', i.e. mainly the products of the later 'Delhi' school, the second. These were combined with 'revolutionary' design derived from Beardsley and the Yellow Book, and a gauzy British watercolour method with many washings and soakings. Abanindranath continued for some sixty years to produce his sentimental adaptations, and around him an influential school grew up, including Nandalal Bose, who taught at Shantiniketan for many years, and Rahman Chugtai, far the best painter of this school, who opted for Pakistan when partition came. Some of their pupils, when they were young, travelled with Lady Herringham to Ajanta, and there helped to produce the copies which first brought the splendour of the Ajanta murals to the attention of the world.

Break in 'Victorian Night'

A few knowledgeable critics were able even at first actually to approve the work of the Bengal school as art, but only for nationalist reasons. For it represented the first serious attempt to produce an 'Indian' art since the Victorian academic night had come down. Its infiuence extended widely in India, and the heads of most of the major art schools during the twenties and thirties were alumni of this school. Its influence spread outside India both into Japan, where Count Okakura was attempting a similar revival of native traditions, and to the West where Edmund Dulac absorbed it. Even today much of the art of the Indian Academy is based upon it, and echoes of its style are often found in official art of all kinds. It provided the background for later generations of rebels. For its tenuous relationship with the older Indian artistic traditions, and its poor grasp of artistic problems became steadily more obvious. This weakness is all the more surprising in that Rabindranath Tagore, whose own horizons were broad, and who opposed the narrow revivalism of Gandhi in favour of cultural openness, was himself closely concerned with the movement, and had to some extent planned the course Abanindranath should follow. Rabindranath, however, seems to have become impatient and in 1925 urged that India's artists should not remain narrowly nationalistic. Later he expanded his own public activities to include painting. By cultivating a version of the post-surrealist 'automatic' method he executed a long series of drawings and watercolour paintings, in a loose, rhythmically swerving line with massed hatching and blobs, whose imagery was taken not from 'Indian legend', but from his own unconscious fund. He thus pointed a lesson which Indian art has taken a very long time to learn—Indian painters do not have to labour at being Indian; they are so already Rabindranath's pictures had great success in Europe, but it was many years before they were appreciated at home.

Return to Roots; Jamini Roy

Many artists did attempt to go back to the grass roots of Indian art. They did not need like Gauguin to travel thousands of miles to find their inspirational paradise; but they nevertheless came to the vestigial traditions practised by the humble, submerged classes of India, as if they were something exotic. At the same time they expressly hoped that their art should be socially recognised, not a solitary adventure. These attempts, however, were slow to earn recognition. Jamini Roy is an example. He admired the Santals, then a happy aboriginal people living outside the constricted world of Hindu society, and attempted to find a purely stylistic parallel to his idealistic rejection of the apparatus of 20th century sophistication in adopting about 1928 a manner derived from the style of the surviving Patua and Kalighat painters. He went so far as to make his pictures corporate products like their exemplars, pupils and members of his household executing different phases of the work. Jamini Roy has gradually become a powerful influence, and his style has contributed its quota to the orthodox academic styles of modern India, though many imitators of his drastic simplifications do not avoid banality.

Amrita Sher Gil

Another of the recently canonized artists of the Indian academy is Amrita Sher Gil, a half Indian oil painter who settled in India when her style was already formed on the model mainly of Gauguin without benefit of any specific study of Indian art. The life of village India touched her feelings deeply and she produced, before she died at the age of 28 in 1941, a series of canvases, many of them large, hymning in a simplicist style, 'with acknowledgements' to Ajanta, the ordinary people of India. It is clear to a non-Indian eye that the Indian scene remained to her something exotic which she painted as an outsider. Since independence, however, her subject matter—groups of women, resting men, village life—reflecting as it does the general political concern with the condition of the peasant masses, has provided the iconography for a great deal of 'official' Indian painting. As well, the search for political unity has been accompanied by a corresponding search for artistic unity. The belief that in the 20th century it was possible of set purpose to create a 'national style' of art has actually conditioned patterns of artistic development. Thus a group of recognizable academic styles has been created, compounded out of elements that have earned political respectability, and the urge towards conformity in Indian society has been satisfied. N. S. Bendre and K. K. Hebbar are perhaps the best exponents of such styles, importing selected characteristics of older Indian art into their decoratively brusque treatment of Amrita Sher Gil's subject matter.

The New Art

With the growth of artistic self-confidence a generation of artists matured who reacted against the limitations both of Indian conservative society and the new national academic style of art. Self-confidence encouraged experiment, and after independence it was no longer either 'subservience' or 'treachery' to look for inspiration to a West at odds with the same academic values as India had rejected. India is not yet a country deeply conscious of the value of live art, and the modern Indian academy continues to exhibit in Delhi all shades of derivative work. But by now the canonical subject matter from Indian life or legend executed in strong 'Indian' colours, with enough dressing of modernism of one kind or another to avoid the charge of reaction, has become jejune. A number of the better artists of the established generation have tried to make it the material for abstract development (as Picasso and Braque did with Harlequin and guitar). Husain's vaguely sexual groups, B. Raval's entwined cattle, K. S. Kulkarni's village groups, set out this way; Ceylon's George Keyt has similarly adapted Picassoist interpenetration of lines to erotic Indian themes. But Indians still demand of art sentimental prettiness and tasteful undulating formulae, and thus even these efforts have been suffocated, and the artists have been obliged to conform.

Renewed Western Influence

This process is, of course, the consequence of the study of modern Western art, either in the original or in art-publications. The unjustly neglected brother of Abanindranath Tagore, Gagendranath, was the first seriously to attempt to absorb the experimental painting of the school of Paris during the twenties and thirties, when such interest in the West was not politically approved, producing some interesting adaptations of cubism. Today many artists have set out to assimilate elements from the language of one or other of the better known Europeans with interesting consequences. The Bombay painter Gaitonde has taken up Klee's spidery linearism, others have adapted Dubuffet's *art brut*, and Jean Arp's smooth, erotic forms are favoured by a number of sculptors. Satish Gujral has adopted a Mexican manner derived mainly from Orozco. It cannot, however, be denied that the present state of patronage in India makes it impossible for experimental art to flourish. Few artists make a living from art alone; but the successful are still those who can blend elements from the canonised 'patriotic' styles, spice them with 'modernism', and retain the required sentiment. None has actually been able to evade one slick formula or another and recover the unselfconscious directness of the best painting of the Indian past.

It is of the nature of modern art to make a disruptive assault on the viewer's feelings, but the innate tendency of the Indian mind towards generalization softens the expression of adopted formal languages. For this reason the greatest successes of modern Indian art have been gained by Indians who have settled in the West for longer or shorter periods of time. Living in an artistic environment which values above all 'originality' and individualism they have found that their intrinsic Indianness has been stimulated and sharpened. They are sometimes accused in India of having ceased to be Indian artists. They have indeed rebelled against the social and artistic conservatism prevailing at home; most of them remember their student days under their Indian academic mentors with horror. But many have become artists of world stature, and other younger artists are following their example. The painters Avinash Chandra and F. N. Souza live in London, Raza and A. Padamsee mainly in Paris, M. B. Samant in Rome, New York and London, but it is they who have done Indian art the greatest service; for through the cult of individualism they have found their Indian selves, and have been able unselfconsciously to absorb only those elements of Indian artistic tradition with which they felt themselves to have the closest affinity. They have discountenanced the nationalist assumption that good art can be the product of even the best intentioned political aspirations. They are free to experiment as 'shockingly' as they wish with traditional Indian symbolism as a means of genuine personal expression, just as European artists are with elements from many exotic arts. And they have been able to sell enough work to live as artists. It is most probable that their contribution to the modern world-wide investigation of visual imagery will be recognized as of the very highest importance. It cannot, however, be said that Indian artists in India are influencing the art of Asia as a whole. Even in Ceylon a distinctive type of art, not derived from India's, has evolved. Ivan Peries, the Deraniyagalas and George Claessen have discovered their artistic problems in direct consultation with Western painting, mainly by residence in the West. The Indonesian Affandi owes nothing to Indian examples. At the moment it seems that the influence of Indian art is being spread through cosmopolitan contacts in the cities of Europe and America.

Architecture

In architecture India has yet to find a style, or produce a distinguished practitioner. Until virtually the last decade most of the major public works on Indian soil have been designed by Europeans. There was a very pleasant style of stuccoed architecture, with distinct echoes of Mogul building, evolved in the 19th century under the British, for villas, resthouses and hotels. The buildings are wide-fronted, simply rectangular, with deep arcaded verandahs and moulded string courses. They are everywhere. Especially beautiful examples survive in Madras and Delhi. Modern houses for Government officials or villas for the wealthy often recall them.

Twentieth-century work of Indian design is marked by the same revivalist spirit as the other arts. Such revivalism has not so much developed surviving patterns as selfconsciously incorporated motives from the classical epochs of Indian architecture, and little of it can be called really successful. Amongst the more interesting of these attempts may be mentioned temples in Benares and Christian churches in various parts of India which are 'salads' of architectural motives from different epochs. Shrish Chatterjee, the noted Bengali architect, has designed many houses incorporating motives from India's architectural past. On the wooded slopes of hill stations like Darjeeling, modern variants of traditional types of house have been built for wealthy families—alongside houses under a strong Scandinavian influence. Works by European architects have been tinged with this same spirit. Lutyens at Delhi was not guiltless, and works like Koenigsberger's Victory Hall in Bangalore, executed in the local grey granite employed eaves profiles in concrete derived from local classical prototypes.

Especially interesting are the local housing projects carried out under the community development programme started in 1952 to house the peasant population. Foreign architects like Jane Drew have contributed designs for such mass-produced houses, but many designs have been evolved by official architects based upon local traditional house-types, and here, perhaps, important developments may best be expected. In this programme the

Central Building Research Institute, Roorkee, has played a leading part. At this level of simplicity the issue of conscious revivalism is not insistent, and the application of mass-production methods provides a genuine reason for architectural simplifications. The ancient ogival chaitya arch can be used to frame the door of an economically built community centre without giving aesthetic offence. Many of these housing projects consist of complete new villages, planned as entities. The villagers have been encouraged to use their traditional decorative skills on their new homes.

In the sphere of major construction, such as university buildings, scientific institutes, hospitals and schools the international language of financial austerity has been adopted. Pure rectilinear construction, often in reinforced concrete frame and brick screen (derived from the doctrines of de Stijl), has produced some handsome if stark buildings like the administrative offices of the Council of Scientific Industrial Research, New Delhi, or the Central Building Research Institute, Roorkee. Occasionally such buildings may be enriched with traditional motives, e.g. rosettes, but bare concrete is the rule.

The most characteristically Indian functional feature of these buildings, which seems likely to provide the best basis for architectural development and plastic interest, is the deeply recessed or sharply projecting window frame, intended to exclude the sun. A larger opening may be shielded by a jali, a kind of openwork boxing of stone, brick or concrete, whose pattern can be made an integral part of the proportional system of the structure. It is this feature that was especially developed in the design, by a committee of Europeans and Indians led by Le Corbusier, of the city of Chandigarh, the new state capital of the Punjab, begun in 1953. A wide variety of cofferings and projections add textures to the rectilinear elevations, and here and there screens, sometimes of plain catenary arches, some inverted, provide ornamental features. The enterprising spirit behind Chandigarh will certainly offer inspiration and stimulus to the whole of Asia.

BIBLIOGRAPHY

W. G. Archer. *India and Modern Art.* (Allen and Unwin, London, 1959.)

W. G. Archer and M. Archer. *Indian Painting for the British, 1770–1880.* (Oxford Univ. Press, London, 1955.)

P. Brown. *Indian Architecture (Islamic).* (Taraporevala, Bombay, n.d.) *Indian Painting under the Mughals.* (Oxford Univ. Press, London, 1924.)

K. Khandalavala. *Amrita Sher Gil.* (New Book Co., Bombay, n.d.)

A. Mookerji. *Modern Art in India.* (Oxford Book and Stationery Co., Calcutta, n.d.)

P. S. Rawson. *Indian Painting.* (Tisné, Paris and New York, 1961.)

V. Smith. *Fine Art in India and Ceylon.* (Oxford Univ. Press, London, 1930.)

CURRENT PERIODICALS

Marg. (Bombay.)

Design. (Bombay.)

The March of India. (Delhi.)

BIOGRAPHICAL NOTE

PHILIP S. RAWSON. Keeper, Gulbenkian Museum of Oriental Art, University of Durham, and Lecturer at the University. Previously Assistant Keeper of the Ashmolean Museum, Oxford and Lecturer in the History of Indian Art at the School of Oriental and African Studies, University of London. For many years Lecturer in the History of Art (Eastern and Western) at the Universities of Durham, Oxford and Birmingham. UNESCO Visiting Expert in Museology posted to Indian Grants Commission, 1964. Author of many books and articles on Indian and Japanese painting.

CHINESE ART

by

PETER C. SWANN

Ceramics

Art in China began in the third millennium B.C. From this period date the earliest ceramics made by neolithic peoples in the area. They produced a number of types of ware, the most notable being a buff pottery fashioned by hand but sometimes finished on a slow wheel. The designs painted in red and black on these jars are bold and skilful. They are almost invariably geometric and probably were associated with fertility beliefs. They are strikingly similar both in design and shape to some neolithic wares made in Eastern Europe. However, it seems that there were no contacts between East and West in these early days. The culture which the Chinese developed in the Yellow River Basin area during the third and second millennia B.C. must have arisen independently and with few direct external influences.

Throughout the centuries the Chinese perfected the art of ceramics, making it one of their greatest contributions to the world's store of art. By the middle of the second millennium B.C., they were producing a very fine wheel-turned burnished black ware with an extremely thin body (Lung-shan type). They took the first steps towards the invention of pure porcelain in the 3rd century B.C. with a type of highly-fired porcelainous stoneware known as Yüeh which was slowly perfected over the following thirteen centuries until about the 9th–10th century when pure porcelain was first produced— about eight hundred years before the West was able to discover its secret.

The potters enlarged the range of colours of their glazes from olive brown or green to a three-coloured ware comprising green, cream and brown typical of the 7th–10th centuries. During these centuries cultural influences from Persia and India influenced all the crafts including ceramics, notably in shape and decoration. However, most experts consider that the Chinese made the finest ceramics the world has seen in the Sung Dynasty from the 10th to 13th centuries. During that period shape, glaze, colour and decoration united into a rare perfection. The shapes have delicate assurance, the glazes are subtle, the freehand decoration is invariably powerful but discreet. They are always alive.

Perhaps the most familiar of all Chinese porcelain is the underglaze blue-and-white which, in its export varieties, flooded the Western world from the 16th century onwards. This ware was first produced in the 14th century and has continued down to the present day in much debased forms. The finest was made during the 15th century for imperial use. A whole industrial city grew up in Ming times (1368–1644) to supply the demand for Chinese porcelains. Technical standards continued to improve until in the 18th century a wide range of plain (monochromes) and decorated wares (famille verte, famille noire, famille rose) were the envy of the civilised world. No problems of shape, decoration or colour seem to have been too difficult for the potters. Once the various European eastern trading companies established themselves in the late 16th century, European families were able to order vast sets of table-ware decorated with their individual coats of arms at a fraction of the cost they would have been in Europe. The trade in porcelain and tea resulted in an adverse balance of trade which the West was only able to redress by shipping opium in ever-increasing quantities.

METALWORK

In metalwork, the Chinese produced their finest from about 1300 B.C. down to about the 9th century A.D. The early bronzes were mostly ritual vessels for use in connection with ceremonies of ancestor worship. The finest from a point of view of both workmanship and religious power were made during the second half of the Shang Dynasty from about 1300–1000 B.C.). Their decorations are zoomorphic and geometric with a powerful animal mask predominant. The casting is of a fineness which even today defies repetition. During the following centuries down to about the 3rd century B.C. the styles tended to become more decorative and less awesome than in the earlier period. From the 3rd century the finest workmanship was reserved for the decorated backs of bronze mirrors. Gold and silver and semi-precious gem inlays were popular and sometimes the precious metals were used alone though comparatively few of these have survived. China during these centuries was expanding from its birthplace on the Yellow River and a number of provincial bronze styles can be identified.

From about the 3rd century A.D. onwards bronze was used mainly for statues to serve the Buddhist faith. These ranged in size from about an inch to over life-size and were often gilded. Japan, which adopted Buddhism from China, has alone preserved some of the large T'ang style bronze statues. During the T'ang Dynasty (618–907) very elegant bowls and cups were made in gold and silver to satisfy the tastes of a luxury-loving court. Iron was used for casting large figures in the Sung and Ming periods and some of these have great power. Metals were always used extensively in subsequent periods but, although the craftsmanship in the objects the Chinese made was often of a very high standard, the actual artistic taste shows a steady decline in standards. The only exceptions are cloisonné (introduced from the Middle East) and enamels inspired by Limoges and made at Canton.

JADE

Jade and lacquer are perhaps the two most characteristically Eastern materials. Even the neolithic Chinese seem to have venerated jade, but it was first used for really artistic purposes during the Shang period when small objects of white jade schematically carved to represent animals were extensively used on dress. Various coloured jades were used for the blades of ceremonial swords and daggers. Many have been excavated from the tombs.

Larger pieces were sometimes used for musical chimes. From this very hard and intractable material which first came from Central Asia and Siberia and later from Burma, the hands of patient workmen have produced some of the most remarkable objects of Chinese culture. We know little about the products in jade from the 3rd to 17th centuries A.D., but in the 18th century the Ch'ing or Manchu court lapidaries produced a flood of objects ranging from vessels of every shape to hat stands, from tiny jewelry to imperial sceptres in which all the possibilities of jade were explored. Huge boulders of green Burmese jade were carved to represent miniature mountains complete with landscapes, dwellings and inhabitants. An 18th-century interest in archaeology led to the manufacture of jade vessels inspired by the shapes and designs of early bronzes. Throughout their history the Chinese have always regarded the material as having all the symbolic virtues which we associate with diamonds and pearls.

Lacquer

Lacquer is made from the sap of a tree indigenous to the Far East; it was used very early in China's history. There are a few Shang bronzes with what appears to be a lacquer inlay. However, it was not used extensively for small vessels like drinking cups and containers such as cosmetic boxes until the centuries just before Han times. In the Han Dynasty (*circa* 200 B.C.–200 A.D.) it was an extensive industry throughout the whole of the East. The early pieces are generally dark brown with red painted decoration. In T'ang times lacquer was very popular and even Buddhist statues were made from it. The most familiar type is the cinnabar red carved lacquer which is manufactured by applying coat after coat of lacquer on a wood or hemp base. When a sufficient thickness has been built up the whole was carved deeply with floral or landscape designs. The finest of these were produced during the Ming centuries when the boldness and balance of the designs were in harmony. The red lacquer boxes, trays, bottles etc. produced from about 1700 display the same technical care and skill but the designs tend to be overcrowded to the extent of fussiness.

Sculpture in Stone

Sculpture in stone began in China during the Han Dynasty. A few isolated marble pieces from Shang tombs are of interest but of small artistic merit and can hardly count as sculpture proper. The Chinese mastered the art of carving stone under the inspiration of the Buddhist faith which entered China in the first centuries A.D. From India, the birthplace of Buddhism, came the idea of carving temples out of the living rock. The Chinese emulated the Indians and carved huge shrines containing myriads of sculptures both large and small at a number of sites like Yün-kang, Lung-mên, Mai-ch'i-shan and P'ing-ling-ssu. The style was at first an extension of that found in the central Asian oases which acted as stepping stones for the religion in its progress eastwards. Quite rapidly the Chinese, from about 500 A.D., created an individual style in which the bodies of the images, instead of being only very lightly clad as in the Indian examples, became heavily swathed in robes which tumble in regular cascades over the figures and down over the pedestals on which they sit. This very spiritual style did not last very long. In the T'ang Dynasty, as communications with India improved, so strong waves of Indian influence brought Indian sculptural ideals of sensuality and graceful movement which completely conquered the Chinese sculptors. Later, in the Sung, when communications with China were again cut off, the Chinese developed their own personal and graceful, almost indolent, styles of Buddhist statuary. They also produced very naturalistic priest and lay figures. The standards of monumental sculpture declined rapidly from the Ming Dynasty onwards—seemingly with the decline in the influence of Buddhism itself.

However, before leaving sculpture altogether, one must mention one of the most attractive aspects of the Chinese ceramic craft. This is the glazed and unglazed funerary figures. Starting at the end of the Han Dynasty, *ca.* 200 A.D., the huge output of figures for burial includes some of the most attractive objects in the whole of Chinese art. The culmination of this art was in the T'ang Dynasty when the craftsmen produced animals of all types, Buddhist religious figures, notably guardians, a whole range of delicately modelled figures, servants, musicians, dancers, travellers of many races, all of which bring the atmosphere of the period vividly to life. The horses and camels are among the world's masterpieces of animal sculpture. The art of figure modelling for the grave continued in Ming times (1368–1644) at a lower artistic level and then petered out, but the Chinese gift for modelling was continued in the *blanc-de-chine* figures of Fukien province kilns which from the 15th century onwards produced a very large number of most sensitively carved figures—notably of Kuan-yin, the Goddess of Compassion. These continued until the 18th century, but the late Ming figures are outstanding.

Painting

We have hitherto discussed mainly what the Chinese consider to be the crafts. The only real art for the Chinese is that of painting with its allied form of calligraphy. The art of painting goes back to pre-Han times, but of this almost nothing has survived. From the Han centuries we have a number of paintings on tiles taken from tombs and on bronzes. A large number of stamped brick tiles have survived and these provide a great deal of information concerning the skills which the Chinese artisans must have had in the art. In the form of rubbings they show an art of silhouette and movement, two permanent qualities of Chinese painting. In the centuries following the Han, Chinese artisans gained much experience in painting Buddhist subjects including early landscapes. The finest of these either perished in persecutions of the faith or from other disturbances or neglect over the centuries. Our main source of information on the art from Han to T'ang comes from the Buddhist site of Tun-huang in the far west of China. This was the last outpost before the Chinese pilgrims set out across Central Asia towards India and the first centre of Chinese civilisation on their return. Here in soft cliffs are many cave temples with painted clay figures and painted walls. Already the art is well advanced. Japan preserved at Nara the finest Chinese-style early Buddhist wall paintings until quite recently when they were destroyed by fire.

As early as the 4th–5th centuries the Chinese started to think seriously about painting and their first theorists like Hsieh Ho outlined the essentials of the art. His main canon was that a painting should have the 'life breath', that it should be alive and full of movement. From his time onwards a vast library on the art has grown up. Artists were favoured at the court and lavishly rewarded for their services. The T'ang was the great period of figure painting and a few examples have survived, but towards the end of this period the Chinese created an art of pure landscape painting, many centuries before the West. The great development in the art of landscape painting took place in the centuries from about 900 to 1350. This included a short period (907–960) following the T'ang when the country was divided. Faced with the dangers of political life serious-minded men turned to the eternals of nature, some of them expressing their thoughts in noble landscapes. As in ceramics, the Sung also is considered to be the finest period in painting. A whole galaxy of painters explored every aspect of landscape from the lofty, austere and detailed works of the first half of the Sung period to the poetic, evocative, romantic landscapes of the second half.

During these centuries the technique of brushwork was minutely studied and a whole repertoire of strokes were assembled for the representation of every aspect of nature—different rocks, trees in the various seasons, mountains in the mist, water in every mood, etc.

It was left to the scholars of the late Ming Dynasty to develop what the Sung created into a system which threatened to destroy the art. In this period the scholars took over the leadership of the art, especially landscape painting. The scholar administrator was expected to pass his spare time in some artistic or literary way—poetry, belles-lettres, historical studies or the arts of painting and calligraphy. They themselves emphasised that painting should be the work only of amateurs and be a vehicle for the expression of their lofty sentiments. Anything professional was anathema to them and they castigated even first class painters if there was any suspicion of professionalism about them. For their part, these literary painters created many splendid landscapes but some tended to be dry and studied rather than warm and sincere reactions to the splendours of nature. From them stems the close connection of painting and poetry and many of these paintings carry long poetry or prose passages which are intended to add another dimension to the enjoyment of a picture as well as demonstrating calligraphic skill and literary erudition.

Fortunately painting could not be put into a strait-jacket and the rules and strictures of the amateur scholar-painters created their own reaction. Throughout Chinese painting there have always been a number of eccentric painters who refused to obey the rules but who produced memorable works. From the 16th century onwards a number of individualists, either by bold brushwork or by their genuine reaction to nature itself, produced works of intense life and brilliance. From this time onwards the art of painting split into two broad schools, the one which followed the tradition of the scholar painters and the other which stressed the need for a man to see and feel for himself the emotions which he wishes to express. The men who followed the individualist line generally found themselves out of office and though they were supposed to be amateur and never to paint for money, there seems little doubt that their work was highly sought after and that they lived by it. The nineteenth century produced comparatively little great work but since 1900 a number of notable painters are showing that the art is not dead, that it is coming to grips with Western influences and producing fine paintings of originality and inspiration. These tend to look more to the individualists than to the scholar-painters, but the styles are recognisably new and personal. A number of Chinese painters working in America and in Europe are also producing original work which is often more in the internationally accepted modern styles than that of their colleagues in China itself, where anything too Western would be frowned upon. It may be predicted that Chinese painting is about to enjoy a revival.

Calligraphy

The one aspect of Chinese art which unfortunately Westerners have fought shy of is certainly that of calligraphy. Fine examples of calligraphy are mounted, hung and admired as much as painting. The Chinese characters are written with the same brush and ink as are used for monochrome painting. Starting as pictograms in the Shang Dynasty the Chinese script acquired its present form just over two thousand years ago. The characters themselves are a very abstract form of art. The Chinese script has always been highly venerated both for its artistic qualities and as the vehicle for learning. A number of different styles have been developed, a formal script, a so-called 'grass' style which is very abbreviated and cursive, a style for carving seals, etc. The calligraphy of the individualist painters is very wild or deliberately eccentric. Calligraphy does, in fact, reveal very well the character of the writer and it does not need a great deal of experience for a foreigner to be able to appreciate it as art.

BIBLIOGRAPHY

J. Cahill. *Chinese Painting.* (Skira, Geneva, 1958.)

Cheng Te-k'un. *Archaeology in China,* 3 vols. (Cambridge Univ. Press, London, 1959 onwards.)

W. B. Honey. *Ceramic Art of China and Other Countries in the Far East.* (Faber, London, 1945.)

Sherman E. Lee. *A History of Far Eastern Art.* (Thames and Hudson, London, 1964.)

A. Sickman and A. Soper. *The Art and Architecture of China.* (Penguin, London, 2nd ed., 1960.)

O. Siren. *Chinese Painting: Leading Masters and Principles,* 7 vols. (Lund Humphries, London, 1956-1958.)

M. Sullivan. *An Introduction to Chinese Art.* (Faber, London, 1961.)

P. C. Swann. *Chinese Painting.* (Zwemmer, London, 1958.)

W. Watson. *Ancient Chinese Bronzes.* (Faber, London, 1962.)

W. Willetts. *Chinese Art.* (Penguin, London, 1958.)

BIOGRAPHICAL NOTE

Peter C. Swann. B. 1921, London. Educated at London, Leiden and Oxford Universities; studied history and subsequently Japanese in war-time naval service. After the war returned to Oxford to study Chinese and specialized in the arts of Japan and China. Studied in U.S.A. and Japan, 1950-51. Editor of *Oriental Art*: Keeper of Department of Eastern Art, Ashmolean Museum, Oxford. Author of *An Introduction to the Arts of Japan* (Cassirer, Oxford, 1958), *Chinese Painting* (Zwemmer, 1958) and *Art of China, Korea and Japan* (Thames and Hudson, London, 1963) and editor of *Hokusai* (Faber and Faber, London, 1959) and (with Yukiro Yashiro) *2,000 Years of Japanese Art* (Thames and Hudson, London, 1958).

JAPANESE ART

by

HUGO MUNSTERBERG

The Jomon and Yayoi Periods

Of all the existing artistic traditions, the Japanese is by far the oldest, for it can trace its beginnings back to the fifth millennium B.C. when Jomon art originated. Not only is this neolithic pottery civilization more ancient than that of China and India, but it is also highly original, owing no debt to the ceramic culture of the mainland. The forms used by the Jomon potters are often fantastic and highly expressive, depending for their effect on sculptural relief rather than on painted designs or beauty of shape. Strangely enough, there are striking similarities between Jomon ware and certain neolithic pottery of pre-historic America such as the ceramics of the mound builders, and it is also interesting to note that the Jomon idols are far closer to the fertility deities of pre-historic Europe than anything found on the Asian mainland.

Jomon culture flourished for about four thousand years, lasting from around 4500 B.C. to the time of Christ, and then lingering on for several more centuries in the northernmost districts of the country. It was followed by a bronze age culture called Yayoi (named after the quarter of Tokyo where the earliest examples were found), which was brought to Japan from the mainland. The advent of these peoples marked the beginning of the Japanese nation and civilization as we know it today. The use of natural materials, the love of simplicity and restraint, and the subtle beauty of formal relationships were already found in the art of this period, as is well illustrated by the Shinto shrines, such as those of Ise and Izumo, which though not built at that time nevertheless faithfully reflect the style and technique of the period. Related to Yayoi art and developing out of it is the art of the subsequent grave mound period during which the grave figures known as Haniwa were made.

Chinese Influence

Following the pre-historic age, Japan entered a period during which her art was deeply influenced by the art of the continent. Under the impact of Buddhism, new artistic forms appeared, first from Korea and then from China, which were completely to transform the culture of Japan. If there is any validity in the widely held conception that all Japanese art is basically derived from that of China, then it applies most specifically to the Asuka, Nara and early Heian rules, that is roughly between 600 and 900 A.D. when the art of Japan was little more than a provincial reflection of the great art of Sui and T'ang China. The Buddhist temple, the religious sculptures representing the various Buddhist deities, and the wall and scroll paintings originated at this time which the Japanese today look back upon as the golden age of their religious art. A monastery such as Horyuji with its magnificent temples, its wall paintings, and its ancient bronze and wood images has no equivalent today in China, even if it was conceived as an imitation.

Only in the Muromachi period (1333-1573), especially during the 15th century, was the influence of China as strong as in 600–900 A.D. Through Zen Buddhism, continental civilization once again reshaped the culture of Japan. Many things which today both Japanese and foreigners think of as typically Japanese—tea ceremony, ink painting, flower arrangement, rock gardens, and Zen Buddhism itself—were brought from China to Japan where they flourished and developed long after they had ceased to play a vital role in Chinese civilization. The outstanding Muromachi artists, such as the 15th century painter Sesshu, travelled to China to study and collect the masterpieces of Sung and Yuan painters, and it was the landscape of China rather than that of their own country which they rendered in their scrolls. The culture of the continent was considered far superior to that of Japan, and the Ashikaga rulers tried to have their court reflect its elegance and sophistication. Although China continued to play an important role, especially during the Tokugawa rule of the 17th and 18th centuries, never again was the prestige of Chinese culture to be so great.

The Heian, Momoyama and Edo Periods

Compared to these periods of Chinese domination, other periods of Japanese art owe very little to Chinese inspiration. It was during these times that the native artistic genius developed most fully, and made its unique contribution to the art of the world. Above all the Heian period (900-1200) and the Momoyama period (1573-1615) reflect this distinctly native Japanese spirit, and much of the Edo period (1615-1868) is also very Japanese in character. The two art forms which exemplify this best are the narrative scrolls of the Heian period, which fittingly enough are known as Yamato-e or Japanese painting, and the decorative screen painting of the Momoyama and Early Edo periods, which with its use of gold leaf and bold, decorative colours is completely different from any painting which ever existed in China. Both these qualities, the narrative and the decorative, are also found in the coloured woodcut of the Edo period, the Ukiyo-e, or painting of the Floating World. Although the Japanese looked down upon these prints because they dealt with the low life of the Yoshiwara district with its courtesans, tea house girls and Kabuki actors, the instinct of the West was right when it hailed it as a great and typically Japanese art, and today, under Western influence, the Japanese themselves have learned to appreciate Ukiyo-e as one of their most original art forms. The work of men like Moronobu, Harunobu, Kiyonaga, Utamaro, Sharaku, Hokusai and Hiroshige exerted a profound influence on the art of both the Impressionists and the Post-Impressionists. To the Japanese, however, even finer than the masters of the woodblock prints are the great decorative painters, above all Sotatsu and Korin who excelled in the colourful, decorative screen painting which had originated during the Momoyama period. Not only was their style typically Japanese, but their choice of subject was characteristic of the native tradition, for they chose scenes from Japanese literature instead of Chinese legends, and they painted views of their own country instead of imaginary Chinese landscapes.

The Role of Art in Everyday Life

Perhaps the greatest difference between the arts of China and Japan lies in the role they play in their respective civilizations. The artistic tradition of China is, of course, very great and ancient, one of the most remarkable the world has ever known and in many respects superior to that of Japan. But art in China was always a matter for a small élite, especially the court and the scholars, and the great mass of people, peasants as well as middle class artisans and merchants, had no relationship with it. It is for this reason that Chinese porcelain, which had been so brilliant under the imperial patronage of the Sung, Ming and Ch'ing rulers, declined when an impoverished court could no longer subsidize it, and it is for this reason that the average Chinese house or restaurant is so ugly. In Japan, on the other hand, art has always been a part of life, permeating the entire fabric of Japanese society. Although the individual Japanese masterpieces may not equal those of China, the aesthetic quality of daily life is much higher. The concern with aesthetic values is not only the affair of a few cultured people, it reaches down to ordinary levels so that even in the house of a peasant one may find handsome, well made objects which are true works of art. Forms such as Ukiyo-e were distinctly middle class in origin, catering for the rich merchants of Edo rather than the literati and courtiers. The flower arrangement in a modest house, the village shrine with its sensitive use of material, the small rock garden in a courtyard—these are the aspects which make Japanese civilization the most artistic in the world: art is part of daily life.

Perhaps the most remarkable expression of this is the Japanese house. It is no pure chance that in spite of the tremendous impact of Western art and Western civilization, the Japanese have kept to their native traditions when it comes to domestic architecture. In its present form the Japanese house originated during the 17th century, that is early Edo, but its beginnings can be traced back to the Heian period. It is built largely of wood, a material well suited to withstand the earthquakes of Japan, though the choice is probably also dictated by an instinctive preference for wood as a building material. In fact the colour and texture of the natural wood, which is never covered with paint, is from a Japanese point of view one of the most attractive features of the house. The forms are always extremely simple, using a geometric design which makes a plain but attractive exterior. The interior is very open, with sliding screen partitions separating not only one room from another, but also the interior from the exterior. This flowing space and openness towards the outside is the quality modern architects have admired most in the traditional Japanese architectural design. This quality also creates a closeness to nature. Instead of the building dominating or standing in contrast to its natural setting, as is so often the case in the West, the Japanese architect tries to blend the building with its surroundings, and often more care is spent on the garden setting than on the building itself.

The Japanese have, in fact, always looked upon garden architecture as one of their most important art forms.

If one were to name one field in which the Japanese have been supreme, it would not be painting, or sculpture, or even architecture, outstanding as their contribution has been, it would be the crafts. It is in this field above all others that the Japanese, both in the quality of their production and in the variety of their output, have been unique masters. This is true not only of their ceramics and textiles, or of such typically Japanese specialities as their lacquers which are the finest the world has known, but also of various art forms which Westerners would not even think of such as flower arranging, paper folding, basket making and even rope tying. All these crafts are pursued with a skill, a dedication and an aesthetic awareness which are usually reserved for the so-called fine arts. It is significant that the Japanese did not differentiate between fine arts and crafts—they did not even have a word to distinguish the two, a distinction which by the way even in the West is relatively recent, dating from the 16th century. To the Japanese any object which is well made and reveals aesthetic sensibility is a work of art, showing the taste and skill of its maker, and to this day a famous potter such as Hamada is regarded as equal to any painter and far superior to any sculptor or architect; the latter almost always remain anonymous in traditional Japanese art. Here again the close connection between art and life is emphasized, for crafts such as pottery and weaving are not only thought of as works of art but as objects for daily use which help to make life more enjoyable.

This aesthetic awareness which touches even the ordinary is perhaps best illustrated by the folk art of Japan. Here, in an art form created by peasants and by artisans of small country towns, we have one of the finest manifestations of Japanese artistic sensibility. Made for practical purposes, these objects are often of great beauty. In Japan alone this kind of popular art exists even today, although modern industry has made serious inroads upon it, so that it survives only in the most backward and isolated regions of the country. During the Edo period and all through the 19th century, this art was one of the most important and popular aspects of Japanese creativity, and the finest of the folk works were equal to the best things made by the celebrated craftsmen of the big urban centres. The ceramic wares, the folk textiles, the lacquer bowls and cups, the many kinds of baskets, the bamboo utensils, the metal work, the hand-made paper, the folk toys and above all the peasant houses are true manifestations of an all but universal artistic awareness which never existed in China and cannot be matched in any other country. Today when folk art is gradually being replaced by mass produced objects made in the modern factories of Tokyo and Osaka, the Japanese themselves have begun to re-evaluate it, and art critics and collectors are praising the honesty, simplicity and beauty of these works by the unknown artists of rural Japan.

The Strength of Native Culture

Because of the vital role of art, as well as the all-pervading aesthetic sensibility, Japan is the only country in Asia whose art has not been overwhelmed by the art of the West. Not that Europe and in recent years America has not been a tremendous influence on the art of Japan (modern Japanese painting and sculpture have become little more than a reflection of the School of Paris), yet in spite of this, certain more traditional and purely Japanese features have survived, and in domestic architecture and the crafts where the native tradition was most alive, Western influence has hardly been felt. In China and India the enfeebled tradition could not withstand the impact of a Western art which brought with it all the prestige of the aggressive Western civilization; but in Japan the native culture was able to survive this onslaught, creating new art forms which embodied both modern and traditional elements. Certainly in pottery Japanese artists today are generally acknowledged to be the best in the world, and the influence of their work is felt in Europe and America. Oil painting has of course become very popular, but both the representational oil painters such as Umehara, and the abstract ones such as Okada, reflect their Japanese heritage. The print makers and the craftsmen produce works which attempt, often successfully, to create a synthesis of native Japanese sensibility and modern Western taste. Next to Paris and New York, Tokyo has emerged as a third art centre where the best of Japanese and foreign art is displayed, and a real contribution is made to the art of our time.

Influence on the West

The image which the West has had of this Japanese contribution has changed very much over the years. When Japanese art was first discovered, it was the porcelain of the Arita potters which under the names of Kakiemon and Imari ware became very popular in Europe and inspired the European porcelain industry. Later, after Japan had been opened by Commodore Perry, coloured woodblock prints and decorated enamel wares aroused the enthusiasm of Western art lovers. In fact at the end of the century this became a veritable craze, known as Japonoiserie. After the Second World War, beginning with the American occupation of Japan, there began a third period of Japanese influence during which modern architects and artists discovered yet other aspects of the Japanese tradition. Now it is not the refined porcelains or decorated enamel wares which enjoy favour, but the crude pottery made for the tea ceremony, such as Raku and Shino ware, and the simple peasant works. Instead of the Buddhist temples and the ornate shrines at Nikko, it is now the Katsura Detached Palace and the traditional Japanese house which find ardent champions in the West, which sees in them the same kind of aesthetic values which Western artists are trying to embody in their own work. Future generations, in re-examining the art of Japan, will no doubt find other aspects which will prove valuable and rewarding to them.

BIBLIOGRAPHY

T. Akiyama. *Japanese Painting*. (Skira, Geneva, 1961.)
A. D. Ficke. *Chats on Japanese Prints*. (Ernest Benn, London, 1915.)
J. Hillier. *Japanese Masters of the Colour Print*. (Phaidon, London, 1955.)
J. E. Kidder. *Masterpieces of Japanese Sculpture*. (Tuttle, Tokyo, 1961.)
H. Munsterberg. *The Arts of Japan*. (Tuttle, Rutland and Tokyo, 1957.)

H. Munsterberg. *The Folk Art of Japan.* (Tuttle, Rutland and Tokyo, 1958.). *The Ceramic Art of Japan.* (Tuttle, Rutland and Tokyo, 1964.)
R. Paine and A. Soper. *Art and Architecture in Japan.* (Penguin, London, 1955.)
L. Warner. *The Enduring Art of Japan.* (Harvard Univ. Press, Cambridge, Mass., 1952.)
T. Yoshida. *Japanese Houses and Gardens.* (Praeger, New York, 1955.)

BIOGRAPHICAL NOTE

HUGO MUNSTERBERG. B. 1916, Berlin. Became a citizen of U.S.A. in 1935. Educated at Harvard University (A.B., 1938 and Ph.D., 1941). Taught at Michigan State University, 1946-52 and at International Christian University, Tokyo, 1952-56; now Professor of Art History at the State University of New York. Author of ten books and numerous articles on Far Eastern art.

SOUTH-EAST ASIAN ART

by

ANTHONY CHRISTIE

Indian Influence

Lying as they do between India and China, the countries which constitute South-East Asia have not unnaturally been influenced by both. The majority of the peoples now inhabiting them seem to have originated in China, either in the coastal regions or in the area to the south of the Yangtze. The main external cultural influences, on the other hand, have come from India; in Vietnam alone do we find almost overwhelming Chinese influence, the result of nine hundred years of Chinese domination and the presence of a people closely related to the Chinese themselves. No Indian state exercised suzerainty over any part of South-East Asia, yet not only Indian religions but also Indian political ideas came to predominate in Burma, Thailand, Malaya, Laos and Cambodia, as well as in many of the islands which today constitute the Republic of Indonesia. With them came iconographies and artistic concepts which served the secular and spiritual needs of the many states which preceded those of modern South-East Asia. Thus it has been claimed that the greatest achievements of Indian art are to be found overseas, at Angkor Wat and Borobudur, in the jungles of Cambodia and the plains of central Java. There developed in the various countries of South-East Asia a series of artistic traditions which owed their origins and much of their basic repertories to India, but such traditions were centred on the courts where a greater or lesser degree of indianization was *de rigueur*.

Outside these centres, native arts and crafts continued to flourish: pottery, bark-cloth, textiles (some woven from pre-dyed threads, others wax-resist dyed or embroidered), confections in feathers, rattans or plaited leaves, modelling and carving in wood and stone. It was the existence of these older traditions and their persistence in peripheral areas which influenced the local treatments of Indian themes to distinguish Khmer from Burmese, Thai from Indonesian, Javanese or Sumatran from Balinese. Sometimes these older traditions emerged as the dominant element; sometimes there was a reaction from trends which seemed to deviate too far from Indian artistic propriety as defined in the Sanskrit texts available to South-East Asian orthodoxy. Then there would be a period of archaism in which the artistic styles of the courtly centre would show a reversion towards what was conceived of as a purer, more proper form (though its by then remote Indian origin might remain unrecognized by those who urged its acceptance).

It is difficult to claim for any of the artistic achievements of South-East Asia that they are certainly of native origin. Even the famous *batik* cloths of Indonesia (in which wax is used to reserve areas of the textile while the rest is immersed in dye) and the *ikat* technique (in which threads dyed at predetermined points prior to weaving are used for the warp and, less often, for the weft as well) may have originated in India. As in other arts and crafts, there were local improvements in technique. It is in terms of what they achieved in other peoples' arts rather than in originality of conception that the artists of South-East Asia must be assessed.

The Bronze Age

The use of metal, whether bronze or iron, did not reach South-East Asia until well into the first millennium B.C., while the use of stone axes, adzes, digging implements and the like persisted in some marginal areas until the 19th century; in New Guinea until the present-day. Once metallurgical techniques had reached the area however there was an astonishing efflorescence and for one or two centuries before and after the beginning of the Christian era a range of objects in bronze (the alloy often containing a high admixture of lead) was produced which showed a notable degree of artistic as well as technical attainment.

Bronze objects, including drums, have long been known from South-East Asia; the first drum entered a European collection in the 17th century. But none had been found *in situ* until 1927 when a Bronze Age dwelling site and cemetery were discovered at Dong-son in northern Vietnam. This village has given its name to the whole bronze-using culture of South-East Asia, although there is evidence to suggest that in Burma, at least, there was a different bronze-using tradition employing an alloy without the high lead content to manufacture objects in a style clearly distinguishable from the Dong-son.

A wide range of objects of Dong-son culture has been found, of which the most remarkable are the bronze kettledrums of all sizes, from miniature models used as grave-goods to great ceremonial drums with a head more than a metre in diameter. The whole of the surface of the drum-head is covered with designs arranged in concentric rings. The decorations are both geometric—triangles, spiral and tangent and the like—and naturalistic—birds, animals, reptiles, fishes and human figures, often in elaborate feathered costumes. Human figures are portrayed dancing, playing upon mouth organs, castanets and drum or gong-chimes, pounding rice, or travelling, perhaps as war-parties, in canoes. Their long-houses are also depicted. The weapons shown include bows and curious foot-shaped axes, examples of which are known from Dong-son sites. The bodies of the drums have somewhat similar decorations. All motifs are in linear style, sometimes with hatching. All the decorations were cut into the stone moulds in which these astonishing instruments were made.

Although the idea of using metal, and the actual metallurgical techniques, were introduced from outside, almost certainly from China, the drums and the décor as a whole, with the possible exceptions of some filler motifs, were native South-East Asian products. There is, on the other hand, little evidence of statuary in metal at this period; only one figure is known from the Dong-son culture. One or two other bronze figurines are known from Indonesia, but their exact provenance and dating is most uncertain. On the other hand, a site in Yunnan, Shih Chai Shan, has recently furnished evidence for a bronze-using culture, extremely rich in figure casting, which has links with that of Dong-son. We may expect therefore to find evidence for such art in South-East Asia proper as archaeological investigation proceeds.

At first the imagers seem to have been content to copy small images of Indian origin. These same images may also have served as models for their fellows who worked as stone-carvers. Later local traditions developed and the work was no longer confined to small pieces; the head of a Vishnu from the West Mebon, Angkor, dating from the middle of the 11th century is almost one-and-a-half metres high. This was made by the same *cire-perdue* process used in the production of the small Khmer figurines which have long been prized by collectors and museum curators. The bronze-casters' skill was also in demand for the production of the gong-chimes and metallophones which figure so strongly in the orchestras of Java, Bali and parts of mainland South-East Asia.

Side by side with the bronze tradition went a skill in jewellery and goldsmithery which served both for adornment of the gods and for the decking of their worshippers. Sites from the Mekong Delta furnish evidence for jewellery, including much work in tin, dating from early in the Christian era. The use of goldleaf to embellish carved woodwork and stone developed as did the use of glass mosaic. Bronze statues of deities were also gilded.

In the Indonesian world at least the blacksmith held an honoured place as the maker of the *keris*. He was addressed as *Mpu*, a title of honour accorded also to poets among others. The keris is more than a weapon: it is a magical and symbolic object which embodies its owner; its forging is a ceremonial act and its ornamentation a work of creative art in which the cutting and folding of normal and meteoric irons, with repeated reforging, which may be combined with gold-wire inlaying, produce an elegant blade set in a handle carved to represent a mythical creature or a heroic figure, or elegantly embellished with incised tendrils and other natural motifs.

Use of Wood

Techniques of working in stone were already established before the coming of Hinduism and Buddhism. What was new was the demand for buildings in that material, for the native faiths of South-East Asia required only simple shrines for which, as for royal and chiefly dwellings, wood, with bamboo and palm thatch, was deemed the proper material. Ceremonial buildings and long-houses of many tribal peoples in South-East Asia are still constructed with these materials, and richly carved and coloured.

Royal buildings and monasteries were built by master carpenters who also served as architects. Their principal tool was based upon an adze, in which the blade was hafted in such a way as to be capable of rotation through 360 degrees in a plane at right-angles to the shaft. This tool in various sizes is still the basic implement of the woodworker in many parts of South-East Asia, where a cutting tool with an adze has always been standard, rather than the axe blade typical of western Eurasia and palaeolithic Africa. (This form is probably related to the widespread use of bamboo whose siliceous skin is more easily cut by a blade with an adze-pattern edge than with an axe.) Split bamboo woven into patterns served as walling for these buildings, whose framework was either of tree trunks or bamboos fixed with wooden pegs and lashed with rattans. Later, carved wood panelling took the place of the woven walls, and the pillars were decorated with lacquer (the use of which seems to have been introduced from China), or with glass mosaic or gold leaf. Gold leaf was also applied to the carved wood and to the accent pieces on the gable ends and ridge poles.

Intricately carved hilts of swords and daggers, as well as spoons and other domestic items, are commonly to be found among the tribal peoples. These, with the ornate buildings on monastic and royal sites both ancient and modern, as well as those in tribal areas, suggest that wood and other forest products are the materials best suited to the artistic genius of the peoples of South-East Asia.

Architectural Variety: Indonesia

The approach to the nature of sacred buildings varies throughout South-East Asia. The *stupa* (shrine), which somewhat resembles a pointed helmet in shape, is the typical sacred building throughout the Buddhist world. In Java, however, there are no stupas, with the exception of the best known of all Indonesian monuments, the 9th-century Chandi Borobudur. This building with its great open galleries, their walls covered in relief carvings of the Buddha's life and previous lives, and stories to illustrate the search for the true Doctrine, its square platforms giving way to round ones crowned with lattice stupas and culminating in a single austere central stupa, and with the outer walls of each of its sides set with ritually determined figures of future Buddhas, is in all probability a dynastic centre as well as a place of Buddhist worship. It is tempting to see its form as reflecting some older type of religious symbolism, perhaps to be linked with the Dong-son culture.

Elsewhere in Java the preference is for the single building, with a smaller shrine facing it to house the deity's sacred mount: Shiva's bull; the garuda on which Vishnu rides. Such pairs could then be grouped in sets as at Prambanan and given a further cosmic significance by being installed in an enclosure to represent the world's encircling mountains and ocean. In Sumatra on the other hand, there is evidence for the existence of conventional stupas, while in Bali the houses of the gods are conceived of most often as unoccupied thrones, open to the sky, on to which the god can be invited with appropriate rites and ceremonies. These thrones may be grouped in courtyards with buildings serving various functions in the rites. It was in Bali too that there developed a style of genre carving as part of the decoration of a temple site: ultimately this gives rise to such things as a panel representing an official on his bicycle whose wheels and sprockets develop tendrils and leafy sprays, or a party of Dutchmen going for a picnic in their motorcar.

There have grown up in the present century a number of centres where carvers worked on wooden figures specifically designed as objets d'art. Alongside traditional religious pictures and images, pictures too came to be produced in styles which owed much to the influence of European artists who settled in Java. These illustrate what is so typical of South-East Asian art: the way in which the local genius imposed its own patterns upon imported cultures to produce truly indigenous styles and systems.

The Mainland

This process can be seen on the mainland of South-East Asia also. Among the Chams of central Vietnam, brick-built towers, apparently conceived of as separate entities and juxtaposed without any regard to structural synthesis, were typical. But when the idea of building a tower sanctuary spread from the Chams to the Khmers in the 6th and 7th centuries, the latter were able first to translate the structure into stone and then to set about the process of elaborating a complex relationship between the separate towers, ultimately to produce the symbolism of Angkor Wat with its outer walls and moats, its inner courtyards and water-tanks, culminating in the quincuncial inmost shrine which was the world axis, Sumeru the world-mountain. This symbolism, well developed in Indian cosmological systems, is found also throughout South-East Asia where it is expressed in a number of forms of which the temple is only the most obvious.

Elsewhere in the region, both stupa and temple developed along local lines. At Pagan in central Burma well over 6,000 separate shrines of Buddhist intention were constructed in the period 1000-1280, all of them in brick and the largest of immense size. Here there developed styles of mural painting and the use of glazed panels with figures in relief to exemplify the Doctrine for the worshippers.

What happened at Pagan serves to exemplify the typical pattern of artistic development in South-East Asia. Indian influences reached central Burma through the Mons, a people related to the Khmer further to the east who occupied lower Burma and parts of central Thailand at the end of the 5th century. Other influences came from India to Burma across the frontier with Assam and reached the Pyu, a Tibeto-Burmese people who preceded the Burmans in South-East Asia by several centuries. There grew up a hybrid culture upon which the coming of the Burmans in about the 10th century acted as a catalyst to produce a new national tradition out of which modern Burmese culture has evolved. The main roots were Indian, though native elements can be traced in it at every stage. During the Pagan period Chinese influences made themselves felt, and one major introduction, that of lacquer, became a characteristically Burmese craft. After the fall of Pagan the various artistic developments and the architectural styles which evolved then set the pattern for the future. Such changes which took place subsequently were small and it was only with European influence that any marked changes were to be seen. But these were largely derivative and there has not yet been time for a non-traditional Burmese art to emerge. Much the same comment can be made about the other countries of South-East Asia, though in each there have been certain developments of interest.

Thailand and northern Vietnam produced during the 13th and 14th centuries local ceramic industries of some scale and importance, established under Chinese influence. The best known are those of Sukhodaya and Sawankalok (14th-15th centuries.) The wares of the former are mostly in decorated glazed stone and resemble those of Tzu-ch'ou in China, while the wares of the latter more closely resemble those of Luang-ch'uan. This reference back to China is characteristic of Vietnam, and it is noteworthy that when the Emperor Gia Long (1802-1819) set about establishing national unity in his country, he took China as his model, and made his capital at Hue a copy of the so-called Forbidden City at Pekin. The Nguyen Dynasty tombs were modelled, though poorly, on those of the Ming Dynasty.

The Filipino Style

In the Philippines alone has there been a real emergence of a new artistic tradition with the growth of schools of painting which, though obviously influenced by the Ecole de Paris, have not been swamped by it. Filipinos paint in styles which can properly be called 'Filipino' and not simply 'traditional', exhibit locally and see their pictures bought by their fellow-countrymen, not because they are required for religious or ritual ends but because they are paintings. There are signs that a similar pattern is emerging in parts of Indonesia.

The Present Situation

These signs of change notwithstanding, the arts in South-East Asia are, in general, still in the traditional phase. Their primary function is social, and where they have emerged as purely 'artistic' the trend has been towards a copy of Western styles. Sometimes, in the interest of nationalism, there has been a deliberate harking back to classical models which in any case have remained the ideal of the majority of the cultured classes. The growth of popular art and cinema, radio and television must clearly alter this; to some extent the traditional culture, centred upon the court circle, has always been the preoccupation of the 'gentry'. But it has been this group, for instance in Java among the *priyayi* (an essentially urban class of bureaucrats), which has tended to set the tone for the whole and it is from them that Indian influence has reached out into villages. Thus although in Java probably only the *priyayi* really believe that the shadow theatre, the gamelan orchestra, the traditional myths (*lakon*), classical dancing and poetry and hand-made *batik* represent the only proper art, there are very few Javanese who do not share in this belief to a surprisingly large degree. So it is elsewhere in South-East Asia.

BIBLIOGRAPHY

A. H. Christie. 'The Sea-Locked Lands' in *The Dawn of Civilization*. (Thames and Hudson, London, 1961).

A. B. Griswold. 'Burma' in *Burma, Korea; Tibet*. (Methuen, *Art of the World* series, London, 1964.)

B. P. Groslier. *Indochina*. (Methuen, *Art of the World* series, London, 1962.)

F. A. Wagner. *Indonesia*. (Methuen, *Art of the World* series, London, 1959.)

BIOGRAPHICAL NOTE

Anthony Christie, M.A., was educated at the Universities of Manchester and London, where he is now Lecturer in the Art and Archaeology of South East Asia and the Islands in the School of Oriental and African Studies.

LITERATURE

MODERN INDIAN LITERATURE

by

KHUSHWANT SINGH

IN the last two decades since India has been independent there has been a tremendous outburst of literary activity in all vernacular languages. Book Trusts have been set up in many States to organize translation of foreign classics intothe provincial languages. These translations and works of eminent Indian authors are published at very low prices. The States also have literary academies which award prizes to writers and poets who have produced works of merit during the year. At New Delhi, the Sahitya Akademi does on a national scale what the State Academies and Book Trusts do on the provincial. The President and the Prime Minister take a keen interest in its affairs. Every year one work from each of the fourteen major languages is chosen and its author awarded a Rs.5,000 (£375) prize. The presentation is made by the President at a public function attended by foreign diplomats, cabinet ministers, civil servants and the literati. All India Radio, with its vast network of broadcasting stations, is a great patron of men of letters. A large number of poets and novelists are on its payroll and practically every Indian who writes earns something from broadcasting. A.I.R. organizes discussions on subjects like the contemporary novel, modern trends in poetry, problems of translation etc. which are relayed at peak listening hours. To these three Government-subsidized agencies—Book Trusts, the Sahitya Akademi and All India Radio—goes the credit for stimulating interest in literature. More has been published, produced and recited in the last decade than ever before in the history of the country. Hardly a month goes by, according to some enthusiastic critics, without a 'Bengali Shakespeare', or a 'Tamilian Scott' bursting in the literary firmament. By the time their works are made available to others in English (which is still the only language common to all educated Indians) the new discovery has been forgotten.

THE LANGUAGE SITUATION

Three aspects of this officially inspired renaissance in literature deserve attention. In the first place, there is a revival of Sanskrit as the classical language *par excellence*. What Greek and Latin are to European littérateurs, Sanskrit is becoming to the Indian. With Sanskrit has come a renewal of interest in Hindu religious literature: the Vedas, Upanishads, the epics Ramayana and Mahabharata (which includes the celebrated Bhagavadgita) and the works of ancient scholars, notably the poet-dramatist Kalidas (circa 3rd century A.D.). Secondly, Arabic, Persian and Urdu which may be loosely described as the languages of the Muslims are on the decline. Apart from

Kashmir and a few Muslim seats of learning like Aligarh, Osmania University at Hyderabad, the theological Seminary at Deoband in Uttar Pradesh, these languages are ceasing to be taught as subjects for examinations. Even Urdu which is recognized as one of the major languages of India is on the way out. At one time the centres of Urdu learning were Lucknow, Delhi and Hyderabad—all in India. Today they are at Lahore and Karachi in Pakistan. Thirdly, English is being replaced by Hindi as the language of communication. This has not only lowered the standard of English taught in the universities and prejudiced the future of the Indo-Anglian writers but is also gradually shutting off Indians from live contact with contemporary English and European literature.

The Novel

Who are the prominent writers of modern India? In the last eight years the Sahitya Akademi has honoured sixty-eight novelists, dramatists and poets for significant contributions to the literature of their respective languages. Fortunately many of the prize-winning works have been translated into English, but the English translations strangely do not bear testimony to the greatness claimed by the protagonists of contemporary Indian literature. It has however to be conceded that a translation can seldom, if ever, do justice to poetry—and poetry is the most popular form of literature in India. We can however presume that any great work of prose will stand the test of translation—provided the translator knows his job. Many Indians know the English language well, and it can be further presumed that the translations sponsored by the Sahitya Akademi have been handled by competent men. UNESCO and the Asia Society of New York have also financed translations of works of contemporary Indian writers into English. The fate of these translations is at least one indication of the quality of the original. A few short stories have found their way into *avant garde* English and American magazines. Of the dozen or more Indian novels only two, *Umrao Jan Ada*, a biographical novel of the life of a courtesan of Lucknow by Mohammed Ruswa and *Chemmeen* by Thakazhi Sivasankar Pillai of Malabar have found English publishers. If the opinions of readers of publishing houses are to be accepted—a not altogether unreasonable criterion of judgment—modern India has produced very little prose of any quality. In India itself it is now reluctantly admitted that the present is an age of mediocrity.

There are many reasons for the failure to produce good writers. The leisured rich upper middle class which produced Rabindranath Tagore and Sir Mohammed Iqbal has ceased to exist. The best brains, including the creative, are absorbed by the civil service and commerce. Those who fail to get better jobs take to journalism—and writing. The Indian writer is academically ill-equipped, his vocabulary limited and his knowledge of contemporary literature of other parts of the world extremely hazy. This is evident from his writing. It lacks subtlety, humour and appreciation of nature. No Indian has been able to paint his country's landscape for the simple reason that he does not know the names of the flora and fauna. Nevertheless, to be a 'progressive' is *de rigueur*. To keep up with the literary Joneses he will inject in his narrative heavy doses of Communist propaganda or chunks of sexy cheese-cake and describe it as psycho-analytical. And if he cannot affix either the Marxist or the Freudian label to his writing, he will claim that it is 'existentialist'.

An equally strong reason for the poverty of the Indian novel is the absence of tradition. It is claimed by Sanskritists that the novel as a literary form was known to the classical writers before the Muslim invasions which began in the 7th century A.D. Even if that be true, there is little doubt that for over a thousand years no Indian language has produced a novel of any significance and we can therefore start from scratch with its introduction under British rule.

The earliest attempts by Indians were patterned after the popular British novelists of the time, notably Sir Walter Scott. Bankim Chandra Chatterjee was inspired by *Ivanhoe*. He was followed with greater success by Sarat Chandra Chatterjee. Neither of the Chatterjees, nor even Rabindranath Tagore who was so great a poet, succeeded as novelists. Tagore's best known *Gora*, which tells the story of an English foundling brought up in a Bengali home, fails to do justice to the theme. The greatest novelist of northern India, Prem Chand, who wrote both in Hindi and Urdu, is admired more for his language, his portrayal of Indian life and his patriotism than for the story element of characterization. What makes Prem Chand tedious is his didacticism—a temptation few Indians can resist—which turns his story into a sermon. Prem Chand's best known novel, *Godan*, translated under the auspices of UNESCO, failed to find a publisher in Europe or the United States.

In the last fifteen years India has not produced a great novelist—or even a great novel. All languages have, however, a string of good second-raters. Three themes recur in most of them. Transfer of power from British to Indian hands is still a very popular subject. Most novels of this genre tell of the wickedness of British rule; a few however are nostalgic about the Raj. Vatsayan, who was at one time a terrorist, has written this up in the form of an autobiography, *Shekhar* (Hindi); Yashpal who was a Communist has done the same from the Marxist angle in his *Desh Drohi*—Traitor (Hindi). It is also the theme of many English novels: Mulk Raj Anand's *Two Leaves and a Bud;* R. K. Narayan's *Waiting for the Mahatma;* Nayantara Sehgal's *Chocolate and Prison Cake;* Kamala Markandaya's *Some Inner Fury;* Abbas's *Inquilab*.

The partition of India and the massacres that followed the setting up of Pakistan have produced a spate of novels in northern Indian languages and English: Yashpal's *Jhoot Sach*—False Truth (Hindi), Amrita Pritam's *Pinjar*—the Skeleton (Punjabi) and most of Kartar Singh Duggal's post-partition novels and short stories. It is significant that despite the flood of hate-propaganda let loose by the Governments of India and Pakistan and the press of the two countries, neither the Indian nor the Pakistani writers have been contaminated by it. Partition literature is full of compassion and objectivity.

Now that memories of the British Raj have begun to fade, novelists have begun to write of poverty and rustic backwardness without exploiting it as propaganda against foreign rule. The most distinguished writer of this school was the late Bibhuti Bhushan Bandopadhya whose novels of the Bengal village life have been so admirably filmed by Satyajit Ray in the trilogy, *Pather Panchali*, *Aparajito* and *Apur Sansar*. The leading Bengali novelists of today, Tara Shankar Bannerjee, Manik Bandopadhya and Premen Mitra also write of the poorer sections of Bengalis—but with a socialist objective. Pillai's *Chemmeen*—The Shrimp (Malayalam) is perhaps the most successful novel in a vernacular language. It tells of the lives of Muslim fisher folk of the Malabar coast. Two Hindi novels with the same theme have been widely acclaimed: Phaneshwar Nath Renu's *Maila Anchal* (The Soiled Apron) in the dialect of the Bihar villagers and Mohan Rakesh's *Band Andherey Kamrey* (Closed, Dark Rooms) of the life in Delhi's bazaars.

Drama

Although India has a dramatic tradition going back several centuries, this has been restricted to an unsophisticated form of folk theatre or dramatization of religious epics like the Ramayana and the Mahabharata. Till 1947 not one Indian city had a theatre or troupe of professional actors. The only chance playwrights had of displaying their talents was by raising casts of amateurs and putting on plays in community halls. All India Radio gave playwrights their first real opportunity—but only for plays suited to broadcasting. In recent years theatres have been built in Calcutta, Bombay, Poona and Madras. At the Tagore Centenary celebrations in 1962, the Government announced a plan to build theatres in all large towns. In another few years the buildings will be completed. One hopes they will create schools of playwrights and actors.

The Short Story

Next to poetry, the most popular medium of expression is the short story, and the standard achieved in most languages is high. Even Tagore, who failed as a novelist, excelled in this medium. His most popular is *Kabuliwala*, a sentimental story of the attachment between a Bengali child and a Pathan money-lender. Prem Chand is also more renowned for his stories than for his novels. One of his most moving stories tells of a diminutive Hindu Babu who, in order to make himself out as a hero to his wife, made up stories of the way he stood up to his English boss. The climax is reached when the Englishman actually insults the Babu and so compels him to play out his heroic role. The Prem Chand tradition has been developed by Urdu writers—Rajinder Singh Bedi, Krishen Chandra, and Ali Abbas Hussaini.

Poetry

In a country where paper came late into common use, the practice grew of committing long passages to memory and reciting them to audiences. And poetry being a more spontaneous form of expression not dependent on learning, the peasant and the worker made his contribution with more uninhibited zeal than the erudite.

The most time-honoured institution in the cultural life of India is the poetic symposium—*Mushaira* or *Kavi Sammelan*. It exists in all linguistic groups and is the one place where an outsider can feel the true literary pulse of a language. The attendance at the annual Indo-Pakistan *Mushaira* where leading Urdu poets from the two countries meet is frequented by over 10,000 men and women. The leading Urdu poet of the day, Pakistan's Faiz Ahmed Faiz, will draw as large a crowd as the top film star of the Indian screen. Faiz's poems are sung in the streets and in the houses of courtesans.

The giants of Indian poetry have not been gone long enough to give us the chance to judge the stature of the present generation of poets. The names of Rabindranath Tagore (Bengali), Sir Mohammed Iqbal (Urdu and Persian), Vir Singh (Punjabi) and Vallathol (Malayalam) are still uttered with awe and their successors consequently treated with condescension. Bengal has not produced any one of the calibre of Tagore, but it has a string of excellent minor poets: Nazrul Islam, Sudhin Datta (d. 1960), Budha Deva Bose and Premen Mitra. Hindi has its traditionalists: 'Nirala' (d. 1962), Mahadevi Varma and Sumitra Nandan Pant as well as 'Experimentalists' like Vatsayan and Suman. The *Kavi Sammelan* where a certain amount of stage-craft, a good voice and ability to recite are at a premium has its own favourites: Bacchan—who leads the revolt against Sanskritized Hindi (and has translated a lot of Shakespeare)—and Dinkar.

Punjabi, which is often dismissed as a rustic dialect or a bastard offspring of Hindi and Urdu has more vigour than either of its 'parents'. The two outstanding figures of Punjabi poetry are Mohan Singh and Amrita Pritam—both recipients of the Sahitya Akademi's awards. Mohan Singh has gone through the 'Marxist' phase and is now only a passionate idealist who can put his emotions in powerful words. In a recently published poem he expressed his 'revolutionary' sentiment:

The pitch-black within the pitcher has burst
Spilling the milk-white of the moonlight;
'Tis time we talked of a new dawn
And gave up the gossiping of the night.

I grant that autumn's touch
Hath robbed some leaves of their sap.
Sorrow not for what is lost and gone
With hope anew fill thy lap.

How long on the ancient vault of heaven
Idle fantasies draw and hold them dear?
Come let us caress the earth's tresses
Come let us talk of something near.

Amrita Pritam is now the rage of littérateurs in both the Punjabs—the Pakistani and the Indian. She is more spontaneous than erudite; she does not experiment in new forms and there is always a nostalgic strain of the old Punjabi ballad in her poems. The love for bejewelled phrase, the lilt of words often wafts her away from the central theme. But she remains eminently readable. Amrita's good looks make her the biggest draw at Punjabi poetic symposia. In a poem—one of her own favourites—the lover addresses his sweetheart:

Awake, my love!
Thy eyes are heavy with dreams,
Dreams of days gone by,
When breezes were with odours woven.
(Does that make thee sigh?)
Out of the black of the moonless night
Let a myriad stars thy tresses light.

Indian Writers in English

Many Indians write English uncommonly well. Nehru, Radhakrishnan, Krishnamurthy and Nirad C. Chaudhuri have made their mark as writers of good, forceful prose. The phenomenon does not extend to the works of fiction where with some notable exceptions the Indian novelists have been content to cultivate the use of Indianisms. Some good novels have however been written. Govind Desani's *All About H. Hatterr*—(a brilliant piece of Joycean verbosity), R. K. Narayan's *The Guide* and *The Financial Expert;* Raja Rao's *Kanthapura* and *Serpent and the Rope*; Kamala Markandaya's *Nectar in a Sieve* and Ruth Jhabvala's *To Whom She Will* are amongst those that may live.

The performance of Indian poets in English has been a dismal one. First, there were the syrupy outpourings of the Dutt sisters and Sarojini Naidu's Lo-and-behold style of verse. They were followed by a host of poets who imitated Tagore where the meaning of words was lost in the haze of a mystic twilight. Then came the 'moderns' who deleted capital letters and punctuation, scissored their flamboyant prose and called it poetry. An exception to the general poverty of poetic talent is the young Dom Moraes—a Bombay born Goan whose only language is English and who has made his home in England. At twenty-one Moraes won the Hawthornden Prize for poetry with his collection of poems *A Beginning*. Since then he has produced two more collections—both acclaimed by English writers. Moraes' personal situation and loneliness is expressed in the following verse:

I have grown up, I think, to live, alone,
To keep my old illusions, sometimes dream,
Glumly, that I am unloved and forlorn.
Runaway from strangers, often seem
Unreal to myself in the pulpy warmth of a sunbeam.
I have grown up, hand on the primal bone,
Making the poem, taking the word from the stream,
Fighting the sand for speech, fighting the stone.

BIBLIOGRAPHY

Mulk Raj Anand. *The Coolie.* (Lawrence and Wishart, London, 1936.) *The Village.* (Jonathan Cape, London, 1939.)

Bhabani Bhattacharya. *So Many Hungers.* (Gollancz, London, 1947.)

Nirad C. Chaudhuri. *Autobiography of an Unknown Indian.* (Macmillan, London, 1951.) *Passage to England.* (Macmillan, London, 1959.)

Contemporary Indian Short Stories (Series I). (Sahitya Akademi 1959.)

Govinda V. Desani. *All About H. Hatterr.* (Saturn Press, London, 1949.)

Ruth P. Jhabvala. *To Whom She Will.* (Allen and Unwin, London, 1955.)

Kamala Markandaya. *Nectar in a Sieve.* (Putnam, London, 1954.)
Dom Moraes. *A Beginning.* (Parton Press, London, 1957.)
R. K. Narayan. *The Guide.* (Methuen, London, 1958.)
Thakazhi Sivasankar Pillai. *Chemmeen,* trans. R. Narayana Menon. (Harper Brothers, New York, 1962.)
Balchandra Rajan. *Too Long in the West.* (Heinemann, London, 1961.)
Santha Rama Rau. *Remember the House.* (Gollancz, London, 1956.)
Rabindranath Tagore. *Stories from Tagore.* (Macmillan, London, 1927.)
Khushwant Singh. *Train to Pakistan.* (Chatto and Windus, London, 1956.)
Who's Who of Indian Writers. (Sahitya Akademi, 1961.)

BIOGRAPHICAL NOTE

KHUSHWANT SINGH. Educated in England; practised law at Lahore till partition. Thereafter with the Indian Ministry of External Affairs (posted in Canada and London), All India Radio and the Planning Commission (edited *Yojana*). In 1958 the Rockefeller Foundation gave him a long-term grant to carry out research in Sikh history which resulted in a two-volume *History of the Sikhs* (Princeton Univ. Press, Princeton, N.J., 1963–), *Ranjit Singh—Maharajah of the Punjab* (Allen and Unwin, London, 1963) and *The Fall of the Kingdom of the Punjab* (Orient Longmans, 1962.) Indian delegate to Writers' Conference, Edinburgh Festival, 1962, and leader of the Indian delegation at the meeting of Asian Writers organized by PEN International at Manila in December 1962.

MODERN PAKISTAN LITERATURE

by

FAIZ AHMED FAIZ

In Pakistan, as in India, literature through the ages spoke in two voices, the polished, ornamental voice of the imperial or feudal courts, and the homely, unaffected voice of its many peoples, mainly composed of poor peasantry. There were, of course, corridors of communication between the two and some margin of co-mingling, but close, promiscuous inter-mingling—never. Each voice mirrored a world sufficient unto itself, the world of prince and courtier, a world of fancy and conceit, splendrous and cruel, of jewelled words, murderous loves, and treacherous jealousies; and the world of the itinerant minstrel, and the wandering saint, a world of earthly sorrows and divine compensation, of land and harvest, birth, marriage and death, of tribal feats, of mourning and festivity. What separated the two worlds was not social distance alone, but the spoken word itself. For the courts, Hindu, Muslim or British, spoke in the 'classics,' Sanskrit, Persian, English, and the people spoke in many tongues, according to the land of their birth, east, west, north or south, Pashto, Punjabi, Brij or Bengali. The two worlds persisted until the end of the social system which gave them birth, and this was in the middle of the 19th century, when the British finally abolished the fiction of the last imperial Mogul court in Delhi, and the reality of most of the feudal principalities. In the process they also bundled out bard and saint, the court poet and feudal protégé and set the best of them to manufacture something completely new which belonged neither in the feudal nor in the folk world of old. In the institutions founded by the new rulers, in Calcutta, Delhi and Lahore, literary practitioners laboured over creating a new literary ethos, mainly based on Matthew Arnold, a new poetry based on Wordsworth, Tennyson and Longfellow, and a new fiction based on Walter Scott, Jane Austen and Thackeray. This 'modern movement' naturally soon outgrew its prescribed specifications. Writers asked to forget the sake and the wine-cup, the candle and the moth, the rosebud mouth and the magic eye, and to concentrate instead on the splendours of Nature and the urgency of social reform, performed their chores so well that what began as a formal literary exercise ended up as passionate social-awareness, irrevocably committing the writer to a political purposefulness he had never known before. The best of them have remained so 'committed' ever since.

Tagore and Iqbal

The early decades of the 20th century saw the culmination of this process in the work of two giant figures, Rabindranath Tagore in the East, and

Sheikh Mohammed Iqbal in the West, who dominated the literary landscape of un-divided India until the late twenties. Unlike the earlier writers of the 19th century, their acquaintance with Western literature was not perfunctory and externally guided, but masterful and absorbed. They were, therefore, neither copyists nor imitators, but original creators of a completely new synthesis between ancient tradition and modern practice and thought. Each added to his own literature, Urdu and Bengali, new dimensions of experience and expression, and thus liberated the later writers from the limitations which their ancestors never even attempted to transcend.

Tagore, soft-eyed and lyrical, even partially bridged the gulf between the folk and classical traditions of old and brought to his verse not only the high polish of phrase, but also the simple lilt of the fisherman at his net, and the peasant at his plough. But then his task was easier than Iqbal's because in the East the spoken and the literary language is the same, namely Bengali, while in Western Pakistan the literary language, Urdu, which Iqbal wrote in, although closely allied to the spoken languages of the region, Pashto, Sindhi and Punjabi, is not spoken as a mother tongue except by a very small minority of the people. Perhaps wisely then, Iqbal, hard-voiced and discursive, did not attempt to depart from the high classicism of his forebears.

Before Independence

In the twenties wave after wave of rebellious sentiment swept over the sub-continent, each relating to a different field of social experience, but all contributing to a collective mood of iconoclasm, euphorical romanticism and colourful dreams. This was the period when the Indian Nationalist movement gathered momentum, the hey-day of literary journalism, the Indian summer of the short-lived national theatre, when the gay lyricism of Hafeez, Akhtar Sherani, Hasrat Mohani, was born; it produced the brilliant wit of 'Pataras' (A. S. Bokhari), the biting polemical verse of Zafar Ali Khan, the wonderful rhetoric of Nazar-ul-Islam, the eloquence of Abul Kalam Azad, and a host of modern 'ghazal' writers, Asghar, Jigar, Fani and others. It saw the birth of romantic fiction, mainly through the pen of Yaldrum, Niaz and Mirza Saeed, and added to the sense of political and social emancipation, it brought to literature a new daring in experiment, a new freedom in the exploration of experience, and an impatience, not only with the ancient classics, but also with the modern dominant influences, particularly of Tagore and Iqbal.

Beginning with the thirties, and during the long and bitter years of the Great Depression before the Second World War, this rebelliousness hardened and solidified into a conscious and organized politico-literary movement, the movement of the Progressive Writers. This school inherited, on the one hand, the social awareness of the great social reformist writers of the 19th century, and on the other the literary experimentalism of the twenties. But the new writers found that neither of these answered either to the intensity of their personal suffering or to the reality of the social situation around them. They found no counterpart in the earlier writing for the new urban working-class, for the humiliation and the deprivations they had to pass through, for the rise of Fascism in Europe, and the Spanish Civil War.

This produced a literature which was varyingly bitter protest, stark realism, strident satire or tender humanism and lacerating self-pity.

Parallel to this a contrary subjectivist movement also flourished which concentrated on a personal idiom to convey details of personal emotional exploration. This was a period of the rise and perfection of the short story, the political lyric, of free verse and extremely sensitive literary criticism. Most of the established writers in Pakistan today, both in the East and the West, began their career somewhere around these years, beginning with the middle thirties and ending with the coming of independence in 1947. The names which rose to celebrity during this period included among others Jasimuddin, Abul Mansur Ahmed, Farukh Ahmed, Motahar Hussain, Sayed Walliullah, Ahsam Habeeb in Bengal, and Rashid, Faiz, Miraji, Ghulam Abbas, Minto, Krishan Chander and Bedi in the Punjab. This was perhaps the period of our literature's closest communication with Western writing through the medium of contemporary leftish English and American writings on the one hand, and the earlier French symbolist writings on the other. Western literary names which have dominated, from time to time, the mental landscape of the Indo-Pakistan writers is a fascinating study by itself. The series begins, as was said earlier, with the Victorian and pre-Victorian writers towards the end of the 19th century, when the modern movement of Indian literature began. This was followed by a brief ascendancy of the aesthetes Pater, Oscar Wilde, Loti, Gautier in the twenties, and in the thirties by the great Russian realists, the Angry Young Men of the time, Auden, MacNeice, Isherwood, the Americans Dos Passos and Sinclair, and by the newly-discovered Baudelaire, Rimbaud and Verlaine.

By and large, the literature of this period is a record of hope and despair, of fortitude and suffering, of loneliness and identification, of violent cynicism and equally violent social protest. But the whole of it is informed by the light of a unified dream, the dream of personal and social salvation, symbolized in the image which continues to dominate our writing to the present day, the image of dawn, or morning, which meant Freedom. This freedom came in 1947, and Pakistan was born.

Independence

But the new freedom was scarred by bloodshed and social and political confusion. The writing in Pakistan since independence faithfully reflects this confusion. Only a fraction of it carries the mood of fulfilment; the rest is either a continuation of the conflicting mood and temperament of the previous two decades with such amendments and modifications as the new environmental realities dictated, or, on a smaller scale, the expression of new emotive and experiential elements peculiar to this period.

The first of the latter is a body of nostalgic prose and verse mainly produced by the refugees who came to settle in West Pakistan after forcible eviction from their homes across the border. In poetry their nostalgia finds expression in the revival of the classical 'ghazal' form based on the sad and mournful lyrics written by the great masters of Urdu during the fading twilight of the Mogul Empire when the country was wracked by civil wars, the British invasion and marauding warriors of all descriptions and the poor poet of the time trudged from one tottering feudal court to another, in search of a living. In prose it took the form of stories, novelettes, and at least one outstanding novel, which described with loving detail the sleepy feudal ways of the zamindaris and townships of Oudh, and its surroundings, and lamented the demise of a way of life which the rough and tumble of a newly liberated country would no longer permit. Of these the evocative 'shikar' stories of Abul Fazl Siddiqui and the verse of a large number of younger writers, too numerous to name, provide excellent examples. It found its most outstanding exposition, however, in Quratul Ain Hyder's voluminous novel *Aag ka Darya* (The River of Fire), a rather complex composition, part allegory, part historical documentation and part autobiography. The novel seeks to trace the cultural, intellectual and emotional evolution of successive generations of young men and women from the time of Buddha to the present day, through a group of central figures who are transformed into their comparable counterparts in each succeeding epoch by suitable changes of name and habitat. The novel perhaps does not quite come off as a work of fiction because the devices employed by the writer to expound her thesis are a little too transparent, but it remains, nevertheless, a fine documentary on the various modes of sensibility that countless generations of the sub-continent have known; it displays a profound understanding of the intellectual and cultural movements in various historical periods and its description of the contemporary events immediately preceding and following independence are exquisitely beautiful.

Another theme, not entirely new, but never so consciously and deliberately propounded, is an array of religious, or pseudo-religious motifs. Unlike the nostalgic theme which is confined almost exclusively to the refugee writers in West Pakistan, the religious theme finds an echo in both East and West Pakistan alike, and is not confined to any age or cultural group. In fiction this particular thematic preoccupation has given rise to a kind of picaresque novel extolling the exploits of ancient Muslim heroes, real or legendary, in lands and periods glamorized by time and distance. In poetry it takes the form of heroic epics, moral homilies, hymns and eulogies. It is difficult to deny the sincerity of purpose in this particular form of writing, but then little of it carries the fine emotional rapture of the ancient mystics, or the profound intellectual content of Iqbal, and understandably, therefore, it has had little impact on the general body of contemporary writing.

A much more positive contribution, however, has come from the revival of interest in folk literatures of various regions, particularly in West Pakistan, and a renewal of creative writing in the regional spoken languages, Pashto, Sindhi, Balochi and Punjabi. Some of these literatures have a distinguished literary heritage, particularly in mystic and heroic verse, but the tradition has languished for nearly a hundred years or more, partly because of the ascendancy of Urdu, and partly because of the almost total discouragement of these languages in the educational system devised by the British administration. New writing in these languages, therefore, by lyricists like Abdul Ghani Khan in Pashto, by socio-political rhetoricians like Azad Jamaldini in Balochi and Ustad Daman in Punjabi, carry a vigour and freshness which is somewhat uncommon among their contemporaries following established literary traditions.

The main stream of contemporary writings, however, still follows the furrows already ploughed by the writers of the thirties and the early forties. There is, however, a difference. Many of the older writers, for instance, exhausted much of their anger and their pain during the long years of bitter waiting before independence came and their recent writings convey a sense of ideological fatigue and emotional attenuation, which contrasts strangely with their earlier work. There is a similar sense of satiety and impoverishment attaching to the well-worn verse and story themes, of starving clerks enamoured of rich men's daughters, unemployed idealists turned petty criminals, of the peasant who cannot pay his taxes and the refugee who cannot pay his rent. This does not apply to all the established writers, of course, and some of them, like N. M. Raschid, have even returned to consistent writing after long lapses of silence. The main compensation, however, is provided by a brand-new team of younger writers, particularly in East Pakistan, who have attained maturity after independence. Their main forte, at the moment, appears to be satire, and their main target, instead of the foreign colonial power of old, is the new Establishment. And for this again these new writers have discovered a new medium as well—drama. The Establishment might mean either the religious charlatan or theological dogmatist, finely satirized by Sayed Walliullah in *Bohi Pir*, or an impersonal repressive force equally powerfully lashed by Munir Chaudhuri in *Qabr*, or the new agencies of big money satirized in Nurul Momin's *Nemesis*. Finally, there are the Angry Young Men, a bunch of young people based in Lahore, writing in both Urdu and Punjab, who are experimenting with completely unorthodox forms.

The Theatre

The revival of dramatic writing and the theatrical arts is one of the most interesting post-independence developments in both East and West Pakistan. In undivided India a number of professional theatrical companies suddenly came to flourish in the early years of the present century and went into decline with equal speed towards the end of the twenties. The reasons for this dramatic rise and fall were almost purely commercial. The large British communities in big towns like Calcutta, Bombay and Madras had brought the tradition of amateur theatricals with them which suggested to some enterprising Parsi businessmen of the time the obvious lucrative possibilities of organized entertainment for the new urban citizenry. So they set about manufacturing their own version of the Western theatre—a rather weird mixture of melodrama, vaudeville, 'morality' play and operetta rolled into one. Even though these adventurous pioneers were mainly interested in mass entertainment and had little use for literary or artistic values as such, the good money they paid attracted to their enterprise considerable talent from diverse fields—writers, composers, musicians and stage actors. Some of the plays written for this theatre, therefore, had considerable literary merit in spite of their rather fantastic formal structure. It created besides a new music and a new spoken idiom by an imaginative synthesis of the classical and popular forms, a legacy which its successor, the sound film, found invaluable. And it was the sound film which put the old Indian theatre to sleep when its financial patrons transferred their money and affection to this new attraction from the West.

The theatre, however, did not entirely die. In Calcutta, contemporaneously with the Urdu or Hindustani plays written for the commercial theatre, a more catholic and more sophisticated drama also came to be written, not by professional hacks, but by such revered celebrities as the great Tagore himself. It is this tradition of the literary rather than the commercial drama which has been transplanted to Dacca by the new writers of East Pakistan most of whom were educated in Calcutta and knew the Calcutta stage.

In West Pakistan it was different. With some rare exceptions, the best of Urdu writers never took the same interest in drama as in poetry or fiction and after the decline of the professional theatre the only Urdu writings in this genre were short broadcast plays written for the sound radio. The best of these came from the pen of former theatre enthusiasts like Imtiaz Ali Taj and Rafi Peerzada, but because of the inherent limitations imposed by the medium itself as well as the official expediencies of the State Radio, the scope and influence of radio drama remained rather severely restricted. The stage and drama movement which has taken shape in West Pakistan in the last few years thus appears to have only one link with the past and this was provided neither by eminent writers nor by the professional theatre, but by amateur groups, more notably by the Dramatic Society of Government College, Lahore. It was mainly this institution which provided the nucleus of writers, actors and producers for the new amateur theatre now successfully performing at Lahore and Karachi with the financial and technical sponsorship of the Pakistan Arts Council. These groups unlike their contemporaries in East Pakistan are more interested in the stage and production rather than in the literary side of the new experimental theatre and the bulk of their productions have been adaptations of Western successes old and new—Ibsen, Chekhov, Shaw, O'Neill—rather than original writings. The only notable exception perhaps was *Lal Qila se Lalu Khet Tak* by Khwaja Mueenud Din, a bitter exposé of the plight of immigrant refugees which owed its success to the brilliant direction of Zia Mohyeddin who later made a name for himself in the Oxford Playhouse production of *A Passage to India*. There is no doubt that the continuing success of this amateur experiment will attract before long more creative and original contributions.

Space has permitted only the outline of a very intricate composition to be sketched in, a composition which is for ever unfinished because of its inner dynamic vitality, constantly reaching out in new directions towards new points of expression and communication. Contemporary writing in Pakistan today gives ample demonstration of this manifold and dynamic vitality.

BIBLIOGRAPHY

G. Allana. *Introducing Pakistani Poetry.* (Pakistan Writers' Guild, Karachi.)
A. S. Bokhara. *Urdu Writers of Our Time.* (Pakistan PEN Publications, Karachi.)
Jatra or Bengali Folk Drama. (The Pakistan Quarterly, Karachi.)
Poems by Faiz. Trans. V. G. Kiernan. (Indian People's Publishing House, Delhi.)
Poems by Iqbal. Trans. V. G. Kiernan. (John Murray, London, 1955.)

Poems by Nazrul Islam. (Pakistan Publications, Karachi.)
Quratul Ain Hyder. *The Exiles.* (Pakistan PEN Publications, Karachi.)
Rashed Hussain. *Ballads of East Pakistan.* (The Pakistan Quarterly, Karachi.)
Abdul Latif. *The Influence of English on Urdu Literature.* (Writers Emporium, Bombay.)
Sarwar Morshed (ed.) *Contemporary Writing in East Pakistan.* (New Values Publications, Dacca.)
M. Sadiq. *Twentieth Century Urdu Literature.* (Taraporewala and Co., Bombay.)
Dr. Shahidullah. *Muslim Bengali Literature.* (Bengali Academy, Dacca.)
S. A. Vahid. *Iqbal—His Art and Thought.* (John Murray, London, 1959.)

BIOGRAPHICAL NOTE

Faiz Ahmed Faiz, poet, critic and journalist, born Sialkot (West Pakistan) 1911, was educated at the Scottish Mission High School, Sialkot, and at Government College, Lahore. He began his career as a teacher of English language and literature in 1935 and taught at various institutions in Lahore. After the outbreak of the Second World War he joined the Indian Army in 1942, was decorated (M.B.E.) and resigned in December 1946 with the rank of Lieut.-Colonel. In February 1947 he took up the editorship of the English daily, *The Pakistan Times*, and later the chief editorship of a chain of publications brought out by the same concern, *Progressive Papers Limited.* Resigned in April, 1959, when the concern was taken over by the military Government in Pakistan. Later in the same year he assumed the General Secretaryship of the Pakistan Arts Council and re-organized it into a multi-purpose cultural organization. He also worked as a trade union and social welfare organizer, broadcaster and film script writer. Selections of his verse have appeared in translation in English, Czech, Russian, Chinese, Hindi and Bengali.

MODERN CHINESE LITERATURE

by

CYRIL BIRCH

LITERARY activity in China on the eve of the Japanese invasion in 1937 was extraordinary in its variety and promise. There had been twenty years of conscious effort to fashion from the modern spoken language and from the models offered by recent European practice a literature which would replace the rejected classical tradition. Now, with novels like Mao Tun's *Midnight* and Lao She's *Rickshaw Boy*, with the plays of Ts'ao Yü and the poetry of Pien Chih-lin and Tsang K'o-chia, the 'new literature' had come of age.

The war itself saw some fine work, short stories by Chang T'ien-yi, or *Winter Night* which is probably the best novel of the prolific Pa Chin; but its general effect was to depress the standards so recently attained. The pressure of events was too great, the need for mass communication too obvious to permit much creative life at a level higher than the production of patriotic propaganda. First to suffer were the more experimental and 'difficult' modes of verse; the stylish contemplative essay was next to disappear. As the war dragged on, the advocates of proletarian literature tended to dominate the scene to an ever greater extent.

This process was only accelerated by the rise to national power of the Communist Party in the years following the war with Japan. By the time of the establishment of the People's Republic in 1949, practically all major Chinese writers had accepted not only Communist rule but the general line of Marxist literary theory. Apart from one outstanding novel, *The Whirlwind* by Chiang Kuei, writing on Taiwan in the years of Chinese Nationalist rule has tended towards nostalgic or escapist fantasy; outside China, probably the only creative writer of the front rank is Eileen Chang, who left the mainland in 1952 and is now domiciled in the U.S.A.

PARTY GUIDANCE

The decisive step in the formulation of the literary theories of the Chinese Communists and their imposition on writers was taken in May 1942 when a series of 'talks' was held in Yenan. The policies laid down by Mao Tse-tung himself during these meetings with leading writers have been merely elaborated since that date, notably by the authoritative critic Chou Yang. Cornerstones of the directives are the subordination of creative activity to the requirements of national policy; the satisfaction of the cultural and educational needs of the masses of workers, peasants and soldiers as the primary objective; and the necessity for the creative artist to 'make himself one' with these masses. The 'down to the countryside' movement was instituted to cilitate the latter process. Although writers have no doubt profited from ›ells of sojourn and productive labour in the villages (or, in later years, on ›e Korean front or in factories) to gather material and to develop a com- .and of more naturalistic dialogue, it would appear that participation in the .ovement has sometimes been imposed as a disciplinary measure.

The primary national organization of writers in Communist China is the /riters' Union, whose chairman is the leading pre-war novelist Mao Tun. his Union is affiliated with the general Federation of Literary and Art /orkers, whose president is the poet and dramatist Kuo Mo-jo. Neither of ›ese two men has been very productive of creative work since 1949. 'ational congresses of the Federation were convened in 1949, 1953 and 1960. . is principally at these congresses that stock is taken of recent achievement . the cultural field and that, for writers in particular, announcement is .ade of those items of policy which in their future work they should be ›ost concerned to expound and interpret.

The seal of official approval is conferred on a writer by publication of his 'ork in one of the leading literary periodicals such as the monthly *People's iterature*, or in book form by a major publishing house such as the Authors' ›ress or the People's Literature Press, or by the selection of his work for ublication in translated form by the Foreign Languages Press. Distribution f approved work is widespread: the first printing of a new novel by an stablished writer may run to a hundred thousand copies. Magazines or ublishing houses independent of Communist Party control no longer exist. 'he most authoritative critical journal is the *Literary Gazette*. All the above- ›entioned institutions are centred in Peking; there is also a wide network of rovincial and local branch presses and literary journals. All of these func- on as organs of control. In case of need, however, campaigns are mounted gainst works or writers considered pernicious. Major attacks have been .unched in both literary periodicals and the national press against the critic [u Feng, the leading woman novelist Ting Ling and the poet Ai Ch'ing mong numerous others.

THEMES

'he quality of literary work produced under such party guidance has uctuated. Emphasis in the years preceding 1949 was on the exposure of the ark side of pre-Communist society, and several successful pieces were added › a tradition of social criticism which dates back to the nineteen twenties. .mong these works were Ting Ling's novel of the land reform, *The Sun hines Over the Sang-kan River*, awarded a Stalin Prize, and the *yangko* play (a ›oken drama incorporating a type of folk-dance currently popular) *The Vhite-Haired Girl*, the product of a team of writers headed by Ho Ching-chih. .fter 1949 writers were urged to turn from exposure of past evils to glorifica- on of the achievements of the new society. The early years of the People's .epublic saw a mass of stereotyped productions by new and old writers.

Accepted and secure Communist writers did however succeed in creating ıodels for the new literature. As the land reform gave place to the co- perative movement in the countryside, novels like *Three Mile Bend* (by Chao hu-li) and later *Great Changes in a Mountain Village* (by Chou Li-po) reflected and interpreted this development and in the process created lively images o village life under the new regime. Liu Pai-yü, Ai Wu and others wrote i racy if melodramatic fashion of the heroism of Chinese troops in the Korea War. Less successful were the efforts to celebrate the industrial advances of th time: Ts'ao Ming's novel *Energy* remained supreme in this field until th appearance in 1957 of Ai Wu's *Steeled and Tempered.* Attempts in fictior drama and verse to portray convincing 'model workers' suffered most fror the harsh stamp of the stereotype. With what appears to be increasin frequency writers have tended to go back to the pre-Communist period fc their material, to treat themes from the early history of the Party (e.g. under ground work in Shanghai), episodes from the war against Japan or the Civi War, or even as a last standby the villainous landlords of former days.

For poets as for novelists public concerns have replaced personal. Lov and death, to consider two themes we might expect to clutch at the poet' heart, have been studiously neglected, unless the love is of a young village for the hard-working girl by his side in the fields, or the death is in action the self-sacrifice of a warrior. Lyrical eulogies of the blessings of socialisn are now at the centre of poetic production. These may be highly topical almost instantaneously celebrating a record harvest or the completion of a new dam. Or they may be on the popular theme of contrast, such-and-suck a place revisited, its former decay and misery transformed now into greer crops and happy laughter, the glories of its ancient historical past recalled and outshone by the achievements of its modern industry.

Technique

In form and diction there is the greatest conceivable variety, and skilfully worked poems are by no means rare. Pre-Communist poets had pioneerec the introductions of neologisms, even of political jargon, into lines which would still sound Chinese. The trend since 1949 has been away from thei irregular or varied metre, back to the more compact, regular line, based ir fact on the seven-syllable, four-beat line which was a staple of classica poetry as well as of much folk verse. The scrupulously restricted and refinec classical vocabulary has of course yielded place to an absolute license tc incorporate peasant diction or Marxist terminology into a more readily intelligible modern syntax; and in partial consequence of this the preciou classical economy and power of suggestion are no longer to be found. On the contrary, some of the most highly-acclaimed productions have been long narrative poems or ballads by T'ien Chien, Li Chi and others.

Poetic drama, on the other hand, has been at a standstill in comparison with the creation of new plays of the socialist realistic type. Although much discussion, under the head of 'reform of the traditional drama', was devoted to the improvement of production techniques and the editing out of 'feudal ideology', the major interest of playwrights has been in the field of purely spoken plays. Typical themes are socialist reconstruction (*Dragon's Beard Ditch*), production problems (*Taming the Dragon and Tiger*), and the revision of social attitudes (*The Test*). The dialogue of such plays, as indeed of much fiction also, represents real advance in the direction of natural, lively speech.

An important role in the undertaking to reach the most extensive public as been played by those who have worked to resuscitate folk forms. Some f these forms belonged in the past to an exclusively oral tradition, often cal in scale, and have become widely-known for the first time in modern roductions on contemporary themes. Many local variants of the traditional rama have been thus popularized, as have ballads, 'drum songs', 'dialogues' nd other short prose or verse items collectively known as *ch'ü-yi*. Well-known terary figures such as Lao She and Chao Shu-li have utilized folk forms, but ie great mass of material is the work of men otherwise unknown.

In addition to the specifically popular forms themselves, all genres have ome heavily under the influence of the popular literature of the past, notbly of such classic novels as *The Men of the Marshes*. Heroes of myth and gend, recalls of the narrative techniques of the market-place storytellers, and ferences to events and personages from the traditional stage are thickly attered through recent writings, even though (as is the case for instance ith the novels of Chou Li-po) the overall pattern may well be modified om the work of a Soviet Russian writer.

The 'Hundred Flowers' and the 'Great Leap Forward'

nstances can be found of a more sophisticated mode of writing which ttempts to depict more realistically the problems posed by life in a Comiunist society. The time of the greatest relaxation of control was the spring nd summer of 1957, when in the 'Hundred Flowers' period the Chinese ommunist leadership invited criticism. Writers previously silent then pubshed pieces strikingly different in content and style from the general run of opular entertainments and eulogies of the regime. Several stories printed i the issue of *People's Literature* for July 1957 were subsequently attacked for ieir destructive criticism of the behaviour of party cadres or for their egative attitude towards the new morality. Though not of outstanding uality, these stories had plausibility, sincerity and attempted elegance.

The subsequent repression, in the 'Anti-Rightist' movement, gave place in urn to the excesses of the 'Great Leap Forward' begun in 1958. Writers rove to keep pace with the claims of huge increases in agricultural and idustrial production by announcing ambitious quotas for their own creative ens. Although few of these quotas can have been filled, an unprecedented henomenon was the 'multi-million poem' movement launched at this time. mateur poets, worker and peasant and soldier poets were published in stronomical quantities. The typical 'do-it-yourself' poem of the new iovement was very short, of jingling metre and rhyme, and devoted to the oastful celebration of a single facet of production in field or factory. The omplementary development in prose was the 'short short story', a vignette gain on a theme to glorify some unprecedented feat of production.

In theoretical terms, the somewhat hysterical fervour of writing of this ind is justified by reference to 'revolutionary romanticism' as a necessary omplement to socialist realism. Whilst the realist-romantic argument dates ack in modern Chinese literature at least as far as the 1921 opposition of uo Mo-jo and Mao Tun, revolutionary romanticism appears to be an nevitable concomitant of the militant and obligatory optimism with which ommunist China marches towards its future.

BIBLIOGRAPHY

China Quarterly, London, January-March, 1963, and articles in earlier issues by S. H. Ch'e Cyril Birch and others.

Chinese Literature, Peking (English-language quarterly.)

C. T. Hsia. *A History of Modern Chinese Fiction.* (Yale Univ. Press. New Haven, 1961.)

Mao Tse-tung on Art and Literature. (Foreign Languages Press, Peking, 1960.)

TRANSLATIONS IN ENGLISH

All Men are Brothers (version by Pearl Buck of the popular classic *The Men of the Marshes* (Heritage Press, New York, 1948.)

Eileen Chang. *The Rice-Sprout Song* (Scribner, New York, 1955.) *Naked Earth* (Hong Kon 1956.)

Lao She (Lau Shaw). *Rickshaw Boy.* (Reynal and Hitchcock, New York, 1945.)

BIOGRAPHICAL NOTE

CYRIL BIRCH. B. 1925, Bolton, Lancashire; educated Bolton School and the University London. Began the study of Chinese in the School of Oriental and African Studies, Un versity of London, 1942. Served (mainly in Calcutta) in the Intelligence Corps of th British Army, 1944-47. Lecturer in Chinese, School of Oriental and African Studies, 194 60; presently Associate Professor of Oriental Languages in the University of California a Berkeley. Ph.D. in Chinese Literature 1954; publications include *Stories from a Min Collection* (London: Bodley Head, 1958), *Chinese Myths and Fantasies* (London: Oxfor University Press, 1960) and articles on traditional and recent Chinese literature in *Bullet of the School of Oriental and African Studies, Asia Major, China Quarterly* and elsewhere.

MODERN JAPANESE LITERATURE

by

DONALD KEENE

APANESE critics are usually at pains to distinguish 'post-war literature' from e more general category of 'literature since the war.' By 'post-war literature' ey mean the writings of authors who had not published prior to 1945, articularly those of an anti-traditional or even revolutionary bent. The xperiences which all Japanese writers have undergone since 1945 have been extraordinary, however, that with few exceptions even the works of the lder generation of writers must be treated under the heading of post-war terature.

When the war ended in 1945 almost all writers were in the embarrassing osition of having publicly supported a thoroughly discredited cause. Even riters on the extreme left had turned out blatantly patriotic compositions praise of the militaristic activities of the ultranationalists. The Governent enlisted the talents of most writers, sending them abroad to the farung regions conquered by the Japanese Army so that they might comemorate the victories. The poets especially had demonstrated great nthusiasm for the outbreak of the 'holy war' in December, 1941, and roughout the war vied with one another to celebrate the fall of Manila nd Singapore, or to hurl imprecations at the Americans and English. oné Noguchi, who at one time had enjoyed something of a reputation in the Vest for his fragile little English lyrics, declared in a poem entitled 'Slaughter em! The Americans and English are our Enemies!' that he hoped his ld American and English friends were already dead; if not, he announced, We'll slaughter you, friendship and all!' Hardly a year later, Japanese riters were denouncing with equal fervour everything to do with the war.

The 'Modern Literature' Group

he American Occupation ruled over Japan from August 1945 until April 952, but exerted surprisingly little pressure on literature. Initially, the merican authorities, afraid of a recrudescence of militarism, prohibited he sale of certain patriotic books as well as the performance of traditional lays which extolled the feudal morality. This concern was sometimes pushed comical extremes, but despite minor irritations, writers in Japan enjoyed nprecedented freedom. The freedom for some meant that they could ublish with impunity works of near pornography, after decades of puritanial restrictions; for others it meant a renewing of the 'proletariat' literature novement. One important result of the new literary activity was the foundaion in January, 1946 of the magazine *Modern Literature* (*Kindai Bungaku*), an event cited frequently as marking the true beginning of post-war literature. The *Modern Literature* group consisted at first chiefly of left-wing writers, but in a few years came to include outstanding men of many divergent opinions. The seriousness of these writers' absorption with literary problems, rather than any particular views which they expressed, gave the magazine its great prestige. Typical novelists of the group included Rinzo Shiina (born 1911), an existentialist markedly influenced by Dostoievsky; Hiroshi Noma (born 1915), a Communist whose novel *Zone of Emptiness* (1952) gave a brutally realistic portrayal of wartime army life; and Shinichiro Nakamura (born 1918), a writer of psychological fiction in the French tradition.

The Pre-War Generation

The general public could not respond with much enthusiasm to the work of these writers during the difficult years immediately following the war. The new novels were often couched in a deliberately ungainly Japanese idiom, as if to emphasize the differences between the authors and their romantic forebears. The outspoken and even exclusive concern of some novelists with social or philosophical problems seriously weakened the literary appeal of their books, and innumerable writers of less lofty principles were ready to meet the demand for entertainment, if necessary with pornography. The literature of greatest merit continued to be provided by the pre-war generation. Junichiro Tanizaki (born 1886) began serial publication of his major novel *The Makioka Sisters* in 1943, only to have the Government ban further publication after two episodes appeared, on the grounds that this was literature unsuited to wartime Japan. He continued to work on this novel during the war at his country retreat, and the publication of the three volumes of the completed work in 1946-47 marked the first important post-war literary achievement. Since then Tanizaki has produced a steady flow of novels and other writings, all acclaimed by the general public, who consider him to be the outstanding living Japanese writer. One will search in vain for Tanizaki's name, however, in accounts of post-war literature written by up-to-date critics, who dismiss as survivals of a distant past even such indisputable post-war creations as the sensational *The Key* (1956), and the hardly less surprising *Diary of an Old Lunatic* (*Futen Rojin Nikki*, 1962).

Another active figure of the older generation is Yasunari Kawabata (born 1899). He has never enjoyed the popularity of Tanizaki, no doubt because his novels are more complex and indirect, but in retrospect he may appear to have been a superior writer. *Thousand Cranes* (1951) and the extraordinary *Sleeping Beauties* (*Nemureru Bijo*, 1961) have demonstrated his continuing mastery of literary craftsmanship.

The 'Between' Generation

Between the older established writers and those of the *Modern Literature* group was the in-between generation of writers who had begun to publish before the war but achieved their reputations afterwards. Outstanding among them was Osamu Dazai (1909-1948), whose novels *The Setting Sun* (1947) and *No Longer Human* (1948) still attract many new readers, especially gamon high school and university students. Dazai's desperation and nihilism are tinged with a sense of humour which makes his descriptions of the nightmarish Japan immediately after the end of the war vivid even today, when most of the innumerable other accounts of the period have lost their immediacy. *No Longer Human*, in its strongly autobiographical manner, has also influenced much subsequent writing. The 'I novel', as autobiographical fiction has been known in Japan since the 1880's, though often seemingly about to disappear as a serious literary form, retains its importance today thanks to Dazai and others, and is considered not merely an acceptable kind of writing but a particularly important one. The very lack of structure or recognizable plot is taken as proof of purer literary qualities, and writers who have 'pandered' to the general preference for carefully plotted works may be restored to the ranks of serious writers if they publish an 'I novel', preferably one which suggests that the author speaks for a whole generation of unhappy, aimless souls.

The loneliness and isolation of the intellectuals, a favourite theme of serious novels, was given notable expression in the novel *Solitude in the Open Square* (*Hiroba no Kodoku*, 1951) by Yoshie Hotta (born 1918), believed by some critics to have inaugurated a new literary era. This novel deals with the uncertainties of a Japanese intellectual during the Korean War, in face of ideological conflicts represented by Communists, Americans and deracinated Chinese.

The Coming of Prosperity

The Korean War brought prosperity to Japan and thereby terminated the period of novels devoted largely to descriptions of shabbily clothed men scrounging for food in bombed-out sites. When Yukio Mishima (born 1925) published his first novel *Confessions of a Mask* (1949), concerned mainly with the narrator's inability, owing to his abnormal sexual inclinations, to make love to a woman, the critics assumed that this was another instance of the familiar post-war theme of impotence caused by malnutrition. But with the first post-war prosperity it became possible for authors to leave the grim realities of daily life and write with greater detachment and artistry. Shohei Ooka (born 1909), who first gained a literary reputation with the publication in 1948 of his photographically vivid *Prisoner's Record* (*Furyoki*), later distilled his wartime experiences into the unforgettable novel *Fires on the Plain* (1951), an example of a development observable also in the works of many lesser writers.

The best of the specifically post-war writers is probably Yukio Mishima, both for the extraordinary variety of his novels and plays, and for the conscious literary craftsmanship with which he has infused every work. Mishima has been most widely translated of the post-war Japanese authors, no doubt because he combines to best advantage a Western-trained sensibility with a Japanese eye for detail. His novel *The Sound of Waves* (1954) was conceived of by Mishima as a Japanese reworking of *Daphnis and Chloë*. He deliberately chose overly familiar characters and situations, but gave them new life by surrounding them with an unmistakeably Japanese atmosphere. He thereby transformed the ancient Greek tale, and used it to demonstrate his belief that the hidden, dark aspects of human life, which had furnished him with themes for his earlier works, were not the entire truth about men. In h later *Temple of the Golden Pavilion* (1956) Mishima returned with brillia success to darker themes, describing in Dostoievskian terms the crime of Zen priest. Perhaps his most finished novel is *After the Banquet* (1960), a wor which occasioned a legal suit for invasion of privacy by the aged politicia who served as the model for the leading character.

Drama

Mishima's career is unusual for Japan in that some of his best works have bee written for the stage. The modern Japanese drama has been much slowe than the novel to achieve maturity, largely no doubt because writing for th stage is economically unfeasible as a career. Mishima's success as a noveli has permitted him to indulge his exceptional talents for the theatre. H inimitable feeling for dialogue, apparent in the novels, is his greatest dramati asset. Although he favours modern subjects, he has cast some of his work into the form of the traditional No plays.

Another leading playwright, Tsuneari Fukuda (born 1912), has written in tellectual comedies, employing European techniques and conventions t depict modern Japanese society in a manner for which no Japanese pre cedents existed. Fukuda has also written historical tragedies, works in whic his experiences as the leading contemporary translator of Shakespeare seen to be reflected. His knowledge of English is probably also responsible for hi disregard of normal Japanese syntax in some of his dialogue, in the attemp to achieve the greater force of English expression.

Junji Kinoshita (born 1914), whose most successful plays have been base on Japanese folklore, represents still another aspect of the post-war theatre Dissatisfied with the standard Tokyo speech, Kinoshita has created a specia patois for his folk-plays, not one spoken in any particular region, but con taining elements easily understood throughout Japan. His *Twilight Cran* (1949), the most popular post-war play, has been adapted also for the N stage and as an opera. Kinoshita's use of traditional folk materials contrast with Mishima's use of traditional forms and Fukuda's use of traditiona historical materials, but each reflects a desire to incorporate some of the ric theatrical past of Japan in modern works. The playwrights thus diffe strikingly from the novelists, few of whom evince any interest in the tradi tional Japanese literature.

Poetry

Japanese poetry since the war has not shown as much activity as fiction o the theatre. Three main varieties are still composed: the *tanka*, the classica verse form which originated before the 8th century; the *haiku*, a shorter form which gained popularity in the 17th century; and the modern poem, written since the 19th century, originally in imitation of European examples. Much of the important production in all three forms continues to be writter by poets whose reputations were established before the war. The number o amateur poets has increased notably since the war, leading to wider circula- tions for poetry magazines, but the public as a whole remains indifferent to modern poetry. The most significant development since the war in the traditional varieties of poetry was occasioned by the publication in 1946 of an article by Takeo Kuwabara, a professor of French at Kyoto University, entitled 'A Second Class Art', in which he declared that the modern haiku had little value as a medium for expressing contemporary thought, and was no more than a second-class, dilettantish diversion. The article aroused a great storm, and has induced many younger *haiku* poets to reconsider the potentialities of their art, but despite all attacks, the composition of *haiku* remains a favourite national pastime.

The Demand for Literature

Quite apart from the consideration of individual excellences and of the various trends since the war, one must note the amazing ferment of literary activity in Japan. There are literally hundreds of magazines devoted to various forms of literature; each newspaper daily publishes two or three serialized novels as well as a poetry column; and best-selling novels sell two or three hundred thousand copies. This activity gives employment to thousands of writers and many poets. The demand for literature extends to foreign works; hardly a European novel of importance has not been translated at least once, and some have gone through several renderings. Japanese writers, through these translations, have shared in most of the European literary movements since the war.

Inexpensive book prices in part account for the huge sales of popular fiction. Production costs, though rising, are still considerably lower than in Europe. Books are not only cheap, but handsomely printed and bound. Illustrated art books published in English have in particular increased the international reputation of Japanese printers and engravers.

The financial rewards for publication have been generous to the popular writers. On several occasions since the war novelists have enjoyed the highest incomes of any Japanese, and they often live in a luxury rare by normal Japanese standards. A well-known writer's face is almost as familiar as a film star's, and the details of his life are eagerly sought by the popular magazines. Japan, in short, is an excellent country in which to be a writer.

Not surprisingly, only a small part of the huge output of post-war Japanese writings has been of genuine literary merit, but that small part compares favourably with that produced elsewhere in the world. Modern Japanese literature is little more than seventy years old, but in this short time, particularly since 1945, it has established itself as one of the important branches of the literature of the world.

BIBLIOGRAPHY

Kobo Abé. *The Woman in the Dunes*, trans. E. Dale Saunders. (New York, Knopf, 1964.)

Osamu Dazai. *No Longer Human*, trans. Donald Keene. (Peter Owen, London, 1959.) *The Setting Sun*, trans. Donald Keene. (Peter Owen, London, 1956.)

Yasunari Kawabata. *The Thousand Cranes*, trans. E. G. Seidensticker. (Secker and Warburg, London, 1959.)

Yukio Mishima. *After the Banquet*, trans. Donald Keene. (Knopf, New York, 1963.) *Confessions of a Mask*, trans. Meredith Weatherby. (New Directions, Norfolk, Conn., 1958.) *Five Modern No Plays*, trans. Donald Keene. (Knopf, New York, 1957.) *The Sound of Waves*, trans. Meredith Weatherby. (Knopf, New York, 1956.) *The Temple of the Golden Pavilion*, trans. Ivan Morris. (Knopf, New York, 1959.)

Shohei Ooka. *Fires on the Plain*, trans. Ivan Morris. (Knopf, New York, 1957.)
Jiro Osaragi. *Homecoming*, trans. Brewster Horwitz. (Knopf, New York, 1959.) *The Journey*, trans. Ivan Morris. (Knopf, New York, 1960.)
Junichiro Tanizaki. *The Key*, trans. Howard Hibbett. (Knopf, New York, 1961.) *The Makioka Sisters*, trans. E. G. Seidensticker. (Knopf, New York, 1957.)
The Old Woman, the Wife and the Archer (three short novels), trans. Donald Keene. (Constable, London, 1962.)

BIOGRAPHICAL NOTE

DONALD KEENE was born in New York in 1922. He was educated at Columbia, Harvard and Cambridge Universities. After teaching for five years at Cambridge University, he returned to Columbia where he is now Professor of Japanese. His writings on modern Japanese literature include the anthology *Modern Japanese Literature* (1956); 'Literary and Intellectual Currents in Postwar Japan' in *Japan Between East and West* (1957); *Modern Japanese Novels and the West* (1961).

MODERN INDONESIAN AND MALAYSIAN LITERATURE

by

T. WIGNESAN

MODERN literature in the forms known to 19th-century Europe, America and Russia was not introduced to Indonesia, Malaya and Singapore until after the First World War. The Dutch-educated Indonesians introduced the novel in the twenties; in poetry free verse, introduced by Mohd Yamin in the journal *Jong Sumatra*, was used in Roestam Effendi's *Petjikan Permenungan* (1928) to break the stranglehold of the traditional quatrain. Malay writers in Malaya made less effort to abandon traditional literary forms and relied on Indonesian innovations. The Malayan novel was often laden with verse interpolations and made a diatribe on prevailing conditions such as *adat*, the traditional law governing conduct (Marah Rusli's *Sitti Nurbaja*), emancipation of women (Alisjahbana's *Lajar Terkembang*—Unfurled Sails), and mixed marriage and family life (Moeis's *Salah Asuhan*—Wrong Upbringing). The present-day novelist is hampered by this heritage.

The short story was introduced to Indonesia, Malaya and Singapore only after the Second World War by Dutch- and English-speaking writers. Until about 1950 there was little significant literature in Chinese, Tamil or English in the area, though in Indonesia a number of writers used Javanese, Sundanese and other native languages before the Second World War.

Modern Malay literature received its decisive impetus in 1928 at the Congress of Young Indonesians; Malay was chosen as the national language —which it has since remained—and its recognition forced in spite of support given by the Dutch East Indies Government to Dutch and other native languages. In Malaya and Singapore most writers were content to use English, but the example of the Indonesians and the political struggles after the Second World War prompted the Malay community to write into the Independent Constitution that by 1967 Malay will become the national language. Malay writers in British Malaya and Singapore, however, had little contact with writers in Dutch Indonesia, and not until after Indonesian independence did writers from both sides of Singapore meet at three congresses, the last of which was held in 1956; meanwhile, Chinese, Tamil and English became established as the literary languages in Malaya and Singapore, writers being inspired by the literatures of China, India and Britain. Many Chinese, Tamil and English writers met for the first time at the Malayan Writers Conference held in Singapore in 1962. Present signs are that Malaysian writers are beginning to realize a common objective in drawing together the various communal literatures.

Literature in Malay

After the Second World War Indonesian writers found themselves in a situation unique in their history. The Japanese regime and the revolution against the Dutch had awakened their national consciousness. Apart from this, there was renewed and eager discussion among the intellectual 'groups' of the whole question of the development of the arts in Indonesia. The controversy among the leaders of the Pudjangga Baru group (Alisjahbana, Sanusi and Armyn Pane, and Dr. Yamin) over the formation of an Indonesian culture distinct from Hindu tradition and *adat* was taken up by the younger Gelanggang, which found a refreshing voice in Chairil Anwar—a 'Beatnik' with genuine nationalistic ardour. The Gelanggang manifesto urged an open-minded policy: the Indonesian ethos must be sought in 'the people' rather than in external features.

With his poems *Deru Tjambur Debu* (Rumbling Mixed with Dust) and *Kerikel Tadjam dan Jang Terempas dan Jang Putus* (Sharp Gravel, The Plundered and the Wrecked), Chairil Anwar (1922-47) had already stamped the Indonesian personality with an indomitable spirit of individuality and paved the way for L'art pour l'art as a guiding principle against other organizations like the Lekra which sought to use literature for the purpose of inculcating socialist views, making art subservient to the welfare of the community. Throughout Chairil's poetry of doom and pessimism (influenced by Marsman, Slauerhoff and Nietzsche), there lurked a vein of hope for his people that was full-blooded and eternal in value. Witness his oft-quoted poem *AKU* (I Am What I Am):

When my time arrives
I wish nobody will cry
Not even you
You needn't weep for me
I'm only a wild animal
Expelled from its herd
Let the bullets strike me deep
I'll still growl and rush ahead
Poison and wound run with me
I'll flee
Till pains and sorrows have gone
Nothing bothers me anymore
And I shall live a thousand years longer

(trans. in *Education and Culture*, 1951)

By his close association with some of postwar Indonesia's best poets, Asrul Sani, Rivai Apin, Sitor Situmorang and playwright Utuy T. Sontani (*Tiga Menguak Takdir*—Three Warding Off Fate, and *Flaming Earth Anthology*), he has become an irresistible force in contemporary Indonesian letters. The Malayan poets Masuri (*Awan Puteh*) and Tongkat Waran (*Gelumbong*) who began to use the sajak (free verse) form mainly after the war, write much in the wake of the Angkatan '45 of Indonesia (see *Puisi Melayu Baru* I and II—New Poetry and *Modern Malay Verse*, 1963). Postwar Malay literature has seen a far greater amount of poetry and short stories, mostly appearing in magazines and newspapers, than plays and novels. Poetry is still geared to awakening the people to a national consciousness, by a simple method of direct statement, without pretence; sometimes with a sentiment that borders on naïvety, though some have learnt eagerly, but inexpertly, from Eliot and the Indonesian-born Du Perron . . . Tongkat Waran, pen-name of Usman Awang, conveys the tone of his generation:

> O human beings in every continent,
> Listen, listen to the beating of a giant heart!
> Our longing to live together is the song that thunders
> From the fluttering flags of prosperity and peace!
>
> (from *News from Asia, Modern Malay Verse*, 1963)

Malay poets still imitate modern Western techniques—a necessary process since traditional Malay forms seriously limit their scope and sometimes cause embarrassing self-consciousness. The Malay short story tends to be unsuccessful because it has few models, foreign short stories being seldom translated into Malay (some, however, have read Maupassant and Chekhov diligently). It still deals excessively with *adat* or inartistically seeks social and political justice.

The presence of numerous rival literary factions does not prevent a sense of direction in modern Malay literature. The impact of Western culture on the structure of an essentially Hindu and Muslim society has prompted writers to seek a new order that does not reject the past completely but makes it resilient and progressive. Malay writers are quick to criticize corruption and immorality in society and government. Utuy T. Sontani in his play *Awal dan Mira* castigates the post-independence Government for abandoning the ideals of the revolution. Perhaps the most impressive attack on contemporary Indonesian life has been made by Mochtar Lubis in his novel *Twilight in Djakarta* (1963), in which a pattern of short stories and sketches is woven into time sequences.

The foremost novelist is Pramudya Ananta Tur whose *Sparks of the Revolution* (short stories), *Keluarga Gerilja* (Guerilla Family) and *Those Who Are Crippled* (long novel) and a host of other novels and stories produced in the late forties are a vivid testimony of the life, suffering, frustration and fear of a people fighting to emerge as an independent nation. Idrus's *Surabaja*—a criticism of some aspects of the revolution—*From Ave Maria to Another Way to Rome*, *Aki* (Grandfather) and *Underground Notes* bring him within the new generation of writers who are sincerely working out a new dynamic way of life for themselves. Likewise too with Achdiat K. Mihardja's novel *Atheis* (Atheist). The Malayan novelists, Ahmad Lutfi, Ishak bin Haji Mohammad and Harun bin Mohammad Amin have not improved either the form or the content of their novels. Most of their novels are short, like Lutfi's first moral series, which have often been described as pornographic (they contain bedroom scenes). Ishak, a politically committed socialist, uses his novels as instruments (through his proliferous editorial commentary) to work social justice. His novels, in the form of transparent satires (*Putera Gunong Tahan* and *Anak Mat Lela Gila*), are mainly directed against the Malay bureaucrats and the aristocracy enjoying the protection of the British, though in his later novels (*Judi Karen*, *Budak Becha* and *Pengantin Baru*) he is fired with a zeal for demanding an exemplary socialist life. Ishak and Lutfi, good campaigners for moral and political uplift, fail as novelists because they are too eager to change their society, and freely indulge in direct exhortations throughout their novels, a serious drawback that tends to hold the Malay novel from developing.

Literature in Chinese

Pre-war Malayan Chinese writers were expatriates from China who chiefly excelled in traditional verse and classical Chinese prose, often getting into difficulties with modern Chinese prose, and as a result of the Sino-Japanese War, they turned to the local scene for their material in an attempt to arouse the local Chinese by writing about their exile and nostalgia for China. After a hushed, oppressed silence during the war, a new generation of writers emerged and, unlike some of the earlier generation, this new generation grew up in the Chinese tradition through the influence of the Chinese schools. But despite this, they have managed to derive their literary inspiration mainly from the Malayan milieu. By the beginning of the fifties, the new generation of writers had found an outlet and readership in Malaya and Singapore. Previously, their work was directed to an indefinite audience in China (because local editors were unco-operative) and was conditioned by the tastes and trends in China. Three factors make for their identification and assimilation in their new-found home. (i) The Emergency in Malaya made the Chinese writers there more conscious of their responsibilities as partners in this polyglot society. (ii) The Communist regime in China caused an embargo to be placed on the literature coming from China, thus forcing them to turn to their own environment. (iii) By 1950, thirty years of expatriate Chinese education made local Chinese newspaper and magazine editors eager to publish them.

Among the foremost of the postwar generation are Wei Yun and Miao Hsiu, both of whom had come to Malaya from China before the war. Wei Yun, who matured in China, has produced, in the latter half of the fifties, a novel, a novelette, and three collections of short stories that take the Malayan milieu for their background. He writes with deep feeling and compassion for those who fall victim to their own biological compulsion and social displacement ('The Dusk' and 'Water Devils'). The English-educated Miao Hsiu, whose work remains true to the social history of the late thirties and early forties, uses his self-taught Chinese with greater facility than Wei Yun. The poets writing in the past seventeen years are, however, severely handicapped, mainly because the modern Chinese language is changing. The poets who show promise are Wei Pei-hua (an Indonesian Chinese), Chung Ch'i, Tu Hung, Chien Shih, Yet Tung and Yuan Tien, primarily because they reject the attitude of their predecessors whose cant essentially was the socio-political revolution's in China. Wei Pei-hua who is free of this sentiment, which spoils much of Chinese verse, is original though his style is laboured. Tu Hung's outstanding lyrical talent, however, becomes diffuse and sentimental in his collection, *Rubber Trees Blossom*.

With the short story the Chinese writer is at his best. Yu Mo-wo's three collections (*Threads*, *Padi Seed* and *Modern Ways*), together with Hsieh

K'o's four good collections (*For the Next Generation*, *Besieged City*, *Scenes of Singapore*, and *Returned Student*) occupy an important place in Chinese prose. Other short story writers include Yun-li Feng, Tiao Wen Mei, Ma Yang, Cheng Yen, Chai Yung and T'u Hung. Two recent novellas—*Atap Hut* by Ho Chin and *Green Creeper* by Sung Ya—are well worth reading. The *Atap Hut* examines the nature of the Chinese school system in Malaya and points the way to progressive reform. The theme of adolescent love, often pathetically worked by Malayan writers, is again laboriously attempted in *Green Creeper*. Though drama is quite popular, the stage is held by an experienced playwright from China, Li Synko, whose only rival is the young Malayan Chinese, Lin Chen.

Literature in Tamil

Creative writing in Tamil is confined to the fifties, and the bulk of it has either been broadcast or published in the local newspapers. The Tamil writers come very strongly under the influence of classical (Indian) literature, and they seek no innovation in their verse forms (being content with variations of the *Vennba*-quatrain). Their main motif is theistic moral preachment; they glorify the powers of Nature (Perumal's *Accusation*, N. Palanivelu's *Art, Man and Nature*); they point out the inviolability of the Hindu family institution (A. Shanmugam's *Doll*, Hassan Gani's *Chalanam*, K. Perumal's *Devotee* and *Stop and Go*, T. S. Shanmugam's *Thalir*). As a predominantly Dravidian community, they portray the greed and the sanctimonious authority of the Brahmin class (K. Perumal's *Kalakkanaku*): they invariably exhort their fellowmen to rise with love and honour for their land (K. Perumal's *Dawn of Independence*), or they reflect the severity of their social needs and conditions. Tamil poetry is meant to be spoken or sung rather than printed, and its effervescence is sometimes quite overpowering. The art form of the short story, as it is known to the West, is non-existent; Tamils do not know how to end, and invariably try to draw a moral. The stories are usually plain narrations without the more consummate characterizations found in the American or European short story. Tamil radio-plays are remarkable for the homespun humour—quaint speech patterns and rhythms, traceable in their dialects. The versatile K. Perumal epitomizes in his short plays, parables, poems, stories and essays the best of Tamil writing.

Literature in English

One remarkable fact about the Malayan English writers is that almost all of them are Chinese by race, the exception being S. Rajaratnam. The English writers are invariably better informed (for obvious reasons) about developments in Western literature, and perhaps by virtue of this knowledge produce poetry and short stories that compare favourably with other post-colonial literatures.

The work that stands out in all Malaysian and Indonesian literature is Wong Phui Nam's collection of poems *How the Hills are Distant* (included in *Bunga Emas*—see bibliography). A Malaysian intellectual stands at the confluence of the major cultural streams that have meandered their way to a standstill in present-day Malaysia. Committed to self-expression amongst a people virtually devoid of intellectual tradition, he is stifled in an atmosphere of complacent degeneration. For Wong Phui Nam the gods have died; he wearies of the task of sustaining an illusory belief he himself has created.

> This is a time to endure
> camping upon the lonely beaches,
> content not to take much stock
> by shooting stars, auguring the advent of sails.
>
> (from *How the Hills are Distant*)

Most of the poets are graduates in the English university system; consequently, their poetry is influenced by Yeats (Edwin Thumboo), Patrick Kavanagh (Goh Poh Seng), Dylan Thomas (Oliver Seet). An exception is the Zen Buddhist Tan Han Hoe who uses a form of the *tanka* and *haiku* to contain his boundless poetic energy.

Almost all the short story writing is in the realistic and naturalistic tradition of late nineteenth-century America. S Rajaratnam, maturing in the thirties in England, wrote short stories (*Locusts, Famine, Drought, What has to be*) that are essentially tracts of socialism, indictments of the forces at work to punish the peasant, the underdog and the poor. He is concerned with their day-to-day problems, their hopeless birth, their degrading death, their inveterate clinging to life, their search for food, water and health, their fear of wild life, locusts, drought and even rain. His characters are simple people—over-wrought, oppressed, troubled and perplexed by the cruelty of nature, and only have themselves to hold on to, as unprotesting pawns, only occasionally moving meekly against their fate.

The short story has come to stay in English mainly through the work of Lee Kok Liang's *Mutes in the Sun and Other Stories*. Like a true scion of his socialist 'fathers', he attempts to portray the agony of the impoverished land. The varied minutiae of the lives of his Chinese community in the North-Western States of Malaya are quite convincingly put together to give a semblance of reality, though he makes ample use of fantasy, symbolism, and a rather unreal set of characters who are the victims of their own biological blamelessness. Lee's concern or pity for the malformed, ill-thought-of imbeciles, spastics, idiots and cretins is almost obsessive. Local colour is the prominent motif of his stories.

Awang Kedua in his stories (*A New Sensation*, *Cone*, *Bees on the Stairs*) tries to purify the degenerate life of the older generation. His use of signs and symbols is indicative of his puritanical moral code, a method that seems to stem from the earlier forms of the sermon in the Christian Church.

Finally, there is the novelist Janet Lim (*Sold for Silver*—the autobiography of a fallen woman in the Malayan underworld) and Chin Kee Onn (*The Silent Army*, *The Grand Illusion*, *Malaya Upside Down*) whose novels although primarily based on fact and Malayan wartime and Emergency history, appear to be rather documentary constructions. What they lack by way of imagination, character delineation, plot structure and purpose, they make up for with compelling dramatic situations.

The Literary Market

Few writers have become permanently self-supporting by writing. Some, like Ananta Tur, take jobs to supplement earnings from writing even though they have netted handsome royalties. Many are employed in journalism, teaching, publishing and Government literary institutions and information services—the Dewan Bahasa dan Pustaka and the Balai Pustaka, official literary bureaus of Malaysia and Indonesia respectively, and the Dewan Bahasa dan Kebudayaan Kebangsan, Singapore's Language and Culture Institute. Almost all the Tamil writers work in the Government's radio and information services or with newspapers. The Chinese writers, however, have a harder life. There is no copyright law among the Chinese, and the publishers exploit the writer—all that they give the author is a mere hundred copies or so (the Dewan Bahasas allow a reasonable royalty on the first 5,000 copies to Malay authors). These Chinese writers struggle along quietly, either as poorly-paid teachers and journalists or petty businessmen. The Malayan English writers by virtue of their university education enjoy comparatively cosy, middle-class existence.

The Dutch-created Balai Pustaka, a propaganda body under the Japanese, was reconstituted in 1948 under the Republic, and once more became Indonesia's leading publishing house. It reprinted books of lasting value and also those of new Indonesian writers, mainly in Bahasa Indonesia (national language) and to a lesser degree in Javanese and Sundanese. Besides providing a livelihood for many writers, the importance of the Balai Pustaka in contemporary Indonesian literature may be gauged by its increasing activity—production figures for the years '48, '49 and '50 amount to 128 editions, or, in numbers of books, respectively: 183,500, 430,800 and 603,000. These editions covered modern literature (over fifty new publications and about ninety reprints), classical literature (also books in the regional languages), cultural, political and social sciences, popular scientific and technical books and children's books. It may well be useful to reflect that the level of literacy, under 10 per cent prewar, is now well over 65 per cent.

Among the influential post-Second World War periodicals in Indonesia are the weekly *Vitzicht* (1945-6) published by the Dutch-Indonesian Government Information Service; the fortnightly *Orientatie* (1947-54)—contributors included J. Boon (Vincent Mahieu), M. Balfas, H. B. Jassin, G. J. Resink, Beb Vuyk, Asrul Sani (*My Friend Cordiaz*) and Idrus (*From Ave Maria to Another Way to Rome*); and after independence, *Education and Culture* published by the Ministry of Education and Culture, and the magazines *Mimbar Indonesia*, *Siasat* (Strategy), *Indonesia* and the Malayan *Hiburen*.

In Malaya and Singapore the Dewan Bahasas are mainly occupied with Government publications and the promotion of the Malay language, and their literary output is meagre (*Puisi Melayu Baru I* and *II*—New Poetry). On the other hand, an overabundance of local and foreign publishing firms rule and ruin the writer. Local branches of London publishers have brought out much contemporary writing in Malay. Almost all Chinese writers can find their way into print, and pirating is not unprofitable. Tamil writers continue to be much in demand by radio and newspaper. Until recently most writers in English had to seek overseas magazines; now an enterprising local publishing house, Rayirath (Raybooks), publishes literary works.

BIBLIOGRAPHY

INDONESIA

Fiction

Idrus. *Surabaja* (sketches). (Merdeka Press, Djakarta, 1947.) *The Surono Family* (drama). (Lukisan Pudjangga, Medan, 1948.) *Dari Ave Maria Kedjalan Lain Ke Roma* (anthology: novelette, short stories and sketches). (Balai Pustaka, Djakarta, 1948.)

Mochtar Lubis. *Twilight in Djakarta.* (Hutchinson for Congress of Cultural Freedom, London, 1963.)

Ananta Tur. *Sparks of the Revolution* (short stories). (Gapura, Djakarta, 1950.) *Kelurga Gerilja.* (Pembangunan, Djakarta, 1950.) *On the Bekasi River.* (Gapura, Djakarta, 1951.) *Na. Dancing in the Streets.* (Balai Pustaka, Djakarta, 1951.) *Those Who Are Crippled.* (Balaio Pustaka, Djakarta, 1951.)

Poetry

Ahmed Ali (ed.) *The Flaming Earth* (anthology). (Friends of the Indonesian Republic Society, Karachi, 1949.)

Chairil Anwar. *Deru Tjapur Debu.* (De Brug, Amsterdam and Pembangunan, Djakarta, 1949.) *Kerikel Tadjam dan Jang Terempas dan Jang Putus.* (Pustaka Rakjat, Djakarta, 1950.)

H. B. Jassin (ed.) *Gema Tanoh Air* (anthology of poetry and prose). (Balai Pustaka, Djakarta, 2nd ed., 1951.)

Tiga Menguak Takdir (three poets). (Balai Pustaka, Djakarta, 1950.)

MALAYSIA

Fiction

Lee Kok Liang. *Mutes in the Sun and Other Short Stories.* (Raybooks, Kuala Lumpur, 1963.)

Janet Lim. *Sold for Silver.* (Fontana, London, 1960.)

Chin Kee Onn. *The Silent Army.* (Corgi, London, 1954.) *The Grand Illusion.* (Corgi, London, 1961.)

T. Wignesan (ed.) *Bunga Emas* (anthology). (Anthony Blond, London, 1964.)

Poetry

Ee Tiang Hong. *I of the Many Faces.* (Privately published, Singapore, 1960.)

Edwin Thumboo. *Rib of Earth.* (Privately published, Singapore, 1956.)

T. Wignesan. *Tracks of a Tramp.* (Raybooks, Kuala Lumpur, 1961.)

SOURCES

Publications of the Embassy of the Republic of Indonesia (Cultural Department) in New Delhi and London.

Wang Gung Wu. 'A Short Introduction to Chinese Writing in Malaya' in *Bunga Emas* (see above).

BIOGRAPHICAL NOTE

T. WIGNESAN. B.1933, Kuala Krai, Malaya. Studied and taught in Malaya, 1951-55 and in Europe, 1955-61. Now foreign correspondent of *Straits Times,* Singapore.

POLITICAL AFFAIRS

POLITICAL INSTITUTIONS AND PARTIES IN ASIA

THE states of Asia present a wide variety of political systems. Some are heavily influenced by Western models; some are more characteristically Asian; but all contain a mixture of Eastern and Western elements. Democracy is sometimes said to be a peculiarly Western concept. That may have been the case originally; but it has since been generally adopted in Asia also, and it is used as a political slogan or standard in Asian countries even where the regime would not measure up to Western criteria. Accordingly, it is useful to distinguish in the first place those Asian states which may be classified as democratic in the ordinary sense of the word. There are six of these: India, Pakistan, Ceylon, Malaysia, Japan and the Philippines.

INDIA: THE WESTMINSTER MODEL

India is widely regarded as the mainstay of democracy in Asia, with good reason since it is by far the largest of the democratic countries. A breakdown of the Indian political system would have correspondingly serious repercussions. The system is strongly influenced by the former British connection, and is based upon the Westminster model. There is a bicameral parliament and cabinet government. Elections for the lower house (Lok Sabha) are by universal suffrage in single-member constituencies. Political life generally bears close resemblances to that of Britain where many Indian politicians received part of their education. But there are also differences. That the head of state is an elected president, not a hereditary monarch, has little practical significance as in both cases their function is very largely ceremonial. But the Indian upper house (the Council of States) is also elected, not hereditary, and the electorate in this case is composed of the Legislative Assemblies of the 16 States that go to make up the Union of India.

The size of the country, both in area and in population (440 million in 1961) and the existence of strongly marked regional distinctions led to the adoption of a federal system. The powers and functions of government are divided by the Constitution between the centre and the States. Although the Constitution leans rather more towards central authority than towards State autonomy—permitting the centre to take over the government of any State in time of crisis, as has happened in Kerala—the States have real powers which they guard jealously. Regional consciousness and loyalties are strong, and are buttressed by linguistic differences. There are 14 major languages, among which Hindi, the official language, is the most widespread; but it does not spread far into the south of India. Consequently, the attempt to end the use of English for official purposes has evoked protests and resistance from the south which would find itself at a disadvantage in the use of Hindi. Even Prime Minister Nehru was obliged to yield to the pressure of linguistic nationalism. Under his successor, Shastri, the centre has become appreciably weaker in relation to the States.

The Indian National Congress, however, still constitutes a cohesive force. That organization was built up under the leadership of Gandhi and Nehru as the instrument of independence. After that object was achieved, it continued as the main political organization of the country. It has been challenged and sometimes defeated in some of the States, but has retained an overwhelming majority at the centre through successive general elections. The opposition—Communist, Socialist, right-wing Jan Sangh and a sprinkling of others—has been too disparate to unite against it. But there is a danger to the Congress in the cracks and schisms which are appearing within its organization, and in the fact that while repeatedly winning a majority of seats at general elections, it has never had an overall majority of votes.

Pakistan and Ceylon

Pakistan also has the problem of regional rivalries, made more severe by the physical separation of the two halves of the country with 1,000 miles of Indian territory lying between. There too, regionalism is reinforced by language differences: the national language Urdu belongs to the Western region while the Eastern region speaks Bengali. A federal solution was attempted in the first Constitution after independence, but it took a long time to complete and longer still to put into full operation. Meanwhile the political situation deteriorated, until in 1958 General Ayub Khan, then Minister of Defence, took over the Government and instituted a military dictatorship. But this was a temporary, transitional phase, preparing the way for a remodelling of the Constitution which was proclaimed in 1962.

The new regime was modelled more on Paris than on Westminster. It substituted for cabinet government a presidential system influenced by General de Gaulle, with the difference that it introduced indirect election not only for the Presidency but also for Parliament. This system, to which Ayub Khan gave the name of Basic Democracy, was designed to eliminate the hitherto prevalent manoeuvring and corruption of the political parties.

Unlike India, Pakistan's politics were not a continuation of the independence movement. The leaders of that movement, the Muslim League, did not long survive the establishment of the state, and although the League itself continued as a political party, it was soon only one of many and went into a decline. Ayub Khan aimed to establish firm and stable government, and to clean up the party system. He was only partly successful. Many active politicians of the earlier regime were debarred from politics for a period, but the parties refused to disappear, and although constricted by the system of Basic Democracy, in the 1965 Presidential election they showed that there was still a good deal of life in them. The parties managed to sink their differences in favour of a joint candidate, Miss Jinnah, the sister of the founder of the state. Ayub Khan won easily, but there were moments when the issue appeared to hang in the balance, and the conduct of the election clearly showed that Pakistan, after the military interregnum, was again to be counted among the democratic states of Asia.

Ceylon's political system, which was also based on the Westminster model, has remained essentially unchanged since independence, although it has been subject to severe strain because of the friction between the Sinhalese majority and Tamil minority who objected strongly to the institution of Sinhalese as the sole official language. The Tamil claim for a federal system has been resisted, and the state remains unitary; but there is a multiplicity of political parties, because of a strong tendency towards splintering, so that the Government has usually been a coalition. Two parties, however, have alternated in the dominant position. The United National Party formed the Government after independence and again after the 1965 general election. In the interval the Government was led by the Sri Lanka Freedom Party under the leadership of S. W. R. D. Bandaranaike, who split away from the UNP and formed a Left-wing coalition. When he was assassinated by a Buddhist monk his widow took over both the leadership of the party and, after an electoral victory, the office of Prime Minister, until defeated by Dudley Senanayake.

Malaysia

Malaysia, like India and Ceylon, also follows the Westminster model, except that the government is federal and there is an admixture of traditional elements. The constituent States of the Federation are represented in the Second Chamber or Senate, but there is also a third Chamber called the Conference of Rulers which has some limited functions, among them that of providing the Head of State. Malaysia was constituted in 1963 by joining Singapore and the two North Borneo territories of Sarawak and Sabah with the Federation of Malaya. The largest element in the new state was the Federation of Malaya, which had achieved independence in 1957. The Malayan constitution of that date was adopted as the basis for the new state of Malaysia. There was political as well as constitutional continuity. The Government of Malaya had, since its inception, been in the hands of the Alliance composed of the United Malays National Organization, the Malayan Chinese Association and the Malayan Indian Congress. The Prime Minister and leader of the Alliance was Tungku Abdul Rahman, a Malay prince, who became Prime Minister of the new Malaysia. The political complexion of this Government tends to be conservative. But in Singapore where the population is predominantly Chinese, the Prime Minister, Lee Kwan Yew, is Chinese and leads the People's Action Party which is moderate left-wing. In Sarawak and Sabah the ethnic structure of the population is different from Singapore and from the mainland, and political alignments also differ. The Chief Ministers of Sarawak (Stephen Kalong Ningkan-Iban) and Sabah (Donald Stephens-Kadazan) are members of indigenous communities which are neither Malay nor Chinese.

The Philippines and Japan

The Philippines, as might be expected of a former American dependency, has for its political system followed not the Westminster but the Washington model. Its constitution bears a close resemblance to that of the United States, except that it is not federal. Like the United States also, its politics are dominated by two parties (Nationalists and Liberals) in which the personality of the leader is more significant than differences of ideology. The Liberal candidate, Macapagal, was elected President in 1961, defeating President Garcia who led the Nationalists. Although the Philippines' political system is constantly criticized for its corruption, it appears stable.

Japan's constitution is also of American origin, but not on American lines. It was drafted and adopted during the American Occupation, but it provided for a system of cabinet government. It also stipulated that Japan would never maintain armed forces, a clause which has subsequently caused embarrassment to both the U.S. and the Japanese Governments. Another sensitive point was the position of the Emperor. Under the constitution he is given the role of 'symbol' of the state under the sovereignty of the people, which makes his position like that of the British monarch. With one brief interlude in 1947-48 Japan has had a continuous succession of right-wing governments under a variety of names. The opposition, with the exception of that interlude, has been the Socialist Party, also with some variation of title resulting from internal schisms. Broadly, however, Japan has a two-party system divided on a doctrinal basis between left and right, and a number of minor parties, among which the most significant are the Democratic Socialists and the Communists.

Communist Regimes

The six countries so far examined have political systems which, although differing in their institutions, are recognizably democratic in their operation. Together they have a population of more than 700 million.

Of the remaining Asian countries three—China, North Korea and North Vietnam—are Communist and comprise a population of about the same size, mostly Chinese. Although control by the Communist Party is a feature common to all three countries and in each case the Communist Party is organized according to the standard pattern, there are some subsidiary differences. In North Korea the controlling body is called the Korean Workers' Party which resulted from an amalgamation of the Communist Party and the New People's Party, producing a party which is numerically large in proportion to the population. In North Vietnam also, the Communists operate under the title of the Workers' Party (Dang Lao Dang) and tolerate the existence of one or two minor parties so long as they conform. The constitution adopted in 1960 had special provisions for the authority of the President, designed to accommodate the veteran Vietnamese Communist leader Ho Chi Minh. Similarly the Chinese constitution of 1964 instituted the position of Chairman of the Chinese People's Republic for Mao Tse-tung, to which Liu Shao-chi has succeeded. There is a whole hierarchy below of congresses and councils built up like a pyramid on a system of indirect election. But in China as in other Communist states, the formal processes mask the reality. Elections are simply endorsements of candidates whose nomination is decided by the Communist Party. If at lower levels the Party permits flexibility, its ultimate control is unimpaired.

Military Dictatorships

The other states of Asia, which are neither democratic nor Communist, amount to eleven in all, and comprise a population of some 230 million. They fall into various categories. First there are the military dictatorships.

In Burma General Ne Win in 1962 ended the democratic system which had existed under the premiership of U Nu. Since that time the Army has been in control of the country both administratively and politically through the organization of the Burma Socialist Programme Party and the repression of its opponents.

South Vietnam also falls into this category since the assassination of President Diem in 1963. There are, however, the differences that the conflicts within the ruling military junta are more in evidence, and that the machinery of civilian administration remains in being.

Thailand also qualifies as a military dictatorship. There is a constitution, and there have been elections. But the standard way of changing the government is not by the ballot-box but by *coup d'état.* The present regime was instituted when Marshal Sarit overthrew Marshal Pibul Songgram in 1958. His successor as Prime Minister is General Thanom Kittikachorn in whose hands effective power resides.

There are two states that combine elements of military dictatorship with elements of democracy. One of these is Formosa which has a constitutional system and elections which have been attested as free. Yet it is difficult to conceive that Generalissimo Chiang Kai-shek would permit himself to be voted out of office, and it is not clear that the inhabitants of Formosa would have voted for him if he and the remnants of his armies had not descended upon the island.

The other state combining elements of military dictatorship with a measure of democracy is South Korea. The United Nations vouched for the elections held in 1948 which preceded the establishment of the Republic of Korea with Syngman Rhee as President. Then came the Korean War, and in 1960 the overthrow of Syngman Rhee. The constitution was amended to curb the power of the President, and a new government was formed as the result of elections. But this government was overthrown by a military coup in 1961 and a new constitution adopted in the following year restoring the power of the Presidency occupied by General Pak. There have been elections which gave a majority to General Pak's Democratic Republican Party. Government therefore appears to rest on electoral endorsement, but with the threat of military sanctions in the background.

In Laos also the role of military force in relation to government is very apparent, but in this case there is no unity of command. There is division between the right-wing faction led by General Phoumi, the centre or neutralist faction led by Prince Souvanna Phouma, and the left-wing pro-Communist faction led by his half-brother Prince Souvannouong. But in Laos, as in South Vietnam and South Korea, it would be unrealistic to expect a fully functioning democratic system, as in addition to the impediments shared with other Asian countries, all three are in a state of war or threat of war. In that situation even mature democracies may become repressive.

Civilian Dictatorship

There is a fourth group of countries in which traditional forms of government are prominent. Laos might also come into this category, since the rôle of the Princes in the factionalism and feuding is partly traditional despite the modern-sounding 'neutralist' and 'pro-Communist' labels. The string of states on the northern frontier of India—Nepal, Sikkim and Bhutan—provide clearer examples of traditional rule by monarchs, although in the case of Nepal it is the result of a restoration. There was a brief period of democratic government after the revolt which overthrew the Ramas; but then the alliance between the King and the democratic parties broke down and monarchical rule was instituted.

Cambodia, too, is governed essentially in traditional style even though it has a modern constitution and the effective ruler of the country—Prince Norodom Sihanouk—refused to remain King and has repeatedly resigned the Premiership. Such is his status in the country that elections regularly produce an overwhelming victory for the candidates that support him. In theory the voters could exercise other choices; in practice they prefer not to, and their preference is positive, not dictated by intimidation. Cambodia is a close approximation to a benevolent despotism with the despot having the willing submission of his subjects. This could be regarded as a form of democracy, though a very exceptional one.

Indonesia

Indonesia somewhat resembles Cambodia; President Sukarno is to some extent a popular autocrat. His power is more limited than Sihanouk's, since he is dependent on the mutually antagonistic forces of the Army and of the Communist Party. Nor does he command the same degree of popular support, as is shown by the rebellion which broke out against his regime in 1958 and by his need to suppress and arrest his political opponents. His position is more like that of Ne Win in Burma, except that he was already President when he overthrew the democratic system in Indonesia in 1959 and instituted what he calls 'guided democracy', in which government is carried on by his balancing of counterposed forces. Several political parties maintain their existence, but the Communist Party is acknowledged to be the strongest (the Masjumi having been banned) and the system hinges on the person of Sukarno who retains popular support with his oratorical gifts, as well as the glamour of having been an architect of Indonesia's independence.

Conclusions

It is impossible to generalize about an area with half the world's population. The systems of centrally controlled regimes and those of parliamentary democracy are furthest apart, but even the distance between the democratic regime supported by traditional forms of rule under which the Federation of Malaysian States is governed is far apart from the system of 'guided democracy' that applies in neighbouring Indonesia. It would be rash in these circumstances to draw any final conclusions about the prospects of Asia's political institutions and parties. Some parts of the political vacuum that was created by the withdrawal of the European colonial powers have yet to be filled effectively. Here the final political pattern has not yet emerged. Military disturbances are outward signs of this state of suspense.

On the whole, the countries which have modelled their institutions on Westminster and the Capitol, have been able to uphold the principles of parliamentary democracy which most newly emerging countries proclaim as their ultimate goal. In the face of national or international crises these countries have revealed great resilience. Some of them have been fortunate in being led into independence by leaders who had gained their experience in the struggle against the colonial country that had modelled them during the most formative years of their lives. Others have been less fortunate.

The successor states of the former French, Dutch and Japanese colonial empires were less well equipped than the Indian sub-continent to fill the seats vacated in the political arena. In these parts of Asia the uncertainties as to the future pattern of political institutions and parties are greatest. They provide the main temptation in the area for rivalling political forces and the chief justification for those who maintain that the newly emerging countries of Asia are not ready for a form of parliamentary control. Yet even here the signs are many of lively liberal forces that refuse to accept without challenge and indefinitely autocratic regimes, military or civilian.

The model which now applies to the world's largest country has its attraction elswhere in Asia. At the same time the setbacks in the rate of economic progress of both China and Russia and the ideological disputes which have destroyed the monolithic structure of the Communist camp have not been lost on Asian countries. The search for indigenous rather than alien cures of political ills is most fervent in the countries whose political moulds are not yet hard. Some must crack before they can hold their contents.

Much will depend on the way India and Japan go. As long as these two countries adhere to their present internal balance between central and regional authority and between governing party and opposition, the non-Communist parts of Asia seem to have a fair prospect of moving, though not without setbacks, towards political institutions not all too different from those which have stood the test of time in Western parliamentary democracies.

BIBLIOGRAPHY

A. Doak Barnett (ed). *Communist Strategies in Asia.* (Praeger, New York, 1963.)

George McT. Kahin (ed). *Major Governments of Asia.* (Cornell Univ. Press, Ithaca, New York, 2nd ed., 1963.)

George McT. Kahin (ed). *Governments and Politics of Southeast Asia.* (Cornell Univ. Press, Ithaca, New York, 2nd ed., 1964.)

Saul Rose (ed). *Politics in Southern Asia.* (Macmillan, London, 1963.)

Hugh Tinker. *India and Pakistan.* (Praeger, New York. 1962.)

PAN-ASIANISM

by

C. P. FITZGERALD

PAN-ASIANISM is neither an old nor an indigenous Asian idea. It is not ancient, since the very concept of the continent of Asia is not an Asian, but a European idea, formulated by the Greeks, taken over by the Romans, and handed down to modern Europe. To the Greeks it was natural to divide their world into the three regions which lay west, east and south of the Aegean Sea. So Europe originally meant mainland Greece and countries west and north of it, Asia meant what is now Turkey and Syria, Africa meant Egypt and Libya. Nothing beyond these regions was really known or named. The Macedonian conquest and the later Roman conquests enlarged the idea of Asia; it now stretched away to the confines of India and to whatever lay beyond, of which only imperfect knowledge percolated to the West. Africa was enlarged until it came to mean what it does to-day, although almost all the southern three-quarters of the continent was still unexplored.

These geographical concepts were thus formed in Europe by Europeans; they were not familiar to the peoples of Asia, who did not divide their known world in this way. In ancient times the Chinese were not aware of what countries lay far to their west. When they gained some knowledge of them they distinguished India, known as Shen Tu, then Yin Tu; Persia, known as An Hsi, later P'o Ssu; and the Roman Orient first known as Ta Ts'in, later as Fu Lin. In still later times these divisions came to correspond very broadly with the regions of Hindu, Persian, and Arabian Muslim cultures. Indians also saw the world as India in the middle, a Chinese world to the east, and a Muslim world to the west.

After the rise of Islam, Muslims tended to see the world as divided into three parts, Islam, the Christian West, and the infidel East. The spread of Buddhism throughout the Far East did not lead to any great change in these ideas. The Chinese saw Eastern Asia as either influenced by their culture, and thus in theory 'tributary' to the great central Empire, or barbarian, as were the nomad peoples to the north and the mountain and jungle peoples to the south and west. South-East Asia became predominantly a region of Buddhist religion, but as part of the area, the old Annamite Kingdom, was under Chinese cultural influence, while the rest was inspired by Indian, at first Hindu, culture, Buddhism, when it first replaced Hinduism, tended to take the colour of the underlying civilization, whether Chinese or Indian, and did not unify these countries in a new synthesis.

There was very little unity at all in what the Europeans thought of as

'Asia'. Chinese and Indians were (and are) as far apart in culture and in outlook as either were from the European peoples. The nomadic North, Mongolia, Siberia, and Turkestan, remained a world apart, the reservoir from which destructive invaders poured out upon the civilizations of the South. The Muslim West felt no unity with the infidels of the East, who were not even 'People of the Book'—the Bible—which although seen by Muslims as an incomplete revelation, was none the less held to be the Word of God. The idea that some bond united all these peoples in opposition, or in contradistinction, to the peoples who lived north of the Mediterranean and Black Seas was utterly strange and unknown to Asians before the 19th century.

Origin of Pan-Asianism

The origin of the notion of Pan-Asianism may perhaps be traced to the first European peoples who came by the sea route to southern and eastern Asia, the Portuguese and Spaniards. Both nations had had a long history of conflict with the Muslims: when they rounded the Cape, or crossed the Pacific to the Philippine Islands, they found in these new lands of Asia both Muslim rulers and also pagan peoples. It was natural to distinguish them sharply from Christian nations at home in Europe. The Muslims were traditional enemies, the pagans should be won for Christ. Since the Portuguese maritime empire touched upon many diverse peoples from Indians at Goa, Sinhalese at Colombo, Malays at Malacca right round to the Chinese at Macao, the newcomers tended to see them all as 'Asians'. Very gradually the Asian peoples themselves came to adopt this classification.

The idea was rather new, even in Europe. In the Middle Ages, during the Crusades, the Franks, struggling to maintain their precarious Kingdom of Jerusalem, had been very willing to seek allies beyond the Muslim world which hemmed them in. Envoys from the lay rulers and also from the Pope attempted to get into touch with the still pagan Mongols who had swept through Asia to the borders of Europe and Africa. There is no evidence that Western Europeans thought of these strangers from the Further East as having anything in common with the Muslims of the Near East. They were pagan, so could perhaps be converted to Christianity and become invaluable allies. Had they been converted they would have become part of Christendom.

In the early centuries of growing contact between the non-Muslim part of Asia—India and China—and Europe, the Western world did not conceive of itself as superior in any respect, except religion. The manufactures and luxuries of the East far surpassed those of the West. The huge Empires of Ming China and Mogul India were states beside which the greatest kingdoms of Europe were but small. The civil service of China represented a degree of state organization and control which no European power had attained since the fall of the Roman Empire. The one comforting defect about these great states and peoples was that they were pagan, or infidel. All their glory was overshadowed by the darkness of unbelief. The European enterprise in the East became a double one, to purchase the luxuries and refined products of the Asian world for resale at a handsome profit at home, and to win these peoples for Christ.

This situation did not outlast the 17th century. The Mogul Empire declined, and even if the Chinese Empire under the early Manchu rulers remained apparently very strong, it became evident in many parts of Asia that the Europeans had the upper hand in wars. Technical innovation, fostered perhaps by the important role of sea-borne trade in the European world, soon outstripped the level attained in Asia, which had a few centuries earlier been higher than that of Europe. By the middle of the 18th century the men who voyaged to the East had acquired the idea that European civilization was superior in other ways than possession of religious truth. The increasing European impact coincided with, and in part caused a period of decline and confusion in the great communities of Asia. India fell into weakness, which facilitated European encroachment. China had passed the peak of the Manchu Dynasty's power and vigour. In South-East Asia division and political incoherence gave advantage to the sea-borne invader.

The 19th century saw the Europeans turn from trade to conquest. The process had begun in India after Plassey, and gathered momentum in the next century. It was partly, but only partly, inspired by the old 'dream of empire', the inheritance which the West had derived from the conquests of Alexander and the Roman proconsuls. Much more was it due to the simple necessity of imposing order on chaos, or the protection of trading ports. Most of the European nations expanding into the Asian countries would have preferred empires of the Portuguese type, a chain of fortified ports dominating the trade but not the administration of vast hinterlands. The decline of the Asian kingdoms and empires made this development impossible. In India, Malaya, Indonesia and Indo-China the Western powers were led step by step into annexation and the imposition of protectorates, which latter expedient steadily became in practice indistinguishable, except in form, from outright annexation.

This policy soon created a growing dilemma. The Asian lands were vast; militarily they had become insignificant antagonists, but for the colonial powers they still presented formidable administrative problems. When the British had absorbed India, they shrank from conquering China also; the decline of the Turkish Empire was as much an embarrassment as an opportunity. For while the nations of Western Europe had intruded by the sea route into Asia in search of trade, and stayed to rule, the Russians had expanded into Northern Asia, not as traders, but as conquerors and settlers. Russian conquests followed the old Roman pattern. Before the second half of the 19th century was much advanced the Western Europeans became more afraid of ultimate Russian ambitions than of the remnant strength of the independent Asian states.

The Rise of Japan, Revolution and Nationalism

The reaction of Asia to this double invasion, by sea and by land, was slow and confused. Up till nearly the end of the 19th century it found no positive or concrete expression. The main centres of such resistance as existed were negative: the Asian peoples did not respond to missionary zeal; conversion to Christianity remained statistically very small even in the 'pagan' societies; in Muslim lands it was microscopic. The second, more unfortunate, form of resistance was the slow response to Western technical superiority. It is true that the new colonial empires did not actively encourage economic progress or technical advance except where it showed a profit to them, or made political control easier. They built railways, but did not foster heavy industries. Yet in those parts of Asia, such as China, which remained independent, progress was if anything slower than in the colonial empires. Only Japan met the challenge by an all-out effort of modernization. This Japanese reaction was to a great extent an application of the American political adage 'if you can't beat them, join them.' Japan sought to win recognition as an equal of the Western powers by adopting their techniques in industry and warfare, and by making such more superficial changes in her political system as would entitle her to 'join the club'.

The Japanese were really anxious to escape the growing stigma of being classed as an Asian people, except in the inescapable geographical sense. Yet it was their example and success which inspired the Pan-Asian movement. Up to the end of the 19th century no Asian people had successfully withstood a European people in arms. There had been local successes, heroic resistances, but always final defeat. It had become an axiom that the West must always win. The policy of the few remaining independent states was to walk a tight rope between the conflicting ambitions of the Western powers—'playing off one barbarian against another' was the Chinese version, far from successful. The able King of Siam, Chulalangkorn, followed a plan of balancing French and British power while permitting some cautious modernization. His success was in part at least due to his own personal quality. Where such leadership was absent the results were usually fatal. Persia survived because Russia and Britain could not agree upon how to divide the spoil. Afghanistan survived for much the same reason. The break-up of Turkey would have precipitated a European war, and was consequently undesirable. The partition of China, frequently threatened, was avoided more by the daunting magnitude of the task and the certainty of inter-European rivalry than by the feeble defence policy of the declining Manchu Court.

In 1905 Japan went to war with imperial Russia and won a resounding victory. It is true that Russia, fighting at the end of an immense line of communications, menaced by internal unrest, and lacking effective sea power, fought at great disadvantage. This made no difference to the effect produced, which went far further than Japan herself either wanted or expected. The Japanese hoped, rightly, that their victory would make them finally and for ever accepted as a Great Power. They did not want the leadership of Asia in an anti-European movement, they wanted to be counted among the Great Powers, who were in fact all Western peoples. But elsewhere in Asia the result was seen in other terms. The Asians could 'do it' if they only acquired the means and the skill to carry on modern warfare. The means were modern armaments, the skill could be learned, the obstacles were lack of money and an inefficient and outworn political system.

Thus the first result of the victory of imperial Japan was an immense impulse to revolution in Asia. The old dynasties must go, either in favour of reformed monarchy or republic, opinions varied, but there rapidly appeared a new solidarity among revolutionary parties in different parts of Asia.

The Congress movement in India included both Hindus and Muslims, and Hindus later gave support to the purely Muslim Khalifat movement, intended to save Turkey from partition by the European powers. There were contacts, slight but not without importance, between young Turks and Chinese republican plotters. The Young Turkish revolution of 1908 was by some Chinese regarded as a model.

The Asian intellectual of the early 20th century was now more often a 'returned student' than one who had been educated only at home in his native land. He was returned from England, America, France, Germany or Japan. There he had met and mixed with other Asian students, Chinese, Indians, Indonesians, Malays, Egyptians and many others. He had found that they saw their own problems just as he saw his. The enemy was Europe, but Europe was also the teacher. The Europeans in spite of their divisions and rivalries stood together, particularly in respect of colonial problems and unrest. It seemed obvious that cohesion and co-operation among Asian nationalists would be more effective than isolated and independent movements. Moreover the Asian countries were very large; most of them had not in the past had clearly defined sensitive frontiers, as in Europe, nor minorities from a neighbouring nation who could divide the loyalties of the nascent nationalist movements. It seemed that Indians and Chinese, Indonesians and Indo-Chinese could co-operate without any fear of rivalry. So the idea of Pan-Asia was born in these circles, essentially an emigré idea matured in foreign surroundings, under the strong influence of an alien culture and political system.

This is no doubt the main reason why Pan-Asianism has always been a theory rather than a practical policy adopted by governments. Asian nationalists spoke in favour of Pan-Asia; they acted, when they came to power, in furtherance of their national interests without finding Pan-Asianism much help in the task. The problems of the early Chinese Republic were not usefully related to the problems of Indian nationalism, Indonesian nationalism, or Arab independence. The enemies might all be Europeans but they were of different nations, with differing policies. For China it was soon Japan, not any European nation, which presented the most menacing front.

It was while the nationalist movements in Asia were still far from power and victory that Pan-Asianism made its greatest appeal to their members. Then all were equally among the dispossessed and despised. As they came to power they found that the actual problems of achieving complete independence were not closely connected with events in other Asian countries. In the period between the two wars the rise of Communist movements in Asia further weakened the Pan-Asian concept. The Communist parties opposed the Pan-Asian idea; it was un-Marxist. It was the solidarity of all workers, the black, the brown, the white and the yellow in opposition to all Capitalists, of whatever colour or race, which they preached as the solution for the problems of Asia, just as much as for the problems of Europe, South America, and any other region. Pan-Asianism was divisive and therefore reactionary; the toilers of Asia needed to be freed from their own aristocratic or bourgeois exploiters as much as from European masters, and the working class of the West was in the same state of servitude.

The Defeat of Japan and the Decline of Pan-Asianism

The policy of Japan in the Second World War was the last positive attempt to use Pan-Asianism as a political factor, and the failure of that policy and the defeat of Japan gravely discredited the whole theory. The Japanese Co-Prosperity Sphere was based on the idea that the Asian peoples freed from European colonial rule could be induced to accept Japanese leadership if it was dressed up in this Pan-Asian garb. Japan would lead Pan-Asia; for was it not Japan who had first upset the tradition of Western military victory, and was now following this up with further, shattering blows against the European domination in Asia? There can be no doubt that for a while this policy met with some success. Nationalists did co-operate with the Japanese, in Burma, in Indonesia, in Indo-China, and to some extent in Malaya also. The extremist wing of the Indian movement did the same.

But there was always one awkward exception, and of the largest size. China was the enemy of Japan, the ally of the West. In vain the Japanese tried to represent their puppet regime in Nanking as the true Government of China, their opponents, whether Nationalist or Communist, as 'Asian traitors'. The mass of the Chinese people both at home and overseas made it quite clear that they were utterly unconvinced, and felt no solidarity with the friends of Japan.

The defeat of Japan ended the Co-Prosperity Sphere, and all outward manifestations of Pan-Asianism. It was now the United States of America which emerged as the champion and friend of the newly liberated Asian peoples. American intervention brought an end to Dutch attempts to delay or arrest the independence of Indonesia. American opinion undoubtedly hastened the British into giving India and Pakistan, Ceylon and Burma, self-government or independence. America took over from France the protection of the new states of Indo-China, but upheld their right to national independence.

At the same time the real division of opinion in Asia became fixed on new lines. There were those who believed that colonialism could best be rooted out by destroying Capitalism; the Communists. There were those who sought both to oppose Communism and to gain national independence at the same time; the nationalists. The issue is still in debate; colonialism has almost wholly vanished, but its disappearance has not solved the problems in the way the ardent revolutionaries expected.

The Bandung Conference

The latest, probably the last, Pan-Asian occasion was the Conference at Bandung in Indonesia in 1955. All Asian states, Communist and non-Communist, sent delegations. Some of the outstanding leaders of Asia, Mr. Nehru, Chou En-lai, Col. Nasser, attended in person. No Western power sent a delegation, or was invited. President Sukarno of Indonesia delivered the opening address, speaking in English, with great eloquence. It was a passionate denunciation of colonialism, at the same time a paean of triumph that the dragon was slain. In the course of his speech he had occasion to refer to the assembled delegates as 'we of the coloured peoples'. It was evident from their startled movement that the Turkish delegates had never thought of themselves in this light. When it came to passing resolutions which could have a political implication, the conference could not give effect to any unanimous opinion. Colonialism was condemned, easily, because all had once suffered from it, but suffered no longer. But between Communists and anti-Communists, between non-aligned states and the allies of the United States of America, there could be no real meeting place. Thus the conference concluded with an air more of an Irish wake than a meeting to draw up a blue-print for the future. The funeral of colonialism was joyfully celebrated, but the heirs to the estate had no common plan for their inheritance and were in some cases sharply divided in their views as to how the assets should be allocated.

Since Bandung Pan-Asianism, under any other name, is seldom mentioned. The Afro-Asian bloc in the United Nations Organization is a wider grouping, and is far from a solid bloc. The division between Communist, non-aligned, and Western-allied Asian states constitutes the reality of present Asian international relations. These three groups have little in common, are composed of diverse peoples from widely separated parts of the continent, not even closely corresponding to the ancient divisions between the Chinese Far East, the Hindu South, and the Muslim West of Asia. Pan-Asianism was a reaction against a European attitude, itself outmoded. It has therefore withered as the concept to which it was opposed has also faded from the minds of European men.

BIBLIOGRAPHY

K. M. Panikkar. *Asia and Western Dominance.* (Allen and Unwin, London, 1959.)

G. B. Sansom. *The Western World and Japan.* (Cresset Press, London, 1950.)

Benjamin Schwartz. *In Search of Wealth and Power—Yen Fu and the West.* (Harvard Univ. Press, Cambridge, Mass., 1964.)

BIOGRAPHICAL NOTE

C. P. Fitzgerald. B. 1902, London; educated at Clifton College, Bristol. Lived in China 1923-39, with brief breaks, and for four years after the war, 1946-50. Has subsequently paid two visits to China (1956 and 1958). Leverhulme Fellowship for anthropological research in China, 1936-39. Worked at Tali, Yunnan province. Representative of the British Council in North China, 1946-50. Author of many books on China, including *The Birth of Communist China* (Penguin, London, 1955), *China: A Short Cultural History* (Cresset Press, London, revised ed., 1961) and *The Chinese View of their Place in the 1965 World* (The Royal Institute of International Affairs, London, 1964.)

POLITICAL INNOVATIONS IN ASIA

by

GUY WINT

SINCE the end of the war, the experience of the countries of Asia in handling political institutions has been imitative rather than creative. It has been remarkable what skill has been shown in adapting Western institutions for their needs. But the Asian countries have not used much ingenuity or imagination in the creation of new ones.

Among the Communist states there has been the imitation of Russia. In China, it is true, Mao Tse-tung has faced quite different problems from Russia, and has sought, usually without admitting what he is doing, to give the machinery of state a different twist from the Russian. But formally he has not yet been a great innovator. Neither in North Korea nor North Vietnam has there been any very novel development.

Among South-East Asian states the model has been the free world. The Philippines has a constitution borrowed from the United States; Malaya borrows from Westminster, though it has had to adjust this to provide for a form of federation. No constitution deserves special attention, except the one of South Vietnam which, rather like Kuomintang China of the past, combines a veneer of liberal institutions familiar in the West with the reality of single party dictatorship.

In 1962 Burma passed under the dictatorship of Ne Win, and ceased to be governed by an imitation of the Western parliament. Ne Win is said to be so much concerned about the possibility of a nuclear war that he wishes to detach Burma from the influence both of China and of the West. Burma is ruled by a hierarchy of councils in which popular election plays a part; but the chairman of each council, the man who effectively controls their action, is always an Army officer. The details of the operation of this political system are obscure.

In general the absence of political writing in the other countries is as remarkable as the absence of political innovation. They are thrown back on other models—Russian or Western—because they have not generated their own ideas.

There have however been significant innovations in the institutions of three Governments, those of India, Pakistan and Indonesia. There has also been interesting speculation in Ceylon.

INDIA

In India the outstanding event has been the great success (up to the time of writing) of the system adopted in 1947. That in turn was the elaboration of the system devised by the British, and which was embodied or was forecast in the Government of India Act 1935. In one respect however India is making a notable advance. This is the so-called Panchayet Raj. It is an attempt to give the peasant actual control of the lower reaches of administration, the part which comes closest to him. The Panchayet is the village council, and this is directly elected. The development of the system has been hastened by the considerable success and influence of the Community Development Projects, which are an attempt to stimulate rural development by making grants of capital available for projects in which the people as a whole show genuine interest, and which they are willing to further by personal sacrifice and effort. For this purpose the Panchayet obviously forms a very useful executive instrument. It will be some time before the whole of India has its Panchayets.

India is the place where a very considerable change was meditated in the years preceding independence, but, because of the way in which independence was in fact achieved, did not actually come about. When Mahatma Gandhi was the dominant figure in Congress, the nationalist view was that parliaments and the parliamentary type of government did not suit the needs of India. A completely new system, of Village Councils genuinely expressing the will of the people, was to be put in their place. But when the time came, Gandhi had ceased to be the controlling force (though he remained the keeper of the country's conscience) and the party leaders of Congress found it convenient to maintain their sophisticated political machinery. After the death of Gandhi the Gandhians, though they continued to exist as a wing of Congress, lost ground at first. But in time two forces appeared among them which seemed likely to give Gandhism a new lease of life and to make it influential in India's political development. One was Vinoba Bhave and his Bhoodan movement. The other was the ideas of Jaya Prakash Narayan.

Vinoba Bhave was in Gandhi's lifetime one of the most dedicated disciples of Gandhi. He lived as austerely as Gandhi, and like him refused to possess any property. Like him too he was a firm believer in non-violence. In the years after independence he became extremely depressed at the spread of Communism and with it the cult of violence among the poor. He discovered that his way of life gave him immense power with the people, and he initiated a scheme of land gifts by the well-to-do to the poor. This was followed by a scheme of gifts of service. Thereby a great network was built up of people who were pledged by vow to a form of service, and in this he saw the best antidote to Communism. And so it was, but the weakness of the enterprise lay in the organization. There was no adequate scheme for settling the gifts of land upon the poor, or in fact of sorting out the genuine gifts from bogus ones, such as other people's land or waste land, which many landlords donated freely.

Jaya Prakash Narayan is the former leader of the Indian Socialist Party. He had a distinguished fighting record during the war-time clash of the Socialists with the Government. He resigned from the Socialist Party to join Vinoba Bhave because he felt that at the time India needed missionaries of ideas rather than men of action. Jaya Prakash is the son of a peasant and the first major political leader who came neither from the Westernized intelligentsia nor from the administrative classes in the Princely States. He has prepared long manifestoes attacking at all vulnerable points the present system, and he has proposed a drastic recasting of the country's policy. He argues that India and the West are different worlds, and that institutions which may suit the West are not suited to India, either to its psychology or its present needs. He criticizes the parliamentary system of government on the grounds that it necessitates nation-wide political parties, which, by their nature, divide the country and carry new and unnecessary conflicts into society, especially the villages. These parties, he says, are creations of the towns, in which only 20 per cent of the Indian people live, and they know little of the realities of the Indian village. To the villager, the structure of parliamentary democracy is something remote and unmanageable.

In the place of the present system of government, Jaya Prakash Narayan proposes a new constitution which would tilt the focus of political activity from the town to the villages. Rather infelicitously, he calls this 'communitarianism'. The basic unity would be the village community with a village council directly elected by the suffrage of all inhabitants. Villages would be grouped into units of about 150 villages; the councils for these, to be called the Panchayet Samithi, would be indirectly elected by the basic village councils. In Jaya Prakash's view, a very surprising amount of the ordinary business of government could be transacted by these councils. His hope is that the established political parties could be deterred, either by the law or agreement, from contesting the elections for the councils.

Jaya Prakash, though urging a sweeping change, is not an irresponsible anarchist, and accepts that superior units of government must exist, both provincial governments and a central government. The central government would maintain the army: Jaya Prakash is less of a pacifist than Gandhi. But the powers of the superior organs would be devolved upwards from below, and would be limited by law.

Jaya Prakash has recently lived aloof from day by day politics. But his ideas have been making headway. He enjoys great esteem in the public opinion polls which show the popularity of leaders in India.

Pakistan

Pakistan has had a more restless and troubled political history than India. From 1958 it was under military government; it has now ended, but the search for a stable constitution is still in mid-career. Pakistan began its political history in 1947 with a constitution of the Westminster type. In course of time this broke down, partly because the political parties proved unstable and lacked strong leadership. (In Asia, generally, parliament only thrives where there is a strong political party.) Serious concern was felt for the state and its economic system: corruption became widespread. The parliamentary regime was finally discredited by a squalid fracas on the floor of a provincial legislative assembly which resulted in the death of the Deputy Speaker. The Army struck, and declared parliament abolished and the parties prohibited.

In form the new regime was a military dictatorship. But it was very unlike military juntas of the classical type. After the first few days the Army was little in evidence. It existed as a sanction and a threat in the background Under its protection Pakistan was ruled by its civil servants. It was very like the system of government in the heyday of British power in India. The Army insisted on certain reforms, and they were executed, including the purge of the Civil Service, which thus redeemed itself from corruption. Reform took place in all branches of the Government and social organization. But sooner or later the regime had to face the task of achieving a long-term settlement and giving the country a new constitution. The principal figures in this venture were President Ayub Khan and Manzur Quadir, his Foreign Secretary. Mr. Quadir had had no previous experience of politics until he was brought into the Government by President Ayub. He had been a fashionable lawyer, and was noted as a rather eccentric thinker about social problems.

These two men started, like Jaya Prakash Narayan, from the principle that the root evil in their system of politics was the parliamentary party; it was this which determined all features of politics, and determined them in a way which had little relation to the needs of the country as a whole. It brought to the top such undesirable elements as had reduced Pakistani politics to contempt, and bred inefficiency and corruption. It divided the country into factions fighting over issues with which they had no intimate concern. In place of the previous party system, they set themselves to produce politics of a new type, served by a new type of politician. To this end, they decreed the formation of what they called Basic Democracy, local councils handling local affairs. No less than 80,000 were brought into being. In the election of these councils, political parties were to be allowed no part, and in this way Ayub Khan and Manzur Quadir sought to exclude the old-style politician and also to foster a type of politics redolent of the countryside more than of the town. Candidates were to be local men, known intimately to the voters.

In 1962 President Ayub went a step further and tried to regularize the system by crowning it with a national parliament elected by the basic democracies. This, however, led to difficulties which are not yet overcome. His intention was that the candidates should be as independent of party as those which form the basic democracies. But, in fact, though candidates pretended to be independent, it was an open secret that many of them represented the former political parties. When they came together in the parliament, they acted together as cohesive groups, and Ayub had little choice except to recognize the reconstitution of the parties. At least, he did not decide to make an issue of it and to fight the parliament over the parties' existence.

Thus the political party had edged itself back into the centre of politics. The next move was an attempt at the restoration of the full parliamentary system. In January 1965 there took place a Presidential election. The old-style political parties combined and put up Miss Jinnah as a candidate. At first her popularity was evidently more than President Ayub had expected. But the election took place in two stages. The first was the election of Basic Democrats; these then proceeded to elect the President. In the result, President Ayub's calculations proved correct; the Constitution had been so made that a quite different result was produced from what might have been by direct election. President Ayub won comfortably.

INDONESIA

The other country where there has been innovation is Indonesia. The system there is called 'Guided Democracy'. This replaced in 1957 the previous type of government which had been the parliamentary system. President Sukarno was dissatisfied with cabinets created by the manoeuvres of the parties in parliament. He argued that they led to great waste of talent, since the majority parties excluded the minority ones. He wanted to have permanent representation in the cabinet of all the interests which he thought it in the public welfare to have recognized. And this representation was to be on a permanent or slowly changing basis, and not as evanescent as the fortune of parties in parliament. He therefore set up an executive consisting of representatives of all the parties and freed it from the liability of overthrow by the national parliament.

That was the theory of the 'Guided Democracy'. In practice it worked out to strengthen greatly the power of the President. Sukarno included in his cabinet only the representatives of the parties—and groups—which he favoured. The principal constituents were the Nationalists and the Communists. The great Conservative Party of the Muslims—the Masjumi—was excluded, and indeed, was forbidden to function.

The Indonesian experiment, though great claims had been made for it, was really less radical than the innovation in Pakistan, which struck at the political party, and made that responsible for the shortcomings of politics. But the Indonesian system was based on the party. It was an attempt to make the government more representative and more lasting by building upon the party structure. But it freed the parties from the danger of eclipse or of defeat by their competitors at the polls, and their consequent exclusion from office and their being doomed to running a fractious opposition.

CEYLON

There remains Ceylon. This has not actually made any innovation at all. It is governed, more or less regularly, by the parliamentary constitution which was given to it by the British upon receiving independence. But its political life has not been a happy one, as is shown by the turmoil, the communal riots, and the extreme demagogy that have occurred since the fall of the U.N.P. party in 1956.

A popular Prime Minister, Mr. Bandaranaike, who ended by being murdered, proposed before his death a scheme of reform. This was less drastic than it seemed, and also less novel, because in some respects it looked back to the Constitution of Ceylon which had actually been in force for a time, and is associated with the Donoughmore Commission; but it is none the less interesting. He wanted parliament divided into committees rather than parties, each committee having executive powers to carry out parliament's decisions. He believed that the parliamentary system was immensely wasteful by leaving at least half the members in opposition; and he sought to provide work for all members. Every individual member of parliament would take an effective, active role in the government of the country. The whole parliament would divide up into committees, to which would be allotted the administration. The composition of these committees would be determined by general agreement, or by drawing of lots. As a result, representatives would be known by their individual capacity and their importance would not be estimated by their attitude as party men.

Here again is an attempt at reforming the party system. It is this which most Asian thinkers have taken as the vital element, the pivot on which the whole political system turns. Other countries are likely to follow suit. The most likely centre of change is at present India, which is hardly likely to continue for long with its present Constitution intact.

BIBLIOGRAPHY

Sydney D. Bailey. *Parliamentary Government in Southern Asia.* (Hansard Society, London, 1953.)

A. Gledhill. *Fundamental Rights in India.* (Stevens, London, 1955.)

G. McTurnan Kahin. *Nationalism and Revolution in Indonesia.* (Cornell Univ. Press, Ithaca, New York, 1962.)

Beatrice Lamb. *India: a World in Transition.* (Pall Mall Press, London and Dunmow, 1963.)

Leslie Palmier. *Indonesia and the Dutch.* (Oxford Univ. Press, London, 1962.)

R. L. Park and Irene Tinker. *Leadership and Political Institutions in India.* (Princeton Univ. Press, Princeton, N.J., 1959.)

The Burma Socialist Programme Party, The System of Correlation of Man and his Environment. The Philosophy of the Burma Socialist Party. (Rangoon, 1963.)

Hugh Tinker. *India and Pakistan.* (Pall Mall Press, London and Dunmow, 1962.)

Tarzie Vittachi. *The Brown Sahib.* (André Deutsch, London, 1962.)

L. Howard Wriggins. *Ceylon: Dilemmas of a New Nation.* (Princeton Univ. Press, Princeton, N.J., 1960.)

BIOGRAPHICAL NOTE

GUY WINT. B. London, 1910. Educated at Dulwich College, Oriel College, Oxford, and Berlin University. Member of St. Antony's College, Oxford since 1957. Formerly leader-writer for *The Manchester Guardian*: now writes for *The Observer* on Asian affairs. His publications include *Spotlight on Asia* (Penguin, London, 1955), (with Peter Calvocoressi) *Middle East Crisis* (Penguin, London, 1957), *Common Sense About China* (Gollancz, London, 1960) and *China's Communist Crusade* (Praeger, New York, 1965).

THE ROLE OF THE MILITARY IN ASIA

by

ASLAM SIDDIQI

ASIAN nations have emerged independent in a troubled world. Political subordination was a great shame; they are therefore keen to win international acceptance and respect. One of the ways is to adopt the democratic form of parliamentary government and to set up a welfare state. Other aspirations, ideological, traditional and social, are not lacking. The nations of Asia thus generally set themselves a difficult task to fulfil.

These undertakings usually prove too onerous. Asians lack the experience to organize political parties which is so necessary to run a parliamentary government. Their raw administrations deteriorate and public affairs suffer. The welfare state proves a mere dream. The people soon get frustrated and learn to disbelieve and disrespect their leaders.

Of this situation the Communists take advantage. Subversion starts working silently and ceaselessly. The Communists look around for 'nation-wide crises' and for 'the ruling classes, passing through governmental crises' so that they may 'overthrow the government' (Lenin). Law and order pose a grave problem. The demand for military equipment and personnel becomes more pressing. Defence grows into a financial burden and holds up economic development. Initially the military forces are called in to control situations of emergency; but soon they feel constrained to stay on, wishing to remove the chronic national maladies in order to build a secure base for economic development and national security.

THE 'LEADER-FOLLOWER' RELATIONSHIP

The Asians hold national independence very dear. Its consolidation largely depends on economic development. This is possible only by accepting the laws of industrial economy. For Asia, this choice amounts to a social revolution. The Asians have to adapt themselves to the new economy and in the process face the inevitable crises. Otherwise they must remain subservient, economically and politically, to other powers.

Asian societies are conglomerations of closed primary communities spread out in numerous villages. The people are narrow in their outlook and parochial in their loyalties. They have communal but no public spirit. They therefore organize themselves around individuals. Such organizations inevitably lack a national outlook. Besides, there are intrinsic flaws. These political organizations lack programmes, public support and funds. Their leaders, the politicians, are constantly jockeying for positions and abusing their influence. When in power, they manipulate economic controls in order to buy support. The result is corruption and general deterioration in administration. There is much talk, critical and even abusive, of other parties and the Government, but little action. The concept and the role of the loyal opposition is little known and less appreciated. The processes of democracy thus inevitably lead to general frustration and chaos. Such a dangerous situation cannot last in any society. Somebody has to take control. The Asian nations have thus got to find leaders who can safeguard independence and also cope with the problems of economic development.

The nature of leader-follower relationship in Asia is thus of paramount importance. In a primary society individuals meet as whole persons and, therefore, every aspect of the personality comes under scrutiny. They have common interests and purposes and the tendency to act together. The dynamic basis of such a society is a common ideal. It demands in its leader a reference-model, whom it can follow and even idealize. He must have integrity and character, and be above suspicion or at least reproach.

In a secondary society, full personalities do not come into contact. The association of individuals is for special purposes and narrowed down by social barriers. Personal loyalty is lacking. Democratic processes and politicians are the creations of the secondary society; they tend to demolish the ideals of the primary society. Political propaganda and open criticism of political opponents make the integrity of all suspect. Politicians thus lose respect and fail to provide the leadership that primary societies urgently need.

For leadership, there is also a functional test. 'The more clearly perceived the goal and the more visible is progress towards it, the more follower emphasis there will be on the functional competence of the leader.'[1] In Asia the goals are all too clear. Most of the politicians lack functional competence which is demonstrated by deterioration in administration, corruption, stagnation and even retrogression. The military personnel, on the contrary, establish their competence by controlling emergencies and national calamities. Under colonial rule, the people moreover get accustomed to carrying out orders. They therefore associate efficiency with the military way of doing things. The military officers are aloof from the public and have no reputations to live down. Their training and professional work give them a national outlook. In the primary society, the military leader thus has a clear advantage over the politician. Once he gets a chance, he stays in power. 'The leader-follower relation most likely to become established in a free situation is the relation that is reciprocally rewarding to both the follower and the leader.'[2]

Military Leaders

The military leaders have generally lived up to the expectations of the people. On 8th October, 1958, President Mohammad Ayub Khan took over

[1] *Readings in Social Psychology* (New York: Henry Holt & Co., 1952), p. 340.
[2] Ibid, p. 339.

power in Pakistan. He said, 'There is total administrative, economic, political and moral chaos in the country, which cannot be tolerated in these dangerous times. A perfectly sound country has been turned into a laughing stock.' The national pride was hurt. He took immediate and vigorous steps to reform almost all aspects of national life. Land reforms combined with improved farming methods have increased agricultural production faster than population growth. In the economic field, the success is equally brilliant. The implementation of the Second Five-Year Plan has in several fields exceeded targets. Reviewing the financial affairs of Pakistan, the London *Times*[1] remarked, 'The improvement in the national accounts during the four years of military rule has been little short of miraculous.' In June, 1962 military rule was withdrawn.

In Burma, parliamentary democracy floundered in 1958 because of the sharp differences among the political parties. General Ne Win set up a military caretaker regime which continued in office till 1960. He then restored power to the political parties. But they could not function long. They again clashed and brought about an administrative breakdown. In March, 1962, General Ne Win again took over power. This time, the aim was not to caretake but to bring about administrative and economic revolutions.

An elaborate programme is under way to build society on a 'Burmese way to Socialism'. The immediate goals are physical security, administrative efficiency and increased agricultural productivity. Security Councils have been set up at village, town, district and division levels in order to meet local needs and also to implement Central Government programmes and projects. The Burma Economic Development Corporation which is the major productive organ in the fields of commerce and industry, has been fairly successful. The State Agriculture Marketing Board has the monopoly of purchasing rice and selling it abroad. The Government has taken over all public transport and enforced strict standards of efficiency. Radical reforms in the educational system have been introduced. The emphasis is on vocational and technical training. General Ne Win has, however, yet to find a non-military channel for communication with the people at large so that the regime may rest on a sure base.

In Thailand, there is no alternative to the military rule. Its contact with the West has been slight and therefore the democratic form of parliamentary government has not a very great appeal. National integrity has always been precarious. Laos wants the rich north-east region of Thailand to secede and join it. Laotian agents are continually busy in subversion, training guerillas, engaging in border skirmishes and carrying on 'revolutionary' activities. The region is thus in a state of tension and turmoil. Law and order and national integrity constitute difficult problems and do require strong men to tackle them. Since 1947, several military coups have taken place. On 20th October, 1958, Field-Marshal Sarisdi Dhanarajta assumed full powers.

Field-Marshal Sarisdi Dhanarajta has adopted vigorous measures to diversify agriculture, to develop industry and commerce and to improve irrigation works. This has strengthened the national economy and raised the

[1] October 29th, 1962.

living standard slightly. He has also implemented the North-east Development Plan in order to integrate the north-east region more firmly with Thailand. Stringent measures have been adopted to check Communist activities and subversion. The results are encouraging. On the occasion of the third anniversary of cabinet formation in 1962, the Field-Marshal said, 'Come have a look at it: come prove it for yourself; come see what we have done, and what good it will bring.'

General Park Chung Hee took over power in South Korea on 16th May, 1961, in order to 'eliminate accumulated evils and corruption' and to 'drive out so-called leaders who brought misery to the people; and the country to the brink of ruin'. On 5th January, 1962, he said, 'In the domestic sector, we have wiped out corruption and other evils and consolidated the ground-work for efficient Government administration.' He also announced that the Government would implement energetically a Five-Year Plan of economic development. In December, 1962, martial law was withdrawn.

There are variants of the direct military regime. The fundamental difference between a politician and a military leader is that whereas the former has to resort to questionable and even corrupt practices in order to win and retain the support of a political party, the latter has the support of a disciplined party of the armed forces. The military leader has no party problems and hardly has any need to adopt dishonest ways. In identifying the nature of power, it is thus important to know the structure of the party and its role.

In Indonesia, President Sukarno continues to play off the military against the political leaders. The armed forces consist largely of former fighters for national independence and enjoy considerable prestige. They seem to lack functional competence and prefer to operate through a civilian. There has been consequently only slight success in removing 'economic bottlenecks and shortages'.

A strong party has a role very much like the military. There is seldom open criticism which shakes public confidence and creates trouble in primary societies. In India, the Indian National Congress plays this role. Mr. Nehru's 20 years in jail gave him a prestige which no other Indian could have. During the Sino-Indian clash, the Congress members were threatened with 'stern disciplinary action' for criticizing the Government or the party leadership—which is, however, not as strong today as it was under Nehru. Nevertheless, the National Congress plays a role the military have in some other Asian countries.

Authoritarianism has thus, directly or indirectly, found its way into the Governments of Asia.

Power Confrontation in Asia

Asia is yet to find a balance of power. World War II and the withdrawal of colonial powers have virtually created a power vacuum. India and Japan have the resources to grow into sizeable military powers but they are not yet developed. There seems to be only one centre of power in Asia, namely, Peking. In fact, China and the Soviet Union have under their immediate control almost the entire territory once described as the 'geographical pivot of history'. The preconditions for world domination by these two Communist allies therefore exist. Such a state of affairs is hardly conducive to peace. It must keep Asian nations and others in jitters.

At present, the two Communist countries control a frontier across Asia which runs from Greece to the Pacific along the Soviet border with Turkey, Iran and Afghanistan and then along the Chinese border with Pakistan, India, Burma, Indo-China, the Pacific and Korea. Facing this land frontier is a string of bases along the rim of Asia, which are controlled by the United States and other Western powers. The present situation is that a huge land power is facing a sea power. This confrontation is powerfully influenced by the development of air and space weapons and the nuclear powered submarine which tend to tilt the balance in favour of the land power.

Under the present circumstances, any outward pressure of China in the Far East must be felt first of all by Korea, Hong Kong and Singapore. For the West, they are no more than outlying pickets. Next targets could be Japan and Formosa. Both of them can be powerfully supported from the American base in Okinawa. The Pacific itself is well manned by the American bases in Midway, Wake, Guam and Luzon. With Singapore in Chinese hands, the situation in the Indian Ocean would be precarious. Aden and Gan are the only two British bases from which naval operations could be conducted. Nationalization of the Suez has made it impossible for the British Navy in the Mediterranean to render any help in the Indian Ocean. Most of South and South-east Asia is under Chinese pressure. There were boundary disputes with Burma and Nepal. With India, there is open war. About 11 million Chinese help advance mainland China's policies. The Soviet Union has also penetrated into Afghanistan. Her threat to Iran and Turkey is constantly present. The historical urge of the Soviet Union to take over a warm water outlet, in particular the Straits of Dardanelles and the Gulf of Persia, still remains unsatisfied. She has the means, political, economic and military, to exert pressure on other countries in order to advance her interests.

To strengthen its position in this power confrontation in Asia, the United States of America has sponsored SEATO and CENTO and offered military arrangements to Asian nations. Turkey, Iran and Pakistan are members of CENTO. Pakistan, Thailand, the Philippines, Australia and New Zealand are members of SEATO. Cambodia, Laos and South Vietnam are the Protocol States. Japan, the Philippines, Formosa and South Korea have Mutual Defence and Security Treaties with the United States. Australia and New Zealand are members of ANZUS. There are also a number of American military bases in the Asian region.

The Mutual Security Act is the main enabling legislation for American Military Aid. In the case of Asia, Congress has added the condition that 'in furnishing military assistance in Asia, the President shall give the fullest assistance, as far as possible, directly to the free peoples in that area, in their creation of a joint organization, consistent with the Charter of the United Nations, to establish a programme of self-help and mutual cooperation designed to develop their economic and social well-being, to safeguard basic rights and liberties, and to protect their security and independence'. Several countries, including India, benefit from this Act.

The military leaders of Asia appreciate that the world has shrunk; and accumulation of military power anywhere is dangerous. They, therefore, support the forces which try to set up some sort of balance of power in Asia. They cooperate with the United States and thus contribute to world peace. This stability is actually a precondition for the economic development of Asia. It helps all. Politicians, however, exploit the situation. They have developed the policy of neutralism which has flourished in Asia only because of the presence of the American military power. It is again the politicians' attitude of sacrificing the nation for the party, and the world for the country, which jeopardizes the balance. As internal problems eliminate the Asian politicians, so the armed clashes like the Sino-Indian war will wipe out the neutralists. Nationally and internationally, the military leaders in Asia thus contribute to stability, security and the cause of peace.

Rival Military Dogmas

The military in Asia has also a role far more important than the immediate one. Asia provides a battle-ground for the encounter of civilizations—Western Democracy and Communism. The ancient civilizations of Asia are not mere spectators. They are already trying to pick and choose. How far they succeed, only the future can tell. The military has, however, a key role in this process. Asians are determined to stay independent, internally and externally. This demands efficient military forces. They can be secured only by adopting new techniques. Certain consequences follow. 'In adopting the rudiments of the Western military technique, the Imam had introduced into the life of his people the thin end of a wedge which in time would inexorably cleave their close-compacted traditional Islamic civilization asunder. Every historic culture pattern is an organic whole in which all the parts are interdependent so that, if any part is prised out of its setting, both the isolated part and the mutilated whole behave differently from their behaviour when the pattern is intact. The broken pattern tends to reconstitute itself in a foreign environment into which one of its components has once found its way.'[1] The military is 'the thin end of a wedge' or 'the isolated part of a culture pattern'. What dogma of war the military adopts is of paramount importance for the future of Asia.

Western war technology and techniques are rapidly improving. Their improvement has almost reached a dead end. In Western dogmas of war, weapons are supreme. Immense resources, financial and technical, are required to produce them. No Asian nation can buy these prohibitively costly weapons; it may, however, beg and borrow. But this leads to dependence, which the Asians hate. A vicious circle is thus set up which there is no way to break. Moreover, Western weapons and war techniques have so developed in destructiveness and intricacy that they have lost flexibility. In the words of General Maxwell D. Taylor they constitute 'the uncertain trumpet' which would not inspire the people to fight. Asians also find them unsuitable. In

[1] Arnold Toynbee: *Civilization on Trial* (New York: Meridian Books, Inc., 1958), p. 170.

November 1962, Mr. Nehru ascribed the Indian collapse in the Sino-Indian clashes in the Himalayas to inefficient British techniques and unsuitable weapons. India has, therefore, raised the armed militia as a part of the regular armed forces. This marks a break with the Western war techniques.

The dogma of the protracted war, propounded by Mao Tse-tung, has, however, great fascination for the Asians. They feel hopeful when Mao Tse-tung declares, 'Weapons are an important factor in war but not the decisive one: it is man and not material that counts. The contest of forces is not only a contest of military and economic power, but also one of the power and morale of man. Military and economic power must be controlled by men'.[1] The speed with which Mao captured China in 1949 astonished all, including Stalin. In the Korean War in 1952, the Chinese acquitted themselves quite well. Lieutenant-General James M. Gavin writes, 'The real tragedy of Korea was that this great nation, with its scientific resources and tremendous industrial capacity, had to accept combat on the terms laid down by a rather primitive Asiatic power.'[2] He deplores that the fighter-bombers failed to provide effective tactical air support and that 'even horse cavalry divisions were able to move the length of North Korea and participate in the battles'. In the Sino-Indian clashes in 1962, 'swift attack and withdrawal', 'swift concentration and dispersal' and 'quick decision', resulted in a collapse of the Indian forces. This dogma has thus repeatedly proved its efficacy in the battlefield. It has almost revolutionized the concept of war. A regular army with guerillas as its auxiliaries gains considerably in hitting power and in collecting intelligence. All Communist states maintain their own guerilla formations. Even the United States has started training irregular fighters. The techniques of guerilla warfare have thus come to stay.

Guerilla warfare admirably suits Asia's primary societies. The members of such societies are bound by loyalties which the strains of war strengthen. The Asian nations can produce or procure only rudimentary weapons which are good enough for the guerilla fighter. Their battles are mostly defensive which helps build morale. Nationalism is another morale builder. The large populations of Asian nations provide adequate numbers of superb man-weapons. Their quality in general is such that according to General Alfred M. Gruenther it takes ten men in conventional forces to nullify one guerilla fighter. Even nuclear weapons will not be able to exterminate the guerilla fighters. In fact, they alone will be able to operate after a nuclear holocaust. The protracted or guerilla warfare has thus clear advantages. Its adoption, however, has consequences not confined to the battlefield alone. It creates an attitude of mind which may considerably influence Asia's future.

Limitations of Military Methods

To the Asian nations, the military, no doubt, provides stability and, in a restricted sphere, functional competence. But the basic task is to effect an economic revolution. 'The economic structure of society,' Engels said, 'always forms the real basis from which, in the last analysis, is to be explained the whole superstructure of legal and political institutions as well as of the

[1] *On the Protracted War* (Peking, 1954), p. 56.
[2] *War and Peace in the Space Age* (New York: Harper and Brothers, 1958), p. 123.

religious, philosophical and other conceptions of each historical period.' To change the economic structure therefore demands the incessant effort of the entire nation in all fields of human activity. It cannot be a command performance. It is not within the competence of the military or any other section to bring about such a radical change. A nation-wide effort has to be made at all levels.

The military forces which turn their attention from the frontiers to the inside of the country find themselves confronted with an intricate and an unusual situation. They do restore law and order and check subversion and other anti-social practices. They also provide steadiness to national affairs. But the real cause of national chaos lies deeper. Crises are inevitable in the course of economic transformation. Asians seek to accomplish in years what the Europeans took centuries to do. The problems that the military have therefore to face are far too many, far too intricate. Decisions have to be taken and actions enforced in fields not their own. Here lies their peril as also their opportunity.

Inflated by their success, most of the military leaders develop aggressive self-confidence. They refuse to see the other viewpoint, and enforce their own at point of sword. By training, they are 'offensive' minded. 'Fall on the enemy in numbers and masses: therein lies salvation', advises Marshal Foch. The 'enemy' is the man with a different viewpoint. In the interests of 'salvation', the sword becomes omnipotent. But the sword is apt to inflict fatal injuries upon those who wield it with the slightest clumsiness or misjudgement. 'When an individual or a Government or a community that has command of military power mistakes the limits of the field within which this power can be used with effect, or misconceives the nature of the objectives which it is possible to attain by means of it, the disastrousness of this aberration can hardly fail to make itself conspicuous through the seriousness of the practical consequences.'[1] Such mistakes are often made. Nations get divided and so do the military forces. The sword again proves the arbiter; and the strong men have to yield place to the stronger men. Such is the rule of the sanctuary of Diana Nemarensis where a candidate for the priesthood could only succeed to office by slaying the priest, and having slain him, retained office until he himself was slain by a stronger or craftier. Nations blighted by such strong men are lost.

But the strong men who understand and respect the limits of the military power, may prove saviours of the Asian nations. The primary societies of Asia are on the move. Internally, they have to face the strains and stresses of economic transformation; externally, the environment is not too friendly. They do need protection and assistance which strong men promise to provide. Their success consists in giving this protection and assistance the form of institutions, acceptable to the people at large. If they can additionally reconstitute the pattern of culture of which they have selected a part or revive and adapt their own cultural pattern to contemporary conditions, then they have amply justified themselves. This phenomenon however is not very frequent.

[1] Arnold Toynbee: *A Study of History*, Vol. IV. (London: Oxford University Press, 1951), p. 504.

The role of the military in Asia is thus a precarious one. The situation is such that risks have to be taken. The military leaders only symbolize the urgent need of steadiness in the course of an economic revolution. If helped in their venture, Asian nations may go forward and fulfil the large task they have set themselves. If not, they will fall by the roadside and prove sources of chronic danger to world peace.

BIBLIOGRAPHY

William Gutteridge. *Armed Forces in New States.* (Oxford Univ. Press, London, 1962.)

Joseph E. Johnson (ed). *The Role of the Military in Underdeveloped Countries.* (Princeton Univ. Press, Princeton, N.J., 1962.)

Arnold Toynbee. *A Study of History*, Vol. IV. (Oxford Univ. Press, London, 1954.)

Mao Tse-tung. *On the Protracted War.* (Foreign Languages Press, Peking, 1954.)

Survival. Journal published by the Institute of Strategic Studies, London.

BIOGRAPHICAL NOTE

ASLAM SIDDIQI. Author of *Pakistan Seeks Security* (Longmans, Pakistan Branch, Lahore, 1960) and *A Path for Pakistan* (Pakistan Publishing House, Karachi, 1964), etc. Regular contributor to specialized journals. Active member of Pakistan Institute of International Affairs. Deputy Director, Central Institute of Islamic Research, Pakistan.

COMMUNISM IN ASIA

by

RICHARD HARRIS

History of Communism in Asia

Communism has a history of over forty years in Asia from the time it was imported in the years following the Russian revolution. During those forty years it has gradually become domesticated. Chinese ideological differences with the Soviet Union have given this process a push forward; the whole world Communist movement has become polycentric. Such differences were indeed inherent from the moment when, flouting Stalin's wishes, the Chinese Communists triumphed. It is misleading however to deduce from this that Chinese leadership has been substituted for Russian leadership in Asia; the process whereby Communism has been domesticated has been influenced by the differences to be found within the various civilizations of Asia. Only in a broad sense can generalizations be made about Communism in the whole continent.

It is in its early history, when it was imported from the West, that such generalizations are valid. There is no need to quote Lenin's dicta about imperialism or an assault on the West by way of the East to explain what happened; it was a natural sequence. Just as imperial rule brought to these countries the political and economic outlook of the West, so the new Western political doctrine of Marxism was imported, either by Asians who went to study in the West and became associated with the Communist movement there, or by Western revolutionaries who went to the East as missionaries for their revolutionary faith. In the early days these European Communists were as much leaders as the imperial rulers themselves. Communist parties in Asia thus began, to borrow a Communist term, as semi-colonial parties, led by Asians whose impulse towards Western ways divorced them from their own country, advised by Westerners who had no knowledge or sympathy for the conditions facing these countries in their own revolutionary course.

The first Communist party in Asia to escape from this Western tutelage and rebuild itself on native foundations was the Chinese, which was one, though only one, of the reasons for its final success. No other Communist party achieved this shift before the war and thus no party, with the exception of the Vietnamese, was able to catch the tide of anti-imperialism and ride to power with its backing. The refounding of these parties has come since the war; in India gradually and still far from complete; in Indonesia after the total failure of the revolt at Madiun in 1948. Burma still has Communist guerillas surviving from the past though an 'above ground' movement exists. Ceylon has never quite escaped the past; Malaya, with its strong Chinese element, is a special case.

The post-war new-style Communist party differs from the old-style Comintern party. Its emphasis is national rather than international. It must have leaders who are not over-Westernized and divorced from their own culture. It recognizes that the peasants can be a revolutionary force in Asia if properly harnessed and it accepts the corollary that Communist victory can never be achieved through an urban proletariat. Finally Communism must accommodate itself after some fashion to the country's religious and cultural traditions. It must not seem opposed to the national spirit. Only then has it any hope of gaining a mass following.

Any further generalization about Communism in Asia is dangerous and indeed misleading since its growth depends on factors that differ from country to country, factors which favour its growth far more in some countries than in others; factors such as climate, population pressure on resources, the balance of religious and secular interests in society, the legacy of Western rule, the intellectual energy within the culture and so on. On the other hand it is not necessary to consider each country as an entirely separate case if a broad development can be charted.

Divergence of Communism in Asia

An important development of Asian Communism is its divergence, an outcome of the differences in its civilizations. Though South Asia is not one coherent civilization East Asia is and if its Communist parties are examined it will be seen that they differ, already, from those of South Asia. Communism in Asia followed something of a common pattern in its beginnings because its parties were semi-colonial and thus influenced by Europe. For a time, in the first years of independence after the war, pan-Asian feeling was transposed to pan-Asian Communist feeling. But this was no better founded than was the early semi-colonial stage; and just as the gulf between China and Russia has demonstrated the independence of a national East Asian Communist party, so the gulf between China and India, revealed in the border issue, illustrates the gulf between these two civilizations. The pan-Asianism of Bandung is no longer possible after the conflict between China and India; the pan-Asian Communism of fifteen years ago is no longer possible either. It is easier therefore to divide this account into sections dealing with East Asia and South Asia.

East Asia

East Asian civilization includes China, Japan, Korea and Vietnam. These countries are linked to China by the influences they have derived from its civilization over two thousand years; through China's direct rule or suzerainty, as in the case of Vietnam and Korea, or from the direct borrowings and exchanges with Japan. Chinese learning was the classic base for all these countries. Chinese philosophy moulded their political thought, especially when the Chinese language was accepted as the fundamental equipment of the scholar. And although there were profound differences as well, it may be said that Chinese political institutions and Chinese political thought have been part of the inheritance influencing these countries to-day.

This coherence in East Asian civilization, a coherence established by doctrines to which the convenient label Confucianism has been given, impelled it to resist the incursion of Western power with more vehemence and more confidence in its own superiority—above all in China's case—than South Asia did. And since its own state systems, if not directly Confucianist, were by tradition authoritarian, looking to an emperor or to a bureaucracy as a source of political and ideological authority, the influence of the West was difficult to incorporate piecemeal. In China in this century, Communism could seem a total substitute for Confucianism as a system for the organization of man in society. It is therefore its claim as a total philosophy, as a new creed on which to refound these societies that Communism has an appeal. It is a new system to replace the old, though a system to be translated into East Asian terms. In none of these countries is religious tradition or a religious hierarchy strong enough to be a barrier to the import of Communism. In a society where intellectual leadership has always operated through an authoritarian system East Asian Communism is a creed that appeals because it offers a central truth. A country that orders its society in accordance with prescribed truth about the nature of man and his relationships in society expresses its Communist faith in accordance with these traditions. Communism in East Asia has a total, ideological appeal; in South Asia its appeal is pragmatic and piecemeal. With these general observations we can turn to the state of East Asian Communist parties.

JAPAN

Just as Japan differs more from the East Asian pattern than the two smaller countries which grew up in China's shadow, so the Japanese Communist Party differs from the others. For one thing, the modernization of Japan after the Meiji Restoration of 1868 was a partial, but within its limits, wholehearted acceptance of Western ways. The Japanese Communist Party, which was founded under direct stimulation from the Comintern in 1922, was thus too late to play in Japanese life the same role as the Chinese Communists in China, as thinkers who offered a resolution of the conflict between East Asian and Western values. In large part Japan had already taken that choice and the Communists could thus make little headway with national sentiment. In so far as a national sentiment tried to assert itself in reaction to this Westernization there grew up the spurious creed which justified militarist expansion, veneration of the Emperor, the Shinto religion and other supposedly hallowed Japanese beliefs. This pre-war blind alley phase in Japan's development naturally militated against Communist success, quite apart from the brutal suppression of Communists by most Japanese Governments before the war.

With Japan's defeat the Communist Party could expand again in an atmosphere in which all Western ideas were equally welcome. Some of its leaders had been in exile, among them Sanzo Nosaka, the present Chairman of the Party, who had been with the Chinese Communists in Yenan. Under the American Occupation the Party was free to enter political life and by 1949 its membership had grown to 230,000 and it won 35 seats in the lower house of the Diet. But it had still not, like the Chinese Communist Party, been transformed into a native model. Land reform and economic progress under the Occupation reduced even further the possibility of any mass movement from below. Progressive Westernization—and the existence of the Japanese Socialist Party—removed its chances of offering a compact ideology for Japan's post-war renewal. Besides this, or perhaps because of it, the Japanese Communists still suffered from internal differences. One struggle was between the use of violent as against parliamentary methods; another was the conflicting traditions in the party between its Comintern-dominated past and those of its leaders influenced by a Chinese outlook. During the fifties membership fell sharply. The left-wing of the Japanese Socialists seemed to offer more hope for change in Japan. In the 1955 elections, the first to be held after the end of the Occupation, the Party won only two seats; in the 1963 elections it won only 5 seats. The Party has gone over to the Chinese side in the Sino-Soviet dispute, though a small faction led by Yoshio Shiga broke away over the Party's hostility—in keeping with the Chinese—to the nuclear test ban treaty.

Japan has gone so far along the Western path, not merely in advanced technology and in Western style institutions, but into acceptance of Western ideas, as to leave extremism and a total ideological solution no chance. Attempts to revive the right-wing ideology in numerous small parties are no more likely than Communism to be an answer to Japan's problems. Such parties still exist while the country moves uneasily from an East Asian into a wholly Western pattern. And there is always still the possibility that an accommodation with China could again bring Japan back into an East Asian world of thought. Otherwise the prospects for Communism in Japan seem poor.

Korea

Korean Communism grew up in the 1930's largely among exiles opposed to the Japanese occupation of their country. Some were with the Chinese Communists in Yenan, a few in the West, but most in the Soviet Union. It was thus possible for the Soviet-trained Kim Il-song to be raised to power at the head of the Korean Laodong Party in the northern part of the country occupied by the Russians. The assault on South Korea showed the Stalinist character of the party and its defeat after U.N. intervention much reduced the chance of Communism ever gaining a following in the south. Since the armistice the Government in the north has restored its devastated territory and rebuilt its industry. Conflicts within the Party have necessarily reflected affiliations with either China or the Soviet Union and as the Sino-Soviet split has grown wider the Koreans have gradually come down on the Chinese side, though trying not to offend the Russians. While South Korea remains under a determined anti-Communist dictatorship and all contact between north and south is refused—by the south—the country seems likely to remain divided. Progress in the north had attained a fair standard of living and an effective industrial base by 1965 but this did not serve as an attraction to the south as it was still accompanied by a Stalinist discipline. Nor has the south evolved or shown much sign of evolving a political system and ideas which might eventually win over the north. The Korean Communists have come out on the Chinese side in the Sino-Soviet dispute and Mr.

Kosygin's visit early in 1965 made no fundamental difference to their position.

Vietnam

The Vietnamese Communist Party was founded in 1930 and enjoyed the leadership of the only man of comparable political stature to Mao Tse-tung in China—Ho Chi Minh. The party was severely repressed under French rule, began to build up its cells in the countryside during the war years, and, as the dominant element in a nationalist coalition, the Vietminh, was able to proclaim itself as a provisional government at the war's end. In South Vietnam its strength was not enough to resist the allied reoccupation, but in the north the French negotiated with Ho Chi Minh's government. Eventually after a long struggle negotiations at Geneva led to the partition of Vietnam into a Communist North and an anti-Communist South. Under a declaration of the conference elections to unify the country were to be held by 1956, but the government of Ngo Dinh Diem, supported by the Americans, was unwilling to enter into discussions with the North and no elections were held. In 1957 and 1958 there were signs of revolt from Communist cells surviving in the South which expanded, after a repressive campaign by Diem, into full-scale guerilla warfare in 1959. By 1960 this came under the political direction of the North and the war had reached a critical point with talk of negotiations early in 1965.

After attempting to remain neutral in the Sino-Soviet dispute the North Vietnamese Communists finally came down on the Chinese side, though avoiding any outright attacks on the Russians. A Russian mission headed by Mr. Kosygin visited Hanoi in January 1965 and the joint communique with its mention of peaceful coexistence suggested that the Vietnamese were keeping one foot in the Russian camp. While pro-Chinese ideologically, the Vietnamese are at the same time determined to remain independent of China. Economic errors and difficulties with the intellectuals have hindered the regime in the North. It is nevertheless interesting proof of the East Asian desire for a total solution of ideological problems that in the South many of the young dedicate themselves to the Communist cause apparently little influenced by the failings shown in practice by the Northern regime in its eight years' rule.

China

Founded in 1921 the Chinese Communist Party grew slowly, wasted its energies in fruitless strikes and armed actions, was thrown out of the alliance by the Kuomintang and only began to gain strength when guerilla armies set up liberated areas with the backing of peasant revolutionaries. Of such areas the largest and most successful was led by Mao Tse-tung in Kiangsi province. The evacuation and concentration of these liberated areas in north-west China (1934-36) gave the Chinese Communists a base from which they spread during the war years and won victory in the civil war in 1949.

Before it ever came to power therefore Chinese Communism had won confidence in itself as an independent military force and as the ruler of nearly 100 million peasants; above all, in the view of Mao Tse-tung and his colleagues, it was able to interpret Marxism-Leninism creatively in Chinese terms. When it took power in 1949 it was a largely home-grown movement, able to capture Chinese patriotic loyalty. In the fifteen years since then the Chinese Communists have remained remarkably united, even through the extreme difficulties and obvious failure of their policies during the past three years. Signs of apathy among its eighteen million members are no more than could be expected. The zeal of the early years could hardly have been sustained. The basic belief in a Chinese interpretation of Marxism is unshaken. This tendency has been much strengthened by the differences with the Russians over co-existence and world revolution. It would be reasonable to forecast therefore that the sinicizing of Communism will continue, that its rigours will be modified (with some older Chinese traditions flavouring the mixture), that if prudent state relations with the Russians are restored nevertheless the severance of Communist party relations will remain, and that Chinese policy will follow its own path.

The belief that its influence will be great in Asia needs sceptical examination. For one thing its attitudes and methods are alien to those of South Asia. It has never had any close association with the Indian Communists; its cultivation of the Indonesian Communists will not necessarily mean stronger Chinese influence in Indonesia. The adherence to the Chinese line of such small parties as the Burmese and Thais adds little to Chinese power; indeed, during their dispute with the Russians the Chinese have shown rather more interest in the competition for the allegiance of nationalist-revolutionary movements than in Communist parties as such.

South Asia

South Asian Communism still has more in common with European Communism than it has with East Asian Communism. It began with the same handicaps of semi-colonial status and while the international character was still dominant in 1948 began attempts to gain power by violence in India, Burma, the Philippines, Malaya and Indonesia. The relics of this warfare still drag on in some countries but for the most part their Communist parties have now come out in new colours. They are self-consciously 'national' parties, unwilling to allow that they are in any way bound to the dictates of international Communism. They are ready to accommodate themselves to regional, linguistic, religious or caste differences, as the Indian Communist party shows. The tendency is for these parties to accept the argument for peaceful change wherever a democratic system allows them to function and this may continue in spite of Chinese arguments favouring violent revolution. It might be said that the Communists of South Asia represent themselves to the electorate as just like any other party only more devoted to the electors' interests, more dedicated and uncorrupt and more efficient and progressive.

It may be a long time before this appeal goes very far. In many of these countries the early years of independence have been succeeded by a reaction, natural enough in countries severed by imperialism from much of their past, towards religion, language, culture and customs that modify the accepted progressive, Western standards with which they began their independent lives. This militates against Communist success and at most, Communists can hope only for regional success. A preference for friendship with the Russians—as against East Asian Communists—seems likely to survive.

India

The further the Party has got from universalism and the closer to the realities of Indian life the better it has done. It was elected to power for a time in Kerala and may succeed there again. The Sino-Soviet dispute and the border conflict with China helped to split the Party into left and right wings. In 1965 the arrest of many left-wing leaders damaged what little chances the Party had of making headway in India after Mr. Nehru's death.

Indonesia

The PKI is the largest party in Asia outside China. It was rebuilt after the failure of the Madiun rebellion in 1948. Its membership had then sunk to 5,000 but under the leadership of D. N. Aidit from 1951 onwards it has been built up to over two and a half million (1965). Its strength is largely in Java where it has built its success on mass organizations, particularly for peasants and women, which offer some substitute for a decaying social structure. The party has supported the Chinese in the dispute with the Russians but has not been as hostile to the Russians as the Chinese and will probably wish to keep on good terms with Moscow. The Indonesian Communists are anxious to avoid a close affiliation with China that might harm their national image in their country. Latterly, in skilful support of President Sukarno they have advanced to an almost impregnable position in the 'guided democracy' he leads.

Malaysia

Communism here is a Chinese and hence an East Asian phenomenon, temporarily obscured by the unity of Communists, whether Chinese or Malay or Indian, in opposition to Malaysia and in support of the Indonesian Communist Party in sympathy with Indonesia's confrontation of Malaysia. The young Chinese educated in Sarawak, Singapore and (rather less) in Malaya provide recruits, but a relatively progressive and economically successful society militates against any mass basis for Communism.

Buddhist South-east Asia

In Burma Communists still survive as guerillas though now harassed by a military government. Communist infiltration into left-wing parties goes on but has not been very effective. In Thailand a military dictatorship represses Communism severely, though in 1964 a patriotic front under probably Communist leadership was active in the north-east. In Cambodia Prince Sihanouk has a small left-wing opposition with a tiny Communist leadership but without hope of growth. This leaves Laos as the only problem country. The Pathet Lao began life as a nationalist guerilla movement in 1946, was reorganized by the Vietminh in the war against the French in 1951 and has since had a small Laotian Communist leadership and a much larger and more influential Vietnamese Communist backing. East Asian and South Asian Communism are here confused. Not until Laos can separate itself from the influence of North Vietnam will the weakness of Laotian Communism be exposed.

Asia and the Sino-Soviet Dispute

The issues in this dispute may be summarized as follows: whether imperialism is fundamentally warlike or whether its nature has changed at all since Lenin's day; whether coexistence is thus possible or can be only a temporary expedient; whether the result of nuclear war—threatened by imperialism—will be capitalist collapse and Communist gain, or whether both would suffer equally in the holocaust; whether Communist parties can gain power by peaceful means and should prefer these means; whether Yugoslavia's position outside the Communist camp is a permanent threat to its health; whether and in what form aid should be given to revolutionary movements and the conflict this makes with aspirations for world peace; and the nature of bourgeois nationalist governments and the aid that should be given them.

Throughout South and South-east Asia independent governments now exist making many of these issues irrelevant. Where they are relevant to the Communist parties of Asia, such as in the means to power—whether by guerilla warfare or parliamentary democracy or otherwise—then the Communist parties want to be left alone to decide for themselves. That is the first thing to be said about the dispute: that it has accelerated the tendency for each party to assert its independence in its national role and methods. The second fact arises from this: an abhorrence of the kind of split that is likely to be reflected in their own parties and to damage them severely. Whatever may appear on the surface therefore there is an underlying current of neutralism towards the split, both over the issues being argued and the effects the split may have.

Having said this, something of a line-up can be detected in the three zones of East, South-east and South Asia. In East Asia as we might expect, the devotion to ideology and a way of philosophical thinking derived from China makes for sympathy with the Chinese case. The North Koreans and Japanese parties are firmly on the Chinese side though both have been careful to avoid offending the Russians more than was necessary. The North Vietnamese tried to remain neutral but have more or less committed themselves to the Chinese side.

In South-east Asia, with the exception of Indonesia, the Communist parties are not large, but they share a common and inherited attitude of caution and respect towards China which means that, given the choice, it is the Chinese side they come down on. The Indonesian party, much cultivated over the years by Peking, and in the early stages of the dispute wholly on the Chinese side, has lately seen how dangerous a split in its own ranks could be. The Indonesians thus urge a settlement and a carefully prepared conference; though they still side generally with the Chinese this is a hook they want to get off for fear they might hang on it.

In South Asia, the most westward-looking part of Asia, a pro-Chinese wing has emerged in the Ceylon party whereas the left-wing of the Indian party might be better described as such than as pro-Chinese.

Throughout much of South and South-east Asia Russian influence can be exerted through economic aid and the supply of arms; and where this operates, those Communist parties that seek to take a national role are unlikely to spoil their chances by too great an attachment to the Chinese. The conclusion seems to be therefore that just as the Communism of East Asia is in a class by itself, it will be in that cultural area alone that lasting support for the Chinese position will be found. An 'Eastern Church' exists in all but name.

Conclusion

Pan-Asian feelings have died away as Asian countries revert to their own individuality. The great gulf between East Asia and South Asia has been dramatically underlined by the dispute over the India-China border. A Communism continually moulded by East Asian tradition will survive in China, Korea and Vietnam, detached from the Communism of Eastern Europe. In South Asia, as and when political conditions allow it, Communist parties will stand for election and may gain a solid following. In no one country do they seem likely to achieve power in this way (still less in any other way) in the foreseeable future, though the example of Kerala may be repeated in local or regional Communist power which might well one day come about in parts of Java.

Communist Parties in Non-Communist Countries in Asia

Country	Name of Party	Membership	Pro-Soviet	Pro-Chinese
India	Communist Party of India (CPI)	165,000 (split)	*	*
Nepal	Communist Party of Nepal	3,000 (split)	*	*
Pakistan	Communist Party of Pakistan	2,500		
Ceylon	Communist Party of Ceylon (CCP)	2,000 (split)	*	*
Taiwan	—	negl.		
Hong Kong	Communist Party of Hong Kong (section of Chinese CP)	unknown		*
Japan	Communist Party of Japan (JCP)	150,000		
South Korea	—	negl.		
Burma	Communist Party of Burma—Red Flag (CPB)	500		*
	Burma Communist Party—White Flag (BCP)	1,000		*
	National United Front (NUF)	unknown	*	

Country	Name of Party	Membership	Pro-Soviet	Pro-Chinese
Thailand	Thai Communist Party . .	unknown		*
	Chinese Communist Party (Thailand)	unknown		*
Cambodia	Pracheachon Party . . .	100		*
Laos	Workers' Party (Phak Khon Ngan —PKN)	100		*
	Neo Lao Hak Xat (NLHX) .	3,000		*
	Pathet Lao (armed forces) .	20,000		*
South Vietnam	National Front for the Liberation of South Vietnam (NFLSV) .	unknown		*
	People's Revolutionary Party .	unknown		*
Malaya	Malayan Communist Party (MCP)	500		*
Singapore	Malayan Communist Party (MCP)	2,000		*
Sarawak	The Communist Organization (CCO)	1,000		*
Indonesia	Indonesian Communist Party (PKI)	2,500,000		*
Philippines	Filipino Communist Party (PKP)	2,000		

BIBLIOGRAPHY

J. H. Brimmell. *Communism in South-East Asia.* (Oxford Univ. Press. London, 1959.)

Michael Edwardes. *Asia in the Balance.* (Penguin, London, 1962.)

Donald Hindley. *The Communist Party of Indonesia 1951-1963.* (Cambridge Univ. Press, London, 1965.)

Gene D. Overstreet and Marshall Windmiller. *Communism in India.* (Cambridge Univ. Press, London, 1959.)

L. W. Pye. *Guerilla Communism in Malaya.* (Oxford Univ. Press, London, 1956.)

Stuart R. Schram (ed. and trans.) *The Political Thought of Mao Tse-tung.* (Pall Mall Press, London, 1964.)

Benjamin I. Schwartz. *Chinese Communism and the Rise of Mao.* (Oxford Univ. Press, London, 1951.)

BIOGRAPHICAL NOTE

RICHARD HARRIS. B. 1914 in China and lived there until 1928. Returned to China on war service, 1945; with British Embassy in China, 1947-50; joined *The Times* as correspondent in Hong Kong, 1951-53, and Singapore 1953-55. Since 1955 leader-writer on Asian affairs for *The Times*, London. Author of *Independence and After* (Oxford Univ. Press, London, 1962). Has also taken part in broadcasting and television on Asian subjects.

THE SOUTH-EAST ASIA TREATY ORGANIZATION

by

HUGH TOYE

THE South-East Asia Treaty Organization is an alliance of states located in or having interests or responsibilities in South-East Asia, formed in 1954 after the end of the Indo-China War as an earnest of continued Western resistance to the spread of Communism in the area. The nations concerned are the United States, Great Britain and France by reason of post-colonial obligations, the Philippines, Thailand and Pakistan by reason of location, and Australia and New Zealand by reason of propinquity. Although it remains in 1965 a useful organ of defence co-operation, policy disagreements between its Western members in recent years have reduced its credibility. This development has to some extent been counteracted by bilateral arrangements between certain of its members.

WAR IN INDO-CHINA AND THE GENEVA CONFERENCE, 1954

1954 was an anxious year for the West in the Orient. The war against Communist insurgency was only beginning to be won by the British in Malaya. The Communist grip on North Korea had been confirmed by the outcome of the Korean War in 1953. Communist insurgency was still rampant in the Philippines. The United States, moral and material backers of the French in Indo-China ever since Communist Chinese recognition of the Vietminh in 1950, were to be saved only by their hard-headed Congressmen from U.S. Air Force intervention to avert a French defeat at Dien Bien Phu. It seemed to many that the consequences of that defeat, the surrender of North Vietnam to Communism and of the other newly independent Indo-Chinese states to neutralism, would lead to the progressive collapse of freedom throughout the region. Mr. Dulles, the United States Secretary of State, found neutralism immoral. 'The loss of Indo-China,' said President Eisenhower, 'will cause the fall of South-East Asia like a set of dominoes.'

These were the circumstances in which on the eve of the Geneva Conference of 1954, Mr. Dulles began to promote the idea of a collective arrangement 'within the framework of the United Nations, to assure the peace, security and freedom of South-East Asia and the Western Pacific.' France in the agony of her defeat raised no objection. Britain, who was to assume with Russia special responsibilities with regard to Indo-China as co-chairman of the Geneva Conference, sought to ensure that Mr. Dulles' initiative should not prejudice either a peaceful settlement at Geneva or the chances of the Colombo Powers—India, Pakistan, Burma, Ceylon and Indonesia—joining in the proposed collective arrangement.

Preliminary discussions took place during the Conference itself. The agreements on peace in Indo-China with which it ended in July 1954 confirmed Mr. Dulles' worst fears, although the price demanded for peace was less than the French had expected and was considered reasonable by the British. The Communists were, however, clearly not prepared to participate on practicable terms in any reciprocal guarantee of what had been agreed. It was the more urgent to underwrite the settlement as soon as possible with a definitive treaty.

Differences of view on the importance of associating the Colombo Powers in the new pact had meanwhile been part cause of some disharmony between Britain and the United States during the Conference. The United States never wholly accepted the British view that a South-East Asian defence organization without these nations could not be fully effective. In the event Mr. Nehru, who welcomed the Indo-Chinese settlement but wished to do nothing to antagonize the Chinese, expressed uncompromising opposition. Partly for this very reason Pakistan, alone of the Colombo powers, became a member of the South-East Asia Treaty Organization when it was founded at Manila on 8th September, 1954.

Terms and Functions of SEATO

The Treaty came into force after due ratification on 19th February 1955. It was conceived as a regional organization under the terms of the UN charter. The area it covered was defined as the general area of South-East Asia and of the South-West Pacific south of latitude 21° 30° north—a provision which excluded Formosa and Hong Kong—with the addition, of course, of the territory of Pakistan. The signatories agreed 'separately and jointly, by means of continuous and effective self-help and mutual aid,' to 'maintain and develop their individual and collective capacity to resist armed attack and to prevent and counter subversive activities directed from without against their territorial integrity and political stability' and to co-operate in developing their economies to promote economic progress and social well-being. In the event of armed attack against any of their territories in the treaty area, or against the territory of any state designated by protocol to the treaty whose government invited or consented to their intervention, each signatory agreed that it would 'act to meet the common danger in accordance with its constitutional processes'. The states designated in the protocol were Laos, Cambodia and South Vietnam, who were regarded as being under the protective umbrella of the new alliance though they themselves could not join it.

The governments of member nations agreed that they would be represented on the Council of SEATO, as it soon came to be called, by their Foreign Ministers. The first Council meeting took place at Bangkok in February 1955, and it was at Bangkok that in the following year the permanent secretariat of the Organization was established. It was agreed that the Council would meet once a year or more often if necessary and that its decisions would be taken by unanimous agreement. The Thai statesman Mr. Pote Sarasin took office as Secretary-General in 1957. He was replaced by Mr. K. Supramongkhol in 1964.

Between Council meetings continuing consultation was maintained at Bangkok by designated representatives with ambassadorial rank, and a parallel body, the military advisers, was made responsible to the Council on military matters. A permanent military planning office was set up at Bangkok in 1957. Its work includes the standardization of service procedures, the planning of military exercises, and specialist meetings dealing with intelligence, counter-subversion, logistics, communications and cartography. The Asian members have received considerable military and civil training assistance under the treaty both by bilateral arrangements and through specialist schools set up in their countries.

Three other specialized committees work at Bangkok under representatives of the Council. A committee of security experts keeps the security authorities of member states in contact and enables them to pool experience. A committee of economic experts reviews for members the economic implications of their defence commitments under the Treaty. A committee on information, cultural, education and labour activities provides expert advice in these fields. Public Information, Research Services and Cultural Relations Offices have also been established.

Unsolved Problems

The political and military situation in Indo-China caused, as we have seen, the formation of SEATO. It continued to be its chief preoccupation, for the three Indo-Chinese states, Laos, Cambodia and Vietnam, each left the Geneva conference-table with an unsolved problem. Laos had been cast for the role of neutral buffer between Thailand and North Vietnam, a role which her internal instability made it impossible for her to play. Cambodia, whose internal problem was quickly mastered by her royal national leader Prince Sihanouk, feared the revival of the dual threat from Thailand and Vietnam which had been quiescent during French colonial rule. Vietnam, partitioned into Communist North and non-Communist South, was left to reunify herself by free general elections in 1956, a solution never accepted by South Vietnam or by the United States.

The situation in Laos was of immediate concern to SEATO because of the long open border between Laos and Thailand. The threat to Thailand had, indeed, always been SEATO's central issue. In the summer of 1954, before the Organization came into existence, Thailand had notified the Security Council of the United Nations of her anxiety at the approach of the North Vietnamese to her frontiers by their invasion of Laos, and had subsequently accepted substantial assistance from the United States in order to double her military forces. Thailand's fears had deep historical roots. They rested in the ancient, bitter enmity between the closely related Thai-Lao and Thai-Siamese peoples and the Vietnamese, which in its turn was founded on the confrontation between Indian-influenced and Chinese-influenced kingdoms in Indo-China which has been going on for almost two thousand years.

When the French came to Indo-China in the second half of the 19th century, this ancient conflict had reached the point where Thailand—which had absorbed Laos—had become the protagonist of the Indian-influenced side, and faced the Chinese-influenced Vietnamese in a long struggle for power over Cambodia. France restored the integrity of Cambodia and rescued a small part of Laos from Thailand. Five-sixths of the Lao population, however, and most of the old Laotian territory, remained in Thailand. In compensation, French Laos was given areas in the mountains to the east which had long served as a neutral buffer between Thailand and Vietnam, or whose people had other traditional objections to domination by the Lao. The potentially anti-Lao population in the hills was a little more numerous than the Lao himself, who inhabitated the more easily accessible valleys.

While France held the ring, the innate instability of Laos did not matter. But as French power finally departed, the ethnic contradiction built into the fabric of the country by the accidents of history made it impossible for Laos to achieve the internal harmony which the neutral role assigned her by the Geneva Conference demanded. The North Vietnamese were able to use the fears and suspicions of the anti-Lao hillmen to prolong their hold on northern Laos. The Lao population in their turn looked to the influence of the five to seven million Lao in Thailand. The United States and then SEATO took up position on the side of Thailand; the Communist world was automatically ranged on the other. Laos could not be an effective buffer; it needed only the occasion to become a full-scale battleground. This was the root cause of Thailand's anxiety in 1954; not her anti-Communist sentiment, but the ingrained mutual hostility between her people and the Vietnamese.

Undeclared Wars

Matters came to a head in May 1962, when in spite of limited United States and Thai help to their friends in Laos, substantial Vietnamese support seemed likely to bring the Communist faction to the borders of Thailand at a moment when a new Geneva Conference was attempting to re-establish Laotian neutrality and stability. Although French disagreement prevented SEATO action as such, owing to the unanimity rule, other SEATO powers under the leadership of the United States responded individually to Thailand's appeal for help by moving troops and aircraft to the threatened area. These forces were withdrawn within a few months, but their presence and the implication that effective SEATO action was no longer prevented by the unanimity rule did much to reassure Thailand during the subsequent difficulties in Laos.

By the end of 1964 the complexities of the still-unsolved Laotian problem were becoming more and more entangled with that of North and South Vietnam. This too had become critical, for South Vietnam's rejection of general elections, as constituting too great a risk of Communist domination, had been followed by the formation on her soil of a Communist guerilla movement backed by North Vietnam. The increasing strength of the Vietcong, as it is called, had led to ever greater involvement of the United

States in support of the non-Communist South Vietnamese Government. Finally in February 1965, when over twenty thousand United States advisers and immense financial support had failed to stem the Vietcong tide, United States aircraft began to attack targets in North Vietnam. By this act the United States took into her own hands the issue of peace or war not only in Vietnam but in Indo-China as a whole. SEATO is thus deeply concerned with the outcome.

The nature of the SEATO alliance had however meanwhile changed in several directions. In 1957 Malaya, which under the British had both enjoyed the protection of SEATO and provided some of the bases for Commonwealth action in support of the alliance, became independent. This substantially reduced SEATO territory. Malaya did not join SEATO but the bases remained available for SEATO purposes subject to the veto implicit in Malayan sovereignty. The much more important Singapore base remained available under similar conditions when Singapore attained independence as part of Malaysia in 1963. But Malaysia too stayed outside SEATO. Thus the undeclared war waged by Communist-inclined Indonesia on the newly integrated Malaysian state since 1963 was also none of SEATO's concern, although effective Commonwealth participation in SEATO was clearly bound up with Malaysia's survival, and although three SEATO members became actively engaged on one side and a fourth, the Philippines, inclined to sympathy with the other.

Events on the Himalayan border between India and China in 1962 had led at the same time to changes in the attitude of Pakistan. When Pakistan became a member of SEATO in 1954 she was in no danger from Communist China in spite of her own Himalayan border, and the danger from Russia through Afghanistan was remote. She was however deeply concerned with the threat from India, with whom she was still bitterly at odds over Kashmir. Although the United States made it quite clear that in her view SEATO was an anti-Communist alliance and that it was only against Communist aggression that the United States was automatically committed, Pakistan's membership was motivated partly by her wish for allies in case of a war with India.

CENTO BETWEEN SEATO AND NATO

The Pakistani decision in September 1955 to adhere to the Central Treaty Organization (CENTO), then known as the Baghdad Pact, was more clearly directed towards the threat from the Communist world. CENTO was the third of the great regional pacts to come into existence, binding together Turkey, Iran, Iraq, Pakistan and Britain in terms somewhat similar to those of NATO and SEATO, with the backing of the United States. Turkey provided the link to the west through her simultaneous membership of NATO, and Pakistan to the east as a member of SEATO. The Iraqi revolution in 1958 led to the withdrawal of Iraq from CENTO and to the removal of the headquarters from Baghdad to Ankara, where in March 1959 bilateral agreements for mutual security and defence were signed by the United States with Iran, Pakistan and Turkey.

Through her two great alliances Pakistan was provided with ample assurance against attack by Russia and China, but in her quarrel with India over Kashmir she had always felt alone. In 1962 India's long-smouldering border disagreement with China burst into flame. The Indians were sharply defeated and turned to the West for help. Britain and the United States responded promptly and the pro-Chinese slant of India's non-alignment was at an end. For Pakistan the important point was that India, without being a member of SEATO or CENTO, had received substantial Western help which she might use against Pakistan when the danger from China receded. Pakistan's reaction was to mend her bridges with China, although this has not so far affected her membership of SEATO and CENTO.

From the changed position which followed the return to power of General de Gaulle in 1958, France, too, no longer viewed the South-East Asian problem in the old simple terms of containment of Communism. The formation of SEATO in 1954 had followed hard on the heels of the Vietminh victory over France in Indo-China, a war in which China materially supported the Vietminh. It was natural that the French should view Communist China as an enemy. Ten years later, however, General de Gaulle, ever more critical of United States handling of the situation in Vietnam, gave point to his criticism by a cordial rapprochement with China. His new attitude did not yet entail a withdrawal from SEATO, although his refusal to act with SEATO in the successive Laotian crises, and his recent decision to be represented only by an observer at the SEATO Council Meeting in 1965, show how far circumstances have changed. The West, he said, should leave the people of the area to settle their quarrels themselves, and also to settle freely the question of their relations with China. This implied agreement to the Chinese claim to a natural hegemony in South-East Asia was not at all to the taste of SEATO as a whole.

SEATO in Changed Circumstances

Nevertheless, there is no doubt that the nature of the threat to SEATO is different from what it was in 1954. When SEATO was founded it was assumed that China would seek by all means to spread Communism throughout South-East Asia, and that she would be implicitly backed by Russia in this aim. Now that the Sino-Soviet dispute seems to have invalidated this assumption, the short-term military threat from China has become less likely, in spite of her recent acquisition of a nuclear capability. Some Chinese have even shown a more immediate preoccupation with their border with Russia than with what they see as the threat to themselves in the south.

In these circumstances it may well be asked what useful purpose SEATO serves. The area of concern contains two active wars in which its members are engaged: SEATO is involved in neither. Two of its members have entered into cordial relationships with the Communist power against whom the organization was constructed.

The answer lies partly in intangibles. Much has been achieved at the grass roots of international co-operation. The day-to-day work on common problems at Bangkok, the liaison, the training and intelligence exchanges have had immense value. The close collaboration between intelligence services and border control officials, the adoption of common police methods, the examination and analysis of propaganda techniques, the lending of experts, have been and will continue to be of great importance. The possibility of disagreeing without necessarily being disagreeable, the forum of discussion and compromise that membership of a great organization brings, are themselves contributions to stability.

The capital fact is, however, the substantial degree of unanimity that remains, exemplified by the recent adoption of a common attitude to the war in Vietnam by all the members of SEATO except France. As the widening Sino-Soviet rift leads statesmen to re-examine the foundations of their policies in the Orient, the measure of agreement within SEATO is perhaps more significant than the differences of view.

MILITARY DEFENCE FORCES IN ASIA

TABLE 1

Country	Gross National Product ($ per head of population)	Defence Expenditure ($ per head of population)	Defence Expenditure Total (million $)	Defence Expenditure (per cent of GNP)	Armed Forces Total (millions)	Armed Forces (per cent of males 15-64 years)
			COMMUNIST COUNTRIES			
Soviet Union	n.a.	(140)	(32,500)	n.a.	3·30	6·3
Soviet Union in Asia	n.a.	n.a.	n.a.	n.a.	n.a.	n.a.
China	n.a.	n.a.	n.a.	n.a.	2·45	1·3
N. Korea	n.a.	n.a.	n.a.	n.a.	0·35	11·7
N. Vietnam	n.a.	n.a.	n.a.	n.a.	0·25	5·4
			NON-COMMUNIST COUNTRIES			
			SEATO/CENTO			
Pakistan	74	3	225	4·5	0·25	1·0
Thailand	93	3	90	3·5	0·08	1·0
Philippines	190	2	70	1·9	0·06	0·8
			U.S. MUTUAL DEFENCE			
Japan	504	8	765	1·6	0·24	0·8
S. Korea	(105)	5	150	6·0	0·60	8·6
Taiwan	115	12	145	10·0	0·60	18·5
			NON-ALIGNED COUNTRIES			
India	73	n.a.	1,970	5·1	0·87	n.a.
Indonesia	69	n.a.	980	n.a.	0·41	n.a.
Malaya	241	n.a.	90	4·1	0·05	n.a.

TABLE 2

Country	Form of Military Service	Land Forces (thousands)	Sea Forces (thousands)	Air Forces (thousands)
		COMMUNIST COUNTRIES		
Soviet Union	conscription	2,200	460	500
Soviet Union in Asia	conscription	n.a.	n.a.	n.a.
China	conscription	2,250	136	90
N. Korea	conscription	325	7	20
N. Vietnam	conscription	250	2	n.a.
Pathet Lao		26	—	—
Viet Cong		20	—	—
		NON-COMMUNIST COUNTRIES SEATO/CENTO		
Pakistan	voluntary	230	8	20
Thailand	conscription	50	21	13
Philippines	voluntary	25	6	9
S. Vietnam	conscription	210	15	20
		U.S. MUTUAL DEFENCE		
Japan	voluntary	175	35	39
S. Korea	voluntary and conscription	550	44	15
Taiwan	conscription	400	62	82
		NON-ALIGNED COUNTRIES		
India	voluntary	870	16	28
Indonesia	conscription	350	35	27
Malaya	conscription	19	2	n.a.

n.a.—not available
( )—estimate

Source: The Institute for Strategic Studies—*The Military Balance 1964-65*, London 1964

BIBLIOGRAPHY

Collective Defence in South-East Asia. (Royal Institute of International Affairs, London, 1956).
Brian Crozier. *South-East Asia in Turmoil.* (Penguin, London, 1965.)
Saul Rose (ed.) *Politics in Southern Asia.* (Macmillan, London, 1963.)
The South-East Asia Treaty Organization. (Central Office of Information, R. 5569, London, April, 1963.)

BIOGRAPHICAL NOTE

HUGH TOYE. B. 1917. Educated at Queens' College, Cambridge. Has spent several years in the Far East, including Indo-China, in the course of military service. Now temporarily Research Fellow at Nuffield College, Oxford. Author of *The Springing Tiger*, a study of S. C. Bose (Cassell, London, 1959.)

CHINA'S 'ALGEBRA OF REVOLUTION'

by

W. A. C. ADIE

THE BANDUNG CONFERENCE AND THE TEN PRINCIPLES

IN April 1955 the first attempt was made by the leaders of some 'non-aligned' Asian and African countries to formulate a political platform acceptable to all of them. They met at Bandung, Indonesia and drew up Ten Principles of Peaceful Coexistence as a code of international behaviour for developing nations. Several of these Principles referred to the Charter of the United Nations. The emphasis of this first Afro-Asian Conference, originally proposed by the non-aligned Colombo Powers, was mainly on economic cooperation among the participating countries on the basis of mutual interest, respect for mutual sovereignty, and non-alignment *vis-à-vis* the Great Powers.

By April 1965, when the tenth anniversary of the Conference was celebrated in Djakarta, much of the original concept had been transformed. Of the sixty countries invited to Djakarta only thirty-six were represented at the opening ceremony; delegates included only one foreign head of state (Prince Sikanouk of Cambodia) and three Communist prime ministers: Chou En-lai, Kim Il-song of North Korea and Pham-Van-Dong of North Vietnam. As the Japanese Kyodo news agency put it, these celebrations were meant to 'steal the thunder' of the second Afro-Asian Conference to be held in Algiers. President Sukarno called for a reconsideration of the first of the ten Bandung principles—respect for the purposes and principles of the UN Charter; this set the tone for the Sino-Indonesian approach to the Algiers meeting.

During the celebrations Sukarno laid the foundations for a building to house the Conference of New Emerging Forces (CONEFO) and he made clear that this conference, which he hopes to convoke in August 1966, is backed by China. Chou En-lai, whose diplomacy contributed so much to the success of the first Bandung Conference, also called for alteration of the Ten Principles and suggested that CONEFO could become a revolutionary and progressive alternative to the United Nations. During the preparations for the Second Afro-Asian Conference, the order of priorities adopted by the first was reversed; practical economic cooperation came last after subjects like decolonization and prohibition of nuclear tests.

The considerable shift in alignments since the doctrine of non-alignment was first adopted has largely been due to the attempts of the Communist Powers, especially Russia and China, to take over the whole idea of Asian,

Afro-Asian and non-aligned movements and conferences and use them for their own purposes. Thanks to the cold war and the schisms in the Communist bloc, the emergent nations' movement towards solidarity and mutual cooperation has disintegrated towards a split between nations supporting the ideals of the 'non-aligned' conferences of Belgrade and Cairo and nations in alignment with Peking.

Policies of China and the Soviet Union

China, for reasons connected with its own revolutionary history, reiterates that emancipation and economic development for emergent countries can never come from international organizations or big powers, and that disarmament and relaxation of international tension will not increase aid and produce world peace, that on the contrary permanent peace can be won only by purging the world in mass revolutionary war and building on the ruins. The Peking leaders cast Asia and its African and Latin American allies in the same rôle, on a world scale, as that performed by the peasant masses in China's revolutionary war: as the Chinese villagers were then united under the leadership of Mao Tse-tung in and by struggle against 'imperialism and its lackeys' in the towns, so now the 'world countryside' is to be united under the leadership of Mao's China in and by the struggle against 'United States imperialism and its lackeys' in the highly industrialized countries—including the 'revisionist' Soviet Union.

Just before the First Afro-Asian Conference at Bandung, Madame Sun Yat-sen published an article entitled 'Five Cardinal Principles' which claimed that the Soviet Union and China based their relations with each other on these 'Five Principles'. First invoked in 1954 to set Nehru's seal on Mao's occupation of Tibet, the Principles were: mutual respect for each other's territorial integrity and sovereignty, mutual non-aggression, mutual non-interference in each other's internal affairs, equality and mutual benefit, peaceful coexistence. At that time Stalin's successors had reappraised their policy towards such 'national-bourgeois' leaders as Nehru, Nasser and Sukarno; China was assigned a leading rôle in drawing them by diplomacy and example into a sort of economic co-prosperity sphere relying on Soviet weapons for defence; eventual economic, administrative and social Sovietization was the aim.

In order to harness the neutralist and pacifist sentiments of the emergent peoples of Asia and Africa for the new stage of the cold war—a great outflanking movement through the 'world countryside'—the World Peace Council (WPC), the Communist front organization for the exploitation of anti-European policy and national liberation movements, set up 'Afro-Asian Solidarity Committees' at a so-called 'Asian Nations conference for the relaxation of international tension' held in New Delhi. These later developed into the Afro-Asian People's Solidarity Organization (AAPSO). The Communists publicized this conference as a preparation for the Asian-African Conference; it was attended by a large Chinese delegation and by Soviet members of the WPC bureau, although Russia was not invited to Bandung. The Indian Government issued a denial that this meeting had any standing in relation to the Bandung Conference.

At Bandung, Chou En-lai radiated reasonableness, eclipsed Nehru and charmed Nasser; the AAPSO headquarters were set up in Cairo, not Delhi and trade and diplomatic relations were soon established between Cairo and Peking. It looked as if China was indeed playing her part in a combined operation to harness the 'Bandung Spirit'. But after 1956 it became clear that Moscow and Peking were projecting rival interpretations of this 'spirit' which reflected ideological conflict underlined by rivalry for control of the territories, resources and subject peoples of Central Asia and the 'Third World'.

In Moscow, Khrushchev emphasized that the Soviet Near and Far East had a special part to play in his plans for attracting other countries of the East to his 'world economic system of socialism'. In Peking, Liu Shao-ch'i and others assigned a similar task to the minority areas of China. They emphasized the importance of their independent strategic resources. They also stressed the close connection between United Front work in the non-Chinese areas within China's frontiers and the work of extending China's 'international united front' beyond them. In South-East Asia, it was hoped that Buddhist and Islamic organizations and the overseas Chinese would act as a link to promote this front.

At this time Mao Tse-tung probably still hoped to solve his problems, including Formosa, by kid-glove methods, assuming that he enjoyed overwhelming popular support. His followers' task was to 'help' the non-Communist Chinese to 'raise their ideological level'; they would accept Communism with a minimal use of violence on either side. Similarly with the rest of the world; Chou En-lai and his colleagues have often said that '90 per cent of the world's population want revolution', and that it is China's 'special destiny' to help all those who are not yet 'liberated'—this includes all independent countries which have 'bourgeois-nationalist' governments, such as Indonesia.

Like the Russians, the Chinese handle their relations with the Afro-Asian world as an extension of their drive to 'help' the minority areas of Central Asia, and changes in the nature of the United Front within China have been closely linked with changes in relations with outside countries, notably India and the Soviet Union itself. These in turn have affected the whole atmosphere of Asian relations. With the 'sharpening of the class struggle' against supposed counter-revolutionaries in China, both the international Communist movement and the movement for Asian solidarity have been split into two. The main reason for this has been the nature of the Chinese revolution. In Mao's 'algebra of revolution' armed struggle is indispensable in order to have a 'main enemy' against whom others (secondary enemies) must willy-nilly join the Communists in a United Front; then the stress of enemy pressure and alternate doses of 'unity' and 'struggle' are used to assimilate these allies to the Communist core.

When the Chinese and then the AAPSO established themselves in Cairo, the AAPSO became the scene of an inconclusive struggle for control between the Chinese, the Russians and the Egyptians who supplied the Secretary-General. It soon became clear that the Chinese regarded their links with the Arab countries as primarily a means of access to areas where armed struggle could be encouraged, especially Algeria; the Arab leaders, Nasser's friend Tito and the Soviet leaders were opposed to the escalation of armed struggles in the area.

During the Middle East crises of 1956, 1957 and 1958 and in Iraq in 1959, the Chinese appeared eager to embroil the Soviet Union in an 'anti-imperialist war' and to encourage local armed risings. Nasser declared a 'holy war' against Communism and Khrushchev dissociated himself from China's militant talk of 'volunteers'. The Peking press told Nasser that if he wanted to promote Arab unity he should support 'the people of Algeria, Jordan, Oman, etc. now under direct imperialist aggression'—that is, promote armed struggles—and hinted that otherwise he would end up like Chiang Kai-shek. *Red Flag* denounced the UAR's slogan 'neither East nor West' as a 'step towards going over to the enemy'. During the CPC 10th Anniversary celebrations in October 1959, Peking published an attack on Nasser by the Syrian Communist leader, Bakhdash, which described him as a reactionary dictator and tool of the Bank of Egypt, if not of 'imperialism'. The Egyptian Foreign Office sent word to the twenty-five nations of the Bandung Conference suggesting that they reduce their representation at Peking to that of chargé d'affaires as a mark of protest against Chinese aggression against Tibet, India, Laos 'and now the UAR'.

In fact, by this time the original 'Bandung Spirit' had largely evaporated. Nehru had revealed China's activities on the Indian border and shortly afterwards a Tass communiqué dissociated the Soviet Government from China on this issue too. China had also faced Nepal and Burma with border claims, and quarrelled with Indonesia over her discrimination against the overseas Chinese; the Chinese press called this 'currying favour with US imperialism'.

These accusations of 'going over to the enemy' reflected Peking's recasting of the international united front. It was not a mere reappraisal of the neutralist leaders but a practical operation of revolutionary algebra to change their standpoint. Under struggle, they must move closer to China or be 'exposed' as stooges of the enemy, like the Dalai Lama. This operation against the neutralists abroad was the corollary of the tougher measures taken for the ideological transformation of non-Communist Chinese and of the Tibetans and other minority peoples, after the 'hundred flowers' period of free speech in 1957 had revealed an unexpectedly serious opposition to the Communist Party's rule within China.

Having carried 'struggle' to the extreme and thereby brought about Chinese international isolation, Peking now switched towards emphasis on 'unity' in both internal and foreign policy and rapidly mended its fences with Burma, Nepal and outer Mongolia; but the reconciliation with Indonesia, sealed by the visit of Ch'en Yi to sign a treaty of friendship, soon acquired a wider significance. The joint Communiqué issued after his talks with Sukarno called for 'a second Asian-African Conference in the shortest possible time'. Peking now began to use Djakarta more and more as Moscow had originally tried to use Peking, as a catspaw for operations in the Afro-Asian world. Like Mao, however, Sukarno had his own purposes.

In 1960 the Chinese leaders began to consider Africa, especially tropical

Africa, as the centre of the world revolution. They failed to have the AAPSO secretariat moved to Conakry, but after the fact-finding tour of Africa by a Chinese delegation to the AAPSO meeting there in June 1961, Peking increasingly used its Asian contacts, especially Indonesia and Ceylon, as a means of extending its influence in the continent. China's entry on the African scene was marked by the massacre of Arabs in the Zanzibar revolution. Although China probably had little to do with that event, she has profited from it since. But it is not clear whether her purpose is to supplant the Arabs, Indians, Soviets and Europeans in Africa or to secure valuable raw materials. As the *Peking Review* has pointed out, the Congo produces many minerals used to make thermonuclear and other weapons.

Soon after the opening of the Sino-Soviet cold war in April 1960, Mao Tse-tung began to edge the Soviet Union out of Asian and African organizations, with the help of his Indonesian allies. Battle was openly joined at the Afro-Asian writers' conference in Cairo. Soviet delegates told Asians: 'the Chinese pretend America is the enemy, but really it is ourselves'. The Chinese told the Africans: 'These Europeans are all the same'. In April 1963 Sino-Soviet polemics disrupted the AAPSO conference at Moshi, Tanganyika; and President Nyerere warned against the neo-colonialist tendencies of socialist as well as capitalist countries. In the same month a conference held at Djakarta set up an 'Afro-Asian Journalists Association' to rival the Soviet-controlled 'International Organization of Journalists'. In June the Sino-Indonesians took over the Afro-Asian Writers' Bureau; they have subsequently taken over the permanent bureau of the Afro-Asian Lawyers Conference in Conakry and tried with varying success to organize Front organizations for scientists, youth, workers, lawyers, 'peace-fighters', etc. The ultimate aim is to establish an 'Afro-Asian Permanent Secretariat' in Djakarta to replace the AAPSO and its subsidiaries the Afro-Asian Economic Seminar and Women's Bureau.

Cairo Conference, 1964 and Second Afro-Asian Conference

All this activity was in preparation for a Second Bandung Conference and ultimately, perhaps, for CONEFO, which are expected to embody the 'great unity' of Afro-Asian and Latin American peoples under China's leadership, much as the Chinese People's Political Consultative Conference embodies the 'great unity' of China's people with Mao Tse-tung. In the last two years it has become increasingly clear that these conferences are seen by the Chinese as both a means and an alternative to the transformation according to Peking's requirements of the world Communist apparatus (now represented as a tool of the Soviet Revisionists) and of the United Nations (still allegedly manipulated by the American imperialists).

At the end of 1963 Chou En-lai made a 72-day tour of ten African countries, Burma, Pakistan and Ceylon; on return he reported that the tour had served to prepare for the second Afro-Asian meeting, at which 'concrete measures must be taken for the liberation of nations still under colonial rule.' At that time most of Chou En-lai's hosts were more interested in the coming second non-aligned conference in Cairo (5-11th October, 1964) to which forty-seven countries sent substantial delegations. The conference adopted nine principles of coexistence and called on all nations not to produce, acquire or test nuclear weapons. China exploded her first atomic device six days later, and a *People's Daily* editorial welcomed Sukarno's demand for 'confrontation' instead of coexistence.

China's militant attitude again reflected her internal situation; a return to the tense political atmosphere of 1958-60 had followed concessions to 'capitalist' economic methods which arrested the economy's downward spiral but encouraged ideological deviations. With the escalation of the war in Indochina, China multiplied her military preparations while Chou En-lai made strenuous efforts at the Bandung Anniversary celebrations to cement the international Communist front. The postponement of the Second (Algiers) Afro-Asian Conference was a setback to Chou En-lai's diplomacy.

ASIAN POLITICAL CONFERENCES, 1946-65

1946—Conference at Delhi convened by Jawaharlal Nehru for discussion of Asian affairs. Pan-Asianism given a trial run, but not regarded as a practicable ideal. Conference notable for clash between India and Kuomintang representatives of China over rival views on status of Tibet.

1949—Conference of Asian countries called at Delhi to give moral support to Indonesians after Dutch attempt to suppress Indonesian Republic.

1954—Conference of Colombo Powers (India, Pakistan, Burma and Ceylon) at Colombo. Stormy discussions between India and Pakistan over Kashmir. Conference led to widening of idea of Asian conferences and produced the Bandung Conference.

1955—'Asian Nations Conference for the relaxation of international tension' convened in Delhi before the Bandung Conference by WCP, an organization dominated by Soviet and pro-Soviet Communists. Recognized as an attempt to exploit Bandung idea for Soviet purposes, and repudiated by India and Indonesia.

1955—Bandung Conference of Asian and African powers. Conceived as an international demonstration in favour of non-alignment. Struggle for primacy between India and China; China entered on period of respectability and diplomatic initiative. Soviet Union excluded from conference as being a non-Asian country. Anti-Communist front by Ceylon and Turkey proved on the whole a failure.

1961—Conference at Belgrade of non-aligned powers. Held in the shadow of resumption of atom tests by Soviet Union. Western hopes that conference would roundly condemn the Communists were disappointed. Nehru and Tito dominant figures.

1964—Cairo Conference of non-aligned countries; forty-seven participants adopted nine principles of coexistence and called on all nations not to produce, acquire or test nuclear weapons.

1965—Algiers Conference, planned for July, postponed to November owing to revolution in Algiers. This conference intended as the sequel to Bandung; but whereas original Bandung Conference stressed loyalty to the Charter of the United Nations, this conference was expected to be a demonstration against the United Nations. Of special interest was attempt by China to exclude Soviet Union once more, and counter-attempt by Soviet Union to gain admittance. Indonesia, which played a leading part in making arrangements for the conference, tried to exclude Malaysia.

BIOGRAPHICAL NOTE

W. A. C. Adie, M.A. Formerly worked on Far Eastern and South-East Asian affairs at the Foreign Office and at posts in the area. Now Senior Research Fellow at St. Anthony's College, Oxford, engaged in research on recent and contemporary history of China. Author of articles in *China Quarterly*, *Political Quarterly*, *Political Studies*, etc. (London) and member of the Royal Institute of International Affairs Working Group on China and the World.

MINORITIES AND DISPUTED AREAS

MINORITY GROUPS IN ASIA

by

EDMUND LEACH

ALMOST without exception the frontiers of the present-day sovereign states of South and South-East Asia are the product of political bargains and administrative arrangements made by the European colonial powers during the 19th and early 20th centuries. Such frontiers pay scant regard to the ethnic peculiarities of the populations which they contain. For example, at least 60 quite different languages are spoken by the inhabitants of modern Burma and some of these correspond to cultural differences quite as radical as those which separate an Englishman from a Turk.

As British experience shows, the political problems which such ethnic differences entail are not easily predictable. The English ultimately assimilated the Cornish and achieved a political synthesis with both the Welsh and the Scots yet failed altogether to come to terms with the Irish. Similar puzzles present themselves all over Asia. A great variety of factors may be relevant, the numerical size of the 'minority' and the level of its political sophistication being among the more obvious. As to the latter, the incompatibility of Buddhist Sinhalese and Hindu Tamils in Ceylon or the relations between Chinese and Malays in the Federation of Malaya are issues of quite a different order from those posed by the tribal minorities of Burma or by the Nagas of Assam in relation to the Government of India. It is the circumstances of 'tribal' minorities of the latter kind which I wish briefly to consider in this essay.

MINORITIES

Several general points need to be stressed. In the first place this problem of the tribal minorities is no minor matter. Minorities of this kind exist in every Asian country; they number, in all, many millions of individuals; and in many countries, Burma, Thailand, Malaya and Indonesia for example, the map area inhabited by the tribal peoples is substantially greater than that occupied by the politically dominant majority.

Secondly it must be understood that within these tribal areas the number of distinguishable linguistic groups is very large. If each group is to be considered as a separate ethnic unit deserving special attention on its own then certainly the problems posed by the tribal minorities become insuperable. But that is not really how things are. All over Asia the smaller linguistic groups are ceasing to be distinguishable as separate entities; they are either disappearing altogether by assimilation with the dominant majority or else they are coalescing into self-conscious minority nations. In the borderlands of Burma and Assam the minorities which really matter are those which appear in news reports under such labels as Naga, Kachin, Chin, Karen. Originally these terms were merely category labels used by foreigners to describe a mixed collectivity of very small culturally distinct groups; it is only the political accidents of the past 25 years which have moulded the populations concerned into incipient nations. Thirty years ago there were no Nagas; there were only Angami, Ao, Rengma, Sema, Konyak and so on, all busily engaged in perennial mutual hostilities. To-day the inhabitants of the Naga Hills are aware of themselves as Nagas and on that account they constitute a genuine political force of serious dimensions. In the essay which follows it is with tribal minorities of this latter scale that I am concerned.

At this level the common assumption that the adjective 'tribal' is equivalent to 'primitive' or 'backward' needs to be treated with caution.

It is true that, in general, the tribal peoples occupy inaccessible parts of the country, and on that account they are, quite literally, 'backwoodsmen'. A certain primitiveness follows automatically from the lack of communications; these are people who exist on the margins of the world economic system; compared with those of even the least sophisticated townsman their standards of life are elementary; by suitably selected photographs journalistic propaganda can readily make it appear that the typical tribesman is a naked savage. Even so it does not follow that such tribesmen are ill-qualified to take advantage of changing political and economic circumstance. The quality of the educated élite among the tribal peoples is often as good or better than that on which the central government has to rely.

History is relevant here. When the European colonial regimes were first elaborated during the 19th century the tribal peoples of East Asia appeared pre-eminently 'primitive'. Precisely on this account, they received a disproportionate amount of charitable aid. Most colonial governments paid exaggerated respect to local religious prejudice. But 'religious' in this context referred only to the acknowledged major religions—Christianity, Hinduism, Buddhism, Islam. The religions of the tribal minorities were deemed to be mere superstition and deserved no protection. The great surge of 19th century Christian missionary endeavour was therefore diverted towards the primitives. In the eyes of the administration the Christian conversion of a Buddhist or a Muslim might entail all sorts of unforeseeable political consequences, but surely the conversion of a cannibal or a headhunter could only be for the good? Maybe; yet in the long run this too had political consequences. The well financed schools of the Christian missions often provided an education vastly superior to anything contained in the traditional system of the 'civilized' major groups.

Today the leaders of the tribal minorities are almost invariably mission trained Christians of considerable educational attainment. They frequently display an almost European contempt for the ignorant stupidity of their 'heathen' political overlords. In consequence, the cultural gulf which now separates the tribal minorities from their nominal masters is much wider than it was in the original pre-missionary phase of colonial expansion. The prospect is lamentable. The opposition of Christian versus Buddhist or of

Christian versus Muslim offers truly formidable obstacles to any attempted cultural synthesis or assimilation.

Another relevant historical detail is that in some (but not all) cases the colonial authorities systematically recruited military police from the 'tribals' rather than from the majority population. In Burma, for example, before 1940, locally recruited military and military police were drawn from the Kachin, Chin and Karen tribal minorities but none at all from the majority Buddhist population of Burmese and Shans. Similarly in Indonesia the bulk of the Dutch colonial army was recruited from the Eastern Islands in the vicinity of Amboina where most of the population are of Papuan extraction and converts to the Dutch Reformed Church. Government policy was plainly designed to range these dark skinned Christians in opposition to the Indonesian Muslim population which is heavily concentrated in the Island of Java.

Questions of Sovereignty

Although the successor governments are less dependent upon the loyalty of tribal soldiers, the military competence of tribal minorities still has widely ramifying political implications. For example the paradox by which Indonesia pursued a chauvinistic policy towards Western New Guinea at a time when the Government's control over Indonesia proper was only notional was certainly influenced by the potential threat which an otherwise unemployed Amboinese soldiery might offer to the internal security of the State. Or again there is the Burma case. At the coming of independence the Commander-in-Chief of the Burma Army was a highly qualified Karen graduate of the British Military Academy. His later dismissal coincided with the disbandment of a substantial (Karen) section of the Burma Army. This in turn helped to perpetuate the insurrectionist movement among the Karen minority, but it also increased the dependence of the central Government upon the loyalty of the other main tribal minorities (Kachin and Chins). The semi-autonomous Kachin and Chin regions were then provided with lavish budgetary assistance from central funds. Since the coup d'état of 2 March 1962 Burma has had a military government headed by a Chairman of the Revolutionary Council and the office of President of the Burma Union has been abolished. It is however a mark of the political importance of the minorities that prior to this event a Kachin had been appointed President and titular Head of the State.

Yet although education and military advantage often place the leaders of the tribal minorities on a par with the leaders of the political majority there are basic problems which remain unresolved. These stem from a fixed belief that the tribal minorities are, in their very essence, both primitive and inferior.

Despite all the fine talk of Asian freedom and 'emancipation from the slave mentality of the colonial epoch' the central governments of countries such as India, Burma and Indonesia have tended to inherit the prejudices and administrative habits of their British and Dutch predecessors. Colonial administrators treated tribal peoples with ruthless severity. The military punitive expedition seldom achieved any useful purpose but it was the stock response of all colonial governments to any form of 'trouble' in tribal areas. The successor governments tend to react in an identical manner with equal lack of effect. Indeed the indications are that, over the past few years, certain governments, that of India in particular, have been *more* prone than their colonial predecessors to resort to military sanctions against the tribal peoples of their border zones.

The issue of national frontiers is very relevant here. The tribal peoples are frequently located in mountainous regions lying between the major states—the sub-Himalayan area between Assam and west China is a case in point. During the colonial period many such regions were left 'unadministered', that is to say they were designedly treated as buffer zones, a tacitly neutral no-man's-land which the Great Powers could conveniently leave alone. In such circumstances the tribal peoples enjoyed, in practice if not in theory, a large measure of independence. In contrast, the successor states are pre-occupied, to an exaggerated degree, with questions of sovereignty. Because of this, the precise details of political frontiers have come to assume an ominous importance. The territorial claims of the Indian Government in the North-East Frontier are no different from those of the previous British Raj but, whereas the British were often enough satisfied with a notional frontier on a notional map the Indians have felt themselves obliged to establish effective administration up to the very limits of their territory to the clear detriment of the tribal peoples concerned.

It is true that closer administration brings benefits in the form of better communications, medical services, education, trade and so on but this is true of all colonial enterprise. In any particular case these advantages have to be weighed against the countless difficulties which ensue from the intensification of ethnic solidarity. The Indian Government may plead in all honesty that its attitude towards the tribal peoples is one of high moral purpose, that it aims to bring civilization and economic development to the primitive peoples of Eastern Assam. But this is an old story. With all the hindsight of history one might still say that the French sought to bring civilization and economic development to the peoples of North Africa. Unfortunately nationalist consciousness pays no heed to good intentions of this kind.

The political fate of L'Algérie française has considerable relevance for any assessment of the prospects of Asian minorities. The currently existing nations of Southern Asia have proudly achieved their statehood by throwing off the shackles of colonial domination. Yet, in respect to the tribal peoples, they have simply taken over the role of the former colonial powers. Vis-à-vis the tribal minorities most of the central governments continue to act as if they themselves were colonial imperialists. Good works are imposed by force. Yet one may predict that where administrative policies of tutelage and apartheid depend upon military sanction then in the long run political nemesis is certain. In any tribal situation a policy of military coercion has the automatic consequence of consolidating a nationalist opposition out of the confusion of pre-existing tribal loyalties. In such circumstances (unless, as in Russia, the central authorities are prepared to be quite exceptionally ruthless) the long term advantage seems to lie with the advocates of political independence even when economic factors seem to indicate precisely the opposite. The political realities of Africa in 1962 in no way correspond to economic common sense, and the fact that an independent Naga State would be an economic absurdity does not necessarily imply that such a state will never come into being.

The Balkanization of Asia into a vast array of petty independent sovereignties seems undesirable from almost every point of view yet the existence of the tribal minorities offers a constant threat of this kind of development. How far such Balkanization proceeds will depend in part upon how well the civilian politicians of the existing state manage to keep their military under control. Every act of military suppression postpones still further the prospects of cultural assimilation. A series of military incidents has occurred in South-East Asia in the last few years.

If the tribal minorities are to play their part in a larger statehood they must be treated with respect. Military restraint is not enough; it is also necessary that the civil administrators of such regions learn to behave as civil servants and cease to parade themselves as imitation European nabobs and pukka sahibs. The problems posed by the minorities would largely disappear if the central governments concerned devoted their energies to civilizing the administration instead of civilizing the population.

Since Western New Guinea has become a part of Indonesia, the policy of military confrontation which was there so successful is being directed against the newly born Malaysia. In this new set of disputes in which the sovereign Governments of Malaysia, Indonesia and the Philippines are all involved the politicians again seek justification for their actions in the historical circumstances of the colonial past rather than in the facts of the present ethnic situation. The Indonesians no doubt have right on their side when they argue that there is no logical sense in drawing a political frontier through the middle of Borneo; but on the other hand, if Borneo were to become a political unity, there is no obvious reason why it should be ruled by Javanese just because the latter happen to be political successors to the Dutch. It would appear that one factor of major importance in this confused area is that the Indonesian army contains large 'tribal' elements which have little loyalty to the concept of Indonesia as such and which must on that account be kept fully employed. It also deserves note that the policy of 'confrontation' results in large Indonesian military garrisons being stationed in West Borneo and Sumatra, two regions where the bulk of the local population belongs to the 'tribal' category and is notoriously unsympathetic to its Javanese rulers. To a Sumatra Batak tribesman the Indonesian soldier must look very like a military policeman.

The Scale of the Minority Problem

The official census statistics for Asian countries are neither satisfactory nor comparable. Figures relating to 'minority' communities are especially defective. There are various reasons for this. Minorities tend to be located in inaccessible areas to which census enumerators do not penetrate; there is no agreed principle according to which minorities should be classified; figures are falsified outright for political reasons. The figures cited below are not comparable with one another but give some indication of the dimensions of the problem.

India 1951 Census. Nine major language groups accounted for 325 million out of a total of 356 million. 47 other language groups were listed in which the speakers numbered more than 100,000 per group. 720 language groups were listed in which speakers numbered less than 100,000 per group.

There is no way of assessing the total of those who might rate as 'tribal minorities' in the terms of this essay. Supporters of the controversial Nagas claim that they number 'about a million'; the census admits only that they number more than 212,000.

Indonesia 1953 Census. Of a total of 88 million, 52 million are concentrated in the politically dominant islands of Java and Madura. The remaining 36 millions are divided into about 100 different major culture groups dispersed over hundreds of different islands.

Malaya 1955 Estimate. Population classified as 3 million 'Malaysians', 2·3 million Chinese, 0·7 million Indians and Pakistanis. The term Malaysian is here a very wide category including a number of substantial minorities who are not Malays in any ordinary sense.

Thailand 1952 Census. Claims that 94 per cent of a population of 23 million are of Thai culture, 2·8 per cent Chinese and 3 per cent Malay. Apparently the tribal minorities of the northern hill country were not enumerated at all.

Burma 1956 Estimate. Of a total of 20 million roughly 60 per cent Burmese, 6 per cent Arakanese, 7 per cent Shan, 9 per cent Karen, 10 per cent Mon, 6 per cent Kachin, Chin etc.

Ceylon 1953 Census. Roughly: $5\frac{1}{2}$ million Sinhalese, 1 million Ceylon Tamils, $\frac{1}{2}$ million Ceylon Muslims, 1 million Indians (without Ceylon citizenship).

Laos and Vietnam. All published figures must be discounted as items of political propaganda. In Laos the numerical total of the numerous tribal minorities appears to be at least equal to that of the politically dominant Thai.

BIBLIOGRAPHY

F. G. Baily. *Tribe, Caste and Nation*. (Manchester Univ. Press, Manchester, 1960.)

Verrier Elwin. *A Philosophy of NEFA*. (Sachin Roy, Shillong, 1959.)

Julian F. Embree and Lilian O. Dotson. *Bibliography of the Peoples and Cultures of Mainland South-East Asia.* (Yale Univ. Press, New Haven, 1950.)

Raymond Kennedy. *Bibliography of Indonesian Peoples and Cultures*, 2 vols. (Yale Univ. Press, New Haven, revised ed., 1955.)

Edmund Leach. *The Frontiers of 'Burma'*. *Comparative Studies in Society and History*, Vol. III, No. 1. (Mouton, The Hague, 1960.)

H. N. C. Stevenson. *The Hill Peoples of Burma.* (Burma Pamphlets No. 6: Longmans, Calcutta, 1944.)

B. Ter Haat. *Adat Law In Indonesia*. (Institute of Pacific Relations, New York, 1948.)

P. D. R. Williams Hunt. *An Introduction to the Malayan Aborigines.* (Government Press, Kuala Lumpur, 1952.)

BIOGRAPHICAL NOTE

EDMUND RONALD LEACH. Reader in Social Anthropology in the University of Cambridge. Fellow of King's College, Cambridge. Author of *Social and Economic Organisation of the Rowanduz Kurds* (1940), *Social Science Research in Sarawak* (1948), *Political Systems of Highland Burma* (1954), *Pul Eliya: A Village in Ceylon* (1961), *Rethinking Anthropology* (1962), and numerous papers in anthropological journals. Graduated from Cambridge (Clare College) with a first class degree in Engineering (Mechanical Sciences) in 1932. During the period 1937-39 studied social anthropology at the London School of Economics under Professors B. Malinowski and Raymond Firth. Spent a brief period in Iraq in 1938. In 1939 was engaged in fieldwork among the Kachins of Northern Burma. Much of the war spent on 'irregular' activities in Northern Burma. In 1946 returned to L.S.E. and completed a Ph.D. In 1947 spent six months in Borneo carrying out research on behalf of the Colonial Office. Was engaged in fieldwork in Ceylon in 1954 and again in 1956.

THE PROBLEM OF KASHMIR

by

MATINUZZAMAN ZUBERI

THE State of Jammu and Kashmir has five political divisions—Jammu, the Kashmir Valley, Ladakh, Baltistan, and Gilgit. It has a population of over four million, an overwhelming majority of whom are Muslims; Hindus are mainly concentrated in Jammu and Buddhists in Ladakh.

HISTORY BEFORE THE PARTITION OF INDIA

Kashmir was the largest of the Princely States of India before partition. The Maharaja was an absolute autocrat. A system of forced labour combined with a complete lack of any means of expressing their grievances had reduced the people of Kashmir virtually to serfs. Muslims were especially discriminated against, being almost entirely excluded from Government posts and the State Army. In 1931, when the restlessness of the people found expression in a State-wide revolt led by Sheikh Mohammad Abdullah, who had just returned from the Aligarh Muslim University, thousands were thrown into prison without trial.

In 1932 Abdullah founded the All Jammu and Kashmir Muslim Conference. He realized, however, that if the struggle against Dogra princely rule were to succeed, it needed positive support from all sections of the people. Abdullah was brought into contact with the Indian National Congress and realized that the struggle of the Kashmiris was gradually becoming an integral part of the wider struggle for freedom in India. Accordingly, the movement was renamed the All Jammu and Kashmir National Conference and in June 1939 was thrown open to all communities. In 1944 it formulated the 'New Kashmir' plan, which advocated the abolition of landlordism and the convening of a Constituent Assembly based on adult franchise to frame a new constitution for the State.

When the movement became intercommunal in character, Ghulam Abbas, formerly one of its prominent members, parted company with Abdullah and in 1944 revived the Muslim Conference which was drawn towards the ideology of the All India Muslim League. In the same year, the National Conference became a member of the All India States Peoples' Conference, a sister organization of the Congress whose aim was to secure political rights for the people of the Princely States. Thus, the ideological struggle between the Congress and the Muslim League was carried over to Kashmir.

In 1946 the National Conference started the 'Quit Kashmir' movement, demanding the termination of autocratic rule in the State, and in May,

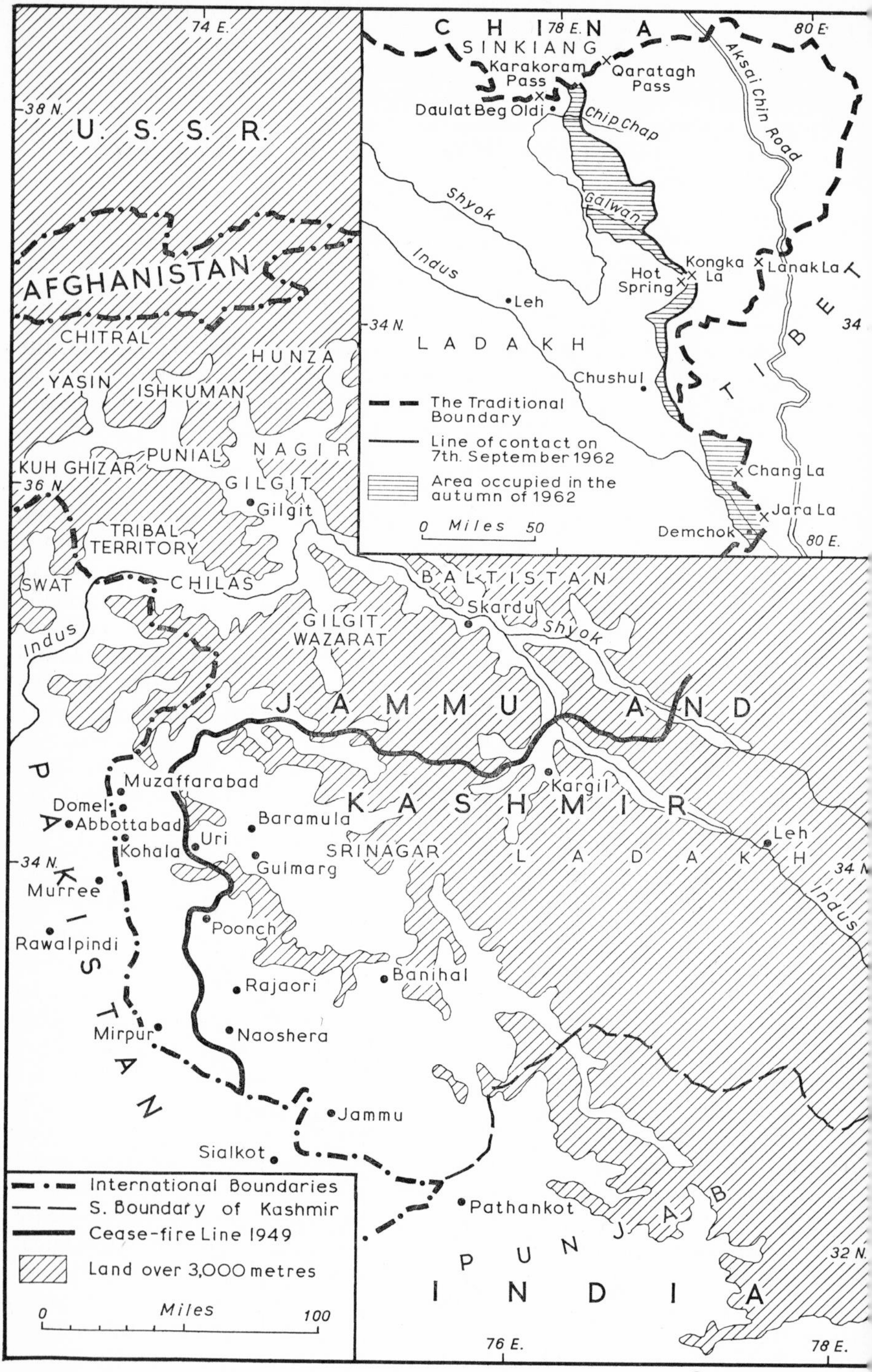

74 E.
38 N.
U. S. S. R.
AFGHANISTAN
CHITRAL
HUNZA
YASIN
ISHKUMAN
NAGIR
PUNIAL
KUH GHIZAR
36 N.
GILGIT
Gilgit
TRIBAL TERRITORY
SWAT
CHILAS
Indus
GILGIT WAZARAT
BALTISTAN
Skardu
Shyok
JAMMU AND KASHMIR
PAKISTAN
Muzaffarabad
Domel
Abbottabad
Kohala
Uri
Baramula
Kargil
Leh
SRINAGAR
LADAKH
34 N.
Murree
Gulmarg
Poonch
Rawalpindi
Banihal
Rajaori
Mirpur
Naoshera
Jammu
Sialkot
Pathankot
PUNJAB
INDIA
32 N.
76 E.
78 E.
International Boundaries
S. Boundary of Kashmir
Cease-fire Line 1949
Land over 3,000 metres
0 Miles 100
CHINA
SINKIANG
78 E.
80 E.
Karakoram Pass
Qaratagh Pass
Daulat Beg Oldi
Chip Chap
Aksai Chin Road
Shyok
Galwan
Indus
Hot Spring
Kongka La
Lanak La
Leh
34 N.
LADAKH
TIBET
Chushul
The Traditional Boundary
Line of contact on 7th. September 1962
Area occupied in the autumn of 1962
Chang La
Jara La
Demchok
0 Miles 50
80 E.

Abdullah, along with other National Conference leaders, was arrested. While in jail, he was elected as Nehru's successor to the Presidentship of the All India States Peoples' Conference, a position which he held until July 1948, when the organization was merged with the Congress. The close links between the National Conference and the secular nationalist movement in India have profoundly affected the development of the Kashmir problem.

The Muslim Conference tried to benefit from the temporary eclipse of its rival by co-operating with the Maharaja and opposing the popular demand for responsible government in the State. Such co-operation was, however, short-lived. Having arrested the National Conference leaders the Maharaja turned his attention to the Muslim Conference, and Abbas and his supporters were arrested on a charge of violating the law prohibiting mass demonstrations. Such was the political situation in Kashmir on the eve of partition.

Kashmir and the Partition of India

The Indian Independence Act of 18th July, 1947 failed to provide for the future of the Princely States, merely stating that British suzerainty, together with all treaties and engagements in force, would lapse on 15th August. A separate States Ministry was created for each Dominion, and by 15th August only three States had not decided upon their future status; one of these was Kashmir.

The Maharaja of Kashmir was in a difficult position: being a Hindu, he must have realized that accession to Pakistan might cost him his throne, while accession to India was bound to lead to the transfer of power to the National Conference. He therefore played for time, and when Lord Mountbatten went to Kashmir in June 1947 to hasten a decision, he avoided serious discussion. Mountbatten afterwards stated publicly in Britain:

> 'Had he acceded to Pakistan before 15th August 1947, the future government of India had allowed me to give His Highness an assurance that no objection whatever would be raised by them. Had His Highness acceded to India by 14th August, Pakistan did not then exist and therefore could not have interfered. The only trouble that could have been raised was by non-accession to either side, and this was unfortunately the very course followed by the Maharaja'.

On 12th August the Maharaja, in an attempt to maintain the *status quo*, sent identical telegrams to the new Governments of India and Pakistan asking for the conclusion of 'Standstill Agreements' with both countries. On 15th August a Standstill Agreement was concluded with Pakistan, providing for the continuation of the administrative arrangements for communications, supplies, posts and telegraphs. No formal agreement was concluded with India, although it was given effect in practice. However, these arrangements did not create the rights and obligations arising from an act of accession. The absence of a formal agreement with India was interpreted by Pakistan as an indication that Kashmir would ultimately accede to her, and it was later even assumed that the Standsill Agreement somehow covered defence and external affairs. That the Maharaja could simultaneously have asked both India and Pakistan to enter into arrangements involving control of defence and external affairs can certainly be dismissed as impossible. Pakistan's assumption of Kashmir's final accession to her was partly based on the fact that her lines of communication lay through Pakistan, while she had no all-weather road links with India.

Relations between Pakistan and Kashmir deteriorated rapidly. Kashmir complained of a shortage of essential supplies guaranteed by the Standstill Agreement. Refugees in thousands were pouring across the new frontiers of India and Pakistan, and Jammu became a refugee highway.

Amidst this chaos there occurred the Poonch Revolt. Poonch had been ruled by a Hindu Raja who had, after a lawsuit, been deposed by the Maharaja of Kashmir. Subsequently, the much more oppressive Kashmiri taxation system had been extended to Poonch and the people had risen in a no-tax campaign. When Dogra troops were sent to repress it, the militant Poonchis (traditional recruits for the Indian Army) crossed the frontier and returned with arms supplied by their Pakistani supporters. Thus, the movement flared into a full-scale rebellion to overthrow Dogra rule—the 'Azad (Free) Kashmir' movement—and set in motion a series of incidents culminating in the invasion of Kashmir.

Invasion and Accession

Realizing that he could no longer cope with the situation in the State without the help of the National Conference on 29th September, the Maharaja released Abdullah. The latter declared: 'Our first demand is the complete transfer of power to the people of Kashmir. Representatives of the people in a democratic Kashmir will then decide whether the State should join India or Pakistan'. While a delegation of the National Conference was trying to enlist the support of Pakistani leaders for Abdullah's demand for 'freedom before accession', full-scale invasion of Kashmir started on 22nd October.

Tribesmen from the North-West Frontier Province of Pakistan marched across West Punjab and advanced rapidly towards Srinagar. They were joined by Pakistani soldiers 'on leave' under the leadership of Major General Akbar Khan, later Chief of Staff of the Pakistan Army. Looting, burning and abduction took place, claiming both Muslim and Hindu victims, and on the evening of 24th October the Government of India received a desperate appeal for help from the Maharaja. V. P. Menon, Secretary of the Indian States Ministry, flew to Srinagar to clarify the situation. Mehr Chand Mahajan, who became Prime Minister of Kashmir on 15th October, summed up the situation in his book *Accession of Kashmir*: 'We had decided by the 25th evening to go to India if we could get a plane, or else to go to Pakistan for surrender'. Menon reported to the Defence Committee that military help was urgently needed. Mountbatten took the view that as Kashmir had not yet acceded to India, it would be improper to send Indian troops there. If, on the other hand, the Maharaja acceded to India, Kashmir would become an integral part of India and Indian troops could then be sent to defend it from further aggression. Mahajan and Abdullah also implored the Indian Government for immediate military assistance.

Menon next flew to Jammu accompanied by Mahajan. He advised the Maharaja, who had left Srinagar in unseemly haste, to offer accession to India. The Maharaja in fact did so, enclosing an Instrument of Accession with a letter to Mountbatten in which he asked for military aid from India. Mountbatten accepted the accession.

In a separate letter, Mountbatten told the Maharaja that it was his Government's wish that 'as soon as law and order have been restored in Kashmir and its soil cleared of the invader, the question of the State's accession should be settled by a reference to the people'. This letter has been the subject of great controversy. Pakistan has maintained that it makes Kashmir's accession conditional upon the verdict of the people and that as the Indian Independence Act did not envisage conditional accession, it is null and void, and that anyway the Maharaja had no authority to execute an instrument of accession after his flight from Srinagar. India, on the other hand, insists that it was a personal letter from Mountbatten in reply to the Maharaja's covering letter and does not form part of the acceptance of the Instrument of Accession, that that document is in no way different from those executed by some 500 other States in India, has no conditions attached to it and does not state that the accession is provisional, and is therefore a document complete in itself.

The Indian view is that legally the document had to be signed by the Maharaja; but it was supported by the largest political organization in the State, the National Conference, which occupied a position similar to that of Congress in India and the Muslim League in Pakistan. Constitutionally India was under no obligation to commit herself to ascertaining the wishes of the people of Kashmir, but with her declared hostility to feudal arbitrary rule and her close links with the popular movement in Kashmir, did not relish the idea of finding herself in a position where she became an ally of the Maharaja against his people. She therefore made this unilateral offer and insisted that despite critical conditions in the States popular rule should be established immediately. Accordingly, an Emergency Administration headed by Abdullah was established, thereby bringing about a revolutionary transfer of power from the Maharaja to the people, the first popular government that the State had ever had. India also maintains that her unilateral offer to seek the will of the people, which in no way affected the legality of accession, was to be implemented only *after* the expulsion of the invaders and the restoration of law and order in the State.

With the constitutional accession of Kashmir, a contingent of Indian troops flew into Srinagar on 27th October, just in time to halt, at the very edge of the airstrip, an advance party of the invaders. During the critical days between 22nd and 27th October the National Conference maintained a remarkable degree of order with the help of a local militia. Thus the invaders, who certainly did not want Kashmir's accession to India, not only forced the hesitant Maharaja to make up his mind, but also acted as a catalytic agent in bringing about the overthrow of autocratic rule and the establishment of a popular government.

Pakistan suspected elaborate planning behind the Indian airlift and Jinnah ordered his C-in-C, General Gracey, to send Pakistani troops to

Kashmir immediately. This Gracey was not prepared to do without the approval of Field-Marshal Auchinleck, who was responsible for superintending the partition of the former Indian Army. Auchinleck told Jinnah that such an act of invasion would involve the immediate withdrawal of every British officer from the Pakistan Army, whereupon Jinnah withdrew his order. As for the hastily improvised airlift of Indian troops, the three British Cs-in-C of the Indian Army, Air Force and Navy have denied that it was planned.

On 30th October the Pakistan Government issued a statement alleging that Kashmir's accession to India was 'based on fraud and violence'. On 1st November Mountbatten conferred with Jinnah, who repeated the charge. The rest of their discussion is best summarized by Mountbatten's press attaché in his book *Mission with Mountbatten*: 'The argument then got into a vicious circle. Mountbatten agreed that the accession had been brought about by violence but the violence came from the tribes, for whom Pakistan, and not India, was responsible. To this Jinnah would retort that in his opinion it was India who had committed violence by sending in the troops.' When Mountbatten told Jinnah that the prospect of the tribesmen entering Srinagar was now remote, the latter suggested that both sides withdraw simultaneously. Mountbatten asked how Pakistan could ensure the withdrawal of the tribesmen, to which Jinnah replied: 'If you do this I will call the whole thing off.'

Kashmir and the United Nations

On 1st January 1948, after months of futile negotiations, India submitted a formal complaint to the Security Council under Chapter VI of the Charter. She requested the Council to ask Pakistan 'to prevent Pakistan Government personnel, military and civil, from participating in or assisting the invasion of Jammu and Kashmir State' and to deny to the invaders access to and use of her territory for operations in Kashmir. Pakistan lodged a series of countercharges and emphatically denied any complicity in the invasion of Kashmir, claiming that the Pakistan Government had 'continued to do all in their power to discourage the tribal movement by all means short of war'.

On 17th January the Council called upon India and Pakistan to desist from any action which might increase tension and to inform the Council immediately of 'any material change in the situation'. Three days later the Council authorized the appointment of a three-member Commission, one member each to be nominated by India and Pakistan, the third selected by the nominees, to investigate the situation and to mediate. Later the Commission was enlarged to five members. India nominated Czechoslovakia, Pakistan Argentina, and the Council appointed Belgium, Colombia and the United States. Had the Commission, proposed in January, been despatched without delay instead of reaching the sub-continent as it did only at the beginning of July, it might have succeeded in bringing about an early cease-fire in the snow-covered regions of Kashmir; by the time it arrived the snow had melted and the big spring offensive had already started.

The UN Commission and the Resolutions of August 1948 and January 1949

The Commission was informed by the Pakistan Foreign Minister that the Pakistan Army had at the time three brigades of regular troops in Kashmir, and that troops had been sent into the State during the first half of May. This action, it was claimed, was taken as a measure of self-defence. The Governor of the North-West Frontier Province told the Commission that the movement of the tribesmen into Kashmir had in fact to be canalized through his province in order to avoid the serious risk of outright war within the territory of Pakistan. It was further admitted that the Azad Kashmir forces were under the over-all command and tactical direction of the Pakistan Army. The Commission was now confronted with a situation not visualized by the Security Council during its debates—a clash between the regular armies of India and Pakistan. Its failure to inform the Council immediately of this alarming development and to request fresh instructions has been the cause of many obstacles to settlement of the Kashmir problem.

On 13th August, the Commission adopted a Resolution consisting of three parts. Part I dealt with the establishment of a cease-fire. It did not mention the Azad Kashmir forces; responsibility for implementing the cease-fire was put exclusively on the High Commands of India and Pakistan. Part II set out the principles of a Truce Agreement, beginning with the recognition that the presence of Pakistani troops in Kashmir constituted 'a material change in the situation since it was presented by the Government of Pakistan before the Security Council'. It accordingly provided that (1) all Pakistani troops as well as tribesmen and other Pakistani nationals were to be withdrawn from Kashmir; (2) the territory thus evacuated was to be administered by 'the local authorities under the surveillance of the Commission'; (3) when the Commission had notified that the tribesmen and Pakistani nationals had withdrawn, 'thereby terminating the situation which was represented by the Government of India as having occasioned the presence of Indian troops' in Kashmir, and that Pakistani forces were also being withdrawn, India would 'begin to withdraw the bulk' of her forces 'in stages to be agreed upon with the Commission'; (4) pending acceptance of the conditions for the final settlement, India was permitted to 'maintain within the lines existing at the moment of the cease-fire' a minimum force which in agreement with the Commission was considered necessary to assist local authorities in the maintenance of law and order. Part III stated that after acceptance by India and Pakistan of a Truce Agreement, both countries would 'enter into consultations with the Commission' to determine conditions for the free expression of the will of the people of Kashmir.

India accepted the Resolution on 20th August with the following reservations to which the Commission gave its unqualified acceptance: (1) that the sovereignty of the Jammu and Kashmir Government over the area evacuated by Pakistani troops would not be brought into question; (2) that no recognition would be given to the Azad Kashmir authorities; (3) that the time when the withdrawal of Indian forces was to begin, the stages in which it was to be carried out and the strength of the Indian forces to be retained in the State would be decided only by India and the Commission; (4) that the size of the Indian force to be retained in Kashmir should be conditioned by the need to ensure its security against external aggression; and (5) that Part III of the Resolution did not in any way recognize the right of Pakistan to have any part in the plebiscite. With regard to the strategic Northern Area of Gilgit and Baltistan, which had not been covered by the Resolution, Nehru requested that, after the withdrawal of Pakistani forces, the responsibility for the administration of this region (from which he was prepared to exclude Gilgit) should revert to the Kashmir Government and that for its defence to the Government of India. The Commission assured him that this question would be considered.

Pakistan, unenthusiastic, demanded clarification, her main objective being to bring about a 'balanced and synchronized' withdrawal of Indian and Pakistani troops without the disbandment of the Azad Kashmir forces. The Commission concluded that Pakistan was 'unable to accept the Resolution without attaching certain conditions beyond the compass of this Resolution, thereby making impossible an immediate cease-fire and the beginning of fruitful negotiations'. The Commission submitted its first report to the Council in November 1948 but the problem was not really explored. Another opportunity for a complete reappraisal of the problem was, therefore, lost and the Council merely asked the Commission to proceed with its efforts to bring about a cease-fire in Kashmir.

On 11th December the Commission drafted proposals for a plebiscite which were supplementary to the August Resolution. Their main feature was that the United Nations Secretary-General was to nominate a Plebiscite Administrator who would be formally appointed to office by the Government of Jammu and Kashmir.

India's acceptance of these proposals was based on a series of assurances received from the Commission. These were: (1) that India could not be expected to discharge any of her responsibilities regarding the plebiscite until there was satisfactory evidence that Pakistan was carrying out her obligations under Part II of the August Resolution; (2) that the Commission did not contemplate that the Plebiscite Administrator should undertake any administrative functions in regard to the plebiscite until Parts I and II of the Commission's Resolution of 13th August had been implemented; (3) that, in view of the fact that the Azad Kashmir forces now consisted of 32 armed battalions under the operational command of the Pakistan Army, there would be 'large-scale disarming' as well as disbanding of these forces; (4) that 'any political activity which might tend to disturb law and order could not be regarded as legitimate'; it was made clear that this assurance precluded any appeal to religious fanaticism; and (5) that should the Plebiscite Administrator find a plebiscite to be impracticable, the way would be open to consider other methods for ensuring the free expression of the will of the people of Kashmir.

Pakistan accepted the proposals after her fears regarding the selection and appointment of the Plebiscite Administrator had been removed by the Commission's assurance that Pakistan, along with India, would be consulted in his selection, and that he would be exclusively responsible for the organization of the plebiscite.

With the acceptance by India and Pakistan of these proposals, a Cease-fire Agreement came into force on 1st January 1949. An agreement on the demarcation of the cease-fire line was finally reached on 27th July. A group of United Nations Military Observers has been patrolling the cease-fire line ever since.

The December proposals were embodied in the Commission's Resolution of 5th January 1949. The very first sentence of these proposals reaffirmed the August Resolution. The manner in which this crucial Resolution was accepted by India and Pakistan had far-reaching consequences during the Truce negotiations. While India had accepted it on the basis of precise written assurances, Pakistan had imposed conditions which amounted to rejection and had later subscribed to it only indirectly. In its anxiety to bring about a cease-fire which depended upon Pakistan's adherence to the August Resolution, the Commission failed to clarify the nature of Pakistan's eventual 'acceptance' of it. Its reports reveal that Pakistan continued to insist on her own interpretation.

On 24th March 1949 the United Nations Secretary-General nominated an American, Admiral Chester Nimitz, as the Plebiscite Administrator, an unfortunate choice in view of later developments. India had in fact proposed the appointment of the President of the International Red Cross to this post, a proposal favoured by the Colombian member of the Commission, but other delegations had 'explicit instructions' to urge that the Plebiscite Administrator should be a United States citizen. A diplomatic 'victory' virtually undid all the work the Commission had accomplished.

Negotiations for a Truce Agreement

Three interrelated problems presented insurmountable difficulties and wrecked the efforts of the Commission and all the United Nations Mediators to bring about a Truce Agreement: (1) disposal of the Azad Kashmir forces, (2) withdrawal of the regular forces, and (3) the Northern Area.

Disposal of the Azad Kashmir forces. The Resolution of 13th August, while taking note of the presence of Pakistani troops in Kashmir, did not mention the Azad Kashmir forces. The Commission had unanimously agreed that 'it should avoid any action which might be interpreted as signifying *de facto* or *de jure* recognition of the Azad Kashmir Government'. India relied on the assurance that 'large-scale disarming' of Azad forces would take place as a prerequisite to the holding of a plebiscite. She pointed out that these forces, hardly distinguishable from the Pakistan Army, now consisted of 32 battalions, which, according to the Commission's own Military Adviser, represented 'a formidable force'. This had changed the military situation since the Resolution was accepted by India; she, therefore, insisted that the phasing of the withdrawal of the 'bulk' of Indian troops from Kashmir depended on the progress made with the disarmament of Azad Kashmir forces. Pakistan, on the other hand, maintained that this question was not relevant to the Truce negotiations and that any disbandment of these forces was conditional upon a reduction in the Kashmir State forces and a withdrawal of Indian troops beyond that of the 'bulk' authorized by the Resolution. The Commission rejected her contention that the main objective of the proposed Truce Agreement was to create a military balance between the forces on either side. It stressed the crucial importance of the disposal of the Azad forces in relation to the withdrawal of Indian troops and concluded that if it had been 'able to foresee that the cease-fire would be prolonged throughout the greater part of 1949 and that Pakistan would use that period to consolidate its position in the Azad territory', this question would have been dealt with in Part II of the Resolution.

Withdrawal of the regular forces. India maintained that the timing and staging of the withdrawal of the 'bulk' of her forces and the strength of her troops to be retained in the State were matters for settlement between herself and the Commission only. Her stand on this crucial issue was based on the terms of the Resolution and the Commission's assurances. Pakistan, on the other hand, wanted the withdrawal of her forces to be synchronized with that of the 'bulk' of Indian troops, and in support of her stand she referred to an assurance that such a synchronization could be arranged between the respective High Commands and the Commission. But the Commission explained that its reference to synchronization was meant to ensure 'the establishment of a time sequence' for the two withdrawals after the acceptance of Truce Terms; it could not accept the Pakistani contention that the withdrawal of her forces was conditional on her agreement to the Indian withdrawal plan because this would have been incompatible with its Resolution.

The Northern Area. India relied on the Commission's assurance that although this area was not mentioned in the August Resolution, her demand to re-establish control over it could be considered in its implementation. Pakistan, on the other hand, maintained that as her forces effectively controlled it when the Resolution was drafted, the region did not require any special treatment and that Part II of the Resolution applied equally to all parts of the State where the armed forces of India and Pakistan faced each other. But the Commission was inclined to the view that Pakistan had consolidated her military control over the area between August 1948 and January 1949. It conceded that the Indian demand was 'based on legal claims', but in view of the changed military situation it could not be a party to an arrangement which would have resulted in an extension of conflict.

The deadlock was now complete. The greatest single obstacle to a Truce Agreement was the reorganization of the Azad Kashmir forces into 32 well-equipped battalions; it transformed the military situation and made the withdrawal of regular forces more difficult to achieve within the framework of the Resolution. The Commission had to admit that 'the situation in the State has changed; the Resolutions remain unchanged'. Abandoning its mediatory role, the Commission finally proposed compulsory arbitration by Admiral Nimitz on all points of dispute regarding the Truce Terms. Pakistan accepted the proposal but India maintained that the issues at stake were primarily political in character and did not lend themselves easily to arbitration, and that the main issue of the disbandment of the

Azad Kashmir forces was 'not a matter for arbitration but for affirmative and immediate action'. The Commission admitted in its final report to the Security Council in December 1949 that its ambiguous clarifications and sometimes contradictory assurances had partly contributed to the deadlock.

The Dixon Report

Even at this stage the Security Council failed to discuss the substance of the Kashmir problem. After an 'informal mediation' by General McNaughton, the Canadian Member of the Council, which tended to eliminate the Commission's assurances regarding the Azad Kashmir forces and the Northern Area, the Council asked Sir Owen Dixon, an Australian jurist, to bring about the demilitarization of Kashmir and to make any suggestions which might contribute to a solution.

Dixon stated in his report that 'when the frontier of the State of Jammu and Kashmir was crossed on . . . 20th October 1947, by hostile elements, it was contrary to international law, and . . . when, in May 1948, . . . units of the regular Pakistan forces moved into the territory of the State, that too was inconsistent with international law'. This statement by a jurist of international repute implied a recognition of the Indian case that Kashmir was constitutionally a part of India and that she had been a victim of agression; but Dixon drew no practical conclusions. He proposed several schemes for the demilitarization of Kashmir which were unacceptable to India as they ran counter to the Commission's assurances. Concerned to avoid another refugee problem, he then suggested a combination of partition and plebiscite in the Valley. This was presented in two forms: (1) a plebiscite by sections and the allocation of each section according to the result of the vote, or (2) regions where there was no doubt about the will of the people should be allocated to India or Pakistan without any vote being taken, the plebiscite to be 'confined only to the uncertain area'. India was willing to discuss the second variation of Dixon's scheme with one addition—that the demarcation proposed in it should pay due regard to geographical features and to the requirements of an international boundary, and the Indian Prime Minister was prepared to attend a conference with his Pakistani counterpart to discuss such a settlement. Pakistan, however, refused to accept a proposal which went back on the idea of a plebiscite for the entire State. In order to obtain Pakistan's acceptance to his partition and plebiscite proposal, Dixon suggested the establishment of an administrative body under the Plebiscite Administrator in the limited plebiscite area; but then India could not agree to the supersession of the Government of the State for the duration of the plebiscite.

The Graham Reports

The Security Council did not explore the possibility of implementing Dixon's new proposals, but instead in April 1951 appointed Dr. Graham, of the United States Ministry of Labour, as the new Mediator. Graham tried to bring about the demilitarization of Kashmir 'in a single, continuous process' within three months; but the three months became two years of fruitless negotiations. Between 1951 and 1953 he submitted to the Security Council five reports, the last of which recommended negotiations between the two countries. The main cause of Graham's failure was the fundamental conflict between India and Pakistan over their obligations under the Resolution of August 1948. While the Security Council tried to reconcile these differences at five-yearly intervals, the Kashmir situation, both in its local and international aspects, was completely transformed. The deadlock is now as complete as it was at the beginning of the Truce negotiations in 1949.

Developments within Kashmir

Abdullah's new Government, which replaced his Emergency Administration in March 1948, embarked upon a programme of economic and social reforms. The Instrument of Accession was superseded by Article 370 of the Indian Constitution which preserved the special status of Kashmir and prescribed a flexible procedure for the gradual application of the Constitution to the State. In accordance with the 'New Kashmir' plan of 1944, a Constituent Assembly was convened on 31st October 1951 which further clarified Kashmir's constitutional relationship with India. The Security Council took the view that the decisions of the Assembly could in no way affect the international commitments of India regarding the future disposition of the State. India, however, maintained that so long as Kashmir was constitutionally an integral part of Indian territory, the convening of the Assembly was a purely internal matter; her international commitments simply meant that in case the verdict in a plebiscite went against India, Kashmir would be relieved of its constitutional links with her.

The Assembly proposed the termination of hereditary rule and the abolition of landlordism without compensation. These sweeping reforms profoundly affected the interests of the Hindu landed aristocracy of Jammu. The Praja Parishad, a party representing these vested interests and having close links with Hindu communal organizations in India, accordingly started an agitation for the complete integration of Kashmir, demanding the total application of the Indian Constitution, which makes it obligatory for the State to compensate for compulsory acquisition of property. The Delhi Agreement of 24th July 1952, however, sanctioned the abolition of Dogra rule and preserved the special status of Kashmir, enabling the agrarian reforms to be implemented. Abdullah, the chief architect of the Agreement, triumphantly declared: 'This is not a paper agreement but a union of hearts which no power on earth can loosen'. On 14th November 1952, Karan Singh, son of the last Maharaja, was unanimously elected by the Assembly as the first Head of State for a period of five years. The Parishad revived its agitation with greater intensity. Abdullah, rumoured to be leaning towards an independent status for Kashmir and to have found encouragement from foreign powers, delayed full implementation of the Delhi Agreement. This led to a split in his Cabinet; three of his colleagues accused him of deliberately trying to rupture Kashmir's relationship with India. On 9th August 1953 Abdullah was arrested and Bakhshi Ghulam Mohammad, his Deputy since 1948, formed a new administration. In

May 1954 further provisions of the Indian Constitution were applied to Kashmir. The State Constitution, which came into force on 26th January 1957, declares that Kashmir 'is and shall remain an integral part of the Union of India'. Bakhshi remained in power for a little over ten years; his present successor, Ghulam Mohammad Sadiq, has proposed the elimination of the remaining symbols of Kashmir's special status in the Indian constitutional framework.

But on the other side of the Cease-fire Line Pakistan has consolidated her position, directly administering Gilgit and Baltistan and indirectly controlling the Azad Kashmir area. There has been a great increase in the number of incidents along the Cease-fire Line.

Kashmir, the United Nations and the Great Powers

The period immediately following Graham's fifth report began hopefully. The Prime Ministers of India and Pakistan entered into direct negotiations and on 21st August 1953 issued a joint communiqué declaring that the question of Kashmir should be settled in accordance with the wishes of the people of the State. They agreed that the Plebiscite Administrator should be appointed by the end of April 1954; and that committees of experts should be set up to advise the Prime Ministers on the best way of bringing about the demilitarization of Kashmir. But differences immediately appeared. India pressed for the appointment of an Administrator from a small country so that the Kashmir problem could be isolated from Big Power rivalries. The whole question was radically altered in Indian eyes when Pakistan signed a Mutual Defence Assistance Agreement with the United States in May 1954 and later joined the Western-sponsored military pacts. Admiral Nimitz himself resigned in September 1954 from an office which he was never able to exercise.

The mediation of the United Nations in Kashmir was almost entirely based on the initiative of the Western Powers. While not formally committing themselves on the substance of the question, they were generally more favourable to the Pakistani point of view. The strategic importance of Kashmir in the context of the cold war and the growing divergence between the foreign policies of India and Pakistan furthered these tendencies. The one-sided character of the intervention of the United Nations in Kashmir was underlined by the non-participation of the delegates of the Soviet bloc in the Security Council debates. Apart from raising some procedural points, they invariably abstained from voting on the Council's Resolutions. The first major Soviet intervention came in January 1952 when the Soviet delegate suggested that the people of Kashmir should be given an opportunity to decide the question of the State's constitutional status by themselves without outside interference. Soviet policy was finally clarified when Khrushchev said in Dec. 1955 that the question of Kashmir 'as one of the States of the Republic of India' had already been decided by the people of Kashmir. Since then the Soviet Union has maintained that Kashmir is 'an inalienable part of the Republic of India'.

The Kashmir problem has been further complicated by the direct involvement of China as a result of the construction of the strategic road in Ladakh linking Tibet with Sinkiang. While not formally clarifying her stand on the Kashmir question, Chou En-lai gave the impression on a number of occasions that China accepted India's basic position in Kashmir. After the Chinese attack on India in the autumn of 1962, however, Sino-Pakistan relations improved considerably. Having gained a third of the State in Ladakh, China was now willing to exploit Indo-Pakistan differences to her advantage. Pakistan, disenchanted with her Western allies who rushed military assistance to India and never questioned her sole responsibility for the defence of Ladakh which is, after all, part of Kashmir, was only too eager to make India's difficulty her opportunity to redress the Kashmir account. On 2nd March 1963 Pakistan and China signed an agreement providing for the demarcation of the border of the northern area of Kashmir. This agreement proved fatal to the Indo-Pakistan ministerial talks then in progress to settle all outstanding problems between the two countries.

The Resolutions of August 1948 and January 1949 still remain the basic terms of reference for the Security Council's attempts to settle the Kashmir problem; but its deliberations have been increasingly divorced from the rapidly changing situation in the area. Graham's fifth report, submitted in March 1953, was not considered by the Council until 1957, when it requested Gunnar Jarring, the Swedish delegate, to settle Indo-Pakistan differences. Like his predecessors, he too failed in his mission. Graham made another effort to resolve the deadlock. His report, submitted in March 1958, was not considered by the Security Council until 1962. The Council has always tended to reaffirm its previous resolutions without giving due consideration to the new factors brought to its attention by its own mediators. The reports of the Commission have been buried under a series of resolutions which, while endorsing the two basic Resolutions, have marked a retreat from them. The warnings about the effects of a bitter plebiscite campaign on the minorities in India and Pakistan have been completely ignored. The practical problem of reconstituting the Kashmir electorate of 1947 has been brushed aside. As exercises in sheer frustration the Security Council's records could hardly be improved upon. It has failed to take note of the Chinese occupation of Ladakh, a third 'partition' of the State which undermined the whole basis of mediation by the United Nations. With the barren hills of Ladakh humming with military activity, demilitarization of Kashmir has become a farce, and the Kashmir problem can no longer be considered in the context of Indo-Pakistan relations alone.

There is no obvious solution acceptable to both India and Pakistan. Kashmir being only one of a complex of issues which have plagued the two countries since independence, only a determined effort to forge new ties of friendship will be able to heal the old wounds of partition. The Kashmir problem is linked with the fate of the minorities in India and Pakistan, and any disturbance in the *status quo* would not only have widespread domestic repercussions but would also add to Himalayan tensions.

BIBLIOGRAPHY

C. B. (Baron) Birdwood. *Two Nations and Kashmir.* (Robert Hale, London, 1956.)

Michael Brecher. *The Struggle for Kashmir.* (Ryerson Press, Toronto, 1953.)

Alan Campbell-Johnson. *Mission with Mountbatten.* (Robert Hale, London, 1950.)

Josef Korbel. *Danger in Kashmir.* (Princeton Univ. Press, Princeton, N.J., 1954.)

M. C. Mahajan. *Accession of Kashmir to India* (*The Inside Story*). (Institute of Public Administration, Sholapur.)

V. P. Menon. *The Story of the Integration of the Indian States.* (Longmans, London, 1956.)

Sheikh Mohammed Abdullah. 'Kashmir, India and Pakistan'. (*Foreign Affairs*, April, 1956.)

Publications by the Government of India: *Jammu and Kashmir* (1948). *Twelve Months of War in Kashmir* (1948). *Pakistan's War Propaganda Against India* (1951). *Indo-Pakistan Relations.* (1951). *Kashmir* (1954).

Publications by the Government of Pakistan: *India's War Propaganda Against Pakistan* (1951). *India's Threat to Pakistan* (1951).

Reports of the United Nations Commission for India and Pakistan: S/1100, November 1948; S/1196, January 1949; S/1430, December 1949.

Reports of the United Nations Mediators (1950-58): S/1453, 1950 (Report of General A. G. L. McNaughton). S/1791, 1950 (Report of Sir Owen Dixon). S/2375, 1951; S/2448, 1951; S/2611, 1952; S/2783, 1952; S/2967, 1953; S/3894, 1958 (six Reports of Dr. Frank Graham). S/3821, 1957 (Report of Gunnar V. Jarring).

BIOGRAPHICAL NOTE

M. Zuberi. B. 1930. Studied at the Muslim University, Aligarh, India (B.A., 1949; M.A. in Political Science, 1951). Thereafter Lecturer in Politics at Aligarh University. Scholarship to Balliol College, Oxford; Senior Scholarship at St. Antony's College, Oxford. Now writing a study of British policy in Asia during the late 19th and early 20th centuries with special reference to the defence of the Indian Empire.

THE NAGAS

by

KHUSHWANT SINGH

THE north-eastern frontier of India is inhabited by a large number of Indo-Mongoloid tribes of whom the Nagas are the most important. The Nagas are not one people but over a dozen different tribes speaking different languages. Dr. J. H. Hutton, an acknowledged authority on the subject, says:

'It is generally assumed in a vague sort of way that those tribes which are spoken of as Nagas have something in common with each other which distinguishes them from the many other tribes found in Assam and entitles them to be regarded as a racial unit in themselves . . . The truth is that, if not impossible, it is exceedingly difficult to propound any test by which a Naga tribe can be distinguished from other Assam or Burma tribes which are not Nagas.'

It is assumed that the conglomeration of what have come to be known as associated Naga tribes number almost one million people living in India (Assam-NEFA, Nagaland proper and Manipur) and in Burma. The majority of the Nagas, between 60 and 80 per cent, are Christians; the remainder are Buddhists or Animists.

The origin of the word 'Naga' is obscure. Sanskritists believe that it is derived from *naga*—meaning hill—and therefore refers to the 'people of the hills'. (It has no connection with *naga*—snake.) The late Dr. Verrier Elwin, the Indian Government's expert on Indian tribes, was of the opinion that it is derived from *nok*, meaning people in several Tibeto-Burman dialects.

The world has known little about the Nagas' customs and manners except their practice of head-hunting. The introduction of Christianity and the spread of literacy has brought about revolutionary changes. No cases of head-hunting have been reported since 1958. Naga boys and girls attend schools and colleges in ever-increasing numbers; many have gone abroad for further studies or research to British and American universities.

Historical Background and British Occupation

The earliest records of Nagas go back to the 13th century when a Shan chief subjugated their territory. The Ahoms (the dynasty from which Assam derives its name) extended their sway over the Naga tribes and took tribute from them. The Nagas rose against the Ahoms several times during the 16th and 17th centuries, but later entered into matrimonial alliances with them by giving their daughters in marriage to Ahom princes. A Mogul chronicler who visited Assam in 1662 wrote that although the Nagas did not pay taxes to the Assamese ruler, 'yet they accept his sovereignty and obey some of his commands'.

The first contact with the British was in 1832—eight years after the termination of the Anglo-Burmese war. That year the Raja of Manipur again subjugated the Naga tribes and occupied Kohima. The British, who were unhappy about the Manipur incursion, conceded that the Raja had some sort of *de facto* control over the hills.

The Nagas resisted British intrusion into their regions with the same determination they had shown towards other strangers. They raided British-occupied areas and had to suffer retaliation—destruction of their villages, granaries and standing crops. The British Government's attitude towards the Nagas vacillated between an aggressive 'mission of civilization' alternating with a policy of 'leave well alone' to preserve the tribes as museum pieces. The chief determining factor was always finance.

In the latter half of the 19th century a cautious forward policy was resumed. In 1866 an outpost was established at Samaguting with a school and a dispensary. In 1877, Kohima was established as the headquarters of the administration with a sub-headquarters at Wokha. A police force was established and house-tax levied. This was the beginning of effective administration which in 1881 was regularized as the Naga hills district. In 1888 yet another sub-headquarters was opened among the Aos at Mokokchung. By and large the Nagas accepted the Pax Britannica with good grace.

The Nagas During the World Wars

The Nagas remained loyal to the British during the World Wars. In the First, about 2,000 men (half of them Semas) volunteered for the Labour Corps in France. In the Second, Naga partisans worked for the Allies behind enemy lines after the Japanese had over-run Naga territory. Field Marshal Slim paid them handsome tribute in his book *Defeat into Victory* as

> '. . . the gallant Nagas whose loyalty, even in the most depressing times of the invasion, never faltered. Despite floggings, torture, execution and the burning of their villages they refused to aid the Japanese in any way or to betray our troops. Their active help to us was beyond value or praise. They guided our columns, collected information, ambushed enemy patrols, carried our supplies, and brought in our wounded under the heaviest fire—and then, being the gentlemen they were, often refused all payment.'

However, a small number which included Mr. A. Z. Phizo (an Angami Naga and later the President of the Naga National Council) collaborated with the Japanese invaders and the Indian National Army of Subhas Chandra Bose and were with them in the capture of Kohima.

The Naga Demand for Autonomy

In the 1920s the Nagas started becoming politically conscious and began to talk of independence. The Indian National Congress, specifically Mahatma Gandhi, encouraged the Naga freedom movement. In 1929, a delegation representing the 'Naga Club' presented a memorial to the Simon Commission demanding to be 'left alone' to determine their own future whenever the British decided to quit India. In 1930 southern Naga tribes rose in revolt under Jadunam of Zeliang. Jadunam was captured and hanged but his sister 'Rani' Gaidilu continued the struggle. She was arrested and spent 18 years in gaol. She was freed by the Indian Government and granted a life-pension.

When transfer of power from British to Indian hands seemed imminent, the Nagas reconsidered their position. One section was for some form of association with India. The Naga National Council, a radical section consisting largely of Christians, formed in February 1946, was pledged to the establishment of an independent, sovereign Naga state. Its leader was Mr. Phizo.

Negotiations were started between the Indian Government and representative Naga organizations. The spokesman for the Government was the governor of Assam, Sir Akbar Hydari. In June 1947 a nine-point Ten-Year Agreement was signed between the Government and the Nagas. The preamble stated:

> 'That the right of the Nagas to develop themselves according to their freely expressed wishes is recognized . . . The general principle is accepted that what the Naga National Council is prepared to pay for, the Naga National Council should control. The principle will apply equally to the work done as well as staff employed. . . '

The provisional terms of the Ten-Year Agreement stated that the judiciary, agriculture, the legislature and Tax, Education and Public Works Departments, all came under the supervision and control of the Naga National Council.

The ninth point of the Agreement dealt with the all-important right of self-determination. It read:

> 'The Governor of Assam, as the Agent of the Indian Union, will have a special responsibility for a period of ten years to ensure the due observance of the agreement; at the end of this period the Naga National Council will be asked whether the above agreement is to be extended for a further period or a new agreement regarding the future of the Naga people arrived at.'

The clause was interpreted differently by the Indians and Naga moderates on one side and the Naga radicals on the other. The moderates and Indians believed that association with the Indian Union was implied; the radicals did not read that into the clause. A Naga delegation of radicals met Mahatma Gandhi on 19th July 1947 and later Prime Minister Nehru. While the Mahatma in his usual conciliatory language gave the Nagas assurances of independence, Mr. Nehru in his equally forthright language stated that 'independence' meant no more than autonomy and the right to continue their way of living without outside interference. The moderates who later re-grouped themselves as the 'Naga People's Convention' agreed to co-operate with the administration.

The attitude of the Naga radicals and the Indian bureaucracy hardened towards each other. Mr. Phizo became the undisputed leader of the Naga National Council. He was arrested. And as could have been anticipated, he came out of gaol with enhanced prestige amongst his own people and greater bitterness against his gaolers. In May 1951 Mr. Phizo organized a plebiscite on the issue of an independent Nagaland and later announced that the Nagas had recorded a 100-per-cent vote in its favour. The Indian Commissioner in charge described the plebiscite as a farce. Relations between the Naga supporters of Mr. Phizo and the Indian Government became worse. Mr. Phizo's supporters abstained from going to Indian schools, colleges and hospitals. They boycotted the general elections of 1951. The match was applied to this inflammable situation by an incident at Kohima in October 1952. A procession of Naga demonstrators clashed with the police; casualties resulted on both sides. Amongst the dead was a judge of the Angami Tribal Court. A commission of enquiry exonerated the police officer concerned. This further angered the extremists. When Mr. Nehru came to visit Kohima in March 1953, the Deputy Commissioner declined permission for a memorial to be presented to him; the Nagas demonstrated their resentment by walking out of the meeting arranged in his honour.

The Assam authorities proceeded to take action against the supporters of the Naga National Council. Fighting broke out in 1955. The rebels succeeded in importing arms from neighbouring states or capturing them from Indian patrols. They almost succeeded in overwhelming the local militia. Regular units of the Indian Army were sent in. While the Army was under instructions to take limited action, the rebels were able to muster their strength. Under the command of 'General' Kaito they raised and trained a volunteer militia of over 40,000 men. Whatever else the Indian Army did to suppress this revolt, it was unable to check gun-running across the borders.

The fighting continued with increasing bitterness and became particularly acute in 1956 and 1957. The Indian Army demanded a freer hand. The rebels complained of atrocities against non-combatants. In 1958 Mr. Phizo escaped from India and in the summer of 1960 made a dramatic appearance in London. He succeeded in eliciting the support of the influential Sunday paper *The Observer* and the Reverend Michael Scott who was held in great esteem by the Indians for his excellent work for the coloured peoples of South Africa. In his turn, the Reverend Scott elicited the support of Mr. Jaya Prakash Narain, one of the most outspoken and honest of India's contemporary statesmen.

The Indian Government realized that it had allowed local bureaucrats to let matters go too far. Mr. Nehru took personal interest in the Naga problem. On 1st August 1960 he announced in the Indian Parliament that the Nagas would be given complete autonomy and Nagaland would become the sixteenth state of the Indian Union. He said: 'Our policy has always been to give the fullest autonomy and opportunity of self-development to the Naga people, without interfering in any way in their internal affairs or way of life.'

The State of Nagaland and the Naga National Council

In June 1962 an autonomous Nagaland, the sixteenth state of the Indian Union, came into existence with Mr. Shilo Ao as the Chief Minister. Nagaland is 6,236 square miles with a population of about 400,000 Nagas belonging to thirteen tribes. The Naga National Council boycotted the Shilo Ao

Government and intensified its underground activities. Hostilities continued unabated with all the ghoulish atrocities connected with guerilla warfare. Ultimately a three-man 'Peace Mission' consisting of the Chief Minister of Assam, Mr. Badri Prosad Chaliha, Reverend Michael Scott and Jaya Prakash Narain made contact with some of the fighting Nagas and arranged a cease-fire. Negotiations between the Naga National Council and the Indian Government, represented by Mr. Gundevia, of the External Affairs Department, were resumed under the auspices of the Peace Mission.

The differences between the Indian point of view and that of the Nagas in revolt are being gradually narrowed down. The Indian Government contend that Naga territory has always been geographically a part of India and was inherited by them from the British; that Nagaland is too small to be economically or politically viable as an independent state: that it is strategically important to India in its defence against Communist China; and that the present recalcitrant attitude of a section of the Nagas is due to anti-Indian propaganda of Christian missionaries and the English who now have no responsibilities in the region. The rebels refute Indian contentions. They claim that they are a Mongoloid race with nothing in common with any of the Indian races, and that being largely Christian now they have little in common with the idolatrous Hindu; that they were never a part of India and were able to maintain autonomy even during British rule; that as an independent people they will be in a better position to safeguard the frontiers of India. Whilst it is realized by both parties that the resumption of hostilities will have disastrous consequences, a settlement of the dispute is not yet in sight.

BIBLIOGRAPHY

Verrier Elwin. *Nagaland.* (Adviser's Secretariat, Shillong, 1961.)

Karl Eskelund. *The Forgotten Valley.* (Alvin Redman, London, 1959.)

Sir Edward Gait. *A History of Assam.* (Thacker, Spink and Co., Calcutta and Simla, 2nd ed., 1926.)

Ursula Graham Bower. *Naga Path.* (John Murray, London, 1950.)

C. von Fuerer-Haimendorf. *The Naked Nagas.* (Methuen, London, 1939.)

J. H. Hutton. *The Angami Nagas.* (Macmillan, London, 1921.) *The Sema Nagas.* (Macmillan, London, 1921.)

George N. Patterson. 'The Naga Revolt'. (Royal Central Asian Journal, London, January, 1963.)

R. Reid. *History of the Frontier Areas bordering on Assam from 1883-1941.* (Shilling, 1942.)

L. W. Shakespear. *History of Upper Assam, Burmah and North Eastern Frontier.* (Macmillan, London, 1914.)

David Snellgrove. *Himalayan Pilgrimage.* (Bruno Cassirer, Oxford, 1961.)

BIOGRAPHICAL NOTE

Khushwant Singh. Educated in England; practised law at Lahore till Partition. Thereafter with the Indian Ministry of External Affairs (posted to Canada and London), All India Radio and the Planning Commission (edited *Yojana*). Long-term grant from Rockefeller Foundation to carry out research in Sikh history (1958) which resulted in a two-volume *History of the Sikhs* (Princeton Univ. Press, Princeton, N.J., 1963–), *Ranjit Singh—Maharaja of the Punjab* (Allen and Unwin, London, 1963) and *The Fall of the Kingdom of the Punjab* (Orient Longmans, 1962). Indian delegate to Writers' Conference, Edinburgh Festival, 1962, and leader of the Indian delegation at the meeting of Asian writers organized by P.E.N. International at Manila, December 1962.

PAKHTUNISTAN

by

GUY WINT

PAKHTUNISTAN has become one of the areas of debate in Asia. It is the region inhabited by Pathans—Pashto speakers—which lies on the borders of Pakistan and Afghanistan. Its area has never been defined exactly. Its claim to autonomy has been put forward since the war ended by various Pathan leaders in the area, and they are backed by the Afghan Government, but no maps exist with hard and fast boundaries. The claims put forward often grotesquely exceed the area in which Pathans are in a majority; and at the same time they usually omit any part of the Southern province of Afghanistan, in which there reside Pathans who are racially exactly the same as the Pathans of Pakistan.

The problem of the Pathans has been inherited from British days. Under the British the Afghans recognized an international line dividing Afghanistan from British territory called the Durand Line. On the British side of the line the Pathans who were tribally organized were divided into those of administered and unadministered territories. The administered territory formed six districts of the North-West Frontier Province. With some exceptions these districts were governed in the same way as the districts of the Punjab onto which they abutted. The unadministered Pathans lay between these settled districts and the Durand Line. In these no organized magistracy existed and there was no collection of revenue. The Government limited its interest to imposing peace along the roads. For the rest it relied on its influence with the tribespeople, exerted through the tribal chiefs.

The system underwent certain changes with the setting up of Pakistan in 1947. Previously there had been a constant state of war along the frontier. The unadministered tribespeople raided the settled areas, and intermittent military operations had to be undertaken to repress these raids. Pakistan, acting on the ideas of Mr. Jinnah, sought a rapprochement with the tribal people emphasizing that there was now no religious difference between them and the new Government. A military withdrawal was ordered from all the posts the Government occupied in the tribal region. The Government promised to respect the independence of the unadministered area, to continue the payment of subsidies which had been paid by the British Government as a kind of danegeld, and began a scheme, which only reached a substantial size in the late '50's, for economic development. On the whole the policy has been extremely successful. The region has been quieter than at any time within historical memory.

However, in spite of such an enlightened policy, the Pakhtunistan movement developed. It was fermented by Afghanistan which, in 1947, had refused to recognize the Durand Line. It put forward the demand that the Pathans should be independent; over the long run it doubtless wished that they should be annexed to itself, and it advanced the claims of the Pathans to include as wide a stretch of Pakistan territory as was possible. In appealing for support of the movement it made much of the historical tension which has always existed between the Pathans and the Punjabis.

It was argued on behalf of the Pathans that in a plebiscite which had been held before the independence of India to decide on their future they had been called on to vote either for Pakistan or India. They had not been given the opportunity to vote for an independent Pakhtunistan.

The Afghan Government has continued to support the movement, chiefly by backing ambitious or disgruntled tribal chiefs; the principal among these is Abdul Ghaffar Khan, a former Gandhian leader. It has smuggled in arms, conducted propaganda, dispersed large sums of money, and has kept up a radio war. In 1961 it sent into Pakistan an armed force of volunteers, though the fact that these were regular troops was camouflaged. On the whole these efforts have failed. Nothing was more striking than the lukewarm support which the Afghan leaders received. Pakistan's rule, its respect for tribal independence, and its economic policy are popular. They have attached the tribal territory firmly to itself. Pakistan is vigilant, but the number of political prisoners is not high.

The Afghan backing of the movement has led to constant ill-feeling between Pakistan and Afghanistan. At one stage, the Pakistan embassy was burned in Kabul. In 1961 Pakistan broke off diplomatic and trade relations with Afghanistan on the grounds that Afghan officers stationed in the frontier region were openly inciting the people to revolt. In 1963 there was a change of government in Afghanistan which promised a milder policy. Mediation by Persia brought Pakistan and Afghanistan together again and Pakistan improved matters by releasing Abdul Ghaffar Khan from prison, but it is too early to say whether Afghanistan has given up promoting the cause of Pakhtunistan.

BIOGRAPHICAL NOTE

GUY WINT. B. London, 1910. Educated at Dulwich College, Oriel College, Oxford, and Berlin University. Member of St. Antony's College, Oxford since 1957. Formerly leader-writer for *The Manchester Guardian*; now writes for *The Observer* on Asian Affairs. His publications include *Spotlight on Asia* (Penguin, London, 1955); (with Peter Calvocoressi) *Middle East Crisis* (Penguin, London, 1957); *Common Sense About China* (Gollancz, London, 1960) and *China's Communist Crusade* (Praeger, New York, 1965.)

THE OVERSEAS CHINESE

by

LOIS MITCHISON

THERE are between 12 and 13 million overseas Chinese, the exact number depending on how much of his ancestry has to be Chinese before a person thinks himself, or is thought by others, to be Chinese. Small communities in the United States, the Caribbean, Peru, Britain, India and Australia account for a few hundred thousand of the overseas Chinese, but much the biggest groups are in South-East Asia.

In Malaya, with 2,365,000 Chinese out of a total population of 6,250,000, the Chinese are the biggest racial group. Singapore (1,300,000 out of a total population of 1,600,000) is largely a Chinese city, and there are proportionately smaller, but still sizeable Chinese communities, in every other South-East Asian country. In the North Borneo parts of Malaysia one person in four is Chinese (250,000 out of a total population of a million), in Thailand one person in ten (2½ million out of a 28 million population), in Indonesia there are 2,250,000 Chinese, in South Vietnam 780,000, about 600,000 in North Vietnam, 10,000 in Laos, 230,000 in Cambodia, 270,000 in the Philippines, and 320,000 in Burma.

Nearly all the overseas Chinese have come from the four south China provinces of Kwantung, Kwangsi, Fukien, and Hainan Island. During the 19th and early 20th centuries the land shortage and the political troubles in the south led to large-scale emigration of young men.

For almost the whole period of the Empire Chinese who left their country without imperial permission were looked on as criminals, and 18th-century emperors appealed to South-East Asian governments to return Chinese immigrants so that they could be executed.

GOVERNMENT PROTECTION OF OVERSEAS CITIZENS

In 1909, just before the revolution, the Chinese Court passed a new nationality edict recognizing children of Chinese fathers as Chinese wherever they were born. This act was the legal foundation for the post-revolutionary attempts of succeeding Chinese governments to protect their overseas citizens.

Dr. Sun Yat-sen and the Kuomintang leaders after him recognized the overseas Chinese as financially and politically valuable to China, and Chinese diplomats protested to other Asian governments at what they considered to be ill-treatment of local Chinese. Very few of these protests however carried any weight because the Chinese governments of the time were patently unable to back them forcefully.

The Communists also promised protection to the overseas Chinese. But again this protection was seldom forthcoming, partly because the Communists did not have diplomatic relations with many South-East Asian countries. On the other hand there were new facilities for those overseas Chinese who wished to return to China to study or to retire, or who wanted to invest money there. Overseas Chinese were given eight per-cent interest on their investments in the new government's corporations, and were allowed to hold more land in the villages than the normal Chinese.

Assimilation

To begin with South-East Asian governments welcomed the Chinese for the trade and new skills they brought. Later the colonial powers, particularly Britain in Malaya, France in Indo-China, and Holland in Indonesia, found Chinese communities useful buffers between themselves and the ambitions of the local people. Moreover Chinese immigrants were docile and industrious labourers on the new colonial enterprises. The shipping of labourers to Malayan rubber plantations and tin mines was called 'the pig trade'.

In the newly independent and nationally conscious countries that emerged in South-East Asia after the Second World War there was considerable suspicion and resentment of the Chinese communities for political and economic reasons. South-East Asians were particularly afraid that China would use the overseas Chinese as a fifth column to overturn the governments of their countries. South-East Asian governments passed numerous laws, more or less effectively enforced, to restrict the commercial supremacy of the Chinese and to hurry on their assimilation with the local populations.

The great majority of Chinese emigrants have always planned to return to China with their fortunes made. They looked on South-East Asian countries as second best places to live, inhabited by inferior people. They sent back their savings to support the families they had left in China, and to buy themselves land and a house to return to. While they lived abroad they kept up Chinese habits, ate Chinese food, and wore Chinese clothes.

Nevertheless some Chinese failed to make their fortunes, or found they preferred their new countries. This happened most often during the 18th and early 19th centuries when a strong imperial government in China had to be heavily bribed if the penalties against returning emigrants were not to be enforced. In countries with Buddhist populations, like Thailand and Burma, the Chinese took local wives and their grandchildren were assimilated to the general population. In Indonesia and Malaya, Muslim countries, assimilation was more difficult, and half-Chinese communities grew up with their own traditions and married among themselves.

After the First World War assimilation to the local populations or to locally based groups of half-Chinese became less common, because Chinese families for the first time allowed women to emigrate from China to join their husbands overseas, and set up completely Chinese homes overseas. Chinese schools too, which used textbooks printed in China to teach the Chinese language, geography, and history rather than local languages and local geography and history, became increasingly popular with overseas Chinese parents.

Overseas Chinese were among Dr. Sun Yat-sen's most valuable supporters, and after the revolution of 1911 there was growing concern among the overseas communities about political changes in China. As merchants and shopkeepers, in ambition or in actuality, overseas Chinese were not naturally sympathetic to Communism, and they were shocked by violence during the land reform movements and the purges. But many of them were proud of China's new position as an internationally feared power, and some of the younger Chinese were converted to Communism after studying at mainland universities.

Economic Power

The overseas Chinese have an importance out of proportion to their numbers because they control so much of the commerce and industry of South-East Asia. Few of them have settled as farmers, unless they grow crops like pineapples or rubber which demand more steady labour and skill than the local farmers are prepared to give. But every sizeable town in South-East Asia has a large quarter where all shops and factories are Chinese; and even in the country, the cross-roads Chinese shop is also the repair shop for lorries and anything else mechanical that goes wrong, and the local Chinese merchant or his relative arranges for the sale of the crops, seeds, and fertilizers.

By a treaty negotiated with the Indonesian Government, the Indonesian Chinese had to choose between Chinese and Indonesian citizenship—the first official Chinese acknowledgment that a Chinese could ever cease to be a Chinese citizen. Meanwhile Chinese officials urged other overseas Chinese either to become citizens of the countries they were living in, or at least respect its policies, laws and customs, and allow their children to learn its language and history.

Most South-East Asian governments have tried to restrict this economic power of the Chinese in their countries. Since Bangkok was almost paralysed by a Chinese strike in 1910, the Thai, and other governments later, have done their best to cut down on the economic power of their Chinese. Industries and occupations have been reserved for local people, and then sometimes de-reserved as the government found it could not manage without Chinese enterprise. A much publicized example of large-scale economic restriction was in Indonesia in 1959 and 1960 when the government decided to replace Chinese shops by Indonesian co-operatives. The Chinese were forcibly moved out of the rural areas; but there were too few Indonesians to replace them, and many country people, deprived of their ordinary traders, suffered almost as much as the Chinese families concerned.

Policy of the Communist Government

Since the Bandung Conference of 1955 Communist China appears to have given up any previous ambition she may have had to revive the old Chinese imperial domination of South-East Asia. Chinese interest is concentrated on South America, the Middle East, and the emerging countries of Africa rather than on her immediate neighbours to whom she has, on the whole, been conciliatory and friendly.

In this friendly policy South-East Asian suspicion of the overseas Chinese has been an embarrassment to China; and it has also sometimes been embarrassing when overseas Chinese have returned to the mainland as students or to retire. Trained in bourgeois habits and often used to some degree of free speech and action they find Communist austerity and the total direction of every aspect of life by the state hard to accept, and their subversive ideas may infect other Chinese.

However the Communist Government knows that if it fails to provide some facilities for overseas Chinese in China, and fails to make at least token protests to other governments on their behalf, the Kuomintang in Taiwan (Formosa) will benefit from increased support. Paradoxically weight has been added to Taiwan protests on behalf of the local Chinese in Vietnam, the Philippines, and Indonesia by the promptitude with which they were followed by rival protests from Peking. Moreover at present, while the Communist Government is particularly short of foreign exchange, the overseas Chinese remittances and investments are particularly valuable.

Peking might be able to use the China-oriented loyalties of the overseas Chinese communities to back internal Communist revolutions in the countries where they live, or to support direct Chinese invasion. But in most countries Peking could not count on complete support from the communities, and there is no suggestion that at present the Communist Government wants to use the overseas Chinese as a fifth column. (In Malaya Peking did not back the internal Communist revolt, which was mainly recruited from the local overseas Chinese, by anything more than occasional expressions of sympathy.)

This danger of the use of the overseas Chinese as a fifth column will recede in the future, as the ties between China and the overseas Chinese weaken. When the Taiwan question is settled there will be no need for Peking to protest in order that the Kuomintang should not seem more zealous than the Communists for all Chinese interests. Investments and remittances from the overseas Chinese are bound to fall off as few new emigrants leave China, and the generation abroad that remembers their home country dies.

Meanwhile South-East Asian policies of assimilation have time on their side. Memories of China will dim. Entirely Chinese schools and newspapers are already being shut down, and pressure is mounting on those Chinese who want to stay in profitable occupations to take the nationality of the country where they are living. As the South-East Asian governments gain in political experience less draconian laws, rousing less resentment and xenophobia among the local Chinese, will probably be passed, and those that are passed will be more easily enforced.

BIBLIOGRAPHY

J. H. Brimmell. *Communism in South-East Asia.* (Oxford Univ. Press, London, 1959.)

Morton H. Fried (ed.). *Colloquium on the Overseas Chinese.* (Institute of Pacific Relations, New York, 1958.)

D. G. E. Hall. *A History of South-East Asia.* (Macmillan, London, 1955.)

George McT. Kahin (ed.) *Governments and Politics in South East Asia.* (Cornell Univ. Press, Ithaca, New York, 1959.)

Lois Mitchison. *The Overseas Chinese.* (Bodley Head, London, 1961.)

Victor Purcell. *The Chinese in Southeast Asia.* (Oxford Univ. Press, London, 1951.) *The Chinese in Malaya.* (Oxford Univ. Press, London, 1948.)

Lucien W. Pye. *Guerilla Communism in Malaya. Its Social and Political Meaning.* (Princeton Univ. Press, Princeton, N.J., 1956.)

William G. Skinner. *Chinese Society in Thailand.* (Cornell Univ. Press, Ithaca, New York, 1957.) *Leadership and Power in the Chinese Community of Thailand.* (Cornell Univ. Press, Ithaca, New York, 1958.)

Virginia Thompson and Richard Adloff. *Minority Problems in Southeast Asia.* (Stanford Univ. Press, Stanford, California, 1955.)

BIOGRAPHICAL NOTE

Lois Mitchison first went to Asia as a university teacher in Pakistan and travelled widely in India and Ceylon. She worked as a foreign correspondent for *The Guardian* in Asia, and later as a free-lance writer, visiting China and most countries in South-East Asia. Her articles and photographs have been published in *The Guardian*, *Neue Zürcher Zeitung*, *New Statesman*, and *Glasgow Herald*, and she has broadcast on the Asian, African and Home Services of the B.B.C. After a working visit to West Africa she wrote *Nigeria: Newest Nation* in 1960 (Pall Mall Press, London), and *The Overseas Chinese* in 1961 (Bodley Head, London).

ASIA AND THE WORLD

THE INDIAN PERSONALITY

by

RAGHAVAN IYER

> 'India will not lead the world in science, in industry, or luxury living, but she may well make invaluable contributions to mankind's understanding of itself and the human art of living . . . In the past, light came from the East; in the future it will come again. But this time it will be a rainbow ray through a prism, one face of which was made in the West.'
>
> PERCIVAL SPEAR

PHILOSOPHERS today rightly debunk the notion of national character, as well as the dogma of historical inevitability. It can be both misleading and harmful to talk, for example, of the Israeli or the Irish or the Italian personality. The distortion and danger are even greater when we talk of the Indian personality for at least two reasons. First of all, it has often been questioned whether India was ever a single cultural entity; much has been made of its bewildering diversity. Secondly, despite the emphasis on its enormity and variety, there has been a long-standing and deceptive mystique shrouding the sub-continent. Today, the traditional mystique wears a modern dress; the ancient land of Aryavarta has become a new nation, a sovereign republic after centuries of subjection by alien rulers. The emphasis abroad is now upon poverty, not riches; discontent, not fatalism; material uplift rather than spiritual exaltation; India's new international status instead of its age-old cultural stature. Fresh clichés are rife: the leader of the uncommitted world, the beacon of democracy in Asia, the alternative to China and its desperate rival, the exemplar of 'planning by consent'. Indians themselves are often the victims of the facile phrases coined by foreigners. But even the international personality of India is still peculiarly difficult for foreigners to comprehend. The new epithets, no less than the old, obscure the truth as much as they reveal it.

'The Indian personality' is both extremely old and very new; herein lies its distinctiveness and its perplexity. Traditional India, like classical Greece, is essentially timeless—one of the chief sources of human wisdom and inspiration. It was not merely the home of the Hindu-Buddhist religious heritage, the oldest philosophical schools and conceptual systems, a complete world-view and an exacting, rounded, way of life. It was, in fact, a world in itself, seemingly self-sufficient, smugly indifferent to the valuations of other peoples. It was ethnocentric in the strict sense; it was not aware of its insularity, especially as its image of itself enclosed and transcended the entire globe. Its dominating concepts were *moksha* and *tapas*, enlightenment and austerity, but it found place in practice both for the heroic outlook and the monastic ideal, enshrined in its two popular epics which even now live in the minds of millions of peasants. Society was split into compartments by caste and competition was anathema, but it was held together loosely and precariously by a shared concept of *dharma* or obligation under the Moral Law. Truth, love and compassion were incarnated respectively—as Vinoba has recently pointed out—in the personalities of Rama, Krishna and Buddha. Detachment and non-violence were held in high esteem and at times degenerated into apathy and passivity. *Satya* and *ahimsa*, truth and non-violence, were translated by Asoka in the 3rd century B.C. into practical applications of tolerance and civility. Even the worldly came to respect those who set the example of non-possession (*aparigraha*) and renunciation. These ideals and values were disseminated with the spread of Indian cultural influences by traders, missionaries and settlers in South-East Asia and the Far East. In India itself the impact of the Buddhist Reformation upon a decadent Hinduism was deep but short-lived. The weaknesses as well as the strength of Indian tradition were revealed as waves of Muslim invaders came into the country and created successive empires until the British unified the subcontinent and exposed it to the far-reaching impact of the modern West.

The Strength of Tradition

The strength of Indian tradition lay in its absorptive, assimilative character and in the elusive, essentially non-doctrinal and undogmatic nature of Hinduism, reinforced by the stability of small, self-enclosed village communities. There was a continuity of cultural life, though not as significant as has been claimed by some writers. Carlyle's 'everlasting yea' was the theme-song of Indian tradition, the basis of its genuine universality but also the main source of its weakness. Hard choices were evaded, immediate problems were shelved rather than solved, and the country suffered from its fatal inability to say 'No' to social abuses, anarchic tendencies, laxity in administration and in dispensing justice, internal feuds and violent intrigue. There were remarkable experiments in co-existence—between races, religions and languages—but also between universalism in theory and segregation in practice. The saving grace of tradition lay in that there arose from time to time exceptional individuals who displayed in their lives the potency of persisting ideals of detachment, gentleness, and concord. But these oases were few and far between in the spreading desert of indolence, cowardice and suspicion. Traditional India was too weak and divided to offer effective resistance to its invaders from afar, and it was considerably demoralized though not destroyed by centuries of alien rule.

During the nationalist movement against British imperialism, Indians were led to take pride in their ancient past and to stress the grandeur of their cultural heritage. Now that India has risen to take its place among the largest nation-states, the emerging national self-consciousness has almost freed the Indian personality from the burden, but also the spell, of bygone glory. The 'me-too'-ism and the messianic streak that were injected by the modernists and revivalists into the nationalist movement have diminished but not disappeared. These elements in the Indian personality are now focussed upon the present and future achievements of a nation caught in the throes of economic and social change. Salvationist creeds secure acceptance more readily when they are couched in a secularist and utilitarian language. The gospel of progress—often presented in the naive forms once fashionable in the West—suits the new nationalist temper. Dams, atomic reactors, military prowess, technical innovations, the rule of law under the Constitution, democratic planning, non-alignment—all these things matter more to the Indian intelligentsia than temples and monuments, epics and folk-songs, *dharma* and *moksha*. But behind the modernist creeds that command enthusiasm there is a self-conscious eclecticism that comes easily to the inheritor of Indian tradition, however indifferent he may be to his national legacy.

It would be tempting to view the Indian personality as confused, insecure and schizoid, torn between an ineradicable pride in the past and a blinding obsession with the present status and advance of the new republic. Indians have no doubt not found as yet a balance between their desires and their limitations, their hopes and fears, the claims of tradition and the increasing demands for social change and economic growth. It is also true that the Westernized élites, alienated from the way of life of the rural masses and from the sources of Indian culture, hold the initiative today before a retreating orthodoxy and the divided, defensive traditionalists. Further, Mahatma Gandhi's re-interpretation of traditional concepts of *ahimsa*, *tapas*, *dharma*, *aparigraha* is less influential in moulding the thinking of policy-makers than Nehru's conception of a socialistic pattern of society, a casteless and egalitarian order in which the highest priority is given to 'modernization' and material advancement. Yet the very concern with the removal of rural poverty and the attempt to restore village panchayats owe their original inspiration to Gandhi. It would indeed be rash to conclude from the experience of a decade and a half that the seeming conflict between traditional values and 'modernization' has already been settled in favour of the latter. Nor is it meaningful to assert that the Indian personality has been rendered neurotic and schizoid by the complex and continuing interaction between indigenous and imported ideas, values and institutions.

If the Indian personality seems today to be distorted by its ambivalent response to the impact of the West, it could be differently viewed by placing it in the context of the cultural dialogue that began early in the 19th century and reached its high watermark with Gandhi and Tagore. The significance of this dialogue cannot be seen if we subscribe either to the 'sponge' theory of some Indian writers or to the 'historicist' dogmatism of some Western commentators. Both these attitudes express an essential truth but dilute its significance by effusive exaggeration and illicit inferences. The 'sponge' theorists are right to stress the assimilative power and the continuity of Indian culture but they ignore the high cost of assimilation. They also tend to overlook the fact of Indian resistance—to Buddhism and Islam, to the intrusion of alien influences,[1] and especially to the powerful inroads made by the West into the mental make-up and the self-awareness as well the self-confidence of the modern Indian. The historicists are justified in asserting that the impact of the industrial civilization and secular culture of the West

[1] It was the power of Hindu resistance which made Nobili fail in India, whereas Ricci succeeded in making Christianity acceptable to the élite in China.

upon the life of traditional society is different in kind, and not merely in the degree of intensity, from that made by the earlier invasions of India. It is, however, naive to think that the cultural deposit of thousands of years can be suddenly swept away by the factory system and the machine age, and that India cannot find its own way of preserving its soul while adapting its society.

Dialogue between Reformers and Revivalists

It would be absurd to insist that the profound impact of the West has affected the Indian personality in the same way as it changed the Russian or the Chinese or the Japanese. The fact that India, unlike Russia, China, Japan or Turkey, came directly under Western rule and influence for over a century, resulted in a distinctive dialogue between the reformers and the revivalists. This dialogue was unique in that its leading participants, the Westernized and the traditionalists alike, had to come to terms with the sources of strength and weakness of the Western impact as well as of Indian tradition. The reformers in India—Roy, Ranade, Gokhale, Tagore, Nehru—could not go as far as Westernizers in Russia like Chaadayev, for example, in actually despising their traditional society, despite its cultural decadence. Similarly, the revivalists in India—Dayananda, Vivekananda, Tilak, Bankim Chandra, Aurobindo—did not go as far as a Slavophil like Gogol, for instance, in debunking Western civilization or in denying that there was anything at all of any value in the impact of Western culture. Even Dayananda could freely concede the 'virtues of the Europeans'. There was an unreality and an extremist flavour about the dialogue between Westernizers and traditionalists in Russia or China which could not be found in 19th century India directly under British rule. With Western education India imported the spirit of the European Renaissance and Reformation—critical, curious, and anti-authoritarian—which permitted a fresh look at traditional values and institutions and even facilitated a rediscovery of the Indian classics. As a result, the cultural dialogue in India for almost a century has been marked, on the whole, for its reasonableness and moderation, despite the occasional lapses into messianic dogmatism or romantic obscurantism. These two vices may still be detected in India today—among self-styled 'progressives' and very vocal communalists. But the pattern of the new Indian personality at its finest has already emerged—a few remarkable men and women, rooted in Indian culture, responsive to the best that the West has to offer, able and willing to appreciate the art and music as well as the literature and thought of India and the West.

In his perceptive essay on 'Hindu Protestantism', Ranade showed the importance for the modern Hindu of a selective approach and a re-appraisal of his ancestral religion. Although this is a new attitude of mind, it may truly be said to be in the best tradition of Hinduism itself and perhaps even to be required among its sophisticated adherents. With the ending of imperial rule by foreigners belonging to a different, even a rival, religion, there is less need than ever to be defensive about corrupt Hindu practices or touchy about Hindu rituals. In general, the Indian is now freer than before to be as unorthodox or eclectic as he chooses in calling himself Hindu or Muslim, Buddhist or Christian, Zoroastrian or Sikh or Jain. Under the impact of the

West, the religions of India have undergone a process of self-criticism and self-renewal, a process initiated by Western education and the challenge of foreign missionaries and intensified during the heyday of the Theosophical Movement in the eighties and nineties of the last century.

In the twenties Mahatma Gandhi introduced an ethical current into Indian life which has crucially affected the Indian personality. India began to experience, as Europe did in the 17th century, the consequences of a decisive shift in emphasis from the *via contemplativa* to the *via activa*, from *Moksha* to *Dharma*, from the cycle of withdrawal (*nirvritti*) to that of involvement (*pravritti*). Gandhi also pointed out, in a celebrated controversy with Tagore, that Indians had to learn from the West to say 'No' to injustice, oppression and exploitation in the political and social spheres. The habit of saying 'Yes' to everything sprang from a deep-seated universalism but it soon became a form of mental laziness, passivity and moral abdication. Tagore and Gandhi were agreed that narrow nationalism was a menace and that Indian freedom should be sought as an integral part of a new world order. The difference between them was a matter of emphasis, in regard to priorities and methods. Gandhi stressed that life is made up of affirmations and rejections and the latter are as morally significant as the former. Without non-violent non-cooperation in regard to despotism, however benevolent, there could be no genuine cooperation or goodwill to all men.

With the ending of alien rule and the martyrdom of Gandhi, a muddled mood of unreality, the old habit of wishful thinking, began to re-assert itself in the formulation of domestic as well as foreign policy. Nehru courageously and consistently said 'No' to casteism, provincialism, communalism as well as to authoritarian devices, thus laying the foundations of a secular State and a democratic polity. He also said 'Yes' to planning and socialism, liberal and egalitarian principles, and, above all, to peaceful methods of social change. His concern was with securing a national consensus in regard to the immediate tasks and larger ideals of the new republic. In this he did achieve considerable success but only at the cost of bypassing, rather than removing, the divisive and separatist tendencies embedded in Indian society. He also tried to maintain the dynamism and tempo, the moral momentum of the national movement. Here his inevitable failure has been more apparent than such success as he undoubtedly achieved. The problems of poverty, inequality and factionalism are too intractable to be solved merely through committing the country to worthwhile social goals or to well-intentioned political and economic policies. The Indian personality today is deeply involved—intellectually and emotionally—in its fine affirmations and firm rejections, but it lacks the will to translate them into effective action. Further, with the ending of British rule, extremist and unreal attitudes towards the West are emerging both among the Westernizers and the traditionalists.

Nehru moulded the new international personality of India even more powerfully than its internal self-image. Behind the phraseology of his foreign policy—non-alignment, peaceful co-existence, *Pancha Shila*—there lay a recognition of the need to preserve the nation's effective independence; to create a climate and even an area of peaceful conduct in which to pursue national tasks; to learn from the experience of Western as well as Communist nations in transforming Indian society; to further the aspirations of other dependent and under-developed countries; to reduce the dominant influence of the Big Powers in the United Nations as well as to mediate between the ideological blocs in explosive situations. These concepts have influenced the attitudes of other new states to a remarkable degree, and even the two blocs have slowly come to accept their authenticity and force if not their validity and implications. Unfortunately, India has been far less successful in coming to terms with the fact that it has willy-nilly stepped into the shoes of a Big Power in its own geopolitical context. Further, while Nehru displayed a genuine Gandhian friendliness to all peoples, he did not show Gandhi's willingness to understand the attitudes of those inimical to India, and even more, he failed, unlike Gandhi, to take the proper measure of his foreign antagonists. Again, the fine affirmations of the Indian personality have become a substitute for an effective and coherent policy in regard to world affairs or the United Nations and especially in the matter of national defence. One of the odd consequences of an abstract faith in non-alignment is the concrete co-existence within the same government of politicians and officials who lean towards either of the two ideological blocs. This has hindered the formulation of an effective policy, especially in relation to India's neighbours.

Gap between Exhortation and Example

All this points to inherent traits of the Indian personality—the tendency to mistake affirmations for achievements, the failure to face up to the implications of hard choices, the habit of regarding the promises of one's own or of others as tantamount to performance, exulting in the willingness of the spirit to the extent of overlooking the weakness of the flesh, a preoccupation with what might be or even with what ought to be unmatched by a careful examination of existing reality. In India the inherited faith in universal brotherhood and the concern with cosmic justice have all too often meant the neglect of the immediate neighbourhood. The higher the standards set, the more glaring the gap between exhortation and example. There is nothing surprising about this; what is sad is the apparent indifference to the growth of the gap, the same insensitivity with which Indians so often charged their former rulers. Again, it is not so strange that the Indian personality should be more concerned with Western opinion than with Asian opinion; this is the natural consequence of the hypnotic spell exercised by Western imperialism. It is also easy to see why the pan-Asian sentiments generated early in the century and repeated soon after independence should have rapidly evaporated with the emergence of SEATO and the developments in Communist China. What is more difficult to explain is the failure to appreciate the place of India in the immediate context of South Asia or the importance of its cultural and religious links with Tibet, South-East Asia and the Far East. Increasingly, in the coming decades the Indian cannot help focussing his vision eastwards rather than exclusively westwards.

Altogether, it would be only a superficial appraisal of the Indian personality that would merely stress its present predicament. Although it has its roots in the mature wisdom of a rich philosophical and cultural heritage, it has still not come of age in its new manifestation. If the Indian personality seems to be effervescent and volatile, tossed between abstract idealism and concrete cynicism, this is because it has still to gain the confidence that comes from experience in a new environment. It must find a way of recovering the toughness and the will-power that marked even the leading liberals of the last century and certainly the nationalist movement at its height in the decades before independence. The finest examples of the Indian personality in the present age are not visionaries or machiavellians, but practical idealists whose actions speak louder than their words—men like Gandhi and Vinoba and Karve. Such men have cared little for the cynicism of the outside world and incarnated their ideals while toiling at their chosen tasks. They did not mistake enthusiasm for idealism or cynicism for worldly wisdom. Their failures did not lead them to abandon their principles or their ideals, but only to a rigorous self-examination and a greater concentration of endeavour. Such men may be few, but their influence is far-reaching and will continue to be, as long as the acceptance of a *guru* remains a vital element in Indian life. The tradition of the *guru* has no doubt been much abused, but at its best it uniquely fulfils the function of transmitting ideals and providing ethical continuity to society.

As the inheritors of a living heritage, tested by time, Indians owe it to themselves not to succumb to the ephemeral fashions laid down by foreigners. Equally, as the citizens of a new republic, they owe it to the coming generations that they do not slavishly copy the patterns of thought and conduct that have emerged in the older states. If the Indian personality is to retain its distinctiveness and explore its hidden possibilities it must deepen its roots in its ancestral soil and mature its conception of the new society that could emerge in the foreseeable future.

BIBLIOGRAPHY

Mulk Raj Anand. *Contemporary Indian Civilization.* (Asia Publishing House, London, 1962.)

Vera Micheles Dean. *New Patterns of Democracy in India.* (Harvard Univ. Press, Cambridge, Mass., 1959.)

Theodore de Bary and others (ed.) *Sources of the Indian Tradition.* (Columbia Univ. Press, New York, 1958.)

Selig S. Harrison. *India—The Most Dangerous Decades.* (Princeton Univ. Press, Princeton, N.J., 1960.)

N. V. Sovani and V. M. Dandekar (eds.) *Changing India.* Essays in Honour of D. R. Gadgil. (Asia Publishing House, London, 1962.)

Percival Spear. *India—A Modern History.* (Univ. of Michigan Press, Ann Arbor, 1961.)

Arnold Toynbee. *One World and India.* (Oxford Univ. Press, London, 1960.)

BIOGRAPHICAL NOTE

RAGHAVAN IYER. Educated in Bombay and Oxford (First Class Honours in Modern Greats, President of the Oxford Union.) Spent a year with the Indian Planning Commission. Formerly Fellow and Lecturer in Politics, St. Antony's College, Oxford. Visiting Porfessor at the Universities of Oslo, Chicago and Ghana. Edited *South Asian Affairs* (Chatto and Windus, London, 1960) and *The Glass Curtain Between Asia and Europe* (Oxford Univ. Press, London, 1965). Now teaches at the University of California and is also associated with the Centre for the Study of Democratic Institutions, Santa Barbara.

THE CHINESE PERSONALITY

by

RICHARD HARRIS

THE world has not yet got the feel of China's international personality; it is still insubstantial, puzzling, disturbing. The world is anxious to come to terms with China yet after sixteen years of Communist rule the dialogue has scarcely begun. Partly, this might be explained by the American hostility that keeps China out of world councils. Partly it is due to the suspicion and secretiveness of Chinese as of other Communists. But is this secretiveness Communist or Chinese? Are there aspects of China's international personality which Asia has understood no better than the West? And is there an unwillingness on the part of the Chinese to make themselves understood? Their leader Mao Tse-tung, to take one obvious example, has not travelled as Nehru, Sukarno and all other Asian leaders have done. Never having left China before he came to power he has been to Moscow only twice since. He has visited no other Communist country and no Asian country whatsoever, though he has had ample opportunity and might have created a favourable effect if he had gone. Here is one clue to the Chinese personality: an unwillingness to go out and meet the other man, to open up, to act upon others from choice. Chinese influence may be powerful but it has been exerted in precisely the opposite way, by drawing in not by outgoing.

CIVILIZATION WITHIN THE WALLS

To attempt to explain this personality needs an understanding of the centuries that have gone to its making. China has long existed as a civilization within its own walls, within the 'four seas' in Confucius' phrase, where 'all men are brothers'. The sense of Chineseness was fixed on a civilization, the Chinese never thought of themselves as one nation state among others; it was made stronger by the fact that China never came into contact with any civilization equal to her own—beyond the walls roamed barbarians to be appeased or conquered—or civilized. The belief in Chinese superiority, so amply justified through many hundred years of Chinese history, remained intact when Western incursion finally forced on China a knowledge of Christendom. At last barbarians who could not be drawn in and given the Chinese imprint had won the day. That great quality of Chinese civilization—to mould, to shape and to transform invaders—had always worked before but only within the walls. The question we must ask now is whether the Chinese personality can be exerted effectively outside the Chinese walls.

It is necessary first to point out that this civilization was distinctive in it humanist and rational foundations. Confucianism as moral example was th doctrine of an élite ruling class. Religion has never really rivalled thi doctrine (since the T'ang dynasty) nor has China ever had a religiou hierarchy. This gives to Chinese Communism (and to Chinese idealism in an form it has taken) a sense of zealous self-righteousness (something to mak any European Communist visitor feel shallow); and here, too, one shoul note that China has not lived with other doctrines unless it be the withdrawa and rejection of the world which both Taoism and Buddhism have stood for Chinese civilization was thus seen as potentially universal as well as superior

A unique language insulated this belief, emphasizing the sense of enclosur and exclusiveness. And lastly there was the effect of Chinese social solidarity The free, lone, self-reliant, creative individual is not a product of Chines culture. His upbringing drives him into the group and cultivates his sense o obligation to it. Freedom of choice has hardly existed. This has made for natural reserve in the expression of opinion; the normal process of argu ment and debate natural to a democracy is under-developed. Distinctive ness is inhibited; outward conformity is encouraged; unity and harmony ar the keystones of the Chinese outlook.

Communism

This was the outlook struck by the traumatic experience of Wester incursion in the 19th century. It was not until the end of that century tha Chinese defences really began to crumble: only in the early years of thi century were Chinese thinkers attacking the foundations of their ow culture. The flag of surrender was finally run up by the younger generatio in the May 4th movement of 1919 when the Chinese past was declare to be rotten and a complete renewal seemed necessary. At this moment o maximum cultural self-abasement China seemed ready to accept in tot the doctrines and culture as well as the technology of the West. Yet it wa just at this point in history that a doctrine that might fulfil Chinese needs fo total renewal was brought home to them by the Russian revolution of 1917

Marxism soon made headway among Chinese intellectuals. The genera tion that was abolishing Confucius relished an alternative doctrine of th nature of man and society, the more so because it was a doctrine that wa both fashionably Western and yet seemed a jump ahead of what the Wes itself was importing; besides it was a doctrine that was anti-imperialist an satisfying to China's national temper; and, if the deeper roots of Chines thought were turned up, it also satisfied China's need for a universal creed Marxism promised a future world harmony. As the begetter of worl harmony China could come into the world only through such a doctrine anything less was inadequate.

The alien aspects of Communism were soon replaced by Chinese remould ing of the manner if not the matter. By the 1930s the Chinese Communis Party had a completely Chinese look; Mao and his Hunanese colleague were Chinese revolutionaries, not Comintern exports; heirs of the Taiping and any others they liked to claim as forebears. Only after coming to powe in 1949 were these men presented with some of the contradictions of thei outlook. The split with the Soviet Union has lately thrown them into prominence. Is China simply a partner in a world Communist revolutionary movement or first among equals? Is China the creative leader of world Marxism? In short, how can the dichotomy of Communism as against Chineseness, of Chinese superiority as against Chinese equality among other nation states, be resolved? The contradictions may be denied in theory; they are observable in practice. They remain the clues to China's international personality. Does not the very fact of China reshaping Communism in a distinctively Chinese mould make of it something exclusive to China (bringing in ideas from older Chinese tradition) and thus alien from the universal creed of an internationalist like Lenin? The more Chinese Chinese-Communism becomes the less meaning it can have for the non-Chinese world. A new doctrinal wall is going up.

Three Faces

So much for China's outlook on the world; but there is China herself to be restored first. Before considering China in Asia it is worth noting her attitude to the restoration of her old authority. Only a century divides Ch'ien Lung's magisterial dismissal of Macartney in 1793 and the shame of China's defeat by Japan in 1895 and her spoliation by European scrounging of concessions. Chinese rage has thus been coming slowly to the boil for a century; rage at this humiliation of a once great and still proud people, determined to regain control of territories like Formosa, Manchuria, Sinkiang and Tibet and quite unwilling to listen to any plea that these territories are not solely China's affair. A century of shame has to be wiped out and Mao and this generation that was young when the treaty ports were in their heyday perhaps care more for this than any external achievement. On this home ground China is unyielding, fierce, quick to take offence, ready to issue its three hundred and seventy-fifth serious warning to the United States for having violated Chinese territorial waters with as much vehemence as the first. The conflict on the Indian border shows how those unwilling to listen sympathetically to the Chinese case can be treated.

As it expresses itself internationally the Chinese personality might be said then to have three faces. There is the angry humiliated country standing up for its rights; there is the suave promoter of coexistence seen at Bandung; and there is the frigid dismissal of the Western world, mixing Communist self-righteousness with old style Chinese contempt, prophesying the utter downfall of capitalism.

Playing the game of coexistence—not for that reason any less honest within its limits—the new China begins to look very much like the old. Delegations come from small and relatively powerless South-east Asian countries and are received politely. Border agreements are initialled, trade agreements signed and the visitors sense a patronizing benevolence. They, after all, are paying tribute; it is a political tribute to China's restored power and in return their neutralism is gift enough. They may not recognize the universal authority of the Chinese Emperor as their forebears did but acknowledgement of some kind is part of the relationship.

When it comes to a country with the cultural and political impact of

India then China cannot make herself understood (or India either). An underlying contempt is scarcely veiled. The Himalayas are not only a frontier in dispute, they divide two radically different civilizations. India is not part of China's historical awareness and where national pride is at stake the Chinese have shown themselves as intemperate and careless of the effects of their behaviour as they might have done with an admitted enemy.

And so China, this great and admirable civilization, will go on domesticating its Communism and find its friends among its own cultural kinsmen. The Chinese can communicate with the Japanese well enough and vice-versa. And the same is true of the Koreans and Vietnamese. They are all part of the civilization of which China is the mother. These last two may be small and may have been dominated at various times in the past by China, but their jealous sense of independence does not preclude a recognition of where they feel most at ease. The Chinese doctrinal divergence from the Russians may have embarrassed these countries initially; they have not yet worked out their new relationships and still exist in divided countries, totally severed from their southern halves. Yet the signs are already appearing. There have been references to the East Asian front of the Communist world and we may reasonably forecast that this front will be firmer doctrinally than the European revisionist front, subsisting by its own lights.

In face of apparent Chinese belligerence and uncompromising doctrine this forecast of a China virtually enclosed within its own walls must seem strangely obtuse. Surely this expanding power, once it has overcome its present setbacks, will stride forward again towards the future that will one day make it a power to rival any that now exist. So it may; other countries have developed talents and vigour and then lost them again. The Chinese personality may change; China may become an effective influence and thus a power in all Asia. Yet there is the history to deny it and it is a long one. If the Chinese are developing a new personality in keeping with their new power and their new outlook there are no signs of it yet.

BIBLIOGRAPHY

C. P. Fitzgerald. *The Birth of Communist China.* (Pelican, London, 1955.)

Mu Fu-sheng. *The Wilting of the Hundred Flowers.* (Heinemann, London, 1962).

Robert J. Lifton. *Thought Reform and the Psychology of Totalism.* (London, Victor Gollancz, 1961.)

Victor Purcell. *China.* (London, Ernest Benn, 1962.)

Ssu-yu Teng and John K. Fairbank. *China's Response to the West.* (Harvard University Press, London, Oxford University Press, 1954.)

BIOGRAPHICAL NOTE

RICHARD HARRIS. B. 1914 in China and lived there until 1928. Returned to China on war service 1945; with British Embassy in China, 1947-50; joined *The Times* as correspondent in Hong Kong, 1951-53, and Singapore, 1953-55. Since 1955 leader writer on Asian affairs for *The Times*, London. Author of *Independence and After* (Oxford Univ. Press, London, 1962). Has also taken part in broadcasting and television on Asian subjects.

THE JAPANESE PERSONALITY

by

R. P. DORE

DELINEATING *the* personality of the Japanese people has been a favourite pastime of foreign observers at least since St. Francis Xavier in the 16th century described those qualities which seemed to him to make the Japanese people 'the best of all among unbelievers' and the most ripe for conversion. The Japanese themselves have also been given to introspective analysis of the essential Japanese spirit, particularly at times when conflict with the outer world has given them reason to emphasize their unique Japaneseness.

It was a common assumption until the beginning of this century that the supposedly unique features of Japanese personality and culture were biologically determined; and leopards cannot change their spots. Thus the French sociologist Le Bon declared that although many a Japanese had acquired all the outward marks of Western civilization this was a mere 'varnish' which was 'quite superficial and has no influence on his mental constitution'.[1] It was with a sense of daring that Sidney Gulick, the missionary author of one of the first attempts at a full-length analysis of the Japanese character, started from the assumption that 'the main differences between the great races of mankind today are not due to biological but to social conditions'.[2] This however—except for the more fanatical Japanese nationalists of the thirties who claimed the benefit of direct descent from the gods—has been the assumption of most subsequent writers on the subject. There is, to be sure, no obvious reason for denying that, just as the basic physical similarity between, say, the average Japanese and the average Englishman is modified by marginal differences in stature, bone structure, pigmentation, etc., there might also—again in terms of mean values in the ranges of variation exhibited by the two populations—be marginal differences in those genetically determined dispositions which affect the development of temperament and character. But the presence in the United States of large numbers of sons and grandsons of Japanese immigrants no less 100 per cent American than the descendants of European immigrants should effectively dispose of any suggestion that biological heritage has a major importance in determining national differences.

What, then, *are* the differentiating factors? Gulick, the American missionary, explained what he considered to be the typically Japanese personality characteristics simply as signs of 'backwardness' in the scale of evolutionary development. The suspiciousness, the fickle enthusiasm for current fads, the

[1] *The Psychology of Peoples*, 1898, p. 37.

[2] *The Evolution of the Japanese*, fourth ed., 1905, p. 21.

ambition and conceit, the submissive acceptance of fate, indirectness of speech and repression of emotions which he discerned in the Japanese were all the heritage of a feudal past which the forces of progress would—he hoped—soon eliminate. The pagan Lafcadio Hearn had a similar explanation for his rather different version of the Japanese 'race-character'—the charm, the kindliness, grace of manners, peacable cooperativeness and loyal self-denial which would—he feared—disappear with rapid social evolution.[1]

The Pursuit of Duty

The anthropologists who made appreciations of the Japanese character for the guidance of American policy-makers during the Second World War worked with a different set of assumptions. The most whole-hog Freudian of them all, Weston LaBarre, had a simple key to the whole puzzle. The Japanese were the victims of 'severity and cruelty in treatment during the period of cleanliness training' in infancy. This resulted in their exhibiting as a people all the traits corresponding to the clinical description of the typical 'anal-compulsive' personality type—the secretive hiding of emotions, perseverance, conscientiousness, self-righteousness, fanaticism, perfectionism, ceremoniousness, ritual cleanliness, hypochondria, and of course sado-masochism.[2] Other writers were less obviously the victims of wartime tendencies to view the enemy as the devil incarnate, and less monocausal in their explanations. Geoffrey Gorer, for instance, also concentrated on the experiences of early childhood and ascribed somewhat similar results to toilet training, but he also stressed two other themes. The first was the nature of the child's emotional relations with his parents (which were supposed to give him a tendency to divide the world into the softer, yielding, feminine half towards which he can act aggressively with impunity and the male half which demands submissive compliance); and the second, the importance placed on bodily self-control and precise conformity to etiquette which was explicitly taught as a means of avoiding shaming mockery from others and so retaining one's position as an esteemed member of one's group.[3] Ruth Benedict, the most subtle and urbane of these wartime writers, followed some of the same themes, but gave greater importance to the explicit ethic taught in schools and enshrined in proverbs and the everyday language of moral discourse. Her book[4] was, in effect, an elaboration of the epitomization of the Japanese character given in Nitobe's pre-war version of the 'international prize competition for an essay on the elephant' story. (According to Nitobe, the Japanese entry bore the title, 'The duties and domestication of the elephant.') Thus, in Benedict's interpretation the Japanese character was in large measure the product of explicit training in the need for self-sacrificing pursuit of duty—of duty towards the Emperor, the nation, the family, status superiors and personal benefactors, and of the duty to maintain

[1] *Japan: An Interpretation*, 1904.

[2] 'Some observations on character structure in the Orient', *Psychiatry*, 8 (1945) pp. 319-42, reprinted in B. S. Silberman, *Japanese Character and Culture*, 1962.

[3] 'Themes in Japanese culture', *Trans. New York Academy of Sciences*, Sect. II, 5, (1943) pp. 105-24. Repr. in Silberman, *op. cit.*

[4] *The Chrysanthemum and the Sword*, 1946.

ne's good name in order to retain the esteem of one's group—a pre-ccupation which made shame rather than guilt the major moral sanction. ince the duties were particular duties relating to particular spheres of onduct and particular social relations, large areas of life were left free for nnocent sensual enjoyment, untroubled, if there was no conflict with duty, y any sense of guilt. And this dichotomy was exemplified and reinforced by he discontinuity of childhood training—the indulgence of early childhood ontrasting with the sudden requirement of conformist responsible behaviour ater on. The Japanese had, in short, with their stress on particular duties ather than generalized principles of conduct, a 'situational ethic' which nade them a well-disciplined moral people in familiar situations, but lacking n guide-lines for behaviour when—as in wartime—they were faced with ew ones.

Clearly the evolutionists struck closer to the truth than the 'potters and veaners' in their explanation of Japanese national character, if only because he latter jumped too easily to false conclusions about how the Japanese wean nd pot. (An anthropologist who made a study of toilet training in a Japanese own in 1952 came to the conclusion that there was such individual variety of nethod as to make generalization impossible.[1]) Consider, for instance, one spect of the Japanese noted by many observers as differentiating them from Anglo-Saxons; a lesser willingness to take individual initiatives involving the isk of failure, and a tendency to be more uneasily anxious in competitive ituations and more overwhelmingly mortified by the shame of failure. One an think of a number of good reasons why this sort of sense of honour is most ikely to be found in a closed stratified society such as Japan before 1870 or medieval Europe for that matter), a society in which a man's status and ccupation was largely determined by birth and in which even in the cities nen's lives were lived in small communities. Where there was little possibility f overt competition for position and occupational opportunities men rarely nad the chance to experience—and get used to the experience of—being lefeated or rejected. Again, failure in another sense, being accused of not iving up to the expectations implicit in one's hereditarily-assigned role, was he more totally damaging to a man's self-respect in that there was little ossibility of moving on and starting afresh. Equally, where life was not egmented into different spheres of work and recreation and family life, the mbarrassment of failure in one sphere could not be compensated for by etaining the regard and affection of members of quite separate spheres. One's small community contained all one's life activities; it judged one as a whole man, and there was small chance of escape. The more open, mobile ociety of modern Japan, where schools and employers recruit by selective ompetition and where leadership in politics and trade unions and women's nstitutes is decided by competition for votes, is likely to breed different per-onalities. The unusual aspect of Japan was that until 1945 the change in ersonality which one might expect to follow from the changing structure f society was slowed down by deliberate Government policy. Elements of the eudal code of personal relations—particularly the emphasis on duty and the

[1] Betty Lanham, 'Aspects of child care in Japan,' in D. Haring, ed., *Personal Character and he Cultural Milieu*, 1956, reprinted in Silberman, *op. cit.*

punctilious fulfilment of obligations to superiors—were reformulated in the late 19th century into an officially sanctioned 'uniquely Japanese moral code' and instilled into every Japanese in the schools, in the army, through the press and through the radio—a feature the importance of which Ruth Benedict justly recognized.

Even in 1945, however, it was already doubtful whether it made any sense to talk of *the* typical Japanese personality. It is even more doubtful today after nearly 20 years of freedom from the incubus of state indoctrination in the 'Japanese spirit' and after a decade of the most rapid industrialization the world has ever seen. An industrial nation of 95 million people is bound to be so differentiated by regional, class and individual variation that any generalization must admit of very large exceptions. The modern Japanese jazz musician probably has much more in common with an English jazz musician than he has with a Japanese civil servant. It still remains possible that the difference between the average Japanese and the average English jazz musician, and the differences between the average Japanese and the average English civil servant, lie in a consistent direction. Thus, to take a hypothetical example, a patient sociologist who invented a scale of 'politeness' might find that the following proportions of his samples were by his criterion 'polite people'.

	Japanese	British
Jazz musicians	40 per cent	30 per cent
Civil servants	80 per cent	70 per cent

It is only in this limited statistical and comparative sense that one can legitimately talk of national character. Thus, the assertion 'the Japanese are a polite people' has to be interpreted 'most Japanese are more polite than is usual among their counterparts in my (the asserter's) country'.

The National Character

This being said, what are the characteristics which, in this limited sense, might still be said to differentiate the Japanese from other people? It seems clear that some parts of the Western stereotype of Japan now have to go. The 'mere imitators lacking in originality' notion derives from the 19th century when Japan was quite clearly hell-bent on catching up with the West. Now that she has in large measure caught up, Japanese are beginning to make their own fair share of original contributions to science and technology as they have always done in the field of art. Nevertheless such stereotypes are persistent, not least among the Japanese themselves. In 1958 a large national sample was asked to choose from a list of adjectives all those which they thought could justly be used to describe the Japanese people. The adjectives, and the proportion of the sample choosing each of them, were as follows; rational (12 per cent), diligent (55 per cent), freedom-loving (15 per cent), *tampaku* (something like 'unemotional', 'frank', 'indifferent') (19 per cent), persevering (48 per cent), kind-hearted (50 per cent), originally creative (8 per cent), polite (47 per cent), cheerful (23 per cent), idealistic (33 per cent).

Such stereotypes are unlikely to be an accurate mirror of reality. On the other hand, they probably have some foundation in reality even if it is the reality of a generation ago. My own list of the features which (in the limited statistical and necessarily comparative sense indicated above) differentiate the modern Japanese from the modern Englishman would be somewhat as follows. For each characteristic one may choose either the approving or the pejorative term according to taste (as in the declension: 'I am a man of principle, you are obstinate, he is bigoted.') The Japanese, then,

are less self-confident and more neurotically preoccupied with retaining the good opinion of others.	have a keener sense of personal honour and are less complacently self-righteous.
are more imitative.	have a more realistic willingness to learn from others.
are more ambitious.	have a keener desire for self-improvement.
are more slavishly diligent.	are less afraid of hard work.
are more submissive to superiors.	have a more realistic appreciation of the need to cooperate in society.
are less willing to stand up for individual rights.	are less selfish.
are more dishonest and indirect in speech.	are more sensitive to, and less willing to offend, the feelings of others.
are less men of principle.	are more willing to forego the pleasures of self-assertion in the interests of social harmony.
have less sense of social responsibility to remove abuses in their own society.	are less busybody, with a more tolerant willingness to live and let live.
are more childishly naive.	have more good-humoured cheerfulness.
are more introverted.	are shier about imposing their views and feelings on strangers.
are more sentimental.	show greater affectionate warmth and quicker emotional responses in intimate relations.

How many of these qualities—assuming that they really do characterize the modern Japanese—will be modified by further social change, and how far they will remain a permanent part of the Japanese variant of industrial man it is difficult to predict. Equally problematical is their meaning for the future place of Japan in the world. In the short run, at least, the qualities of drive and willingness to learn seem to promise that Japan's rapid economic progress will continue. The limits placed on self-assertiveness might suggest that the cohesiveness of Japanese society will continue to be able to contain disruptive social conflict. (Though this is not necessarily the case; the same trait can help reinforce the cohesiveness of sectional groups within the nation and so harden the lines of division which exist.) The continued sensitivene to the good opinion of others suggests that, now that Japan is no longer abl to force grudging admiration by the aggressive display of strength, her leade will continue to follow a policy of international cooperation and punctiliou observance of her obligations to her chosen allies—whoever, at the time, the happen to be.

BIBLIOGRAPHY

Frank Gibney. *Five Gentlemen of Japan. Portrait of a Nation's Character.* (Victor Gollanc London, 1953.)

I. Kawasaki. *The Japanese Are Like That.* (Tuttle, Tokyo, 1956.)

E. O. Reischauer. *The United States and Japan,* Part III. (Harvard Univ. Press, Cambridg Mass., 1957.)

BIOGRAPHICAL NOTE

R. P. Dore. Professor of Sociology with special reference to the Far East at the Londo School of Economics and Political Science and the School of Oriental and African Studie Formerly taught at the University of British Columbia. Author of *City Life in Japan* (Uni of California Press, Berkeley and Los Angeles) and *Land Reform in Japan* (Oxford Uni Press, London, 1959). B.A. in Modern Japanese at London University.

THE IMPORTANCE OF ASIA TO RUSSIA AND THE WESTERN WORLD

by

K. M. PANIKKAR

ASIA covers a very large area of the land surface of the world. It contains over half of its population. In essential resources for industrial production it is richer than the other continents. Naturally, in an era when the world is organized into camps, the control of Asia, its space, its manpower and its natural resources can tilt the balance of power.

Before the Second World War, all Asia outside Japan was divided into two almost equal parts, one forming part of the territories of the Soviet Union and the other under the authority or influence of the Western powers. A line from the Black Sea border of Turkey along Iran, Afghanistan, the Pamirs and China to the Pacific marked the boundary. The area to the north was a part of Soviet Russia, occupied, administered and developed as part of a federated union of states. The great Western powers shared the area to the south of this line which, before the war, contained no less than 1,250 million people.

Britain, basing her power on her Indian Empire, spread her authority into the Far East. Her outstretched arms spread into Tibet and into Sinkiang. France had, in the second half of the century, built herself an empire in the valley of the Mekong and the Meenam. From there she sought to extend her influence over south China. The Dutch ruled over the Indonesian archipelago and controlled its immense riches. Even America, after the occupation of the Philippines, became for a short time an Asian power. The areas of the Middle East were equally under European influence if not direct authority. Iran maintained a precarious independence as a buffer state between the British and the Russians, subject to the pressure of both. The oil-rich Arab kingdoms and principalities were areas of British and American influence. Palestine was ruled by the British under a mandate, while Syria and Lebanon were under French authority. Turkey had opted out of Asia and claimed to be a part of Europe.

The area under Russian control had a different history. In the 19th century the Czarist empire had, by slow but determined steps, moved on to the Pamirs, the frontier of Britain's Indian Empire. In the process she had annexed the Muslim Khanates and territories in the historic Central Asian region. Across the steppes of Siberia, she had planted colonies of Russians even in Czarist times. In the period between the Revolution and the Second World War the Soviet Union followed in its Asian territories a vigorous programme of economic development as a defence against Nazi attack.

A basic difference between the Western and the Russian approach to the Asian countries needs to be emphasized. The importance of Asia to the Western powers lay mainly in trade, development and utilization of economic resources, political authority and use of man-power for purposes of warfare. They were not interested in colonization in the strict sense, in peopling the areas of Asia with men of Western stock. The case was different with Russia, as we shall see later. In none of the Asian countries under Western occupation was there a settled European population or even a considerable number of people of mixed blood.

The period following the Second War witnessed the withdrawal of the Western nations from Asia. Within a period of ten years ending with 1957 practically every portion of Asia over which the Western nations exercised political authority was liberated.

But this withdrawal did not affect the Soviets except in Manchuria where, in agreement with the People's Republic of China, such rights as she possessed over the Manchurian railway and Port Arthur were surrendered shortly after the Communist revolution in China. Not only did the Soviet Union not have to withdraw from the vast areas of Asia into which she had overflowed but she affirmed in unequivocal terms her position as a great Asian state. In his famous speech at Srinagar in 1954 Mr. Khrushchev claimed that China and India, along with the Soviet Union, constituted the three great powers of Asia.

Asia and the West

The importance of Asia to the West, in spite of the elimination of political power, is very considerable. The West draws a good deal of its industrial raw material from the countries of Asia. A substantial portion of the oil supply of the West comes from the Arabian peninsula, Iraq, the trucial sheikhdoms and Indonesia. The investment of the West in the half of Asia outside Communist control is considerable and, in fact, is greater than at the time of imperial authority. In India, for example, British investment at the time of independence amounted to only £155 million. In 1959 it was over £300 million, or had doubled itself. America was practically an unknown factor in South and South-East Asia outside the Philippines in the period before the Second World War. Today she has a major share in investment and trade.

But this is not a position which is stable as the Asian countries are not content to remain the suppliers of raw material or markets for capital goods and manufactured products. Nor do they desire to be, for long, areas of profitable investment. India, the largest of the non-Communist countries, has already progressed a good way towards the creation of a self-sustained industrial economy: the other countries will also tread the same path. While non-Communist Asia of over 900 million (with Japan) will continue to be a major trading partner of the West, it is obvious that the future interest of the West in those regions will not continue in the field inherited from the days of colonialism. A return to political authority, economic dominance, restriction of production to raw materials or industry under the control of the West, as at one time in Shanghai and Calcutta, would be clearly impossible.

There is a sphere, however, where the importance of Asia to the West is a growing one. It is necessary to recognize that non-Communist Asia has to a large extent become integrated with the culture of the West. Education in all these countries is being developed largely in cooperation with Europe and the U.S.A. The universities of the former British Empire in Asia are linked with their counterparts in countries of the Commonwealth. They also maintain close relations with America. In matters of scientific research there is a great deal of exchange between Europe and countries like India and Japan. The literature and artistic life of new Asia, outside the Communist world, is also closely connected to movements in the Western world.

Asia and Russia

The importance of Asia to Russia lies in other factors. The original colonial position, especially in the Central Asian area, has been transformed already by a large-scale migration of people. The following figures of population in the two major areas of this region will show the magnitude of the transformation that has already taken place. The Republic of Kazakhstan is an immense territory lying between lower Volga, Sinkiang and Mongolia. It has an area of 1,263,000 square miles, or nearly the same as India. Its population, however, is only 10 million of which in 1956 over 35 per cent was of Russian stock. With the immense development schemes that the Soviets have in hand, it is obvious that in a few years the population of Kazakhstan will not only go up by leaps and bounds but that it will soon have a majority of people of Russian stock. Again Turkmenistan with an immense area has a population of only a million and a half of which 20 per cent are already Russians. Siberia, which is much larger in size than the whole of Europe, is overwhelmingly Russian in the composition of its population. Thus over vast areas of Asia constituting more than half of the continent, Russia is fast ceasing to be a colonial power. It is becoming part of the Russian homeland. In the former colonial territories of Central Asia, the integration of the local proletariat with the fast growing Russian population is itself a major factor. Besides, the economic and social developments of these areas have modernized their traditional economies and helped to create a society which has broken away from Muslim traditions. These areas in fact constitute Russia's New Frontier, the great challenge to the constructive ability of the Soviet Union.

But apart from the areas which form part of the USSR, there are two other sectors of Asia which are of importance to the Soviets. There is the Communist bloc of Asian countries—the People's Republic of China, Mongolia, North Korea and North Vietnam, which between them have seven hundred million people. What is the importance of this area to Russia? This would be best appreciated by imagining what the position would be if China, instead of going Communist, had reorganized herself effectively and been a member of the Western bloc. It is the change that has taken place in China and the Communist countries of Asia that has brought the Pacific areas within the Communist challenge. It is not necessary to emphasize that but for the growth of Communist Asian states Soviet power would have been effectively contained and limited as before the Second World War.

The problem of Asia's importance to Russia has another dimension and that is the position of the non-Communist half of the continent. To the south of the Soviet and Chinese territories lies a continental area which together with Japan, Indonesia, Ceylon and Taiwan has a population of over 900 million. It is difficult to over-estimate the importance of this area both to the West and to Russia. Apart from what may be called the long term interest of converting every country to the gospel of Communism, the importance of this area to the Soviet Union lies in the fact that the Western end from Turkey to Pakistan lies close to the sparsely populated Central Asia. Also from the eastern border of India to the South China Sea the territory is a battle ground where an expanding Communism faces the peoples of South-East Asia. The Soviet Union is for the time being content, so far as this area is concerned, to ensure that the states of South-East Asia should not be used as military bases by the Western bloc. She, therefore, supports a policy of non-involvement, such as is followed by India, Nepal, Burma and Indonesia and extends to them technical and economic support.

The 'Battle for Souls'

The importance of this area to the West has already been briefly discussed. Basically it is that the countries and peoples of non-Communist Asia constituting over a third of the world's population should not fall under Communist influence and be lost to the free world; for the West realizes full well that if South and South-East Asia fall within the Communist orbit, the ultimate victory of Communism would be assured. To the West, therefore, it is the freedom of the non-Communist half of Asia that is important.

Thus a battle for souls is being waged in Asia with Russia entrenched in her Asian territories and China in her sphere of influence, and the West associated in economic development, technical and educational spheres. The West also shares with this area a common, though perhaps a weakening, liberal tradition, which has played a notable part in shaping its present life.

BIBLIOGRAPHY

G. F. Hudson. *Questions of East and West.* (Odhams, London, 1953.)

K. M. Panikkar. *Asia and Western Dominance.* (Allen and Unwin, London, revised ed., 1959.)

BIOGRAPHICAL NOTE

KAVALAM MADHAVA PANIKKAR: Vice-Chancellor, Jammu and Kashmir University; ex-M.P. (Rajya Sabha); D. Litt. (Delhi), LL.D. Member of the National Academy of Letters, India. B. 1895; d. 1963. Educated at Madras, Oxford; Scholar of Christ Church. Career: Editor, *Hindustan Times*, New Delhi; Minister, Patiala State; Prime Minister, Bikaner State; Member, Constituent Assembly of India; Vice-President, Royal India Society, London; Vice-President, Indian Council for Cultural Relations; Member, Indian Academy of Letters; Ambassador in China (1948-52); Ambassador in Egypt (1952-53); Member, States Reorganization Commission (1954-56); Ambassador in France (1956-59); Member, Rajya Sabha (Upper House of Parliament) (1959-61). Invited to deliver lectures at the Universities of Paris, Oxford, St. Gallen (Switzerland), and at Indian universities. Author of numerous books on Asia; has also published novels, plays and poems in Malayalam.

THE WORLD AND ASIA

BRITAIN'S ATTITUDE TOWARDS ASIA

by

GEOFFREY HUDSON

LATE in the 19th century a visitor to the House of Commons, surprised at the emptiness of the chamber when a debate was supposed to be going on, was told that this was because the subject was 'only India'. It was indeed notorious how little interest the British electorate and its parliamentary representatives took in the affairs of the country whose inhabitants composed a large majority of the total population of the British Empire. The political passions that were aroused over Irish Home Rule, Welsh Disestablishment or the House of Lords, were not stirred by the actions of Viceroys or the problems of the Frontier.

THE HERITAGE OF EMPIRE

This indifference was not due to any distaste or aversion from imperial power; the convinced anti-imperialists, though always vocal, never exerted a really strong political influence. It was rather that the Empire was taken for granted; it was an accepted part of the natural order of things that Englishmen should go out and govern Asia, that Scotsmen should make money there and that Irishmen should soldier there. Asia had become a part of the normal and familiar background of English social life. The East India Company and the 'nabobs', the Indian Civil Service and the retired 'Anglo-Indian', the Indian Army colonel whose temper was excused on the ground of long exposure to a tropical sun, Dr. Watson injured at Maiwand and returning to share lodgings in Baker Street with Sherlock Holmes—all were a part of the English scene because of Britain's 'dominion over palm and pine' and it was hardly possible to imagine it otherwise. But because Asia was so far off—many months in the days of sail round the Cape and still weeks away in the age of steam by 'Ports', because the British who actually went there were so few, and because empire-building drew so little directly on the national resources and energies of Britain, policies in Asia were not of intimate concern to the British nation as a whole; they were best left to the experienced few who understood what they were about. The Empire was the affair of specialists; it ran on its own. Eastern wars were financed from the profits of Eastern trade or the revenues of administered territories, the British Raj was sustained by the Indian sepoy and the British volunteer regular, and it was not until the Second World War that British conscripts were drafted to service in India and Malaya—an innovation which in itself produced a new mood of questioning about the significance of the white man's burden.

The traditional British attitude towards imperial commitments in Asia needs to be understood if there is to be a comprehension of the current outlook after the period of decolonization and disengagement. For several reasons the renunciation of the imperial heritage has been relatively easy for the British nation. Because the Empire and its agencies of power were so loosely attached to the central core of British nationhood, their liquidation involved no tearing of deep roots or bitter traumatic experience. Because Britain was victorious in both world wars, cessions of power could be made from strength; the Empire was not dissolved through military defeat by an external enemy. Because of the strength of the tradition of liberal political thought going back to Macaulay and beyond, there was a general acceptance of the idea that the task of the Empire was to prepare subject peoples for independence, even though officials might disagree with their pupils' own estimates of their progress in capacity for self-government. Because protracted resistance to nationalist movements was avoided and there was a minimum of bloodshed—the 'Emergency' in Malaya was not a struggle against Malayan nationalism—the transfers of power were peaceful and, with rare exceptions, amicable relations could be established with the new rulers. Thus the process of decolonization came to be regarded by a majority of the British people more as the accomplishment of a purpose than as an enforced deprivation.

The Commonwealth

There has been, nevertheless, a continuing involvement in Asian affairs which is hardly in accordance with the formal termination of all imperial responsibilities. Asia has indeed been too long a factor in British history for countries which were a part of the Empire to be suddenly regarded as foreign states. All the newly independent Asian territories except Burma have become members of the Commonwealth, and although this association involves neither automatic obligations of alliances nor restrictions on national sovereignty, there can be no doubt that a sense of special relationship with other members of the Commonwealth remains a factor of real importance in British politics. It is not confined to one party; it is a natural inheritance of the party of Disraeli and Salisbury, but it is also strong in the Labour Party, as shown by the latter's willingness to maintain commitments 'east of Suez' even at the expense of Britain's strategic position in Europe. The Labour Party indeed can rightly regard itself as the creator of the new Commonwealth, since its period of office from 1945 to 1952 saw the first extension of membership to nations which were neither of British settler origin nor of monarchical constitution.

Although the Commonwealth may seem to some observers to be no more than a fiction for disguising the real disintegration of the British Empire, it has involved Britain in commitments in Asia which can hardly be explained but for the fact that the territories concerned were recently under British rule. Malaya only became independent in 1957, and it seemed natural to the British Government that its defence should continue to be guaranteed by Britain even after it had attained sovereignty, even though it was hardly anticipated what a severe conflict this obligation was soon to involve. India, determined to be neutral and free from all entangling alliances, received no defence guarantee from Britain, but when a broken Indian army was being chased down into the plains of Assam by a Chinese invasion, there was a remarkable surge of enthusiasm in Britain for helping in the defence of India, despite the fact that there was no longer any imperial frontier in the Himalayas. This willingness to be involved in dangerous situations far removed geographically from Britain as an offshore island of Europe cannot be explained by the relatively small material economic interests at stake in the area; it reflects rather an attitude formed by history. It was their own work that the British instinctively moved to protect, whether in Malaysia or India. What was to be defended against Indonesian *confrontation* was the creation of Raffles and six generations of British administrators in the Straits Settlements and the Malay States, of the Brookes in Sarawak and the British North Borneo Company in Sabah; it was from these elements that Malaysia was formed. What was to be defended in India was a frontier which in relation to the Chinese Empire of the Ch'ing Dynasty had received its final definition from the British Raj.

Sukarno, who claims to represent the 'new emerging forces' of Asia and declared as long ago as 1945 that Malaya must be included in his Greater Indonesia, denounces the Malaysian Federation as a device of 'neo-colonialism' and its government as a puppet of the British without whose military aid it would soon be overwhelmed by the superior power of Indonesia; the Chinese accuse India of trying to maintain a frontier created at China's expense by aggressive British imperialism and of subservience to British and American protectors without whose backing India would have to submit to the superior power of China in the disputed frontier zone. It is true that most of the established frontiers of the newly independent nations of Asia and Africa date from the colonial period, but this very fact means that the former metropolitan power feels a sense of identification with the territorial entity which it has defined, and if its relations with the successor state are good, it desires to keep the inheritance intact. Thus Britain has been willing to concede independence to the inhabitants of former British-governed territories in the Malay Peninsula and Borneo, but not to acquiesce in the grabbing of these areas by the successor state to the former Dutch East Indies. Britain has likewise yielded her sovereignty in India to Indian nationalism, but supports the Indian national Government in the contention that its frontier with China is what Britain held it to be when power was handed over in 1947.

Britain's Commonwealth links are, however, an embarrassment rather than otherwise when the conflict is not between a Commonwealth partner and an external power but between two members of the association. Over a period of eighteen years Britain has been unable to do anything to reconcile India and Pakistan in their quarrel over Kashmir. Pakistan hoped that her participation in the CENTO and SEATO alliances would give her an advantage over neutralist India in Britain's political affections, but London has never been willing to antagonize India on behalf of Pakistan. America likewise has refrained from taking sides. The Communist powers, on the other hand, have suffered from no such inhibitions. The Soviet Union has openly and emphatically championed India's cause over Kashmir, while Communist China has entered into an informal alliance with Pakistan against India. Neither India nor Pakistan has severed its ties with Britain and America, but both tend to look towards their respective Communist sponsors for the active political support in their mutual conflict which they cannot expect from London or Washington. In spite of all the help he received from Britain and America in the days after the disaster in Assam in 1962, Nehru publicly attributed the Chinese withdrawal to Russian pressure, though there has never been any evidence whatever that this was the reason for it. Similarly Pakistan, although retaining membership of both the CENTO and SEATO alliances, now appears to rely upon China rather than her Western partners to aid her against an Indian attack. This situation is an unpleasant one for Britain and tends to diminish the prospects of whole-hearted co-operation with either of the successor states to British India. It has always been the British hope that India and Pakistan would compose their differences sufficiently for them to organize a joint defence for the sub-continent and perhaps ultimately achieve a degree of political re-unification which would make India-Pakistan a power comparable to China in the affairs of Asia. But such a future depends on a settlement of the Kashmir issue and of that there is no sign so far; it has remained one of the most intractable and embittered disputes in the whole range of international affairs.

China

Failing a restoration of the political unity which the Indian sub-continent possessed before 1947, a united and modernized China, under whatever social regime, must be the strongest indigenous power of Asia, and the Chinese People's Republic today certainly holds this position. British policy towards China since the Pacific war has been based on a clear recognition that British armed power in the Far East, which was at its maximum in the opening years of the present century (before the advent of the Dreadnought battleship rendered Hong Kong obsolete as a naval base), has virtually ceased to exist, that the surviving colonial territory of Hong Kong is held only on sufferance, and that whatever Western presence still remains in the China Seas is not British but American.

Britain has therefore tried both to establish the best possible relations with China, whether under Kuomintang or Communist rule, while at the same time co-ordinating policy with the United States. This has proved extremely difficult because of the Korean War of 1950 and the events which followed from it. Down to the summer of 1950, when the Communist North Korean army invaded South Korea, the British and American Governments on the whole saw eye to eye on policy towards China; both were ready to abandon the Kuomintang regime in China if it were losing the civil war and to accept a Communist victory. Britain early in 1950 recognized the Communist authority in Peking as the *de jure* Government of China, thereby withdrawing recognition from the Kuomintang Government which continued to hold out on its island stronghold of Formosa,

The British Foreign Office was given to understand that America would soon act likewise, but that the domestic political situation in the United States made it inexpedient for the Truman Administration to do so before the mid-Congressional elections of November 1950. In the meantime the Korean war broke out and the American plus United Nations intervention was followed by the hostile counter-intervention of Communist China. Britain was America's partner in the United Nations action, but the political effect of the war in the two countries was very different. For Britain it was a small military involvement in a remote country undertaken in accordance with obligations under the United Nations Charter and to be limited in scope as far as possible. For America, on the other hand, it involved not only a much larger commitment of troops, with heavy casualties in three years of hard fighting, but a great surge of emotional antipathy towards the new regime in China which forced American policy to move into a course opposite to the one it had been taking.

Unlike the British, who had never felt any sense of political intimacy with China, the Americans had imagined themselves to have a special relationship with the Chinese people assuring a perpetual amity between the two countries; it was therefore a terrible shock when Mao Tse-tung after setting up the People's Republic went off to Moscow and concluded a military alliance with the Soviet Union, and the Truman Administration was blamed for not having done more to prevent a Communist victory in China. Its position in the face of its critics was a weak one, for American intervention in Europe to check the expansion of Soviet power had been justified as a policy of 'containment of Communism'; it thus had a general ideological character which was not needed by British policy with its traditional concept (abhorrent to Americans) of the balance of power, and, being a matter of universal principle, could not be confined to Europe, so that the war in Korea came more and more to be regarded in America as part of an anti-Communist crusade. As a consequence of this the protection of American arms was extended to Chiang Kai-shek's regime in Formosa, and it was recognized as still the *de jure* Government of China; this excluded any diplomatic relations with Peking even after the fighting in Korea was over, and it became also America's fixed policy to oppose the transfer of China's seat in the United Nations to a representative of the People's Republic. Britain, on the other hand, refused to be committed to any support for the regime in Formosa, urged the seating of Communist China in the United Nations and only refrained from anti-American lobbying on the matter when it became clear that a bloc of Britain and the Soviet Union in support of Peking could mean the rupture of the Anglo-American alliance.

British and American policies in the Far East therefore continued to diverge without ever coming to an outright collision; a crisis on China's seat in the United Nations was avoided by getting the question shelved whenever it came up on the agenda. Public opinion in Britain regarded the American attitude as doctrinaire and unrealistic and tended to indulge in unduly optimistic forecasts of the improvement in the Far Eastern situation to be expected from the admission of Communist China to the United

Nations; Americans charged Britain with complacency, opportunism and a lack of will to oppose the advance of Communism in Asia.

Hong Kong

British possession of Hong Kong was a factor in British policy in so far as it was potentially a hostage to China for a certain minimum of (from the Chinese point of view) British good behaviour. If Britain were to line up too closely with America, Hong Kong could be attacked, and it was not considered strategically tenable any more than it had turned out to be in 1941; if, on the other hand, the Chinese were to attack it without British provocation, it would inevitably have the effect of driving Britain and America together. It was therefore in China's interest to leave Hong Kong alone as long as British and American policies were divergent, and in Britain's interest, as long as Britain had a stake in Hong Kong, not to identify her policy too closely with America's. The Chinese Communists also derived certain advantages in the matter of foreign currency from trading with and through Hong Kong, but the political have probably been more important than the economic considerations as motives for Peking's forbearance over Hong Kong in spite of its obviously obnoxious character as a survival from the age of Western imperialism in China.

South-East Asia

To the south of China Britain has officially supported American operations in defence of South Vietnam in spite of mounting criticism of American policy there in wide sections of British opinion and fears that the war may escalate into armed conflict between the Great Powers. Britain's defence of Malaysia is bound up with the American cause in Vietnam, not only because the United States may be expected to refuse any support over Malaysia to a Britain which repudiates America in Vietnam, but also because an American defeat in Vietnam would probably cause Thailand to change sides and enable Peking to give direct support to the Chinese Communists of Malaya, whose revolutionary movement there has been fermenting underground since the end of the guerilla campaign in 1960. It is recognized in British official quarters, if not on the left wing of the Labour Party, that Britain cannot pursue a policy of defending the independence and integrity of Malaysia while at the same time trying to remain above the battle in Vietnam.

The basic common purpose of both British and American policies in South-East Asia is to preserve the independence of a group of states friendly to the West which would otherwise through Communist subversion or military invasion be brought under the domination of China. The issue is complicated in various ways; neither the Indonesian confrontation of Malaysia nor the military infiltration into South Vietnam is a direct action of China, and some Western statesmen have even speculated on the possibility of building barriers against China with Sukarno and Ho Chi-minh But if the residual Western presence is once eliminated from South-East Asia, it will not be long before Chinese power is extended southward to the Straits of Malacca.

BIBLIOGRAPHY

G. F. Hudson. *Questions of East and West.* (Odhams, London, 1953.) *Europe and China: A Study of their Relations in History before 1800.* (Edward Arnold, London, 1931.) *The Far East in World Politics.* (Oxford Univ. Press, London, 2nd ed., 1939.)

BIOGRAPHICAL NOTE

GEOFFREY HUDSON. Fellow of All Souls College, Oxford, 1926-54. Served in the Research Department of the Foreign Office, 1939-46. Worked part-time on the editorial staff of *The Economist,* 1946-54. Fellow and Director of Far Eastern Studies at St. Antony's College, Oxford, since 1954. Advisory Editor of *The China Quarterly* since 1960. Author of *Europe and China: a Survey of their Relations in History to 1800* (Edward Arnold, London, 1931) and *The Far East in World Politics* (Oxford Univ. Press, London, 2nd ed., 1939).

THE AMERICAN ATTITUDE TOWARDS ASIA

by

GEORGE E. TAYLOR

THE general outlines of the American approach to Asia today were made clear by President Truman two days after the opening of the Korean War. In this statement he announced that the United States would build a military cordon around Communist China in order to prevent the further extension of Communist influence through the use of force. This decision led to the dispatch of a military mission to Taiwan to rebuild the army of the National Republic of China and to the strengthening of American military forces in Japan, Korea, Okinawa, the Philippines, and on the high seas. Military supplies and economic support for local forces were to be increased in all allied countries. At the same time the United States proceeded to negotiate a peace treaty with Japan and to sign bilateral mutual security arrangements with the Philippines, Taiwan, and South Korea, and later with an independent Japan. It also became a member of regional alliances, such as ANZUS and SEATO, and the co-signer of the Manila Charter, a pale imitation of the Atlantic Charter. As the United States owns no territory in the Western Pacific, its military position is tied in very closely with its political alliances and depends particularly on the agreements on the maintenance of military bases.

President Truman also made it clear that United States economic aid would be used to strengthen the economies not only of allies of the United States but also of those countries that were committed to neither side. New techniques were invented and new organizations created to provide economic aid. The Mutual Security Administration, now the Administration for International Development, was set up to coordinate the many different organizations that had grown up for the purpose of extending economic aid. The United States came to accept the important principle that aid should be provided, if acceptable, on the assumption that a country that is able to take care of its major economic problems is likely to have a more responsible political outlook than one that is not. Anything that can be done, therefore, to assist the newly independent states of Asia to remain independent, even if they are highly critical of the Free World, is well worth the investment.

The general pattern established by Truman remains, although changes have been made in the way in which policy is applied. The commitment of 20,000 American military personnel in South Vietnam even before the 1965 conflagration was a logical application of the Truman policies, but it would not necessarily have been undertaken by another administration. The same is true of the acceptance of the responsibility for what is called 'counter-insurrection', the name given to the doctrines and operational techniques of countering Communist guerilla warfare. The ten-year struggle of the British in Malaya against Communist terrorists and of the Americans and Filipinos against the Hukbalahap uprising in the Philippines contributed valuable experience, but the decision to make counter-insurrection the responsibility, on the highest level, of the Department of Defense should have been made much earlier. The rapid response to India's call for arms and equipment was also within the pattern of policy laid down at the time of the Korean conflict.

Post-War Commitments

The decades following World War II have probably seen greater changes in the American position in Asia than has any other comparable period in the history of American relations with that part of the world. After fighting a war with Japan, the United States took over the main burden in fighting another war with China and North Korea and is now heavily involved in a struggle in South Vietnam to preserve for the peoples of South-East Asia the opportunity to live in comparative freedom. If the Founding Fathers would be surprised to find the Republic involved in 'entangling alliances' with the powers of Europe, they would be even more bewildered by the commitments that Americans have made to so many Asian states. The mistakes that have been made in this massive readjustment in Asia are minor, however, when considered in the light of the scale and appropriateness of the approach. The United States has adjusted its policies to the post-war situation in Asia—the liquidation of imperialism, the rise of Communist China, the problems of the new nations, the Korean War, and Communist subversion in South-East Asia—with speed, flexibility, and conviction.

Why was this possible? While there was nothing inevitable about the adoption of current policies, they are all logical extensions of the American approach to Asia that developed during the 19th and 20th centuries. Largely owing to the late but vigorous American response to the challenge from the Communists and to the separate but related problems of the underdeveloped part of the world, the United States has stumbled and staggered into the leadership of a vast coalition of highly diverse nations. In doing so it has called on its resources of tradition and experience, if not always to the fullest measure, at least in measure sufficient to enable it to take the initiative. Think what might have happened if those trends in American history that came to the fore during the 1930s had been dominant after 1945. What if the United States had withdrawn from Europe and Asia, if there had been no Marshall Plan, no NATO, no foreign economic assistance, no rebuilding of a defeated Japan, no support of South Korea and no United States military presence in the Western Pacific?

The unique qualities of the American approach to Asia spring from the facts of American history and geography. While it is hard to determine where Europe ends and Asia begins, America is separated from Asia proper by thousands of miles of ocean. The nations of Europe have had vigorous contacts with their Asian neighbours in the Near East, hence their familiarity with Turkic, Persian, Arabic, and Semitic languages and cultures. The Orient, in this sense of the term, has made a major contribution to European civilization. The American relationship with Asia began without a history. The first contact was at Asia's easternmost end. That is why, when Americans think of Asia, they think first of China and Japan, the countries with which they had their most important economic and political relations. At the same time, having no fear of Asia, for no Asian armies had ever threatened their sioil, Americans saw the countries of Asia, not as treacherous and powerful foes, but as potential allies against the prevailing influence of the great mercantilis- empires of Europe. From the time of their earliest contacts, therefore, Amerit cans presented themselves to the Chinese and Japanese as former subjects of European imperialism, therefore as natural allies in the struggle against it.

The American attitude towards imperialism, which has much to do with present policies, is closely connected with another peculiarly American attitude: the assumption that all Asians are intrinsically capable of self-government and that, given the opportunity, they will wish to adopt American values and institutions. A typical example of this aspect of the American approach was the Occupation of Japan. Here a deliberate effort was made to shift the internal balance of forces in favour of democracy by changing property and social relationships in town and countryside and by rewriting the constitution. There is something very American about this sort of effort to change the society of a defeated country. It is definitely part of the American revolutionary tradition to assume that certain representative institutions and political forms are better than any other. Americans take the view that the world will be safer for democracies if it is full of democracies. Behind all this, there is a fundamental and unwavering faith in the political judgment of a well-informed electorate. It is assumed that, given a free press and uninhibited channels of communication, universal suffrage, and representative institutions, democracy is within reach of all.

While it is easy to satirize the crude and sentimental aspects of the American dream when translated to China or any other Asian country, it is folly to overlook its political dynamism. This urge to impose on other countries the social and political ideals of the American Republic is the most distinctive feature of the United States approach to Asia. It came to be the American objective during the occupation of the Philippines; it was the main objective of the Occupation of Japan; and it determined the conditions of United States aid to Chiang Kai-shek in 1946, conditions that he either refused or could not meet. Americans have tended to discount the good side of imperialism—the establishment of law and order, public health and education, communications and industry—because of the denial of independence, on which, for obvious historical reasons, they put a high premium. Americans have always tended to identify themselves with the colonial peoples rather than with the imperial masters because independence, to the American, comes first.

Support of Colonial Peoples

There is the view that Americans are hypocritical in their denunciation of colonial empires and in their oft-proclaimed support of colonial peoples.

There are those who point to the utter disregard of the rights of the American Indian, the conquest of the continent at the expense of Mexico, and the annexation of Hawaii. In point of fact, however, it is difficult to demonstrate that the United States has been one of the great colonial empires. Even Lenin said of the United States, 'She has no colonies'. What, then, of the Philippines? While many of the forces that drove the United States into the Philippines are identical with those that explain the expansion of the European powers—trade, resources, national security, and 'the white man's burden'—the United States added to the theory and practice of imperialism a new concept—that of a self-liquidating colony. The drive of the 'manifest destiny' school was strong enough to support the ruthless conquest of the Philippines but not strong enough to establish a colony on the usual pattern. So while the conquest of the Philippines was a violation of the intent of the American Constitution (until the Supreme Court ruled otherwise) and a deviation from the anti-colonial attitudes of the American people, it was also a deviation from the standard pattern of colonial control as exercised by the European powers. It has often been pointed out that when the United States gave independence to the Filipinos in 1946, it retained its naval and air bases in the Philippines, whereas when Britain left India, she withdrew unconditionally. To Americans, the conditions attached to Philippine independence do not seem illogical because the military bases were all that the United States wanted in the first place, and the Filipinos did not have to fight for their independence. The acquisition and governing of the Philippines were incidental to the main purpose.

Americans are more willing to agree now than they were before that imperialism is not entirely evil. Yet resentment against British imperialism is taking an unconscionable time to die because it combined for over a century political principles and national interest. It is impossible to understand some of Franklin D. Roosevelt's actions without realizing that Roosevelt, a strong navy man, was at one time more suspicious of the post-war intentions of British imperialists than he was of Soviet Communists. That is why he was capable of the cavalier suggestion that Mr. Churchill return Hong Kong to the Chinese but was agreeable to the proposition that the Soviet Union be given the same rights and interests in Manchuria as were claimed by the Tzars in 1904. He may not have understood Soviet intentions, but he had been brought up with the traditional American disapproval of British imperialism. It must be remembered that the general principles of national strategy, most of which were laid down in the first 50 years of American contact with the Far East, were devised with the British Empire very much in mind. American strategy was, first, to promote freedom of the seas, free trade, and equality of commercial opportunity in order to undermine mercantilism; second, to limit the expansion of the British Empire by supporting the independence of self-governing oriental states, such as China and Japan; third, to secure naval bases in the Pacific in preparation for the anticipated naval struggle with the British and other fleets in the Western Pacific waters. For a variety of reasons, the strategy succeeded. The political and economic doctrines of the new Republic were diametrically opposed to those prevailing at the time, but because they had been derived from 18th century English liberalism, the American colonists had allies in the United Kingdom. There were many English traders who approved of the American position on international trade and put pressure on the British Government to adopt it. They finally got their way after the Reform Act of 1832, when the new Parliament abolished the monopoly of the East India Company trading with China. From this time on, British and American economic policies were competitive, but parallel, both, for example, supporting the Open Door policy.

Anglo-American Rivalry

In spite of Anglo-American agreement on the Open Door and many other matters there, has always been a political rivalry between the two countries on policy towards China. The reasons for this go back as far as the Anglo-Chinese War, 1839-42, when the United States, disapproving the British method of opening up China, stayed neutral. The neutrality, however, was in favour of China. The head of the leading American firm in Canton suggested to Daniel Webster that it would be useful if the United States could, in a quiet way, 'without infringing upon the courtesy due to Britain', help the Chinese in their defence against further British aggression. The American Commissioner, Caleb Cushing, presented the Chinese with technical books on the building of fortifications. In order to cultivate Chinese goodwill, Mr. Cushing informed the Chinese that the United States had asserted her independence from England and that whereas the British were well established in India, the United States had no colonies anywhere near China.

There are some American historians who feel that the United States in the 19th century played an ignominious role by refusing to share in the military operations against China while accepting all the benefits for which others expended their blood and treasure. But United States policy put restraints on what was thought to be the British intention. This opposition was clear to Disraeli, who told the House of Commons in 1857, the year before the Anglo-French expedition against Tientsin, that the offer of Lord Hastings to conquer China with 20,000 men in the first decade of the century might have succeeded then but would have been far too dangerous to attempt in the middle of the century when such a course might have involved the United Kingdom in a war with the Russian Empire and the American Republic. China, like Japan, owes her political survival in part to United States policy.

The other aspect of United States national strategy was the policy of building up naval strength in the Pacific. This is clearly illustrated in the opening of Japan in 1853. The Navy, which felt that a conflict with the British Navy was inevitable, pressed for the opening of Japan while the British and French were involved in the Crimean War. It was essential, the Navy felt, to secure bases on the Great Circle Route to China for repairs and supplies in the conflict with the British fleet. The American diplomat, Townsend Harris, secured a commercial treaty with Japan, not by the use of force, but by persuading the Japanese that they could not possibly avoid opening up their country to foreign commerce and that if they signed a reasonable treaty with the United States, it could be the pattern for treaties with other countries, so that Japan could in this manner avoid the fate of China. By the end of the century, Navy doctrines had been formalized. The insistence upon bases in the Pacific had much to do with the American decision to take the Philippines in 1898 and to annex Hawaii at the same time. Indeed, if the Navy had had its way, the American flag would have flown on many other Pacific Islands.

It is easy to see how the same American policies that promoted Japanese independence also brought about United States support of China's political and territorial integrity. China came to be the key to the balance of power in Eastern Asia mainly because its weakness invited aggression. In order to remove this weakness, the United States opposed every empire—the British, the Russian, the Japanese, and now the Soviet—that appeared to seek a predominant position in China. But, more important, the United States projected on to China, after 1928, its own concept of a strong, united, and democratic China. The level of political expectation rose all the higher because the Comintern had apparently failed to achieve its hope for a strong, united, communistic China.

There is probably more agreement today between the United Kingdom and the United States on policies in Asia than there has been at any time in history. This is partly due to the disappearance of colonialism as an issue. It is also due to the challenge of the Sino-Soviet bloc and the desperate need for common policies with which to meet it. There is also the joint acceptance of responsibility for aid and assistance to the under-developed parts of the world and cooperation in meeting it. The United States and the United Kingdom are both members of the Colombo Plan. They cooperated in the Korean conflict, and more recently, in the crisis between India and China. It would seem that the only major difference in policy today is over the recognition of Communist China and the admission of that regime to the United Nations.

Recognition of Communist China

There are differences of opinion in the United States as well as in the United Kingdom as to the wisdom of their respective policies towards Peking, but ever since the Korean conflict, there has been no way in which the United States could recognize Peking even if it wished to do so. If the Chinese Communists had conquered Taiwan in 1949, as they expected to do, the United States might well have recognized Peking as the *de facto* government of China. But this did not happen. With the opening of the Korean War, the United States felt it advisable to protect Taiwan, partly to secure lines of communication, partly because no one could tell where the War would lead. This action led directly to a commitment to support the National Government of China and to a mutual defence treaty by which the United States is legally bound to defend Taiwan. There is now no way of recognizing Peking unless Peking is willing to agree to the independent status of the National Government, which, to date, it is not.

The very common charge that United States policy towards Communist China is dictated entirely by disappointment and emotion hardly does credit to the policies of a great power. The United States has always considered the granting or the withholding of recognition a political weapon, as have most other countries, and under present circumstances, it is assumed that there would be no particular advantage to the United States in recognizing Peking, while there would be very serious disadvantages in so doing. Recognition on Peking's terms would demoralize many of America's allies by casting doubt on her stated purposes, encouraging the left, and making it all the more risky for Asian anti-Communists to come out in the open. It is dangerous to give the impression of vacillation and indecision. There are conditions, no doubt, under which the United States might well recognize Peking, but those conditions are not in existence now. The United States can afford to wait until Peking needs United States support so desperately that it is willing to accept United States conditions. There are actually some advantages in having the United Kingdom, an ally, represented in Peking. Recognition by the United Kingdom presumably brings all the advantages that recognition might hold, while non-recognition by the United States brings the moral advantages of discrimination against the regime that has attacked the United Nations and is attempting to bring about revolutions in neighbouring countries. It also leaves the way open for the growth of an alternative political centre of attraction among the anti-Communist Chinese on Taiwan or elsewhere.

Projection of Democratic Ideals

The importance of the recognition issue is that it reflects the one major difference between the United States and the United Kingdom in their approach to Asia. The imperialist issue is no longer important, the naval rivalry has merged into collective security, the economic rivalry is insignificant. But the Americans are unwilling to give up their hope that some day, under some conditions, the Communist regime in China will pass away, and in the meantime it is important to keep the record straight by supporting the 'legitimate' government of China. The American dream is an aggressive projection of the ideals of democracy, American style, in the belief that they will ultimately prove more attractive than any alternative. When policy has been formulated in this spirit, the results have not been unrewarding. There is the Philippines with free elections, free press, independent judiciary, system of public education. Some credit can be taken for the fact that the Philippines is a staunch ally. The Occupation of Japan may be said to have succeeded most in those areas in which the Japanese themselves were ready for change, such as the elimination of militarism and the emancipation of women, but the most far-reaching change was the carrying out of a land reform. In the Korean War, insistence upon the right of prisoners to choose whether or not they would return to Communist control was a political and psychological victory, even it it was not fully exploited. The patient handling of India's political leaders and the very considerable aid given to that country have not gone unrewarded. Furthermore, the United States takes Asia very seriously as a subject for research and teaching in its schools and universities. The United States takes the study of Asia much more seriously than does any other Western country, and certainly more seriously than Asian countries take the United States. A people who advocate idealistic political principles are necessarily open to a critical examination of their own practices, and

Asians have given a good deal of attention to the problems of race relations in the United States. Such criticisms, however, can be taken as a tribute to the political dynamism of democratic principles, for the criticism proceeds in terms of Western rather than Asian values. The American Republic has changed its friends and its policies, but it is difficult to improve upon the ideals of the Founding Fathers as the basis for national strategy. The problem for America is not to imitate the tactics of others or to invent new ones, it is to be true to American democratic traditions.

BIBLIOGRAPHY

S. F. Bemis. *A Diplomatic History of the U.S.* (Holt, New York, 4th ed., 1955.)

Dorothy Borg. *American Policy and the Chinese Revolution, 1925-28.* (Macmillan, New York, 1947.)

Tyler Dennett. *Americans in Eastern Asia.* (Macmillan, New York, 1922.)

Foster R. Dulles. *China and America: The Story of Their Relations Since 1784.* (Princeton Univ. Press, Princeton, N.J., 1946.)

John K. Fairbank. *The United States and China.* (Harvard Univ. Press, Cambridge, Mass., 2nd ed., 1962.)

Herbert Feis. *The Road to Pearl Harbor.* (Princeton Univ. Press, Princeton, N.J., 1962.)

Russell Fifield. *Woodrow Wilson and the Far East.* (Crowell, New York, 1952.)

A. W. Griswold. *The Far Eastern Policy of the U.S.* (Harcourt Brace, New York, 1939.)

Townsend Harris. *The Complete Journal of Townsend Harris.* (Doubleday, New York, 1930.)

Geoffrey F. Hudson. *Europe and China: A Survey of Their Relations from the Earliest Times to 1800.* (Edward Arnold, London, 1931.)

Harold R. Isaacs. *New Cycle in Asia.* (Macmillan, New York, 1947.)

George F. Kennan. *American Diplomacy 1900-1950.* (Univ. of Chicago Press, Chicago, 1951.)

William L. Langer. *The Diplomacy of Imperialism.* (Knopf, New York, 2nd ed., 1950.)

Military Situation in Far East: Hearings Before the Committee on Armed Services and the Committee on Foreign Relations, United States Senate, Eighty-Second Congress, First Session. (Washington, D.C., 1951.)

Nathan A. Pelcovits. *Old China Hands and the Foreign Office.* (Columbia Univ. Press, New York, 1933.)

Edmund Stillman and William Pfaff. *The New Politics, America and the End of the Postwar World.* (Coward McCann, New York, 1961.)

The United States and the Far East, American Assembly. (Graduate School of Business, Columbia University, New York, 1956.)

U.S. Navy: U.S. Strategic Bombing Survey (Pacific). *Interrogations of Japanese Officials,* 2 vols. (Government Printing Office, Washington, D.C., 1946.)

BIOGRAPHICAL NOTE

GEORGE E. TAYLOR. Born and educated in England; B.A., M.A. and D.Litt. from Birmingham University. Studied at Johns Hopkins and Harvard Universities from 1928 and thereafter became a naturalized citizen of U.S.A. Harvard-Yenching Fellowship for study of Chinese language and history, 1930. In China and Far East, 1930-39. Joined University of Washington, 1939. During war Deputy Director of Office of War Information in charge of Pacific Operations; Director of Office of Information and Cultural Relations for the Far East in U.S. State Department, 1945-46. Travelled extensively in Far East, 1951-52. Member of U.S. Delegation to SEATO conference, Philippines, 1957, and to meeting of NATO Study Group on Asian and African languages, London, 1958. Author of several books, including *The Far East in the Modern World* (with Franz Michael: Methuen, London, 1956) and *The Philippines and the United States: Problems of Partnership* (Praeger, New York, 1964.)

THE AUSTRALIAN ATTITUDE TOWARDS ASIA

by

C. P. FITZGERALD

EARLY in the 19th century a party of convicts, transported to Australia, escaped from custody and started to travel north in the belief that they would be able to reach China—overland. Apart from the probability that they would have been sadly disappointed by their reception if they had been able to accomplish such a journey, the story illustrates the general ignorance of uneducated persons of the true situation of Australia, and at the same time the realization that it was, indeed, a very great way from Europe. In the century and more that followed Australians had little desire to voyage to China or any where else in Asia: if they could afford to travel overseas they came 'home' to the United Kingdom, to visit relatives, to see for themselves the land from which their fathers, or grandfathers, had emigrated.

Asia remained a sealed book. It was largely under the safe rule of the European colonial powers, of which their own Britain was the greatest; and Britannia Ruled the Waves. There was no conceivable danger from Asia; Asians were backward; they were not Christians. They were therefore a suitable field for missionary endeavour, and many Australians took part in that enterprise. Some of them came back to retire in their homeland. They were much in demand to speak of their experiences, raise money for the missionary work, and in this way they exercised a real influence over the mind of the rising generation. It was necessarily a rather one sided and even distorted picture of Asia which was received. A great continent of pagans—or 'heathen'—as yet barely touched by the light of the Gospel. A region which could not hope to progress until that light shone more widely; a land of toiling millions, benighted and poverty-stricken masses of humanity. Missionaries did not come into close contact with the educated and ruling classes of Asia, and when they did, they found these people uncooperative, obstructive and opposed to the work of the missions. They were therefore just as benighted as their uneducated countrymen, with less excuse.

These notions have not yet wholly faded from the consciousness (or perhaps the unconscious) of many of the older generation, not excluding the eminent. They persisted in spite of the existence of a small but competent group of Australians who really did know Asia and followed its politics with close attention. Such men as George Morrison, correspondent of the London *Times* in Peking for many years at the end of the 19th and early 20th century; W. Donald, who was the intimate adviser of General Chiang Kai-shek in the years before the war; and many of lesser fame in business, mining and industry could have been the formers and leaders of an informed public opinion. In fact they exercised little or no influence upon opinion in their homeland. They only rarely returned to it; their contacts were increasingly with Europe or America. Effective policy towards Asia was not made in Australia; capital for enterprises in Asia was not raised in Australia.

British and American Protection against Japan

Until a few years before the outbreak of the Second World War Australia had no independent diplomatic representation overseas, and no Ministry of External Affairs. Parliament and public left the conduct of foreign affairs to Whitehall. As far as Asia was concerned this did not matter, as there was only one Asian state which could have any significance for Australia either as a threat or as an ally; Japan. For a long period Japan was the ally of Britain, and therefore a friend. When this situation came to an end and Japan gradually became a threat, Australia responded very slowly to the change. Yet it is significant that among the very few diplomatic missions sent to a foreign power in the years shortly before the Second World War, Japan was one. Informed people were aware by 1938-39 that Japan was on the march, her ambitions far-reaching, and that Australia was in a very exposed position. The ease with which Japan had flouted foreign privileges in China, derided the protests of the powers, and employed force and violence without incurring any penalty opened the eyes of thinking men to the very real dangers ahead.

The general public remained unaware, confident and indifferent. If there was trouble, Britain would protect her kith and kin. British sea power was so strong a tradition that only close students of the changing world could assess its present limitations. Australians were generously ready to spring to arms to defend the 'home country'. The traditions of Flanders and Gallipoli lived vividly in the national memory, enshrined in the national day, Anzac Day, which for most still had (and has) a far greater significance than the commemoration of the first settlement of the Continent, or the foundation of the Commonwealth of Australia. But war to Australians had essentially this chivalric, detached, remote quality. Patriotic men enlisted to fight for the Empire in some far-off foreign land. They fought for principles, not for self-defence. No one really ever supposed that the Germans or the Turks could or would invade Australia. Few Germans were then found in Australia; it is very doubtful whether more than a very few individuals of the thousands who landed at Gallipoli had ever before set eyes on a Turk.

When invasion nearly came in the Second World War, when the Japanese had seized Malaya, landed in New Guinea, launched their naval power to take command of the Western Pacific, and only been checked at the last moment by the Battle of the Coral Sea, Australia experienced a traumatic shock. It became known that the military had had to base their plans on the 'Brisbane Line', which would have yielded the northern sparsely inhabited half of the continent to the invader without resistance. American sea power saved Australia. The historical fact is well known, but all its consequences have yet to sink into the general understanding of Australians.

The war left the Australian people with a sense of gratitude to America, but much more strongly with a sense of fear and horror of Japan. This is often attributed mainly to the sufferings of Australian prisoners of war, captives of a people whose military tradition did not admit clemency. But this was not all; underlying it was the realization that the Japanese had destroyed a dream, and violated a sacred shrine: the dream of Australia's perfect security behind the shield of Britain's Navy; the shrine of the Just War fought for pure patriotism and high principle, far away, in strange lands, against impersonal foes from remote nations.

The Japanese were not far away, they had come right down to New Guinea, an Australian territory. The war was not only for principles, but for survival; the penalty for defeat was not severe casualties and a heroic rear-guard action, but invasion, conquest, perhaps permanent subjugation. Such had indeed been the fate of many peoples, for varying lengths of time. Those who have had the experience never forget it: conquest, partial or total, marks a watershed in the national history. If permanent, as with the Normans, it takes centuries to complete the fusion of the two peoples, to eradicate the last vestiges of privilege stemming from victory, of bondage stemming from defeat. It may be that the Japanese could never have conquered Australia, or held it if they had at first overrun the defence; but to the Australians this was certainly not apparent, and is in any case speculative. What was certain was that Asia could never be ignored in future. Japan might be defeated, occupied, disarmed; but who could guarantee that she would not rise again within a generation, just as Germany had risen.

The answer to this question was, and is, 'America'. The second lesson of the Second World War was that America was the only force in the world which could, if she would, save Australia, and protect Australia. But this lesson is learned much less easily, and is far less welcome. Attachment to Britain is strong, especially in the age group from which political leadership comes. It is not easy to recognize that Britain cannot now fulfil her traditional role. If the fact is recognized, it is not easy, nor politically wise, to over-emphasize it. To accept American preponderance in the Western world, and total domination of the Pacific Ocean, is comforting so long as it is certain that America won't forget her white cousins on the Western side. But from time to time it becomes uneasily apparent that American ideas on Asia and the aspirations of Asians are not always in harmony with Australian sentiment.

The New Asia

In the post-war world Australia was faced with an entirely new Asia. Japan, the one real terrible danger, was eliminated. But so, all too soon, were the old colonial empires, which had hitherto put the whole of South-East Asia into a kind of political cold storage. It was with London, The Hague or Paris that one used to deal if ever the affairs of Malaya, Indonesia or Indo-China impinged on Australian interests. Now it was with new men in new places, all unfamiliar. Everything was changed; China had been the ally in the war, distant, ineffective, vaguely romantic, but a friend. Very soon the Australians were being told, above all by the Americans, that the new Communist China was the enemy, far worse than Japan, ideological as well as military. It was more than hinted that Australian fears of Japan were outmoded and unreal; they should be taking heed of the new danger and assessing the new enemy. But the Australian people have been very slow to learn this lesson; in fact, very many of them repudiate the teaching.

Australia accepted, with reluctance, the lenient terms imposed on Japan at San Francisco. The rearming of Japan, even on a limited scale, is viewed with deep suspicion. On the other hand the thesis that China is the new enemy is not widely accepted outside the right wing of both the Liberal (conservative) and Labour Parties. In the first group, the knowledge of servicemen of what war they are bound to prepare for influences opinion; in the second the strong proportion of Roman Catholics in the Labour Party influences the view of China from an ideological rather than a practical or military standpoint. A majority of Australians are not under these special influences. The country, although not at present ruled by the Left, has always had a Left outlook. Communism as such may be unattractive, but there is a widespread knowledge that the Asian working class had been oppressed, ill-paid, and down-trodden; that the Chinese revolution was due to these facts and not to some 'Communist conspiracy.' The mass of the Australian people still hold their own colonial past in bitter memory; they are not unresponsive to others who feel the same.

There thus work in the Australian mind two rather contradictory impulses in respect of Asia: fear and sympathy. The old missionary village-hall lecturer has left his mark, sometimes in an unexpected way. The toiling millions may not be yet converted; but the modern Australian tends to remember their existence, both to fear their potential strength, and to feel concerned at their low standard of living. He is more alarmed by their poverty than distressed by their unbelief. If the poverty can be relieved, the pressure for revolutionary change can be eased, and thus the fear of violent upheavals, aggressive wars, and possible invasions reduced. Fear and sympathy dictate to many a similar approach; Australia's task in Asia is to assist development.

There is a considerable resistance to the approach which is dictated more by fear than sympathy. To contain Communism without trying to discover what makes Asians inclined to follow that doctrine; to form military alliances which bolster up very undemocratic regimes, but which seem none the less unable to win enthusiastic support from Asians; to many Australians, broadly, but not only, those of the Left, all this seems wrong-headed. There is thus a further dilemma facing Australians in their approach to the new Asia. The history of the last war has shown, beyond dispute, that Australia depends on America for her survival in a major war. But much of American policy in the East of Asia has seemed either unsound or positively contrary to Australian interests. Nor is this confined to matters concerning China and Communism.

Western New Guinea

Australia feared that Japan was being let off too lightly; although trade with Japan now flourishes, many still feel that American policy towards that country wholly ignored Australia's point of view. Indonesia has been an uneasy neighbour for Australia: her closest Asian neighbour, but unstable, with a large Communist Party, a rickety economy, and unsatisfied claims on Western New Guinea. Western New Guinea is divided from Eastern, Australian New Guinea, by a meridian of longitude, a line without reality in geographical terms, undemarcated, and unrelated to tribal boundaries or ethnic divisions. The Australians felt that if this territory was to become Indonesian just because it had been part of the Dutch Empire, then there was no reason in logic or geography why Indonesia would not claim Eastern New Guinea also. In any case they had little confidence in the ability of the Indonesian state to develop, govern and improve the trackless jungles of a most difficult region. Their own, not very clearly formulated plans for the future development of Eastern New Guinea, in which English would be the language of education and democracy the form of government, might be prejudiced by the creation of an artificial Indonesian nationalism in Western New Guinea. Therefore the Australian Government, with the support of the Opposition, and the undoubted backing of the electorate, upheld Dutch sovereignty and hoped it would continue.

President Sukarno was determined to gain Western New Guinea. When diplomacy failed he resorted to covert but increasing use of force, aided by the rearmament of his army and air force with Russian war material. It became obvious that the Dutch could not resist this pressure for long. New Guinea, and the ambitions of Indonesia in New Guinea, are questions very real to Australians. The campaign to keep the Japanese out of southern New Guinea was a heroic chapter in the war annals of Australia. Here was a matter where Australia conceived she had a vital interest at stake, where reliance on the American alliance should decide the issue, where that power was essential if Indonesian ambition was to be restrained.

But the United States of America had never taken up a defined attitude on the question of Western New Guinea. Australia had never obtained any promise from America in respect of this country, had not demanded—or had been refused—such a quid pro quo for accepting other American policies in the East of Asia. When early in 1962 it became clear that Indonesia and Holland would soon be at war, America stepped in to enforce mediation, under the chairmanship of an American diplomat. The result was an agreement which yields the territory to Indonesia, after a transitory and doubtless unreal condominium with the United Nations. By the middle of 1963 Indonesia was to be firmly in possession. Within a few months Indonesia opened her policy of confrontation directed against the new Federation of Malaysia, a policy intensified in 1964 and still continued. The Australian Government has increasingly been compelled to manifest its complete disapproval of this aggressive policy.

Possible Future Policies

Australia has three possible policies which could be pursued in respect of Asia. She could adopt a form of neutralism, sever her alliance with America by leaving the SEATO and ANZUS pacts, recognize Communist China, and thus endeavour to follow in the South-West Pacific the line which India has made her own. Such a transformation has had few advocates in Australia, and recent events in India are not likely to have made more Australians ready for such a policy.

Australia can also continue with the policy now followed by the present Liberal-Country Party coalition Government, but which the Labour Opposition would at least modify. This is to rely upon the American alliance and the British Commonwealth, with the emphasis on the American alliance. Communist China must not be recognized, although Britain does so. Australia does trade with China, travel and cultural exchange is free, but in deference to American opinion no move is made to regulate diplomatic relations, and an envoy from Formosa remains in Canberra, although no Australian mission has been established in Taipeh. The Labour Party has declared that it would recognize China, and perhaps also withdraw from or modify Australian commitments to send troops to Asia under the SEATO pact. Probaby the majority opinion in the country acknowledges that the American alliance is the only policy possible, even while increasingly recognizing that American aid is conditional on serving American interests, and that these are not always identical with Australian interests. With this recognition goes a determination to develop friendship with Asian countries in every non-political way possible. That this attitude betrays a secret doubt can hardly be concealed.

A third policy would, no doubt, be the most logical, a kind of Western Pacific counterpart of the European Community: an alliance between Australia, New Zealand and Japan, the three developed capitalist countries of the Western Pacific. The Philippines and the emergent Greater Malaysia could be also included. This combination could be strong enough to defend itself without exclusive reliance on America, and independent enough to follow its own policies where America was either not interested or not willing to take a stand in opposition to local nationalism (as in Western New Guinea).

The real obstacle to such a development is the abiding fear and hostility to Japan still very much alive in the Australian electorate. Many Australians know that this would be a solution for their dilemma, a situation which would neither compromise their friendship with the parent countries of the West nor jeopardize their hope of making lasting friends with the countries of Asia. It is politically impossible at this time, but it may well be that the logic of events and the developing power structure of post-war Asia will push Australia gradually towards this possibility.

Australia has only had to take real account of Asia since the end of the Second World War. During this period many very great changes have occurred, with extreme rapidity. It is hardly surprising if public opinion is still floundering in the wake of events, and political parties still uncertain of their footing. There is a marked cleavage between the views of the older and younger generations, many of the latter being ready to give an exaggerated mportance to relations with Asia, without taking full account of the real ties which must bind Australia to America and the West. 'Australia is part of Asia' may be a geographical fact (although not one accepted by geographers) but Australians are certainly not Asians either by descent or by culture. No attitude which ignores either the geographical propinquity, or the racial and cultural affinity, can adequately serve as an Australian response to the problems which the new Asia presents to a community of some ten million people of European descent inhabiting a continent located in the South-West Pacific.

BIBLIOGRAPHY

W. Macmahon Ball. *Nationalism and Communism in East Asia.* (Melbourne Univ. Press, Melbourne, 1952.)

John Burton. *The Alternative.* (Morgan's Publications, Sydney, 1954.)

G. Greenwood and N. Harper (ed.) *Australia in World Affairs.* (F. W. Cheshire, Melbourne, 1957.)

Donald Horne. *The Lucky Country.* (Penguin, Sydney, 1964.)

R. N. Rosecrance. *Australian Diplomacy and Japan, 1945-1951.* (Melbourne Univ. Press, Melbourne, 1961.)

BIOGRAPHICAL NOTE

C. P. Fitzgerald. B. 1902, London; educated Clifton College, Bristol. Lived in China from 1923 to 1939, with brief breaks, and for four years after the war, 1946-50. Has subsequently paid two visits to China, 1956 and 1958. Leverhulme Fellowship for anthropological research in China, 1936-39. Worked at Tali, Yunnan province. After the war representative of the British Council in North China, 1946-50. Author of many books on China, including *Birth of Communist China* (Penguin, London, 1955), *China: A Short Cultural History* (Cresset Press, London, revised ed., 1961) and *The Chinese View of their Place in the 1965 World* (The Royal Institute of International Affairs, London 1964.)

THE SOVIET ATTITUDE TOWARDS ASIA

by

G. E. WHEELER

AT THE end of the 15th century the Russians, a people of European origin who had been under Mongol domination for 250 years, were concentrated to the west of the Ural mountains. Russian penetration into Asia did not begin until 1483, but by the end of the 17th century it had spread right across Siberia to the Pacific. Early in the 18th century expansion moved southwards, and by the end of the 19th century more than one third of the total territory of Asia was under Russian domination. The population of much of the Asian territory thus occupied was sparse and was soon outnumbered by Russian settlers, except in the southern region bordering on Persia, Afghanistan and China. At the 1959 census the Asian peoples of the Soviet Union amounted only to about thirty-one million, or less than one-sixth of the total population. Thus, although a far greater part of Soviet territory lies in Asia than in Europe, the mainly European make-up of the population enables one to speak of the Soviet Union's 'attitude towards Asia'.

At the outbreak of the Revolution in 1917, Russia's imperialist aspirations in Asia had not been fully realized. These aspirations were described in a confidential report written to the Tsar in 1916 by Kuropatkin, then Governor General of Turkestan, as including the annexation of most of Northern Persia and of a large part of Western China (Northern Sinkiang), Northern Mongolia and Northern Manchuria. Russian ambitions also involved control of the Dardanelles and thus of the Eastern Mediterranean.

The Soviet conception of the 'political division' of Asia is set forth in the Soviet Geographical Encyclopaedia published in 1960. This, briefly, is as follows: *West Asia*—the Asian part of the Middle East plus Turkey and Afghanistan; *South Asia*—the Indian sub-continent including Ceylon and Nepal; *East Asia*—China, Korea and Japan; *South-East Asia*—Burma, Thailand, Cambodia, Laos, Vietnam, Malaysia, Indonesia and the Philippines; *Central Asia*—the Mongolian People's Republic, and 'parts' of China (i.e. Sinkiang and Tibet).

During the first ten years after the Revolution Soviet policy towards Asia passed quickly through two phases and entered a third one. The first phase has been described as 'the period of renunciation'. This involved the apparent abandonment of the internal and external imperialist position previously held by Russia: a declaration of 1917 accorded to all the nationalities of the former Empire absolute equality and the right to secede; other declarations and a series of treaties and agreements with Asian countries renounced all the concessions, privileges and extraterritorial rights formerly exercised by the Russian State. This new principle of renunciation was enunciated at the Second Congress of the Third International held in July and August 1920, which was followed in September of the same year by a pan-Asiatic Conference in Baku at which 37 Asian countries were represented.

The first effects of the new attitude were considerable, particularly in the countries bordering the Soviet Union: it was felt in some quarters that Russia was no longer a menace, and even that her aid might be enlisted in breaking free from the rule and restrictions on liberty and independence exercised by other imperialist powers. There is no doubt that the new principles propounded by the revolutionary leaders were informed to some extent by genuine fervour and sincerity. When, however, they found themselves confronted with the hard facts of internal government and foreign relations they were constrained to revert to the traditional lines of Russian policy and action in Asia.

It soon became clear that the actual grant of self-determination to the subject peoples of Asiatic Russia would in all probability involve the loss to the Russian State of the vital oil of Transcaucasia and the cotton of Central Asia. The early declarations about national equality and religious freedom had given rise to a movement among Muslim Communists aiming at the creation of a kind of Asian Communism which proposed to develop on lines quite different from those of Marxism-Leninism. This movement was officially condemned as 'counter-revolutionary' and rigorously suppressed. By 1924 Moscow had decided upon a new administrative structure in the more populous parts of Soviet Asia which, while affording some semblance of national self-government, would in fact keep the political, economic and military control of the Asian nationalities as firmly in the hands of the central government as it had been under Tsarist rule.

Once the new regime had gained full control of the Asian territory occupied by the Tsarist Empire, it began to concern itself with re-establishing the former spheres of Russian influence ostensibly with the object of spreading the doctrines and principles of Communism. It immediately encountered growing opposition in the form of new nationalist regimes which were of upper or middle class origin and feared the effect which Communist or Socialist doctrines might have on the illiterate masses. In the Middle East Soviet penetration was virtually brought to a halt by the strong governments which developed in Turkey and Persia and by the mandatory system established in the newly emerging Arab states. In the Far East opposition did not develop until later; but by 1930, Soviet policy in Asia began to occupy what might be called a defensive position, from which, however, it has not hesitated to advance, if only temporarily, whenever opportunity offered.

It will now be convenient to examine the course of Soviet policy in the different areas of non-Soviet Asia listed above.

West Asia[1]

In the Middle East the Soviet Government's earliest efforts were directed towards gaining control of the nationalist movements in Turkey and Persia. These efforts were unsuccessful. There was little Soviet influence in the Arab countries until after the Soviet Union's entry into the war on the side of Britain in 1941. This gave the USSR a respectable introduction to the Arab world and resulted in Soviet diplomatic representation in most of the Arab states. Until 1955, however, all the so called 'bourgeois nationalist' governments in the Middle East were classed as reactionary and as subservient to the West.

The total failure of the Soviet-organized separatist movement in Azerbaijan in 1945-46 caused a serious setback to Soviet influence in Persia and a period of strained relations ensued which was not eased until 1962. Soviet-Turkish relations followed much the same pattern: the tension which followed Soviet territorial claims on Turkey in 1945 was partly reduced in 1953 and virtually disappeared after 1960.

From 1955, and particularly after the Twentieth Party Congress in 1956, the Soviet Government changed its attitude towards 'bourgeois nationalist' governments and concentrated on supporting the so-called National Liberation movements. Exploiting the anti-British feeling which resulted from the Suez incident in 1956, the Soviet Government tried to gain control of the pan-Arab nationalist movement. But after 1958 it apparently decided to deal with the Arab states individually rather than as parts of a concerted Arab movement.

Soviet policy had made some progress in Afghanistan up to the fall of King Amanullah in 1929, when the Soviet Government made an unsuccessful attempt at military intervention on his side. After this, Soviet influence sank to a very low ebb but began to recover in the 1950s, since when technical and economic aid without any attempt at Communist propaganda or political interference has put Soviet relations with Afghanistan on a better footing than at any time since the Revolution.

South Asia

Soviet influence hardly existed in the Indian sub-continent before the legalization of the Indian Communist Party in 1942 and its progress was further delayed by Soviet failure to grasp the reality of Indian independence which ensued after the transfer of power in 1947. It was wrongly assumed that this independence was only nominal, that Nehru and the Congress Party were stooges of the British and that both India and Pakistan would remain under British control.

It was not until the early 1950s that the Soviet Government began to understand that Indian and Pakistan independence was genuine and that India was able and ready to receive Soviet technical and financial aid. At the end of 1955, Khrushchev (then First Secretary of the Communist Party) and Bulganin (then Prime Minister) toured India, Burma and

[1]Although the Middle East falls outside the scope of this book, the area must be taken into account here for complete understanding of the activities of the Soviet Union elsewhere in Asia.

Afghanistan and, after recording agreement on a wide range of international problems, made arrangements for Soviet financial aid in building a steel plant at Bhilai with an annual output of a million tons, and in a number of other projects. This aid has been steadily continued although it has never approached the proportions of aid from the West.

Up to the beginning of 1965 the Soviet Government had carefully refrained from any open expression of sympathy over the Sino-Indian frontier dispute, although India was granted some military aid by the Soviet Union. Similarly, the Soviet Union avoided taking sides on the subject of Tibet. Since the early 1950s the emphasis in Soviet propaganda directed towards India has been more on the power and progress of the Soviet Union as a state than on the advantages of Communism. Soviet concern with the Indian Communist Party appears to have diminished. No particular interest was shown either in the appointment of a Communist Government in Kerala in 1956 or in its subsequent replacement. The serious split of the Party in 1964 into pro-Soviet and pro-Chinese factions and the success of the latter in the February, 1965 Kerala elections introduced a new factor.

The Soviet attitude towards Pakistan has been much less friendly than towards India, mainly because of Pakistan's closer ties with the West. A Pakistan Communist Party was formed in 1948 but proscribed in 1954. Relations showed signs of improving in the early 1960s but their progress was complicated by the friendly attitude adopted by Pakistan towards China. Over Kashmir the Soviet Government at first adopted a pro-Indian attitude but since 1960 the blame for the impasse has been shifted from Pakistan to Britain and America.

East Asia

In the early years of the Revolution the Soviet Government had to contend with four virtually independent forces in China—the Peking Government, the Chinese revolutionaries under Sun Yat Sen operating from Canton, the Manchurian warlord General Chang Tso Lin and the provincial administration of Sinkiang. In 1924 agreements with Peking and Chang Tso Lin followed the early Soviet mood of renunciation, while at the same time securing partial Soviet control of the Chinese Eastern Railway. As a result of these agreements Soviet influence throughout China was greatly increased; but as elsewhere in Asia, the more moderate nationalist and revolutionary elements began to fear the effect of Communism on the masses, and coups staged against Soviet organizations in both north and south China resulted in the eventual collapse of Soviet influence by the end of 1927. A precarious Soviet control was maintained over the Chinese Eastern Railway, but after a serious military clash in 1931 with Japan, whose imperialist designs included the control of the whole of Manchuria, the Soviet Government sold the railway to the new Japanese puppet state of Manchukuo. The clash between Soviet and Japanese imperialism over China might have resulted in open war but for the outbreak of World War II.

After Japan's defeat in 1945 the Soviet Union's position in the Far East was better than it had ever been before. But the rapid rise of Chinese Communism and the final success of the Chinese Communist Revolution in

1949 opened an entirely new chapter in Sino-Soviet relations. It soon became apparent to both sides, and later to the world in general, that the superficial bond of a common ideology was more than counter-balanced by cultural differences and national state rivalries which lay deep in history. Some Soviet influence was maintained by Chinese dependence on Soviet technical and economic aid, but by 1960 all the Soviet technicians and advisers had been withdrawn from Chinese territory and Soviet influence in China was at an end. The state of tension between the two countries which began to develop in 1959 showed no signs of easing by the beginning of 1965 when China seemed to be challenging not only the Soviet Union's leadership of the Communist world but the whole Soviet position in Asia..

After World War II, the Soviet Union regained from Japan all the rights and territories which Russia had lost in the Russo-Japanese War of 1904; but the subsequent Soviet attitude towards Japan was conciliatory.

South-East Asia

The Soviet attitude toward South-East Asia has followed much the same pattern as elsewhere. The first phase of fostering militant revolution came to an end in 1927; but a new 'forward policy' emerged in 1935 which was directed towards obtaining support in the South-East Asian countries against Russia's traditional enemy Japan. After the defeat of Japan, the Soviet Union lent its support to the series of Communist insurrections which broke out in Burma, Malaya and Indonesia. After the end of the Korean War the Soviet Union began to represent itself as the promoter of international peace as opposed to the South-East Asia Treaty Organization organized by the West which was represented as intent on war. The Bandung Conference of 1955, although not primarily anti-Western in its inspiration, offered opportunities for Communist exploitation. Since, however, the Soviet Union did not qualify for participation in the Conference as an Asian state, China was able to draw ahead of the Soviet Union in what came to be known as the Bandung Movement.

As a result of the Twentieth Party Congress of 1956 traditional Soviet policy of support for revolutionary movements began to be replaced by one of support for 'bourgeois nationalist' governments in their alleged 'national-liberation' struggle against the West. Indonesia has so far been the largest recipient in South-East Asia of Soviet economic and technical aid, but aid projects have also been undertaken in Burma, Ceylon and Cambodia. In spite of the widening of the Sino-Soviet rift since 1962 and China's obvious interest in bringing pressure on the uncommitted countries of South-East Asia, there had been no open manifestation of Soviet-Chinese rivalry in this area up to the beginning of 1965.

Central Asia

Outer Mongolia, or the Mongolian People's Republic, is the only region on the Asian mainland where Russia's traditional aspirations have been to some extent realized. Although the first Soviet military intervention in Mongolia in 1921 was with Chinese consent, China later objected strongly to the sovietization of Mongolia and under the 1924 agreement the Soviet Union recognized it as an integral part of China. China recognized Mongolia's independence in 1945 and this recognition was confirmed by the Communist Government in 1950. Soviet influence is still strong, but since the development of the Sino-Soviet rift Mongolia has become even more precariously poised between the two powers.

After the Russian Revolution, Soviet economic control over the province of Sinkiang greatly increased and at various times Soviet armed forces entered the province at the request of the Chinese Governor in order to quell revolts by the predominantly Muslim population. After the reassertion of Chinese Central Government control in 1942, Soviet influence began to decline. A commercial agreement with the Chinese Communist Government in 1951 seemed to assure continuation of Soviet economic privileges. By 1964, however, all Soviet consuls and other representatives had been withdrawn and Russian influence in Sinkiang stood lower than at any time since the signing of the Treaty of Peking in 1860.

The Soviet Government has always refrained from expressing any opinion on the Chinese seizure of Tibet; but on Soviet maps Tibet is still shown as an integral part of China.

General Policy of the Soviet Government

From the above it will be seen that while the Soviet Union has improved her position in the Pacific by the acquisition from Japan of the southern half of Sakhalin and the Kurile Islands, her territorial position on the Asian mainland has not changed except in the creation of a satellite state in Mongolia. On the other hand, by the beginning of 1965 the Soviet Union's prestige as a powerful, and even as a beneficent state had greatly increased in many of the independent countries of Asia. Since 1956 the ostensible Soviet attitude towards national governments, whether 'bourgeois' or otherwise, has been one of respect coupled in many instances with effective economic and technical aid. Such governments are still urged to pursue anti-Western policies, but these are not now regarded as a pre-requisite for good relations with the Soviet Union.

Since 1956 or even earlier, Soviet moral and material support of local Communist Parties as a spearhead of revolution has been greatly reduced. The recent splitting of some of these Parties into pro-Soviet and pro-Chinese factions has restricted their potential value as Fifth Columns. Soviet propaganda in Asian countries is nowadays conducted independently of these Communist Parties and is concerned more with the positive achievements of the Soviet regime than with the advantages of Communism. An important contribution to the advancement of Soviet policy is being made by the intensive study of Asian political, cultural and economic affairs conducted in Soviet academic institutions.

In general it can be said that the present Soviet attitude towards Asia is one of extending Soviet national interests by peaceful means coupled with the recognition of existing frontiers and governments. This situation has been brought about by various factors; the realization that subversion and armed intervention do not as a rule pay; opposition by the Western powers; the Soviet Union's improved economic condition; and the assumption by China of the Soviet Union's earlier role of Communist aggressor and fisher in troubled waters. This does not mean that formal Soviet support of working-class movements in Asian countries has been or will shortly be discontinued. Nor does it mean that outside action, and particularly by China, might not bring about a reversion to former Soviet methods.

BIBLIOGRAPHY

J. H. Brimmell. *Communism in South East Asia.* (Oxford Univ. Press, London, 1959.)

D. J. Dallin. *The Rise of Russia in Asia.* (Hollis and Carter, London, 1950.)

W. Z. Laqueur. *The Soviet Union and the Middle East.* (Routledge and Kegan Paul, London, 1959.)

Prince Andrei A. Lobanov-Rostovsky. *Russia and Asia.* (Univ. of Michigan Press, Ann Arbor, 1951.)

G. D. Overstreet and M. Windmiller. *Communism in India.* (Univ. of California Press, Berkeley and Los Angeles, 1959.)

G. E. Wheeler. *The Modern History of Soviet Central Asia.* (Weidenfeld and Nicolson, London, 1964.)

A. S. Whiting. *Sinkiang: Pawn or Pivot?* (Michigan State Univ. Press, East Lansing, 1958.)

BIOGRAPHICAL NOTE

GEOFFREY WHEELER. Director of the Central Asian Research Centre, London, since 1953. Served for 33 years in the Army and Indian Political Service; Counsellor in the British Embassy in Tehran, 1946-50. Author of *Racial Problems in Soviet Muslim Asia* (Oxford Univ. Press, 2nd ed., 1962) and Joint Editor of *Central Asian Review.*

THE SINO-SOVIET CONFLICT

by

DAVID FLOYD

IN 1949 Mao Tse-tung led his peasant armies to final victory over the Kuomintang, and on 1st October he proclaimed the establishment of the People's Republic of China. On the very next day the Soviet Government announced its recognition of Mao's Communist regime, and Russia's satellites in Eastern Europe and Asia quickly followed suit. With the addition of China's 600 millions the 'socialist camp' had more than trebled in size overnight.

THE TREATY OF FRIENDSHIP

Before 1949 was out Mao had arrived in Moscow for talks with Stalin, and on 14th February, 1950 the two leaders concluded a 30-year Treaty of Friendship, Alliance and Mutual Assistance. That these two great nations bestriding Europe and Asia, both now committed to the cause of Communism, should link themselves together for their mutual advantage seemed an entirely natural development. Indeed, to a world already bemused by the post-war advance of Communism into Europe, its extension to the shores of the Pacific seemed to be part of an inevitable process. The Sino-Soviet alliance seemed to be based on the surest of foundations and in 1950 few people would have forecasted that it would have crumbled in less than a decade.

But it is now known that major differences of opinion on policy had developed between Moscow and Peking by 1956, that there was serious conflict between the Russian and Chinese Communist parties by the end of 1957, and that by the summer of 1959 relations between the Soviet and Chinese Governments had reached deadlock. In the course of 1960 the conflict and rivalry between Russians and Chinese came into the open for all to see, and since then relations between the two Governments and Parties have steadily worsened in a welter of mutual recrimination and open hostility. Out of the torrent of words hurled between Moscow and Peking after 1960 it is now possible to trace with some precision the course of Sino-Soviet relations since 1950.

The meeting between Mao and Stalin at the beginning of 1950 was not a meeting of old friends. Stalin had based his policy towards China ever since the twenties on support for the Nationalist Kuomintang led by Chiang Kai-shek and had steadily discouraged the Chinese Communists from attempting to seize power, doubtless foreseeing the problems that a strong Communist regime in China would create for the Soviet Union. But Mao chose to ignore Stalin's advice, trusting in his own judgment and ability. In 1950, therefore, Stalin had no choice but to accept the situation with as good a grace as he could muster, and Mao had no one else to whom he could turn for the aid he needed urgently for the restoration of China's battered economy. The alliance was at best a *mariage de convenance*.

Stalin's policy towards his new ally was primarily one of containment, and he treated this country of 600 millions in basically the same way as he had treated the nations of Eastern Europe which Soviet armies overran at the end of the war. It took Mao two months to obtain Stalin's agreement to a niggardly loan of 300 million dollars spread over five years and his promise to withdraw Russian troops from Manchuria, Port Arthur and Dairen by the end of 1952. And Mao had to accept Russia's continued presence in Sinkiang and her control of Outer Mongolia.

Within months of the signing of the 1950 Treaty, war broke out in Korea. This conflict dominated the situation for the remainder of Stalin's life, pushed the question of Sino-Soviet relations into the background and involved the Chinese in a military effort so costly as to outweigh any aid the Russians may have been able to give the Chinese economy.

The Post-Stalin Period

When Stalin died in 1953 his successors took immediate steps to reduce tension in Soviet relations with the rest of the world, Communist and non-Communist. They went out of their way to raise the Chinese leaders to equality of status within the Communist world; they increased the scope of their economic aid; they undertook to eliminate the Soviet military presence in China and to dissolve the Sino-Soviet mixed companies which Stalin had set up. They made a visible effort to appease the Chinese.

The period from 1954 to 1959 was in fact the heyday of the Sino-Soviet alliance. Under Khrushchev's rule the Soviet Government made a substantial contribution towards the expansion of the Chinese economy, and by the beginning of 1959 was committed to the construction in China of over 200 industrial plants and to the supply of industrial equipment costing almost £1,000 millions. This was to provide the basis of China's industrialization and represented a considerable diversion of effort by the hard-pressed Soviet economy, apparently accepted by Khrushchev as the price which Russia had to pay to maintain the 'unity' of the Communist world and her own leadership of it. What he did not expect was that the Chinese would regard the economic aid as no more than the Soviet Union's fulfilment of her 'proletarian duty' and that they would still expect to have a major say in the formation of policy in the Communist world.

At the beginning of 1956 the Soviet Communist Party held its 20th Congress at which Khrushchev proclaimed his revision of Communist teaching on the subjects of war and revolution. This was the ideological basis for reducing the militancy of Communist policy in the nuclear age. On the same occasion Khrushchev made his violent denunciation of Stalin, presumably to underline the extent of the Soviet Union's break with the policies of the past. There was some opposition to Khrushchev's 'revisionism' within his own party, but in the summer of 1957 he eliminated his main opponents and from the beginning of 1958 appeared to be in complete control.

The Chinese leaders quickly let it be known that they disagreed with Khrushchev. On more than one occasion in 1956 Mao Tse-tung told the Russians that he considered Khrushchev's assessment of Stalin to be mistaken and that 'Stalin's merits outweighed his faults'. Also in 1956 the Chinese published two major theoretical articles in which they offered a more balanced assessment of Stalin's role and took Marshal Tito, the Yugoslav leader, to task for his opposition to 'Stalinist elements' in other Communist parties. Such an attitude, the Chinese said, could lead only to 'a split in the Communist movement'. The Russians thus found themselves in the position of having assumed responsibility for the industrialization of a vast, backward country, the leaders of which, far from acknowledging their backwardness and dependence, seemed bent on dictating policy to their benefactor. The more the Russians gave, the more demanding the Chinese became.

The Moscow Conference of World Communist Parties, 1957

The first major confrontation between the Russian and Chinese leaders took place at the Moscow meeting of the world's Communist parties in November 1957, which was also the first international meeting of Communist leaders since the Second World War and which was intended to set the stamp of approval on Khrushchev's new strategy. The importance of the meeting was heightened by the facts that it coincided with the 40th anniversary of the Russian Revolution and that the Russians had just launched their first space satellite.

The Chinese delegation to the conference was led by Mao Tse-tung himself, who showed no disposition at all to accept Khrushchev's ideas of 'peaceful coexistence' and 'peaceful transition to socialism'. On the contrary, he saw in Soviet nuclear power and in the advance of Communism every reason for greater, not less, militancy. On the eve of the conference Mao had extracted from the Soviet Government an undertaking to assist China in the acquisition of an atomic weapon—the prize, presumably, which Khrushchev had to pay for Mao's continued maintenance of the façade of 'unity'. For Mao, it meant that the 'East Wind' was now unquestionably stronger than the 'West Wind'.

The Chinese did their best to impress their views on the conference. But they did not command sufficient influence among the other Communist parties, and they had to content themselves with some concessions to their views in the final Declaration. At that stage the Chinese had everything to gain from keeping the movement united. Mao could not hope to assume leadership of the movement, and he was quite ready to acknowledge Soviet priority, so long as he could influence policy and so long as the flow of Soviet economic and military aid continued.

The End of the Alliance

1958 was probably the critical year in the development of Sino-Soviet relations—the year in which the Russians realized clearly what Mao's aims were. Khrushchev made a hasty visit to Peking in July for a meeting with Mao which produced a brief détente between the two countries. Though neither side has revealed what happened in 1958, it seems probable that Mao was pressing for Soviet support for an assault on Formosa and that Khrushchev refused. Nevertheless, or perhaps as a form of compensation or reassurance, Khrushchev committed the Soviet Union to giving the Chinese further substantial economic aid in February 1959.

But according to the Chinese account (which the Russians have not denied), on 20th June 1959 the Soviet Government formally revoked the Agreement on Technology for National Defence under which it had undertaken *inter alia* to provide the Chinese with a sample atomic bomb. At some point in the first half of 1959, therefore, the Soviet Government must have taken a decision, not only to withhold atomic weapons and atomic know-how from the Chinese (for they had, as far as we know, not honoured their undertaking of 1957), but to make it clear to the Chinese that they had no prospects of ever receiving such aid from the Soviet Union. What exactly persuaded the Russians to take this step is still not clear, though it must be assumed they became convinced that, if the Chinese once acquired atomic weapons, they would inevitably supplant the Russians as leaders of the world revolution and possibly embroil the Communist world in conflict with the West. Whatever the reasons for it, the decision of 20th June 1959 marked the end of the alliance. It indicated a degree of mutual distrust which made the alliance meaningless and a further development of the conflict inevitable.

Events followed quickly in 1959. At the Lushan Plenum of the Chinese Communist Party in August Marshal Peng Teh-huai and other leading Chinese Communists believed to be pro-Soviet and to have opposed Mao's line were dismissed. In September the Chinese invaded the territory of India, a country with which Khrushchev had made great efforts to improve relations. Placed in a dilemma by the Chinese action, the Soviet Government issued a carefully worded statement which fell far short of supporting their Chinese allies in their adventure. Later in the month Khrushchev, fresh from talks with President Eisenhower in America, went to Peking for what proved to be his last meeting with Mao Tse-tung. At the end of his visit, which was obviously unproductive, he spoke publicly of the dangers of 'testing by force the stability of the capitalist system'. Khrushchev had apparently provoked Mao's ire by urging on him the desirability of seeking a peaceful solution of the Formosa problem and accepting a 'two Chinas' policy, which was heresy to the Chinese Communists.

By the beginning of 1960, therefore, the Russians and Chinese were visibly at odds over two major issues—the Sino-Indian border and Formosa—and each side began to make public statements clearly aimed at rallying support for its own view. At meetings of the Warsaw Pact Organization and the World Federation of Trade Unions the Chinese delegates advocated policies manifestly at variance with Khrushchev's 'peaceful coexistence'. And in April, on the 90th anniversary of Lenin's birth, the Chinese published a long doctrinal article entitled 'Long Live Leninism!' which in effect outlined their objections to Khrushchev's 'revisionism' and depicted the Chinese as the defenders of the pure Communist faith. Khrushchev replied to the Chinese criticisms in a speech to the Third Congress of the Rumanian Communist Party in Bucharest in June 1960. He restated his contention that the future of the world depended to a large extent on relations between Russia and America, and he ridiculed those who merely repeated Lenin's words without taking account of changes in the world situation. As far as the outside world was concerned the Russians and Chinese were still shadow-boxing; but in fact they were already engaged in active rivalry. Khrushchev tried to turn the Rumanian congress into an international conference which would approve the Russian line and condemn the Chinese. But the Chinese delegate, Peng Chen, put up a vigorous opposition which led to hard words being exchanged between him and Khrushchev. The latter's failure to carry the day led to the summoning of another world conference—the meeting of 81 Communist parties—in Moscow in November 1960.

The Widening Rift and the Fall of Khrushchev

While relations between the parties were steadily deteriorating in increasingly heated 'ideological' exchanges, relations between the Chinese and Soviet governments were also increasing in tension. By the summer of 1960 the flow of Russian technicians and their families leaving China had reached such proportions as to make it apparent that the Russians were severely curtailing their economic aid. By 1961 the volume of Soviet exports to China had dropped to little more than one-third of the 1959 level.

At the meeting of the 81 parties in Moscow in November 1960 there was no longer any attempt to conceal the extent of the gulf between the Russian and Chinese points of view. The leaders of the more important parties were drawn into the debate, which dragged on throughout the month. The Chinese made an uncompromising bid for the leadership of the whole Communist movement and were outspoken in their criticisms of what they regarded as the Russians' attempt to impose their views and policies on world Communism. Although the conference eventually managed to produce an enormously long and verbose statement of policy which attempted to paper over the cracks and satisfy both sides to the dispute, neither side had any illusions about the question of Sino-Soviet 'unity'.

Subsequent developments were not concerned with the restoration of 'unity' but with manoeuvring by both sides over the form which their split should take. The Chinese maintained a flow of polemics which increased steadily in frankness, and they gloated openly about Khrushchev's setback in the Cuban crisis at the end of 1962. The Russians were on the whole less vocal, though they organized public heckling of Chinese delegates to various international meetings in 1963. This public squabbling became so embarrassing to the rest of the Communist leaders that pressure grew for efforts to be made towards a reconciliation. After much hesitation on the part of both Russians and Chinese and further acrimonious polemics, representatives of the Chinese and Russian Communist parties met in Moscow in July 1963 for discussions in which, as far as is known, both sides simply repeated the views which they had aired *ad nauseam* already.

The meeting was suspended *sine die:* the Russians and Chinese had nothing more to say to each other.

Following the failure of the 1963 meeting the Chinese continued their anti-Soviet polemics, which were aimed ever more directly at the person of Khrushchev, and intensified their efforts to win the support of other Communist parties, especially in Asia. Meanwhile Khrushchev became committed to the idea of holding a further international conference, at which he hoped for condemnation of the Chinese. A preliminary meeting was called for December 1964, but Khrushchev fell from power some weeks before it was due to take place, and one of the reasons for his fall was undoubtedly the *impasse* into which he had led the Russians in their handling of the Chinese. His successors eventually held the 'preparatory' meeting in March 1965, but without the Chinese and their supporters. The meeting was clearly only a face-saving operation which did nothing to reduce Sino-Soviet tension or to further the unity of the Communist movement. It did, however, demonstrate that the Chinese Communists had a substantial, if not decisive, following among the world's Communists and that the Communist movement had in fact already split into Eastern and Western parts.

Khrushchev's successors, Brezhnev and Kosygin, revealed some desire at least to 'normalize' relations with China and appeared ready to increase the volume of trade exchanges. But the Chinese soon realized that the new leaders had no intention of abandoning the general line of Khrushchevian 'peaceful coexistence' or of accepting Chinese guidance in matters of foreign policy. It was not long therefore before the Chinese were denouncing them with almost the same ferocity as they had denounced Khrushchev himself. If Khrushchev had mishandled the Chinese tactically, his 'general line' was no mere personal whim but was rooted deep in the history of relations between Russia and China.

The Sino-Soviet Border

At the end of 1962 Khrushchev, stung by the Chinese Communists' criticisms of his handling of the Cuban crisis, reproached the Chinese for the 'patience' with which they accepted the continued occupation of Hong Kong and Macao by 'imperialist' powers. This provoked the Chinese to remind the Russians that Britain and Portugal were not the only powers that had imposed 'unequal treaties' on China in the past: Tsarist Russia had also carried out 'unbridled aggression' against China. But it was the policy of Peking to maintain the status quo until conditions were judged ripe for the treaties to be renegotiated. Was it really the Russians' intention, the Chinese asked, to raise all the questions of unequal treaties? 'Has it ever entered your heads what the consequences would be?' With these ominous words a new element—the question of the 4,000-mile Sino-Soviet border—was introduced publicly into the dispute between the two nations.

In fact, according to the Russians, the Chinese had raised the question of Soviet territorial acquisitions much earlier. On his visit to Moscow in 1957 Chou En-lai was said to have told Khrushchev that 'the Soviet Union had taken too much territory, ranging from Japan in the East to China, the Middle East, Eastern Europe and Finland'. But it was not until 1963 that there was any suggestion that the two countries might come to blows over territorial issues.

The area of potential dispute is large. In the course of centuries of expansion eastwards, Russia had taken some 700,000 square miles of territory formerly claimed by China. By the Treaty of Peking (1850) alone, China ceded 133,000 square miles of territory to Russia, and the Treaty of Aigun (1858) accounted for another 185,000 square miles. As late as 1954 a map appeared in a Chinese text-book showing the Maritime Province of the Soviet Union and large parts of Soviet Central Asia as Chinese territory.

At about the same time public tension increased on both sides of the Sino-Soviet border. In September 1963 the Chinese accused the Russians of conducting 'large-scale subversive activities' in the Ili region of Sinkiang and of forcing tens of thousands of Chinese citizens to go to the Soviet Union. The Russians alleged in reply that the Chinese had been violating the Soviet frontier systematically since 1960.

The question of the frontier was raised again in the acrimonious polemics of 1964, when the Chinese reaffirmed their willingness to reach a negotiated settlement on the basis of the existing treaties, but accused the Russians of stirring up trouble in the frontier areas. The Soviet attitude was that any points of dispute along the frontier were of a minor nature and could be easily settled. For this purpose a Soviet delegation went to Peking in February 1964, but apparently failed to reach any agreement with the Chinese, who were reported to have tabled claims to 580,000 square miles of Soviet territory.

Mao Tse-tung himself put new heat into the dispute in July 1964 when, in conversation with Japanese journalists, he accused the Soviet Union roundly of expansionism and added: 'About 100 years ago the area east of Baikal became Russian territory and since then Vladivostok, Khabarovsk, Kamchatka and other places have been Soviet territory. We have not yet requested a settling of this account. As for the Kurile Islands, this question is clear for us. They must be returned to Japan.' Mao also accused the Soviet Union of taking Mongolia under its control and of concentrating troops on the Chinese border. Whatever the Chinese intention in raising these questions, there were signs that the Soviet Union did not treat them lightly. In 1963 Soviet frontier guards along the whole of the border with China appear to have been reorganized and steps taken to improve defences against a possible Chinese attack.

Towards the end of 1964 a map was published in China which for the first time showed over 1,000 miles of frontier between Manchuria and the Far Eastern territories of the Soviet Union as being undefined. The Chinese clearly had no intention of letting the territorial question drop, even though they were careful to stress that their claims were long-term and to avoid backing them by a threat of force. Their immediate object appeared to be to exploit the situation to the maximum discomfiture of the Soviet Union rather than to recover actual territory.

Rival Powers

Thus by 1965 the Soviet Union and China confronted each other as two rival imperialist powers, rather than as two 'progressive', liberating Communist powers jointly committed to the overthrow of 'Western imperialism'. The Russians were preoccupied with their own internal problems—the problems of a backward nation that had been industrialized too quickly—and with the problem of holding their East European empire together. The Chinese already had a substantial following in Asia and had begun to look to the West for the economic aid which they knew would not be forthcoming from the Russians. Despite some resumption of trade between the two countries, relations between the Soviet Union and China were in 1965 minimal, strictly formal and governmental. If it seemed unlikely that the Soviet and Chinese leaders would be so misguided as to allow their relations to descend to the level of open conflict, there seemed little hope that any real warmth would be restored to their relations or that real life could be injected into the framework of the Treaty of 1950.

History had proved to be stronger than ideology, which alone would have made Russians and Chinese natural allies. But history made them natural rivals, and that is what they remain.

BIBLIOGRAPHY

Max Beloff. *The Foreign Policy of Soviet Russia, 1929-1941.* (Oxford Univ. Press, London, 1949.) *Soviet Policy in the Far East, 1944-1951.* (Oxford Univ. Press, London, 1953.)

Howard L. Boorman and others. *Moscow-Peking Axis: Strengths and Strains.* (Harper Brothers, New York, 1957.)

Robert R. Bowie and John K. Fairbank (eds.) *Communist China, 1955-1959: Policy Documents with Analysis.* (Harvard Univ. Press, Cambridge, Mass., 1962.)

Zbigniew K. Brzezinski. *The Soviet Bloc: Unity and Conflict.* (Praeger, New York, 1961.)

Edward Crankshaw. *The New Cold War: Moscow v. Peking.* (Penguin, London, 1963.)

David Floyd. *Mao against Khrushchev. A Short History of the Sino-Soviet Conflict.* (Pall Mall Press, London and Dunmow, 1964.)

William E. Griffith. *The November 1960 Meeting: A Preliminary Reconstruction.* (The China Quarterly, London, 1962.)

Alice Langley Hsieh. *Communist China's Strategy in the Nuclear Era.* (Prentice-Hall, New Jersey, 1962.)

G. F. Hudson, Richard Lowenthal and Roderick MacFarquhar. *The Sino-Soviet Dispute (Documents and Commentaries).* (The China Quarterly, London, 1961.)

J. M. Mackintosh. *Strategy and Tactics of Soviet Foreign Policy.* (Oxford Univ. Press, London, 1962.)

Klaus Mehnert. *Peking and Moscow.* (Weidenfeld and Nicolson, London, 1964).

Günther Nollau. *International Communism and World Revolution: History and Methods.* (Praeger, New York, 1961; Hollis and Carter, London, 1961.)

Harry Schwartz. *Tsars, Mandarins and Commissars.* (Gollancz, London, 1964.)

Donald S. Zagoria. *The Sino-Soviet Conflict 1956-1961.* (Princeton Univ. Press, New Jersey, 1962.)

BIOGRAPHICAL NOTE

David Floyd. B. 1914; educated at Oxford University. After military service in the Second World War, which took him to Moscow, he served in the British embassies in Moscow, Prague and Belgrade. In 1952 he joined the staff of the London *Daily Telegraph* to deal with the affairs of the Communist world and has made frequent visits to Russia and the Communist countries of Eastern and Southern Europe. Author of *Mao Against Khrushchev: A Short History of the Sino-Soviet Conflict* (Pall Mall Press, London and Dunmow, 1964) and *Rumania: Russia's Dissident Ally* (Pall Mall Press, 1965), and of some translations from the Russian.

A WHITE RUSSIAN VIEW OF COMMUNIST CHINA[1]

by

EUGENE BAJKOWSKI

SOME of the most authentic and objective reports on living conditions on the Chinese mainland and relations between Peking and Moscow have come from the relatively large groups of 'White' Russian refugees who were allowed to leave Manchuria for the free world in 1962-63. Considerable numbers have been resettled in Australia with the assistance of the Commonwealth and State Governments and the Australian Council of Churches.

Not all the Russian refugees are willing to speak about their experiences under the Communist Government in China. But the ones that have shaken off the haunting fears of Communist vengeance—and who have no relatives or close friends left behind—have provided one of the most valuable sources of information about China in recent years.

Most of these Russian refugees had settled down in Manchuria shortly after the Russian Revolution. Most of the older generation—including a very large proportion of Amur, Transbaikalian and Orhenburgh Cossacks—had fought in the defeated White Armies during the long and bitter years of the Russian Civil War, which had not ended in the Far East until the beginning of 1924. The younger age groups were born in Manchuria and had lived there all their lives.

Although there was relatively little intermarriage between the Russian settlers and the Chinese population, racial relations were on the whole good. It is interesting to note that the Russian refugees who were able to leave Manchuria in 1962-63 bear no grudges against the Chinese as a people, despite the fact that they had been persecuted for years by the Chinese Communist authorities and had lost all their property in Manchuria. On the whole the persistent efforts of the Peking authorities to incite the local population against Russian settlers in the rural areas in Manchuria have been unsuccessful. The Communists had more success in the industrial centre of Harbin and some smaller cities and towns. Here the large influx of destitute peasants, originally brought in to expand the industrial labour force, made it easier for the Communist authorities to blame everything on the 'White Devils'. A large proportion of the hastily created new industrial labour force had come from central and northern China where there had been little contact with foreigners over the past twelve years.

As relations between the Soviet Union and Communist China gradually

[1] See *Note* on page 550.

deteriorated after the death of Stalin the Chinese Communist 'cadres' began using Soviet specialists, technicians and advisers as scapegoats for all the shortages and deficiencies which had developed after the collapse of ambitious industrialization and collectivization drives.

Although in some cases Soviet advisers were responsible for occasional breakdown and planning errors they were on the whole good technicians. However, it was relatively easy to direct the mounting resentment of the Chinese city masses against them because of the vast difference in pay scales and the standard of living. This resentment was then indiscriminately transferred to the 'White' Russians, who were normally somewhat better off than the Chinese population. Anti-foreign agitation and calculated exploitation of traditional Chinese national prejudices and phobias were an established policy of the Peking regime.

Descriptions given by Russian refugees from Manchuria often add colour to previous reports. The effects of the 'pig-iron drive' of 1958-59, during which much of the rural labour force left the fields to produce pig-iron in small clay stoves, have been described by many.

A highly qualified Russian accountant—a former businessman with a prosperous export-import firm built-up from scratch after settling down in Harbin in the early twenties—describes how all city transport was suspended in this great Manchurian industrial centre. Factory workers had to walk to and from their jobs because buses, lorries and even pushbikes were worked round the clock bringing in iron ore, scrap metal and firewood from the outer suburbs and adjoining rural areas to district and block 'foundries'. Streets were dug up in search of iron ore and metal scraps. Parties of young 'cadres' roamed the city streets pulling out metal doors, window frames, collecting pots and pans, taking down iron roofs, confiscating metal objects from private dwellings. Work on all other city projects had stopped and iron and steel girders from new building sites were pulled down and tossed into the smelting pots, sometimes replaced by great bonfires. A heavy smog hung over the city, causing a large number of deaths. Most city stores stopped trading and supplies of food and essential articles rapidly dwindled. Schools were closed down. University lectures were suspended as students and professors dug and smelted and stoked the fires. The only iron grills left untouched were those in the closely guarded city gaols. But the prisoners were deprived of their tin mugs and plates.

Within a month Harbin had the look of a city stricken by a hurricane and stripped by an invading army. Thousands of houses stood partly roofless, glass from broken windows mixed with refuse on the streets. All wooden fences, benches and many telephone poles were gone. Bursts of wind stirred up clouds of ash dust, polluting fresh water supplies. Railway stations were stripped of all 'surplus' wooden or iron equipment. Streets were dug up and filled with rain water. Parks were criss-crossed with uneven trenches. All the trees in the area were cut down, and still the madness continued.

The Lost Harvest

Field work was practically suspended and peasants were being driven from early morning to late at night digging and smelting. Irrigation work was neglected. When harvest time came Peking ordered that field work be limited to reaping essential food grains. Everything else was to be covered by a thin layer of earth and left in the fields for a fortnight.

This was tragic for Manchuria and north China, which had a bumper harvest of Chinese cabbages, cucumbers, sweet potatoes and pumpkins. The central authorities in Peking did not bother to instruct the local 'cadres' to adapt their instructions to local climatic conditions. China is a vast country with large variations in climate, and when Peking realized its error it was too late to save the crops, which form part of the staple diet for Manchuria and most of north China.

The first winter frosts were early and severe and the bumper harvest was all but lost. Since all labour in the communes was directed by military-like 'command posts' controlled by the local and district 'cadres' no one was allowed to make any prior arrangements for food supplies.

The Peking authorities then suspended the pig-iron drive in the central and southern areas and rushed labour into the fields. A large proportion of the non-grain crops was harvested and attempts were made to rush them to the north, where famines began. But China's weak communications system could not stand the double strain of the pig-iron drive and rushed food deliveries. Bottle-necks developed and a large proportion of the harvested crops rotted away near railway sidings or in storage heaps. The local population was not allowed to use them, as they were earmarked for deliveries to city centres and relief supplies.

Transport bottlenecks also frustrated the scheduled delivery of winter clothing to the peasants in the 'people's communes'. Russian settlers have described how entire villages rapidly died of hunger or were frozen to death during the bitterly cold nights. An elderly Russian farmer who lived near the Manchurian centre of Mailar described how eighty hungry villagers in a small rural commune with 110 members died during a winter night huddled together for warmth around a makeshift storehouse with some grain and half-frozen vegetables, a bit of winter clothing and straw. The storehouse was guarded by a platoon of the 'public security army' armed with rifles. Most were in their summer uniforms and the villagers, too weak to rush them, had vainly hoped they would be driven away by the bitter cold.

In the morning the guard—which had several cases of severe frostbite—was relieved by a fresh and adequately clothed unit which remained in the village for several days and prevented the survivors from removing the clothing of their dead relatives. This 'belonged to the people'.

A number of riots flared up in Manchuria but they were quickly suppressed. On the whole the people were too hungry and too weak to offer any sustained opposition. The Government advised them to eat grass and certain roots, but only after feeding the farm animals. Slaughter of farm animals was punishable by death. A number of communes had pigs. These, too, died as there was no food for them and disease broke out when the villagers began eating carrion.

Then the campaign was suddenly called off and a new series of purges started. When the first shipments of 'home-made iron' reached the great Anshan steelworks in Manchuria, it was soon discovered the entire effort was wasted. The quality of home-baked pig iron was far too poor for steel smelting. It was too poor even for re-smelting into higher-grade pig iron. The same experience was repeated in Mukden, Kaileng, Lunghai, Henyang, Changsha, Shanghai, Nanking, Wuchang and other industrial centres in Manchuria and China proper.

Many heads billed as scapegoats were eagerly sought out by the Communist leaders. But this failed to stem the flood of other tragedies that followed.

Famine and Disease

Much of the grain crop in the year of the pig-iron drive was used for sowing or had to be exported to the USSR in payment for China's mounting industrialization debts. Industrial workers in the major cities were put on reduced rations. All free sale of food was prohibited.

The rural population was put on a monthly ration of 26 pounds (din) of coarse corn flour and about an ounce of vegetable oil a month. Children received less. Even as a theoretical ration this was almost below the subsistence level—but not infrequently this could not be drawn as supplies failed. The village storehouses were emptied by the Government long before.

Russian refugees are careful to point out that they were much better off than their Chinese neighbours. Despite persistent and often brutal police reprisals, they did not join the 'people's communes' and were allowed a certain minimum of private property.

Normally they were allowed to keep as much land and as many domestic animals as a Chinese village commune of roughly the same area and population. Their property was not pooled as was the case with the Chinese. Remaining outside the communes the Russian farmers had more freedom in their work. They had to deliver fixed quotas of their produce but not their entire output as the Chinese village communes.

An average Russian family was allowed to keep one cow, one horse, several pigs and chickens, perhaps a goat. Any additions to the quota—such as calves—had to be surrendered at a fixed price paid in cash, which was valueless in rural areas without ration forms.

Another important concession was exemption from the long morning and evening political meetings and freedom from exhausting militia training and military discipline.

Their isolation from the world was pretty complete. People who had wireless sets were often gaoled and reading any non-Chinese newspapers—not only the Soviet press but even the Chinese-sponsored Russian language news-sheet issued in Harbin—was actively discouraged. Travel outside the immediate vicinity of the settlement was prohibited. Any trip to a district centre or to Harbin required a special visa. Strangely, mail was not normally interfered with although it was often late. On the whole police observation was intense and contact with the Chinese often dangerous because of the Communist police's 'rumour-mongering' mania. Such a charge could bring up to ten years of forced labour—and death for a Chinese. There was no supply of new clothing. Even the coarse blue cloth could only be purchased in cities and the rural population, including the Russians, had to have special permits to buy it. The annual cloth ration was three yards a person.

HARBIN, SHENYANG (MUKDEN) AND OTHER TOWNS IN MANCHURIA

Following the collapse of agricultural production in 'people's communes' famine conditions soon spread to Harbin, Shenyang (Mukden), Hailar, Tsitsihar and other large centres in Manchuria (officially designated by the Chinese as the North-Eastern Provinces—Tung-Pei).

Transport difficulties caused by the 'pig-iron drive' were aggravated by large scale floods, particularly in the Sungari and Noni river valleys. Sungari floods often reached the proportions of a major disaster with bridges washed away by the fast-moving brownish water and numerous villages flooded. Fresh water supplies were polluted and all drinking water had to be boiled.

The Ministry of Communications decided to cancel special transport priorities for deliveries of home-made pig iron ingots to the steelworks, but food supplies—particularly from the Central-Eastern and South-Eastern Provinces—were held up by the floods. Air transport facilities provided by the People's Liberation Army Air Force and the Chinese National Airways Corporation were wholly inadequate.

At first the trickle of food brought to city centres under heavy security troops guard was supplemented by issues from local stockpiles. Industrial workers had priority, followed by the local Russian population (Soviet experts were, of course, in a special category) and a handful of Poles, Czechs and other foreigners still living in Manchurian towns. The Association of Soviet Citizens (which compulsorily federated all 'White' Russians holding so-called 'Sovzagranvids'—in effect second-class passports, which were of little practical value) was allowed to have its own bakery in Harbin, supplied from State grain stores with a small but regular grain ration. Black markets flourished despite exorbitant prices and severe penalties. Army and police units, however, were given adequate food rations, ensuring their loyalty to the Government.

Russian migrants have reported that at this stage dismissal from the Communist armed or police forces became almost as severe a punishment as the death sentence. A dismissed soldier usually starved in disgrace and many preferred suicide.

By 1961 all Manchuria was in the grip of famine. The pig iron and 'people's communes' debacle and continuous severe floods foiled all attempts by the Peking Government to improve the situation. Even the famous campaign to eliminate sparrows, as vicious parasites which consumed grain in the fields, backfired. Birds preyed on insects and when they were gone the fields were taken over by swarms of insect parasites.

Peking decided to import considerable quantities of food grains and stopped food distribution from the stockpiles. The population was in a disastrous situation as only a small proportion of food grain imports reached them. The rest was used to feed the armed and police forces, to supplement depleted stockpiles, for sowing and even for re-export for political purposes.

In the autumn of 1961 Harbin was a sprawling industrial centre of 3,500,000 people.

Despite strict police control and a general restriction on travel to the cities from rural areas, the population swelled daily, as famine-stricken peasants kept arriving illegally hoping that there was more food in the big centres.

Illegal residents often ended up in the huge 'corrective labour' camps in north-eastern Manchuria. The death rate in these penal colonies set up in the mining and timber industry areas is said to have been higher than in Soviet concentration camps.

Prolonged malnutrition resulted in a dreaded disease popularly called 'the famine sickness'. The victims had swollen red faces, swollen joints and enlarged stomachs, accompanied by frequent fits of faintness. The only cure was intensive feeding with such foods as pork, eggs and milk. Soon the health authorities prohibited hospitalization of victims of the 'famine sickness'. And in fact it was useless, unless adequate food rations could be provided. The only attention these people received was from the corpses collection section of the city health authorities. Russians from Harbin tell of the stricken Chinese roaming the streets in vain search of scraps of food and then collapsing and dying on the streets. No one stopped or turned around when a victim collapsed and died. Police merely summoned the corpses collection detail.

As the disease spread Harbin was allocated a 'survival quota' of 20,000 a mon h. This meant that the local health authorities were authorized to draw up a list of 20,000 victims who were given the forced feeding treatment.

The cure was simple: each of the lucky 20,000 selected for survival by the Communist city authorities was given special ration cards. This normally entitled him to two eggs, a glass of milk, some better quality bread, half a pound of meat (usually pork) and some rice or millet each day. As a rule this food had to be consumed at specially established centres operated by the city health authorities. This was to prevent the patient from sharing his ration with the starving members of his family or with his friends. Any traffic in these ration cards was extremely severely punished. Lost cards were not replaced, which usually meant death. Russian migrants point out the essential decency of the starving Chinese population. They quote several examples of destitute people finding lost ration cards and returning them to the owners, who had often lost them in a fit of dizziness.

As a patient was fed back to health—or died—his place was given to another lucky candidate. It is difficult to establish the criterion of selection—Communist industrial workers and skilled technicians had some preference, but their normal rations were usually such that they did not fall victim to the dreaded disease. The others were selected largely at random, after being vetted by the public security bureau for their ideological background. The Communist State had no desire to aid the survival of potential enemies.

By the end of 1960 the situation in Manchuria became so desperate that a special committee was formed in Peking, and given wide powers to find at least a temporary solution. Its members included leading representatives of the People's Liberation Army and People's Security Forces, the Central Committee of the Chinese Communist Party, the Standing Committee of the Chinese National People's Congress and top officials of the agricultural and industrial ministries. It is rumoured that violent arguments broke out from the start, although the sessions were held in secret and nothing was reported in the press.

By this stage relations between the USSR and the Chinese People's

Republic were very strained and a mass recall of Soviet technicians was well under way. Some were dismissed by the local Chinese authorities, which became very sensitive to the least suggestion of criticism. As the Soviet Union began to hold up deliveries of industrial goods and spare parts to China, Manchuria's industrial output began to sag. All joint Soviet-Chinese enterprises were taken over by Peking. Reprisals against local Russians holding 'Sovzagranvids' were followed by harassing of the few remaining Soviet experts and even of the Soviet consular officials. Russians going to the Soviet Consulate-General in Harbin were frequently seized by the security police and closely questioned. A number were arrested and held incommunicado.

Relations with some satellite countries also worsened. The Czechoslovak Communist authorities demanded payment on a number of old credits and requested that deliveries of Chinese goods under new trade contracts be maintained strictly according to schedule. Warsaw was hostile because of the continuation of Stalinist policies and also because the Chinese had persistently failed to live up to their obligations of supplying 50 per cent of the ships for the joint Sino-Polish shipping line established as early as 1952. Rumania wanted payment for its oil deliveries.

The handful of Poles remaining in Manchuria apparently received the most considerate treatment of all the foreigners. The Communist Polish Embassy in Peking had always been anxious to establish itself as the protector of all people of Polish extraction in China. It did not hesitate to intervene before the Chinese authorities if Poles were arrested or molested—even if the persons concerned were hostile to the regime ruling in Warsaw.

Moreover, Polish ships provided the only existing sea link between Manchuria and Japan, calling regularly at Dairen. And Peking's debts to Polish shipyards in Gdansk, Gdynia and Szczecin steadily mounted. Russian migrants say that Polish Communist papers from Warsaw often provided the least biassed source of information about the outer world. Poles used to get them pretty freely from the Peking Embassy and were allowed to keep them, though not to pass them on or discuss them with the Chinese or Russians. Such magazines as *Panorama Slaska*, *Przekroj* or *Swiat* are said to have regularly driven the Communist police to fits of fury—in their outward appearance, and occasionally in their content, they resembled too much the 'fascist, capitalist Western yellow press'.

The End of Manchuria's Industrialization

By the end of January 1962 the special committee on Manchurian affairs had completed its long, secret deliberations. Relations with the Soviet Union were approaching a crisis. Deaths from hunger were reaching catastrophic proportions.

Even more dangerous was the starved apathy of the peasants in the communes. Despite all the efforts of the 'cadres' the collective cooking, feeding and washing centres did not work. The elimination of family links resulted in a general breakdown of discipline. People lost the will to work, and there is little that can be done with a Chinese peasant who has reached such a stage of despair that he prefers to die rather than work. Driven out with red flags to the fields the peasants moved about like shadows, and practically did no work. All this was felt during the bitter, hungry winter of 1961-62.

In February 1962 the Peking Government published a long decree issued by the Central Committee of the Chinese Communist Party. It duly blamed nature, Western capitalists and warmongers, revisionist traitors allegedly centred in Belgrade and domestic enemies for the 'passing and severe difficulties' and said that certain drastic steps had to be taken to 'ensure the people's final victory'. After claiming that 'the basic aims of the establishment of the "people's communes" and of industrialization had been achieved', the statement listed a number of errors due to overzealousness and announced that a major reform would be undertaken in Manchuria.

Almost immediately the State-controlled stores released huge quantities of consumer goods and canned foods on the market throughout Manchuria. The prices were from four to twelve times higher than those paid for rationed articles. Some of the items released had little immediate use for the starving population—for instance the 'Churin Department Store' in Harbin began selling grand pianos, harmonicas, etc. A good deal of expensive furniture was thrown on the market.

Whatever was offered for sale was snapped up by crowds of eager buyers. No restrictions were placed on the quantity or value of articles sold. Harbin's population, long accustomed to empty shelves and almost reconciled to a system under which getting hold of an electric bulb or of a sewing needle was a major problem, lost no time buying whatever was available.

One saw people struggling under the load of ten water buckets or carting away a wheelbarrow loaded with tinned food and musical scores. The main idea was to spend all one's savings on some kind of consumer goods. Food was in high demand, followed by locally-produced vodka. But anything else was bought too, particularly household utensils and furniture. The population was convinced that soon this unique spree would be over and lean years would be back for good.

On the whole, the people had accumulated considerable sums of money. Industrial and administrative workers were well paid in cash—it was a different story that they could not buy anything with their earnings unless they possessed special ration coupons given as a rare and special reward by the Communist authorities. Money, as such, could buy little, if anything. Ration cards were the things that mattered. And those who had contacts in the villages knew that peasants would not sell any food for money.

In a little over a month the great sale was over. Almost immediately the Peking Government disclosed the next steps adopted on the recommendation of the special committee on Manchurian affairs. Simultaneously the Central Committee of the Chinese Communist Party issued a policy statement, calling for a vigorous effort in agriculture. Priority was shifted from industrialization to food production. It was said that the planned stage in industrialization was reached, especially in Manchuria, and that further progress depended on 'a total mobilization of forces on the food production front'.

City communes were suspended. They were never very successful and existed more on paper than in reality. In Harbin the drive to establish district communes confined itself to setting up great community lavatories and knocking down any partitions or fences which had survived the fuel collection gangs of the 'pig-iron-at-home' days.

Conditions in the villages were also slightly relaxed. The peasants were allowed a slightly greater margin of personal property and their rations were somewhat improved. They were also allowed to buy some consumer goods for cash—a rare privilege in Manchuria. The drive to enlarge the size of rural communes to encompass entire districts (hsians) was suspended.

Never loath to jump from one extreme to the other, the Peking Govern ment decided to transfer all 'surplus' industrial labour and city population to rural communes to aid the agricultural drive.

A ten-point 'new economic programme' was announced for Manchuria. It was a drastic admission of the failure of the industrialization drive. Some 50 per cent of Manchuria's industrial undertakings were put in mothballs and the workers dismissed. Of Manchuria's eight new sugar mills only two remained in normal operation. That was as much as could be run without Soviet, Polish and Czechoslovak experts and technicians and with the skilled labour and raw materials available. River craft shipyards, general engineering works in Harbin, a number of specialized equipment plants which could not work without spare parts and foreign technicians, were 'put on the conservation list'. Hundreds of small workshops in Harbin were amalgamated or closed down. Almost all the heavy industry enterprises which depended largely on Soviet deliveries or Soviet experts were shut down or substantially reduced their output.

A considerable proportion of these plants were set up without any real hope of operating profitably until China could develop its own raw material base and train adequate numbers of skilled labour. This is always a slow process, requiring capital and time. Rushing masses of untrained labour from the rural areas is no substitute, and often leads to grave difficulties. This was the case in the USSR, and then in Poland, Rumania, Bulgaria, Hungary and even in East Germany. In China this policy led to a real disaster because of the country's extremely small initial industrial base and the negligible rate of capital accumulation.

Another grave problem was the fact that the few consumer goods which were produced were stockpiled under the severe rationing system or were kept away from the market by inbuilt distribution difficulties.

Factories were not paid until their goods were sold. Goods were not sold as a matter of policy or because of failures in the distribution system. Credit difficulties mounted, despite the rather limited scope of China's money economy. This was partially solved by the mass sellout in February 1962. Moreover, the great consumer goods spree wiped out an important pocket of concentration of money in private hands. The Government then played yet another trick.

The Depopulation Drive

Following the closing down of the factories in Manchuria the Peking Government ordered the return of all those who had arrived in the cities after 1953 back to their ancestral villages. Very few exemptions were made, limited to key personnel in plants which continued operation, and some party workers.

Time given for the transfer was strictly limited. Transport was provided—but only for the evacuee and whatever goods could be carried by the person himself. One of the simple ways in which the authorities ensured that most of the goods were left behind was by making the evacuees walk a considerable distance on foot carrying their belongings. Even the lucky ones with push-bikes often had to give in because their homes were hundreds of miles away.

Thousands tried to stay behind. Thousands ran away from the evacuation transports and found their way back into Harbin. Some were punished by deportation to forced labour camps but most were left to their own devices, in the end 'voluntarily' applying, even pleading, for transport to the villages. They simply could not stay in centres like Harbin without employment. And no work was available. Selling their possessions was useless at this stage. Strict checks prevented people taking goods out of city areas and within the cities no one would buy anything except food. State stores would not buy back the goods they had so recently sold at high prices. Food reappeared and even restaurants opened. But the unemployed had no money and no ration cards. They had to find their way to their old villages or die in the cities. There was no private employment and no Government jobs were available. So they trekked away sadly or committed suicide. Their treasured possessions, which they had snapped up only a few weeks ago, were abandoned and soon found their way to the Government stockpiles.

The latest arrivals from Harbin say that the food situation has indeed improved, although rations are still small. State-owned restaurants dispense meals without ration cards, but they are very expensive and poorly patronized. The population look healthier, although their appearance remains drab. The city itself is largely in a state of disrepair. Most of the weaker people have died off—either during the famine or on their way back to the villages. As yet there are no signs that another industrialization drive is about to begin in Manchuria.

By and large the mass influx of city dwellers into the rural areas has not improved things greatly. The Chinese Communist Party still believes in the blue ants theory—anything can be accomplished with great labour masses. Peking still sends thousands of people into the villages—students are sent from high schools and universities, academic and administrative staff are sent out into the fields, cities send great teams for Sunday field work.

But supplies of farm machinery, fertilizers and capital for irrigation and soil conservation are still inadequate. The output of the newly drafted and often inexperienced farm labour is low. Relations between the new arrivals, members of the rural communes and party 'cadres' are bad. Many party leaders are still in the dark about basic agricultural processes. Rations are inadequate and morale is low.

Peasants are now allowed to rear a few pigs and even cultivate small strips for themselves. But they are still distrustful, as it has happened that zealous 'cadres' laid hands on this newly-won private property to supplement the official delivery quotas during the various 'socialist competitions'.

Little Possibility of a Revolution

The Russian refugees are almost unanimous that, although the vast majority of the people oppose the domestic policy of the Chinese Communist Party, the possibility of a well organized anti-Communist revolution is remote.

Isolated revolts are not unusual. They are quickly and ruthlessly crushed. The whole locality is then punished. But a major uprising requires adequate planning and good organization. It also requires enthusiasm and faith in the future. These elements are now lacking on the Chinese mainland. People are hungry and tired. They are thoroughly terrorized and secret police control is efficient. The Communist authorities act quickly and ruthlessly. Indoctrination is incessant and isolation from the outside world almost complete. At this stage the people in the villages are grateful for a bit of peace, an extra bowl of rice and a few slices of vegetables. They need time to recover. Moreover, the Chinese are a people that can wait.

There are anti-Communist organizations active in the maritime provinces of eastern China, but their impact is apparently small at the moment. The Communist police spying and denunciation system is efficient. Particular stress is laid on indoctrinating children and youths and setting them against their parents. It is not unusual for children to denounce their parents, for wives to report their husbands. In these circumstances any anti-Communist activity is extremely difficult.

Sino-Soviet Relations

The steadily mounting and increasingly vicious ideological disputes between Peking and Moscow are reflected in day to day life. Albania, Peking's odd ally in Communist Europe, is the great hero of the tightly-controlled press. Yugoslavia is the main villain, although some Yugoslav journalists occasionally stay in Peking for considerable periods of time.

Russian migrants are frequently lectured on the erroneous ways of revisionist traitors, and no anti-Stalinist remarks are tolerated. Stalin's portraits still adorn public halls. As early as 1961 there was police interference with Soviet technicians and experts. In 1962 direct action was taken against Soviet-sponsored organizations of the Russian migrants. In Harbin the entire committee of the Association of Soviet Citizens was arrested and held incommunicado for several weeks. Two officials, including the chairman, were officially reported as having committed suicide. The Association has now been closed and its property taken over by the Harbin city authorities.

All the property of the historic Russian Orthodox Mission in Beiguan, near Peking, has long since been taken over by the newly established Chinese Orthodox Church, which was in turn forced to 'donate' most of it to 'the people'. The few remaining Russian Orthodox priests are virtually barred from saying mass. In Harbin a few small chapels are still open and services are conducted by Chinese Orthodox clergy, who are being subjected to increasingly violent persecution. Chinese Catholics, who persevere in their allegiance to Rome, are treated as criminals. Exception is made for the few remaining Poles who are occasionally allowed to hear mass in primitive circumstances. This is again attributed to the protection of the Polish Communist diplomats in Peking. Chinese Communists regard their Warsaw post as the most important one in Europe after Moscow—it is, inter alia, the scene of the only official contacts between Peking and Washington through the medium of the Peking and United States ambassadors to Warsaw—and do not mind giving in on a few minor points.

The Communist security police raided the Soviet Consulate-General in Harbin, seizing documents and arresting the consular staff. One report said that a consular official resisted the raid and shot dead two armed Chinese Communist policemen who broke into the premises. The Soviet Consulate-General in Shanghai was closed down, although there were no reports of violence. The Soviet Consulate in Tientsin and representations in Hankow and Canton have also been closed down.

There was one fortunate aspect of deterioration in Sino-Soviet relations as far as the Russian migrants were concerned. For many years the Soviet representatives in Manchuria held wide powers over the local Russians. No one could leave for abroad without the Soviet Consulate-General's consent. Severe pressure was brought down to force Russians to go to the USSR. A number succumbed to it, having no alternative.

However, when the Peking-Moscow dispute became public, the local Chinese Communist authorities removed the local Russians from the *de facto* jurisdiction of the Soviet representatives. Their consent was no longer required to leave. Moreover, Peking suddenly decided that it would be well rid of these troublesome 'White' Russians. In a way this was part of the great 'de-Russianization' drive in Manchuria, in which Russian cultural, economic and political influence was always very strong.

NOTE

This chapter is based on information obtained by the author from White Russian refugees recently arrived in Australia from Manchuria. This information was collated with that obtained from Soviet and non-Soviet journalists, politicians and diplomats who visited or lived in China after 1949, and with further information gathered from extensive reading in four languages. The author has published a number of articles based on the same sources in periodicals.

BIBLIOGRAPHY

Eugene Bajkowski. 'The White Russian Refugees.' (*The Bulletin*, Sydney, 10 November, 1962.)

Chang Yen. 'A Tale of Co-ops.' (*China Reconstructs*, No. 9, Peking, September, 1957.)

Chow Ching-Wen. *Ten Years of Storm. The True Story of the Communist Regime in China.* (Holt, Rinehart and Winston, New York, 1960.)

C. W. L. Chin-ming. 'Economic Planning and China's Industrialization.' (*Economic Review*, journal of Sydney University Economics Society, Sydney, Vol. IV, 1958.)

Kirby, E. Stuart (ed.) *Contemporary China.* (Hong Kong Univ. Press, Hong Kong, 1956.)

Knell Rings for Communist Regime. (Cosmorama Cultural Enterprise, Hong Kong, 1963.)

Tang-Min-chao. 'China's Agricultural Leap.' (*China Reconstructs*, Peking, No. 11, November, 1958.) 'The Leap Forward Continues'. (*China Reconstructs*, No. 11, November, 1959.)

BIOGRAPHICAL NOTE

EUGENE A. BAJKOWSKI. B. 1931, Harbin, Manchuria, of Polish parents. Educated at Colleges of St. Jeanne d'Arc and St. Francis Xavier, Shanghai and at Universities of London and Cambridge. Crossed China from the Soviet frontier to Shanghai, 1949; lived in Shanghai, 1949-52. Since 1952 has lived in Australia; became a naturalized Australian citizen, 1958. Graduated in Economics from University of Sydney, 1958. Financial editor of *The Bulletin*, Sydney, 1959-62; also editor of *The Wild Cat Monthly* (financial publication), 1959-61; Australian correspondent of *The Petroleum Times*, London, from 1960. Currently a Research Officer in the Commonwealth Treasury.

ASPECTS OF SOCIETY

PROBLEMS OF DEVELOPMENT IN ASIA

by

WERNER KLATT

DEVELOPMENT is as painful a process as the change from boyhood to manhood. There are now well over twenty countries in Asia that are undergoing this change, and nothing—short of war—will stop it. Leaders of countries emerging from the colonial past insist on a rapid change from what they see as social backwardness and economic stagnation to mobility and growth, even if aware that this might cause more distress than happiness. The clash between traditional forms of life and dynamic societies which occurred during colonial rule has left behind a ferment that cannot be stopped. As a result the end products of Western society seem desirable even if the intellectual and technical processes that made them possible appear less worthy of acceptance or imitation.

It would be presumptuous to think that the representatives of developed countries are necessarily qualified to solve the problems of developing ones. The problems of the latter are unique in kind and unprecedented in scale. In fact, both developed and underdeveloped countries are facing a new phenomenon, and it may be that only few are qualified to provide answers —partial answers at best—to the many questions which are raised in the course of development. Because of the high degree of specialization of modern society, most experts have become technicians in a highly departmentalized world; yet what is needed is a universal approach to the problems of change. The economist who refuses to concern himself with the significance of tabus is bound to fail, as is the engineer who disregards the role of a racial minority. The life of nations and individuals is undergoing many changes; if major errors of judgment are to be avoided, it has to be studied in all its aspects, and in its reaction to many forms of outside interference.

The literature on matters of development has grown as fast as the problem itself. It is no longer possible to do justice to it in brief. Leaving aside all matters of detail, one may distinguish between those authors who are guided by the desire for orderly processes of balanced development and those who emphasize the need for tensions in a process of growth which is bound to be erratic and disorderly in the best of circumstances. Within this framework of alternatives there is place for an almost unlimited amount of advice ranging from a concentration of effort on improving agriculture to a selection of targets in the steel, cement and engineering industries, or from a preference for a widely dispersed programme of basic education to the creation of a highly centralized planning apparatus.

In its most extreme forms the argument boils down to the age-old controversy between revolutionaries and revisionists. One must be prepared, however, for both evolution and revolution; where the former fails, the latter is bound to take its place. Stagnation is marked by a series of vicious circles; to break any one of them amounts to breaking with the *status quo*. This is bound to cause stresses and strains, be they political, social or economic. By no means all traditional institutions are incapable of adjustment to new circumstances, however. The more existing patterns are utilized in any process of change, the smoother it is likely to be. To be acquainted with such patterns is a prerequisite of success in any attempt to change them.

Rural Basis

Throughout Asia society is still based on farming as the chief occupation of the majority and on the village as the traditional form of society. This is true even of Japan and of Soviet Central Asia where urbanization and industrialization have dislodged from their previous positions both agriculture and rural society. Its closely knit pattern is broken where plantations have been superimposed on the broad basis of subsistence farming, but the latter still prevails in more than one million villages of Asia. The pattern of farming, though by no means unalterable, is fixed by circumstances in most instances. The production of food grains for consumption on the farms and for sale in the markets forms the basis; all else tends to be of marginal significance except in the relatively rare cases where the production of a cash crop has led to specialization. Whilst the cultivators are not necessarily hostile to new ideas, most farm operations have not changed for centuries. The art of animal husbandry is largely unknown; nor does fruit and vegetable gardening take up more than an insignificant part of the land used. As a result the diet, like the farm pattern, tends to be monotonous.

The application of modern farm requisites is limited to the relatively few farms that specialize. In many villages four-fifths of the farm produce is excluded from any cash transaction. Though local transport services are increasingly widening the horizon, the village community remains largely a world of its own. In Japan and Taiwan (Formosa) rural self-administration and social mobility resulted from fairly drastic agrarian reforms which were carried out in the wake of the last war. Elsewhere in Asia some of the excesses of landlordism and money-lending may have been eliminated, but the polarization of the village community has not yet been broken everywhere. Thus the way of life in the villages is often still circumscribed by a code of behaviour to which all but the very few conform, anchored to the expanded family and the village shrine. Traditional loyalties are rarely questioned.

If the picture which emerges is one of uniformity and conformity, this should not be taken to mean that there is no individuality and colour. There is plenty of both, particularly in areas where different races and religions exist side by side. Leaving on one side Confucianism which is a philosophical concept and a way of life rather than a religion, Buddhism probably more than any other Asian belief is capable of accommodating itself to the requirements of a changing society. Against this, Islam, though closest to Christianity, seems to cling most tenaciously to an established code of conduct. Muslims do not allow pigs on their farms nor pork on their tables; they thus deprive themselves of the best scavenger of household refuse. Elsewhere in Asia the Hindu attitude towards cattle represents one of the most insurmountable barriers to advance in farming and food supplies.

It is to nobody's advantage to gloss over the damage that tabus towards livestock and towards women can cause to development in Asia. The exclusion of women from work in the fields and from public life is the most serious handicap to the rate of change, since the next generation is largely the product of maternal efforts in countries in which primary and secondary education is still the privilege of the few rather than the custom of the many. It would be wrong to conclude that religious beliefs are invariably 'enemies of the people'. Those who hold this view may ponder with profit the changes which Christianity has undergone since it was first conceived 2,000 years ago. At the same time it cannot be denied that development only begins where religious beliefs are brought into line with secular interests.

Without the rationalization of theological concepts and the secularization of political thought there is no prospect of social and economic advance nor of modern forms of government. Those who desire the end products of Western society may be reminded that Europe's communities accepted the changes brought about by renaissance, reformation, counter-reformation and enlightenment before they became what they are today, willing to abandon conformity and to take the risks that this entails. Racial, like religious, minorities are a factor of importance in Asian society and its change. Where race barriers are maintained, the prospects of general advance are limited, although the racial minority in its struggle for survival may do well for itself. Whilst religious minorities are often secluded from the world, racial minorities tend to be down-to-earth. The Chinese in South-East Asia have shown this more than any other minority. Where they have been allowed to integrate, they have brought advantages to themselves and to their host country. Many of the towns of Asia would not exist if it were not for the trading communities of migrants from other lands.

Urban Ambitions

The towns of Asia are the centres of change. Some 90 million people now live in 40 towns, each of which gives a home of sorts, if not work, to more than one million people. There are many more millions of urban dwellers who live in towns of less than one million inhabitants. The majority of them are labourers. The middle classes are still thinly spread in Asian societies. The towns are the refuge of those who choose to escape the villages where opportunities are limited. No wonder that towns in Asia often give the appearance of villages that have grown beyond their bamboo or cactus fences without having lost the characteristic features of rural communities. The process of urbanization progresses with frightening speed; in some towns the number of inhabitants has doubled within one decade. The towns attract those with the greatest initiative, but they also accept those who will be redundant in any society. Thus the towns are not only the centres of change but also the receptacles of the unwanted and the hotbeds of extremism. Among the intellectual leaders are many who are dissatisfied with the economic backwardness around them and impatient for social and political change. They find little in their country's past that they regard as worth keeping. It would be asking too much of them to expect them to recognize the assets of their colonial past, such as the infra-structure left behind, including a language that gives them access to the world of science and technology and to the United Nations. In their quest of the future they usually regard industrialization as the universal remedy for all social and economic ills and they see in planning the mechanism by which to fulfil their personal and national ambitions. They tend to associate private enterprise with imperial rule and farming with the monotony which they left behind when they chose the city as their home and their place of work.

As the life span of a generation is still short in Asia, its intellectual élite and its ruling groups are young by Western standards; they should not be misjudged on account of their age. They are usually earnest in their desire to lift their country in one great swoop from medieval backwardness into the twentieth century. They are passionately patriotic, at times chauvinistic and xenophobic. When things go wrong, they are readily accused of corruption; more often than not it is a case of nepotism rather than corruption, a relapse into the mentality of the villager who prefers a member of the family to the outsider. As skills are in short supply, they tend to take on more than they are qualified to carry out. As most of them have been educated in Western academic institutions, or institutions modelled on them, all too often they judge their own problems with eyes trained on Western targets. They are apt to travel too much in Europe and America, and too little in their own countries. As a result they sometimes overlook indigenous opportunities and rely too heavily on Western 'panaceas'.

Degrees of Development

The problems of development that the political, administrative and managerial élite has to face vary considerably from country to country. Historical experience and national environment, natural resources and human skills are among the factors that account for considerable differences in the degree of development and the chances of further advance. International comparisons are handicapped by a lack of data; they are also invidious as they may be wrongly considered as value judgments rather than as mere tools to assess the degree of development achieved and the possibilities that lie ahead. As Chester Bowles has said: 'Economic progress measured in statistical terms of steel production, irrigation water, improving health standards and literacy is only one facet in the critical competition. An even more important measure for the long haul may be the sense of participation, of belonging, of community purpose that accompanies the material gains.'[1] Without certain indicators no comparison is possible, however; in using them one should leave no doubt that every indicator implies an asset and a liability at

[1] Philip W. Thayer (ed.). *Nationalism and Progress in Free Asia.* (Baltimore, 1956).

the same time. If it is taken as a criticism of the past, it should be read also as a challenge for the future.

In most cases Japan figures as the country with the largest number of points. This is not surprising. Japan can legitimately be regarded as the most advanced country in Asia—socially, economically, and politically. This is not necessarily identical with being the happiest country. At the other end of the scale stands Pakistan; it might be displaced by Indonesia or one or another small Asian country if factual documentation were sufficient to permit of a comparison. This is not to say that Pakistan is a particularly unhappy community; development is not synonymous with happiness, but it is an aim of the leaders' policy. In any event, the differences are great enough to deserve recording; in some cases they are startlingly great.

Japan has a density of population of over 250 per square kilometre; Pakistan's density is slightly more than 100. Japan's population increases by less than 1 per cent a year; in Pakistan the rate of growth of the population is over 2 per cent. Two-thirds of Japan's population live in towns as against one-seventh in Pakistan. The gross national product, as calculated by the statistical office of the United Nations, is over $500 per head (£180) in Japan as against less than $75 (£27) in Pakistan. Japan's gross national product has increased annually by almost 10 per cent in recent years; in Pakistan the increase has been less than 3 per cent. In Japan a little over one-half of the gross national product is accounted for by private consumption; in Pakistan it absorbs three-quarters. In Japan, one-third of the gross national product falls on fixed capital investment; in Pakistan it is less than half as much. In Japan the amount of energy available per head of population is equal to almost 1,400 kilos (or nearly 1.5 tons) of coal; in Pakistan it is equal to 75 kilos. The corresponding figures for steel available per head of population are almost 250 kilos (or one-quarter ton) and less than 10 kilos respectively. In Japan the yield of paddy (rice) per hectare is over 5 tons; in Pakistan it is 1·5 tons. The corresponding figures for the milk yield per cow are 1·2 tons and 0·4 tons respectively. In Japan over 400 newspapers and over 300 radio and television sets are available per 1,000 inhabitants; in Pakistan, five newspapers and four radio sets. In Japan over 90 per cent of all children between the ages of 5 and 19 years are enrolled in schools; in Pakistan, one-quarter of all children in this age group. Finally, in Japan, on average, one medical doctor looks after 1,000 inhabitants; in Pakistan he looks after 10,000.

Development Measures

The difference between the levels of development demonstrated in the two cases of Pakistan and Japan are so wide as to justify a narrowing of the gap without one country necessarily imitating the other. In fact, all countries in Asia have development plans aiming at economic growth and designed to reduce the gap between themselves and other, more advanced countries. Only Russia and China, both of which have the most highly centralized forms of state planning in Asia, have been obliged in recent years to abandon their long-term plans and to replace them temporarily by annual plans. Other countries have been more fortunate in that they have been able to uphold their plan targets, but no country has succeeded in fulfilling its plan in all its detail; nor is this essential. In most cases plans are no more than expressions of intent; nor should they be more. However, only in a few cases are they comprehensive—as they should be—that is to say, they cover all major aspects of development and anticipate as well the effects of the changes planned. There are, of course, not the same needs everywhere. A country such as Burma, that is richly endowed and not overpopulated by present standards, is clearly less exposed to tensions as a result of development than say West Bengal (India) or Java (Indonesia) where the pressure of the growing population on limited resources has reached explosive proportions. To be met effectively the so-called population explosion needs to be defined in quantitative and geographical terms.

Irrespective of regional peculiarities, certain measures may be singled out for the attention and consideration of planners in developing countries; but it must be understood that they should not be regarded as *panaceas*. Each case must be judged on its own merit; and each measure must be considered, in conjunction with other measures, as to its likely impact on existing social and economic patterns. As all Asian societies except Japan are agrarian in character, no single measure is likely to release social and economic forces as effectively as a reform of land ownership and tenure including the level of land rents and interest rates. This reform should not be interpreted as a measure designed to create an egalitarian society; but by eliminating justified grievances it would be likely to contribute to the development of intensive forms of farming, including animal husbandry, without which the growing urban population must go short of protein in its diet. Any improvement in the average diet and thus in the condition of health is likely to require an annual growth of farm output of 3 per cent or more. Where plantation crops earn foreign exchange, the industry deserves to be kept competitive and not to be starved of capital investment.

In view of the current high rates of growth of population, most countries in Asia may find it a task beyond their means to employ more than the natural increase of population outside agriculture. At present prices it costs at least $2,000 (£700) to absorb a man outside agriculture; it may cost as much as $3,000 (£1,100). As this outlay may prove too great an undertaking, most countries in Asia are likely to remain predominantly agrarian in character for many years to come. As productivity tends to be at least twice as high in industry as in agriculture, however, any human, physical and financial resources available beyond the needs of agriculture are best utilized outside it. In order to husband them, the non-agricultural sector must be so designed as to absorb a maximum of labour at a minimum of financial outlay. It will therefore be advisable to concentrate on investment in industries that are capital extensive rather than intensive; the industries that serve a large domestic market deserve special attention in this respect.

To generate growth a modern industrial sector is necessary. Here the choice is particularly difficult, and the temptation to select impressive targets for reasons of prestige may be irresistible. Expert advice is particularly wanted here, yet badly lacking at times. The demand on indigenous and foreign capital, on knowledge and initiative will be heavy; yet at this stage of development the shortage of entrepreneurs, technical and managerial skill and, last but not least, capital often presents almost insurmountable obstacles. Unless it is accepted that the capital required is provided, at least initially, by the taxpayers of other countries, domestic financial resources will have to be mobilized in large sums and handled with great care. Even so, the creation of a modern industry is bound to entail a period of reduced rather than improved standards of living. All development processes are painful and costly, but some are more painful and costly than others. To be successful the modern industrial sector of a developing society requires not only the contributions of engineers and economists, but also the co-operation of sociologists, demographers, anthropologists and the specialists of many other disciplines of current knowledge. There is no limit, in fact, to the help required by countries engaged in the process of development.

BIBLIOGRAPHY

P. T. Bauer. *Economic Analysis and Policy in Underdeveloped Countries.* (Routledge and Kegan Paul, London, 1965.)

Eugene R. Black. *The Diplomacy of Economic Development.* (Harvard Univ. Press, Cambridge, Mass., 1960.)

N. S. Buchanan and H. S. Ellis. *Approaches to Economic Development.* (The Twentieth Century Fund, New York, 1955.)

A. K. Cairncross. *Factors in Economic Development.* (Allen and Unwin, London, 1962.)

Sally H. Frankel. *The Economic Impact on Under-developed Societies.* (Blackwell, Oxford, 1953.)

John Kenneth Galbraith. *Economic Development.* (Harvard Univ. Press, Cambridge, Mass., 1964.)

Albert O. Hirschman. *The Strategy of Economic Development.* (Yale Univ. Press, New Haven, 1958.)

Bert F. Hoselitz (ed.). *The Progress of Underdeveloped Areas.* (University Press, Chicago, 1952.)

W. Klatt *et al. The Fertiliser Industry of the Asia and Far Eastern Region.* (Mimeograph, Rome, 1960.)

Simon Kuznets. *Six Lectures on Economic Growth.* (Harvard Univ. Press, Cambridge, Mass., 1964.)

William A. Lewis. *The Theory of Economic Growth.* (Allen and Unwin, London, 1955.)

H. Mint. *The Economics of Developing Countries.* (Hutchinson, London, 1964.)

Gunnar Myrdal. *Economic Theory and Under-developed Regions.* (Duckworth, London, 1957.)

Ragnar Nurkse. *Problems of Capital Formation in Underdeveloped Countries.* (Blackwell, Oxford, 1955.)

W. W. Rostow. *The Progress of Economic Growth.* (Clarendon Press, Oxford, 1960.)

Eugene Staley. *The Future of Underdeveloped Countries.* (Harper, New York, 1954.)

BIOGRAPHICAL NOTE

DR. W. KLATT, O.B.E. is an Economic Adviser and a student of economic and agrarian affairs in Europe and Asia. He has been a consultant to United Nations agencies on several occasions. He has undertaken a number of surveys in various Asian countries. He has written for journals in England, America and the Continent and is the editor of and a contributor to a symposium, *The Chinese Model. A Political, Economic and Social Survey* (Hong Kong Univ. Press, Hong Kong, 1965.)

INDICATORS OF DEVELOPMENT IN ASIA

Table 1
General Indicators

Country	Population Density (persons per sq. km.)	Population Increase (per cent per year)	Urban Population (per cent of total)	Age Groups under 14 and over 65 (per cent of total)	Illiteracy Rate (per cent of over 10 years)	School Enrolment (per cent of 5-19 years)
India . . .	148	1·9	18·0	n.a.	77	31
Pakistan . .	102	2·1	13·0	48·0	72	26
Ceylon . .	159	2·8	15·5	44·5	24	74
Thailand . .	54	2·6	12·0	46·0	14	58
Malaya . .	56	3·1	42·5	47·0	29	62
Taiwan . .	315	3·1	n.a.	46·5	16	74
Philippines .	98	2·1	35·5	46·5	24	70
Hong Kong .	3,304	2·7	76·5	44·0	9	66
Singapore. .	2,982	2·9	63·0	44·5	31	77
Japan . . .	257	0·9	63·5	36·0	negl.	91
Comparison						
USSR . .	10	1·7	48·0	38·0	negl.	78
UK . . .	219	0·8	78·5	35·5	negl.	85
USA . . .	20	1·6	70·0	41·0	negl.	102

Table 2
Social Indicators

Country	Private Consumption (per cent of GNP)	Food and Drink (per cent of private consumption)	Calorie Intake (per day)	Protein Intake (grammes per day)	Urban Housing (persons per room)	Physicians (per thousand inhabitants)
India . . .	n.a.	n.a.	2,060	56	2·7	0·20
Pakistan . .	75	n.a.	2,120	56	3·1	0·12
Ceylon . .	73	60	2,120	47	2·3	0·22
Thailand . .	73	51	2,120	45	n.a.	0·13
Malaya . .	65	57	2,400	54	3·0	0·16
Taiwan . .	67	56	2,440	59	n.a.	0·65
Philippines .	78	50	2,000	45	n.a.	0·14
Hong Kong .	n.a.	n.a.	n.a.	n.a.	n.a.	0·36
Singapore. .	n.a.	51	n.a.	n.a.	n.a.	0·43
Japan . . .	52	44	2,360	70	1·4	1·08
Comparison						
USSR . .	n.a.	n.a.	(3,000)	(85)	1·5	n.a.
UK . . .	65	41	3,280	88	0·8	1·08
USA . . .	63	26	3,090	91	0·7	1·28

n.a.—not available
( ) —estimate
Sources: UN Statistical Yearbook 1963; UN National Accounts 1963; ILO Labour Statistics 1963; FAO Production Statistics 1963

TABLE 3
AGRICULTURE AND EDUCATION

Country	Agricultural Working Population (per cent of total working population)	Rice Yield (tons per hectare)	Milk Yield (tons per cow)	Education Expenditure (per cent of GNP)	Newspapers (per thousand inhabitants)	Radio and TV Receivers (per thousand inhabitants)
India	70	1·38	0·40	2·4	11	7
Pakistan	75	1·51	0·42	1·2	5	3
Ceylon	53	1·66	n.a.	4·5	37	38
Thailand	82	1·48	0·50	2·5	11	12
Malaya	58	2·53	0·47	n.a.	67	41
Taiwan	50	3·31	2·78	3·3	66	72
Philippines	58	1·25	n.a.	3·2	16	24
Hong Kong	7	1·72	(2·80)	n.a.	226	65
Singapore	8	2·50	(2·80)	n.a.	286	90
Japan	30	5·26	1·22	6·5	416	329
Comparison						
USSR	39	1·05*	1·70	1·5	181	237
UK	5	4·35*	3·10	4·2	490	520
USA	7	1·69*	3·18	6·2	321	1,306

TABLE 4
DEVELOPMENT INDICATORS

Country	Gross Nat. Product ($ per head of population)	Gross Nat. Product (growth rate per cent in 'fifties)	Fixed Capital (per cent of GNP)	Industry, Mining, Construction (per cent of GNP)	Energy** Consumption (kilos per head)	Steel Consumption (kilos per head)
India	73	3·5	(15)	18	161	14
Pakistan	74	2·7	(15)	15	75	7
Ceylon	129	3·7	14	n.a.	118	19
Thailand	93	5·4	18	20	77	11
Malaya	241	4·1	15	15	260	37
Taiwan	115	7·1	17	26	568	29
Philippines	191	5·2	13	23	169	13
Hong Kong	258	n.a.	n.a.	n.a.	517	130
Singapore	361	n.a.	n.a.	n.a.	722	n.a.
Japan	504	9·9	34	38	1,388	242
Comparison						
USSR	n.a.	9·0	n.a.	n.a.	3,046	334
UK	1,288	2·7	16	n.a.	4,948	332
USA	2,691	2·8	16	37	8,263	488

n.a.—not available
( )—estimate
*—wheat
**—coal equivalent

Sources: UN Statistical Yearbook 1963; UN National Accounts 1963; ILO Labour Statistics 1963; FAO Production Statistics 1963

ASIA'S POPULATION PROBLEM

by

S. CHANDRASEKHAR

TODAY the total world population has exceeded the 3000 million mark. The world's population has been increasing at a faster rate during the last fifty years, especially during the last two decades, than ever before in human history. According to some 'guestimates' there were probably no more than ten to fifteen million people in the whole world at the end of the Stone Age. At the birth of Christ the population had probably increased to about 250 million. By 1650 A.D. it was about 500 million and a century later, in 1750, about 695 million. In 1850 total population had passed the 1000 million mark to become 1091 million, and half a century later, that is at the beginning of the 20th century, it rose to 1500 million. But during the last sixty years (1900-60) the world population has doubled and become 3000 million. Thus it took man many thousands of years to multiply to 1000-1500 million but it took only a little more than half a century to double that number—an incredible and unprecedented rate of increase.

Every year more than a hundred million babies are born and 50 million people of all age groups die, leaving a net yearly addition of some 50 millions to the existing population. And now the United Nations estimates that at the current rate of increase the world might have over 6000 million by 2000 A.D.! Thus, 'viewed in the long-run perspective, the growth of the earth's population has been like a long thin powder fuse that burns slowly and haltingly until it finally reaches the charge and then explodes.'

GROWTH OF ASIA'S POPULATION[1]
(IN MILLIONS)

Year	1650	1750	1800	1850	1900	1950[2]	1962
Asia's population	327	475	597	741	915	1,384	1,764[3]
Total world population	545	728	906	1,171	1,608	2,509	3,135
Percentage of Asia's population to world total	60·0	65·2	65·9	63·3	56·9	55·1	56·3

[1] Source: the figures for 1650 to 1900 are A. M. Carr-Saunders' estimates.
[2] *Demographic Year Book* (New York, United Nations, 1963), pp. 32-5.
[3] Of this, some 1,670 million are the subject of this chapter; the remaining 94 million live in the Middle East (including Afghanistan). The population of Soviet Central Asia, Siberia and the Soviet Far East is excluded.

Of the world's 3000 million people, Asia claims over one half, and this huge population is confined to about a fifth of the total world area. Asians are today increasing faster than Europeans (this was not true in the more distant past) and since Asia's population is a young one, the potential for rapid population growth is great. At the current rate of increase Asia may have to take care of 60 per cent of the total world population by 2000 A.D.—an increase she can hardly afford in the light of her present standard of living and at the current rate of her economic development.

Asia possesses the two most densely populated countries in the world: China with over 700 millions (if her published 1953 census figures and birth and death rates between 1954 and 1960 are assumed to be correct) and India with her 460 millions (based on the 1961 census). Between them, China and India account for more than one milliard people. Only three other countries in Asia are of major importance from the point of view of population numbers—Japan, Pakistan and Indonesia. Although it is difficult to generalize about so large an area since in almost everything both extremes are possible, major trends and predominantly common features can be pointed out.

Density

Asia as a whole is the second most densely populated continent in the world. Despite the fact that nearly 80 per cent of the Asian population is rural, the density per square mile in some Asian countries is higher than the density of some thickly populated European countries. While in the United States the density per square mile is 50 and in Europe 220, it is 820 in Taiwan and 670 in Japan. The density per square mile in India and Pakistan is 384 and 265 respectively. It is even higher in East Pakistan where the majority of the Pakistanis live. And certain areas within some of the Asian countries are even more densely populated. Kerala (1125 per square mile), and West Bengal (1031 per square mile) in India, Java (1050 per square mile) in Indonesia are examples of extremely dense settlements.

Agrarian Economy

Asia's population is predominantly rural and consequently agrarian. All Asian countries except Japan depend on agriculture for the meagre livelihood of a majority of their people. The man-land ratio in Asia is so adverse and the pressure of population on the soil so great that agriculture is, by and large, more a pathetic and sentimental way of life than a successful business or commercial proposition. In almost every Asian country between 70 and 80 per cent of the population is dependent on the soil for a livelihood. Hunger, particularly in India and Communist China, is almost endemic.

The problems of Asian agriculture are well known—too well known to need any pointed discussion. In some parts of the continent the outmoded, feudalistic land revenue system gives little right to the tiller of the soil. Variations of absentee landlordism and the share-cropping system with all their drawbacks still continue in many regions. The peasant is illiterate and ignorant of all that may be called modern scientific agriculture. The traditional methods he employs are quasi-primitive and yield no worthwhile results. He is in poor health, largely the result of his insanitary and unhygienic rural environment, poor diet and the want of rural medical aid. He is perennially in debt as he has little or no resources to improve himself or his livestock. He is usually in the grip of the usurious village money-lender unless the government can give him credit. And last, no matter what his resources, unwanted children keep arriving at regular intervals, depressing his already poor level of living.

As for his land, it is a fragmented and subdivided bit of a plot, uneconomic in size to become a successful agricultural proposition. From year to year the cultivator is dependent upon the availability of good seed, natural manure or fertilizer, seasonal rainfall or government irrigation, factors often beyond his control. Then there are problems of pest control, soil erosion, storage and marketing. It is true that in recent years the governments in most Asian countries have been dedicated to improving the general welfare of the peasant, but the pace of reform has been slow, and where reforms have been revolutionary, as in Communist countries, the long-range outcome for both the peasants and production has been disastrous. The problem of food—adequate nutrition in quantity and quality for the people—continues to be a major problem in most Asian countries.

Young Population

An examination of the age structure of those Asian countries for which reliable age statistics are available reveals that Asia's population is predominantly young. On the whole, roughly two persons in every five are under 15 years; about 55 per cent are 15-59, and about one in twenty is 60 years or over. This has two undesirable consequences. One is that the number of dependants per adult is relatively large. For the economy as a whole the number of gainfully employed is disproportionately small in relation to the two unproductive groups who are dependent on them—children and old people. Secondly in view of Asia's current birth rate, the age structure is favourable for large additions in the future to the existing massive population.

Per Capita Income

Asia, with about 18 per cent of the world's land surface and 55 per cent of the world's population, receives only 12 per cent of the world's income. The per capita income of a vast majority of Asians is below the poverty line. It ranges between 50 and 120 U.S. dollars and is in striking contrast to the per capita income of some $2000 in the United States and Canada and about $1000 in Europe excluding the Soviet Union. This low income is both the cause and consequence of the misery of the underdeveloped countries in Asia.

Literacy and Education

As for literacy and primary education, more than half the world lives in unlettered darkness. While Asia claims more than half the world's population, her share of illiterates is disproportionately high. The illiteracy rates range from 75 per cent in India to 4 in Japan. Leaving aside the adult illiterates, all the Asian countries find it impossible to provide educational resources to catch up with the birth rate. The governments are simply unable to provide trained teachers and textbooks, school buildings and equipment to take care of the children reaching school-going age every year.

High But Declining Death Rates

The tremendous increase in the world's population and particularly the population of Asia in recent years is due to man's increasing control over disease and death. The effectiveness of death control is not uniform all over the world, for while the death rate in the Soviet Union and most countries of North-West Europe is about 10 per 1000, the rates in Asia are relatively high —about 30 to 35 per 1000 in Burma and Nepal, 20 in India and Indonesia; they are about 10 in Ceylon and Japan only.

However, during the last decade and more the death rates in many Asian countries have begun to decline thanks to the work of the World Health Organization, American technical aid, Colombo Plan assistance and the efforts of the various national governments in providing a modicum of modern sanitation and environmental hygiene, health education, wonder drugs and basic health services. In Ceylon, for instance, between 1945 and 1955 the death rate was cut by more than 40 per cent; in India within a few years by 33 per cent. What is more, once underground drainage, potable water supplies, modern conservancy measures and up-to-date preventive, diagnostic and curative medical services are made available, the death rates in even the most under-developed Asian countries will register even more dramatic declines.

The infant mortality rate, which is considered a sensitive index of a community's level of living and cultural milieu, is also declining in many Asian countries. While in North-Western Europe, Canada and the United States of America the infant mortality rate is between 20 and 25 per 1000 live births, the rates in Asian countries, which were considerably above 100 before the Second World War, have dropped to 98 in India and Indonesia, 67 in Ceylon, 41 in Japan and 35 in Taiwan in recent years. The rates are still high in Burma and the Philippines, about 150 and 110 respectively. Even the lower rates are uncivilized and there is room for considerable further decline. However, it must be remembered that in some parts of Asia the rates were between 150 and 200 only twenty-five years ago.

High Birth Rates

The average world birth rate during 1955-60 was estimated to be about 35 per 1000 population. On a continental basis, Africa has the highest estimated birth rate of 45 per 1000. Asia has the next highest birth rate of about 40 per 1000.

Within Asia birth rates range from 50 per 1000 in Burma to 40 per 1000 in Malaya and India and about 35 per 1000 in Ceylon and Thailand. Regionally during the last decade the birth rates have ranged between 42 per 1000 in West Asia to 35 in East Asia.

Thus with a definitive decline in the death rate and a high and near stationary birth rate, the survival rate is high, yielding huge net annual additions to the existing population. For instance, the population of India alone increased by more than 77 millions during the decade 1951-61.

The Problem

The population problem of Asia is partly a legacy of European imperialism. The balance sheet of Western colonialism in Asia is a mixed one. Asia lost her political freedom and with it the chances of rapid economic development as her raw materials were taken off to feed hungry machines in Europe, while the manufactured products were dumped on Asian markets with the aid of preferential tariffs. But, on the other hand, Europe brought a measure of peace, democratic political institutions and above all a revolution in health and modern science and technology. The abolition of internecine struggles and wars and the control of epidemics and famines brought down the death rate. But at the same time the Europeans interfered little with the indigenous cultural mores conducive to a high birth rate. And so with a declining death rate, a high birth rate and a poor agrarian economy without any industrialization, Asia was reduced to poverty. The seeds of Asia's current population explosion were sown more than a century ago by well-meaning British, French and Dutch administrators.

Thus today the basic economic and social problem in Asia is really demographic, for here more people means more poverty and vice versa. How can Asia raise the standard of living (which means more of food, clothing, housing, education and other goods and services for everybody) and cut down the still relatively high death rate (which means keeping alive more people and taking care of them), when it is so difficult to support the existing population even at a low standard of living, *if* the population continues to increase by about 30 millions every year?

Asia cannot lower her level of living any further. Nor can anyone suggest raising the death rate! From the Asian point of view, the way out appears to be rapid economic development with foreign aid and a drastic reduction in the birth rate. Planned internal migration whenever possible and the exploration of outlets for Asian emigration to thinly populated regions of the world may help some, but the major emphasis must be on rapid economic development and birth control.

Population Policies

Four major countries in Asia—Japan, India, China and Indonesia—have attempted to formulate national population policies. These policies have been carried out with varying degrees of success.

Japan was faced with a desperately serious population problem at the end of the Second World War, with the loss of her empire and the repatriation of her overseas nationals. Actually population pressure was a serious problem for Japan before the last war and was one of the factors that turned her into a belligerent nation. With a war-shattered economy, Japan had to support some 78 million on an area the size of the state of California. To meet this situation, Japan passed in 1948 the Eugenic Protection Law which 'authorizes voluntary and even compulsory sterilization in certain cases, the public sale of contraceptives which had hitherto been forbidden, and the performance of abortion in the event that continued pregnancy or parturition is likely to harm the mother's health on account of physical or economic reasons'. Japan thus reversed her pre-World War II pro-natalist population policy. Today, officially a million (and unofficially about two million) abortions are performed in Japan every year. Japan's population increased from 78 million in 1947 to 93.3 million in 1957. But the annual number of births fell from 2.7 to 1.6 million during the same period. That is, Japan's birth rate dropped from 34 per 1000 in 1947 to 17 in 1957. The country's birth rate was halved in ten years.

With her high literacy and education rates, disciplined national consciousness and adequate medical resources (more than 763 health centres in 1960) Japan has been able to reduce her birth rate through the drastic, costly and unhappy method of induced abortion.

India, where the problem is not as pressing as in Japan, embarked on an official policy of population control in 1951 when the Government Planning Commission was set up. The Government realized that a rapidly growing population in an under-developed agrarian country like India is more a hindrance than a help in raising the nation's standard of living, for with a high birth rate every increase in national effort was being used up to maintain the existing low standard of living.

But, unfortunately, non-Catholic, secular India lost nearly a decade foolishly experimenting with the safe period or rhythm method of birth control because of the Gandhian ideology of the then Minister of Health. (Mahatma Gandhi was opposed to scientific contraception.)

Today the Government of India has taken a progressive stand on this question and is in favour of all mechanical, chemical and surgical methods of family planning. It has been found, however, that under backward rural conditions conventional contraceptives are not successful as they require a clinical consultation, some knowledge of the physiology of reproduction and a relatively high level of living. Indian experience shows that sterilization or surgical methods of permanent conception control (vasectomy for fathers and salpingectomy for mothers) is really the answer to effectively curb population growth. Therefore, today several states of the Indian Union have embarked on a programme of subsidized voluntary sterilization.

A rough calculation shows that India's birth rate can be halved if about five fathers or mothers out of every thousand of the total population undergo sterilization. India's vital statistics are none too reliable but the latest statistics show that the death rate is definitely declining while the birth rate is stationary at a high level, yielding a net annual addition of some nine million to the existing population. It is hoped that India can stabilize her population at no more than 500 millions.

As for Communist China, her population today is over 700 million if her published statistics are accurate and reliable and not padded as her production figures are. Among all the under-developed countries China has been the *locus classicus* of the Malthusian dilemma. But when the Communists conducted the country's first census and discovered that the mainland's population in 1953 was around 583 million, they apparently found the figures an occasion for jubilation. Later, however, the plight of the economy, and particularly the food situation, was so bad that the country became a surprising convert to family planning. For nearly two years an intensive and unconventional campaign in favour of birth control was waged all over the country through all the available mass media. But at the end of 1958 the country reversed its stand on ideological grounds. Marx won, Malthus was overthrown, and the traditional Communist dogma that over-population is a vicious figment of the bourgeois imagination asserted itself.

Following the agricultural failures of 1960-2, rising population again became a major problem and the campaign for family planning was officially resumed. By 1964 the most popular method in urban areas was the I.U.D. ring—unperfected in China, in contrast to its success in Hong Kong, where cheap manufacture has been achieved. In 1965 the oral pill was under trial and in demand. The spread of education in all parts of China and the extensive control of the People's Communes would seem to make it possible for any technical achievements in birth control to become effective comparatively rapidly in Asia's most highly populated country.

Indonesia, with an area of 569,000 square miles, has to support more than 95 million people. Indonesia's population problem is in a sense regional and not national. The density on the main island of Java is very high, whereas many outer islands are relatively sparsely populated. Java contains about one-eleventh of the area of Indonesia but about two thirds of the entire population. While the land in the outer islands is probably less fertile than that in Java, it is good enough to carry many millions. So even before Indonesia became free, emigration of peasant families to Sumatra and Borneo was organized, but the cost per settler was high and the Javanese farmer was not too willing to migrate to neighbouring underdeveloped islands. In recent years there has been some talk of pursuing settlement schemes in other Indonesian islands but nothing substantial has come of it. Apart from the theoretical schemes of redistributing the Indonesian population among the various islands, the Government has given no thought to any policy of population control, possibly on the assumption that there is plenty of land in the country as a whole.

More recently Indonesia demanded from the Dutch the return of the western half of New Guinea, now called West Irian. This region has an area of 180,000 square miles and an estimated population of some 750,000. From the demographic point of view, Indonesia needs this land provided she can successfully colonize it with the Javanese.

As for other Asian countries, Pakistan, with a population of 97 millions, has embarked under President Ayub Khan on a policy of population control. Birth control clinics have been opened in both wings of the country but the Muslim masses have not been attracted to them as yet. Ceylon is also officially in favour of population control but determined Government efforts are not visible. Formosa, Hong Kong and Singapore have active voluntary family planning associations which are doing useful work with some Government encouragement.

On the other hand Burma and also Thailand, for reasons best known to their Governments, consider themselves under-populated or at any rate free from population pressure. The levels of living in these countries are not particularly high in relation to other Asian countries, and there is no reason to suppose that their per capita incomes would increase if there were more people.

Conclusion

The solution to Asia's population problem lies as much in population control as in economic and social development. While every Asian country is trying to modernize its agriculture and embark on planned large-scale industrialization, only a few have tried to curb their population growth.

However, the successful and widespread implementation of planned parenthood implies not only a reasonable standard of living but, more important, women's social emancipation. Once the women of Asia are liberated from ignorance and apathy, and education in the liberal sense of the word becomes widespread among the people of Asia, a new awareness of the dignity and worth of the individual is bound to dawn.

And last, no Asian country can develop its resources without substantial aid from the advanced Western nations. Such aid should not be confined to agricultural and industrial development alone but must extend to all the available 'know-how' on health and family planning. In the long run, Asia must be enabled to lower both her birth and death rates to civilized levels. When every Asian woman delivers two babies instead of the four or six she delivered before, and when every Asian farmer grows two ears of corn where one or none grew before, Asia's demographic and economic problems will be solved. A relatively rich Asia is bound to have beneficent repercussions even on the affluent West, for prosperity like peace is indivisible.

BIBLIOGRAPHY

George W. Barclay. *Colonial Development and Population in Taiwan.* (Princeton Univ. Press, Princeton, N.J., 1954.)

Census of India, 1951. Part I-A. Report. (Govt. of India, New Delhi, 1953.)

Census of India, Paper No. 1 of 1962. 1961 Census. (Govt. of India, New Delhi, 1962.)

S. Chandrasekhar. *China's Population: Census and Vital Statistics.* (Oxford Univ. Press, London, 2nd ed., 1959.) *Red China: An Asian View.* (Praeger, New York, 1962.) *Population and Planned Parenthood in India.* (Allen and Unwin, London, 2nd ed., 1961.) *Hungry People and Empty Lands.* (Allen and Unwin, London, 3rd ed., 1955.)

Chu Chong-Lwan. 'Korean Economy and Population Problem'. (*Korea Journal*, Seoul, November, 1961, Vol. I, No. 3.)

Ansley J. Coale and Edgar M. Hoover. *Population Growth and Economic Development in Low-Income Countries.* (Princeton Univ. Press, Princeton, N.J., 1958.)

Kingsley Davis. *The Population of India and Pakistan.* (Princeton Univ. Press, Princeton, N.J., 1957.)

Demographic Year Book. (United Nations, New York.)

Dennis Kux. 'Growth and Characteristics of Pakistan's Population.' (*Population Review*, Madras, January 1962, Vol. 6, No. 1.)

John Robbins. *Too Many Asians.* (Doubleday, New York, 1959.)

Irene Täuber. *The Population of Japan.* (Princeton Univ. Press, Princeton, N.J., 1958.)

Warren S. Thompson. *Population and Progress in the Far East.* (Univ. of Chicago Press, 1959.)

Justus M. van der Kroef. 'Cultural Aspects of Indonesia's Demographic Problem.' (*Population Review*, Madras, January, 1960.)

Guy Wint. *Spotlight on Asia.* (Penguin, London, 1955.)

BIOGRAPHICAL NOTE

PROFESSOR SRIPATI CHANDRASEKHAR received his training from the Madras Presidency College, the University of Madras, and Columbia and New York Universities. After lecturing for two years in American universities he became Professor and Head of the Department of Economics, Annamalai University, South India, 1947-51. Director of Demographic Research, UNESCO, Paris, 1948-49. Professor and Head of the Department of Economics, Baroda University, Baroda. Nuffield Fellow, London School of Economics, 1953-55. Director, Indian Institute for Population Studies, 1956 onwards. Visiting Professor of Demography, University of Missouri, 1957, University of Pittsburgh, 1961. Has lectured before numerous universities in the U.S.A., Canada, U.K., Scandinavia, Middle East, Africa and South-East Asia. Has been a delegate to numerous international conferences. Is a member of several national and international learned bodies. Is a member of the Demographic Advisory Committee of the Government of India and the International Union for the Scientific Study of Population. Elected a Member of Parliament (Upper House) at New Delhi, 1964. Appointed Professor of Demography, University of California, Riverside, 1965.

LABOUR IN ASIA

by

WERNER KLATT

MOST of the working men and women in Asia are engaged in agricultural pursuits. Outside Japan—the only country that has progressed beyond the stage of agrarian backwardness—the rural population accounts for at least three out of four, sometimes even four out of five of the total population. As Louise Howard said in her book on farm labour: 'For millions of persons born in rural districts there is no escape from an agricultural career'[1]. The villages provide a home not only for those who till the land, but also for indigenous craftsmen and local traders. Much of the non-agricultural occupation is thus centred in hamlets and country towns rather than capital cities which accommodate primarily the administrative, academic, commercial and military sections of society, but little industry. In most parts of Asia the age of the congested areas holding the proletariat of modern industry is yet to come. This is not to say that Asia is a continent of bucolic peace and rural prosperity. On the contrary; even where it is not overcrowded by present, or indeed by any standards of production and productivity, the countryside is at best a backwater of development; at worst it provides back-breaking toil and the hazards of intestinal disease.

PREDOMINANCE OF FARM LABOUR

The predominance of the villager in general and the agriculturist in particular is overwhelming. The share of cultivators, tenants and farm labourers in the total labour force accounts normally for two-thirds, but in some of the least industrialized areas for as much as three-quarters of the labour force. Any survey of its size, its forms of employment and of any changes in its composition would therefore be incomplete without an assessment of the agricultural sector. However much they may despise life on the land, even administrators, intellectuals, traders and industrialists are closely tied in their mentality and in their relations to the villages from which they are often removed by not more than one generation.

Surveys of agricultural labour and of rural working conditions are still relatively scarce in some parts of Asia, as indeed they are throughout the world; yet the planning of social and economic change is closely linked to an understanding of the rural communities and their role in society. Often even basic statistical data cannot be had easily. Certain salient features are, however, so pronounced as to provide an impression, at least in qualitative, if not in quantitative terms. Frequently one-fifth to one-quarter of the village

[1] L. E. Howard, *Labour in Agriculture* (London, 1935).

population is engaged in non-agricultural activities. This section usually embraces the local rebels as well as the innovators. From here stems the beginning of social mobility; here can be found the ancestors of the foremen of factories, if not the entrepreneurs, exporters, officers and civil servants. The division between agricultural and non-agricultural pursuits is rarely rigid, except where the rules of caste prescribe men's status in life and death. Trading and handicraft are by necessity tied closely to the needs and the opportunities of the village community. Occupational choices are thus interwoven and interchangeable.

Even within agriculture the lines of division between cultivators, tenants and labourers are fairly fluid. Generalizations are more dangerous here than elsewhere, but in the rice economies of South and South-East Asia the farm labourers seem to account for between one-third and two-fifths of the total agricultural labour force. Its magnitude and composition is, of course, determined largely by the size of the holding. The smaller the farm, the more it depends on family labour. In some communities the owner-occupiers and tenants try to maintain a social status different from that of the labourers, but any such segregation tends to break down. Where the land available is limited and much sought after, cultivators and tenants may have to seek supplementary manual work to support themselves and their families. There are also agricultural workers who own some land and who thus stand somewhere between the landless labourer and the owner-occupier, tenant or share cropper. However, the labourer turned owner is as rare a specimen in Asia as is the lord of the manor.

During the depression of the late twenties many cultivators lost their land and became labourers. Where agrarian reforms have been carried out meanwhile, it has been one of their purposes to eliminate some of the worst features of landlordism and money-lending. Where these reforms have been successful, as in Japan, the village community has become more homogeneous than it was in the past in its social composition, in its economic interest, and in its political affiliation. In this situation tenants tend to gain by comparison with owners, and labourers sometimes gain by comparison with both.

Hidden Unemployment

Where modern Western society is plagued by urban unemployment, Eastern society's greatest blot is the underemployment in the rural communities. As the last of the various Indian famine reports pointed out, 'perhaps the most important, and in many ways the most intractable of all rural economic problems is that of underemployment.'[1] It is sometimes concluded that the withdrawal of farm labour and its transfer into industry is an easy process able to solve both rural underemployment and industrial growth. In fact, the position is too complex to lend itself to ready solutions. There is chronic as well as seasonal underemployment, and much of the disguised unemployment does not express itself in complete idleness but in work with insufficient or unsatisfactory tools that make for low productivity and excessive input of labour.

[1] Famine Enquiry Commission's Final Report (Madras, 1945).

The extent of rural unemployment is clearly related to the amount of land available and the form of farming chosen. Where paddy (rice) is grown on wet ground and wheat, pulses and oilseeds are grown on dry land, some 200 working days are needed under present conditions on ten acres of land; to this have to be added the days taken up for repairing the house, the bunds, the implements; for collecting firewood and fodder and carrying farm products to the market. This adds up to almost uninterrupted employment from one end of the year to the other. There is not enough work, however, for the breadwinner and not enough food for his family, if the holding is substantially smaller than ten acres, and this applies in many, if not most, instances throughout Asia; often even five acres can be considered a gift of the gods.

In these circumstances underemployment and poverty can be averted only if the level of intensity of farming can be raised or supplementary or alternative employment can be found outside agriculture. Within farming, output and productivity cannot be raised substantially without the application of farm requisites additional to those available at present. Supplementary mechanical power and commercially produced plant nutrients are the most prominent among the many requisites by which a new lease of life can be given to the farming communities of Asia. Badly needed animal protein cannot be produced without additional supplies of fodder, the chief by-product of double cropping and mixed farming. Once animal husbandry plays its full part, it is bound to create new jobs on the farms, but this development has to await the growth of an industrial labour force that is yet to come in most of Asia. Thus farm and factory are two aspects of one and the same phenomenon.

As a result of improvements in transport facilities, villagers in Asia find it easier than in the past to secure supplementary employment and thus additional income, but these activities rarely contribute substantially to reducing seasonal unemployment, which is more marked in plantations than in subsistence farming; yet the plantations have brought a sense of labour discipline and an understanding of the money economy without which industrialization is unthinkable. Even allowing for supplementary earnings, total farm income is rarely large enough to provide more than a bare subsistence; sometimes it is less than that. In typical Asian farming communities some 75 to 80 per cent of the total net income is spent on food, the remainder being divided fairly evenly between clothing, shelter and other daily necessities. Two-thirds to three-quarters of the food bill is accounted for by cereals which provide the bulk of the daily calorie intake. Whilst the diet is overburdened with starchy foods, its content of animal protein is low. After weaning, the consumption of milk is insignificant. Its absence in the diet of the adult causes shortages of calcium and riboflavin. Where rice is highly milled, the diet lacks thiamin as a result of which cases of beri beri can be found. Short stature, low body-weight and high frequency of stomatitis are the nutritional marks of societies in need of occupational change.

Occupational Changes

The workers employed in Asia's industry and commerce are the brothers and sisters, the sons and daughters of those remaining in the villages. Their problems are similar and they are interrelated. Some take temporary employment but return to their farm plots during harvest time. The industrial workers thus react to their new environment not unlike their rural relatives; yet their new conditions of work are far removed from their previous mode of life. The disruption caused by physical and mental dislocation is as violent in Asia as it has been in urban communities elsewhere in the world. Its by-products are reminiscent of Europe's industrial past. Some of the tenements of Asian industrial and urban centres bring to mind the worst features of early industrialization in Europe, but remarkably good housing and modern social services can be found in the most developed of the under-developed countries of Asia. If the political instability in many parts of Asia is taken as a sign of immaturity, this diagnosis is correct in so far as it describes the end of an old-fashioned rural society with its own built-in equilibrium and the beginning of the painful growth of new forms of living and working together in conditions where the monotonous, regular rhythm of the machine takes the place of the irregular, yet no less powerful rhythm determined by sun-rise and sun-set, by dry season and by wet.

The non-agricultural labour force of Asia may seem small if related to all those described in the official records as gainfully employed; yet in absolute numbers it represents a formidable force by any standards. Admittedly the statistical counts are neither complete nor accurate. The records of the International Labour Office, which was founded in 1919 and now advises on questions of labour on behalf of the United Nations, show almost 50 million workers employed in mining, construction and manufacturing industries in the countries of Asia outside the Sino-Soviet bloc. There are many more outside these industries who have not been counted; they represent the potential on which entrepreneurs in all walks of urban life can draw. Urban labour includes not only factory hands, but also white-collar workers, as well as labourers in transport, trade and communications. The administrative grades often carry not only better remuneration, but also higher social status than the other groups. Whilst they provide a large portion of the élite of Asia, the members of the trading communities are often of alien origin and thus find it difficult to integrate in the indigenous labour force.

The flow of migrants from the rural areas to the urban centres of Asia has gained momentum since the end of the last war, when transport and communications began to provide the preconditions of mobility on an unprecedented scale. As a result the process of urbanization has been faster in Asia than it was at a similar stage of industrial development in Europe. Many towns of Asia have become the receptacles of the rural under-employed. Urban unemployment may thus be seen as the other side of over-population, at present levels of production, in the villages.

On the whole the new recruits to industry in Asia have shown a remarkable degree of adaptation to alien conditions. To be sure, there have been serious difficulties in some industries and there are still some to be overcome. Only the impatient or the rapacious, however, would have reason to be dissatisfied. Where indigenous skills were not dislodged as a result of the international division of labour, the training of industrial recruits has been easiest. At the middle layer of the industrial—as indeed of the administrative—hierarchy it seems most difficult to train large numbers fast enough. The programmes of international organs, such as the Technical Assistance Board of the United Nations or the Consultative Committee of the Colombo Plan, have provided some assistance in the training of suitable industrial staff, but the Western expert is not automatically the most suitable teacher of Asian managerial or engineering personnel. Much suitable human skill exists, yet uncovered, in Asian villages and small towns that are rarely visited by government officials or their foreign advisers; it will pay handsome dividends to tap this.

The Status of Labour

As the supply of unskilled and semi-skilled labour usually surpasses the urban and industrial demand, workers are in a weak bargaining position. As a result, wages and working conditions tend to be unsatisfactory by Western standards. Even so, industrial workers of low skill usually earn twice as much and skilled workers may earn more than three times as much as agricultural labourers. This does not necessarily mean that urban living standards are correspondingly higher than those obtaining in villages where a large part of the income accrues as part of the subsistence economy and thus is cheap if not free of charge. As earnings are low, women have to earn in addition to men. Of this a great deal can be seen in Asia. The working women of Asia carry, as a rule, an even heavier burden than men. Except during the last stages of pregnancy, women of working class origin, apart from running their households, are in fact invariably engaged in some form or other of paid employment. Child labour, though forbidden in several countries of the area, is not entirely unknown either. In these conditions absenteeism from work is frequent; it should not be seen as either a sign of income saturation or of laziness. On the whole Asian workers are industrious, though ill-paid. They have yet to reach the social and economic status that industrial workers have gained for themselves in Western society.

As private savings are small or non-existent, the opportunities for private large-scale capital investment are limited in Asia. In these circumstances the State steps in on many occasions which remained the preserve of the individual entrepreneur in the Western world for a century or more. The State is thus becoming rapidly the largest employer even where it is not the only one—as in the Soviet Union and in China. It is thus not surprising that labour relations and the struggle for the rights of the working man have taken forms in Asia that are distinct from those known in the older industrial countries of the world; for example, government legislation regulating conditions of work and labour relations has been introduced in several Asian countries at an early stage of industrial development. As a result civil servants have tended at times to regard labour matters—not unlike those concerning the co-operatives—as the prerogative of government departments rather than that of independent arbitration machinery. These tendencies have been encouraged in Asia by the weakness of organized industrial labour.

Asian Trade Unions

The trade unions in Asia are numerically second to none, but they include, according to an estimate of the International Confederation of Free Trade Unions (ICFTU) 'not more than one-quarter of the trade union potential in the non-Communist countries of Asia'[1]. Some 20 Asian trade union organizations from 12 territories in Asia and representing more than 7 million members are affiliated to the ICFTU which maintains, through its Asian Regional Organization (founded in 1951), close relations with the Asian trade unions and labour associations. It also maintains in Calcutta a training college for labour organizers and trade union officials; it holds conferences and seminars throughout the region; and it has sent good-will missions from time to time to territories where intractable difficulties within the trade union movement seemed to justify the despatch of experienced officers of the international organization. A good many non-Communist labour unions have remained outside the international framework provided by the ICFTU, particularly in Japan, Indonesia and Burma; whilst their total membership is uncertain, it is unlikely to add more than 6 million to the total non-Communist trade union membership. The numerical strength of the Communist and Communist-dominated organizations in Asia does not exceed 2 millions; they are affiliated to the World Federation of Trade Unions (WFTU) which has had to face certain internal difficulties lately due to the Sino-Soviet ideological dispute.

Japan, being the country with the largest industrial labour force in Asia, has almost 8 million workers who are organized in trade unions; this number falls little short of the membership of the Trade Union Congress of Great Britain. India has approximately 4 million trade union members, Pakistan claims half a million and Ceylon, Malaysia and South Korea have approximately one-quarter of a million each. Hong Kong and Taiwan (Formosa) each have half as much as that. Whilst amalgamation progresses among trade unions in the Western world, Asian trade unions are marked by a tendency towards fragmentation, if not fratricide. In Japan as elsewhere, industrial workers are frequently organized according to place of work rather than occupation. Some 40,000 unions share the total membership and the average is thus a mere 200 members per union. In fact the two main unions, the General Council of Trade Unions (Sohyo) and the Japanese Trade Union Council (Zenro), neither of which is affiliated to the ICFTU, though Sohyo enjoys observer status, absorb the bulk of Japan's organized industrial labour force. Sohyo draws its membership principally from workers in public enterprises, whilst Zenro operates mainly among workers employed by private industry.

In India the average membership per union is 400. In many cases more than one union operates on the factory floor. The two largest unions are both affiliated to the ICFTU. The Indian National Trade Union Congress

[1] ICFTU, Report to the Seventh World Congress (Berlin, 1962).

(INTUC) is nearing the 2 million mark in membership, whilst Hind Mazdor Sabha (HMS) has less than half as many members. Elsewhere in Asia trade unions have a hard time, if they are not in fact restricted in their activities, as in Pakistan. In Ceylon, Malaysia, Hong Kong and Formosa they are fairly effective organs. Nowhere in the area do farm labourers represent more than a tiny section of organized labour. Most rural districts have not yet seen a trade union organizer.

The concept of political independence is not yet generally accepted by the unions in Asia. Several of them are clearly associated in the mind of the public with political parties, and work in the unions is often undertaken in the interest of political advance rather than of negotiation and arbitration. In spite of certain shortcomings, however, the trade unions in Asia represent an important factor in public life. The more effective of them are on the road to fulfilling functions not dissimilar to those undertaken by their counterparts in Europe and North America.

BIBLIOGRAPHY

Abdul Aziz and W. Klatt. 'The Development and Utilization of Labour Resources in South East Asia' in Philip W. Thayer (ed.), *Nationalism and Progress in Free Asia.* (Johns Hopkins Press, Baltimore, 1956.)

Tadashi Fukutake. *Man and Society in Japan.* (Univ. of Tokyo Press, Tokyo, 1962.)

Louise E. Howard. *Labour in Agriculture. An International Survey.* (Oxford Univ. Press, London, 1935.)

International Labour Organization. *Agricultural Wages and Incomes of Primary Producers.* (International Labour Office, Geneva, 1949.) *Basic Problems of Plantation Labour.* (International Labour Office, Geneva, 1950.)

W. Klatt. *Land and Labour in Burma.* (Mimeograph, Rangoon, Burma, 1956.)

Radhakamal Mukerjee. *The Indian Working Class.* (Hind Kitabs, Bombay, 1951.)

Surendra J. Patel. *Agricultural Labourers in Modern India and Pakistan.* (Current Book House Bombay, 1952.)

B. Ramamarti. *Agricultural Labour. All-India Agricultural Labour Enquiry* and *Report on the Second Agricultural Labour Enquiry.* (Government of India, Delhi, 1954 and 1960.)

R. H. Tawney. *Land and Labour in China.* (Allen and Unwin, London, 1932.)

BIOGRAPHICAL NOTE

Dr. W. Klatt, O.B.E. is an Economic Adviser and a student of economic and agrarian affairs in Europe and Asia. He has been a consultant to United Nations agencies on several occasions. He has undertaken a number of surveys in various Asian countries. He has written for ournals in England, America and the Continent and is the editor of and a contributorj to a symposium, *The Chinese Model. A Political, Economic and Social Survey* (Hong Kong Univ. Press, Hong Kong, 1965.)

AGRICULTURAL AND NON-AGRICULTURAL LABOUR FORCE IN ASIA

Country	Economically Active Population (per cent of total population)	Population engaged in Agricultural and Non-Agricultural Pursuits (per cent of total employed population)		Industrial Workers in Mining, Manufacture, Construction (million)
South Asia				
India . . .	43	70	30	21·5
Nepal . . .	49	93	7	0·1
Pakistan . .	33	75	25	2·9
Ceylon . . .	37	53	47	0·4
Central Asia				
Tibet . . .	n.a.	n.a.	n.a.	n.a.
Mongolia . .	n.a.	n.a.	n.a.	n.a.
Russian Central Asia . . .	n.a.	n.a.	n.a.	n.a.
Far East				
China . . .	n.a.	n.a.	n.a.	n.a.
Taiwan . . .	30	50	50	0·4
Hong Kong .	39	7	93	0·6
Japan . . .	50	30	70	14·5
South Korea .	32	58	42	0·9
North Korea .	n.a.	n.a.	n.a.	n.a.
Russian Siberia and Far East	n.a.	n.a.	n.a.	n.a.
South-East Asia				
Burma . . .	n.a.	n.a.	n.a.	n.a.
Thailand . .	53	82	18	0·6
Cambodia . .	n.a.	(70)	(30)	n.a.
Laos . . .	n.a.	n.a.	n.a.	n.a.
South Vietnam .	n.a.	n.a.	n.a.	n.a.
North Vietnam .	n.a.	n.a.	n.a.	n.a.
Malaya . . .	34	58	42	0·3
Singapore . .	n.a.	8	92	
Sarawak . .	n.a.	(70)	(30)	0·1
Sabah . . .	n.a.	85	15	
Indonesia . .	34	72	28	2·6
Philippines . .	38	58	42	1·4

n.a.—not available
( ) —estimate

Source: ILO, *Yearbook of Labour Statistics*, Geneva, 1964

TRADE UNIONS IN NON-COMMUNIST COUNTRIES IN ASIA

Country	Name of Trade Union	Membership (in thousands)	ICFTU Affiliate (+) Observer (*)	WFTU Affiliate (+)
India	Indian National Trade Union Council (INTUC)	1,850	+	
	Hind Mazdoor Sabha (HMS)	700	+	
	All-India Trade Union Congress (AITUC)	500		+
Nepal	All-Nepal Trade Union Organization	10	+	
Pakistan	All Pakistan Confederation of Labour	325	+	
Ceylon	Ceylon Workers' Congress	315	+	
	Ceylon Trade Union Federation (CTUF) (pro-Chinese)	unknown		+
	Federation of Trade Unions of Ceylon (FTUC) (pro-Soviet)	unknown		+
Taiwan	Chinese Federation of Labour (CFL)	160	+	
Hong Kong	Hong Kong and Kowloon Trade Union Council	125	+	
	Hong Kong Federation of Trade Unions (communist-supported)	unknown		
Japan	General Council of Trade Unions of Japan (SOHYO)	6,100 (together with SANBETSU)	*	
	Japanese Federation of Industrial Unions (SANBETSU)		*	
	Japanese Trade Union Congress (ZENRO KAIGI)	1,130	+	
	Japanese Federation of Free Trade Unions (SODOMEI)	400	+	
	Japanese Postal Union (ZENTEI)	200	+	
	Coalminers; Traffic, Metal and Broadcasting Workers	135	+	
South Korea	Federation of Korean Trade Unions	240	+	
Burma	Trade Union Congress, Burma (TUC B)	unknown		
Thailand	No workers' associations	—		
South Vietnam	Union Ouvrière du Vietnam (UOV)	50	+	
	Confédération des Syndicats des Travailleurs du Vietnam	unknown		
Malaysia	Malayan Trade Union Congress (MTUC)	230	+	
	Singapore Association of Trade Unions (SATU)	unknown		
	National Trade Union Congress, Singapore (NTUC)	unknown		
Indonesia	Gabungan Serikat Buruh Islam	1,000	+	
	Kongress Buruh Islam Merdei (KBIM)	60	+	
Philippines	Philippine Trade Union Council	80	+	
	Katipunang Manggagawong Philipino (KMP)	500		

THE POSITION OF WOMEN IN ASIA

by

TAYA ZINKIN

Asia is many places, many traditions, many religions; the way women are treated varies from country to country far more than it does in Europe which has one unifying culture based upon the Bible. Yet, even in Europe, the position of women is far from uniform: Swiss women cannot vote, Spanish women are still heavily chaperoned while Swedish women enjoy sexual equality. In Asia the differences are infinitely greater. There are Buddhist countries and Muslim countries, there are countries where Hinduism, Taoism, Christianity or Marxism are practised, and religion profoundly affects the way women are treated.

Moreover, within one and the same religious tradition there can be differences even more far-reaching than those between Switzerland, Sweden and Spain. For instance there is practically nothing in common in the way women are treated in say, Indonesia where they are pretty fancy-free, and West Pakistan where they are still largely kept in purdah. Indeed, within the same country, and the same religious tradition, there are differences too. Thus purdah is practically unknown in East Pakistan and the position of the Indonesian woman varies from island to island and even within the same island from place to place, while the women of India enjoy quite different status and rights not only according to their religion but also according to their caste. There is nothing in common between the way a Brahmin lady and her Nair neighbour behave in Malabar since the two are governed by totally different rules and traditions. The Brahmin lady may be kept indoors, she can only marry once, her husband is her master and he can marry as often as he likes while the Nair lady who is governed by the laws of matriarchy rules the roost, owns the property, marries as often as she fancies, though one husband at a time, and treats men like drones.

In such a medley of traditions and influences, one cannot generalize about the position of women in Asia. However, it is possible to generalize about two things: there is a basic difference between the position of women in Asia and the West, and forceful influences have been brought to bear upon that position in recent years.

Tradition and Western Influence

First, Asian homes have, in most parts of Asia, been joint-family homes in contrast to the West where the family unit living under the same roof has always been relatively limited since the days of the cave civilization. In much of Asia it has been the custom for all the married sons to remain in the paternal house with their wives, children and grand-children, three or even four generations fanning themselves out under one roof. Such a system can only operate if there is a minutely detailed code of behaviour based on a rigidly laid down, accepted and enforced hierarchy, particularly for the women. The position of Asian women, in addition to the place given them by their religions, has therefore been largely conditioned by the existence and the needs of the joint-family. That too many cooks spoil the broth is an old Asian discovery; there is only one cook in the Asian home, the senior-most woman, the others are merely helpers or scullery maids according to their seniority which can readily be calculated in terms of the number of their living sons, and the seniority of their husband. Whereas in the West the dominant woman is the wife, in Asia it is the mother, indeed the grandmother, the matriarch who is always, everywhere, even in Japan where women do not count, profoundly respected. I shall never forget the middle-aged Muslim university professor invited to represent his country at the United Nations wiring home for permission to accept; he wired his illiterate mother, not his matriculate wife.

Next, the influences which are being brought to bear upon the position of women in Asia all come from the West, from the writings of John Stuart Mill or Karl Marx, from the dedication of Emma Pankhurst and Florence Nightingale. The promoters of female emancipation in Asia have been Asian men, not Asian women. Asian women have not had to fight for their rights, the fighting has been done for them by men like Ram Mohan Roy, Gandhi, Nehru, Ayub Khan, Sun Yat-sen or Mao Tse-tung. Indeed, it can be said that equality has often been forced upon the women of Asia before they were ready for it. For every woman who wanted and welcomed change, there were many who feared it because they realized obscurely that change can only be achieved at the expense of the security and warmth which tradition bestows even upon the most barbarous practice, for there is always an element of security in certainty. The bird launching itself from the safety of its nest for its first trial flight must feel much of the same panic as the Asian woman discarding her purdah or choosing her own husband. For both, the woman and the bird, the sky is the limit, but there are those who crash to the ground. And there are enough love marriages which go wrong in societies where marriages have always been arranged, to remind pioneers of the risks of transition. Yet, under pressure from the men, the women of Asia are being made to spread their wings wider and wider all the time. Indeed, it is possible to say that the position of women has changed more drastically in the East in the post-war decades than it has in the West in the last century.

India

In India, women begin with the great advantage that Hinduism bestows upon them an honoured place. Many of the most important Hindu deities are Goddesses; the Gods are monogamous and faithful. Women are described in the religious books as the sacred field in which men are born; there is no Pauline slur on sex, no Islamic hint that women are there for men to enjoy.

For Hindus, the enjoyment is mutual and it is the husband's sacred duty to please his wife. When the Lord Krishna tells the hero Arjuna to fight, he calls him 'son of Kunti'; Western heroes are usually known after their fathers. There have been educated women, philosophers and poets from the earliest times, and some queens rode with their armies to war.

Women in India have been respected more than anywhere in the world. While the War of Troy was fought to avenge Paris's honour, the great war of the Mahabharata was fought to avenge an insult done to the Pandava Queen. However, perhaps because women were so profoundly respected,. they came to be overprotected and lost their civic rights in the process- From the day of their birth to the day of their death, they were the re. sponsibility of a man, first their father, then their husband, then their sons This tutelage applied mostly to high caste Hindu women; other women had varying degrees of freedom and independence. Many hill women are polyandrous.

Forty years ago Gandhi took a solemn pledge to make women the legal equals of men in every way. By the time Gandhi came onto the scene widows were no longer allowed to commit suttee, child marriage was restricted, and girl infanticide was forgotten. But women still were legal minors and had no redress if they were badly treated. Gandhi's first step to emancipate women was to draw them into politics, because half the strength of any nation lies with its women. The women responded to Gandhi's call with amazing celerity whether they were educated or not and courted arrest by their tens of thousands in the non-cooperation campaigns.

It was therefore only natural that, at independence, women should find themselves in politics and rising easily to positions which are still only rarely, in the West, within reach of their sisters. There are women ministers, ambassadors, governors of provinces, vice-chancellors of universities, senior administrators and directors of private businesses. Moreover, to emancipate women legally, the Congress Government piloted through a new Hindu Code whose object was to reform Hindu law to give women the same rights as men. Only fear of upsetting Muslim sensitivity prevented Mr. Nehru's making monogamy obligatory for all and putting through an India, instead of a Hindu, Code. As a result of the new law Hindu women can divorce for much the same reasons as in Britain, and they have almost the same rights in inheritance as men. And Hindu men are able to claim alimony when divorce is pronounced in their favour. Equality can hardly go further.

In addition, women are given many advantages; the Congress Party makes it a point to reserve 15 per cent of its candidatures to Parliament and the State Assemblies for women. The Government, other things being equal, recruits women in preference to men; there are half a million women employed by Government if one includes teachers and nurses as well as clerks, and a few of them have reached high positions in the administrative grade. All this has been possible because women have taken to education like flies to honey. At the turn of the century one could have counted the number of girls at university on the fingers of both hands; in 1960 there were over 200,000 and the number shoots up every year.

The Role of Education: The Indian Example

Education is the key to emancipation in every way. Not only does it open the door to economic independence, but it also cracks the crust of the joint-family. An educated daughter-in-law is not likely to kow-tow to an illiterate mother-in-law for long, she sets up a separate household. Indeed, hardly a decade ago, urban young couples were still expected to stay in the joint family, at least until they had children; today even before they get married they look for accommodation of their own and no evil tongue wags unduly. Even in the villages girls are becoming increasingly literate and correspondingly more demanding. As a result of education, both in the towns and the villages there is a shift in the way marriages take place. In the past marriages used to be arranged by the parents of the couple and their respective astrologers. Today marriages are no longer arranged, they are, more and more, prepared, that is the boy and the girl have an increasing say in what they expect their parents to lay on for them. Even petty clerks want literate wives because they want a wife they can talk to, and because an educated wife has become a status symbol. Parents now find it cheaper to educate a girl than to give her a full dowry; each year their daughter spends at school knocks the price of the groom down. While the groom wants a wife he can talk to, the bride has set views on what she expects from her husband; the more educated she is, the more set her views and narrow the parental choice. 'She wants a husband from our own subcaste and from our own town, he must be tall, handsome—of course—play tennis, twist, be fond of Western classical music and have a senior position as a steel engineer with the Government' wailed a friend telling me of his daughter's tall order. 'I begged her to go out and find a husband for herself but she would not hear of it, despite her degree in sociology, she is too old fashioned!' More and more girls are being too old-fashioned in this very modern sort of way. They are, down to the village lass, more and more inclined to exercise their ancient right of veto, for once they can read and write they acquire a new confidence, especially when arguing with parents who are still illiterate.

Educating women is the quickest way to transform the marriage pattern from a blind arrangement to a carefully planned operation, as a glance at the matrimonial ads in the newspapers shows—'Wanted husband for Arora school teacher age 27, good family, dowry seekers need not apply'. Less than a score of years ago a spinster of 27 was unheard of, people used to marry their crippled daughters to trees rather than let them remain single. Today girls in the cities get married in their mid twenties, who in the past would have been married off in their teens. And nobody seems to be surprised when girls work, and continue to do so after they are married and have children. Some work because they have to, others because they like to. My husband had to fight to be permitted to employ the first woman junior administrator in the Bombay Secretariat at the beginning of the War; he did not struggle in vain. The Secretariats in India are now largely staffed by women, who can be found at all the echelons from typist to head of a department, from Research Officer to Collector of a District. And in business too, women have been taking strides as wide as Puss in Boots. The days when a British traveller could be so depressed by what he saw in India that he was spurred to write 'the only thing female that is respected is the cow' have gone. Indeed, the thing which strikes the traveller today is the extent to which the women are coming into their own. There is no Indian equivalent to the misogynism which keeps women out of clubs in Britain and away from senior positions in America. Indian women may pay respect to their men, walk behind them, not contradict them in public—but nobody is under any illusion about who in the end takes the decisions; it seldom is the man.

Pakistan

The experience of the rest of the Indian sub-continent has been rather less dramatic, but the tendency is the same. In Pakistan—at least in the West—women began with a situation much more loaded against them than it was in India. West Pakistan was the home of purdah in its extreme form. And the middle class, which was the breeding ground of emancipation, was much weaker in Pakistan than in India. But the tendency in Pakistan was the same. In the educated élite, though it was so much smaller than that of India, the same feminine aspirations were found, there was the same growth of feminine public opinion, and the same capitulation by the males. This tendency was shown vividly during the military rule of Ayub Khan when the Government boldly tried to reform the marriage law and virtually abolished polygamy. The old masculine forces are still powerful, backed as they are by religion and the mullahs and feminism has to struggle, even to consolidate what it has already gained; but the gain among the small enlightened circle is real and far-reaching, and it is a circle which is likely to become wider and wider.

China and Communist Asia

That is one part of Asia. The part which is Communist has had a different experience. Whereas the non-Communist part has moved forward in the emancipation of women by the actions primarily of society, encouraged and registered by the acts of Government, it is Government itself which has been the great force in the Communist countries. The centre of achievement is China. The Communist Government, it is true, inherited legislation from its Kuomintang predecessor by which the whole legal structure of the family had been altered. A law of 1931 was of staggering enlightenment in matters of inheritance, divorce, and equality of women in property rights. But this law was never put in force. It was left to the Communist Government to show that female emancipation could be made a reality in China. The succession of laws which it has made are all of them admirable—laws against concubinage, bigamy, child betrothal, and sales of daughters and wives, laws banning arranged marriages and match-makers, and substituting marriage by choice, laws governing the ownership and management of family property.

At first these new regulations were accompanied by a vigorous propaganda to encourage their use by discontented women. This resulted in an extraordinary increase of the divorce rate in China. In 1951 it was one third as high as in the United States. Faced with this the Government went into reverse, and its influence was used to frown on casual marriage.

In all that has taken place in China, and in the countries under similar influence in Asia, the decisive role of Government has been obvious. What has the Government done? What is Governmental influence? That is the decisive thing. Under Governmental pressure these countries have advanced far towards a system of sexual equality. It is curious, therefore, that when one looks at politics, both at the apparatus of day by day political action, and at the ideas which are put into public circulation, women have played a disproportionately small part. They have not yet achieved that measure of political power which theoretically is theirs. They hold a disproportionately small share in public life (there are few women ministers and high civil servants), smaller, for example, than is found in India. The change has come about because the men, impelled by an ideal, have voluntarily abandoned the superior position that they held, and have invited women to staff the public life. But the women have not yet moved in in force. When they do so, and when they make their influence felt in Chinese society, by tradition strongly patriarchal, they will have brought about one more Chinese revolution.

BIBLIOGRAPHY

Dymphna Cusack. *Chinese Women Speak.* (Angus and Robertson, London, 1959.)
Mi Mi Khaing. *Burmese Family.* (Longmans, Bombay, 1946.)
M. N. Srinivas. *Marriage and Family in Mysore.* (New Book Company, Bombay, 1942.)
Barbara E. Ward. *Women in Asia.* (UNESCO Publications, 1963.)

BIOGRAPHICAL NOTE

Taya Zinkin. B. 1918. Studied medicine in Paris; researched in bio-chemistry at the University of Wisconsin. Lived in India from 1945 to 1960. From 1950 to 1960 correspondent from India for *The Economist* and *The Guardian*, and from 1955-60 for *Le Monde.* Author of *India Changes!* (Chatto and Windus, London, 1958), *Rishi* and *Rishi Returns* (Methuen, London, 1960 and 1961), *Caste Today* (Oxford Univ. Press, London, 1962), *Reporting India* (Chatto and Windus, London, 1962), *India* (Oxford Univ. Press, London, 1963) and (with Maurice Zinkin) *Britain and India: Requiem for Empire* (Chatto and Windus, London, 1964).

WOMEN'S DRESS IN ASIA

by

LADY MOOREA WYATT

WHETHER for good or evil Western dress is slowly spreading over the world. For some extraordinary reason this is equated with progress.

In the West women uncover their legs but not their bosom—at least not all of it. In much of the East they have tended to show their bosom but not their legs and even in China, where skirts are revealingly slit up the side, too much thigh indicates a good time girl.

Two respectable ladies I saw shopping in Bombay would have been arrested in England and jailed in Spain for the transparency of their blouses. But those rolls of spare tyre bulging nakedly between blouse and skirt are considered neither ugly nor indecent—merely comfortable and cosy. Saris stay up far more easily over fat than bone and a rounded stomach is a help.

Why should bare legs be more 'advanced' than bare breasts? Western standards are being imposed on the East. Our magazine camera men and film units are having the effect of the apple in the Garden of Eden. In Malabar and Bali bare bosoms are rapidly becoming old-fashioned. The Asian way of life is also changing in many areas and whereas kimonos or saris at home are charming, in a factory they may be dangerous. As women take a more active part in modern life, their dress must and does change.

THE INDIAN SUB-CONTINENT

Indian children usually wear cotton dresses till they are thirteen or fourteen and many girl students at universities now wear shorts and shirts for games and tight jeans much of the rest of the time, but as during a journey through India from Kashmir to Kerala, from Bombay to Madras, I saw not one single pair of these trousers (tight or otherwise) I assume they revert to national dress on finishing their studies.

The older generations of women still play squash, tennis and other games in saris by tucking the floating end into their waistband. There are no Indian women athletes of international fame. Could there be some connection? At the 1962 Commonwealth Games Great Britain, Australia, New Zealand and Rhodesia sent about 200 women competitors. Pakistan sent three and the Indian female contribution would have been on the same scale had it not been withdrawn at the last moment.

The 'sari' is either a silk or cotton length of cloth five-and-a-half to six yards long and 45 or 52 inches wide. Sometimes there is an extra yard woven on to make the blouse or 'choli', but often this is made from other material.

The cloth is wrapped once round the lower half of the body and tightly knotted (everything depends on that knot) at the waist. Then, leaving a length to hang over the left shoulder, the rest of the six yards are pleated in the front and tucked into the waistband. There is one danger. A charming young student told me that on her first day at College she left her dress too long and, when going up the steps to the inaugural lecture, tripped over her hem pulling these yards of pleats out of her waistband. This accident does not often occur, but some women guard against it with a safety pin.

In many ways the sari is an extremely practical article of dress. Indian women claim that they can dress in sixty seconds, taking thirty seconds for the sari and thirty seconds for sandals (chappels), blouse (choli) and, occasionally, a long petticoat. Brassières are a comparatively new innovation, rarely worn by poor women, never under those evening blouses which are fastened only by a thin ribbon tied across the back, and are hardly necessary under some day blouses which like a couturier evening dress are shaped to provide sufficient support.

It is claimed that in the 44-lb. air baggage allowance it is possible to take sixty saris and accessories. Many Indian women own several hundred saris.

There are few dressmakers and no maternity clothes.

Considering that all Indian women have black hair, almost invariably long and drawn straight back from the face, and that the sari is almost uniformly worn by adults, it is astonishing how very different they manage to look. If the narrator of the Arabian Nights had been an Indian girl, she would probably have worn a different hairstyle on each of the thousand and one nights.

A recent exhibition in Bombay showed hundreds of Indian arrangements. The front was brushed back with or without a centre parting and then elaboration began: three or four feet of hair twisted and turned, some in thin baby snakelike plaits, others in one thick luscious pigtail, into intricate designs usually with jewellery and/or sweet-smelling jasmine flowers. The lady attendants changed their own hair three and four times a day during the exhibition's run, never repeating the same style twice.

In the southern Indian state of Kerala girls wash their hair every day, not with shampoo but vegetable oils or 'ritha' (soap nuts). Then they decorate it with elaborate flower arrangements freshly made even at that early hour in the morning and dry it hanging down their backs on the way to school.

There is no demand for hairdressers and, except in the largest towns, the existing few are primitive. A German lady in Goa had a permanent wave. The curlers were removed and she was presented with her bill. 'But what about my set?' 'You don't need temporary curls now, we have given you permanent ones', and home she had to go to set her own hair.

Eastern fashion is colour not line. The variations on wearing a sari are so slight as to be hardly noticeable to an 'outsider'. No Dior dramatically dropping hemline. Although the Punjabi national dress (worn also by unmarried women in other regions) of knee length tunic ('kurta') over trousers ('salwar') has adopted the sack, princess and empire lines, it still remains tunic and trousers. At present the better the figure the tighter the fit.

Attempts have been made to modernize the choli but it has reverted to old styles, the only essential being a tight fit in sleeves and bodice whether cut to the diaphragm or, as in Bengal, to the waist, which is considered less chic.

The 1962 colour fashion was shot silk—no patterns or borders—with choli and handbag to match. As Indian women neither renew their make-up nor smoke, their bags would hardly suffice for evening in a western country.

The high cost of imported cosmetics (home manufactured are inferior) has restricted the use of make-up to eyes and a trace of lipstick. But the Hindu caste mark which used by its shape, size and colour to show to which sect the wearer belonged, is now used as a beauty spot. It is made by dipping a finger into black or red paste or powder and pressing it on the forehead. Only married women wear a mark in their hair.

Indian jewellery is often enormous, with earrings so heavy they need as well as the usual wire or clip a thin chain round the ear to support their weight. In Kashmir even peasant women working in the fields wear earrings hanging to their shoulders. The Indians have never perfected precious stone cutting, but use rough, uneven gems, and till only about fifty years ago pale emeralds, rubies and sapphires were backed by bright green, red and blue metal paper to deepen their tones—thus a deep rich green emerald removed from its setting could prove a disappointment, if not a swindle.

One of the most famous crafts is Jaipur work, a combination of jewels and enamel, which is more expertly finished than most gold and silver jewellery. These Jaipur necklaces, with stones one side and brightly coloured enamels the other, are fastened at the back by a sliding silk tassel.

There is a very ornate jewel to be worn only by the bride on her wedding day. Five rings—one on each finger and one on the thumb—are attached by small chains to a medallion on the back of the hand and that, also by chains, to a bracelet. But many Indian rings have curious small holes in them and I suspect have been detached from these wedding day jewels.

Small hands and arms are considered of great beauty and bracelets are almost vital even to the poorest girl. According to one manufacturer, a fashion in glass bangles can last as little as ten days. These bracelets must be as tight a fit as possible and a ritual is enacted by the girl and her jeweller. She sits with her arm raised while he carefully eases the tightest possible bracelet over her hand. If it slips on too easily she will not buy it. If he breaks it then she need not pay, but both are expert and he wastes more time than money.

There are also jewels worn on one or other side of the nose and anklets, but these are rapidly going out of fashion.

Variations on the sari occur among Parsees, Sinhalese and Pakistanis. The Parsee life and outlook are more Europeanized than those of other Indians—also affecting their clothes. They have short, dressed hair, evening shoes instead of flat sandals, Cartier-type jewellery and make their saris of Western brocade and evening dress material, fastening them with a brooch on the right shoulder. Sinhalese, who also favour the right shoulder, wear the 'kandian' sari, draped with a frill across the left side. Sarongs are also widely worn in Ceylon.

In Pakistan there is a separate two-and-a-half yard drape often worn over the head. Another Pakistani dress is the 'gharar', which is covered by a tunic.

A sari version worn by poor working classes in some parts of India is the 'marati', which is nine yards long and fifty-two inches wide. This yardage is draped, leaving an end to pull between the legs forming loose trousers, which on working women can be pulled up almost to the knee.

Cold Kashmir has its own peasant costume—a long, loose, chain-stitch embroidered shirt-cum-coat for men and women, with V-neck and enormous wide sleeves so that in winter the wearer pulls his arms inside to clutch his small charcoal transportable stove. This is nursed day and night, and in the winter it is central heating, hot water bottle and additional cooker combined.

Burma

Burmese dress has been influenced by Indians, Siamese, Portuguese—who introduced velvet—British and recently by the Chinese and, unlike the Indian sari, has changed through the last few centuries almost as radically as Western fashion.

The wired, stand-out-on-the-hip jackets, crowns, hair ornaments, hair waxings—padded and shaped as stiffly as French eighteenth-century powdered wigs, only black instead of white—now appear only in theatres. Modern Burmese costumes consist of blouse and skirt or 'longyi'. To visualize this skirt imagine a sack, beautifully coloured, open at both ends, reaching from waist to ankle, or mid-calf, and loose enough to contain two people. The spare material is pulled out usually to the right, then folded across the front and firmly tucked into the waist. For decorum it should reach mid-calf in daytime and ankle length at night, but teenagers leave home with a long skirt and hitch it up to their knees as soon as they are away from their parents. Sadly, the home-made wrap-over is being replaced by a sewn pleat and the new longyi is put on with a clip like a skirt.

The blouse 'angyi' is nearly always thin and often transparent, but never of the same material as the skirt. White is more popular than colours.

In Burma fashion changes only on the upper half of the body and recently the blouse shape has been Chinese, with mandarin collar, side fastening and frogging. The previously wide sleeves are now tight, either short or long. Stoles—'pawa' if gauzy and transparent or 'dabet' if in heavy material—were definitely 'in' for 1963. Completely visible brassières are waist length, embroidered or of lace and generally part of the costume. Richer ladies even wear real gold shoulder straps—which sounds dreadfully uncomfortable.

Although city make-up has become Western, country women continue to use their ancient formula for manufacturing a fine paste to cover face and body. This 'thanakha' is made from ground sandalwood, which gives a matt creamy-golden colour and a delicious faint scent from the wood.

Hair is often cut short, but still washed in oils extracted from tree bark. However, even when it reaches—as it often does—the ground, it is no longer waxed into the stiff stand-away shapes of the eighteenth and nineteenth centuries, but piled neatly into a smooth coil on top of the head.

Bikinis are not yet accepted by the richer women, but one-piece bathing suits are worn by girls and married women. Poorer Burmese women bathe in public with complete decency. The longyi is fastened above the breast while they wash under a pump or swim, then another clean dry longyi slips over the wet one and the change is complete.

China

The Chinese in the People's Republic of China ask one question—'Is it practical?' If the answer is 'yes' then that's the fashion. Hence the 'Lenin' or 'boiler' suit worn all over the country by both sexes and all ages. This is jacket and trousers. In cold areas the jackets are quilted, with silk padding inside. (This padding looks like coarse cotton wool but is pure silk.) Shoes are also padded, hats are worn only for warmth and fur coats and often gloves, too, have the fur inside.

Under this suit some Chinese, especially the older generation, wear a rich brocade shirt, but only remove their jacket if no political advisers are present. Only the old wear jewellery—a jade ring, or small gold or diamond stud earrings.

Until a few years ago serviceable material was rationed to two feet per person every six months. Expensive silks and brocades, however, were rationed only by price and now, especially in Central and Southern China where fashion has always moved faster than in the freezing North, V.I.P.s are wearing a loose cut version of the 'cheong sam' (Chinese dress) on formal occasions. And judging by recent magazine and newsreel films Western dress is gradually infiltrating into China. It is an interesting thought that till the 1930s all women wore a tight corset to flatten their breasts and many bound their children's feet.

Hong Kong and Formosa

In Hong Kong and Formosa the women have adapted their traditional clothes to Western style. Hem lines rise and fall with Dior; but the slit, mandarin collar and frogging for buttons and button holes still remain. As the hem varies, so must the slit. The longer and tighter the skirt, the higher the slit has to be to allow movement.

In Hong Kong dressmakers and Western materials are cheap; a working girl may buy between twenty and thirty dresses a year. Hairstyles, jewellery, make-up and accessories are more influenced by America through films than Europe.

Japan

Although the tea ceremony, traditional flower arrangement and cooking are still taught at Japanese finishing schools, the under-twenty-fives no longer wear kimonos. Their clothing and hairstyles come from American films, except on their wedding day when, if it is a traditional ceremony, they wear a white kimono with long flowing train and elaborate hair arrangement—now inevitably achieved by a wig.

The wide, stiff, breast flattening sash 'obi' is thirteen yards long, taking about fifteen minutes to tie, unlike the modern pre-tied, clip-on-in-two-seconds version now used by women at home. The bustle effect on the original is made by folds of material—in the modern time-saving substitute by a small pad or cushion.

The great majority of Japanese women go to work in Western dress, then change when they return home in the evening. These everyday kimonos are ankle length and have three-quarter, not too full, sleeves, to facilitate movement as all Japanese women cook. European women are often surprised to find themselves the only female at a dinner party, as despite their costume revolution Japanese wives take no part in their husband's social life and executives' wives live almost entirely at home.

In summer the 'tabi' (socks) are made of cotton, in winter of velvet, and are divided between the big and the other toes for the 'geta' sandals' thong. Woollen and nylon stockings are also made in this shape, but there is no demand for shoe sizes larger than four.

Nearly all valuable jewellery was broken up and melted down during the last war so, except for the modern costume variety, is non-existent. Only geishas, who maintain tradition in life and clothes, wear hair ornaments of coral or semi-precious stones in their elaborate waved and lacquered hair.

Peasant costume consists of 'mompei' which are baggy trousers worn with a hip length kimono-shaped jacket and small headscarf to keep the sweat out of the eyes. Hats and raincoats are of straw and when the wearers are working in the rain look like thousands of small round thatched ricks.

South Koreans like Japanese have adopted Western styles for work but most women retain their national dress ('chima-chokori') at home and for formal occasions. The only fashion changes are in the length of the bodice and width of the sleeves which always remain long. Flat rubber shoes (the same shape for both feet) and long thick socks are worn under the ground-touching skirts.

Malaysia and Indonesia

The same work-play, Western-Eastern mixture as that adopted in Japan and Korea applies also to Malaysia, Indonesia, Thailand and the Philippines.

Although Chinese and Indian Malaysians maintain their own dress at home, for official functions everyone now wears the Northern Malay 'sarong-kabaya' (skirt-blouse) of which the sarong is always long but the knee-high slit moves to front, back or side according to the latest fashion. In recent years sarongs and blouses have been machine-made and zip-fastened except for the widely worn 'baker-kurong' consisting of a knee-length dress over a sarong which is always hand-sewn and brightly coloured.

Considering that 90 per cent of Indonesians are Muslims, it is surprising that there are two women cabinet ministers, that there is equal pay for equal work, and that all the younger generation wear Western dress except for formal occasions such as weddings.

Indonesia is said to have more costumes than inhabited islands, but since independence women are encouraged to wear dresses from all regions. For instance Javanese now adopt Sumatrans' black blouse and trousers if they so wish, and vice versa, which previously would have been considered eccentric.

As in other Asian countries Western make-up is expensive, so, apart from lipstick, it is rarely worn, but older women still make traditional rice face-powder scented and coloured by flowers.

Javanese brides add to the universal style of long hair pinned into a bun by painting curves and points of trompe l'œil hair on their foreheads with blacking.

Country women still wear large straw hats, blouses and sarongs which are washed in tea leaves to preserve their bright colours. But all attempts to adapt the national costume for modern life have so far failed. Indonesians wear all-East or all-West but never a modification or mixture whereas in Thailand and the Philippines the national dress has been Westernized while still retaining some original features.

Thailand and Philippines

Under Queen Sirikit's influence Thailand evening dresses of the privileged minority might have come from Paris—except that all are made in Thai silk, sometimes embroidered or woven with gold and silver. Silk is so cheap in the manufacturing areas that few use any other material. The 'panung', a trouser skirt almost universal fifty years ago, is now nearly obsolete.

Brides wear colours, even brilliant orange, and as headdress a circle of plain cord joined to another circle on the bridegroom's head symbolizing their union.

Philippine costume has undergone dynamic changes through the centuries. Having started as a mixture of Malay and Chinese, it had become Spanish by the beginning of the 18th century under Mexican and South American influence; it then became isolated for a period from the West, and by the 19th century it had developed an individuality which has been retained despite renewed Western communication.

However closely evening dresses follow foreign fashion, they always have butterfly sleeves. These transparent, embroidered and heavily starched elbow-length sleeves which stand up and away from the shoulders are now often detachable.

South Vietnam and Laos

In South Vietnam and Laos fashion is independent of Western trends; most women wear national costume most of the time. Their black and often wavy hair hangs loosely on the shoulders of thin calf-length gowns with stiff high collars ('aó daì') which partly cover full black or white trousers ('quân') made in silk or synthetic fabrics.

In the capital of South Vietnam and the surrounding countryside palm-leaf hats are worn, tied under the chin.

There is little ready-made about Laotian dress. Hair worn in a bun on the right side of the head is decorated with a reddish gold chain. The bodice or 'phetu' is a self-draped stole, pinned over the left shoulder but leaving the right side bare. The only sewing occurs in the skirt, not as you might suppose at the sides but round the bottom, because the hem-like border is always of a different material and never woven in one piece with the skirt ('sinh'). This crossover sinh is supported by the usual tuck-in system as gold belts are more for ornament than use.

Dress and Industrial Advance

All over Asia dress trends go with industrial advance, but not necessarily with equality of rights for women. In Japan, where women's position is socially and economically inferior to men's and where politics as a formal career is inconceivable, nearly all the under-twenty-fives wear only Western dress. But in Burma, where for hundreds of years law, medicine and business have been open professions to women, and where there is near equality of inheritance (wills are non-existent and a wife or husband inherits full estate on the other's death, and when both parents die property is divided equally between children of both sexes) and near equality in marriage and also in divorce (even in the now rare polygamous marriages the first wife can if she objects to her husband taking a second wife sue for a divorce and partition of property)—with all this freedom Burmese women have chosen to retain their national dress. This is approximately true also of India, where women's rights are so rapidly improving. And the boiler suits of China have their obvious implication.

The trend to the West is like a rising graph with occasional drops. The hard fight for tradition will be lost—but extremely slowly.

BIOGRAPHICAL NOTE

Lady Moorea Wyatt is the daughter of the Earl of Huntingdon and is married to Woodrow Wyatt, M.P. She spent some years in the theatre before her marriage. She has written for a number of magazines on travel and fashion.

THE INTELLIGENTSIA

THE ASIAN INTELLECTUAL

by

EDWARD A. SHILS

The Problems of the Asian Intellectuals

The intellectuals of Asia, like their counterparts everywhere, are defined by the relative elaborateness of their intellectual activities, professional and vocational, such as those of university teachers, scientific research workers, literary men, theologians and journalists; or avocational, such as are sometimes found among businessmen, politicians, civil servants, physicians and engineers. The level of development of the intellectual classes, and their intellectual institutions, differs profoundly from country to country in Asia. At the one extreme is Japan with its many universities and research institutions, and with a vast output of science and scholarship, an impressive literary productivity, a tremendous and prosperous press and publishing industry and a dense and well-organized bookselling business; and India and Pakistan with great numbers, occasionally high quality and a profuse though disorganized system of intellectual institutions, through Burma, Indonesia and the Philippines, and the smaller countries like Laos and Cambodia with small bodies of intellectuals and very motley institutional systems.

The Asian intellectual classes, of all countries, including even Japan, have in common the recent and exogenous origin of their modern culture. All the Asian countries, unlike most of Africa, have a rich tradition of religious-philosophical culture, well developed in written form and cared for by a class of professional custodians. In Asia, modern culture, introduced from the West, had, by the beginning of the 20th century, developed an elaborate set of institutions, universities, learned societies, periodicals, etc., through which modern culture was reproduced and applied to indigenous problems and traditions. Together with these there developed a considerable indigenous personnel, well schooled in the techniques and outlooks of modern culture. Japan and India were in the forefront. In Japan, of course, the initiative was Japanese, in India, Indian and British initiatives were intermixed. In China too, mixed initiatives were giving rise to a modern intelligentsia, academic, journalistic and literary. In the other parts of South and South-East Asia under foreign rule, numbers were much smaller, but still some persons with a modern education—mainly lawyers and businessmen—existed to express an indigenous demand, to serve as a pressure group for the establishment of advanced modern higher educational institutions, and as a public for modern intellectual works, preponderantly of metropolitan origin. All these intelligentsias, large and small, with well equipped and well functioning institutions or poorly equipped and poorly functioning, a century old in their rooting in Western culture or relatively recent, all faced, and still face, certain common problems and have certain common responses. Nationalism, populism, xenophilia and xenotropism generally, xenophobia and nativistic revivalism, inferiority feelings, curiosity and resentment in the face of the metropolitan culture are found throughout the continent. Countries like Japan, which retained their sovereignty throughout, as well as those which were ruled by Western powers, manifested these attitudes.

The Scientific-Technological Void

In their occupational structure, the intellectual classes of the formerly colonial territories still bear the marks of their colonial inheritance as well as of the present economic backwardness of their countries. In the colonial period, except in India, the highest administrative posts were reserved for expatriates, but the middle ranks of administration afforded numerous opportunities for indigenous, educated persons. High posts for scientists and technologists in industry and in governmental technical services were similarly reserved and few in number. There was little advanced scientific research and teaching, the poverty of the population meant a low effective demand for medical services. Outside the service of government, the main opportunity for the educated to deploy their skills with a prospect of substantial financial reward was in the legal profession. As a result, the educated classes in almost all the Asian countries, except Japan, are markedly skewed in the direction of the arts subjects—literature, languages, history—and the social sciences, while the scientific and technological categories are rather poorly represented. Japan and, latterly and incipiently, China are the only Asian countries which, possessing a modern industrial system and a more or less modern system of mass communications, have an intellectual class in which the technological component resembles that of the advanced Western countries.

The governments of most of the Asian countries have, in recent years, tried to establish or develop further technological education, medicine and scientific research. Yet the fact remains that indigenously established industry, except in Japan, and, to a much lesser extent, China, is both rudimentary and reluctant to give a prominent place to technologists, scientists and engineers. (In India, for example, which is one of the more advanced countries of Asia, one-third of all engineers are employed in industry and two-thirds in government departments where, in some Western countries, the proportions are four-fifths in industry and one fifth in government departments.)

Since government departments are still the major employers of highly educated persons, the old tradition persists. It is indeed reinforced by the simple fact that the powerful drive to education, so characteristic of the new states of Asia, encounters no resistance from the arts faculties—more students can always be crowded into the lecture halls and standards are less exacting—whereas the scientific, medical and technological departments limit admissions more or less proportionately to the space available in laboratories.

(Furthermore, since the latter are much more expensive to construct and equip than lecture halls, the expansion proceeds more slowly.)

Discouraging Conditions

In income and wealth the Asian intellectual is generally a very poor man. Recruitment into the intellectual professions in Asia, although markedly biassed in favour of persons of middle class origin, is really too wide to remain a monopoly of the offspring of the wealthy classes. Intellectuals are therefore dependent on their earned income—often gained in several occupations concurrently practised—and supported by kinsmen in accordance with the traditions of the extended family system. Civil servants at the level of permanent secretaries and other members of the highest categories, some very successful physicians and lawyers, a handful of journalists and university professors, a small number in business, similarly small numbers of literary men, especially those who write for films, have incomes which permit them to live in what could be called, according to Western criteria, a middle class manner. The mass of journalists, secondary school and college teachers, literary men who write in the vernacular, most lawyers and doctors, although much better off than the masses of their countrymen, live in relative poverty. In their housing they are crowded far past the point where privacy of any sort is possible; they are unable to purchase books. Those with regular employment and income in the profession of their choice are the fortunate ones. At the bottom are the educated who have never been able to find a position corresponding even to very modest aspirations. About a tenth find no employment at all on the completion of their university studies, and this period of unemployment may persist for several years. Great numbers of the educated unemployed ultimately do find posts which, even though they are not what was sought, are sufficient for a scant livelihood. This is common to all the underdeveloped countries of Asia and even Japan, as a result of the tremendous expansion of university studies, has a moderate amount of intellectual unemployment.

This situation is most pronounced in India which had numerous universities before independence and a corresponding surplus of graduates. It has also become true of countries whose higher educational system has taken definite shape only since independence. Few governments have taken any steps to cope with the unemployment of the educated.

In all these countries, intellectual unemployment is an urban phenomenon. Unwillingness to accept posts as village teachers and community development workers, because of the lack of amenities and low salary, is fostered by the extended family system.

The traditional intellectuals—monks, priests—live in their traditional mendicant poverty, perhaps even less well than they lived under the colonial regime because of the diminution of patronage and charity resultant on reforms in land ownership and the diminution of the princely orders. Despite the political concessions made to them by governments in Pakistan, Ceylon and Burma and the flattery which, almost everywhere except Japan and the Communist states, is directed towards the traditional culture and its custodians, Asian governments have done very little to improve the economic lot or even the institutional provision for traditional intellectuals.

Intellectual Institutions

The three major Asian countries, Japan, India and China, are the only ones which have a relatively highly developed system of intellectual institutions. The Japanese system is the only one which has a full range of well-working universities, technical colleges, secondary schools, teacher training institutions, scientific and technological laboratories, libraries, museums, bookshops, broadcasting and television services, daily and periodical press, scientific press and book reviewing system.

The Indian system of intellectual institutions is, by virtue of its differentiatedness and amplitude, the most advanced of any underdeveloped country. It is less self-sustaining than the Japanese; it depends, like that of practically all underdeveloped countries, on government subvention and sponsorship. This is a consequence of the small size of the public willing and able to pay for intellectual goods and services. The literary market is very much smaller in India than it is in Japan. The supportive capacity of this small market is further diminished by the fragmentation of the country into a multitude of heterogeneous non-communicating cultures. The situation is no better in many of the other countries, in contrast with Japan where the public is linguistically homogeneous. For these reasons, journalism and literary institutions, which suffer in any case from inadequate professional, commercial and technical traditions, are further impeded by poverty.

The universities of most Asian countries are usually overcrowded and understaffed (often by part-time teachers), their libraries are small and dirty. The scientific research carried on in universities almost everywhere except Japan is scant in quantity and seldom important in quality. The publication of books and periodicals is ill-organized and often unscrupulous; the system of book distribution is haphazard. Scientific research outside Japan, China and India is very poorly provided for. Relatively little was inherited from the colonial regimes and, although the new governments have created many research institutions, their performance has generally been meagre—as could have been expected in situations where the tradition of modern scientific research has not been well implanted and where highly qualified personnel have been in short supply.

Modernity and Tradition

The culture of the intellectual classes of most of the Asian countries is of a threefold composition. There is, first, the modern culture which involves an appreciation of the validity of science and of a rational, non-magical approach to the problems of individual life and social organization; it involves knowledge of some of the main works of modern culture in science, literature, history, and a continuous contact with some stream of modern culture. The second culture is a mixture of the traditional and indigenous with the modern. It is a culture which entails familiarity with the lately metropolitan languages and an acquaintance with some of the main works in it; much of this second culture is in the indigenous language. The products of this culture are an unstylized, matter-of-fact intermingling of indigenous traditional and exogenous modern. The third culture is the traditional religious-philosophical culture.

Higher civil servants, the more important university teachers, scientists, engineers, outstanding lawyers, physicians, editors of leading newspapers and their more prominent correspondents, some politicians, are the major participants in the modern culture. The second, mixed culture, is shared largely by elementary and some secondary school teachers, particularly in rural areas and small towns, journalists in vernacular newspapers or in the provincial press, middle and lower rank civil servants, and most politicians, particularly those outside the central political élite. The traditional culture is carried by priests and monks, practitioners of indigenous or folk medicine, and religious teachers; although increasingly the bearers of the first and second cultures are taking their share in certain selected aspects of the third culture.

Since the acquisition of independence by the newly sovereign states, the balance has shifted somewhat more in the direction of the second class, from the first class which for so long had, jointly with the foreign ruler, played so vital a part in the implantation of the seeds of modernity in their societies. Even now the first class still occupies the central position of influence in their respective societies, in the higher civil service, in the law courts, in the leadership of the political parties, in the army, in journalism and in the universities. Since, however, the new regimes of Asia are either democracies, or populistic oligarchies, the second class and the third too have come forward to greater prominence and influence. In Japan, even the extremes of nationalism and hostility towards the West among the intellectuals have however not in recent years resulted in any marked upsurge of cultural revivalism.

Of course, in no Asian country is even the first class, the modern or 'Westernized' intellectuals, so modern or 'Westernized' that they preserve no traces of the indigenous traditional culture in their outlook, in their tastes and social relationships, in their self-identification, or in their loyalties. At the other end of the continuum, there must be very few in the third class who are entirely untouched by modern Western ideas and practices, and who do not respond in some way to their challenge.

The first class is often referred to as a class of 'Brown Englishmen' or 'Brown Frenchmen' or 'Brown Sahibs', as 'uprooted intellectuals, suffering from schizophrenia', as men 'suspended between two worlds belonging to neither.' They are alleged by their critics, often less educated politicians or littérateurs from their own circles, as being 'out of touch with the people'.

These criticisms notwithstanding, most of the Westernized intellectuals in the Asian countries retain in their outlook, in their family relationships and in their tastes, a great deal of their indigenous culture. Many of them know a great deal about their indigenous culture too, often more than the less well educated politician, whose education, such as it is, was also a modern Western education and whose indigenous culture is more a matter of espousal than of knowledge. The 'Westernized intellectuals' of Asia usually know more about the higher content of the traditional culture than their peasant fellow-countrymen with whom they are so often and so unfavourably compared. They are also more attached to the national idea than most of the rest of their fellow nationals in their country, they are likely to be less sectional, less regional, less communal, less caste-bound. Not that the 'Westernized intellectuals' are entirely free from these sectional attachments, they are just more free than most of their fellow countrymen.

Ambivalence and its Consequences

Their attachment to their country and their appreciation of its past and its traditions generally coexist with some disbelief in the traditional, indigenous view of the world and of man's place on earth. They are, generally, more secular in their understanding of the world, more hedonist in their conception of a good life, more equalitarian in principle, more accepting of science, technology, progress and the potentialities of human initiative in changing society. This complex of beliefs has proved to be fairly compatible with a considerable degree of embeddedness in traditional familial institutions and the retention of indigenous elements in their style of life. Internal strain and conflict, at least on the level of consciousness, do not always result, nor need they do so. Yet, so deeply has this self-image of a 'split personality', alienated from its society, penetrated into the consciousness of the modern Asian intellectual that it has become a secondary *malaise*. Their feeling of being *à l'écart* with respect to populistic and demagogic politics since independence has led many to accept as true the charge of 'being out of touch with the people'.

The intellectuals of the second class are much less afflicted by this problem. They do not possess so much modern culture that they feel themselves under attack when 'uprooted intellectuals' are being criticized. Most of their cultural life is lived in the medium of their mother tongue and its literature. So much of their professional activity as school teachers, local officials, journalists and authors is carried on in it and so unintense is their concern with the modern culture conducted in English or French that they feel no conflict or remorse. It does not occur to them to look on themselves as alienated. They are too concerned with local problems which always have an indigenous accent.

The traditional intellectuals, at least the more sensitive and more alert among them, feel themselves on the defensive, under pressure from the secularizing tendency of the 'Westernizing' intellectuals and higher civil servants of the big cities. Even where Buddhism or Islam is established as the state religion or where the state is designated as a Buddhist or Islamic state, the traditional intellectuals know that this has been achieved against the resistance of the political, administrative and intellectual élite of the country. The conflict in which they are engaged is an external conflict, not an internal one within their own minds.

Creativity and Intellectual Independence

In its modern culture, much of Asia is still uncreative. In Japan the novel flourishes; in India there are some literary men of genuinely high quality. There are some interesting painters. On the whole, the tendency is towards reproduction rather than creation. In mathematics and the natural sciences, Japan has become a fully modern culture. In India there has been some work of high quality in physics and Indians abroad have done distinguished work in this and in related fields. In India, research in the natural sciences is carried on on a large scale but the quality of the scientific output in India, throughout practically all the fields of science, is not generally thought to be up to a very high international standard. The situation in Pakistan seems even poorer, both quantitatively and qualitatively. In both of these countries, which, with Japan and China, are the most advanced in modern culture in Asia, there is a very marked tendency for some of the ablest young scientists to emigrate from their countries, temporarily, if not permanently, to Western Europe or North America. Throughout South-East Asia, scientific research scarcely exists. In the social sciences creative, and even routine, work at a high standard of proficiency is still scant. Valuable work is being done in the historiography of the region, and in the study of the indigenous traditional cultures. In these fields, the leading Asian scholars are now beginning to enter into collegial equality with metropolitan scholars.

The modern intellectuals of most Asian countries depend for their intellectual sustenance on the output from Western Europe and North America, and the level of intimate knowledge of this output is often very high. It is perhaps even too high for its own dignity, being impelled sometimes by a preoccupation with the culture of the old imperial metropolis almost as much as by a love of its intrinsic substance. Even in Japan, which in many fields of work is a full-fledged member of the world intellectual community, there is a strong xenotropic tendency. This preoccupation with the West as an intellectual metropolis is intimately connected with the continuation of substantial intellectual dependence on the West. Except for Japan, which has a very productive modern culture, nearly as self-sustaining as any modern culture in the world, Asian intellectual life continues to suffer from a many-faceted intellectual dependence on the old metropolitan centres.

The problem becomes acute in connection with the medium of instruction in the universities and the availability of textbooks. Practically all the other countries must still use textbooks in English or French, or textbooks which are translations and adaptations of European or American textbooks. Since, except in Japan, China and Indonesia, the medium of instruction has in the main been the metropolitan language, the situation could scarcely be otherwise. The introduction of a local medium of instruction, for which there is powerful motivation, is moving ahead. National self-regard, persistent preoccupation with colonialism, considerations of populistic politics and a conviction of the anomaly of the high culture of the country being conducted in a language foreign to the mass of the population, all give impetus to the drive, and only strong determination by educators and high administrators is able to hold it in check, while slowly yielding to the inevitable pressure.

The present and the oncoming generations of students face a situation in which they must either conduct their higher education in a language which they have very imperfectly mastered—owing to unsatisfactory language instruction—or, if they are instructed at a university in their mother tongue, they still have to depend for their reading on literature in a foreign language or on a very inferior kind of literature produced in their mother tongue. The consequences of this linguistic interregnum for the quality of culture of the Asian intellectuals are apparent. Their contacts with the more creative metropolitan culture will be attenuated before their own cultures have become creative. The high points of intellectual cultivation and urbanity attained in the Asian societies by a small proportion of the intellectual class will undoubtedly be maintained, but the proportion of those at the heights will be reduced while the proportion of the second class of intellectuals will increase very markedly, and many of the latter will therefore have to be drawn on to occupy roles such as university teaching, journalism and higher civil service.

The linguistic interregnum must, for a time, hamper the creativity of the indigenous modern culture, and thus will prolong the period of dependence. At the same time the metropolitan culture which comes to the Asian countries is dilapidated by the promotion of indigenous culture and the ramshackle quality of schools and universities, bookshops and libraries, periodicals and newspapers.

This cultural dependence has always carried with it overtones of inferiority. The response to this inferiority almost everywhere among Asian intellectuals has a propensity towards revivalism. This has entailed, in the new states, an effort to rehabilitate the indigenous culture, to make it more prominent and more appreciated. Among the most Westernized intellectuals, there has been a quickening of interest in the traditional artistic, architectural and religious inheritance. Here and there there are efforts to modernize by reformulation in the modern idiom and to discover points of continuity between the cultural inheritance and the aspirations towards modernity.

Intellectuals in Politics

The political life of the Asian states, except Japan, is in many important respects the creation and the affair of the modern educated class. The political élites of the new states of Asia were constituted almost exclusively from the parties and groups which had been in opposition under the colonial regime. The longer history of the Indian political movement and the relatively early and large supply of educated and cultivated lawyers, business men, publicists and social workers permitted the formation of a political élite of mature men. Similarly, the longer experience of the Indian movement for a larger share in government—and ultimately for self-government and its much larger scale—permitted the emergence of a differentiated body of specialized politicians, party organizers and 'bosses'. In the other countries of Asia, the movement was of more recent growth and tended to draw on a younger generation, particularly from the student population.

The political leaders in Asia—except for Japan, where an older aristocracy and plutocracy could provide personnel for politics—were drawn from the modern intellectual class. There were indeed few other groups from which a political élite could be drawn. Landowners and merchants lacked civic spirit and national concern; the latter were often alien in race and culture, and they and the landowners prudently sought to avoid incurring the displeasure of the colonial rulers. Teachers in government schools and colleges and civil servants were barred from public political agitation, unless they were ready to give up their coveted stability of employment. Hence mis-employed educated young persons, some of the prosperous lawyers and physicians, and more of the less successful lawyers with time on their hands supplied the personnel of political agitation. The tradition, endemic in the oriental religions, which authorizes the religiously learned and devoted to eschew the daily comforts and routine responsibilities of this world and to live from the charity of others, both impelled many of the intellectuals to turn towards the higher cause of politics and enabled them to live in a calling which offered no significant income.

The political intellectuals of Asia, particularly those who came into politics after the First World War, were to a man nationalist and anti-imperialist. Anti-imperialism tended almost automatically to be anti-capitalist and therefore, by implication, socialist. Asian intellectual politics have also become increasingly populist; the more insistent on complete independence, and the less they were inclined towards the piecemeal enlargement of the sphere of self-government, the more populist they tended to be. For the most part they were culturally modernist and anti-traditional as well, although the need to provide a cultural legitimation for nationalist political aspirations led to a more affirmative attitude towards selected elements of the traditional indigenous culture. Finally, the politics of the intellectuals in Asia before independence were oppositional and agitational, and often merely obstructive since, with the exception of a short period in India in the second half of the 1930's, there was no constitutional possibility for a nationalist political movement to assume power as long as the foreign ruler remained.

With the attainment of independence, the political outlook of the intellectuals retained much of its earlier content. Those who took over the responsibilities of government became professional politicians to a greater extent than before. As members of the government, they had regular incomes. They also had to pay more attention to their party machinery; this entailed for the major parties, to a greater extent than before independence, the creation of a party apparatus, which required full-time, regularly paid political employment.

This led to a fissure in the ranks of the intellectuals between those who now had a stake in the new government and its supporting institutions and those who remained outside. The former soon lost their oppositional disposition; the latter retained it and even deepened it.

The routines and the pitfalls of governing have produced a type of man and a type of rhetoric which fits poorly with the Asian intellectual's reverence for selflessness and for a pattern of life in accordance with a high, quasi-religious, ideal. The result has been disillusionment with politics. In some cases the disillusionment is accompanied by a greater realism and a resigned reconciliation with the breed of politician available and with the rigours of the politician's task; in others disillusionment has led to alienation from politics, not only in action but in sentiment and belief. De-politicization is the end-product.

What is striking about the Asian intellectuals, given the importance of the political culture of the European thirties which is so important in their political tradition, their anti-imperialism, their collectivistic outlook in economic matters and their fluctuating anti-Western impulses, is that so few of them have become active Communists or even sympathizers with the Communist Parties in their countries. Fellow-travelling is certainly common among Asian intellectuals—it is in a sense the 'natural' political outlook of the Asian intellectual—but membership and active support of Communist parties, legal and illegal, is certainly not widespread.

No discussion of the politics of the Asian intellectual can overlook the importance of the university student and even of the high school student. In the independence movements, they supplied many of the lower-rank agitators. Demonstrations, which are an essential part of Asian politics, almost always draw heavily on student support.

To cite a few instances: the Japanese students are of an extreme and passionate turbulence, of which the wild demonstrations prior to the projected visit of former President Eisenhower to Japan gave only one instance. In Burma, the government of General Ne Win recently felt called upon to destroy physically the Student Union because there was a nest of student agitation. The restless demonstrativeness of the Indian students has often been noted in political as well as non-political events. In Pakistan the students, even in the more repressive phase of General Ayub's military government, reconciled themselves to the regime less passively than any other section of Pakistani society. In South Korea student demonstrations played an important part in bringing down the government of Dr. Syngman Rhee.

The tradition is an old one, as old as the independence movements and modern higher education in Asia. Adolescent rebelliousness, the decline of traditional authority, the impoverished conditions of student life, the lack of prospects, economically, of the students on graduation, youthful idealism have been significant factors. The deliberate machinations of party politicians, especially among the opposition within and outside the ruling parties, aggravate the situation.

The Prospect

In the coming decades, the intellectuals of the Asian countries are bound to increase in number. The rapid expansion of the university population throughout Asia guarantees that there will be more university teachers, and that from among the growing number of graduates there will be an indeterminate number who will follow intellectual occupations or who will develop and pursue intellectual interests avocationally. It is also likely that the governmental cultural bureaucracy—in communications, in the administration of academies, etc.—will increase. The belief in the need for technologists and applied scientists will also increase facilities, create posts and undoubtedly attract many persons.

The vocational opportunities will undoubtedly be outnumbered by the aspirants with the formal qualifications of university degrees and diplomas. The rate of economic development of the Asian countries is not likely to be great enough to absorb all who aspire to follow an intellectual occupation. There is bound to be an increase in those in lesser administrative and clerical posts and a large number who feel themselves mis-employed.

The large numbers who enter into government service in one form or another will not greatly enhance the status of the intellectual in Asia. Government service, aside from the security it confers, is not such a claim to deference now as it was before independence. There are too many people in it with a marginal economic existence; it is no longer believed to be the only proper place for young men of the highest intelligence, and the low esteem in which politicians are held will not enhance the reputation of those who staff their governments.

Teaching in colleges and universities is likewise not likely to increase in prestige, insofar as income and dignity of employment are sources of such prestige. The large numbers of students, the indifferent quality of the instruction which they seem destined to receive in the near future, and the undistinguished intellectual output of university staff will also not enhance their position in their respective societies.

What then are the chances for greater creativity where there has been little recently, or for the development of a higher standard of performance, which, even though not creative in a deep sense, would markedly raise the average level of intellectual attainment? Regarding the former: in literature, in painting or in the arts generally, such a development is not inconceivable. The improvement of performance in the non-artistic spheres of cultural life, of scientific and scholarly research, of university teaching, of journalism, of the learned professions, is more subject to policy, and therefore to wise policy, than in the artistic sphere. Much depends on the leadership of the universities. The difficulties which the near future will inherit from the present will be very great. Throughout India, Pakistan, Burma, the Philippines and Indonesia, the universities are in a bad way. In China, they have no opportunity to exercise leadership. Only in Japan have some universities managed to distinguish themselves from the motley of mediocrity, and therewith maintained, at least in certain fields of science and scholarship, a standard which reminds the deficient of their deficiencies. Yet, in the rest of non-Communist Asia, the situation is not hopeless. The human material is there. Many outstandingly intelligent young Asians manage, despite their university systems, to come through to qualify themselves, and to do excellent post-graduate work overseas. (Many, of course, are so poorly trained that, when sent overseas, they are incapable of doing competent work.) Many of them who do good work overseas are wasted in all sorts of ways when they return home. Sheer difficulty in finding fitting employment is one source of waste; another is life in an unstimulating intellectual environment in isolation from other talented men and women of their own generation and interests. There are no reasons, other than political hesitation, bureaucratic indifference and the jealousy of older mediocrities in prominent positions, why this waste of talent should be allowed to go on. A little more courage by politicians, a little more alertness on the part of bureaucrats, a little more generosity on the part of the elders, would make it possible for one or a few high grade universities in the more populous countries, one high grade regional university in the French-speaking countries of South-East Asia, to emerge. It would not be necessary, to attain this end, to change the open admissions policy which is now followed and which is one of the factors in the dilapidated condition of intellectual life of this area. All it would require is a little determination to concentrate resources more circumspectly than is done at present. Such a concentration helps to explain the superiority of Japanese intellectual life. If this were done, there would be grounds for hope that the intellectual life of the Asian societies would find a new centre of gravity. The civil service which depends on the universities would be immensely benefited, economic policies would be improved, public criticism would be better informed and more realistic. The formation of a highly qualified specialized corps of scientifically trained technologists would be furthered. Science and scholarship would become sufficiently productive and small but effective intellectual communities would grow up. Intellectual dependence and provinciality would begin to fade. The Asian intellectuals would begin to become equal members in the world-wide intellectual community.

BIOGRAPHICAL NOTE

EDWARD A. SHILS. B. 1911; Professor of Social Thought at the University of Chicago. His publications include *The Intellectual between Tradition and Modernity: The Indian Situation* (Mouton, The Hague, 1961) and *Political Development in the New States* (Mouton, 1963); joint editor (with Talcott Parsons) of *Toward a General Theory of Action* (Harper and Row, New York, 1962.)

EDUCATION IN ASIA

by

JOHN VAIZEY

THE development of Asian education has been held back by the extreme poverty afflicting the majority of Asian countries. It is only in the last few years that they have been enabled even to conceive of the possibility of mass education, and it is still the case today that in Asia as a whole roughly half the population is denied any opportunity of being educated.

There are of course wide variations between the different regions. In South Korea *all* children between the ages of 6 and 12 go to school; Ceylon and Thailand are almost as advanced in the percentage of their school-age children at school, while in all sectors of education Japan leads the rest of Asia. In other countries—India, Pakistan, South Vietnam, Indonesia, for instance—only half the child population has the chance of receiving any education at all.

Geographical Dispersion and Linguistic Variation

Within the Asian continent there are immense variations between the different countries in size, population and development, but most Asian countries have something between three-quarters and four-fifths of their population in rural areas; not only this, but the rural population in these countries is split up into thousands of tiny communities, each isolated, and poverty-stricken in the extreme. There are in India 443,000 such communities of less than 200 people, and the position is paralleled in Burma, Malaya, Pakistan, Laos, Indonesia and many other Asian countries. The situation is further complicated by the fact that the population is also split up by innumerable differences of race, custom and language, which create additional difficulties for social and economic contact. India, for instance, has well over a hundred separate dialects of speech, while there are at least a dozen major literary languages. Indeed, most Asian countries are multilingual, with from two to twelve major written languages, apart from the many varieties of spoken tongue.

Primary education, therefore, faces these two immense problems—the geographical isolation of a large proportion of the population in small groups, and serious complications of language. Even when children have been provided with a school they have at the very beginning to overcome tremendous language barriers to learn the basic skills of reading and writing. This must often be done in a language other than the one in which they speak, and often too in one where the script itself is extremely difficult to master.

These difficulties exist, of course, throughout the population, but as with any underdeveloped area there are some groups—the rural population, the poor, and girls—which are more under privileged than the rest of the population. It is particularly unfortunate that women should be handicapped in much of Asia not only by the economic poverty which keeps them uneducated, but also by social and religious taboos which exercise strong pressures against their emancipation.

Shortage of Teachers

One of the major difficulties in providing opportunities for basic education for the whole population is the chronic shortage of teachers, and in other parts of the world women make up a large percentage of the teaching force. It is here that the Asian countries fall behind. In almost all of them women have an inferior status, and there is strong prejudice against educating them, even where schools do exist. Every country, with the exception of the Philippines and South Korea, is very short of teachers, and foreign nationals, even if they could be recruited in sufficient numbers, cannot possibly fill a gap which must eventually be filled by the Asians themselves.

Here again there are striking differences between regions. In the Philippines (where the teacher shortage does not exist) there are many more women than men teachers; in Ceylon the numbers are equal. But at the other extreme India and South Korea have only 20 female teachers to every hundred men. In these and many other countries the status of women is still very low, and new ideas come slowly. But it is vital that these countries come to appreciate as soon as possible the important contribution which educated women can make to a country's social, cultural and economic progress. The education of women could, too, be a factor in stemming the population flood, by dispelling ignorance and giving women new standing and dignity outside the home. It could have a vitalizing effect even within the confines of the home, since it is generally known that a child is greatly influenced by his mother—the only person with whom he is in close contact during his early formative years. Women too can provide a cheaper teaching force, since they are paid less, and the opportunities for advancement elsewhere are more limited for them. The education of women then is vital to Asian development. Only when they emerge to take their proper place in the economic and cultural life of their country can it begin to realize the full extent of progress possible.

The low status of women, however, is not the only hindrance to the recruitment of sufficient teaching staff. Many educated Asians are unwilling to work in jobs which they feel to be inappropriate to their social status. This is partly a function of the wage or salary level; the employment of educated and trained people is inhibited in some sectors because the conventional salary acceptable to a graduate is more than he is worth to the firm which would employ him. Teaching suffers in this way from its low standing and relatively poor pay, and many whose training would fit them to teach remain unemployed. In India, for example, there are three million unemployed graduates; there are also large numbers of unemployed intellectuals in Pakistan; and this situation is mirrored throughout many of the countries of Asia.

Another facet of the problem of status is that it is almost impossible to recruit educated people to teach in village schools; those qualified to teach tend to live in towns and are unwilling to return to the country where they feel their social standing would be lowered and where, in addition, they are likely to encounter difficult conditions for their work.

Those who do go into teaching are quickly attracted away to posts which hold a higher social status. Government service, for instance, provides an alternative which carries both a higher salary and a far greater degree of prestige.

Financing Expansion

Educational development in Asia depends on the possibilities of raising additional revenue or of diverting expenditure from other services; and in countries so poor as these this presents a formidable problem. Educational expansion conflicts with other urgent and competing claims on the limited resources available, and puts a strain on budgetary resources.

Training schemes must be developed to meet the ever-swelling demand for teachers, and it is here that foreign aid funds can be wisely invested. Special teacher training programmes have been started in Laos and Malaya, while in India Literacy Village, in Lucknow, has been set up as a centre training people to teach reading and writing. Three new polytechnic institutes have been developed in Pakistan to train teachers for technical schools, thus giving a new impetus to technical schools in other parts of Pakistan, and in South Vietnam a technical education teacher training centre has been established at Phutho.

In China, between the years 1950 and 1953 the primary school enrolment increased by over 75 per cent, and by 1960 87 per cent of children aged 7 to 12 were attending school. Even in the primary classes, however, political training is included, as also are extra-curricular activities. In the secondary classes an increasing amount of time is spent in production—for example, in small factories—and vocational secondary schools are organized by individual Ministries, teaching 'not only to understand theories, but also to carry out actual operations'. The Chinese are emphasizing secondary vocational education and higher technical education to combat the shortage of intermediate technical personnel.

Aids and Equipment

But it is important too in creating the fullest possible impact with limited resources to attempt to increase the range of each teacher. Any auxiliaries to the teaching process which are not too demanding in terms of skill and specialized requirements are welcomed in a situation of teacher shortage. The most feasible method in Asia at present would appear to be teaching by radio, which is already done on a nation-wide scale in Japan. Films and television are expensive in that they require costly equipment and skilled technicians, but radio is far less demanding in equipment or human skill, and it seems possible that when this method is adopted the well-organized system of Japanese school-broadcasting could be used as a model for emerging Asian countries.

But besides teacher training and the effective use of trained skills, the construction of new school buildings is an important aspect of the educational programme of the Asian countries. The immensity of this task can be measured by the vast numbers of small but separate communities scattered in their thousands throughout Asia, many of which are without school or teacher. Some remarkable progress has been made during the last ten years; but the need is still tremendous, and the population is increasing at such a rate that it is often difficult, even with the utmost stretching of resources and careful deployment of labour, to maintain existing standards, let alone to make any kind of progress.

Wastage

Yet expansion of population is not the only setback to a real increase in the growth of the education system. In addition the wastage rate of school-children in many countries is unfortunately very high. Apart from Malaya and South Korea, every Asian country has a drop-out rate of at least fifty per cent of children enrolled in the first year. In Pakistan only two per cent of these eventually attain any sort of educational qualification. This of course means that money and energy directed towards a child's education are largely wasted.

There are many explanations for this wastage. The sheer hard work of struggling to learn to read and write in a language which is completely different from the dialect in which they speak inevitably deters large numbers of children who perhaps make an effort for a year or two, but eventually become discouraged and dispirited, and drift away from school. In addition the great use made of child labour in most of the Asian countries, particularly in rural areas, keeps many children out of school at particularly busy periods of the year.

Above all, it is easy for a child to drop away from school when there is no environmental stimulus to encourage him to persevere. Many children live in small peasant communities, where there is no direct and obvious incentive to learn even the basic skills of reading and writing. The community lives at a bare subsistence level from its agriculture, using methods which have been handed down from father to son. Since there is no outlet for any use of skill—no books, no paper, no form of mass communication which might provide intimations of the wider world—it is extremely difficult to give a child from such a background any appreciation of how education can help him to make his life more useful.

Further difficulties arise from the fact that any educational traditions which do exist are dominated by the tradition of the prevailing religion. In Asian religions the oral tradition lays great stress on the ability to memorize; this is directed towards the learning of prayers, ceremonial rituals and similar religious functions. But such habits have a stultifying effect on the true learning process, and are at odds with Western methods of modern education, which emphasize initiative and an intelligent critical approach to problems.

Such methods of teaching, however, require aids such as pictures, books and tools, which are all too often rarities in the Asian school. Because of the complications of language books are difficult and costly to produce; the basic teaching tools are often regarded as luxuries by Asian schools with their paucity of equipment.

University Education

Within the wider context of higher education, the Asian countries are playing their part in the rapid expansion which is taking place throughout the world. In the last ten years there has been a 25 per cent increase in the number of graduates in the Asian countries, and this rapid expansion of higher education characterizes much of the educational development of Asia today. In many Asian countries it outstrips the expansion of primary and secondary education.

In the universities the language problem mentioned above is intensified, in that many courses are conducted in Western languages which few students have mastered sufficiently to use as a tool for abstract or analytical thinking. But language difficulties are not the only cause of the lowered standards in some Asian universities. Often the rigid curriculum of the schools, which still predominates in many of these countries, stultifies the student's creative ability. Many of those who enter the university are thus in fact incapable of benefiting from the higher education they receive, and their presence lowers the general standards of learning in the college. Added to this is the fact that many students finish their secondary school course in their early teens, and enter the university at the age of fourteen or fifteen. There have, however, been proposals to prolong the secondary school period in India from 11 to 17, for students who wish to transfer to higher education. In this proposal is the implicit acceptance of the fact that in a well-developed educational system the three stages of education—primary, secondary and higher—should be organically related, each planned to lead on from the next.

Another important facet of higher education is the fact that many students study abroad, and so co-ordination between the educational levels is necessary if they are to take their places as equals in foreign universities with their Western counterparts. This opportunity is particularly important for those from countries where facilities for higher education are not adequately developed.

China, in her higher education programme, emphasizes technical and scientific subjects to the extent of over-specialization in the universities. Figures for university education from Communist China are distorted and confused, but certain features of the education system are prominent. One of these is the system of the integration of work and study introduced by the Communist regime. This integration appears to have been carried out fairly smoothly in subjects such as engineering, agriculture and medicine, where labour has some relation to studies, but it apparently met with strong opposition from students in such fields as the arts, history and philosophy. Chinese students seeking advanced degrees until recently went to the USSR to further their studies, whereas before the Communists came into power they usually went to Europe, America or Japan.

Japan has the most developed system of higher education in Asia. Here too there has been a phenomenal increase in the number of students at institutes of higher education—in 1951 there were over 310,000 students, while at the time of writing the figure has risen to over 2 million. This very rapid increase is due to the establishment of junior colleges, which make up an important part of the Japanese higher education system, much as they do in the United States of America.

Adult Education

Adult education in Asia poses different problems in many ways from those arising in the education of young people, for it is primarily concerned with enormous masses of illiterate men and women. If the problems of organizing primary, secondary and university education in most of the Asian countries seem immense, how much larger are those arising from the task of educating an enormous population of illiterate adults, whose lives are taken up by their work or homes, who exist largely at subsistence level, and who often have no incentive to make the tedious and necessary first efforts at becoming literate. Nevertheless, despite the difficulties, progress is being made in most of the Asian countries towards achieving a functionally literate population, able to compose short letters, to read notices, government announcements, and news, and able to play useful parts as workers, parents and citizens. The corner stone of this progress has been the training of the population in social education, combining instruction in the mechanical skills of literacy with teaching in such things as hygiene, housecraft, and home nursing.

The basic problem, then, in providing adult education is that of teaching vast scattered populations who are largely illiterate. In many Asian countries this has been achieved by the method of literacy campaigns, usually organized by a department of the central government; these, when thoughtfully worked out with the needs of adults in mind, are meeting with success. In Burma the Mass Education Council was formed in 1949 with the purpose of providing a fundamental education for the general population. The Council runs classes in the rural areas, each class being set up by an organizer specially trained in the work of teaching people to improve their social and educational condition. A similar development can be noted in other areas.

One of the main difficulties, however, in organizing such literacy campaigns, is the need to provide an incentive to attract the adult population. In no Asian country is adult education compulsory, and unless classes can be made instructive and attractive people either do not attend at all, or else gradually drop away in discouragement. It is here that the importance of combining social education with instruction in literacy is seen. In both India and Pakistan, the first attempts at literacy campaigns met with little success. Poorly paid teachers were virtually compelled to conduct classes in reading and writing, using dark unattractive rooms, and without the aid of any mass-media either during the classes or as a follow-up programme. So even those who persevered quickly relapsed into illiteracy. In India adult education is now known as 'social education', and includes training in hygiene, agriculture, the responsibilities of citizenship, and crafts, all of which have a direct bearing on the individual's daily life, and all of which, therefore, help to make the programme meaningful to him. Travelling theatres, lectures and radio programmes have been introduced to stimulate interest, and the aim is to enrich adult life and encourage active participation rather than produce narrowly literate adults.

Other countries, too, have found that the use of mass-media is of great importance in their adult education campaign. The Adult Education Division of the Ministry of Education in Thailand contains a section for audio-visual education, which produces films for adult education. Such media are also used in the Philippines, and in Ceylon, where there is a special branch of the Education Department—the Audio-Visual and Adult Education Branch. Besides organizing adult education in general, this department arranges special rural broadcasts, and film shows by mobile cinema units which tour the rural areas. Japan, with her well-developed education programme and high standard of literacy, is even more advanced in the use of educational aids in her adult education programme—also called 'social education' here. This is looked upon as a follow-up of the compulsory education of Japanese children, and is conducted, much as in England, through groups using local facilities such as libraries and museums, and through correspondence courses.

But the difficulty of encouraging active participation in the literacy campaigns is intensified by the lack of workers in the field; although plans are often made for teachers to train substitutes to take over from them in the different areas the problem is still immense. In India rural training colleges (Janta Colleges) have been set up to train women for social education in rural areas, in an attempt to cope with the teacher shortage. Here too, as in Thailand and many other of the Asian countries, ordinary teachers work in the evening at adult education classes; but the scheme is handicapped by insufficient personnel. In Ceylon, too, the adult education movement is held back for this reason, despite the high literacy rate for Asia of 75 per cent found there.

In some places the prevailing religion is a help in providing personnel to staff the adult education drive. In Burma and Thailand the monks of the Buddhist monasteries play an important part; the tradition demands that every man should enter the priesthood for several months, and should become literate either before or during that time. Elsewhere private agencies help to support the work of the central government, by providing financial aid, by promoting their own schemes, and by training workers in the field. In Malaya, for example, evening classes for adults are organized by private bodies in addition to Government departments, while in Ceylon the Association of Women's Institutes—a private organization—is mainly responsible for providing social training for countrywomen.

But teacher-training schemes and the help of private agencies are not sufficient to provide the enormous numbers of teachers required, and other means have to be sought in addition. Some countries have found that the method known as 'each-one-teach-one' helps to solve the problem of teacher shortage. In this method school pupils who have already become proficient at reading and writing act as teachers, passing on these basic skills. This method is used, for example, in the Philippines, where half the adult population has never attended school. It has also been used to great effect in China.

In nearly all the Asian countries there exist, in addition, schemes for adult education directed towards the adult who wishes to improve his technical education, or to acquire new training in specific skills. This training is also usually organized by the central government, and varies from country to country in the number of courses offered, and the level attained. In Hong Kong and Japan there are Evening Institutes offering adult classes in languages, commercial and technical subjects. Other countries, such as the Philippines, Formosa, and Ceylon, offer evening classes in more elementary subjects such as carpentry, sewing, weaving or typing. Such classes are often attached to the day school in the area. Yet again in other areas, as in China and in Cambodia, apprenticeship schemes exist for technical education.

But vocational training must be built on a sound basis, and the fact remains that the adult education movement in nearly all the Asian countries is still mainly concerned with the problem of illiteracy. New schemes for adult education have to overcome apathy and prejudice, and the whole system is still severely handicapped by shortage of trained staff and lack of finance.

Priorities

This brings us to the question of priorities. It is impossible for any of the Asian countries, with their limited resources in terms of money and teachers, to attempt at once a full programme of education for the whole population. What has to be decided is the extent to which different levels and kinds of education should be developed, and in different areas the 'target group' towards whom education would be most wisely directed will differ. In some areas priority may be given to agriculture as the main means of economic growth. In such a case the development of new agricultural techniques would be vital, and rural education would figure largely in the country's education programme. In other countries the need may be for literate clerks to staff the administration, or for workers who have mastered simple skills of a technological nature. It is for each country to direct its education towards the provision of the type of skilled personnel needed in its economic growth, and it is here that the evaluation of manpower requirements can play a major part in determining the course of a country's development.

Yet there do exist very strong pressures towards mass education. Even in cases where this appears economically unsound it seems likely that the Asian countries will gradually have to find their way round those difficulties in the path of providing a simple basic education for the great majority of the population. It is a responsibility which cannot be ignored.

BIBLIOGRAPHY

Ronald S. Anderson. *Three Epochs of Modern Education.* Bulletin 1959 No. 11. (U.S.A. Office of Education, 1959).

Britannica Book of the Year 1962. *World without Want.*

G. P. Dartford. *Problems of Malay Education.* (O.Ed. Vol. XXIX No. 1, April 1957).

Nicholas de Witt. *Soviet Professional Manpower.* (Harvard University, Washington D.C., 1955).

O.E.E.C. Policy Conference on Economic Growth and Investment in Education, Washington 1961. Paper III 'The Strategy of Educational Supply' by J. Vaizey, and 'Manpower Planning and Education' by P. Pant.

Phi Delta Kappa. Vol. 39 No. 1: M. Justus van der Kroef, *Education in Indonesia.* Vol. 39 No. 3, December 1957: Special Issue on problems and promises of education in Asia.

Science and Freedom, No. 19, June 1961. *Academic standards and the new universities of South-East Asia.*

Thomas Nicholas Siquerai. *Modern Indian Education.* (Oxford Univ. Press, London, 1960.)

K. C. Vyas. *The Development of National Education in India.* (Bombay, Vora and Co., 1954).

UNESCO. *Education and Progress* (1961). *Manual of Educational Statistics* (1961). *The Needs of Asia in Primary Education* (1961). *Compulsory Education in Cambodia, Laos and Vietnam* (1955). *World Survey of Education*, I, II, III (1961). *Current School Enrolment Statistics* (September, 1962). *International Yearbook of Education* (Vol. XXV, 1963.)

BIOGRAPHICAL NOTE

JOHN VAIZEY was a Scholar of Queens' College, Cambridge, where he took Firsts in Economics. He taught Economics at Cambridge, where he was a Fellow of St. Catharine's College, and later at Oxford, where he was a Lecturer. He then became Director of the Research Unit in the Economics of Education, attached to the University of London Institute of Education. He is an economic consultant to the Organization for Economic Co-operation and Development, UNESCO, and the United Nations, and has worked full-time for all three. He is at present Official Fellow and Tutor of Worcester College, Oxford. Author of several books, including *The Cost of Education* (Allen and Unwin, London, 1958), *The Economics of Education* (Faber and Faber, London, 1962), *Education for Tomorrow* (Penguin, London, 1962) and *The Control of Education* (Faber and Faber, London, 1963).

BOOKS IN ASIA

by

MICHAEL FODOR

In the varied circumstances of Asian countries there are superficially similar conditions: shortage of paper and printing machinery; problems of typography; lack of copyright laws; difficulties of distribution and much mistrust pervading everything and everybody. Each of these is due basically to a variety of causes; climate, language, religions differing from region to region, country to country and also within national boundaries.

A high degree of education, unless it is part of a coherent programme for social as well as economic development, cannot be achieved. In the Western world as well as in the more advanced newly developing countries, schools, industrial development, and libraries are chronologically close to one another. Historically the introduction of compulsory education and the first library acts, authorizing the expenditure of public funds on the maintenance of free libraries for the general public, are closely related in England. An educational programme, without the backing of easily available purposeful reading material will be wasted to an extent which in terms of agriculture and food production would mean a famine of country-wide magnitude. Books and information must be readily available to the general reader as well as to the administrator, to the large industrial concern as well as to the university professor or student. This is the backbone of a well informed, democratic, continuously developing society.

While it is now accepted in Asian countries that the eradication of illiteracy is the responsibility of governments, there is all too little understanding of the importance of books and libraries in this context. Libraries have been, at all times in history, the store houses as well as the fountainheads of human knowledge and experience. Almost as accurately as with a seismograph, the widening base of general enlightenment can be measured and equated to the circle of people for whom books and libraries have been available. Nevertheless, even the meagre numbers who now pass through some form of education in Asia are almost immediately handicapped by the shortage of all forms of printed information relevant to their everyday life and work. The availability of this type of literature is taken for granted in the West. The professor and the administrator in Asia are expected to do their own bibliographic research. This is a waste of their talent and time. Most of this secondary but specialised work ought to be delegated to librarians. Present conditions result in a lack of accuracy, and information which ought to be available is not unearthed because the work is not done by a documentation specialist. Research and administration suffer. When one man is trying to do two jobs neither is done accurately. Take an example from the earlier part of this century. Countries where the rapid industrial, social and economic progress has had the support of the indigenous publishing and book trade, libraries and bibliographical services, are Japan, China and the Soviet Union. Great efforts are now being made to bring Soviet literature on technical subjects into the hands of Western scientists. At the same time the Russians are well advanced in the field of fast and accurate translation of the latest Western publications and their scientists have obviously reaped the benefits of this.

In most Asian countries the problems attendant on the question of textbooks are fraught with politics. The three colonial languages, French, Dutch, and, in particular, English, have left behind the retreating powers their own problems. The advantages of inheriting a major universal language have to be balanced against a desperate shortage of teachers. Probably such an advantage will initially have to be abandoned, since there are not enough teachers using even the local languages to deal with the ever increasing numbers of children of school age. Even before we were conscious of the population explosion, it must be remembered that very few children in Asia ever went to school. The governments of newly independent countries have an understandable desire to achieve on this score two points:—(i) to put the maximum possible number of children through some form of schooling, and (ii) provide the schools, at a minimum cost, with textbooks conforming to the ideals and aspirations of the national government. Where are the textbooks to come from? The translation and editing of books from foreign sources is cumbersome. It entails the expenditure of hard-earned foreign exchange. It also requires men capable of such an intricate task. The Burma Translation Society (Sarpay Beikman Institute) in Rangoon, and the Official Language Department of the Government of Ceylon are two bodies, created by their respective governments, for such work. Incidentally the work helps to produce authors able to write their own texts, by far the most effective manner of dealing with the problem.

With foreign assistance a multitude of unco-ordinated activities are going on, waiting for the unification and guidance of their efforts. The American Government assists translation programmes in several countries of Asia; the production of cheaper, paper-backed books is being assisted in Burma and South India by the Ford Foundation; UNESCO is helping to establish book promotion agencies in Ceylon and in Pakistan, which work under the supervision of the national governments; the Asia Foundation of San Francisco, UNESCO and the British Council are assisting towards library development; the Government of India sponsors the Indian National Book Trust. All these activities are gradually making Asia self-sufficient in books.

Shortcomings of the Book Trade

Existing shortcomings cannot, however, be laid at the door of any single person, group or government. In South Asia, for example, in the previously British territory of Burma, Ceylon, India and Pakistan, only one country, India, has a modern Copyright Act. The Pakistan Copyright Act is in fact the Indian Act of 1914 which was itself based on the British Act of 1911. It is hardly necessary to dwell on the changes since those days which would require a revision consonant with present day needs. It would also be desirable to bring any new copyright legislation into line with the Universal Copyright Convention, the related Berne Union and the most recent Neighbouring Rights Convention. Such modernization would in the long run benefit Asian authors as much as authors from any other part of the world. Is it possible that since independence, Asian countries, long rich in literature, have forgotten their previous zeal for emphasizing their national cultural heritage? Undoubtedly, so far as the preservation of works of new and past authors is concerned, a national library is the best repository. Yet there is hardly an Asian country where the serious student can adequately study or research in his own history. Japan and India are possible exceptions, while Ceylon, though it has an exceptional collection of books, has long neglected it. For some time to come students will still have to come to London, Paris and other Western centres of learning to discover their own origins.

Printing works, book shops and libraries only appear to serve their functions. Their efforts are far short of national needs. Nevertheless their inadequacies are accepted and there is too little understanding by those in positions of authority of how far a lack of training in printing, book-shop management and publishing is hindering the national effort along other sectors of development. Training is often ignored as something that is unnecessary, expensive and time consuming, in surroundings where the existing ways appear to serve just as well. With only rare exceptions, cost accounting, print planning and sales are haphazard and mostly left to chance; sales and distribution are held back by mistrust; difficulties of postal and other forms of communication and lack of credit facilities prevent expansion of trade. Machines are left to run dry for want of a penny-worth of oil; shops lose business for lack of organization and men are paid starvation wages because they are graduates and not self-styled business men. Books are literally locked up on shelves beyond the reach of borrowers in libraries so that they may not be disarranged or, worse still, borrowed and not returned. In a case like this the librarian has to replace the book out of his own low wages under regulations imposed by higher authority.

There is too little individual renunciation in the book world of the small immediate profit, for the much richer advantages to be gained personally and nationally by a little concerted effort and the observation of professional ethics. There is a multitude of competing associations all claiming to represent a nation-wide body of printers, publishers or sellers. This frequently prevents even willing governments from taking professional advice on some matter of policy concerning the book trade. In Pakistan the Government has insisted that a single association should represent each component part of the book world—printers, sellers, publishers, librarians and authors; nevertheless such bodies often prove to be little more than a registered address and an official letter head. It does not help matters that frequently two or more trade functions are performed by one person under the same roof. Too ofteu the caste- and religion-bound customs prevent educationally qualified persons from practising their desired professions. Authors, printers, publishers, sellers and librarians are almost invariably looked down on by the frequently less cultured but wealthier or high bred. Teachers, too, are included in this segregation which contains those whose services may be bought with cash or simply demanded by authority. The obvious answer is unity in professional associations, which demands certain sacrifices and is therefore difficult to implement. The dilemma of such a course for the manufacturing component of the trade is clear, demanding as it does a self-imposed limitation of immediate profit and concerted action with would-be competitors. The dilemma of the librarian is less clear. This is the point where training and professional qualifications assert themselves. We in the West are only a short step in advance of Asia. Present conditions in librarianship naturally relate training to other professional training courses which have long traditions of university learning, but with one vital difference. No one in their right mind would trust a lawyer or doctor, no matter how many degrees and diplomas he had, if one were not sure that, by tradition, the practitioner had hospital or court room experience as part of the training in addition to his university-found theoretical knowledge. Yet, in Asia, this is precisely the case, especially so among librarians, who should have realized that for the performance of professional work at least equal parts of theory and practice are needed. It would be up to the profession as a whole to put forward a revised scheme of study. Unfortunately, both individuals and associations are suffering under the delusion that by ignoring practical work, by hiding it or delegating it to a lower uneducated servant class, they would all the sooner be accepted as representatives of a truly learned profession. Before the world around them and the professions themselves can observe a changed image, a serious reappraisal will have to take place in the training programmes presently in existence in the Asian book world.

Libraries

India has a comprehensive library development plan which is included in the continuing series of five-year plans. Perhaps the largest plan of its kind in Asia, it is usefully studied for its comprehensive nature, its achievements and its shortcomings. Public libraries in Asia offer to the basically literate a chance to read for profit or pleasure as they choose. School and public libraries lack sufficient recognition, although they are equally valuable and necessary to the growth and health of an educated and useful population. The usefulness of libraries is less obvious and has less publicity value than such projects as dams, power stations or steel mills.

By the end of the first five-year plan period in 1956, nine of the States of the Indian Union, with considerable financial assistance from the Union Government, had begun to set up State Central Libraries. A number of States were also in the process of establishing smaller District Libraries in conformity with the prescribed national standard. At the end of the second five years in 1961, India had a complete system of State Central Libraries, although some were rather weakly linked in the system. Most districts had had a library by this time. Somewhat earlier, in 1959, an Advisory Committee reported to the Union Ministry of Education that the nation had a coverage of libraries of various sizes and competence numbering 32,000, with a stock of 7,100,000 books. As there are approximately 32,000 Districts in India this seems to confirm the plan's intention of having at least one library per

District. However, the Committee further stated that the country as a whole spent less than five million rupees on this service, or about one and a quarter American cents per head of population. The book stock provided an average of one volume for every fifty citizens. Elsewhere in the Report the Committee describes most of these libraries as 'small stagnating pools of books'. Other statistics of reading habits revealed that up to twenty persons read, between them, only one book per year. At about the same time, British public library statistics showed a national reading average of nine and a half books per person per year, though it must be admitted that 80 to 85 per cent of the Indian population was illiterate and therefore could not have read even if they had wanted to. Incidentally the State Central Libraries assist in the production of the Indian National Bibliography.

A closer indication of what is aimed at and what, in relation to the size of the problem, might be achieved, may be judged better from the experiences of the State of West Bengal. There library development is recognized as part of the State's Social Education Programme. Two important prerequisites are admitted, namely, that library development is created both for social development and also for the support of general educational work of the State along three lines:—

1. Establishment of libraries where previously there were none.
2. Assistance to selected existing 'public' libraries based on subscription.
3. Creation of new, and development of existing libraries, in higher secondary schools.

The State Central Library in Calcutta is the controlling and co-ordinating body and had for a start in 1961 some 30,000 books in its own stock. Around this centre are fifteen Districts of the State of West Bengal each with its own library, and an additional four libraries covering the bigger of more thickly populated Districts. The 19 units have some 135,000 books. Smaller libraries, serving localities within a few miles' radius, exist in 24 further points. They have between them a network of 120 branch libraries and 500 so-called rural libraries serving the basic administrative 'thana', or police service area. Including some 2·5 million books belonging to various subscription libraries there are about 2·75 million books available to an estimated population of over 26 millions, of whom it is admitted that less than 2 million might benefit from the existing service.

However libraries may be organized in Asia, it is the sector of public libraries, allowing free access of the user to books, that needs to receive most attention in the future. The existence of other types of libraries, if not actually approved, has at least received de facto recognition. Nobody would venture to suggest that university libraries are not necessary. Efforts such as in Bengal and the similarly well-intentioned legislation of Madras State, India; the work of the school library system in Indonesia; the system of a publicly financed network of village libraries in Ceylon, serving the second most literate population of Asia after Japan; all these still add up to only a little less than apathy and failure. Only too frequently governments to whom the people look for leadership and motivation of action have too many more urgent problems facing them. They rather short-sightedly fail to ensure that amidst the often highly-planned exploitation of national resources, less than sufficient priority is given to the availability of reading materials in the local languages. They forget that, in the race towards technological advance, human resources have to be cultivated in order to achieve the aimed-at harvest of material resources. In the Delhi Public Library, which owes its existence to joint sponsorship by UNESCO and the Indian Government, as a regional pilot project, a minor percentage only of the book stock is in the local languages.

The Future

For the future the book world of Asia might well concentrate its efforts and attention on the younger rather than the older sections of its potential market. For several reasons, historical, political and economic, in spite of great improvements in public health, the expectation of life is still far shorter in Asia than in the West. Partly for this reason and also because of a realization that available funds simply do not cover the needs of all that is planned, there is a growing concentration towards the development of educational facilities at the primary level, at the expense of adult or literacy education. The blunt truth, it appears, is that adult education, with the exception of selected cases, is simply not value for money in Asia. The newly literate adult has too short a working life to offer a return. On the other hand even a rather sketchy primary education provides greater return in the circumstances when children continue to be required to start working as early as possible. For this reason much more effort is required to improve standards of book production, and the Indian Government can take pride in the establishment of a group of five strategically placed schools of printing. This will eventually lead to an improvement in printing, though neither in India, nor elsewhere in Asia, can we look forward to an appreciable rise in standards, so long as both paper and printing machinery have to be imported from the West. This adds a further burden to the already precarious resources of foreign exchange. Unhappily, this dearth of quality is most regrettable in the field of text-books, where the shoddy book in the child's hand leaves a lastingly bad impression, with the inevitable loss to the trade of a potential customer.

For the foreseeable future, paper continues as the basic raw material of all forms of reading material. Even in the West present resources are barely sufficient to cope with an ever-increasing demand. Because of potential requirements due to the increasing educational facilities in newly developing areas, there is a much greater effort towards the exploitation of the natural resources of cellulose in Asia. In West Pakistan a survey was completed in 1962 to assess the commercial feasibility of using waste from sugar refining as a possible base for a first paper mill in that half of Pakistan, and government sanction has recently been granted for this project. Karnaphuly paper, produced in East Pakistan from local bamboo, is sufficient in quantity to meet existing needs of newsprint in Pakistan and allow some for export. This quality of paper can also serve as a cheap form of book paper but it is unsatisfactory because the print shows through on both sides of the page. Thailand, South Vietnam and Ceylon now produce paper in various, though small quantities. Art and other qualities of paper are coming on the Asian markets too, and for the future there are several projects under way. In Indian Kashmir, based on a Russian survey, two further mills are proposed, while three other mills, in Maharastra State, are included in the present five-year plan and will help to ease the shortage in spite of the highly-geared production in existing mills.

Turkey romanized its script some thirty years ago and it is reported that China is considering a similar course of action. Much study on the printed forms of Asian languages has still to be done in order to condense, simplify and standardize them. Although the Urdu script used in West Pakistan is similar to Persian, there is still considerable prejudice in West Pakistan against simplifying Urdu script in such a way as to make possible the printing of Urdu from machine-set metal type, as used in Iran and Afghanistan. Even in the present day the majority of Urdu language books, as well as newspapers, are hand-written on to litho transfers, page by page, and column by column. No educational or printing reform can be carried out in this region until the problem of script reform has been settled and accepted. Indian languages, Burmese, Ceylonese and Thai have all reached the stage of being simplified enough to allow the use of machine-set type. Indonesian has been romanized ever since the Dutch administration.

In closing, we may observe that, in spite of the fact that the overall picture of books in Asia appears gloomy, we may still feel encouraged. These are but the birth pangs of progress, and the many isolated efforts to improve conditions are hastening the process of development, virtually pushing history.

BIBLIOGRAPHY

Ministry of Education, India. *Advisory Committee for Libraries Report.* (New Delhi, 1959.)

UNESCO. *Information Bulletin on Reading Materials.* (Issued quarterly by the Regional Centre for Reading Materials, Karachi.) *Books for the Developing Countries.* (*Reports on Mass Communication No. 47*), Paris, 1965.)

United States Information Agency, Research and Reference Service. *Communications fact books series.* (Washington, D.C., various dates.)

BIOGRAPHICAL NOTE

MICHAEL FODOR. B. 1927, Hungary. Educated in England; has worked among books and with books for the past fifteen years and recently spent three years travelling in South Asia on a UNESCO book production project. Now a Reference Librarian at the Central Office of Information, London.

SCIENCE IN ASIA

by

ALAN MACKAY

In Asia are to be found societies at all stages of development, from those which have still hardly produced a settled agriculture, to those which are at work applying automation to industry and television to higher education. The limitations on economic development have always been social rather than technological. For this reason, perhaps, scientists have tended to radical political views. There has, in fact, always been a reservoir of technology waiting to be applied and, behind it, a corpus of scientific results waiting to be developed. With today's efficiency of communication, a knowledge of science and technology can be diffused almost instantaneously, so that the social limitations are more and more evident. It is characteristic of the developing countries that they have set up institutes of scientific information early in their careers. The USSR, China, Japan and India all have institutes which integrate the handling of scientific information more rapidly than is done in most Western countries.

Science comprises two basic activities. The first is *science as an intellectual activity* (which does not mean that the use of the hands is excluded), the struggle to explain and understand the universe. There has been scientific thought, in the modern sense of Einstein's definition, since the earliest times—the incident of David and the Priests of Bel, recounted in the Apocrypha (Bel and the Dragon, vv. 1-23), could be instanced. Progress has been almost continuous since the times when the urges of early man to feel at home in his environment were temporarily satisfied by mythologies, in which familiar phenomena had names but remained capricious and uncontrolled. Steadily, mythology has retreated from physics, chemistry, meteorology and, in our own period, from biology. We may expect that in the future it will desert religion, sociology and other branches of psychology which relate to the individual and collective behaviour of man. Nietzsche observed 'It is all over with priests and gods when man becomes scientific'. It is characteristic of the present stage of science that advances are being made into the fields of the hitherto less exact sciences with the full panoply of experiment, mathematics and logic. Subjects at present investigated include economics, animal behaviour, linguistics, palaeography and archaeology—most earlier considered to be the preserves of the humanist or naturalist.

We now have societies, the USSR and China, which claim to base their operation on a scientific theory of the development of human society, rejecting religion and attaching extreme importance to scientific progress. By highly selective processes they have been able to leap ahead in certain spheres, such as nuclear physics, while neglecting wide areas of development to which other societies, such as Japan, attribute importance. The priority given by China to the explosion of a nuclear device is an example of such a difference in approach.

The drive to understand nature is accompanied by a trend towards controlling nature; at first, by bribing the gods in charge, and later, by direct understanding. The slogan 'We do not seek favours from Nature. We must wrest them from her' (Michurin) is not a universal characteristic of societies. In places such as Indonesia, where the maintenance of life has been easier than in Russia, the philosophical tendency has been towards a symbiosis with nature, which has perhaps hindered a genuine understanding, or has at least retarded examination by scientific methods. It is now realized in most countries that for controlling nature—technology—it is necessary to have pure science working ahead; that technology depends on apparently pure theorizing.

The second of the activities of science is the *application of known principles in new situations*. In this, a certain class must be distinguished—the practitioners who have skills of various kinds. They include engineers, doctors, economists, teachers, etc. who have had educations very similar to that of the scientist, but who work in technical professions. What such people do is not, in the strict sense, science, but, in the developing countries their role is really the more important and cannot be neglected in discussing science. They are experienced in dealing with things, situations and people in an objective and rational manner. Schiller put it: 'For one, science is an exalted goddess; for another, it is a milch cow which provides him with butter'. Pure and applied science will, in what follows, be considered together as science.

In Asia, only Japan, China and India have developed any appreciable scientific activity for their own purposes. Their societies are very different but they are all seeking to use the same tool for raising their living standards. Each will be considered in turn.

JAPAN

Japan was the first nation in Asia to adopt modern science and technology and, in these fields, remains far ahead of any other Asian country. Progress has been extremely rapid since Japan emerged from a state like that of Europe in the middle ages, only a century ago. Probably science is advancing in Japan faster than in the United States but slower than in the USSR. In all respects science in Japan is comparable to that in France or Germany. As regards chemistry, a useful index of the state of science, of the world's output in 1960, 8 per cent of papers came from Japan; 27 per cent from the United States; 19 per cent from the USSR; 14 per cent from the British Commonwealth. The quality of Japanese scientific papers is high.

Japan is almost unique in having changed from a feudal society, through industrialization, extreme militarism and Fascism, and defeat in war, to a modern patriarchal-capitalist society, without revolution or civil war. Originally, technology was consciously adopted as an adjunct to military and commercial conquest. Now it is the foundation of business, which is a more popular activity than war. Since the defeat of 1945, the bases of power have not seriously changed except for the decline of the military faction, but now the Zaibatsu (industrial combines) have the policy of encouraging a booming consumer market at home (formerly the home demand was kept down to the barest subsistence level); this has been accompanied by a perceptible democratization and a spreading of industrial and political power. Both Government and industry realize that it is necessary to have a body of pure science providing a supply of new ideas for development. The basic scientific services are organized by the Government and some planning, by consent, of the national economy takes place. The more profitable manufacturing fields are left to private industry.

The chief policy-determining body is the Council for Science and Technology, which includes Prime Minister, Finance Minister, Education Minister, Director-General of the Economic Planning Agency, the Director-General of the Science and Technics Agency, the President of the Science Council of Japan and three scientific counsellors. It has a standing committee with governmental, industrial and university members. The Science Council of Japan (formed in 1949) consists of 210 members elected by some 132,000 qualified scientists (including doctors and engineers). It is an organization in which science policy in its social, political, ethical and organizational aspects can be discussed, and through which scientists in general can have some voice in public affairs.

The Science and Technics Agency (formed in 1956) is the chief executive organ and is responsible for the administration of certain national institutes, for the supervision of the Atomic Energy Bureau, for planning and promoting research activities and arranging for the utilization of the results, for training scientists and technicians and for the utilization of natural resources (through its Resources Bureau). It comprises a secretariat, a planning bureau and a promotion bureau, besides the departments mentioned.

It has recently been realized that the level of basic science is too low and efforts are being made to raise the expenditure from 1 per cent to 2 per cent of the national income. Present difficulties include the low salaries paid to scientists and university teachers generally, which lead to losses to other countries, particularly to the United States. In exchange for technical 'know-how', foreign companies have acquired an extensive interest (perhaps 5 per cent) in basic Japanese industry. Part of the sums now used for the licences of foreign patents could be better employed in supporting research in Japan. Even in the transistor industry an insufficient part of the profits have been put back into semi-conductor research, but some improvement is now taking place. In general it is difficult to find private capital for projects not likely to give an immediate return. Nevertheless, Japan has a rapidly expanding economy and a 10 per cent annual increase in the national income will probably be maintained.

China

China has undergone a thorough revolution which has entirely changed the basis of its society. A totalitarian Communist state is now being established in which economic development depends on what is physically possible and not on the artificial limitations which obtain in other economies where there are competing sectional interests. Because China is the last country to have started on whole-hearted industrialization backed by science, it has the advantage of being able to use the latest techniques. It is only a question of applying them and of raising the physical and human resources for doing so.

There were always some scientists in China—it is estimated that in 1950 there were 688 natural scientists with higher degrees and about 10,000 with first degrees. The first years after 1949 were spent in having a stock of cadres trained abroad, most in the USSR. About 7,000 students had gone abroad for training by 1957. The organization of science did not really get under way until 1956 when the appropriation for science jumped from $15 million in 1955 to $100 million. In 1960 it was estimated at roughly 1 per cent of the national income. The money spent on science doubled every 15 months from 1951 to 1961. As there is an enormous distance to go before saturation effects set in, there is no reason why this rate of increase should not continue until China has at least the same fraction of engineers and scientists as the more advanced countries. Taking the modest figure of 1 per cent of the population (which will then be about 1,000 million) this will be 10 million. In 1962 the total of those graduating was 170,000 of whom 59,000 were in engineering, 20,000 in agriculture and forestry, 17,000 in medicine and 11,000 in the natural sciences. This increase brought the total of all those graduating since 1949 to 900,000 of whom 290,000 were engineers. The figure of 10 million may thus be reached by 2000 A.D. (The world total of scientists and engineers was about three million in 1956.)

The primary object of the Government is to establish a modern industrial economy. This has to be done almost entirely independently, since the aid, in per capita terms, which any other country could give would be small. Only absolutely essential items can be imported. It is clear that the amount of money spent on science has been limited only by what can be used. Skilled manpower is above all the determining factor in the initial stages, and all possible efforts were made to start with as large a number as possible, by inviting overseas Chinese to return, by the secondment of Russian experts and by getting Chinese trained abroad. These sources are now not important compared with the numbers being trained at home. The Chinese system has now 'taken-off' and is self-sustaining.

The Chinese Academy of Sciences is responsible for basic science to back technology and some pure science is carried out. Proper arrangements for preserving the long-term balance between pure and applied science appear to have been made. For example, although the training of doctors has to be as rapid and as standardized as possible, special facilities are made for the training of selected students for future medical research; these are given an 8-year medical course with special emphasis on fundamental chemistry and biology. The Academy takes about 27 per cent of the total science budget and operates 105 institutes with a research staff of 7,000. Special efforts are made to apply new techniques boldly, risking failure for the sake of possibly spectacular results (as in the Victorian period in Britain).

A Twelve-year Plan (1956-67) for science was formulated in 1956 under the supervision of the Science Planning Commission. It comprised (a) 57 major tasks and (b) a development scheme for all branches of science (even topology). The aim is that science in China should reach the international level by 1967. Each part operates under four heads: (1) the scientific and technical problems to be investigated, (2) the establishment of research and training institutes, (3) the training of scientific and technical personnel and (4) international cooperation.

Only a nation as determined, as disciplined and as industrious as the Chinese could carry out the programme of scientific and industrial development which has been envisaged. Only internal political disaster or foreign military intervention could prevent it. The expressed intention that China should become, in 50 years from 1949, a modern industrial nation of 1,000 million presages one of the most significant and dramatic events in history. Science will be an agent of this transformation.

India

It is important to indicate the volume of scientific and industrial activity in India, the poorest of the countries which can be considered as having an appreciable development in these directions. The annual per capita steel consumption (in Kg.) is a useful index. The 1962 figures are:

India	14	UK	332
China	20	USSR	334
Japan	242	USA	488

The Indian economy has competing public and private sectors but economic development is under the control of the Government, which is carrying out a series of five-year plans, the first being for the period 1951-56. Planning is by consent and the intent of the Congress Party is towards democratic socialism. The effect of Governmental activities is very limited, as the annual per capita revenue was only Rs 25 for the central Government plus a further Rs 25 for the States' budgets. This compares with a per capita income of Rs 286 (1961). It is hoped to raise the income to Rs 540 by 1976 but it increased by only 14 per cent from 1951 to 1961, because the population grew by 22 per cent over the same period.

Control of the population is the overriding requirement at the present stage of development. There is very considerable unemployment and underemployment. Family limitation has, therefore, a priority as great as that of science, and Rs 270 million were allocated for such services during the third five-year plan (1961-66). As more than half the population is still illiterate and extremely poor, the difficulties in introducing effective measures are immense.

Control of the animal population is as important as control of the human population, since one unproductive cow can eat as much as 10 people. Religious beliefs hinder the rational use of animals and their products—meat, milk, dung and bones. At present the dung is burnt, the animals are too ill-nourished to provide milk, meat is taboo and the bones are exported—all practices which impoverish the land and the people.

There is every intention of using science to raise the standard of life in

India, but the scale of application in relation to the tasks is small. Moreover, many problems are not technical but are 'pseudo-problems' connected with dietary taboos, religions and social customs and habits of thought. Much of the energy available is expended on political, linguistic and religious conflicts. Personal leadership, both in science and in government, plays a somewhat destructive role, in that when the personalities change, the institutions are also seriously affected. This follows perhaps from the shortage of outstandingly capable people at all levels. Reluctantly, some of the deficiencies in the Indian economy and science must be attributed to the Indian temperament and traditions which have not seemed to encourage efficiency in dealing with objective reality.

The target is a 'take-off' to a self-sustaining economy by 1970. Professor Rostow uses this expression 'when the economy and society of which it is part transform themselves in such ways that economic growth subsequently is more or less automatic'. Science is really the only activity which is expanding fast enough to overtake the rate of increase in population, so that, in spite of its limited scale, science is relatively well supported by the Government. During the second five-year plan (1956-61) a considerable expansion occurred as the relationship between scientific progress and economic development was realized.

Most links between organizations engaged in science are consultative and not executive. The principal organization for the administration and planning of scientific and technical development is the Council for Scientific and Industrial Research (CSIR). CSIR operates the principal laboratories and coordinates almost all other scientific work. It accepts contract research from industry. The Government, either through CSIR or directly, provides services—information, standards, personnel registers and resources surveys—which make the application of science more efficient. Many of the institutions follow British models. A small part of science is concerned with advancing world science—in all there have been 14 Indians who have been Fellows of the Royal Society—a further part is concerned with keeping ahead in applied scientific fields, such as atomic energy, which may be expected to be useful later in the national economy, but the bulk of the work is the adaptation of known techniques to local conditions.

There is no direction of manpower—the total scientific manpower does not even seem to be known—but there is a register of scientific and technical personnel which contains 179,000 names, 6,860 those of Indians abroad (1962). Qualified people who do not contemplate changing their jobs may perhaps not be included and the national total could be twice this figure. At present about 28,000 science and engineering students graduate each year. By 1966 this figure may rise to 35,000. The less-qualified of them find some difficulty in finding suitable work in India and a pool has been organized to provide retaining stipends for them as a temporary measure. Those in the pool are attached to an institute while waiting, perhaps for a year, to be placed. In 1963 there were 1,300 in the pool.

The organization of science in India is British in form but socialist in intention. Characteristic Indian forms have yet to be developed from the examples to be seen in the rest of the world.

The USSR in Asia

A large part of the territory of the USSR lies in Asia. Contacts with the other countries are not great but scientifically, as politically, the influence of the USSR is enormous. The USSR and the 'capitalist' countries offer the two great alternatives to the developing countries. Some suggest that it is not necessary to choose—'If capitalism made science possible, then science in its turn makes capitalism unnecessary' (J. D. Bernal). In number (though not necessarily in content) of chemical papers published, the USSR is expected to overtake the United States in about 1965.

Within the Soviet Union, there are two huge Asian regions, Siberia and Central Asia. These areas are not densely populated, although there is a large indigenous population in Central Asia, and every encouragement is being given to their settlement and development by people from the West of the USSR. Enormous industrial and agricultural schemes are in progress—the Bratsk Hydro-electric Station and the other stations on the Angara ladder, for example. Parallel to the growth of industry and population, scientific activity in these regions is growing too. At present 50 per cent of the scientific work of the USSR is concentrated in Moscow and Leningrad, but great efforts at decentralization are being made. The most significant is the construction of the Academic Township at Novosibirsk, organized by the Siberian Section of the Academy of Sciences, and there is to be a similar centre in Irkutsk. Fourteen universities serve the Asian parts of the USSR, that at Novosibirsk being developed after a new pattern with emphasis on inter-disciplinary studies.

There are Academies of Science in the Republics of Uzbekistan, Kazakhstan, Kirgizia, Tadzhikistan and Turkmenistan. In all, these operate 105 institutes in which work about 1,200 scientists having higher degrees (Ph.D. and D.Sc.). The general standards of science and education in Siberia and Central Asia are on almost the same level as in the European parts of the USSR and are far higher than in the neighbouring countries.

The Asiatic part of the USSR cannot be considered separately from the rest. The ethnically Asian peoples are having to develop on modern lines and have the same educational, medical and industrial level as the others. Although the Asian societies are being completely integrated into a modern super-state, they have preserved some of their national characteristics.

Science in the USSR is planned through the State Committee for the Coordination of Scientific Research which pays increasing attention to the development of the Asian parts of the country. It is probable that many of the atomic energy and rocket establishments are located in Siberia and Central Asia.

Conclusions and Summary

There are isolated individuals all over Asia contributing to the world stock of scientific knowledge. In only a few countries, however, are there the conditions—a developing technology and an educated population—which permit the whole-hearted application of the results of scientific work. The rational application of science is only possible on a large scale in certain kinds of economic and political systems. Three examples are given:

In *China*, where, by totalitarian methods, science and technology are being applied on a potentially gigantic scale, both short- and long-term measures are being taken in conjunction with total planning. The initial level of science was very small indeed but the rate of increase is very high.

Japan has a high level of industry and education, but a moderate amount of scientific activity, which is hampered by the sacrifice of long-term plans to immediate profit. The economy is a strictly capitalist one and scientific planning is with the consent of industry.

India has a low level of scientific activity and a technology which, while planned, is not self-sustaining like Japan, nor ruthlessly controlled as in China. The economy is nominally socialist, with private sectors in both large- and small-scale industry. Agriculture is almost entirely in the private sector.

When political conditions are unsuitable, the intervention of more developed countries and international agencies can only achieve a temporary amelioration of living conditions. Only intervention which aims at the raising of the educational and industrial level of the mass of the population and the productivity of agriculture is likely to be of long-term benefit. Foreign aid directed towards enabling the indigenous populations to do more and more for themselves can make an important contribution.

BIBLIOGRAPHY

General
J. D. Bernal. *World Without War.* (Routledge and Kegan Paul, London, 1958.)
Ruth Gruner (ed.) *Science and the New Nations.* (Basic Books, New York, 1961.)
D. J. de S. Price. *Science since Babylon.* (Yale Univ. Press, New Haven, 1962.)
World Federation of Scientific Workers. *Scientific World.* (London, 1957 and onwards.)

China
American Association for the Advancement of Science (AAAS). *Sciences in Communist China.* (Washington, 1961.)
China Quarterly. No. 6, pp. 19-169. (1961.)
D. Wilgress. 'China's Leap Forward in Science'. (*Discovery*, November, 1960.)

Japan
Hideomi Tsugi. *Historical Development of Science and Technology in Japan.* (Tokyo, 1961.)
A. L. Mackay. 'Science in Japan'. (*Impact* (UNESCO), No. 12, 1962.)
Science and Technics Agency, Tokyo, Reports.

India
Information Service of India, London. Annual Reports.
Council of Scientific and Industrial Research, New Delhi. Reports.

USSR
N. de Witt. *Education and Professional Employment in the USSR.* (NSF, Washington, 1961.)

BIOGRAPHICAL NOTE

Alan Mackay is a Lecturer in Physics at Birkbeck College (University of London); he has specialized in crystallography since taking his first degree at Cambridge in 1947. He has worked in the USSR and in Yugoslavia on exchange schemes and in 1961 visited scientific institutions in Japan for three months with a travel grant from the Royal Society. The past, present and future relations of science and society have been a major spare-time interest. He has written on symmetry, documentation and translation problems and the history of science besides crystallographic topics.

ACUPUNCTURE
A Traditional System of Chinese Medicine

by

FELIX MANN

Before the West, with its recently developed system of scientific medicine, made an impact on China, the health of the nation depended on the practitioners of traditional Chinese medicine.

The Chinese doctor did not practise surgery, indeed, under the Manchu he was not allowed to. As a result the scope of the Western missionary doctors, who were also surgeons, was not inconsiderable; for they were able to cure, or at least excise, certain disease processes which the traditional doctor was unable to influence.

Thereafter the two systems of medicine continued side by side, but entirely independent of one another, not learning from one another's experience. The traditional Chinese doctor was able to cure a vast number of both mild and severe diseases, many of which are refractory to the methods of scientific Western medicine. He was unable, though, to explain in a Western scientific way how or why his methods worked. The small nucleus of Western-trained Chinese doctors had the advantage of being able to explain scientifically at least a part of what they were doing, but on the other hand had the disadvantage of only being able to treat a smaller range of diseases.

The present Chinese Government has rectified this situation, with its policy of 'walking with both feet', by making it mandatory for all Chinese medical students to study both Western scientific medicine and their own traditional Chinese medicine, of which acupuncture is the most typical representative. In addition, the elder doctors who knew only Western medicine, are studying the rudiments of acupuncture; while the old traditional Chinese acupuncturist is studying at least the basic conceptions of Western scientific medicine. The number of medical students trained has been vastly increased and both forms of medicine are now practised in Chinese hospitals.

Basic Conceptions of Traditional Chinese Medicine

Chinese medicine is founded on a careful and yet imaginative observation of the various changes that take place in nature. It was noticed that certain illnesses were prevalent in certain localities, that certain diseases occurred at specific times of the year, or that a disease contracted at a certain season might be dormant and then manifest itself in another season. A way of life was evolved which fitted in with the variations that took place during the course of the year and thus it was possible to avoid a certain proportion of disease.

This is summed up in a sentence of one of the classical writers. 'The sages followed the laws of nature and therefore their bodies were free from strange diseases; they did not lose anything that they had received by nature and their spirit of life was never exhausted.' (Nei Jing, written about 300 B.C.).

One of the basic Chinese observations was that of polarity of Yin and Yang. Expressed in terms of physics it means that every action has an equal and opposite reaction. This law, well known to physicists, says, for example, that it is impossible to generate a positive charge without, at the same time, having a negative charge of electricity, or that if there is a dextro-rotary chemical compound there must also be a levo-rotary one. The Chinese applied this principle of opposites of Yin and Yang to the principles of biology with the resultant enrichment of medicine.

The Chinese developed several methods of treatment: acupuncture, herbal medicine, medical gymnastics, medical breathing exercises, massage, bone-setting etc. The basic principles pervading all these systems are the same, and best exemplified by acupuncture which is the most highly evolved and effective over the largest range of diseases.

ACUPUNCTURE

Acupuncture (Zhen Jiu) consists of the insertion of a fine needle for about a tenth of an inch into certain strategic spots on the body. It is, for example, well known that someone who has an ordinary headache usually develops a tender nodule at the junction of the back of the head and the neck, and that if this point is pressed the pain will be relieved. Or, for example, in someone who has gout, if a certain place is massaged on his foot, the excruciating pain will disappear within minutes. If a careful examination is made, tender spots appear regularly in certain places in all diseases, even if the diseases are of the painless type. The correlation is not simple, for the tender places do not always appear in the same place for the same disease. It is this system of tender points on the surface of the body which has been evolved by the Chinese into a most complicated system whereby both diagnosis and cure are possible.

Simplified forms of acupuncture exist amongst the Eskimos in Alaska, who use sharp stones; amongst the Indians of the Columbian-Venezuelan border, who shoot little arrows into appropriate points by instruments which are halfway between a blow-pipe and a bow; among native African doctors, who scratch certain parts of the body and then rub herbs into them; amongst Arabs, who cauterize with a red-hot iron a point on the ear to successfully cure sciatica. The Egyptian papyrus Ebers of 1450 B.C. mentions twelve vessels, which possibly could refer to acupuncture; and, of course, cautery was practised in mediaeval Europe in specific places to treat specific diseases. Whether all these systems developed indigenously, or were spread from China, is unknown, but they are certainly very primitive in comparison to acupuncture as practised in China.

The Meridians

It was found that the thousand or so acupuncture points that are scattered over the whole surface of the body are fundamentally divisible into twelve systems. All the points of one system are connected to one another by a line called a meridian.

These twelve meridians correspond to the twelve important organ systems as used in Chinese medicine. The meridian of the heart, for example, runs from the region of the heart, down the arm to end in the little finger, which is roughly the course along which pain is felt during a heart attack; the liver meridian runs from the big toe, where one has gout, up the inside of the leg to end near the region of the liver.

There are of course many more structures in the body, but it is nevertheless found from the point of view of Chinese medicine, that the body can be divided into these twelve meridian-organ systems, and every disease manifests itself in one or more of these. The eyes, for example, are not one of the basic twelve organs, but the eyes are very often dependent on the liver, and the spasmodic blindness that may occur during severe attacks of migraine can be successfully cured by treating the liver—not by treating the eyes at all. Other eye diseases may though be dependent on other of the basic twelve organ-meridians.

Chinese Diagnosis

In China, a good physician was one who diagnosed disease by just looking at a patient, a second-grade one had to feel the pulses, while a third-grade one had also to make an ordinary physical examination, while it was only a really bad one who had to ask a patient what was wrong. To be able to do this required extremely keen observation of the subtle variations in the patient's colour, the tone of his voice, the way he walked or held himself, the way his eyes sparkled, the way he talked quite apart from what he said, etc., etc., just as an artist who looks at a cloud does not see a uniform grey but an interplay of the shades of many colours. Likewise the Chinese doctor is able to diagnose health and disease by the methods of an artist rather than those of a laboratory.

The most typically Chinese form of diagnosis is that of the so-called pulse diagnosis. In this, the pulse at the radial artery of the wrist is divided into twelve segments, each segment corresponding to one of the basic organs. In addition each of these twelve places may have one of 28 qualities, whereby the type of disturbance in each organ may be diagnosed. The resultant diagnosis may, though, be very different from the Western diagnosis, for where the Western doctor may, for example, diagnose a duodenal ulcer, the acupuncturist may diagnose an under-active kidney. In this case, from the point of view of the acupuncturist, the duodenal ulcer is only a symptom of secondary importance to the under-activity of the kidney, for if the kidney is under-active the acid-base balance of the body may be disturbed, resulting in hyper-acidity, which may show itself as an excess of acidity in the stomach and thus a resultant duodenal ulcer. This, of course, is only one of the many different causes of a duodenal ulcer.

Preventive Medicine

The Chinese consider that a good doctor prevents a disease, while a bad doctor has to wait until the patient becomes ill before treating him.

'The sages did not treat those who were already ill; they instructed those who were not ill. They did not want to rule those who were already rebellious; they guided those who were not yet rebellious.

'To administer medicine to diseases which have already developed and to suppress revolts which have already developed is comparable to the behaviour of those persons who begin to dig a well after they have become thirsty, and to those who begin to cast weapons after they have already engaged in battle. Would these actions not be too late?' (Nei Jing from Veith).

The rationale behind this is as follows:—Before a disease develops, particularly the more chronic diseases, there is a stage lasting several months or possibly years, when there is a mild physiological disturbance in the body, but which is not yet severe enough for the patient to notice his symptoms, or the Western-trained doctor to diagnose objectively. The acupuncturist, though, by his very sensitive methods of diagnosis, particularly by the pulse diagnosis, is able to notice those slight physiological disturbances and then to treat them immediately. The Chinese doctor saw his patient at regular intervals and corrected any mild physiological disturbances before they became severe enough to be noticed as obvious diseases. He was thus able to prevent many diseases. It is for this reason that the Chinese doctor was paid by the patient when he was healthy; payment stopped when the patient became ill, i.e. when the doctor had failed.

Mode of Action of Acupuncture

The Chinese have a most complicated system of traditional physiology which can only be touched on here. They say that Qi, the energy of life, circulates together with blood through the meridians, disease resulting when the blood, or the Qi, does not reach a part of the body or is in excess, or if the balance between Qi and blood has been disturbed. The needle prick helps to promote the flow of Qi by removing obstacles or by attracting Qi to the site of the needle puncture. The Qi is divided into two types, the Ying Qi, which flows along the meridians, and the Wei Qi, which forms a protective layer in the sub-cutaneous fat and acts as a protection against 'invading evil influences'. It is particularly this Wei Qi which is disturbed in rheumatic diseases. There are many other substances and bodily fluids, which according to Chinese conception perform various physiological functions in the body.

According to Wogralik there are collections of specialized nerve endings at the acupuncture points. These are stimulated by the acupuncture needle, the impulse travelling up the fibres of the autonomic nervous system to the lower centres of the brain and from there back along other fibres of the autonomic nervous system to the diseased region of the body.

Kim Bong Han has found special egg-shaped cells at acupuncture points, which are connected to one another by bundles of hollow cells, corresponding to the course of the meridians and also connected to the appropriate internal organs.

Niboyet, Brunet, and many others have found that the electrical skin resistance at acupuncture points is less than that of the surrounding skin. They therefore claim that they can find the acupuncture points electrically.

My own research suggests that the meridians of acupuncture have evolved from the lateral line system of the fish. At least, the main lateral line follows a similar course to the meridian of the gall bladder; and in the fish, Alosa finta, the main lateral line goes via the internal ear and swim bladder to the region of the common bile duct. The acupuncture points themselves could easily be equivalent to the collections of neuromasts (sensitive nerve cells) that occur in the lateral line. Both the meridians and acupuncture points on the one hand, and the lateral lines and neuromasts on the other, serve as regulatory systems so that an evolutionary development is not beyond possibility.

BIBLIOGRAPHY

G. Bachmann. *Die Akupunktur eine Ordnungstherapie.* (Haug, Ulm, 1959.)

A. Chamfrault. *Traité de Médecine Chinoise.* (Coquemard, Angoulême, 1954.)

F. B. Mann. *Acupuncture: The Ancient Chinese Art of Healing.* (Heinemann, London, 1962.) *The Treatment of Disease by Acupuncture.* (Heinemann, London, 1963.) *The Meridians of Acupuncture.* (Heinemann, London, 1964.)

G. Soulié de Morant. *L'Acuponcture Chinoise.* (Lafitte, Paris, 1957.)

I. Veith. *The Yellow Emperor's Classic of Internal Medicine.* (Williams and Wilkins, Baltimore, 1949.)

BIOGRAPHICAL NOTE

Dr. Felix Mann, a London physician, was trained at Cambridge University and Westminster Hospital. He first studied acupuncture in Munich, Vienna and Montpellier; thereafter he learnt Chinese and went to Peking, Nanking and Shanghai. He now practises acupuncture almost exclusively, is President of the Medical Acupuncture Society, and teaches other doctors acupuncture.

MASS MEDIA

THE ASIAN PRESS

by

E. J. B. ROSE

MANY people of Asia outside China are not yet reached by any of the modern media of mass communication. In a population of approximately 900 million the total circulation of all daily newspapers is 50 million, of which 40 million are sold in Japan. Whereas in Japan every two persons have one newspaper between them, in India and Indonesia a hundred people may have one newspaper between them.

In some countries the figures fall startlingly below even the overall low average. Thus in Pakistan which has a population approaching 100 million, total newspaper circulation is not more than 600,000, or little more than the circulation of newspapers in the Philippines with a population of one quarter of its size.

Burma and Thailand are fairly representative countries with 250,000 and 300,000 daily newspapers sold in populations of 23 and 28 millions; but even in a relatively developed country like Ceylon, with a circulation of over 350,000 newspapers, a great part of the 11 million citizens never see a daily newspaper.

FACTORS LIMITING CIRCULATION

There are various economic factors which at the moment set a limit to the circulation of the press. Chief among these is of course the poverty of the people and the price of the newspaper. In India a month's subscription to a newspaper is the equivalent of one day's salary of an average worker. The cost of a cheaper newspaper in India is the equivalent of twenty minutes of labour. In Thailand, a morning paper costs 1 tekel. For 1.50 tekels a man can buy a bowl of noodles which is sufficient for his midday meal.

The result is that newspapers are passed from hand to hand and the average newspaper may be read by at least seven people. In Hong Kong and Singapore readership may be as high as 30 a paper as the teashops rent out newspapers to their customers. In the shops, where there is little work to do, the paper is passed from the owner down through the employees and, when it has been read fully by the apprentice, it is exchanged for another newspaper with the neighbouring shop. In India and elsewhere newspapers are read aloud to groups of illiterates in the villages.

A second limiting factor is the low level of literacy but poverty and illiteracy cannot fully account for the position in a country like India. The latest UNESCO survey estimates literacy at 25 per cent which would give a figure of over 100 million literates but the total circulation of all daily newspapers in all languages is barely more than 5 million. Supposing that half the literate population could not afford to buy a newspaper this would still leave more than 10 million families able to read and able to pay who at present do not buy a daily newspaper.

All governments in Asia are giving high priority to education and it is estimated that literacy rates in many countries are rising by 8 per cent a year. There is therefore going to be an ever-widening reading public which at present is not being reached by the press. It is not being reached chiefly because publishers are not producing the kind of newspaper which appeals to the new literate and to the rural worker. This is largely a matter of skills but there are also other causes which lie in the recent colonial past.

The Vernacular Press

The future rests with the vernacular press in Asia. English is a fading language and the standard of English is in many places declining. In Burma 99 per cent of those who fail to matriculate fail in English. In many countries English is no longer used as a medium of instruction and children now only begin to learn English at ten whereas formerly it was taught in the first grade.

However in most countries which were formerly under British rule the local language press is at present the poor relation of the English press. This is particularly true in India, Malaysia and Pakistan. Even in Rangoon where the bulk of the newspaper circulation is in Burmese two of the three leading newspapers are produced in English. In Malaysia where over half the population is Malay hardly one-third of the newspaper circulation was, until very recently, in the Malay language.

In almost none of these ex-British countries has the language press got a strong economic base. Nor has it yet developed a character of its own. The English language press, very often modelled on the old British nineteenth century pattern, is too political and is addressed to a small élite of businessmen, civil servants and intellectuals. It lacks vitality. The language press mistakenly follows this pattern. Too much emphasis is placed on the leading article. Many language papers are in fact the direct descendants of the English eighteenth-century pamphlet. They can be disguised as newspapers because of the existence of news agencies which enable them to put news on their front and back pages, but the quality of this news, its interest for their readers and the criteria for its selection are doubtful.

Nevertheless this position is bound to change with the national awakening, the growth of literacy and as new skills are acquired. Mass circulations, when they come, will only be attained in the vernacular press.

It must not be forgotten that in some countries the press, as we know it, is not yet 20 years old. This is the case in Indonesia and Pakistan. Before 1947 there were very few Muslim journalists in India and the press of Pakistan has suffered from lack of traditions as much as from shortage of skilled workers. In India under British rule the native press was largely agitational in character; the papers were run at a loss, the editor was supported by his family and was an honoured member of the community whether in or out of gaol. After liberation all this was to change. Newspapers had to become commercial propositions and very often passed into the hands of businessmen who found them a useful adjunct to their other activities. These men have not been primarily concerned with the profession of journalism and have not promoted it. Not only in India but in most of Asia the pay and conditions of employment in journalism are wretched; the journalists's morale is often very low, the standing of the profession suffers and it is hard to maintain good ethical standards.

Some of the problems of the language press in Asia spring from the nature of the languages themselves and these are mainly production problems. All news agency copy is supplied in English and has to be translated in the newspaper. This imposes an added burden on the budget as most newspapers have to employ several translators.

As the body type of most of the scripts is a minimum of nine point—in most cases it is twelve point or nearly twice the size of the body type in an English language paper—and as the languages are wordier than English and in translation run as much as 50 per cent longer than the corresponding English text, it will be seen that the amount of space available for agency news in a six or eight page paper is severely restricted.

In the process of translating and condensing almost all background information gets cut out and the resulting text may easily be distorted.

Technical Problems and Presentation

There are very great contrasts within the continent of Asia—ranging from the most modern methods of production in Japan, where the *Asahi Shimbun* of Tokyo produces an edition by facsimile 900 miles away in Hokkaido through a television process, to the Urdu newspapers in West Pakistan and north India which are still in the pre-Caxton age. On Urdu papers there is not even hand setting of type; the newspapers are written by calligraphers and then produced by lithography. The Hokkaido edition of the *Asahi* is printed within seconds of transmission of the signals from Tokyo; the first two pages of an eight page Urdu paper have to be 'composed' nearly 24 hours before press time.

Between these extremes there are many successful newspapers and many interesting experiments. Some of the largest circulations in South and South-East Asia are in the language press. In almost all cases, except for the Chinese papers in Singapore and Hong Kong, these successful papers are written in simple direct language and carry a certain amount of entertainment features. They are not heavily political. One Tamil paper published in Madras has raised its circulation from 8,000 to 150,000 in ten years through adapting the techniques of the popular tabloid press in the West; all stories in the paper are short and tightly written; the content is on the whole sensational and is sensationally presented. In the same state of Madras there are two weekly family magazines, again in Tamil; each sells more than 100,000 copies and each must have more than half a million readers. Out of 100 pages only eight are given to politics; the rest contain short stories, serials, much of Tamil traditional culture and features for the home.

Much research and development is needed in evolving typewriters, teleprinter keyboards and mechanical methods of setting type in the various scripts. Much is already being done. However the future for many papers may perhaps lie with cold-type and some form of photo composition. The many difficult scripts are an obstacle to literacy and to modern production methods; the real expansion of the vernacular press may come when newspapers go over to romanized script as was done in Indonesia after the war and is now being successfully pioneered by one newspaper in Malaysia. Such a reform, though badly needed, would be a most radical step in many countries and should first be taken in the schools. The Chinese are simplifying the characters of their script, of which some 3-4,000 are still needed, however, for full understanding; this could mean a great leap forward to literacy. For other languages to convert to romanized script would be a far simpler operation.

Japan

Japan is the shining exception in Asia. With one newspaper for every two persons in the population Japan has the highest density of newspaper readership of any country in the world except Britain. Two newspapers in Tokyo, each selling six million copies a day, have the largest daily circulations in the world. These circulations are achieved through intensive methods of distribution and because there is a *cachet* attached to reading a Tokyo newspaper. But the provincial newspapers do not allow themselves to be dominated by Tokyo and there are several papers published in the provinces with circulations of over one million.

The editorial standard of the multi-millionaire papers is remarkably high as is the overall standard of literacy throughout the country. But for the problem of language the Japanese press might well offer technical assistance to the rest of the press of Asia. It is certain that new and cheaper methods of production will be evolved in Japan for the benefit of a future Asian press.

China

If Japan is a special case Communist China is a world of its own. The whole business of communication is strictly controlled in the interest of the Party and the Government and follows the Leninist pattern perfected in the Soviet Union, with some variations which are peculiar to China.

The total circulation of newspapers is estimated to be 12 million daily. This may seem to be a low figure in a population of 700 millions but it must be related to the highly developed system of public reading groups which the Communists have organized and which they strictly supervise. The schools have adopted newspaper reading as part of their official curricula; and Government agencies, mass organizations, military units, commercial firms, industrial enterprises and collective farms have organized newspaper reading groups in which literate persons read the papers to those who are illiterate. The Government carries out periodical tests to make sure that in fact the newspapers are being effectively read.

In Communist China the Government decides when, where and how many newspapers should be founded. The Government also decides who or what organizations are to be responsible for editing them. It also decides among what groups of people the various newspapers should respectively seek circulation.

Thus in recent years the Government has been concentrating on founding a regional press directed to the rural population; for example a directive issued by the Central Committee of the Party in 1956 called for the establishment of 360 new regional newspapers as a means of strengthening the Party's ideological leadership at a time when agricultural collectivization was being vigorously promoted. Up till then there had been, as in most other countries in Asia, far too much concentration of newspapers in the large cities.

In addition to the newspapers with twelve million circulation there are countless handwritten wall-newspapers in villages, factories and in all units of the armed forces.

A most interesting feature of publishing in China is that newspapers have to try to pay their way. Subscription rates are set to cover the cost of the newsprint. The press can even take advertisements for publishing houses and certain commercial enterprises. There is very tight managerial control and a good revenue from job printing. The national dailies do in fact pay their way. In this respect the Chinese system differs almost completely from that in most other Communist countries.

Distribution over great distances is one of the greatest problems facing the press in all developing countries. In China the newspapers are distributed through the post offices. Postmen deliver and also renew and open new subscriptions. They exercise considerable pressure on the public. They also help to organize reading groups.

There is the most rigid control over the contents of the press in China. This control is exercised through selection and indoctrination of the staffs who are appointed by the Party (far more effective than censorship); through ground rules, directives and scrutiny of the press. Most news comes from the central New China News Agency. The control is in fact as nearly perfect as it can be working through human material. But it has its disadvantages. The papers are far too full of propaganda; they tend to neglect items of human interest. They are therefore dull and monotonous and to that extent not as effective an instrument of Government as they might otherwise be.

Government Control and Freedom

In the rest of Asia, while there is nothing to compare with the systematic thought control practised in China there are now only four countries where the press is free. These countries are India, Japan, Malaysia and the Philippines. In Malaysia, however, the Government is sensitive to criticism and the press finds it prudent not to be too critical; it operates a form of self-censorship; and in India few papers are financially strong enough to be indifferent to the revenue from Government advertising. Government influence particularly at the state level is often exercised through this form of patronage. However in spite of this and other kinds of pressure the Indian press does operate in a climate of freedom. Elsewhere in Asia the situation of the press has deteriorated in the last ten years. The scene is familiar and repetitive. Military dictatorships, police states, 'guided democracy' have crippled or crushed the independent press. There have been some victories by the press, notably in Japan, India and most recently in South Korea but a press that was relatively free has been subjected in Burma, Indonesia, Thailand and Pakistan. In Formosa there is virtually no native press and the

Chinese publications have never known freedom. In other countries what press there is is completely subservient.

As elsewhere in the world, the strongest supporter and competitor of the press in Asia is broadcasting; but as the number of intellectuals grows and the politically conscious gain influence, the press is bound to increase in volume and to improve in content. It may never become as important, however, as it is in Europe and America.

BIBLIOGRAPHY

World Press, Newspapers and News Agencies. (UNESCO, Paris, 1964.)

BIOGRAPHICAL NOTE

E. J. B. Rose. Educated Rugby and New College, Oxford. Literary Editor of *The Observer* 1948-51. First Director of the International Press Institute, Zurich, from 1951 to 1962. Under his direction the IPI launched a programme of Technical Assistance to the Asian Press in 1960 following a survey of the needs conducted by him in 1958.

BROADCASTING IN ASIA

by

H. R. HOWSE

Few generalizations are possible in considering any aspect of Asia, which only has real meaning as a loose, geographical designation. The following points, however, although not true of broadcasting in all countries in the area, are to be noted as having some general validity; they are inter-related. The first point to be noted is the rapidity with which broadcasting has developed or is developing in these countries; the second is the special importance attached to broadcasting and to radio in particular in most Asian countries; and finally, and not surprisingly in the context of political beliefs and the political situation in many countries of Asia, the usually strict governmental control of this particular medium of communication even in countries where the press is free.

The Transistor Revolution

With the main exception of Japan, which, as in so much else, is out on its own in this field, broadcasting was still very much in its infancy in most countries in the area until the Second World War when it began to make its mark. Even then, sets were relatively few, and there could not have been, for example, as many as a million sets in the whole of China by 1947. As to transmitting stations, post-war growth has been, until recently, more rapid than the increase in the number of receivers. To continue with China as an example, by 1959 the Central People's Broadcasting Station in Peking was claiming that radio transmitting power was five times greater than the total transmitting power in the twenty years of Kuomintang rule from 1928 to 1947. While the authorities in the Chinese People's Republic have devoted particular attention to the rapid development of broadcasting along with all other means of communication, governments in other countries, too, although giving it less priority, have been quick to realize its importance. The first post-war impetus to broadcasting came from the assumption of power of new governments not only in China, but also in the former dependent territories in Asia. In China a target of nation-wide coverage was set for 1962. Development plans in such countries as India, Pakistan and Malaysia have included special provisions for the building of additional transmitting stations. In Thailand and the Philippines, for commercial as well as for political reasons, radio stations have sprung up like mushrooms in recent years. Throughout Asia (including the Middle East) according to figures issued by UNESCO, the total of transmitters increased from less than 450 in 1950 to more than 1,200 in 1962.

A second impetus to the development of broadcasting—and one more far-reaching in its effects—has come more recently still from the introduction of the transistorized receiver, now available relatively cheaply. This has brought radio to the remotest village in, say, north-east Thailand or East Pakistan. In much of still predominantly rural Asia nowadays, the first purchase when a sum of money comes to a villager's hand is a transistor radio. Even in China where radio is predominantly a means of social control and where wired systems of broadcasting have naturally been developed for the communes, the individual radio set is a prized possession. A Chinese resident in Peking until comparatively recently has equated the 'refrigerator, washing-machine and car' chain of status symbols in the West with 'fountain pen, radio set and bicycle' in China. Radio factories in Shanghai, for example, began producing transistor sets in 1963 and sales of radio sets all over China in 1964 increased the 1952 figure by seventeen times. Accurate figures for radio set ownership in general are impossible to obtain for most countries in the area, let alone a breakdown into transistorized receivers, mains sets and wired sets. However, a comparison of reasonably sound figures for June 1960 with figures for December 1963 gives some indication of the effect of the transistor revolution in Asia:

Estimated Radio Sets (including Wired Sets) in Thousands

	June 1960*	December 1963
India	2,150	4,000
Pakistan	275	475
Ceylon	305	415
Hong Kong	175	395
Japan	15,600	26,500
Burma	110	160
Malaya	270	630
Singapore	190	300
Indonesia	825	1,510
Philippines	555	1,200

* Differing sources and years taken account for any discrepancies between the above figures and those given in Part One.

The main locomotive of this transistor set revolution has been Japan whose export of all kinds of radio sets in 1962 was no less than 19 million of which about 68 per cent were transistorized radios. Whilst the main market was the United States, nearly 1·25 million sets went to Asian countries such as South Korea, Thailand, Cambodia, South Vietnam, the Philippines and Indonesia. By 1963, this latter figure had risen to 1·7 million of which 1·5 million were transistor sets. Many governments in the area, increasingly conscious of the importance of radio, have encouraged the spread of listening facilities by such means as importing kits for local assembly (in Pakistan, Thailand and Indonesia for example), by the assisted import of sets and, in a few instances, even by distributing sets free. In the Communist countries in the area, there has been a steady increase in the installation of wired broadcasting systems, particularly in North Vietnam and above all in China where it is now claimed that 95 per cent of counties and cities have their own radio rediffusion stations with 80 per cent of the communes and 60 per cent of production brigades having a broadcasting service. Even in China, however, there has obviously been both a need and a demand for individual sets, particularly in urban areas, and their manufacture has increased rapidly in the last few years.

Radio Sets and Broadcasting Coverage

UNESCO suggests five radio sets per hundred people as a minimum of adequacy. In the twelve years from 1950 to 1962, when the transistor revolution had only begun to take effect, the figure for the whole of Asia rose from one set per hundred people to two sets per hundred. One year later, however, it had risen to over three sets per hundred. This ratio of course varies tremendously for individual countries from Japan's near-saturation point at one end of the scale to Pakistan's 0·5 per hundred at the other. Thailand, Malaysia, Brunei, Hong Kong and Taiwan all have over the minimum figure of five sets per hundred people and Ceylon, the Philippines and South Korea are now near this figure. The two giants of Asia, India and China have only approximately 1 and 1·3 sets per hundred people respectively and Indonesia, next in size of population, has roughly the same ratio as China. It must be remembered, however, that even where the number of sets is still low, the prevalence of family, group and community listening, particularly in rural areas, means that there are far more pairs of ears to one set than there could ever be pairs of eyes to a newspaper, even if rates of literacy were uniformly high.

This pattern of wide variation in the distribution of radio sets in Asia is repeated in the variation of broadcasting coverage within Asian countries. At one end of the scale is again Japan with over 400 transmitters and 99·5 per cent coverage of the country and at the other, countries such as Pakistan, where, in the West, for example, there is transmitter coverage of only about 20 per cent of the territory and 50 per cent of the population, and Burma with only five transmitters. Coverage in the smaller, more compact countries such as Malaysia and Ceylon is good but in countries such as Thailand, where there are more than 80 radio stations, or the Philippines where there are 140, haphazard growth in which the commercial element has been a strong factor has resulted in coverage of remote areas still presenting problems. In China, the strong Central People's Broadcasting Station in Peking is backed up by regional stations in all provincial centres and now, with well over 200 transmitters, nation-wide coverage has been attained in a loose sense; in remote areas this has been achieved by such localized arrangements as monitoring teams, local broadcasting centres and receiving stations and, more recently, radio listeners' centres.

Nation-wide coverage naturally presents formidable problems in countries as large as China and India or as geographically fragmented as Pakistan with its two wings, and Indonesia with its thousands of islands. India's aim is to achieve coverage of 77 per cent of the country with medium-wave by 1970 and development plans in Pakistan include the provision of additional, more powerful transmitters. Indonesia has increased its number of regional stations on the six main islands to over 30 during the last few years and there are now some 70 transmitters in the country, but the area to be covered is vast. Whilst medium-wave is being used increasingly throughout Asia, both the size and the topography of many of the countries in the area give a continuing importance to short-wave. Indonesia, for example, does not use medium-wave at all, but broadcasts solely on short and the so-called 'tropical' wave bands. China, India, Pakistan, Burma, Vietnam, Laos, Malaysia and most other countries in the area use short as well as medium waves. Even in Japan, where as in Hong Kong, F.M. (frequency modulation) broadcasting has been introduced, there is one commercial station which still broadcasts on short-wave to a potential audience of some 5-6 million short-wave listeners.

In many countries, added to the problem of obtaining nation-wide coverage is that of having to broadcast in several major languages as well as making special provision for broadcasts to ethnic minorities. All-India Radio, with the most complex linguistic task of all, has to broadcast in 16 major languages, 51 local languages and 82 tribal dialects. Even small countries face this problem. Radio Malaysia in Kuala Lumpur provides broadcasts in several Chinese dialects and Tamil as well as in the national language, Malay and English; the V.T.V.N. in South Vietnam, in addition to Vietnamese, broadcasts in three Chinese dialects, Khmer and Thai as well as in several minority languages from local stations. As against this, in some countries the dictates of policy lead to the main weight being given to broadcasts in one language in order to spread uniformity, as in China and Indonesia, for example, where P'u T'ung Hua (literally 'common speech' and the term now used for what Westerners have been accustomed to refer to as 'Mandarin') and Bahasa Indonesia respectively are the main vehicles for broadcasting, although in each case, at the local level, some broadcasting in local dialects and local languages still continues and obviously will continue until complete uniformity is attained. Although, in the Philippines, there is some broadcasting in a number of local dialects, concentration in the main on English and Tagalog has done much to spread both and the latter in particular.

External Broadcasting

Along with the development of domestic radio broadcasting, there has been a marked increase in external broadcasting both within and into Asia. In this field it is China, with her proselytizing mission and her use of radio not only as a massive instrument of propaganda but almost, in certain areas, as a substitute for diplomacy, which has set the pace. Indeed, China's development of external broadcasting has set the pace not only in Asia, but internationally. In the 15 years since the Communist Government came to power in China, her external broadcasts have risen from 17½ hours weekly in five Chinese dialects for Overseas Chinese in 1950 to over 900 hours weekly in most Asian languages, several African languages, English, Arabic, Spanish, French and, increasingly as the Sino-Soviet dispute has developed, Russian. The BBC, in comparison, broadcasts just over 600 hours weekly in its External Services. Only Radio Moscow with more than 1,000 hours weekly broadcasts more than China. It is significant that no less than 46 per cent of China's external broadcasting (not including broadcasts to Taiwan) is directed to Asia on medium as well as short waves. Including broadcasts to Taiwan, China directs over 562 hours per week to Asia. As would be expected, other targets of special importance to China are Africa and Latin America. China's broadcasting effort within Asia is strongly backed up by North Vietnam with 77 hours weekly in Asian vernacular languages and North Korea with almost 200 hours. Radio Moscow broadcasts over 350 hours weekly to Asia.

From the West, the Voice of America broadcasts most with over 312 hours a week; the BBC, some of whose news and programmes, not only in English but also in vernacular languages such as Japanese, Chinese, Vietnamese and Thai, are rebroadcast by various local stations in Asia, has just over 113 hours and Australia, increasingly conscious of its geographical position and a most active founder member of the Asian Broadcasting Union, also has an effective service to Asia of 243 hours weekly in English, French and several Asian languages. West Germany and Egypt with increasing broadcasts in Asian languages are the latest entrants into the field. Within Asia, apart from the Communist countries already mentioned, Radio Japan, the international service of N.H.K. (the BBC of Japan), All-India Radio, Radio Pakistan, and Radio Republik Indonesia have all been building up their external services in the last few years. Japan, for example, broadcasts over 160 hours per week in various languages for Asia. There is also an extensive service of external broadcasts in Asian languages by the Voice of the Orient in the Philippines. External broadcasts to near neighbours have become important, too, for South Vietnam, Malaysia, Cambodia, Laos and Thailand and, in South-East Asia in particular, political conflict has led to the establishment of several clandestine stations.

Television[1]

Against this understandable background of concentration on the development of radio, as well as that of the economic situation and the predominantly rural nature of most Asian societies, it is not surprising that the development of television has been, with the exception of Japan, both slow and of modest proportions. Although television was not introduced in Japan until 1953, it has since developed with remarkable rapidity. N.H.K., a public broadcasting service, first started its regular Television Service on 1st February, 1953 to no more than 866 viewers in the whole country, and commercial television began later the same year. There are now some sixteen million television sets in the country and Japan is second only to the United States in the number of television viewers. In addition to N.H.K.'s nationwide General Television Service and its Educational Television network, started in 1959, there are 46 commercial companies with 176 television stations. Both N.H.K. and a commercial company, N.T.V., have been transmitting programmes in colour for the past five years although the number of colour receivers remains small; 91 per cent of homes in urban areas and 69 per cent of homes in rural areas, however, have ordinary

[1] Differing sources and years taken account for any discrepancies between the following figures and those to be found in Part One.

television sets. The standard of programmes, especially educational, bears comparison with any in the world.

Japanese experience and skill, along with that of Western nations, has been a material factor in assisting the development of television in other parts of Asia. The first country on the Asian mainland to introduce television was in fact Thailand where there are now about 200,000 sets and where viewing is no longer confined to the capital, Bangkok. The Philippines with some 70,000 sets and six television stations, and South Korea with three stations and some 50,000 sets, follow Thailand in their rate of television development. Hong Kong has had a wired service for some years now and a wireless service is likely to start soon. Malaysia (some 30,000 sets) has television in both Singapore and Kuala Lumpur and a television service was inaugurated in 1962 in Indonesia where there are now some 30,000 sets. Cambodia launched experimental television on a limited basis in 1961 and the number of sets today is only 1,000. Taiwan, with some 20,000 sets, has two television stations. In China, television began in Peking in 1958 and there are now eleven other cities with a regular television service and twelve more cities where television is at the experimental stage. Sets, in public places as opposed to private homes, number some 30,000. In India, too, most television sets at the time of writing are community ones (about 1,000) in New Delhi, where television has been in use for social education and the teaching of chemistry, physics and English for schools. Since January 1965, there has been an entertainment programme broadcast by All-India Radio Television Unit in the Delhi area. The Government of India is currently considering the whole future of broadcasting with particular reference to the introduction of television on a much wider scale. In Pakistan, there is a television station in Lahore (800 sets) and in Dacca (600 sets) and plans are in hand for the operation, on a part-Government part-commercial basis, of television stations in five cities in East and West Pakistan.

Television in Asia, Japan apart, is thus confined to a handful of cities and towns. Pressures, however, are building up for its further development, and the powerful combination of prestige, educational need, urban demand for entertainment, commercial opportunity and the desire of governments to have this new means of communication at their disposal, make it likely that its development will be accelerated in future. China is already making good use of the medium in the field of higher education, but several other developing countries in Asia have begun television with high hopes of its potential as an educative medium only to find that its cost, which so often can be met only by the introduction of a strong commercial element, results in primacy being given to entertainment. The danger that arises when television is solely a government enterprise, however, is best illustrated at its most extreme by looking at a less laudable aspect of television in China than its use there for higher education: the Deputy Director of the Broadcast Research Institute in Peking has described television as 'an excellent instrument for propaganda and culture', and continues, 'Television is able to penetrate into the everyday life of the people . . . in the field of propaganda, television has far greater advantages than other propaganda media'.

Importance of Broadcasting and Government Control

With the exception—but only in the special sense of authoritativeness—of China and Japan, where, for reasons of cultural tradition, it is still the written word which carries the weightiest authority, broadcasting is now the most important medium of communication in Asian countries. It is, first of all, the quickest means of reaching the largest number of people. This primacy of broadcasting as a direct means of communication and information is perhaps best illustrated by reference to the present sequence of coups d'état and attempted coups d'état in South Vietnam: on each occasion the radio station in Saigon was the first objective to be seized and it was by radio broadcasts that each new authority first sought to establish itself.

In China where, as would be expected, State and Party control and exploitation of the media of mass communication is more complete and more systematic than in any other country in Asia, the Central People's Broadcasting Station's own description of its main function as a means of strengthening links between the centre and the regions, the Party, Government and the working people illustrates in an extreme form a second aspect of the importance of broadcasting in Asia. So does the Central People's Broadcasting Station's stated aim of 'strengthening the patriotic education of the masses'. In China, radio has been widely and consciously used as a means of spreading to the whole country ideological and Governmental campaigns initiated at the centre, ranging from the propagation of Mao Tse-tung's thought, campaigns against revisionism and campaigns to emulate the model hero, Lei Feng, to land reform, the formation of communes and the extermination of sparrows. More fundamentally perhaps, it has also been an important means of spreading and maintaining China's revitalized national consciousness.

Whilst this direct and systematic use of broadcasting as a powerful element in the apparatus of State and, above all, Party, is naturally confined to the three Communist Governments in Asia, its role in relation to national cohesion in, for example, such countries as Indonesia with its scattering of islands and Pakistan with its two separate wings, is not difficult to appreciate. Its allied role in relation to remote areas and ethnic minorities in several countries in the areas has already been touched upon and its special importance in the divided countries of Asia, Korea and Vietnam, where it is the sole direct means of communication—if that is not too flat a word for radio warfare—between North and South needs no emphasis.

A third aspect of the importance of broadcasting in Asia arises from its special value as a means of information and education in predominantly rural societies where literacy is still a problem. In India and Pakistan great attention has been paid to the provision of special programmes for farmers and Malaysia's rural development plans have had much support from radio. Particularly in recent years, most broadcasting stations in Asia have been giving considerable thought to the further development of rural broadcasting and the provision of effective 'farm' broadcasts. The same is true of schools broadcasts and educational broadcasts for adults, although in some areas, including Hong Kong and South Vietnam, there is still no schools broadcasting as such. In Thailand where not only the Public Relations Department but many other Government agencies, too, are involved in broadcasting, both the Ministry of Agriculture and the Ministry of Education have their own broadcasting stations, the latter broadcasting not only to schools but also to teachers and adults. In television, also, the demand for educational programmes usually exceeds the supply except in Japan.

The stress on the social and political aspects of the importance of broadcasting in the foregoing reflects the attitudes of many governments in the area, but the entertainment value of the medium also has to be noted. In China, radio plays, stories, music and opera afford relaxation to the listener but, with politics totally in command, most broadcasts even in this field are not without their political point. The proportion of light entertainment in broadcasting is particularly high in Thailand and the Philippines where most stations are operated on a commercial basis and it is also a major component of broadcasting in Malaysia and Hong Kong. In areas such as these radio sets which are rarely switched off, particularly in 'coffee shops' and concentrations of population, provide a constant background of pleasurable noise. Even where broadcasting primarily meets this less demanding need, however, there is an increasing recognition of its overriding importance in the socio-political field.

Whereas in the context of British tradition and practice, the social and political implications of broadcasting and its potential influence led to its being developed as a public service, insulated against government control, so, in the Asian context, the same factor has led to its being developed strictly under government control, again with the main exception of Japan. In India, Pakistan, Nepal, Burma, Vietnam, Laos, Cambodia, Indonesia and China, broadcasting is totally financed and controlled by government agency. In Malaysia (except for commercially operated wired services in Malaya and Singapore) and Ceylon, control is by government but there is a commercial element in some of the broadcasts as an aid to financing operations. In Thailand several government departments, the army and the police all operate radio stations on a commercial basis, and in the Philippines a government station co-exists with numerous commercial and private stations. Hong Kong has both government and commercial radio as do Taiwan and South Korea. Politically, however, the broadcast voice—Japan apart—is the voice of government throughout the area even in countries such as India, Malaysia and Ceylon where there are opposition parties and where the press can and does voice opposition.

The Asian Broadcasting Union

Finally, no outline of broadcasting in Asia could omit the most recent significant development within broadcasting in Asia—the formation of the Asian Broadcasting Union. For some years now, there has been an increasing trend towards co-operation between fellow broadcasting organizations in Asia and, after a series of earlier annual broadcasting conferences, the Asian Broadcasting Union was inaugurated on 1st July 1964 and had its first General Assembly Session at Sydney in November 1964. N.H.K. Japan provides the first President of the A.B.U., All-India Radio and the United Arab Republic Broadcasting Corporation provide the first Vice-Presidents and the Australian Broadcasting Commission the first Secretary-General. Other founder members were Radio Pakistan, Radio Malaya, the Philippines Broadcasting Service, Thai National Broadcasting, Broadcasting Corporation of China (i.e. Taiwan), the Korean Broadcasting System, Vietnamese National Broadcasting Service, the New Zealand Broadcasting Corporation, Turkish Radio and T.V. Administration and Radiodiffusion Nationale Lao. Broadcasting in Asia has already developed fast and far and the formation of the A.B.U. augurs well for its continued development in the future.

BIBLIOGRAPHY

BBC Handbook, 1965. (BBC, London.)
Franklin Houn. *To Change a Nation.* (Crowell, New York, 1961.)
NHK (Japan Broadcasting Corporation) *Handbook, 1964*. (Tokyo.)
'The Use of Radio in China'. (*China Quarterly*, London, April, 1960.)
World Communications. (UNESCO, Paris.)
World Radio T.V. Handbook. (World Radio-Television Handbook Co., Hellerup, Denmark.)

BIOGRAPHICAL NOTE

H. R. Howse. Graduate in Chinese of the School of Oriental and African Studies, London University. He has worked for many years in various parts of South-East Asia and the Far East in the information and educational fields. In 1947 he was Army Public Relations Officer in Hong Kong. From 1949 to 1955, as a member of the Malayan Civil Service, he worked in Malaya in the information and educational fields. Since 1956 he has worked at the BBC and is at present Assistant Head of the BBC Far Eastern Service.

CINEMA IN ASIA

by

B. D. GARGA

Towards the close of the last century when most of Asia was under Western domination—political, economic and intellectual—*la cinématographie lumière* arrived in the Orient. The prestige of the European was already enormous with the advent of the railway engine and the Suez Canal. The 'moving shadow' confirmed it.

Between then and now nearly three-quarters of a century has elapsed. But the Oriental's adulation of the 'marvel of the century' (as M. Lumière chose to advertise his invention) has remained unabated. The extent of this popularity can best be gauged from the fact that today, it is Asia, and not the West, that leads the world in film production. While in Europe and America television has successfully lured people back to their living rooms, in Asia more people visit the cinemas than ever before.

Some 20 countries in Asia produce feature films and their total output is increasing every year. The first three places in world output in 1961 were held by Japan (535 films), India (324) and the tiny British Crown Colony of Hong Kong (302). In the same year China and Korea together produced over 100 features, the Philippines 97, and Burma and Pakistan 72 and 48 respectively. Even smaller countries like South Vietnam, Singapore, Ceylon and Thailand have sizeable film industries.

Notwithstanding the size and scope of the Asian cinema, by and large, it has remained isolated from the mainstream of artistic trends in Europe. Not until Ikira Kurosawa's masterpiece *Rashomon* won the grand prix at the Venice Film Festival in 1951 did Japan break onto the world scene. Similarly, little was known of the Indian cinema until the appearance of Satyajit Ray's *Pather Panchali* at Cannes in 1955.

Japan

Though Japan became known to the outside world only with the 'discovery' of *Rashomon*—which indeed was remarkable for its intensity of feeling, the classic formalism of its images, and its ritualistic acting—films of immense artistic merit were produced long before that. Kinugasa, Ozu, Mizoguchi, Heniosuke, Gosho and Shimizu, all well-known directors, made films true to their *milieu*. But this is not to deny the existence of an overwhelming number of films of dubious merit—pseudo-French romances, American style crime and science-fiction stories—all of which, apart from the growing home consumption, find a ready market among overseas

Chinese and in South-East Asia, an area long dominated by the Hollywood film.

There are some 7,200 cinema houses in Japan with a total seating capacity of over 3 million. In 1960 well over 1,000 million persons attended cinema shows, representing 11 visits per person. About 85 per cent of the total production is divided between the five major film producing companies, i.e. Shochiku (the first to produce a talking picture as well as a colour film in Japan), Toho (concentrating on technical innovations and trick photography), Daiei (which produced *Rashomon*), Toei (specializing in period films and samurai themes), and Nikkatsu (established recently—the most modern), whereas the remaining 15 per cent is accounted for by affiliates of these five companies and a few independent producers.

The 'Big Five' not only produce but distribute and control all the main cinema circuits in the country. The cinemas are graded in six categories. Each film (an average film is shot in about a month, sometimes even less, though directors like Kurosawa, Kinoshita or Imai take much longer) as it leaves the studio is shown for a week in Grade A houses, the next week in Grade B, and so on. This practice is widely different from other Asian countries as well as the West, where a film continues to be shown as long as there is an audience for it.

Japanese films are generally classified in one of the two main categories: *Jidaigeki*, or historical films, and *Gendaigeki*, or contemporary films. The historical category accounts for forty per cent of the total production and is greatly influenced by the Kabuki theatre, not only in themes but in acting as well. *Seven Samurai*, *Ugetsu*, *Gate of Hell* and Kurosawa's more recent *Yojimbo* are a few examples of this *genre*. The *gendaigeki* or contemporary type, though less known in the West, is more popular in Japan. *Children of Hiroshima*, *The Rickshaw Man*, *Street of Shame* and *The Island*, show as much of modern Japan as De Sica's *Bicycle Thieves* did of modern Italy.

India

Like Japan, India too has a thriving film industry, second in world output, third in capital investment, fourth in respect of wages paid and fifth in terms of employment in the national industrial sector. In addition, India has the world's largest domestic market. With over half a million villages still unlit by the 'silver beam', the saturation point—which in Europe has long been reached—is not likely to be reached for decades to come.

In terms of filmic material India, with its incredible contrast and contradictions, is a film maker's dream come true. Life is lived here at once in the 20th century B.C. and 20th century A.D. The wooden plough used four thousand or more years ago by the ploughmen of Mohenjo Daro jostles with the most modern agricultural outfit. In the shadow of the latest Le Corbusier structures stand rows of mud huts that might have belonged to an era when man first came out of the caves to live in greater privacy. And yet, except for Satyajit Ray, few other Indian film directors have had the courage and the vision to realise the immense wealth of material they are heir to, all of it awaiting interpretation.

Films in India are produced in about a dozen languages (Hindi, Urdu,

Marathi, Gujarati, Tamil, Telugu, Malayalam, Kanarese, Bengali, Assamese and Oriya), their length varying between 13,000 feet (the average length of a European film is about 8,000 ft.) to 17,000 ft. Most cinemagoers prefer lengthy films. Traditionally, Indians are used to long sessions in diversion and entertainment. Ten-act plays are not uncommon, nor are the dusk-to-dawn performances of *Kathakali* and *Ram Leela* dramas.

Efforts to free the Indian cinema from its routine, functional grip have been made in Hindi films by K. A. Abbas (*The Children of the Earth* and *Munna*), Bimal Roy (*Two Acres of Land*), Raj Kapoor (*Keep Awake*) and Guru Dutt (*Sahib Bibi Aur Ghulam*); in Bengali by Satyajit Ray (*Apu* Trilogy), Ritwick Ghatak (*Ajantrik* and *Meghe Dhaka Tara*), Tapan Sinha (*Louha Kapat* and *Kshudhita Pashan*, based on Tagore's *Hungry Stones*) and Mrinal Sen (*Baishe Sravan*); in Marathi by Raja Paranjpe (*Pedgaonche Shahane*), Anant Mane (*Chimani Pakhare*) and Madhukar Pathak (*Prapanch*). No winds of change, however, blow in the south, where, to use René Clair's succinct phrase, cinema is still at the 'canned theatre' level.

As in Hollywood, a more recent trend in the Indian cinema has been the production of costly costume films, employing big stars (some of whom reportedly receive as much as a million rupees), regiments of shapely girls and muscular men, hundreds of horses and elephants and whole new townships. A recent film *Mughal-E-Azam*, a quasi-historical romance took 500 shooting days and cost 20 million rupees. 'Colossal proportions,' said Bernard Shaw, 'make mediocrity compulsory.' They do.

In comparison, Satyajit Ray's austere masterpieces, made on a shoestring budget and shot in no more than 30 working days, prove that it does not require millions to make an artistic film; in fact, it is almost axiomatic that the more money a film costs, the worse it is apt to be.

Hong Kong

Hong Kong, which produces some 300 feature films a year, is probably the world's cheapest place for film production. The average cost of a film there is around £8,000, the leading actress consuming most of it (some of them receive as much as £4,000). Hong Kong's film industry is virtually under the control of two Singapore Chinese who own a chain of more than 350 film theatres throughout South-East Asia. Loke Wan Tho, Cambridge-educated tin and rubber magnate, and Run Run Shaw, a shrewd and colourful businessman from Shanghai, produce, exhibit and export about half of Hong Kong's annual production.

Although a large proportion of films produced in Hong Kong are in Mandarin, which is the official spoken dialect in Communist China, few, if any, locally produced pictures are ever shown on the mainland. With Communist China imposing a blanket ban on the import of Hong Kong films, Singapore, Malaya, Taiwan and the Philippines have become the main overseas market for them. Traditional themes from Cantonese operas constitute the backbone of these films. Modern themes are more often than not artless adaptations of Hollywood films. With a growing Western influence over this tiny eastern colony, Suzie Wong has come to be something of a symbol of its acquired culture.

THE REST OF ASIA

Thematically, the mainland films are different only in the sense that they concern resistance heroines, youthful martyrs and child pioneers. According to an official report, in 1949, at the time of the Revolution, some 47 million people visited the cinema-theatres; in 1960, the admissions totalled some 4,000 million in all of its 15,000 theatres.

Philippines, Indonesia, Thailand and Pakistan are other countries where films are produced in ever increasing numbers. Most of these films, though vastly popular within the countries concerned, are undistinguished artistically. The Filipino cinema has still not shed its colonial past, and most of its films appear to be pale copies of Latin American films. The Indonesian cinema, dependent as it is on Government subsidy, is free from any controversial comment. Thai films, strangely enough, are the most highly Westernized in the whole of Asia. A little while ago, however, Prince Bhanu, fourth in the line of succession to the throne, directed a very interesting film, *The Brothers*, a story of political intrigue and corruption. But this was an exception from the rule. In Pakistan, which produced 42 films in 1961, the tendency is to imitate successful Indian films.

Of the smaller film producing countries such as Malaya, Burma, and Ceylon, each is still wrestling with its numerous problems of form and content. The Ceylonese cinema, for instance, is very largely a projection of the Tamil film. In fact, not long ago most of the Sinhalese films were shot in Madras. In 1957, Lester James Peries, who had spent several years in England making experimental films, shot the first real Ceylonese film, *Rekawa*. It failed at home but brought its producer enough funds from abroad to enable him to embark on his next, *Sandesaya* (Message), a historical film tracing a rural rebellion against the Portuguese. It ended on a distinctly Buddhist note: rejection of violence. Thereafter Peries started work on a film, *Gam Peraliya* (The Changing Village), on the decline and fall of a rural middle class family. Apart from this one director, most Ceylonese production is inconsequential.

Notwithstanding the artistic *gaucherie* of much of the Asian film, in the universal grey of the average Asian's life cinema provides a bright patch. What is more, with its amazing capacity to educate, enlighten and entertain, the cinema in Asia has a very special role to play.

BIBLIOGRAPHY

J. L. Anderson and D. Richie. *The Japanese Film: Art and Industry.* (Charles E. Tuttle Co., Tokyo, 1957).

B. D. Bharucha (edited by). *Indian Cinematograph Year Book, 1938.*

B. V. Dharap (edited by). *Motion Picture Year Book of India, 1940.*

Far Eastern Film News, Tokyo.

B. D. Garga. *A History of Indian Film.* (*Filmfare*, November 7th, 1958 —March 27th, 1959.)

Government of Japan. *Film Education in Japan.* (Department of Education, Tokyo, 1937.)

J. E. Harley. *Worldwide Influence of the Cinema.* (University of South Carolina, Los Angeles, 1940.)

Japan Motion Picture Almanac, 1958, 1959.

Arthur Knight. *The Liveliest Art.* (Macmillan, New York, 1957.)

Proceedings of the Motion Picture Congress, 1939.

UNESCO. Report of the Commission on Technical Needs in Press, Film and Radio, Following a Survey in Seventeen Countries, 1948.

BIOGRAPHICAL NOTE

B. D. Garga. Filmologist and historian of the Indian cinema; director and producer of documentary films. Has written extensively in India and abroad on films, having done research for a decade in various film archives. At present preparing a history of the Indian cinema.

ECONOMIC AFFAIRS

INDIA'S POST-WAR ECONOMIC RECORD

by

V. K. R. V. RAO

THE Indian economy was not in particularly good shape when India regained her political independence in 1947. Quite apart from the damage done to the economy by the Second World War and that resulting from partition, the country was faced by its long period problem of mass poverty. India's per capita income in 1948-49, for which year an estimate was made by an official committee, was one of the lowest in the world, being only Rs.250 or less than £19 a year. The structure of the economy as well as its habits clearly showed the presence of under-development. Thus, agriculture and allied activities accounted for 72·4 per cent of the working force. Of the 65·7 million rural households 14·4 millions owned no land while another 36 millions had an average holding of about two acres and less than 7 per cent of the households had a holding of more than 15 acres each. The total number of workers employed in factories was only 2·9 millions or about 7·2 per cent even of the non-agricultural labour force. Urban population was only 17·3 per cent of the total population. Coal output was 92 tons and power 5·1 kw per 1,000 of the population; oil hardly figured in domestic output, while even imports were only of the order of 2,473 litres per 1,000 of the population. Steel output was less than 3 tons per 1,000 of population; and machinery was conspicuous by its virtual absence in domestic output. Even imports of iron and steel manufactures and machinery accounted for a value of no more than Rs. 4·4 or about 7 shillings per head of population. Domestic savings and investment were estimated at about 5 per cent of gross national product which on a capital output ratio of 3 : 1 and the current rate of population growth, could hardly suffice to hold the per capita national income from falling, while there was but little significant injection of foreign capital to enhance the rate of economic growth. A low basic level of economic activity, a high rate of population growth, a pre-industrial economic structure, and a small rate of economic growth were the salient features of the Indian economy. Writing in December 1954, I characterized the position as 'a static economy in progress' and concluded that 'if the static character of the economy is to be altered, it is evident that developmental effort must be on a far vaster scale than anything seen during the twenty years ending with 1950-51'. It is against this background that we should view the Indian economic record in post-independence India.

The first three years following independence were largely devoted to the task of national integration, building up of our republican constitution, and dealing with the imminent tasks of relief and rehabilitation of the millions of refugees that flowed into the country after partition. With the enactment of the Constitution and the proclamation of the Indian Republic in January 1950, Government could turn to the economic problem. And that it did in a big kind of way. The Indian Planning Commission was appointed in March 1950 and was given the task of formulating plans for the deliberate development of the Indian economy with a view to doubling the per capita national income within a period of 22 to 25 years. Behind this task were the Directive Principles of economic policy embodied in the Constitution which visualized 'an economic and social order based on equality of opportunity, social justice, the right to work, the right to an adequate wage, and a measure of social security for all citizens'. No rigid economic or social framework was prescribed and there was a studied absence of dogmatism or ideological fixation.

THE FIRST FIVE-YEAR PLAN

India's first five-year plan was modest both in its nature and in its dimension. In the words of the Commission in the outline of the first five-year plan that it presented before the country: 'The problem before the country is, firstly, to rectify the disequilibrium in the economy caused by the War and partition, and, secondly, to initiate the development of certain basic resources so as to lay the foundation of more rapid economic growth in the future. The rehabilitation of displaced persons links up with both these aspects. Further, in finding solutions to this twofold problem, considerations of social justice and the need for a progressive re-orientation of the economy along the lines suggested in the Constitution have to be borne in mind.' Moreover, the Commission did not have a clean slate upon which to write its first plan. The immediate post-war period had already seen the undertaking of a number of schemes in the field of irrigation and power and these were in varying states of execution. There were also the urgent problems of rehabilitation from the damage caused by the war and partition. The immediate task became therefore one of bringing order out of chaos.

India's first five-year plan started on the whole under favourable auspices. While the Korean boom sent up the domestic level of prices it also brought the country a large favourable balance of payments. In addition, there was available a substantial portion of the sterling balances that the country had built up during the War, which could be used for obtaining the foreign resources needed for economic development. Moreover, a good deal of spade work had already been done in regard to the planning and programming of many of the projects included in the first plan and all that was needed was direction, financing and implementation. The volume of investment planned for the five-year period was modest, amounting to Rs.3,520 crores or £2,640 million. Of this, about 51 per cent represented what the private sector was supposed to undertake and hardly figured as an integral part of planned development. The real planning was in the public sector where an investment of £1,470 million over five years became the responsibility of Government. Agriculture, including community development, irrigation claiming the lion's share, accounted for 31 per cent of the planned investment. Transport and communications accounted for 27 per cent, power for 13 per cent, social services for 23 per cent, and industry led the tail with an allocation of about 4 per cent of the total investment. The bulk of the finances needed were to be found from domestic resources and sterling balances, with foreign aid and deficit financing playing only marginal roles in the drama. The targets set were modest: the national income was to be increased by 11 per cent, the per capita income by 5·5 per cent and domestic saving was to reach about 7 per cent from its pre-plan level of 5-6 per cent. Nature was also friendly and the first plan period saw two favourable monsoons which led to bumper harvests in its concluding years. The plan thus got over-fulfilled. National income rose by 17·5 per cent at the end of the plan instead of the targeted figure of 11 per cent; and per capita income by 10·5 per cent instead of 5·5 per cent. Prices actually recorded a decline, sterling balances still remained a substantial nest-egg, deficit finance was significantly below what the planners had been prepared to acquiesce in, and there was no balance of payments problem. Truly, planning was not only successful but also appeared to be painless; and the country saw the close of the first plan period with a great feeling of optimism and self-confidence. There were, of course, some blemishes in the picture. Even the modest industrial target was not achieved, land reforms got blocked up in legal tangles and unwillingness of the landed interests to give up their privileged positions, and the community development programme, while releasing a new wave of expectations in the rural areas, did not succeed in sufficiently canalizing it in positive channels of self-reliance and economic betterment. All the same, the total picture looked good and the country set out on its second five-year plan with a feeling of accomplishment.

The Second Five-Year Plan

The second plan was formulated on a more ambitious scale; and it was more of a plan in the orthodox sense of the word than the first plan. Emphasis was now shifted to industry; and not just industry, but basic industry, steel, cement, coal, power and oil which provide the sinews of industrial development and machine tools, machine building, heavy engineering and heavy chemicals which give the country its growth potential in the physical sense and will set it on the road to a self-sustaining and self-accelerating economic development. To get the economy to 'take off' became the objective; and there was readiness to make more use of deficit financing as also eagerness to make more use of foreign aid. The strategy of the second plan was to make investment not only more massive but also more growth-oriented and more based on foreign resources and leave consumption goods to small scale and cottage industries and less capital-intensive methods of production. The volume of investment contemplated, including what is called current outlay or current expenditure of a developmental character, was Rs.7,700 crores or £5,775 million of which £2,325 million was expected to be in the private sector. Governmental investment was placed at £3,450 million over the five-year period. This time, agriculture, including irrigation and power, accounted for only 30 per cent of the public outlay as against 44 per cent in the first plan's proportion in the public outlay; social services recorded a decline from 23 per cent to 18 per cent. The most significant change was in the investment in industry and minerals in the public outlay. This increased from 4 per cent to 20 per cent and out of a total that was double that of the first plan. There was also a big rise in the investment in industry in the private sector. Mainly because of this emphasis on industry, there was a big increase in foreign exchange requirements, the total deficit in the balance of payments being estimated at £825 million. After allowing for a withdrawal from our sterling balances to the tune of £150 million, the plan estimated the foreign aid required at £675 million as against the foreign aid of £153 million used for the first plan. In absolute terms, foreign aid requirements were thus estimated at more than four times that actually used in the first plan period. Domestic resources, in spite of a substantial increase in their absolute amount, also showed a larger gap with the result that deficit financing was now placed at £900 million or more than three times the amount used for the first plan. National income was expected to rise by 25 per cent as against the realized increase of 17·5 per cent during the first plan period, thus showing the longer gestation period of the investment contemplated during the second plan and the consequent rise in the capital-output ratio. Per capita income was expected to increase by about 18 per cent as against the 11 per cent achieved during the first plan period. Domestic saving was expected to rise from 7 per cent to 9·7 per cent, investment increasing faster from 7·3 per cent to 10·7 per cent.

The second plan was thus not only bigger in both the effort it required and the targets it put forward, but also in its dependence on both deficit financing and foreign aid. The plan also required a more careful and detailed measure of planning and programming and in a field, namely, basic and heavy industries, in which the country did not have enough experience. The second plan quickly ran into difficulties. Laxity in the administration of licensing and import controls led to a much larger volume of private investment and private imports than the plan contemplated. Import prices rose partly on account of the Suez crisis and partly on account of growing full employment and inflationary conditions abroad and swelled our foreign exchange requirements. Plan estimates of expenditure on investment turned out to be gross under-estimates in some major projects with the result that some of the investments contemplated had to be postponed, while others cost much more than had been anticipated. Agricultural production failed to increase, especially during the first three years of the second plan period; and domestic prices of both food grains and raw materials rose with inevitable repercussions on public expenditure, both developmental and non-developmental, and on exports. Deficit financing on the vast scale provided for in the plan added to the difficulties of the situation more especially as output failed to rise to the anticipated extent. The country was faced with a balance of payment crisis almost from the first year of the second plan period; sterling balances were drawn upon well beyond the amount visualized in the plan document, making it necessary to amend the law for lowering the statutory foreign exchange reserves of the Indian currency, and foreign aid was asked for and resorted to on a much bigger scale than originally contemplated. Imports of food grain had also to be increased substantially under PL 480 agreement with the United States in order to exercise a curb on rising domestic prices and augment the country's food supplies. Altogether, the second plan woke up the country to the real implications of planning for a rapid rate of economic growth and made the people realize that economic development was in some respects like war involving sweat and toil, if not also tears.

It must be added however that the second plan did not prove a failure, as anticipated by some. It proved the country was capable of responding to the economic challenge even as in the year 1962 the people showed themselves capable of responding to the psychological challenge posed by Chinese aggression. While over-all achievement was less than targeted and there were short-falls in output and postponements in investment, what was accomplished was nevertheless truly impressive. National income rose by 20 per cent and food production increased by 15 million tons in five years. The index of mineral production showed an increase of 42 per cent and that of organized industry 39 per cent. Some of the major basic and heavy industries increased their output in startling fashion, basic industrial chemicals by 143 per cent, fertilizers by 149 per cent, basic metals by 84 per cent, machinery by 170 per cent and petroleum products by 57 per cent. During the same period, imports of machinery of all kinds rose by nearly 40 per cent. The number of villages covered by community development and national extension services increased from 143,000 to 364,000; the number of pupils in primary schools from 23·9 million to 34·8 million, in high schools from 8·5 million to 9·5 million and in universities from 574,000 to more than one million. Progress was particularly rapid in engineering and technology, the number of pupils in engineering colleges practically doubling itself during this period, with admission capacity reaching the figure of 13,860 for degree and 25,570 for diploma courses in engineering and technology. During the second plan period the economy had become both advanced and diversified and added substantially to its growth capacity.

The Third Five-Year Plan

The third five-year plan was formulated against this background of both achievement and experience. While larger than the second five-year plan, the third plan contemplated a more moderate rate of increase over the previous plan as compared to that of the second plan over the first plan. The total investment it envisaged was £9,031 million, of which the public sector accounted for £6,000 million. Agriculture, power and irrigation now accounted for 30 per cent of the investment outlay as compared with 25 per cent in the second plan. Organized industry and minerals claimed 25 per cent as against 23 per cent in the second plan, while transport and communications were given a smaller share at 17 per cent as against 21 per cent in the previous plan. Social services were also lower at 16 per cent as against 19 per cent in the previous plan. Except for the increased emphasis on agriculture and power indicated by the rise of 5 per cent, the accent still remained on industry, and heavy industry at that, except that minerals, particularly iron ore and petroleum, were now given greater importance. There was a larger degree of dependence on foreign aid, the amount of aid visualized, including PL 480 funds, being £2,400 million as compared with £1,054 million in the second plan. In contrast, there was a drastic reduction in the volume of deficit financing provided for in the third plan as compared to that in the second plan, the figure being £412 million as contrasted with £900 million in the second plan. The third plan also required a great deal of project preparation and programming because of its emphasis on minerals and industry. National income was expected to rise by 30 per cent as against the realized increase of 20 per cent in the second plan period, and domestic savings were expected to reach about 11·5 per cent of the national income as against 8·5 per cent at the end of the second plan period, with net investment reaching 14·5 per cent from the 11 per cent reached at the end of the second plan period. The third plan has also started facing difficulties from the outset; and investments and achievements so far have not been up to targets, notably in agriculture and some of the heavy engineering and heavy chemical industries. However, it is too early to say what achievement will turn out to have been at the end of the third plan period. What is clear, however, is that the stresses and strains experienced during the second plan period continued into the third plan period as well.

A general view of the growth of the economy during the first and second five-year plan periods may be obtained from some selected indicators set out in the report on the third plan. We give below the percentage increase in 1960–61 over 1950–51 in some of these selected indicators:

Index of agricultural production	41
Index of industrial production	94
Food grain production	46
Oilseed production	39
Sugarcane production	43
Cotton production	76
Jute production	21
Cotton textiles	33
Iron and steel	138
Machinery (all types)	403
Chemicals	188
Iron ore	134
Coal	69
General education—No. of pupils	85
Technical education—No. of pupils	239
National income	42
Population	21
Per capita income	16

Conclusions

The Indian economic record during the first decade of planning is therefore not an unsatisfactory one. But it still remains far below what the Indian economy requires because of the low basic levels from which the planning has been started and the large leeway the country has to make up before the population as a whole can be assured of a minimum acceptable standard of living. The strategy of development followed, however, has been on the right lines. Investment patterns have been geared in the main to the building up of the social and economic overheads without which it is not possible to release for utilization the creative economic energies of the country. Irrigation, power, fuel, transport, steel, chemicals, machine tools, machinery and scientific and technical education have all received their due emphasis and it is but inevitable that the public sector has had to play the major role in this process, while the bulk of the benefit accrues equally inevitably to the private sector because of the mixed economy that provides the framework for our economic development. The snag, however, lies not in faulty strategy, but in administrative failings and in inadequacy of both domestic effort and foreign aid when viewed in the context of the requirements for making a massive impact on the economy. There is also the vexed problem of a high rate of population growth and, accompanying it, that of finding productive employment for a labour force increasing in terms of millions every year. All the same, there is no need to be pessimistic about the future of the Indian economy. On the contrary, the achievements so far are truly massive against the background of the economic stagnation that preceded the introduction of planned development in the Indian economy. The record shows, however, the difficulty of forcing the pace and the enormity of the social and economic discipline that it entails on the part of both the classes and the masses in the country. In one sense, we in India have added to our economic burden by sticking to democracy and a free society. But the cost is worth incurring when the stakes are high. With luck, a more massive domestic effort on our part, and a more understanding and more generous policy of aid by our foreign friends, the Indian economy is sure to reach the take-off stage by the end of the current decade, though it will still continue to be faced by balance of payments problems. It should not however take more than 5 or at most 10 years from then to give the country a tolerable minimum standard of living and set it securely on the road of self-sustaining and self-accelerating growth, which indeed is the goal of all planned economic development

BIBLIOGRAPHY

Government of India, Planning Commission. *First Five Year Plan. Second Five Year Plan. Third Five Year Plan.* (New Delhi.)

W. A. Lewis. *Principles of Economic Planning.* (Dobson, London, 1949.) *Theory of Economic Growth.* (Allen and Unwin, London, 1955.)

W. Malenbaum. *Prospects for Indian Development.* (Allen and Unwin, London, 1962.)

W. B. Reddaway. *The Development of the Indian Economy.* (Allen and Unwin, London, 1962.)

M. R. Sinha (ed.) *A Decade of Economic Development and Planning in India.* (Asian Studies Press, Bombay.)

H. Venkatasubbiah. *Indian Economy Since Independence.* (Asia Publishing House, London, 2nd ed., 1961.)

BIOGRAPHICAL NOTE

DR. V. K. R. V. RAO, founder and first Director of the Delhi School of Economics, resigned after three years from the post of Vice-Chancellor of the University of Delhi to return to academic work. He then became the Director of the Institute of Economic Growth, Delhi, an all-India institution specializing in advanced studies and research in problems of economic growth and development. He is the Chairman of the Advisory Board on Programme Evaluation of the Planning Commission, New Delhi, and the Chairman of the Steering Committee of the UNESCO Research Centre for Social and Economic Development in the ESCAFE region. He was the Chairman of the United Nations Sub-Commission on Economic Development for four years. Recently, he has been appointed a Member of the National Planning Commission. He has written a number of books on economics and is known for his pioneering work on India's national income.

THE ECONOMY OF INDIA

by

TAYA ZINKIN

A Rural Economy

India is a country of poor peasants. Five-sixths of the population live in the countryside. Three out of four depend on agriculture. Four in five of those who live off the land own something; but a half of all the farmers own an acre or less, and large estates are so few that if everything over 30 acres were confiscated, only about 10 per cent of the land would become available.

The average size of a farm varies with the part of the country and the quality of the land. Three acres is quite a good holding of coconuts and areca nuts and rice in Kerala; 15 is only just enough in the dry millet lands of the Deccan. Taking the country as a whole, five acres is about the mean.

With holdings of this size, poverty, by European standards, is inevitable. Moreover, yields are low; eight cwts. of wheat per acre, 10 cwts. of paddy, are in India very reasonable yields. In England, the farmer expects to get three times as much wheat from his acre, and the Japanese farmer gets three times as much paddy from his.

Most of what is grown is used for the subsistence of farmer and family. Only one-third of the foodgrains grown is sold, the rest is eaten by the farmer and his family. This does not always make for the most efficient use of land; a man will grow millet when it would be much more profitable to grow cotton or groundnuts because he wants to be sure of his food.

Five acres at 800 lbs. of wheat to an acre must mean poverty. Naturally the Indian income per head is only 10*s*. per week. In the countryside indeed, it is lower than 10*s*., for people are slightly better off in the small towns, and very much better off in the big ones, especially in the great cities of Bombay, Madras, Calcutta and Delhi—each of them bigger than any English town except London—where incomes are at least twice the national average.

Although the farmer grows mainly foodgrains, these are not his only crops. He gets his protein mainly from pulses, though he does also eat some animal protein, mainly goat or chicken and, in the coastal or riverain areas, fish; he does not eat beef, and India has very little mutton or lamb. India also grows some 5,000,000 bales of cotton a year and over 5,000,000 bales of jute, enough to keep going the world's largest jute industry and its second largest cotton textile industry.

The small size of Indian farms is the result of a combination of two circumstances, the pressure of population on the land and very labour-intensive agricultural techniques. Until 1920 or so, the population grew slowly. It may have been little larger in 1900 than in 1800, and between 1890 and 1920 it hardly grew at all. But since 1920 it has been growing at an increasing pace, which is now probably more than two per cent per year and, up to now, most of this increase has had to find its place on the land. The percentage of the population living in towns may well be no higher now than 150 years ago.

This concentration on the land is made worse by the Hindu and Muslim laws of inheritance. Every son is entitled to a share of the family estate. If there are four acres and four sons, each son gets one acre; and once a man has some land, he tends to be tied to his village. Land gives so much prestige that nobody will cut himself off from his village if he can help it. Every factory, even today, has to face a large demand for leave from its employees as soon as the harvest season comes round.

This fragmentation of ownership, however, only exacerbates a tendency already inherent in Indian techniques of cultivation. The plough animal over most of India is the bullock—in paddy land it is sometimes the buffalo. Even on light dry land a pair of bullocks cannot manage more than 15 acres or so; in heavy or wet land they can manage less still; and in areas like Orissa or Tanjore, where the cattle are poor, one may need more than one pair to plough the same field; one can sometimes see as many as eight pairs operating in tandem. And each pair of bullocks requires a ploughman. Methods of transplantation and of harvesting are similarly extravagant of labour. At transplanting each paddy plant has to be put in separately; this requires whole teams of women for every field. At harvest each stalk is either pulled out or cut with a little sickle, individually. This too requires whole teams of men and women for every field.

The Indian peasant is skilled in his own tradition; and he is much quicker than is generally believed to accept profitable innovations. But many of his methods are basically inefficient. He treats the cow as sacred; so there are two cattle for every three people, many cattle give neither milk nor labour, and the Indian rice areas swarm with the world's poorest animals. He is only beginning to learn how to select his seed; proper seed-farms did not exist until recently. He uses most of his cowdung for fuel; he has no option, he cannot get coal and most villages are lacking in wood. Chemical fertilizers are a new idea, and, though demand now exceeds supply, this is because the supply is still so pathetically small, a few hundred thousand tons in terms of nitrogen per year. Erosion is, in all the unirrigated areas, an ever present threat. Cereals are grown on the same land year after year; the farmer very often ploughs downhill instead of along the contours; the rains come in torrents and cut great gullies out of the bare slopes. Not nearly enough legumes are grown for a proper rotation. Most animal breeding is casual, without any deliberate selection of the sire.

The poverty that comes from too small holdings and too little application of modern methods is compounded by the high charges the peasant has to pay when he borrows or rents or sells. Tenancy has been greatly reduced of late years by legislation enabling the tenant to buy his landlord out; but a good deal—just how much nobody knows—still remains, and despite laws prescribing lower levels, the tenant still usually pays half his crop as rent. Moneylenders now have to be licensed, and interest is limited by law; but most borrowing is still from patrons or relations or shopkeepers or merchants, and at rates well above the legal maximum: 18 per cent to 25 per cent is frequent, anything under 12 per cent exceptional. There are co-operative societies for the giving of credit, and the Government has been pouring funds into them, but they still do only a small part of all rural lending. This is partly because so many of the rural population are not creditworthy by any reasonable business standards, partly because so much of the borrowing is for unproductive purposes. A man will hesitate to put himself deeply in debt for fertiliser or to build a well. He cannot hesitate if he has a daughter to marry, a son's thread ceremony to perform, or a mother's funeral to conduct. These social obligations are expensive. A wedding can easily cost a year's income.

The peasant also loses when he comes to sell. He needs money quickly when his harvest comes in. He has the land revenue to pay, his creditors may be pressing, he has things he wants to buy. So prices dip at harvest time, and the frequent unscrupulousness of the merchant means that the simpler farmers do not even get the whole of the lower price. Even if the merchant is totally honest, the price in the village is bound to be low. The collection of many small parcels and their storage over several months is an expensive business, especially when, as happens very often, the peasant does not take his crop to market but expects the merchant to come and fetch it in the village. This is particularly expensive because communications are bad. Most villages are not on a road of any sort. When the rains come, they are cut off; and even when there is no rain, there are usually two or three unbridged streams between them and the main road; the strain of pulling a load up the banks of these streams is severe, so the bullock carts carry less than they would if the roads were good.

Nature, too, is against the villager. Many soils are light, and exhausted by hundreds of years of cereal growing. When there is water, there is often too much; the rain pours down, inches in a day, and there are floods. But most of the time, over most of the countryside, there is not enough water. Crops fail, or are not as good as they might have been because the rain was inadequate, or did not come at the right time, or was too heavy when it did come. Some 70 million acres are now irrigated, and along the coasts, especially, there are areas whose rain is reasonably certain. But even in the irrigated areas, the water can fail if there is no rain in the catchment areas away in the hills; and the unirrigated areas of uncertain rainfall are still perhaps three-quarters of the total.

Traditionally, the Indian peasant provided for extra sons by reclaiming new land. In some areas this process was still in full swing in the 1930s. But now it is virtually finished. Over half of India's land surface is now arable; in most States the forest has been reduced well below what is desirable, and many villages have no pasture land left at all. There is still some room for reclamation, but it is no longer of the old sort. Now it involves tractors and a major effort by the State to make ravines cultivable, or to get rid of Khans grass. For more people to be able to get a living from the land in future, agriculture will have to become more intensive. There will have to be more fertilizer, better seed, more water, more artificial insemination in the flocks and herds, more changing over from farming for subsistence to farming for cash.

For this to happen more knowledge and more capital must be applied to the land. Better seed means seed-farms and money to buy it with. More fertilizers means fertilizer factories, and again money to buy them with. More artificial insemination means more veterinary surgeons, more good sires, more veterinary clinics, and, in due course, money to pay a fee with. More water means more wells, more dams, more canals, and money to pay the water rate with. All of it means more activity by Government. There has to be more extension work; the Government was talking of covering the whole of India by 1963. There has to be more credit, without which the farmer will not be able to pay for the fertilizer, the seed, the wells, or any of the other hundred and one improvements, from gully-stopping to orchards, which his land may need. More credit means more co-operative societies, and more Government money for them so that they will have enough to lend. The talk is of several hundred million pounds by 1966—there was virtually no Government money in the co-operative movement in 1947.

Poorest of all in the countryside are the agricultural labourers. Just how many of them there are is hard to say. Most small owners, and nearly every tenant, also do some agricultural labour. When a man has no work to do on his own land, he ekes out his living by working on somebody else's land; when there are two brothers sharing a farm hardly big enough for one, one or other will spend much of his time working for other people. On the other hand, many of those who return themselves in a census as labourers probably have at least a cottage-garden; a considerable proportion will have half an acre or so of their own or perhaps on lease. But the number of those who are predominantly labourers must be approaching twenty million; those who do some agricultural labour may be three times that or more.

The lot of the agricultural labourer, like everything else, varies a good deal from one part of the country to another. In parts of the Punjab, where irrigation has just been provided and labour is still scarce, a man may earn 4*s*. a day and have work for virtually as many days as he wishes. In parts of Madras or Kerala where population has been rising rapidly and no new land has come under cultivation he may earn 1*s*. 6*d*. a day and count himself fortunate if he works 180 days a year, though this will be supplemented by work at lower rates for the wife and children at such peak times as harvest.

The peasant spends two-thirds of his income on food alone though much of this of course is not expenditure in the market sense of the word but home grown produce consumed in the home. After that, and after ceremonies and taxes, he does not have much left over for anything else. He buys salt from the town, perhaps sugar, almost certainly kerosene and matches, probably soap; sometimes he will have a cup of tea or coffee; occasionally he may buy a newspaper or visit a cinema or go on a pilgrimage by train or to town by bus, or get a rim for his cart-wheel or a sari for his wife. That is virtually all. His demands on the rest of the economy are limited in the extreme; which is why the rest of the economy is so small.

India has, it is true, a very considerable railway system, over 40,000 miles of line connecting up every major centre; and this railway system is so heavily loaded that it is one of the few left in the world which still makes a profit. India has a cotton textile industry which produces more than seven billion yards of cloth a year (including handloom production), a jute industry which produces a little over a million tons of jute cloth a year, a steel industry which will soon produce six million tons of steel a year, and growing chemical and engineering industries. But that is the whole of India's modern industry. In relation to the country as a whole it is tiny. All factory employment put together is less than one-fiftieth of total employment. Industry is still a few small islands in a very large ocean, important in perhaps a dozen cities, and that is all.

Inadequate Infrastructure

India does not even have yet an adequate infrastructure. The railways are heavily overloaded; they cannot move all the coal which is produced, and low priority traffic often has great difficulty in moving at all, while a third class passenger coach is the nearest human equivalent to a sardine tin known. Electric power, although it doubles every five years or so, is still only a fraction of that available per head in Western countries, and is quite inadequate; there is hardly any part of the country which has not suffered severely from power cuts over the last few years, and which does not anticipate more power cuts to come. The road system is improving, but it is still equally inadequate. Many major rivers are still unbridged; the asphalted part is often wide enough only for one vehicle; only the major roads are asphalted at all. Buses and lorries manage somehow to get their passengers and goods even over dirt tracks without culverts; but wear and tear is enormous, and makes worse the already high costs resulting from punishing high taxation.

Motor vehicles are not alone in paying high taxes. Although the percentage of the national income which goes in tax is very low, about seven per cent, this is because the people are poor, not because the taxes are low. India has a combination of taxes on the rich—income-tax, super-tax, capital-gains-tax, wealth-tax, gifts-tax, estate-duty—equalled elsewhere only by Ceylon. A rich Indian cannot pay all his taxes and be left with anything to spend unless he is very good at making capital gains. Nor are indirect taxes light. Everything is taxed (except salt because of the memory of Gandhi's salt march), everything from kerosene to soap, from steel to cooking fat; and taxes are high; between municipal octrois and State sales taxes and Central excises 25 per cent is a frequent level, and on such necessities as cloth and sugar it is usually higher still. Not much except foodgrains and certain handicraft articles is exempt from tax, and even that is not universal.

Although taxes are high, revenues are low. The State is poor; or perhaps one should say the States, for India is a federation, where the centre has the main taxes and controls the economy as a whole but where the States are entitled to such important taxes as the sales tax and the land revenue, together with a share of certain central taxes, and look after such vital subjects as education, health, agriculture and law and order.

The poverty of the State reflects itself in many ways. The armed forces are small for a country of 450,000,000 people, and the part with modern equipment is smaller still. The need to increase them to meet the Chinese threat is placing a crushing burden on the economy. It will be the end of the '60s before all children even in the age group 6–11 are at school; at present more than half the girls get no education at all; and it is a rare villager who gets to secondary school, let alone to university, though a large percentage of townsmen do both. Most villagers see a doctor only in an epidemic or when seriously ill; there is rarely a doctor in the village, and the nearest dispensary is normally some miles away. They see a nurse more seldom still; there is only one trained nurse for every 30,000 people. Social services are virtually confined to clerical staff and factory labour. They get a health service and provident funds, though not unemployment pay. The rest of the population gets nothing, except for a very modest beginning with old age pensions in Andhra; though the hospitals are free, when there is a hospital.

Development

The most serious effect of the poverty of the State and the community, however, is upon development. It is difficult for a poor country to make the savings which are necessary for development. It is almost equally difficult for it to find the money to develop the many specialized skills development needs.

In 1947 in India probably about five per cent of the national income was saved. This was just about enough to ensure that the increase in population—already then over 1 per cent per annum—did not lead to a positive drop in standards; it was not enough to provide for any improvement. Income per head in India in 1950 may well have been no higher than in 1880. There has been a steady effort all through the '50s to increase savings, but even now they are not more than 8 or 9 per cent of the national income. Moreover, three-quarters of the savings are invested directly by the people who make them. Most Indians, perhaps as many as 80 per cent, are self-employed, as peasants, as shopkeepers, or as craftsmen; when they save, they put the money straight back into their own enterprises. The shopkeeper buys more stock or gets a bigger shop; the craftsman may take in an assistant or two; the peasant digs a well, or makes some contour bunds, or buys a new pair of bullocks. All of them build themselves houses, even if only of mud and wattle, or timber and bamboo; the really successful villager may build in brick or stone. This habit of self-finance extends into industry. About half of the profits of companies after tax are ploughed back, and this is the major source of company finance, though it is increasingly easy for a company with a progressive profit record or a well-known foreign collaborator to raise money in the market.

The Government gets about one-fifth of total savings; some of this comes from savings certificates, but much of it is the result of the legal requirement that provident funds must be invested in Government securities and of the Government's ownership of the Life Insurance Corporation, the Reserve Bank (the Central bank) and the biggest commercial bank. Government also makes a profit on certain of its enterprises, notably banks and railways.

Modern skills are nearly as difficult as savings. What managers India has got are, on the whole, good, but in an economy which is now really beginning to expand, they are inevitably scarce. In chemicals and engineering and steel, where in the past the Indian industry was very small, there are very few people with the necessary training and experience, and each new factory means a new training programme. Moreover, the Indian universities before the war produced overwhelmingly arts graduates. Only since the war has it become the fashionable thing for the bright young man to do physics or engineering. Engineering colleges, science faculties, polytechnics and medical colleges are now being built as fast as the staff can be found for them, but it will be late '60s at the earliest before management ceases to be a bottleneck.

Nor is management the only bottleneck. There are equally serious difficulties lower down, at the level of the foreman, the fitter, and the overseer of public works; and this bottleneck is even harder to cure, for so much of the training has to be practical and on the job. It takes longer to make a good overseer than a good engineer.

The most backward area of all in the Indian economy is small industry, under which name one may include both the handicrafts and such artisan professions as motor repairing or very small scale engineering. This is traditional in its methods, badly lacking in modern equipment, and very short of capital. There is very considerable Government assistance, for the small industrialist through such measures as industrial estates, special advisory services, and special financing arrangements, for the handicraftsman through training schemes, tax preferences and sometimes limitations on the big business right to expand. This special assistance has had some success. Handloom weaving, for instance, which had been declining for a century, is now beginning to expand again.

The Five-Year Plans

This burgeoning, like the extension service in agriculture or the new colleges, is one of the results of India's new five-year plans. The first plan began in 1951. Two have been completed so far, and the third began in 1961. Achievement already is very considerable. The national income increased by 40 per cent over the ten years of the first two plans, and this included an increase in agricultural production of very nearly as much. There are now over one million students at university, four times as many as pre-war, and roughly as many in proportion to the population as in Great Britain, though standards are of course lower; most students do pass degrees. The death rate has been nearly halved, and malaria brought under control by a nation-wide campaign of DDT spraying. Millions of acres have been contour-bunded, hundreds of thousands of holdings have been consolidated, there is a bigger demand for fertilizer than the Government can satisfy, absentee landlords have been got rid of, a stable industrial labour force has been created, industrial peace has been largely preserved by an elaborate structure of compulsory arbitration. The figure for steel production increased from one to six million tons by 1963. There have been some promising discoveries of oil, four refineries have been built, and two more are building. A machine industry has been established. India now makes most of its own textile and sugar machinery, and nearly all its own diesel engines, for instance. Production of chemicals has grown threefold and India now produces most of the standard chemicals like sulphuric acid or chlorine or caustic soda for itself. Banking has been pushed into the smallest towns, life insurance is being sold throughout the middle classes, the co-operative movement has been reorganized, the range of taxation has been greatly widened. In short, an economy which had been stagnant for centuries is, at last, getting off the ground in a way that is obvious not only in the figures, but to the naked eye. Wherever one goes around India, one can see new power stations, new roads, new bridges, new schools, new dams, new electrified railways, new dispensaries, new factories, new contour bunds, new canals, taller crops and better cattle.

Development of this sort very rapidly acquires its own momentum. Every year the national income increases, savings increase, the number of the specially skilled increases, the taxable capacity increases, the effect of the extension services increases. There is a benevolent as well as a vicious circle in economics, and India is now firmly turning on this bright circle. All of this, however, requires large amounts of foreign exchange for the import of machinery and raw materials. The need for these goes up and up; India's capacity to pay for them does not. India's main exports are tea, cotton textiles, and jute textiles, and for all of these world demand is sluggish. Nor is it easy to find new exports. India's new industries can rarely export; their costs are too high or their quality is too low or their products are too urgently needed at home. Agriculture no sooner increases its production than the cotton or rice or ground-nuts or whatever it may be is absorbed by the insatiable demand at home. The Government of India's calculation is that its foreign exchange deficit over the years 1961–66 will be of the order of £2,500 million; and it seems likely that deficits of this order will continue well into the '70s. If this foreign exchange is not found, India's rate of progress will slow down until it is barely able to provide for the growth of population; or, alternatively, India will have to become more totalitarian in order to squeeze the necessary sacrifices of consumption out of its population. But if the foreign exchange is found there is no reason why this century should not see the end of India's age-old problem of poverty. India will still not be rich, in the Western way; but it may at least be moderately comfortable.

THIRD PLAN TARGETS

	1960–61	1965–66
Food gains production (in million tons)	76	100
Nitrogenous fertilizer consumed (thousand tons of N)	230	1,000
Area irrigated (in million acres)	70	90
Co-operative advances to farmers (in million £)	150	397
Steel ingots (in million tons)	3·5	9·2
Aluminium (in thousand tons)	18·5	80·0
Machine tools (value in million £)	4·2	22·5
Sulphuric acid (in thousand tons)	363·0	1,500·0
Petroleum products (in million tons)	5·7	9·9
Mill made cloth (in million yards)	5,127·0	5,800·0
Other than mill made (in million yards)	2,349·0	3,500·0
Iron ore (in million tons)	10·7	30·0
Coal (in million tons)	54·6	97·0
Exports (in million £)	480·0	640·0

THIRD PLAN TARGETS (*contd.*)

	1960–61	1965–66
Power (in million kilowatts)	5·7	12·7
Railway freight carried (in million tons)	154·0	245·0
Vehicles on the road (in thousands)	210·0	365·0
Students in school (in millions)	43·5	63·9
Hospital beds (in thousands)	186·0	240·0
Practising doctors (in thousands)	70·0	81·0
Food (in calories per capita per day)	2,100	2,300
Cloth (in yards per capita per year)	15·5	17·2
Cement (in million tons)	8·5	13·0

PRODUCTION OF MAJOR CROPS

Foodgrains (in million tons)	76·0	100·0
Oilseeds (in million tons)	7·1	9·8
Sugarcane (in million tons)	8·0	10·0
Cotton (in million bales)	5·1	7·0
Jute (in million bales)	4·0	6·2
Tea (in million lbs)	725·0	900·0

TRANSPORT AND COMMUNICATION

Railway new lines (in miles)	800	1,200
Railway new double lines (in miles)	1,300	1,600
Railway freight carried (in million tons)	154·0	245·0
Post offices (in thousands)	77·0	94·0
Telegraph offices (in thousands)	6·5	8·5
Telephone connections (in thousands)	460·0	660·0

PRIVATE SECTOR INVESTMENT IN MILLION £

Agriculture including irrigation	637
Power	35
Transport	175
Village and small industry	244
Large and medium industry and minerals	825
Housing and other constructions	844
Inventories	450
Total	3230

FOREIGN EXCHANGE REQUIREMENTS IN MILLION £

Payment for imports of capital goods and equipment required for the plan	1425
Components, balancing equipment etc. to increase production of capital goods	150
Refinancing of maturing obligations	375
Total (excluding PL480 imports of £450,000,000)	1950

To the above must be added a considerable though indefinite requirement for arms.

There are signs that when it comes to framing the fourth five-year plan more attention will be given to agriculture than has been done in the past; that food, fertilizers and defence will get the lion's share and that many prestige projects will be trimmed unless India is forced to enter into the atomic arms race by China's atomic threats.

BIBLIOGRAPHY

F. G. Bailey. *Caste and the Economic Frontier.* (Humanities Press, New York, 1958.)

C. Bettelheim. *L'Inde indépendante.* (Armand Colin, Paris, 1962.)

T. S. Epstein. *Economic Development and Social Change in South India.* (Manchester Univ. Press, Manchester, 1962.)

W. Malenbaum. *Prospects of Indian Development.* (Allen and Unwin, London, 1962.)

W. B. Reddaway. *The Development of the Indian Economy.* (Allen and Unwin, London, 1962.)

The Third Five Year Plan. (Planning Commission, Government of India, New Delhi, 1961.)

M. Zinkin. *Development for Free Asia.* (Chatto and Windus, London, 1961.)

BIOGRAPHICAL NOTE

TAYA ZINKIN. B. 1918. Studied medicine in Paris; researched in bio-chemistry at the University of Wisconsin. Lived in India from 1945 to 1960. Correspondent from India for *The Economist* and *The Guardian*, 1950-60 and for *Le Monde*, 1955-60. Author of *India Changes!* (Chatto and Windus, London, 1958), *Rishi* and *Rishi Returns* (Methuen, London, 1960 and 1961), *Caste Today* (Oxford Univ. Press, London, 1962), *Reporting India* (Chatto and Windus, London, 1962), *India* (Oxford Univ. Press, London, 1963) and (with Maurice Zinkin) *Britain and India: Requiem for Empire* (Chatto and Windus, London, 1964)

THE ECONOMY OF CHINA

by

WERNER KLATT

CHINA is undergoing a process of change the like of which has probably never been experienced in modern history. The degree of success or failure of the experiment, carried out under the strict control of the Communist Party which has ruled the country since 1949, will affect directly more than a quarter of the human race. It is bound to have an impact also beyond the borders of China in countries recently freed from Western colonial rule and bent on solving their political, social and economic problems without giving the appearance of Western tutelage. The Chinese model, being Asian in its practical application even if European in its doctrinal origin, tends to have its attraction where the Soviet variant of Communism is suspected of being only another form of domination by whites over non-whites.

The Chinese pattern is watched with all the more interest as it represents an attempt to turn an overpopulated, underdeveloped agrarian society, in the shortest possible space of time and with the minimum of foreign assistance, into the third most highly industrialized nation on earth. Unlike Russia which had experienced some of the birth pains of industrialization when it entered the phase of Communist revolution, China showed all the marks of economic backwardness and social stagnation of an underdeveloped country when the Communists dislodged the Kuomintang from its seat of power.

OVERRIDING POLITICAL CONSIDERATIONS

Born a child of the revolution, China's economy cannot deny its political parentage. It would thus be futile to describe development during the last decade as if it was an economic phenomenon free of political overtones. Some observers believed for a good many years that Chairman Mao, the founder of the new China, was a mere agrarian reformer. By now there can be no doubt about the solid Marxist training of all the leading Chinese Communists. This is not to say that they applied uncritically the formulae of the Soviet textbooks in their own revolutionary situation. On the contrary, they displayed a large measure of originality when faced with problems which none of the European Communist leaders could have anticipated.

This is not the place to argue whether and to what extent the Chinese model is a mere variant of the Soviet one. The Chinese leaders unquestionably consult the Soviet precedent whenever they are faced with a new problem. At the same time they have shown much ingenuity on more than one occasion when instigating institutional changes of their own in a specifically Chinese situation. The creation of the communes is only the most eminent and the most recent case in point. The short history of Communist China's development provides many other instances.

Wartime Destruction

When the Chinese Communists came to power in 1949, they inherited a country which had been disrupted by many years of war and civil war. Moreover, Manchuria, the only industrial base of the country, where investment had been increased five-fold during the ten years of Japanese occupation, was largely depleted of its industry. Industrial equipment was dismantled and removed when the Soviet Army entered the country. In the rural areas China had suffered more from lawlessness and lack of security than from the destruction of transport and communications; the most important part of an infra-structure was still in its infancy at the time of the Communist seizure of power. The majority of the population was able to live and work in the villages provided rivalling war-lords allowed it to do so.

At least four-fifths of the population were villagers and the bulk of them worked on the land, the non-farm population being engaged in local handicraft and trade rather than industry and commerce which was limited to a few urban areas along the seashore. After years of war and internal strife farming operations were not at their best. In particular irrigation canals had been neglected all too long. Even so output per acre was higher than in most other parts of Asia outside Japan. Against this, productivity of labour was as low as elsewhere in Asia. Farming provided little beyond the meagre subsistence level maintained by the producer. Inequalities in rural areas were great as the polarization of the village community had reached extreme forms. Landlords and tenants were worlds apart.

The true picture of the level of production in 1949 will probably never be known, but even if it had not declined as much as Communist statements maintained later on, there can be no doubt that it was low by previous standards. Its recovery was dependent upon the restoration of law and order so long absent from rural areas and urban centres of production. The Communist leadership made this its first task. It was of course a Communist type of law and order that was created. Side by side with the establishment of political and administrative control, the stabilization of prices, the introduction of a unified tax system, the repair of industrial plant and transport equipment, and the redistribution of land, violent campaigns were directed against landlords, industrialists and traders, many of whom were treated as counter-revolutionaries. The 'anti-campaigns' against the enemies of the revolution and their excesses were intensified after the outbreak of the Korean war in 1950.

Period of Restoration

During the period of restoration, from 1949 to 1952, China's economic policy was governed by the Common Programme which had been adopted by the Chinese People's Political Consultative Conference in September 1949. Five years later it was superseded by the Constitution of the Chinese People's Republic which was adopted by the National People's Congress in September 1954. During the period of transition certain concessions were made to existing institutional conditions, but the ultimate aim was the 'socialist' transformation of agriculture, handicraft, industry and commerce and in particular the creation of the 'socialist' industrialization of the country. This meant that expropriation of foreign and indigenous capital, industrialization of the heavy type and collectivization of agriculture represented the overriding political targets of Communism in China. Whereas in the first stages of the revolution a policy of a united front was pursued and collectivization was rejected as an immediate aim, the ultimate pattern of the economic policy was never in doubt.

By the end of the period of restoration institutional changes were well under way; they had followed familiar Communist patterns. As to economic performance, the Chinese Communists claimed that pre-war peak levels of output had been surpassed by 16 per cent in the case of producer goods and by 32 per cent in consumer goods. Whilst these were exaggerated claims, by the end of 1952 the pre-war level of output had on balance been restored. China was thus ready to embark on a programme of 'transition to socialism' which was expected to take three five-year plan periods, i.e. from 1953 to 1967. The plan was to be worked out by the State Planning Committee (later named State Planning Commission) under the powerful chairman of the North-East Administrative Region, Kao Kang. Later a National Economic Commission was created to supervise the drafting and implementation of the annual portions of the Plan. A State Statistical Bureau set up in 1952 was to supply the planners with the necessary statistical documentation.

The First Five-Year Plan

Although work on the first five-year plan had begun in 1951 it was not ready for adoption by the State Council until the middle of 1955, two-and-a-half years after the plan era had been officially inaugurated. Statistical services were far from perfect and statistical data were subject to extensive revisions until the end of 1954. The plan when eventually published showed the marks of the Soviet pattern. In fact the Soviet Union was mentioned explicitly as the model for China. Nearly 60 per cent of all investment was earmarked for industry, and nearly nine-tenths of this amount was allocated to heavy industry, little over one-tenth being available for the development of consumer industries. Less than 8 per cent of total investment was set aside for agriculture, forestry and water conservation. It was not surprising in these circumstances that an annual rate of growth of nearly 18 per cent was expected in heavy industry against little more than 4 per cent in agriculture.

Shortly after the publication of the first five-year plan Mao Tse-tung asked for the rapid collectivization of agriculture which had hardly recovered from the effects of a drastic land reform. The planners had not allowed for a major institutional change of this kind to be carried out before the end of the first plan. It led almost immediately to difficulties in food supplies which necessitated strict rationing in cities as well as villages. This was only the first major unplanned dislocation of production in the countryside. Others were to follow during the second plan.

Reliability of Statistics

So as not to create a misunderstanding about the significance of data quoted in this essay, something will have to be said about the nature of

Chinese statistics. As in Russia, they are regarded as a political instrument of the Communist regime rather than a technical device with which to record and assess economic and social processes. As statistics are considered of vital importance to the state, their disclosure has been made a capital offence (by decrees on the suppression of counter-revolutionary activities and on the security of state secrets). In trying to penetrate the partial blackout of information on economic development, Western observers have thus to rely on the very limited amount of factual information released by the Chinese authorities. This was regarded on the whole as free from deliberate falsification until the end of 1957, but even then data on industrial production or foreign trade in physical units could be trusted more than farm statistics, aggregate value data, or indices of gross production, labour productivity and national income.

China does not publish statistical yearbooks or reports of the kind now generally available in countries of the Soviet bloc. As statistical services are extended, there is a tendency towards increased secrecy in reporting. Discrepancies are generally regarded as due to obscurity in methodological concepts and statistical definitions rather than deliberate distortions, but a caveat has to be entered here with regard to the year 1958 when the attempt was made to establish a network of primary statistical units throughout the rural districts of China. This move coincided with the 'Great Leap Forward' and led to 'mass participation' in statistical work under Party leadership. Statistics became a tool in the hands of local political cadres instead of being handled by trained men of professional integrity. All statistical progress reports suffered from a strong upward bias, if they were not outright fabrications.

The revised agricultural targets for 1958, the first year of the second five-year plan, called for doubling the grain output within one year; the plan results not surprisingly recorded an all-time record harvest of 375 million tons compared with 175 million tons in 1957. The disaster that was to follow this gross exaggeration, though dismissed as improbable by some observers at the time, could be foreseen. After half the crop had been consumed, statistical recounts were ordered which yielded a revised grain estimate of 250 million tons, a figure which was probably still overstated by at least 12 per cent. Similar exaggerations occurred in other sectors of the mass production drive, such as in small-scale iron and steel production. Since 1958 Chinese statistical reports have become less and less frequent. The volume of data flowing from Peking can be regarded as a measure of success or failure not only of the statistical services, but of the whole system of economic planning. In the absence of official data, economic analysis of the current five-year plan has become even more hazardous than in the past.

The Second Five-Year Plan

Draft proposals for the second five-year plan due to start in 1958 were made known by Li Fu-chun, chairman of the State Planning Commission, at the congress of the Chinese Communist Party held in 1956. The new plan was even more ambitious than its predecessor. Material production of industry, handicraft and agriculture was to increase in five years by as much as

75 per cent compared with the plan figure of 51 per cent in the previous plan. The emphasis was even more than before on the increased output of producer goods whose share in total industrial production was expected to rise from 38 per cent as planned for 1957 to 50 per cent in 1962. Consumer goods were to decline correspondingly from 62 per cent previously to 50 per cent at the end of the second plan. These were ambitious targets which were said to require twice the amount of capital investment set aside during the first plan when it absorbed between one-fifth and one-quarter of the nation's total efforts.

When the plan was due to start early in 1958, no detailed targets were known. Like its forerunner it represented little more than an expression of intent. The political leadership saw it within the wider framework of its economic policy which was to aim, within fifteen years, at overtaking Britain in the output of iron, steel and other important industrial products. During the last years of the first plan the economy had been so seriously overtaxed that the pace of economic development had to be slowed down and intellectuals and professionals had to be given a period of grace. As Mao's advice to 'let a hundred flowers bloom' had led to outspoken criticism on a large scale, new ways had to be found to mobilise the bourgeoisie as well as the masses in the interest of the second plan.

The Soviet leaders had shown the way when they replaced bureaucratic centralism by decentralized forms of control. The sweeping institutional changes that were introduced in China during the first year of the second plan were an adaptation rather than an imitation of the Soviet model. They were nevertheless ill-conceived since the economic planners had in no way provided for them. The new course was introduced by Liu Shao-chi, the Party's theoretician, at the second session of the eighth Party Congress held in 1958. Representing the wing of the Party which wished to forge ahead without making concessions to public sentiments, Liu asked for a great leap forward in economic development through mass participation on a nation-wide scale. This led to feverish activities which were directed by local Party cadres and which were aimed at achieving the production targets of the second plan in the course of one year instead of five. By the autumn of 1958, some 600,000 small-scale furnaces were reported to have been set up, employing over a million people with no previous experience in industrial processes. The steel target of the year was raised from 6·2 million tons early in 1958 to 8 million tons in the summer and nearly 11 million tons, or twice the output of 1957, in the autumn of 1958. At the end of the year it was claimed that gross industrial output had increased by 65 per cent within the preceding twelve months.

The 'Great Leap Forward'

The targets set for agriculture were no less fantastic. Some 100 million cultivators were apparently organized for the purpose of building irrigation canals which were to raise the acreage under wet crops by 30 per cent within one year. At the same time home-produced fertilizers were to be manufactured, deep ploughing, close planting and other new farm techniques were to be introduced on a massive scale. The direction and control of labour in a campaign of such vast dimensions required forms of organization for which there was no precedent in the history of Communism. In the autumn of 1958, the so-called People's Communes were created, and by the end of the year over 700,000 agricultural producer co-operatives (set up as recently as 1957) were reported to have merged into some 26,000 communes with an average of almost 5,000 rural families and 10,000 acres of land. Urban communes were to be set up on a similar pattern.

Much has been written in the last few years about the principal features of the communes, their multi-character within the setting of the second five-year plan and the 'Great Leap Forward'. Apart from mobilizing surplus labour for the dual purpose of raising the output of industry without impeding farm production, the communes were designed to effect drastic changes in the structure of Chinese society, in family relations, and in the values and loyalties of the individual. Whereas it is still too early to draw the final balance sheet of this mass experiment in social engineering, there can be no doubt that the price paid, in human terms, has been heavy indeed. The dislocation of work in the fields at the height of the paddy harvest set in motion a downward trend in agriculture which has only recently been brought to a standstill. The resentment caused was such that a halt had to be called in 1959 which led to a period of economic and organizational retrenchment which has only just been ended. Since 1960 the communes have ceased to control agriculture. Administrative authority is now vested in the production brigades which supervise, much like the former agricultural producer co-operatives, on average some 250 households. Work in the fields is done under contract by production teams, consisting as a rule of some 40 households. Private plots and rural markets which were eliminated in 1958 are allowed again so as to provide incentives to the cultivators. However, in three successive years of poor yields caused by bad weather and political mismanagement farm production fell well below the level reached in 1957. This level was surpassed for the first time in 1964.

At first the Chinese Communist leaders were so certain of success that they claimed a major shortcut on the way towards Communism to be possible owing to the creation of the communes. This led to an ideological clash with the Soviet Union with whom relations had not been any too cordial since the time of the uprisings in Eastern Europe. China, preoccupied with the completion of her first plan and the drafting of the second, was pained to see $1,000 million worth of Soviet aid go to unreliable European members of the bloc; all the more so as, though badly in need of foreign aid herself, she was in fact re-paying short-term Soviet trade credits. The second plan was thus designed on the assumption that China had to rely on her own resources and could not expect foreign aid for her economic development.

Sino-Soviet Economic Relations

Only the two Soviet loans of February 1950 and October 1954, providing the equivalent of $430 million, are known for certain. Military aid during and after the Korean war was given, but the amount granted remains a closely guarded secret. In addition China accumulated between 1950 and 1955 almost $1,000 million in short-term trade balances. In 1956 she began to repay these and her trading deficit with the Soviet Union turned into a surplus by 1962 of approximately $125 million. In 1964 only a small amount was outstanding on the repayment of the Soviet long-term loans. China's balance of payments position is not known, but the surplus was sufficient to meet the commitments which fell due in 1961 to 1964, when after some poor harvests over $250 million had to be made available each year for the purchase of five million tons of Canadian, Australian and West European grains. In future additional foreign exchange commitments of this kind will have to be met from savings in imports and from earnings through exports of commodities and bullion as well as overseas Chinese remittances. China's trade has been adjusted drastically to the policy of economic retrenchment. Imports of plant equipment have been cut severely so as to make room for foodstuffs. At the same time exports have been kept up fairly well, though their volume is also reduced. Sino-Soviet trade turnover in 1963 amounted to less than one-half of the average of the previous five years. China's exports to the Soviet Union were halved within three years and her imports from the Soviet Union were reduced at the same time to one-fifth. Even so, Soviet Russia's contribution to China's industrial development must not be underrated. Before China was obliged to settle on a policy of economic retrenchment at home and abroad, she had received Soviet plant and factory equipment worth over $2,000 million. Without this, her rapid industrialization would have been impossible.

Apart from machinery, Soviet technicians and know-how were of vital importance since they became available to China at a crucial period of her economic development. All in all, over 10,000 Soviet specialists worked in China at one time or another. The withdrawal of 1,000 to 1,500 technicians at the height of the Sino-Soviet discord aggravated a situation which was precarious in itself. Following the temporary settlement of the dispute the Soviet Union granted China in 1961 a moratorium on her loan services and on the payment for 50,000 tons of sugar; it also returned some industrial specialists to China. There is no evidence, however, of a revival of large-scale Soviet shipments of industrial plant. In their absence China's industrialization programme has to rely on strictly limited domestic resources, and this means that China has to mark time. Her trade and aid commitments to developing countries outside the Soviet bloc which amount at present to approximately $300 million of credits and grants and $450 million trade turnover a year may well be affected by her tight economic position.

Outcome of the Second Plan

As no production data have been published since 1960 and no plan or budget data were made known at the sessions of the National People's Congress held in the spring of 1962, the autumn of 1963 and the winter of 1964, it is difficult to estimate the effects of the current policy on the likely results of the long-term plan. Allowing for yet further mediocre harvests which must be expected by the Chinese authorities, there are bound to be shortfalls in those sectors of the economy which are dependent on the performance of the farming industry. However, as the output of at least some of the basic raw materials and semi-manufactured goods was above the original target set for 1962, there is bound to have been a certain increase in the overall gross industrial output. Against this, farm production has been lagging badly behind the plan. Even an exceptionally good harvest in 1963 would have failed to raise agricultural output substantially above the level attained in 1957, the last year of the previous plan. In fact, the crop of 1963 was only marginally better than the crops which preceded it. This means that the goal set for the total national product is unlikely to have been reached by the end of the second five-year plan period.

The Ten-Point-Programme, outlined by Chou En-lai, the Chinese Prime Minister, at the National People's Congress in 1962, reflected the temporary victory of caution over enthusiasm in economic policy. Agriculture has been given priority over industry, and in the industrial sector the emphasis is on consumer goods which will be required to provide rewards to those at home and abroad who help China out of her current predicament. In this context the emphasis on consumer industries should be seen as interrelated with the aim of expanding foreign trade. Although improved supplies of consumer goods were promised to domestic producers in factories and farms, they are likely to take second place to those of her customers able to supply the foreign exchange badly needed for the purchase of capital equipment and spare parts. Whereas it is not possible to forecast the duration of the current order of economic priorities, references have been made to a new leap forward as soon as circumstances permit. A good harvest may encourage the less patient among China's political leaders. For the time being, however, the interdependence of agriculture and industry is being stressed.

Balance Sheet And Outlook

A balance sheet of China's past achievements and failures and its prospects in the foreseeable future is bound to be tentative and open to revision. The official statistical blackout is to be blamed as much as Western ignorance for any shortcomings in an assessment of this kind. There can be little doubt, however, on a number of important counts. Industrial production, hardly returned to pre-war level in 1952, has more than doubled meanwhile. Whilst this is a notable achievement bringing China within the range of industrializing countries, it amounts to relatively little when the large population is taken into account. In 1962 China produced about 20 kilos of steel per head of its population. The corresponding data for Japan, Soviet Russia, and the United States were over ten, seventeen and over twenty times as large. As was to be expected, the emphasis of China's industrialization programme has been without interruption on heavy industry where the rate of growth has been almost three times as large as in light industry. The discrepancy appears even more pronounced if one considers so important a sector as the metal and machine industry where output has increased almost tenfold within the last ten years. Construction, transport and communication, though lagging, have kept in step with the most vital requirements of a rapidly expanding economy.

By comparison, agriculture which is still the largest and most important sector of the economy has failed lamentably. As a result, its contribution to the nation's total output has declined from almost two-thirds of the gross national product at the beginning of the plan era to little more than one-third ten years later. Even so, the farming industry and the farming community has had to carry the bulk of the burden of the industrialization programme. Poor weather and appalling mismanagement have brought the rate of growth in farming to a virtual standstill. Serious shortfalls in farm output have resulted in the maldistribution of food and in cases of nutritional deficiency, if not malnutrition, in certain periods of the crop season and over certain areas of the country. The end of these difficulties is not yet in sight.

No firm data are available on the investment programme, but the share of gross domestic investment is likely to have increased from one-sixth of the gross national product in 1952 to over one-quarter in 1963. Personal consumption has declined correspondingly from three-quarters of the gross national product ten years ago to less than two-thirds at present. In the course of this decade China has moved a long way on the road towards industrialization. She is still a long way away from becoming an industrial nation. How long this will take cannot be gauged as long as all information concerning the third five-year plan continues to be withheld from foreign observers.

In his report to the National People's Congress held at the end of 1964, Chou En-lai was able to speak of a turn for the better and of a new period of development lying ahead. The period of retrenchment now lies behind, and the years of consolidation have borne fruit. Steel output may now be close on 10 million tons against 5 million tons in 1957 and 13 million tons in 1959. Though a marked recovery has taken place, the claim of an industrial growth rate of 15 per cent in one year may be regarded as an exaggeration. In agriculture 50,000 tractors are available compared with ten times as many in Britain on an acreage that is approximately one-fifteenth of China's. Some 3 million tons of fertilizers are now available equal to 3 kilos (7 lbs) of plant nutrients per acre or one-twentieth of the amount used on farms in Britain.

The priorities laid down early in 1962 continue to determine economic policy in the years ahead. As before agriculture is described as the foundation and industry as the leading sector of the economy. Self-reliance continues to be the yardstick where foreign economic relations are concerned. Once again reference is made to a leap forward, though there is yet no claim that it is to be great. The road of development is thus charted. If and when the new five-year plan (1966-1970) is put into effect with three years' delay, it will be time to review afresh the economic intentions of the leaders of China.

RATES OF ECONOMIC GROWTH

	First Five-Year Plan 1953–1957			*Second Five-Year Plan* 1957–1962		
	target set	achievement claim	achievement actual	target set	achievement claim	achievement actual
Rate of Growth		1952 = 100			1957 = 100	
Gross Agricultural Output	123	125	(115)	135	—	(95)
Gross Industrial Output	190	215	(200)	200	—	(120)
Gross Material Output	151	165	(150)	175	—	(110)
National Income	143	155	(140)	150	—	(100)
Rate of Growth		% per annum			% per annum	
Gross Agricultural Output	4·3	4·6	(2·8)	6·2	—	(−1·0)
Gross Industrial Output	13·7	16·6	(14·9)	14·9	—	(3·7)
Gross Material Output	8·6	10·5	(8·5)	11·9	—	(1·9)
National Income	7·4	9·2	(7·0)	8·5	—	(0·0)

PUBLIC INCOME AND EXPENDITURE

(in 000 million $)

	1949 actual	1952 actual	1957 actual	1959 actual	1960 target	1962 target
Income	n.a.	7·46	13·04	23·00	29·73	n.a.
Expenditure	n.a.	7·17	12·94	22·40	29·73	n.a.
Investment	n.a.	(3·10)	(6·31)	(13·66)	(18·22)	n.a.

INDUSTRIAL PRODUCTION

(in million physical units)

	1949 actual	1952 actual	1957 actual	1959 claim	1962 target	1964 est.
Electricity (000 kwh)	4·3	7·3	19·3	41·5	50·0	33·0
Coal (tons)	31·0	66·5	130·7	347·8	230·0	220·0
Crude Oil (tons)	0·1	0·4	1·5	3·7	5·5	6·0
Iron Ore (tons)	0·6	4·3	19·4	71·0	n.a.	n.a.
Pig Iron (tons)	0·2	1·9	5·9	20·5	n.a.	n.a.
Crude Steel (tons)	0·2	1·3	5·3	13·3	15·5	10·0
Cement (tons)	0·7	2·9	6·9	12·3	13·5	8·0
Timber (cbm)	4·0	10·0	28·0	41·2	32·5	n.a.
Fertilizers (tons)	0·0	0·2	0·6	1·3	5·0	3·0
Cotton Yarn (tons)	0·3	0·7	0·8	1·5	1·5	1·0
Cotton Cloth (000 meters)	1·4	4·0	5·0	7·0	9·0	4·5
Sugar (tons)	0·2	0·5	0·9	1·1	6·0	n.a.

FARM MANAGEMENT
(in millions)

Peasant Families	1950 actual	1952 actual	1957 actual	1959 actual	1960 actual	1962 target
Private Households	94·20	68·30	2·00	(1·20)	(1·00)	none
Mutual Aid Teams	11·30	45·40	none	none	none	none
Agric. Producers' 'Co-ops'	0·00	0·00	119·50	negl.	negl.	negl.
People's Communes	none	none	none	(122·00)	(124·00)	n.a.
Total	105·50	113·70	121·50	123·20	(125·00)	n.a.

AGRICULTURAL PRODUCTION
(in million physical units)

	1949 actual	1952 actual	1957 actual	1959 claim	1962 target	1964 est.
Crops (hectares)						
Grains and Potatoes	101·6	112·3	120·9	121·3	n.a.	n.a.
Soyabeans	8·2	11·5	12·6	12·8	n.a.	n.a.
Cotton	0·3	0·5	0·6	0·6	n.a.	n.a.
Crops (tons)						
Grains and Potatoes	108·0	154·5	185·0	270·5	250·0	190·0
Soyabeans	5·1	9·5	10·0	11·5	12·5	12·0
Cotton	0·4	1·3	1·6	2·3	2·4	2·5
Livestock						
Horses, Donkeys and Mules	15·8	19·6	19·8	(20·0)	n.a.	n.a.
Cattle and Buffaloes	43·9	56·6	65·8	(65·4)	90·0	n.a.
Pigs	57·8	89·8	145·9	(180·0)	250·0	n.a.
Sheep and Goats	42·3	61·8	98·6	(112·5)	170·0	n.a.

AGRICULTURAL ESTIMATES DURING GREAT LEAP FORWARD

	1958			1959		
	target	claim		target		claim
	original	original	final	original	revised	final
Crops (mill. tons)						
Grains and Potatoes	196·0	375·0	250·0	525·0	275·0	270·0
Soyabeans	10·4	12·5	10·5	15·0	15·0	11·5
Cotton	1·7	3·3	2·1	5·0	2·3	2·4
Livestock (mill.)						
Pigs	180·0	200·0	160·0	280·0	180·0	n.a.

FOREIGN TRADE ESTIMATES

(in 000 million $)

	1950	1952	1957	1959	1961	1962	1963
Imports							
Soviet Union	0·4	0·6	0·5	0·9	0·4	0·2	0·2
Other Soviet Bloc	0·1	0·2	0·4	0·5	0·3	0·3	0·2
Total Soviet Bloc	0·5	0·8	0·9	1·4	0·7	0·5	0·4
Developing Countries	0·2	0·2	0·2	0·2	0·3	0·3	0·3
Other Non-Bloc	0·1	0·1	0·2	0·4	0·4	0·4	0·5
Total Non-Bloc	0·3	0·3	0·4	0·6	0·7	0·7	0·8
Total World	0·8	1·1	1·3	2·0	1·4	1·2	1·2
Exports							
Soviet Union	0·2	0·4	0·7	1·1	0·6	0·5	0·4
Other Soviet Bloc	0·1	0·2	0·4	0·5	0·3	0·4	0·4
Total Soviet Bloc	0·3	0·6	1·1	1·6	0·9	0·9	0·8
Developing Countries	0·3	0·3	0·2	0·2	0·3	0·3	0·3
Other Non-Bloc	0·1	0·1	0·3	0·4	0·3	0·3	0·4
Total Non-Bloc	0·4	0·4	0·5	0·6	0·6	0·6	0·7
Total World	0·7	1·0	1·6	2·2	1·5	1·5	1·5

FOREIGN AID ESTIMATES

(in million $)

	1956/7	1958	1959	1960	1961	1962	1963
Aid offered to Bloc							
European Bloc	50·0	—	35·0	—	125·0	—	—
Asian Bloc	40·0	50·0	100·0	155·0	157·0	—	—
Total Bloc	90·0	50·0	135·0	155·0	282·0	—	—
Aid offered to Non-Bloc							
Africa and Middle East	5·0	16·0	—	27·0	40·0	—	90·0
Asia	55·0	43·0	26·0	33·0	133·0	20·0	—
Latin America	—	—	—	60·0	—	—	—
Total Non-Bloc	60·0	59·0	26·0	102·0	173·0	20·0	90·0
Total World	150·0	109·0	161·0	275·0	455·0	20·0	90·0

n.a.—not available
( )—estimate

Sources: Chinese official sources
Estimates

BIBLIOGRAPHY

A. D. Barnett. *Communist Economic Strategy: The Rise of Mainland China.* (National Planning Association, New York, 1959)

J. L. Buck. *Land Utilization in China.* 3 vols. (Nanking University, Shanghai, 1937)

S. Chandrasekhar. *China's Population.* (Hong Kong University Press, Hong Kong, 1959)

K. C. Chao. *Agrarian Policy of the Chinese Communist Party.* (Asia Publishing House, London, 1960)

A. Eckstein. *The National Income of Communist China.* (The Free Press, Glencoe, Illinois, 1961)

W. W. Hollister. *China's Gross National Product and Social Accounts 1950-1957.* (The Free Press, Glencoe, Illinois, 1958)

R. Hsia. *Economic Planning in Communist China.* (Institute of Pacific Relations, New York, 1955)

T. J. Hughes and D. E. T. Luard. *The Economic Development of Communist China 1949-1960.* (2nd ed.) (Oxford University Press, London, 1961)

E. S. Kirby, a.o. *Contemporary China.* Vols. I-IV. (Hong Kong University Press, Hong Kong, 1956 ff)

C. M. Li. *Economic Development of Communist China.* (University of California Press, Berkeley and Los Angeles, 1959), *The Statistical System of Communist China.* (University of California Press, Berkeley and Los Angeles, 1962). Ed. *Industrial Development in Communist China.* (Praeger, New York, 1964)

T. C. Liu and K. C. Yeh. *The Economy of the Chinese Mainland: National Income and Economic Development*, 1933-1959. (Princeton Univ. Press, Princeton, N.J., 1965)

C. F. Remer, a.o. *International Economics of Communist China.* (University of Michigan Press, Ann Arbor, 1959)

W. W. Rostow, a.o. *The Prospects of Communist China.* (John Wiley, New York, 1954)

T. Shabad. *China's Changing Map.* (Praeger, New York, 1956)

T. H. Shen. *Agricultural Resources of China.* (Cornell University Press, Ithaca, N.Y., 1951)

R. H. Tawny. *Land and Labour in China.* (Allen and Unwin, London, 1932)

Y. L. Wu. *An Economic Survey of Communist China.* (Bookmen Associates, New York, 1956)

H. Yin and Y. C. Yin. *Economic Statistics of Mainland China.* (Harvard University Press, Cambridge, Mass., 1960)

JOURNALS

Economic Survey of Asia and the Far East. (Bangkok)

Economic Bulletin for Asia and the Far East. (Bangkok)

Far Eastern Economic Review. (Hong Kong)

Problems of Communism. (Washington)

The China Quarterly. (London)

BIOGRAPHICAL NOTE

DR. W. KLATT, O.B.E. is an Economic Adviser and a student of economic and agrarian affairs in Europe and Asia. He has been a consultant to United Nations Agencies on several occasions. He has undertaken a number of surveys in various Asian countries. He has written for journals in England and America and on the Continent; he is the editor of and a contributor to a symposium, *The Chinese Model. A Political, Economic and Social Survey* (Hong Kong Univ. Press, Hong Kong, 1965).

THE ECONOMY OF JAPAN

by

R. N. WOOD

THE chaotic conditions which accompanied the end of the war make it difficult to assess with any accuracy what defeat meant for Japan in material terms. It is probable, however, that the real national income in 1945-46 had fallen back to the level achieved 15 or 20 years before. The reduction of individual incomes was even more serious, since the 1945 population was much higher than it had been in the mid-twenties. Many people lived on the verge of starvation and, with a major part of the country's economic assets destroyed, it looked as if it would be a long time before recovery.

POSTWAR RECOVERY

The postwar recovery—as in West Germany and Italy—was however remarkably rapid. A great deal of the credit for this must go to the United States, the principal influence in the formation of the policy of the occupation forces (SCAP). Very generous financial assistance was given to the stricken country, and SCAP made every effort to encourage the improvement of living standards. This enlightened policy together with the industry and enterprise shown by the Japanese produced most gratifying results.

Between 1946 and 1953—the year after independence was regained and which is taken here as the end of the postwar recovery period—the national income more than doubled in real terms, bringing an increase of nearly 90 per cent in income per head. In the immediate postwar years there was, it is true, rapid inflation, but increases in production were rapid too and by the end of 1950 inflationary pressures had been reduced to modest proportions.

One of the most significant and successful measures introduced by SCAP was the land reform. This effected a transfer of land ownership from the few big proprietors to numerous peasant smallholders. Although the reform was carried out on strictly orthodox lines, with provisions for compensation for the old land owners, the burden of debt on the peasants was appreciably reduced by inflation. There is no doubt that the changed basis of land tenure has, since the war, contributed greatly to the ever increasing yields of Japanese agriculture (although it may now be time for the matter to be reconsidered). Between 1945 and 1953 total agricultural production increased by two-thirds, despite the fact that 1953 was an unusually bad year. Rice is the main crop, and the growth of its output was the main factor contributing to the overall increase. The most rapid advance, however, was in the production of livestock, which rose nearly six times during this period.

Japan's mineral output is dominated by coal, though there are small quantities of many other minerals. Total mining production rose by 83 per cent between 1945 and 1953. Coal production declined sharply in 1946, however, and over the period production rose by only 53 per cent.

The major growth sector both in the early, postwar period and more especially after 1953 was manufacturing industry. It was here that the effects of defeat in war were felt most acutely. In 1946 the index of manufacturing production was two-thirds lower than it had been in 1945. By 1953, however, it had reached a level 96 per cent above that for the year of Japan's surrender. Progress in basic items such as iron and steel, rolling stock, textiles, and foodstuffs was much more rapid than average—though the machinery industry, to be one of the front runners in the later period, was rather slow to recover.

The postwar progress of manufacturing was closely linked to the success of Japan's exports. Here, too, the enlightened policy of the United States was important, for, in contrast to West European countries, it maintained a liberal attitude to imports from Japan. South-East Asian markets also proved fruitful, with reparations agreements smoothing the path of exports. The total value of exports rose 14 times between 1945 and 1953.

Changes in Economic Structure

While Japan's recovery after the war was remarkable, it is to a large extent overshadowed by the speed of advance since the end of the reconstruction period. Between 1953 and 1964 the gross national product more than doubled in real terms, giving an annual average rate of growth of nearly 10 per cent. No other country in the free world (and probably not in the Communist world either) can boast of such a dynamic achievement. Intensive Government campaigns greatly reduced the birth rate in comparison with the prewar period, so that the increase in total output was not greatly eroded as a result of population growth; the real rise in GNP per head over the period 1953-63 was more than 10 per cent. The rapid rise in production was accompanied and promoted by an upsurge in investment. Gross fixed capital formation in 1963 was $4\frac{1}{2}$ times higher in real terms than in 1953 and amounted to as much as 37 per cent of GNP. Foreign trade, too, expanded very rapidly during this period. Between 1953 and 1963 exports rose nearly $3\frac{1}{2}$ times and imports nearly 3 times.

The swift progress of the last ten years has been accompanied by great changes in economic structure. While in 1953 agriculture, forestry, and fisheries contributed 22 per cent of the domestic output, by 1963 their share had dropped to a mere 13 per cent. Manufacturing, on the other hand, increased its share of the total from 24 per cent in 1953 to 30 per cent in 1963. These changes are reflected, though to a lesser extent, in the employment figures. In 1953 45 per cent of the total labour force was engaged in agriculture, forestry, and fisheries; by 1963 the proportion had shrunk to less than one-third. Over the same period the proportion of the labour force in manufacturing rose from 17 per cent to 24 per cent. There is no doubt that this flow of workers from the countryside into more productive employment in the towns has been one of the major factors in Japan's economic success.

This is not to say that agriculture stagnated. Between 1953 and 1963 the overall index of agricultural production rose by well over half. Government purchases of domestically produced rice rose from 4·0 million tons in 1953 to 6·5 million tons in 1963; in the same period imports dropped from nearly 1 million tons to less than 200,000 tons. Freak weather conditions seriously affected the 1963 wheat harvest; between 1953 and 1962, however, production rose 2½ times. The swift advance here, and also in livestock, milk, and egg production reflects the changes in dietary habits, which are still going on.

As has already been said, the land reform made a major contribution to the rise in agricultural production by giving the peasants a stake in the soil. Many of the individual holdings are small, however, and prevent the fullest and most economic use of new machinery and techniques. A programme for larger holdings and increased mechanization has been started in a number of communities with the emphasis on commercial crops and dairy products. Larger-scale operations are essential not only to boost agricultural output further, but also to enable a sufficient number of workers to move to employment in the towns and so prevent industrial labour costs from rising unduly.

Since 1953 mining has been, perhaps, the least successful of the major industrial sectors. To a large extent this reflects the problems of the coal industry, the main traditional centre of which is the southern island of Kyushu. Much of the coal is of poor quality, while the seams are narrow and have become increasingly difficult to work. Total mineral production rose by only one-third between 1953 and 1963; coal production increased by a mere 11 per cent. Output of coal from Kyushu did little more than stagnate, though production from the northern island of Hokkaido expanded quite fast. Hitherto the Government has been prepared to protect coal mining, partly to conserve foreign exchange and partly for social and political reasons. In future, however, it is intended to rely increasingly on petroleum, the bulk of which has to be imported. Coal miners are putting up a stiff fight against closures and 'rationalization', but many of them are likely to become redundant.

Manufacturing Industry

It is manufacturing industry, of course, which has been the star turn of the Japanese economy. Between 1953 and 1963 manufacturing production increased fourfold. There have naturally been big differences in the performance of the various sectors. Traditional, light manufactures, such as cotton textiles, ceramics, food products, etc., have lost ground to technically advanced, heavy industries. Production of cotton fabrics, for example, rose by only one quarter between 1953 and 1963.

The rather mediocre performance in these areas was offset by some quite outstanding results in others. Machinery production in 1963 was nearly eight times above that for 1953. The main growth sector here was the electrical machinery industry. Production of television sets rose from 14,000 in 1953 to 5 million in 1963; production of transistors which did not really get under way until 1957, rose from 5·7 million then to over 250 million in

1963. The record of these items is rivalled in the non-electrical sector by the performance of motor cars, motor cycles and scooters, and trucks.

The chemical industry has also gone ahead very fast, particularly on the organic side. Japan's progress with synthetic resins and non-cellulose based plastic materials has been astounding, and it now produces as wide a range of these products as any other country in the world. Synthetic textiles have been the only really buoyant part of the textile industry, and have greatly enhanced overall results there.

Wholesale and retail trade remains one of the least modernized sectors of the economy. Retailing, in particular, is characterized by a large number of very small enterprises and, though department stores are increasing in importance, they still account for only a small proportion of total sales. In many spheres of domestic trade there are large numbers of middle men, with few resources, often with large debts, existing on minuscule profit margins. In wholesaling, however, there are also some very big firms, such as Mitsui, Mitsubishi and Sumitomo, which are connected with the large cartels (zaibatsu).

Government Policy

Government expenditure lagged behind advances in trade and industry in the fifties, but has accelerated in recent years. Between 1953 and 1963 Central Government outlays—including those of public corporations and special institutions—rose $2\frac{1}{2}$ times. Even so, many basic facilities relying on Government support, such as roads, ports, sewerage and housing have become increasingly inadequate to cope with the rapidly expanding economic and social needs.

The Government's impact on the economy has been more in the direct influence it has exerted on private industry. There are indications, however, that the opportunities for this sort of Government interference may be reduced. Its most powerful weapons in controlling the private sector have derived from its power to regulate foreign trade and exchange. Since Japan possesses hardly any of the raw materials necessary to support its industry, it is argued that its balance of payments is likely to be subject to greater strains than elsewhere. This is usually put forward as justification for the structure of trade and exchange controls. Probably more important, however, have been the Government's wish to regulate competition and to control the domestic economy, and its fear lest too large a part of Japan's assets should fall under foreign control. Under pressure from other industrial countries the authorities are liberalizing the external restrictions. This process has now gone some distance, though a significant number of items is still subject to restrictions. Further liberalization is planned, however, and as these defences disappear, so will the Government's power over private industry diminish.

The Future

Japan's progress has been remarkable. What of its future? In 1961 the Government published its Long-Range Economic Plan, setting out the targets for the sixties. The plan calls for the following objectives to be reached by 1970 (increase over 1956-58 given in brackets): national income per head

£207 (2·4 times), gross domestic capital formation £2,958 million (2·8 times), exports £3,329 million (3·5 times), and imports £3,534 million (3·2 times). These targets may look ambitious in relation to economic performance elsewhere. Viewed against the background of Japan's own progress they are by no means unreasonable. Indeed, owing to the extraordinary rate of growth achieved in the years 1959-61, Japan has begun the plan far ahead of the start-line envisaged by the planners.

Nevertheless there are a number of factors which suggest that expansion may now proceed more slowly than in the recent past. First, labour is likely to become scarcer. Even if more efficient methods release more people from the land, the flow is likely to be less rapid than in the past. Moreover, as the economy becomes more complex, the problem of providing workers with the appropriate skills will become more acute. This calls for reforms of the educational and employment systems, and the setting up of adequate re-training programmes, all of which will take time. Second, much of Japan's progress since the war has been based on the adaptation of new, often foreign techniques. As a result the technical gap between Japan and the richer nations has now been very greatly narrowed. The pace of technical advance in future may, therefore, be slower and provide a less strong expansionary impetus. Third, the economy has so far been powered mainly by the private sector. Large amounts will now have to be spent on improving the basic economic infrastructure, and the returns may be smaller and slower to accrue than those earned by private industry.

Although there may be a gradual downtrend in the growth rate during the sixties, however, the targets of the plan should be met without too much difficulty. Japan's still looks one of the world's most ebullient economies, and it would be surprising if its total output were growing much less than five or six per cent a year by the end of the decade.

BIBLIOGRAPHY

G. C. Allen. *Japan's Economic Recovery*. (Oxford Univ. Press, London, 1958.)

J. B. Cohen. *International Aspects of Japan's Economic Situation.* (Council of Foreign Relations, London, 1957.) *Japan's Postwar Economy.* (Indiana Univ. Press, Bloomington, 1958.)

S. S. Kuznets (ed.) *Economic Growth: Brazil, India, Japan.* (Duke Univ. Press, 1955.)

S. Okita. *The Rehabilitation of Japan's Economy and Asia.* (Ministry of Foreign Affairs, London, 1956.)

S. Takahata. *Quo Vadis, Japan?* (Institute of Pacific Relations, Kyoto, 1954.)

The Japanese Economy. (Economist Intelligence Unit for Federation of British Industries, London, 1962.)

BIOGRAPHICAL NOTE

R. N. Wood. Graduated from Oxford in Politics, Philosophy and Economics, 1958. Rockefeller Studentship in International Studies, London School of Economics and Political Science, 1958-9. Now Manager of Asian and Middle Eastern Department, Economist Intelligence Unit, London.

BUDDHIST ECONOMICS

by

E. F. SCHUMACHER

'Right Livelihood' is one of the requirements of the Buddha's Noble Eightfold Path. It is clear, therefore, that there must be such a thing as Buddhist Economics.

Buddhist countries, at the same time, have often stated that they wish to remain faithful to their heritage. So Burma: 'The New Burma sees no conflict between religious values and economic progress. Spiritual health and material well-being are not enemies: they are natural allies.'[1] Or: 'We can blend successfully the religious and spiritual values of our heritage with the benefits of modern technology.'[2] Or: 'We Burmans have a sacred duty to conform both our dreams and our acts to our faith. This we shall ever do.'[3]

All the same, such countries invariably assume that they can model their economic development plans in accordance with modern economics, and they call upon modern economists from so-called advanced countries to advise them, to formulate the policies to be pursued, and to construct the grand design for development, the Five-Year Plan or whatever it may be called. No one seems to think that a Buddhist way of life would call for Buddhist economics, just as the modern materialist way of life has brought forth modern economics.

Economists themselves, like most specialists, normally suffer from a kind of metaphysical blindness, assuming that theirs is a science of absolute and invariable truths, without any pre-suppositions. Some go as far as to claim that economic laws are as free from 'metaphysics' or 'values' as the law of gravitation. We need not, however, get involved in arguments of methodology. Instead, let us take some fundamentals and see what they look like when viewed by a modern economist and a Buddhist economist.

There is universal agreement that the fundamental source of wealth is human labour. Now, the modern economist has been brought up to consider 'labour' or work as little more than a necessary evil. From the point of view of the employer, it is in any case simply an item of cost, to be reduced to a minimum if it cannot be eliminated altogether, say, by automation. From the point of view of the workman, it is a 'disutility'; to work is to make a sacrifice of one's leisure and comfort, and wages are a kind of compensation for the sacrifice. Hence the ideal from the point of view of the employer is to have output without employees, and the ideal from the point of view of the employee is to have income without employment.

[1] This and subsequent reference numerals in the present chapter indicate titles in the list of sources given on page 701.

The consequences of these attitudes both in theory and in practice are, of course, extremely far-reaching. If the ideal with regard to work is to get rid of it, every method that 'reduces the work load' is a good thing. The most potent method, short of automation, is the so-called 'division of labour' and the classical example is the pin factory eulogized in Adam Smith's *Wealth of Nations*. Here it is not a matter of ordinary specialization, which mankind has practised from time immemorial, but of dividing up every complete process of production into minute parts, so that the final product can be produced at great speed without anyone having had to contribute more than a totally insignificant and, in most cases, unskilled movement of his limbs.

Work

The Buddhist point of view takes the function of work to be at least threefold: to give a man a chance to utilize and develop his faculties; to enable him to overcome his ego-centredness by joining with other people in a common task; and to bring forth the goods and services needed for a becoming existence. Again, the consequences that flow from this view are endless. To organize work in such a manner that it becomes meaningless, boring, stultifying, or nerve-racking for the worker would be little short of criminal; it would indicate a greater concern with goods than with people, an evil lack of compassion and a soul-destroying degree of attachment to the most primitive side of this worldly existence. Equally, to strive for leisure as an alternative to work would be considered a complete misunderstanding of one of the basic truths of human existence, namely, that work and leisure are complementary parts of the same living process and cannot be separated without destroying the joy of work and the bliss of leisure.

From the Buddhist point of view, there are therefore two types of mechanization which must be clearly distinguished: one that enhances a man's skill and power and one that turns the work of man over to a mechanical slave, leaving man in a position of having to serve the slave. How to tell the one from the other? 'The craftsman himself,' says Ananda Coomaraswamy, a man equally competent to talk about the Modern West as the Ancient East, 'the craftsman himself can always, if allowed to, draw the delicate distinction between the machine and the tool. The carpet loom is a tool, a contrivance for holding warp threads at a stretch for the pile to be woven round them by the craftsmen's fingers; but the power loom is a machine, and its significance as a destroyer of culture lies in the fact that it does the essentially human part of the work.'[4] It is clear, therefore, that Buddhist economics must be very different from the economics of modern materialism, since the Buddhist sees the essence of civilization not in a multiplication of wants but in the purification of human character. Character, at the same time, is formed primarily by a man's work. And work, properly conducted in conditions of human dignity and freedom, blesses those who do it and equally their products. The Indian philosopher and economist J. C. Kumarappa sums the matter up as follows:

> 'If the nature of the work is properly appreciated and applied, it will stand in the same relation to the higher faculties as food is to the physical body. It nourishes and

enlivens the higher man and urges him to produce the best he is capable of. It directs his freewill along the proper course and disciplines the animal in him into progressive channels. It furnishes an excellent background for man to display his scale of values and develop his personality.'[5]

If a man has no chance of obtaining work he is in a desperate position, not simply because he lacks an income but because he lacks this nourishing and enlivening factor of disciplined work which nothing can replace. A modern economist may engage in highly sophisticated calculations on whether full employment 'pays' or whether it might be more 'economic' to run an economy at less than full employment so as to ensure a greater mobility of labour, a better stability of wages, and so forth. His fundamental criterion of success is simply the total quantity of goods produced during a given period of time. 'If the marginal urgency of goods is low,' says Professor Galbraith in *The Affluent Society*, 'then so is the urgency of employing the last man or the last million men in the labour force.' And again: 'If . . . we can afford some unemployment in the interest of stability—a proposition, incidentally, of impeccably conservative antecedents—then we can afford to give those who are unemployed the goods that enable them to sustain their accustomed standard of living.'[6]

From a Buddhist point of view, this is standing the truth on its head by considering goods as more important than people and consumption as more important than creative activity. It means shifting the emphasis from the worker to the product of work, that is, from the human to the sub-human, a surrender to the forces of evil. The very start of Buddhist economic planning would be a planning for full employment, and the primary purpose of this would in fact be employment for everyone who needs an 'outside' job: it would not be the maximization of employment nor the maximization of production. Women, on the whole, do not need an 'outside' job, and the large-scale employment of women in offices or factories would be considered a sign of serious economic failure. In particular, to let mothers of young children work in factories while the children run wild would be as uneconomic in the eyes of a Buddhist economist as the employment of a skilled worker as a soldier in the eyes of a modern economist. In either case, a 'productive' person would be thought to be unproductively used from the Buddhist point of view.

While the materialist is mainly interested in goods, the Buddhist is mainly interested in liberation. But Buddhism is 'The Middle Way' and therefore in no way antagonistic to physical well-being. It is not wealth that stands in the way of liberation but the attachment to wealth; not the enjoyment of pleasurable things but the craving for them. The keynote of Buddhist economics, therefore, is simplicity and non-violence. From an economist's point of view, the marvel of the Buddhist way of life is the utter rationality of its pattern—amazingly small means leading to extraordinarily satisfactory results.

Standard of Living

For the modern economist this is very difficult to understand. He is used to measuring the 'standard of living' by the amount of annual consumption, assuming all the time that a man who consumes more is 'better off' than a man who consumes less. A Buddhist economist would consider this approach excessively irrational: since consumption is merely a means to human well-being, the aim should be to obtain the maximum of well-being with the minimum of consumption. Thus, if the purpose of clothing is a certain amount of temperature comfort and an attractive appearance, the task is to attain this purpose with the smallest possible effort, that is, with the smallest annual destruction of cloth and with the help of designs that involve the smallest possible input of toil. The less toil there is, the more time and strength is left for artistic creativity. It would be highly uneconomic, for instance, to go in for complicated tailoring, like the modern West, when a much more beautiful effect can be achieved by the skilful draping of uncut material. It would be the height of folly to make material so that it should wear out quickly and the height of barbarity to make anything ugly, shabby or mean. What has just been said about clothing applies equally to all other human requirements. The ownership and the consumption of goods is a means to an end, and Buddhist economics is the systematic study of how to attain given ends with the minimum means.

Modern economics, on the other hand, considers consumption to be 'the sole end and purpose of all economic activity', taking the factors of production—land, labour, and capital—as the means. The former, in short, tries to maximize human satisfactions by the optimal pattern of consumption, while the latter tries to maximize consumption by the optimal pattern of productive effort. It is easy to see that the effort needed to sustain a way of life which seeks to attain the optimal pattern of consumption is likely to be much smaller than the effort needed to sustain a drive for maximum consumption. We need not be surprised, therefore, that the pressure and strain of living is very much less in, say, Burma than it is in the United States, in spite of the fact that the amount of labour-saving machinery used in the former country is only a minute fraction of the amount used in the latter.

Pattern of Consumption

Simplicity and non-violence are obviously closely related. The optimal pattern of consumption, producing a high degree of human satisfaction by means of a relatively low rate of consumption, allows people to live without great pressure and strain and to fulfil the primary injunction of Buddhist teaching: 'Cease to do evil; try to do good.' As physical resources are everywhere limited, people satisfying their needs by means of a modest use of resources are obviously less likely to be at each other's throats than people depending upon a high rate of use. Equally, people who live in highly self-sufficient local communities are less likely to get involved in large-scale violence than people whose existence depends on world-wide systems of trade.

From the point of view of Buddhist economics, therefore, production from local resources for local needs is the most rational way of economic life, while dependence on imports from afar and the consequent need to produce for export to unknown and distant peoples is highly uneconomic and justifiable only in exceptional cases and on a small scale. Just as the modern economist would admit that a high rate of consumption of transport services between a man's home and his place of work signifies a misfortune and not a high standard of life, so the Buddhist economist would hold that to satisfy human wants from far-away sources rather than from sources nearby signifies failure rather than success. The former might take statistics showing an increase in the number of ton/miles per head of the population carried by a country's transport system as proof of economic progress, while to the latter—the Buddhist economist—the same statistics would indicate a highly undesirable deterioration in the *pattern* of consumption.

NATURAL RESOURCES

Another striking difference between modern economics and Buddhist economics arises over the use of natural resources. Bertrand de Juvenal, the eminent French political philosopher, has characterized 'Western man' in words which may be taken as a fair description of the modern economist:

> 'He tends to count nothing as an expenditure, other than human effort; he does not seem to mind how much mineral matter he wastes and, far worse, how much living matter he destroys. He does not seem to realise at all that human life is a dependent part of an ecosystem of many different forms of life. As the world is ruled from towns where men are cut off from any form of life other than human, the feeling of belonging to an ecosystem is not revived. This results in a harsh and improvident treatment of things upon which we ultimately depend, such as water and trees.'[7]

The teaching of the Buddha, on the other hand, enjoins a reverent and non-violent attitude not only to all sentient beings but also, with great emphasis, to trees. Every follower of the Buddha ought to plant a tree every few years and look after it until it is safely established, and the Buddhist economist can demonstrate without difficulty that the universal observance of this rule would result in a high rate of genuine economic development independent of any foreign aid. Much of the economic decay of South-East Asia (as of many other parts of the world) is undoubtedly due to a heedless and shameful neglect of trees.

Modern economics does not distinguish between renewable and non-renewable materials, as its very method is to equalize and quantify everything by means of a money price. Thus, taking various alternative fuels, like coal, oil, wood or water power: the only difference between them recognized by modern economics is relative cost per equivalent unit. The cheapest is automatically the one to be preferred, as to do otherwise would be irrational and 'uneconomic'. From a Buddhist point of view, of course, this will not do; the essential difference between non-renewable fuels like coal and oil on the one hand and renewable fuels like wood and water-power on the other cannot be simply overlooked. Non-renewable goods must be used only if they are indispensable, and then only with the greatest care and the most meticulous concern for conservation. To use them heedlessly or extravagantly is an act of violence, and while complete non-violence may not be attainable on this earth, there is none the less an ineluctable duty on man to aim at the ideal of non-violence in all he does.

Just as a modern European economist would not consider it a great economic achievement if all European art treasures were sold to America at attractive prices, so the Buddhist economist would insist that a population basing its economic life on non-renewable fuels is living parasitically, on capital instead of income. Such a way of life could have no permanence and could therefore be justified only as a purely temporary expedient. As the world's resources of non-renewable fuels—coal, oil and natural gas—are exceedingly unevenly distributed over the globe and undoubtedly limited in quantity, it is clear that their exploitation at an ever increasing rate is an act of violence against nature which must almost inevitably lead to violence between men.

The Middle Way

This fact alone might give food for thought even to those people in Buddhist countries who care nothing for the religious and spiritual values of their heritage and ardently desire to embrace the materialism of modern economics at the fastest possible speed. Before they dismiss Buddhist economics as nothing better than a nostalgic dream, they might wish to consider whether the path of economic development outlined by modern economics is likely to lead them to places where they really want to be. Towards the end of his courageous book *The Challenge of Man's Future*, Professor Harrison Brown of the California Institute of Technology gives the following appraisal:

> 'Thus we see that, just as industrial society is fundamentally unstable and subject to reversion to agrarian existence, so within it the conditions which offer individual freedom are unstable in their ability to avoid the conditions which impose rigid organization and totalitarian control. Indeed, when we examine all of the foreseeable difficulties which threaten the survival of industrial civilization, it is difficult to see how the achievement of stability and the maintenance of individual liberty can be made compatible.'[8]

Even if this were dismissed as a long-term view—and in the long term, as Keynes said, we are all dead—there is the immediate question of whether 'modernization', as currently practised without regard to religious and spiritual values, is actually producing agreeable results. As far as the masses are concerned, the results appear to be disastrous—a collapse of the rural economy, a rising tide of unemployment in town and country, and the growth of a city proletariat without nourishment for either body or soul.

It is in the light of both immediate experience and long-term prospects that the study of Buddhist economics could be recommended even to those who believe that economic growth is more important than any spiritual or religious values. For it is not a question of choosing between 'modern growth' and 'traditional stagnation'. It is a question of finding the right path of development, the Middle Way between materialist heedlessness and traditionalist immobility, in short, of finding 'Right Livelihood'.

That this can be done is not in doubt. But it requires much more than blind imitation of the materialist way of life of the so-called advanced countries.[9] It requires, above all, the conscious and systematic development of a Middle Way in technology, of an 'intermediate technology', as I have called it,[10, 11] a technology more productive and powerful than the decayed technology of the ancient East, but at the same time non-violent and immensely cheaper and simpler than the labour-saving technology of the modern West.

REFERENCES

1. *Pyidawtha, The New Burma.* (Economic and Social Board, Government of the Union of Burma, 1954, p. 10.)
2. *Ibid.*, p. 8.
3. *Ibid.*, p. 128.
4. Ananda K. Coomaraswamy. *Art and Swadeshi.* (Ganesh and Co., Madras, p. 30.)
5. J. C. Kumarappa. *Economy of Permanence.* (Sarva-Seva-Sangh-Publication, Rajghat, Kashi, 4th ed., 1958, p. 117.)
6. J. K. Galbraith. *The Affluent Society.* (Penguin, 1962, pp. 272-273.)
7. Richard B. Gregg. *A Philosophy of Indian Economic Development.* (Navajivan Publishing House, Ahmedabad, 1958, pp. 140-41.)
8. Harrison Brown. *The Challenge of Man's Future.* (The Viking Press, New York, 1954, p. 255.)
9. E. F. Schumacher. 'Rural Industries' in *India at Midpassage.* (Overseas Development Institute, London, 1964.)
10. E. F. Schumacher. 'Industrialisation through Intermediate Technology' in *Minerals and Industries*, Vol. 1, no. 4. (Calcutta, 1964.)
11. Vijay Chebbi and George McRobie. *Dynamics of District Development.* (SIET Institute, Hyderabad, 1964.)

BIOGRAPHICAL NOTE

E. F. SCHUMACHER. B. 1911, Bonn; emigrated to England in 1937. Educated at the universities of Bonn and Berlin, Oxford (Rhodes Scholar), and Columbia, New York. After several years in business, farming and journalism joined the British Control Commission for Germany in 1946 as Economic Adviser. Economic Adviser of the National Coal Board, London, since 1950 and Director of Statistics since 1963. In 1955 seconded to United Nations as Economic Adviser to the Government of the Union of Burma; in 1962 invited by the Indian Government to advise the Indian Planning Commission on problems of Indian development policy. Has travelled widely in Europe, America and Asia and published many articles and several books on economic and philosophical subjects. In November 1963 received an honorary doctor's degree from the Technical University of Clausthal, West Germany.

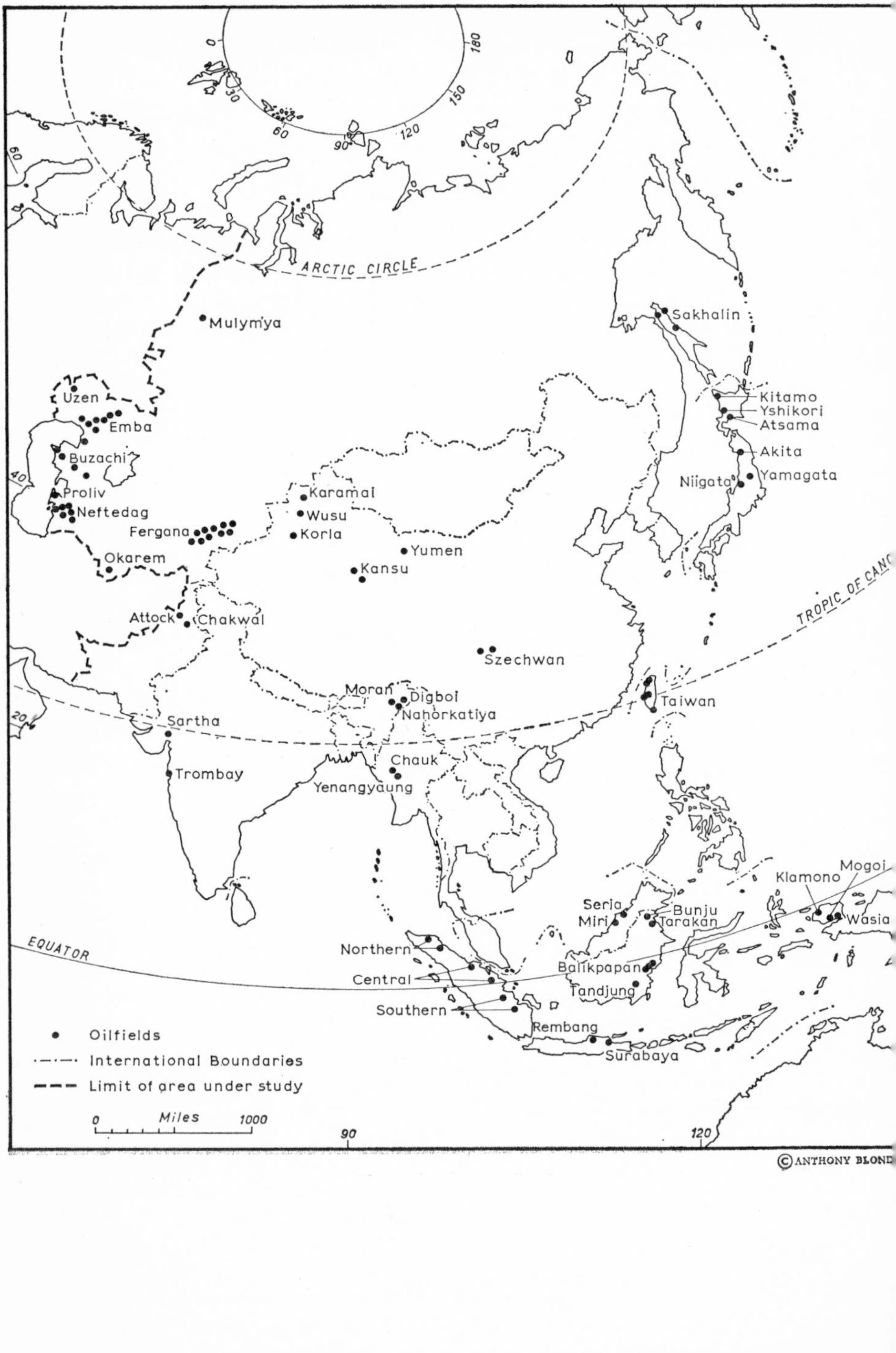
ARCTIC CIRCLE
TROPIC OF CANC
EQUATOR
Mulymya
Uzen
Emba
Buzachi
Proliv
Neftedag
Fergana
Okarem
Karamai
Wusu
Korla
Yumen
Kansu
Attock
Chakwal
Szechwan
Moran
Digboi
Nahorkatiya
Sartha
Trombay
Chauk
Yenangyaung
Sakhalin
Kitamo
Yshikori
Atsama
Akita
Niigata
Yamagata
Taiwan
Seria
Miri
Bunju
Tarakan
Klamono
Mogoi
Wasia
Northern
Central
Southern
Balikpapan
Tandjung
Rembang
Surabaya
Oilfields
International Boundaries
Limit of area under study
0 Miles 1000
60
40
20
90
120
0
30
60
90
120
150
180

OIL IN ASIA

by

LORD BANGOR

In the rapidly expanding and developing countries of Asia oil is playing a vital part in raising standards of living, improving means of communication, and providing power for fast-growing industries. In addition, in countries where oil is being produced, oil revenues are making important contributions to national economies.

Few Asian countries, however, are large scale oil producers. Indonesia, the largest, has for several years been trying to find a formula that would enable oil companies to go ahead with development plans which could do so much to help the country's economic struggle.

In West Irian (New Guinea) oil has been produced since the war, but supplies are dwindling and it seems unlikely, despite the large investment in the Klamono field, that the situation will improve.

In Borneo British/Dutch companies have for long been drilling offshore. Success has at last rewarded their efforts and, after years of steady decline in oil output, Brunei has a new lease of life.

China has developed new oilfields, but is still greatly dependent on supplies from the Soviet Union. Japan, whose post-war 'economic miracle' is largely based on petroleum, has found a large oilfield in the Persian Gulf, but at home there is only minor production.

Burma has not yet recovered from the destruction of the war years. The Government has recently bought out the company responsible for local production since the last century and taken over the enterprise. Future developments will be watched with interest.

India has only small production despite heavy foreign investment in exploration and in recent years the Government has turned increasingly to the Soviet bloc for help in the oil search, with results yet to be assessed.

Pakistan, where oil companies have also spent many millions of pounds in a mainly unsuccessful search, has also accepted Russian loans to be spent on Soviet technical aid in further exploration. In East Pakistan, however, a British/Dutch/Pakistan enterprise has found substantial gas fields which should soon be supplying much of the industrial needs of Dacca and Chittagong, just as the output of the Sui gas field in Western Pakistan (discovered in 1952 by a joint Pakistan Government and British private exploration venture), has almost wholly replaced oil in meeting industrial fuel requirements.

In many other Asian countries repeated disappointments do not seem to have quenched hopes that success may some day be achieved. Exploration continues, with varying degrees of intensity, in the Philippines, Thailand, Papua and elsewhere.

Raising Living Standards

The growth of refining facilities in the region has been even more notable. Plants are now either on stream or in course of development in India, Pakistan, Singapore, Malaya, Borneo, Indonesia, Burma, Thailand, the Philippines, Japan, China, Taiwan and Korea. Before the war only two or three of these countries could have been listed in this context.

But it is the part that oil has played in raising living and industrial standards in Asian countries that is probably most important. In recent years the major oil companies have not only provided by far the greater part of the financial resources needed to expand production and refining facilities. They have developed distribution networks which have brought petroleum products within the reach of many more millions of people and greatly increased consumption.

The impact of this expenditure is apparent in the development of Asian highways, the improvement in housing, and the growth in agricultural production. Petroleum-based fertilizers are enabling more food to be grown to feed populations that are rapidly rising almost everywhere. Kerosene is bringing warmth, light and better cooking (and fishing) facilities to countless people formerly denied them. Gasoline- and diesel-powered trucks are transporting crops to market and children to schools along roads only recently constructed.

Airliners—depending on petroleum for their fuel, whether powered by jet or piston engines—take off from bitumen-surfaced runways to carry Asian business men from one capital to another, or out into the kampongs or barrios, enabling journeys that formerly took days to be completed in hours. Detergents are now used in regions where new standards of cleanliness and hygiene have made possible a degree of freedom from disease that would hardly have been believed possible in the thirties.

Indeed, while it is fairly common knowledge that there has been a revolution in living standards and in industrial and agricultural productivity through Asia in the last 20 years, the part oil has played in the transformation is by no means widely appreciated.

History

An interesting feature of the oil industry in the Far East is its extreme antiquity. Burmese oil is mentioned in Chinese writings of the 13th century. It had become a leading commodity in national and international trade many decades before James Young had begun his experiments for refining mineral oils in England, or the first oil well had been drilled in the U.S.A.—events which heralded the birth of the modern oil industry. The Burmese wells were not drilled but dug by hand—to depths of several hundred feet—and lined with timber. The oilfields, lying along the Irrawaddy River, were worked by the Twinzayos, hereditary heads of a group of twenty-four families. The oil was distributed throughout the entire country, large quantities being transported down the River to Rangoon. In the middle of the last century,

Burmese oil was even exported to England for manufacture into lubricants and paraffin wax.

In ancient China, where oil was discovered in the province of Szechuan in the course of working brine deposits, a system of drilling was evolved which closely resembled the 'cable-tool' or 'percussion' method of drilling used by the American oil pioneers in the latter half of the 19th century. The Chinese are believed to have drilled for oil more than two thousand years ago; although their only form of power was human or animal, the surprising average depth of these wells was over 1,500 feet and one well reached 3,000 feet.

In addition to the oil industries of Burma and China, which, though by modern standards very small, were comparatively highly developed, there was a widespread use of seepage oil throughout the Far East. On the island of Timor, for instance, a burning gas seepage similar to the 'Eternal Fires' of Baku has long been an object of veneration; in Japan a strange 'Flaming Water' was discovered in the Niigata district in the reign of Emperor Tenji (668-672 A.D.) and seepage oil was used as fuel by countless generations of Indonesians and Japanese. With this background, it was inevitable that the Far East should be one of the first areas to be developed by the modern oil industry, and before the end of the 19th century commercial production had been established in several areas. In 1938 Indonesia (which together with Western New Guinea, then comprised the Netherlands East Indies), was the world's fifth largest producer, and Burma and British Borneo were also important oil exporters. Although extensive war damage was suffered by the oil industry in all these areas, it was possible to resume production in Indonesia in many of the fields and in British Borneo, and by 1950, only five years after the end of the war, output for the Far East as a whole was running above the pre-war level.

Indonesia

A large number of oilfields have been discovered in Indonesia but the output from most of them is small. Production comes from fields in Sumatra, Kalimantan (formerly Dutch Borneo) and Java. Total production from these three centres, together with some oil produced in Ceram, amounted in 1938 to between 7,000,000 and 8,000,000 tons a year. War damage in Indonesia was immense—it was estimated at £62 million. Much of it was self-inflicted to prevent the oil going to the Japanese. Immediately after the war the oil companies were unable to return to some of the oilfields owing to the unsettled political situation. In 1946 total oil production had dwindled to a mere 300,000 tons. But by 1964 it had risen to over 23,500,000 tons—about three times the pre-war figure—and the rate of output is still increasing.

Sumatra

This is the most important and the oldest oil-producing island in Indonesia. Commercial production began as long ago as 1893 but many of the oilfields have been discovered in the last thirty years. Oil has been found in three separate areas: in the Pangkalan Brandan district in North Sumatra where the original discovery was made; in South Sumatra, where oil was also found before the end of the last century, and in mid-Sumatra, where some oilfields were discovered shortly before World War II and where further discoveries have been made in recent years. All these oilfields lie to the east of the high mountain range nearly 1,000 miles long, which forms the backbone of Sumatra; it is not expected that oil in commercial quantities will be found to the west of the mountains where they descend sharply to the sea. Production comes mostly from comparatively shallow depths, although in the south oil has also been found at about 7,000 feet. In 1949, production in the south already exceeded the pre-war level of output. In the north, up to the end of 1959, the oil industry was unable to recommence operations: now Government and Japanese oil interests have concluded an agreement to develop these fields—formerly worked by British and Dutch interests.

Kalimantan

In addition to the oil discoveries in Brunei and Sarawak, in British Borneo, oil has been found in three different areas in that part of Borneo which was formerly Dutch, but is now part of Indonesia and is known as Kalimantan. The first is in Tarakan Island, off the north-east coast: Tarakan crude oil is a most unusual type which can be used as diesel or boiler fuel after simple dehydration. A second oil-producing area lies to the north of Balik Papan on the east coast. Both these areas have been in production for many years, and oil is recovered mostly by pumping. In the third area at Tandjung, 120 miles to the south-west of Balik Papan, oil was only discovered in 1938 and production began regularly at the end of 1961 when a 150-mile pipeline to the refinery at Balik Papan came into operation. Since the war, production has been resumed in the Tarakan field, but in 1964 amounted to less than half the pre-war output.

Java and Ceram

Here, as in Sumatra and Kalimantan, the oil industry dates from the end of last century. Java has two main producing areas, at Rembang in the centre of the island and at Surabaya on the east coast, which together produced almost 900,000 tons in 1938. Ceram also had a small output in pre-war years. Owing to political circumstances, post-war rehabilitation of the oil industry has been delayed considerably, and although reconstruction has begun in Java, where 1964 output was less than 200,000 tons, up to the end of the same year no progress had been possible in Ceram.

West Irian

Seepage oil was observed in Western New Guinea (now 'West Irian') early in this century, and oil prospecting was carried out, but without success. In 1936 a mixed British, Dutch and American company began prospecting for oil in the Vogelkop, the peninsula forming the extreme north-western end of New Guinea, and in the same year discovered the Klamono oilfield. The oil, at a depth of a few hundred feet, was found to be a heavy asphaltic type. In 1940 two other oilfields were discovered in New Guinea—the Wasian and Mogoi fields—also in the Vogelkop. Commercial production began in the

Klamono field at the end of 1948, but the other two fields did not start production until 1954 and in 1962 showed negligible returns.

West Irian is one of the best examples imaginable of the kind of difficulties that can beset an oil company developing an oilfield. The climate is fearful. As much as 120 inches of rain in a single month have been recorded. It took two years to airmap the 400,000 square mile concession—under normal conditions this would have taken a few weeks. The terrain varies from high mountains to swamp and it is in the latter that oil has been discovered. It is very difficult to transport heavy equipment to such country and many wells had to be drilled by light, man-powered rigs carried in by bearers. From the Klamono oilfield it was necessary to lay a pipeline to the harbour at Sorong, a former missionary settlement. The distance between the two is only 30 miles but it took two years to build a road and lay the pipeline. The other oilfields are even less accessible.

After all the effort put into the development of these New Guinea oilfields, it is disheartening to record that production has already declined below the former peak level and further exploration was abandoned in 1960.

Refining

About 10 per cent of the refining capacity of the Far East is in Indonesia. The refineries are at Pladju and Sungei Gerong in South Sumatra; at Balik Papan in Kalimantan; and at Wonokromo and Tjepu in Java. A great deal of the then existing refining capacity in Indonesia was destroyed in the war. By 1964 refining capacity had risen to 14,000,000 tons a year.

Papua

In Papua test drilling has been going on since the war but so far without finding oil in commercial quantities.

Borneo

Borneo possesses two commercial oilfields. The smaller one at Miri in Sarawak was discovered in 1910 and reached its peak between the years 1926 and 1930 when it was producing at the rate of 700,000 tons a year. Production then began to decline until by the outbreak of war it had sunk to some 200,000 tons. Meanwhile the far more important Seria field in Brunei was discovered in 1929 and by 1938 its production rate had risen to 700,000 tons a year. World War II played havoc with oil production in British Borneo, to a large extent, as in Indonesia, as a result of deliberate sabotage by the oil company to deny the oil to the Japanese. When the Japanese retreated in 1945 they left most of the wells on fire and the rehabilitation of the oilfields was a formidable task. Nevertheless by 1956 production had reached a peak of 5,600,000 tons, provided almost entirely by the Seria field —Miri has now sunk to a mere 50,000 tons a year. Since 1956 the yield has gradually declined and Seria is now producing at the rate of less than 4,000,000 tons a year. This field runs for eight miles along the sea coast and $1\frac{1}{2}$ miles inland, with offshore wells drilled from jetties and barges anchored off the coast. Exploration work is being pushed ahead and is now largely concentrated on offshore waters where results so far have been encouraging.

The rapid stepping up of output at Seria immediately after the war was of great value on account of the shortage of oil supplies in general at that time and of the slow recovery of the industry in other parts of the Far East, mostly as a result of political disturbances. Today, though yields have fallen off somewhat, Borneo remains one of the important oil producers of the Far East.

Refining

In the 1930's there was a large refinery in operation at Lutong in Sarawak. It was destroyed during the war but has since been replaced by a new and larger plant. This processes about 2,300,000 tons of crude oil a year. The rest of Borneo's production is exported, chiefly to Australia and Japan, though small quantities also go to Western Europe.

Burma

The oilfields of Burma lie along the Irrawaddy River about 300 miles from its estuary. Chauk and Yenangyaung are the most important. Power drilling was started as early as 1889 but a number of hand-dug wells were still in operation up to the outbreak of the last war. In 1938 production was just over 1,000,000 tons a year. This came almost entirely from pumping wells. Production costs were high, but against this the crude oil was of very good quality. The industry was almost totally destroyed in the war and output even by the mid-fifties had only risen to just over 200,000 tons. By 1959 it had increased to over 500,000 tons and 1964 saw a further rise to 620,000 tons. Exploratory drilling has recently started again.

Refining

Reconstruction of the refinery at Rangoon was completed in 1957 and the plant, now operating at full capacity, is fed by river barge. Refining capacity in 1964 was 1,235,000 metric tons.

India

Traces of oil were noted in Upper Assam over a century ago but an attempt to drill for oil in 1867 was unsuccessful. The first success was recorded in 1890 with the discovery of the Digboi oilfield. When the Indian sub-continent was partitioned in 1947, Upper Assam, with its oil resources, became part of India. Exploration was carried out and in 1953 an important oil discovery was made at Nahorkatiya. Further drilling confirmed that this field has large resources but it has not yet been developed fully. In 1955 another find was made at Moran, but this has not yet been brought to commercial production.

In order to speed up commercial development of the newly discovered oil resources a project was drawn up to provide pipelines and a refinery. A 260-mile 16-inch crude line connecting the Assam fields to a refinery at Gauhati Nunmati came into operation in the first half of 1962. A 460-mile 14-inch line from Gauhati Nunmati to Barauni, on the Ganges, was completed in April 1964 and feeds the refinery there which also came on stream that year. A parallel product line is being built from Gauhati Nunmati to Siliguri.

In western India the first major discovery of oil was made at Ankleshwar; commercial production started in 1962. Ankleshwar is now India's largest producer.

Refining

India has long been refining oil, her plants operating mainly on imported crude oil. There are two refineries at Trombay Island, Bombay, with a combined capacity of 6½ million tons a year and other small plants at Vizagapatam and Digboi. The Nunmati plant, with an annual capacity of 750,000 tons, came into operation early in 1962. The refinery at Barauni started operating in 1964. India's total refining capacity in 1964 was 10,645,000 tons.

PAKISTAN

When the sub-continent was partitioned, part of the Punjab was allotted to Pakistan. Oil exploration here began in the 1860's but it was not till 1915 that an important oil discovery was made at Khaur. Other oilfields have since been found at Dhulian (1934), Joya Mair (1944), Balkassar (1946) and Kharsal (1956). Khaur and Dhulian are now on a steady decline but production is still increasing in the Joya Mair and Balkassar fields. When Kharsal is in operation it is expected that the total yield of all the fields will amount to about 600,000 tons—about one fifth of Pakistan oil consumption.

Natural Gas

The first major natural gasfield to be discovered in Pakistan was at Sui, in Baluchistan and about 350 miles from Karachi. A pipeline was laid from Sui to Karachi and it came into operation in 1955. A second line from Sui to Multan and nearby centres in the north-east came into operation in 1958. Gas has been found more recently at Uch to the west of Sui but so far there has been no commercial production from this field. An important gas field has also been found at Titas in East Pakistan. A scheme is being discussed to build a pipeline to transport the gas to Dacca and eventually to Chittagong. There is also similar gas production at Sylhet which supplies a fertilizer plant at Fenchungi.

Refining

A long-established oil refinery at Rawalpindi in West Pakistan handles about 300,000 tons of crude oil a year—enough to cope with local output until fairly recently. A far larger refinery was officially opened in November, 1962, near Karachi. It had an initial capacity of 1½ million tons of crude oil a year, which was later increased to two million tons.

JAPAN

Petroleum was known in Japan as far back as the year 1600 and distillation was first successfully carried out in 1850. In 1870 crude oil production was officially recorded in Government statistics. In the last 90 years many small oilfields have been discovered. The most important are on the main island of Honshu.

Production

In 1964 Japanese domestic production amounted to some 800,000 tons. Japan formerly held an oil concession from the U.S.S.R. in the northern part of Sakhalin Island but this was cancelled in 1944. She also lost control of the shale deposits at Fushun in Manchuria and natural gasfields in Formosa. In 1958 Japan started development overseas with the establishment of the Arabian Oil Company which is developing the Khafji field in the Persian Gulf. This field has proven reserves of some 800 million tons. Crude oil from Khafji has been shipped to Japan since 1961. Another Japanese enterprise abroad is in Indonesia with the North Sumatra Oil Development Co-operation Company. In 1962 the estimated production figure was some 800,000 tons and the target for the near future is about two million tons.

Consumption

Japanese consumption has risen to a fabulous degree since 1950, when it was about two and a quarter million tons. By 1964 the figure had sky-rocketed to 60,000,000 tons.

Refining

To meet this increased consumption the rise in refining capacity in Japan has been no less spectacular. Some thirty refineries have sprung up all over the country and from being virtually nil at the end of the war, refining capacity had reached a rate of over 80 million tons a year by 1964.

China

Chinese production in 1964 is considered to have been in the region of 7 million tons. This figure includes oil from shale and coal. Most of this production came from the province of Kansu in north-west China. Petroleum and natural gas in small quantities have also been found and produced in other parts of China, including the province of Szechuan, scene of China's ancient wells. In certain areas of the north the discovery of large oil reserves has been reported recently.

Owing to the comparatively low level of oil consumption in most Asiatic countries, the total requirements of the Far East (including Australasia) before the war amounted to only about 13,000,000 tons a year. Although the Far East produced about the same amount of oil as was used there, the area was both an importer and exporter of oil. A large proportion of oil used in Japan came from California. India obtained large imports from Persia and Bahrain. Indonesia exported oil to Australia and to neighbouring countries.

At the end of the war there was a wide gap between supply and demand caused by war damage and post-war disruption. The reduction in exports from the United States compelled the Far East to rely on increasing supplies from the more distant Middle East. The considerable expansion in production in the Far East that has now been achieved has greatly eased the position and this is of great importance to the development of the local economy.

Future Prospects

It remains true that as an oil-producing region Asia is still considerably less important than the four other main regions—the United States, the Middle East, the Caribbean and the Soviet Union. But there are extensive areas in the East yet to be explored, and the intensity of the search may be expected to increase from year to year.

While the physical obstacles to success are often considerable, the political difficulties encountered are sometimes even more challenging. It is accepted on all sides that the proper development of natural resources—of which oil is one of the most vital—is a matter with which governments must be closely concerned.

As understanding grows of the problems that must be faced, it may be that governments which stand in great need of foreign capital for their countries' economic development will allow it to come in on reasonable terms, giving the investor a fair deal and adequate security for his investment. Given these conditions, oil exploration (and production, if the search is successful) can go ahead to the general benefit.

The alternative to the orderly deployment of foreign risk capital is often excessive dependence on industrial aid from foreign governments with its unavoidable political implications.

In the years to come oil will play a still greater part in helping to feed, clothe, transport, keep in health and provide employment for Asia's fast growing populations. There is little fear of shortage either of crude oil or of manufacturing resources, but great problems of logistics, research and capital availability have to be faced—problems that can be solved only by wise and far-seeing co-operation between governments and companies. In the long run, there is every reason to believe that the countries of Asia will take the fullest advantage of the benefits that oil can bring to modern living.

SOURCES

The material in this contribution was gathered from the Petroleum Information Bureau and from personal knowledge. Shell International Petroleum Company assisted with suggestions about content.

BIOGRAPHICAL NOTE

Lord Bangor. As Edward Ward, a Reuter correspondent in China before World War II. Joined BBC in 1938; one of its first war correspondents covering the war in Finland, Middle East, Abyssinia and Greece. Covered Japanese surrender in Hong Kong and Chinese war in Manchuria. Travelled for the BBC over most of the world after the war and obtained some knowledge of the oil industry during travels in Texas in 1950, and later in Iraq, Nigeria, the Sahara and Venezuela. Succeeded to the title of Viscount Bangor in 1950. Has directed the Petroleum Information Bureau in London since 1961.

DEVELOPMENT AID TO ASIA

by

WERNER KLATT

WITHOUT aid there would be no development worth its name in Asia. Outside Japan, Asia consists of countries that are marked by their lack of economic development, industry and social services. They are described as backward, underdeveloped or pre-industrial. Whilst none of these terms is entirely fitting, and some have an unfortunate ring of paternalism, most of the countries of Asia have certain features in common which are absent in the case of fully developed industrial societies. One of the most important characteristics is the role played by farming as the most frequent form of economic activity, and by village life as the most prominent form of society.

Economic and social change is associated with urbanization and industrialization. These are costly processes which are enforced by dictatorial regimes where they are carried out with great speed and paid for out of the forced savings of the cultivators. This is the form of development which has been chosen by the Communist regimes of China, North Korea, North Vietnam, Mongolia and Tibet. Elsewhere in Asia, economic development, though instigated as a matter of urgency, has been carried out at a less frantic pace and it has been financed to a large extent through contributions from abroad.

MULTILATERAL AID

The forms of development aid are so manifold that it is impossible to give a complete picture within the compass of a brief review. The two principal types to be distinguished are multilateral and bilateral aid, the former being channelled through international organs, such as the agencies of the United Nations and the Colombo Plan, whilst the latter is usually given on the basis of agreements between the governments of the donor and the recipient country. To this has to be added the not insignificant contribution which is made to development by private capital investment.

Foreign trade is, of course, the oldest form of economic assistance. Development aid ought to be considered, therefore, in relation to foreign trade transactions which are often the outward sign of aid programmes being implemented. This is particularly so in the case of bilateral aid offers made by countries of the Sino-Soviet bloc which implement their development programmes as a rule through barter trade transactions.

The largest foreign contributor to the economic progress of Asian countries is the United States, which ranks ahead of all other countries in both multilateral and bilateral development programmes. The next largest contributor is Britain. In recent years Germany has entered the sphere of economic development aid on a rapidly increasing scale, but her aid is directed primarily to countries in Africa. Japan deserves also to be mentioned here.

The World Bank

Of the international organs that have contributed towards economic progress in developing countries of Asia, the World Bank deserves to be singled out because of the size and nature of its development programme. The principal objectives of the World Bank, founded in 1944 as a specialized agency associated with the United Nations, are implicit in its official title:— International Bank for Reconstruction and Development. When the most immediate post-war tasks of reconstruction had been fulfilled, the World Bank turned its attention towards aiding the economic growth of developing countries.

The World Bank has made well over three hundred loans to sixty countries, totalling nearly US $7,000 million. It obtains funds for these loans from capital subscribed by its seventy-five member countries, from sales of Bank bonds in the various capital markets of the world, and from net earnings on its operations. In addition, sales of portions of Bank loans to other investors and repayments of loans permit the Bank to recover its funds and thereby serve to reduce the amount which the Bank must obtain from other sources for its lending operations.

From its very beginning, the World Bank's emphasis has been on serving as a bridge for the movement of private capital into international investment. This explains why many of its financial resources and more than half its loans have come from private investors. The larger part of this investment has come from outside the United States.

From its inception the World Bank has operated a lending policy patterned on the practices of private investment banks. Thus, in making loans it must give due consideration to the possibilities of repayment. The loans must be for productive purposes and, whether given to government agencies or private enterprises, must carry the guarantee of the government of the country in which they are placed. Before considering a loan the Bank must satisfy itself that the proposed project is economically justified, that the plans for carrying it out are sound and that the borrower will be able to meet payments of interest and principal on the loan when they fall due. The Bank must also determine that the borrower cannot obtain the loan from private sources on reasonable terms, within the prevailing market conditions. The rate of interest charged on Bank loans is based on the rate which it would itself have to pay to borrow money at the time the loan is made, plus a commission charge which is allocated to a Special Reserve, and a small charge to meet administrative costs. In practice, the long-term lending rate of the Bank varies between five and six per cent.

Normally World Bank loans cover only the foreign exchange costs of a project. The Bank feels that it can best serve the interests of its developing member countries by concentrating its loans on basic services, such as electric energy and transportation, without which economic progress is almost impossible. These projects, because of their high costs and low returns, tend to attract little private investment.

At the same time, the Bank has sought to promote the development of private industry. In some cases it has made loans directly to private industries, by contributing to projects such as the production of steel in India and by helping national development banks which use the World Bank's funds for their own lending operations. However, the requirement of a governmental guarantee for all its loans has limited the Bank's action in the field of private investment.

International Finance Corporation

Governments are reluctant at times to guarantee loans to particular private enterprises which, on their part, sometimes fear official interference as a result. To overcome these difficulties, the International Finance Corporation was established in July, 1956. Over sixty nations became members of IFC which has funds close on US $100 million and shares its President and Executive Director with the World Bank.

IFC performs a particularly useful function in the field of underwriting stock issues, since in many of its member countries, capital markets, where they exist at all, are not yet fully developed. In Asia it has made investments in India and in Pakistan in companies producing cement, steel, pumps, refractory bricks and textiles.

International Development Association

The need for outside capital has been increasing faster than the ability to service conventional loans. Some countries have already begun to draw close to the limit of the debt they can prudently assume on conventional terms. It was awareness of this problem which led to the founding of the International Development Association as an affiliate of the World Bank. The establishment of IDA came after many years of discussions of the desirability of accelerating economic growth in the less developed areas by adding international funds, repayable on other than conventional terms, to the flow of development capital. By 1962, over sixty countries had joined IDA and had subscribed a total of over US $900 million. More than 80 per cent of IDA's subscribed funds is in convertible form. Ten Asian countries have joined IDA.

IDA is closely linked with the World Bank. The President of the World Bank is *ex officio* President of IDA, and the officers and staff of the Bank serve as officers and staff for IDA. A project submitted for IDA financing is expected to meet the same technical, economic, financial and administrative standards as the World Bank itself would look for if the Bank were making a loan for that project on conventional terms.

It is IDA's primary purpose to provide development capital for countries whose balance of payments prospects would not allow them to incur external debts on conventional terms. Thus most of the IDA credits have been extended for projects which are of a type traditionally financed by the World Bank, but IDA is allowed to finance projects in the field of social investment which the Bank has hitherto not undertaken. In the past IDA has assisted municipal water supply projects in Taiwan and it is investigating the possibility of assisting school construction programmes in some countries. Development credits have been extended for fifty years without interest, amortization to begin after a ten-year period of grace, thereafter, in most cases, one per cent of the principal being repayable annually for ten years and three per cent during the final thirty years.

United Nations Credits to Asia

Throughout Asia and the Far East[1] some fourteen countries (Burma, Ceylon, Taiwan, India, Indonesia, Japan, Korea, Laos, Malaysia, Nepal, Pakistan, Philippines, Thailand and Vietnam) are members of the World Bank; ten of them (all except Burma, Indonesia, Laos and Nepal) are members also of the Bank's affiliate, the International Development Association. Total lending in the area by the two institutions amounts to over US $2,000 million. Up to 1962 nine had received loans, amounting to well over a quarter of all the World Bank's loans and over half of all development credits extended by the International Development Association. The emphasis has been on the development of basic services. Loans for transportation by road, rail, sea and air amounted to over two-fifths of the total. Electric power and industrial development each accounted for a little more than a fifth, and most of the remainder had been devoted to agriculture, which also benefited from increased transport and electricity services.

The World Bank and IDA have granted loans for railways in Burma, India, Japan, Pakistan and Thailand; for ports in all these countries except in Japan, and in addition in Taiwan and the Philippines; for roads in India and Japan; and for a natural gas pipe-line in Pakistan.

Seven countries have borrowed from the Bank or IDA so as to finance electric power projects. The loans have helped to finance fifteen major dams and hydro-electric stations, eleven thermoelectric stations, many thousands of miles of transmission lines, and extensive distribution facilities. When all the projects are complete, they will add over three million kilowatts to the total generating capacity of countries in Asia and the Far East.

Bank loans for agriculture have helped to increase food production in India through the reclamation of lands, while IDA credits have financed irrigation and drainage schemes. In Pakistan, a Bank loan financed heavy machinery used to prepare land for settlement in the Thal irrigation areas, and IDA credits are helping to pay for a pilot irrigation project and a major scheme to restore waterlogged and salty land to full production. In Japan, the Bank made a loan for equipment to clear and stock new farms established in remote areas, and for imported cattle. A Bank loan to Thailand helped to increase rice production in the Central Plain.

Most of the Bank's lending for industry in Asia and the Far East has been used to finance the expansion of the iron and steel industries of India and Japan. Between them, the two countries have borrowed well over US $300 million for this purpose, installing inter alia six blast furnaces, five strip or

[1] This term, which includes Afghanistan, is used here as it appears in many of the sources upon which this chapter is based, and in many cases it is impossible to separate figures for Afghanistan from those for other countries of the area.

plate mills, seven converters and two open-hearth furnaces. Coal production in India will be expanded with the help of a Bank loan and IDA credit. In Pakistan, a Bank loan helped to pay for construction of a paper mill. In addition, the Bank and IDA have extended loans and credits amounting to near US $100 million to development banks interested in small industrial companies in India, Pakistan and Taiwan.

A Bank loan of US $90 million was made to Pakistan towards the cost of works to be carried out under the terms of the settlement of the dispute between Pakistan and India over the use of the waters of the Indus River and its tributaries.

In addition to its lending, the Bank has provided survey missions, whose reports on Ceylon, Malaya and Thailand provide valuable information and advice. Bank missions have kept in particularly close touch with the economic problems of India and Pakistan and have given advice to their governments on various aspects of their development plans and on setting up development banks. Last, but not least, the Bank has concerted the efforts of developed countries to provide aid to the two countries under the auspices of the 'Aid to India' and 'Aid to Pakistan' consortia.

United Nations Technical Assistance

The deployment of credits and loans on development projects has disclosed a gap at the pre-investment stage that needed closing. The United Nations Special Fund which started its work early in 1959 with an initial fund of some US $26 million was charged with creating conditions which make capital investment either feasible or effective. Its assistance consists mainly of surveys, research and demonstration, and its emphasis is on water, irrigation, power and soil surveys. Approximately one-third of the Special Fund's contributions have been earmarked for Asia and the Far East. In Thailand an investigation was financed into the silting conditions in Bangkok harbour which was to provide the data necessary for investment in remedial works to be undertaken by the port authority. Other pre-investment schemes include survey work on hydraulic projects in Taiwan, soil surveys in East Pakistan and mineral surveys in West Pakistan.

Whereas the normal minimum sum involved in schemes of the Special Fund amounts to US $250,000, the projects of the Technical Assistance Programme of the United Nations and eight of its specialized agencies rarely surpass one-fifth of that sum. The programme has been in operation since 1948 and its main functions are to arrange for experts to visit countries in need of advice; to provide for fellowships for training of experts from developing countries; and to provide equipment required in the course of these activities. A Technical Assistance Board is responsible for the coordination and supervision of the programme.

Since its inception, over US $300 million have been expended, some 10,000 experts have been provided and 20,000 fellowships have been awarded. The Food and Agriculture Organization and the World Health Organization usually have the heaviest call on the funds of the technical assistance programme. Much of the work of the experts is concentrated on what is nowadays called 'impact' projects, assistance which—like that financed by the Special Fund—will pave the way for later development. Emphasis is placed on eliminating illiteracy and promoting vocational education; on improved human and animal health; on improved strains of plants and increased use of farm requisites; on surveys of natural resources; on feasibility studies in industry; and on training of technicians, foremen, managers and administrators. In recent years some US $10 million have been expended under this programme in countries of Asia and the Far East, involving 1,000 each of foreign experts and national trainees.

A special form of assistance provided by the World Bank is the training it provides to officials of its member countries. In all, some sixty officials from twelve Asian countries have attended the six-month courses of the Economic Development Institute in Washington, D.C., which was established in 1955 with the object of improving the quality of economic management in government in developing countries. Another sixty officials have undergone training at the Bank itself.

The Economic Commission for Asia and the Far East (ESCAFE) has played an increasingly active part in matters of technical assistance and the aid programmes of the United Nations. Its annual economic surveys, the reviews of specific aspects of economic development in its quarterly economic bulletins and the reports of its committees are among the indispensable sources of factual information on Asia. They also provide food for thought on a wide range of problems, of which development aid, though not the least important topic, is only the most recent subject for discussion among Asian planners, managers, economists and their foreign experts.

The Colombo Plan

The survey of multilateral aid would be incomplete without mention being made of the Colombo Plan, the only multilateral programme which applies to Asian countries only. It was created early in 1950 for the furtherance of economic development in South and South-East Asia, and a consultative committee was set up to consider the needs and to assess the resources available and required in the area. Development programmes of the original South and South-East Asian members (India, Pakistan, Ceylon, Malaya and British Borneo) were drawn up and compared for the six years starting from July 1951, and technical cooperation was instigated from that date. In the meantime, the Colombo Plan has been extended twice, to be continued until 1966 on the understanding that the period of a further extension be considered in 1964. In the meantime the organization has been joined from within the region by Burma, Cambodia, Nepal, Indonesia, Laos, South Vietnam, Singapore, Sarawak, Thailand and the Philippines. The members from outside the region, i.e. the United Kingdom, Canada, Australia and New Zealand have been joined by the United States and Japan.

The original plans of the South-East Asian member countries were marked by their emphasis on the development of agriculture and transport, each of which were to take a share of one-third of the total estimated cost of their plans, the remainder being shared almost equally between the cost of social services (housing, health, education) and industrialization (industry, mining, fuel and power). It was assumed that by far the largest portion of the cost of each plan would have to be met by each country itself. The contributions of the developed member states of the Commonwealth rested in (a) their willingness to provide experts and training facilities; (b) Britain's willingness to release close on £250 million from the sterling balances of the member countries in South-East Asia. During the first ten years of the plan approximately £250 million were spent on experts, trainees and equipment and more than 1,700 experts and over 15,000 training places were supplied. During the same period some £2,850 million from indigenous and foreign sources were committed in the area of South and South-East Asia on economic development projects, and marked progress was achieved in most countries of the area. At the same time sterling reserves were withdrawn at an unexpectedly fast rate and requirements of foreign aid proved to be much larger than anticipated originally.

Aid Programmes of the United States

Without massive bilateral aid Asia would be in a bad way. As it is, the bulk of credits and grants is of the bilateral kind, and the overwhelming portion of these is American in origin. The American aid programme can be traced to the outbreak of hostilities in Korea, although this gave only a new urgency to problems which had been recognized before that event. In 1950 the activities of the Economic Cooperation Administration, the United States aid organization which had previously operated in Europe, were expanded to Asia and other continents. The importance of technical and economic assistance was underlined in Point IV of President Truman's inaugural address of January 1949 which was to give its name to American aid throughout the world. The need for an expansion of this feature of American foreign policy was underlined in Gordon Gray's report to the President on 'Foreign Economic Policies' and that of the International Development Advisory Board which, under the chairmanship of Nelson Rockefeller, issued 'Partners in Progress'.

An important part of the foreign policy of the United States in this sphere has been the emphasis on creating conditions that will stimulate the investment of private capital in the areas earmarked for economic and technical assistance. In Asia it has been operated under different names, for the purpose of relief, reconstruction and development, including a wide variety of goods and services ranging from surplus farm produce to most modern capital equipment, and from teachers in primary education to specialists in computers and physicists familiar with the application of atomic energy for civilian uses. In strategically vulnerable areas, such as South Korea, South Vietnam and Taiwan, a large part of the assistance was given under the Mutual Defence Assistance Act. Even where these projects have satisfied American security requirements in the first instance, they have benefited at the same time the recipient countries, in that they aimed at creating stability, provided scarce raw materials and equipment, saved foreign exchange and thus improved living standards. Even so, the results seemed not always to justify the expenditure, and therefore American, like other Western, aid has sometimes come under fire both at home and abroad.

The history of American aid to Asia is too long and varied to be recounted herein any detail except to recall that in March 1961 President Kennedy in a message to Congress redefined it under the following headings: (a) all forms of economic aid to be administered by a single agency; (b) military assistance to be separated from economic aid; (c) aid to be allocated for a period of five years instead of a year-to-year basis; (d) cooperation to be established with other donor nations; (e) aid to be given to nations willing to help themselves by their own economic and social efforts. A new Agency for International Development (AID) took the place of the former International Cooperation Administration (ICA) and it absorbed the Development Loan Fund. The President was authorized to enter into long-term commitments and to spend US $7,200 million on development loans over a period of five years, subject to annual appropriations.

In the meantime, Congress has had second thoughts and the appropriation for 1963 at US $2,600 million was considerably less than the President had requested and also less than had been appropriated in the fiscal year 1962. As to the future, General Clay's report on United States aid is likely to keep Congress in a critical mood; it has led to further economies. Even so, the American aid programme is of extraordinarily large proportions and surpasses anything ever done before in this sphere. Since the end of the Second World War more than US $30,000 million have been appropriated to Asia and the Far East (excluding the Middle East), of which 70 per cent were for economic projects and 30 per cent of a military nature. Of the economic aid, over two-thirds were grants and less than one-third loans. The chief recipients were South Korea, India, Taiwan, Japan, South Vietnam and Pakistan—in that order. The programme reveals the priorities which have prevailed in the past and which have now been exposed to criticism.

British and European Aid

Compared with American orders of magnitude Britain's foreign aid programme may seem modest. Just the same, since the end of the Second World War some £335 million have been allocated by the Exchequer to countries of Asia and the Far East. Of this sum approximately 65 per cent were offered as loans and 35 per cent were grants-in-aid. About two-fifths of the total was earmarked for India and almost one-third for Burma and Malaya together, Pakistan and other countries of the area sharing the remainder. Public and private projects range from government cover for a steel mill built by an industrial consortium in India to the provision of research staff for Burma and of arms during the emergency in Malaya.

In recognition of the importance of technical assistance to donor and recipient alike, all forms of aid of this kind were brought in 1961 under a single government agency, the Department of Technical Cooperation.

In 1964 the Government created a Ministry of Overseas Development under a Cabinet Minister who was given over-all control of all aid operations.

Of other countries in Europe, France and West Germany are the principal donors, but both specialize mainly in areas other than Asia and the Far East, although a German industrial consortium has set up a steel mill in India. The European community has made some contributions of a general nature which are of significance also to the area under review. Under the auspices of the

Organization for Economic Cooperation and Development (OECD—formerly OEEC) surveys have been undertaken of the flow of international capital from public and private sources which suggest that earlier estimates, published under the auspices of the United Nations, have underestimated the flow of resources from developed to developing countries.

The world total now runs at an annual rate equivalent to almost US $9,000 million. Of this total, the share of Asia and the Far East may be estimated to be nearly 50 per cent. It used to be higher, but the recent emergence of independent countries in Africa has shifted the priority of aid programmes in favour of the latest claimants. Even at the high rates of financial assistance quoted it is estimated that only two-thirds of the minimum requirements of the developing countries in foreign capital are being met at present. Unfavourable terms of trade and increasing debt services absorb a substantial and growing portion of the financial assistance of developing countries, and high rates of growth of population swallow much of the economic progress that is made.

In recognition of past shortcomings of Western aid programmes, the Development Assistance Committee of the Organization for Economic Cooperation and Development, in its first annual review of 1962, made some timely recommendations, e.g. the need for (a) securing public support for expanding aid programmes; (b) coordinating aid efforts to ensure their fullest effect; (c) linking aid to long-term development objectives; (d) increasing the earnings of foreign exchange of the developing countries by providing expanding markets for their products, including manufactured goods, in developed countries. Thus the awareness is growing that attention must be devoted, more than in the past, to the effectiveness of aid as against its mere size. This recognition has been brought about in part by a critical analysis in recent years of the methods practised in developing countries by members of the Soviet bloc.

Sino-Soviet Aid

Soviet interest in developing countries is of fairly recent date. Even today, aid—like trade—is a residual rather than an essential part of Soviet foreign policy. However, since Stalin's death and more specifically since 1956 when the Soviet Union experienced its 'Indian mutiny' within its realm, the awareness of the problems of development has grown to the extent that the concept of 'peaceful coexistence' has replaced that of 'socialism in one country'.

Soviet publications claim that not only has Russia grown, within less than five decades following the revolution, from a backward country to a great power, but in particular it has developed tribal areas, kept by the Czarist regime under conditions of feudal servitude, ranging from the areas of the small peoples of the extreme north to the territories of the aborigines in the Caucasian mountains. Although much of this is part of the national folklore rather than the historical record, it meets with a certain response in some of the newly emergent countries. Where Russia is regarded as too remote or too European, China's more recent experiment in development sometimes has a special appeal. This was at least so prior to the Sino-Indian border incidents and the failures of the Chinese 'Great Leap Forward' (see chapter entitled 'The Economy of China', p. 677). In time, China may yet recover its appeal in Asia.

There is a certain affinity between the developing countries and the Sino-Soviet bloc which has its origin in their predominantly rural character; their preoccupation with farming pursuits; their urbanization and industrialization through planning as conscious attempts to break with the medieval past; and, last but not least, their hostility to certain undesirable features of Western capitalism and colonial rule, if not to these phenomena as such. In these circumstances the attraction which the Sino-Soviet bloc and its aid have, is hardly surprising. Its contribution to development in Asia and the Far East has been smaller than the publicity given to it seems to imply.

Since Soviet economic aid was started in 1954, offers to developing countries equivalent to over US $6,000 million have been made by members of the bloc. Of this total, Asia's share accounts for approximately half, the principal recipients being India (US $1,350 million) and Indonesia (US $650 million). Indonesia also received a substantial part of the military aid offered to Asia.

Projects, like countries, are highly selected, more than half of the economic aid offered being earmarked to go to industrial projects where the emphasis lies with plants processing indigenous raw materials and manufacturing producer and capital goods. The largest project of this kind is the much publicized Bilai steel mill in India. Prestige projects, such as a sports stadium, a tourist hotel, or a technological institute have also received a good deal of public attention, but there are also less conspicuous, though no less useful projects, such as cement factories and sugar mills.

The actual financial outlay for Sino-Soviet economic aid has been relatively small. Although official figures are not published, it can be estimated at hardly more than US $1,000 million, or one-third of the offers made between the beginning of 1954 and the end of 1964. Military offers have been met from Soviet armament depots at a faster rate than non-military commitments, but here data are even less readily available and less reliable than in the sphere of economic aid.

As is usual, plant equipment is accompanied by technicians of whom there are at present some 4,500 from Soviet bloc countries operating in Asian countries. Simultaneously Asian students have been trained at universities and technical colleges throughout the Soviet bloc. Their present numbers are unlikely to total more than 2,500. Linguistic difficulties form a barrier for technicians and trainees even where other obstacles are ignored.

As Soviet bloc aid consists of credits only and is thus repayable in full, there is a close correlation between the trends of trade and aid. At present Sino-Soviet bloc trade with developing countries in Asia and the Far East runs at an annual rate of less than US $600 million in either direction, consisting of an exchange of industrial capital goods against agricultural and mineral raw materials. These are small transactions when compared with those of the traditional commercial partners of Asia. In fact, Sino-Soviet trade transactions, like aid disbursements, amount to a mere five per cent of the corresponding operations of non-Communist countries.

Even so, the Soviet—like the American—aid programme seems to have been the subject of a careful political reappraisal leading to a temporary decline in offers in 1962 due to certain strains in Russia's economy. In 1964 approximately US $500 million were offered to Asian countries from the Sino-Soviet bloc. China, with limited resources, made no offers of economic aid in 1962. Its foreign policy seems to favour revolutionary developments in preference to regimes composed of members of the 'national bourgeoisie' of developing countries.

Conclusion

Aid to developing countries is part and parcel of the conflict of a divided world. Seen from the developing countries, there is a *prima facie* case for taking economic aid irrespective of any political aspects of importance to the donor. The inclination in favour of non-alignment, though strong, has however been weakened in South and South-East Asia since the fallacy of this concept has become manifest in the recent past. As a result the rivalry between the industrial West and the Soviet bloc is recognized increasingly as a fact of life, of which economic aid has become an indispensable part.

Table 1

World Bank and International Development Association. Loans and Credits to Asia. 1944–1963

(U.S. $ million)

	South Asia	S.E. Asia and Far East	Total
Economic Aid:			
Bank Loans	1,100	750	1,850
IDA Credits	150	—	150
Total	1,250	750	2,000
thereof:			
India	950	—	950
Japan	—	500	500
Pakistan	250	—	250
Thailand	—	150	150
Others	50	100	150
Total	1,250	750	2,000
thereof:			
Transport	550	300	850
Industry	300	150	450
Power	250	200	450
Agriculture	100	50	150
Others	50	50	100
Total	1,250	750	2,000

Sources: World Bank Reports (published and unpublished)

TABLE 2

UNITED STATES. ECONOMIC AND MILITARY AID TO ASIA. 1945-1962
(U.S. $ million)

	South Asia	S.E. Asia and Far East	Total
Economic Aid:			
Loans	4,285	2,052	6,337
Grants	2,975	12,615	15,590
Total	7,260	14,667	21,927
Military Aid	63	8,807	8,870
Grand Total	7,323	23,474	30,797
thereof:			
Korea	—	5,674	5,674
Taiwan	—	4,524	4,524
Vietnam (Indochina)	—	3,431	3,431
India	4,718	—	4,718
Japan	—	3,824	3,824
Pakistan	2,227	—	2,227
Philippines	—	1,851	1,851
Thailand	—	869	869
Indonesia	—	881	881
Laos	—	328	328
Cambodia	—	367	367
Afghanistan	237	—	237
Others	141	1,725	1,866
Grand Total	7,323	23,474	30,797

Sources: International Co-operation Administration, U.S. Foreign Assistance 1945-1961. Agency for International Development, U.S. Foreign Assistance 1945-1963. Washington 1963.

TABLE 3

UNITED KINGDOM. ECONOMIC AND TECHNICAL ASSISTANCE TO ASIA. 1945/46–1963/64
(£ million)

	Loans	Grants	Total
Economic and Technical Aid:			
South Asia	180·6	1·2	181·8
S.E. Asia and Far East	19·1	74·1	93·2
Unspecified	15·4	44·6	60·0
Total	215·1	119·9	335·0
thereof:			
India	145·4	2·9	148·3
Malaysia	14·7	41·7	56·4
Burma	4·4	32·4	36·8
Pakistan	35·2	3·4	38·6
Unspecified	15·4	39·5	54·9
Total	215·1	119·9	335·0

Sources: Central Statistical Office, Annual Abstracts of Statistics, 1961 to 1964. London 1961 to 1964.

TABLE 4
SINO-SOVIET BLOC ECONOMIC AND TECHNICAL AID TO ASIA. 1954–1964
(U.S. $ million)

	South Asia	S.E. Asia and Far East	Total
Economic Aid Offers			
Loans	1,800	850	2,650
Grants	250	100	350
Total	2,050	950	3,000
thereof:			
Soviet Aid	1,600	400	2,000
East European Aid	350	300	650
Chinese Aid	100	250	350
Total	2,050	950	3,000
thereof:			
India	1,350	—	1,350
Indonesia	—	650	650
Afghanistan	550	—	550
Others	150	300	450
Total	2,050	950	3,000
Economic Aid Drawings			
Loans	700	200	900
Grants	50	50	100
Total	750	250	1,000
	1960	1962	1964
Economic Experts	1,600	4,000	4,500
Students Trained	2,000	3,500	2,500
Foreign Trade Agreements	40	45	45
Foreign Trade Turnover (U.S. $ million)	800	1,000	1,200

Sources: National Statistics. Estimates as at March 1965.

BIBLIOGRAPHY

BOOKS

R. L. Allen. *Soviet Economic Warfare.* (Public Affairs Press, Washington, 1960.)
H. J. P. Arnold. *Aid for Developing Countries.* (Bodley Head, London, 1962.)
F. C. Benham. *The Colombo Plan and Other Essays.* (Royal Institute of International Affairs, London, 1961.) *Economic Aid to Underdeveloped Countries.* (Oxford Univ. Press, London, 1961.)
J. S. Berliner. *Soviet Economic Aid.* (Praeger, New York, 1958.)
A. A. Jordan. *Foreign Aid and the Defence of South East Asia.* (Praeger, New York, 1962.)
M. Kovner. *The Challenge of Coexistence.* (Public Affairs Press, Washington, 1961.)
R. F. Mikesell and J. N. Behrman. *Financing World Trade and the Sino-Soviet Bloc.* (Princeton Univ. Press, Princeton, N.J., 1958.)
A. Nove and D. Donnelly. *Trade with Communist Countries.* (Hutchinson, London, 1960.)

Official Papers

Commonwealth Consultative Committee. *The Colombo Plan for Co-operative Economic Development in South and South East Asia.* Cmd. 8080. (London, 1950.) *The Colombo Plan, The Tenth Report.* Cmd. 1600. (London, 1961.)

ESCAFE. *Economic Surveys of Asia and the Far East.* Vols. I-XV. 1947-1961. (Bangkok, 1948-1961.) *Economic Bulletins for Asia and the Far East.* Vols. I-XII. 1950/51-1962/63. (Bangkok, 1950-1963.)

H.M. Government. *Technical Cooperation.* Cmd. 1698. (London, 1962.) *Technical Assistance from the United Kingdom for Overseas Development.* Cmd. 1308. (London, 1961.)

O.E.C.D. *The Flow of Financial Resources to Less Developed Countries, 1956-1963.* (Paris, 1962.)

U.S. Congress. *Economic Policies Towards Less Developed Countries.* (Washington, 1961.) *United States Foreign Policy: Asia.* (Washington, 1959.)

U.S. Department of State. *The Sino-Soviet Economic Offensive in the Less Developed Countries* (Washington, 1958.) *Communist Economic Policy in the Less Developed Areas.* (Washington 1960.)

U.S. Government. *ICA, U.S. Foreign Assistance.* (Washington, 1962.) *AID, U.S. Foreign Assistance.* (Washington, 1962.) *Mutual Defence Assistance Control Act of 1951. First to Fifteenth Reports to Congress.* (Washington, 1951-1962.)

United Nations. *ECOSOC, International Flow of Long-Term Capital and Official Donations 1959-1961.* (New York, 1962.)

United Nations. *Yearbook of the United Nations, 1961.* (New York, 1963.)

BIOGRAPHICAL NOTE

Dr. W. Klatt, O.B.E. Economic Adviser and a student of economic and agrarian affairs in Europe and Asia. Has been a consultant to United Nations Agencies on several occasions. Has undertaken a number of surveys in various Asian countries. Has written for journals in England and America and on the Continent; editor of and a contributor to a symposium, *The Chinese Model. A Political, Economic and Social Survey* (Hong Kong Univ. Press, Hong Kong, 1965.)

TOURISM IN ASIA

by

DICK WILSON

EVER since Marco Polo and Friar Odoric astonished mediaeval Europe by their accounts of travelling in Asia, the East has fascinated outsiders. The rich colours of Asian life and the variety of its cultures today attract hundreds of thousands of tourists annually, and the travel trade has become an important part of the local economies. Japan earns as much from tourism as from her steel or cotton cloth exports; India's tourist receipts represent one-twentieth of her entire export earnings; tourism is second only to the textile mills as breadwinner for Hong Kong. In 1964, year of the Tokyo Olympic Games (first to be held on Asian soil), something like £200 million was spent by tourists in Asia, and the Orient is fast competing with the Caribbean and Europe for the favours of the American tourist.

This is the continent of the Forbidden City of Peking, the Taj Mahal, Angkor Wat, the island of Bali, the Himalayas and Mount Fuji. Here are hibiscus, orchids, bougainvillea, magnolias, sampaguita and thousands of other exquisite flowers; here are the *sari*, *kimono*, *cheongsam*, *lunggyi*, *barong Tagalog* and dozens of delightful national costumes; here are Buddhism, Hinduism and all the world's religions in societies now undergoing all the stress and stain of modernization. Asia is a natural tourist wonderland.

It is only in the 1960's that tourism has become fully accepted as an industry in Asia. Most of the Government departments of tourism, acting collectively within the Pacific Area Travel Association (PATA), designated 1961 as the first 'Visit the Orient' year. Since then facilities have constantly improved in almost every country, though they are still below European or North American standards, and an annual increase in tourism of between 10 per cent and 15 per cent has been the common experience.

Most Asian countries report that about a third of their visitors are American, another third European or Australian, and the rest from neighbouring Asian lands. Unfortunately, shortage of foreign exchange obliges their Governments to restrict the natural travel urge of many Japanese, Chinese, Indians and Indonesians. Hong Kong attracts more travellers than any other country in Asia, partly because it is a travel centre for Overseas Chinese and a bottleneck through which almost everyone crossing the Pacific to or from Asia has to pass (the reputation of its shops usually tempting you to stay a few days there *en route*). Thailand is the third most visited Asian country, partly for the similar reason that Bangkok, its capital, is a hub of the East Asian air network. But Japan and India are the countries where visitors spend more than a casual few days, and where a long holiday can be immensely rewarding. The table below shows some recent statistics for tourism in these four areas.

CHIEF ASIAN TOURIST AREAS

	Number of Tourist Arrivals (in Thousands) in			Percentage of whom American	Estimated receipts (in £ Millions)
	1962	1963	1964		1964
Hong Kong	253	316	399	28	48
Japan	278	305	353	55	22
Thailand	120	195	224	40	12
India	134	141	157	22	20

Note: Some of these figures are estimates, calculated from data supplied by the country concerned, and not in every case strictly comparable. They provide a rough guide only.

ACCOMMODATION

The legendary hotels of the Somerset Maugham era—Hong Kong's Peninsula, Frank Lloyd Wright's Imperial in Tokyo, the Raffles in Singapore and Bombay's Taj—are now complemented by such completely modern luxury establishments as the Okura in Tokyo, the Mandarin in Hong Kong and the Indonesia in Djakarta. You would not pay much less than £5 for a night in these hotels, and you might not guess, except by looking out of the windows, that you were outside London or New York. In most cities, however, there are modest but adequate Western-style rooms to be got for £2-3. The best hotels are given below after the names of the cities in which they are found. Visitors willing to try the traditional Japanese-style inn (*ryokan*) with its rush-matting and paper screens, the Korean inns with their heated floors (*ondol*), or the Chinese hotels which flourish everywhere east of Calcutta, will both economize and be educated—except in Tokyo where the *ryokan* are designed for rich Japanese and are often more expensive than the Western-style hotels. Language is usually the barrier keeping Western travellers to the Western-style hotels where English (French in Vietnam, Cambodia and Laos) is fully understood. For a less demanding visitor cheap but good accommodation is offered in many cities by the YMCA, YWCA, the Salvation Army and the Youth Hostel Association. The countries formerly under British rule (India, Pakistan, Ceylon, Burma and Malaysia) preserve in the smaller towns the *dak* bungalows, Government resthouses and circuit houses which tourists can use at little cost provided they can announce their intentions by letter in advance. An American student shoe-string globe-trotter reports that he survived in Asia on £1 a day, except in Japan where he needed twice that amount. Hospitality is generous in Asia, and the prevalence of servants in its less-developed economic conditions makes it common for a visitor to be invited to stay with friends.

WEATHER

There are three fairly distinct weather zones in Asia. *Temperate* Asia (above the 30° latitude, that is to say North China, Korea and Japan, Nepal and the nothern parts of India and Pakistan) is like Europe or North America; the winter is cold, the summer slightly humid and so the best seasons for visiting are spring (April to June) and autumn (September to November). *North Tropical* Asia (from 5° to 30° north, or between the latitudes of Shanghai and Penang) comprises India, the South-East Asian peninsula (except Malaya), the Philippines, South China, Taiwan and Hong Kong. Here heavy rains occur in the summer between June and September, which is thus uncomfortably hot and wet. Winter is considered the most pleasant season, and September to April are the best months. Light clothing will suffice here unless one climbs up to the hill stations. *Equatorial* Asia, i.e. Malaysia and Indonesia, has a different monsoon pattern with rain in the winter; April to September is the recommended tourist season, but those from temperate regions will find this region hot and humid at the best of times. No need of woollen clothes here.

Transportation

Phineas Fogg had some anxious hours in the East, but today over 40 international airlines and a larger number of shipping lines girdle Asia. All the major world airlines cross the continent, and almost every country has its own national airline. The Russian and Czech airlines also now serve South Asia. The cheapest single air ticket from London to Delhi is £140, to Tokyo £240. A P and O berth from London to Bombay (the voyage lasts a fortnight) costs upwards of £100, and Messageries Maritimes can ship you from Marseilles to Bombay for £70. These days several firms run overland coaches to India from London or Paris via Ankara and Teheran. The traveller with time to spare could spend a week on the Trans-Siberian railway between Moscow and Peking: £25 upwards, or about £70 upwards if you start at Paris and go through to Hong Kong (it is the Chinese visa that is difficult to get). Japan, China and India have good rail systems, and you can also travel by rail between Malaysia, Thailand and Cambodia. The Asian Highway, unfortunately, is cut in two by Burma, which rigorously refuses road entry; otherwise you could go by Land Rover from Delhi to Singapore. Border-crossing by land tends to be difficult in South-East Asia.

Visas

Asian Governments have not, unhappily, reached the stage where common sense and the rewards of tourism might lead them to cut through the baffling red tape of entry procedures. Americans need no visa for Ceylon, Malaysia, the Ryukyus, South Vietnam or Thailand. British Commonwealth citizens are equally privileged in Ceylon, Hong Kong, India, Malaysia and Pakistan—and Britons in Japan. Many West Europeans do not need visas for Ceylon, Japan, Malaysia and Pakistan. But in all other cases a prior visit to an Embassy or Consulate to have one's passport visa-ed is necessary. Some countries offer a short stay of between 24 and 72 hours to anyone without a previous visa, sometimes insisting however on the traveller's having a confirmed onward reservation and ticket; Burma, the Philippines, South Korea, South Vietnam, Taiwan and Thailand were in this position in 1964. These regulations frequently change, however, and an intending visitor should make further enquiries. China and Burma are notoriously difficult countries to get visas for, but others usually give a visa freely to *bona fide* tourists. In some countries an exit permit is required before leaving.

Health

Most Asian Governments require valid smallpox and cholera vaccination certificates, and also one for yellow fever for arrivals from Africa or Latin America. Typhoid and poliomyelitis injections are recommended. Malaria is not now a serious risk for the normal visitor (though he will find mosquitoes a trial and will probably want an insect repellent lotion in tropical and equatorial Asia), and water is safe to drink in most Asian cities these days. Entero-vioform tablets are nevertheless useful to carry against minor stomach disorders.

Money

Travellers' cheques, letters of credit and sterling or US dollar currency are the best forms for your money. You should be prepared for strict regulations about declaring your money and keeping records of all exchanges, save in Hong Kong, Japan, Malaysia, the Philippines and Thailand where foreign exchange control is more lax. Some Asian countries, notably Cambodia, Laos and Indonesia, have weak currencies and artificial exchange rates immensely frustrating for visitors: special rates are often available, however, for *bona fide* tourists staying at Government hotels. Customs inspection can be quite rigorous in India and China and you may have to record the number of your camera or transistor radio as a check against selling it inside the country. In some countries currency obtained in the free money market is unwelcome.

Shopping

Most of your normal needs will be available in shops, though not always your favourite imported brand. It is wise to stock up at home (or in such entrepot ports as Aden, Bangkok, Hong Kong and Singapore) on film, drugs and cosmetics which are particularly difficult in China, India and Indonesia. Souvenirs, handicrafts and bargains—especially in silk, lacquerware, wood carvings and brassware—are abundant, however. You will not forget a browse in Bangkok's Thieves' Market (Nakorn Kasem), Peking's Tung An bazaar, Delhi's Chandni Chowk, the Bogyoke Market in Rangoon or Cat Street in Hong Kong. Hong Kong is good for suits and dresses (the tailor will make them up in 24 hours, but will do a better job if you can give him three or four days) and also for watches and duty-free European or American goods—but there are few fixed prices there. Americans require a special certificate of origin to show that their purchases in Hong Kong did not originate in mainland China. No one should miss the chance of visiting a Tokyo department store (Mitsukoshi, say, or Takashimaya).

Attractions

Festivals are an important feature of traditional Asian life, and a visitor is unlucky not to see one. The Chinese New Year (in January or February, depending on the moon) is celebrated everywhere east of Calcutta with firecrackers and performances. In India Dussehra (October) and Diwali (November) are the main festivals, while in Thailand and Burma the April water festival (known as Songkran and Thingyan respectively) is exciting. Other events to look out for are the Easter Week festivities in the Philippines; the Perahera at Kandy in Ceylon (August); the Bon (lantern festivals) all over Japan in July; and the Dragon Boat Races in Hong Kong in June. Hunting is good in Asia: Indian tiger *shikars* are cheaper than African, and Nepal, Pakistan and Thailand also offer excellent game facilities. Japan has fine fishing and game birds. Golfers and swimmers will not be frustrated, except in China. Night life is of a high standard in Tokyo, while the nightclubs in Bangkok, Hong Kong and Manila provide cheaper, less professional but equally enjoyable entertainment. Filipino musicians man the bands all over the Continent.

Tourist Agencies

The Pacific Area Travel Association (153 Kearny Street, San Francisco) can be helpful, and individual Asian Government tourist organizations are increasingly represented in American and European cities. The Japan National Tourist Organization, the Government of India Tourist Office and the Hong Kong Tourist Association, for instance, all have offices in London, New York, San Francisco, Chicago, Sydney and Melbourne. India and Japan are also represented in Paris, Frankfurt and Toronto (and Japan further in Geneva). All these will answer enquiries, as indeed will most travel agents. Intending tourists should not hesitate to utilize the Government-run tourist agencies (the Japan Travel Bureau in Japan, NITOUR in Indonesia and China Travel Services in China) which are exceptionally courteous and efficient in making arrangements.

Burma

Frequent air and occasional sea services from Calcutta and Singapore—and air from Bangkok—will deliver you to Rangoon (Strand Hotel), the somewhat seedy but interesting capital of Burma. There are also flights from China via Kunming and Mandalay. Rangoon's chief monument is the Shwedagon, a Buddhist pagoda covered with a million pounds' worth of gold plate. Up-country the centre is Mandalay, capital of the former Burmese Kings and noteworthy for the Mahamuni pagoda. Pagan, Ava and Amarapura have ruins in varying stages of decay, each of interest. Security conditions make it difficult to travel into the border regions, but a tour of the Shan States (with a climate like Kenya's) is worth while; go on the Inle Lake and see the leg-rowers.

Cambodia

Prince Sihanouk's current quarrels with his Thai and Vietnamese neighbours make the entry into Cambodia more difficult than usual. There are air services from Bangkok, Saigon and Hong Kong, but the road/rail journey from Thailand and South Vietnam is subject to interruption. In Phnom Penh (Hotel Le Royal) the Royal Palace and National Museum deserve visits; the city is elegant and modern. But the principal attraction in Cambodia is Angkor where the ruins of a complete Khmer civilization, flourishing from the 9th century A.D. until the Thai conquest in 1431, were 're-discovered' by a French naturalist in 1860. Four centuries of neglect in the jungle preserved the most complete example of Hinduistic architecture in the world. You reach the site via Siem Reap, the nearest town (direct flights from Bangkok, also train and bus from Phnom Penh; stay at the Grand Hotel, still French-managed). The ruins, which extend over 60 square miles, can be seen by trishaw and land rover, and three days should be spared. Angkor Wat is the grandest site, with a magnificent bas-relief frieze of the Ramayana. The Bayon, Angkor Thom and the distant Banteai Srei ought to be seen, as well as the Ta Prohm temple which has been left as Henri Mouhot found it a century ago, to show how the jungle had overgrown and undermined the masonry. The Classical Khmer Dance Troupe performs occasionally in the moonlight beside the ruins. French is necessary to get the best out of Cambodia.

CEYLON

The island can be reached by rail-ferry from India, and there are frequent air and sea services from India and Singapore. Colombo (Galle Face and Mount Lavinia Grand Hotels) is a pleasant city, with a seashore playground at Mount Lavinia. Nuwara Eliya is a cool hill station inland where the heat can be escaped. Kandy, the ancient capital, is notable for its Temple of the Tooth and botanical gardens. The ancient Buddhist ruins at Anuradhapura and Polonnaruwa, and the wall paintings at Sigiriya, ought to be seen.

CHINA

China can be reached by air and train from Moscow, by air from Rangoon, and by ships calling at Shanghai and other ports, but the most common entry is by air or ship to Hong Kong, thence over the border by train to Canton, thence by train or air to other Chinese cities. China Travel Service (6 Queen's Road Central, Hong Kong) handles all these arrangements. Peking (Peking and Hsinchiao Hotels) needs a week even for the energetic tourist. The Forbidden City of the old Emperors, with its golden roofs and six great halls (Supreme Harmony, Complete Harmony, Preserving Harmony, Heavenly Purity, Union and Earthly Tranquillity) is the principal monument. Visitors should also see the Tien An Men Square with its twin Museums of Chinese History and Revolution, the Summer Palace and, further off, the Great Wall and Ming Tombs. Shanghai (Peace Hotel) is still a most interesting city, and the centre for the parks and lakes of Soochow and Hangchow. Internal travel is by air (mainly Viscounts and Ilyushins) and train. Few Western visitors get into China, whose Government is suspicious of foreigners, but there are more opportunities since the Pakistan International Airlines began services in 1964 to Canton and Shanghai. All travel in China is Government-organized, but you are not made to feel shadowed all the time these days. Americans are not given permission by their Government to enter China.

Mongolia is sandwiched between China and Russia, and can be approached by air or train either way (also by air from Delhi).

Taiwan is one hour by jet from Hong Kong, and is also served by air from Tokyo and by ships. The Portuguese called it the Beautiful Island, and its scenery is unrivalled. From Taipei (Grand Hotel, President or Ambassador) go to the Sun Moon Lake and see some aboriginal life. Tainan, the former capital, is interesting. The Government encourages tourists.

Hong Kong

The liveliest city in the East, Hong Kong (Mandarin, Hilton, Peninsula and a dozen more hotels of good class) is also the busiest travel centre. Tourists like to patronize the floating fish restaurants at Aberdeen, ascend the funicular Peak Tram for a view of the harbour (which rivals Rio's), stroll along the sleezy Wanchai waterfront made famous by Suzie Wong, swim at Repulse Bay and tour the New Territories (views of the Chinese frontier, an old walled village, traditional agriculture). But shopping is the main draw: in a virtually duty-less free port, Hong Kong's shops are famous throughout Asia. They work on a small profit margin and bargain prices can be obtained—but you can also be overcharged if you are vague about the real value of your purchase.

Macao (Bela Vista Hotel), the tiny Portuguese colony, is four hours by ferry (fifteen minutes by seaplane) from Hong Kong and affords a quiet contrast with sleepy streets and old colonial-style architecture.

India

Like China, India is a continent and a civilization to itself; unlike China, however, it allows the foreigner to roam as he pleases (save in some border regions). The four big cities provide the bases for visiting the main regions.

The visitor who depends on alcoholic nourishment should remember that many parts of India prohibit drinking, and he should obtain an All-India Liquor Permit along with his visa at his local Indian Embassy. Delhi and Calcutta are more tolerant, but getting a drink in Madras and Bombay can be a trial.

West: Bombay (Nataraj and Taj Mahal Hotels), the usual port of entry from Europe, is the cleanest and most Western of India's cities. See the Elephanta cave temple across the bay, and strike inland to the renowned Ellora and Ajanta rock temples.

North: Delhi (Ashoka and Intercontinental Hotels) comprises Lord Curzon's 'deserted cities of dreary and disconsolate tombs' with ruins of seven empires (culminating in the Moguls) and memories of British imperial rule. The Red Fort and Jama Masjid are the best monuments, apart from the modern Government buildings. Air, car or rail trips should be made from Delhi to Agra (for the Taj Mahal which will not disappoint, and the more distant Fatehpur Sikri ruins of 1569), Khajuraho (10th-11th-century temples with erotic sculpture), Banaras (Holy City of the Hindus, who bathe in the sacred waters of the Ganges and lay their bodies at last on the burning *ghats*), Jaipur (the pink city) and Kashmir. Kashmir is the pride of the sub-continent, with superb mountain scenery (also Asia's best golfcourse at Gulmarg) and the Mogul gardens of Shalimar, though more expensive than the rest of India (stay in Srinagar's Oberoi Palace Hotel).

East: Calcutta (Great Eastern and Oberoi Grand Hotels), the dirtiest and most depressing city in the world, is the centre for the Bengal-Bihar industrial areas, for East Pakistan, for Nepal and Darjeeling. From Calcutta you should also try to see Patna, centre of the Buddha country, and the Temple of the Sun God at Konarak. Darjeeling (Oberoi Mount Everest Hotel) is the centre of the Himalayan foothills, full of Tibetan émigrés, splendidly-costumed Nepalese and Bhutanese noblemen, panoramas of Kanchenjunga and Everest—but you need a permit from Calcutta before going. This is also the way to enter Sikkim or Bhutan, the two semi-independent kingdoms between India and Tibet, but permission from the Indian External Affairs Ministry is needed—and rarely granted. To reach Darjeeling and the Himalayas, fly from Calcutta to Bagdogra and then take a car (there is also a narrow-gauge railway from nearby Siliguri into Darjeeling).

South: Madras (Connemara Hotel) is the base from which to strike at the Dravidian South, totally different from India's Aryan North. Go to the 7th-century rock-cut shore temples of Mahalaburipam, see the sun rise at Cape Comorin, try to be in Mysore for the Dusserah festival in October, and do not miss the coconut palms of Kerala.

Nepal

Though an independent sovereign state, this beautiful and charming kingdom is accessible only through India (by air from Calcutta or Delhi, via Patna, or by a tough rail/bus journey from Raxaul on the border) and is, in effect, a part of one's Indian tour. Pick up your visa (24 hours needed) in Delhi or Calcutta. Kathmandu (Royal Hotel, run by the legendary Russian dancer, Boris) is full of mediaeval street façades and elaborately carved windows. Take a jeep to the smaller towns of Bhatgaon and Patan and fly to the next valley, Pokhara, for lake and mountain views.

Indonesia

Twelve airlines serve Djakarta (Hotel Indonesia) from Singapore, Hong Kong and Bangkok, and ships also call. Your internal travelling in Indonesia is best put in the hands of NITOUR, the Government tourist agency. Try to see Jogjakarta, the centre for the 10th-century Buddhist carvings at Borobodur and for the Ramayana Wayang Ballet at Prambanan (performed during each week of the full moon between June and October). Bandung is also a scenic city. Outside Java travel is sometimes difficult, but make every effort to fly to Bali (Bali Hotel in Denpasar) and spend a few days in a museum-piece society where dance is a part of daily life (try to see a cremation ceremony and the *ketchak* or *ape-dance*, and be prepared for bare bosoms). In Sumatra a journey to Lake Toba from Medan is recommended.

Japan

Tokyo (Okura, Imperial, Hilton, New Otani and a score of other excellent hotels) is the world's largest urban complex. It is a relatively modern city and there are few important monuments, but the visitor should not miss the Ginza entertainment district (now rivalled by Shinjuku) and should see a *Kabuki* drama, *Noh* play and *sumo* wrestling if in season. The best day or weekend trips are to Kamakura (with the great open-air Buddha which filmgoers saw in *Round the World in Eighty Days*), Nikko (scarlet-and-gold 7th-century Shinto shrines among the cedars), Hakone (the lake by Mount Fuji, which you can climb in 5½ hours in the summer only) and anywhere in the Boso or Izu peninsulas. For summer climbs and winter skiing in the Japan Alps, take the train to Matsumoto. In northern Japan, the old city of Sendai and the aboriginal Ainus of Hokkaido, the northernmost island, are worth a visit.

In the south, Osaka is the commercial and industrial centre and close to the two ancient capitals, Kyoto and Nara. Kyoto distils for the visitor the essential Japan, with superb temples (Honganji, Kiyomizu, Kinkakuji) and a fine castle (Nijo), Japan's best *geisha* schools in Gion and Pontocho, sophisticated coffee-shop and night-club society and good shopping for traditional wares. Nara, the 8th-century capital, is smaller, with a famous deer park; see the Todaiji housing the biggest bronze Buddha in the world), the Kasuga shrine and Horyuji. The inland sea of Seto (centre: Hiroshima) is the favourite holiday ground of the Japanese themselves; try to see the delightful islet of Miyajima. If you can spend some weeks in Japan, travel about in efficient buses and trains, staying in *ryokan*—the Japanese-style inns where you will be introduced to the *ofuro* (Japanese hot bath) and the delicacies of Japanese cuisine. But take a Japanese phrase-book, since English is not well understood.

Korea

Few tourists go to North Korea (reached from Peking or Irkutsk by air, or by occasional ships from Japan). South Korea, however, welcomes visitors and is so scenic that even the scars of war do not reduce its attractiveness. Seoul (Bando Hotel) has enchanting dilapidated mediaeval palaces (Kyongbok, Toksu) and is the base for the old Kings' tombs and Walker Hill, the GI-oriented recreation and amusement centre. Try to visit Kyongju, further south, for the old Buddhist temple of Pulguk-sa, and also the mountain vistas of Mt. Sorat.

Laos

Vientiane (Setha Palace and Lan Xang Hotels for diplomats, Constellation for journalists) can be reached by air from Bangkok, Phnom Penh or Saigon also by train or car from Bangkok with ferry over the Mekong River. It has some picturesque temples, but there is more sightseeing in Luang Prabang (one hour's flight), the religious and royal capital.

Malaysia

Many airlines serve Kuala Lumpur and Singapore (which is also Asia's biggest shipping centre), and you can ride by train from Bangkok. Kuala Lumpur (Merlin Hotel) is a modern city with the best contemporary architecture in Asia. You will find more history at Malacca (early Dutch and Portuguese colonial buildings) and Penang (a holiday island with beaches, botanical gardens and a famous snake temple). The cooler Cameron Highlands are well-equipped for walking, golf and tennis. Singapore (Singapura and Raffles Hotels) is a city of tremendous, slightly decaying appeal: visit the Great World amusement centre, the Death House in Sago Lane and other quarters of its Chinatown. Daily flights take you to the two Borneo states, Sabah and Sarawak, and also to independent Brunei (ships also). There is no organized tourist industry in Borneo but the primitive charm of *dayak* life and the longhouses appeal to visitors.

Pakistan

Over sixteen airlines serve Karachi (Metropole and the new Intercontinental Hotels), and West Pakistan can be reached by ship, by road from Iran, rail from Afghanistan and by all three methods from India. Karachi itself has little to see but a drive to Thatta and Hyderabad is interesting. Lovers of antiquity should see the major prehistoric sites at Mohenjodaro and Harappa, as well as the early Buddhist relics at Taxila. Lahore is a city of gardens; visit the Shalimar Gardens of Shah Jahan and the Badshahi Mosque. Rawalpindi is near the newly-building capital, centre for the excellent hill stations. Peshawar (near the Khyber Pass), Quetta and the Pathan tribal life of the far north-west all demand notice.

East Pakistan is less well served by transport, Dacca (Shabagh Hotel) not being an international air centre. Most visitors proceed from Calcutta; there are frequent flights from Karachi, and infrequent ones from Rangoon, Kathmandu and Canton. Ships call at Chittagong, and there is road or rail entry from India. East Pakistan (or East Bengal) is little developed, and possesses few important monuments save a handful of mosques. There is a fine beach at Cox's Bazaar.

Philippines

Manila (Manila Hotel) is well served by airlines and steamship companies; it is a racy, Americanized, Latin city with a taste for violence—you should be careful about casual taxi rides. See the Old Intramuros of the Spanish period, the Cathedral and the one surviving early church. Drive to Baguio for cooler temperatures, golf and riding—and see at Banaue the legendary 2,000-years-old rice terraces. Legaspi is the town for the perfect-coned Mayon volcano, Cebu for Mactan Island where Magellan met his death. In Mindanao, the southern island, enjoy the whiffs of Arab influence still evident at Zamboanga, where the Muslim Zoros ply their brightly-coloured *vinta* boats. Ferries and planes are available from island to island.

Thailand

Bangkok (Erawan and Rama Hotels) is the hub of South-East Asian air routes, and is also patronized by ships (there is rail and road access from Malaysia). It is a sprawling city with bad roads and traffic jams, but there is enough to see to last a week. The Royal Palace and Temple of the Emerald Buddha come first on the list, followed by the early morning river tous (Temple of the Dawn, the royal barges, the floating markets) and exhibitionr of Thai boxing (in which feet are used as well as fists) and classical Thai dance. Bangkok is the United Nations headquarters for Asia, and an important diplomatic centre. Hua Hin is its seaside resort. A visit to Ayuthya, the old ruined capital, is rewarding, but the best expedition is to Chiengmai, capital of northern Siam, by train or air. Here are picturesque temples, in a quiet hilly area where tribal life is to be observed; there is an adequate Station Hotel. Seekers of the exotic will attend the elephant round-up, usually involving two hundred beasts, organized every November by the Tourist Organization of Thailand (TOT) at Surin, in the north-east. This brief summary does little justice to Thailand, which has an exceptionally strong charm and where almost every activity of life is pleasurable. Tourists also like its shopping—Thai silks, antique or forged Buddha heads, lacquerware and rubbings.

Vietnam

North Vietnam is rarely visited, access being by train or air from China, ship from Hong Kong or air from Phnom Penh. South Vietnam, by contrast, encourages tourism although fewer travellers have been attracted as the civil war has enlarged in scope. Saigon (Caravelle Hotel), a French city with the Chinese Cholon alongside it, is a sophisticated place. Patronize the pavement cafés of Tu-Do (Liberty) Boulevard, still known by its old name of Rue Catinat; see the National Museum; go to Cap St Jacques and Loughai for long white beaches (of which the most magnificent, however, is at Nhatrang, some 250 miles north). Dalat is the hill resort, with pines, lakes and a zoo. The imperial tombs and palace at Hue, the former imperial capital, are worth inspecting. But satisfy yourself about security conditions before going outside Saigon.

BIBLIOGRAPHY

Nigel Cameron. *To the East a Phoenix.* (Hutchinson, London, 1960.)
Fodor's Guide to Japan and East Asia. (MacGibbon and Kee, London, 1962.)
A Handbook for Travellers in India, Pakistan, Burma and Ceylon. (John Murray, London, 1965.)
Martin Hürlimann. *Traveller in the Orient.* (Thames and Hudson, London, 1960.)
Japan: The Official Guide. (Japan Travel Bureau, Tokyo, 1964.)
Frederick Joss. *Of Geishas and Gangsters.* (Odhams, London, 1962.)
New Horizons World Guide. (Pan American World Airways, 1964.)
Sacheverell Sitwell. *The Red Chapels of Banteai Strei.* (Weidenfeld and Nicolson, London, 1962.)
Travellers' Digest. (British Overseas Airways Corporation.)
Daniel Wolfstone (ed.). Golden Guide to South and East Asia. (Far Eastern Economic Review, Hong Kong, 4th ed., 1963.)
George Woodcock. *Faces of India.* (Faber and Faber, London, 1964.)

BIOGRAPHICAL NOTE

Dick Wilson. B. 1928. Educated at Universities of Oxford and California (Berkeley). Lectured at Dacca University, Pakistan, 1954; on staff of *The Financial Times*, London, 1955-8; Editor of *The Far Eastern Economic Review*, Hong Kong, 1958-64. Now a freelance writer on Afro-Asian affairs and travels frequently in Asia. Ramon Magsaysay Award for Journalism and Literature (1964). Author of *The Colombo Plan Story* and (under the pseudonym of 'Daniel Wolfstone'), *The Golden Guide to South and East Asia.*

PART FOUR

APPENDIX

POST-WAR TREATIES AND AGREEMENTS

INDIA

INDIAN INDEPENDENCE ACT, 1947 (ABRIDGED)

Act[1] to make provision for the setting up in India of two independent Dominions (18th July 1947).

Be it enacted by the King's most Excellent Majesty, by and with the advice and consent of the Lords Spiritual and Temporal, and Commons, in this present Parliament assembled, and by the authority of the same as follows:—

SECTION 1

As from the fifteenth day of August, nineteen hundred and forty-seven, two independent Dominions shall be set up in India, to be known respectively as India and Pakistan.

SECTION 2

(1) Subject to the provisions of subsections (3) and (4) of this section, the territories of India shall be the territories under the sovereignty of His Majesty which, immediately before the appointed day, were included in British India except the territories which, under subsection (2) of this section, are to be the territories of Pakistan.

(2) Subject to the provisions of subsections (3) and (4) of this section, the territories of Pakistan shall be:

(a) the territories which, on the appointed day, are included in the Provinces of East Bengal and West Punjab, as constituted under the two following sections;

(b) the territories which, at the date of the passing of this Act, are included in the Province of Sind and the Chief Commissioner's Province of British Baluchistan; and

(c) if, whether before or after the passing of this Act but before the appointed day, the Governor-General declares that the majority of the valid votes cast in the referendum which, at the date of the passing of this Act, is being or has recently been held in that behalf under his authority in the North West Frontier Province are in favour of representatives of that Province taking part in the Constituent Assembly of Pakistan, the territories which, at the date of the passing of this Act, are included in that Province.

(3) Nothing in this section shall prevent any area being at any time included in or excluded from either of the new Dominions, so, however, that;

(a) no area not forming part of the territories specified in subsection (1) or, as the case may be, subsection (2), of this section shall be included in either Dominion without the consent of that Dominion; and

(b) no area which forms part of the territories specified in the said subsection (1) or, as the case may be, the said subsection (2), or which has after the appointed day been included in either Dominion, shall be excluded from that Dominion without the consent of that Dominion.

(4) Without prejudice to the generality of the provisions of subsection (2) of this section, nothing in this section shall be construed as preventing the accession of Indian States to either of the new Dominions.

[1] Similar Acts were published on 10th December 1947 providing for the independence of Ceylon and Burma, the former within the British Commonwealth, the latter outside.

SECTION 3

(1) As from the appointed day the Province of Bengal, as constituted under the Government of India Act, 1935, shall cease to exist and there shall be constituted in lieu thereof two new Provinces, to be known respectively as East Bengal and West Bengal.

(2) If, whether before or after the passing of this Act, but before the appointed day, the Governor-General declares that the majority of the valid votes cast in the referendum which, at the date of the passing of this Act, is being or has recently been held in that behalf under his authority in the District of Sylhet are in favour of that District forming part of the new Province of East Bengal, then, as from that day, a part of the Province of Assam shall, in accordance with subsection (3) of this section, form part of the new Province of East Bengal.

(3) The boundaries of the new Provinces aforesaid and, in the event mentioned in subsection (2) of this section, the boundaries after the appointed day of the Province of Assam, shall be such as may be determined, whether before or after the appointed day, by the award of a boundary commission appointed or to be appointed by the Governor-General in that behalf, but until the boundaries are so determined:

(a) the Bengal Districts specified in the First Schedule to this Act, together with, in the event mentioned in subsection (2) of this section, the Assam District of Sylhet, shall be treated as the territories which are to be comprised in the new Provinces of East Bengal;

(b) the remainder of the territories comprised at the date of the passing of this Act in the Province of Bengal shall be treated as the territories which are to be comprised in the new Province of West Bengal.

SECTION 4

(1) As from the appointed day the Province of the Punjab, as constituted under the Government of India Act, 1935, shall cease to exist and there shall be constituted two new Provinces, to be known respectively as West Punjab and East Punjab.

(2) The boundaries of the said new Provinces shall be such as may be determined, whether before or after the appointed day, by the award of a boundary commission appointed or to be appointed by the Governor-General in that behalf, but until the boundaries are so determined:

(a) the Districts specified in the Second Schedule to this Act shall be treated as the territories to be comprised in the new Province of West Punjab; and

(b) the remainder of the territories comprised at the date of the passing of this Act in the Province of the Punjab shall be treated as the territories which are to be comprised in the new Province of East Punjab.

SECTION 5

For each of the new Dominions, there shall be a Governor-General who shall be appointed by His Majesty and shall represent His Majesty for the purposes of the government of the Dominion:

Provided that, unless and until provision to the contrary is made by a law of the Legislature of either of the new Dominions, the same person may be Governor-General of both the new Dominions.

SECTION 6

(1) The Legislature of each of the new Dominions shall have full power to make laws for that Dominion, including laws having extra-territorial operation.

(2) No law and no provision of any law made by the Legislature of either of the new Dominions shall be void or inoperative on the ground that it is repugnant to the law of England, or to the provisions of this or any existing or future Act of Parliament of the United Kingdom, or to any order, rule or regulation made under any such Act, and the powers of the Legislature of each Dominion include the power to repeal or amend any such Act, order, rule or regulation in so far as it is part of the law of the Dominion.

(3) The Governor-General of each of the new Dominions shall have full power to assent in His Majesty's name to any law of the Legislature of that Dominion and so much of any Act as relates to the disallowance of laws by his Majesty or the reservation of laws for the

signification of His Majesty's pleasure thereon or the suspension of the operation of laws until the signification of His Majesty's pleasure thereon shall not apply to laws of the Legislature of either of the new Dominions.

(4) No Act of Parliament of the United Kingdom passed on or after the appointed day shall extend, or be deemed to extend, to either of the new Dominions as part of the law of that Dominion unless it is extended thereto by a law of the Legislature of the Dominion.

(5) No Order in Council made on or after the appointed day under any Act passed before the appointed day, and no order, rule or other instrument made on or after the appointed day under any such Act by any United Kingdom Minister or other authority, shall extend, or be deemed to extend, to either of the new Dominions as part of the law of that Dominion.

(6) The power referred to in subsection (1) of this section extends to the making of laws limiting for the future the powers of the Legislature of the Dominion.

Section 7

As from the appointed day:

(a) His Majesty's Government in the United Kingdom have no responsibility as respects the government of any of the territories which, immediately before that day, were included in British India;

(b) the suzerainty of His Majesty over the Indian States lapses, and with it, all treaties and agreements in force at the date of the passing of this Act between His Majesty and the rulers of Indian States, all functions exercizable by His Majesty at that date with respect to Indian States, all obligations of His Majesty existing at that date towards Indian States or the rulers thereof, and all powers, rights, authority or jurisdiction exercizable by His Majesty at that date in or in relation to Indian States by treaty, grant, usage, sufferance or otherwise; and

(c) there lapse also any treaties or agreements in force at the date of the passing of this Act between His Majesty and any persons having authority in the tribal areas, any obligations of His Majesty existing at that date to any such persons or with respect to the tribal areas, and all powers, rights, authority or jurisdiction exercizable at that date by His Majesty in or in relation to the tribal areas by treaty, grant, usage, sufferance or otherwise:

Provided that, notwithstanding anything in paragraph (b) or paragraph (c) of this section, effect shall, as nearly as may be, continue to be given to the provisions of any such agreement as is therein referred to which relate to customs, transit and communications, posts and telegraphs, or other like matters, until the provisions in question are denounced by the Ruler of the Indian State or person having authority in the tribal areas on the one hand, or by the Dominion or Province or other part thereof concerned on the other hand, or are superseded by subsequent agreements.

Section 8

(1) In the case of each of the new Dominions, the powers of the Legislature of the Dominion shall, for the purpose of making provision as to the constitution of the Dominion, be exercizable in the first instance by the Constituent Assembly of that Dominion, and references in this Act to the Legislature of the Dominion shall be construed accordingly.

(2) Except in so far as other provision is made by or in accordance with a law made by the Constituent Assembly of the Dominion under subsection (1) of this section, each of the new Dominions and all Provinces and other parts thereof shall be governed as nearly as may be in accordance with the Government of India Act, 1935; and the provisions of that Act, and of the Orders in Council, rules and other instruments made thereunder, shall, so far as applicable, and subject to any express provisions of this Act, and with such omissions, additions, adaptations and modifications as may be specified in orders of the Governor-General under the next succeeding section, have effect accordingly:

Provided that:

(a) the said provisions shall apply separately in relation to each of the new Dominions and nothing in this subsection shall be construed as continuing on or after the appointed day any Central Government or Legislature common to both the new Dominions;

(b) nothing in this subsection shall be construed as continuing in force on or after the appointed day any form of control by His Majesty's Government in the United Kingdom over the affairs of the new Dominions or of any Province or other part thereof;

(c) so much of the said provisions as requires the Governor-General or any Governor to act in his discretion or exercize his individual judgment as respects any matter shall cease to have effect as from the appointed day;

(d) as from the appointed day, no Provincial Bill shall be reserved under the Government of India Act, 1935, for the signification of His Majesty's pleasure, and no Provincial Act shall be disallowed by His Majesty thereunder; and

(e) the powers of the Federal Legislature or Indian Legislature under that Act, as in force in relation to each Dominion, shall, in the first instance, be exercizable by the Constituent Assembly of the Dominion in addition to the powers exercizable by that Assembly under subsection (1) of this section.

(3) Any provision of the Government of India Act, 1935, which as applied to either of the new Dominions by subsection (2) of this section and the orders therein referred to, operates to limit the power of the legislature of that Dominion shall, unless and until other provision is made by or in accordance with a law made by the Constituent Assembly of the Dominion in accordance with the provisions of subsection (1) of this section, have the like effect as a law of the Legislature of the Dominion limiting for the future the powers of that Legislature.

SECTION 9

(1) The Governor-General shall by order make such provision as appears to him to be necessary or expedient:

(a) for bringing the provisions of this Act into effective operation;

(b) for dividing between the new Dominions, and between the new Provinces to be constituted under this Act, the powers, rights, property, duties and liabilities of the Governor-General in Council or, as the case may be, of the relevant Provinces which, under this Act, are to cease to exist;

(c) for making omissions from, additions to, and adaptations and modifications of, the Government of India Act, 1935, and the Orders in Council, rules and other instruments made thereunder, in their application to the separate new Dominions;

(d) for removing difficulties arising in connection with the transition to the provisions of this Act;

(e) for authorizing the carrying on of the business of the Governor-General in Council between the passing of this Act and the appointed day otherwise than in accordance with the provisions in that behalf of the Ninth Schedule to the Government of India Act, 1935;

(f) for enabling agreements to be entered into, and other acts done, on behalf of either of the new Dominions before the appointed day;

(g) for authorizing the continued carrying on for the time being on behalf of the new Dominions, or on behalf of any two or more of the said new Provinces, of services and activities previously carried on on behalf of British India as a whole or on behalf of the former Provinces which those new Provinces represent;

(h) for regulating the monetary system and any matters pertaining to the Reserve Bank of India; and

(i) so far as it appears necessary or expedient in connection with any of the matters aforesaid, for varying the constitution, powers or jurisdiction of any legislature, court or other authority in the new Dominions and creating new legislature, courts or other authorities therein.

(2) The powers conferred by this section on the Governor-General shall, in relation to their respective Provinces, be exercizable also by the Governors of the Provinces which, under this Act, are to cease to exist; and those powers shall, for the purposes of the Government of India Act, 1935, be deemed to be matters as respects which the Governors are, under that Act, to exercize their individual judgment.

(3) This section shall be deemed to have had effect as from the third day of June, nineteen hundred and forty-seven, and any order of the Governor-General or any Governor made on

or after that date as to any matter shall have effect accordingly, and any order made under this section may be made so as to be retrospective to any date not earlier than the said third day of June:

Provided that no person shall be deemed to be guilty of an offence by reason of so much of any such order as makes any provision thereof retrospective to any date before the making thereof.

(4) Any orders made under this section, whether before or after the appointed day, shall have effect:

(a) up to the appointed day, in British India;
(b) on and after the appointed day, in the new Dominion or Dominions concerned; and
(c) outside British India, or, as the case may be, outside the new Dominion or Dominions concerned, to such extent whether before, on or after the appointed day, as a law of the Legislature of the Dominion or Dominions concerned would have on or after the appointed day,

but shall, in the case of each of the Dominions, be subject to the same powers of repeal and amendment as laws of the Legislature of that Dominion.

(5) No order shall be made under this section, by the Governor of any Province, after the appointed day, or, by the Governor-General, after the thirty-first day of March, nineteen hundred and forty-eight, or such earlier date as may be determined, in the case of either Dominion, by any law of the Legislature of that Dominion.

Section 10

(1) The provisions of this Act keeping in force provisions of the Government of India Act, 1935, shall not continue in force the provisions of that Act relating to appointments to the civil services of, and civil posts under, the Crown in India by the Secretary of State, or the provisions of that Act relating to the reservation of posts.

(2) Every person who:

(a) having been appointed by the Secretary of State, or Secretary of State in Council, to a civil service of the Crown in India continues on and after the appointed day to serve under the Government of either of the new Dominions or of any Province or part thereof: or
(b) having been appointed by His Majesty before the appointed day to be a judge of the Federal Court or of any court which is a High Court within the meaning of the Government of India Act, 1935, continues on and after the appointed day to serve as a judge in either of the new Dominions,

shall be entitled to receive from the Governments of the Dominions and Provinces or parts which he is from time to time serving or, as the case may be, which are served by the courts in which he is from time to time a judge, the same conditions of service as respects remuneration, leave and pension, and the same rights as respects disciplinary matters or, as the case may be, as respects the tenure of his office, or rights as similar thereto as changed circumstances may permit, as that person was entitled to immediately before the appointed day.

(3) Nothing in this Act shall be construed as enabling the rights and liabilities of any person with respect to the family pension funds vested in Commissioners under section two hundred and seventy-three of the Government of India Act, 1935, to be governed otherwise than by Orders in Council made (whether before or after the passing of this Act or the appointed day) by His Majesty in Council and rules made (whether before or after the passing of this Act or the appointed day) by a Secretary of State or such other Minister of the Crown as may be designated in that behalf by Order in Council under the Ministers of the Crown (Transfer of Functions) Act, 1946.

Section 11

(1) The orders to be made by the Governor-General under the preceding provisions of this Act shall make provision for the division of the Indian armed forces of His Majesty between the new Dominions, and for the command and governance of those forces until the division is completed.

(2) As from the appointed day, while any member of His Majesty's forces, other than His Majesty's Indian forces, is attached to or serving with any of His Majesty's Indian forces:

(a) he shall, subject to any provision to the contrary made by a law of the Legislature of the Dominion or Dominions concerned or by any order of the Governor-General under the preceding provisions of this Act, have, in relation to the Indian forces in question, the powers of command and punishment appropriate to his rank and functions; but

(b) nothing in any enactment in force at the date of the passing of this Act shall render him subject in any way to the law governing the Indian forces in question.

SECTION 12

(1) Nothing in this Act affects the jurisdiction or authority of His Majesty's Government in the United Kingdom, or of the Admiralty, the Army Council, or the Air Council or of any other United Kingdom authority, in relation to any of His Majesty's forces which may, on or after the appointed day, be in either of the new Dominions or elsewhere in the territories which, before the appointed day, were included in India, not being Indian forces.

(2) In its application in relation to His Majesty's military forces, other than Indian forces the Army Act shall have effect on or after the appointed day as if His Majesty's Indian forces were not included in the expressions 'the forces', 'His Majesty's forces' and 'the regular forces'.

(3) Subject to the provisions of subsection (2) of this section, and to any provisions of any law of the Legislature of the Dominion concerned, all civil authorities in the new Dominions, and, subject as aforesaid and subject also to the provisions of the last preceding section, all service authorities in the new Dominions, shall, in those Dominions and in the other territories which were included in India before the appointed day, perform in relation to His Majesty's military forces, not being Indian forces, the same functions as were, before the appointed day, performed by them, or by the authorities corresponding to them, whether by virtue of the Army Act or otherwise, and the matters for which provision is to be made by orders of the Governor-General under the preceding provisions of this Act shall include the facilitating of the withdrawal from the new Dominions and other territories aforesaid of His Majesty's military forces, not being Indian forces.

(4) The provisions of subsections (2) and (3) of this section shall apply in relation to the air forces of His Majesty, not being Indian air forces, as they apply in relation to His Majesty's military forces, subject, however, to the necessary adaptations, and, in particular, as if for the references to the Army Act there were substituted references to the Air Force Act.

SECTION 13

(1) In the application of the Naval Discipline Act to His Majesty's naval forces, other than Indian naval forces, references to His Majesty's navy and His Majesty's ships shall not, as from the appointed day, include references to His Majesty's Indian navy or the ships thereof.

(2) In the application of the Naval Discipline Act by virtue of any law made in India before the appointed day to Indian naval forces, references to His Majesty's navy and His Majesty's ships shall, as from the appointed day, be deemed to be, and to be only, references to His Majesty's Indian navy and the ships thereof.

SECTION 14

(1) A Secretary of State, or such other Minister of the Crown as may be designated in that behalf by Order in Council under the Ministers of the Crown (Transfer of Functions) Act, 1946, is hereby authorized to continue for the time being the performance, on behalf of whatever government or governments may be concerned, of functions as to the making of payments and other matters similar to the functions which, up to the appointed day, the Secretary of State was performing on behalf of governments constituted or continued under the Government of India Act, 1935.

(2) The functions referred to in subsection (1) of this section include functions as respects the management of, and the making of payments in respect of, government debt, and any enactments relating to such debt shall have effect accordingly:

Provided that nothing in this subsection shall be construed as continuing in force so much of any enactment as empowers the Secretary of State to contract sterling loans on behalf of any such Government as aforesaid or as applying to the Government of either of the new Dominions the prohibition imposed on the Governor-General in Council by section three hundred and fifteen of the Government of India Act, 1935, as respects the contracting of sterling loans.

(3) As from the appointed day, there shall not be any such advisers of the Secretary of State as are provided for by section two hundred and seventy-eight of the Government of India Act, 1935, and that section, and any provisions of that Act which require the Secretary of State to obtain the concurrence of his advisers, are hereby repealed as from that day.

(4) The Auditor of Indian Home Accounts is hereby authorized to continue for the time being to exercize his functions as respects the accounts of the Secretary of State or any such other Minister of the Crown as is mentioned in subsection (1) of this section, both in respect of activities before, and in respect of activities after, the appointed day, in the same manner, as nearly as may be as he would have done if this Act had not passed.

Section 15

(1) Notwithstanding anything in this Act, and, in particular, notwithstanding any of the provisions of the last preceding section, any provision of any enactment which, but for the passing of this Act, would authorize legal proceedings to be taken, in India or elsewhere, by or against the Secretary of State in respect of any right or liability of India or any part of India shall cease to have effect on the appointed day, and any legal proceedings pending by virtue of any such provision on the appointed day shall, by virtue of this Act, abate on the appointed day, so far as the Secretary of State is concerned.

(2) Subject to the provisions of this subsection, any legal proceedings which, but for the passing of this Act, could have been brought by or against the Secretary of State in respect of any right or liability of India, or any part of India, shall instead be brought:

(a) in the case of proceedings in the United Kingdom, by or against the High Commissioner;

(b) in the case of other proceedings, by or against such person as may be designated by order of the Governor-General under the preceding provisions of this Act or otherwise by the law of the new Dominion concerned,

and any legal proceedings by or against the Secretary of State in respect of any such right or liability as aforesaid which are pending immediately before the appointed day shall be continued by or against the High Commissioner or, as the case may be, the person designated as aforesaid:

Provided that, at any time after the appointed day, the right conferred by this subsection to bring or continue proceedings may, whether the proceedings are by, or are against, the High Commissioner or person designated as aforesaid, be withdrawn by a law of the Legislature of either of the new Dominions so far as that Dominion is concerned, and any such law may operate as respects proceedings pending at the date of the passing of the law.

(3) In this section, the expression 'the High Commissioner' means, in relation to each of the new Dominions, any such officer as may for the time being be authorized to perform in the United Kingdom, in relation to that Dominion, functions similar to those performed before the appointed day, in relation to the Governor-General in Council, by the High Commissioner referred to in section three hundred and two of the Government of India Act, 1935; and any legal proceedings which, immediately before the appointed day, are the subject of an appeal to His Majesty in Council, or of a petition for special leave to appeal to His Majesty in Council, shall be treated for the purposes of this section as legal proceedings pending in the United Kingdom.

Section 17

(1) No court in either of the new Dominions shall, by virtue of the Indian and Colonial Divorce Jurisdiction Acts, 1926 and 1940, have jurisdiction in or in relation to any proceedings for a decree for the dissolution of a marriage, unless those proceedings were instituted before the appointed day, but, save as aforesaid and subject to any provision to the contrary which may hereafter be made by any Act of the Parliament of the United Kingdom or by any law of the Legislature of the new Dominion concerned, all courts in the new Dominions shall have the same jurisdiction under the said Acts as they would have had if this Act had not been passed.

(2) Any rules made on or after the appointed day under subsection (4) of section one of the Indian and Colonial Divorce Jurisdiction Act, 1926, for a court in either of the new

Dominions shall, instead of being made by the Secretary of State with the concurrence of the Lord Chancellor, be made by such authority as may be determined by the law of the Dominion concerned, and so much of the said subsection and of any rules in force thereunder immediately before the appointed day as require the approval of the Lord Chancellor to the nomination for any purpose of any judges of any such court shall cease to have effect.

(3) The reference in subsection (1) of this section to proceedings for a decree for the dissolution of a marriage includes references to proceedings for such a decree of presumption of death and dissolution of a marriage as is authorized by section eight of the Matrimonial Causes Act, 1937.

(4) Nothing in this section affects any court outside the new Dominions, and the power conferred by section two of the Indian and Colonial Divorce Jurisdiction Act, 1926, to apply certain provisions of that Act to other parts of His Majesty's dominions as they apply to India shall be deemed to be power to apply those provisions as they would have applied to India if this Act had not passed.

Section 18

(1) In so far as any Act of Parliament, Order in Council, order, rule, regulation or other instrument passed or made before the appointed day operates otherwise than as part of the law of British India or the new Dominions, references therein to India or British India, however worded and whether by name or not, shall, in so far as the context permits and except so far as Parliament may hereafter otherwise provide, be construed as, or as including, references to the new Dominions, taken together, or taken separately, according as the circumstances and subject matter may require:

Provided that nothing in this subsection shall be construed as continuing in operation any provision in so far as the continuance thereof as adapted by this subsection is inconsistent with any of the provisions of this Act other than this section.

(2) Subject to the provisions of subsection (1) of this section and to any other express provision of this Act, the Orders in Council made under subsection (5) of section three hundred and eleven of the Government of India Act, 1935, for adapting and modifying Acts of Parliament shall, except so far as Parliament may hereafter otherwise provide, continue in force in relation to all Acts in so far as they operate otherwise than as part of the law of British India or the new Dominions.

(3) Save as otherwise expressly provided in this Act, the law of British India and of the several parts thereof existing immediately before the appointed day shall, so far as applicable and with the necessary adaptations, continue as the law of each of the new Dominions and the several parts thereof until other provision is made by laws of the Legislature of the Dominion in question or by any other Legislature or other authority having power in that behalf.

(4) It is hereby declared that the Instruments of Instructions issued before the passing of this Act by His Majesty to the Governor-General and the Governors of Provinces lapse as from the appointed day, and nothing in this Act shall be construed as continuing in force any provision of the Government of India Act, 1935, relating to such Instruments of Instructions.

(5) As from the appointed day, so much of any enactment as requires the approval of His Majesty in Council to any rules of court shall not apply to any court in either of the new Dominions.

Section 19

(1) References in this Act to the Governor-General shall, in relation to any order to be made or other act done on or after the appointed day, be construed:

- (a) where the order or other act concerns one only of the new Dominions, as references to the Governor-General of that Dominion;
- (b) where the order or other act concerns both of the new Dominions and the same person is the Governor-General of both those Dominions, as references to that person; and
- (c) in any other case, as references to the Governors-General of the new Dominions, acting jointly.

(2) References in this Act to the Governor-General shall, in relation to any order to be

made or other act done before the appointed day, be construed as references to the Governor-General of India within the meaning of the Government of India Act, 1935, and so much of that or any other Act as requires references to the Governor-General to be construed as references to the Governor-General in Council shall not apply to references to the Governor-General in this Act.

(3) References in this Act to the Constituent Assembly of a Dominion shall be construed as references:

(a) in relation to India, to the Constituent Assembly, the first sitting whereof was held on the ninth day of December, nineteen hundred and forty-six, modified:

(i) by the exclusion of the members representing Bengal, the Punjab, Sind and British Baluchistan; and

(ii) should it appear that the North West Frontier Province will form part of Pakistan, by the exclusion of the members representing that Province; and

(iii) by the inclusion of members representing West Bengal and East Punjab; and

(iv) should it appear that, on the appointed day, a part of the Province of Assam is to form part of the new Province of East Bengal, by the exclusion of the members theretofore representing the Province of Assam and the inclusion of members chosen to represent the remainder of that Province;

(b) in relation to Pakistan, to the Assembly set up or about to be set up at the date of the passing of this Act under the authority of the Governor-General as the Constituent Assembly for Pakistan:

Provided that nothing in this subsection shall be construed as affecting the extent to which representatives of the Indian States take part in either of the said Assemblies, or as preventing the filling of casual vacancies in the said Assemblies, or as preventing the participation in either of the said Assemblies, in accordance with such arrangements as may be made in that behalf, of representatives of the tribal areas on the borders of the Dominion for which that Assembly sits, and the powers of the said Assemblies shall extend and be deemed always to have extended to the making of provision for the matters specified in this proviso.

(4) In this Act, except so far as the context otherwise requires:

references to the Government of India Act, 1935, include references to any enactments amending or supplementing that Act, and, in particular, references to the India (Central Government and Legislature) Act, 1946;

'India', where the reference is to a state of affairs existing before the appointed day or which should have existed but for the passing of this Act, has the meaning assigned to it by section three hundred and eleven of the Government of India Act, 1935;

'Indian forces' includes all His Majesty's Indian forces existing before the appointed day and also any forces of either of the new Dominions;

'pension' means, in relation to any person, a pension whether contributory or not, of any kind whatsoever payable to or in respect of that person, and includes retired pay so payable, a gratuity so payable and any sum or sums so payable by way of the return, with or without interest thereon or other additions thereto, of subscriptions to a provident fund;

'Province' means a Governor's Province;

'remuneration' includes leave pay, allowances and the cost of any privileges or facilities provided in kind.

(5) Any power conferred by this Act to make any order includes power to revoke or vary any order previously made in the exercise of that power.

SECTION 20

This Act may be cited as the Indian Independence Act, 1947.

JOINT STATEMENT BY INDIA AND PAKISTAN ON BORDER PROBLEMS

New Delhi, 12th September, 1958

On the invitation of the Prime Minister of India, the Prime Minister of Pakistan visited New Delhi from September 9th to 11th. During this visit, the Prime Ministers of Pakistan and India discussed various Indo-Pakistan border problems with a view to removing causes of tension and establishing peaceful conditions along the Indo-Pakistan border areas.

The Prime Ministers had frank and friendly discussions about these border problems. They arrived and agreed settlements in regard to most of the border disputes in the eastern region. They also agreed to an exchange of enclaves of the former Cooch Behar State in Pakistan and Pakistan enclaves in India.

Some of the border disputes, namely, two regarding the Radcliffe and Bagge Awards in the eastern region, and five in the western region, require further consideration.

The Prime Ministers agreed to issue necessary instructions to their survey staff to expedite demarcation in the light of the settlements arrived at and to consider further methods of settling the disputes that are still unresolved. In regard to the Husainiwala and Suleimanke disputes, the Foreign Secretary of the Pakistan Government and the Commonwealth Secretary of the Government of India, will, in consultation with their engineers, submit proposals to the Prime Ministers.

The Prime Ministers agreed that when areas are exchanged, on agreed dates, as a result of settlement and demarcation of these disputed areas, an appeal should be made to the people in the areas exchanged to continue staying in their present homes as nationals of the State to which the areas are transferred.

The Prime Ministers further agreed that, pending the settlement of unresolved disputes and the demarcation and exchange of territory by mutual agreement, there should be no disturbance of the status quo by force and peace conditions must be maintained in the border regions. Necessary instructions in this regard will be issued to the respective States and to the local authorities on the border.

The Prime Ministers agreed to keep in touch with each other with a view to considering various steps to be taken to further their common objective of maintaining and developing friendly and co-operative relations between their two countries.

AGREEMENT BETWEEN INDIA AND PAKISTAN CONCERNING MINORITIES

New Delhi, 8th April, 1950

A. The Governments of India and Pakistan solemnly agree that each shall ensure, to the minorities throughout its territory, complete equality of citizenship, irrespective of religion, a full sense of security in respect of life, culture, property and personal honour, freedom of movement within each Country and freedom of occupation, speech and worship, subject to law and morality. Members of the minorities shall have equal opportunity with members of the major community to participate in the public life of their Country, to hold political or other office, and to serve in their Country's civil and armed forces. Both Governments declare these rights to be fundamental and undertake to enforce them effectively. The Prime Minister of India has drawn attention to the fact that these rights are guaranteed to all minorities in India by its constitution. The Prime Minister of Pakistan has pointed out that similar provision exists in the Objectives Resolution adopted by the Constituent Assembly of Pakistan. It is the policy of both Governments that the enjoyment of these democratic rights shall be assured to all their nationals without distinction.

Both Governments wish to emphasise that the allegiance and loyalty of the minorities is to the State of which they are citizens, and that it is to the Government of their own State that they should look for the redress of their grievances.

B. In respect of migrants from East Bengal, West Bengal, Assam and Tripura, where communal disturbances have recently occurred, it is agreed between the two Governments:

(1) That there shall be freedom of movement and protection in transit.

(2) That there shall be freedom to remove as much of his movable personal effects and household goods as a migrant may wish to take with him. Movable property shall include personal jewellery. The maximum cash allowed to each adult migrant will be Rs. 150 and to each migrant child Rs. 75.

(3) That a migrant may deposit such of his personal jewellery or cash as he does not wish to take with him with a Bank. A proper receipt shall be furnished to him by the Bank for cash or jewellery thus deposited and facilities shall be provided as and when required, for their transfer to him subject, as regards cash, to the exchange regulations of the Government concerned.

(4) That there shall be no harassment by the Customs authorities. At each Customs post agreed upon by the Governments concerned, liaison officers of the other Government shall be posted to ensure this in practice.

(5) Rights of ownership in or occupancy of the immovable property of a migrant shall not be disturbed. If, during his absence, such property is occupied by another person, it shall be returned to him, provided that he comes back by the 31st December, 1950. Where the migrant was a cultivating owner or tenant, the land shall be restored to him, provided that he returns not later than the 31st December, 1950. In exceptional cases, if a Government considers that a migrant's immovable property cannot be returned to him, the matter shall be referred to the appropriate Minority Commission for advice.

Where restoration of immovable property to the migrant who returns within the specified period is found not possible the Government concerned shall take steps to rehabilitate him.

(6) That in the case of a migrant who decides not to return, ownership of all his immovable property shall continue to vest in him and he shall have unrestricted right to dispose of it by sale, by exchange with an evacuee in the other Country, or otherwise. A committee consisting of three representatives of the minority and presided over by a representative of the Government shall act as trustees of the owner. The Committee shall be empowered to recover rent for such immovable property according to law.

The Governments of East Bengal, West Bengal, Assam and Tripura shall enact the necessary legislation to set up these committees.

The Provincial or State Government, as the case may be, will instruct the District or other appropriate authority to give all possible assistance for the discharge of the Committee's functions.

The Provisions of the sub-paragraph shall also apply to migrants who may have left East Bengal for any part of India, or West Bengal, Assam or Tripura for any part of Pakistan prior to the recent disturbances but after the 15th August, 1947. The arrangement in this sub-paragraph will apply also to migrants who have left Bihar for East Bengal owing to communal disturbances or fear thereof.

C. As regards the Province of East Bengal and each of the States of West Bengal, Assam, and Tripura respectively, the two Governments further agree that they shall:

(1) Continue their efforts to restore normal conditions and shall take suitable measures to prevent recurrence of disorder.

(2) Punish all those who are found guilty of offences against persons and property, and of other criminal offences. In view of their deterrent effect, collective fines shall be imposed, where necessary; special courts will, where necessary, be appointed to ensure that wrongdoers are promptly punished.

(3) Make every possible effort to recover looted property.

(4) Set up immediately an agency, with which representatives of the minority shall be associated, to assist in the recovery of abducted women.

(5) Not recognise forced conversions. Any conversion effected during a period of communal disturbance shall be deemed to be a forced conversion. Those found guilty of converting people forcibly shall be punished.

(6) Set up a Commission of Enquiry at once to enquire into and report on the causes and extent of the recent disturbances and to make recommendations with a view to preventing recrudescence of similar trouble in future. The personnel of the Commission which shall be presided over by a Judge of the High Court, shall be such as to inspire confidence among the minority.

(7) Take prompt and effective steps to prevent the dissemination of news and mischievous opinion calculated to rouse communal passion by press or radio or by any individual or organisation. Those guilty of such activity shall be rigorously dealt with.

(8) Not permit propaganda in either Country directed against the territorial integrity of the other or purporting to incite war between them and shall take prompt and effective action against any individual or organisation guilty of such propaganda.

D. Sub-paragraphs 1, 2, 3, 4, 5, 7 and 8 of C of the Agreement are of general scope and applicable, according to exigency, to any part of India or Pakistan.

E. In order to help restore confidence, so that refugees may return to their homes, the two Governments have decided:

(1) To depute two Ministers, one from each Government, to remain in the affected areas for such period as may be necessary;

(2) To include in the Cabinets of East Bengal, West Bengal and Assam a representative of the minority community. In Assam the minority community is already represented in the Cabinet. Appointments to the Cabinets of East Bengal and West Bengal shall be made immediately.

F. In order to assist in the implementation of this Agreement, the two Governments have decided apart from the deputation of their Ministers referred to in E, to set up Minority Commissions, one for East Bengal, one for West Bengal and one for Assam. These Commissions will be constituted and will have the functions described below.

(1) Each Commission will consist of one Minister of the Provincial or State Government concerned, who will be chairman, and one representative each of the majority committees from East Bengal, West Bengal and Assam, chosen by and from their respective representatives in the provincial or state legislatures, as the case may be.

(2) The two Ministers of the Government of India and Pakistan may attend and participate in any meeting of any Commission. A minority Commission or any two minority Commissions jointly shall meet when so required by either Central Minister for the satisfactory implementation of this Agreement.

(3) Each Commission shall appoint such staff as it deems necessary for the proper discharge of its functions and shall determine its own procedure.

(4) Each Commission shall maintain contact with the minorities in Districts and small Administrative headquarters through Minority Boards formed in accordance with the Inter-Dominion Agreement of December, 1948.

(5) The Minority Commissions in East Bengal and West Bengal shall replace the Provincial Minorities Board set up under the Inter-Dominion Agreement of December, 1948.

(6) The two Ministers of the Central Governments will, from time to time, consult such persons or organisations as they may consider necessary.

(7) The functions of the Minority Commission shall be:

(a) To observe and to report on the implementation of this Agreement and, for this purpose, to take cognisance of breaches or neglect.

(b) To advise on actions to be taken on their recommendations.

(8) Each Commission shall submit reports, as and when necessary to the Provincial and State Governments concerned. Copies of such reports will be submitted simultaneously to the two Central Ministers during the period referred to in E.

(9) The Governments of India and Pakistan, and the State and Provincial Governments, will normally give effect to recommendations that concern them when such recommendations are supported by both the Central Ministers. In the event of disagreement between the two Central Ministers, the matter shall be referred to the Prime Ministers of India and Pakistan who shall either resolve it themselves or determine the Agency and procedure by which it will be resolved.

(10) In respect of Tripura, the two Central Ministers shall constitute a Commission and shall discharge the functions that are assigned under the Agreement to the Minority Commissions for East Bengal, West Bengal and Assam. Before the expiration of the period referred to in E, the two Central Ministers shall make recommendations for the establishment in

Tripura of appropriate machinery to discharge the functions of the Minority Commissions envisaged in respect of East Bengal and Assam.

G. Except where modified by this Agreement, the Inter-Dominion Agreement of December, 1948, shall remain in force.

Signed: Jawaharlal Nehru (Prime Minister of India)

Liaquat Ali Khan (Prime Minister of Pakistan)

New Delhi, 8th April, 1950

AGREEMENT BETWEEN INDIA AND CHINA CONCERNING TIBET

PEKING, 19TH APRIL, 1954

The Government of the Republic of India and the Central People's Government of the People's Republic of China:

Being desirous of promoting trade and cultural intercourse between the Tibet region of China and India and of facilitating pilgrimage and travel by the people of China and India;

Have resolved to enter into the present agreement based on the following principles:

(1) Mutual respect for each other's territorial integrity and sovereignty;

(2) Mutual non-aggression;

(3) Mutual non-interference in each other's internal affairs;

(4) Equality and mutual benefit;

(5) Peaceful co-existence.

ARTICLE 1

The High Contracting Parties mutually agree to establish trade agencies:

(I) The Government of India agree that the Government of China may establish trade agencies at New Delhi, Calcutta and Kalimpong.

(II) The Government of China agree that the Government of India may establish trade agencies at Yatung, Gyangtse and Gartok.

The Trade Agencies of both parties shall be accorded the same status and same treatment. The Trade Agents of both parties shall enjoy freedom from arrest while exercising their functions, and shall enjoy in respect of themselves, their wives and children who are dependent on them for their livelihood freedom from search.

The Trade Agencies of both parties shall enjoy the privileges and immunities for couriers, mail bags and communications in code.

ARTICLE 2

The High Contracting Parties agree that traders of both countries known to be customarily and specifically engaged in trade between the Tibet region of China and India may trade at the following places:

(1) The Government of India agree to specify (1) Yatung, (2) Gyangtse and (3) Phari as markets for trade; the Government of India agree that trade may be carried on in India including places like (1) Kalimpong, (2) Siliguri and (3) Calcutta, according to customary practice.

(2) The Government of China agree to specify (1) Gartok, (2) Pulanchung (Taklakot), (3) Gyalima-Khargo, (4) Gyanima-Chakra, (5) Ranura, (6) Dongbra, (7) Puling Sumdo, (8) Nabra, (9) Shangtse and (10) Tashigong as markets for trade; the Government of India agree that in future when in accordance with the development and need of trade between the Ari district of the Tibet region of China and India, it has become necessary to specify markets

for trade in the corresponding district in India adjacent to the Ari district of the Tibet region of China, it will be prepared to consider on the basis of equality and reciprocity to do so.

ARTICLE 3

The High Contracting Parties agree that pilgrimages by religious believers of the two countries shall be carried on in accordance with the following provisions:

(1) Pilgrims from India or Lamaist, Hindu and Buddhist faiths may visit Kang Rimpoche, (Kailash) and Mavam Tse (Manasarowar) in the Tibet region of China in accordance with custom.

(2) Pilgrims from the Tibet region of China of Lamaist and Buddhist faiths may visit Banaras, Sarnath, Gaya and Sanchi in India in accordance with custom.

(3) Pilgrims customarily visiting Lhasa may continue to do so in accordance with custom.

ARTICLE 4

Traders and pilgrims of both countries may travel by the following passes and route:—

(1) Shipli La Pass
(2) Mana Pass
(3) Niti Pass
(4) Kungri Bingri Pass
(5) Darma Pass
(6) Lipu Lekh Pass.

Also the customary route leading to Tashigong along the valley of Eick Gatasangpu (Indus River) may continue to be traversed in accordance with custom.

ARTICLE 5

For travelling across borders, the High Contracting Parties agree that diplomatic personnel, officials and nationals of the two countries shall hold passports issued by their own respective countries and visaed by the other party except as provided in paragraphs 1, 2, 3 and 4 of this article.

(1) Traders of both countries known to be customarily and specifically engaged in trade between the Tibet region of China and India, their wives and children, who are dependent on them for livelihood and their attendants will be allowed entry for purposes of trade into India or the Tibet region of China, as the case may be, in accordance with custom on the production of certificates duly issued by the local Government of their own country by its duly authorized agents and examined by the border checkposts of the other party.

(2) Inhabitants of the border districts of the two countries, who cross borders to carry on petty trade or to visit friends and relatives, may proceed to the border districts of the other party as they have customarily done heretofore and need not be restricted to the passes and route specified in Article 4 above and shall not be required to hold passports, visas or permits.

(3) Porters and mule-team drivers of the two countries, who cross the border to perform necessary transportation services, need not hold passports issued by their own country, but shall only hold certificates good for a definite period of time (good for three months, half a year or one year) duly issued by the local Government of their own country or by its duly authorized agents and produce them for registration at the border checkpost of the other party.

(4) Pilgrims of both countries need not carry documents of certification but shall register at the border checkpost of the other party and receive a permit for pilgrimage.

(5) Notwithstanding the provisions of the foregoing paragraph of this article, either Government may refuse entry to any particular person.

(6) Persons who enter the territory of the other party in accordance with the foregoing paragraphs of this article may stay within its territory only after complying with the procedures specified by the other party.

ARTICLE 6

The present Agreement shall come into effect upon ratification by both Governments and shall remain in force for eight years. Extension of the present agreement may be negotiated by the two parties if either party requests for it six months prior to the expiry of the agreement and the request to by the other party.

Signed: N. Raghavan (Plenipotentiary of the Government of the Republic of India)

Chang Han-fu (Plenipotentiary of the Central People's Government of the People's Republic of China)

Peking, 19th April, 1954

JOINT STATEMENT BY PRIME MINISTERS OF INDIA AND CHINA

New Delhi, 28th June, 1954

1. H.E. Chou En-lai, Prime Minister and Foreign Minister of the People's Republic of China, came to Delhi at the invitation of H.E. Jawaharlal Nehru, Prime Minister and Foreign Minister of the Republic of India. He stayed here for three days. During this period the two Prime Ministers discussed many matters of common concern to India and China. In particular they discussed the prospects of peace in South-East Asia and the developments that had taken place in the Geneva Conference in regard to Indo-China. The situation in Indo-China was of vital importance to the peace of Asia and the world and the Prime Ministers were anxious that the efforts that were being made at Geneva should succeed. They noted with satisfaction that some progress had been made in the talks at Geneva in regard to an armistice. They earnestly hoped that these efforts would meet with success in the near future and that they would result in a political settlement of the problems of that area.

2. The talks between the Prime Ministers aimed at helping, in such ways as were possible, the efforts at peaceful settlement that were being made in Geneva and elsewhere. Their main purpose was to arrive at a clearer understanding of each other's points of view in order to help the maintenance of peace, both in co-operation with each other and with other countries.

3. Recently India and China have come to an agreement in which they laid down certain principles which should guide the relations between the two countries. These principles are:
(1) Mutual respect for each other's territorial integrity and sovereignty;
(2) Non-aggression;
(3) Non-interference in each other's internal affairs;
(4) Equality and mutual benefit; and
(5) Peaceful co-existence.

The Prime Ministers reaffirmed these principles and felt that they should be applied in their relations with other countries in Asia as well as in other parts of the world. If these principles are applied not only between various countries but also in international relations generally, they would form a solid foundation for peace and security and the fears and apprehensions that exist today would give place to a feeling of confidence.

4. The Prime Ministers recognised that different social and political systems exist in various parts of Asia and the world. If, however, the above-mentioned principles are accepted and acted upon and there is no interference by any one country with another, these differences should not come in the way of peace or create conflicts. With the assurance of territorial integrity and sovereignty of each country and of non-aggression, there would be peaceful co-existence and friendly relations between the countries concerned. This would lessen the tension that exists in the world today and help in creating a climate of peace.

5. In particular, th. Prime Ministers hoped that these principles would be applied to the solution of the problems in Indo-China where the political settlement should aim at the creation of free, democratic, unified and independent States, which should not be used for aggressive purposes or be subjected to foreign intervention. This would lead to a growth of self-confidence in these countries as well as to friendly relations between them and their

neighbours. The adoption of the principles referred to above would also help in creating an area of peace which, as circumstances permit, could be enlarged, thus lessening the chances of war and strengthening the cause of peace all over the world.

6. The Prime Ministers expressed their confidence in the friendship between India and China which would help the cause of world peace and the peaceful development of their respective countries as well as the other countries of Asia.

7. These conversations were held with a view to help in bringing about a greater understanding of the problems of Asia and to further a peaceful and co-operative effort, in common with the other countries of the world, in solving these and like problems.

The Prime Ministers agreed that their respective countries should maintain close contacts so that there should continue to be full understanding between them. They appreciated greatly the present opportunity of meeting together and having a full exchange of ideas leading to a clear understanding and co-operation in the cause of peace.

KASHMIR

INSTRUMENT OF ACCESSION OF JAMMU AND KASHMIR STATE

26TH OCTOBER, 1947

Whereas the Indian Independence Act, 1947, provides that as from the fifteenth day of August, 1947, there shall be set up an independent Dominion known as INDIA, and that the Government of India Act, 1935, shall with such omissions, additions, adaptions and modifications as the Governor-General may by order specify, be applicable to the Dominion of India;

And whereas the Government of India Act, 1935, as so adapted by the Governor-General, provides that an Indian State may accede to the Dominion of India by an Instrument of Accession executed by the Ruler thereof;

Now therefore I Shriman Indar Mahandar Rajrajeshwar Maharajdhiraj Shri Hari Singhji Jammu Kashmir Naresh Tatha Tibbet adi Deshadhipathi Ruler of JAMMU AND KASHMIR State in the exercise of my sovereignty in and over my said State do hereby execute this my Instrument of Accession and

1. I hereby declare that I accede to the Dominion of India with the intent that the Governor-General of India, the Dominion Legislature, the Federal Court and any other Dominion authority established for the purposes of the Dominion, shall, by virtue of this my Instrument of Accession, but subject always to the terms thereof, and for the purpose only of the Dominion, exercise in relation to the State of Jammu and Kashmir (hereinafter referred to as 'this State') such functions as may be vested in them by or under the Government of India Act, 1935, as in force in the Dominion of India on the 15th day of August 1947, (which Act as so in force is hereinafter referred to as 'the Act').

2. I hereby assume the obligation of ensuring that due effect is given to the provisions of the Act within this State so far as they are applicable therein by virtue of this my Instrument of Accession.

3. I accept the matters specified in the Schedule thereto as the matters with respect to which the Dominion Legislature may make laws for this State.

4. I hereby declare that I accede to the Dominion of India on the assurance that if an agreemen is made between the Governor-General and the Ruler of this State whereby any functions in relation to the administration in this State of any law of the Dominion Legislature shall be exercised by the Ruler of this State, then any such agreement shall be deemed to form part of this Instrument and shall be construed and have effect accordingly.

5. The terms of this my Instrument of Accession shall not be varied by any amendment of the Act or of the Indian Independence Act, 1947, unless such amendment is accepted by me by an Instrument supplementary to this Instrument.

6. Nothing in this Instrument shall empower the Dominion Legislature to make any law for this State authorising the compulsory acquisition of land for any purpose, but I hereby undertake that should the Dominion for the purposes of a Dominion law which applies in this State deem it necessary to acquire any land, I shall at their request acquire the land at their expense or if the land belongs to me transfer it to them on such terms as may be agreed, or, in default of agreement, determined by an arbitrator to be appointed by the Chief Justice of India.

7. Nothing in this Instrument shall be deemed to commit me in any way to acceptance of any future constitution of India or to fetter my discretion to enter into arrangements with the Government of India under any such future constitution.

8. Nothing in this Instrument affects the continuance of my sovereignty in and over this State, or, save as provided by or under this Instrument, the exercise of any powers, authority and rights now enjoyed by me as Ruler of this State or the validity of any law at present in force in this State.

9. I hereby declare that I execute this Instrument on behalf of this State and that any reference in this Instrument to me or to the Rulers of the State is to be construed as including a reference to my heirs and successors.

Given under my hand this 26th day of October nineteen hundred and forty-seven.

Signed: Hari Singh,
(Maharajdhiraj of Jammu and Kashmir State)

I do hereby accept this Instrument of Accession.

Dated this twenty-seventh day of October nineteen hundred and forty-seven.

Signed: Mountbatten of Burma,
(Governor-General of India)

RESOLUTION OF UNITED NATIONS SECURITY COUNCIL

17TH JANUARY, 1948

The Security Council:

Having heard statements on the situation in Kashmir from representatives of the Governments of India and Pakistan;

Recognizing the urgency of the situation;

Taking note of the telegram addressed on 6th January by its President to each of the parties and of their replies thereto; in which they announce their intention to conform to the Charter;

Calls upon both the Government of India and the Government of Pakistan to take immediately all measures within their power (including public appeals to their people) calculated to improve the situation and to refrain from making any statements and from doing or causing to be done or permitting any acts which might aggravate the situation;

And further requests each of those Governments to inform the Council immediately of any material change in the situation which occurs or appears to either of them to be about to occur while the matter is under consideration by the Council, and consult with the Council thereon.

RESOLUTION OF UNITED NATIONS COMMISSION FOR INDIA AND PAKISTAN

13TH AUGUST, 1948

The United Nations Commission for India and Pakistan:

Having given careful consideration to the points of view expressed by the representatives of India and Pakistan regarding the situation in the State of Jammu and Kashmir; and

Being of the opinion that the prompt cessation of hostilities and the correction of conditions the continuance of which is likely to endanger international peace and security are essential to implementation of its endeavours to assist the Governments of India and Pakistan in affecting a final settlement of the situation;

Resolves to submit simultaneously to the Governments of India and Pakistan the following proposal:

PART I

Cease-Fire Order

A. The Governments of India and Pakistan agree that their respective High Commands will issue separately and simultaneously a cease-fire order to apply to all forces under their control in the State of Jammu and Kashmir as of the earliest practicable date or dates to be mutually agreed upon within four days after these proposals have been accepted by both Governments.

B. The High Commands of the Indian and Pakistani forces agree to refrain from taking any measures that might augment the military potential of the forces under their control in the State of Jammu and Kashmir.

(For the purpose of these proposals forces under their control shall be considered to include all forces, organised and unorganised, fighting or participating in hostilities on their respective sides.)

C. The Commanders-in-Chief of the forces of India and Pakistan shall promptly confer regarding any necessary local changes in present dispositions which may facilitate the cease-fire.

D. In its discretion and as the Commission may find practicable, the Commission will appoint military observers who, under the authority of the Commission and with the co-operation of both Commands, will supervise the observance of the cease-fire order.

E. The Government of India and the Government of Pakistan agree to appeal to their respective peoples to assist in creating and maintaining an atmosphere favourable to the promotion of further negotiations.

Part II

Truce Agreement

Simultaneously with the acceptance of the proposal for the immediate cessation of hostilities outlined in Part I, both Governments accept the following principles as a basis for the formulation of a truce agreement, the details of which shall be worked out in discussion between their representatives and the Commission.

A

1. As the presence of troops of Pakistan in the territory of the State of Jammu and Kashmir constitutes a material change in the situation since it was represented by the Government of Pakistan before the Security Council, the Government of Pakistan agrees to withdraw its troops from that State.

2. The Government of Pakistan will use its best endeavour to secure the withdrawal from the State of Jammu and Kashmir of tribesmen and Pakistani nationals not normally resident therein who have entered the State for the purpose of fighting.

3. Pending a final solution, the territory evacuated by the Pakistani troops will be administered by the local authorities under the surveillance of the Commission.

B

1. When the Commission shall have notified the Government of India that the tribesmen and Pakistani nationals referred to in part II A2 hereof have withdrawn, thereby terminating the situation which was represented by the Government of India to the Security Council as having occasioned the presence of Indian forces in the State of Jammu and Kashmir, and further, that the Pakistani forces are being withdrawn from the State of Jammu and Kashmir, the Government of India agrees to begin to withdraw the bulk of its forces from that State in stages to be agreed upon with the Commission.

2. Pending the acceptance of the conditions for a final settlement of the situation in the State of Jammu and Kashmir, the Indian Government will maintain within the lines existing at the moment of the cease-fire the minimum strength of its forces which in agreement with the Commission are considered necessary to assist local authorities in the observance of law and order. The Commission will have observers stationed where it deems necessary.

3. The Government of India will undertake to ensure that the Government of the State of Jammu and Kashmir will take all measures within its power to make it publicly known that peace, law and order will be safeguarded and that all human and political rights will be guaranteed.

C

Upon signature, the full text of the truce agreement or a communiqué containing the principles thereof as agreed upon between the two Governments and the Commission will be made public.

PART III

The Government of India and the Government of Pakistan reaffirm their wish that the future status of the State of Jammu and Kashmir shall be determined in accordance with the will of the people and to that end, upon acceptance of the truce agreement, both Governments agree to enter into consultations with the Commission to determine fair and equitable conditions whereby such free expression will be assured.

LETTER FROM PRIME MINISTER OF INDIA TO CHAIRMAN IN REPLY TO UNITED NATIONS COMMISSION'S RESOLUTION OF 13TH AUGUST, 1948

NEW DELHI, 20TH AUGUST, 1948

1. On 17th August, my colleague, the Minister without Portfolio, and I discussed with you and your colleagues of the Commission now in Delhi the Resolution which you had presented to us on the 14th instant. On the 18th, I had another discussion with you, in the course of which I tried to explain to you the doubts and difficulties which members of my Government, and representatives of the Government of Kashmir whom we consulted, had felt as the result of a preliminary but careful examination of the Commission's proposals.

2. During the several conferences that we had with the Commission when it first came to Delhi, we placed before it what we considered the basic fact of the situation which had led to the conflict in Kashmir. This fact was the unwarranted aggression, at first indirect and subsequently direct, of the Pakistan Government on Indian Dominion territory in Kashmir. The Pakistan Government denied this although it was common knowledge. In recent months, very large forces of the regular Pakistan Army have further entered Indian Union territory in Kashmir and opposed the Indian Army which was sent there for the defence of the State. This, we understand now, is admitted by the Pakistan Government, and yet there has been at no time any intimation to the Government of India by the Pakistan Government of this invasion; there has been a continual denial and the Pakistan Government have evaded answering repeated inquiries from the Government of India.

In accordance with the Resolution of the Security Council of the United Nations adopted on 17th January, 1948, the Pakistan Government should have informed the Council immediately of any material change in the situation while the matter continues to be under the consideration of the Council. The invasion of the State by large forces of the regular Pakistan Army was a very material change in the situation, and yet no information of this was given so far as we know to the Security Council.

The Commission will appreciate that this conduct of the Pakistan Government is not only opposed to all moral codes as well as international law and usage, but has also created a very grave situation. It is only the earnest desire of my Government to avoid any extension of the field of conflict and to restore peace, that has led us to refrain from taking any action to meet the new situation that was created by this further intrusion of the Pakistan Army into Jammu and Kashmir State. The presence of the Commission in India has naturally led us to hope that any arrangement sponsored by it would deal effectively with the present situation and prevent any recurrence of aggression.

3. Since our meeting of 18th August, we have given the Commission's Resolution our most earnest thought. There are many parts of it, which we should have preferred to be otherwise and more in keeping with the fundamental facts of the situation, especially the flagrant aggression of the Pakistan Government on Indian Union territory. We recognize, however, that if a successful effort is to be made to create satisfactory conditions for a solution of the Kashmir problem without further bloodshed, we should concentrate on certain essentials only at present and seek safeguards in regard to them. It was in this spirit that I placed the following considerations before Your Excellency:

(1) That paragraph A3 of Part II of the Resolution should not be interpreted, or applied in practice, so as:

(a) To bring into question the sovereignty of the Jammu and Kashmir Government over the portion of their territory evacuated by Pakistan troops;

(b) To afford any recognition of the so-called 'Azad Kashmir Government'; or

(c) To enable this territory to be consolidated in any way during the period of truce to the disadvantage of the State.

(2) That from our point of view the effective insurance of the security of the State against external aggression, from which Kashmir has suffered so much during the last ten months, was of the most vital significance and no less important than the observance of internal law and order and that, therefore, the withdrawal of Indian troops and the strength of Indian forces maintained in Kashmir should be conditioned by this overriding factor.

Thus at any time the strength of the Indian forces maintained in Kashmir should be sufficient to ensure security against any form of external aggression as well as internal disorder.

(3) That as regards Part III, should it be decided to seek a solution of the future of the State by means of a plebiscite, Pakistan should have no part in the organization and conduct of the plebiscite or in any other matter of internal administration in the State.

4. If I understood you correctly, A3 of Part II of the Resolution does not envisage the creation of any of the conditions to which we have objected in paragraph 3(1) of this letter. In fact, you made it clear that the Commission was not competent to recognize the sovereignty of any authority over the evacuated areas other than that of the Jammu and Kashmir Government.

As regards paragraph 3(2), the paramount need for security is recognized by the Commission, and the time when the withdrawal of Indian forces from the State is to begin, the stages in which it is to be carried out and the strength of Indian forces to be retained in the State, are matters for settlement between the Commission and the Government of India.

Finally, you agreed that Part III, as formulated, does not in any way recognize the right of Pakistan to have any part in a plebiscite.

5. In view of this clarification, my Government, animated by a sincere desire to promote the cause of peace, and thus to uphold the principles and prestige of the United Nations, have decided to accept the Resolution.

REPLY FROM CHAIRMAN OF UNITED NATIONS COMMISSION TO LETTER FROM PRIME MINISTER OF INDIA OF 20TH AUGUST, 1948

New Delhi, 25th August, 1948

I have the honour to acknowledge the receipt of your communication dated 20th August. 1948, regarding the terms of the resolution of the United Nations Commission for India and Pakistan which the Commission presented to you on 14th August, 1948.

The Commission requests me to convey to Your Excellency its view that the interpretation of the Resolution as expressed in paragraph 4 of your letter coincides with its own interpretation, it being understood that as regards point 3 (1) (a) the local people of the evacuated territory will have freedom of legitimate political activity. In this connection, the term 'evacuated territory' refers to those territories in the State of Jammu and Kashmir which are at present under the effective control of the Pakistan High Command.

The Commission wishes me to express to Your Excellency its sincere satisfaction that the Government of India has accepted the Resolution and appreciates that spirit in which this decision has been taken.

RESOLUTION OF UNITED NATIONS COMMISSION FOR INDIA AND PAKISTAN

5th January, 1949

The United Nations Commission for India and Pakistan;

Having received from the Governments of India and Pakistan, in communications dated 23 December and 25 December, 1948, respectively, their acceptance of the following principles which are supplementary to the Commission's Resolution of 13 August, 1948:

1. The question of the accession of the State of Jammu and Kashmir to India or Pakistan will be decided through the democratic method of a free and impartial plebiscite.

2. A plebiscite will be held when it shall be found by the Commission that the cease-fire and truce arrangements set forth in Parts I and II of the Commission's Resolution of 13 August, 1948, have been carried out and arrangements for the plebiscite have been completed.

3. (a) The Secretary-General of the United Nations will, in agreement with the Commission, nominate a Plebiscite Administrator who shall be a personality of high international standing and commanding general confidence. He will be formally appointed to office by the Government of Jammu and Kashmir;

(b) The Plebiscite Administrator shall derive from the State of Jammu and Kashmir the powers he considers necessary for organizing and conducting the plebiscite and for ensuring the freedom and impartiality of the plebiscite;

(c) The Plebiscite Administrator shall have authority to appoint such staff of assistants and observers as he may require.

4. (a) After implementation of Parts I and II of the Commission's Resolution of 13 August, 1948, and when the Commission is satisfied that peaceful conditions have been restored in the State, the Commission and the Plebiscite Administrator will determine, in consultation with the Government of India, the final disposal of Indian and State armed forces, such disposal to be with due regard to the security of the State and the freedom of the plebiscite;

(b) As regards the territory referred to in A2 of Part II of the Resolution of 13 August, final disposal of the armed forces in that territory will be determined by the Commission and the Plebiscite Administrator in consultation with the local authorities.

5. All civil and military authorities within the State and the principal political elements of the State will be required to co-operate with the Plebiscite Administrator in the preparation for and the holding of the plebiscite.

6. (a) All citizens of the State who have left it on account of the disturbances will be invited and be free to return and to exercise all their rights as such citizens. For the purpose of facilitating repatriation there shall be appointed two Commissions, one composed of nominees of India and the other of nominees of Pakistan. The Commissions shall operate under the direction of the Plebiscite Administrator. The Governments of India and Pakistan and all authorities within the State of Jammu and Kashmir will collaborate with the Plebiscite Administrator in putting this provision into effect;

(b) All persons (other than citizens of the State) who on or since 15 August, 1947, have entered it for other than lawful purpose, shall be required to leave the State.

7. All authorities within the State of Jammu and Kashmir will undertake to ensure, in collaboration with the Plebiscite Administrator, that:

(a) There is no threat, coercion or intimidation, bribery or other undue influence on the voters in the plebiscite;

(b) No restrictions are placed on legitimate political activity throughout the State. All subjects of the State, regardless of creed, caste or party, shall be safe and free in expressing their views and in voting on the question of the accession of the State to India or Pakistan. There shall be freedom of the press, speech, and assembly and freedom of travel in the State, including freedom of lawful entry and exit;

(c) All political prisoners are released;

(d) Minorities in all parts of the State are accorded adequate protection; and

(e) There is no victimization.

8. The Plebiscite Administrator may refer to the United Nations Commission for India and Pakistan problems on which he may require assistance, and the Commission may in its discretion call upon the Plebiscite Administrator to carry out on its behalf any of the responsibilities with which it has been entrusted.

9. At the conclusion of the plebiscite the Plebiscite Administrator shall report the result thereof to the Commission and to the Government of Jammu and Kashmir. The Commission shall then certify to the Security Council whether the plebiscite has or has not been free and impartial.

10. Upon the signature of the truce agreement the details of the foregoing proposals will

be elaborated in the consultations envisaged in Part III of the Commission's Resolution of 13 August, 1948. The Plebiscite Administrator will be fully associated in these consultations:

Commends the Governments of India and Pakistan for their prompt action in ordering a cease-fire to take effect from one minute before midnight of 1 January, 1949, pursuant to the agreement arrived at as provided for by the Commission's Resolution of 13 August, 1948; and

Resolves to return in the immediate future to the subcontinent to discharge the responsibilities imposed upon it by the Resolution of 13 August, 1948 and by the foregoing principles.

CHINA

AGREEMENT BETWEEN CHINA AND NEPAL CONCERNING BOUNDARY BETWEEN THE TWO COUNTRIES

PEKING, 21ST MARCH, 1960

[The full details regarding the delineation of the agreed boundaries between the two countries were written into a later agreement signed at Peking, 5th October, 1961.]

The Government of the People's Republic of China and His Majesty's Government of Nepal having noted with satisfaction that the two countries have always respected the existing traditional customary boundary line and lived in amity: with the view to bringing abouts the formal settlement of some existing discrepancies in the boundary line between the two countries and the scientific delineation and formal demarcation of the whole boundary line, and to consolidating and further developing friendly relations between the two countries, the two Governments have decided to conclude the present Agreement under the guidance of the Five Principles of Peaceful Co-existence and have agreed upon the following:

ARTICLE 1

The Contracting Parties have agreed that the entire boundary between the two Countries shall be scientifically delineated and formally demarcated through friendly consultations, on the basis of the existing traditional customary line.

ARTICLE 2

In order to determine the specific alignment of the boundary line and to enable the fixing of the boundary between the two countries in legal form, the Contracting Parties have decided to set up a Joint Committee composed of an equal number of delegates from each side and inform the Committee, in accordance with the provisions of Article 3 of the present Agreement, to discuss and solve the concrete problems concerning the Sino-Nepalese boundary, conduct surveys of the boundary, erect boundary markers, and draft a Sino-Nepalese treaty. The Joint Committee will hold its meetings in the capitals or other places of China and Nepal.

ARTICLE 3

Having studied the delineation of the boundary line between the two countries as shown on the maps mutually exchanged and the information furnished by each side about its actual jurisdiction over the area bordering on the other Country, the Contracting Parties deem that, except for discrepancies in certain sections, their understanding of the traditional customary line is basically the same. The Contracting Parties have decided to determine concretely the boundary between the two countries in the following ways in accordance with three different cases:

1. Sections where the delineation of the boundary line between the two countries on the maps of the two sides is identical.

In these sections the boundary line shall be fixed according to the identical delineation on the maps of the two sides. The Joint Committee will send out joint survey teams composed of an equal number of persons from each side to conduct survey on the spot and erect boundary markers.

After the boundary line in these sections is fixed in accordance with the provisions of the above paragraph, the territory north of the line will conclusively belong to China, while the territory south of the line will conclusively belong to Nepal, and neither Contracting Party will any longer lay claim to certain areas within the territory of the other party.

2. Sections where the delineation of the boundary line between the two Countries on

the maps of the two sides is not identical, whereas the state of actual jurisdiction by each side is undisputed.

The Joint Committee will send out joint survey teams composed of an equal number of persons from each side to conduct survey on the spot, determine the boundary line and erect boundary markers in these sections in accordance with the concrete terrain features (watersheds, valleys, passes etc.) and the actual jurisdiction by each side.

3. Sections where the delineation of the boundary line between the two countries on the maps of the two sides is not identical and the two sides differ in their understanding of the state of actual jurisdiction.

The Joint Committee will send out joint teams composed of an equal number of persons from each side to ascertain on the spot the state of actual jurisdiction in these sections, make adjustments in accordance with the principles of equality, mutual benefit, friendship and mutual accommodation, determine the boundary line and erect boundary markers in these sections.

Article 4

The Contracting Parties have decided that, in order to ensure tranquillity and friendliness on the border, each side will no longer dispatch armed personnel to patrol the area on its side within twenty kilometres but only maintain its administrative personnel and civil police there.

Article 5

The present Agreement is subject to ratification and the instruments of ratification shall be exchanged in Kathmandu as soon as possible.

The present Agreement will come into force immediately on the exchange of the instruments of ratification and will automatically cease to be in force when the Sino-Nepalese boundary treaty to be signed by the two Governments comes into force.

Done in duplicate in Peking on the 21st day of March, 1960, in the Chinese, Nepalese and English languages, all texts being equally authentic.

Signed: Chou En-lai
(Plenipotentiary of the Government of the People's Republic of China)

B. P. Koirala
(Plenipotentiary of His Majesty's Government of Nepal)

Peking, 21st March, 1960

AGREEMENT BETWEEN CENTRAL PEOPLE'S GOVERNMENT OF CHINA AND LOCAL GOVERNMENT OF TIBET ON MEASURES FOR THE PEACEFUL LIBERATION OF TIBET

Peking, 23rd May, 1951

In the latter part of April 1951, the delegates with full powers of the local government of Tibet arrived in Peking. The Central People's Government appointed its own representatives with full powers. As a result of these talks, both parties agreed to conclude this Agreement and guarantee that it will be carried into effect.

1. The Tibetan people shall unite and drive out imperialist aggressive forces from Tibet; the Tibetan people shall return to the big family of the Motherland—the People's Republic of China.

2. The local government of Tibet shall actively assist the People's Liberation Army to enter Tibet and consolidate the national defence.

3. In accordance with the policy towards nationalities laid down in the Common Programme of the Chinese People's Political Consultative Conference, the Tibetan people have the right of exercising national regional autonomy under the unified leadership of the Central People's Government.

4. The central authorities will not alter the existing political system in Tibet. The central authorities also will not alter the established status, functions, and powers of the Dalai Lama. Officials of various ranks shall hold office as usual.

5. The established status, functions, and powers of the Panchen Ngoerhtehni shall be maintained.

6. By the established status, functions, and powers of the Dalai Lama and of the Panchen Ngoerhtehni are meant the status, functions and powers of the Thirteenth Dalai Lama and of the Ninth Panchen Ngoerhtehni when they were in friendly and amicable relations with each other.

7. The policy of freedom of religious belief laid down in the Common Programme of the Chinese People's Political Consultative Conference shall be carried out. The religious beliefs, customs, and habits of the Tibetan people shall be respected, and lama monasteries shall be protected. The central authorities will not effect a change in the income of the monasteries.

8. Tibetan troops shall be reorganised by stages into the People's Liberation Army, and become a part of the national defence forces of the People's Republic of China.

9. The spoken and written language and school education of the Tibetan nationality shall be developed step by step in accordance with the actual conditions in Tibet.

10. Tibetan agriculture, livestock raising, industry, and commerce shall be developed step by step, and the people's livelihood shall be improved step by step in accordance with the actual conditions in Tibet.

11. In matters related to various reforms in Tibet, there will be no compulsion on the part of the central authorities, the local government of Tibet should carry out reforms of its own accord, and when the people raise demands for reform, they shall be settled by means of consultation with the leading personnel of Tibet.

12. In so far as former pro-imperialist and pro-Kuomintang officials resolutely sever relations with imperialism and the Kuomintang and do not engage in sabotage or resistance, they may continue to hold office irrespective of their past.

13. The People's Liberation Army entering Tibet shall abide by all the above-mentioned policies and shall also be fair in all buying and selling and shall not arbitrarily take a single needle or thread from the people.

14. The Central People's Government shall conduct the centralised handling of all external affairs of the area of Tibet; and there will be peaceful coexistence with neighbouring countries and establishment and development of fair commercial and trading relations with them on the basis of equality, mutual benefit, and mutual respect for territory and sovereignty.

15. In order to ensure the implementation of the Agreement, the Central People's Government shall set up a military and administrative committee and a military area headquarters in Tibet, and apart from the personnel sent there by the Central People's Government, shall absorb as many local Tibetan personnel as possible to take part in the work.

Local Tibetan personnel taking part in the military and administrative committee may include patriotic elements from the local government of Tibet, various districts, and leading monasteries; the name list shall be drawn up after consultation between the representatives designated by the Central People's Government and the various quarters concerned, and shall be submitted to the Central People's Government for appointment.

16. Funds needed by the military and administrative committee, the military area headquarters, and the People's Liberation Army entering Tibet shall be provided by the Central People's Government. The local government of Tibet will assist the People's Liberation Army in the purchase and transport of food, fodder, and other daily necessities.

17. This Agreement shall come into force immediately after signatures and seals are affixed to it.

BOUNDARY AGREEMENT BETWEEN CHINA AND PAKISTAN

PEKING, 2ND MARCH, 1963

Following is the full text of the agreement between the Government of the People's Republic of China and the Government of Pakistan on the boundary between China's Sinkiang and the contiguous areas, the defence of which is under the actual control of Pakistan. Signed in Peking on 2nd March, 1963.

The Government of the People's Republic of China and the Government of Pakistan,

Having agreed with a view to ensuring the prevailing peace and tranquillity on the border, to formally delimit and demarcate the boundary between China's Sinkiang and the contiguous areas, the defence of which is under the actual control of Pakistan, in a spirit of fairness, reasonableness, mutual understanding and mutual accommodation and on the basis of the ten principles as enunciated in the Bandung conference;

Being convinced that this would not only give full expression to the desire of the peoples of China and Pakistan for the development of good-neighbourly and friendly relations, but also help safeguard Asian and world peace;

Have resolved for this purpose to conclude the present Agreement and have appointed as their respective plenipotentiaries the following:

For the Government of the People's Republic of China: Chen Yi, Minister of Foreign Affairs;

For the Government of Pakistan: Zulfikar Ali Bhutto, Minister of External Affairs:

Who, having mutually examined their full powers and found them to be in good and due form, have agreed upon the following:

ARTICLE 1

In view of the fact that the boundary between China's Sinkiang and the contiguous areas the defence of which is under the actual control of Pakistan has never been formally delimited, the two Parties agree to delimit it on the basis of the traditional customary boundary line including national features and in a spirit of equality, mutual benefit and friendly co-operation.

ARTICLE 2

In accordance with the principle expounded in Article 1 of the present Agreement, the two Parties have fixed, as follows, the alignment of the entire boundary line between China's Sinkiang and the contiguous areas, the defence of which is under the actual control of Pakistan:

(1) Commencing from its northwestern extreme at height 5,630 metres (a peak, the reference co-ordinates of which are approximately longitude 74° 34′ E and latitude 37° 03′ N), the boundary line runs generally eastward and then southeastward strictly along the main watershed between the tributaries of the Tashkurgan River of the Tarim River system on the one hand and the tributaries of the Aunza River of the Indus River system on the other hand, passing through the Kilik Pass, the Mintaka Pass, the Kharchanai Pass (named on the Chinese map only), the Mutsfilga Pass (named on the Chinese map only) and the Parfik Pass (named on the Pakistan map only), and reaches the Khumjerab (Yutr) Pass.

(2) After passing through the Khumjerab (Yutr) Pass, the boundary line runs generally southward along the above-mentioned main watershed up to a mountain top south of the Daban Pass, where it leaves the main watershed to follow the crest of a spur lying generally in a southwesterly direction, which is the watershed between the Akfilga River (a nameless corresponding river on the Pakistan map) on the one hand, and the Taghdumbash (Ofrang) River and the Kelimansu (Ofrang Tilga) on the other hand; according to the map of the Chinese side, the boundary line, after leaving the southeastern extremity of this spur, runs along a small section of the middle line of the bed of the Kelimansu to reach its confluence with the Kelechin River. According to the map of the Pakistan side, the boundary line, after leaving the southeastern extremity of this spur, reaches the sharp bend of the Shaksgam or Muztagh River.

(3) From the aforesaid point, the boundary line runs up the Kelechin River (Shaksgam or Muztagh River) along the middle line of its bed to its confluence (reference co-ordinates

approximately longitude 7,602′ E, latitude 36° 26′ N) with the Shorbulak Daria (Shimslal River or Braldu River).

(4) From the confluence of the aforesaid two rivers, the boundary line, according to the map of the Chinese side, ascends the crest of a spur and runs along it to join the Karakoram Range main watershed at a mountain-top with reference co-ordinates approximately longitude 75° 54′ E and latitude 36° 15′ N, which on this map is shown as belonging to the Shorbulak Mountain. According to the map of the Pakistan side, the boundary line from the confluence of the above-mentioned two rivers ascends the crest of a corresponding spur and runs along it, passing through height 6,520 metres (21,390 feet), till it joins the Karakoram Range main watershed at a peak (reference co-ordinates approximately longitude 75° 57′ E and latitude 36° 03′ N).

(5) Thence, the boundary line, running generally southward and then eastward, strictly follows the Karakoram Range main watershed which separates the Tarim River drainage system from the Indus River Drainage system, passing through the East Mustagh Pass (Muztagh Pass), the top of the Chogri Peak (K2), the top of the Broad Peak, the top of the Gasherbrum Mountain (8,058 metres), Indirakoli Pass (named on the Chinese map only) and the top of the Teram Kangri Peak, and reaches its southeastern extremity at the Karakoram Pass.

(6) The alignment of the entire boundary line, as described in section 1 of this Article, has been drawn on the 1/one million scale map of the Chinese side in Chinese and the 1/one million scale map of the Pakistan side in English, which are signed and attached to the present Agreement.

(7) In view of the fact that the maps of the two sides are not fully identical in their representation of topographical features, the two Parties have agreed that the actual features on the ground shall prevail so far as the location and alignment of the boundary described in Section 1 is concerned; and that they will be determined as far as possible by joint survey on the ground.

Article 3

The two Parties have agreed that:

(1) Wherever the boundary follows a river, the middle line of the river bed shall be the boundary line, and that:

(2) Wherever the boundary passes through a pass the water-parting line thereof shall be the boundary line.

Article 4

(1) The two Parties have agreed to set up, as soon as possible, a Joint Boundary Demarcation Commission. Each side will appoint a Chairman, one or more members and a certain number of advisers and technical staff. The Joint Boundary Demarcation Commission is charged with the responsibility in accordance with the provisions of the present Agreement, to hold concrete discussions on and carry out the following tasks jointly:

(2) To conduct necessary surveys of the boundary area on the ground, as stated in Article Two of the present Agreement, so as to set up boundary markers at places considered to be appropriate by the two Parties and to delineate the boundary line on the jointly prepared accurate maps.

TREATY BETWEEN CHINA AND BURMA CONCERNING BOUNDARY BETWEEN THE TWO COUNTRIES (EXTRACTS)

Peking, 1st October, 1960

The Chairman of the People's Republic of China and the President of the Union of Burma:

Being of the agreed opinion that the long-standing question of the boundary between the two countries is a question inherited from history, that since the two countries successively won independence, the traditional friendly and good-neighbourly relations between the two countries have undergone a new development, and the fact that the Prime Ministers of the two countries jointly initiated in 1954 the Five Principles of Peaceful Co-existence among nations with different social systems as principles guiding relations between the two countries has all the more greatly promoted the friendly relations between the two countries and has created conditions for the settlement of the question of the boundary between the two countries;

Noting with satisfaction that the Government of the People's Republic of China and the successive Governments of the Union of Burma, conducting friendly consultations and showing mutual understanding and mutual accommodation in accordance with the Five Principles of Peaceful Co-existence, have overcome various difficulties, and have eventually reached a successful and overall settlement of the question of the boundary between the two countries; and

Firmly believing that the formal delimitation of the entire boundary between the two countries and its emergence as a boundary of peace and friendship not only represent a milestone in the development of friendly relations between China and Burma, but also constitute an important contribution towards the safeguarding of Asian and world peace;

Have resolved for this purpose to conclude the present Treaty on the basis of the Agreement on the question of the boundary between the two countries signed by Premier Chou En-lai and Prime Minister Ne Win on January 28th, 1960 and appointed their respective plenipotentiaries as follows:

Chou En-lai, Premier of the State Council, for the Chairman of the People's Republic of China, and U Nu, Prime Minister of Burma, for the President of the Union of Burma,

Who, having mutually examined their full powers and found them in good order, have agreed upon the following:

Article 1

In accordance with the principle of respect for sovereignty and territorial integrity and in the spirit of friendship and mutual accommodation, the Union of Burma agrees to return to China the area of Hpimaw, Gawlum and Kangfang (measuring about 153 square kilometres, 59 square miles, and as indicated on the attached map) which belongs to China; and the People's Republic of China agrees to delimit the section of the boundary from the junction of the Nam Hpa and Nam Ting Rivers to the junction of the Nam Hka and the Nam Yung Rivers in accordance with the notes exchanged between the Chinese and the British Governments on June 18th, 1941, with the exception of the adjustment provided for in Articles 2 and 3 of the present Treaty.

Article 2

In view of the relations of equality and friendship between China and Burma, the two Parties decide to abrogate the 'perpetual lease' by Burma of the Meng-Mao Triangular Area (Namwan Assigned Tract) which belongs to China. Taking into account the practical needs of the Burmese side, the Chinese side agrees to turn over this area (measuring about 220 square kilometres, 85 square miles, and as indicated in the attached map) to Burma to become part of the territory of the Union of Burma. In exchange, and having regard for the historical ties and the integrity of the tribes, the Burmese side agrees to turn over to China to become part of Chinese territory the areas (measuring about 189 square kilometres, 73 square miles, and as indicated on the map) under the jurisdiction of the Panhung and Panlao tribes, which belong to Burma according to the provision in the notes exchanged between the Chinese and the British Governments on June 18th, 1941.

Article 3

For the convenience of administration by each side and having regard for the intratribal relationship and production and livelihood needs of the local inhabitants, the two Parties agree to make fair and reasonable adjustments to a small section of the boundary line as defined in the notes exchanged between the Chinese and British Governments on June 18th, 1941, by including in China Yawng Hok and Lungnai villages and including in Burma Umhpa, Pan Kung, Pan Nawng and Pan Wai villages, so that these boundary-line-intersected villages will no longer be intersected by the boundary line.

ARTICLE 4

The Chinese Government, in line with its consistent policy of opposing foreign prerogatives and respecting the sovereignty of other countries, renounces China's right of participation in mining enterprises at Lufang of Burma as provided in the notes exchanged between the Chinese and the British Governments on January 18th, 1941.

ARTICLE 5

The Contracting Parties agree that the section of the boundary from the High Conical Peak to the western extremity of the Sino-Burmese boundary, with the exception of the area of Hpimaw, Gawlum and Kangfang, shall be fixed along the traditional customary line, that is, from the High Conical Peak northwards along the watershed between the Taping, the Shweli and the Nu Rivers and the section of the Tulung (Taron) River above western Chingdam village on the one hand and the Nmai Hka River on the other, to a point on the south bank of the Tulung (Taron) River west of western Chingdam village, thence across the Tulung (Taron) River above western Chingdam village and the Tsayul (Zayul) River on the one hand, all the upper tributaries of the Irrawaddy River excluding the section of the Tulung (Taron) River above western Chingdam village on the other, to the western extremity of the Sino-Burmese boundary.

ARTICLE 6

The Contracting Parties affirm that the two sections of the boundary from the High Conical Peak to the junction of the Nam Hpa and the Nam Ting Rivers and from the junction of the Nam Hpa and the Nam Ting Rivers and from the junction of the Nam Hka and the Nam Yung Rivers to the southeastern extremity of the Sino-Burmese boundary at the junction of the Nam La and Lanchang (Mekong) Rivers were already delimited in the past and required no change, the boundary being as delineated in the maps attached to the present Treaty.

ARTICLE 7

(1) In accordance with the provisions of Articles 1 and 5 of the present Treaty, the alignment of the section of the boundary line from the High Conical Peak to the western extremity of the Sino-Burmese boundary should be as follows [six paragraphs follow].

(2) In accordance with the provisions of Articles 1, 2, 3 and 6 of the present Treaty, the alignment of the section of the boundary line from the High Conical Peak to the south-eastern extremity of the Sino-Burmese boundary shall be as follows [18 paragraphs follow].

(3) The alignment of the entire boundary line between the two countries described in this Article and the location of the temporary boundary marks erected by both sides during joint survey are shown on the 1/250,000 maps indicating the entire boundary and on the 1/50,000 maps of certain areas, which are attached to the present Treaty.

ARTICLE 8

The Contracting Parties agree that wherever the boundary follows a river, the mid-stream line shall be the boundary in the case of an unnavigable river, and the middle line of the main navigational channel (the deepest water course) shall be the boundary in the case of a navigable river. In case the boundary river changes its course, the boundary line between the two countries shall remain unchanged in the absence of other agreements between the two sides.

ARTICLE 9

The Contracting Parties agree that:

(1) Upon the coming into force of the Treaty, the Meng-Mao Triangular Area to be turned over to Burma under Article 2 of the present Treaty shall become territory of the Union of Burma.

(2) The area of Hpimew, Gawlum and Kangfang to be returned to China under Article 1 of the present Treaty and the areas under the jurisdiction of the Panlung and Panlao tribes to be turned over to China under Article 2 shall be handed over by the Burmese

Government to the Chinese Government, within four months after the present Treaty comes into force;

(3) The areas to be adjusted under Article 3 of the present Treaty shall be handed over respectively by the Government of one Contracting Party to that of the other within four months after the present Treaty comes into force.

ARTICLE 10

After the signing of the present Treaty, the Chinese-Burmese Joint Boundary Committee constituted in pursuance of the agreement between the two countries on the question of the boundary between the two countries of January 28th, 1960, shall continue to carry out necessary surveys of the boundary line between the two countries, to set up new boundary markers and to examine, repair and remould old boundary markers, and shall then draft a protocol setting forth in detail the alignment of the entire boundary line and the location of all the boundary markers, with detailed maps attached showing the boundary line and the location of the boundary markers. The above-mentioned protocol, upon being concluded by the Governments of the two Countries, shall become an annex to the present Treaty and the detailed maps shall replace the maps attached to the present Treaty.

Upon the conclusion of the above-mentioned protocol, the tasks of the Chinese-Burmese Joint Boundary Committee shall be terminated and the Agreement between the two Parties on the Question of the Boundary between the two Countries of January 28th, 1960, shall cease to be in force.

ARTICLE 11

The Contracting Parties agree that any dispute concerning the boundary which may arise after the formal delimitation of the boundary between the two countries shall be settled by the two sides through friendly consultations.

ARTICLE 12

The present Treaty is subject to ratification and the Instruments of Ratification shall be exchanged in Rangoon as soon as possible.

The present Treaty shall come into force on the day of the exchange of Instruments of Ratification.

Upon the coming into force of the present Treaty, all past treaties, exchanged notes and other documents relating to the boundary between the two Countries shall be no longer in force, except as otherwise provided in Article 10 of the present Treaty with regard to the Agreement between the two Parties on the question of the Boundary between the two Countries of January 28th, 1960.

Done in duplicate in Peking on October 1st, 1960, in the Chinese, Burmese and English languages, all three texts being equally authentic.

U.S.S.R.

TREATY OF FRIENDSHIP, ALLIANCE AND MUTUAL ASSISTANCE BETWEEN THE U.S.S.R. AND CHINA

MOSCOW, 14TH FEBRUARY, 1950

The Presidium of the Supreme Soviet of the Union of Soviet Socialist Republics and the Central People's Government of the Republic of China;

Filled with determination jointly to prevent, by the consolidation of friendship and co-operation between the Union of Soviet Socialist Republics and the People's Republic of China, the re-birth of Japanese imperialism, and the repetition of aggression on the part of Japan or any other State which should unite in any form with Japan in acts of aggression;

Imbued with the desire to consolidate lasting peace and universal security in the Far East and throughout the world in conformity with the aims and principles of the United Nations Organisation;

Profoundly convinced that the consolidation of good-neighbourly relations and friendship between the Union of Soviet Socialist Republics and the People's Republic of China meets the fundamental interests of the peoples of the Soviet Union and China;

Resolved for this purpose to conclude the present Treaty and appointed as their plenipotentiary representatives:

The Presidium of the Supreme Soviet of the Union of Soviet Socialist Republics: Andrei Yanuarovich Vyshinsky, Minister of Foreign Affairs of the Union of Soviet Socialist Republics;

The Central People's Government of the People's Republic of China: Chou En-lai, Prime Minister of the State Administrative Council and Minister of Foreign Affairs of China;

Who, after exchange of their credentials, found in due form and good order, agreed upon the following:

ARTICLE 1

Both High Contracting Parties undertake jointly to take all the necessary measures at their disposal for the purpose of preventing a repetition of aggression and violation of peace on the part of Japan or any other State which should unite with Japan, directly or indirectly, in acts of aggression. In the event of one of the High Contracting Parties being attacked by Japan or States allied with it, and thus being involved in a state of war, the other High Contracting Party will immediately render military and other assistance with all the means at its disposal.

The High Contracting Parties also declare their readiness in the spirit of sincere co-operation to participate in all international actions aimed at ensuring peace and security throughout the world, and will do all in their power to achieve the speediest implementation of these tasks.

ARTICLE 2

Both the High Contracting Parties undertake by means of mutual agreement to strive for the earliest conclusion of a peace treaty with Japan, jointly with the other Powers which were allies during the Second World War.

ARTICLE 3

Both High Contracting Parties undertake not to conclude any alliance directed against the other High Contracting Party, and not to take part in any coalition or in actions or measures directed against the other High Contracting Party.

ARTICLE 4

Both High Contracting Parties will consult each other in regard to all important international problems affecting the common interests of the Soviet Union and China, being guided by the interests of the consolidation of peace and universal security.

ARTICLE 5

Both the High Contracting Parties undertake, in the spirit of friendship and co-operation and in conformity with the principles of equality, mutual interests, and also mutual respect for the State sovereignty and territorial integrity and non-interference in internal affairs of the other High Contracting Party—to develop and consolidate economic and cultural ties between the Soviet Union and China, to render each other every possible economic assistance, and to carry out the necessary economic co-operation.

ARTICLE 6

The present Treaty comes into force immediately upon its ratification; the exchange of instruments of ratification will take place in Peking.

The present Treaty will be valid for thirty years. If neither of the High Contracting Parties give notice one year before the expiration of this term of its desire to denounce the Treaty, it shall remain in force for another five years and will be extended in compliance with this rule.

Done in Moscow on 14th February 1950, in two copies, each in the Russian and Chinese languages, both texts having equal force.

AGREEMENT BETWEEN THE U.S.S.R. AND CHINA ON THE CHINESE CHANGCHUN RAILWAY, PORT ARTHUR, AND DALNY

MOSCOW, 14TH FEBRUARY, 1950

The Presidium of the Supreme Soviet of the Union of Soviet Socialist Republics and the Central People's Government of the People's Republic of China state that since 1945 radical changes have occurred in the situation in the Far East, namely: Imperialist Japan suffered defeat; the reactionary Kuomintang Government was overthrown; China has become a People's Democratic Republic, and in China a new People's Government was formed which has united the whole of China, carried out a policy of friendship and co-operation with the Soviet Union, and proved its ability to defend the State independence and territorial integrity of China, the national honour and dignity of the Chinese people.

The Presidium of the Supreme Soviet of the Union of Soviet Socialist Republics and the Central People's Government of the People's Republic of China maintain that this new situation permits a new approach to the question of the Chinese Changchun Railway, Port Arthur, and Dalny.

In conformity with these new circumstances, the Presidium of the Supreme Soviet of the Union of Soviet Socialist Republics and the Central People's Government of the People's Republic of China have decided to conclude the present agreement on the Chinese Changchun Railway, Port Arthur, and Dalny.

ARTICLE I

Both High Contracting Parties have agreed that the Soviet Government transfers gratis to the Government of the People's Republic of China all its rights in the joint administration of the Chinese Changchun Railway, with all the property belonging to the Railway. The transfer will be effected immediately upon the conclusion of a peace treaty with Japan, but not later than the end of 1952.

Pending the transfer, the now existing position of the Soviet-Chinese joint administration of the Chinese Changchun Railway remains unchanged; however, the order of filling posts by representatives of the Soviet and Chinese sides, upon the coming into force of the present Agreement, will be changed, and there will be established an alternating filling of posts for a definite period of time (Director of the Railway, Chairman of the Central Board, and others).

As regards concrete methods of effecting the transfer, they will be agreed upon and determined by the Governments of both High Contracting Parties.

ARTICLE 2

Both High Contracting Parties have agreed that Soviet troops will be withdrawn from the jointly utilized naval base of Port Arthur and that the installations in this area will be handed over to the Government of the People's Republic of China immediately upon the conclusion of a peace treaty with Japan, but not later than the end of 1952, with the Government of the People's Republic of China compensating the Soviet Union for expenses incurred in the restoration and construction of installations effected by the Soviet Union since 1945.

For the period pending the withdrawal of Soviet troops and the transfer of the above installations, the Governments of the Soviet Union and China will appoint an equal number of military representatives for organizing a joint Chinese-Soviet Military Commission which will be in charge of military affairs in the area of Port Arthur; concrete measures in this sphere will be determined by the joint Chinese-Soviet Military Commission within three months upon the coming into force of the present Agreement and shall be implemented upon the approval of these measures by the Governments of both countries.

The civil administration in the aforementioned area shall be in the direct charge of the Government of the People's Republic of China. Pending the withdrawal of Soviet troops, the zone of billeting of Soviet troops in the area of Port Arthur will remain unaltered in conformity with the now existing frontiers.

In the event of either of the High Contracting Parties being subjected to aggression on the part of Japan or any State which should unite with Japan and as a result of this being involved in military operations, China and the Soviet Union may, on the proposal of the Government of the People's Republic of China and with the agreement of the Soviet Government, jointly use the naval base of Port Arthur in the interests of conducting joint military operations against the aggressor.

ARTICLE 3

Both High Contracting Parties have agreed that the question of Port Dalny must be further considered upon the conclusion of a peace treaty with Japan.

As regards the administration in Dalny, it fully belongs to the Government of the People's Republic of China.

All property now existing in Dalny provisionally in charge of or under lease to the Soviet side, is to be taken over by the Government of the People's Republic of China. For carrying out work involved in the receipt of the aforementioned property, the Governments of the Soviet Union and China appoint three representatives from each side for organizing a joint commission which in the course of three months after the coming into force of the present agreement shall determine the concrete methods of transfer of property, and after approval of the proposals of the Joint Commission by the Governments of both countries will complete their implementation in the course of 1950.

ARTICLE 4

The present Agreement comes into force on the day of its ratification. The exchange of instruments of ratification will take place in Peking.

Done in Moscow on 14th February 1950 in two copies, each in the Russian and Chinese languages, both texts having equal force.

Signed: A. Y. Vyshinsky
(By authorization of the Presidium of the Supreme Soviet of the Union of Soviet Socialist Republics)

Chou En-lai
(By authorization of the Central People's Government of the People's Republic of China)

TREATY OF FRIENDSHIP AND MUTUAL ASSISTANCE BETWEEN THE U.S.S.R. AND THE MONGOLIAN PEOPLE'S REPUBLIC

MOSCOW, 27TH FEBRUARY, 1946

In connexion with the ending of the ten-year term of the Protocol on Mutual Assistance concluded between the Union of Soviet Socialist Republics and the Mongolian People's Republic, the Presidium of the Supreme Soviet of the U.S.S.R. and the Presidium of the

Little Khural of the Mongolian People's Republic decided to change the Protocol of 12th March 1936, quoted below, into a Treaty of Friendship and Mutual Assistance to be valid for ten years:

The Governments of the Union of Soviet Socialist Republics and the Mongolian People's Republic, proceeding from the relationship of consistent friendship which has existed between the two countries since the liberation with the aid of the Red Army of the territory of the Mongolian People's Republic in 1921 from the White Guard detachments which had contact with the troops that invaded the territory of the U.S.S.R.;

and directed by the desire to secure peace in the Far East and to strengthen further the friendly relations existing between them;

hereby formulate in this Protocol the gentlemen's agreement existing between them since 27th November 1934, which provides for mutual support by all possible measures in averting and forestalling any threat of military attack as well as for mutual assistance and support in case of attack on the U.S.S.R. or on the Mongolian People's Republic by any third party.

Article 1

In the case of a menace of attack on the territory of the Union of Soviet Socialist Republics or on the Mongolian People's Republic by a third State, the Governments of the Union of Soviet Socialist Republics and the Mongolian People's Republic undertake immediately to discuss jointly the situation arising and to take all such measures as might be necessary to safeguard the security of their territory.

Article 2

The Governments of the Union of Soviet Socialist Republics and the Mongolian People's Republic undertake in the case of military attack on one of the Contracting Parties to render each other every assistance including military assistance.

Article 3

The Governments of the Union of Soviet Socialist Republics and the Mongolian People's Republic deem it self-understood that the troops of one of the Parties stationed by mutual agreement on the territory of the other Party, in fulfilment of the undertaking under Articles 1 and 2, will be withdrawn from the territory in question without delay when the necessity for this is over, as was the case in 1925 in regard to the withdrawal of Soviet troops from territory of the Mongolian People's Republic.

The present Treaty comes into force as from its ratification, which must be effected within as short a time as possible. The exchange of ratification instruments will take place in Ulan Bator.

Unless one of the High Contracting Parties one year prior to the expiration of the term of the present Treaty gives notice of its desire to denounce the Treaty, it will remain valid for the next ten years.

Done in Moscow, 27th February 1946, which corresponds to the 27th day of the Second Moon of the 36th year of the Mongolian Calendar, in two copies, each in the Russian and Mongolian languages, both texts being equally valid.

JAPAN AND KOREA

TREATY OF PEACE WITH JAPAN (EXTRACTS)

San Francisco, 8th September, 1951

Whereas the Allied Powers and Japan are resolved that henceforth their relations shall be those of nations which, as sovereign equals, co-operate in friendly associations to promote their common welfare and to maintain international peace and security, and are therefore desirous of concluding a Treaty of Peace which will settle questions still outstanding as a result of the existence of a state of war between them;

Whereas Japan for its part declares its intention to apply for membership in the United Nations and in all circumstances to conform to the principles of the Charter of the United Nations; to strive to realize the objectives of the Universal Declaration of Human Rights; to seek to create within Japan conditions of stability and well-being as defined in Articles 55 and 56 of the Charter of the United Nations and already initiated by post-surrender Japanese legislation; and in public and private trade and commerce to conform to internationally accepted fair practices;

Whereas the Allied Powers welcome the intentions of Japan set out in the foregoing paragraph;

The Allied Powers and Japan have therefore determined to conclude the present Treaty of Peace, and have accordingly appointed the undersigned Plenipotentiaries, who, after presentation of their full powers, found in good and due form, have agreed on the following provisions:

CHAPTER I—*PEACE*

Article 1

(a) The state of war between Japan and each of the Allied Powers is terminated as from the date on which the present Treaty comes into force between Japan and the Allied Power concerned, as provided for in Article 23.

(b) The Allied Powers recognize the full sovereignty of the Japanese people over Japan and its territorial waters.

CHAPTER II—*TERRITORY*

Article 2

(a) Japan, recognizing the independence of Korea, renounces all right, title and claim to Korea, including the islands of Quelpart, Port Hamilton and Dagelet.

(b) Japan renounces all right, title and claim to Formosa and the Pescadores.

(c) Japan renounces all right, title and claim to the Kurile Islands, and to that portion of Sakhalin and the islands adjacent to it over which Japan acquired sovereignty as a consequence of the Treaty of Portsmouth of September 5th, 1905.

(d) Japan renounces all right, title and claim in connection with the League of Nations Mandate System, and accepts the action of the United Nations Security Council of April 2nd, 1947, extending the trusteeship system to the Pacific Islands formerly under mandate to Japan.

(e) Japan renounces all claim to any right or title to or interest in connection with any part of the Antarctic area, whether deriving from the activities of Japanese nationals or otherwise.

(f) Japan renounces all right, title and claim to the Spratley Islands and to the Paracel Islands.

Article 3

Japan will concur in any proposal of the United States to the United Nations to place under its trusteeship system, with the United States as the sole administering authority, Nansei Shoto south of 29° north latitude (including the Ryukyu Islands and the Daito Islands), Nanpo Shoto south of Sofu Gan (including the Bonin Islands, Rosario Island and the Volcano Islands) and Parece Vela and Marcus Island. Pending the making of such a proposal and affirmative action thereon, the United States will have the right to exercise all and any powers of administration, legislation and jurisdiction over the territory and inhabitants of these islands, including their territorial waters.

ARTICLE 4

(a) Subject to the provisions of paragraph (b) of this Article, the disposition of property of Japan and of its nationals in the areas referred to in Article 2, and their claims, including debts, against the authorities presently administering such areas and the residents (including juridical persons) thereof, and the disposition in Japan of property of such authorities and residents, and of claims, including debts, of such authorities and residents against Japan and its nationals, shall be the subject of special arrangements between Japan and such authorities. The property of any of the Allied Powers or its nationals in the areas referred to in Article 2 shall, insofar as this has not already been done, be returned by the administering authority in the condition in which it now exists. (The term nationals whenever used in the present Treaty includes juridical persons.)

(b) Japan recognizes the validity of dispositions of property of Japan and Japanese nationals made by or pursuant to directives of the United States Military Government in any of the areas referred to in Articles 2 and 3.

(c) Japanese owned submarine cables connecting Japan with territory removed from Japanese control pursuant to the present Treaty shall be equally divided, Japan retaining the Japanese terminal and adjoining half of the cable, and the detached territory the remainder of the cable and connecting terminal facilities.

CHAPTER III—*SECURITY*

ARTICLE 5

(a) Japan accepts the obligations set forth in Article 2 of the Charter of the United Nations, and in particular the obligations

(i) to settle its international disputes by peaceful means in such a manner that international peace and security, and justice, are not endangered;

(ii) to refrain in its international relations from the threat or use of force against the territorial integrity or political independence of any State or in any other manner inconsistent with the purposes of the United Nations;

(iii) to give the United Nations every assistance in any action it takes in accordance with the Charter and to refrain from giving assistance to any State against which the United Nations may take preventive or enforcement action.

(b) The Allied Powers confirm that they will be guided by the principles of Article 2 of the Charter of the United Nations in their relations with Japan.

(c) The Allied Powers for their part recognize that Japan as a sovereign nation possesses the inherent right of individual or collective self-defence referred to in Article 51 of the Charter of the United Nations and that Japan may voluntarily enter into collective security arrangements.

ARTICLE 6

(a) All occupation forces of the Allied Powers shall be withdrawn from Japan as soon as possible after the coming into force of the present Treaty, and in any case not later than 90 days thereafter. Nothing in this provision shall, however, prevent the stationing or retention of foreign armed forces in Japanese territory under or in consequence of any bilateral or multilateral agreements which have been or may be made between one or more of the Allied Powers, on the one hand, and Japan on the other.

(b) The provisions of Article 9 of the Potsdam Proclamation of July 26th, 1945, dealing with the return of Japanese military forces to their homes, to the extent not already completed, will be carried out.

(c) All Japanese property for which compensation has not already been paid, which was supplied for the use of the occupation forces and which remains in the possession of those forces at the time of the coming into force of the present Treaty, shall be returned to the Japanese Government within the same 90 days unless other arrangements are made by mutual agreement.

CHAPTER IV—*POLITICAL AND ECONOMIC CLAUSES*

Article 7

(a) Each of the Allied Powers, within one year after the present Treaty has come into force between it and Japan, will notify Japan which of its prewar bilateral treaties or conventions with Japan it wishes to continue in force or revive, and any treaties or conventions so notified shall continue in force or be revived subject only to such amendments as may be necessary to ensure conformity with the present Treaty. The treaties and conventions so notified shall be considered as having been continued in force or revived three months after the date of notification and shall be registered with the Secretariat of the United Nations. All such treaties and conventions as to which Japan is not so notified shall be regarded as abrogated.

(b) Any notification made under paragraph (a) of this Article may except from the operation or revival of a treaty or convention any territory for the international relations of which the notifying Power is responsible, until three months after the date on which notice is given to Japan that such exception shall cease to apply.

Article 8

(a) Japan will recognize the full force of all treaties now or hereafter concluded by the Allied Powers for terminating the state of war initiated on September 1st, 1939, as well as any other arrangements by the Allied Powers for or in connection with the restoration of peace. Japan also accepts the arrangements made for terminating the former League of Nations and Permanent Court of International Justice.

(b) Japan renounces all such rights and interests as it may derive from being a signatory Power of the Conventions of St. Germain-en-Laye of September 10th, 1919, and the Straits Agreement of Montreux of July 20th, 1936, and from Article 16 of the Treaty of Peace with Turkey signed at Lausanne on July 24th, 1923.

(c) Japan renounces all rights, title and interests acquired under, and is discharged from all obligations resulting from, the Agreement between Germany and the Creditor Powers of January 20th, 1930, and its Annexes, including the Trust Agreement, dated May 17th, 1930, the Convention of January 20th, 1930, respecting the Bank for International Settlements, and the Statutes of the Bank for International Settlements. Japan will notify to the Ministry of Foreign Affairs in Paris within six months of the first coming into force of the present Treaty its renunciation of the rights, title and interests referred to in this paragraph.

Article 9

Japan will enter promptly into negotiations with the Allied Powers so desiring for the conclusion of bilateral and multilateral agreements providing for the regulation or limitation of fishing and the conservation and development of fisheries on the high seas.

Article 10

Japan renounces all special rights and interests in China, including all benefits and privileges resulting from the provisions of the final Protocol signed at Peking on September 7th, 1901, and all annexes, notes and documents supplementary thereto, and agrees to the abrogation in respect to Japan of the said protocol, annexes, notes and documents.

Article 11

Japan accepts the judgments of the International Military Tribunal for the Far East and of other Allied War Crimes Courts both within and outside Japan and will carry out the sentences imposed thereby upon Japanese nationals imprisoned in Japan. The power to grant clemency, to reduce sentences and to parole with respect to such prisoners may not be exercised except on the decision of the Government or Governments which imposed the sentence in each instance, and on the recommendation of Japan. In the case of persons sentenced by the International Military Tribunal for the Far East, such power may not be exercised except on the decision of a majority of the Governments represented on the Tribunal, and on the recommendation of Japan.

Article 12

(a) Japan declares its readiness promptly to enter into negotiations for the conclusion with each of the Allied Powers of treaties or agreements to place their trading, maritime and other commercial relations on a stable and friendly basis.

(b) Pending the conclusion of the relevant treaty or agreement, Japan will, during a period of four years from the first coming into force of the present Treaty

(1) accord to each of the Allied Powers, its nationals, products and vessels

(i) most-favoured-nation treatment with respect to customs duties, charges, restrictions and other regulations on or in connection with the importation and exportation of goods;

(ii) national treatment with respect to shipping, navigation and imported goods, and with respect to natural and juridical persons and their interests—such treatment to include all matters pertaining to the levying and collection of taxes, access to the courts, the making and performance of contracts, rights to property (tangible and intangible), participation in juridical entities constituted under Japanese law, and generally the conduct of all kinds of business and professional activities;

(2) ensure that external purchases and sales of Japanese state trading enterprises shall be based solely on commercial considerations.

(c) In respect to any matter, however, Japan shall be obliged to accord to an Allied Power national treatment, or most-favoured-nation treatment, only to the extent that the Allied Power concerned accords Japan national treatment or most-favoured-nation treatment, as the case may be, in respect of the same matter. The reciprocity envisaged in the foregoing sentence shall be determined, in the case of products, vessels and juridical entities of, and persons domiciled in, any non-metropolitan territory of an Allied Power, and in the case of juridical entities of, and persons domiciled in, any state or province of an Allied Power having a federal government, by reference to the treatment accorded to Japan in such territory, state or province.

(d) In the application of this Article, a discriminatory measure shall not be considered to derogate from the grant of national or most-favoured-nation treatment, as the case may be, if such measure is based on an exception customarily provided for in the commercial treaties of the party applying it, or on the need to safeguard that party's external financial position or balance of payments (except in respect to shipping and navigation), or on the need to maintain its essential security interests, and provided such measure is proportionate to the circumstances and not applied in an arbitrary or unreasonable manner.

(e) Japan's obligations under this Article shall not be affected by the exercise of any Allied rights under Article 14 of the present Treaty; nor shall the provisions of this Article be understood as limiting the undertakings assumed by Japan by virtue of Article 15 of the Treaty.

Article 13

(a) Japan will enter into negotiations with any of the Allied Powers, promptly upon the request of such Power or Powers, for the conclusion of bilateral or multilateral agreements relating to international civil air transport.

(b) Pending the conclusion of such agreement or agreements, Japan will, during a period of four years from the first coming into force of the present Treaty, extend to such Power treatment not less favourable with respect to air-traffic rights and privileges than those exercised by any such Powers at the date of such coming into force, and will accord complete equality of opportunity in respect to the operation and development of air services.

(c) Pending its becoming a party to the Convention on International Civil Aviation in accordance with Article 93 thereof, Japan will give effect to the provisions of that Convention applicable to the international navigation of aircraft, and will give effect to the standards, practices and procedures adopted as annexes to the Convention in accordance with the terms of the Convention.

CHAPTER V—*CLAIMS AND PROPERTY*

Article 14

(a) It is recognized that Japan should pay reparations to the Allied Powers for the damage and suffering caused by it during the war. Nevertheless it is also recognized that the resources of Japan are not presently sufficient, if it is to maintain a viable economy, to make complete reparation for all such damage and suffering and at the same time meet its other obligations.

CHAPTER VII—*FINAL CLAUSES*

Article 23

(a) The present Treaty shall be ratified by the States which sign it, including Japan, and will come into force for all the States which have then ratified it, when instruments of ratification have been deposited by Japan and by a majority, including the United States of America as the principal occupying Power, of the following States, namely Australia, Canada, Ceylon, France, Indonesia, the Kingdom of the Netherlands, New Zealand, Pakistan, the Republic of the Philippines, the United Kingdom of Great Britain and Northern Ireland and the United States of America. The present Treaty shall come into force for each State which subsequently ratifies it, on the date of the deposit of its instrument of ratification.

(b) If the Treaty has not come into force within nine months after the date of the deposit of Japan's ratification, any State which has ratified it may bring the Treaty into force between itself and Japan by a notification to that effect given to the Governments of Japan and the United States of America not later than three years after the date of deposit of Japan's ratification.

Article 24

All instruments of ratification shall be deposited with the Government of the United States of America which will notify all the signatory States of each such deposit, of the date of the coming into force of the Treaty under paragraph (a) of Article 23, and of any notifications made under paragraph (b) of Article 23.

Article 25

For the purposes of the present Treaty the Allied Powers shall be the States at war with Japan, or any State which previously formed a part of the territory of a State named in Article 23, provided that in each case the State concerned has signed and ratified the Treaty. Subject to the provisions of Article 21, the present Treaty shall not confer any rights, titles or benefits on any State which is not an Allied Power as herein defined; nor shall any right, title or interest of Japan be deemed to be diminished or prejudiced by any provision of the Treaty in favour of a State which is not an Allied Power as so defined.

Article 26

Japan will be prepared to conclude with any State which signed or adhered to the United Nations Declaration of January 1, 1942, and which is at war with Japan, or with any State which previously formed a part of the territory of a State named in Article 23, which is not a signatory of the present Treaty, a bilateral Treaty of Peace on the same or substantially the same terms as are provided for in the present Treaty, but this obligation on the part of Japan will expire three years after the first coming into force of the present Treaty. Should Japan make a peace settlement or war claims settlement with any State granting that State greater advantages than those provided by the present Treaty, those same advantages shall be extended to the Parties of the present Treaty.

Article 27

The present Treaty shall be deposited in the archives of the Government of the United States of America which shall furnish each signatory State with a certified copy thereof.

In faith whereof the undersigned Plenipotentiaries have signed the present Treaty.

Done at the City of San Francisco this eighth day of September, 1951, in the English, French and Spanish languages, all being equally authentic, and in the Japanese language.

MUTUAL DEFENCE ASSISTANCE AGREEMENT BETWEEN JAPAN AND THE U.S.A.

TOKYO, 8TH MARCH, 1954

The Government of the United States of America and the Government of Japan:

Desiring to foster international peace and security within the framework of the Charter of the United Nations, through voluntary arrangements which will further the ability of nations dedicated to the purposes and principles of the Charter to develop effective measures for individual and collective self-defence in support of these purposes and principles;

Reaffirming their belief as stated in the Treaty of Peace with Japan signed at the city of San Francisco on September 8th, 1951 that Japan as a sovereign nation possesses the inherent right of individual or collective self-defence referred to in Article 51 of the Charter of the United Nations;

Recalling the preamble of the Security Treaty between the United States of America and Japan, signed at the city of San Francisco on September 8th, 1951, to the effect that the United States of America, in the interests of peace and security, would maintain certain of its armed forces in and about Japan as a provisional arrangement in the expectation that Japan will itself increasingly assume responsibility for its own defence against direct and indirect aggression, always avoiding any armament which would be an offensive threat or serve other than to promote peace and security in accordance with the purposes and principles of the Charter of the United Nations;

Recognising that, in the planning of a defence assistance programme for Japan, economic stability will be an essential element for consideration in the development of its defence capacities, and that Japan can contribute only to the extent permitted by its general economic condition and capacities;

Taking into consideration the support that the Government of the U.S.A. has brought to these principles by enacting the Mutual Defence Assistance Act of 1949, as amended, and the Mutual Security Act of 1951, as amended, which provide for the furnishing of defence assistance by the United States of America in furtherance of the objectives referred to above; and

Desiring to set forth the conditions which will govern the furnishing of such assistance, have agreed as follows:

ARTICLE I

(1) Each Government, consistently with the principle that economic stability is essential to international peace and security, will make available to the other and to such other governments as the two Governments signatory to the present Agreement may in each case agree upon, such equipment, materials, services or other assistance as the Governments may authorize, in accordance with such detailed arrangements as may be made between them. The furnishing and use of any such assistance as may be authorized by either Government shall be consistent with the Charter of the United Nations. Such assistance as may be available by the Government of the U.S.A. pursuant to the present Agreement will be furnished under those provisions, and subject to all those terms, conditions and termination provisions of the Mutual Defence Assistance Act of 1949, the Mutual Security Act of 1951, acts amendatory and supplementary thereto, and appropriation acts thereunder which may affect the furnishing of such assistance.

(2) Each Government will make effective use of assistance received pursuant to the present Agreement for the purposes of promoting peace and security in a manner that is satisfactory to both Governments, and neither Government, without the prior consent of the other, will devote such assistance to any other purpose.

(3) Each Government will offer for return to the other, in accordance with terms, conditions and procedures mutually agreed upon, equipment or materials furnished under the present Agreement, except equipment and materials furnished on items requiring reimbursement, and no longer required for the purposes for which it was originally made available.

(4) In the interest of common security, each Government undertakes not to transfer to

any person not an officer or agent of such Government, or to any other government, title to possession of any equipment, materials, or services received pursuant to the present Agreement, without the prior consent of the Government which furnished such assistance.

ARTICLE 2

In conformity with the principle of mutual aid, the Government of Japan agrees to facilitate the production and transfer to the Government of the U.S.A. for such period of time, in such quantities and upon such terms and conditions as may be agreed upon of raw and semi-processed materials required by the U.S.A. as a result of deficiencies or potential deficiencies in its own resources, and which may be available in Japan. Arrangements for such transfers shall give due regard to requirements for domestic use and commercial export as determined by the Government of Japan.

ARTICLE 3

(1) Each Government will take such security measures as may be agreed upon between the two Governments in order to prevent the disclosure or compromise of classified articles, services or information furnished by the other Government pursuant to the present Agreement.

(2) Each Government will take appropriate measures consistent with security to keep the public informed of operations under the present Agreement.

ARTICLE 4

The two Governments will, upon the request of either of them, make appropriate arrangements providing for the methods and terms of the exchange of industrial property rights and technical information for defence which will expedite such exchange and at the same time protect private interests and maintain security safeguards.

ARTICLE 5

The two Governments will consult for the purpose of establishing procedures whereby the Government of Japan will so deposit, segregate, or assure title to all funds allocated to or derived from any programmes of assistance undertaken by the Government of the U.S.A. so that such funds shall not be subject to garnishment, attachment, seizure or other legal process by any person, firm, agency, corporation, organisation or government, when the Government of Japan is advised by the Government of the U.S.A. that any such legal process would interfere with the attainment of the objectives of the programme of assistance.

ARTICLE 6

(1) The Government of Japan will grant exemption from duties and internal taxation upon importation or exportation of materials, supplies or equipment imported into or exported from its territory under the present Agreement or any similar Agreement between the Government of the United States of America and the Government of any other country receiving assistance, except as otherwise agreed to, and exemption from and refund of Japanese taxes, as enumerated in the attachment Annex E, so far as they may affect expenditures of or financed by the Government of the U.S.A. effected in Japan for procurement of materials, supplies, equipment and services under the present Agreement or any similar Agreement between the Government of the U.S.A. and the Government of any other country receiving assistance.

(2) Exemption from duties and exemption from and refund of Japanese taxes as enumera-ated in the attached Annex E will apply, in addition, to any other expenditures of or financed by the Government of the U.S.A. for materials, supplies, equipment and services for mutual defence, including expenditures made in conformity with the Security Treaty between the U.S.A. and Japan or any foreign aid programme of the Government of the U.S.A. under the Mutual Security Act of 1951, as amended, or any acts supplementary, amendatory or successory thereto.

ARTICLE 7

(1) The Government of Japan agrees to receive personnel of the Government of the

United States of America who will discharge in the territory of Japan the responsibilities of the latter Government regarding equipment, materials and services furnished under the present Agreement, and who will be accorded facilities to observe the progress of the assistance furnished by the Government of the U.S.A., under the present Agreement. Such personnel who are nationals of the U.S.A. including personnel temporarily assigned, will, in their relationships with the Government of Japan, operate as part of the Embassy of the U.S.A. under the direction and control of the Chief of the Diplomatic Mission, and will have the same privileges and immunities as are accorded to other personnel with corresponding rank in the Embassy of the U.S.A.

(2) The Government of Japan will make available, from time to time, to the Government of the U.S.A. funds in yen for the administrative and related expenses of the latter Government in connection with carrying out the present Agreement.

Article 8

The Government of Japan, reaffirming its determination to join in promoting international understanding and goodwill, and maintaining world peace, to take such action as may eliminate causes of international tension, and to fulfil the military obligations which the Government of Japan has assumed under the Security Treaty between the United States of America and Japan, will make, consistent with the political and economic stability of Japan, the full contribution permitted by its manpower, resources, facilities, and general economic condition to the development and maintenance of its own defensive strength and the defensive strength of the free world, take all reasonable measures which may be needed to develop its defence capacities, and take appropriate steps to ensure the effective utilization of any assistance provided by the Government of the U.S.A.

Article 9

(1) Nothing contained in the present Agreement shall be construed to alter or otherwise modify the Security Treaty between the U.S.A. and Japan or any arrangements concluded thereunder.

(2) The present Agreement will be implemented by each Government in accordance with the constitutional provisions of the respective countries.

Article 10

(1) The two Governments will, upon the request of either of them, consult regarding any matter relating to the application of the present Agreement or to operations or arrangements carried out pursuant to the present Agreement.

(2) The terms of the present Agreement may be reviewed at the request of either of the two Governments or amended by agreement between them at any time.

Article 11

(1) The present Agreement shall come into force on the date of receipt by the Government of the U.S.A. of a written notice from the Government of Japan of ratification of the Agreement by Japan [the Agreement entered into force on 1st May, 1954].

(2) The present Agreement will thereafter continue in force until one year after the date of receipt by either Government of a written notice of the intention of the other to terminate it, provided that the provisions of Article 1, paragraphs 2, 3 and 4, and arrangements entered into under Article 3, paragraph 1 and Article 4 shall remain in force unless otherwise agreed by the two Governments.

(3) The Annexes to the present Agreement shall form an integral part thereof.

(4) The present Agreement shall be registered with the Secretariat of the United Nations.

In witness whereof the representatives of the two Governments, duly authorized for the purpose, have signed the present Agreement.

Done in duplicate in the English and Japanese languages, both equally authentic, at Tokyo, this eighth day of March, one thousand nine hundred and fifty four.

Signed: John M. Allison (U.S.A.) — Katzuo Okazakik (Japan)

TREATY OF MUTUAL COOPERATION AND SECURITY BETWEEN JAPAN AND THE U.S.A.

WASHINGTON, 19TH JANUARY, 1960

The United States of America and Japan:

Desiring to strengthen the bonds of peace and friendship traditionally existing between them, and to uphold the principles of democracy, individual liberty and the rule of law,

Desiring further to encourage closer economic cooperation between them and to promote conditions of economic stability and well-being in their countries,

Reaffirming their faith in the purposes and principles of the Charter of the United Nations, and their desire to live in peace with all peoples and all governments,

Recognizing that they have the inherent right of individual or collective self-defence as affirmed in the Charter of the United Nations,

Considering that they have a common concern in the maintenance of international peace and security in the Far East,

Having resolved to conclude a treaty of mutual cooperation and security,

Therefore agree as follows:

ARTICLE 1

The parties undertake, as set forth in the Charter of the United Nations, to settle any international disputes in which they may be involved by peaceful means in such a manner that international peace and security and justice are not endangered and to refrain in their international relations from the threat or use of force against the territorial integrity or political independence of any state, or in any other manner inconsistent with the purposes of the United Nations.

The parties will endeavour in concert with other peace-loving countries to strengthen the United Nations so that its mission of maintaining international peace and security may be discharged more effectively.

ARTICLE 2

The parties will contribute toward the further development of peaceful and friendly international relations by strengthening their free institutions, by bringing about a better understanding of principles upon which these institutions are founded, and by promoting conditions of stability and well-being. They will seek to eliminate conflict in their international economic policies and will encourage economic collaboration between them.

ARTICLE 3

The parties, individually and in cooperation with each other, by means of continuous and effective self-help and mutual aid will maintain and develop, subject to their constitutional provisions, their capacities to resist armed attack.

ARTICLE 4

The parties will consult together from time to time regarding the implementation of this Treaty, and, at the request of either party, whenever the security of Japan or international peace and security in the Far East is threatened.

ARTICLE 5

Each party recognizes that an armed attack against either party in the territories under the administration of Japan would be dangerous to its own peace and safety and declares that it would act to meet the common danger in accordance with its constitutional provisions and processes.

Any such armed attack and all measures taken as a result thereof shall be immediately reported to the Security Council of the United Nations in accordance with the provisions of Article 51 of the Charter. Such measures shall be terminated when the Security Council has taken the measures necessary to restore and maintain international peace and security.

Article 6

For the purpose of contributing to the security of Japan and the maintenance of international peace and security in the Far East, the United States of America is granted the use by its land, air and naval forces of facilities and areas in Japan.

The use of these facilities and areas as well as the status of United States armed forces in Japan shall be governed by a separate Agreement under Article 3 of the Security Treaty between the United States of America and Japan, signed at Tokyo on February 28th, 1952 as amended, and by such other arrangements as may be agreed upon.

Article 7

This Treaty does not affect and shall not be interpreted as affecting in any way the rights and obligations of the parties under the Charter of the United Nations or the responsibility of the United Nations for the maintenance of international peace and security.

Article 8

This Treaty shall be ratified by the United States of America and Japan in accordance with their respective constitutional processes and will enter into force on the date on which the instruments of ratification thereof have been exchanged by them in Tokyo.

Article 9

The Security Treaty between the United States of America and Japan signed at San Francisco on September 8th, 1951, shall expire upon the entering into force of this Treaty.

Article 10

The Treaty shall remain in force until in the opinions of the Governments of the United States of America and Japan there shall have come into force such United Nations arrangements as will satisfactorily provide for the maintenance of international peace and security in the Japan area.

However, after the Treaty has been in force for ten years, either party may give notice to the other party of its intention to terminate the Treaty, in which case the Treaty shall terminate one year after such notice has been given.

In witness whereof the undersigned plenipotentiaries have signed this Treaty. Done in duplicate at Washington in the English and Japanese languages, both equally authentic, this 19th day of January, 1960.

For the U.S.A.: Christian A. Herter
Douglas MacArthur, 2nd
J. Graham Parsons

For Japan: Nobusuke Kishi
Mitsujiro Ishii
Aiichiro Fujiyama
Tadashi Adachi
Koichiro Asakai

Agreed Minute to the Treaty of Mutual Cooperation and Security. Japanese Plenipotentiary:

While the question of the status of the islands administered by the United States of America under Article 3 of the Treaty of Peace with Japan has not been made a subject of discussion in the course of treaty negotiations, I would like to emphasize the strong concern of the Government and People of Japan for the safety of the people of these islands since Japan possesses residual sovereignty over these islands. If an armed attack occurs or is threatened against these islands the two countries will of course consult together closely under Article 4 of the Treaty of Mutual Cooperation and Security. In the event of an armed attack, it is the intention of the Government of Japan to explore with the United States of America measures which it might be able to take for the welfare of the islanders.

UNITED STATES PLENIPOTENTIARY:

In the event of an armed attack against these islands, the United States Government will consult at once with the Government of Japan and intends to take the necessary measures for the defence of these islands, and to do its utmost to secure the welfare of the islanders.

C.A.H.
N.K.

KOREAN ARMISTICE AGREEMENT (SUMMARY)

PANMUNJOM, 27TH JULY, 1953

The undersigned, the Commander-in-Chief, United Nations command, on the one hand, and the Supreme Commander of the Korean People's Army and the Chinese People's Volunteers, on the other hand, in the interest of stopping the Korean conflict, with its great toll of suffering and bloodshed on both sides, and with the objective of establishing an armistice which will ensure a complete cessation of hostilities and of all acts of armed force in Korea until a final peaceful settlement is achieved, do individually, collectively, and mutually agree to accept and to be bound and governed by the conditions and terms of armistice set forth in the following paragraphs, which said conditions and terms are intended to be purely military in character and to pertain solely to the belligerents in Korea.

Military Demarcation Line and Demilitarised Zone

(i) A Military Demarcation Line shall be fixed and both sides shall withdraw to two kilometres from this line so as to establish a Demilitarised Zone between the opposing forces. A Demilitarised Zone shall be established as a buffer Zone to prevent the occurrence of incidents which might lead to a resumption of hostilities. The demarcation line is that drawn up jointly by Staff Officers and shown on a map attached to the Agreement.

(ii) Neither side shall execute any hostile act within, from, or against the Demilitarised Zone. Movement across the Demarcation Line or on the Demilitarised Zone will be strictly controlled except for members of Commissions and Inspection Teams set up by the Agreement in connection with its implementation and supervision.

Concrete Arrangements for Cease-Fire and Armistice

(i) The Commanders of the opposing sides shall order and enforce a complete cessation of all hostilities in Korea, by all armed forces under their control to be effective 12 hours after the signature of the Armistice.

(ii) The Commanders of both sides shall within 72 hours withdraw all military forces, supplies, equipment, from and destroy all fortification in the Demilitarised Zone. A similar withdrawal is to be operated in Korean coastal waters and coastal islands off Korea within 10 days. Off the west coast of Korea, the Agreement provides for the retention under the control of the United Nations forces of certain island groups to the south of latitude 38° 57′ north.

(iii) The Commanders of both sides shall cease the introduction into Korea of reinforcing military personnel and cease the introduction or reinforcing of arms, aircraft and ammunitions with the following exceptions: (a) rotation—i.e. the replacement of units or personnel by other units or personnel, on a man-for-man basis up to 35,000 men per month; (b) replacement of destroyed, damaged or expended arms, aircraft and ammunition on a piece-for-piece basis.

(iv) The Commanders of both sides shall provide 'full protection and all possible assistance and co-operation', together with logistic support to the Commissions and Inspection Teams set up by the Agreement.

(v) The Armistice Agreement shall apply to all the opposing ground, naval and air forces under the military control of each side.

(vi) The Agreement provides for the setting up of a Military Armistice Commission composed of 10 senior officers, five being appointed by each side. This Commission will be assisted by 10 (or less) Joint Observer Teams, each composed of between four and six officers, half of whom are to be appointed by each side. The general function of the Military Armistice Commission will be to supervise the implementation of the Armistice Agreement and to settle through negotiations any violations of this Armistice Agreement. The Commission's Headquarters will be located at Panmunjom, it will 'operate as a joint organisation without a chairman' and adopt its own rules of procedure. The commission will direct the operations of the Joint Observer Teams. It will report the results of its investigations of violations of the Armistice Agreement to the Commanders of the opposing sides and it may recommend amendments or additions to the Agreement 'designed to ensure a more effective Armistice'.

(vii) The Agreement further sets up a Neutral Nations Supervisory Commission composed of four senior officers, one each appointed by Sweden, Switzerland, Czechoslovakia and Poland. This commission shall be initially assisted by 20 Neutral Nations Inspection Teams who will be responsible only to the Supervisory Commission. The functions of the Neutral Nations Supervisory Commission will be to supervise, observe, inspect and investigate the 'rotation' of troops, and the reinforcement and replacement of war material (see (iii) above) and to conduct special investigations into violations of the Agreement at the request of the Military Armistice Commission. The Supervisory Commission will report the results of its work to the Military Armistice Commission. The Supervisory Commission's inspection of the rotation of troops and replacement of war material will be effected at the following 'ports of entry':

(a) In United Nations controlled territory;
(b) In Chinese and North Korean controlled territory.

Arrangements Relating to Prisoners of War

(i) The release and repatriation of prisoners of war held in the custody of each side, at the time this Armistice Agreement becomes effective, is to be effected in accordance with the terms of the separate Agreement signed on 8th June, 1953 (see below). The release and repatriation of such prisoners of war shall be effected in conformity with lists which have been exchanged and have been checked by the respective sides prior to the signing of this Armistice Agreement.

(ii) Both sides agree not to employ in acts of war in the Korean conflict any prisoners of war released and repatriated as a result of the Agreement.

(iii) Subject to the provisions of the terms of reference of the Neutral Nations Repatriation Commission, the release and repatriation of all prisoners shall be completed within a time limit of 60 days after this Armistice Agreement becomes effective. Within this time limit each side undertakes to complete the repatriation of all of the prisoners of war in its custody at the earliest practicable time.

(iv) The Agreement designates Panmunjom as the principal place where prisoners of war will be delivered and received by both sides, and sets up a Committee for Repatriation of Prisoners of War (of six officers, three being designated by each side) to be responsible for co-ordinating and supervising the exchange of prisoners, under the general direction of the Military Armistice Commission.

(v) Provision is also made by the Agreement for joint Red Cross teams composed equally of representatives of the National Red Cross Societies of each side to undertake necessary and desirable humanitarian services in connection with the exchange of prisoners.

(vi) The Commanders of both sides are to provide within 10 days of the signature of the Agreement (a) complete data on prisoners of war who have been captured or have escaped since data was last exchanged; (b) complete information on prisoners of war who have died while in captivity.

(vii) The Agreement lays down that facilities shall be provided for all (Korean) civilians to return to the part of Korea (north or south of the military demarcation line) in which they resided before 24th June, 1950. A similar provision is made for the free movement of foreign nationals. Such movements are to be aided and controlled by a special Committee for Assisting the Return of Displaced Civilians.

[The Agreement signed on 8th June on the prisoner of war repatriation issue was in the form of terms of reference for the Neutral Nations Repatriation Commission. The setting up of such a commission and its membership had been previously agreed.]

Terms of Reference of the Neutral Nations Repatriation Commission

General Terms of Reference

1. In order to ensure that all prisoners of war have the opportunity to exercise their right to be repatriated following an armistice, Sweden, Switzerland, Poland, Czechoslovakia and India shall each be requested by both sides to appoint a member to a Neutral Nations Repatriation Commission which shall be established to take custody in Korea of those prisoners of war who, while in the custody of the detaining powers, have not exercised their right to be repatriated. The Neutral Nations Repatriation Commission shall establish its headquarters within the demilitarised zone in the vicinity of Panmunjom, and shall station subordinate bodies of the same composition as the Neutral Nations Repatriation Commission at those locations at which the Repatriation Commission assumes custody of prisoners of war. Representatives of both sides shall be permitted to observe the operations of the Repatriation Commission and its subordinate bodies to include explanations and interviews.

2. Sufficient armed forces and any other operating personnel required to assist the Neutral Nations Repatriation Commission in carrying out its functions and responsibilities shall be provided exclusively by India, whose representative shall be the umpire in accordance with provisions of the Article 132 of the Geneva Convention [Article 132 of the Convention provided for two parties who are in dispute as to whether there has been any violation of the Convention, to appoint an umpire to decide on the procedure to be followed in an enquiry on the alleged violation], and shall also be chairman and executive agent of the Neutral Nations Repatriation Commission. Representatives from each of the other four powers shall be allowed staff assistants in equal number not exceeding fifty (50) each. The arms of all personnel provided for in this paragraph shall be limited to military police-type small arms.

3. No force or threat of force shall be used against the prisoners of war specified in paragraph 1 above to prevent or effect their repatriation, and no violence to their persons or affront to their dignity or self-respect shall be permitted in any manner for any purpose whatsoever. This duty is enjoined on and entrusted to the Neutral Nations Repatriation Commission. This Commission shall ensure that prisoners of war shall at all times be treated humanely in accordance with the specific provisions of the Geneva Convention, and with the general spirit of that Convention.

Custody of Prisoners of War

4. The Agreement provides that all prisoners of war who do not exercise their right of repatriation after the conclusion of an Armistice shall be handed over by the detaining side to the Commission, within at most 60 days.

5. The Neutral Nations Repatriation Commission, after having received and taken into custody all those prisoners of war who have not exercised their right to be repatriated, shall immediately make arrangements so that, within 10 days after the Neutral Nations Repatriation Commission takes over custody, the nations to which the prisoners of war belong shall have freedom and facilities to send representatives to the locations where such prisoners of war are in custody to explain to all the prisoners of war depending upon these nations their rights and to inform them of any matters relating to their return to their homelands, particularly of their full freedom to return home to lead a peaceful life.

The number of these representatives is not to exceed 7 per 1,000 prisoners with a minimum of five representatives, and all interviews with prisoners of war are to be conducted in the presence of a representative of each member nation of the Commission and of the detaining side.

Disposition of Prisoners of War

6. Any prisoner of war who, while in the custody of the Neutral Nations Repatriation Commission, decides to exercise the right of repatriation, shall make an application requesting repatriation to a body consisting of a representative of each member nation of the Neutral Nations Repatriation Commission. If the application is approved, the prisoner in question is to be repatriated.

7. Ninety days after transfer of custody of prisoners of war to the Commission, access of representatives to captured personnel shall terminate, and the question of disposition of the

prisoners of war who have not exercised their right to be repatriated shall be submitted to the political conference recommended to be convened in Paragraph 60 of the draft Armistice Agreement, which shall endeavour to settle this question within 30 days, during which period the Neutral Nations Repatriation Commission shall continue to retain custody of those prisoners of war. Any prisoners of war, who within 120 days after the Neutral Nations Repatriation Commission has assumed their custody have not exercised their right to be repatriated and for whom no other disposition has been agreed to by the political conference, shall be changed from prisoner of war status to civilian status by declaration of the Neutral Nations Repatriation Commission.

Thereafter, according to the application of each individual, those who choose to go to Neutral Nations shall be assisted by the Neutral Nations Repatriation Commission and the Red Cross Society of India. This operation shall be completed within 30 days, and upon its completion, the Neutral Nations Repatriation Commission shall immediately cease its functions and declare its dissolution. After the dissolution of the Neutral Nations Repatriation Commission, whenever and wherever any of those above-mentioned civilians who have been relieved from prisoner of war status desire to return to their fatherlands, the authorities of the localities where they are shall be responsible for assisting them in returning to their fatherlands.

Other Provisions

8. After the Armistice Agreement becomes effective, the terms of this Agreement shall be made known to all prisoners of war who, while in the custody of the detaining side, have not exercised their right to be repatriated.

9. The interpretation of this Agreement shall rest with the Neutral Nations Repatriation Commission. The Neutral Nations Repatriation Commission and/or any subordinate bodies to which functions are delegated or assigned by the Neutral Nations Repatriation Commission shall operate on the basis of majority vote.

10. The Agreement will come into effect after accession to it by the five nations named to the Commission and at the same time as the coming into effect of an Armistice.

[Other paragraphs deal *inter alia* with Red Cross services for prisoners of war, freedom of press coverage, and logistical support both for prisoners of war and for the Commission.]

Recommendations to Governments Concerned on Both Sides

In order to ensure the peaceful settlement of the Korean question, the military commanders of both sides hereby recommend to the Governments of the Countries concerned on both sides, that within three (3) months after the Armistice Agreement is signed and becomes effective, a political conference of a higher level of both sides be held by representatives appointed respectively to settle through negotiations the questions of the withdrawal of all foreign forces from Korea, the peaceful settlement of the Korean question, etc.

Miscellaneous

(a) Amendments and additions to this Armistice Agreement must be mutually agreed to by the Commanders of the opposing sides.

(b) The paragraphs of this Armistice Agreement shall remain in effect until expressly superseded either by mutually acceptable amendments and additions or by provision in an appropriate agreement for a peaceful settlement at a political level between both sides.

SOUTH-EAST ASIA

FINAL DECLARATION OF THE GENEVA CONFERENCE ON THE RESTORATION OF PEACE IN INDO-CHINA

GENEVA, 21ST JULY, 1954

[Members of the Conference were Cambodia, China, Democratic Republic of Vietnam, France, Laos, State of Vietnam, U.K., U.S.A. and U.S.S.R.]

(1) The Conference takes note of the agreements ending hostilities in Cambodia, Laos and Vietnam and organizing international control and the supervision of the execution of the provisions of these agreements.

(2) The Conference expresses satisfaction at the ending of hostilities in Cambodia, Vietnam and Laos; the Conference expresses its conviction that the execution of the provisions set out in the present declaration and in the agreements on the cessation of hostilities will permit Cambodia, Laos and Vietnam thenceforth to play their part, in full independence and sovereignty, in the peaceful community of nations.

(3) The Conference takes note of the declarations made by the Governments of Cambodia and of Laos of their intention to adopt measures permitting all citizens to take their place in the national community, in particular by participating in the next general elections, which, in conformity with the constitution of each of these countries, shall take place in the course of the year 1955, and in conditions of respect for fundamental freedoms.

(4) The Conference takes note of the clauses in the agreements on the cessation of hostilities in Vietnam prohibiting the introduction into Vietnam of foreign troops and military personnel as well as of all kinds of arms and munitions. The Conference also takes note of the declarations made by the Governments of Cambodia and Laos of their resolution not to request foreign aid, whether in war material, in personnel or in instructors, except for the purpose of the effective defence of their territory and in the case of Laos, to the extent defined by the agreements on the cessation of hostilities in Laos.

(5) The Conference takes note of the clauses in the agreement on the cessation of hostilities in Laos to the effect that no military base under the control of a foreign state may be established in the regrouping zones of the two parties, the latter having the obligation to see that the zones allotted to them shall not constitute part of any military alliance and shall not be utilized for the resumption of hostilities or in the service of an aggressive policy. The Conference also takes note of the declarations of the Governments of Cambodia and Laos to the effect that they will not join in any agreement with other states if this agreement includes the obligation to participate in a military alliance not in conformity with the principles of the Charter of the United Nations or, in the case of Laos, with the principles of the agreement on the cessation of hostilities in Laos, or, so long as their security is not threatened, the obligation to establish bases on Cambodian or Laotian territory for the military forces of foreign Powers.

(6) The Conference recognises that the essential purpose of the agreement relating to Vietnam is to settle military questions with a view to ending hostilities and that the military demarcation line is provisional and should not in any way be interpreted as constituting a political or territorial boundary. The Conference expresses its conviction that the execution of the provisions set out in the present declaration and in the agreement on the cessation of hostilities creates the necessary basis for the achievement in the near future of a political settlement in Vietnam.

(7) The Conference declares that so far as Vietnam is concerned, the settlement of political problems, effected on the basis of respect for the principles of independence, unity and territorial integrity, shall permit the Vietnamese people to enjoy the fundamental

freedoms, guaranteed by democratic institutions established as a result of free general elections by secret ballot In order to ensure that sufficient progress in the restoration of peace has been made, and that all the necessary conditions obtain for free expression of the nation's will, general elections shall be held in July, 1956, under the supervision of an international commission composed of representatives of the member States of the International Supervisory Commission, referred to in the agreement on the cessation of hostilities. Consultations will be held on this subject between the competent representative authorities of the two zones from July 20th, 1955, onwards.

(8) The provisions of the agreement on the cessation of hostilities intended to ensure the protection of individuals and of property must be most strictly applied and must, in particular, allow everyone in Vietnam to decide freely in which zone he wishes to live.

(9) The competent representative authorities of the Northern and Southern Zones of Vietnam, as well as the authorities of Laos and Cambodia, must not permit any individual or collective reprisals against persons who have collaborated in any way with one of the parties during the war, or against members of such persons' families.

(10) The Conference takes note of the declaration of the Government of the French Republic to the effect that it is ready to withdraw its troops from the territory of Cambodia, Laos and Vietnam, at the request of the Governments concerned and within periods which shall be fixed by agreement between the parties except in the cases where, by agreement between the two parties, a certain number of French troops shall remain at specified points and for a specified time.

(11) The Conference takes note of the declaration of the French Government to the effect that for the settlement of all the problems connected with the re-establishment and consolidation of peace in Cambodia, Laos and Vietnam, the French Government will proceed from the principle of respect for the independence and sovereignty, unity and territorial integrity of Cambodia, Laos and Vietnam.

(12) In their relations with Cambodia, Laos and Vietnam, each member of the Geneva Conference undertakes to respect the sovereignty, the independence and the territorial integrity of the above-mentioned states and to refrain from any interference in their internal affairs.

(13) The members of the Conference agree to consult one another on any question which may be referred to them by the International Supervisory Commission, in order to study such measures as may prove necessary to ensure that the agreements on the cessation of hostilities in Cambodia, Laos and Vietnam are respected.

MALAYSIA AGREEMENT (ABRIDGED)

London, 9th July, 1963

The United Kingdom of Great Britain and Northern Ireland, the Federation of Malaya, North Borneo, Sarawak and Singapore:

Desiring to conclude an Agreement relating to Malaysia agree as follows:—

Article 1

The Colonies of North Borneo and Sarawak and the State of Singapore shall be federated with the existing states of the Federation of Malaya as the States of Sabah, Sarawak and Singapore in accordance with the constitutional instruments annexed to this Agreement and the Federation shall thereafter be called 'Malaysia'.

Article 2

The Government of the Federation of Malaya will take such steps as may be appropriate and available to them to secure the enactment by the Parliament of the Federation of Malaya of an Act and that it is brought into operation on 31st August, 1963 (and the date on which the said Act is brought into operation is hereinafter referred to as 'Malaysia Day').

ARTICLE 3

The Government of the United Kingdom will submit to Her Britannic Majesty before Malaysia Day Orders in Council for the purpose of giving the force of law to the Constitutions of Sabah, Sarawak and Singapore as States of Malaysia.

ARTICLE 4

The Government of the United Kingdom will take such steps as may be appropriate and available to them to secure the enactments by the Parliament of the United Kingdom of an Act providing for the relinquishment, as from Malaysia Day, of her Britannic Majesty's sovereignty and jurisdiction in respect of North Borneo, Sarawak and Singapore so that the said sovereignty and jurisdiction shall on such relinquishment rest in accordance with this Agreement and the constitutional instruments annexed to this Agreement.

ARTICLE 5

The Government of the Federation of Malaya will take such steps as may be appropriate and available to them to secure the enactment before Malaysia Day by the Parliament of the Federation of Malaya of an Act for the purpose of extending and adapting the Immigration Ordinance, 1959, of the Federation of Malaya to Malaysia and of making additional provisions with respect to entry into the States of Sabah and Sarawak; and the other provisions of this Agreement shall be conditional upon the enactment of the said Act.

ARTICLE 6

The Agreement on External Defence and Mutual Assistance between the Government of the United Kingdom and the Government of the Federation of Malaya of 12th October, 1957 and its annexes shall apply to all territories of Malaysia, and any reference in that Agreement to the Federation of Malaya shall be deemed to apply to Malaysia, subject to the promise that the Government of Malaysia will afford to the Government of the United Kingdom the right to continue to maintain the bases and other facilities at present occupied by their service authorities within the State of Singapore and will permit the Government of the United Kingdom to make such use of those bases and facilities as the Government may consider necessary for the purpose of assisting in the defence of Malaysia, and for Commonwealth defence and for the preservation of peace in South-East Asia.

ARTICLE 7

(1) The Federation of Malaya agrees that her Britannic Majesty may make before Malaysia Day Orders in Council for the purpose of making provision for the payment of compensation and retirement benefits to certain overseas officers serving, immediately before Malaysia Day, in the public service of the Colony of North Borneo or the Colony of Sarawak.

(2) On or as soon as practicable after Malaysia Day, Public Officers' Agreements shall be signed on behalf of the Government of the United Kingdom and the Government of Malaysia; and the Government of Malaysia shall obtain the concurrence of the Government of the State of Sabah, Sarawak or Singapore, as the case may require, to the signature of the Agreement by the Government of Malaysia so far as its terms may affect the responsibilities or interests of the Government of the State.

ARTICLE 8

The Governments of the Federation of Malaya, North Borneo and Sarawak will take such legislative, executive or other actions as may be required to implement the assurances, undertakings and recommendations signed on 27th February, 1963, in so far as they are not implemented by express provision of the Constitution of Malaysia.

ARTICLE 9

The provisions of this Agreement relating to Common Market and financial arrangements shall constitute an Agreement between the Government of the Federation of Malaya and the Government of Singapore.

ARTICLE 10

The Governments of the Federation of Malaya and of Singapore will take such legislative or other actions as may be required to implement the arrangements with respect to broadcasting and television in so far as they are not implemented by express provision of the Constitution of Malaysia.

ARTICLE 11

This Agreement shall be signed in the English and Malay languages. In case of doubt the English text of the Agreement shall prevail.

Done at London this Ninth Day of July, Nineteen Hundred and Sixty Three, in five copies of which one shall be deposited with each of the Parties.

TREATY OF FRIENDSHIP BETWEEN INDONESIA AND CHINA

DJAKARTA, 1ST APRIL, 1961

The Government of the People's Republic of China and the Government of the Republic of Indonesia, out of the desire to maintain and further develop cooperation and friendly relations between the two countries and, in accordance with the spirit and the ten principles of the 1955 Asian-African Bandung Conference as well as the five principles of peaceful co-existence, have decided to conclude the present treaty and have appointed as their respective plenipotentiaries:

The Government of the People's Republic of China: Marshal Chen Yi, Vice-Premier of the State Council and Minister of Foreign Affairs of the People's Republic of China;

The Government of the Republic of Indonesia: Dr. Subandrio, Second Deputy Chief Minister and Minister of Foreign Affairs;

Who, having examined each other's credentials and found them in good and due form have agreed upon the following:

ARTICLE 1

The contracting parties respect each other's independence, sovereignty and territorial integrity so as to maintain and develop the friendly relations between the two countries.

ARTICLE 2

The contracting parties agree to continuously consolidate the diplomatic and consular relations between the two countries in accordance with the principles of reciprocity and international practice.

ARTICLE 3

The contracting parties will, when they deem it necessary, designate delegates to meet to exchange views on questions of common interest and consider methods and ways of co-operation on the above-mentioned questions.

ARTICLE 4

The contracting parties agree to develop and further strengthen the economic and cultural ties between the two countries in the spirit of friendship and co-operation and in accordance with the principles of equality and mutual benefit and of non-interference in each other's internal affairs.

ARTICLE 5

Should any dispute arise between the contracting parties, they shall settle it by consultation through diplomatic channels and other ways agreed upon by both parties in a spirit of fraternal and sincere friendship.

ARTICLE 6

The present treaty shall be ratified by the contracting parties in accordance with their respective constitutional procedures and shall come into force upon the date of the exchange of the instruments of ratification, which shall take place in Peking.

ARTICLE 7

The present treaty shall remain in force for a period of ten years but each contracting party has the right to notify the other to terminate this treaty, and the treaty shall cease to be in force six months after the day of such notification.

ARTICLE 8

The present treaty is done in duplicate in the Chinese and Indonesian languages, both texts being equally authentic.

In faith hereof, the plenipotentiaries of the contracting parties have affixed their signatures on the present treaty.

Done in Djakarta on the first day of April Nineteen Hundred and Sixty One.

COLOMBO PLAN FOR COOPERATIVE ECONOMIC DEVELOPMENT IN S. AND S. E. ASIA: CONSTITUTION OF COUNCIL FOR TECHNICAL COOPERATION

LONDON, SEPTEMBER, 1950

PREAMBLE

The Governments of Australia, Canada, Ceylon, India, New Zealand, Pakistan and the United Kingdom having considered:

(a) the urgent need for further technical assistance, additional to that available from other sources, to promote economic development in South and South-East Asia with a view to raising the living standards of the peoples of the area,

(b) the desirability of developing further cooperation and enterprise in the provision of technical assistance, and

(c) the need for fullest cooperation with the United Nations and other agencies providing technical assistance in the area, with a view to encouraging and speeding the provision of technical assistance from all sources,

have resolved that a scheme should be organized to provide assistance up to a maximum value of £8 million sterling over the three years commencing 1st July, 1950, and that, for the purpose of this work, a Council for Technical Cooperation in South and South-East Asia should be set up with the following constitution.

A—FUNCTIONS

1. The purpose of the Council for Technical Cooperation is to assist in the economic development of South and South-East Asia by the provision of technical assistance.

2. The Council will organize the provision of such assistance as the following:

(i) (a) Training of personnel from countries in the area in countries where suitable instruction is available, and the despatch of missions abroad to study the latest techniques or practices;

(b) Experts, instructors and advisory missions to assist in planning, development or reconstruction, or for use in public administration, in health services, scientific research, in agricultural, industrial, or other productive activities and in the training of personnel;

(c) The provision of equipment required for training or use by technical experts in the region.

(ii) Where any cooperating Government considers that the provision of technical assistance requires the establishment, equipment, extension or endowment of training or other institutions in the countries of the region not available under any other scheme, such facilities may be contributed as technical assistance. It will be for the country requested to provide assistance to decide whether such assistance should be afforded.

3. The Council will investigate any obstacles or difficulties that reduce or prevent the availability or best use of technical assistance, and will use its best endeavours to remove or mitigate all such obstacles or difficulties.

4. For the guidance of cooperating Governments the Council will endeavour to agree on

the general conditions such as remuneration and allowances which might best apply to experts and others who are employed in various countries of South and South-East Asia and to trainees, whenever sent out of their own country.

B—Organization

5. The Council will consist of one representative of each cooperating Government. The Council may at any time admit to its membership a Government which applies to cooperate under the Scheme.

6. The Council will establish headquarters in Colombo where it will normally meet as often as business requires. It may, however, meet from time to time at any other convenient place in the area.

7. Each cooperating Government will meet the expenses of its representatives on the Council.

8. To assist the Council in the performance of its duties a Bureau will be established consisting of a Director and such other Staff as the Council may appoint.

9. Under the control of the Council, the Director of the Bureau shall organize the development of the Technical Co-operation Scheme.

10. The Director shall submit for approval by the Council an estimate of expenditure for each year ending 30th June.

11. Contributions by each Government to meet the working expenses of the Council for any year will, unless otherwise determined by the Council, be in the same proportion as the contributions to the Technical Cooperation Scheme for that year.

12. The Council will make appropriate provision for the maintenance and audit of its accounts.

13. The Council will take into account the known views of cooperating Governments unable from time to time to be represented at a Council meeting. Any increase in the membership of the Council or changes in its constitution or office of Director will be made only after proposals have been discussed and agreed between all cooperating Governments. The estimated working expenses of the Council and the proportion in which these expenses will be borne by cooperating Governments will also be discussed and agreed between them. The Council will proceed in the cooperative spirit which is the keynote of the Scheme and endeavour at all times to reach agreement without formal rules of procedure.

C—Administration

14. The Director of the Bureau shall maintain and make available to all cooperating Governments an up-to-date record of all sources of technical assistance available to the area through any international or national agency.

15. The Director of the Bureau shall establish liaison immediately with the United Nations and the specialized agencies, and with all other organizations or countries not members of the Scheme, which are presently affording technical assistance within South and South-East Asia, or which may in future decide to do so.

16. Each cooperating Government will supply the Director of the Bureau with a statement of the types of technical assistance which it can make available, and will from time to time supplement and revise such information.

17. Cooperating Governments seeking technical assistance under the Scheme will state their requirements to the Director of the Bureau, and will provide such relevant information as may be required to deal with them, including particulars of any application made to any other agency.

18. On receipt of a request for technical assistance, the Director of the Bureau shall give every assistance in documenting the request and bringing it to a successful conclusion.

19. Cooperating Governments to whom requests for assistance are transmitted will advise the Director of the Bureau, as soon as possible, of any assistance that can be arranged, and he shall be responsible for putting the Governments in touch either direct or through the Council.

20. In the furtherance of the work of the Council, members of the Council, the Director of

the Bureau or members of the Staff may visit any cooperating country with the agreement of the Government concerned.

21. The Director shall prepare for the Council periodical progress reports of the Scheme at such intervals as the Council may require. For this purpose each cooperating country will maintain contact with the Director on the progress of requests for technical assistance under the Scheme.

D—Operation of the Scheme

22. Technical assistance provided under the Scheme will be arranged on a bilateral basis by agreement between cooperating Governments, and the terms and conditions upon which assistance is provided will, in every case, be solely a matter for the Governments concerned. Bilateral arrangements do not exclude joint schemes where more than two cooperating countries are involved.

23. In order to ensure, in the interests of the area, the best use of resources available, a contributing Government will, in the normal course, be expected to bear, to the fullest extent possible, as a charge against its contribution to the Scheme, the costs of basic salaries of persons whom it makes available under the Scheme, and the Government to whom experts are made available will, in the normal course, be expected to bear, to the fullest extent possible, the local costs of the experts, including subsistence and travelling.

24. In order to assist cooperating countries to secure training for personnel additional to that already available from existing sources, the cooperating countries will normally accept personnel for training on the following basis: So far as practicable the country from which the trainees are sent will defray the costs arising in respect of the trainees in their own country; and, so far as practicable, the Government of the country providing training will bear all costs of training arising within its own territories, including allowances for the maintenance of trainees.

25. The allocation of costs suggested in paragraphs 23 and 24 is intended only as a pattern for the guidance of cooperating Governments and these provisions do not in any way detract from the clear understanding that in every case such arrangements will be solely a matter for the Governments concerned as provided in paragraph 22.

26. Governments will make special efforts to encourage the training of personnel in the trainee's own country, and for this purpose other cooperating Governments will devote as large a proportion of their contribution as is practicable to provide teaching staff and material facilities.

27. Any cooperating Government may, as a contribution under the Scheme, offer to defray the costs of obtaining technical assistance or training facilities, including endowment of existing institutions, in any other country. In the event that the facilities needed to satisfy an application for technical assistance cannot be provided because they are only available either in a country whose Government's contribution to the Scheme is exhausted or in a non-participating country, the Council shall endeavour to arrange for the costs to be met from the uncommitted part of the contribution offered by other cooperating Governments, bearing in mind the desirability of maintaining reasonable equality in the extent to which contributions are fully utilized.

28. Costs met by a cooperating Government in respect of technical assistance received by it will not be regarded as a contribution under the Scheme.

29. To ensure an adequate record of the progress of the Scheme and also of the appropriate distribution of the expenses incurred, the Council will keep accounts of the expenditure incurred by each cooperating Government under the Scheme. For this purpose each cooperating country will forward a periodical statement to the Director showing, for the period in question, particulars of the expenditure incurred and chargeable under the Scheme.

SECURITY TREATY BETWEEN AUSTRALIA, NEW ZEALAND AND THE U.S.A.

SAN FRANCISCO, 1ST SEPTEMBER, 1951

The Parties to this Treaty,

Reaffirming their faith in the purpose and principles of the Charter of the United Nations and their desire to live in peace with all peoples, and all Governments, and desiring to strengthen the fabric of peace in the Pacific Area,

Noting that the United States already has arrangements pursuant to which its armed forces are stationed in the Philippines, and has armed forces and administrative responsibilities in the Ryukyus, and upon the coming into force of the Japanese Peace Treaty may also station armed forces in and about Japan to assist in the preservation of peace and security in the Japanese Area,

Recognising that Australia and New Zealand as members of the British Commonwealth of Nations have military obligations outside as well as within the Pacific Area,

Desiring to declare publicly and formally their sense of unity, so that no potential aggressor could be under the illusion that any of them stand alone in the Pacific Area, and

Desiring further to co-ordinate their efforts for collective defence for the preservation of peace and security pending the development of a more co-operative system of regional security in the Pacific Area,

Therefore declare and agree as follows:

ARTICLE 1

The Parties undertake as set forth in the Charter of the United Nations, to settle any international disputes in which they may be involved by peaceful means in such a manner that international peace and security and justice are not endangered and to refrain in their international relations from the threat or use of force in any manner inconsistent with the purposes of the United Nations.

ARTICLE 2

In order more effectively to achieve the objective of this Treaty the Parties separately and jointly by means of continuous and effective self-help and mutual aid will maintain and develop their individual and collective capacity to resist armed attack.

ARTICLE 3

The Parties will consult together whenever in the opinion of any of them the territorial integrity, political independence or security of any of the Parties is threatened in the Pacific

ARTICLE 4

Each Party recognises that an armed attack in the Pacific Area on any of the Parties would be dangerous to its own peace and safety and declares that it would act to meet the common danger in accordance with its constitutional processes.

Any such armed attack and all such measures taken as a result thereof shall be immediately reported to the Security Council of the United Nations. Such measures shall be terminated when the Security Council has taken the measures necessary to restore and maintain international peace and security.

ARTICLE 5

For the purpose of Article 4, an armed attack on any of the Parties is deemed to include an armed attack on the metropolitan territory of any of the Parties, or on the island territories under its jurisdiction in the Pacific or on its armed forces, public vessels or aircraft in the Pacific.

ARTICLE 6

This Treaty does not affect and shall not be interpreted as affecting in any way the rights and obligations of the Parties under the Charter of the United Nations, and the responsibility of the United Nations for the maintenance of international peace and security.

ARTICLE 7

The Parties hereby establish a Council, consisting of their Foreign Ministers and their Deputies, to consider matters concerning the implementation of this Treaty. The Council should be so organised as to be able to meet at any time.

ARTICLE 8

Pending the development of a more comprehensive system of regional security in the Pacific Area and the development by the United Nations of more effective means to maintain international peace and security, the Council, established by Article 7, is authorised to maintain a consultative relationship with States, Regional Organizations, Associations of States and other authorities in the Pacific Area in a position to further the purposes of this Treaty and to contribute to the security of that Area.

ARTICLE 9

This Treaty shall be ratified by the Parties in accordance with their respective constitutional processes. The instruments of ratification shall be deposited as soon as possible with the Government of Australia, which will notify each of the other signatories of such deposits. The Treaty shall enter into force as soon as the ratifications of the signatories have been deposited.

ARTICLE 10

This Treaty shall remain in force indefinitely. Any Party may cease to be a member of the Council established by Article 7 one year after notice has been given to the Government of Australia, which will inform the Governments of the other parties of the deposit of such notice.

ARTICLE 11

This Treaty in the English language shall be deposited in the archives of the Government of Australia. Duly certified copies thereof will be transmitted by that Government to the Governments of each of the other signatories.

In witness whereof the undersigned plenipotentiaries have signed this Treaty.

Done at the city of San Francisco this first day of September, One thousand, nine hundred and fifty one.

SOUTH-EAST ASIA COLLECTIVE DEFENCE TREATY (EXTRACTS)

MANILA, 8TH SEPTEMBER, 1954

[On 8th September, 1954 Australia, France, New Zealand, Pakistan, the Philippines, Thailand, the United Kingdom and the U.S.A. signed at Manila a pact of 'continuous and effective self-help and mutual aid,' which established a collective defence system in South-East Asia.]

ARTICLE 4

(1) Each party recognises that aggression by means of armed attack in the treaty area against any of the parties or against any state or territory which the parties by unanimous agreement may hereafter designate would endanger its own peace and safety, and agrees that it will in that event act to meet the common danger in accordance with its constitutional processes. Measures taken under this paragraph shall be immediately reported to the Security Council of the United Nations.

(2) If in the opinion of any of the parties the inviolability or the integrity of the territory or the sovereignty or political independence of any party in the treaty area or of any other State or territory to which the provisions of paragraph (1) of this article from time to time apply is threatened in any way other than by armed attack or is affected or threatened by any fact or situation which might endanger the peace of the area, the parties shall consult immediately in order to agree on the measures which should be taken for the common defence.

(3) It is understood that no action on the territory of any State designated by unanimous agreement under paragraph (1) of this article or on any territory so designated shall be taken except at the invitation or with the consent of the government concerned.

ARTICLE 5

The parties hereby establish a council on which each of them shall be represented to consider matters concerning the implementation of this treaty. The council shall provide for consultation with regard to military and any other planning as the situation obtaining in the treaty area may from time to time require.

ARTICLE 6

This treaty does not affect and shall not be interpreted as affecting in any way the rights and obligations of any of the parties under the Charter of the United Nations or the responsibility of the United Nations for the maintenance of international peace and security. Each party declares that none of the international engagements now in force between it and any other of the parties or any third party is in conflict with the provisions of this treaty and undertakes not to enter into any international engagement in conflict with this treaty.

ARTICLE 7

Any other State in a position to further the objective of this treaty and to contribute to the security of the area may by unanimous agreement of the parties be invited to accede to this treaty. Any State so invited may become a party to the treaty by depositing its instrument of accession with the Government of the Republic of the Philippines which shall inform each of the parties of the deposit of each such instrument of accession.

ARTICLE 8

As used in this treaty, the treaty area is the general area of South-East Asia including also the entire territories of the Asian parties and the general area of the South-West Pacific not including the Pacific area north of 21° 30′ N. lat. The parties may by unanimous agreement amend this article to include within the treaty area the territory of any State acceding to this treaty or otherwise to change the treaty area.

ARTICLE 10

This treaty shall remain in force indefinitely but any party may cease to be a party one year after its notice of denunciation has been given to the Governments of the other parties.

APPENDIX

The United States of America in executing the present treaty does so with the understanding that its recognition of the effect of aggression and armed attack and its agreement with reference thereto in Article 4, paragraph (1), apply only to Communist aggression, but affirms that in the event of other aggression or armed attack it will consult under the provisions of Article 4(2).

FINAL COMMUNIQUE OF ASIAN-AFRICAN CONFERENCE

Bandung, 24th April, 1955

The Asian-African Conference, convened upon the invitation of the Prime Ministers of Burma, Ceylon, India, Indonesia, and Pakistan, met in Bandung from the 18th to the 24th April, 1955. In addition to the sponsoring countries the following 24 countries participated in the Conference.

Afghanistan	Liberia
Cambodia	Libya
People's Republic of China	Nepal
Egypt	Philippines
Ethiopia	Saudi Arabia
Gold Coast	Sudan
Iran	Syria
Iraq	Thailand
Japan	Turkey
Jordan	Democratic Republic of Vietnam
Laos	State of Vietnam
Lebanon	Yemen

The Asian-African Conference considered problems of common interest and concern to countries of Asia and Africa and discussed ways and means by which their people could achieve fuller economic, cultural and political co-operation.

A. Economic Co-operation

1. The Asian-African Conference recognised the urgency of promoting economic development in the Asian-African region. There was general desire for economic co-operation among the participating countries on the basis of mutual interest and respect for national sovereignty. The proposals with regard to economic co-operation within the participating countries do not preclude either the desirability or the need for co-operation with countries outside the region, including the investment of foreign capital. It was further recognized that countries outside the region, through international or under bilateral arrangements, had made a valuable contribution to the implementation of their development programmes.

2. The participating countries agreed to provide technical assistance to one another, to the maximum extent practicable, in the form of: experts, trainees, pilot projects and equipment for demonstration purposes; exchange of know-how and establishment of national, and technical knowledge and skills in co-operation with the existing international agencies.

3. The Asian-African Conference recommended the early establishment of the Special United Nations Fund for Economic Development; the allocation by the International Bank for Reconstruction and Development of a greater part of its resources to Asian-African countries; the early establishment of the International Finance Corporation which should include in its activities the undertaking to equity investment; and encouragement to the promotion of joint ventures among Asian-African countries in so far as this will promote their common interest.

4. The Asian-African Conference recognised the vital need for stabilising commodity trade in the region. The principle of enlarging the scope of multilateral trade and payments was accepted. However, it was recognized that some countries would have to take recourse to bilateral trade agreements in view of their prevailing economic conditions.

5. The Asian-African Conference recommended that collective action be taken by participating countries for stabilising the international prices of and demand for primary commodities through bilateral and multilateral arrangements, and that as far as practical and desirable, they should adopt a unified approach on the subject in the United Nations Per-

manent Advisory Commission on International Commodity Trade and other international forums.

6. The Asian-African Conference further recommended that Asian-African countries should diversify their export trade by processing their raw materials, wherever economically feasible, before export; that intra-regional trade fairs should be promoted and encouragement given to the exchange of trade delegations and groups of businessmen; that exchange of information and of samples should be encouraged with a view of promoting intra-regional trade, and that normal facilities should be provided for transit trade of land-locked countries.

7. The Asian-African Conference attached considerable importance to shipping and expressed concern that shipping lines reviewed from time to time their freight rates, often to the detriment of participating countries. It recommended a study of this problem, and collective action thereafter, to induce the shipping lines to adopt a more reasonable attitude. It was suggested that a study of railway freight of transit trade might be made.

8. The Asian-African Conference agreed that encouragement should be given to the establishment of national and regional banks and insurance companies.

9. The Asian-African Conference felt that exchange of information on matters relating to oil, such as remittance of profits and taxation, might eventually lead to the formulation of common policies.

10. The Asian-African Conference emphasised the particular significance of the development of nuclear energy for peaceful purposes for the Asian-African countries. The Conference welcomed the initiative of the Power principally concerned in offering to make available information regarding the use of atomic energy for peaceful purposes; urged the speedy establishment of the International Atomic Energy Agency which should provide for adequate representation of the Asian-African countries on the executive authority of the Agency; and recommended to the Asian and African Governments to take full advantage of the training and other facilities in the peaceful uses of atomic energy offered by the countries sponsoring such programmes.

11. The Asian-African Conference agreed to the appointment of Liaison Officers in participating countries, to be nominated by their respective national Governments, for the exchange of information and ideas on matters of mutual interest. It recommended that fuller use should be made of the existing international organisations, and participating countries who were not members of such international organisations but were eligible, should secure membership.

12. The Asian-African Conference recommended that there should be prior consultation with participating countries in international forms with a view, as far as possible, to furthering their mutual economic interest. It is, however, not intended to form a regional bloc.

B. Cultural Co-operation

1. The Asian-African Conference was convinced that among the most powerful means of promoting understanding among nations is the development of cultural co-operation. Asia and Africa have been the cradle of great religions and civilisations, which influenced other civilisations and cultures while themselves being enriched in the process. Thus the cultures of Asia and Africa are based on spiritual and universal foundations. Unfortunately, contact among Asian and African countries was interrupted during the past centuries. The peoples of Asia and Africa are now animated by a keen and sincere desire to renew their old cultural contacts and develop new ones in the context of the modern world. All participating Governments at the Conference reiterated their determination to work for closer cultural co-operation.

2. The Asian-African Conference took note of the fact that the existence of colonialism in many parts of Asia and Africa, in whatever form it may be, not only prevents cultura co-operation but also suppresses the national cultures of the people. Some colonial powers have denied to their dependent people basic rights in the sphere of education and culture, which hampers the development of their personality and also prevents cultural intercourse with other Asian and African peoples. This is particularly true in the case of Tunisia, Algeria, and Morocco, where the basic right of the people to study their own language and culture has been suppressed. Similar discrimination has been practised against African and coloured peoples in some parts of the Continent of Africa. The Conference felt that these policies amount

to a denial of the fundamental rights of man and impede cultural advancement in this region and also hamper cultural co-operation on the wider international plane. The Conference condemned culture in some parts of Asia and Africa by this and other forms of cultural suppression.

In particular the Conference condemned racialism as a means of cultural suppression.

3. It was not from any sense of exclusiveness or rivalry with other groups of nations and other civilisations and cultures that the Conference viewed the development of cultural co-operation among Asian and African countries. True to the age-old tradition of tolerance and universality, the Conference believed that Asian and African cultural co-operation should be developed in the larger context of world co-operation.

Side by side with the development of Asian-African cultural co-operation, the countries of Asia and Africa desire to develop cultural contacts with others. This would enrich their own culture and would also help in the promotion of world peace and understanding.

4. There are many countries in Asia and Africa which have not yet been able to develop their educational, scientific and technical institutions. The Conference recommended that countries in Asia and Africa which are more fortunately placed in this respect should give facilities for the admission of students and trainees from such countries to their institutions. Such facilities should also be made available to the Asian and African people to whom opportunities for acquiring higher education are at present denied.

5. The Asian-African Conference felt that the promotion of cultural co-operation among countries of Asia and Africa should be directed towards:

(i) the acquisition of knowledge of each other's country;

(ii) mutual cultural exchange; and

(iii) exchange of information.

6. The Asian-African Conference was of opinion that at this stage the best results in cultural co-operation would be achieved by pursuing bilateral arrangements to implement its recommendations and by each country taking action on its own, wherever possible and feasible.

C. Human Rights and Self-Determination

1. The Asian-African Conference declared its full support of the Fundamental Principles of Human Rights as set forth in the Charter of the United Nations and took note of the Universal Declaration of Human Rights as a common standard of achievement for all peoples and all nations.

The Conference declared its full support of the principle of self-determination of peoples and nations as set forth in the Charter of the United Nations and took note of the United Nations resolutions on the rights of peoples and nations to self-determination which is a pre-requisite of the full enjoyment of all fundamental Human Rights.

2. The Asian-African Conference deplored the policies and practices of racial segregation and discrimination which form the basis of government and human relations in large regions of Africa and in other parts of the world. Such conduct is not only a gross violation of human rights, but also a denial of the fundamental values of the civilisation and dignity of man.

The Conference extended its warm sympathy and support for the courageous stand taken by the victims of racial discrimination, especially by the peoples of African and Indian and Pakistani origin in South Africa; applauded all those who sustain the cause; re-affirmed the determination of Asian-African peoples to eradicate every trace of racialism that might exist in their own countries; and pledged to use its full moral influence to guard against the danger of falling victims to the same evil in their struggle to eradicate it.

D. Problems of Dependent Peoples

1. The Asian-African Conference discussed the problems of dependent peoples and colonialism and the evils arising from the subjection of peoples to alien subjugation, domination and exploitation.

The Conference is agreed:

(a) in declaring that colonialism in all its manifestations is an evil which should speedily be brought to an end;

(b) in affirming that the subjection of peoples to alien subjugation, domination and exploitation constitutes a denial of fundamental human rights, is contrary to the Charter of the United Nations and is an impediment to the promotion of world peace and co-operation;

(c) in declaring its support of the cause of freedom and independence for all such peoples; and

(d) in calling upon the Powers concerned to grant freedom and independence to such peoples.

2. In view of the unsettled situation in North Africa and of the persisting denial to the peoples of North Africa of their right to self-determination, the Asian-African Conference declared its support of the rights of the people of Algeria, Morocco and Tunisia to self-determination and independence and urged the French Government to bring about a peaceful settlement of the issue without delay.

E. Other Problems

1. In view of the existing tension in the Middle East caused by the situation in Palestine, and of the danger of that tension to world peace, the Asian-African Conference declared its support of the rights of the Arab people of Palestine and called for the implementation of the United Nations resolutions on Palestine and the achievement of the peaceful settlement of the Palestine question.

2. The Asian-African Conference, in the context of its expressed attitude on the abolition of colonialism, supported the position of Indonesia in the case of West Irian based on the relevant agreements between Indonesia and the Netherlands.

The Asian-African Conference urged the Netherlands Government to reopen negotiations as soon as possible to implement their obligations under the above-mentioned agreements and expressed the earnest hope that the United Nations would assist the parties concerned in finding a peaceful solution to the dispute.

3. The Asian-African Conference supported the position of Yemen in the case of Aden and the Southern parts of Yemen known as the Protectorates and urged the parties concerned to arrive at a peaceful settlement to the dispute.

F. Promotion of World Peace and Co-operation

The Asian-African Conference, taking note of the fact that several States have still not been admitted to the United Nations, considered that for effective co-operation for world peace, membership in the United Nations should be universal, and called on the Security Council to support the admission of all those States which are qualified for membership in terms of the Charter. In the opinion of the Asian-African Conference the following among the participating countries, viz. Cambodia, Ceylon, Japan, Jordan, Libya, Nepal, a unified Vietnam, were so qualified.

The Conference considered that the representation of the countries of the Asian-African region on the Security Council, in relation to the principle of equitable geographical distribution, was inadequate. It expressed the view that as regards the distribution of the non-permanent seats, the Asian-African countries which, under the arrangement arrived at in London in 1946, are precluded from being elected, should be enabled to serve on the Security Council, so that they might make a more effective contribution to the maintenance of international peace and security.

2. The Asian-African Conference having considered the dangerous situation of international tension existing and the risks confronting the whole human race from the outbreak of global war in which the destructive power of all types of armaments, including nuclear and thermo-nuclear weapons, would be employed, invited all the attention of all nations to the terrible consequences that would follow if such a war were to break out.

The Conference considered that disarmament and the prohibition of the production, experimentation and use of nuclear and thermo-nuclear weapons are imperative to save mankind and civilisation from the fear and prospect of wholesale destruction. It considered that the nations of Asia and Africa assembled here have a duty towards humanity and civilisation to proclaim their support for disarmament and for the prohibition of these weapons and to appeal to nations principally concerned and to world opinion, to bring about such disarmament and production.

The Conference considered that effective international control should be established and maintained to implement such disarmament and prohibition and that speedy and determined efforts should be made to this end.

Pending the total prohibition of the manufacture of nuclear and thermo-nuclear weapons, this Conference appealed to all the Powers concerned to reach an agreement to suspend experiments with such weapons.

The Conference declared that universal disarmament is an absolute necessity for the preservation of peace, requested the United Nations to continue its efforts and appealed to all concerned speedily to bring about the regulations, limitation, control and reduction of all armed forces and armaments, including the prohibition of the production, experimentation and use of all weapons of mass destruction, and to establish effective international control to this end.

G. Declaration on the Promotion of World Peace and Co-operation

The Asian-African Conference gave anxious thought to the question of world peace and co-operation. It viewed with deep concern the present state of international tension, with its danger of atomic world war. The problem of peace is correlative with the problem of international security. In this connection, all States should co-operate, especially through the United Nations, in bringing about the reduction of armaments and the elimination of nuclear weapons under effective international control. In this way, international peace can be promoted and nuclear energy may be used exclusively for peaceful purposes. This would help answer the needs particularly of Asia and Africa, for what they urgently require are social progress and better standards of life in larger freedom. Freedom and peace are interdependent. The right of self-determination must be enjoyed by all peoples, and freedom and independence must be granted, with the least possible delay, to those who are still dependent peoples. Indeed all nations should have the right freely to choose their own political and economic systems and their own way of life in conformity with the purposes and principles of the Charter of the United Nations.

Free from mistrust and fear, and with confidence and goodwill towards each other, the nations should practice tolerance and live together in peace and with one another as good neighbours and develop friendly co-operation on the basis of the following principles:

1. Respect for fundamental human rights and for the purposes and principles of the Charter of the United Nations.
2. Respect for the sovereignty and territorial integrity of all nations.
3. Recognition of the equality of all races and of the equality of all nations, large and small.
4. Absention from intervention or interference in the internal affairs of another country.
5. Respect for the right of each nation to defend itself, singly or collectively, in conformity with the Charter of the United Nations.
6. (a) Abstention from the use of arrangements of collective defence to serve the particular interests of any of the big Powers.
   (b) Abstention by any country from exerting pressures on other countries.
7. Refraining from acts or threats of aggression or the use of force against the territorial integrity or political independence of any country.
8. Settlement of all international disputes by peaceful means, such as negotiation, conciliation, arbitration or judicial settlement as well as other peaceful means of the parties' own choice, in conformity with the Charter of the United Nations.
9. Promotion of mutual interests and co-operation.
10. Respect for justice and international obligations.

The Asian-African Conference declares its conviction that friendly co-operation in accordance with these principles would effectively contribute to the maintenance and promotion of international peace and security, while co-operation in the economic, social and cultural fields would help bring about the common prosperity and well-being of all.

The Asian-African Conference recommended that the five sponsoring countries consider the convening of the next meeting of the Conference in consultation with the participating countries.

BIBLIOGRAPHY OF AMERICAN PUBLICATIONS

BIBLIOGRAPHY OF AMERICAN PUBLICATIONS

This bibliography lists American editions (i.e. published in the U.S.A. and its dependencies) in print of titles for which British Commonwealth editions are entered in the bibliographies included in Parts Two and Three of this book. It is compiled from Books in Print: an Index to the Publishers' Trade List Annual, *R. R. Bowker, New York (up to 1964) and* Cumulative Book Index: World List of Books in the English Language, *H. W. Wilson, New York (up to 1964).*

H. Alexander. *Consider India.* (Taplinger, New York, 1961.)

G. C. Allen. *Japan's Economic Recovery.* (Oxford Univ. Press, New York, 1958.)

B. Amritananda. *Buddhist Activities in Socialist Countries.* (China Books and Periodicals, San Francisco, Calif., 1961.)

M. R. Anand. *Is There a Contemporary Indian Civilization?* (Taplinger, New York, 1962.)

J. L. Anderson and D. Richie. *Japanese Film.* (Charles E. Tuttle, Rutland, Vt., 1959.)

M. and W. G. Archer. *Indian Painting for the British 1770–1880.* (Oxford Univ. Press, New York, 1955.)

H. J. P. Arnold. *Aid for Developing Countries.* (Dufour Editions, Chester Springs, Pa., 1962.)

F. G. Bailey. *Tribe, Caste and Nation.* (Humanities Press, New York, 1960.)

A. L. Basham. *The Wonder that was India.* (Grove Press, New York, paperback ed., 1959.)

P. T. Bauer. *Economic Analysis and Policy in Underdeveloped Countries.* (Duke Univ. Press, Durham, N.C., 1957.)

F. C. Benham. *The Colombo Plan and Other Essays.* (Oxford Univ. Press, New York, 1956.) *Economic Aid to Underdeveloped Countries.* (Oxford Univ. Press, New York, 1961.)

J. D. Bernal. *World Without War.* (Monthly Review Press, New York, 1959.)

L. Binder. *Religion and Politics in Pakistan.* (Univ. of Calif. Press, Berkeley, Calif., 1961.)

M. Brecher. *Nehru.* (Beacon Press, Boston, Mass., paperback ed., 1962.)

J. H. Brimmell. *Communism in South East Asia.* (Oxford Univ. Press, New York, 1959.)

P. Brown. *Indian Architecture, Islamic Period.* (Tudor, New York, 1963.)

W. K. Bunce. *Religions in Japan.* (Charles E. Tuttle, Rutland, Vt. 1959.)

J. E. Buck. *Land Utilization in China.* (Paragon Book Reprint Corp., New York, 1964.)

A. K. Cairncross. *Factors in Economic Development.* (Praeger, New York, 1962.)

K. Callard. *Pakistan, a Political Study.* (Macmillan, New York, 1957.)

G. M. Carstairs. *The Twice Born.* (Indiana Univ. Press, Bloomington, Indiana, 1958.)

K. Chao. *Agrarian Policies of Mainland China, 1949-56.* (Harvard Univ. Press, Cambridge, Mass., 1957.)

Prince C. Chakrabongse. *Lords of Life.* (Taplinger, New York, 1960.)

A. Chakravarty (ed.). *Tagore Reader.* (Macmillan, New York, 1961.)

S. Chandrasekhar. *China's Population.* (Oxford Univ. Press, New York, 2nd ed., 1960.)

N. C. Chaudhuri. *Passage to England.* (St. Martins Press, New York, 1960.)

T. H. E. Chen. *Thought Reform of the Chinese Intellectuals.* (Oxford Univ. Press, New York, 1960.)

A. H. Christie. 'The Sea-locked Lands' in *The Dawn of Civilization*, ed. S. Piggott. (McGraw-Hill, New York, 1961.)

Collective Defence in South East Asia. (Oxford University Press for Royal Institute of International Affairs, New York.)

C. Collins. *Public Administration in Hong Kong.* (Institute of Pacific Relations, Univ. of British Columbia, Vancouver, 1952.)

E. Conze. *Buddhism: Its Essence and Development.* (Peter Smith, Gloucester, Mass.) (Trans.) *Buddhist Scriptures.* (Penguin, Baltimore, Md., 1959.)

R. J. Coughlin. *Double Identity: The Chinese in Modern Thailand.* (Oxford Univ. Press, New York, 1960.)

C. D. Cowan. *Nineteenth-Century Malaya.* (Oxford Univ. Press, New York, 1961.)

G. H. Creel. *Chinese Thought from Confucius to Mao Tse-tung.* (Univ. of Chicago Press, Chicago, 1953.)

O. Dazai. *No Longer Human*, trans. Donald Keene. (New Directions, New York, 1958.) *Setting Sun.* (New Directions, New York, 1947.)

E. Dening. *Japan.* (Praeger, paperback ed., 1960.)

P. D. Devanandan. *The Gospel and Renascent Hinduism.* (Friendship Press, New York, 1959.)

S. C. Dube. *Indian Village.* (Humanities Press, New York.)

M. Edwardes. *Asia in the Balance.* (Peter Smith, Gloucester, Mass., 1962.)

C. Eliot. *Hinduism and Buddhism*, 3 vols. (Barnes and Noble, New York, 1954.) *Japanese Buddhism.* (Barnes and Noble, New York, 1959.)

G. B. Endacott. *A History of Hong Kong.* (Oxford Univ. Press, New York, 1958.)

T. S. Epstein. *Economic Development and Social Change in South India.* (Humanities Press, New York, 1962.)

K. Eskelund. *Forgotten Valley.* (Taplinger, New York, 1961.)

B. H. Farmer. *Ceylon: A Divided Nation.* (Oxford Univ. Press, New York, 1963.) *Pioneer Peasant Colonization in Ceylon.* (Oxford Univ. Press, New York, 1957.)

A. D. Ficke. *Chats on Japanese Prints.* (Charles E. Tuttle, Rutland, Vt.)

L. Fischer. *The Story of Indonesia: Old Land, New Nation.* (Harper and Row, New York, 1959.)

C. P. Fitzgerald. *China, A Short Cultural History.* (Praeger, New York, 4th revised ed., 1962.)

Fodor's Guide to Japan and East Asia. (David McKay, New York, 1962, revised annually.)

S. H. Frankel. *The Economic Impact on Underdeveloped Societies.* (Harvard Univ. Press, Cambridge, Mass., 1953.)

J. K. Galbraith. *The Affluent Society.* (Houghton Mifflin, Boston, 1958.)

M. K. Gandhi. *An Autobiography.* (Beacon Press, Boston, Mass., paperback ed., 1957.)

B. G. Gokhale. *The Making of the Indian Nation.* (Taplinger, New York, 2nd ed., 1960.)

G. Greenwood and N. Harper (eds.). *Australia in World Affairs, 1956-60.* (Institute of Pacific Relations, Univ. of British Columbia, Vancouver, 1963.)

Sir P. Griffiths. *Modern India.* (Praeger, New York, revised ed. 1962.)

A. B. Griswold. 'Burma' in *Art of Burma, Korea and Tibet.* (Crown, New York, 1964.)

B. P. Groslier. *The Art of Indochina.* (Crown, New York, 1962.)

W. Gutteridge. *Armed Forces in the New States.* (Oxford Univ. Press, New York, paperback ed., 1962.)

D. G. E. Hall. *Burma.* (Rinehart, New York, 1950.) *A History of South-East Asia.* (St. Martins Press, New York, 2nd ed., 1964.)

E. Hambro. *Problem of Chinese Refugees in Hong Kong.* (Oceana, Dobbs Ferry, N.Y., 1955.)

M. ul Haq. *Strategy of Economic Planning: A Case Study of Pakistan.* (Oxford Univ. Press, 1963.)

B. Harrison. *South East Asia: A Short History.* (St. Martin's Press, New York, 1954.)

D. Hindley. *The Communist Party of Indonesia 1951-63.* (Univ. of Calif. Press, Berkeley, Calif., 1964.)

P. J. Honey. *Communism in North Vietnam.* (MIT Press, Cambridge, Mass., 1963.)

D. Howarth (ed.). *My Land and My People* (Autobiography of the 14th Dalai Lama). (McGraw-Hill, New York, 1962.)

G. F. Hudson. *Europe and China: A Survey of their Relations from the Earliest Times to 1800.* (Beacon Press, Boston, Mass., 1961.)

G. F. Hudson and others. *The Sino-Soviet Dispute.* (Praeger, New York, 1961.)

M. Hürlimann. *Traveller Through the Orient.* Published as *Journey Through the Orient.* (Viking Press, New York, 1960.)

J. H. Hutton. *Caste in India.* (Oxford Univ. Press, New York, 3rd ed., 1961.)

D. Insor. *Thailand.* (Praeger, New York, 1963.)

Sir W. I. Jennings. *Constitutional Problems in Pakistan.* (Cambridge Univ. Press, New York, 1957.) *The Economy of Ceylon.* (Oxford Univ. Press, New York, 2nd ed., 1951.)

F. Joss. *Of Geisha and Gangsters.* (Transatlantic Arts, Florida, 1962.)

G. McT. Kahin. *Nationalism and Revolution in Indonesia.* (Cornell Univ. Press, Ithaca, N.Y., 1952.)

R. K. Karanjia and J. Nehru. *The Mind of Mr. Nehru.* (International Publications Service, New York, 1961.)

Y. Kawabata. *Thousand Cranes.* (Alfred A. Knopf, New York, 1959.)

I. Kawasaki. *The Japanese Are Like That.* (Charles Tuttle, Rutland, Vt., 1955.)

D. Keene. *Living Japan.* (Doubleday, Garden City, N.Y., 1959.) (Trans.) *The Old Woman, The Wife and The Archer: Three Modern Japanese Short Novels.* (Viking Press, New York, 1961.)

J. Kennedy. *A History of Malaya.* (St. Martin's Press, New York, 1962.)

M. M. Khaing. *Burmese Family.* (Indiana Univ. Press, Bloomington, Ind., 1962.)

J. E. Kidder. *Masterpieces of Japanese Sculpture.* (Charles E. Tuttle, Rutland, Vt., 1961.)

J. Kirkup. *These Horned Islands.* (Macmillan, New York, 1962.)

E. S. Kirby (ed.). *Contemporary China,* 5 vols. (Oxford Univ. Press, New York, 1958-62.)

W. Kolarz. *Religion in the Soviet Union.* (St. Martin's Press, N.Y., 1962.)

A. Lamb. *The China-India Border.* (Oxford Univ. Press, New York, paperback ed., 1964.)

D. Lancaster. *The Emancipation of French Indo-China.* (Oxford Univ. Press, New York, 1961.)

K. S. Latourette. *History of the Expansion of Christianity,* 7 vols. (Harper and Row, New York, 1937-45.)

O. Lattimore. *Nomads and Commissars.* (Oxford Univ. Press, New York, 1962.)

S. E. Lee. *A History of Far Eastern Art.* (Prentice-Hall, Englewood Cliffs, N.J., 1964.)

W. A. Lewis. *Theory of Economic Growth.* (Richard D. Irwin, Homewood, Ill., 1955.)

R. J. Lifton. *Thought Reform and the Psychology of Totalism.* (W. W. Norton, New York, 1961.)

Chiu-mei Lin (Janet Lim). *Sold for Silver.* (World Publishing Co., Cleveland, Ohio, 1958.)

E. Lipper. *Eleven Years in Soviet Prison Camps.* (Henry Regnery, Chicago, Ill., 1951.)

E. Luard. *Britain and China.* (Johns Hopkins Press, Baltimore, Md., 1962.)

E. F. C. Ludowyk. *The Story of Ceylon.* (Roy, New York, 1963.)

M. Lubis. *Twilight in Djakarta.* (Vanguard Press, New York, 1964.)

D. N. Majumdar. *Caste and Communication in an Indian Village.* (Taplinger, New York, 1959.)

J. M. Maki. *Government and Politics in Japan.* (Praeger, New York, paperback ed.)

W. Malenbaum. *Prospects for Indian Development.* (Free Press, New York, 1962.)

F. B. Mann. *Acupuncture.* (Random House, New York, 1963.)

Mao Tse-tung on Guerilla Warfare, trans. S. B. Griffith. (Praeger, New York, 1961.)

K. Markandaya. *Nectar in a Sieve.* (New American Library, New York.)

B. B. Misra. *The Indian Middle Classes.* (Oxford Univ. Press, New York, 1961.)

L. Mitchison. *The Overseas Chinese.* (Dufour Editions, Chester Springs, Pa., 1961.)

I. Montagu. *Land of Blue Sky.* (Dufour Editions, Chester Springs, Pa., 1956.)

P. Moon. *Divide and Quit.* (Univ. of California Press, Berkeley and Los Angeles, 1961.)

F. Mu. *The Wilting of the Hundred Flowers.* (Praeger, New York, 1963.)

G. Myrdal. *Economic Theory of Underdeveloped Regions.* Published as *Rich Lands and Poor.* (Harper and Row, New York, 1958.)

C. A. O. van Nieuwenhuijze. *Aspects of Islam in Post-Colonial Indonesia.* (Gregory Lounz, New York, 1957.)

S. Nikhilinanda. *Hinduism: Its Meaning for the Liberation of the Spirit.* (Harper and Row, New York, 1958.)

D. T. Niles. *Upon the Earth. The Mission of God and the Missionary Enterprise of the Churches.* (McGraw-Hill, New York, 1962.)

T. J. Norbu. *Tibet is My Country.* (E. P. Dutton, New York, 1961.)

R. Nurkse. *Problems of Capital Formation in Underdeveloped Countries.* (Oxford Univ. Press, New York, 1953.)

G. D. Overstreet and M. Windmiller. *Communism in India.* (Univ. of California Press, Berkeley, Calif., 1959.)

R. T. Paine and A. Soper. *Art and Architecture of Japan.* (Penguin, Baltimore, Md.)

L. H. Palmier. *Indonesia and the Dutch.* (Oxford Univ. Press, New York, 1962.)

K. M. Panikkar. *Asia and Western Dominance.* (Hillary House, New York, rev. ed., 1959.) *A Survey of Indian History.* (Taplinger, New York, 4th ed., 1964.)

C. N. Parkinson. *British Intervention in Malaya, 1867-1877.* (Oxford Univ. Press, New York, 1960.)

P. S. R. Payne. *The White Rajahs of Sarawak.* (Funk and Wagnalls, New York, 1960.)

M. Perham. *Lugard: The Years of Authority 1898-1945.* (Oxford Univ. Press, New York, 1960.)

L. Pye. *Guerilla Communism in Malaya.* (Princeton Univ. Press, Princeton, N.J., 1956.)

S. Radhakrishnan. *Indian Philosophy*, 2 vols. (Humanities Press, New York.) *The Hindu View of Life.* (Macmillan, New York, 1927.)

B. Rajan. *Too Long in the West.* (Atheneum, New York, 1962.)

H. G. Rawlinson. *India: a Short Political History.* (Praeger, New York, paperback ed., 1965.)

W. B. Reddaway. *The Development of the Indian Economy.* (Richard D. Irwin, Homewood, Ill., 1962.)

W. D. Reeve. *The Republic of Korea: A Political and Economic Study.* (Oxford Univ. Press, New York, 1963.)

E. O. Reischauer and J. K. Fairbank. *East Asia: The Great Tradition.* (Houghton Mifflin, Boston, Mass., 1960.)

C. Robequain and others. *The Economic Development of French Indo-China.* (Oxford Univ. Press, New York, 1944.)

W. W. Rostow. *Process of Economic Growth.* (W. W. Norton, New York, rev. ed., 1960.)

S. Rose (ed.) *Politics in Southern Asia.* (St. Martin's Press, New York, 1963.)

G. B. Sansom. *The Western World and Japan.* (Alfred A. Knopf, New York, 1950.) *Japan: A Short Cultural History.* (Appleton-Century-Crofts, New York, rev. ed., 1962.) *History of Japan*, 3 vols: *To 1334, 1334-1615, 1615-1867.* (Stanford Univ. Press, Stanford, Calif., 1958, 1961, 1963.)

S. R. Schram (ed. and trans.). *The Political Thought of Mao Tse-tung.* (Praeger, New York, 1963.)

Y. Semyonov. *Siberia: Its Conquest and Development.* (Taplinger, New York, 1963.)

C. Sen. *Tibet Disappears.* (Taplinger, New York, 1960.)

O. Siren. *Chinese Painting, Leading Masters and Principles*, 4 vols. (Ronald Press, New York, 1958.)

D. E. Smith. *India as a Secular State.* (Princeton Univ. Press, Princeton, N.J., 1963.)

V. Smith. *History of Fine Art in India and Ceylon*, revised K. Khandalavala. (Tudor, New York, 3rd revised ed., 1963.)

V. A. Smith. *The Oxford Student's History of India*, ed. H. G. Rawlinson. (Oxford Univ. Press, New York, 15th ed., 1951.) *Early History of India*, revised S. M. Edwardes. (Oxford Univ. Press, New York, 4th ed., 1957.) *Oxford History of India*, 3 vols., ed. P. Spear. (Oxford Univ. Press, New York, 3rd ed., 1958.)

W. C. Smith. *Islam in Modern History.* (New American Library, New York, 1959.)

N. V. Sovani and K. Dandekar (eds.). *Changing India.* (Taplinger, New York, 1961.)

O. H. K. Spate. *India and Pakistan.* (E. P. Dutton, New York, 1953.)

E. Staley. *Future of Underdeveloped Countries.* (Praeger, New York.)

I. Stephens. *Pakistan.* (Praeger, New York, 1963.)

R. Storry. *A History of Modern Japan.* (Penguin Books, Baltimore, Md., 1960.)

M. Sullivan. *An Introduction to Chinese Art.* (Univ. of California Press, Berkeley, California, 1961.)

D. T. Suzuki. *Zen and Japanese Culture.* (Pantheon Books, New York, 1959.)

E. F. Szczepanik. *The Economic Growth of Hong Kong.* (Oxford Univ. Press, New York, 1958.)

R. H. Tawney. *Land and Labour in China.* (Octagon Books, New York.)

H. Thomsen. *New Religions of Japan.* (Charles E. Tuttle, Rutland, Vt., 1963.)

H. Tinker. *Union of Burma.* (Oxford Univ. Press, New York, 3rd ed., 1961.) *India and Pakistan, a Political Analysis.* (Praeger, New York, 1962.)

A. J. Toynbee. *A Study of History*, vol. 4. (Oxford Univ. Press, New York, paperback ed., 1962.)

G. T. Trewartha. *Japan: A Physical, Cultural and Regional Geography.* (Univ. of Wisconsin Press, Madison, Wis., 1947.)

S. A. Vahid. *Iqbal, His Life and Thought.* (Humanities Press, New York, 1959.)

H. Venkatasubbiah. *Indian Economy since Independence.* (Taplinger, New York, 2nd revised ed., 1961.)

B. H. M. Vlekke. *Nusantara: A History of Indonesia.* (Quadrangle, Chicago, Ill., revised ed., 1960.)

F. A. Wagner. *Art of Indonesia.* (Crown, New York.)

W. Watson. *Ancient Chinese Bronzes.* (Charles E. Tuttle, Rutland, Vt., 1962.)

G. E. Wheeler. *The Modern History of Soviet Central Asia.* (Praeger, New York, 1964.)

G. E. Wheeler. *Racial Problems in Soviet Muslim Asia.* (Oxford Univ. Press, New York, 2nd ed., 1962.)

W. Willetts. *Chinese Art,* 2 vols. (George Braziller, New York, 1958.)

A. Winnington. *Tibet.* (International Publishers, New York, 1957.)

R. Winstedt. *Malaya and its History.* (Hillary House, New York.)

World Radio TV Handbook. (Heinman Imported Books, New York.)

S. A. Zenkovsky. *Pan-Turkism and Islam in Russia.* (Harvard Univ. Press, Cambridge, Mass., 1960.)

M. Zinkin. *Development for Free Asia.* (Oxford Univ. Press, New York, rev. ed., 1963.)

M. and T. Zinkin. *Britain and India.* (Johns Hopkins Press, Baltimore, Md., 1964.)

T. Zinkin. *Caste Today.* (Oxford Univ. Press, New York, paperback ed., 1962.) *India Changes!* (Oxford Univ. Press, New York, 1958.)

INDEXES

INDEX OF CONTRIBUTORS

INDEX

Compiled by Roger F. Pemberton, M.A.,
Member of the Society of Indexers

Cross-references *from* main headings are *to* main headings. Cross-references *from* sub-headings are *to* sub-headings in the same group, except those followed by '*m. h.*', indicating 'main heading'. References to statistical tables are indicated thus: *e.g.* '724 (*table*)', except under the main heading 'Statistics'. Page references to the Appendix are in italics.

A.—27

A.—28*

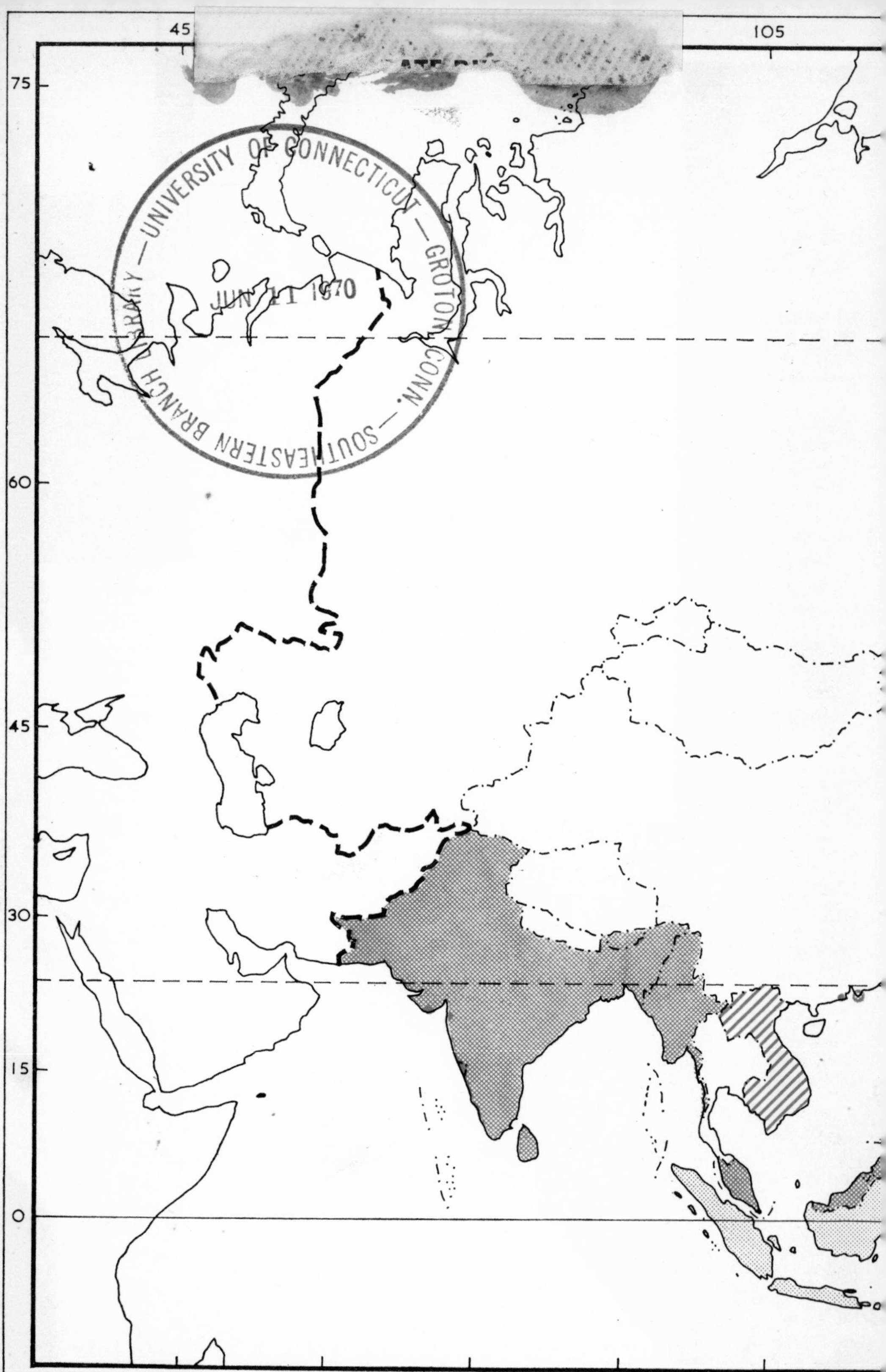
45
105
75
60
45
30
15
0
45
60
75
90
105